CONSTITUTIONAL & ADMINISTRATIVE LAW

This book is supported by a Companion Website, created to keep *Constitutional & Administrative Law* up to date and to provide enhanced resources for both students and lecturers.

Key features include:

- termly updates
- self-assessment tests
- links to useful websites
- links to 'ebooks' for introductory and further reading
- revision guidance
- guidelines on answering questions

www.routledgecavendish.com/textbooks/1845680332

CONSTITUTIONAL & ADMINISTRATIVE LAW

Sixth Edition

Hilaire Barnett, BA, LLM

Queen Mary,
University of London

Routledge·Cavendish
Taylor & Francis Group

Sixth edition first published in 2006
by Routledge-Cavendish
2 Park Square, Milton Park, Abingdon, Oxon OX14 4RN

Simultaneously published in the USA and Canada
by Routledge-Cavendish
270 Madison Ave, New York, NY 10016

Reprinted 2007

*Routledge-Cavendish is an imprint of the
Taylor and Francis Group, an informa business*

© Hilaire Barnett   2006
Previous editions published by
Cavendish Publishing Limited
First edition   1995
Second edition   1998
Third edition   2000
Fourth edition   2002
Fifth edition   2004

Typeset in Palatino by RefineCatch Limited, Bungay, Suffolk
Printed and bound in Great Britain by MPG Books Ltd, Bodmin, Cornwall

British Library in Cataloguing Publication Data
A catalogue record for this book is available from the British Library

Library of Congress Cataloging in Publication Data
A catalog record has been requested

ISBN10: 1-84568-033-2 (pbk)
ISBN10: 1-84568-066-9 (hbk)

ISBN13: 978-1-84568-033-6 (pbk)
ISBN13: 978-1-84568-066-4 (hbk)

For Matthew

PREFACE

The United Kingdom's constitution, while of ancient origins, remains both dynamic and vibrant. As every public lawyer is only too aware, nowadays, the proper boundaries of constitutional and administrative law are both increasingly wide and subject to debate. In compiling any textbook on this subject, one of the principal preliminary tasks lies in defining the scope of material to be included and the approach to be adopted in relation to that material. The task of writing is made more problematic by the many and varied depths in which, and the means by which, the subject is taught both in the United Kingdom and overseas. Full time students, part time students, students on long distance learning programmes and students combining both constitutional and administrative law within a one year course, all have differing needs. The aim in this book has been to provide sufficient detail to meet all such needs in a user-friendly manner.

As emphasised in the introductory chapters, the study of the United Kingdom's constitutional and administrative law involves rather more than a learning of rules of law, and necessarily encompasses – over and above an understanding of legal rules – an understanding of history, government, politics and conventional practices which form the foundations of the contemporary constitution. As a result, any constitutional and administrative law textbook must incorporate sufficient information relating to such matters so as to enable students to view the constitution in its historical, political and conventional context. In this book, I have addressed the subject in this manner in order to provide a rounded, contextual explanation of the United Kingdom's constitution, which goes beyond pure law while also adequately covering the law.

As previously, the text is divided into seven main parts. Part I provides a general introduction to the scope of constitutional law, the sources of the constitution and the structure of the United Kingdom. In Part II, the fundamental concepts of the constitution are considered: the rule of law, separation of powers, the royal prerogative and parliamentary sovereignty. In Part III, the European Union and Community is discussed. The material is divided into two chapters. Chapter 8 considers the evolution, aims and structure of the Union and Community and the principal institutions and their respective powers. In Chapter 9, the sources of Community law and the relationship between national and Community law are discussed.

In Part IV, the structure of government is discussed, Chapter 10 considering the role of Prime Minister, Cabinet and the Civil Service, Chapter 11 discussing the concept of responsible government and ministerial responsibility and Chapter 12 the devolution of power to the Northern Ireland Assembly, Scottish Parliament and Welsh Assembly and local government.

Part V is devoted to the United Kingdom Parliament: Westminster. Chapter 13 discusses the electoral system, and Chapter 14 introduces the reader to the House of Commons. Chapters 15 and 16 are devoted to parliamentary procedures for the scrutiny of legislative proposals and scrutiny of government administration. The House of Lords, its role, functions and the current reform proposals are considered in Chapter 17. Parliamentary privilege is discussed in Chapter 18.

Part VI focuses on the individual and the state, covering civil liberties, police powers and the protection of human rights. The subject of state security is discussed in Chapter 25. Part VII introduces administrative law. Judicial review of administrative action comprises two chapters, the first dealing with the role and scope of judicial review and procedural matters; the second analysing the grounds for judicial review. The complementary role, functions and powers of Commissioners for Administration are considered in Chapter 28.

Revising the text for a new edition always presents challenges. On this occasion it has been the sheer volume and range of new legislation. In addition to the Constitutional Reform Act 2005, there have been major reforms relating to immigration and asylum, the police and police powers and state security. As this text goes to print, an investigation is taking place into the link, if any, between financial donations and the granting of peerages; a major Cabinet reshuffle has taken place; and a Home Secretory has been sacked over the release of foreign criminals from prison who should have been deported. All these, and other developments will be reported on the website which accompanies this text. In preparing this edition I have been fortunate to have had the unstinting support of Justin Fuller who has made the task so much easier. As ever, any errors remain my sole responsibility. My thanks as ever to Sonny Leong and his team at Routledge-Cavendish, with whom as before it has been a pleasure to work.

I would also like to thank all the students, past and present – both at home and, particularly, in the Far East – who over the years have deepened my understanding of the difficulties they face in studying such a rich, varied and essentially protean subject as that of the constitution of the United Kingdom. Family and all friends are again owed a large and unquantifiable debt of gratitude, not just for all their support, but also for allowing me the necessary time and solitude in which to update the text.

Hilaire Barnett
School of Law
Queen Mary, University of London
May 2006

CONTENTS

PART I – GENERAL INTRODUCTION

PART II – FUNDAMENTAL CONSTITUTIONAL CONCEPTS

PART III – THE EUROPEAN COMMUNITY AND UNION

PART IV – CENTRAL, REGIONAL
AND LOCAL GOVERNMENT

PART V – PARLIAMENT

PART VI – THE INDIVIDUAL AND THE STATE

TABLE OF CASES

TABLE OF LEGISLATION

TABLE OF STATUTORY INSTRUMENTS

DIRECTIVES, TREATIES AND CONVENTIONS

Decisions

Directives

Regulations

Treaties and Conventions

PART I

GENERAL INTRODUCTION

CHAPTER 1

INTRODUCTION:
THE SCOPE OF CONSTITUTIONAL LAW

Constitutional law is concerned with the role and powers of the institutions within the state and with the relationship between the citizen and the state. The constitution is a living, dynamic organism which at any point in time will reflect the moral and political values of the people it governs, and accordingly, the law of the constitution must be appreciated within the socio-political context in which it operates.

The study of the constitution of the United Kingdom involves acquiring an understanding of a variety of historical, legal, philosophical and political factors which have, over the centuries, shaped the organisation of the state. The United Kingdom appears to be almost unique in not having a constitution which is conveniently set out in a single written document. Israel and New Zealand share this constitutional feature. However, not too much weight should be given to the 'unwritten' nature of the constitution. Under all constitutions, not all of the rules will be written, and still less will they be collected within a single document.

In the United Kingdom, by contrast with most other states, the constitution is the product of many centuries of continuous and, mostly, gradual, peaceful evolution. With the exception of the constitutional turmoils of the seventeenth century,[1] the United Kingdom's constitutional development has an unbroken history dating from 1066. Accordingly, historical origins form the background for the study of the contemporary constitution, and no meaningful appreciation of the present constitution can be acquired without understanding this historical backcloth which reveals the moral and political influences that have shaped the constitution as it exists today. That said, it must always be remembered that the principal emphasis of study is on the contemporary constitution of the United Kingdom rather than on the many centuries of development which underlie it. With that point in mind, it is necessary to draw on historical sources and events with a view to understanding the contribution made to an evaluation of the many constitutional issues which present themselves today.

It is particularly true of the United Kingdom's constitution, which is more the product of evolution than conscious rational thought, that it is difficult to see clearly the demarcation lines between constitutional law, history, philosophy and political science. In order, therefore, to study the United Kingdom's constitution successfully, it is necessary to gain an insight into the history, politics and political philosophy which underpin the constitution. This task is not easy, particularly as many students will come to constitutional law without a background in history, politics or political philosophy. It is, however, an essential component of constitutional study, without which the structure, law and policies of the state cannot be understood. More than any other area of legal study except jurisprudence, constitutional law in the United Kingdom involves far more than a

---

1   See in particular Chapters 2, 6 and 7.

learning of legal rules. Indeed, it may be said, without exaggeration, that the non-legal rules and practices within the constitution are at least as important – if not more important on many occasions – as the legal rules. For example, in analysing and evaluating the extent to which the individual citizen enjoys constitutional protection of individual rights, it is necessary to appreciate the timeless and tireless quest to ensure the legal protection of the rights of individuals. This study involves, *inter alia*, an appreciation of natural law and social contract theories[2] which underpin the constitutional limitations on government power in order that the rights of individuals are protected against the power of the state.

Also, by way of example, the study of the constitutional relationship between the government and the legislature today encompasses a knowledge of the political backcloth, the rules of parliamentary practice and the non-legal or conventional rules which apply in a given situation. By way of further illustration, when studying the legislative supremacy of parliament, it is of fundamental importance to grasp that, in terms of classical constitutional legal theory, the power of parliament – in the absence of a written constitution – is omnipotent or sovereign.[3] However, the constitutional and legal fact that parliament has the ultimate law making power within the state, does not mean that there are no restraints on what parliament may do. The law making powers of parliament, while theoretically and legally unlimited, are in fact constrained by the electorate to which parliament is accountable, and by economic, moral and political necessities. In terms of accountability to the electorate and the limits which this imposes on parliament's powers, it is necessary to appreciate the philosophical and historical foundations of democracy and the idea of individual rights. Notwithstanding the lack of a codified constituent document, under the constitution of the United Kingdom, the principles on which the government operates today are precisely those which govern the relationship between the government and the people under a written constitution. Here, an understanding of the idea of 'social contract'[4] makes it possible to understand the complex relationship between 'sovereign power' and the power of the people to determine who holds that sovereign power and the manner in which it may – and may not – be exercised.

Nowadays, the 'supremacy' of parliament in the United Kingdom must also be considered against the United Kingdom's membership of the European Union,[5] which has significant implications for the classical doctrine of sovereignty. Since 1972, when the United Kingdom acceded to the European Community,[6] the United Kingdom has in many respects ceased to be an autonomous, independent state and has become a member of an ever-expanding European political, economic and legal order, the impact of which reaches to the heart of the constitution. In legal terms, it is undeniable that the United Kingdom

---

2   See Chapters 4 and 19.
3   See Chapter 7.
4   See Chapters 4 and 19.
5   See Chapters 8 and 9.
6   The original three Communities are now referred to as the European Community. This forms a major part of the European Union, which came into being under the Treaty on European Union 1992 (the Maastricht Treaty).

Parliament could decide to withdraw from the European Union. It is, however, arguable that, in light of the non-legal restraints – political and economic – there exists little real power to withdraw from the Union. The non-legal restraints are in fact more important in this regard than the simple legal rule that parliament is sovereign in its law making powers.

To illustrate further the distinction between absolute legal power and practical power, in terms of law, the Crown has the right to appoint the Prime Minister of its choice, and the power to dissolve parliament when it chooses.[7] To know these rules, however, is not to know very much, for the legal powers of the Crown are restricted – constrained – by non-legal, 'conventional' rules which determine the conditions under which the Crown has a discretion to exercise its powers. In order, therefore, to understand issues such as the appointment of a Prime Minister and the rules regulating the dissolution of parliament, it is necessary to understand the conventional rules which have developed over time and have taken on binding force.

THE CONCEPT OF CONSTITUTIONALISM[8]

'Constitutionalism' is the doctrine which governs the legitimacy of government action. By constitutionalism is meant – in relation to constitutions written and unwritten – conformity with the broad philosophical values within a state. Constitutionalism implies something far more important than the idea of 'legality' which requires official conduct to be in accordance with pre-fixed legal rules. A power may be exercised on legal authority; however, that fact is not necessarily determinative of whether or not the action was 'constitutional'. The doctrine of constitutionalism suggests, at least, the following:

(a) that the exercise of power be within the legal limits conferred by parliament on those with power – the concept of *intra vires* – and that those who exercise power are accountable to law;

(b) that the exercise of power – irrespective of legal authority – must conform to the notion of respect for the individual and the individual citizen's rights;

(c) that the powers conferred on institutions within a state – whether legislative, executive or judicial – be sufficiently dispersed between the various institutions so as to avoid the abuse of power; and

(d) that the government, in formulating policy, and the legislature, in legitimating that policy, are accountable to the electorate on whose trust power is held.

In summary, constitutionalism suggests the limitation of power,[9] the separation of powers[10] and the doctrine of responsible accountable government. It is against these conceptual and practical requirements that the constitution of the United Kingdom must be studied and evaluated.

---

7   See Chapter 6.
8   See Bogdanor, 1988, 'Introduction'; McAuslan and McEldowney, 1985, pp 11 ff.
9   See Chapter 4.
10   See Chapter 5.

WHAT IS A CONSTITUTION?

In lay terms, a constitution is a set of rules which governs an organisation. Every organisation, whether social club, trade union or nation state, which has defined objectives and departments or offices established to accomplish those objectives, needs a constitution to define the powers, rights and duties of the organisation's members. This set of rules, in addition to regulating the internal working of the organisation, will also make provision for the manner in which the organisation relates to outside bodies. It can therefore be said that a constitution looks to both internal and external regulation of the body to which it relates.

In addition to the function of defining powers and duties and relationships with other bodies, a constitution fulfils two related purposes – those of definition and evaluation. In its defining function, the constitution is both descriptive and prescriptive (or normative). Differently expressed, the constitution will both define the manner in which the rules in fact operate and dictate what ought to happen in a given situation. As such, the rule or normative statement in question sets a standard of conduct or behaviour which is regarded as correct and which is expected to be adhered to by those to whom the rules are addressed. These constitutional rules – whether written or unwritten – facilitate the stability and predictability of behaviour. Further, when such normative rules exist, they provide a standard against which actual conduct can be judged or evaluated. If the accusation is made that members of an organisation have acted 'unconstitutionally', the speaker is claiming that those accused have acted in a manner which breaches the required standards of behaviour as laid down in the body of generally accepted pre-determined normative rules. In this sense, a constitutional rule, in addition to being descriptive, normative and predictive, is evaluative and judgmental.

When examining the rules of any organisation, it becomes apparent that individual rules have differing levels of importance and, moreover, that rules may have differing degrees of specificity or generality. The manner in which the rules are expressed may also differ; some may be written down, whereas some may be discernible only through observation of actual conduct. And thus it is with the constitution of a state, and particularly that of the United Kingdom, in which the sources of constitutional law are varied. The legal sources are represented by a mixture of statute and judicial precedent, and these legal sources are supplemented by the binding, non-legal, conventional rules and practices.[11] The rules of constitutional law will also reveal differences in the manner in which they may be changed to adapt to changing circumstances. Under a written constitution, the constitution will itself define the procedure for amendment and may provide for varying degrees of ease or difficulty in amendment in relation to particular rules. The rules regarded as the most important are characterised by the greatest degree of difficulty in the process of amendment. Under the United Kingdom's constitution, by way of contrast, the manner in which constitutional

---

11 See Chapter 2.

change is effected will be dependent not upon clearly defined written rules but, rather, by accepted constitutional practice which has evolved over time.

DEFINING CONSTITUTIONS

Professor KC Wheare defines the constitution of a state as:

> ... the whole system of government of a country, the collection of rules which establish and regulate or govern the government. [1966, p 1]

An older definition, that of Thomas Paine, reveals a more complex set of ideas:

> A constitution is not the act of a government, but of a people constituting a government, and a government without a constitution is power without right ... A constitution is a thing antecedent to a government; and a government is only the creature of a constitution. [1792, Pt II, p 93]

From this second definition, it can be discerned that a constitution is something which is prior to government, or, as Paine expresses it, 'antecedent' to government, giving legitimacy to the government and defining the powers under which a government may act. As such, the constitution sets limits both to the powers which can be exercised and to the manner in which they may be exercised. Accordingly, the constitution defines the legality of power. This notion is particularly apposite in a country with a written constitution and a Supreme Court which is conferred with jurisdiction to rule on the legality of government action. Under such a constitutional arrangement, it can be said that everything which the government does is either lawful or unlawful depending upon whether or not the contested conduct is held to be 'constitutional' or not. Under a largely unwritten constitution, the position is less clear-cut, and it may often be the case that conduct will be adjudged to be 'unconstitutional' and yet not be 'unlawful'. This distinction will be returned to in a subsequent discussion of the legal and non-legal sources of the constitution. At this introductory stage, it need only be noted that the unwritten nature of the United Kingdom's constitution has given rise to argument as to whether or not a constitution – as generally understood in the majority of states – exists. Sir Ivor Jennings, author of *The Law and the Constitution*, offers a balanced evaluation of this apparent paradox:

> If a constitution means a written document, then obviously Great Britain has no constitution. In countries where such a document exists, the word has that meaning. But the document itself merely sets out rules determining the creation and operation of governmental institutions, and obviously Great Britain has such institutions and such rules. The phrase 'British constitution' is used to describe those rules.[12]

CLASSIFYING CONSTITUTIONS

When looking for the salient characteristics of the constitution, it is helpful to bear in mind the range of possible classifications which can be applied to any

---

12 Jennings, 1959b, p 36. See also McIlwain, 1958; Ridley, 1988.

constitution. Professor KC Wheare identifies the following classifications (1966, Chapter 1):

(a) written and unwritten;

(b) rigid and flexible;

(c) supreme and subordinate;

(d) federal and unitary;

(e) separated powers and fused powers; and

(f) republican and monarchical.

Written and unwritten constitutions

A written constitution is one contained within a single document or a series of documents, with or without amendments, defining the basic rules of the state. The origins of written constitutions lie in the American War of Independence (1775–83) and French Revolution (1789). More recent written constitutions derive from the grant – or devolution – of legislative power from previously imperial powers to former colonies and dominions,[13] whether secured as a result of peaceful settlement or violent revolution.[14]

The feature which characterises all states with a written constitution is that there has been a clear historical break with a previously pertaining constitutional arrangement, thus providing the opportunity for a fresh constitutional start. As Wheare explains:

> If we investigate the origins of modern constitutions, we find that, practically without exception, they were drawn up and adopted because people wished to make a fresh start, so far as the statement of their system of government was concerned ... The circumstances in which a break with the past and the need for a fresh start come about vary from country to country, but in almost every case in modern times, countries have a constitution for the very simple and elementary reason that they wanted, for some reason, to begin again ... This has been the practice certainly since 1787 when the American constitution was drafted, and as the years passed, no doubt imitation and the force of example have led all countries to think it necessary to have a constitution. [1966, p 4]

The absence of any such break in continuity in British history, from 1066 to the current time,[15] more than any other factor, explains the mainly unwritten nature of the United Kingdom's constitution.

The characterisation of constitutions into 'written' and 'unwritten' is, however, too limited, for such classification tells neither the whole constitutional story nor necessarily makes the constitution accessible to those seeking to understand it. A written constitution will provide the basic rules, but, for an understanding of the

---

13 See eg the South Africa Act 1909, the British North America Act 1867 (now the Constitution Act 1867) and the Canada Act 1982.

14 See eg the Nigeria Independence Act 1960 and the Zimbabwe Act 1979. See also de Smith, 1964, Chapter 5.

15 With the exception of the seventeenth century constitutional upheavals (see Chapters 6 and 7).

whole constitutional picture, it is also necessary to examine subsequent interpretations of the constitution contained in case law and the political practices which reveal the actual operation of the constitution. At the heart of this matter lies one simple fact: all constitutions – howsoever defined and categorised – are dynamic organisms. They are dependent for much of their meaning and relevance on the societal framework which surrounds them. Nowhere is this more apparent than in relation to individual rights and liberties. The vast majority of states have adopted both written constitutions and Bills of Rights stipulating the inviolable rights of citizens – nevertheless, the political reality for many citizens' rights around the world is very different from the formally drafted constitution. Irrespective of whether or not a state has a written constitution and a Bill of Rights, it must be recognised that the actual protection of individual rights, as with so much of the constitution, is explained not solely by reference to written rules. Regardless of the form in which rights are protected, in any society, it will be the democratic political process, political practice and norms of acceptable governmental conduct that, while not having the force of law, provide constitutional standards which determine the respect accorded to individual rights.[16] These constitutional features also establish standards against which the probity of official conduct may be measured. It is for this reason that a true understanding of constitutions and the concept of constitutionalism requires a deeper understanding than that provided for by an analysis of the formal written rules.

Rigid and flexible constitutions

This classification rests primarily on the question whether or not constitutions can be amended with ease. The framers of a written constitution, endeavouring to provide a comprehensive legal framework for the state, will naturally seek to protect its constitutional provisions from subsequent repeal or amendment. Towards this end, all or many of the rules will be 'entrenched', that is to say the constitution will stipulate stringent procedures to be followed in any attempt to amend the provision in question. As will be seen later, entrenchment may take several forms, but its central characteristic is that it either prevents, or makes difficult, amendment or repeal. By way of example, the federal Commonwealth of Australia Constitution Act of 1900 specifies the procedure to be adopted for its own alteration. An amending Bill must pass through at least one House of Parliament by a specified majority and the proposed amendment must be endorsed in a referendum which approves the measure by an overall majority in at least four of the six states.[17] Between 1900 and 1990, 42 proposals for constitutional amendment had been put forward. Of these, only eight were approved by a majority of electors nationally and a majority of electors in a majority of states. In this regard, it has been observed that 'constitutionally speaking, Australia is a frozen continent'.[18] As a further example, under the

---

16 See Bogdanor, 1988.
17 Commonwealth of Australia Constitution Act 1900 (UK), s 128.
18 Sawer, 1967, p 208. See Lee, 1988.

United States' constitution, constitutional amendments may be proposed either by a two-thirds majority of both Houses of Congress or, following a request by the legislatures of two-thirds of the States, by the convention summoned by Congress. To be accepted, the proposed amendments must then be approved by the legislatures of three-quarters of the states, or by conventions in three-quarters of the states. Between 1813 and 1913, only three amendments had been accepted; between 1913 and 1933 six amendments; and by 1951, only one further amendment.[19]

The United Kingdom's constitution, by comparison with the constitutions of the United States and Australia, represents the height of flexibility. Under the doctrine of parliamentary sovereignty examined in Chapter 7, parliament is the supreme law making body and can pass any law, by a simple majority vote in parliament, on any subject matter whatsoever. Moreover, no court may hold an Act of Parliament to be void.[20] Note for now, therefore, that under the United Kingdom's constitution, no legal constraints can – under the traditional doctrine of sovereignty – fetter parliament's powers.[21] Of particular importance in this regard is the fact that no parliament may lay down irreversible rules regulating future legislative procedures which must be followed. The constitutional importance of this lies in flexibility. It has been argued, controversially, and continues to be argued, that the legislative supremacy of parliament is constrained by various constitutional devices and acts of constitutional importance. However, it is significant that none of these challenges has yet succeeded in limiting parliament's theoretical power.

The issue of flexibility, however, should not be exaggerated. That there are no legal restraints on what parliament does, does not mean that there are no non-legal constraints. In practical terms, such 'extra-legal' constraints may be as important as legal controls. By way of illustration of the distinction between legal and non-legal constraints, Sir Ivor Jennings offers the example of parliament passing an Act which bans smoking in the streets of Paris. As he states, there is nothing in the constitution which prevents parliament from doing precisely that: 'If it enacts that smoking in the streets of Paris is an offence, then it is an offence' (1959b, p 170). The relevant Act so passed would be valid and recognised by the English courts. However, the Act would be totally ineffective and ignored by the courts and everyone else in France. Equally, as Jennings states, 'if Parliament enacted that all men should be women, they would be women so far as the law is concerned'. Sir Leslie Stephens, writing in the nineteenth century,[22] asks what restrains parliament from passing an Act providing that all blue-eyed babies be put to death? The response to this question is that in legal-theoretical terms, of course parliament could pass such a law, but in political terms, it neither could nor would do so, for ultimately, parliament is dependent upon the support of the electorate.

---

19 See Wheare, 1963, Chapters 4 and 12.
20 *Edinburgh and Dalkeith Railway v Wauchope* (1842); *Sillars v Smith* (1982).
21 Complications arise in relation to the European Community and Union, to be examined in Chapters 8 and 9.
22 See *The Science of Ethics*, 1882.

Supreme and subordinate constitutions

This constitutional category overlaps in many respects, although not totally, with the classification into federal and unitary states. A 'supreme' constitution refers to a state in which the legislative powers of the governing body are unlimited. Conversely, a subordinate constitution is one whose powers are limited by some higher authority.[23]

Federal and unitary constitutions

In many states, for example, the United States of America, Canada, Australia and Malaysia, there exists a division of powers between central government and the individual states or provinces which make up the federation. The powers divided between the federal government and states or provinces will be clearly set down in the constituent document. Some powers will be reserved exclusively to the federal government (most notably, such matters as defence and state security); some powers will be allocated exclusively to the regional government (such as planning and the raising of local taxation); and others will be held on the basis of partnership, powers being given to each level of government with overriding power, perhaps, reserved for central government. The common feature of all federal states is the sharing of power between centre and region – each having an area of exclusive power, other powers being shared on some defined basis. Equally common to all federations is the idea that the written constitution is sovereign over government and legislature and that their respective powers are not only defined by the constitution but are also controlled by the constitution, which will be interpreted and upheld by a Supreme Court.

The constitution of the United Kingdom presents a very different arrangement from that outlined above. The state is unitary and there is no defining written constitution controlling the powers of government or of the legislature.[24] Instead of a written constitution, there exists a sovereign legislative body, which represents the ultimate law making power in the state. Power is given to the Northern Ireland, Scottish and Welsh legislatures and to local government, under Acts of the United Kingdom Parliament, to fulfil defined functions such as the provision of services and raising of local revenue to finance such services. However, no power is given to the regions or to local government other than that decreed by parliament. Regional parliaments and assemblies and local authorities are entirely creatures of Acts of Parliament, and any power given can subsequently – subject only to political acceptability to the electorate – be withdrawn. An illustration of this point can be seen in relation to the statutory abolition of the Greater London Council and other Metropolitan Borough Councils in 1985, under the Local Government Act of that year. An example on a larger scale can be seen in the grant of limited legislative authority to the Northern Ireland Assembly under the Government of Ireland Act 1920. The law

---

23 See Chapter 7 for discussion in relation to New South Wales (Australia) and South Africa.
24 But note the issue of devolution to Northern Ireland, Scotland and Wales; see below, p 15, and see further Chapter 12.

making power given in 1920 was later revoked by the United Kingdom Parliament by the Northern Ireland Constitution Act 1973. Similarly, during the 1970s, the Labour government planned to devolve limited legislative power to Scotland and Wales, and Acts of Parliament were passed to this effect (Scotland Act 1978; Wales Act 1978). Neither of those Acts was, however, brought into force, and legislative power in relation to both Scotland and Wales thus remained with the Westminster Parliament.[25] In 1998, however, devolution of power was again on the constitutional agenda. The Scotland Act 1998, Government of Wales Act 1998 and Northern Ireland Act 1998 each involve a decentralisation of power, although ultimate sovereign power remains with the Westminster Parliament.[26]

Separated powers and fused powers

The separation of powers is a fundamental constitutional concept which will be discussed more fully in Chapter 5. With respect to the classification of constitutions, the concept here requires outline consideration. The doctrine is of great antiquity, dating back at least to Aristotle.[27] John Locke, Viscount Bolingbroke and Baron Montesquieu gave further expression to the idea.[28]

The essence of the doctrine is that the powers vested in the principal institutions of the state – legislature, executive and judiciary – should not be concentrated in the hands of any one institution.[29] The object of such separation is to provide checks on the exercise of power by each institution and to prevent the potential for tyranny which might otherwise exist. A constitution with clearly defined boundaries to power, and provisions restraining one institution from exercising the power of another, is one in conformity with the doctrine of separation of powers. This arrangement is most readily achievable under a written constitution, although it is arguable whether, under any constitution, a pure separation of powers is possible, or indeed desirable, a point which will be returned to later. At the other end of the spectrum of constitutional arrangements from a nearly 'pure' separation of powers is a totalitarian state or a purely monarchical state. Under such a constitution will be found a single figure, or single body, possessed with the sole power to propose and enact law, to administer the state, and both to apply and to adjudicate upon the law.

Under the largely unwritten constitution of the United Kingdom, the separation of powers is difficult to ascertain and evaluate. There is undeniably a distinct legislative body, executive, and judiciary, each exercising differing powers. On further examination, however, it will be found that, in practice, there are so many exceptions to the 'pure' doctrine that the significance of separation of

25 The phrase 'Westminster Parliament' refers to the United Kingdom Parliament. Westminster is the geographical area in which parliament is sited.
26 The Northern Ireland Act 2000 temporarily suspended the operation of the Northern Ireland Assembly and Executive. See further Chapter 12.
27 384–323 BC; see *The Politics*.
28 Locke, 'Second treatise of civil government', 1690, Chapter XII, para 143; Bolingbroke, 1748; Montesquieu, 1748, Bk XI.
29 See Vile, 1967, Chapter IV.

powers is called into question. Suffice to say at this introductory stage that it is a doctrine which is respected under the constitution, despite many apparent anomalies.

Republican and monarchical constitutions

A republic is a state having as its figurehead a (usually) democratically elected President, answerable to the electorate and to the constitution. Presidential office is both a symbol of statehood and the repository of many powers. In the name of the state, the President will enter into treaties, make declarations of war, and represent the state on formal international and domestic occasions. Additionally, as with the President of the United States of America, the President has responsibility for proposing legislation to give effect to the political programme which gave him the mandate of the people. The President, however, has no formal power to initiate legislation, and it is the Congress of the United States which will ultimately determine the acceptability of legislative proposals. It may well be that the elected President is from a different political party than that which dominates Congress.[30] When that political situation pertains, the prospect of successful implementation of Presidential election promises is weakened, and although the President has a veto power over legislation passed by Congress, that veto can be overridden by Congress voting with a two-thirds majority.

Looking at the United Kingdom as an example of a sophisticated Western democracy based on constitutional monarchy, the position of the head of state is very different.[31] Queen Elizabeth II is the head of state, and all acts of government are undertaken in the name of the Crown. This statement implies that great power is accorded to the Queen. In reality, however, and with the exception of important residual powers, this is not the case. As with the President of the United States of America, the Queen is the figurehead – the symbol of nationhood – on a domestic and international level. The Crown also represents the continuity of the state. From an historical constitutional viewpoint, it matters little which leader of which political party at any one time occupies the office of Prime Minister, or whether he or she is a Labour or Conservative Prime Minister, for he or she will be exercising all powers in the Queen's name. Unlike the position of the head of state under the United States' constitution, however, the Queen is, by definition, unelected and unaccountable to the electorate in any democratic sense. The Crown enjoys enormous legal-theoretical power but little practical power, save in exceptional circumstances.

The legal powers held by the Crown are, for the most part,[32] exercised in her name by the elected government of the day. The rules which restrict the monarch's powers are for the most part non-legal. The restrictions comprise the all-important conventional rules of constitutional practice which regulate so much of the United Kingdom's constitution. Thus, for example, the Crown has the legal

---

30 As was the position under President Clinton (Democrat) and Congress (Republican).
31 See Chapter 10.
32 See, however, Chapter 6 for discussion of the circumstances under which this theoretical power may become real power.

power to withhold royal assent from Bills passed by parliament but, by convention, this assent will never be withheld (and has not been withheld since 1708) unless so advised by the government.

In addition to representing the symbolic figurehead, the role of the Crown may be said to be protective. The Queen, it has been said, has the power to 'warn and advise' the Prime Minister of the day.[33] Queen Elizabeth II, since her accession in 1952, has seen many Prime Ministers, both Conservative and Labour, enter and leave office. Throughout that 54 year reign, the Queen has quietly influenced government,[34] and garnered vast experience in domestic, international and particularly Commonwealth affairs. That experience represents a wealth of knowledge at the disposal of the government in power. While the role of the monarchy is a matter for contemporary debate, the continuity and longevity of monarchy remains a distinguishing feature of the United Kingdom's constitution.

CHARACTERISTICS OF THE
UNITED KINGDOM'S CONSTITUTION

From the discussion of classification above, some conclusions can now be reached about the characteristics of the United Kingdom's constitution. In summary, it can be said that it:

(a) is largely unwritten in character;

(b) is flexible in nature;

(c) is supreme;

(d) is unitary in structure, but with some powers devolved to a Scottish Parliament, to a Welsh Assembly, to the Northern Ireland Assembly and to local government;

(e) exhibits mainly but not completely separated powers; and

(f) is monarchical.

Each of these features will become clearer as we examine the constitution in more detail.

THE CONSTITUTION IN FLUX

The absence of a written constitution, allied to the doctrine of parliamentary sovereignty, enables constitutional change to be brought about within the United Kingdom with the minimum of constitutional formality. The constitution has evolved in a pragmatic and gradual manner over the centuries. At the current time, however, the constitution is undergoing more major change than in previous decades. The last and greatest constitutional change occurred in 1973

---

33 Bagehot, 1867, Chapter II.
34 See Macmillan, 1961–63; Wilson, 1971.

when the United Kingdom joined the European Communities.[35] Joining the Community, which has now evolved as but one part of the wider European Union, involved not only entering into an agreement which affected the economic life of the country, but also joining a unique legal order under which rights and obligations in matters regulated by the treaties are ultimately defined and enforced by the European Court of Justice. Moreover, the Treaties on European Union mark new and significant developments within the European Union in relation to economic, monetary and political union and the evolution of common policies in relation to co-operation in judicial and policing matters, home affairs and security and foreign affairs policies.

It was the general election of 1997 which presaged further significant constitutional change. The incoming Labour government had committed itself to several constitutional reforms. Devolution of limited, but nonetheless wide ranging, law making powers to Scotland and Wales was the first issue to be addressed by the government.[36] An elected 'strategic authority' for London was also on the agenda, as was regional devolution in England. Reform of the membership of the House of Lords, the 'upper House' of the United Kingdom's bicameral parliament, has already been effected, although the ultimate role and powers of the Lords remains to be determined. The settlement reached in April 1998 with regard to Northern Ireland culminated in devolved powers to a new Northern Ireland Assembly. The government was also committed to the better protection of rights and freedoms, and in order to achieve this objective, the Human Rights Act 1998 'incorporated' rights protected under the European Convention on Human Rights into domestic law, thereby for the first time providing a 'code' of human rights The Human Rights Act marks a change in perception about freedoms and rights among the British people who, by contrast with citizens living under written constitutions and Bills of Rights, have hitherto been largely unaware of their rights and freedoms.

Further reform was effected by the Constitutional Reform Act 2005 which reforms the office of Lord Chancellor, establishes a new Supreme Court physically separated from parliament and provides for the House of Lords to elect its own speaker, an office formerly held by the Lord Chancellor. The Act is discussed further in Chapters 2 and 5.

---

35 Now European Community; see further Chapters 8 and 9.
36 On devolution to Northern Ireland, Scotland and Wales, see Chapter 12.

CHAPTER 2

SOURCES OF THE CONSTITUTION

As has been seen in Chapter 1, the United Kingdom's constitution is classified as 'unwritten'. However, while there is no single constituent document, many constitutional sources are of a written nature, albeit not conveniently compiled within any one document. In order to give meaning to the constitution as a whole, it is necessary to study the many fundamental documents, statutes and cases together with the non-legal conventional rules which surround and give meaning to the legal rules. In undertaking this exercise, it must be remembered that what is being sought is not a rote-learned catalogue of sources, but rather a broad appreciation of the constituent elements of the constitution.

DEFINITIONAL DIFFICULTIES

Defining the scope of sources which are correctly labelled 'constitutional' under an unwritten constitution is an inherently difficult exercise. Were the United Kingdom to have a written constitution, all of the rules now contained within various sources would be contained within it. By this means, a clear picture would be obtained as to those rules which the framers of the constitution regarded as being of 'constitutional importance'. In the absence of such a document, matters are less clear-cut and doubt exists as to precisely which rules – statutory, common law or conventional – are correctly defined as 'constitutional' rules. As Geoffrey Marshall explains:

> [N]o easy logical limit can be set to the labour of the constitutional lawyers ... any branch of the law, whether it deals *prima facie* with finance or crime or local government, may throw up constitutional questions. [1971, p 6]

The disadvantage of such a lack of precision may be illustrated in relation to the legal protection of civil liberties and human rights before the Human Rights Act 1998. Hitherto, in the United Kingdom, having neither a domestically enforceable Bill of Rights nor a written constitution, doubts as to such sensitive matters had been resolvable under an application under the European Convention on Human Rights.[1] However, because Convention rights were not enforceable in the domestic courts until the Human Rights Act 1998, no local court could provide a remedy for alleged abuses of rights unless statute or common law provided a remedy. As a result, an individual citizen seeking to discover precisely what legal rights he or she had was obliged to scrutinise the statute book, the text of the European Convention on Human Rights, and case law. The Human Rights Act 1998 remedied this deficiency by conferring jurisdiction on domestic courts of law to rule on Convention rights.

---

1   See Chapter 19.

It is even more difficult, in the absence of a written constitution, for the citizen to discern, at a conceptual level, precisely what is and what is not a 'constitutional issue'. As Marshall observes, all legal issues in the United Kingdom are potentially capable of being interpreted as constitutional issues. That fact is not, however, reassuring to the student of the constitution who is trying to define its scope and limits.

To illustrate this definitional difficulty, questions as to the status of many and differing statutes may be briefly examined.

Employment law

Statutes regulating relations between workers and employers define the extent to which an employee is free to withdraw his or her labour, to act in support of a dispute between him or herself and his or her employer, and to act in support of other workers in support of a dispute with employers. Such matters raise the fundamental question of the individual's right to withdraw his or her labour and the conditions under which this is lawful. Are such statutes 'constitutional' in nature?

Pornography

Also by way of illustration, in the United Kingdom, the Obscene Publications Act 1959 (as amended), an ordinary Act of Parliament having no particular 'constitutional status', provides the legal rules relating to pornographic literature. In contrast, in the United States of America, legal challenges to the availability of and access to allegedly pornographic material fall under the First Amendment to the Constitution.[2] The subject of pornography in the United States may accordingly be classified as a clearly constitutional issue, being regarded as a question of freedom of 'speech'.

Abortion

In the United Kingdom, the right to abortion is defined under the Abortion Act 1967 (as amended). In the United States of America, by contrast, the right to abortion falls under the constitutional right to privacy provisions of the constitution. The constitution of the Republic of Ireland prohibits abortion under its right to life provisions, and a recent challenge to that prohibition was launched under the guise of restrictions on equal access to information and the right to free movement to receive services under the law of the European Community.[3]

These examples are not intended to lead to an analysis of the substantive legal and constitutional issues, but rather demonstrate a very real and important point of principle. That point is that under a written constitution, a particular issue may be defined as a 'constitutional' issue. Under an unwritten constitution, matters are

---

2   *Roth v US* (1957).
3   *The Society of the Unborn Children Ireland Ltd v Grogan* (1991). See Spalin, 1992.

far less certain. Pornography and abortion are clearly regarded as constitutional matters in some jurisdictions.

There are obvious limitations to the utility of merely listing statutory and common law sources of the constitution. It is, however, important at an early stage of study to be familiar with the major statutory sources of the constitution.

LEGAL SOURCES

The Magna Carta

One starting point is the Magna Carta of 1215.[4] Historically, the Magna Carta represented a formal settlement between the Crown and the barons. The Charter represented settlement of the grievances of citizens and challenged the untrammelled powers of the King. The settlement provided for freedom of the Church, and the right of merchants to be free from exorbitant taxation. Today, the document's importance lies in its declaration of the confirmation of the liberties enjoyed by 'freemen of the realm' and their future protection, and in the protection to be given to the enjoyment of these liberties by the requirement for trial by jury:

> No freeman shall be taken or imprisoned, or be disseised of his freehold, or liberties, or free customs, or be outlawed, or exiled, or any other wise destroyed; nor will we pass upon him, nor condemn him, but by lawful judgment of his peers, or by the law of the land. We will sell to no man, we will not deny or defer to any man either justice or right. [Holt, 1965, Chapter XXIX]

While of little legal importance today – for much of the original Magna Carta has been repealed – the document has symbolic value as an early assertion of the limits of monarchical power and the rights of individuals.

The Petition of Right 1628

The Petition of Right 1628 arose as a result of *Darnel's Case* (the *Five Knights' Case*) (1627), where the defendants had been convicted and imprisoned for refusing to pay a loan imposed by King Charles I. The Petition forbade such loans, taxes and other monetary demands without the consent of parliament. The Petition, while still in force, was superseded by the Bill of Rights 1689.

The Bill of Rights 1689

The background

The Bill of Rights 1689 is of greater contemporary constitutional importance than the Magna Carta and the Petition of Right. The source of the Bill of Rights lies, in large measure, in the tensions between Roman Catholicism and the state, originating with the conflict between the Holy See of Rome and Henry VIII (1509–47). The Succession Act, Act of Supremacy and the Treason Act 1534 had

---

4   Magna Carta, Statute 25 Edw I (1297). See Holt, 1965.

established the supremacy of the King as head of the Church of England and destroyed formal papal authority in England. Catholicism did not die out, but over the next 150 years, suspicion and fear of 'popery' remained high at a public level. The death of Charles II in 1685 heralded the succession of James II, an avowed Roman Catholic, who nevertheless publicly declared himself bound 'to preserve this government both in Church and state as it is now by law established'.[5] Despite such assurances, in subsequent years James II strove to remove discrimination against Catholics and to place Catholics in prominent public administrative offices at both central and local level. Prominent Anglicans, dismayed by James's promotion of Catholicism, entered into negotiations with William of Orange, the Protestant husband of James's daughter Mary, with a view to their seizing the throne. In the absence of a male heir, Mary was next in line to the English Crown. However, in 1688, James's wife gave birth to a son, thus providing a Catholic heir. In July of that year, James dissolved parliament. William of Orange landed in England with his army on 5 November 1688 and James II fled the country, landing in France in December 1688.

The 'Convention' parliament

William summoned an assembly of peers, previous Members of Parliament and aldermen of London. William, not yet king, had no legal power to summon the assembly, and the assembly itself had no legal powers. The assembly advised Prince William to summon a Convention of peers and commoners. The Convention, meeting in January 1689, declared that James II had subverted the constitution and abdicated and that, accordingly, the throne was 'vacant'. The House of Lords subsequently agreed with the Convention, and on 13 February 1689, the Crown was offered to William and Mary. The Convention then proceeded to declare itself to be the parliament of England. The parliament had no authority to issue such a declaration: the only lawful manner in which a parliament can come into being is by Writ of Summons from the Crown, and it is for this reason that the Convention parliament is widely regarded as having no law making powers:

> ... it is difficult for a lawyer to regard the Convention Parliament as a lawfully constituted assembly. By whom was it summoned? Not by a king of England, but by a Prince of Orange. Even if we go back three centuries, we find no precedent ... If, when the Convention met, it was no Parliament, its own act could not turn it into a Parliament. The act which declares it to be a Parliament depends for its validity on the assent of William and Mary. The validity of that assent depends on their being king and queen; but how do they come to be king and queen? Indeed, this statute very forcibly brings out the difficulty – an incurable defect. [Maitland, 1908, pp 284–85]

Nevertheless, the Convention parliament passed the Bill of Rights, which incorporated the Declaration of Right which set out the terms under which the Crown was offered to William and Mary. The Convention parliament continued in being until 1690 when a new parliament, correctly summoned by the Crown, met.

---

5   Quoted in Lockyer, 1985, p 351.

William and Mary's accession was not to be unconditional.[6] The Declaration of Right sought to resolve the actual and potential tensions between Crown and parliament, Church and state. The terms of the Bill of Rights marked a sharp alteration in the balance of power between Crown and parliament – in parliament's favour.[7]

The substance of the Bill of Rights

The principal provisions of contemporary importance are:

Article I	the pretended power of suspending ... or executing laws by the Crown without parliamentary consent is illegal;
Article IV	the levying of money for use of the Crown under the prerogative without parliamentary consent is illegal;
Article VI	the raising or keeping of an army in peacetime without parliamentary consent is illegal;
Article VIII	elections of Members of Parliament ought to be free;
Article IX	freedom of speech and debates in proceedings in parliament ought not to be impeached or questioned in any court or place out of parliament;
Article X	excessive bail ought not to be required, nor excessive fines imposed, nor cruel and unusual punishments inflicted;
Article XI	jury trial is available; and
Article XIII	for the redress of grievances, parliament ought to meet frequently.

Subsequent to the Bill of Rights – and to give effect to its provisions – the Crown and Parliament Recognition Act 1689 gave statutory force to the Bill of Rights, and the Meeting of Parliament Act 1694 provided that parliament must be summoned to meet at least once in three years.

The Act of Settlement 1700

The Act of Settlement 1700 clarified the line of succession to the throne. The Act also provided for security of tenure for the judiciary 'during good behaviour',[8] thus ending the power of the Crown to dismiss judges at will. In relation to succession to the throne, the Act tied the succession to Protestant heirs, thus prohibiting accession to the throne by persons who are Roman Catholics, or who marry a Roman Catholic.

The Treaty of Union 1706

The Treaty of Union also has enduring constitutional effect. The Treaty united England and Scotland under a single parliament of Great Britain. Prior to the

6   As had been that of Charles II in 1660.
7   In Scotland, the Claim of Right 1689.
8   On the independence of the judiciary, see Chapter 4.

Treaty, each country enjoyed independent sovereign status. Scotland had its own parliament and its own system of private law. Decades earlier, James VI, King of Scotland and subsequently King of England (as James I (1603–25)), had attempted but failed to bring about a union between Scotland and England. By the late seventeenth century, negotiations were continuing with a view to ending the historical conflicts between the two countries,[9] and the Treaty of Union represented the culmination of this process. See further Chapter 7.

The major provisions of the Treaty of Union 1706

For current purposes, the most important provisions are as follows:

Article I	that the two kingdoms of England and Scotland shall be united in one kingdom by the name of Great Britain;
Article II	that succession to the united throne be according to the Act of Settlement 1700;
Article III	that there be a single parliament;
Article XVIII	that no alteration be made in laws which concern Scottish private rights except for the evident utility of the subjects; and
Article XIX	that the Court of Session in Scotland remain 'in all time being as now constituted', and that lower courts remain subject to alteration in their powers by parliament.

The European Communities Act 1972

The European Communities Act 1972, as amended, together with the European Treaties, regulates the United Kingdom's membership of the European Union and continues to have immense significance for the constitution of the United Kingdom (see Chapters 8 and 9 and, further, below). The law of the European Union and Community represents an increasingly significant source of constitutional law. By acceding to the European Community, and subsequently the Union, the United Kingdom has undertaken the obligation to accept the law of the Union. To understand the constitutional implications of membership of the European Union, it is necessary to understand the scope of the Treaties and the law making institutions, and the manner in which laws are made and enter into force within the legal systems of the Member States. It is also necessary to understand clearly the relationship between European law and domestic law and the question of which law has supremacy should a conflict between them arise. Under the traditional doctrine of parliamentary sovereignty, the law of the United Kingdom Parliament alone has sovereign power. The perception of the European Court of Justice – the highest court of the European Union – is much different. As will be seen, the European Court has long asserted the supremacy of Community law[10] over the laws of Member States, thus providing a fertile source for constitutional speculation about the Diceyan theory of sovereignty.

---

9   For a succinct account of the history, see Maitland, 1908, pp 331–32.
10   *Costa v ENEL* (1964).

The royal prerogative

The prerogative powers of the Crown are those powers which arise out of the common law and which are unique to the Crown. Two definitions may be given by way of introduction. To Dicey, the prerogative powers were 'the residue of arbitrary and discretionary powers legally left in the hands of the Crown' which, being exercised by the government in the name of the Crown, entails 'every act which the executive government can do without the authority of an Act of Parliament' (1885, p 425).

Blackstone, in his *Commentaries*, offers a more limited definition:

... that special pre-eminence which the King hath over and above all persons, and out of the ordinary course of the common law ... And ... only applied to those rights and capacities which the King enjoys in contradistinction to others.

The prerogative will be discussed in detail in Chapter 6.

Acts establishing devolution

The Acts establishing a Scottish Parliament and Welsh Assembly and re-establishing a Northern Ireland Assembly have decentralised the process of government and law making, giving greater national autonomy to Northern Ireland, Scotland and Wales.

The Human Rights Act 1998

The Human Rights Act 1998, which incorporates the rights enshrined in the European Convention on Human Rights and Freedoms into domestic law, represents a fundamental change in the domestic protection of rights. The impact of the Human Rights Act 1998 has already been felt across wide areas of domestic law and provides citizens for the first time with a code of rights which are enforceable in the domestic courts rather than in the European Court of Human Rights in Strasbourg.

The Constitutional Reform Act 2005

The Constitutional Reform Act 2005 introduces changes in three principal areas. The Act reforms the office of Lord Chancellor, transferring his powers as head of the judiciary to the Lord Chief Justice and providing for the House of Lords to elect its own speaker. In addition the Appellate Committee of the House of Lords is to be removed to a location separate from parliament and is to be renamed the Supreme Court.

Further illustrations

Further statutes of major constitutional importance – and the list is by no means exhaustive – include the following:

(a) the Statute of Westminster 1931 gave statutory force to the conventions regulating relations between the sovereign United Kingdom Parliament and legislatures of the Dominions;

(b) His Majesty's Declaration of Abdication Act 1936 varied the succession to the throne established under the Act of Settlement 1700;

(c) the Regency Acts 1937–53 provided that if the Sovereign is under the age of 18, regal powers shall be exercised through a Regent appointed under the Acts;

(d) the Royal Titles Act 1953, which founded a challenge from Scottish lawyers to its compatibility with the Act of Union,[11] provided that the Sovereign may by Proclamation adopt such a style and titles as she may think fit;

(e) the Treaty of Union with Ireland Act 1800, the Government of Ireland Act 1920, the Ireland Act 1949 and the Northern Ireland Constitution Act 1973 have all reflected the changing constitutional relationship between Ireland, Northern Ireland and the United Kingdom.

Throughout history, the judiciary has, through case law, defined the relationship between the institutions of the state – the Crown, the executive, parliament and the judiciary – and defined the relationship between the state and the individual. As with statutory sources of the constitution, the entire study of constitutional and administrative law concerns the examination and analysis of judicial precedents. The relationship between the judiciary and parliament is discussed in detail in Chapter 5, but note at this introductory stage the following points. With the rise in parliamentary supremacy in the seventeenth century, the role of the judges changed significantly, and it has long been accepted that the *dictum* of Coke CJ in *Dr Bonham's Case*, to the effect that the judges could declare an Act of Parliament void, does not – if indeed it ever did[12] – represent the law. The judiciary today has no power to question the validity of an Act of Parliament.[13] However, whilst Acts of Parliament are unchallengeable as to their validity, delegated or secondary legislation is not immune from such review. Furthermore, the judges have the power to review the legality of acts of persons and organisations acting under powers conferred by Act of Parliament in order to ensure that they act *intra vires* the powers conferred by parliament. Note also that, in relation to the conduct of its business, parliament claims many privileges and immunities. As will be seen, judicial deference to parliament extends to the judges declining jurisdiction over any matter of parliamentary privilege, other than to rule whether or not a matter is in fact a matter of privilege. Article IX of the Bill of Rights 1689 confers the absolute privilege of freedom of speech in parliamentary proceedings. Accordingly, a Member of Parliament is free from any threat from the law of defamation by any person harmed by his exercise of free speech.[14]

The extent to which judges have been able to protect individual rights under the common law has – in the light of parliament's supremacy – been limited. Traditionally, the United Kingdom had no Bill of Rights in so far as such a document provides a written source of protection for certain fundamental rights

---

11 *MacCormick v Lord Advocate* (1953). See further Chapter 7.
12 See Plucknett, 1926; Thorne, 1938.
13 *Edinburgh and Dalkeith Railway v Wauchope* (1842); *Pickin v British Railways Board* (1974). But see Chapters 7 and 9 on the position in relation to the law of the European Community.
14 See *Church of Scientology of California v Johnson-Smith* (1972); Mummery, 1978; Leopold, 1981.

and freedoms. In the absence of such guaranteed protection – protection which would prevail even against an Act of Parliament – the citizen remained dependent either upon ad hoc statutory provisions – such as the Habeas Corpus Acts (1679, 1816, 1862), the Race Relations Act 1976 or the Sex Discrimination Act 1975 – or upon judicial protection under the common law (see Chapters 19–22). By way of introductory illustration, the contrasting cases of *Entick v Carrington* (1765) and *Liversidge v Anderson* (1942) may be cited. In the former case, the court ruled that a general warrant issued by a Home Secretary for the entry into private property and seizure of allegedly seditious material was contrary to law and amounted to a trespass to property. This bold assertion of judicial power to rule on the legality of acts of the executive and to control such acts is in stark contrast to the ruling in *Liversidge v Anderson*. Here, in the context of a challenge to the legality of detention without warrant under the order of the Home Secretary, the House of Lords held that the courts could not, in times of emergency, review the Home Secretary's belief that detention was justified. Such conflicting outcomes demonstrate that reliance on judicial protection from executive action, under common law, is by no means certain, let alone guaranteed. The Human Rights Act 1998, however, now enables citizens to challenge the legality of government action against the provisions of the Convention. As will be discussed in Chapter 19, the Act does not empower the courts to challenge the validity of Acts of Parliament, but rather preserves parliament's traditional sovereignty by empowering the courts to make declarations of incompatibility between a statute and Convention requirements. Thereafter, it is for the government and parliament to change the law if it wishes to comply with the Convention requirements.

NON-LEGAL SOURCES OF THE CONSTITUTION

Constitutional conventions

> The short explanation of the constitutional conventions is that they provide the flesh which clothes the dry bones of the law; they make the legal constitution work; they keep it in touch with the growth of ideas.[15]

Constitutional conventions form the most significant class of non-legal constitutional rules.[16] A clear understanding of their nature, scope and manner of application is essential to the study of the United Kingdom's constitution. Conventions supplement the legal rules of the constitution and define the practices of the constitution. Conventions, as Jennings states, 'provide the flesh which clothes the dry bones of the law' and represent the 'unwritten maxims' of the constitution. Conventions apply to virtually all aspects of the constitution, and for this reason it is, in part, unrealistic and unsatisfactory to attempt adequately to consider their role in a 'vacuum'. Nevertheless, given their central importance,

---

15 Jennings, 1959a, pp 81–82.
16 See, *inter alia*, Dicey, 1885, Chapter 14; Jennings, 1959a, Chapter 3; Marshall and Moodie, 1971, Chapter 2; Marshall, 1984, esp Chapters 1 and 13; Munro, 1999, Chapter 3.

conventions must be considered at this early stage, while bearing in mind that many and varied further illustrations will emerge throughout the course of study.

Conventions defined

Conventions are defined by AV Dicey as:

> ... conventions, understandings, habits or practices which, though they may regulate the ... conduct of the several members of the sovereign power ... are not in reality laws at all since they are not enforced by the courts. [1885, p clii]

Marshall and Moodie offer an alternative definition:

> ... rules of constitutional behaviour which are considered to be binding by and upon those who operate the constitution but which are not enforced by the law courts ... nor by the presiding officers in the Houses of Parliament. [1971, pp 23–24]

A number of important questions arise concerning these non-legal rules, namely:

(a) What are the characteristics of a conventional rule?

(b) What is the source or origin of the rule?

(c) In what manner are conventions distinguishable from laws?

(d) Who is bound by the conventional rules?

(e) What is the consequence of a breach of the rule?

(f) Does the distinction between law and convention really matter?

(g) What is the attitude of the courts to conventional rules?

(h) How do conventions change?

(i) How best can these rules be analysed and understood?

(j) Should conventions be codified?

Each of these questions, many of which overlap, must be addressed and answered.

Conventions illustrated

Before turning attention to the task of further analysis, some examples of constitutional conventions will aid understanding. Each of these conventions will be discussed in greater detail later in this book. The number given at the end of each paragraph indicates which chapter should be referred to for further detail:

(a) Acts of Parliament are technically enacted by the Queen in Parliament – the Crown, Commons and Lords. The Queen has the legal right to refuse to give royal assent to Bills passed by the House of Commons and Lords. By convention, the Queen must assent to such Bills unless advised to the contrary by her government (6);

(b) the Queen will appoint as Prime Minister the leader of the political party with the majority of seats in the House of Commons (6);

(c) the Prime Minister must be a member of the House of Commons (6);

(d) the government must maintain the confidence of the House of Commons. If a 'vote of confidence' on a matter central to government policy is lost, the government must resign or advise the Queen to dissolve parliament (6);

(e) the Crown exercises its right to dissolve parliament on the advice of ministers *(6)*;

(f) ministers of the Crown are individually and collectively responsible to parliament *(11)*;

(g) ministers must be members of either the House of Commons or the House of Lords *(10)*;

(h) parliament must be summoned to meet at least once a year *(14)*;

(i) judges shall not play an active part in political life *(5)*;

(j) Members of Parliament shall not criticise the judiciary *(5)*;

(k) the opinion of the law officers of the Crown is confidential *(11)*.

This list is not intended to be exhaustive, but is sufficient to give a flavour of the nature and scope of constitutional conventions.

The binding nature of conventions

The characteristics of conventions are suggested both by Dicey and by Marshall and Moodie. The latter authors correctly introduce the concept of a 'rule', and it is this concept which is central to our understanding and which requires further analysis. What is a rule? A rule may be defined as a statement prescribing the conduct which is required in a given situation and which imposes an obligation on those who are regulated by the rule.[17] The idea of obligation is of prime importance here, for if a person is under an obligation which is recognised by observers of the constitution, and that person fails to act in accordance with the obligation, then that failure will give rise to legitimate criticism which will invariably be phrased in terms of 'constitutionality'. To reiterate, the obligation imposes a standard of conduct which is expected to be followed. The obligation is 'normative': by that is meant that the rule is 'prescriptive' – that it dictates the appropriate form of action in a particular situation. As Sir Ivor Jennings states, conventions 'not only are followed but have to be followed' (1959a, p 2).

Dicey's definition suggests that conventions are of the same quality as 'understandings, habits or practices'. This view is inaccurate in so far as none of these words conveys the idea of obligation – the normative (or prescriptive) – the idea of what ought to be done in particular circumstances.

Conventions distinguished from habits

Conventions are conceptually different from 'habits' or 'practices' in that these concepts do not prescribe or dictate what ought to happen but are merely descriptive of what in fact does happen. To offer a simple but possibly outdated example, consider the statement that 'the English drink tea in the afternoon'. Drinking tea is a habit: the statement is simply reflective of actual observable conduct. There is nothing in the statement which requires that conduct, or which states that it ought to happen. Accordingly, it is a descriptive and not a normative statement. If the English fail to drink tea in the afternoon, or drink coffee instead,

---

17 Hart, 1961, pp 79–88.

that action is not going to give rise to any criticism because a mere habit imposes no obligation. The observation is a statement of what 'is', and not what 'ought to be'. There is no obligation imposed on the English to drink tea and hence no criticism will follow from failure to do so. It is very different with a breach of a constitutional convention, which will invariably give rise to adverse criticism. Conventions are thus distinguishable from habits.

Conventions distinguished from understandings

To what extent is Dicey correct in equating conventions with 'understandings'? Once more, it is helpful to resort to definitions. The word 'understanding' connotes a mutual agreement between relevant actors as to the pertinent subject matter, or the manner in which it is appropriate to respond or react to a given situation. As such, any understanding rests on a meeting of minds, and is capable of being the subject of *mis*understanding, as in cases where the actors, through a lack of understanding of the situation (or as a result of a differing interpretation of the situation), fail to be 'of one mind'. An 'understanding' may well be relied on by the parties, as are conventions. Understandings may also be brought about by some form of previous, or precedent, conduct or mutual recognition: but this is not a prerequisite for their existence or nature. Most importantly, an understanding, while imposing some weak form of moral obligation will not, in the case of failure to comply with its terms, give rise to a sanction in the form of criticism of the same magnitude as that of a breach of a constitutional convention. The explanation for this lies in the fact that an understanding – as opposed to a convention – does not amount to a rule, and accordingly is not obligation-imposing to the same degree as a convention.

Conventions distinguished from practices

The concept of a practice remains for consideration. A practice may be defined as being 'a usual or customary action or proceeding'.[18] A practice, therefore, is the normal manner in which a person or body will react to a factual situation on the basis of some precedent form of conduct. In everyday life – whether in commercial offices or in the professions of medicine or law – it is a commonplace assertion that 'it is our practice to do ...'. That statement conveys the message that past experience of doing something in a particular way is the correct way of proceeding, and that – unless there are justifiable reasons for not so doing – the practice will be adhered to. A practice, therefore, may be distinguished from a mere habit on the basis that it imports a notion of reflectiveness, the idea of the 'right' way of reacting to a situation. How, then, is a practice distinguishable from a convention? The borderline between the two is admittedly fine. It may be, however, that the correct dividing line is drawn on the basis of the concept of obligation and rule, and that it is legitimate to argue that whilst a practice imposes some form of weak obligation – and requires some justification for departure from the practice – the practice is no more than an emergent or potential convention and has not yet acquired the binding characteristic of a rule.

---

18 *Collins' English Dictionary.*

Conventions distinguished from laws

Conventions are distinguishable from laws in a number of important respects. First, the source of a legal rule is, for the most part, identifiable and certain. In searching for a legal rule, its source will normally be found within a judicial decision or within an Act of Parliament. Conventions are far less certain in their origins, and it may at times be difficult to see whether a particular form of conduct is, for example, one of practice or convention. Secondly, the core content of a legal rule will generally have a settled meaning. One often-cited example illustrates the point. In Chapter VII of *The Concept of Law*, Professor HLA Hart offers the example of the correct interpretation of the word 'vehicle' in a statute or delegated legislation (for example, in local authority bylaws). A judge, interpreting the word within the context of a trial concerning an alleged violation of a bylaw prohibiting the use of vehicles in a public park, will be clear, for example, that a motor car, van or armoured truck will fall within the meaning of the word 'vehicle'. But what of a skateboard or its successor, rollerblades? A skateboard shares some of the characteristics of the other examples given: a skateboard is a wheeled object and capable of conveying a person from point A to point B. Is it then a 'vehicle'? Professor Hart makes two important points here. The first point is that to make sense of the word 'vehicle', the word must be placed within its broader context. That is to say, the question must be asked: 'For what purpose was the rule devised?' In other words, can the judge provide an interpretation which is meaningful within the context of the legislature's intention?

The second point, of greater significance to this discussion, is that most words – legal or non-legal – have a 'core of certainty and penumbra of doubt', and that while a motorised wheeled object designed for the carriage of persons and goods is clearly a vehicle, an object designed for purely recreational purposes may, or may not, subject to the court's interpretation of the purpose of the legislation, fall within the meaning of a particular word.

The foregoing discussion can be presented – albeit with recognition of overlaps between, and ambiguities in, the concepts – in the following tabular form:

	Habits	Understandings	Practices	Conventions	Laws
Regularity of conduct	yes	not necessarily	yes	yes	yes
Reflectiveness	no	yes	yes	yes	yes
Degree of obligation imposed	none	weak	strong	absolute	absolute
Sanction attending breach	none	justification required	justification required	charge of unconstitutional conduct	unlawful conduct

Summary of the meaning of constitutional conventions

A constitutional convention is a non-legal rule which imposes an obligation on those bound by the convention, breach or violation of which will give rise to legitimate criticism; and that criticism will generally take the form of an accusation of 'unconstitutional conduct'.

The source of conventions

The question concerning the source of the constitutional convention is in part interwoven with the characteristics of the convention. A conventional rule may be said to exist when a traditional practice has been consciously adopted and recognised by those who operate the constitution as the correct manner in which to act in a given circumstance. A practice will be seen to have become a convention at the point at which failure to act in accordance with it gives rise to legitimate criticism.

Sir Ivor Jennings once suggested that three questions must be asked in order to determine whether a convention exists. First, are there any precedents for the convention? 'Mere practice,' he tells us, 'is not enough. The fact that an authority has always behaved in a certain way is no warrant for saying that it ought to behave in that way.' What more, then, is required? According to Jennings, that turns on the normativity of the practice:

> ... if the authority itself and those connected with it believe that they ought to do so [behave in a certain way], then the convention does exist ... Practice alone is not enough. It must be normative. [1959a, p 135]

Finally, Jennings argues that neither practice nor precedent is sufficient. In addition, there must be a reason for the rule: '... the creation of a convention must be due to the reason of the thing because it accords with the prevailing political philosophy.' This point is supported by JP Mackintosh. Accepting Viscount Esher's view that 'precedent, like analogy, is rarely conclusive' (1915, p 167), Mackintosh argues that precedents have 'no independent existence or validity'. Rather, the precedent represents 'a correct decision or action in certain political circumstances'. Accordingly:

> ... searching for a precedent is really looking for a case where previous exponents of the constitution have solved a similar difficulty in an approved fashion. [Mackintosh, 1977, p 13]

Situations will arise for which there is no apparent precedent and where accordingly there is no firm convention regulating a situation. Mackintosh illustrates this phenomenon by reference to the dilemma in which George V found himself in 1923 when the general election failed to produce a clear majority for any one party, and thus left the King with a real choice as to who should be appointed Prime Minister:

> ... the King noted that 'there are really no precedents for the present situation. I must use my own judgment as each case arises'. [1977, p 13]

Whether the outcome is deemed to be correct or not will depend on the acceptability of that action in light of current political practice.

With this brief discussion in mind, it can be said that, while the meaning and scope of conventions frequently display a lack of certainty, it does not necessarily follow that this is a conclusively distinguishing characteristic from rules of law which may also display uncertainty as to their meaning. Nonetheless, it must be conceded that the requirements of some conventional rules are often difficult to discern. Sir Ivor Jennings cites Mr Stanley Baldwin, Prime Minister during the periods 1912–24, 1924–29 and 1935–37:

> The historian can tell you probably perfectly clearly what the constitutional practice was at any given period in the past, but it would be very difficult for a living writer to tell you at any given period in his lifetime what the constitution of the country is in all respects, and for this reason, that almost at any given moment ... there maybe one practice called 'constitutional' which is falling into desuetude and there may be another practice which is creeping into use but is not yet constitutional. [1959a, p 12]

The effects of breaching constitutional conventions

The question of consequences that flow from a breach of a conventional rule constitutes both a simple and a complex issue. If – as a starting point for discussion – the consequence of breaking a rule of law is examined, two basic points must be recognised. The first point is that a breach of law normally, but not invariably, leads to enforcement of the rule by the courts. The second point is that when a rule of law is breached, the rule remains valid and in force, unless repealed by parliament or overruled by the judges. With conventional rules, the situation is very different. Being non-legal rules, there is no question of a breach of convention being enforced by the courts: the courts do not have the jurisdiction to enforce conventional rules, although they may give recognition to them.[19] However, it is also the case, as Dicey argued, that breach of a convention may lead to a breach of law. The most often cited example offered is that if parliament, in breach of convention, did not meet annually, the consequence would be that money granted on an annual basis by parliament for the maintenance of the armed forces would not be forthcoming. Accordingly, maintenance of the army would become unlawful by virtue of Article VI of the Bill of Rights 1689, which provides that the raising and keeping of an army in peacetime, without parliament's consent, is unlawful. Such consequences are the exception. For the most part, the consequence of violating a conventional rule is political rather than legal.

That said, it is not possible to offer a single consequence. Much will turn on the particular convention 'broken', the extent of the 'breach' and the political mood of the country at the time. Conventions are obeyed because of the potential political difficulties which would arise if a firmly established convention was departed from without constitutional justification.

Two introductory illustrations of the very differing effects of breaching conventional rules are provided by the doctrine of collective ministerial responsibility and the House of Lords.[20]

---

19 *Attorney General v Jonathan Cape Ltd* (1976); *Manuel v Attorney General* (1983).
20 Discussed more fully in Chapters 11 and 17, respectively.

Collective ministerial responsibility

The doctrine of collective ministerial responsibility provides an example of the uncertainties entailed in the scope and binding nature of conventional rules. In two situations the doctrine has been 'waived' in order to respond effectively to political circumstances. In 1932, a coalition government was in office.[21] Following Cabinet disagreements over economic policy, the government adopted an 'agreement to differ', whereby members of Cabinet were free to express their divergent views both in parliament and in public. Within months, the dissident members resigned from the Cabinet and collective responsibility was reinstated. In 1975, the Labour government was divided as to the benefits of continued membership of the European Community. It was decided that the matter should be put to the electorate in a referendum. The Cabinet itself was deeply divided on the question and the Prime Minister decided to 'lift' the convention of collective responsibility in order to facilitate full and free public debate. Thus, a convention was set aside for a particular purpose, for a defined period of time and for a specific matter. The convention remained effective in respect of other matters before the Cabinet, and upon resolution of the issue, the convention was fully reinstated.[22] No adverse political consequences flowed from this, despite criticisms that such a move was unconstitutional. It is arguable whether this action represented a breach of convention at all, but it was clearly a departure from normal constitutional practice.[23] Above all, these situations demonstrate the point that conventions can be adjusted, under certain circumstances which are undefined, to suit the exigencies of a particular situation.

The House of Lords 1908–10

A very different consequence followed a breach of convention by the House of Lords between 1908 and 1910.[24] Prior to the Parliament Act 1911, one major conventional rule regulated the relationship between the House of Lords and the House of Commons in legislative matters and most particularly in financial matters: namely, that the Lords would ultimately give way to the will of the elected House. This convention broke down in 1908 when the House of Lords rejected the Finance Bill of the Commons. After a deadlock between the two Houses, and a threat by the King to 'flood' the House of Lords with sufficient new peers to secure a majority for the Bill, the government introduced the Parliament Bill 1911. The Parliament Act, which will be looked at in detail in Chapter 17, provided that the House of Lords would no longer enjoy equal powers to approve or reject legislative proposals and that its power would be restricted to a power to delay legislation subject to strict time limits.[25] It can be seen from this that where the breach of a convention is deemed to be sufficiently grave, parliament can – in the exercise of its sovereign power – place a convention on a statutory basis.

---

21 See Marshall, 1984, Chapter 4; and see further Chapter 11.
22 The referendum produced a vote in favour of continued membership, although the government had indicated that, in any event, it would not be bound by the result.
23 Two Cabinet ministers resigned over the 2003 Iraq war.
24 See Jennings, 1969, Chapter 12.4.
25 Money Bills, one month; non-Money Bills, two years over three parliamentary sessions.

Further illustrations will present themselves throughout the course of this book: conventional rules are of such fundamental importance that they regulate virtually every aspect of constitutional law. The main point to be understood here is that breaches of conventions have no automatic or defined ramifications.

The differing importance of individual conventions

A related factor which should also be understood is that not all conventions are of equal certainty or importance, and it is in part for this reason that the consequences of a breach will vary. For example, in legal terms, the right to assent or to refuse to assent to Bills passed by parliament rests with the Crown. However, by convention, the Crown must assent to Bills passed by parliament whenever so advised by the Prime Minister. So settled is the convention that the Crown must assent to Bills passed by parliament that it is difficult to foresee circumstances under which it would be broken.[26] Perhaps a political situation could present itself where a Bill had been duly passed by parliament and where the government had a change of heart and, despite parliamentary opposition, refused to present the Bill for assent. Would this represent a breach of convention? Arguably not, for the convention requires that the monarch give assent on the advice of her government. A situation such as this would undoubtedly cause a political furore; but it is doubtful that it would represent unconstitutional conduct on the part of the government, and still less so by the Crown. It could also be asked, speculatively, what the position would be if a Bill was duly passed by parliament, the Bill was presented for royal assent and was refused on the basis that public opinion was so firmly set against the Bill that to assent would amount to defeating the rights of the electorate. Such a situation raises some fundamental questions about democracy and the relationship between the electorate and the elected government. Geoffrey Marshall questions whether the power to refuse assent to legislation is 'now a dead letter', and states that, 'under present constitutional arrangements, it may well be so' (1984, p 22), while recognising that the issue is not closed.

At the other end of the spectrum of the certainty of conventions and their meaning, is the doctrine of individual ministerial responsibility. In essence, individual ministerial responsibility requires that ministers of the Crown are accountable to parliament, and through parliament to the electorate, for their personal conduct and for the conduct of their departments.[27] The doctrine is expressed in practical terms at Parliamentary Question Time, in debates, and in committee proceedings, whereby parliament ensures that ministers explain and, if necessary, defend their actions.[28] In theory, if a minister's personal conduct falls below the high standard required of public figures, he or she should resign. Equally, if the government department under a minister's authority is found to have misused or mismanaged its powers, it is the minister who takes the responsibility in parliament. If the matter is of sufficient gravity and the minister loses the support of his party and Prime Minister, he or she may be forced to

---

26   See Marshall, 1984, p 22.
27   See Chapter 10.
28   See Chapter 16.

resign. But, as with responsibility for personal conduct, there are no hard and fast rules. There exist no fixed criteria from which it can be predicted in advance the consequence which will flow from a breach of convention. In terms of consequences, this convention is the most uncertain of all conventional rules.

Evolution and change

Implicit in the above discussion lies the answer to a further question: how do conventions change? It has been seen that conventions come into being, unlike legal rules, when a habit or practice becomes so established that it imposes obligations on those to whom it applies, and takes on the characteristics of a rule. And so it is with changes in conventions. A convention may change with changing circumstances: individual ministerial responsibility is a prime example of this feature of conventions. Conventions may adapt to meet particular needs, as with collective responsibility in relation to the European Community in 1975, discussed above. Conventions may be breached and placed on a statutory basis, as with the House of Lords in 1911. A legal rule has a relatively fixed and certain quality while in existence. If a legal rule is changed, either by judicial decision or by parliament, the previous rule will be superseded by the new: it will 'go out with a bang'. The same cannot be said of conventions. For the most part, they evolve, adapt in amoeba-like fashion to meet the constitutional needs of the time. It is for this reason that they present the student of the constitution with such a fascinating challenge.

The courts and conventions

Given that conventional rules are non-legal rules, the attitude of the courts towards constitutional conventions is inevitably different from their attitude to legal rules. The courts do not have jurisdiction to adjudicate upon conventions. This is not to say that a court must take no cognisance of conventional rules, but rather, as Dicey asserted, conventions are not 'court enforceable'. The courts will give recognition to conventions, although they are rarely called upon to do so. Two cases are illustrative. The first is that of *Attorney General v Jonathan Cape Ltd* (1976). In 1976, the executors of the late Richard Crossman, a former Cabinet minister, decided to proceed with publication of the diaries he had kept while in government. The diaries included records of Cabinet discussions which, under the doctrine of collective ministerial responsibility, may never be revealed other than under the conditions specified by law or on the authority of the Cabinet Secretary. The government sought an injunction to restrain publication on the basis that Cabinet meetings are, by convention, confidential and that the diaries, accordingly, represented a breach of confidentiality.

This litigation required that the court recognise the convention, and it did so. However, having no jurisdiction over conventional rules, the court could not enforce the convention. The court ruled in favour of the government in relation to the doctrine of confidentiality. In the event, however, the court declined to suppress 'secrets' which were over ten years old. The court ruled that, unless national security was involved, an eight to ten year embargo was the maximum period that such material would be protected.

In 1982, in the Canadian case of *Reference re Amendment of the Constitution of Canada*, detailed consideration was given to the relationship between law and convention. The principal question for decision by the Supreme Court of Canada was whether, as a matter of law, the constitution of Canada could be amended without the consent of the Provinces. A second question was whether the consent of the Provinces was required as a matter of convention. The British North America Act 1867 created the Dominion of Canada and set out the legislative and executive powers of the provincial and federal legislatures. Amendment to the 1867 Act was possible only by a further Act of the Westminster Parliament. At that time, the Statute of Westminster 1931[29] provided, *inter alia*, that the United Kingdom Parliament would not legislate for a Dominion 'unless it is declared in that Act that that Dominion has requested, and consented to, the enactment thereof' (section 4). Section 7 of the Statute, however, prohibited changes to the British North America Act 1867, which affected the competence of provincial or federal legislatures. In 1949, the United Kingdom Parliament passed the British North America (No 2) Act, which gave substantial powers of amendment to the 1867 Act to the Canadian Federal Parliament. However, the power conferred was not absolute, and the Canadian Parliament lacked the competence to enact amendments altering the distribution of powers between the respective legislatures without the request and consent of the provincial legislatures. One of the principles intended to regulate amendments to the constitution, agreed by all the Provinces and set out in a Canadian White Paper in 1965, stated that:

> ... the Canadian Parliament will not request an amendment directly affecting federal-provincial relationships without prior consultation and agreement with the Provinces. This principle did not emerge as early as others but came in 1907, and particularly since 1930, has gained increasing recognition and acceptance. The nature and the degree of provincial participation in the amending process, however, have not lent themselves to easy definition.

It was argued by the Provinces that the 'request and consent' declaration required under the Statute of Westminster meant the 'request and consent' of both the Dominion and the Provinces if the Act were one affecting provincial or federal competence.

By a majority, the Canadian Supreme Court – adopting Jennings's test for the existence of a convention – recognised the constitutional convention that the Canadian Parliament would not request the Queen to lay before the United Kingdom Parliament an Act to amend the constitution of Canada in a manner affecting federal-provincial relationships and their respective powers and rights without first obtaining the agreement of the Provinces. Nevertheless, the court went on to hold that the Diceyan distinction between convention and law remained and that the court could not accordingly go beyond recognition of the convention and enforce it. By a majority, the Supreme Court ruled that consent of the Provinces was not required by law and, again by a majority, that consent was required by convention, but that the convention could not be enforced by a court of law. The court declared:

---

29   See further Chapter 7.

... It should be borne in mind, ... that, while they are not laws, some conventions may be more important than some laws. Their importance depends on that of the value or principle which they are meant to safeguard. Also, they form an integral part of the constitution of the constitutional system.

... constitutional conventions plus constitutional law equal the total constitution of the country.

Is the distinction between law and convention important?

Both Sir Ivor Jennings and John Mackintosh have suggested that the distinction between conventions and laws is ultimately of little significance. In *The Law and the Constitution*, Jennings asserts that:

... there is no distinction of substance or nature. The conventions are like most fundamental rules of any constitution in that they rest essentially upon general acquiescence. [1959b, p 117]

In *The British Cabinet*, John Mackintosh argues that:

There is a distinction between law and convention both from the view of the practical politician and the student of government, but in the long term development of the constitution, it is of no great importance. Both rest on the necessities of political life. Laws can be repealed or conventions changed if this is found to be desirable. The real difference between law and convention is just that there is no formal procedure for enacting or enforcing conventions, though some conventions (for example, the monarch shall not veto laws passed by both Houses; the Prime Minister shall resign if he is defeated on a major issue in the Commons) are as important as any laws and perhaps even more difficult to alter. [1977, p 12]

Such views, while having merit from a political perspective, are overly dismissive from a legal, constitutional standpoint. The significant difference between laws and conventions is well demonstrated in both *Attorney General v Jonathan Cape Ltd* (1976) and *Reference re Amendment of the Constitution of Canada* (1982).[30] In both cases, the lack of a legal remedy is explained by the strict distinction between law and convention.[31] Indeed, in the latter case, judicial approval was given to Professor Colin Munro's view that:

The validity of conventions cannot be the subject of proceedings in a court of law. Reparation for breach of such rules will not be effected by any legal sanction. There are no cases which contradict these propositions. In fact, the idea of a court enforcing a mere convention is so strange that the question hardly arises.

If, in fact, laws and conventions are different in kind, as is my argument, then an accurate and meaningful picture of the constitution may only be obtained if this distinction is made. If the distinction is blurred, analysis of the constitution is less complete; this is not only dangerous for the lawyer, but less than helpful to the political scientist. [1975, p 228]

Should conventions be codified?

One question asked earlier was whether or not constitutional conventions should be codified. Again, no straightforward or simple answer to this question presents

---

30 See also *First Report of the Foreign Affairs Committee*, HC 42 (1980–81), London: HMSO.
31 For a strong, if controversial, argument against this orthodox position, see Allan, 1986.

itself. Much will turn on the perception of the value of the status quo. Much also turns on the constitutional implications of attempting to provide a comprehensive, binding code of constitutional conventions.

The Australian experiment

In Australia, a constitutional crisis in 1975 contributed to the experiment in codification of conventions into an authoritative but non-legally binding text. The crisis involved the prerogative power of the Crown in the person of the Governor General to dismiss the Prime Minister and appoint a caretaker Prime Minister on the condition of ensuring the passage of financial legislation and the holding of a general election. One outcome of the crisis – in which the inherent vagueness of the conventional rules was revealed – was formal consideration of the 'codification' of conventions, albeit in a non-legal form. During the crisis, conventions had been 'creatively interpreted and ignored in a successful attempt to unseat the Labour government during the depths of an international recession'.[32] In 1983, a plenary session of the Constitutional Convention adopted a set of 34 practices which were to be 'recognised and declared' as conventions of the Australian constitution. Among those 'recognised' were the powers of the Crown in relation to the Governor General, and his powers in relation to the dismissal of ministers and powers over parliament, and the relationship between the Prime Minister and the Governor General in relation to the dissolution of parliament.[33]

Professor Charles Sampford analysed the merits and demerits of the codification of conventions. Among the many unanswered questions raised are the following. Under what authority did the Constitutional Convention act? What is the effect of the resolution? Is it merely declaratory of the existing rules? If there is a conflict with the restatement and actual practice, which should be authoritative? Professor Sampford contends that there exist three possibilities here. If the code is followed in preference to conventional practice, then the codification goes beyond clarification and becomes a source of the rules themselves. This raises the question 'why should the old rules and old sources give way to the new?'. The second approach is that the 'declaration' has whatever force the constitutional actors accord to it: it would be absurd if the declaration were to have no authority. Thirdly, it could be argued that the declaration is merely evidence of the rule. This latter possibility, however, is unsatisfactory in so far as the declaration was intended to be 'sole and conclusive evidence for the existence of the recognised convention. This effectively makes the Constitutional Convention a new source for conventions'. Furthermore, what is the position where a convention was agreed to only by a small majority? What then happens to its authority? To what extent will the new conventions be observed? What is the status of those pre-existing conventions which were not 'recognised and declared'? As can be seen, codification is – even if desirable – by no means a simple matter.

32 Sampford, 1987.
33 A previous convention in 1983 had adopted resolutions relating to the conventions regulating the powers of the Queen and the Governor General.

Conclusion

It is clear from the analysis thus far that conventions comprise a set of binding rules, non-legal in nature, which supplement and inform the legal rules of the constitution and which can adapt to meet changing circumstances. Viewed in that light, their primary importance lies in their flexibility. On the other hand, it may be argued cogently that for rules of such importance to be ill-defined, uncertain in application and unenforceable by the courts is, at best, anomalous, and at worst, a threat to the principle of government according to law.

Further considerations intrude upon the discussion. It has been seen that conventions are flexible. In this feature lies much of their value, and it is to be doubted whether, in relation to such a dynamic organism as the constitution, it would be possible to identify, define and formalise conventions in such a manner both to provide a comprehensive code and to allow for subsequent constitutional development. It may prove to be the case that codification would stultify the growth of the constitution. On the other hand, such codification would undoubtedly provide greater insight into the rules regulating government and thereby act as some check on the power of government. Professor SA de Smith[34] states that codification of conventions would purchase certainty at the expense of flexibility, and this point must carry great weight in evaluating the desirability of codification.

The relationship between the government and the courts must also be weighed in the balance in this regard. It has been seen that the courts give recognition to, but cannot enforce, conventions. If the effect of codification were to give jurisdiction to the courts, this would represent a very real and problematic shift in the balance of authority and power between the government and the courts. In Chapter 5, the doctrine of the separation of powers is considered in detail. Enough has been said by way of introduction for it to be apparent that if the courts were to be given jurisdiction to adjudicate upon and enforce, by way of legal sanction, the conventional rules of the constitution, this would impinge greatly upon the concept of the separation of powers.

For these reasons, the loss of flexibility and the separation of powers doctrine, it can be argued that conventions should not be codified.

Authoritative works

Finally and in brief, mention should be made of the writings of eminent jurists such as Blackstone, Dicey, Jennings and later commentators to whose works the actors on the constitutional stage, including the judges, may make reference for elucidation of matters of constitutional law.

---

34   de Smith and Brazier, 1998, Chapter 2.

CHAPTER 3

EVOLUTION OF THE STRUCTURE
OF THE UNITED KINGDOM

The United Kingdom comprises England, Wales, Scotland (which together comprise Great Britain) and Northern Ireland.[1] The Channel Islands and the Isle of Man, while not forming part of the United Kingdom other than for the purposes of nationality law,[2] are represented by the United Kingdom government in international affairs.

While it is correct to speak of the constitution of the United Kingdom, it should not be assumed that there is a single legal system within the constitutionally defined area. The English legal system extends to England and Wales. Scotland has its own system of private law which is distinct from English law. Equally, in Northern Ireland, there exists a quite distinct legal system. Nevertheless, it is the Westminster Parliament which has hitherto legislated for each jurisdiction, and been supreme or 'sovereign'. Change came about in 1998, with devolution of law making powers to a Scottish Parliament, a Northern Ireland Assembly and administrative powers to a Welsh Assembly. Each enjoys limited legislative powers, which must be considered alongside the legislative powers which remain with Westminster. The United Kingdom will remain in being: the object of devolution is to provide more representative and accountable regional government, and to strengthen rather than undermine the union with England.[3]

To understand the constitutional arrangements, it is necessary to revert to history, for the contemporary structure of the United Kingdom is the product of forces of the past. While the 'kingdom' is now 'united', it has not always been so. Rather, the United Kingdom has been forged in part out of conquest (in the case of Wales and what is now the Republic of Ireland) and out of Treaty (for example, with Scotland in 1706). As will be seen, in relation to each part of the United Kingdom, the union with England has not always been smooth, and the history of the United Kingdom is one marked by conflict, with demands at different times in history from Ireland, Scotland and Wales for self-governing status. Devolution – the granting of self-regulating legislative powers – as mentioned above, has become a reality for Scotland and Northern Ireland and, to a lesser extent, Wales.

NORTHERN IRELAND[4]

Northern Ireland has a land area of some 5,000 square miles and a population amounting to three per cent of the United Kingdom population. The constitutional position of Northern Ireland cannot be understood without some

---

1 Interpretation Act 1978, Sched 1.
2 British Nationality Act 1981, s 50(1).
3 Devolution is discussed in Chapter 12.
4 See, *inter alia*, Foster, 1989a, 1989b; *Report of the Royal Commission on the Constitution 1969–73*, Cmnd 5460, 1973, London: HMSO; Calvert, 1968; Bogdanor, 1979; Ranelagh, 1983; Lee, 1990; Hughes, 1994.

appreciation of the history of Ireland as a whole – a matter which remains of contemporary constitutional importance given the recent initiatives to end the sectarian bloodshed and to achieve a lasting constitutional settlement in relation to the status of Northern Ireland. Space does not permit more than a brief overview of the rich and troubled history of Ireland.

Ireland: the early history

Ireland first came under the control of the English in the twelfth century when, in 1155, Henry II (1154–89) had been awarded the overlordship of Ireland by the English Pope, Adrian IV, for the specific purpose of reforming the Irish Church. An Irish Parliament was established by the end of the thirteenth century, although representation was confined to English settlers, thereby excluding the native Irish population. At the time of Henry VII's reign (1485–1509) English rule in Ireland was confined to the Pale, a stretch of coastal land running some 50 miles north of Dublin and 20 miles inland. An early attempt at a form of self-government entailed the Irish Parliament's assertion that Acts of the English Parliament would extend to Ireland only in so far as the Irish Parliament ratified the statute. The outcome of this claim to independence was the reassertion of royal power and the passage of Poyning's Law[5] in 1494, which provided that all Irish legislative proposals must be approved by the King and his Council.

The province of Ulster – then the nine northern counties of Ireland – was largely unaffected by English rule until the sixteenth century, when Elizabeth I (1558–1603) sought to extend her power beyond the Pale. On the advice of the Privy Council, the Queen decided that government in Ireland should be approximated as far as possible to that of England rather than allowing governance on the basis of Ireland's own history and experience. The Queen's decision was to alter the course of history. Beyond the Pale, the 'Irishry' had enjoyed their own language, customs and law. English was now to become the official language and English law and administrative practices were to extend to the whole territory of Ireland. In Munster, in the south, an earlier rebellion against English rule – supported by Spanish and Italian troops and financed by the Pope – started in 1569, and was finally suppressed in 1583.

Relations between the English and the Irish remained uneasy. Ireland adhered to the Roman Catholic faith,[6] whereas the immigrants from Scotland and England were staunchly Protestant. The native tongue was Gaelic, a language neither understood nor spoken by the English. When Hugh O'Neill, the Earl of Tyrone, demanded that traditional rule by chieftains be allowed and that there should be official tolerance of Roman Catholicism, Elizabeth rejected these demands. In consequence of this rejection, a Spanish armada set forth in support of Catholicism. The armada, whilst unsuccessful, heightened the sense of Irish nationalism and antagonism towards the English. In 1603, the rebellion was ultimately suppressed: Tyrone and others fled to France in 'the flight of the Earls'.

---

5   Named after Sir Edward Poyning, the envoy sent by Henry VII to secure obedience to
    English authority.
6   Religious faith was reinforced by missionaries from the Continent.

The province was taken over by the Crown and, in 1607, with the exile of the native aristocracy, was divided into counties on the English model.

One effect of Irish suppression was to further English settlement of the area, with land being confiscated and distributed to English and Scots immigrants. In 1609, under James I (1603–25), a comprehensive scheme of 'plantation' began in Ulster, and by 1622, some 21,000 English, Scottish and Welsh immigrants had settled in Northern Ireland. Fortified towns were built by the incoming settlers as 'control points' across the province.

As the number of Protestant immigrants increased, so too did the potential for religious strife. Immigrants to Ulster changed its character into that of a Protestant society, and the dispossessed Irish found themselves outsiders in their own country. In 1641, the native Irish rebelled against the settlers. Unable to send troops to suppress the rebellion, King Charles I accepted a proposal whereby ten million acres of Irish land would be confiscated and used to repay those who would lend money to suppress the rebellion.

In the Interregnum of 1649 to 1660, during which time England was governed by the Cromwellian Commonwealth, the Treaty of Kilkenny 1649 was agreed, which guaranteed religious toleration and an independent Parliament for Ireland. However, in light of continuing opposition to English rule, Cromwell landed in Ireland in July 1649 with an army intent on suppressing dissent. By May 1652, the conquest was complete. The terms of settlement were set out in the Act for Settlement of Ireland, and included the provision that every Irish landowner would have his estate forfeited unless he could prove that he had shown 'constant good affection to the interests of the Commonwealth of England'. During the Commonwealth, an estimated 36,000 immigrant settlers were given land, much of it in Ulster. An estimated 8,000 Catholic landowners were thus displaced from their lands, to be replaced by English soldiers, who accepted land in lieu of pay, and by those who had lent money to the government for suppression of the rebellion. By 1660, when Charles II was restored to the throne, the share of land owned by native Catholics had declined from 60 per cent to 20 per cent of the total. An attempt – under the Act of Settlement of 1661 – to preserve the land of existing landowners and to restore land to those who had suffered in the Crown's cause was doomed to fail because, quite simply, there was insufficient land to meet the claims. Notwithstanding such attempts to redress past injustices, the Act of Explanation of 1665 declared that, in disputes between Catholics and Protestants, Protestants were to be favoured. The Act of Settlement was to be a continuing source of conflict.

James II, having fled England for Catholic France in 1688, arrived in Ireland in 1689 in an attempt to restore his English Crown. The Irish Parliament – in which, at that time, Roman Catholics formed a majority – repealed the Act of Settlement and restored freedom of religion. In response, William III despatched an army to Ireland, and at the Battle of the Boyne in 1690, James was defeated. Protestants were once again in the ascendancy. Following James's defeat, and the repression which followed, some 12,000 Roman Catholics went into exile.

Throughout the reign of William and Mary (1689–1702), and that of Queen Anne (1702–14), further measures were introduced to confirm Protestant supremacy. Catholics were excluded from parliament, the civil service, armed forces, local government and the professions. An Act of 1728 deprived Catholics of the electoral franchise. Roman Catholics were prohibited from acquiring land and from sending their children to university. On the death of a Catholic, by law his lands were compulsorily divided between all his children, but if there was a Protestant heir, he was to take precedence. By these various means, Catholics were excluded from participation in public life. Some redress occurred in 1792 when the Relief Act allowed Roman Catholics to practise law and to vote, although not to stand for election to parliament which by now had become a Protestant body.

In 1791, the Society of United Irishmen was established in Belfast, with Republicanism – full independence from England for an Irish State – as its political platform. Although the majority of its membership was Protestant, the Society favoured Catholic emancipation.[7] In the north, however, in 1794, the Protestant and staunchly Unionist Orange Order was established. Mounting religious and political instability in Ireland culminated in the Great Rising of 1798.

The Act of Union 1800

In an attempt to quell unrest and reach a lasting settlement, negotiations were undertaken towards establishing political union between Ireland and England. The British Prime Minister, William Pitt, promised full Catholic emancipation. The resulting Act of Union 1800, which came into effect on 1 January 1801, effected the union between Ireland and England on the theoretical basis of equal independence for the two countries. The Kingdom of Ireland and the Kingdom of Great Britain were united under the United Kingdom of Great Britain and Ireland. Irish interests were to be represented in the United Kingdom's House of Lords by 28 Irish peers and four bishops. Representation in the House of Commons was by 100 Irish members. The House of Lords of the United Kingdom was the court of last resort. Demands for the repeal of the Act of Union were soon to be heard from Catholics when the promised emancipation was blocked by George III (1738–1820) – note that the King's veto resulted in Pitt's resignation – and demands made for reforms in relation to land law and education. These claims, in turn, were resisted by Protestants who feared that dissolution of the union and a revived Irish Parliament would favour the Catholics.

The movement towards Home Rule[8]

Following the Napoleonic War in 1815, economic disaster was to strike Ireland. The economy was traditionally heavily dependent upon the potato crop: in the mid 1800s, the crop failed. The effect of famine – starvation and emigration – was to decimate the Irish population.[9] Demands for Home Rule began following the

---

7   Official suppression of the Society took place in 1794.
8   See Morton, 1980; Jalland, 1980; O'Halpin, 1987.
9   In 1841, the population was 8,175,124; in 1881, 5,174,836 and, by 1901, 4,458,775: census figures.

famine when many felt that the British government had taken inadequate steps to deal with the economic crisis. The famine once again heightened demands for independence from England.

Some reforms were introduced: in 1829, a Catholic Relief Act removed discrimination in education and property and provided for Roman Catholic entry to civic and military offices. This emancipation in turn gave rise to increased solidarity in the Unionist communities of the north and to further sectarian violence. In 1836, a paramilitary national police force was set up, to be known from 1867 as the Royal Irish Constabulary.[10]

In 1869, the Anglican Church in Ireland was disestablished,[11] and in 1870 and 1881, Land Acts were introduced to regulate land rents and tenure. Electoral reforms in 1868, 1872 and 1884–85 introduced the secret ballot and extended the franchise. These measures, however, were not enough to quell Irish Catholic discontent. The land question was converted into a full scale campaign for Home Rule for Ireland. Charles Stewart Parnell and Michael Davitt (Member of Parliament for Meath) created the United Irish League, an organisation designed to back Irish Home Rule members of the United Kingdom Parliament. Between 1879 and 1882, a violent campaign against landlords was undertaken. The government's response was to suspend habeas corpus, but at the same time to introduce further land reforms. The violence nevertheless continued: Irish republican leaders were arrested but subsequently released in order to try to stop the bloodshed. In 1881, the brutal murders of the Chief Secretary for Ireland, Lord Frederick Cavendish, and Chief Under Secretary Thomas Burke were to turn public opinion in England against the Irish and put back the cause of Home Rule.

With a total of 100 members, the Irish represented a significant block in the Westminster Parliament. Following the 1885 general election, 85 of the 100 elected members supported Home Rule in Ireland. They proceeded to exercise their power, blocking government legislation and campaigning for Irish independence from Westminster. The Liberal Prime Minister, William Ewart Gladstone,[12] sponsored the cause of Home Rule, but not that of a fully independent Irish State. The aim, for the Liberals, was to introduce constitutional reform which would ensure a degree of autonomy for an Irish Parliament whilst retaining the supremacy of Westminster. By this means, it was hoped that some form of devolution of power would be acceptable to the Unionists.

This compromise solution was one adopted in other attempts at devolution of power from Westminster. In 1867, by the British North America Act, limited powers were devolved to Canada, as was later to be the case in relation also to Australia[13] and South Africa.[14] In each instance, the Westminster Parliament

---

10 Between 1800 and 1921, some 105 Coercion Acts were passed, increasing the powers of the military and police.

11 Irish Church Disestablishment Act 1869.

12 1809–98: Prime Minister 1868–74; 1880–85; 1892–94.

13 Commonwealth of Australia Constitution Act 1900 (UK).

14 South Africa Act 1909.

retained ultimate sovereignty over the laws of each country whilst conferring broad grants of legislative power to the colonial legislature.[15]

Home Rule Bills were introduced in the British Parliament in 1886 and 1893, but both were defeated – the first failing to pass the House of Commons and the latter rejected by the House of Lords. Relations between England and Ireland were to deteriorate throughout the first 20 years of the twentieth century. In 1905, Sinn Fein was established, with strongly nationalist objectives. In the years 1911–12, there was industrial unrest in Ireland. By the outbreak of the First World War in 1914, the scene was set for Civil War in Ireland, an event only postponed by the War.

With Home Rule so firmly on the political agenda, Unionist opposition intensified. For example, on 28 September 1912 (Ulster Day), some 400,000 Ulster Protestants signed the Covenant, committing themselves to use 'all means which may be found necessary to defeat the present conspiracy to set up a Home Rule Parliament in Ireland' and 'to refuse to recognise its authority'.[16] In 1913, the Ulster Volunteer Force (UVF), a private army of over 100,000 men, was formed to protect Unionist interests against Republican demands. The forming of the UVF led directly to the foundation of the Irish Volunteers, the forerunners of the Irish Republican Army (IRA).

The issue of Home Rule for Ireland became, for the British, an issue which demanded the separation of Ulster from the remainder of Ireland, rather than Home Rule for the entire country. A Bill passed through parliament in 1914, but with the outbreak of the First World War was never put into effect, and the intractable issue of separation of north from south was thus delayed.[17] At Westminster, the question of Home Rule had by now become a straight and passionate party political issue, with the Conservatives and Ulster Unionists opposing devolution and the Liberals and Irish members proposing devolution.

The Easter Rising 1916[18]

In 1916, an event occurred which was to prove to be a decisive factor in the Home Rule story. Nationalists in Dublin, under the leadership of Patrick Pearse, James Connolly and Michael Collins, initiated an uprising. On Easter Monday, some 1,600 members of the Irish Volunteers and Irish Citizen Army embarked on a rebellion, proclaiming republican status for Ireland.[19]

Six days later, the rebels surrendered with a loss of life of 132 soldiers and policemen and 397 wounded, and 318 civilian deaths and 2,217 wounded. Three thousand five hundred people were arrested and court-martialled. Fifteen men were executed: 14 in Dublin and one in Cork. While the uprising was unsuccessful, its effect, and the brutal response of the British, was to consolidate

---

15 See, *inter alia*, the Colonial Laws Validity Act 1865 and Chapter 7.
16 Cited by Fitzpatrick, 'Ireland since 1870', in Foster, 1989a, p 191.
17 Attempts were made to implement the Home Rule Bill following the Easter Rising in 1916 but failed.
18 See Thompson, 1967; Martin, 1967; O'Connor, 1989.
19 *The Proclamation of the Irish Republic 24 April 1916*, cited in Hughes, 1994, pp 97–99.

the nationalist cause and to win the support of the Catholic Church. Sinn Fein membership grew and electoral success followed in the 1918 general election, with Sinn Fein members having a majority throughout the country except in the staunchly Unionist area of the north east. Sinn Fein secured 73 seats and 48 per cent of the votes cast. The Unionists secured only 29 per cent of votes.

Civil War: 1919–22

Sinn Fein was banned in 1918, and its leader, Eamon De Valera, arrested. Members of Sinn Fein refused to take their seats in Westminster and instead issued a Declaration of Independence and established the first Irish Parliament – the *Dail Eireann*. Civil unrest again erupted, with the Irish War of Independence[20] lasting until 1921. The war was, essentially, a programme of terrorism directed against the authorities. The government passed the Restoration of Order in Ireland Act in 1920, providing for internment of suspects while at the same time seeking to implement Home Rule. The savagery with which the army and the Royal Irish Constabulary dealt with the troubles provoked disgust and outrage: pressure on the government from public opinion at home and overseas necessitated a truce.

Partition: the Government of Ireland Act 1920

By 1919, it had become clear that there could be no single Home Rule Parliament for a united Republic of Ireland. In light of the continuing and increasing sectarian bitterness and civil unrest, the British government became resigned to a divided Ireland. In 1920, the United Kingdom Parliament passed the Government of Ireland Act under which the country was partitioned, with six of the original nine Ulster counties being separated from the remainder of Ireland.[21] Under the Government of Ireland Act, a Council of Ireland was to be established, having exclusive jurisdiction over a number of all Ireland matters.[22]

Six northern counties,[23] characterised by a majority population of Protestants, were henceforth to be separately represented by a separate parliament from that of southern Ireland. The Act provided for two Home Rule Parliaments, with Westminster retaining ultimate sovereignty:

> Notwithstanding ... anything contained in this Act, the supreme authority of the Parliament of the United Kingdom shall remain unaffected and undiminished over all persons, matters, and things in Ireland and every part thereof. [Government of Ireland Act 1920, s 75]

The Parliament of Southern Ireland – the *Dail* – rejected the Act, and the war of independence continued. In Northern Ireland, however, the Home Rule Parliament opened in 1921. In December 1921, following intensive negotiations, Articles of Agreement were signed by Irish delegates. The Articles provided for the partition of Ireland; for the creation of an Irish Free State with Dominion

---

20   Variously called the Anglo-Irish War, Irish War of Independence or the Black and Tan War.
21   Cavan, Monaghan and Donegal were excluded from the newly created Northern Ireland.
22   Railways, fisheries and contagious diseases in animals.
23   Antrim, Armagh, Down, Fermanagh, Londonderry and Tyrone.

status[24] under the Crown, to be represented by a Governor General. By a narrow majority, the *Dail* accepted the agreement.

The Anglo-Irish Treaty 1921

The Anglo-Irish Treaty gave to southern Ireland (the Irish Free State) self-governing dominion status, equivalent to that of Canada, within the Commonwealth. The Parliament of Northern Ireland was given the choice as to whether or not it should be part of the Irish Free State. When it decided that it should not, the Irish Free State (Consequential Provisions) Act of 1922 provided that the 1920 Act, which regulated the respective powers of the southern and northern parliaments and their relationships with Westminster should cease to apply to any part of the Irish Free State and that its operation was confined to Northern Ireland.

In 1922, the Irish Free State Constitution was published, and ratified by the Westminster Parliament in the Irish Free State (Constitution) Act 1922. War was not to end, however, and on 28 June 1922 the Irish Civil War began, with the IRA leading the campaign against the Treaty. The war ended in 1923, but the anti-treaty forces refused to surrender their arms.[25]

Within the newly separated north, with a Protestant Unionist population of 56.4 per cent of the total, sectarian strife continued. In two years, over 400 people died, the majority being Catholics. The government responded with the Civil Authorities (Special Powers) Act of 1922, which provided for internment of suspected terrorists without trial. The Act was to remain in force until 1972; see further Chapter 25.

The Constitution of the Irish Free State 1937

In 1931, the Statute of Westminster conferred greater freedom on the powers of Dominions. In Ireland, the Prime Minister (the *Taoiseach*), Eamon de Valera (1882–1975), introduced major changes: in 1933, it was announced that Ireland was to become a *de facto* Republic. The Senate – the upper House of Parliament – was abolished; the Governor General was stripped of his powers. In addition, Irish citizens lost their British citizenship. The right of appeal to the Privy Council was abolished.

In 1937, de Valera drafted and published the Constitution of the Irish Free State. The Constitution declared independence from the United Kingdom, declaring in Article I that:

> The Irish nation hereby affirms its inalienable, indefeasible, and sovereign right to choose its own form of government, to determine its relations with other nations, and to develop its life, political, economic and cultural, in accordance with its own genius and traditions.

---

24 As enjoyed by Canada, Australia, New Zealand and South Africa.
25 The same position pertained in 1999.

Under Article 2, the constitution declared Ireland to be a unitary, not divided, state, thus refusing to accept the constitutional position of Northern Ireland as established under the 1920 Act:

> The national territory consists of the whole island of Ireland, its islands and the territorial seas.

Furthermore, it was declared in Article 5 that:

> Ireland is a sovereign, independent, democratic State.

It was not, however, until 1949 that the United Kingdom Parliament was to accept separation and pass the Ireland Act, which formally severed constitutional ties. The Republic withdrew from the Commonwealth in the same year.

Self-government in Northern Ireland 1920–72

From 1920 until 1972, Northern Ireland enjoyed a measure of self-government represented by the parliament at Stormont. The Northern Ireland Parliament had powers to make laws for 'the peace, order and good government of Northern Ireland'. In effect, this meant law and order, the police and lower courts, local government, health and social services, education, planning and internal trade, agriculture and finance.[26] Westminster retained reserved powers and ultimate sovereignty over the territory.[27] Sectarian strife, in addition to the reserved legislative powers, ensured that the United Kingdom government continued to play a role in Northern Ireland.

The Northern Ireland Parliament was bicameral, the House of Commons being elected by the people, the Senate being elected by members of the House of Commons. The Executive was headed by the Governor, appointed by the Crown. In the first elected parliament of 1921, the Unionists held a majority and thus formed the government, a feature which was to be repeated in every election until the constitution was suspended in 1972.

Not only was there a continuous Unionist majority in the House of Commons, but there was also Unionist dominance in local government: a contributing factor to the discontent of the Catholic community. Further disquiet arose over the composition of the Royal Ulster Constabulary, and in particular the force of 'B Specials',[28] all Protestant, which gained a reputation for violence. Catholic membership of the entire police force in Northern Ireland was never to be above 20 per cent of the total. The allocation of public housing also became a matter of discontent. In the attempt to separate Catholics from Protestants, the housing allocated to Catholics proved to be of a poorer standard than that offered to the Protestants. Education was segregated, again on religious grounds. Mutual distrust between the two communities within Northern Ireland intensified as a result of religion.

---

26 See Palley, 1972.
27 Government of Ireland Act 1920, s 75.
28 Part time policemen.

The 'Troubles': 1968–98

In 1968, a campaign of civil disobedience and unrest began. The target for the violence was twofold: the discrimination which existed against Catholics in many sectors of life – such as housing, employment and the local government franchise – and the continued union with the mainland. The civil disturbances led to a Commission of Inquiry which reported a 'widespread sense of political and social grievances for long unaudited and therefore ignored by successive governments of Northern Ireland'.[29] By the summer of 1969, British troops were deployed in support of the police, whose operational control over security matters became subject to military control. In 1970, the Provisional Sinn Fein Party was formed and, in 1971, the Reverend Ian Paisley founded the Democratic Unionist Party. The Civil Authorities Special Powers Act (Northern Ireland) 1922 was used to intern suspected Irish Republican terrorists without trial – a factor which increased rather than decreased sympathy for the nationalist cause. On 30 January 1972, 13 Catholic civilians were shot dead by British paratroopers in the course of a banned civil rights march in Derry (Bloody Sunday). By the end of 1972, 474 deaths had occurred in the escalation of sectarian killings by Protestant murderers and the IRA.

Internment and allegations of ill treatment of detainees led to legal proceedings being initiated against the United Kingdom by the Republic of Ireland government under the European Convention on Human Rights.[30] The Crompton Report of 1971[31] outlined the interrogation methods used as including continuous noise, deprivation of food, water and sleep, and wall standing. Three Privy Counsellors[32] were appointed to examine the procedures. Unable to reach agreement, two differing reports were published.[33] The majority report concluded that the techniques would be acceptable provided adequate safeguards were introduced in relation to their use. Lord Gardiner, however, a former Labour Lord Chancellor, ruled that the procedures used were unlawful:

> If it is to be made legal to employ methods not now legal against a man whom the police believe to have, but who may not have, information which the police desire to obtain, I, like many of our witnesses, have searched for, but been unable to find, either in logic or in morals, any limit to the degree of ill treatment to be legalised. The only logical limit to the degree of ill treatment would appear to be whatever degree of ill treatment proves to be necessary to get the information out of him, which would include, if necessary, extreme torture. I cannot think that Parliament should, or would, so legislate.

The government accepted Lord Gardiner's view, and the interrogation procedures were abandoned. The European Court of Human Rights ruled that the procedures

---

29 *Report of the Cameron Commission: Disturbances in Northern Ireland,* Cmnd 532, 1969, London: HMSO.
30 *Republic of Ireland v United Kingdom* (1978). See further McCrudden, 'Northern Ireland', in Jowell and Oliver, 2000. See also Chapter 24.
31 Cmnd 4823, 1971, London: HMSO.
32 Lord Parker of Waddington, J A Carpenter and Lord Gardiner.
33 *Report of the Committee of Privy Counsellors appointed to Consider Authorised Procedures for the Interrogation of Persons Suspected of Terrorism,* Cmnd 4901, 1972, London: HMSO.

amounted to inhuman and degrading treatment contrary to Article 3 of the Convention on Human Rights but that they did not amount to torture.

Some reforms designed to improve relations between the Catholic community and the Unionists were introduced by the Northern Ireland Parliament. A Northern Ireland Parliamentary Commissioner for Administration was appointed to deal with complaints against public authorities,[34] and a Commissioner for Complaints[35] was established to investigate allegations based on discrimination in employment.

Prorogation of the Northern Ireland Parliament 1972

In 1972, with the violence unabated and the civilian death toll mounting, the United Kingdom government once again assumed responsibility for the province.[36] The Northern Ireland Parliament was prorogued indefinitely and the powers of the Northern Ireland government transferred to a Secretary of State for Northern Ireland. A review of the Special Powers Act and internment was undertaken in 1972.[37] Confirming the need for detention without trial as a short term measure for certain alleged offences, the Committee recommended the introduction of special courts which would sit without a jury: the 'Diplock Courts'.[38]

Power sharing 1973

In 1973, following the prorogation of Stormont and a referendum, a new system of power sharing between the Northern Ireland Assembly and the Westminster Parliament was introduced.[39] Under the Northern Ireland Assembly Act 1973 and the Northern Ireland Constitution Act 1973, an Assembly was to be established, having 78 members elected under the single transferable vote system.[40] The Northern Ireland Constitution Act 1973 provided a statutory guarantee that Northern Ireland should remain part of the United Kingdom until the time at which a majority of the people, voting in a referendum, should determine otherwise.[41] Representation of Northern Ireland at Westminster was increased to 17 Members of Parliament. In a referendum held in 1973[42] on the question of union with the United Kingdom, a majority favoured continuation of the union.[43]

---

34   Parliamentary Commissioner (Northern Ireland) Act 1969.
35   Commissioner for Complaints (Northern Ireland) Act 1969; see Poole, 1972.
36   Northern Ireland (Temporary Provisions) Act 1972.
37   *Report of the Commission to Consider Legal Procedures to deal with Terrorist Activities in Northern Ireland*, Cmnd 5185, 1972, London: HMSO (the Diplock Inquiry).
38   Northern Ireland (Emergency Provisions) Act 1973.
39   *Northern Ireland Constitutional Proposals*, Cmnd 5259, 1973, London: HMSO.
40   See Chapter 13.
41   See Hadfield, 1989.
42   Under the Northern Ireland (Border Poll) Act 1972.
43   Although only 58.7% of the electorate voted.

Direct rule 1974

The breakdown of that system resulted in the Northern Ireland Act of 1974, the result of which was the restoration of direct rule by Westminster over Northern Ireland.

Further attempts were made to dismantle the discrimination which continued to exist in fields of housing and employment.[44] Section 17 of the Northern Ireland Constitution Act 1973 provided that any Northern Ireland legislation which discriminated against persons on the basis of religion or political belief was void.[45] The attempts proved largely ineffective and the Policy Studies Institute reported that the legislation had little impact on the attitudes of employers.[46]

Throughout the 1970s and 1980s, a virtual civil war existed.[47] From 1971 to 1977, 'an average of 252 persons were killed and 3,269 shootings have occurred each year; for the years 1978–81, the averages have fallen, respectively, to 82 and 1,574'.[48] In 1975, a further attempt to devolve power to the province was made when a Constitutional Convention was elected.[49] The attempt failed as a result of the Unionists' insistence that they retain a majority in any new Assembly. The Northern Ireland Act 1982 nevertheless provided for a new Assembly, to be elected by proportional representation, which initially was designed to be a debating and deliberative forum which would, in the future, propose plans for a new form of devolved government in Northern Ireland.[50] The Social Democratic and Labour Party and Sinn Fein members refused to take their seats. Faced with political deadlock, the Assembly was dissolved in 1986. In 1983, the New Ireland Forum was established, in which the major political parties in the south and north were represented. The outcome of deliberations was the Anglo-Irish Agreement, signed by the Prime Ministers of the United Kingdom and the Republic of Ireland in 1985.[51]

The Anglo-Irish Agreement 1985

The Agreement endorsed the principle that no constitutional change concerning the relationship between the north and south could come about other than with the consent of a majority of the people in Northern Ireland. That majority did not currently exist. In the absence of such consent, it was agreed that there should be closer co-operation in relation to security, economic, social and cultural matters and the promotion of reconciliation between the two parts of Ireland. An Inter-governmental Conference was established with a membership drawn from

---

44 See McCrudden, 'Northern Ireland', in Jowell and Oliver, 2000.
45 The Fair Employment (Northern Ireland) Act 1976 makes discrimination in the fields of either public or private employment void.
46 Chambers, 1987; Smith, 1988, cited in McCrudden, 'Northern Ireland', in Jowell and Oliver, 2000.
47 See Gearty, 1991, Chapter 8.
48 Dickson, 1993.
49 Under the Northern Ireland Act 1974.
50 *Northern Ireland: A Framework for Devolution*, Cmnd 8541, 1982, London: HMSO.
51 See Connolly and Loughlin, 1986; Hadfield, 1986; Harvey Cox, 1987; McGarry, 1988.

representatives of both south and north to consider reforms across a range of issues. The British government undertook to consider any recommendations made, although the ultimate sovereignty over Northern Ireland remained firmly in the United Kingdom. Under the Anglo-Irish Agreement, the work of the Inter-governmental Conference was to be reviewed after three years. Reforms implemented since the Agreement included the Fair Employment (Northern Ireland) Act 1989, which aimed at removing discrimination in employment, and the introduction of an independent Commission for Police Complaints.

The Joint Declaration 1993

In 1993, a Joint Declaration was signed by the British and Irish governments. The Declaration recognised and renewed the commitment to preservation of the union with the United Kingdom for as long as a majority of the people of Northern Ireland so wished. The Declaration also, however, indicated for the first time that the British government had 'no selfish, strategic or economic interest' in Northern Ireland, thus officially giving recognition to the neutrality of the government's position over the long term future of the province. In September 1994, the IRA announced a ceasefire of hostilities. The British government responded with cautious optimism. In the same month, and as a response to the ceasefire, the government announced that the ban on live sound broadcasts by members of Sinn Fein would be lifted. The exclusion order on the President of Sinn Fein, Mr Gerry Adams, was also lifted.[52]

In 1995, with the lasting of the ceasefire in Northern Ireland, the prospects for peace in Northern Ireland were higher than at any time in the past. Full negotiations between Sinn Fein and the British government were, however, delayed, in part by a dispute over the terms for negotiation and in part over the refusal of the IRA to relinquish its armoury of weapons[53] in advance of peace talks. The fragile hopes of 1995 were dashed in February 1996 when the IRA bombed Canary Wharf in London, thus ending the ceasefire.

The 1998 peace settlement

The election of the Labour government in May 1997 led to renewed efforts to revitalise the peace talks. In September 1997, following a renewal of the ceasefire by the IRA, and Sinn Fein's renunciation of the use of force, peace talks commenced between all parties. Agreement was finally reached on Good Friday, 10 April 1998.

The agreement centred on five principal points. First, the principle that Northern Ireland would remain part of the United Kingdom was endorsed, and the Republic of Ireland agreed to amend its Constitution to remove its claim to Northern Ireland (Articles 2 and 3). Secondly, a Northern Ireland Assembly of 108 members was to be elected under a system of proportional representation. The Assembly is run by an executive of 12 members. Thirdly, a North-South

---

52   On emergency legislation in respect of Northern Ireland, see Chapter 25.
53   As the IRA refused to do in 1923; see above, p 46.

ministerial council was to be established by the Assembly in order to co-ordinate relations between Ireland and Ulster. Fourthly, a Council of the Isles was to be established, its membership to be drawn from the parliaments at Westminster, Dublin, Edinburgh and the Welsh Assembly. Finally, all participants expressed their commitment to the disarmament of paramilitary organisations, a commitment the fulfilment of which was a condition for the devolution of power.

In order for the agreement to take effect, referendums were held in both the Republic of Ireland and Northern Ireland. In Northern Ireland, the vote in favour of the agreement was 71.12 per cent, with a turnout of 80.98 per cent. In the Irish Republic, 94.40 per cent voted for the agreement, the turnout being 55.47 per cent. In June 1998, elections were held for membership of the Northern Ireland Assembly. The results of the election produced an Assembly with power shared by the four main political parties, with five minority parties winning 18 seats between them.[54]

In 1999, the devolution of power was complete, the Assembly elected and a power sharing executive in place. As noted above, however, the full devolution of power was conditional on agreement being reached over the decommissioning of paramilitary weapons. When the IRA refused to co-operate and it became clear that decommissioning was not to occur, the Assembly was suspended, and power returned to Westminster under the Northern Ireland Act 2000, to be restored once again following further negotiations but once again returned to Westminster. The devolution of power continues to be dependent upon compliance with the agreement and therefore remains fragile.

In 2003 the British and Irish governments issued a Joint Declaration on the achievement of 'security normalisation' in Northern Ireland, including the reduction in troop levels, the removal of army observation posts and de-fortification of police stations. In July 2005 the Irish Republican Army issued a statement that its leadership had ordered an end to its armed campaign. In response the British government undertook to revise the special provisions relating to Northern Ireland security, discussed in Chapter 24, but stated that the special provisions would remain in force until 2007 and could be extended by order until 2008 if necessary.

SCOTLAND[55]

Scotland has a total area of some 30,000 square miles representing an area three-fifths the size of England, with a population of some ten per cent of the United Kingdom total.

---

54 The Ulster Unionists won 28 seats with 21.3 per cent of the vote; the Social Democratic and Labour Party 14 seats with 22.2 per cent of the vote; the Democratic Unionist Party 20 seats with 18.1 per cent of the vote; and Sinn Fein 18 seats with 17.6 per cent of the vote.
55 See, on the origins of devolution in Scotland, *Report of the Royal Commission on the Constitution 1969–73*, Cmnd 5460, 1973, London: HMSO.

The early history

The historical relationship between England and Scotland is one marked by conflict and war resulting from English attempts at seizing sovereignty over Scotland. Perhaps the original force uniting the two countries was the marriage, in 1503, of James IV of Scotland to Margaret, Henry VII's daughter. When Elizabeth I of England died in 1603, without leaving an heir to the throne, Henry VII's great-great-grandson – then James VI of Scotland – succeeded to the throne of England as James I.[56] Despite this union, each country retained its own constitution and parliament and – separated by religious differences and economic rivalry – the two countries were to remain separate for a further century.

In *Calvin's Case* (1608), it was held that persons born in either of the kingdoms, after James's accession to the English throne, held dual nationality, all owing allegiance to the same Crown. James's accession was not, however, to lay past conflicts to rest. James ruled Scotland from London, much of government in practice being conducted by the Scottish Privy Council acting on the King's orders. The Scottish Parliament seldom met and was dominated by the Lords of the Articles, who were royal nominees. Within Scotland, conflict arose in the form of religious dispute with the King, who attempted to curb the power of the Presbyterian Kirk in Scotland, in 1606 exiling one of its leaders, Andrew Melville. In 1608, in the *Five Articles of Perth*, the King ordered certain religious practices to be undertaken which were regarded by the puritans as 'popery',[57] as was the Prayer Book drawn up at James's command in 1619.

It was in the reign of Charles I (1625–49) that open conflict on the religious question emerged. Charles attempted to impose James's Prayer Book on the Kirk (the Scottish Church). The end result, in brief, was that the Scots opponents of his attempted reforms – the Covenanters – played a significant role in Charles's defeat in the Civil War which led to his trial, conviction and execution as 'a tyrant, traitor, murderer and public enemy to the good people of this nation'.[58]

From 1649–60, during the 'interregnum' (the period between the execution of Charles I and the restoration of the monarchy), Scotland was to be ruled by the military, whilst theoretically integrated into the Cromwellian united Republic of England and Scotland. On restoration of the monarchy, religious persecution of the Scottish Presbyterians was rife. The Scottish Parliament, under the control of the Lords of the Articles, proved impotent, and was dissolved by Charles II (1649–85; in exile until 1660). In 1666, provoked by persecution, the Pentland Rising against the Crown occurred. While unsuccessful, it prompted Charles towards greater religious tolerance.

In 1688, when James II (1685–89) was forced to flee England, the Scots took the opportunity to assert their constitutional and religious liberties against William and Mary (1689–1702). The Claim of Right – the Scottish constitutional settlement with the Crown – went much further than its English counterpart, the Petition of

---

56   See Wormald, 1983.
57   Adherence to the Roman Catholic faith.
58   Cited in Lockyer, 1985, p 288.

Right. The Scots claimed that parliament had the right to depose any King who violated the trust on which his powers were held, and William was not to establish his supremacy in Scotland without blood being shed. Rebellious Highland chiefs, who refused to submit to William's authority, were massacred at Glencoe in 1692, as an example to others. Scottish hostility towards the Crown was further exacerbated by the Navigation Acts, which treated Scotland and England as separate entities. As a response, acting alone, and without royal support, the Scots raised revenues for an expedition to Panama. Three expeditions set out but failed, being decimated either by disease or by military opposition from the Spanish Armada. The English, meanwhile, continued to exclude Scotland from its commercial empire. The Scottish response to such discrimination was to declare that Scotland would not be committed to either war or peace by English policy[59] and that the succession to the Hanoverian Crown[60] would not be accepted by Scotland unless and until constitutional, economic and religious liberties were guaranteed to the Scottish people.

The only long term solution to such conflicts of interest was the full union of England and Scotland. The Act of Union with Scotland[61] was passed in 1707, 'abolishing' the respective sovereign parliaments which became united under the title of the Parliament of Great Britain. The Act of Union represented the culmination of years of negotiations between the two countries following centuries of intermittent hostilities. As will be seen in Chapter 7, when union came about, it was to be subject to strict conditions and terms. In particular, the Act of Union protects the separate Scottish legal system – in relation to both private law and the court structure – and provided special protection for the Presbyterian Church. There was, however, to be a common parliament, common flag, taxation and coinage: by this, meaningful political and economic union was secured.

The Wars of Independence between England and Scotland in the Middle Ages, culminating in the recognition of an independent Scotland in 1328, had resulted in a complete break between English law and Scottish law. The Scottish looked to continental Europe for their training and law, and thus adopted the civil law system based originally on Roman law, which had never been fully adopted in England. Under the terms of the union, the highest civil and criminal courts – the Court of Session and the High Court of Justiciary – were to remain outside the jurisdiction of the English courts. The High Court of Justiciary has remained the final court of appeal in Scottish criminal cases, while in civil cases the House of Lords has appellate jurisdiction.[62]

Following the union, Scottish interests were represented by a Secretary of State for Scotland. From 1745, responsibility for Scotland passed to a Secretary of State who also held other responsibilities, such as Home Affairs. In 1885, the office of Secretary for Scotland was established, which, from 1892, became a Cabinet

---

59   Act anent Peace and War 1703.
60   As provided by the Act of Security 1704.
61   See further Chapter 7.
62   By custom, two Lords of Appeal in Ordinary are from Scotland.

post. Administrative devolution to Scotland included Boards created to administer agriculture, fisheries, local government, prisons, health and education, each operating under the supervision of the Scottish Secretary of State.

In 1952, a Royal Commission on Scottish Affairs[63] was appointed to review government functions in relation to Scotland. Further responsibilities were transferred to the Scottish Secretary of State: appointment of Justices of the Peace, animal health, highways and electricity. Subsequently, road passenger transport, ancient monuments, royal parks and palaces have been transferred. The Scottish Office, established in 1945, comprises five departments: Agriculture and Fisheries, Development, Education, Home, and Health. The administration is based in Edinburgh and headed by the Secretary of State, ministers of state and under secretaries.

Responsibility for the administration of the criminal law in Scotland lies with the Lord Advocate who is normally a member of the House of Commons but may, alternatively, be a member of the House of Lords, having been conferred a life peerage. The Lord Advocate has responsibility for aspects of government business affecting Scotland. Representation in parliament was determined by the Act of Union at 45, but has since increased to 72.[64]

The Royal Commission on the Constitution 1969–73[65] recommended the devolution of legislative power to Scotland. As with Wales, the legislation could only come into effect following a referendum which returned a majority of voters in favour, having secured a minimum of 40 per cent of all eligible voters.[66] The results of the referendum in Scotland were 32.5 per cent in favour of devolution, 30.4 per cent against, with 37.1 per cent of voters abstaining. The statutory requirements for an electoral majority being unmet, the Scotland Act 1978 was repealed.[67]

Nevertheless, the devolution issue – particularly in relation to Scotland – had not been finally laid to rest. Following the general election in 1987, the Conservative government, despite having a majority of seats in England, won only ten out of 72 seats in Scotland. The results of the 1992 election, whilst slightly better in terms of government representation, still resulted in Scotland being under-represented in parliament.

The by-election of May 1995, following the death of a Conservative Member of Parliament, resulted in the Scottish Nationalist Party winning the seat. The Conservative government therefore had little electoral support north of the border in general elections or by-elections, a fact which was also reflected in local government elections. This 'democratic deficit' of the Conservative government continued to fuel the fires of the demand for greater devolution of power to

---

63 *Report of the Royal Commission on Scottish Affairs 1952–54*, Cmnd 9212, 1954, London: HMSO.
64 See the Parliamentary Constituencies Act 1986.
65 *Report of the Royal Commission on the Constitution 1969–73*, Cmnd 5460, 1973, London: HMSO, Vol 1.
66 See Bogdanor, 1980.
67 The Royal Commission had not been unanimous in its support of devolution for either Wales or Scotland, and a powerful Memorandum of Dissent was published with the report: *ibid*, fn 67, Vol 2.

Scotland. The 1997 general election resulted in there being no Scottish Conservative Members of Parliament.

Devolution to Scotland[68]

The general election of 1997 presaged the devolution of power to a Scottish Parliament. The government's White Paper, *Scotland's Parliament*,[69] while retaining the sovereignty of the Westminster Parliament (paragraph 4.2), envisaged devolution of law making power to the Scottish Parliament, and a limited power to vary levels of taxation, while also reserving to the United Kingdom Parliament legislative capacity in relation to certain matters. Whether or not powers are devolved or reserved, the Scottish Parliament is entitled to debate all matters (paragraph 2.5). The Scotland Act 1998 gave effect to the proposals for devolution, approved by the people through a referendum. The Scottish Parliament and the Executive are discussed in Chapter 12.

WALES[70]

Wales covers an area of some 8,000 square miles, having a population approximately five per cent of that of the United Kingdom.

The early history

Wales was conquered by the English in 1282, and from 1284,[71] Wales was subject to English law. A rebellion in the early fifteenth century sought to overthrow English rule but, after initial success, collapsed. The enduring union between England and Wales was formally effected by Act of Parliament in 1536.[72] English became the official language for Wales, and use of the Welsh language officially banned, although in 1563 Elizabeth I ordered that the bible be translated into Welsh in order to ensure compliance with the Protestant religion, and by this means ensured that the Welsh language survived.[73] All Acts of Parliament were deemed to extend to Wales. Throughout the nineteenth and twentieth centuries, nationalist feeling increased, with demands for greater recognition and representation of Welsh interests. Nationalism became an overtly political issue at the end of the nineteenth century with the establishment of the Wales of the Future Movement (*Cymru Fydd*), although separatism was not a demand. Welsh Liberals sought national educational institutions[74] and disestablishment of the

---

68 See, generally, Bogdanor, 1997; Bates, 1997.
69 Cmnd 3658, 1997, London: HMSO.
70 See the *Report of the Royal Commission on the Constitution 1969–73*, Cmnd 5460, 1973, London: HMSO, Vol 1.
71 Statute of Rhuddlan 1284.
72 Variously labelled the Laws in Wales Act 1535 and the Act of Union 1536. The Tudor Act of 1542 established the court structure.
73 See now the Welsh Language Act 1967, which provides, *inter alia*, that the Welsh language may be used in legal proceedings in Wales.
74 Intermediate Education Act 1889; Education Act 1902. In 1893, the University of Wales was established by Charter and, in 1896, a Welsh Examination Board established. See further Bogdanor, 1979.

Welsh Church rather than a Welsh Parliament.[75] In 1925, *Plaid Cymru* was established to promote the Welsh language and further Welsh interests and parliamentary representation, although its electoral success was slight.

Administrative decentralisation to Wales has taken place in a number of areas. In addition to education,[76] national insurance was to be separately administered in Wales,[77] and agricultural interests separately represented.[78]

In 1951, the office of Minister for Welsh Affairs was established and, in 1964, the first Secretary of State for Wales was appointed with the responsibility for overseeing the execution of national policy in Wales. In 1969, the Royal Commission on the Constitution recommended by a majority that there should be greater devolution of power to Wales.[79] The scheme envisaged establishing a Welsh legislature (a Senate) with the power to legislate on specifically defined matters. Existing legislation of the United Kingdom Parliament would continue to apply in Wales, but future legislation – provided the subject matter fell within the area of power devolved – would be for the Welsh Parliament. The United Kingdom Parliament would retain power to legislate over certain matters and the United Kingdom government would retain sovereignty and the ultimate power in exceptional circumstances to override legislation passed by the Welsh Senate. The Senate would comprise a single, 100 member chamber, elected on the basis of proportional representation and having a fixed term of four years. Welsh interests would, however, continue to be represented in the United Kingdom Parliament. The Wales Act 1978 gave effect to devolution. However, in order for the Act to come into effect, it was necessary for those voting in favour of devolution to be in a majority of the votes cast and to represent a minimum of 40 per cent of those entitled to vote. The voting in Wales was 11.9 per cent in favour, 46.6 per cent against with 41.7 per cent abstaining. Accordingly, the Act was not to be brought into effect. The Labour government elected in 1997 committed itself to devolution to both Scotland and Wales. In the case of Wales, the proposal was for the establishment of a Welsh Assembly, with principally administrative powers, and subject to the overriding sovereignty of the United Kingdom Parliament. The reforms effected in 1998 are discussed in Chapter 12.

THE BRITISH ISLANDS

The United Kingdom, the Channel Islands and the Isle of Man together comprise the British Islands.[80] Accordingly, while the islands are not part of the United Kingdom, they are part of Her Majesty's dominions. Citizens of the islands are

---

75 Bogdanor, 1979, Chapter 5.
76 In relation to which, a Welsh Department of the Board of Education was established in 1907.
77 National Insurance Act 1911.
78 An Agricultural Commissioner for Wales and an Agricultural Council for Wales were established in 1912.
79 *Report of the Royal Commission on the Constitution 1969–73*, Cmnd 5460, 1973, London: HMSO, Vol 1.
80 Interpretation Act 1978, s 5 and Sched 1.

treated as citizens of the United Kingdom for the purposes of the British
Nationality Act 1981.

The Channel Islands[81]

The Channel Islands comprise the islands of Jersey, Guernsey, Alderney and Sark.
Historically part of the Duchy of Normandy, the Channel Islands remained in
allegiance to the King of England when Normandy was lost by the English in
1204. The islands are organised under two separate Bailiwicks: the Bailiwick of
Jersey and the Bailiwick of Guernsey, which includes Alderney and Sark. Each
Bailiwick enjoys its own legislature, court structure and system of law. Alderney
and Sark, whilst part of the Guernsey Bailiwick, enjoy a large measure of
independence, having their own legislative assemblies.

The States of Jersey comprises 52 elected members and five non-elected
members. The States of Guernsey comprises 61 members. Official links between
the Crown and the United Kingdom government are through the Lieutenant
Governor of the Bailiwicks. The legislature – the States – is headed by the Bailiff
and Deputy Bailiff.

The Isle of Man

The Isle of Man became formally linked with England in 1405. From that time
until 1765, it was ruled by 'Kings' or 'Lords' of Man. Under Acts of Parliament of
1765[82] and 1825,[83] the Westminster Parliament assumed, in the name of the
Crown, the rights of the Lords. In 1958, under the Isle of Man Act of that year,
much control over the Isle was relinquished by Westminster. The Isle enjoys full
powers of self-government and has its own system of courts and law. The head of
the Executive, the Lieutenant Governor of the Isle of Man, is the formal link
between the local administration and the Crown and United Kingdom
government. The parliament (the Court of Tynwald) has executive and legislative
functions. It comprises the Lieutenant Governor, the Legislative Council and the
House of Keys. The lower House – the House of Keys – has 24 members elected
on a constituency basis for a five year term of office. The Legislative Council
comprises the senior Bishop, the Attorney General, a judge and seven members
elected by the House of Keys.

The constitutional relationship between the islands and the United Kingdom

The constitutional position of the islands is thus unique. In some respects, they are like
miniature States with wide powers of self-government ...[84]

---

81 See, *inter alia*, *Report of the Royal Commission on the Constitution*, Cmnd 5460, 1973, London:
     HMSO, Vol 1, Pt XI.
82 Isle of Man Purchase Act 1765.
83 Duke of Atholl's Rights, Isle of Man, Act 1825.
84 *Report of the Royal Commission on the Constitution*, Cmnd 5460, 1973, London: HMSO, Vol 1,
     para 1360.

The Crown has ultimate responsibility for the islands. Under international law, the United Kingdom government is responsible both for the islands' international relations and for their defence. Where legislative measures are to extend to the islands, these are effected through the Privy Council. Acts of Parliament extend to the islands only if the statute expressly so provides, or where the Act applies to all Her Majesty's dominions 'by necessary implication'.[85] The Bailiwicks of Jersey and Guernsey do not accept that either the United Kingdom Parliament or the Queen in Council have the power to legislate for them without the consent of the local legislatures and registration in the Royal Court. Contrary to the accepted doctrine of parliamentary supremacy, the Channel Islands deny that Acts of Parliament or prerogative acts, under Orders in Council, can take effect without local registration.

THE ISLANDS AND EUROPE

The European Community and Union

When the United Kingdom signed the Treaty of Rome, special arrangements had to be effected for the islands.[86] Under Article 227(4) of the Treaty of Rome, the Treaty extends to all territories for which Member States have responsibility for their international relations. Were the Treaty to extend automatically to the islands, it would confer power on the institutions of the Community to legislate for the islands in matters such as taxation – which the United Kingdom Parliament, consistent with the convention, would have no *de facto* power to legislate. Accordingly the islands sought special terms in relation to membership of the Community. The resulting solution was that the United Kingdom government negotiated special status for the islands in relation to the Community: the islands are part of the Community for the purpose of free movement of industrial and agricultural goods but not for the purpose of free movement of persons or taxation provisions.

The European Convention on Human Rights

While the position of the Channel Islands and the Isle of Man vis à vis the European Community is the same, the position is different in relation to the Convention. Initially, the Convention on Human Rights extended to both the Channel Islands and the Isle of Man, and nowadays it continues to apply to the Channel Islands.[87] While the Convention initially applied to the Isle of Man, the case of *Tyrer v United Kingdom* (1978) brought about a change. In this case, the European Court of Human Rights held that judicial birching in the Isle of Man of a juvenile amounted to degrading punishment in violation of Article 3 of the Convention. As a result, the Isle of Man government requested that the right of individual petition under the Convention be withdrawn. The United Kingdom government acceded to the request.

---

85 *Sodor and Man (Bishop) v Derby (Earl)* (1751).
86 See Simmonds, 1970, 1971.
87 See *Gillow v United Kingdom* (1986).

LOCAL GOVERNMENT IN ENGLAND AND WALES[88]

Local government antecedes central government by many centuries. Consideration will be given to local government in Chapter 12. Suffice here to note that the country is divided into local authorities, each having law making and administrative powers as delegated by parliament. Local authorities are entirely creatures of statute: accordingly, the only powers they have are those conferred by the sovereign Westminster Parliament. Increasingly, however, the law of the European Community requires action at local authority level.

With the devolution of legislative power to the Scottish Parliament, Northern Ireland Assembly and Welsh Assembly, and the government's commitment to give further consideration to extending the principle of regional government to English regions, significant changes have occurred to the governmental structure of the United Kingdom.

THE EUROPEAN COMMUNITY AND UNION

The United Kingdom's membership of the European Union represents perhaps the most significant challenge to the constitution. It is no longer possible, realistically, to view the United Kingdom as an isolated constitutional entity. Rather, it must be viewed as a distinctive nation (or union of distinctive nations) within the larger union. The aims and institutions of the Union, its law making powers and the relationship between the law of the United Kingdom and European law will be discussed in Chapters 8 and 9.

THE UNITED KINGDOM AND THE COMMONWEALTH[89]

From Empire to Commonwealth

In the sixteenth and seventeenth centuries, Britain embarked on empire building, although the original expansion of British interests overseas was essentially undertaken by private commercial companies. Where territory was taken over by conquest, it became the property of the Crown.[90] Legal authority over such territories vested in the Crown and political control lay with the Privy Council.

The earliest 'revolution' against colonisation came with the American Declaration of Independence in 1776 in which Britain was deprived of 13 North American colonies. By the end of the nineteenth century, vast swathes of the world's map were 'coloured pink' – that is to say, under British power and control. The relationship between Britain and its colonies may be characterised as the movement from full British sovereignty over the territories through to increasing self-government and independence. In 1865, the Colonial Laws Validity Act was passed by the British Parliament in order to clarify the

---

88   Local government in Scotland and Northern Ireland is differently arranged.
89   See, *inter alia*, Roberts-Wray, 1966; Dale, 1983; Wheare, 1960; de Smith, 1964.
90   *Calvin's Case* (1608).

relationship between British law and colonial law and the capacity of colonial legislatures for self-regulation. While the Act confirmed self-regulating legislative capacity, it also affirmed the principle that such devolved powers were subject to the overriding sovereignty of the imperial parliament.

In 1867, Canada became the first self-governing Dominion (a status implying equality with rather than subordination to Britain), to be followed by Australia in 1900, New Zealand in 1907, South Africa in 1910 and the Irish Free State in 1921. The recognition that the Empire was being transformed into a Commonwealth of Nations came in 1884.

The desire for formal recognition and explication of the constitutional relationship between Britain and the Dominions led to four-yearly Prime Ministerial conferences, which commenced in 1887. The Imperial Conference of 1926 adopted the Balfour Report which defined the Dominions as:

> ... autonomous communities within the British Empire, equal in status, in no way subordinate one to another in any aspect of their domestic or external affairs, though united by common allegiance to the Crown, and freely associated as members of the British Commonwealth of Nations.

The Statute of Westminster 1931 gave formal recognition to this definition. Section 2 of the Act extended the powers of Dominion legislatures to amend or repeal Acts of the United Kingdom Parliament, although this power did not extend to going against the limits on the Dominion's legislative capacity as laid down in the Acts containing that country's constitution.[91]

By the end of the Second World War in 1945, much of the remaining British power had been repossessed by its rightful owners, either through direct resistance to British rule (as in India) or by way of negotiated constitutional settlements between the British Crown and the formerly dependent territory.[92] From this time, what remained of the British Empire was transformed into a loosely defined, voluntary Commonwealth of nations, of which the British monarch represents the formal Head.[93] While the Commonwealth was originally characterised by its members' allegiance to the British Crown, the movement towards republicanism forced a change in direction for the Commonwealth. It was Indian independence that represented the catalyst for change. India had remained a Dominion under the India Act of 1935, until independence in 1947. In 1949, India's desire to become a republic and yet remain within the Commonwealth posed a novel question concerning allegiance to the British Crown. The London Declaration of 1949 revised the position and enabled India to

---

91 See *Harris v Minister of the Interior* (1952); *British Coal Corporation v R* (1935); *Ndlwana v Hofmeyer* (1937); and, further, Chapter 7. The constitutional position in relation to Canada was defined by the British North America Act 1867, which contained no amendment provisions. Accordingly, it remained for the United Kingdom Parliament to amend the Canadian Constitution. This anomalous position was resolved in 1982 by the Canada Act which 'repatriated' the Canadian Constitution. For a challenge to the Act, see *Re Amendment of the Constitution of Canada* (1982), discussed in Chapter 2.

92 The constitutional relationship between the United Kingdom Parliament and Australia was finally resolved in 1986 under the Australia Act, which severed the legislative links with Westminster and terminated appeals from the Australian courts to the Privy Council.

93 See further Dale, 1983; Roberts-Wray, 1966.

enter as the first republican member. Heads of government also agreed, however, that members would continue to recognise the Crown as the 'symbol of their free association and thus Head of the Commonwealth', the position which still pertains.

The Commonwealth today

Unlike the European Union and Community, the Commonwealth is undefined by legal texts; it is not established or regulated by treaty; nor do formal legal procedures regulate its inter-governmental relations. Rather, the Commonwealth is characterised by 'bonds of common origin, history and legal traditions'. The Commonwealth is made up of 54 countries,[94] ranging from monarchies – either under Queen Elizabeth II or national monarchs – to republics.[95] Nowadays, 32 members are republics and five have national monarchies of their own, while 16 are constitutional monarchies which recognise Queen Elizabeth II as Head of State. The total population of the Commonwealth is 1.7 billion. The shared history and traditions of Britain and other Commonwealth members, including legal traditions, provides the basis for this voluntary association of states, which spans six continents and five oceans, and which operates without a formal Charter or Constitution.

The Commonwealth was defined in 1971 at the Commonwealth Heads of Government Meeting (CHOGM) as:

> ... a voluntary association of independent sovereign States, each responsible for its own policies, consulting and cooperating in the common interests of their peoples and in the promotion of international understanding and world peace.[96]

Further, at the 1971 CHOGM held in Singapore, Heads of Government issued the Declaration of Commonwealth Principles. The principles include:

(a) the commitment to international peace in order to ensure the security and prosperity of mankind;

(b) commitments to the liberty of the individual, irrespective of race, colour, creed or political belief and the individual's democratic right to participate in democratic political processes;

(c) a commitment to combating racial discrimination;

(d) an opposition to all forms of colonial domination;

(e) a commitment to removal of disparities in wealth between nations and to raising standards of living; and

(f) a commitment to international co-operation.

These principles were reaffirmed and extended at the Harare CHOGM in 1991, which declared the Commonwealth's commitment to promoting democracy, good government, human rights, the rule of law and gender equality within the

---

94 Nigeria's membership of the Commonwealth was suspended in 1995.
95 See Appendix III, pp 808–09, for a full list of member states.
96 Commonwealth Declaration, 22 January 1971. CHOGMs take place every two years.

context of sustainable economic and social development. Commonwealth members provide assistance to other countries in their transition to democracy by drafting legislation and reviewing electoral procedures.

The Commonwealth Secretariat

The Commonwealth is headed by a Secretary General. Under his stewardship, the Commonwealth Secretariat has been refashioned to enable it better to achieve Commonwealth objectives. The Secretariat was formed in 1965 and now has 12 separate divisions.[97] The operational arm of the Secretariat is the Commonwealth Fund for Technical Co-operation, established in 1971,[98] which, at the request of Commonwealth governments, provides 'technical assistance and expert advice on all issues within the Commonwealth's agenda'.[99]

Appeals from Commonwealth courts to the Privy Council

The Judicial Committee of the Privy Council has jurisdiction to hear appeals from 'dependencies of the Crown'. Deriving from the royal prerogative, the jurisdiction was given statutory force under the Judicial Committee Acts of 1833 and 1844. Appeals may be with special leave of the Privy Council, or without leave. Appeals with special leave are predominantly criminal cases. Appeals against the death penalty represent the majority of appeals.[100]

While before independence colonies had no power to abolish appeals to the Privy Council, on independence, this power arose. As a result, a majority of Commonwealth countries have abolished the right of appeal.

---

97 The Secretariat is funded by an assessed budget (in 1996–97, amounting to £120.4 million), contributed to by member governments on an agreed scale based on each country's population and income. In addition to the assessed budget are the Commonwealth Fund for Technical Co-operation, the Commonwealth Youth Programme, and the Commonwealth Science Council, each of which has its own budget.
98 In 1996–97, the CFTC had an annual budget of £25 million.
99 The CFTC has four principal divisions: the Economic and Legal Advisory Services Division; the Export and Industrial Development Division; the General Technical Assistance Services Division; and the Management and Training Services Division.
100 See *Hector v Attorney General of Antigua* (1990); *Runyowa v R* (1967); *Ong Ah Chuan v Public Prosecutor* (1981); *Riley v Attorney General of Jamaica* (1983); *Pratt v Attorney General of Jamaica* (1994); *Reckley v Minister of Public Safety (No 2)* (1996).

PART II

FUNDAMENTAL CONSTITUTIONAL CONCEPTS

CHAPTER 4

THE RULE OF LAW

Where laws do not rule, there is no constitution.[1]

INTRODUCTION

The rule of law represents one of the most challenging concepts of the constitution. The rule of law is a concept which is capable of different interpretations by different people, and it is this feature which makes an understanding of the doctrine elusive. Of all constitutional concepts, the rule of law is also the most subjective and value laden. The apparent uncertainties in the rule of law and its variable nature should not cause concern, although, inevitably, it will cause some insecurity. In the study of the rule of law, it is more important to recognise and appreciate the many rich and varied interpretations which have been given to it, and to recognise the potential of the rule of law for ensuring limited governmental power and the protection of individual rights, than to be able to offer an authoritative, definitive explanation of the concept.

The rule of law may be interpreted either as a *philosophy* or *political theory* which lays down fundamental requirements for law, or as a *procedural device* by which those with power rule under the law. The essence of the rule of law is that of the sovereignty or supremacy of law over man. The rule of law insists that every person – irrespective of rank and status in society – be subject to the law. For the citizen, the rule of law is both *prescriptive* – dictating the conduct required by law – and *protective* of citizens – demanding that government acts according to law. This central theme recurs whether the doctrine is examined from the perspective of philosophy, or political theory, or from the more pragmatic vantage point of the rule of law as a procedural device. The rule of law underlies the entire constitution and, in one sense, all constitutional law is concerned with the rule of law. The concept is of great antiquity and continues to exercise legal and political philosophers today.

The rule of law cannot be viewed in isolation from political society. The emphasis on the rule of law as a yardstick for measuring both the extent to which government acts under the law and the extent to which individual rights are recognised and protected by law, is inextricably linked with Western democratic liberalism.[2] In this respect, it is only meaningful to speak of the rule of law in a society which exhibits the features of a democratically elected, responsible – and responsive – government and a separation of powers, which will result in a judiciary which is independent of government. In liberal democracies, therefore, the concept of the rule of law implies an acceptance that law itself represents a 'good'; that law and its governance is a demonstrable asset to society.

---

1   Aristotle, *The Politics*, Bk iv, para 1292a31.
2   See, *inter alia*, Fine, 1984; Hutchinson and Monahan, 1987; Neumann, 1986.

CONTRASTING ATTITUDES TO THE RULE OF LAW

It should not be assumed that this acceptance of law as a benevolent ruling force is universally accepted. In differing societies, subscribing to very different political philosophies, the insistence on the rule of law – in the Western liberal sense – has little application. For example, from a Marxist perspective (on which see below, pp 74–75), the law serves not to restrict government and protect individual rights but rather to conceal the injustices inherent in the capitalist system. Accordingly, the concept of the rule of law – denoting some form of morality in law – represents no more than a false idealisation of law designed to reinforce the political structure and economic status quo in society. Echoes of this thesis dominate the more moderate socialist conceptions of the rule of law and the critique of liberalism. It can be argued – from the socialist perspective – that liberalism pays too little regard to true equality between persons and too great attention to the protection of property interests. The liberal domain thus becomes one which, again, masks true social and economic inequality while at the same time proclaiming equality and justice under the rule of law.[3]

The rule of law, as understood in liberal democracies, also has little relevance in a totalitarian state. While it is true that such a state will be closely regulated by law, there will not be government under the law – as adjudicated upon by an independent judiciary – which is insisted upon under the liberal tradition.

In traditional Oriental society, the Western preference for law is an alien notion. By way of example, in relation to traditional Chinese society, David and Brierley write:

> For the Chinese, legislation was not the normal means of guaranteeing a harmonious and smooth-working society. Laws, abstract in nature, could not take into account the infinite variety of possible situations. Their strict application was apt to affect man's innate sense of justice. To enact laws was therefore considered a bad policy by traditional Chinese doctrine. The very exactitude which laws establish in social relations, and the way in which they fix the rights and obligations of each individual, were considered evils, according to the Chinese, not benefits. The idea of 'rights', an inevitable development of the laws themselves, ran counter to the natural order. Once individuals think of their 'rights' there is, it was thought, some form of social illness; the only true matter of concern is one's duty to society and one's fellow men.

> The enactment of laws is an evil, since individuals, once familiar with them, will conclude that they have rights and will then be inclined to assert them, thereby abandoning the traditional rules of propriety and morality which should be the only guides to conduct. Legal disputes become numerous, and a trial, by reason of its very existence, is a scandalous disturbance of the natural order which may then lead to further disturbances of the social order to the detriment of all society. [1966, p 442; and see 3rd edn, 1985, Title III, Chapter 1 for the persistence of traditional ideas]

In Japan, despite the nineteenth century adoption of codes based on French and German models,[4] law, in the Western sense, remained largely irrelevant to traditional Japanese life:

---

3   For a critical account of the liberal tradition see Lustgarten, 1988.
4   Penal Code and Code of Criminal Procedure enacted in 1882; Codes on Judicial Organisation and Civil Procedure 1890; Commercial Code 1899.

Still essential for the Japanese are the rules of behaviour (*giri-ninjo*) for each type of personal relation established by tradition and founded, at least in appearance, on the feelings of affection (*ninjo*) uniting those in such relationships. A person who does not observe these rules is seeking his own interest rather than obeying the nobler part of his nature; he brings scorn upon himself and his family. Apart from the contracts arising between important but depersonalised business and industrial concerns, one does not attempt to have one's rights enforced in a court of law even though this is permitted by the various codes ... [David and Brierley, 1966, p 458; see 3rd edn, Title III, Chapter 2]

As the notion of the rule of law is dependent upon the political foundations of a state, so, too, it is dependent – according to the approach adopted to the concept – upon a nation's economic resources. It may be that law, as a mere regulator of individual behaviour, is perfectly feasible in an impoverished state, and accordingly, a state which maintains law and order, and no more, can conform to a narrow interpretation of the rule of law which insists simply on a citizen's unquestioning compliance with rules of the law. However, if the rule of law implies more than mere regulation by law and is elevated to a theory guaranteeing freedom from hunger and homelessness and entitlement to a basic decent standard of life, then economic conditions are of paramount importance to conformity with the rule of law. Such an approach is adopted by the International Commission of Jurists, which in the New Delhi Declaration of 1959 included – alongside traditional civil and political rights – the realisation of social, economic, cultural and educational standards under which the individual could enjoy a fuller life within the ambit of the rule of law. On the other hand, reasoning such as this is anathema to radical conservatives such as Friedrich von Hayek (1944), who viewed the correct role of government as being best confined to establishing clear, fixed rules of law which ensure maximum economic freedom for individuals, unimpeded either by planning controls or ideas of redistributive justice. From von Hayek's perspective, the rule of law requires no more than the existence of a stable set of minimum rules which are to be applied in a uniform, non-discretionary manner. A legal system is viewed as just – and in conformity with the rule of law – if it exhibits both these features and an absence of discretionary rules or practices.

UNCERTAINTY IN THE WESTERN RULE OF LAW

An understanding and appreciation of the rule of law is both politically and culturally dependent. Moreover, it is also clear that the rule of law has more than one meaning, even within the Western liberal tradition. To some theorists, the rule of law represents an aspirational philosophy; to others, no more than a device under which compliance with law – good or bad in content – is secured. It has been remarked that:

It would not be very difficult to show that the phrase 'the rule of law' has become meaningless thanks to ideological abuse and general over-use.[5]

---

5   Shklar, 'Political theory and the rule of law', in Hutchinson and Monahan, 1987, p 1.

Partly as a result of such 'over-use', some writers have refuted the claim that the rule of law represents anything other than a purely procedural or formalistic device. By way of example, Raz writes that the rule of law:

> ... says nothing about how the law is to be made: by tyrants, democratic majorities, or any other way. It says nothing about fundamental rights, about equality, or justice.[6]

Contrast such views with that expressed in the following statement:

> The rule of law is a rare and protean principle of our political tradition. Unlike other ideals, it has withstood the ravages of constitutional time and remains a contemporary clarion-call to political justice. Apparently transcending partisan concern, it is embraced and venerated by virtually all shades of political opinion. The rule of law's central core comprises the enduring values of regularity and restraint, embodied in the slogan of 'a government of laws, not ... men'. [Hutchinson and Monahan, 1987, p ix]

In light of such divergent assessments, it must be recognised that any attempt to align the rule of law with a broad philosophical doctrine – or indeed with any other interpretation – is likely to meet with opposition from some quarters. Notwithstanding such criticisms, the rule of law retains a secure grasp on political and legal thinking: in the words of Raz (1979), it has 'enduring importance as a central artefact in our legal and political culture'.

THE RULE OF LAW AS PHILOSOPHICAL DOCTRINE

The rule of law is an aspect of ancient and modern natural law thought.[7] In essence, the natural law tradition – of which there are many strands – insists that the authority of law derives not from the power of any political ruler, but from a higher source, either theological or secular. The laws of man must be evaluated against the dictates of this 'higher' form of law. It is impossible to provide more than a mere sketch of the rich history of natural law in Western philosophy and political thought and the legacy it gives to modern constitutions. Nevertheless, a basic understanding of its nature and evolution is instructive, for it reveals the manner in which the requirements of good law – morally worthwhile law – have been stipulated over centuries.

Natural law in ancient Greece and Rome

Aristotle stated in *The Politics* that 'the rule of law is preferable to that of any individual'. The appeal to law as a control over naked power has been apparent throughout history. At a philosophical level, the natural law tradition, whether theological or secular, instructs that the power of man is not absolute, but is rather controlled and limited by the requirements of a higher law. To the ancient Greeks, man was under the governance of the laws of nature – the natural forces which controlled the universe – although this view is more closely aligned to the 'law of nature' than 'natural law' as it came to be understood in later times. However,

---

See Raz, 1979, p 210. On Dicey's influence see below, pp 84 ff; de Smith and Brazier, 1998.
n natural law, see d'Entrèves, 1970; and Finnis, 1980.

from the time of Socrates, Plato (427–347 BC) and Aristotle (384–322 BC), the quest for virtue – or goodness or justice under the law – has been a recurrent theme. Socrates, teacher and philosopher, was accused, tried and convicted by the grand jury of Athens for corrupting youth with his teachings. Despite the possibility of escape, Socrates chose to accept the verdict of death which had been imposed upon him, in order to demonstrate his fidelity to law. When pressed by Crito to escape, Socrates considered the questions which would be put to him by the laws and constitution of Athens were he to succumb to the temptation to escape the penalty of the law:

> Can you deny that by this act [of escaping] which you are contemplating you intend, so far as you have the power, to destroy us, the laws, and the whole state as well? Do you imagine that a city can continue to exist and not be turned upside down, if the legal judgments which are pronounced in it have no force but are nullified and destroyed by private persons? [Crito, in Hamilton and Cairns, 1989, p 50b]

In submitting to death, Socrates was doing nothing other than giving recognition to the supremacy of law: to the rule of law. An early – and famous – formulation of the dictates of natural law was offered by Cicero (106–43 BC):

> True law is right reason in agreement with nature; it is of universal application, unchanging and everlasting; it summons to duty by its commands, and averts from wrongdoing by its prohibitions. And it does not lay its commands or prohibitions upon good men in vain, though neither have any effect on the wicked. It is a sin to try to alter this law, nor is it allowable to attempt to repeal any part of it, and it is impossible to abolish it entirely. We cannot be freed from its obligations by Senate or People, and we need not look outside ourselves for an expounder or interpreter of it. And there will not be different laws at Rome and at Athens, or different laws now and in the future, but one eternal and unchangeable law will be valid for all nations and for all times, and there will be one master and one ruler, that is, God, over us all, for He is the author of this law, its promulgator, and its enforcing judge. [*De Republica,* cited in d'Entrèves, 1970, p 25]

It is from ancient Greek philosophy that natural law enters into Roman law. From the *Corpus Iuris Civilis* (AD 534) is derived *ius civilis, ius gentium* and *ius naturale*. *Ius civilis* denotes the law of the state; *ius gentium* the law of nations; and *ius naturale* 'a law which expresses a higher and more permanent standard'. It is the law of nature (*ius naturale*) which corresponds to 'that which is always good and equitable' (d'Entrèves, 1970, p 24).

Christian natural law thought

The scriptures and gospel provided the basis for Christian natural law thought which developed in the Middle Ages. Natural law was perceived as God-given, communicated to man by Revelation, and remaining absolutely binding upon man and unchanging in its content. As a result, the dictates of natural law take precedence over man made laws. If the demands of the state conflict with the laws of God, the obligation to God must prevail. Undoubtedly, the most powerful writing of the Middle Ages comes from St Thomas Aquinas (1225–74):

> This rational guidance of created things on the part of God ... we can call the Eternal Law.

But, of all others, rational creatures are subject to divine Providence in a very special way; being themselves made participators in Providence itself, in that they control their own actions and the actions of others. So they have a share in the divine reason itself, deriving therefrom a natural inclination to such actions and ends as are fitting. This participation in the Eternal Law by rational creatures is called Natural Law. [*Summa Theologica,* cited in d'Entrèves, 1970, p 43]

In the thirteenth century, Bracton proclaimed that 'the King himself ought not be subject to man but subject to God and to the law, because the law makes him King' (1968–77, f5 b). In 1534, Thomas More (1478–1535) – at the cost of his life – refused to recognise Henry VIII as head of the Church, thereby acknowledging the higher duty of obedience to God rather than the rule of his temporal King.

Natural law and international law

On an international level, natural law thought played a significant role in establishing the overarching dictates of international law. Grotius (1583–1645), for example, maintained that natural law was discernible by man by virtue of his rationality and that a system of natural law would accordingly exist independently of theological perceptions and dictates. In short, natural law would exist even if God did not exist. In addition to the insistence on rationalism, the emphasis of natural law at this time started to focus on the individual, and from this period is discerned the origins of assertions of the rights of man. AP d'Entrèves writes:

... when we read the American or the French Declarations we know that we are confronted with a complete architecture, about the style of which there can be no mistake. It is a political philosophy based upon a particular notion of the individual, of society and of their mutual relationship. [1970, p 57]

The idea of social contract

It is from these beginnings that the theories of social contract and the rights of man derive. The writings of John Locke, Jean-Jacques Rousseau and Thomas Paine are all infused with the doctrine of the inalienability of individual human rights – rights which transcend the law of the state, which cannot be overridden by the state, and which affirm the supremacy of the law of the state with the important proviso that the law of the state is in compliance with natural law.[8]

Natural law and common law

In the West, the sovereignty of law became inextricably linked with the Christian faith. As seen above, in the thirteenth century, Aquinas asserted the overriding obligation to God, as opposed to any temporal power. In England, the break with the Roman Catholic Church in 1535 established Henry VIII as head of the English Church. By assuming supreme power over both spiritual and secular matters, Henry VIII ostensibly broke the logical separation of duty towards God and the duty owed to the King: obedience to the sovereign now became a religious as well

---

8   Locke, 1690; Rousseau, 1762; Paine, 1791, Pt I.

as a political duty. The execution of Sir Thomas More in 1535 is illustrative of the King's reaction to an individual refusal to recognise the absolute supremacy of the King. Nevertheless, natural law thought continued to permeate the common law of England before the settlement of 1688 and the rise of parliamentary sovereignty.

One of the classic exponents of the demand for the King to be subject to the law – rather than above it – was Sir Edward Coke (1552–1634), whose struggle with the King led to his dismissal as Chief Justice in 1616. James I[9] viewed himself as imbued with ultimate power, derived from God under the prerogative. To Coke, laws derived from parliament – comprising the King and the three estates of the realm – the Lords Spiritual, the Lords Temporal and the Commons.[10] The power of parliament was subject to the common law, and hence it was that Coke declared:

> It appears in our books that in many cases the common law will control the Acts of Parliament and sometimes adjudge them to be utterly void; for when an Act of Parliament is against the common right or repugnant or impossible to be performed the common law will control it and adjudge such Act to be void.[11]

When, in 1608, Coke told the King that the common law protected the King, the King regarded his speech as traitorous, proclaiming that 'The King protecteth the law, and not the law the King'.[12] Coke's insistence on the supremacy of common law was not pure natural law thought, but rather the philosophical view of the power of legal reasoning deriving from precedent. Indeed it was the King who claimed natural law as being on his side, claiming that the King was not 'ignorant of any points [of law] which belong to a King to know'.[13] Sir Francis Bacon (1561–1626) favoured the King's view, seeking to limit the power of the judges: it was for the King to formulate policy and make law (*Advancement of Learning*, 1605). Coke's view nevertheless expresses an idea which is central to natural law thought, namely that there is a higher authority – based on moral judgment – than the law of man. The control of the prerogative power of the King was to dominate English constitutional development until 1688. With the settlement of 1688 and the Bill of Rights 1689, the doctrine of parliamentary supremacy over the King, the prerogative and common law was established. Thereafter, there were to be no assertions of any overriding higher law. The judges bowed to the sovereignty of parliament.

---

9   King of Scotland 1567–1625; King of England and Scotland 1603–25.
10 Coke, 1644, Bk IV, Chapter 1.
11 *Dr Bonham's Case* (1610). But see the contrary explanation offered by Thorne, 1938. See also Chapter 7.
12 Bowen, 1957.
13 Bowen, 1957.

THE RULE OF LAW AS POLITICAL THEORY

Liberalism, conservatism and the rule of law

The rule of law has been subjected to analysis by political theorists of all persuasions. From the vantage point of the liberal democrat, the rule of law will ensure the minimum rules in society to enable man to fulfil his life plan according to law, but with the minimum interference of law.

AV Dicey's writing on the rule of law has had a lasting influence on constitutional thought. His writing will be considered in detail below, pp 82 ff. However, Dicey has been criticised by Sir Ivor Jennings for being motivated, in his writings, by his conservative views. Dicey, in expressing his preference for clear and stable rules and the minimum of discretion within the legal process, was, according to Jennings, revealing his conservative preference for certainty within law rather than concern for the law being directed towards social justice which necessarily entails much discretionary power in the application of broad rules. Jennings (1959b, p 311) writes that Dicey was 'concerned not with clearing up of the nasty industrial sections of the towns, but with the liberty of the subject'. For Jennings, Dicey's view that 'Englishmen are ruled by the law, and by the law alone' is 'not enough':

> The powers of Louis XIV, of Napoleon I, of Hitler, and of Mussolini were derived from the law, even though that law be only 'The Leader may do and order what he pleases'. The doctrine involves some considerable limitation on the powers of every political authority, except possibly (for this is open to dispute) those of a representative legislature. Indeed it contains, as we shall see, something more, though it is not capable of precise definition. It is an attitude, an expression of liberal and democratic principles, in themselves vague when it is sought to analyse them, but clear enough in their results. [1959b, p 48]

For Jennings, the doctrine implies, first, that the state as a whole must be regulated by law; secondly, that the separation of powers is implied within the doctrine in order to prevent dictatorship or absolutism. Accordingly, there are incorporated certain basic requirements[14] of the law: equality before the law; clearly defined police powers; clear general rules adjudicated upon by the courts; non-retrospectivity in penal statutes; and the strict construction of penal statutes. Thirdly, the doctrine incorporates the principle of *equality*: a notion which Jennings concedes is as vague as that of the rule of law itself (1959b, p 49). Moreover, and of prime importance, the rule of law implies the notion of *liberty*.

Marxism and the rule of law

Arguments against a formalistic perception of the rule of law adopted by, *inter alia*, Dicey and von Hayek present a formidable target for attack from a Marxist perspective. Where liberalism insists that law is neutral as between persons and classes and favours maximum liberty for all under the law, Marxism insists that law represents the interests of the powerful within society. Law is an ideological

---

14 Cf Raz, 1979, Chapter 11; and Fuller, 1964.

device engaged by those with power to mask the reality of that power in society, and the correlative powerlessness of the ordinary citizen. The rule of law is thus portrayed as a means of subterfuge: it is a mere pretence which hides injustice. Marxism stands in opposition to liberalism and yet, paradoxically, seeks as its end result the complete liberty of man. Law, from a Marxist perspective, is the reflection of economic power within society, a power which is used to exploit the powerless. Thus it is that, under capitalism, the worker is not rewarded with the full value of his labour: rather, he receives a price for his labour to which is added production costs and profits and together comprise the final price of a product. The laws which regulate factories and employment terms are all underpinned by the acceptance of the capitalist ideal. Laws which ameliorate the conditions of the poor do not represent – as appears at first sight – real social justice, but rather they represent a calculated means by which the poor are kept compliant within their powerlessness.[15] Accordingly, the welfare state is but a cynical mask for maintenance of the status quo which defeats the movement towards revolutionary economic and social change:

> Far from hastening the revolution, the welfare state undermines efforts to create working class solidarity. By preventing the fullest development of the material degradation of the working class and by providing a limited immunity from the vicissitudes of economic crises, a welfare state delays the formation of class consciousness and thus prevents a revolutionary situation from arising ... [Collins, 1982, pp 126–27]

Whether law serves to oppress or merely to uphold the economic status quo – and there exists dispute on this matter between Marxists themselves – law, from a Marxist perspective, does not serve the interests of all in society. The rule of law thus becomes a grand slogan under which is hidden the reality of oppression and absence of liberty. The capitalist's insistence on the rule of law is seen as a 'fetishism' which must be removed along with economic oppression (Cain, 1979, Chapter 5). Only when the capitalist system breaks down, and the law which serves it 'withers away', will society become truly free. When that occurs, there will be no need for law and man will achieve true freedom.

Professor Joseph Raz and the rule of law

Professor Joseph Raz approaches the rule of law from a morally neutral but conceptual standpoint, and asserts that:

> The rule of law is a political ideal which a legal system may lack or may possess to a greater or lesser degree. That much is common ground. It is also to be insisted that the rule of law is just one of the virtues which a legal system may possess and by which it is to be judged. It is not to be confused with democracy, justice, equality (before the law or otherwise), human rights of any kind or respect for persons or for the dignity of man. A non-democratic legal system, based on the denial of human rights, on extensive poverty, on racial segregation, sexual inequalities, and religious persecution may, in principle, conform to the requirements of the rule of law better than any of the legal systems of the more enlightened Western democracies. [1979, p 211]

---

15 See Cain and Hunt, 1979.

Raz acknowledges that his claim will 'alarm many', but insists that it presents 'a coherent view of one important virtue which legal systems should possess'. In seeking to elucidate the ideal of the rule of law, Raz draws the analogy between the rule of law and a knife. One quality of a good knife is sharpness. However, the quality of sharpness says nothing as to the use to which the knife might be put: beneficial surgery or murder. Sharpness is morally neutral. And thus it is with the rule of law. However, the purpose of law is to enable citizens to live within the law. Accordingly, there are certain principles that must be respected if that goal is to be fulfilled. For the rule of law to exist in society, certain qualities must be present. The law must be clear if it is to be capable of being obeyed. In *Merkur Island Shipping Corporation v Laughton* (1983), for example, Lord Donaldson MR stated that:

> The efficacy and maintenance of the rule of law, which is the foundation of any parliamentary democracy, has at least two pre-requisites. First, people must understand that it is in their interests, as well as in that of the community as a whole, that they should live their lives in accordance with the rules and all the rules. Secondly, they must know what those rules are ...

Lord Donaldson's view was endorsed by Lord Diplock in the House of Lords:

> Absence of clarity is destructive of the rule of law; it is unfair to those who wish to preserve the rule of law; it encourages those who wish to undermine it. [p 612]

The law must be publicised in order that citizens are aware of its demands; reasonably stable in order that citizens can plan their lives according to law; prospective so that the law does not require the impossible;[16] non-contradictory for the same reason, and, in addition, the courts must be accessible and staffed by an independent judiciary. Compliance with each of these requirements will indicate that a society respects the rule of law. To make such a statement is not to say that the legal system is one which is necessarily morally 'good'. As seen in Raz's illustration with the quality of sharpness in relation to the knife, the fact of sharpness does not dictate the morality of the purposes to which the knife will be put. It is possible, accordingly, for the rule of law to exist without the legal system necessarily pursuing morally good ends.

Professor Lon Fuller and the rule of law

The writing of Professor Lon Fuller (1964) – who stands in contrast to Raz – may be invoked here in order to develop further this idea. Fuller's focus is on the 'morality of law'. For Fuller, the requirements of law, which are substantially the same as those of Raz, lay down the basic minimum requirements, not just of a system in accordance with the rule of law, but for the very existence of a system to which he would accord the label 'legal'. These basic prerequisites form the 'morality of duty' or 'inner morality of law'. These principles provide the basic foundations of a legal system. To draw an analogy with building construction, failure to lay sound foundations will result in the edifice resting on an insecure

---

16 A principle endorsed in *Phillips v Eyre* (1870) and *Waddington v Miah* (1974). See, however, the War Damage Act 1965 and the War Crimes Act 1991 for illustrations of parliament's power to legislate retrospectively.

and fragile base. In addition to a secure foundation, for a legal system to be worthy of recognition – and to impose the duty of obedience upon its members – it must serve the needs of the people. Law does not exist in a vacuum separate from the society it regulates. Recognition of this vital characteristic of law demands that the legal system be directed towards altruistic, beneficial ends. This is the 'morality of aspiration' towards which each valid legal system must strive. Thus, a government must seek to provide the environment in which each citizen may realise to his maximum potential the rational plan of life to which he aspires. Society must be free and directed to the good of each of its members. Any government which fails in a material degree to meet these requirements may fail to deserve the label of a 'legal system'.

The important point here is that Fuller is quite prepared to argue that a system of government which contravened the basic requirements of a 'good' system of law might be recognised as some form of governmental regime but would not be a government according to law, and hence would not be a 'legal' system. In order to deserve recognition as a system of law, the system must respect the very fundamental moral requirements which Fuller identifies.

Professor HLA Hart has argued that even a dictatorial regime with no respect for morality or fundamental rights would be capable of meeting Fuller's requirements (see Hart, 1958). Fuller disputes this, arguing that an evil regime, such as that of Nazi Germany, sooner or later would be compelled to pass retrospective law or secret laws in order to pursue its evil objectives. Moreover, Fuller argues that there is an additional quality of morality which must be present in a system of law: that the law serves the interests of the people it governs. Thus, the law must be pursuing altruistic moral ends if it is to have recognition. If it is not, then Fuller would have no difficulty in denying that a 'legal system' existed at all.

Raz rejects the linkage between the rule of law and morality and claims that Fuller's thesis fails to establish a necessary connection between law and morals. And yet, for some, the distinction may be a fine one.

Friedrich von Hayek and the rule of law

A further perspective of the rule of law is provided by Friedrich von Hayek. *The Road to Serfdom* was written against the background of the Second World War, and expressed von Hayek's fundamental concern with the prospect of the expansion of the state. This von Hayek opposed, other than at a basic level necessary to guarantee freedom, and von Hayek describes the rule of law in the following manner:

> ... stripped of all technicalities this means that government in all its action is bound by rules fixed and announced beforehand – rules which make it possible to foresee with fair certainty how the authority will use its coercive powers in given circumstances, and to plan one's individual affairs on the basis of this knowledge. [1944, p 54]

The idea of a welfare state and the entailed notion of distributive justice which entails the state operating under discretionary rules in order to provide a minimum standard of living was firmly opposed by von Hayek. The rule of law, for von Hayek, should be confined to the provision of clear, certain rules which would enable people to plan their lives in a free society. To require that people should contribute to the less well off in society through a system of graduated taxation, coupled with discretion to determine entitlement and quantum of recipients, violated his perceived ideal state.

Modern expression of many of von Hayek's ideas is to be found in the writings of Robert Nozick, a clear and forceful advocate of the 'minimal state'. Nozick rejects any concept of distributive justice. Instead, he argues for perceptions of justice based on the concept of rights expressed in the name of entitlements. A state of affairs – and hence a state – will be 'just' if it respects the principle of entitlement. As Nozick puts it:

> Things come into the world already attached to people having entitlements over them. From the point of view of the historical entitlement conception of justice in holdings, those who start afresh to complete 'to each according his ...' treats objects as if they appeared from nowhere, out of nothing. [1974, p 160]

Justice therefore lies in the recognition of the justice of holdings. If the manner in which property is acquired is lawful, if the manner in which property is transferred is lawful, the society will be just. To deny the justice of this situation – from a Nozickian perspective – and to argue for the forced redistribution of wealth in society, is to defeat the rights of the individual property holder.

John Rawls's theory of justice and the rule of law

Opposed to von Hayek and Nozick stands John Rawls, whose *Theory of Justice* provides a detailed exposition of, and justification for, the interventionist state committed to distributive justice. In essence, a society will be 'just' if it is organised according to principles established by all its members in the 'original position' behind a 'veil of ignorance'. Suffice to note here that the 'original position' and 'veil of ignorance' relate to a stage of decision making about constitutional arrangements wherein the participants know nothing of their own personal attributes and wants and little of the society in which they live. They will accordingly choose principles of justice which are not self-interested but based on maximising the position of those persons (of whom the decision maker may turn out to be but one) who are in the least enviable position in society. The principles they will choose will be, first, the priority of liberty for all, subject to the need to redistribute goods in society in order to improve the lot of the 'worst off'.

The rule of law, according to Rawls, is 'obviously closely related to liberty' (1973, p 235). Rawls calls for the 'regular and impartial administration of public rules' which is the essence of a just legal system characterised by the 'legitimate expectations' of the people. Several requirements must be met: rules of law must only command action which is possible; those who enact laws must do so in good faith; like cases must be treated alike. Echoing Dicey, Rawls states that there is no offence without a law – *nulla poena sine lege* – and this requirement in turn demands that laws be known, that they be general, and that penal laws should not be retroactive to the disadvantage of those to whom they apply. Finally, the legal system must respect the dictates of natural justice.[17]

'Law and order' and the rule of law: the obligation to obey law

An alternative perception of the rule of law may be labelled the 'law and order' model.[18] This view emphasises the peaceful settlement of disputes without recourse to violence, armed force or terrorism. In legal philosophy, the idea of absolute obedience to law is compatible with the analytical, positivist school of thought which dominated much jurisprudential thought from the nineteenth century until after the Second World War. Positivism is the antithesis of natural law. The primary quest for positivists is to separate legal and moral issues: to distinguish between the 'is' (that which exists as fact) and the 'ought' (that which is desirable). Under positivist theory – which is primarily concerned to explain law as it exists in fact – where valid law exists, that is to say law which is accorded validity under the fundamental constitutional rule in a state, there is an obligation on each citizen to obey that law. Hans Kelsen and other legal positivists regard the duty to obey validly created norms as absolute.[19]

Taken to its logical conclusion, however, the 'law and order' view can lead to the repression of freedom. By way of illustration, it is a common cry of politicians that a demonstration by, for example, trade union members or students, contravenes the 'rule of law'. In a strict sense, any action which involves protest will almost inevitably violate some legal rule – whether it is the rule protested against or otherwise.[20] Public protest, for example, will often involve breach of rules against obstruction of the highway, of the police in the execution of their duty, trespass, or criminal damage, even though those laws are not the object of the protest. It becomes necessary, therefore, to consider – albeit in outline – the nature of an individual's obligation to obey valid law. The fundamental question in this regard lies in the extent to which citizens should be coerced into obedience to 'unjust laws'. Is there an absolute obligation to obey, irrespective of the quality of the law? Is the duty only *prima facie*? Is there ever a duty to disobey the law in pursuit of a higher ideal? Each of these vast and timeless philosophical questions underpins the concept of the rule of law.

Is there a duty to obey law?

To be balanced against the arguments for absolute obedience to law is the legitimacy of protest within society. Since the time of Aristotle, it has been argued that the law must be tempered with equity, which dictates the standards of justice and rightness in society. Law derives its authority from the obedience of the people.[21] Laws must be directed to the 'good', not only to comply with the dictates of morality, but also for the more pragmatic reason of ensuring voluntary

---

17 See, further on this, Chapter 27.
18 See Bradley and Ewing, 1997, Chapter 6.
19 Kelsen, 1961, 1967.
20 On 'direct' and 'indirect' civil disobedience, see Rawls, 1973, Chapter 7.
21 Aristotle, *The Politics*, 1269a.

compliance with law. It may be argued that nowadays in a responsive, democratic state, any dispute as to the rights of individuals and grievances against government action will be dealt with through the provided channels of complaint, for example through the individual's Member of Parliament or through an investigation by the Commissioners for Administration.[22] Alternatively, it may be argued that if many citizens are commonly aggrieved, the media can be employed to influence government and that, ultimately, at least once every five years,[23] the electorate can express its views through the ballot box. None of these avenues, however, may yield the desired result, particularly if the aggrieved individual or group is a minority without popular support.

Is there a right to disobey law?

The question that then arises is whether the individual has a 'right' to disobey the law.[24] A government true to democratic precepts of representativeness and fairness must be sensitive to demands for change. If it fails in that regard, it is at least arguable that demands for change, while entailing technical breaches of the law, should be accommodated within the constitutional framework.

In 1848, Henry Thoreau refused to pay taxes to support the slavery laws and declared: '... the place for a just man in such a community is in jail.'

In the same century, the suffragette movement resorted to unlawful behaviour in the ultimately successful pursuit of the right to enfranchisement – the right to vote.[25] Mahatma Gandhi's peaceful civil disobedience campaign led to the independence of India in 1947. The Civil Rights movement in the United States in the 1950s, led by Martin Luther King, resulted in reforms of the law concerning racial segregation.[26] The tide of protest over American involvement in the Vietnam war had a direct impact on government policy and further raised legal and political interest in civil disobedience. Major social changes of such magnitude would have been impossible without recognition that under certain limited conditions there exists a right of legitimate protest, however inconvenient and uncomfortable this is for governments. The 'law and order' model of the rule of law would fail to respect any such 'right', and the reaction may be one of repression.[27] However, it is not necessary to look to such major societal changes brought about by defiance of law in order to refute the 'law and order' model and proclaim some entitlement to dissent.

John Rawls concedes a right to disobedience in pursuit of changing a society's 'sense of justice', but confines civil disobedience to peaceful protest.[28] Rawls's thesis is founded on the notion of social contract. That concept, as has been seen above, involves the mutual recognition, *inter alia*, of the rights of citizens and the

---

22 See Chapter 28.
23 Under the Parliament Act 1911, the maximum life of a parliament is five years. See further Chapter 14.
24 See Rawls, 1973, Chapter 7.
25 See, *inter alia*, Kent, 1987.
26 *Brown v Board of Education of Topeka* (1954); and see King, 1963.
27 As in Tiananmen Square 1989.
28 Rawls, 1973, Chapter 6.

rights of the state. The extent to which citizens participate in the law making process is critical to an understanding of the extent to which there exists an obligation to obey the law. Participation in the democratic process may, however, be used as a means to deny any right to disobey. That is to say, it may be argued that democratic participation implies the individual's acceptance of all laws within the state. Here we must consider what it is that citizens consent to when electing a government. It seems implausible to argue that we each consent to every action of government throughout a possible five year term of office, irrespective of its merits. However, Professor Plamenatz states that when a vote is cast:

> ... you put yourself by your vote under an obligation to obey whatever government comes legally to power under the system, and this can properly be called giving consent. For the purpose of an election is to give authority to the people who win it and if you vote, knowing what you are doing and without being compelled to do it, you voluntarily take part in the process, which gives authority to those people. [1963, Vol 1, p 239]

This argument surely is contentious and represents a very limited view of the requirement that a government should have moral authority to govern. Richard Wasserstrom (1963), on the other hand, argues that, by the participatory democratic process, a *prima facie* obligation to obey law is imposed, but this *prima facie* duty can be overridden by the demands of conscience.

The appropriate response of the state to acts of civil disobedience is a difficult matter. Professor Ronald Dworkin, for example, argues for official tolerance in the face of dissent and law breaking which is undertaken in pursuit of rights – even where violence is employed.[29] In *Taking Rights Seriously*, Dworkin argues that the state should act with caution in prosecuting civilly disobedient acts. First, the state should respect the stand taken in the defence of rights, even if that stand should prove misguided when the matter ultimately comes before the Supreme Court for a ruling on the validity of the contentious legislation. The decision to prosecute should be decided on the basis of utilitarianism.[30] As Dworkin states in *A Matter of Principle*:

> Utilitarianism may be a poor general theory of justice, but it states an excellent necessary condition for just punishment. Nobody should ever be punished unless punishing him will do some good on the whole in the long run all things considered. [1986, p 114]

By prosecuting disobedience to law, the state upholds the positive law and reinforces it. On the other hand, in prosecuting, the state may reveal the defects in the law and may be seen to be enforcing that for which there exists little or no popular support. By way of example, the acquittal of Clive Ponting on charges of breaching section 2 of the Official Secrets Act 1911[31] is illustrative: the jury

---

29 Dworkin, 1977, Chapters 7 and 8; and see MacGuigan, 'Obligation and obedience', in Pennock and Chapman, 1970.
30 The doctrine which assesses the justification for a particular action according to the overall increase in the sum of benefit to society as a whole.
31 Discussed in Chapter 25.

refusing to convict despite a clear ruling by the judge as to the illegality of Ponting's conduct.[32] It may also be argued that by rigid enforcement the state enhances the moral claims advanced by the civilly disobedient. In part, this was the view adopted by Socrates in submitting to his fate. He drank the hemlock to show respect to the law and constitution of Athens, although he must have known that in so doing he would bring the positive law of the state into disrepute. What he could not foresee was the timeless example that Athens, in executing Socrates, set for humanity.[33]

Is there a duty to disobey?

The converse position must also be considered: if a state violates the requirements of the rule of law, to what extent is it the duty of citizens to disobey the law? Furthermore, what justification, if any, is there for another state or the international community taking action against the 'guilty' state? The Nazi regime in Germany provides the most obvious – but not unique – example. On individual duty, Professor Lon Fuller maintained that the citizen is under no obligation to obey unjust law: 'A mere respect for constituted authority must not be confused with fidelity to law.' Fuller goes further and asserts that an evil regime, which grossly violates the basic precepts of morality, is incapable of creating law at all.[34] In HLA Hart's view, this represents confused thinking on Fuller's part. His preferred approach is to recognise the validity of Nazi laws – however abhorrent in moral terms – but also to recognise that moral obligations can outweigh the legal obligation to obey.[35] In addition to facilitating clarity about law, this approach enables the regime to be held to account for its actions. Simply to deny – as does Professor Fuller – that there was no law during Nazi rule is to remove the basis for international legal sanctions.

AV Dicey and the rule of law[36]

In *Introduction to the Study of the Law of the Constitution*, AV Dicey offered a prosaic description of the rule of law. Here, there are none of the ringing proclamations of the theological or political philosophers. Nevertheless, Dicey's views have continued to exert their influence, despite many challenges, and it is this influence which requires examination.

Dicey argued that the rule of law – in its practical manifestation – has three main aspects:

- no man is punishable or can be lawfully made to suffer in body or goods except for a distinct breach of law established in the ordinary legal manner before the ordinary courts of the land. In this sense, the rule of law is contrasted with every system of government based on the exercise by persons in authority of wide, arbitrary, or discretionary powers of constraint;

---

32 *R v Ponting* (1985); and see Barker, 1990, pp 183–84.
33 See Plato, 'Socrates' defence and Crito', in Hamilton and Cairns, 1989.
34 Fuller, 1958.
35 Hart, 1958, p 593 – a view echoing that of St Thomas Aquinas.
36 See Jennings, 1959b, p 54; Heuston, 'The rule of law', in 1964a, p 40.

- no man is above the law; every man and woman, whatever be his or her rank or condition, is subject to the ordinary law of the realm and amenable to the jurisdiction of the ordinary tribunals; and
- the general principles of the constitution (as, for example, the right to personal liberty, or the right of public meeting) are, with us, the result of judicial decisions determining the rights of private persons in particular cases brought before the courts.[37]

Each of these points requires examination.

Lack of arbitrariness and retrospectivity

The first element of this analysis is self-explanatory. It requires that no one be punished except for conduct which represents a clear breach of law.[38] Designed to deny to governments any right to make secret or arbitrary laws, or retrospective penal laws, and to limit the discretionary powers of government, the rule protects the individual. In order to comply fully with this requirement, laws should be open and accessible, clear and certain. In part, this idea ties in with that of the 'social contract' and the reciprocal relationship between the state and the individual. Under social contract theories, the individual citizen transfers his autonomous individual rights to the government, to be held by that government on trust. To express the matter differently, the citizen owes allegiance to the Crown in return for which he is under the protection of the Crown.[39] The doctrine of allegiance incorporates the idea of obedience to law – both on the part of the citizen and on the part of government. Laws which are arbitrary or secret are incapable of justification on the basis of the mandate of the people and, accordingly, offend against the reciprocal relationship on which constitutional democracy depends. Where wide discretionary powers are conferred on the executive – whether they be in the form of granting power to a minister of the Crown to act 'as he thinks fit' or on civil servants administering the social welfare system – it will be impossible for the individual to know what rights he or she has. Moreover, the delegation of broad discretionary power – albeit on the authority of the sovereign parliament – renders such power difficult, if not impossible, to challenge before a court of law or other adjudicatory tribunal.[40]

If retrospective penal liability is imposed, the individual is placed in the position where his conduct was lawful at the time of his action but, subsequently, he is held responsible as if his conduct was then unlawful. An examination and evaluation of the relevance of this first proposition entails drawing on relevant illustrations from both statute and case law. For example, the courts construe penal statutes narrowly and will be slow to find that parliament intended to impose retrospective liability. So important is the concept of *mens rea* in the criminal law[41] that it will rarely be appropriate for a prosecution to succeed in its

---

37 Diccy, 1885, pp 188, 193, 195, respectively. And see Craig, 1990.
38 The principle of *nulla poena sine lege*.
39 See Chitty, 1820, discussed in Chapter 7.
40 See Smith, 1985.
41 *Sweet v Parsley* (1970).

absence, and it is for this reason that the courts employ the presumption of statutory interpretation against retrospectivity:

> Perhaps no rule of construction is more firmly established than this – that a retrospective operation is not to be given to a statute so as to impair an existing right or obligation, otherwise than as regards matters of procedure, unless that effect cannot be avoided without doing violence to the language of the enactment. If the enactment is expressed in language which is fairly capable of either interpretation, it ought to be construed as prospective only.[42]

In *Waddington v Miah* (1974), the House of Lords interpreted the Immigration Act 1971 in a manner which denied retrospective effect in relation to criminal offences, using, as an aid to construction, Article 7 of the European Convention on Human Rights, which guarantees freedom from retrospectivity. Nonetheless, the presumption will not be available where parliament expressly provides for retrospectivity, as, for example, in the War Damage Act 1965 and the War Crimes Act 1991.[43] In *Burmah Oil v Lord Advocate* (1965), where the House of Lords had awarded compensation for the destruction of oil installations in wartime, the government speedily introduced legislation nullifying the effect of the decision under the War Damage Act 1965. This case demonstrates clearly the subordination of the judiciary to parliamentary supremacy and the limits thereby imposed on the judges' capacity to uphold rights.

Notwithstanding the general prohibition against retrospectivity, there may be instances where a decision which imposes, for example, criminal liability may be upheld by the courts. For example, until 1990, there existed a time honoured exemption from the law of rape for husbands who 'raped' their wives. In the case of *R v R* (1991), however, the House of Lords upheld the conviction of a husband for the rape of his wife, arguing that the rule against liability for rape within marriage was anachronistic. In a challenge to this decision under the European Convention on Human Rights, on the basis that it infringed Article 7 of the Convention, which makes retrospectivity unlawful, the Court of Human Rights ruled that the sweeping away of husbands' immunity from criminal prosecution and conviction for rape represented an evolution towards greater equality between the sexes and was consistent with that equality.[44]

Equality before the law: government under the law

Dicey's second limb emphasises the notion that government itself is subject to law and that everyone, irrespective of rank, whether official or individual, shall be subject to the law,[45] and subject to the same courts. Dicey viewed the French system of special courts to deal with complaints against government as abhorrent, fearing that specially constituted courts would unduly favour the government over the citizen. Dicey has often been interpreted as requiring that there be actual equality in terms of legal rights, powers and capacities. Such an interpretation is,

---

42   Wright J in *Re Athlumney* (1898), pp 551–52.
43   See Chapter 7.
44   *SW v United Kingdom; C v United Kingdom* (1995).
45   See Zellick, 1985.

however, misguided. The idea of equality before the law, irrespective of status, is subject to so many exceptions 'that the statement is of doubtful value'.[46] In so far as equal powers are concerned, it must be recognised that the police have powers over and above the citizen,[47] that ministers have power to enact delegated legislation (but subject to parliamentary approval), that the Crown enjoys immunities under the law, that the government acting in the name of the Crown may exercise prerogative powers which may defeat the rights of individuals,[48] that Members of Parliament have immunity from the law of defamation under the privileges of parliament,[49] and that diplomats enjoy immunities not available to citizens. And, as Sir Ivor Jennings points out, no two citizens are entirely equal:

> ... pawnbrokers, money lenders, landlords, drivers of motor cars, married women, and indeed most other classes have special rights and duties. [1959b, Appendix II, p 11]

Against this catalogue, which is not exhaustive, must be set the extent to which government and public officials are subject to law in the sense of being accountable for their actions before the ordinary courts, for this, indeed, was Dicey's real argument. The doctrine acknowledges the need of a consistent application of the law irrespective of status. No one is immune from criminal prosecution (other than the monarch: 'Against the King law has no coercive power').[50] Official accountability to law is one of the foundations of the rule of law. Following a detailed analysis of Dicey's writing, Professor Jeffrey Jowell concludes that:

> ... its ghost has refused to rest. It rises still to haunt a minister who publishes 'guidelines' that cut across the powers of the statute under which he operates, the minister who penalises local authorities for overspending without giving them a fair hearing, a government department which decides in accordance with a secret code not available to the public, or a Prime Minister who seeks to deprive civil servants of their rights to remain members of a trade union. ['The rule of law today', in Jowell and Oliver, 2000]

Sir Ivor Jennings criticises Dicey's emphasis on government according to law on the basis that it is too narrow an interpretation:

> ... it is a small point upon which to base a doctrine called by the magnificent name of 'rule of law', particularly when it is generally used in a very different sense. [1959b, p 312]

TRS Allan subjects Dicey's analysis to detailed scrutiny, focusing on Dicey's second principle: that of equality before the law.[51] Allan seeks a solution to the apparent paradox presented by Dicey's insistence that both parliamentary sovereignty and the rule of law comprise the fundamental doctrines of the constitution – given that the former concept is inherently capable of damaging the latter. Towards this end, Allan presents a wealth of evidence directed to establishing a middle way between the formalism of the 'principle of legality' and

---

46 Jackson and Leonard, 2001.
47 Under common law and the Police and Criminal Evidence Act 1984.
48 See *Malone v Metropolitan Police Commissioner* (1979), discussed in Chapter 5.
49 See Chapter 18.
50 Maitland, 1908, p 100.
51 Allan, 1985a; 1993, Chapter 2; 2001.

the vagueness of the 'broad political ideal'. In other words, what is sought is an explanation of the means by which the power of sovereignty is restrained or restricted without expounding a 'complete social philosophy' (1985a, p 114). The key to such an understanding, according to Allan, lies in the role of the judiciary and in an acceptance that it is the judges who – in applying the 'juristic principle' of the rule of law – limit the power of parliament. To summarise, Allan draws on the principles of statutory interpretation (non-retrospectivity, clarity, *mens rea* in penal statutes, etc); on the independence of the judiciary as ensured by the separation of powers; on the right of access to the courts for all citizens; and on the judiciary's reluctance for the jurisdiction of judicial review to be limited. By these and other means, Allan seeks to demonstrate that:

> ... the rule of law strengthens democracy by ensuring that government operates only within rules adopted or sanctioned by Parliament ...

and that:

> The constitutional principle of the rule of law serves, however, to bridge the gap between the legal doctrine of parliamentary sovereignty and the political doctrine of the sovereignty of the people. In interpreting statutes in conformity, so far as possible, with general notions of fairness and justice – in seeking to apply those common standards of morality which are taken for granted in the community – the judge respects the natural expectations of the citizen.

> The rule of law therefore assists in preventing the subversion of the political sovereignty of the people by manipulation of the legal sovereignty of Parliament. [1985a, p 130]

In order to evaluate such contrasting views as those expressed above, consideration of some evidence becomes necessary.

Judicial review

Actions for judicial review of administrative action, employing concepts of *intra* and *ultra vires* and the rules of natural justice, ensure that the executive acts within the law. Judicial review – in its infancy in Dicey's time – represents the means by which the sovereignty of parliament is upheld and the rule of law applied. Dicey, writing in 1915, analysed the significance of *Board of Education v Rice* (1911) and *Local Government Board v Arlidge* (1915), claiming that:

> ... each case finally lays down, as far as the courts of England are concerned, a clear and distinct principle by which any department of the government, such for example as the Board of Education, must be guarded in the exercise of powers conferred upon it by statute.[52]

The means by which, and grounds upon which, judicial review may be granted are considered in Chapters 26 and 27. It is sufficient for current purposes to note that judicial review is the means by which administrative authorities – whether ministers of the Crown, government departments, local authorities or others with law making and administrative powers – are confined by the courts within the powers granted to them by parliament. It is for a court to determine – following

---

52   Dicey, 1885, Appendix 2, p 493. On these cases see further Chapter 27.

the granting of an application for judicial review – whether the body in question has acted *intra vires* or *ultra vires* (that is, inside or outside its powers). Judicial review is confined to matters of public, rather than private law. Thus, where a relationship between an aggrieved citizen and a body is based, for example, on the law of contract, judicial review will not lie.[53] It is also necessary – in the interests of good administration – that aggrieved individuals have 'sufficient interest' – or *locus standi* – in the matter to bring it to court.[54] There are numerous grounds on which judicial review may be sought. By way of illustration, a body may act *ultra vires* if it uses its powers for the wrong purpose,[55] or if it abuses its powers,[56] or if it adopts a policy which is so rigid that it fails to exercise a discretion with which it has been invested.[57] The law imposes standards of reasonableness upon administrative bodies, and failure to act in a reasonable manner may cause a body to act *ultra vires*.[58] A body may act *ultra vires* if it is conferred with delegated powers but delegates them further to another.[59] Statute may require that administrators adopt particular procedures in the exercise of these powers: should they not do so, and the procedures are judicially deemed to be 'mandatory' (compulsory) rather than 'directory' (advisory), a body will be held to be acting *ultra vires*. If a public body under a duty to act fails to act at all, the court can order it to do so by a mandatory order. The rules of natural justice must also be observed in decision making: where an individual has a right or interest at stake because of an administrative decision, he is entitled to fair treatment.[60] All of these grounds for review have been rationalised by the House of Lords into three principal categories: irrationality, illegality and procedural impropriety.[61] The powers of the court can only be exercised over a matter which it is competent to determine. This introduces the concept of justiciability,[62] and it is this latter doctrine which most particularly undermines the concept of the rule of law.

In *Council of Civil Service Unions v Minister for the Civil Service*, the House of Lords identified the categories of decision which would be immune from judicial review – that is to say – non-justiciable. Amongst these – and the list is not exhaustive – are the making of treaties, the dissolution of parliament, the appointment of ministers, declarations of war and peace, and matters relating to the granting of honours. What unites these categories is the fact that each involves matters of high policy which is most appropriately determined – in the eyes of the judiciary – not by the courts but by the executive. Where this applies, it may be

---

53 See eg *R v City Panel on Takeovers and Mergers ex parte Datafin plc* (1987); *O'Reilly v Mackman* (1983).
54 See, *inter alia*, *Inland Revenue Commissioner v National Federation of Self-Employed and Small Businesses Ltd* (1982).
55 *Attorney General v Fulham Corporation* (1921).
56 *Webb v Minister of Housing and Local Government* (1965); *Westminster Bank v Minister of Housing and Local Government* (1971).
57 *Padfield v Minister of Agriculture Fisheries and Food* (1968).
58 *Associated Provincial Picture Houses Ltd v Wednesbury Corporation* (1948).
59 *Barnard v National Dock Labour Board* (1953); *Vine v National Dock Labour Board* (1957).
60 *R v IRC ex parte Preston* (1985); *Wheeler v Leicester City Council* (1985).
61 *Council of Civil Service Unions v Minister for the Civil Service* (1985).
62 *Ibid.*

said that the rule of law is undermined by respect for the doctrine of the separation of powers: an ironic consequence.

The doctrine of judicial review nevertheless represents a bedrock for the application of the rule of law, keeping those with law making and discretionary powers within the law. From *Entick v Carrington* (1765) to *R v Secretary of State for the Home Department ex parte Fire Brigades' Union* (1993), wherein Kenneth Baker, the Home Secretary, was held to be acting *ultra vires* when attempting to introduce a new tariff for compensation under the Criminal Injuries Compensation Scheme under the royal prerogative rather than under power conferred by statute, the principle is established and reiterated.

The legal process

For the rule of law to be respected and applied, the legal process – civil and criminal – must exhibit certain features. These features may be categorised as accessibility and procedural fairness.

Accessibility

The law must be accessible to all if rights are to be enforced. Accordingly, there must not only exist a system of courts available locally but the cost of having recourse to the courts must be such that there is real – rather than symbolic – access to the courts. For the law to be attainable, adequate legal advice and assistance must be provided at a cost affordable by all.[63]

The right to a fair trial is protected under Article 6 of the European Convention on Human Rights, and includes the right of the citizen:

> ... to defend himself in person or through legal assistance of his own choosing or, if he has not sufficient means to pay for legal assistance, to be given it free when the interests of justice so require.

In *Granger v United Kingdom* (1990), the defendant had been denied further legal aid to pursue an appeal against conviction. Granger, unable to afford legal representation, acted in person. Representing the Crown were senior government counsel. On an application under the Convention, Granger alleged that he had been denied the protection of law. The Court of Human Rights ruled that the denial of legal aid infringed Granger's rights.

Procedural fairness

Justice and the rule of law demand that, in the conduct of legal proceedings, procedural fairness be observed. Subsumed within this requirement are many subsidiary conditions. The judge must be impartial: *nemo iudex in sua causa*. Where jurors are involved, they, too, must be free from bias. In addition, jurors should be reasonably representative of the society they serve. Evidence gathered by the police must be acquired by lawful means. The evidence admitted into court must

---

63 See, *inter alia*, Smith, Bailey and Gunn, 2002, Chapter 9; Zander, 2003, Chapters 6 and 9; Slapper and Kelly, 2004, Chapter 12.

be both of an admissible nature and fairly presented. The proceedings should be conducted in such a manner as to be intelligible to the parties, witnesses and jurors.[64]

The jury

The precise origins of trial by jury in its modern form are shrouded in mist.[65] It is thought that by the end of the fifteenth century, the jury, as triers of fact, was established in what today would be a recognisable form. Trial by jury for serious criminal offences, and in civil cases where defamation, malicious prosecution, false imprisonment and allegations of fraud are at issue,[66] is regarded as the 'bulwark of our liberties'.[67] The decision of the jury is regarded as conclusive and unimpeachable. Criticisms have long been made of the lack of representativeness of the jury. Several factors militate against representativeness: the accuracy of the electoral register from which jurors are selected; the relative lack of randomness in jury selection; the vetting of jurors;[68] and challenges to members of the jury. Moreover, a wide range of persons are either ineligible for jury service, or disqualified from sitting or may be excused from jury service.[69] When a jury is summoned, the presence of a juror may be challenged 'for cause' – that is, where some fact relating to the juror is known and gives rise to a challenge. Little is known about the individual juror – only the names and addresses are given.[70] This relative anonymity of jurors contrasts starkly with the position in the United States of America, where the selection of a jury entails a prolonged inquiry into the lives and attitudes of prospective jurors. While the process is protracted,[71] it is designed to ensure that the jury ultimately selected will be one free from bias in relation to the defendant. In the United Kingdom, a person may be excused from service on the basis of personal knowledge of the case, bias, personal hardship or conscientious objection to jury service. A juror should not be excused on general grounds such as race, religion, political beliefs or occupation.[72]

Evidence

For the rule of law to be observed, it is of central importance that the evidence before the court be both complete and reliable. Contravention of this requirement undermines the concept of a fair trial. Subsumed within this question is the complex and controversial matter of the manner in which evidence is obtained and the question of admissibility. While the Police and Criminal Evidence Act

---

64 See, *inter alia*, Kafka, 1956; and Keedy, 1951 for illustrations of breaches of this requirement.
65 See Maitland, 1908, pp 115–30. See also Denning, 1982, Pt 2.
66 Supreme Court Act 1981, subject to the proviso in s 69(1) which permits the court to refuse trial by jury in cases of complexity or impracticality.
67 *Ward v James* (1966), p 295, *per* Lord Denning MR.
68 *R v Mason* (1980), *Attorney General's Guidelines on Jury Checks* (1988).
69 Jury Act 1974; Juries' Disqualification Act 1984.
70 Prior to 1973, jurors' occupations were made known.
71 Jury selection for the trial of John de Lorean took five weeks.
72 *Practice Direction* (1988).

1984[73] went some way to improving the safeguards for the accused and was introduced, in part, to rectify deficiencies which had come to light,[74] the cases of the Birmingham Six,[75] the Guildford Four and the Maguire Seven[76] illustrated the deficiencies in the criminal justice system. In each of these cases, the defendants had served long terms of imprisonment for alleged Irish Republican Army (IRA) terrorist acts. In each case, the evidence relied upon was unreliable. Their convictions were quashed by the Court of Appeal following years of campaigning by relatives and friends for a review of their cases. In each case, a serious miscarriage of justice had occurred and as a result the integrity of the criminal justice system tarnished.

At common law, a confession which is improperly obtained is inadmissible.[77] The Police and Criminal Evidence Act 1984 places this rule on a statutory basis, providing that if a confession has been obtained 'by oppression', the court shall not allow the confession to be given in evidence unless satisfied beyond reasonable doubt that the confession – even if true – has not been obtained improperly (section 76).

Whereas the rules on the admissibility of improperly obtained confessions are relatively clear, the admissibility of other evidence obtained by either dubious or unlawful means has proved less clear and less satisfactory. Until 1979, the judges exercised their discretion as to whether or not evidence improperly acquired would be admissible.[78] However, in *R v Sang* (1979), the House of Lords ruled that no discretion existed to exclude evidence which had been obtained by unlawful or improper means. The only basis on which evidence could be excluded would be where the effect of admitting it would prove unduly 'prejudicial' to the defence or 'unfair' to admit it. The fact that the evidence was unlawfully acquired does not amount to 'unfairness' *per se*.[79] The admissibility of such evidence is now governed by section 78 of the Police and Criminal Evidence Act 1984, which provides that the court may refuse to allow evidence if:

> ... it appears to the court that, having regard to all the circumstances, including the circumstances in which the evidence was obtained, the admission of the evidence would have such adverse effect on the fairness of the proceedings that the court ought not to admit it.

Evaluation of Dicey's 'equality before the law'

The evidence for the notion of equality before the law is neither clear nor uncontentious. As with so much of the constitution, there remains room for doubt and argument. Nevertheless, it is submitted that there exists sufficient evidence to suggest that Dicey's approach remains a fruitful avenue for inquiry and exploration. To dismiss – as some writers do – this aspect of Dicey's exposition of

---

73 See, *inter alia*, Zander, 2003.
74 See McConville and Baldwin, 1980.
75 *R v McIlkenny* (1992).
76 See May, J, *Interim Report on the Maguire Case*, HC 556 (1990–91), London: HMSO.
77 *Marks v Beyfus* (1890).
78 *Kuruma Son of Kaniu v R* (1955); *Jeffrey v Black* (1978).
79 See Heydon, 1973; Ashworth, 1977.

the rule of law, is to deprive the student of the constitution of a valuable tool for analysis.

The protection of rights under common law?

The third limb of Dicey's description of the rule of law reveals his preference for common law protection of human rights over and above a specially formulated code of rights, thus demonstrating a faith in the judiciary which is not sustainable nowadays. Evaluation of this aspect of the definition must await analysis of the Human Rights Act 1998 in Chapter 19 and the scope of the protection which it gives to individual citizens.

The Human Rights Act 1998 for the first time 'incorporates' rights protected under the European Convention on Human Rights into domestic law. Accordingly, citizens no longer have to undertake the lengthy process of applying to the Court of Human Rights in Strasbourg, but are able to seek a remedy in the domestic courts. The method of incorporation adopted, however, falls far short of enabling the judges to invalidate or set aside domestic legislation. Instead, the judges of the higher courts are empowered to make 'declarations of incompatibility' with Convention rights. Once such a declaration has been made, it remains for parliament to approve an amendment to the law. As a result, the Human Rights Act, far from elevating individual rights proclaimed in the Convention to a higher status than statute, preserves parliament's sovereign law making and amending power, and also maintains the separation of powers.

Notwithstanding the Act's status, the rule of law is undoubtedly buttressed by the Act: every public body – by no means a simple concept[80] – is required to comply with Convention rights, and to fail to do so is to act unlawfully save where there is no available alternative form of action because of the requirements of primary legislation (section 6). To support rights further, the Act requires that judges interpret primary and secondary legislation 'so far as it is possible to do so in a manner compatible with Convention requirements' (section 3(1)). Coming into effect in Scotland in 1999 and in England in 2000, the impact of the Act has been significant and is having the effect of requiring all public bodies to scrutinise their procedures for Convention compliance, or face legal action.

The rule of law in international dimension

The Universal Declaration of Human Rights of the United Nations, published in 1948, declares that:

> It is essential, if man is not to be compelled to have recourse, as a last resort, to rebellion against tyranny and oppression, that human rights should be protected by the rule of law.

The European Convention also recognises the concept of the rule of law. The preamble states that:

---

80 For discussion see Chapter 19, but note here that s 6(3)(a) and (b) includes courts and tribunals, and 'any person certain of whose functions are functions of a public nature, but does not include either House of Parliament or a person exercising functions in connection with proceedings in Parliament'.

> The governments of European countries which are like-minded and have a common heritage of political traditions, ideals, freedom and the rule of law ... have agreed as follows ...

On an international level, the rule of law is also advanced by the International Commission of Jurists, which strives to uphold and improve the rule of law within the legal systems of its members. The Declaration of Delhi, issued under the auspices of the International Commission of Jurists, affirms the rule of law and its value in promoting the protection of civil and political rights and linked such rights with the development and protection of social and economic rights. The Congress of the International Commission of Jurists met in 1959 in order to 'clarify and formulate a supranational concept of the rule of law'.[81] The Declaration of Delhi 1959 recognised that:

> ... the rule of law is a dynamic concept for the expansion and fulfilment of which jurists are primarily responsible and which should be employed not only to safeguard and advance the civil and political rights of the individual in a free society, but also to establish social, economic, educational and cultural conditions under which his legitimate aspirations and dignity may be realised ...

Such aspirational statements recognise the need for the economic foundations to be such that the dignity of man can be a reality in society. It is meaningless to speak of the rule of law as insisting on decent, or even minimal, standards of living within the context of poverty and disease. In order to secure any such standards, a sufficient level of economic wealth must be achieved. Even where such standards do exist, there will remain resistances to any formulation of social and economic rights as enforceable positive legal rights, for such formulations require the allocation of resources within society. Whereas governments may be willing – indeed obliged – to respect civil and political rights in a democracy, the protection of such rights generally will be effected without significant national resource implications. The protection of freedoms, such as freedom of speech and association, requires no more than a restraint on government. The protection of social and economic rights requires positive action, at a high cost.[82]

CONCLUSION

The rule of law – in its many guises – represents a challenge to state authority and power, demanding both that powers be granted legitimately and that their exercise is according to law. 'According to law' means both according to the legal rules and something over and above purely formal *legality* and imputes the concepts of *legitimacy* and constitutionality. In its turn, legitimacy implies *rightness* or *morality* of law. The law is not autonomous but rests on the support of those it governs. The law is the servant of the sense of rightness in the community, and whilst the rule of law places law above every individual – irrespective of rank and station – it remains, paradoxically, subject to the ultimate judgment of the people.

---

81   Marsh, 'The rule of law as a supranational concept', in Guest, 1961, p 240, and Marsh, 1959.
82   See Aubert, 1983, Chapters 2 and 7.

CHAPTER 5

THE SEPARATION OF POWERS

The separation of powers, together with the rule of law and parliamentary sovereignty, runs like a thread throughout the constitution of the United Kingdom. It is a doctrine which is fundamental to the organisation of a state – and to the concept of constitutionalism – in so far as it prescribes the appropriate allocation of powers, and the limits of those powers, to differing institutions. The concept has played a major role in the formation of constitutions. The extent to which powers can be, and should be, separate and distinct was a central feature in formulating, for example, both the American and French revolutionary constitutions. In any state, three essential bodies exist: the executive, the legislature and the judiciary. It is the relationship between these bodies which must be evaluated against the backcloth of the principle. The essence of the doctrine is that there should be, ideally, a clear demarcation of functions between the legislature, executive and judiciary in order that none should have excessive power and that there should be in place a system of checks and balances between the institutions. However, as will be seen, there are significant departures from the pure doctrine under the United Kingdom's constitution, and it must be conceded that, while the doctrine is accorded respect, it is by no means absolute.

HISTORICAL DEVELOPMENT

The identification of the three elements of the constitution derives from Aristotle (384–322 BC). In *The Politics*, Aristotle proclaimed that:

> There are three elements in each constitution in respect of which every serious lawgiver must look for what is advantageous to it; if these are well arranged, the constitution is bound to be well arranged, and the differences in constitutions are bound to correspond to the differences between each of these elements. The three are, first, the deliberative, which discusses everything of common importance; second, the officials; and third, the judicial element. [Bk iv, xiv, 1297b35]

The constitutional seeds of the doctrine were thus sown early, reflecting the need for government according to and under the law, a requirement encouraged by some degree of a separation of functions between the institutions of the state.

The constitutional historian FW Maitland traces the separation of powers in England to the reign of Edward I (1272–1307):

> In Edward's day all becomes definite – there is the Parliament of the three estates, there is the King's Council, there are the well known courts of law. [1908, p 20]

Viscount Henry St John Bolingbroke (1678–1751), in *Remarks on the History of England*, advanced the idea of separation of powers. Bolingbroke was concerned with the necessary balance of powers within a constitution, arguing that the protection of liberty and security within the state depended upon achieving and maintaining an equilibrium between the Crown, parliament and the people.

Addressing the respective powers of the King and parliament, Bolingbroke observed that:

> Since this division of power, and these different privileges constitute and maintain our government, it follows that the confusion of them tends to destroy it. This proposition is therefore true; that, in a constitution like ours, the safety of the whole depends on the balance of the parts. [1748, pp 80–83]

Baron Montesquieu (1689–1755, living in England from 1729–31) stressed the importance of the independence of the judiciary in *De l'Esprit des Lois* (1748):

> When the legislative and executive powers are united in the same person, or in the same body of magistrates, there can be no liberty ... Again, there is no liberty if the power of judging is not separated from the legislative and executive. If it were joined with the legislative, the life and liberty of the subject would be exposed to arbitrary control; for the judge would then be the legislator. If it were joined to the executive power, the judge might behave with violence and oppression. There would be an end to everything, if the same man, or the same body, whether of the nobles or the people, were to exercise those three powers, that of enacting laws, that of executing public affairs, and that of trying crimes or individual causes.

Here is the clearest expression of the demand for a separation of functions. It has been remarked that Montesquieu's observations on the English constitution were inaccurate at the time, representing more a description of an idealised state than reality.[1] Moreover, it should not be assumed that Montesquieu's preferred arrangement of a pure separation of powers is uncontroversial. Throughout history, there has been exhibited a tension between the doctrine of separation of powers and the need for balanced government – an arrangement depending more on checks and balances within the system (as emphasised by Bolingbroke) than on a formalistic separation of powers. Sir Ivor Jennings has interpreted Montesquieu's words to mean not that the legislature and the executive should have no influence over the other, but rather that neither should exercise the power of the other.[2] Sir William Blackstone, a disciple of Montesquieu, adopted and adapted Montesquieu's strict doctrine, reworking his central idea to incorporate the theory of mixed government. While it was of central importance to Blackstone that, for example, the executive and legislature should be sufficiently separate to avoid 'tyranny', he nevertheless viewed their total separation as potentially leading to dominance of the executive by the legislature.[3] Thus, partial separation of powers is required to achieve a mixed and balanced constitutional structure.

THE CONTEMPORARY DOCTRINE

The separation of powers doctrine does not insist that there should be three institutions of government each operating in isolation from each other. Indeed, such an arrangement would be unworkable, particularly under a constitution dominated by the sovereignty of parliament. Under such an arrangement, it is essential that there be a sufficient interplay between each institution of the state.

---

1   Vile, 1967, pp 84–85.
2   Jennings, 1959b, Appendix I.
3   *Commentaries on the Laws of England* (1765–69), Vol I.

For example, it is for the executive, for the most part, to propose legislation for parliament's approval. Once passed into law, Acts of Parliament are upheld by the judiciary. A complete separation of the three institutions could result in legal and constitutional deadlock. Rather than a pure separation of powers, the concept insists that the primary functions of the state should be allocated clearly and that there should be checks to ensure that no institution encroaches significantly upon the function of the other. If hypothetical constitutional arrangements within a state are considered, a range of possibilities exists:

(a) absolute power residing in one person or body exercising executive, legislative and judicial powers: no separation of powers;

(b) power being diffused between three separate bodies exercising separate functions with no overlaps in function or personnel: pure separation of powers; and

(c) powers and personnel being largely – but not totally – separated with checks and balances in the system to prevent abuse: mixed government and weak separation of powers.

It is to this third category that the constitution of the United Kingdom most clearly subscribes.

DEFINING THE INSTITUTIONS

The executive

The executive may be defined as that branch of the state which formulates policy and is responsible for its execution. In formal terms, the sovereign is the head of the executive. The Prime Minister, Cabinet and other ministers, for the most part, are elected Members of Parliament.[4] In addition, the Civil Service, local authorities, police and armed forces, constitute the executive in practical terms.

The legislature

The Queen in Parliament is the sovereign law making body within the United Kingdom. Formally expressed, parliament comprises the Queen, House of Lords and House of Commons. All Bills[5] must be passed by each House and receive royal assent.

Parliament is bicameral, that is to say there are two chambers, each exercising a legislative role – although not having equal powers – and each playing a part in ensuring the accountability of the government. By way of introduction, it should be noted that membership of the House of Lords is not secured by election and is accordingly not accountable in any direct sense to the electorate. The House of Commons is directly elected, and a parliamentary term is limited under the Parliament Act 1911 to a maximum of five years. In practice, the average life of a parliament is between three and four years. The House is made up of the majority party: the political party which secures the highest number of seats at the election,

---

4   Note that some ministers are drawn from the unelected House of Lords. See further Chapter 17.

5   With the exception provided by the Parliament Acts 1911–49.

which will form the government. The head of that party will be invited by the Queen to take office as Prime Minister. In turn, it is for the Prime Minister to select his or her Cabinet. The opposition parties[6] comprise the remainder of the now 659 Members of Parliament.[7] The official Opposition is the party which represents the second largest party in terms of elected members. In principle, the role of the official Opposition is to act as a government in waiting, ready at any time to take office should the government seek a dissolution of parliament.[8]

The judiciary

The judiciary is that branch of the state which adjudicates upon conflicts between state institutions, between state and individual, and between individuals. The judiciary is independent of both parliament and the executive. It is the feature of judicial independence which is of prime importance both in relation to government according to law and in the protection of liberty of the citizen against the executive. As Blackstone observed in his *Commentaries*:

> ... in this distinct and separate existence of the judicial power in a peculiar body of men, nominated indeed, but not removable at pleasure by the Crown, consists one main preservative of the public liberty which cannot subsist long in any state unless the administration of common justice be in some degree separated both from the legislative and from the executive power. [Vol 1, p 204]

It is apparent, however, that, whilst a high degree of judicial independence is secured under the constitution, there are several aspects of the judicial function which reveal an overlap between the judiciary, parliament and the executive.

THE OFFICE OF LORD CHANCELLOR[9]

The office of Lord Chancellor derives from the Norman Conquest when the King's secretary became known as the royal 'chancellor'. The first Chancellor is recorded in 1068. In the Middle Ages, the primary role of the Chancellor was to preside over parliament. From the fourteenth century, his functions have been both parliamentary and judicial, in the latter role presiding over the Court of Chancery until 1875.

Prior to the Constitutional Reform Act 2005, the office of Lord Chancellor spanned all three institutions of the state – the executive, legislature and judiciary. The Lord Chancellor was a politically appointed member of the Cabinet, the speaker of the House of Lords and the head of the judiciary. Furthermore, as a senior judge the Lord Chancellor was entitled to participate in judicial proceedings, although by convention he would not adjudicate cases which involved the government or were overtly political in nature. As head of the judiciary, with wide-ranging powers relating to the appointment of judges, the

---

6   Conservative, Liberal Democrat, Scottish Nationalists, Ulster Unionists, Democratic Unionists and Plaid Cymru.
7   The number of Members of Parliament was increased to 659 for the 1997 General Election.
8   For consideration of the role of the Opposition, see Chapters 14–16.
9   See, *inter alia*, Heuston, 1964b and 1987; Bradney, 1989; Drewry, 1972. The title Lord Chancellor is first recorded in 1461.

Lord Chancellor acted as the spokesperson for the judges and defended their independence from interference by the executive. Lord Chancellor Birkenhead (1872–1930), for example, defended the link between the head of the judiciary and the Cabinet in 1922:

> ... it is difficult to believe that there is no necessity for the existence of such a personality, imbued on the one hand with legal ideas and habits of thought, and aware on the other of the problems which engage the attention of the executive government. In the absence of such a person, the judiciary and the executive are likely enough to drift asunder to the point of a violent separation, followed by a still more violent and disastrous collision. [1922, Chapter 4]

More recently, Lord Hailsham, Lord Chancellor 1979 and 1987, argued that it is vital that:

> ... the independence of the judiciary and the rule of law should be defended inside the Cabinet as well as in Parliament. The Lord Chancellor must be, and must be seen to be, a loyal colleague, not seeking to dodge responsibility for controversial policies, and prepared to give to Parliament a justification for his own acts of administration. [1975]

However, whatever perceived advantages flowed from the close relationship between the executive and Lord Chancellor these were outweighed by the criticism that the office of Lord Chancellor represented a major breach in the separation of powers, and could not withstand the allegation that the office raised doubts about the independence of the judiciary.[10] As discussed below, the Constitutional Reform Act 2005 reforms the office of Lord Chancellor in a manner which establishes a clearer separation of powers between the executive, legislature and judiciary. The office of Lord Chancellor is retained in name but the powers of the office are radically curtailed. The post is combined with that of the Secretary of State for Constitutional Affairs. The office holder must be 'qualified by experience'[11] but need not be a lawyer, and in future the Lord Chancellor will not exercise any judicial functions nor will he sit as Speaker of the House of Lords. Section 1 of the Act makes explicit reference to the rule of law, stating that the Act does not adversely affect that principle or the Lord Chancellor's existing role in protecting the rule of law. Section 3 imposes a statutory duty on the Lord Chancellor and other ministers of the Crown and those with responsibility for matters relating to the judiciary to uphold the continued independence of the judiciary.

---

10 The requirements of judicial independence were considered by the European Court of Human Rights in *Findlay v United Kingdom* (1997) and *McGonnell v United Kingdom* (2000): see further Chapter 19.

11 Section 2 provides that relevant experience may include experience as a minister, as a Member of either House of Parliament, as a practitioner, as a teacher of law in a university and any other experience that the Prime Minister considers relevant.

THE JUDICIARY

Appointment

The Lord Chief Justice, Master of the Rolls, President of the Family Division, Vice Chancellor, Lords of Appeal in Ordinary and Lord Justices of Appeal are appointed by the Queen.[12] Prior to the Constitutional Reform Act 2005, the appointments were made on consultation with the Prime Minister, who would have consulted the Lord Chancellor. For appointments to the High Court, the candidate must be a barrister of ten years' standing, or a solicitor with rights of audience in the High Court, or a circuit judge of two years' standing. For appointment to the Court of Appeal, the candidate must either be a barrister of ten years' standing, a solicitor with rights of audience in the High Court, or a current member of the High Court Bench.[13]

The socio-economic and educational background of the judiciary has been subjected to much research. In brief, the picture presented is one of a middle and upper class, middle aged, white, predominantly male, judiciary dominated by public school and Oxford or Cambridge University education.[14] The process of selection has traditionally been shrouded in secrecy, with records of eligible candidates, who in practice will be successful practitioners, being maintained by the Lord Chancellor's Department. The criteria for selection are ability, experience, standing, integrity and physical health.[15] It had long been argued that the appointment of judges should be made by an independent Judicial Appointments Commission rather than on the recommendation of the Lord Chancellor alone. The Constitutional Reform Act 2005 has finally brought about reform. The 2005 Act establishes a Judicial Appointments Commission which has responsibility for the recruitment and selection of judges for the courts in England and Wales. The Commission reports to the Lord Chancellor on who has been selected and the Lord Chancellor makes the appointment or recommendation for appointment to the Queen.[16]

The Lord Chief Justice assumes the Lord Chancellor's former functions as head of the judiciary assuming the additional title of President of the Courts of England and Wales and Head of the Judiciary of England and Wales. The Lord Chief Justice of England and Wales, the Lord Chief Justice of Northern Ireland and the Lord President of the Court of Session in Scotland may make written representations to Parliament on matters relating to the judiciary or the administration of justice.[17] Where the functions of the Lord Chancellor have been modified or transferred to the Lord Chief Justice, those functions will generally be

---

12 Supreme Court Act 1981, s 10(1), (2).
13 Courts and Legal Services Act 1990, s 71.
14 See, *inter alia*, Griffith, 1997; Blom-Cooper and Drewry, 1972.
15 *Judicial Appointments*, 1985, London: Lord Chancellor's Department.
16 There is a Northern Ireland Judicial Appointments Commission. The CRA 2005 creates a Northern Ireland Judicial Appointments Ombudsman.
17 In respect of Northern Ireland and Scotland the function is qualified by s 5(2) and (3) in order to respect the devolution settlements with those countries.

exercised either with the concurrence of, or after consultation with the Lord Chancellor.[18]

Tenure

The Act of Settlement 1700 secured a senior[19] judge's tenure of office during 'good behaviour'. More modern expression is given to this protection under the Supreme Court Act 1981,[20] which provides that a person appointed shall hold office during good behaviour, removable only by Her Majesty on an Address presented to her by both Houses of Parliament. Senior judges cannot be dismissed for political reasons. They can be removed by compulsory retirement if they are incapacitated or unable to resign through incapacity.[21] Judges can be dismissed for misbehaviour, and under an Address to the Crown made by the two Houses of Parliament. 'Misbehaviour' relates to the performance of a judge's official duties or the commission of a criminal offence. Not every judge convicted of an offence will be dismissed: six judges have been convicted for driving with an excess of alcohol in their blood but have continued in office. In 1830, Sir Jonah Barrington was removed from office in Ireland under the Address procedure for the embezzlement of monies paid into court. Theoretically, a judge can also be removed by 'impeachment' for 'high crimes and misdemeanours', although this procedure has not been used since 1805[22] and is thought to be obsolete.[23] In Scotland, judges can only be removed on the grounds of misconduct.[24]

The Judicial Pensions and Retirement Act 1993 introduced the retirement age of 70, which may be extended to 75 if in the public interest. From 1959, the retirement ages were set at 75 for a High Court judge and 72 for a circuit judge, although judges appointed before this date were permitted to remain in office.[25]

Salaries

In order further to protect the judiciary from political debate, judicial salaries are charged on the Consolidated Fund.[26] Judicial salaries are relatively high, on the basis that it is in the national interest 'to ensure an adequate supply of candidates of sufficient calibre for appointment to judicial office'.[27]

---

18 See the Constitutional Reform Act 2005, s 15 and Sched 4.
19 Lords of Appeal in Ordinary, Lords Justices of Appeal, Justices of the High Court.
20 Supreme Court Act 1981, s 11(3).
21 *Ibid*, s 11(8), (9).
22 The trial of Lord Melville. The previous trial was that of Warren Hastings in 1788. Two Lord Chancellors, Bacon (1620) and Macclesfield (1725), have been removed by impeachment.
23 Impeachment is not obsolete in the United States of America where President Nixon was threatened with impeachment and resigned and President Clinton was acquitted in impeachment proceedings.
24 Claim of Right 1689, Article 13; *Mackay and Esslemont v Lord Advocate* (1937).
25 As did the late Lord Denning, who retired at the age of 83.
26 Supreme Court Act 1981, s 12(5). The Consolidated Fund provides payments under the Civil List, the salaries of the Speaker, the judiciary, the Comptroller and Auditor General and the Parliamentary Commissioner. The Consolidated Fund Bill is passed without parliamentary debate. See further Chapter 13.
27 HC Deb, Vol 23, Cols 257–61.

Disqualifications

Holders of full time judicial appointments are barred from legal practice,[28] and may not hold paid appointments as directors or undertake any professional or business work. Judges are also disqualified from membership of the House of Commons.[29] Membership of the House of Commons does not, however, disqualify that person from appointment to the Bench.

Immunity from suit

All judges have immunity from legal action in the performance of their judicial functions. Provided that a judge acts within jurisdiction, or honestly believes he is acting within his jurisdiction, no action for damages may lie. A judge is immune from the law of defamation and, even if 'actuated by envy, hatred and malice and all uncharitableness', he is protected.[30] In *Sirros v Moore* (1975), Lord Denning MR and Ormrod LJ ruled that every judge – irrespective of rank and including the lay magistracy – is protected from liability in respect of his judicial function provided that he honestly believed that the action taken was within his jurisdiction.[31] The Crown Proceedings Act 1947 also provides protection for the Crown from liability for conduct of any person discharging 'responsibilities of a judicial nature vested in him' or in executing the judicial process.[32]

Bias or personal interest

A judge is under a duty not to adjudicate on cases in which he has either an interest – whether personal or financial – or where he may be influenced by bias. A fundamental doctrine of natural justice is that 'no man should be judge in his own cause': *nemo iudex in sua causa*.

Financial interests

In *Dr Bonham's Case* (1609) Lord Coke held that members of a board which determined physicians' fines could not both impose and receive the fines, thus giving early judicial expression to the requirement of freedom from bias. Rather more recently, in *Dimes v Grand Junction Canal Proprietors* (1852), the propriety of Lord Cottenham LC adjudicating was challenged on the basis that the Lord Chancellor held shares in the canal company involved in litigation. The House of Lords set aside the decision of the court despite the fact that:

---

28 Courts and Legal Services Act 1990, s 75 and Sched 11.
29 House of Commons Disqualification Act 1975, s 1 and Sched 1.
30 *Sirros v Moore* (1975), p 132, *per* Lord Denning MR. See also *Fray v Blackburn* (1863); *Anderson v Gorrie* (1895). Jury verdicts are similarly protected (*Bushell's Case* (1670)), as are words spoken by participants in legal proceedings (*Munster v Lamb* (1883)). Barristers cannot be sued for negligence in the presentation of a client's case (*Rondel v Worsley* (1969)). For a recent consideration of the scope of immunity by the Court of Appeal see *Heath v Commissioner of Police for the Metropolis* (2004).
31 See Brazier, 1976.
32 Crown Proceedings Act 1947, s 2(5).

No one can suppose that Lord Cottenham could be in the remotest degree influenced by the interest ... It is of the last importance that the maxim that no man is to be judge in his own cause should be held sacred. [p 793]

Thus, the mere existence of a financial interest, even where it does not in fact result in actual bias but may present the appearance of bias, will be sufficient to disqualify a judge from adjudication. The same position prevails in the United States of America,[33] where the issue of financial interests of federal judges is expressly covered by law. The Ethics in Government Act 1978 requires that Supreme Court and Federal judges make a public declaration of 'income, gifts, shares, liabilities and transactions in securities and real estate',[34] a protection which is conspicuously absent in the United Kingdom.

A financial interest in a case which does not go beyond the financial interest of any other citizen does not disqualify judges from sitting. Thus, in *Bromley London Borough Council v Greater London Council* (1983), for example, the fact that all the judges in the Court of Appeal were taxpayers and users of public transport in London did not disqualify them from hearing the case.

Other bias

Judges, like everyone else, may be biased by virtue of race, sex, politics, background, association and opinions.[35] When adjudicating they must, however, be demonstrably impartial. This impartiality involves:

... the judge listening to each side with equal attention, and coming to a decision on the argument, irrespective of his personal view about the litigants ...

and, further:

Whatever his personal beliefs, the judge should seek to give effect to the common values of the community, rather than any sectional system of values to which he may adhere.[36]

Where a judge himself feels that he has a bias against one of the parties to litigation he may disqualify himself from sitting on the case, as did Lord Denning MR in *Ex parte Church of Scientology of California* (1978). There, counsel for the Church requested that he disqualify himself as a result of eight previous cases involving the Church on which he had adjudicated, and in which, in the eyes of the Church, he displayed bias against them.

1989 witnessed the start of a high profile case in which the doctrine of judicial impartiality was re-stated by the House of Lords. Earlier in the year, the former President of Chile, Senator Pinochet, arrived in Britain on a private visit for medical tests. The Spanish government sought the arrest and extradition of Pinochet on charges involving the murder, torture and the hostage-taking of Spanish citizens in Chile between 1973 and 1979. Two provisional warrants for Pinochet's arrest had been granted following the Spanish proceedings.

---

33   28 USC §455(b).
34   See Cranston, 1979.
35   See Griffith, 1997.
36   Bell, 1983, pp 4 and 8.

Pinochet then sought judicial review of the decision to grant an arrest warrant and an order of certiorari to quash the decision.[37] On appeal to the House of Lords, the court ruled – by a majority of three to two judges – that former Heads of State enjoyed immunity from arrest and extradition proceedings in the United Kingdom only in respect of official acts performed in the exercise of their functions as a Head of State. Torture and hostage-taking could not be regarded as part of Pinochet's official functions and therefore were excluded from immunity. In the course of the hearing before the House of Lords, several organisations – including Amnesty International – had been granted leave to intervene and submit evidence to the court. Following the decision, Senator Pinochet's lawyers complained to the Home Secretary that one of the judges, Lord Hoffmann, was a director of the Amnesty International Charitable Trust and, as a result, was disqualified from sitting, on the basis that his participation raised the question of bias: of a judge 'sitting on his own cause'. Senator Pinochet accordingly applied for the decision to be set aside. Lord Hoffmann had been one of the three majority judges. In an unprecedented move, Lord Browne-Wilkinson, convened a differently constituted panel of judges to reconsider the case, reiterating the principle that it was 'of fundamental importance that justice should not only be done, but should manifestly and undoubtedly be seen to be done'.[38] The mere fact of his interest 'was sufficient to disqualify him unless he made sufficient disclosure'.[39]

The *Pinochet* case, spawned further challenges against judges, alleging bias of one form or another. It also led to calls for a register of judges' interests, in which any interests which might raise the question of bias could be recorded and made public, a proposal rejected by Lord Browne-Wilkinson as unworkable: whereas it was generally clear when Members of Parliament's interests conflict with their professional duties, as he put it, 'a judge [unlike Members of Parliament] may be dealing with anything, any local club or society ... there's no end to it'.[40]

THE RELATIONSHIP BETWEEN EXECUTIVE AND LEGISLATURE; LEGISLATURE AND JUDICIARY; EXECUTIVE AND JUDICIARY

In light of the doctrine of separation of powers, it is necessary to evaluate the manner in which, and extent to which, separate functions are allocated between the differing bodies and kept separate. This task is most conveniently undertaken by examining the relationship between first, the executive and legislature, secondly, the legislature and judiciary and, thirdly, the executive and judiciary.

---

37 *R v Evans ex parte Pinochet Ugarte; R v Bartle ex parte Pinochet Ugarte: In re Pinochet Ugarte* (1998).
38 *Per* Lord Hewart in *R v Sussex Justices ex parte McCarthy* (1924), p 259.
39 *In re Pinochet Ugarte* (1999). See Olowofoyeku, 2000.
40 See Gibb, 1999, p 3.

Executive and legislature

The personnel of government

Parliament provides the personnel of government. Ministers of the Crown, including the Prime Minister, must be members of either House of Parliament. By convention, the Prime Minister must be a member of the House of Commons and it is for this reason that Lord Home renounced his peerage in 1963, under the Peerage Act of that year, to revert to being Sir Alec Douglas-Home, Leader of the Conservative Party and subsequently Prime Minister. It is thus immediately apparent that the executive, far from being separated from the legislature, is drawn from within its ranks. It is for this reason that Walter Bagehot in *The English Constitution* denounced the theory of the separation of powers under the English constitution. For Bagehot, this feature of the constitution, however, far from being a dangerous divergence from an ideal separation of powers, had clear merits. To Bagehot, the close relationship between executive and parliament represented 'the efficient secret of the English constitution' which:

> ... may be described as the close union, the nearly complete fusion, of the executive and legislative powers. No doubt by the traditional theory, as it exists in all the books, the goodness of our constitution lies in the entire separation of the legislative and executive authorities, but in truth its merit consists in their singular approximation. The connecting link [between the executive and parliament] is the Cabinet. [Bagehot, 1867, pp 67–68]

There are, however, opposing views. Lord Hailsham, the Lord Chancellor in the 1979–87 parliament, asserted[41] that the current electoral process which, generally, but not invariably, returns a government with a large majority of seats in parliament, contributes to what he termed an 'elective dictatorship' – that is to say, a situation in which the executive controls the legislature. While Bagehot's view may have been tenable at the time in which he wrote, it is nowadays too simplistic and inaccurate a description of the working of the constitution.[42]

Prima facie, this close union of executive and legislature would suggest that the potential for abuse against which Montesquieu warned exists at the heart of the constitution. This would be so if it were to be demonstrated that the executive controls parliament. Judgment on that matter must be suspended until the working of parliament has been examined in detail, in Chapters 14–16. There exist, however, tenable grounds for such an argument, but these must be set against the extent to which procedural mechanisms in parliament avoid an actual or potential abuse of power by the executive. The constitutional principle entailed in this close union between executive and legislature, deriving from historical practice, is that of 'responsible government': that is to say that the powers of government are scrutinised adequately by a democratically elected parliament to whom every member of government is individually and collectively responsible.

---

41 (1976) 120 SJ 693.
42 Richard Crossman (1993) states that Bagehot provides a correct description of Cabinet government as it was between 1832 and 1867; but see the opposing view expressed by Vile, 1967.

Statutory limits on membership

There exist statutory limits on the extent to which the executive can dominate parliament. The House of Commons Disqualification Act 1975 preserves the separation between the executive and legislature by providing that certain categories of people are disqualified from holding parliamentary office. Under section 2, holders of judicial office, civil servants, members of the armed forces and the police and members of foreign legislatures are debarred from office.

The Act also limits the number of government ministers in the House of Commons to 95 (section 2). Despite this limitation, 95 ministers, when considered together with their loyal Parliamentary Private Secretaries,[43] ensures that the government will generally enjoy the automatic support of some 120 Members of Parliament. Where the government has been elected with a strong majority of seats – as in 1983, when the Conservative Party had a majority of 144, and in 1997, when the electorate returned a Labour government with a majority of 179 – it must be conceded that the potential for dominance exists. An evaluation of this matter depends upon the adequacy of parliamentary procedures.

Political and procedural checks on government

The government, it must be recognised, irrespective of the size of its majority of seats in parliament, is dependent upon parliament for its continuance in office. The loss of a vote of confidence on a matter of policy central to a government's programme will cause the government to fall, as occurred in 1979 when the Labour Prime Minister, Mr James Callaghan, was forced to seek a dissolution of parliament and call a general election. Furthermore, parliamentary procedures are devised to secure adequate scrutiny for legislative proposals, and it cannot merely be assumed that the government will always get its legislation through in the form which it envisaged. By way of example, in 1983–84, the Police and Criminal Evidence Bill was substantially amended following pressure from politicians of all parties, pressure groups, academics and lawyers. In 1986, the government – despite having a strong majority in parliament – was forced to abandon its plans for legislation to deregulate Sunday trading due to parliamentary pressure. In 1994, the Conservative government faced unprecedented opposition over membership of the European Community and Union. While the government narrowly won a vote of confidence in the Commons, eight of its own members refused to support the government and the Conservative Party whip[44] was withdrawn. The constitutional effect of losing eight members under the whip was to place the government in the position of a minority government.[45] More recently, in the 2003 to 2004 session, in spite of having a significant majority in the House of Commons, the government won a vote on its Higher Education Bill by a majority of just five votes.

---

43 Who are elected Members of Parliament.
44 The organisational and disciplinary government members who control and co-ordinate parliamentary business. Loss of the whip, in effect, renders Members of Parliament without a political party.
45 In the 1992 election, the government had a majority of 21 seats.

The Opposition

The role of the official Opposition must also be considered. Her Majesty's Loyal Opposition is, constitutionally speaking, a 'government in waiting'. Not only is it the function of the Opposition to question, challenge and oppose the government, but it also puts forward alternative policies and solutions to problems. In order to ensure that there is adequate opportunity for the Opposition to fulfil its constitutional role, 20 days per session are set aside for debate on subjects chosen by the Opposition.[46]

Question Time, debates and select committees

Question Time and debates in parliament ensure the accountability of government to parliament. The administration of the state is scrutinised by a system of select committees in parliament with wide powers of inquiry.

The House of Lords

In addition to checks within the House of Commons, the House of Lords may cause government to modify or abandon proposed legislation. The House of Lords has the power to amend and delay non-Money Bills for approximately a year before the Bill can receive royal assent under the Parliament Acts 1911 and 1949. Rather than risk the delay of legislation, the government may prefer to compromise its proposals and accept proposed amendments from the Lords.

The electorate

Finally, the electorate, in addition to its role in a general election, can also express its displeasure with government policies during a parliamentary term at by-elections and local government elections. In the 1993 county council elections, the government lost control of many of the councils which had been its traditional supporters – clear evidence that no government can afford to ignore the views of the people. Subsequent by-elections confirmed the government's loss of electoral support, as did the general election on 1 May 1997, when the Conservative government suffered a humiliating defeat.

Delegated legislation and the separation of powers

Delegated – or secondary – legislation raises important questions relating to the separation of powers. Delegated legislation refers to laws, rules and regulations, made by government departments, local authorities and other public bodies, under the authority of an Act of Parliament: '... every exercise of a power to legislate conferred by or under an Act of Parliament.'[47]

The principal justification for the delegation of such law making power is efficiency. By granting delegated power, parliament is freed from scrutinising

---

46 Standing Order No 13.
47 *Joint Committee on Delegated Legislation*, HL 184, HC 475 (1971–72), London: HMSO, para 6. See further Chapter 15.

every technical detail of a Bill. Delegated power also enables ministers and others to 'fill in the details' after the parent Act is in force. AV Dicey approved of delegated powers on this basis.[48] Delegated power has, however, been questioned. In 1929, Chief Justice Hewart[49] criticised delegated legislation as being an abuse of power. An Interdepartmental Committee of Inquiry on Ministers' Powers[50] exonerated ministers from this charge and defended both the necessity and desirability of delegated legislation.

In any parliamentary year, some 40 to 50 Acts of Parliament will be passed. The volume of delegated legislation, however, may amount to some 3,000 statutory instruments per year. While general Bills – public and private – are subjected to full parliamentary scrutiny, it will be seen in Chapter 15 that delegated legislation receives far more cursory examination by parliament as a whole. The implication of delegated legislation in constitutional terms is that a legislative function is being exercised by the executive and not parliament. The delegation of law making power is a necessity given the heavy legislative programme and the modern complexity of legal regulation. Provided that parliamentary scrutiny is adequate, and that the courts are vigilant and effective in ensuring that delegated powers are exercised consistently with the law – *intra vires* – it may be concluded that this ostensible breach of the separation of powers is unavoidable, although whether it is subject to adequate scrutiny and control remains questionable.

In addition to the delegation of power to make secondary legislation, Acts of Parliament may on occasion confer on ministers the power to amend primary legislation. Such powers are known as Henry VIII powers and are discussed at p 398 below.

Legislature and judiciary

It has been stated above that parliament is sovereign and that the judiciary is subordinate to parliament. It has also been stated, perhaps paradoxically, that the judiciary is independent. This raises the question of how such apparently conflicting assertions can be reconciled. At the head of the judiciary is the Crown. The Crown represents the 'fountain of justice' and all judicial acts are carried out in the name of the Crown. In law, it is the Crown which appoints all senior judges.

Rules against criticism of the judiciary

To reinforce the independence of judges, convention dictates that there should be no criticism levelled at them from members of the executive – but not from other Members of Parliament. Parliamentary practice prohibits the criticism of judges other than under a motion expressing specific criticism or leading to an Address to the Crown for the removal of a judge. It was not, however, regarded as a breach of conventional rules when the then Prime Minister, Mrs Thatcher, in parliament,

---

48   Dicey, 1885, p 52.
49   Hewart, 1929.
50   Donoughmore-Scott Committee, Cmnd 4046, 1932, London: HMSO.

criticised the light sentence imposed on a child molester.[51] There have, however, been other incidents where judges have been criticised in parliament. In 1977, for example, motions were tabled for the dismissal of judges who had reduced a sentence for rape. Further, a judge who described a rape victim as guilty of contributory negligence was criticised in parliament.[52] The manner in which Members of Parliament are controlled in terms of what they may, or may not, say is through the powers of the Speaker of the House of Commons. These powers will be considered in Chapters 14 and 18.

The subjudice rule

Where civil proceedings are either before a court or awaiting trial, Members of Parliament are barred from raising them in debate. If the matter has not yet reached the courts, debate may be barred if the Speaker considers that there would result a real and substantial danger of prejudice to the trial arising as a consequence. No reference may be made to criminal proceedings from the time of the charge being made until the final appeal is determined.

Parliamentary supremacy and the judicial function

The doctrine of parliamentary supremacy entails the necessary constitutional subordination of judges to parliament and has several implications. First, it is well established that the sovereign parliament can overturn any court decision by way of legislation.[53] Secondly, the judiciary's primary role in relation to the interpretation of statutes is to give effect to the latest expression of the will of parliament.[54]

The Human Rights Act was consciously drafted in such a manner as to preserve the balance of power – and separation of power – between the judiciary and parliament. As will be seen more fully in Chapter 19, this is accomplished by providing that primary (but not secondary) legislation remains immune from judicial invalidation even where that legislation is ruled to be incompatible with Convention rights. Where judges in the higher courts make 'declarations of incompatibility', the matter is referred back to the executive to determine whether, and in what form, amending primary legislation should be enacted by parliament.

Judges as legislators

One of the most debated aspects of the relationship between the legislature and the judges lies in the question: 'Do judges make law?' In constitutional terms, the issue is whether by making law – either by virtue of the doctrine of precedent or through the interpretation of statutes – the judges are usurping the legislative

---

51 HC Deb Vol 34 Cols 123–25, 285–86.
52 *The Times*, 20 and 21 December 1979; *The Times*, 17 January and 1 February 1980; *The Times*, 6 and 21 January 1982.
53 Eg, the War Damage Act 1965.
54 *Vauxhall Estates Ltd v Liverpool Corporation* (1932); *Ellen Street Estates Ltd v Minister of Health* (1934).

function or, in other words, violating the separation of powers.[55]

The role of judges as law-makers must be understood against the backdrop of the long history of the common law – the law common to the whole country, developed by the judges rather than by Act of Parliament. In terms of volume, Parliament only became the principal law-maker in the nineteenth century when the effects of industrialisation required major programmes of legislation, much of it relating to safety at work and employment law, housing, health and relief from poverty. As discussed in Chapter 7, Acts of Parliament are supreme and may overturn the common law, as occurred for example in *Burmah Oil v Lord Advocate* (1965) in which the House of Lords awarded compensation for property loss and Parliament overruled the decision by enacting the War Damage Act 1965. However, when judges make law, Parliament may also 'tacitly' approve the decision by not interfering with it: when this occurs it can be said that the judges and Parliament are acting in a form of constitutional partnership. Parliament may also expressly endorse a judicial decision by incorporating it into statute, as occurred with the amendment to the statutory definition of rape following the House of Lords' decision in *R v R* (1991).[56]

The rules of precedent have been developed by the judges in order to ensure certainty and uniformity in decisions.[57] The need for certainty is expressed in the words *stare decisis*: 'stand by the decided cases'. In essence, decisions of the highest court – the Appellate Committee of the House of Lords[58] – are binding on all the courts lower in the hierarchy. Furthermore, the House of Lords is very slow to go against a previous decision of its own, although since 1966 it has had the power to do so.[59] Decisions of the next highest court – the Court of Appeal – are binding on courts lower in the hierarchy, and the Court of Appeal may only depart from its own previous decisions under limited circumstances.[60] There is thus a structure in place by which the lower courts are controlled by the decisions of the higher courts.

It is of course essential that while the law is certain, it is also able to reflect changes in society. The requisite flexibility is provided within the rules that structure the extent to which judges may depart from previous decisions. It should be noted that not all aspects of a previous case will be binding on a new case before the court. What is 'binding' is the *ratio decidendi* of the precedent case, and the *ratio* may be defined as 'the rule of law upon which the decision is founded', or 'the material facts of the case plus the decision thereon'.[61] Other aspects of the precedent judgments are known as *obiter dicta*: things said 'by the way', which are not binding on future courts but may nevertheless prove to be

---

55 This issue is complex. See, for detailed discussion, Slapper and Kelly, 2004. See also Reid, 1972.
56 See the Criminal Justice and Public Order Act 1994.
57 The detailed rules are outside the scope of this text. See Williams, 2002; Slapper and Kelly, 2004.
58 To be renamed the Supreme Court under the Constitutional Reform Act 2005, when in force.
59 See *Practice Statement* [1966] 1 WLR 1234.
60 As defined in *Young v Bristol Aeroplane Ltd* (1944).
61 There are many complexities in the concept of the *ratio* and further reading is recommended: see Williams, 2003; Goodhart, 1931, p 1.

highly influential in the future. The rules also include the technique of *distinguishing*: the reasoning process through which it can be said that the facts before the court in the instant case can be distinguished from those of a precedent case, thereby making its decision inapplicable.

Taken together, the rules relating to being bound by the higher courts and to the *ratio* and distinguishing produce a high degree of stability, while also allowing for necessary flexibility.

The rules of statutory interpretation, devised by the judges themselves, are designed to limit judicial creativity. Statutory interpretation is not straightforward, even though Acts of Parliament are couched in detailed language in order to maximise clarity and minimise vagueness or obscurity. Despite this attempt to achieve clarity in statutory language, it is artificial to deny that judges 'make law'. Every new meaning conferred on a word, every application of a rule to a new situation, whether by way of statutory interpretation or under common law, 'creates' new law. Judges have themselves abandoned the fiction of the 'declaratory theory' which asserts that they do not 'make' law but merely discover its true meaning. From the separation of powers perspective, judicial law making should cause disquiet only if judges display overtly dynamic law making tendencies. By way of illustration, in *Magor and St Mellons Rural District Council v Newport Corporation* (1965), Lord Denning MR was accused by Lord Simonds in the House of Lords of 'naked usurpation of the legislative function'.

Reviewing Lord Denning's approach, Lord Simonds roundly rejected Lord Denning's broad 'gap filling' attitude to interpretation:

> The court, having discovered the intention of Parliament and of ministers too, must proceed to fill in the gaps. What the legislature has not written, the court must write. This proposition, which restates in a new form the view expressed ... in the earlier case ... cannot be supported. It appears to me to be a naked usurpation of the legislative function under the thin disguise of interpretation. And it is less justifiable when it is guesswork with what material the legislature would, if it had discovered the gap, have filled it in. If a gap is disclosed, the remedy lies in an amending Act.[62]

Lord Denning's contribution to developing the law was marked in many areas. His judicial 'campaign' to protect the occupational rights of deserted wives[63] ultimately led to enactment of the Matrimonial Homes Act 1967, giving statutory protection to rights of occupation in the matrimonial home. Placed within the context of separation of powers and the position of judges as subordinate to parliament, it can be seen that the courts developed the common law to a point where parliament felt it necessary to legislate. *Burmah Oil v Lord Advocate* (1965) further illustrates the point. The government, being dismayed at the implications of the House of Lords' decision over compensation rights for property destroyed in wartime, passed the War Damage Act 1965 to nullify the decision retrospectively. Such is the sovereignty of parliament.

The reference by judges to government publications and records of parliamentary proceedings, for the purposes of interpreting statutes, has

---

62 See Denning, 1979, pp 13–14.
63 *National Provincial Bank v Ainsworth* (1965).

traditionally been regarded as improper. In *Davis v Johnson* (1979), Lord Denning MR stated that privately he looked at *Hansard* in order to establish the true construction of a statute, a revelation not approved of by the House of Lords. The Renton Committee's *Report on the Preparation of Legislation*[64] and the Law Commission's *Report on the Interpretation of Statutes*[65] had both ruled against any relaxation of the rules on the basis, *inter alia*, that such reference was of doubtful benefit, difficult in practice and costly. Exceptions to this rule existed. For example, in *Black-Clawson International Ltd v Papierwerke AG* (1975), the House of Lords accepted that reference could be made to Law Commission reports and to the reports of parliamentary committees in order to establish the defect in the previous law which parliament was seeking to redress. Further, in *Pickstone v Freemans plc* (1989), reference to *Hansard* was regarded as justified for the purpose of determining the purpose of the legislation and government policy. Until the case of *Pepper v Hart* (1992), it had been widely accepted that the courts should not, except under these circumstances, consult materials preparatory to the enactment of the statute or the records of parliamentary proceedings in connection with its passage in order to assist with the task of interpretation. In *Pepper v Hart*, however, the House of Lords conceded the limited right to resort to *Hansard* as an aid to interpretation. The Attorney General had argued that any relaxation in the rules would amount to a questioning of the freedom of speech in debate in parliament contrary to Article IX of the Bill of Rights 1689. Lord Browne-Wilkinson, for the majority, rejected that reasoning, declaring that far from 'questioning the independence of parliament and its debates, the courts would be giving effect to what is said and done there'. For post-*Pepper v Hart* developments, see Chapter 18.

The High Court of Parliament

Parliament has the sovereign power to regulate its own composition and procedure. Under parliamentary privilege – derived from the law and custom of parliament and thus part of the common law – parliament, and not the courts, has jurisdiction to rule on its own powers. Parliament cannot, however – other than by an Act of Parliament – extend its own privileges.[66] The role of the judges in relation to privilege is to rule on its existence and extent. Once the court is satisfied that a particular matter falls within parliament's domain, it will defer to parliament. Accordingly, if, for example, a citizen is defamed by the absolute privilege of free speech in parliamentary proceedings,[67] there is no legal redress. Privilege will thus protect the Member of Parliament from the law of defamation and leave the aggrieved individual without a legal remedy.

Privilege also extends to regulating the legislative process. It is for parliament alone to determine the procedure by which an Act of Parliament should come into being. It is clearly established that, in order to become an Act of Parliament, a Bill must pass its legislative stages in the Commons and Lords (except where the

---

64 Cmnd 6053, 1975, London: HMSO.
65 Law Com No 21, 1969, London: HMSO.
66 *Stockdale v Hansard* (1839).
67 Bill of Rights 1689, Article IX.

Parliament Acts apply) before receiving royal assent. Once that process is complete, it is not for the judiciary to inquire behind the parliamentary roll.[68]

Executive and judiciary

With regard to the relationship between the executive and the judiciary, several matters having implications for the separation of powers require examination: the attitude of the courts in matters entailing the exercise of the royal prerogative; parliamentary privilege; judicial review; the role of judges in non-judicial functions; and the role of the Law Officers of the Crown.[69]

The royal prerogative

Detailed consideration of the royal prerogative will be undertaken in Chapter 6. The royal prerogative has significant implications for the separation of powers. Being the residue of monarchical power, the prerogative is part of the common law and thus amenable to the jurisdiction of the courts. Today, the vast majority of prerogative powers are exercised by the government in the name of the Crown. As will be seen later, the substance of many prerogative powers is political, entailing matters of policy which the judges are not competent to decide or – to phrase it differently – matters which, if ruled on by the judges in a manner inconsistent with the interpretation of the executive, would place the judges in a sensitive constitutional position and leave them open to accusations of a violation of the separation of powers. That is not to suggest, however, that the courts have no role to play with respect to the royal prerogative. The traditional role of the courts is to rule on the existence and scope of the prerogative, but – having defined its existence and scope – to decline thereafter to rule on the exercise of the power. However, in *Council of Civil Service Unions v Minister of State for Civil Service* (1985) (the *GCHQ* case), the House of Lords made it clear that the courts have jurisdiction to review the exercise of executive power irrespective of whether the source of power is statutory or under the prerogative. Having seemingly extended the jurisdiction of the courts in relation to the prerogative, the House of Lords, nevertheless, proceeded to rule that there exists a wide range of 'non-justiciable' matters which should be decided by the executive rather than the courts: a clear expression of the separation of powers.

Law Officers of the Crown

The Law Officers of the Crown – the Attorney General and the Solicitor General – are members of the government. The Attorney General may also be a member of Cabinet. The Attorney General is bound by conventions which serve to limit the overlap in functions. Thus, where his consent to prosecution is required, by convention the Attorney General must avoid party political considerations, and may not take orders from government. This is a particularly delicate matter when

---

68 *Pickin v British Railways Board* (1974).
69 On the Home Secretary's former powers to determine the length of prison sentences and judicial review of his decisions, see the 4th edition of this book, pp 893–96.

essentially political prosecutions are being contemplated.[70] The Law Officers are advisers to government and its ministers, and, by convention, this advice must never be disclosed. In 1986, this convention was breached when Leon Brittan, then Secretary of State for Trade and Industry, revealed advice given on the Westland Helicopter rescue plan.[71]

Judicial review

Judicial review of administrative action is designed to keep those persons and public bodies with delegated powers within the scope of the power conferred upon them by parliament: the doctrine of *intra vires*. Thus, if a minister of the Crown or a local authority or other public body exceeds the power granted, the courts will nullify the decision taken and require that the decision maker reach a decision according to the correct procedure. Judicial review is concerned with the process by which decisions are made, not with the merits of the decision itself, nor with the merits of the legal rules which are being applied by the administrator. From this perspective, it may be said that the judges are upholding the will of parliament in controlling the exercise of powers delegated by it to subordinate bodies. The scope of judicial review has increased considerably – and the rule of law enhanced – since the coming into force of the Human Rights Act 1998.[72] The Human Rights Act, section 6, makes it unlawful for any public body – excluding Parliament but including the courts – to act in a way which is incompatible with the Convention rights protected under the Act. A person who claims that a public authority has acted or proposes to act in a manner incompatible with Convention rights may bring proceedings – including an application for judicial review – against that body.[73]

Judges as fact finders

It has become increasingly common for the executive to appoint judges as chairmen of tribunals of inquiry.[74] That this should be so is unsurprising. Judges are equipped by training and experience to review evidence with impartiality and rigour and to present findings in a logical manner. Inquiries have been conducted by judges into such diverse matters as state security;[75] civil unrest and terrorism;[76] football club disasters;[77] BSE in cattle;[78] arms to Iraq;[79] and the 2003 inquiry into the circumstances surrounding the death of the government weapons inspector Dr David Kelly.

---

70 See *R v Ponting* (1985).
71 See further Chapter 16.
72 On which see Chapter 19.
73 Section 7. Alternatively, Convention rights may be used as a defence against action taken by a public body which is incompatible with Convention rights.
74 See Drewry, 1996.
75 Cmnd 1681, 1962; Cmnd 2009, 1963; Cmnd 2125, 1963.
76 Cmnd 566 (NI), 1972; Cmnd 4801, 1972; Cmnd 5158, 1972; HC 220 (1971–72) (see Boyle, Hadden and Hillyard, 1975, pp 126–29); Cmnd 5847, 1975.
77 Cmnd 9710, 1986; Cmnd 962, 1990.
78 Lord Phillips.
79 See further Chapters 11 and 16.

Many of these inquiries involve sensitive political issues. As a result, it is inevitable that judges will attract criticism from one quarter or another. There exists the potential for charges of political bias in the report, or that the judge has avoided the issue and effected a 'whitewash', or that the inquiry has not been conducted properly. To place judges in the position where criticism is likely to ensue is to create the possibility that their independence and impartiality will be damaged.

CONCLUSION

Some academic constitutional authorities either deny, or minimise, the relevance of the doctrine of separation of powers under the United Kingdom's constitution. Geoffrey Marshall, for example, writes:

> ... the principle is infected with so much imprecision and inconsistency that it may be counted little more than a jumbled portmanteau of arguments for policies which ought to be supported or rejected on other grounds. [Marshall, 1971, p 124]

On the other hand, it has been judicially asserted by Lord Diplock that:

> ... it cannot be too strongly emphasised that the British constitution, though largely unwritten, is firmly based on the separation of powers: parliament makes the laws, the judiciary interprets them.[80]

Equally, Sir John Donaldson MR has stated that:

> ... it is a constitutional convention of the highest importance that the legislature and the judicature are separate and independent of one another, subject to certain ultimate rights of parliament over the judicature ...[81]

As Professor Munro has said, 'there is something of a puzzle here ...'.

The separation of powers is certainly neither an absolute nor a predominant feature of the British constitution. Nevertheless, it is a concept which is firmly rooted in constitutional tradition and thought. Judicial assertions of the importance of the doctrine can be explained in light of the constitutional position of judges in relation to parliament. The concept of separation of powers offers the judiciary a device both for the protection of the independence of the judiciary and against allegations of judicial intrusion into matters more appropriate to parliament or the executive. The reluctance of judges to be drawn into such matters is reflected particularly strongly in relation to matters of the royal prerogative and parliamentary privilege.[82] Accordingly, to deny the relevance of some form of separation of powers would be to misconstrue the evidence. The separation of powers is a principle respected under the constitution which exerts its influence on each of the fundamental institutions of the state. While the separation of powers is ill defined, and is not accorded absolute respect, it ought not to 'be lightly dismissed'.[83]

---

80 *Duport Steels Ltd v Sirs* (1980), p 157.
81 *R v HM Treasury ex parte Smedley* (1985), p 306.
82 See Chapters 6 and 18, respectively.
83 Munro, 1999, pp 195, 328–32.

CHAPTER 6

THE ROYAL PREROGATIVE

The King should not be over man, but under God and the law.[1]

INTRODUCTION

Under the constitution of the United Kingdom, all actions of government are undertaken in the name of the Crown. Any account of the prerogative is an account of power, and the prerogative, historically and contemporarily, concerns the power of the Crown.[2] The prerogative today represents one of the most intriguing aspects of the unwritten constitution. In order fully to appreciate the meaning of the term 'the Crown', an analysis of both who in fact exercises various powers in the name of the Crown, and the source of the power exercised, needs to be examined. The question to be asked is: is the power (to be exercised) a prerogative power or is it the outcome of statute? As will be seen, there is no certainty as to either the existing prerogative powers or the manner in which these may be extinguished. It is, however, clear that no new prerogative powers can be created.

THE PREROGATIVE DEFINED

Blackstone defines the prerogative in his *Commentaries* (1765–69) as:

> ... that special pre-eminence which the King hath over and above all other persons, and out of the ordinary course of the common law, in right of his regal dignity. It signifies, in its etymology (from *prae* and *rogo*) something that is required or demanded before, or in preference to, all others.

Dicey, on the other hand, describes the prerogative in the following manner:

> ... the residue of discretionary or arbitrary authority, which at any time is legally left in the hands of the Crown ... Every act which the executive government can lawfully do without the authority of an Act of Parliament is done in virtue of this prerogative. [1885, p 424]

From these differing definitions, the following can be deduced: first, that these are powers which are inherent in, and peculiar to, the Crown; secondly, that the powers derive from common law; thirdly, that the powers are residual; fourthly, that the majority of the powers are exercised by the executive government in the name of the Crown; and, finally, that no Act of Parliament is necessary to confer authority on the exercise of such powers.

---

1   Bracton (1200–68).
2   On the distinctions between the monarch and the Crown, see Marshall, 1971, pp 17–24.

Joseph Chitty, whose work remains the most comprehensive account of the prerogative, explains the need for prerogative power in the following manner:

> The rights of sovereignty, or supreme power, are of a legislative and executive nature, and must, under any form of government, be vested exclusively in a body or bodies, distinct from the people at large. [1820, p 2]

In Chitty's analysis, the power of the King is but part of a reciprocal relationship between monarch and subject. To the King is owed a duty of allegiance on the part of all subjects; to the subjects is owed the duty of protection.

THE PREROGATIVE BEFORE 1688

The King and parliament

It was for the King to summon parliament and to prorogue it. The King could suspend parliament's sittings and dissolve it. Parliaments were held regularly from 1295, and in 1311, it was decreed that parliament should meet twice a year.[3] In 1330, the first statute was passed requiring that parliament meet at least once a year – and more frequently if necessary. At that time, parliament did not sit for a term of years, but rather was summoned to meet *de novo* each year. The record was by no means constant: there were, for example, no parliaments in the years 1364, 1367, 1370, 1373–76, 1387, 1389, 1392, 1396 or between 1407 and 1410. Under Edward IV (1461–83), only six parliaments met in the course of his 22 year reign. Under Henry VII (1485–1509), there were but seven parliaments, despite the Act of Edward III remaining on the statute book. Whether and when a parliament should meet was much dependent upon the King's need for revenue, for it had been established by the middle of the fourteenth century that it was unlawful for the King to impose direct taxes without parliament's consent. On taxation, see further below, pp 127–29.

In the reign of Henry VIII, between 1491 and 1547, nine parliaments met in 38 years, although one of these lasted for seven years between 1529–36; under Edward VI (1547–53), two parliaments met, the second of which lasted four and a half years. Mary reigned for over five years (1553–58) and parliament met annually throughout her reign. Under Elizabeth I (1558–1603), by way of comparison, a mere ten parliaments met, although one parliament lasted for 11 years. In the reign of James I (1603–25), four parliaments met in 22 years, one lasting for nearly seven years.

The absoluteness of the King's power came to a head in the reign of Charles I (1625–49) when Charles confronted parliament over taxation to meet the cost of war, imprisoning over 70 people who refused to pay the forced loan, including the 'five knights'[4] who sought a writ of habeas corpus against the King. Sir Edward Coke supported members of the Commons who sought to petition the King against unparliamentary taxation, imprisonment without good cause, the billeting of troops and the imposition of martial law. Charles accepted the Petition

---

3   See Maitland, 1908.
4   *Darnel's Case* (1627).

of Right but, faced with continued opposition from parliament, prorogued parliament in June 1628. Parliament was again summoned in 1629 but confrontation was again rife, with the Commons criticising the King's religious policy and refusing to vote supply for the Crown. Charles decided to adjourn parliament in 1629 and there commenced an 11 year period of personal monarchical rule. In 1641, under the leadership of Pym, the 'Grand Remonstrance' was drafted – listing the grievances of the country under the rule of prerogative. While the Commons was divided over the Remonstrance, it represented a starting point in history, one which was to lead to the Civil War, Charles's execution and the rule of Oliver Cromwell under the only Republican constitution Britain has ever experienced.[5]

The Crown and the Council

Members of the King's Council were appointed and dismissed by the King at pleasure. While most matters of government and administration were decided by the Council, the King was under no duty to heed their advice, and, under a strong King, the Council had little real power. Under a weak King, however, real power vested in the Council, and in the course of a King's minority, the 'Council has ruled England'.[6] Under King Edward II (1307–27), the Council became a more formal body, with members being sworn in. The King in Council legislated, raised taxes and dispensed justice. FW Maitland observed that it is difficult to discern, during that time, whether a particular act of government was effected by parliament or the King in Council. From 1386, the proceedings of the Council were recorded, and the Council was established as a permanent part of the machinery of government.

Law making powers of the Crown

Proclamations

In Chapter 2, the constitutional upheavals of the seventeenth century were discussed, and it is in this period of history, and in particular with the constitutional settlement of 1689, that the origins of parliamentary sovereignty are to be discovered. It will be recalled that it was Henry VIII (1509–47) who asserted the power to make law by way of proclamations: '... the most extraordinary act in the Statute Book.'[7] The statute did not affect the common law or existing Acts of Parliament, and it prohibited the use of the death penalty for breach of proclamations. This, nevertheless, left a wide – and ill defined – scope for the Crown to legislate without parliament. The Act was repealed in the reign of Edward VI (1547–53). Its repeal was of great constitutional and symbolic importance in that it denied, by implication, the supremacy of the King over parliament and declared that it was the 'King in Parliament' which represented the lawful legislature. Nevertheless, both Mary I (1553–58) and Elizabeth I

---

5   See Lockyer, 1985, Chapters 12–13.
6   Maitland, 1908, p 200.
7   The Statute of Proclamations 1539. See Maitland, 1908, p 253.

(1558–1603) continued to rule by proclamation. However, when James I (1603–25) asserted his right to rule by proclamation, his assumed power was challenged by an application from the King's Council to the courts. In the *Case of Proclamations* (1611), Chief Coke CJ declared that:

> ... the King by his proclamation or other ways cannot change any part of the common law, or statute law, or the customs of the realm.

> ... the King cannot create any offence by his prohibition or proclamation, which was not an offence before, for that was to change the law, and to make an offence which was not.

> Also, it was resolved that the King hath no prerogative but that which the law of the land allows him.

Dispensing and suspending powers of the Crown

The King's assent was needed for the enactment of statutes, but he also had the power to dispense with statutes and suspend their application. According to Coke, where statute affected the prerogative power, the King could suspend the Act.[8] The conflict between Crown and the courts in the seventeenth century is illustrated by the cases of *Thomas v Sorrell* (1674) and *Godden v Hales* (1686). In *Thomas v Sorrell*, it was declared that the King could not dispense with a penal law made for the good of the public. However, in *Godden v Hales*, the court accepted that the King could dispense with a penal law – under specific circumstances – where that law fell within his jurisdiction. In 1687, James II, intent on removing obstacles to Roman Catholics holding public office, issued a Declaration of Indulgence which condemned the principle of religious compulsion and announced that all penal laws in ecclesiastical matters be suspended. In 1688, he went further, issuing a second Declaration of Indulgence which he instructed all Anglican clergy to read from the pulpit. On an appeal from the seven bishops who questioned the legality of such a dispensing power, James II ordered their arrest on a charge of seditious libel. In the *Seven Bishops' Case* (1688), they were acquitted.

The King and the courts

It was within the King's prerogative to establish new courts of justice. The Court of Star Chamber, exercising extensive criminal jurisdiction with little of the formality of judicial proceedings and without the use of juries, was established either under the Statute of 1487 or under the Crown's inherent prerogative: doubt exists as to its source. Unlike the ordinary courts, the Court of Star Chamber used torture. It became one of the most feared and powerful weapons under the control of the Crown until its abolition in 1641.

The King's claim to dispense justice in his own right and without the judges was dispelled in 1607. In *Prohibitions Del Roy* (*Case of Prohibitions*) (1607), the King sought to settle a dispute concerning land. In the Resolution of the Judges, Coke declared:

---

8   *Case of Proclamations* (1611).

... it was answered by me, in the presence, and with the clear consent of all the Judges of England, and Barons of the Exchequer, that the King in his own person cannot adjudge any case, either criminal, as treason, felony, etc, or betwixt party and party, concerning his inheritance, chattels, or goods, etc, but this ought to be determined and adjudged in some Court of Justice, according to the law and custom of England; and always judgments are given ... so that the Court gives the judgment ...

His Majesty was not learned in the laws of his realm of England, and causes which concern the life, or inheritance, or goods, or fortunes of his subjects are not to be decided by natural reason [which the King claimed] but by the artificial reason and judgment of the law, which law is an art which requires long study and experience, before that a man can attain to the cognisance of it ...

When, in 1617, the King ordered the Court of King's Bench to adjourn proceedings until he had been consulted, Chief Justice Coke refused, declaring that:

Obedience to His Majesty's command to stay proceedings would have been a delay of justice, contrary to the law, and contrary to oaths of the judges.[9]

Coke was dismissed from the Bench.

Whether a writ of habeas corpus would lie against the King was determined in 1627. In *Darnel's Case* (the *Five Knights' Case*) (1627), it was held that, where the King detained a prisoner under special order, the court would not look behind the order. Thus, while the King could not determine cases, he could nevertheless hold a subject free from interference by the judges. The Petition of Right 1628 declared such power to be unlawful, and in 1640, the Habeas Corpus Act guaranteed that habeas corpus would lie against the Crown.

Regulation of trade and defence of the realm

Historically, much of the commerce and trade of the country was under the prerogative of the Crown: according to Sir William Blackstone, the King 'is the arbiter of commerce' (*Commentaries*). But, if such a prerogative ever existed in relation to foreign trade, it was effectively abolished by various statutes and, today, no commentator on the prerogative includes trade and commerce as being within its ambit. The King's duty as to the protection of the realm encompassed the powers to restrict imports of the raw materials of war, and the right to erect ports and havens. As a corollary, the King had the prerogative power of erecting beacons and lighthouses. Under statute, Elizabeth I vested power to erect beacons and lighthouses for the protection of seafarers in Trinity House at Deptford, but the Act did not affect the King's prerogative powers over beacons and lighthouses on the shores of non-coastal waters.

The Crown and taxation

The early history of finance for the Crown is inextricably linked to the notion of the King as ultimate lord of all land. The King was the largest landowner in the Kingdom and exercised his right to collect revenues from the land. In addition,

---

9   *John Colt and Glover v Bishop of Coventry and Lichfield* (the *Commendam Case*) (1617).

the King received profits from legal proceedings in the form of fees paid by litigants and fines. Pardons were also sold. FW Maitland records that in the twelfth century:

> ... the King's revenue was the King's revenue, no matter the source whence it came; it was his to spend or to save, as pleased him best; all was his pocket money; it is to later times that we must look for any machinery for compelling the King to spend his money upon national objects. [1908, p 94]

The granting of supply to the King by parliament from direct taxation had been established in 1215, from which time it was accepted that the King had no power to levy direct taxation without parliamentary consent.[10] The position of indirect taxation was, however, unclear. The power to regulate trade, including the power to establish, open and close ports, was within the royal prerogative. Accordingly, it could be argued that the correlative power to levy taxes on imports and exports was within the power of the Crown. In Mary I's reign, the Queen imposed indirect taxes on the exportation of cloth, and, in Elizabeth I's reign, a tax was imposed on the importation of wine. A legal challenge to this assumed power of the Crown was instigated in James I's reign (1603–25) over the increased taxation on currants. In *Bate's Case* (1606), the Court of Exchequer ruled in the King's favour, accepting that:

> ... commerce and affairs with foreigners, war and peace, the admitting of foreign coin, all treaties whatsoever, are made by the absolute power of the King. The King may shut the ports altogether; therefore he may take toll at the ports.

The indirect taxation issue was again to be tried in the courts in the reign of Charles I, from 1625 to 1649. In 1628, Charles had announced that in future all counties would contribute towards the cost of the navy: the contribution being either in the form of the provision of ships or money in lieu thereof. In 1634, this scheme was put into effect, and thereafter Ship Money was levied annually. Whilst this undoubtedly was within the King's prerogative, it enabled the King to avoid the constitutional convention that there should be no taxation without parliament's approval. In the *Case of Ship Money (R v Hampden)* (1637), Hampden had refused to pay taxes levied by Charles I to raise money for the navy in times of emergency. The King argued that it was for the Crown to determine whether or not an emergency situation existed and that this determination was conclusive of his right to exercise his prerogative power to raise revenue. The courts upheld the power of the Crown.

The Shipmoney Act of 1640 reversed the decision, and Article IV of the Bill of Rights 1689 declared it illegal for the Crown to raise money without parliamentary approval. The King's power included the right to debase the coinage,[11] although Blackstone was doubtful whether such a power was lawful.[12] Establishing markets for trading and granting monopolies over their usage was within the King's power, generating much income for the Crown.

---

10 In the reign of Edward I, 1271–1307.
11 Hale, 1736, Vol 1, p 194.
12 Blackstone's *Commentaries*. See now the Coinage Act 1971 and the Currency Act 1983.

Protest against Charles I's reign by prerogative was fuelled by a rebellion in Ireland, during which an estimated 2,000 English settlers were massacred.[13] The Grand Remonstrance of 1641 listed the grievances of the country ruled under the prerogative. The House of Commons, following debate, voted in favour of the Remonstrance by 159 votes to 148.[14]

In 1685, James II inherited a Crown which was in debt. The question of indirect taxation had not been fully resolved. James, though granting generous sums for the army, requested an increased grant. When parliament refused, in 1685, James prorogued parliament. When James II fled to France in 1688, the throne was offered to William and Mary of Orange under the terms set out in a Declaration of Right. Following acceptance of its terms, the Crown and Parliament Recognition Act 1689 was passed by the Convention established to reach a settlement. Parliament, as then constituted, proceeded to enact the Bill of Rights 1689, providing, *inter alia*, that there should be regular meetings of parliament; that elections should be free; that the Crown's power to raise taxation[15] was subject to parliament's approval, as was the power to maintain an army; that the powers of suspending or dispensing with laws by the Crown[16] were illegal; and, of the greatest significance, that the 'freedom of speech and debates or proceedings in parliament ought not to be impeached or questioned in any court or place out of parliament'.[17]

From this time, the supremacy of parliament over the Crown was established and the prerogative powers of the Crown continued in existence or were abolished or curtailed as parliament determined. No new prerogative powers may be claimed by the Crown: as Diplock LJ stated in *BBC v Johns* (1965): '... it is 350 years and a civil war too late for the Queen's courts to broaden the prerogative.'

Miscellaneous prerogatives

Miscellaneous prerogatives included the right to raise revenue from the demesne lands of the Crown as 'lord paramount of the soil',[18] to the ownership of tidal riverbeds, and to the land beneath a non-tidal riverbed – provided that it had not become a dry riverbed, whereupon the soil is equally owned by the owners of the adjoining banks. Equally, the King, by virtue of his prerogative, was owner of the shores – the land lying between the high and low water mark – of seas and navigable rivers within his dominions. The ancient right of the King to wild creatures, to franchises of forest, 'free chase', park or free warren have been abolished[19] with the exception of the right to royal fish (sturgeon) and swans,

---

13   See Foster, 1989b, Chapter 4.
14   Thus leading to the arrest by the King of one member of the House of Lords and five members of the House of Commons.
15   *R v Hampden* (1637).
16   *Godden v Hales* (1686).
17   Bill of Rights, 1689, Article IX, discussed in Chapter 18.
18   Chitty, 1820, p 206.
19   Wild Creatures and Forest Laws Act 1971.

which is expressly reserved by the 1971 Act. Additionally, the Crown had the right to treasure trove, now regulated under the Treasure Act 1996.[20]

THE PREROGATIVE TODAY

The constitutional questions requiring answer include those relating to the relationship between statute and prerogative and the control, judicial or political, of the prerogative. The most significant question which continues to intrigue and concern constitutional theorists today relates to the very existence and scope of the powers themselves, together with the constitutional implications of this ill defined reservoir of power. As Maitland observed, and as remains true in the twenty-first century, examination of the prerogative is:

> ... set about with difficulties, with prerogatives disused, with prerogatives of doubtful existence, with prerogatives which exist by sufferance, merely because no one has thought it worthwhile to abolish them. [1908, p 421]

Under the United Kingdom's constitutional monarchy, the Queen is part of the legislature: parliament comprises the Crown, Lords and Commons. The Queen is the 'fountain of justice' – and while the Queen has no power to make laws or suspend laws or to act in a judicial capacity,[21] the entire administration of justice is conducted in the name of the Crown.[22] The Queen is Supreme Head of the Church of England.[23] The Queen is Head of State in relation to foreign affairs. The Queen is head of the executive, and all acts of government, whether domestic or foreign, are conducted in the name of the Crown. The right to summon and dissolve parliament remains a legal power vested in the Crown. The Queen is the Fountain of Honour, and all honours in the United Kingdom are conferred by the Crown.

While regal powers are exercised in the name of the Crown by the government of the day, the Crown nevertheless retains important residual powers. Of these, the dissolution of parliament and the appointment of Prime Minister are the most significant. These are discussed below. It must also be recognised that a few powers remain the personal prerogative of the Crown. Illustrations include the grant of honours such as the Order of Merit, and the Orders of the Garter and Thistle. More importantly, there still remains the prerogative notion that the Crown never dies and that the Crown is never an infant (thus ensuring continuity of monarchy), and that the Crown can 'do no wrong', thus placing the Queen outside the jurisdiction of the courts and guaranteeing immunity from prosecution in her own courts. Beyond these limited powers and immunities, the sovereign has, in the words of Bagehot (1867): '... under a constitutional monarchy such as ours, three rights – the right to be

---

20 See MacMillan, 1996, and *Attorney General of Duchy of Lancaster v GE Overton (Farms) Ltd* (1982). Treasure found must be reported within 14 days to the local coroner. Failure to do so will be a criminal offence. A Treasure Valuation Committee has been established which has the duty to value treasure and advise on *ex gratia* payments to the finder.

21 *Case of Proclamations* (1611); Bill of Rights 1689; *Case of Prohibitions* (1607), respectively.

22 See Blackburn, R, 'Monarchy and the Personal Prerogatives' [2004] PL 546.

23 Act of Supremacy 1558. See Leigh, I, 'By Law Established? The Crown, constitutional reform and the Church of England' [2004] PL 266.

consulted, the right to encourage, the right to warn.' In legal theory, however, the position is much different. As Bagehot stated:

> Not to mention other things, she could disband the army (by law, she cannot engage more than a certain number of men, but she is not obliged to engage any men); she could dismiss all the officers, from the General Commander in Chief downwards; she could dismiss all the sailors too; she could sell off all our ships of war and all our naval stores; she could make a peace by the sacrifice of Cornwall, and begin a war for the conquest of Brittany. She could make every parish in the United Kingdom a 'university'; she could dismiss most of the civil servants; she could pardon all offenders. In a word, the Queen could by prerogative upset all the action of civil government within the government, could disgrace the nation by a bad war or peace, and could, by disbanding our forces, whether land or sea, leave us defenceless against foreign nations. [1867, 'Introduction' and pp 287–88]

In order to understand the power of the Crown, it is necessary to look beyond the superficial phrase 'in the name of the Crown'. The actual power which is exercisable by the Crown is limited in two ways. First, by convention, the majority of powers are exercised by Her Majesty's government or Her Majesty's judges in her name. Secondly, the existence and scope of a purported prerogative power is subjected to the scrutiny of the courts: 'The King has no power save that allowed by law.'[24] However, that should not be considered as equivalent to a power to control the prerogative.[25]

THE PREROGATIVE ILLUSTRATED

Before examining the nature, scope and constitutional significance of the prerogative, some examples are necessary to indicate the areas of power which fall under the prerogative. Under the United Kingdom's unwritten constitution, there exists no formal and agreed text as to the prerogative. In order, therefore, to ascertain the contents of the prerogative, an examination of the historical attributes of the Crown and the attitude of the courts to the prerogative is required. It is paradoxical – but undeniable – in a modern democracy, that there is no comprehensive, authoritative 'catalogue' of prerogative powers.[26]

To make an analysis of prerogative powers manageable, they may be separated into two categories:[27] those relating to foreign affairs and those relating to domestic affairs. Under foreign affairs can be subsumed:

- the power to make declarations of war and peace;
- power to enter into treaties;
- the recognition of foreign states;
- diplomatic relations; and
- disposition of the armed forces overseas.

---

24   *Case of Proclamations* (1611).
25   See *Council of Civil Service Unions v Minister for Civil Service* (1985), discussed below, p 142.
26   The most recent authoritative account remains that of Chitty, 1820.
27   As does Blackstone, in his *Commentaries.*

Within the domestic category falls:
- the summoning and dissolution of parliament;
- appointment of ministers;
- royal assent to Bills;
- the granting of honours;
- defence of the realm;
- the keeping of the peace;
- the *parens patriae* jurisdiction of the courts;
- the power to stop criminal prosecutions – *nolle prosequi*;
- reduction of sentences;
- pardoning of offenders;
- regulation of the terms and conditions of the Civil Service; and
- the right to royal fish and swans.

It can be seen from this list, which is by no means exhaustive, that the powers are wide and diverse.

THE PREROGATIVE AND DOMESTIC AFFAIRS

The dissolution of parliament

The dissolution of parliament refers to the process by which an existing parliament is brought to an end with a new parliament coming into being following a general election. The dissolution of parliament lies within the prerogative of the Crown. It is perhaps the most important residual prerogative exercised personally by the sovereign, and represents the greatest potential for controversy. Three aspects of the right to dissolve parliament require consideration: first, whether the Crown has the right to dissolve parliament on its own initiative; secondly, whether the Crown has the right to refuse a dissolution when requested by the Prime Minister or other ministers; and thirdly, whether, by refusing to assent to a Bill contrary to the advice of the Prime Minister, the Crown can indirectly force a dissolution.

Royal dissolution on the initiative of the Crown

The last occasion on which the Crown – on its own initiative – dissolved parliament was in 1835. The dismissal of his government by William IV in 1834–35 reveals the constitutional dangers of the exercise of monarchical power. The government had lost its leader, but was nonetheless viable as a continuing ministry. The King, misjudging the strength of public opinion against the government, forced it out of office only to be replaced by an unsuccessful successor. Bagehot evaluates the 1834–35 situation thus:

> So that the last precedent for a royal onslaught on a ministry ended thus: in opposing the right principles, in aiding the wrong principles, in hurting the party it was meant to help. After such a warning, it is likely that our monarchs will pursue the policy which a long course of quiet precedent at present directs – they will leave a ministry trusted by Parliament to the judgment of Parliament. [1867, p 231]

It has been suggested that 'a royal dissolution in our times would not merely be unpolitical; it would also be unconstitutional'.[28] This view has the support of Sir Ivor Jennings, who argues that, since the dissolution involves 'the acquiescence of ministers',[29] the Queen is accordingly unable to achieve a dissolution without advice. In Jennings's view, 'if ministers refuse to give such advice, she can do no more than dismiss them'.[30] The matter cannot be left there, however, for uncertainty remains over this issue. Walter Bagehot, writing in 1867, observed that the Crown's power to dissolve parliament, other than following a Prime Ministerial request, 'has almost, if not quite, dropped out of the reality of our Constitution' (p 230).

Dicey was of a different view. In Dicey's judgment, the Crown has the right – in extreme circumstances – to 'dismiss a ministry who commands a parliamentary majority, and to dissolve the parliament by which the ministry are supported' (1885, p 433). Dicey continued:

> The discretionary power of the Crown occasionally may be, and according to constitutional precedents sometimes ought to be, used to strip an existing House of Commons of its authority. But the reason why the House can in accordance with the constitution be deprived of power and of existence is that an occasion has arisen on which there is fair reason to suppose that the opinion of the House is not the opinion of the electors. A dissolution is in its essence an appeal from the legal to the political sovereign. A dissolution is allowable, or necessary, whenever the wishes of the legislature are, or may fairly be presumed to be, different from the wishes of the nation.

Dicey recognised, however, that the dissolution of 1834–35 was 'a mistake', the King wrongly interpreting the will of the nation. That judgment is not conclusive of the constitutionality of the King's action, although Dicey conceded that it 'is hard to speak with decision' over that dissolution. As Dicey argued, if there is a constitutional right to appeal directly to the people by dissolving parliament, then that right cannot itself be defeated merely because of a mistaken judgment. The precedent of 1834[31] is cited as authority for the proposition that the Crown has the right to dissolve parliament, other than on the advice of ministers, where the main objective of dissolution is to 'ascertain that the will of parliament coincides with the will of the nation' (Dicey, p 435).

Queen Victoria (1837–1901) was in little doubt that she retained the power to dissolve parliament without the advice of her ministers. Lord Salisbury summarised the consequences of such use of the prerogative:

> A dissolution by the Queen, against the advice of her ministers, would, of course, involve their resignation. Their party could hardly help going to the country as the opponents of the royal authority; or, at least, as the severe crisis of the mode in which it had been exerted ... There must be some hazard that, in the end, such a step would injure the authority of the Queen. It ought not, therefore, to be taken unless there is an

---

28 Markesinis, 1972, p 115; see also Marshall, 1984, Chapter III.
29 In so far as an Order in Council is required, the Lord President of the Council must summon the Council and a Proclamation and writs of summons must be issued, for which the Lord Chancellor has responsibility.
30 Jennings, 1959a, p 413.
31 And the earlier precedent of 1784, when George III dissolved parliament.

urgent reason for taking it. No such reason exists at present. It may ultimately be necessary in order to escape from a deadlock.[32]

Whether such a power continues to exist as a practical reality is, accordingly, in doubt. However, in so far as prerogatives continue in existence until expressly abolished by parliament, in legal-theoretical terms, Dicey's view would appear to be correct. There are, however, principled objections to this position. The power of control over the executive lies within parliament and the parliamentary process. With the parliamentary process of government and opposition functioning correctly, there should never be a situation arising in which an exercise of prerogative power would become necessary. A situation in which the Crown felt obliged to protect the 'sovereignty of the people' against its democratically elected parliament would represent an extreme paradox.

Refusal of dissolution on Prime Ministerial request

Two illustrations of refusal of a dissolution can be drawn from the Commonwealth. In 1926, the Governor General of Canada refused a dissolution to the Prime Minister, Mackenzie King, who resigned. The Governor General wrongly believed that the Leader of the Opposition could form a viable government with the support of parliament. After only four days in office, the incoming government was defeated and the Prime Minister requested, and was granted, a dissolution. A similar situation arose in 1939 in South Africa. In each case, the Governor General was much criticised. It is, however, by no means clear whether the position of a Governor General is identical to that of the Crown. A Governor General is appointed by the Crown, on the advice of Commonwealth ministers, for a fixed term of office. Once appointed, the Governor General acts on the advice of Commonwealth ministers. His position is therefore not identical to that of the monarch, and it cannot be assumed that the precedents of 1926 and 1939 can be invoked unqualifiedly to demonstrate the position of the Queen.[33]

Professor Markesinis questions whether the Crown retains the right – if it ever existed – to refuse a dissolution on the request of a Prime Minister. On the other hand, he states that:

> ... no one in particular was or is quite sure whether a convention has emerged that virtually allows the Prime Minister a free hand in the matter. [1972, p 116]

What does appear clear is that the Crown – if it is to exercise this personal prerogative – must at least have the support of some ministers.[34] The claim that the advice on which the Crown acts to dissolve parliament is Prime Ministerial advice appears to derive only from 1918.[35] However, the situation could arise whereby the Prime Minister wishes a dissolution to take place, but other ministers do not. The Queen would then have to exercise a personal choice. In this regard,

---

32 *Letters of Queen Victoria*, 3rd series, Vol II, pp 297–99, cited in Jennings, 1959a, pp 413–14.
33 See Marshall and Moodie, 1971, Chapter 3.4.
34 See Anson, 1933, Vol 1, p 327.
35 Jennings, 1959a, Chapter XIII.3.

Geoffrey Marshall cites *The Times* newspaper's editorial view, expressed in relation to the Labour government of 1966–70:

> If a Prime Minister defeated in Cabinet, unable to carry his policy in the party meeting, were to ask for a dissolution for the apparent purpose of unnecessarily involving his party in his own downfall, the Queen would have ample grounds for refusing and dismissing him, provided an alternative leader of the majority party was in sight. [1984, p 46]

It is arguable that if there is no discretion remaining, then the prerogative is at least in abeyance, or at most, is no longer truly a prerogative power.[36] Sir Ivor Jennings was of the opinion that, while 'the Queen's personal prerogative is maintained in theory, it can hardly be exercised in practice' (1959a, p 426).

Dissolution following refusal of royal assent

A 'forced' dissolution would inevitably come about if the Queen were to refuse to assent to a Bill against the wishes of her Prime Minister. During the Home Rule for Ireland debate, King George V (1910–36) was encouraged to veto the Home Rule Bill (see Chapter 3 on Home Rule). In legal theory, the Queen has the right to refuse her assent to Bills, but by convention, assent is always given. The right to refuse assent has not been exercised since the reign of Queen Anne in 1704. George V, however, believed that he had the power to refuse assent to the Irish Home Rule Bill under the Parliament Act 1911 in 1913 and 1914.[37] In relation to this, Sir Ivor Jennings states:

> It was assumed by the King throughout that he had not only the legal power but the constitutional right to refuse assent. On the other hand, he recognised that his exercise of the power would involve the resignation of ministers, a dissolution of Parliament, and a general election in which the main issue would be the prerogatives of the Crown. There is something to be said for a power to dismiss an unconstitutional ministry or to dissolve a corrupt Parliament, but nothing to be said for a power to refuse assent to a Bill because the King thinks it wrong. [1959a, p 400]

Doubt exists as to whether the Queen can refuse to give royal assent, dissolve parliament against the government's will, and dismiss the government. No government has been dismissed by the Crown since 1783, although the question arose in 1913–14 over the issue of Irish Home Rule, and the right to dismiss ministers was claimed to exist by George V, but not exercised. Sir Ivor Jennings states:

> The Queen's function is ... to see that the constitution functions in the normal manner. It functions in the normal manner so long as the electors are asked to decide between competing parties at intervals of reasonable length. She would be justified in refusing to assent to a policy which subverted the democratic basis of the constitution, by unnecessary or indefinite prolongations of the life of Parliament, by a gerrymandering of the constituencies in the interests of one party, or by fundamental modifications of the electoral system to the same end. She would not be justified in other circumstances; and certainly the King would not have been justified in 1913. [1959a, pp 403, 407–12]

---

36 Following Blackstone's view that for a prerogative to exist it must be a power unique to the Crown.

37 Jennings, 1959a, Chapter XIII.

On this alleged right to withhold assent to Bills, Geoffrey Marshall speculates as to whether the Queen could refuse to follow the advice of ministers if a Private Member's Bill was approved by both Houses but opposed by government, and whether, if parliament approved a Bill in a manner required by procedural rules, the Queen could refuse assent – but there is no definitive answer to these questions (see Marshall, 1984, pp 21–23).

As can be seen, many doubts surround the prerogative of the dissolution of parliament. It is claimed nowadays that, whilst the dissolution of parliament is technically for the Queen, it is exclusively within the Prime Minister's domain to request a dissolution at a time of his or her choice. Until 1918, when the convention was first challenged, it was thought that the decision rested with Cabinet. However, in 1935, Prime Minister Baldwin asserted his independent right to decide on the date of dissolution, resulting in criticism that the Prime Minister had unilaterally increased the importance of the Prime Ministerial office by assuming the discretionary power of the Crown.[38]

While, for the most part, the timing of a dissolution will be within the Prime Minister's discretion, there may arise situations where the Crown may have a constitutional duty to exercise its powers. By way of example, a minority government – shortly after a general election – might form a pact with an opposition party on whose co-operation it depended for a working majority in parliament. If, as a result of political disagreement, the pact broke down and the opposition party united with other opposition parties, the resultant situation would cause the Prime Minister either to resign or to seek a dissolution of parliament in order to test the support of the electorate. However, if the newly combined opposition parties had a leader who could command a majority in the House of Commons, it is by no means certain that the Queen would grant the dissolution requested. The Queen would, in effect, be confronted by two opposing constitutional principles. The first of these is that the dissolution of parliament is a matter for the Prime Minister and accordingly must be granted. The second principle is that the Queen should appoint as Prime Minister the leader of that party – or parties – which could command a majority in the House of Commons. In such a situation, the Crown clearly would have to exercise its powers of decision making, and might, in the interests of continuity of parliament and the avoidance of another general election, refuse a dissolution and call the leader of the opposition parties to form a government.[39]

The Labour government of 1974 reveals the potential difficulties and uncertainties concerning the power of dissolution. It also reveals the inherent vagueness in the concept of votes of confidence following the loss of which governments – by convention – are expected to seek a dissolution of parliament. The general election resulted in the Labour Party holding 301 seats (37 per cent), the Conservative Party 297 (38 per cent), the Liberal Party 14 and the other parties 23 seats. The Labour Party was accordingly 34 seats short of an overall majority.[40]

---

38 Keith, 1936.
39 See Marshall, 1984, Chapter III; on this specific point, see Brazier, 1982.
40 See Butler, 1989, Chapter II.

Given the indeterminate election result, neither the Labour Party nor the Conservative Party was keen for there to be a dissolution in the near future. The Labour government accordingly made it clear that a defeat in the Commons would not force the government to seek a dissolution, other than where the government had made it clear to all members of the House that it was treating the matter as one of confidence. Between March and October 1974, the government suffered 17 defeats in the Commons.[41] A general election took place in October 1974 when the opinion polls appeared favourable to Labour. The resulting election results produced an overall majority of three seats for the Labour Party.[42]

Between 1977 and 1978, the Labour government entered into a pact with the Liberal Party. While the Labour Party had won a narrow overall majority in the general election of October 1974, by 1976 this majority had been lost. Having failed to reach agreement with the Ulster Unionist Party, the Prime Minister, James Callaghan, entered negotiations with the Liberal Party leader, David Steel, out of which the 'Lib-Lab Pact' was born. The pact did not amount to a coalition government; no Liberals held government posts, nor was the government committed to accommodate Liberal policy within its legislative programme. Despite the government's lack of a majority (from 1976) and its dependency on the Liberal Party for its survival in office, the Party asserted the constitutional right of the Prime Minister – and no one else – to determine the dissolution of parliament. The matter should not be regarded as so certain.

An illustration from the Republic of Ireland

There is no precedent within the United Kingdom from which firm conclusions can be drawn. However, in the Republic of Ireland, the matter has been tested. In November 1994, following a controversial appointment of a former Attorney General (Harry Whelehan) to the position of President of the High Court, the 22 month coalition government of *Fianna Fail* and the Labour Party collapsed. Article 13.2.2 of the Constitution provides that:

> The President[43] may in his absolute discretion refuse to dissolve *Dail Eireann* on the advice of a *Taoiseach* who has ceased to retain the support of a majority in *Dail Eireann*.

It is also clear, however, that the President cannot refuse a dissolution to a Prime Minister who retains the support of a majority in the parliament (*Dail*). Three possible solutions could be sought. First, the President could grant a dissolution on Prime Ministerial request and a general election would take place. Secondly, the opposition parties could try to form a coalition and the President appoint its leader as Prime Minister. Thirdly, the *Fianna Fail* (the governing party) ministers could replace the Prime Minister with another leader who could secure a continued coalition government, in which case neither a dissolution nor a general election would be required. Should the Prime Minister (the *Taoiseach*) lose majority support by losing a formal vote of confidence, he would be obliged to

---

41 Between October 1974 and March 1979, the government was defeated 42 times, three of which were defeats on matters central to government policy.

42 Labour 319, Conservative 277, Liberal 13, others 26.

43 Then Mary Robinson.

resign.[44] When the Deputy Prime Minister, Dick Spring, announced that he would vote against the Prime Minister, Albert Reynolds, in a vote of confidence, the Prime Minister resigned.

After five weeks of political turmoil, John Bruton, Leader of the *Fine Gael* Party, with the support of the Labour and Democratic Left Party, was elected Prime Minister. The new coalition government had a majority of four in the *Dail*. Dick Spring, Leader of the Labour Party, was reappointed as Deputy Prime Minister and Foreign Minister.[45] Thus, the second option had been favoured and a new government – albeit fragile – formed without a dissolution of the *Dail*.

An illustration from Australia

The Australian political crisis in 1975 provides a further example of this uncertain constitutional situation.[46] Under section 2 of the Commonwealth of Australia Constitution Act 1900, the Governor General:

> ... shall have and may exercise in the Commonwealth during the Queen's pleasure, but subject to this Constitution, such powers and functions of the Queen as Her Majesty may be pleased to assign to him.

Section 5 states that:

> The Governor General may appoint such times for holding the sessions of the Parliament as he thinks fit, and may also from time to time, by proclamation or otherwise, prorogue the Parliament, and may in like manner dissolve the House of Representatives.

Section 64 provides that:

> The Governor General may appoint officers to administer such Departments of State of the Commonwealth as the Governor General in Council may establish. Such officers shall hold office during the pleasure of the Governor General.

In October 1975, the Senate refused supply to the government by resolving not to proceed with legislation giving effect to the Labour government's financial programme until the government agreed to a general election for the House of Representatives. When the Prime Minister, Gough Whitlam, refused to accede to this demand, supply was denied. On 11 November 1975 the Prime Minister called on the Governor General, Sir John Kerr, to request that writs be issued for elections to be held for 50 per cent of the Senate seats. Rather than granting the writs, the Governor General informed the Prime Minister that his commission had been withdrawn. In so doing – among other things – the Governor General prevented the Prime Minister from telephoning the Queen, as was his right whilst in office. Subsequently, the Governor General called for the Opposition Leader to act as caretaker Prime Minister, subject to two conditions. The first related to ensuring the granting of supply; the second to advising the Governor General to dissolve both Houses. In the ensuing general election the Opposition Leader, Malcolm Fraser, was returned with a majority of seats and the impasse ended.

---

44   Constitution, Article 28.10.
45   *The Times*, 16 December 1994.
46   Sawer, 1977.

One cause of the problem was the constitution itself, for while ministers must be in the lower House – the House of Representatives – the Senate had been given the power to withhold finance from a ministry formed from the House of Representatives. Compare this situation with the pre-1911 position of the House of Lords in the United Kingdom whereby – by convention – the House of Lords traditionally gave way to the Commons on matters of supply, and now the Parliament Acts 1911 and 1949 which regulate the position. In Australia, there had been no serious conflict until the situation of 1975.[47]

The intervention of – and actions of – the Governor General was much criticised, and whilst acting within his constitutional powers, the Governor General was seen to be directly involved in a political controversy. The criticisms were the greater for the fact that, in so acting, he was dismissing a Labour Prime Minister and the ministry of the House of Representatives and was seen to be favouring the upper House.[48]

David Butler identified four questions implicit in the crises of 1975, two of which have immediate relevance:

(1) What should the Queen have done if Mr Whitlam had the chance to 'phone her to demand the instant dismissal of the Governor General?

(2) Is 'the Governor General in Council' the only power that can dissolve Parliament, necessarily the Governor General and ministers of the Crown: or could the Governor General have called an Executive Council composed of Councillors not currently 'on summons' as ministers?

To neither of these questions were answers forthcoming to David Butler in his discussions.[49] More than anything else, the Australian saga reveals that the constitutional position of the monarch – in the representative form of a Governor General – can be as uncertain under a written constitution as under a largely unwritten one.

Circumstances requiring dissolution

Loss of confidence vote

By convention, a government must resign or seek a dissolution of parliament from the Queen if a confidence vote is lost in the House of Commons. A vote of confidence was described by Prime Minister Ramsey MacDonald in 1924 as being a vote on 'substantial issues, issues of principle, issues which really matter, a matter which strikes at the root of proposals made'. In 1979, the Labour government was forced out of office following a vote of no confidence. The government had been vulnerable to defeat since its election in 1974, having no majority and being reliant on alliances with other parties for its survival. In March 1979 the opposition succeeded in passing a vote of no confidence: the government was defeated by one vote and resigned.

---

47   Hanks, 1996.
48   Hanks, 1996.
49   Butler, 1976.

THE APPOINTMENT OF PRIME MINISTER

In constitutional theory, the Queen – under the royal prerogative – may appoint whomsoever she pleases to the office of Prime Minister.[50] In practice, the position is governed by convention and the Queen must appoint the person who can command a majority in the House of Commons; this, under normal circumstances, will be the leader of the political party which secures the greatest number of parliamentary seats at a general election.[51] Several differing situations present themselves: the government of the day may be returned by the electorate with a majority and the Prime Minister will remain in office. Alternatively, the government may lose the election, and the incoming Prime Minister will be the leader of that political party which commands a majority of seats in the House of Commons. More difficult is the position where the election produces no outright winner, resulting in no one party having an overall majority. Here, the spectre of a 'hung parliament' arises. The situation may also arise where a Prime Minister resigns from old age or ill health during the course of his term of office – as was the case in 1935 (Ramsey MacDonald), 1955 (Winston Churchill) and 1957 (Anthony Eden) – or dies in office (Campbell-Bannerman, 1905–08). Finally, it may be the case that a Prime Minister chooses to retire, as occurred in 1937 (Stanley Baldwin) and 1976 (Harold Wilson).

Appointment of Prime Minister following a general election

Where general elections are involved, for the most part, as will be seen later, the electoral system in the United Kingdom returns a single party with an overall majority, and so no question arises as to whom the Queen should appoint as Prime Minister. It is not out of the question, however, for a different political scenario to present itself. Should the Queen send for the leader of the party having the largest number of seats, or the leader of the party which will hold the balance of power? There is much debate over this issue,[52] but once again no clear cut answer.

In February 1974, the Conservative Party lost the general election by a small number of seats and could command no overall majority in the House of Commons. Following the election results, the Prime Minister, Edward Heath, did not tender his resignation immediately but rather entered into negotiations over the following weekend with the Liberal Party, with a view to forming a political pact which would ensure a majority over the opposition parties. When those negotiations broke down, Mr Heath immediately resigned, and the Queen invited the Leader of the Labour Party to become Prime Minister. The question arising at the time was whether there had been any unconstitutional conduct involved in

---

50 See, *inter alia*, Jennings, 1959a; Marshall and Moodie, 1971; Laski, 1951; Brazier, 1990, Chapters 1 and 2; Marshall, 1984, Chapter II.
51 Under the Prime Minister (Office, Role and Functions) Bill 2001, the power of appointment is placed on a statutory basis.
52 See, *inter alia*, Jennings, 1959a, Chapter II; Marshall, 1984, pp 29–35; Marshall and Moodie, 1971, pp 44–51; Brazier, 1982.

Mr Heath not relinquishing office the moment the election results were known.[53] The answer would appear to be that Mr Heath had the constitutional right to attempt to form a coalition which would avoid the need for a further election.

Appointment of Prime Minister following retirement of the incumbent

When the Prime Minister retires, the government still retains the mandate of the people and hence the choice of the new Prime Minister will be dictated by the wishes of the Party. It may be that there is a 'Prime Minister in waiting' who commands the support of the Party and will hence be appointed without delay. Under such circumstances, it is unrealistic to speak of the Crown having any choice in the matter. Where no Party consensus as to a successor exists, the political process will come into play. Nowadays, each of the major political parties utilises a method of election of its leader, and it is that process which will determine the successor: again, the Queen has no practical 'say' in the matter. It was not always thus.

In 1957, Sir Anthony Eden resigned office, and there was no obvious successor – nor was there in place at that time an electoral process within the governing Conservative Party which would produce a successor. The Queen was thus left with a choice. The Queen consulted elder statesmen of the Conservative Party and acted upon their advice that Harold Macmillan be appointed. Had she not acted upon impartial advice, the Crown could have been damaged by charges of political decision making. One consequence of the 1957 dilemma was that the Labour Party announced its intention to introduce a selection procedure for its leader: a move designed to remove any discretion from the Crown. The Conservative Party did not react in this manner until after the difficulties revealed in 1963. The resignation of Harold Macmillan fell at a time when there were several contenders for leadership of the Party. The matter was resolved by the appointment of Lord Home, a Conservative peer who relinquished his peerage and took a seat in the House of Commons as Sir Alec Douglas-Home. However, the saga emphasised the uncertainties in the choice of Party Leader and an electoral system for the leadership of the Party was subsequently introduced.

THE PREROGATIVE OF MERCY

Nowadays, the prerogative of mercy entails two aspects: the power to grant pardons which in turn has two elements and the power to enter a *nolle prosequi*.

Pardons and commutation of sentence

A complete pardon is used to remove the 'pains, penalties and punishments' which flow from a conviction for a criminal offence, but does not eliminate the conviction itself.[54] The right of pardon does not extend to civil matters. The

---

53 See, *inter alia*, Bogdanor, 1983, Chapters 5–8; Butler, 1983.
54 *R v Foster* (1985).

power is exercisable in England and Wales on the advice of the Secretary of State for the Home Department, who is accountable to parliament. The Crown therefore has no personal involvement in its exercise. Commutation of sentence is a limited – or conditional – form of pardon. The sentence will be reduced on conditions: '... a condemned murderer is pardoned on condition of his going into penal servitude.' As Maitland comments (1908, p 480): 'It is a nice question whether he might not insist on being hanged.' Commutation is distinguishable from remission of sentence. The latter reduces the sentence imposed but does not alter its form.

The prerogative of mercy has traditionally been regarded as unreviewable by the courts. In 1976, in *De Freitas v Benny* (1976), Lord Diplock was to state that:

> At common law, this has always been a matter which lies solely in the discretion of the sovereign, who by constitutional convention exercises it in respect of England on the advice of the Home Secretary to whom Her Majesty delegates her discretion. Mercy is not the subject of legal rights. It begins where legal rights end.[55]

In *Council of Civil Service Unions v Minister for the Civil Service* (1985), Lord Roskill confirmed that the prerogative of mercy was not 'susceptible to judicial review'. However, the case of *Bentley* (1993) suggests a different approach. In 1952, Derek Bentley, aged 19, and with a mental age of an 11 year old, was convicted of the murder of a policeman. At the time, the death penalty was the mandatory sentence for murder. Derek Bentley was hanged in 1953, a mere three months after the murder. His co-defendant, Christopher Craig, who fired the fatal shot at the police officer who died, was also convicted of murder, but escaped execution because he was aged only 16. Despite a recommendation by the jury that mercy be exercised, the Home Secretary decided not to exercise the prerogative. In 1992, the then Home Secretary refused to recommend a posthumous free pardon on the grounds that, while he personally agreed with the view that the death sentence should not have been carried out, it was the long established policy of Home Secretaries not to grant a free pardon unless the person concerned was both 'morally and technically innocent' of any crime and that his review of the case did not establish Bentley's innocence. In an application for judicial review brought by Derek Bentley's family, the court considered the question whether the prerogative of mercy was amenable to judicial review.[56] The applicant sought a declaration that the Home Secretary had erred in law in declining to recommend a posthumous free pardon, and mandamus to require the Home Secretary to reconsider the matter.

Counsel for the Home Secretary argued that the exercise of the royal prerogative of mercy was not reviewable in the instant case, on the basis that the criteria upon which the pardon should be granted was a question of policy, which was not justiciable. Counsel for the applicant argued that the prerogative of mercy is an important feature of the criminal justice system, and that 'it would be surprising and regrettable ... were the decision of the Home Secretary to be immune from legal challenge irrespective of the gravity of the legal errors which

---

55 At p 247. See also *R v Allen* (1862); *Hanratty v Lord Butler* (1971).
56 *R v Secretary of State for the Home Department ex parte Bentley* (1993).

infected such a decision' (p 452 *per* Watkins LJ). The court ruled that the view that 'the formulation of the criteria for the exercise of the prerogative by the grant of a free pardon was entirely a matter of policy which is not justiciable' was 'probably right' (p 453). However, it ruled that the Home Secretary failed to recognise that the prerogative of mercy is 'capable of being exercised in many different circumstances and over a wide range', and should have considered the form of pardon which might be appropriate to the facts of the case. This the Home Secretary did not do, and this failure was reviewable by the courts. The court, citing *Burt v Governor General*, endorsed the view that the prerogative of mercy is now 'a constitutional safeguard against mistakes'. The court also ruled, however, that it had no power to direct the way in which the prerogative of mercy should be exercised, but that it had a role to play by way of judicial review. The court declined to make any formal order, but invited the Home Secretary to reconsider the matter 'in light of the now generally accepted view that this young man should have been reprieved' (p 455).

In 1998, the Court of Appeal, Criminal Division, on a reference by the Criminal Cases Review Commission under section 9 of the Criminal Appeal Act 1995, quashed Derek Bentley's conviction for murder. In a powerful judgment, the Court of Appeal criticised a number of aspects of Bentley's trial. In particular, the court ruled that the then Lord Chief Justice, Lord Goddard, had failed to direct the jury adequately on the standard of proof to be met, had, in effect, reversed the burden of proof from the prosecution to the defence, and had shown partiality to the police's evidence over that of the defence; that the summing up by the Lord Chief Justice represented 'a highly rhetorical and strongly worded denunciation of both defendants and their defence'; and that, by failing adequately to direct the jury on the law then in force as to 'joint enterprises', the judge had 'failed to grapple with that ground of appeal', which should have succeeded. As a result, the effect was to deprive Bentley of the protection that jury trial should have afforded: 'The summing up here was such as to deny Bentley that fair trial which was the birthright of every British citizen.' The Court of Appeal ruled that the conviction had been unsafe, and the conviction for murder was quashed (*R v Bentley* (1998)). Thus, 45 years after the event, Bentley's name was cleared by the courts on the basis that his conviction had been unsafe, the royal prerogative of mercy in the hands of the politicians having failed to provide a remedy.

Nolle prosequi

On proceedings on indictment, the Attorney General, in the name of the Crown, can enter a *nolle prosequi*, the effect of which stops the legal proceedings. The power is not subject to the control of the courts: *R v Comptroller of Patents* (1899). The grant of a *nolle prosequi* does not amount to an acquittal, and accordingly, the accused may be brought before the court on the same charge. The effect of this would be to invite a further application for a *nolle prosequi*.

POWER TO ESTABLISH NON-STATUTORY AGENCIES

The Criminal Injuries Compensation Board was established under the prerogative in 1964. Its objective was to provide compensation for the victims of criminal offences[57] through *ex gratia* payments calculated on the same principles as compensation paid to victims of tort. The Board was reconstituted under statute in 1988,[58] although the provisions had not been brought into force. Was the setting up of the Board in 1964 the exercise of a true prerogative? Reverting to Blackstone's definition, the answer must be negative. The power to establish such a scheme clearly fell within parliament's jurisdiction, as the Criminal Justice Act 1988 proves. However, under Dicey's definition, the government is effectively given a choice in the manner of establishing such bodies: a surely questionable prerogative? In *R v Criminal Injuries Board ex parte Lain* (1967), Lord Diplock stated:

> It may be a novel development in constitutional practice to govern by public statement of intention made by the executive government instead of by legislation. This is no more, however, than a reversion to the ancient practice of government by royal proclamation, although it is now subject to the limitations imposed on that practice by the development of constitutional law in the seventeenth century. [p 886]

Professor HWR Wade denies that this was an exercise of a true prerogative:

> So far as the Crown came into the picture at all, it was exercising its ordinary powers as a natural person, which, of course, includes the power to transfer property, make contracts and so on. Blackstone was quite right, in my opinion, in saying that such powers are not prerogative at all.

> The truth seems to be that judges have fallen into the habit of describing as 'prerogative' any and every sort of government action which is not statutory. It may be, also, that the responsibility for this solecism can be loaded onto that popular scapegoat, Dicey. [1989, p 61]

In 1993, when the relevant provisions of the Criminal Justice Act 1988 had still not been brought into force – despite a statutory obligation being imposed on the Home Secretary by section 171 – the government published a White Paper announcing its intention to implement a different scheme. In June 1993, the House of Lords introduced – and passed – an amendment to the Criminal Justice and Public Order Bill which would have required the Home Secretary to perform his statutory duty under the 1988 Act. The House of Commons removed the amendment.[59] When the Home Secretary introduced changes to the Criminal Injuries Compensation Scheme – claiming to act under the royal prerogative – proceedings for judicial review of his decision were instigated. The outcome was the judicial verdict that the Home Secretary had acted *ultra vires*.[60]

---

57 See Newburn, 1989.
58 Criminal Justice Act 1988, ss 108–17 and Scheds 6–7.
59 For comment see Riddell, 1994, p 9.
60 *R v Secretary of State for the Home Department ex parte Fire Brigades' Union* (1995). For further discussion, see pp 144–46.

THE GRANTING OF HONOURS

Whilst legally still in the hands of the Crown, the effective control over the granting of the majority of honours lies with the executive. The Queen has the personal right to confer the Order of the Garter, the Order of the Thistle, the Royal Victoria Order and the Order of Merit. Otherwise, the conferment of honours is by the Queen, acting on the advice of the Prime Minister who is, in turn, advised by a Political Honours Scrutiny Committee comprising three Privy Councillors.[61] The link between the granting of honours and the financing of political parties has been a matter of concern for decades. This issue is discussed in Chapter 13.

REGULATION OF THE CIVIL SERVICE[62]

The control of the Civil Service is vested in the Crown and civil servants, like ministers, are servants of the Crown. However, the appointments are permanent, subject to 'good behaviour', although, in practice, a civil servant will not be dismissed other than for misconduct.[63] Civil servants have no contractual relationship with the Crown.[64] Salaries and other benefits are prescribed by statute, but for the most part, the Civil Service is governed under the prerogative.[65]

REGULATION OF THE ARMED FORCES

As with the Civil Service, members of the armed forces are regulated under the royal prerogative, and statutory protection of employment in, for example, the Employment Protection (Consolidation) Act 1978, does not apply to members of the armed forces.[66]

The sovereign is Commander in Chief of the armed forces. The Bill of Rights 1689 prohibits the maintenance of an army by the Crown in peacetime without the consent of parliament. The control, organisation and disposition of the forces are within the prerogative and cannot be questioned in a court of law.[67]

---

61 Cmnd 1789, 1922, London: HMSO; see *Parkinson v Royal College of Ambulance* (1925), which led to the passing of the Honours (Prevention of Abuses) Act 1925; and see Wagner and Squibb, 1973. It has been proposed that the Scrutiny Committee be merged with the Independent Appointments Commission to ensure greater scrutiny.

62 See further Chapter 8. The structure and conditions of employment are outside the scope of this work: see Jackson and Leonard, 2001, Chapter 17.

63 Fulton Committee Report, Cmnd 3638, 1971, London: HMSO.

64 *CCSU v Minister for the Civil Service* (1985), p 419.

65 For a detailed and critical analysis of the Civil Service, see Hennessy, 1990.

66 For details of the organisation and control of the armed forces see Jackson and Leonard, 2001, Chapter 18.

67 *China Navigation Company Ltd v Attorney General* (1932); *Chandler v Director of Public Prosecutions* (1964). See also the Crown Proceedings Act 1947, s 11.

THE PREROGATIVE AND FOREIGN AFFAIRS

Acts of State[68]

> An act of the executive as a matter of policy performed in the course of its relations with another state, including its relations with the subjects of that state, unless they are temporarily within the allegiance of the Crown.[69]

Acts of State in relation to foreign states

The recognition of foreign states and government, diplomatic relations – including the sending of diplomats and the reception of foreign diplomats, declarations of war and peace, and the annexation or cession of territory fall within this part of the definition.

Recognition of foreign states

The recognition of foreign states is within the prerogative of the Crown. Several statutes regulate the privilege and immunities enjoyed by heads of foreign states[70] and their diplomatic representatives.[71]

Diplomatic relations

In 1708, the Diplomatic Privileges Act was passed after a Russian Ambassador had been arrested for debt. The Russian Czar, Peter the Great, regarded this action as a criminal offence. The Court of Queen's Bench was uncertain as to the legal position.[72] The Act of 1708 provided that no judicial proceedings could be brought against diplomats or their servants and that it was an offence to commence proceedings.

Under the Diplomatic Privileges Act 1964, diplomatic staff enjoy full immunity – both civil and criminal – whereas administrative and technical staff have immunity for actions taken in the course of their duties but are otherwise civilly – but not criminally – liable for other acts. Members of service staff are immune only in respect of official acts. Whether a particular member of diplomatic staff falls within a certain category is determined by the Foreign Secretary by means of a certificate. The court will determine whether the action performed is within – or without – the individual's official duties.

Where an individual enjoys immunity from the courts, the only redress will be for the Foreign Secretary to request the diplomat's government to recall him as *persona non grata*.

---

68 See Anson, 1933, Vol II, Pt I, Chapter 6.8.

69 Wade, ECS, 1934, p 103.

70 State Immunity Act 1978. On state immunity and its effect on the protection of human rights, see Chapter 19.

71 Diplomatic Privileges Act 1964. On immunities and privilege accorded to international and commonwealth organisations, see the International Organisations Acts 1968 and 1981; Diplomatic Immunities (Conferences with Commonwealth Countries and Republic of Ireland) Acts 1952 and 1961; International Headquarters and Defence Organisations Act 1964.

72 *Mattueof's Case* (1709).

Declarations of war and peace

Where a declaration of war has been made, the status of nationals of the enemy state within the United Kingdom is altered. If the Secretary of State for Foreign and Commonwealth Affairs issues a certificate to the effect that a state of war exists, this must be accepted by the courts.[73]

Annexation and cession of territory

In 1955, the Crown exercised its prerogative power to take possession of the island of Rockall, which subsequently was incorporated into the United Kingdom as part of Scotland.[74] Once territory has been annexed, the Crown has a discretion as to the extent to which it will take over the liabilities of the former government of the state.[75]

The Crown also has the power to alter the limits of British territorial waters.[76] However, while this prerogative seems firmly established, there are doubts as to the power of the Crown – without parliamentary approval – to cede territory and thereby deprive British citizens of their nationality and other rights under United Kingdom law.[77] When the Crown sought to cede Heligoland to Germany in 1890, parliamentary approval was sought. While the law may be doubtful, there is at least a convention that parliament's approval will be sought and granted.

Issue of passports

Consistent with the Crown's power to regulate its boundaries and those who enter and leave is the power to issue passports: again, under Blackstone's definition, this is a questionable prerogative power, for the government is doing no more than what it is free to do under statute and the power has no legal effect as such. Nevertheless, the conventional classification of the right to issue and withhold passports is that of the prerogative. At common law, citizens have the right to enter and leave the realm. It is nevertheless extremely difficult in practice to travel without a passport, which is issued under the prerogative. In *R v Foreign Secretary ex parte Everett* (1989), the court for the first time held that the granting and withholding of passports was subject to review by the courts. The position in the United Kingdom – both uncertain and unsatisfactory – may be contrasted with that in the United States of America where the Supreme Court has held that freedom of travel is a basic constitutional liberty.[78]

The ancient right to issue the writ *ne exeat regno* – forbidding a person from leaving the realm – is declared by Jackson and Leonard (2001), relying on *Felton v Callis* (1969), to be 'obsolescent'. The doctrine of obsolescence has never been one accepted in English law. The rationale for such acceptance in relation to the writ

---

73 *R v Bottrill ex parte Kuechenmeister* (1947).
74 Island of Rockall Act 1972.
75 *West Rand Central Gold Mining Company v The King* (1905).
76 *R v Kent Justices ex parte Lye* (1967); *Post Office v Estuary Radio* (1968).
77 Anson, 1933, pp 137–42; Holdsworth, 1942. See further Chapter 24.
78 See, *inter alia, Aptheker v Secretary of State* (1964); *Kent v Dulles* (1958).

ne exeat regno, and that of impressment into naval service, is that offered by Lord Simon of Glaisdale in *McKendrick v Sinclair* (1972) to the effect that:

> ... a rule of English common law, once clearly established, does not become extinct merely by disuse ... but may 'go into a cataleptic trance' ... and revive in propitious circumstances ... but not revive if it is 'grossly anomalous and anachronistic'.

That it is not obsolete is confirmed by two cases. In *Al Nahkel for Contracting Ltd v Lowe* (1986), the writ was used to prevent a defendant leaving the country to avoid a judgment of the court. In *Parsons v Burk* (1971), an unsuccessful attempt was made to prevent the New Zealand rugby team from leaving the country to play in South Africa.

Treaty making powers

The power to enter into treaties under international law is a feature of the sovereignty of a state. In the United Kingdom, it is generally accepted that such power is an emanation of the prerogative. As such, the entry into treaties is regarded as a matter solely for the executive and not for parliament. A treaty is defined as a written agreement between states governed by international law.[79] It will be seen in Chapter 7 that under the doctrine of parliamentary sovereignty, an Act of Parliament alone can alter domestic law. Accordingly, a treaty – being a creature of international law – cannot alter national law without being given effect by an Act of Parliament.[80] It is for this reason that, *inter alia*, the European Communities Act 1972 was enacted to provide for the entry and application of European Community law into the United Kingdom.

There is debate as to whether treaty making power is truly a prerogative power. Blackstone's definition insists that a prerogative power be unique to the Crown: if it is exercisable by anyone else, it ceases to be a prerogative. The second aspect is – according to HWR Wade – whether the prerogative produces 'legal effects at common law' (1985). It follows, therefore, that a treaty – having no legal effect in the absence of statute – is not a true prerogative. However, the preferred judicial view is in line with Dicey: a prerogative act is any action of government not authorised by statute.

The treaty making power of the executive was challenged in *R v Secretary of State for Foreign and Commonwealth Affairs ex parte Rees-Mogg* (1994). In February 1991, the Heads of Government of the Member States of the European Community signed the Treaty on European Union – the Maastricht Treaty (see Chapter 8). The Treaty was to come into effect on ratification by the Member States. In some countries, ratification was dependent upon the approval of the majority of the people voting in a referendum, as for example in France and Denmark. Under the constitution of the United States of America, treaties are ratified by the President with the advice and consent of two-thirds of the Senators present and voting.

---

79 Vienna Convention on the Law of Treaties, Cmnd 4848, 1969, London: HMSO.
80 *Walker v Baird* (1982); *The Parlement Belge* (1879); *JH Rayner (Mincing Lane) Ltd v Department of Trade and Industry* (1990).

In the United Kingdom, no such constitutional arrangements exist. Under constitutional practice, a treaty need only be approved by parliament if it requires a change in legislation or the grant of public money. Otherwise, the power of parliament is confined to the political process, and in the last resort, the forcing of a government's resignation through the withdrawal of the confidence of the House of Commons. However, a convention has been established whereby parliament approves certain treaties. Under the Ponsonby Rule,[81] the government undertakes to lay every treaty, when signed, for a 21 day period before ratification, and secondly to inform the House of all other 'international agreements and commitments which may bind the nation to specific action in certain circumstances'. The Ponsonby undertaking also included a commitment on the part of government to make time for debate on a treaty if there is a formal demand from the Opposition or other party. The issue raised in *Rees-Mogg* was whether the government had the power to ratify the Maastricht Treaty without the approval of the House of Commons. It was clear that there was substantial opposition to the Treaty on all sides of the House, and the government was not confident that any vote would approve the Treaty. As a result, or as a failsafe device, the Prime Minister announced that, if necessary, the Treaty would be ratified under the prerogative: thus avoiding the risk of parliamentary disapproval. The Queen's Bench Division refused to grant an application for judicial review: the matter was within the prerogative of the Crown. In the long run, the Bill bringing the Treaty into effect in the law of the United Kingdom was passed by the Commons and Lords.

JUDICIAL CONTROL OF THE PREROGATIVE

... the King hath no prerogative, but that which the law of the land allows him.[82]

Statute and the prerogative[83]

Although there is a degree of certainty as to the existence and scope of the prerogatives discussed above, the discussion of all prerogatives must be regarded as overlain with a degree of doubt. Consistent with the doctrine of parliamentary sovereignty, parliament has the right and power to abolish, restrict or preserve prerogative powers. For example, historically, the Crown owed the duty of protection to those under a duty of allegiance to the Crown who were either under the age of majority[84] or suffering mental incapacity. This duty of protection – the concept of *parens patriae* – manifested itself in the wardship jurisdiction conferred on the Court of Chancery.[85] The Law Reform (Miscellaneous Provisions) Act 1949 gave statutory force to the jurisdiction, which was further

---

81 Under Secretary of State for Foreign Affairs 1924. See HC Deb Vol 171 Cols 2001–04.
82 *Case of Proclamations* (1611).
83 Note that the Human Rights Act 1998 provides that prerogative orders (Orders in Council) are not subject to challenge by the judiciary. This appears to confuse s 15 and the distinctive status of Acts of Parliament with the prerogative. See further Chapter 19.
84 Now age 18 (Family Law Reform Act 1969, s 1).
85 Now the Family Division of the High Court.

amended under the Supreme Court Act 1981. The Children Act 1989, while not affecting the entire wardship jurisdiction, removes the right of local authorities to apply to ward a child (section 100). However, the Act also makes provision for local authorities to apply to the court (section 100(4)) for an order under the inherent jurisdiction. The effect of this provision is still unclear, but the constitutional implication is that, whilst the prerogative of *parens patriae* in wardship has been placed on a statutory footing under the 1949 and 1981 Acts, the Children Act 1989 nevertheless recognises and preserves a form of prerogative inherent jurisdiction.

Where an Act of Parliament seeks to regulate a matter previously falling under the prerogative but does not expressly abolish the prerogative, the statute will prevail. In *Attorney General v de Keyser's Royal Hotel Ltd* (1920), the court was faced with a claim for compensation by the owners of the hotel, under the Defence of the Realm Act 1914, for compensation due as a result of occupation by the armed forces in wartime. The government sought to rely on the prerogative under which a lesser, discretionary sum of compensation would be payable. The House of Lords rejected the government's right to rely on the prerogative, holding that, once a statute had been enacted, the prerogative power fell into 'abeyance', that is to say, it was set aside for the duration of the life of the statute. Should the statute be repealed, the prerogative would once more come into operation.

In *Laker Airways v Department of Trade* (1977), statute and prerogative were considered once again. The facts involved regulation of the transatlantic air route. Under the Bermuda Agreement of 1946, the United States and United Kingdom governments agreed that air carriers should be approved by both governments: the 'designation' requirement. In 1971, the Civil Aviation Act was passed by parliament, providing for the licensing of airlines by the Civil Aviation Authority (the CAA). The Act provided that the Secretary of State could give 'guidance' to the CAA as to the policy to be followed in the consideration of licence applications. Mr Freddie Laker had both applied for designation under the Bermuda Treaty and had been granted a licence under the Civil Aviation Act 1971.

A change in government led to a change in policy, and it was decided that British Airways should have a monopoly on the trans-Atlantic route. Accordingly, the Secretary of State issued 'guidance' to the CAA to the effect that Mr Laker's licence should be withdrawn. The Secretary of State also requested that the United States government did not proceed to grant designation to Laker Airways under the Treaty. In an application for judicial review by Mr Laker, it was argued that the Secretary of State's 'guidance' was *ultra vires*. The court agreed, regarding the instruction given to the CAA as beyond the normal meaning of the word 'guidance'. The court also rejected the government's argument that it had the right, under the prerogative, to deny Laker Airways' right to fly the Atlantic route. The government could not, it was held, defeat a statutory right by use of a prerogative power.

In *Council of Civil Service Unions v Minister of State for Civil Service* (1985), the prerogative returned to the courts. The Prime Minister, as the Minister for the Civil Service, by a prerogative order (an Order in Council) terminated the right of workers at the Government Communications Headquarters (GCHQ) to belong to trade unions. The order followed industrial unrest which threatened to disrupt the interception of signals intelligence. The Union challenged the order under judicial review proceedings, claiming that they had a legitimate expectation to be consulted prior to their rights to membership being withdrawn. The Unions won at first instance, but lost before both the Court of Appeal and the House of Lords.

The House of Lords accepted that the terms and conditions of employment of civil servants were within the prerogative powers of the Crown.[86] Their Lordships likewise accepted that the employees had a legitimate expectation to be consulted before their rights were adversely affected. Nevertheless, the government's plea of national security trumped the interests of the union members.[87]

The significance of the *GCHQ* case in relation to prerogative power is twofold. On the question of the reviewability of the royal prerogative, the House of Lords declared that the exercise of the prerogatives of the Crown were, in principle, as reviewable as powers exercised under statute. However, having boldly declared the principle, the court proceeded to qualify the approach by stating that a number of matters would not be subjected to review. Utilising the concept of 'justiciability', the court held that matters such as the appointment of ministers, dissolution of parliament, grant of honours, treaties, and *par excellence* matters of national security were not appropriate subjects for review by the courts. Each of these matters was regarded as involving matters of high policy which it should be for ministers to decide and, by implication, for parliament to control.[88] It remains the case after *GCHQ* that many significant attributes of the prerogative remain immune from judicial review.[89]

The case of *R v Secretary of State for the Home Department ex parte Northumbria Police Authority* (1988) reveals a far less robust judicial attitude towards the control of the prerogative than did the *Laker Airways* case. Once again, the issue involved was the relationship between statute and the prerogative. The Police Act 1964 sets out the respective powers of the Home Secretary, the police authorities and the Chief Constables of police with regard to, *inter alia*, the supply of equipment to police forces (sections 4 and 5).

The Secretary of State, by way of a Circular, advised that the Secretary of State would be making available supplies of riot control equipment to police forces, irrespective of approval by the police authorities. The Northumbria Police Authority sought judicial review of the legality of the Circular. The Home Secretary argued that, as a matter of statutory interpretation, he had power to issue the equipment, and that, independent of the statutory power which he

---

86 On HWR Wade's doubts concerning the accuracy of this classification, see Wade, 1985, p 180.

87 The Labour government has reinstated the right of workers to join trade unions.

88 See also *Patriotic Front – ZAPU v Minister of Justice, Legal and Parliamentary Affairs* (1986), discussed by Walker, 1987.

89 Note, however, that in *R v Ministry of Defence ex parte Smith* (1995), Simon Brown LJ stated, *obiter*, that the question of whether homosexuals were allowed to serve in the armed forces – a matter falling within the prerogative – was not immune from review. There were no operational considerations nor security implications: the courts were qualified to rule on the matter.

claimed, he had the power under the prerogative to issue the weapons. On the point of statutory interpretation, the Court of Appeal held that no monopoly was reserved to the Police Authority and that, accordingly, the Secretary of State had not acted *ultra vires*.

On the prerogative aspect, the court's reasoning was both surprising and interesting. First, the Court of Appeal accepted that the Police Act 1964 left unaffected the prerogative powers to keep the peace. Little evidence was adduced as to the existence of such a prerogative, but nevertheless, Croom-Johnson LJ felt able to hold that he had 'no doubt' that the Crown had such a prerogative. Nourse LJ stated that there was no historical or other basis for denying that a prerogative to keep the peace could be viewed as a 'sister' prerogative to the power to declare war, without making any reference to Blackstone's division of prerogatives into 'foreign' and 'domestic' categories. Recalling that it had never been possible to identify all the prerogatives of the Crown and that their existence could be ascertained only by means of piecemeal decisions, Nourse LJ declared that there had never been 'a comparable occasion for investigating a prerogative of keeping the peace within the realm':

> The Crown's prerogative of making war and peace, the war prerogative, has never been doubted ... it is natural to suppose that it was founded, at least in part, on the wider prerogative of protection ...

> The wider prerogative must have extended as much to unlawful acts within the realm as to the menaces of a foreign power. There is no historical or other reason for denying to the war prerogative a sister prerogative of keeping the peace within the realm ...

More surprisingly, the judge argued that the fact that no evidence existed was almost conclusive proof that it did exist. In the seminal case of *Entick v Carrington* (1765), Lord Camden had asserted that, if there existed authority for the lawful exercise of power, it would be found 'in the books'. It might be thought that in passing the Police Act, parliament considered that it was providing comprehensive regulation of the terms and conditions under which each regulatory body could act. It cannot have been contemplated that, by plea of a previously unconsidered prerogative, the provisions of the Act could be circumvented. Nevertheless, Purchas LJ was clear that:

> ... the prerogative powers to take all reasonable steps to preserve the Queen's peace remain unaffected by the Act and these include the supply of equipment to police forces which is reasonably required for the more efficient discharge of their duties.

The *Northumbria Police Authority* case is indicative of the fine line to be drawn between updating a prerogative and creating a new prerogative. Prerogatives, being a feature of monarchical power are, as Dicey stated, residual. Accordingly, for the judges to give recognition to an alleged prerogative, it must be shown that the prerogative claimed existed before 1688. In *BBC v Johns* (1965), Lord Diplock gave judicial expression to this in the statement: '... it is 350 years and a civil war too late for the Queen's courts to broaden the prerogative.'

In *R v Secretary of State for the Home Department ex parte Fire Brigades' Union* (1995), the matter in issue was whether the Secretary of State, having failed to implement the statutory scheme provided in the Criminal Justice Act 1988, was free to implement a different scheme under the royal prerogative.[90] The scheme introduced a 'tariff' for compensation for injuries at a substantially lower rate than provided for under the statute.

In the Court of Appeal, Sir Thomas Bingham stated that:

... the old non-statutory scheme was established by a proper exercise of prerogative power. In the absence of statute, there would not, in law, have been anything to prevent the Home Secretary exercising his prerogative powers to modify the old scheme or to revoke it and substitute a new one devised on different principles.

Even after the 1988 Act had been passed, he would not have been open to legal challenge had he continued the old scheme without bringing the new statutory provisions into force, so long as his reasons for postponement fell within the wide discretion accorded him.

But was he, while those provisions remained unrepealed, legally free to exercise prerogative powers to establish a scheme radically different from those provisions?

Attorney General v de Keyser's Royal Hotel Ltd (1920) and *Laker Airways Ltd v Department of Trade* (1977) did not concern statutory provisions not brought into force and so provided no direct answer to the question.

Again, the Home Secretary's argument had given too little weight to the overriding legislative role of parliament. It had approved detailed provisions governing the form which, underpinned by statute, the scheme should take. The 1988 provisions were not a discussion paper but a blueprint approved in the most solemn form for which our constitution provided ...

The Master of the Rolls accepted that the Home Secretary had the power to invite parliament to repeal the provisions or to seek enactment of the tariff provisions in statute, or, alternatively, to seek to have the statutory provisions abolished and then implement the tariff provisions under the royal prerogative. But:

... what he could not do, so long as the 1988 provisions stood unrepealed as an enduring statement of parliament's will, was to exercise prerogative powers to introduce a scheme radically different from what parliament had approved ...

Accordingly, the Secretary of State could not avoid the requirements of the 1988 Act and introduce – by means of the prerogative – a different scheme.

The House of Lords ruled, by a majority (Lord Keith of Kinkel and Lord Mustill dissenting), that the decisions of the Secretary of State not to implement the statutory scheme, and to introduce an alternative scheme under the prerogative, were unlawful. The House of Lords refused, however, to rule that the Secretary of State was under a legally enforceable duty to bring the statutory scheme into effect at a particular date.

However, the Secretary of State did not enjoy an unfettered discretion as to whether to bring the scheme into effect, and he could not, through use of the prerogative, defeat the purpose of the statute. Lord Keith, dissenting, argued that the court should not become involved in a matter which was for parliament to

---

90 As announced in the White Paper, *Compensating Victims of Violent Crime: Changes to the Criminal Injuries Compensation Scheme*, Cmnd 2434, 1993, London: HMSO. The scheme was implemented on 1 April 1994.

determine. Lord Mustill was of the same mind, relying specifically on the Bill of Rights 1689:

> Absent a written constitution, much sensitivity was required of the parliamentarian, administrator and judge if the delicate balance of the unwritten rules evolved successfully in recent years was not to be disturbed and all the recent advances undone.
>
> Some of the argument addressed would have the court push to the very boundaries of the distinction between court and parliament established in, and recognised ever since, the Bill of Rights 1689.
>
> Three hundred years had passed since then and the political and social landscape had changed beyond recognition, but the boundaries remained.

Here, within one case, are seen differing considerations weighing on the judges in the House of Lords. The majority decision rests squarely on the rule of law and the preference for statute over the prerogative. The minority view, however, leans far more clearly in favour of the doctrine of separation of powers and the supremacy of parliament in regulating its own affairs and in calling ministers to account.[91]

POLITICAL CONTROL OF THE PREROGATIVE

Political control over the exercise of the prerogative, while preserving the separation of powers between the executive and judiciary, may in practice prove to be inadequate. In theory, the prerogative, as is the case with any other act of government, is capable of being subjected to the full range of parliamentary procedure.[92] Thus, Question Time, debates and select committees may be utilised in order to scrutinise prerogative acts. However, under parliamentary practice, there exist a number of issues on which ministers conventionally decline to provide information, and many of these matters are precisely those which fall within the scope of the prerogative. The dissolution of parliament is a matter for Prime Ministerial determination alone: not even a duty to consult Cabinet is imposed, and the matter will certainly not be for parliamentary scrutiny. Likewise, the grant of honours is a matter not for parliamentary discussion. On matters of the disposition of the armed forces, weaponry for the armed forces, government contracts, judicial appointments, and investigations by the Director of Public Prosecutions, the government will decline to answer questions. Aside from such specific matters, the government may plead such wide notions as national security, confidentiality or the public interest in order to avoid scrutiny.

---

91 Note that, following the decision of the House of Lords, the Criminal Injuries Compensation Act 1995 repealed the Criminal Justice Act 1988, ss 108–17, and made provision for a scheme of payments of a standard amount of compensation calculated in accordance with a tariff prepared by the Secretary of State.

92 This is to be discussed in more detail in Chapters 15 and 16.

CONCLUSION

Under all constitutions, written or unwritten, there will be a number of powers reserved to the executive, powers which are exercisable without the passage of legislation. Such powers may include the entering into treaties, declarations of war and peace, and recognition of foreign states and diplomats. Such powers are referred to as 'inherent executive powers', or 'prerogative power'. Section 2 of the Commonwealth of Australia Constitution Act 1900 confers on the Governor General 'such powers and functions ... as Her Majesty may be pleased to assign to him'. In 1900, these powers entailed the power to summon, prorogue or dissolve parliament, to appoint judges and other public officials. Section 61 of the Constitution confers the executive power of the Commonwealth in the Queen and declares that this executive power is vested in the Governor General. Other powers were expressly assigned to the Governor General in 1954 and 1973, implying that, for such powers to exist, they must be express and cannot exist by implication or by analogy with the prerogative powers of the Crown.

The scope of the powers has been the subject of judicial disagreement in the High Court of Australia, some judges adopting a narrow view of the powers, others a broader interpretation. In *Commonwealth v Colonial Combing Spinning and Weaving Co Ltd* (1922), Higgins J adopted the narrow approach:

> ... the Governor General is not a general agent of His Majesty, with power to exercise all His Majesty's prerogatives; he is a special agent with power to carry out the Constitution and the laws, and such powers and functions as the King may assign to him.

In *Barton v Commonwealth* (1974), Mason J took a broader view that the power conferred under section 61:

> ... enables the Crown to undertake all executive action which is appropriate to the position of the Commonwealth under the Constitution and to the spheres of responsibility vested in it by the Constitution. It includes the prerogative powers of the Crown, that is, the powers accorded to the Crown by the common law.

These two brief examples illustrate the point that, even under a written constitution, the scope of prerogative power is capable of differing interpretations.[93]

Under the United Kingdom constitution, it may be concluded, quite reasonably, that parliamentary control over the exercise of prerogative power is less than adequate. Set alongside or juxtapositioned with the excluded areas of judicial review under the concept of justiciability, it can be seen that there exists a reservoir of power, much of which is undefined or at best ill defined, which is not amenable to either judicial or parliamentary control.

---

93   Marshall and Moodie, 1971, Chapter 3.

REFORM OF THE PREROGATIVE?

It is precisely for the reasons discussed above that, in 1988, the Rt Hon Tony Benn MP introduced a Private Member's Bill to place prerogative powers under statutory authority. That Bill did not proceed through the legislative process but such a proposal requires careful consideration.

The Crown Prerogatives (House of Commons Control) Bill 1988 provided a list of prerogative powers which would require the assent of the House of Commons before having legal effect. Most significant of these are the powers to declare war, to make peace, to recognise foreign governments, to sign or ratify treaties, to grant pardons, to confer honours, and more generally to exercise all other executive powers not conferred by statute. Clause 2 of the Bill conferred on the Speaker of the House the sole responsibility for advising on the dissolution of parliament and the issue of an invitation to a person to attempt to form a government. In respect of both of these matters, the assent of the House of Commons was required and that assent binding on the Crown. The power of the Crown to assent to Bills and of the House of Lords to approve legislation would have been removed under clause 4 of the Bill.[94]

The extent to which such a proposal would clarify questions as to the existence and control of the prerogative is necessarily a matter for speculation. Nowhere in the Bill was the role of the courts mentioned. Once the House of Commons had given its assent to the proposed exercise of power, the courts would be precluded from examining the parliamentary process leading up to that assent.[95] The power of judicial review, however, would remain, and it would be within the courts' jurisdiction to determine whether the power exercised was a power authorised by the assent. It has been seen in relation to the *GCHQ* case that the courts have now developed a category of non-justiciable matters, and the majority of the powers identified in the Bill fall within this category. To that extent, placing the prerogatives under statutory authority would, arguably, make little difference. Remaining powers, covered in the general power 'to issue all other executive powers not conferred by statute', would continue to be reviewable according to their subject matter.

However, the prerogative has been seen to be an elusive constitutional animal which is capable of appearing in novel form under unforeseen circumstances. Recalling the *Northumbria Police Authority* case, it was there seen that the prerogative 'to keep the peace' was pleaded as an alternative to the existence of power within the Police Act 1964: a reserve power claimed as insurance against the court finding that the minister had acted *ultra vires* the statute. That the Court of Appeal upheld the minister's claim was by no means a foregone conclusion, and to do so in the virtual absence of authority and precedent, and with little

---

94 In 2003 the Public Administration Select Committee (PASC) enquired into the use of the prerogative with a view to deciding whether legislation should be introduced requiring the government to seek Parliament's approval before using the prerogative. The PASC was particularly concerned about powers relating to the use of the armed forces, the signing of treaties and the granting or withholding of passports.

95 *Pickin v British Railways Board* (1974).

analysis, was quite remarkable. The *Northumbria Police Authority* case also illustrates the fundamental difficulty of prerogative power: that of identification and definition.

It can be agreed that there is little to suggest that replacing such powers by statute, even if they could be identified, would lead to fewer abuses of power. Further, it may be added that, even if the powers could be identified, given their wraith-like nature, it would be impossible, conclusively, to define their scope and application. For this reason, the prerogative – a paradox in a modern democratic state – is likely to retain its uncertain form, thus leaving to government a residue of largely uncontrolled power.

The royal prerogative and the Human Rights Act 1998

The Human Rights Act 1998 – discussed in detail in Chapter 19 – enables the rights protected under the European Convention on Human Rights to be enforced before the domestic courts. Section 6(1) of the Act makes it unlawful for a public authority to act in a way which is incompatible with Convention rights, thereby extending protection to actions taken under the prerogative. However, section 21 of the Act protects the prerogative by raising the status of Orders in Council made under the prerogative to that of primary legislation. As a result, although the courts may make a declaration that an action is incompatible with Convention rights, the Orders in Council cannot be annulled by the courts and will remain valid in the same way as Acts of Parliament.

CHAPTER 7

PARLIAMENTARY SOVEREIGNTY

INTRODUCTION

The sovereignty, or supremacy, of parliament is 'the dominant characteristic of our political institutions'.[1] Sovereignty as a doctrine has long caused controversy amongst philosophers, lawyers and political scientists and is a concept which assumes – as does the rule of law – differing interpretations according to the perspective being adopted. By way of example, international lawyers are concerned with the attributes which render a state independent and sovereign within the international community. Political scientists are concerned with the source of political power within the state. Legal theorists and constitutional lawyers, particularly in the United Kingdom where the matter remains contentious, are concerned to identify the ultimate legal power within a state.

DIFFERING INTERPRETATIONS OF 'SOVEREIGNTY'

Political and legal sovereignty – from the standpoint of sovereignty within the state as opposed to sovereignty as understood in international law – may be analysed as meaning either the supreme legal authority within a state or the supreme political authority within a state.[2]

Sovereignty as supreme legal authority

It is this interpretation with which AV Dicey and later constitutional writers are concerned. As this meaning is the central focus of our concern in understanding legislative – or parliamentary – sovereignty, consideration will be postponed until other interpretations of the concept have been considered.

Sovereignty as supreme political authority

The essence of this idea is that lawful power and authority must be in conformity with moral dictates: some form of 'higher law' or 'natural law'. Political theorists of the eighteenth century contributed much to an understanding of the idea of ultimate authority. Four broadly similar approaches, each entailing the idea of a 'social contract', may be outlined here.

Thomas Hobbes[3] offered the most extreme version of the social contract theory, arguing that man by nature is incapable of regulating his life in peace and harmony with his fellow man. Hobbes's view of man in a society lacking a restraining all-powerful sovereign was inherently pessimistic, an attitude

---

1 Dicey, 1885, p 39.
2 For a more elaborate categorisation, see Rees, 'The theory of sovereignty restated', in Laslett, 1975, Chapter IV.
3 *The Leviathan*, 1651.

encapsulated in the often quoted phrase that life is 'solitary, poor, nasty, brutish and short'. In order for there to be civil order, it was necessary for each man to surrender to the state his own sovereignty in exchange for security. Such a surrender was revocable only if the state abused its trust. The requirement of obedience to law is strict; and yet there are limits:

> If the Soveraign command a man (though justly condemned) to kill, wound, or mayme himselfe; or not to resist those that assault him; or to abstain from the use of food, ayre, medicine, or any other thing, without which he cannot live; yet hath that man the Liberty to disobey.

Further, Hobbes states that:

> The Obligation of Subjects to the Soveraign, is understood to last as long, and no longer, than the power lasteth, by which he is able to protect them. For the right men have by Nature to protect themselves, when none else can protect them, can by no Covenant be relinquished.

According to Jean-Jacques Rousseau,[4] the citizen enters into a 'contract' with the state, surrendering to the state individual rights in exchange for the protection of the state. The state, according to Rousseau, is thus embodied in the 'general will' of the people and becomes both the agent and ruler of the people in the peoples' name. Rousseau's vision of man differs markedly from that of Thomas Hobbes – far from living in a state of 'war' with one another, men in the 'natural state' of primitive society would have nothing to fight over and would be united in a community of endeavour to secure the essential provisions of life. Man comes together – from necessity – within civil society, and, through participation in the decision making processes, produces a democratic society. Rousseau distinguishes between supreme power – sovereignty – and the government. Sovereignty lies with the people, and is absolute and inalienable. The government's power is less absolute, established to implement the will of the people and accountable to the people. The government is dependent upon the sovereign people for the continuation of its power, and the people retain the right to revoke the power devolved.

Thus, for Rousseau, sovereignty is a concept which entails moral approval and acceptance by the people whose 'collective will' sovereignty represents.[5] Indeed, for Rousseau:

> ... the sovereign, being formed wholly of the individuals who compose it, neither has nor can have any interest contrary to theirs; and consequently the sovereign power need give no guarantee to its subjects, because it is impossible for the body to wish to hurt all its members. We shall also see later on that it cannot hurt any in particular. The sovereign, merely by virtue of what it is, is always what it should be. [p 177]

Thomas Paine advances a social contract theory in which the rights of the individual are given central importance.[6] Paine both influenced and was influenced by the French and American Revolutions. In *Rights of Man*, Paine

---

4   *The Social Contract and Discourses*, 1762.
5   *Ibid*, Bk I, Chapter VII, and Bk II.
6   *Rights of Man*, 1791, Pt 1.

argued that the citizen gives up his rights to the state, but on a conditional basis. The state is placed in the position of trustee of the rights of man, and should that trust be broken, the citizen has the ultimate – or sovereign – right to depose the government. Paine argues that man has natural rights, 'those which appertain to man in right of his existence'. These rights are both individualistic and civil. The former category includes:

> ... all the intellectual rights, or rights of the mind, and also all those rights of acting as an individual for his own comfort and happiness, which are not injurious to the natural rights of others.

By way of distinction:

> Civil rights are those which appertain to man in right of his being a member of society. Every civil right has for its foundation, some natural right pre-existing in the individual. [p 90]

These natural and civil rights are held by government on trust for the people, and should – under an ideal constitution – be protected from governmental abuse by a Bill of Rights. Such an approach is also taken by John Locke, who regards the people, as a collectivity, as holding the sovereign power which is in some sense delegated to the government on trust, and who may accordingly exert their sovereign power to remove the government if it violates its sacred trust.

In *Two Treatises of Government*, John Locke advances powerful arguments for the limits of governmental power and the ultimate political sovereignty of the people. In Book II,[7] Locke argues that men come together in civil society and tacitly consent to be ruled by government directed to 'the peace, safety, and public good of the people'. Hence, the power accorded to government is not absolute, but whilst in existence, the legislative power is the 'supreme power'. Nevertheless, Locke concludes that if the people:

> ... have set limits to the duration of their legislative, and made this supreme power in any person or assembly only temporary, it is forfeited; upon the forfeiture of their rules, or at the determination of the time set, it reverts to the society, and the people have a right to act as supreme, and continue the legislative in themselves or place it in a new form, or new hands, as they think good. [p 242]

Sovereignty, then, is limited and conditional: government holds supreme power on trust for the people. On this view, the authority of the constitution will be dependent upon its conformity with a higher law. As KC Wheare explains:

> This view of government limited by the natural rights of man lies at the basis of the American Constitution and finds a place ... in many modern constitutions. It provides a moral basis upon which a government's actions can be judged and, what is more, upon which the validity of a constitution can be tested. A constitution binds in so far as it is in accordance with natural law. Neither a government nor a citizen may disregard the authority of a constitution except in so far as the action can be justified by the law of nature. This is indeed a 'higher law' than a constitution. [1966, p 65]

---

7   'An essay concerning the true original extent and end of civil government.'

DISTINGUISHING LEGAL AND POLITICAL SOVEREIGNTY

It is often difficult to distinguish clearly between legal and political sovereignty. The distinction is nevertheless one insisted upon by authorities such as Sir Edward Coke, Sir William Blackstone and, in particular, AV Dicey. As with so much of the United Kingdom's constitutional law, contemporary thinking about sovereignty remains influenced by the legacy of Dicey. Dicey's interpretation of parliamentary sovereignty will be examined below (pp 164 ff). At this introductory stage, however, it is necessary to note that Dicey drew a strict separation between legal sovereignty and political sovereignty (as did Coke and Blackstone). In Dicey's view, the people hold political sovereignty whilst legal sovereignty rests with the 'Queen in Parliament'. In large measure, this clear demarcation between the political and the legal is explained by the unwritten nature of the United Kingdom's constitution. In the majority of states having a written constitution, the constitution defines the limits of governmental power. In the United Kingdom, by way of contrast, the powers of government – whilst ultimately dependent upon the electoral 'mandate' – remain unconstrained by any fundamental written document and subject only to parliament's approval. All law making power thus derives, not from the power conferring and power delimiting constitutional document, endorsed by the people, but from the sovereignty of the legislature: parliament.

LEGAL THEORY AND SOVEREIGNTY

Legal theory contributes to an understanding of legal and political sovereignty within the constitution. In the overview of the theories of John Austin, Hans Kelsen and HLA Hart which follow, it will be seen that, in each case, the jurist is seeking an explanation of the source of ultimate authority, its identifying characteristics and the manner in which sovereignty is upheld within a legal order. By revealing the characteristics of valid law, it becomes easier to understand the distinction between laws and other rules in society – such as moral rules – which have binding effect, but which do not have the force – and enforceability – of legal rules.

John Austin

Within every civil society – or polity – there will be found, as a social and political fact, one supreme power. The nineteenth century jurist John Austin[8] was one of the earliest 'modern' theorists to offer an in-depth analysis of sovereignty, and his work – while much criticised by later writers – still marks a useful starting point for analysis of the concept. Austin's theory was an attempt to define law in the positivist tradition.[9] Law is nothing more or less than the commands of the identifiable, illimitable and indivisible sovereign body. The sovereignty conferred

---

8   1790–1859. See *The Province of Jurisprudence Determined*, 1832.
9   Positivism being defined as man made law – as opposed to divine or natural law – enacted by a political superior within the state for the governance of citizens: the law which is posited or laid down.

exhibits itself in the habit of obedience of the people, which in turn is instilled by the fear of sanctions which attach to all laws and thus underpin the legal system. Laws are nothing more nor less than the general commands of this sovereign, to which sanctions are attached.

While the model most closely accords with the criminal statute, it is difficult to endorse in relation to much of the civil law and in relation to those laws which regulate the law making and law enforcing institutions within the state. However, in every state, whether monarchical or parliamentary, unitary or federal, there must be some body which demonstrates the characteristics of a sovereign. For Austin, sovereignty as a legal concept within the United Kingdom lies with the Queen in Parliament: as a political concept, the ultimate sovereignty is vested in the people.

Austin's analysis of both sovereignty and law is somewhat crude. It is difficult, for example, to adapt his idea of sovereignty to a federal state where, to cite but one example, the distribution of power may confer co-equal legislative powers on both the individual provincial legislatures and the federal government and provide for judicial review of the constitutionality of primary legislation.[10] Today, his theory is the more difficult to apply when considered in light of the United Kingdom's membership of the European Union.[11]

HLA Hart

A thorough critique of Austin's analysis is offered by Professor HLA Hart. Hart portrays the legal system as being one of rules rather than commands. For Hart, Austin's jurisprudence is tainted by its overtly coercive nature, as exemplified in the command plus sanction portrayal of law. Austin has missed, according to Hart, an important dimension of law: the concept of a rule. Rules, for Hart, are distinguishable from commands in several significant respects. Legal rules may, as with the criminal law, lay down specific prohibitions, breach of which will be met with punishment. Nevertheless, there are laws that do not exhibit the characteristics of prohibition and sanction. Many rules of law confer the power on individuals and groups to act, but evince no element of coercion: rules of contract, of making wills, of entering into marriage, fall within this category. These rules Hart labels 'power conferring rules': rules which are permissive and the breach of which will result in a 'nullity', a concept which is difficult to conceptualise as an Austinian 'sanction'.

By distinguishing between rules that stipulate prohibitions and rules that confer powers, Hart is able to construct a theory of law which is represented as a union of primary and secondary rules. Each legal rule within the system is identified according to accepted criteria: what Hart calls the 'rule of recognition'. At the apex of the hierarchy of laws – whether bylaws of a local authority, judicial decisions, delegated legislation or statute – is the 'ultimate rule of recognition'. This ultimate rule, while involving some complexity and uncertainty, is mostly explained in the form that 'what the Queen in Parliament enacts is law'.

---

10 As, eg, the Commonwealth of Australia Constitution Act 1900.
11 See further below and Chapters 8 and 9.

Hart analyses the problems surrounding the nature of sovereignty. In *The Concept of Law* (1961), Hart discusses the concepts of *continuing sovereignty* and *self-embracing sovereignty*, an issue which, as will be seen further below, has attracted continuing academic debate. Hart argues that the conventionally understood Diceyan concept of sovereignty is an interpretation which has been accepted as the criterion of legal validity, but that that interpretation is 'only one arrangement among others, equally conceivable' (p 145). The Diceyan view is that parliament enjoys continuing sovereignty – that is to say, that each parliament, irrespective of time, has equal legislative competence to that of any other parliament. However, Hart argues, parliament's sovereignty could be interpreted to be a form of *self-embracing* sovereignty – a sovereignty which would permit the exercise of power to delimit parliament's legislative powers in the future. This power, however, being the ultimate power, would be exercisable only once. Hart draws the analogy with God in the following manner:

> ... on the one hand, a God who at every moment of his existence enjoys the same powers and so is incapable of cutting down those powers, and, on the other, a God whose powers include the power to destroy for the future his omnicompetence. [p 146]

In the former case, God enjoys continuing sovereignty; in the latter, self-embracing sovereignty. Furthermore, neither of these interpretations, Hart instructs:

> ... can be ruled out as wrong or accepted with confidence as right; for we are in the area of open texture of the system's most fundamental rule. Here at any moment a question may arise to which there is no answer – only answers. [p 147]

Hans Kelsen

Hans Kelsen analysed sovereignty both within a state and within the international legal order.[12] Kelsen's theory involves nothing less than an attempt to formulate a scientific global analysis of law. For Kelsen positive, man made, law is best expressed as a 'norm':

> By 'norm' we mean that something ought to be or ought to happen, especially that a human being ought to behave in a specific way. [1967, pp 4–5]

Each norm will be a valid legal rule if it is validated by a higher norm. Thus, a bylaw will be valid if it is properly enacted under an Act of Parliament. A legal decision will be valid provided that the judge is acting within his jurisdiction. An Act of Parliament will be valid if enacted in the constitutionally accepted correct manner. Taken together, the individual legal norms will form a system which itself is validated according to the 'basic norm' or 'grundnorm'. While for Kelsen, unlike Austin, it is not necessary that every legal rule have an attendant sanction, it is crucial that the legal order as a whole is a coercive order:

> As a coercive order, the law is distinguished from other social orders. The decisive criterion is the element of force – that means that the act prescribed by the order as a consequence of socially detrimental facts ought to be executed even against the will of the individual and, if he resist, by physical force. [pp 33–34]

---

12 1881–1973. See *The Pure Theory of Law*, 1967 and *The General Theory of Law and State*, 1961.

At an international level, Kelsen recognises that the existence of a valid national legal order is dependent upon the recognition of the state under international law. Where a revolution occurs within a state, it is international law that will determine the validity of claims to exercise legitimate power and hence law making power. Thus, by this means, it is possible to view law globally.

THE VALIDITY OF LAW AND THE EFFECTIVENESS OF LAW

In addition to identifying the characteristics of valid law, each of the above theorists also seeks to explain the relationship between – and distinctions between – the concepts of validity and effectiveness. The importance of the distinction between validity and effectiveness of law lies in explaining the ultimate source of authority or Sovereignty within a state. One question which frequently arises is whether, if a law is ineffective (perhaps because it is morally disapproved of by a majority of citizens, or because it is regarded as futile), that law loses its validity within the legal order. The commonly agreed position adopted by Austin and Hart is that such a law – provided that it conforms with the constitutional criteria for law – remains valid despite being ineffective. However, it is also a point of agreement that if a legal system were to cease to be effective overall – that is to say, if a state of anarchy existed – then the ultimate sovereign power would be under threat, and would probably be forced to change. The people, in rejecting the ultimate power within the state, would be taking back the power that they had entrusted to the sovereign. Accordingly, it can be seen that the legal sovereign is dependent ultimately upon the political sovereign power in society – the people.

The effectiveness of law, while it does not *per se* determine legal validity, nevertheless interrelates with law's validity. Under the constitutional theory of the United Kingdom, an Act of Parliament does not become invalid under the doctrine of *desuetude* (disuse). As a result, statutes of great antiquity – although never or seldom used – retain the force of law, and may be relied upon at any time.[13] Equally, a statute – of whatever date – is valid if it meets the criteria of validity, irrespective of whether or not it is effective in achieving its objectives. This is the point made by Sir Ivor Jennings in relation to the banning of smoking on the streets of Paris. A more realistic example of the relationship between the effectiveness and validity of law stems from the system of local taxation in the 1980s. The government decided that the existing system of taxation based on the rateable value of properties – irrespective of the number of persons living in the property – was inequitable. Accordingly, the government introduced the Community Charge[14] (or Poll Tax) which levied a flat rate of tax on each person within a local government area. The system was first introduced in Scotland and was met with condemnation and evasion. As a result of its ineffectiveness – based on the rejection of the law by the people – the government was forced to change

---

13 Unless expressly repealed. See eg the Statute Repeals Act 1998, which repeals ecclesiastical leases legislation dating from the early sixteenth century.
14 Under the Local Government Finance Act 1988.

the law. The law did not become invalid as a result of its ineffectiveness: rather, the ineffectiveness created a political reason as to why the law should be repealed.

If that one instance of an ineffective law is extrapolated to the legal system as a whole, the manner in which effectiveness affects validity can be seen more clearly. If a legal system comes under strain to a significant degree, a point will be reached at which there is civil unrest, anarchy or revolution. The law will cease to be effective. The law, however, under the theory of sovereignty, remains valid. At some point on the scale between general effectiveness and more or less total ineffectiveness – and the point cannot be precisely determined – the underlying explanation for the validity of law will cease. Effectiveness, accordingly, can be seen to be the prime condition for meaningful statements about validity.[15]

In a revolutionary situation – as explained by Kelsen – there is a point where the basic norm – or sovereign power – changes. The ultimate validity of law depends on its effectiveness. When there is a revolution, the basic norm may change, brought about by a change in the power structure within a society ultimately creating a new basic norm.

Ultimate validity and effectiveness: an illustration

The relationship between the ultimate validity of a legal system and effectiveness is well illustrated by the position in Rhodesia, as it then was, in the 1960s. Until 1965, the governance of Rhodesia was under the sovereignty of the United Kingdom, with Rhodesia enjoying self-governing powers to the extent allowed under the Constitution of Rhodesia. By convention, the United Kingdom Parliament would not legislate for the colony without the express request or consent of the Rhodesian Parliament. In 1965, however, the Prime Minister of Rhodesia, Mr Ian Smith, issued a unilateral declaration of independence from the United Kingdom and asserted the full right of self-government. The response of the United Kingdom's government was to reassert its own powers, reaffirming its right to legislate for Rhodesia in the Southern Rhodesia Act 1965 and thus overriding the convention. Between 1965 and 1979, when a constitutional conference resulted in full independence being conferred on the renamed Zimbabwe,[16] there was thus doubt as to which parliament represented sovereignty within the state of Rhodesia.

Jurisprudentially, Hans Kelsen had argued that one of the conditions for change in the sovereignty of the state – or, in his phraseology, the 'basic norm' of a state – lay in revolution, whether by act of force or change in the allegiance of the judiciary. The case of *Madzimbamuto v Lardner Burke* (1969) provided the opportunity to test the revolutionary position in relation to sovereignty.

Madzimbamuto had been detained on order of the government of Rhodesia under a provision enacted by the Rhodesian government post-UDI (the unilateral declaration of independence). Challenging the legality of his detention, Madzimbamuto claimed that the Act was *ultra vires* the powers of the Rhodesian

---

15   See Kelsen, 1967, p 214; Hart, 1961, Chapter VI.
16   Under the Zimbabwe Act 1979 and SI 1979/1600.

government. On appeal to the Privy Council, the traditional doctrine of parliamentary sovereignty was affirmed. Lord Reid declared:

> It is often said that it would be unconstitutional for the United Kingdom Parliament to do certain things, meaning that the moral, political and other reasons against doing them are so strong that most people would regard it as highly improper if Parliament did these things. But that does not mean that it is beyond the power of Parliament to do these things. If Parliament chose to do any of them, the courts could not hold the Act of Parliament invalid.

Accordingly, the sovereignty over Rhodesia remained – from the English courts' point of view – that of the United Kingdom Parliament. The Rhodesian government had *de facto* power; *de jure* power remained with the United Kingdom. An impasse was thus reached: to the government of Rhodesia – and ultimately the Rhodesian courts – the alleged sovereignty of the United Kingdom was an irrelevance. To the United Kingdom, however – as illustrated by *Madzimbamuto's* case before the Privy Council – the 'basic norm' of the constitution of Rhodesia remained the sovereign power of Westminster.[17] Nevertheless, from the point of view of the judges within Rhodesia, there was a dilemma: how to react to legislation promulgated by the *de facto* sovereign power. From 1965 to 1968, the Rhodesian courts refused to acknowledge the lawfulness of the Smith government, following the view of the Privy Council that, since the government was unlawful, so too were all of its acts. However, to continue to deny the force of law to any acts of the unlawful government was to produce uncertainty and doubt. The doctrine of necessity was employed by the judges to give legal effect to what was constitutionally invalid. Gradually, the continuing effectiveness of the Smith regime was to result in recognition of the validity of its Acts, thus further revealing the complexities in maintaining a clear separation between the criterion of legal validity and effectiveness.[18]

In a revolutionary situation, a change in the basic norm, or grundnorm, will take place when the judges accept the new source of sovereign power. As JW Harris explains:

> Being merely a hypothesis of juristic thinking, the grundnorm does not change the moment the revolutionaries shoot the King. It cannot change until jurists change their thinking, that is, until lawyers begin to make post-revolutionary assertions to the effect: 'The law in the country now is ...' where 'now' refers to some revolutionary, established source of law. [[1971] CLJ 110]

Kelsen's theory of revolutionary change in the grundnorm has not been universally accepted, but it marks an effort to deal with the difficult issue of change and continuity in a legal order. By way of example, in *The State v Dosso* (1958), the Supreme Court of Pakistan, applying Kelsenian theory, accepted the validity of a coup and that the successful coup conferred sovereign power on the victors. However, in *Asma Jilani v Government of Punjab* (1972), the Supreme Court rejected the notion that any person seizing power could claim the authority of sovereign power. Rather, sovereign power could only be conferred on the

---

17 See, *inter alia*, Harris, 1980, p 125; Raz, 1979, Chapter 7; Stone, 1963; Brookfield, 1969.
18 See Dias, 1968.

successful revolutionary party under the constitution of the state expressing the will of the people through the medium of chosen representatives.[19]

THE ULTIMATE RULE IS EXTRA-LEGAL

When one comes to search for the ultimate higher authority which itself validates the basic norm, a logical impasse is reached. Accordingly, it is necessary to look outside this discrete structural system in order to find the authority which confers ultimate validity. On a domestic basis,[20] we find this validating force in 'juristic consciousness' – in other words, the acceptance of legal validity by the judges. Kelsen's view on the source of ultimate sovereign power is analysed by HLA Hart in *The Concept of Law*. While keen to distinguish his own theory of law from that of Kelsen and that of John Austin, there are similarities between Kelsen's and Hart's view of the ultimate validity within a legal system. For Hart, the ultimate rule of recognition is validated by the sociologically observable fact of official acceptance. By this, Hart means that the officials' – and most importantly the judges' – acceptance of authority can be seen in operation whenever one observes a court of law. A judge may perhaps personally disapprove of a precedent case or of a statutory provision, but his acceptance of its validity is demonstrated by his application of the law. Expressed differently, it is the judges who uphold and reinforce the sovereignty of parliament – the basic norm of the constitution.

In Kelsen's analysis, the 'basic norm' within any state will be the historically traceable first constitution. In many instances, this will prove a workable test. In the United States of America, the Constitution of 1787 will be the basic norm; in the Republic of Ireland, the Constitution of 1937, and in Australia, the Commonwealth Constitution of 1900, as amended. The position in the United Kingdom is less clear cut on this analysis, which will assume importance when considering the status of the Acts of Union with Scotland and Ireland. Since the Norman Conquest in 1066, there has been an unrivalled continuity in constitutional development in the United Kingdom, interrupted by only two major historical events and a fundamentally important, more contemporary, change. The first of these, the Civil War of 1642–46, resulted in the execution of Charles I in 1649, and the abolition of the monarchy and rule by Cromwell until the restoration of the monarchy in 1660. The second significant constitutional change came with the uniting of the sovereign parliaments of Scotland and England under the Act of Union 1706, creating the state of Great Britain, and later the Union with Ireland, 1800, by which Act the state of the United Kingdom came into being. The third change, which has wide ranging implications for the constitution and law, was Britain's accession to the European Community which took effect from 1973. Most recently, devolution to regional assemblies and the incorporation of rights protected under the European Convention on Human Rights under the Human Rights Act 1998 have significant implications for the scope of legislative power which parliament retains while these measures remain in force. These issues are discussed later in the chapter.

---

19 See Iyer, 1973.
20 And Kelsen seeks to establish a global 'pure theory' for law, but that need not be considered here.

SOVEREIGNTY AND WRITTEN CONSTITUTIONS

Where a written constitution exists, it will have come into being either by a grant of independence from a previously sovereign power or through a revolution – peaceful or otherwise. Where the constitution arises from the native authority of the people, it is 'autochthonous':

> ... [the people] assert not the principle of autonomy only; they assert also a principle of something stronger, of self-sufficiency, of constitutional autarky ... of being constitutionally rooted in their own soil. [Wheare, 1960, Chapter 4]

Where autochthony[21] exists, the authority for the constitution arises from the people. The phrase 'We the People' has powerful psychological – and legal – force, and the resultant document, the constitution, will be supreme. As KC Wheare explains in relation to the United States of America:

> The constitution of the United States expresses the essential supremacy of a constitution in a federal government in the passage: 'This Constitution and the Laws of the United States which shall be made in pursuance thereof ... shall be the supreme law of the land; and the judges in every state shall be bound thereby, anything in the constitution or laws of any state to the contrary notwithstanding.' [1963, p 54]

All power entrusted to government comes from the people: it is accordingly understandable that, under such a constitutional arrangement, there is a strongly held belief that government holds its power on 'trust' for the people. It may be said, as a result, that both law making and executive powers are conditionally conferred on those who hold public office, subject to the doctrine of trust which will be enforced by the courts in the name of the people. All constitutions – written and unwritten – exist against the backcloth of historical, political and moral evolution: none exists in a vacuum. However, under a written constitution, this background has a particular significance. The constitution, being the expression of the political morality of its age – updated by the judiciary through interpretative methods – is a constant reflection and reminder of the will of the people and the restraints which that will imposes on government.

Chief Justice Marshall, in *Marbury v Madison* (1803), explained the power of the constitution:

> It is a proposition too plain to be contested that the constitution controls any legislative act repugnant to it; or, that the legislature may alter the constitution by an ordinary act. Between these two alternatives, there is no middle ground. The constitution is either a superior, paramount law, unchangeable by ordinary means, or it is on a level with ordinary legislative acts, and, like other acts, is alterable when the legislature shall please to alter it. If the former part of the alternative is true, then a legislative act contrary to the constitution is not law; if the latter part be true, then written constitutions are absurd attempts, on the part of the people, to limit a power in its own nature illimitable.

It is possible, accordingly, under such a constitutional arrangement, for the constitutional court[22] effectively to redefine the relationship between the

---

21 See Marshall, 1971, Chapter III.4.
22 Howsoever labelled: in the United States of America, the Supreme Court; in Australia, the High Court.

governors and the governed, the state and its citizens. By this means, the
constitution is renewed and reinvigorated. By way of example, the American Bill
of Rights, enacted as amendments to the 1787 Constitution, provides that:

> All persons born or naturalised in the United States, and subject to the jurisdiction
> thereof, are citizens of the United States and of the state wherein they reside. No state
> shall make or enforce any law which shall abridge the privileges or immunities of
> citizens of the United States; nor shall any state deprive any person of life, liberty, or
> property, without due process of law; nor deny to any person within its jurisdiction the
> equal protection of the laws ...[23]

This 'equal protection' clause has been the focus of the development of equal civil
and political rights in the United States of America. In 1896, the Supreme Court
was called upon to determine whether the policy of segregation of black and
white citizens was lawful under the Constitution. The court ruled that 'separate
but equal treatment' laws did not amount to a denial of the equal protection of
law.[24] When, however, in 1954, the question of 'equal protection' came before the
Supreme Court concerning segregation in the schools of the states of Kansas,
South Carolina, Virginia and Delaware, the court was to rule that such 'treatment'
violated the Fourteenth Amendment of the Constitution.[25]

THE SOURCE OF SOVEREIGNTY IN THE UNITED KINGDOM

The sovereignty of parliament is not itself laid down in statute: nor could it be, for
the ultimate law maker cannot confer upon itself the ultimate power. As legal
theorists[26] have demonstrated, when searching for ultimate legal power, there
comes a point of inquiry beyond which one cannot logically move. In order to
understand the ultimate authority of law, whether expressed in terms of the 'basic
norm' (Hans Kelsen) or the 'ultimate rule of recognition' (HLA Hart) or
sovereignty, the inquirer must move beyond the law itself. As has been seen
above, for both Kelsen and Hart, the key to ultimate power lies in its acceptance –
but not necessarily moral approval – by the judges within the legal system.

SOVEREIGNTY AS A RULE OF COMMON LAW

Sovereignty is the fundamental rule of the common law, for it is the judges who
uphold parliament's sovereignty. For as long as the judges accept the sovereignty
of parliament, sovereignty will remain the ultimate rule of the constitution. As
Salmond explains:

> All rules of law have historical sources. As a matter of fact and history they have their
> origin somewhere, though we may not know what it is. But not all of them have legal

---

23 Bill of Rights, Article XIV, s 1, ratified 9 July 1868.
24 *Plessey v Ferguson* (1896).
25 *Brown v Board of Education of Topeka* (1954). The ruling did not end segregation on other
    grounds. See King, 1964; see further the Civil Rights Acts 1964 and 1968.
26 See Kelsen, 1961, p 116; Hart, 1961, p 104. See also Kelsen, 'The function of a constitution', in
    Tur and Twining, 1986.

sources ... But whence comes the rule that Acts of Parliament have the force of law? This is legally ultimate; its source is historical only, not legal ... It is the law because it is the law, and for no other reason that it is possible for the law to take notice of. No statute can confer this power upon Parliament, for this would be to assume and act on the very power that is to be conferred.[27]

Accordingly, the rule that confers validity on legislation is 'logically superior to the sovereign'. The logical consequence of this is stated by HWR Wade:

... if no statute can establish the rule that the courts obey Acts of Parliament, similarly no statute can alter or abolish that rule. The rule is above and beyond the reach of statute ... because it is itself the source of the authority of statute.[28]

The sovereignty of parliament will only be lost under two conditions. The first condition would be where parliament decided – perhaps on the authority of the people tested in a referendum – to abolish its sovereignty and to place its residual authority under that of a written constitution to be adjudicated upon by the judiciary. The second condition would be where the judiciary itself underwent a 'revolution' in attitude, and accepted that parliament was no longer the sovereign law making body and that the judges owed allegiance to an alternative – or different – sovereign power. These points will be returned to when considering challenges to the traditional Diceyan view of sovereignty.

In the United Kingdom, in the absence of a written constitution which asserts the sovereignty of the people and the sovereignty of the constitution – as interpreted by the judiciary – over the legislature and executive, the vacuum is filled by the doctrine of parliamentary sovereignty, or supremacy. Under this doctrine, political sovereignty vests in the people: legal sovereignty vests with parliament over which no legal controls are exerted, but which remains responsible to the electorate for the continued, and regularly renewed, grant of law making and executive authority. The constitution is renewed through the democratic process and the concept of a responsive responsible government, rather than through the means of a Supreme Court reinterpreting the constitution according to judicial perceptions of the mores in society. This is not to suggest that under a written constitution, there is no responsive, accountable and democratic government or that the evolution of the constitution lies solely within the domain of the judges. Rather, the point to be emphasised is that, under a written constitution, there is an additional element in effecting constitutional change. Depending upon the independence, integrity and motivation of the courts, acts of the executive and legislature can be subjected to the control of the constitution.

The origins of parliamentary sovereignty

In Chapter 6, the manner in which the near absolute powers of the Crown[29] were reduced by the courts and parliament was discussed. With the reduction in the King's prerogative powers, there came about the correlative rise in the sovereignty of parliament. From 1688, the supremacy of parliament over the

---

27   Williams (ed), *Jurisprudence*, 10th edn, p 155, cited by Wade, 1955, p 187.
28   Wade, 'Introduction', in Dicey, 1885, 1959 edn.
29   To make laws by proclamation, to rule under the prerogative without parliament, and to participate in the judicial process.

Crown was established. From this time, the prerogative powers of the Crown continued in existence or were abolished or curtailed as parliament determined. No new prerogative powers may be claimed by the Crown, as Diplock LJ stated in *BBC v Johns* (1965).

DICEY AND SOVEREIGNTY

The classical definition of sovereignty, offered from a constitutional law rather than a jurisprudential perspective, is that of AV Dicey (1885). Dicey had been critical of John Austin's account of sovereignty, arguing that Austin confused political and legal sovereignty. From a legal-theoretical point of view, it remains imperative to separate the political from the legal and to recognise that, as matters stand, legal sovereignty remains with the United Kingdom Parliament, although there may be political restraints which effectively inhibit the exercise of those powers. On sovereignty, Dicey stated:

> The principle of parliamentary sovereignty means neither more nor less than this: namely, that Parliament thus defined has, under the English constitution, the right to make or unmake any law whatever; and, further, that no person or body is recognised by the law of England as having a right to override or set aside the legislation of Parliament.

> A law may, for our present purpose, be defined as 'any rule which will be enforced by the courts'. The principle, then, of parliamentary sovereignty may, looked at from its positive side, be thus described: any Act of Parliament, or any part of an Act of Parliament, which makes a new law, or repeals or modifies an existing law, will be obeyed by the court. The same principle, looked at from its negative side, may be thus stated: there is no person or body of persons who can, under the English constitution, make rules which override or derogate from an Act of Parliament, or which (to express the same thing in other words) will be enforced by the courts in contravention of an Act of Parliament. [1885, p 39]

From this description can be deduced three basic rules:

(a) parliament is the supreme law making body and may enact laws on any subject matter;

(b) no parliament may be bound by a predecessor or bind a successor;

(c) no person or body – including a court of law – may question the validity of parliament's enactments.

It is the correctness of this definition which must be tested and evaluated. Having considered the concept of sovereignty in theoretical terms, examination of the manner in which this is translated into a practical legal doctrine is required. Dicey's description of sovereignty will provide the framework for discussion.

Parliament's unlimited law making power

This aspect of sovereignty is the easiest both to explain and to understand: the rule means that there is no limit on the subject matter on which parliament may legislate. Thus parliament may legislate to alter its term of office. In 1716, the life of a parliament was limited to three years under the Act of 1694. Fearing the effects of an election, the government introduced, and parliament passed, the Septennial Act, extending the life of parliament to seven years. The consequence of this Act was to confer authority on the Commons to legislate without the express consent of the electorate: thus usurping the rights of the people.[30] The Septennial Act, under a written constitution such as that of the United States, would be legally invalid. Nevertheless, as Dicey argued, 'Parliament made a legal though unprecedented use of its powers' (1885, p 47). Parliament also extended its own life between 1910 and 1918, and the parliament elected in 1935 was to endure until 1945.[31] Parliament may also legislate to alter the succession to the throne, as with the Act of Settlement 1700 and His Majesty's Declaration of Abdication Act 1936. Parliament may 'abolish' itself and reconstitute itself as a different body, as occurred with the Union with Scotland Act 1706. Parliament may also legislate to alter its own powers, as with the Parliament Acts 1911 and 1949, whereby the powers of the House of Lords in respect of legislation were curtailed. Parliament may grant independence to dependent states, whether dominions or colonies, as with the Nigeria Independence Act 1960 and the Zimbabwe Independence Act 1979. Furthermore, parliament may legislate to limit its own powers in relation to dependent territories, as shown by the Colonial Laws Validity Act 1865 and the Statute of Westminster 1931.[32]

Parliament may also legislate with retrospective effect, as with the War Damage Act 1965. The War Damage Act effectively overruled the decision of the House of Lords in *Burmah Oil Company v Lord Advocate* (1965). In 1942, British troops had destroyed oil installations in Rangoon, with the intention of preventing them from falling into the hands of the Japanese. The British government made an *ex gratia* payment of some £4 million to the company. Burmah Oil sued the government for some £31 million in compensation. The House of Lords held that compensation was payable by the Crown for the destruction of property caused by the exercise of the prerogative power in relation to war. The government immediately introduced into parliament the War Damage Bill to nullify the effect of the decision.

Parliament may legislate with extra-territorial effect; that is to say, it may enact laws affecting the rights and duties of citizens and non-citizens outside the territorial jurisdiction of the United Kingdom. For example, certain offences committed in a foreign state will be triable in this country. Thus, murder, manslaughter, treason, bigamy and tax offences committed abroad will not render the accused immune from prosecution in this country.[33] Parliament may expressly legislate for overseas territory, as in the Continental Shelf Act 1964, under which exploration and exploitation rights of the continental shelf vest in the Crown. However, it is a presumption of statutory interpretation that statutes will not be given extra-territorial effect other than where it is expressly or impliedly provided for under the Act.[34] Such statutes will normally be passed in

---

30 See Priestley, 1771, cited in Dicey, 1885, p 47.
31 Dicey, 1885, p 47.
32 Prolongation of Parliament Act 1944.
33 Law Com No 91, *Territorial and Extra-territorial Extent of Criminal Law*, 1978, London: HMSO.
34 *Treacey v DPP* (1971); *R v Kelly* (1982).

order to give effect to obligations undertaken under an international treaty.[35] The Hijacking Act 1971, for example, gave legislative effect to the Convention for the Suppression on Unlawful Seizure of Aircraft. Section 1 of the Aviation Security Act 1982, which succeeded the Hijacking Act 1971, provides that the crime of hijacking is committed when a person on board an aircraft in flight unlawfully seizes control of the aircraft and exercises control over it by the use of force or by threats. The jurisdiction of the United Kingdom courts, with limited exceptions, extends to an act of hijacking, wherever it occurs, and irrespective of the nationality of the hijacker.[36]

The most often quoted and best remembered examples of parliament's theoretically untrammelled legislative powers are those offered by Sir Ivor Jennings (1959): parliament can legislate to ban smoking on the streets of Paris; parliament can legally make a man into a woman; and Sir Leslie Stephens (1882): parliament could legislate to have a blue eyed babies put to death. These extreme, hypothetical examples illustrate the distinction between what is theoretically possible and what is practically possible, or, to express it differently, the distinction between *validity* and *effectiveness* discussed above. The distinction is important and helps to explain the apparent paradox of unlimited legislative power.

An Act of Parliament will be valid if it has passed through the requisite parliamentary stages and received royal assent. The manner in which the judges deal with this 'enrolled Bill' rule is discussed further below. All that need be noted for now is that, provided an Act of Parliament is 'on the parliamentary roll', it will be held to be good law. That is not to say that every rule making power exercised by parliament results in an 'Act of Parliament' which alone can alter the law, and is thus 'sovereign'.

Acts of Parliament alone are supreme

Resolutions of parliament

Resolutions of either House of Parliament – for example, decisions of the House of Commons – do not have the force of law and cannot alter the law of the land and thereby affect individual rights and duties.[37] For a resolution to have the force of law, it must be placed on a statutory basis.

Proclamations

Proclamations of the Crown, issued under the royal prerogative, do not have the force of law. To understand the status of proclamations, it is necessary to turn to the reign of Henry VIII. Under the Statute of Proclamations 1539, the King was given wide – though not unlimited – power to make law without parliament's consent. The Act was repealed in 1547, although monarchs continued to 'legislate'

---

35 Parliament may, however, legislate contrary to the requirements of international law. See *Mortensen v Peters* (1906); *Cheney v Conn* (1968).

36 See also the Taking of Hostages Act 1982 giving effect to the International Convention Against the Taking of Hostages.

37 *Stockdale v Hansard* (1839); *Bowles v Bank of England* (1913).

by proclamation. The *Case of Proclamations* (1611) clarified the constitutional position. The most significant aspects of the case lay in the findings, first, that the King could not by proclamation create an offence previously unknown to law, and secondly, that the King had only such prerogative power as was granted under law.

Treaties

Treaties entered into under the royal prerogative cannot alter the law of the land. The courts have made it clear that treaties can take legal effect only under the authority of an Act of Parliament.[38] This point will be returned to when the constitutional relationship between the United Kingdom and the European Community is examined in Chapters 8 and 9. It is sufficient to note here that a treaty has no legal force under domestic law unless and until its provisions are incorporated into law by way of statute.

Resolutions, proclamations and treaties are but three species of 'law making' which are distinguishable from statute: and it is the statute alone which will be valid, provided that the required parliamentary procedures have been followed.

Intrinsic and extrinsic limits on parliament's power

As seen above, the criterion of effectiveness underlies the supremacy of parliament and represents one important – albeit extra-legal – constraint on parliament's power. As Dicey says, sovereignty 'is limited on every side by the possibility of popular resistance' (1885, p 79). Leslie Stephens makes the same point and is quoted at length by Dicey:

> Lawyers are apt to speak as though the legislature were omnipotent, as they do not require to go beyond its decision. It is, of course, omnipotent in the sense that it can make whatever law it please, in as much as a law means any rule which has been made by the legislature. But, from the scientific point of view, the power of the legislature is of course strictly limited. It is limited, so to speak, both from within and from without; from within, because the legislature is the product of a certain social conditions, and determined by whatever determines the society; and from without, because the power of imposing laws is dependent upon the instinct of subordination, which is itself limited. If a legislature decided that all blue eyed babies should be murdered, the preservation of blue eyed babies would be illegal; but legislators must go mad before they could pass such a law, and subjects be idiotic before they could submit to it. [p 81]

These views are indicative of the constitutional role of government today. In a representative democracy, the proper purpose of government is to serve the people. In former times, when government was conducted by the King in Council, this was not necessarily the case. But even then, there were limits on monarchical and aristocratic power: ultimately, law cannot be enforced against the will of the governed. Compliance – in the absence of a military or police state – depends for the most part on voluntary acquiescence, not on the application of power. One of Hart's principal objections to Austin's 'command backed by

---

38 See, *inter alia*, *The Parlement Belge* (1879); *AG for Canada v AG for Ontario* (1937); *R v Home Secretary ex parte McWhirter* (1969); *Blackburn v AG* (1971).

sanction' theory of law turns on this point. As Hart explains, the law is largely 'self-enforcing' and 'self-enforced'. By this he means that it rests on acceptance, by and large, by the people. Nowadays, with a more or less democratic House of Commons, the internal and external constraints discussed by Dicey and Stephens coalesce. As Dicey explains:

> The aim and effect of such (representative) government is to produce a coincidence, or at any rate diminish the divergence, between the external and the internal limitations on the exercise of sovereign power.

> Where a Parliament truly represents the people, the divergence between the external and the internal limit to the exercise of sovereign power can hardly arise, or if it arises, must soon disappear. [1885, pp 82–83]

No parliament may be bound by its predecessor or bind its successor

The rationale for this aspect of Dicey's definition of sovereignty lies in the recognition that for a body to be sovereign it must be, in Austin's word, illimitable. For a sovereign body to be subordinate to another body would be a logical contradiction:

> The logical reason why Parliament has failed in its endeavours to enact unchangeable enactments is that a sovereign power cannot, while retaining its sovereign character, restrict its own powers by any particular enactment ... 'Limited sovereignty', in short, as in the case of a parliamentary as of every other sovereign, is a contradiction in terms. [1885, p 68]

It follows, therefore, that each parliament must enjoy the same unlimited power as any parliament before it. No parliament can enact rules which limit future parliaments.[39] It is this aspect of Dicey's definition which gives rise to the most argument and which requires the most careful analysis.

The doctrine of implied repeal

The doctrine of implied repeal provides the mechanism by which the judge gives effect to the rule against parliament being bound by previous parliaments or being able to bind subsequent parliaments, and thereby guarantees contemporary sovereignty. Parliament may, of course, repeal any previous law by expressly declaring that law to be repealed. The position of the judiciary is then clear: they must give effect to the latest expression of sovereign will and judges are not free to apply the earlier statute. The position, however, may not always be so clear cut. Parliament may pass, perhaps through inadvertence, a statute which, while not expressly repealing an earlier Act, is inconsistent with it. When the judges are thus faced with two apparently conflicting statutes, the doctrine of implied repeal will come into play, the judges applying the latest statute in time and deeming the earlier provisions to be impliedly repealed.

Two cases which illustrate the principle in operation are *Vauxhall Estates Ltd v Liverpool Corporation* (1932) and *Ellen Street Estates Ltd v Minister of Health* (1934),

---

39 On the distinction between 'continuing' and 'self-embracing' sovereignty, see above, p 164.

each of which entailed similar facts. Section 7(1) of the Acquisition of Land (Assessment of Compensation) Act 1919 provided that:

> The provisions of the Act or order by which the land is authorised to be acquired ... shall ... have effect subject to this Act and so far as inconsistent with this Act those provisions shall cease to have or shall not have effect ...

The Housing Act 1925 provided for a less generous scheme for compensation on the compulsory acquisition of land than the 1919 Act. In both cases, the plaintiffs argued that section 7(1) of the 1919 Act was binding on the courts and should be applied in preference to the Housing Act 1925. If that claim were to succeed, the constitutional position would be that the provisions of the 1919 Act were effectively 'entrenched' – that is to say, have a superior legal status to that of other Acts of Parliament and therefore binding – on a future parliament. In the *Vauxhall Estates* case, the Divisional Court held that the 1925 Act impliedly repealed the conflicting provisions in the 1919 Act and, in the *Ellen Street Estates* case, the Court of Appeal again ruled that the 1919 Act must give way to the 1925 legislation. Maugham LJ stated that:

> The legislature cannot, according to our constitution, bind itself as to the form of subsequent legislation, and it is impossible for parliament to enact that in a subsequent statute dealing with the same subject matter there can be no implied repeal. If, in a subsequent Act, parliament chooses to make it plain that the earlier statute is being to some extent repealed, effect must be given to that intention just because it is the will of the legislature.[40]

While the implied repeal rule still applies in relation to most statutes, it has been regarded by some senior judges as inapplicable to statutes of major constitutional importance. This view has been expressed in relation to the European Communities Act 1972 and the Human Rights Act 1998: see below for further discussion.

With the doctrines of express and implied repeal firmly in mind, consideration must now be given to the special problems allegedly posed for legislative supremacy by grants of independence, the Acts of Union with Scotland and Ireland, 'manner and form' and 'redefinition' theories. The impact of membership of the European Community and Union also requires careful consideration, as does the recent devolution of power to the Scottish Parliament and the Northern Ireland and Welsh Assemblies, and the Human Rights Act 1998.

---

40 See, however, the earlier case of *Nairn v University of St Andrews* (1909), in which the House of Lords ruled that the Universities (Scotland) Act 1889, which empowered commissioners to make ordinances, *inter alia*, to enable universities to confer degrees on women, did not impliedly repeal the Representation of the People (Scotland) Act 1868, s 27, which provided the right to vote for, *inter alia*, 'every person whose name is for the time being on the register, ... if of full age, and not subject to any legal incapacity'. In *Jex-Blake v Senatus of the University of Edinburgh* (1873), following *Chorlton v Lings* (1868), the court ruled that 'women' were not 'persons' within the meaning to be applied to the right to vote. The House of Lords in *Nairn* ruled that only parliament, in the most express terms, could 'effect a constitutional change so momentous and far-reaching', and it could not be taken to have done so by 'so furtive a process' as this later Act ((1909), *per* Lord Loreburn LC). Given the date of this case, and its positioning in the continuing struggle for women's right to vote, which was so consistently obstructed by the courts, the decision is perhaps best understood within the political climate of the time rather than as an illustration of objective legal analysis.

Grants of independence

The Statute of Westminster 1931 was enacted to give statutory force to the constitutional convention that the United Kingdom Parliament would not legislate for Dominions without their consent. Section 4 provides:

> No Act of Parliament of the United Kingdom passed after the commencement of this Act shall extend, or be deemed to extend, to a Dominion as part of the law of that Dominion unless it is expressly declared in that Act that that Dominion has requested, and consented to, the enactment thereof.

Where parliament confers partial competence on a subordinate legislature, the question arises as to whether the United Kingdom Parliament can revoke that grant of power. The principle that parliament cannot be bound by the acts of its predecessor has already been established. The issue here is the relationship between the sovereign parliament and a parliament dependent for its powers upon Westminster. This issue arose in *British Coal Corporation v The King* (1935). The Judicial Committee of the Privy Council had to determine whether or not the Canadian legislature had the power to regulate or prohibit appeals in criminal matters to the King in Council. A determination of that matter entailed consideration of the scope of legislative competence of the legislature. The relevant Acts were the British North America Act 1867, the Colonial Laws Validity Act 1865, the Statute of Westminster 1931 and the Canadian Criminal Code which prohibited appeal to the courts of the United Kingdom. The Statute of Westminster had removed any legislative incompetence from the Canadian legislature and accordingly the legislature had full power to enact the section in question. It was accepted by the Judicial Committee of the Privy Council that, whilst the power of the Imperial Parliament remained 'in theory unimpaired' and that, 'as a matter of abstract law', section 4 of the Statute of Westminster could be repealed by the parliament of the United Kingdom, in practice it could not be: '... legal theory must march alongside practical reality.' *British Coal Corporation v The King* is, however, no more than a recognition of the extrinsic or practical limitations on the exercise of sovereignty, and not of any legal limitations on parliament's supremacy.

In *Ndlwana v Hofmeyer* (1937),[41] the Appellate Division of the South African High Court adopted the view that such a restriction amounted to a fetter on parliament's powers: '... freedom once conferred cannot be revoked.'[42] Again, however, it is to be noted that such judicial utterances do no more than recognise the practical political restraints which are imposed on parliament, not its legal powers. It is correct, therefore, to view such *obiter* as reflecting the distinction between legal and political sovereignty: a point emphasised by Dicey himself.

The question of the status and effect of section 4 of the Statute of Westminster arose once more in *Manuel v Attorney General* (1982). The issue was whether the Canada Act 1982, passed by the United Kingdom Parliament at the request and consent of Canada, was a valid enactment. The plaintiffs' argument was that the

---

41 See also *Ibralebbe v R* (1964); *Blackburn v AG* (1971).
42 At p 237. See also Owen Dixon, 1935, but cf his later view expressed in *Hughes and Vale Property Ltd v Gair* (1954).

United Kingdom Parliament had no power to amend the Constitution of Canada to the detriment of the native population without their consent. It was argued that section 4 of the Statute of Westminster required not just the consent of the federal parliament but also that of all the provincial legislatures and the native minority population. The application failed: the Statute of Westminster, as interpreted by the Court of Appeal, did not require the actual consent of a Dominion, but rather the mere recital on the face of the request that the United Kingdom legislate for the Dominion. Having thus failed on that point, the plaintiffs proceeded to argue that the conventional rule, which predated the Statute of Westminster 1931, had hardened into a rule of law and was thus as effective as section 4 of the statute. The Court of Appeal rejected that reasoning,[43] maintaining the traditional distinction between conventions and rules of law.

The Acts of Union with Scotland 1706/1707 and Ireland 1800[44]

The Acts of Union, their status and their effect on parliament's sovereignty have provided a fertile source for academic debate which represents a powerful argument against the unlimited freedom of any parliament at any time to legislate as it pleases. The whole debate centres on the notion that the new United Kingdom Parliament was, in the words of Professor JDB Mitchell,[45] 'born unfree'. The idea being conveyed here is that the Acts of Union have some form of 'higher law' status which binds and limits the powers of parliament.

The union with Scotland

As discussed in Chapter 3, prior to the accession to the throne of James I (James VI of Scotland), England and Scotland were both independent sovereign states, each having its own monarch and parliament. With James's accession to the English throne in 1603, the two countries were united under one monarch but retained their sovereign parliaments until 1706. The Treaty of Union 1706 effected, conceptually, the abolition of both parliaments and the birth of the Parliament of Great Britain.

Article I of the Act of Union provides:

> That the two kingdoms of England and Scotland shall upon the first day of May which shall be in the year one thousand seven hundred and seven and for ever after be united into one Kingdom by the name of Great Britain ...

The sovereignty issue has been argued in three cases concerning the Act of Union with Scotland. In *MacCormick v Lord Advocate* (1953), MacCormick sought an injunction against the Lord Advocate, as representative of the Crown, preventing the use of the title Queen Elizabeth II of the United Kingdom of Great Britain. The objection to the use of the title was based on historical inaccuracy[46] and a contravention of Article I of the Treaty of Union which provided for the union of

---

43 See Marshall, 1984, Chapter XII.
44 The English Parliament's legislation was the Union with Scotland Act 1706; the Scottish Parliament's was the Union with Scotland Act 1707.
45 Mitchell, 1963; and see Munro, 1999.
46 Queen Elizabeth I was Queen of England, not of Scotland.

the two countries from 1707. The petition was dismissed, as was the subsequent appeal. Lord Cooper, the Lord President, however, proceeded to discuss the doctrine of sovereignty:

> The principle of the unlimited sovereignty of parliament is a distinctively English principle which has no counterpart in Scottish constitutional law ... Considering that the Union legislation extinguished the Parliaments of Scotland and England and replaced them by a new parliament, I have difficulty in seeing why it should have been supposed that the new Parliament of Great Britain must inherit all the peculiar characteristics of the English Parliament but none of the Scottish Parliament, as if all that happened in 1707 was that Scottish representatives were admitted to the Parliament of England. That is not what was done ...

> I have not found in the Union legislation any provision that the Parliament of Great Britain should be 'absolutely sovereign' in the sense that that Parliament should be free to alter the Treaty at will.

In *Gibson v The Lord Advocate* (1975), the issue tested was whether allowing fishermen of Member States of the European Community to fish in Scottish coastal waters infringed Article XVIII of the Act of Union. Article XVIII provides that:

> ... no alteration be made in laws which concern private right except for the evident utility of the subjects within Scotland.

The claim was dismissed, Lord Keith ruling that the European Community Regulations did not confer rights or obligations on individual citizens and accordingly were matters of public and not private law and, accordingly, that Article XVIII could not be invoked. On the sovereignty question, Lord Keith, however, stated:

> There were addressed to me interesting arguments upon the question of jurisdiction and the competency of the action. These arguments raised constitutional issues of great potential importance ...

> Like Lord President Cooper, I prefer to reserve my opinion what the position would be if the United Kingdom Parliament passed an Act purporting to abolish the Court of Session or the Church of Scotland or to substitute English law for the whole body of Scots law. I am, however, of the opinion that the question whether a particular Act of the United Kingdom Parliament altering a particular aspect of Scots private law is or is not 'for the evident utility' of the subjects within Scotland is not a justiciable issue in this court. The making of decisions upon what must essentially be a political matter is no part of the function of the court, and it is highly undesirable that it should be. The function of the court is to adjudicate upon the rights and obligations of the individual person, natural or corporate, in relation to other persons or, in certain instances, to the state. A general inquiry into the utility of certain legislative measures as regards the population generally is quite outside its competence.

In *Sillars v Smith* (1982), a similar challenge was lodged over the validity of the Criminal Justice (Scotland) Act 1980, on the basis that the United Kingdom Parliament, which had passed the Scotland Act 1978, which created a legislative Assembly for Scotland, had no power to repeal that Act – as had been done – and accordingly, parliament, it was argued, had no power to pass the Criminal Justice (Scotland) Act. The claim was dismissed, the court adopting the classical view expressed in *Edinburgh and Dalkeith Railway Company v Wauchope* (1842) by Lord Campbell:

> All that a court of justice can look to is the parliamentary roll; they see that an Act has passed both Houses of Parliament, and that it has received the royal assent, and no court of justice can enquire into the manner in which it was introduced into parliament, what was done previously to its being introduced, or what passed in parliament during the various stages of its progress through both Houses of Parliament.

Despite the questioning *dicta* of Lords Cooper and Keith on sovereignty, the evidence to date goes clearly against the notion that the Act of Union is legally unalterable. To take but one example, the Protestant Religion and Presbyterian Church Act 1707 provision that 'the true Protestant religion and the worship, discipline and government' of the established church were 'to continue without any alteration to the people of this land in all succeeding generations' was incorporated into the Treaty of Union and declared to be 'a fundamental and essential condition of the ... Union in all times coming'. The Act also required that teachers in universities and schools had to subscribe to the faith. Yet, in 1711, the Scottish Episcopalians Act and the Church Patronage (Scotland) Act were passed to reflect greater religious toleration, and by the Universities (Scotland) Act 1853 and the Parochial and Burgh Schoolmasters (Scotland) Act 1861, the requirement that teachers must subscribe to the Protestant faith was removed. Further changes in the organisation of the Church were made in the Church of Scotland Act 1921.

The union with Ireland

The Act of Union with Ireland 1800 has given rise to similar arguments, although these arguments are even less convincing than those addressed to the Act of Union with Scotland. The Act of Union was declared to 'last forever'. Article 5 provided for a United Church of England and Ireland that 'shall be and shall remain in full force for ever, and that this be deemed and taken to be an essential and fundamental part of the Union'. Nevertheless, in 1869 the Irish Church was disestablished under the Irish Church Act of that year. In *Ex parte Canon Selwyn* (1872), a clergyman sought an order of mandamus against the Lord President of the Council ordering him to petition the Queen for adjudication of the question of whether the giving of royal assent to the Irish Church Act 1869 was contrary to the coronation oath and the Act of Settlement. The coronation oath contained a commitment to maintain a unified and established Church of England and Ireland. The court dismissed the petition on the basis that the statute was supreme and could not be questioned in a court of law.

The Acts of Union[47] provided for the permanent union between Ireland and Great Britain. However, the Ireland Act 1949 recognised the republican status and independence of southern Ireland, thereby terminating the union. The 1949 Act also provided that Northern Ireland:

> ... remains part of His Majesty's dominions and of the United Kingdom and it is hereby affirmed that in no event will Northern Ireland or any part thereof cease to be part of

---

47   The Act of Union (Ireland) 1800; the Act of Union with Ireland Act 1800.

His Majesty's dominions and of the United Kingdom without consent of the Parliament of Northern Ireland. [s 1(2)]

Under the Northern Ireland Constitution (Amendment) Act 1973, the United Kingdom Parliament reiterated the statutory guarantee that Northern Ireland would not cease to be part of the United Kingdom unless and until a majority of voters should determine otherwise. That commitment is reiterated in section 1 of the Northern Ireland Act 1998. However, such assurances, whilst morally and politically binding on the government, do not amount – under Diceyan theory – to a legal restriction on parliament's powers. Parliament remains free, in legal theoretical terms, to legislate contrary to such undertakings, although the political implications of so doing guarantee that parliament will not do so.

AV Dicey and the Acts of Union

AV Dicey had argued that the Acts of Union had no greater legal status than the Dentists Act 1878, or indeed any other unimportant Act.[48] Moreover, as has been seen, Dicey viewed the Acts of Unions as being ordinary Acts of Parliament by which – in the case of the Union with Scotland – the English and Scottish Parliaments 'abolished' themselves, to be reconstituted as the Parliament of Great Britain, and in the case of the Act of Union with Ireland, were reconstituted as the Parliament of the United Kingdom.

Alternative interpretations of the Acts of Union

The power of parliament to 'abolish itself' and be reconstituted as a 'new parliament' is one of the principal matters to which opponents to Diceyan theory address their arguments. Professor JDB Mitchell (1963), for example, questions Dicey's insistence on the equal legal status of Acts of Parliament, distinguishing between rules which create and represent the foundation of the state, and other derivative rules of law: '... the one set of rules creates or is the legal foundation of the state, the other is built upon that foundation.'

The Acts of Union of Scotland and England creating the unified Parliament of Great Britain represents a 'fresh starting point'. In Mitchell's view, the Acts of Union, being antecedent to the Parliament of Great Britain, imposed valid legal limitations on its powers. Conceding that many legislative changes have been made to the provisions of the Acts of Union, Mitchell nevertheless argues that the provisions, at least in relation to the Church of Scotland and the Court of Session, are essential limitations on parliament's powers.

Professor Neil MacCormick also challenges Diceyan orthodoxy.[49] In MacCormick's view, the Acts of Union amounted to a rudimentary written constitution. Adopting Kelsenian terminology, the Anglo-Scottish Treaty of 1706 and the Union with Ireland 1800 represent the 'historically first constitution' of Great Britain and the United Kingdom respectively, and accordingly have a very special status in constitutional law. Harry Calvert (1968) specifically rejects Dicey's view of the effects of the Acts of Union as 'untenable'. Calvert adopts

---

48 Dicey, 1885, p 145.
49 1978; see also 2001.

Professor RVF Heuston's arguments (1964a, pp 20–30) regarding the legal status of the Acts of Union and proceeds to argue that royal assent could be denied – in a departure from constitutional convention – to a Bill purporting to sever the union between Northern Ireland and the rest of the United Kingdom against the wishes of the people, the expression of which has been provided for by statute. Such a severance would, in Calvert's view, be unconstitutional. Accordingly, it would be for the Crown to defeat any attempt to act unconstitutionally:

> [A]t all events, it cannot readily be conceded that a constitutional monarch has no constitutional power to resist being implicated in unconstitutionality by his ministers. The bounds of the British constitution are very widely drawn. There is very little that a Prime Minister, supported by his Cabinet and a majority of the House of Commons, cannot do. But if there is nothing that he cannot do, there is no constitution at all. [1968, p 32]

Manner and form and redefinition theories

Parliament, in the exercise of its sovereign power, may specify particular procedures which must be undertaken in order to enact legislation. It has been seen, for example, that the Northern Ireland Constitution (Amendment) Act 1973 provided that the six counties of Northern Ireland shall not cease to be part of the United Kingdom unless the proposed separation is approved by a majority of the electorate in a border poll (referendum). This may be interpreted to mean either that parliament has specified the procedure – or manner and form – for enacting laws, or that parliament has 'redefined' itself for the purposes of enacting laws, by including in the definition of parliament the electorate of Northern Ireland. Any provision relating solely to procedure but not affecting the composition of parliament may be termed a 'manner and form' provision; whereas when the actual composition of parliament is altered, the appropriate term is 'redefinition'. The Northern Ireland Constitution (Amendment) Act straddles both theories.

The essential question to be asked is whether such provisions, however labelled, are capable of binding a future parliament. If that were to be the case – and, as will be seen, there are supporters for that view – two possible conclusions would follow: first, that parliament has unlimited power – exercisable, as HLA Hart argues (see above, pp 155–56), only at one single point in time, forever after to limit the sovereignty of future parliaments; and, secondly, that future parliaments would be less than sovereign – a contradiction in terms, for it would not then be correct to speak of parliament having unlimited sovereignty.

A seminal case illustrating manner and form theory is that of *Attorney General for New South Wales v Trethowan* (1932). In 1929, the government of New South Wales, Australia, sought to prevent a subsequent government from abolishing the Legislative Council (the upper chamber). An Act of Parliament was passed, amending the Constitution Act 1902, providing that any Bill purporting to abolish the upper House must have the approval of both legislative chambers and of two-thirds of the members of each chamber. Further, there had to be popular electoral support for the abolition, to be determined in a referendum. In addition, to prevent a subsequent parliament ignoring the provisions of the 1929 Act, it was provided that any Bill attempting to repeal the 1929 Act must follow the same procedure: a device known as 'double entrenchment'. In 1930, following an election, the incoming government decided to abolish the upper chamber and to do so by ignoring the provisions of the 1929 Act. Members of the Legislative Council sought an injunction restraining the grant of royal assent to the Bill, and a declaration that such a grant of assent would be unlawful, being *ultra vires* the lower House. The High Court of Australia ruled that the provisions of the 1929 Act could not be avoided, and that royal assent could not be given to the Bill. The matter was referred to the Privy Council which affirmed the judgment of the High Court of Australia.

The constitutional reason underlying the court's rejection of the government's claim that the 1932 Bill could lawfully receive royal assent was that the parliament in New South Wales was a legislative body having subordinate and not supreme power. Such powers as the legislature enjoyed were derived from the sovereign United Kingdom Parliament under the Constitution Acts 1902–29 and the Colonial Laws Validity Act 1865. The Colonial Laws Validity Act 1865 represented a landmark in the clarification of powers between the sovereign United Kingdom Parliament and subordinate colonial legislatures. The Act gave statutory affirmation to the non-legal conventional rule that laws enacted in the colony which were contradictory to statute or the common law of the United Kingdom would not be held to be invalid by the courts of the United Kingdom. The Act further clarified the extent to which the colonial legislature had power to amend its own composition and procedure. Section 5 is the all-important provision for current purposes. It provides that:

> ... every representative legislature shall ... have and be deemed at all times to have had, full power to make laws respecting the constitution, power, and procedure of such legislature; provided that such laws shall have been passed in such manner and form as may from time to time be required by any Act of Parliament, letters patent, Order in Council, or colonial law, for the time being in force in the said colony.

It is this section which dictated the decision in *Attorney General for New South Wales v Trethowan* (1932). The government of New South Wales was not free to introduce the 1932 Bill and attempt to enact it other than in conformity with the requirements of section 5. Section 5 required that the legislature complied with the 'manner and form' provisions in force. The specific 'manner and form' provisions were those laid down in the 1929 Constitution Act, and these requirements could not merely be ignored by the subordinate legislature.[50] In the High Court of Australia in the *Trethowan* case, Rich J denied the proposition that the New South Wales Parliament had unlimited sovereign power.

A similar constitutional arrangement can be seen demonstrated by the South African case of *Harris v The Minister of the Interior* (1952), which tested the validity of the Separate Representation of Voters Act 1951. The South Africa Act 1909, an Act of the United Kingdom Parliament, established the constitution of South Africa. Section 152 of the South Africa Act provided that no repeal or alteration of section 35 (relating to the qualification of Cape coloured voters) should be valid

---

50   The Australia Act 1986 (Commonwealth and UK), s 3(1), provides that the Colonial Laws Validity Act 1865 shall not apply 'to any law made after the commencement of this Act by the Parliament of a State'.

unless the Bill was passed by both Houses of Parliament sitting together, and the third reading was agreed to by not less than two-thirds of the members of each House.

In 1931, the United Kingdom Parliament passed the Statute of Westminster. The Statute of Westminster gave statutory effect to the constitutional convention which previously governed the relationship between the United Kingdom and its Dominions.[51] Section 2 of the Act provided that:

(1) The Colonial Laws Validity Act 1865 shall not apply to any law made after the commencement of this Act by the Parliament of a Dominion.

(2) No law and no provision of any law made after the commencement of this Act by the Parliament of a Dominion shall be void or inoperative on the ground that it is repugnant to the law of England, or to the provisions of any existing or future Act of Parliament of the United Kingdom, or to any order, rule or regulation made under any such Act, and the power of the Parliament of a Dominion shall include the power to repeal or amend any such Act, order, rule or regulation in so far as the same is part of the law of the Dominion.

Section 4 of the Act provided that:

An Act of the United Kingdom Parliament passed thereafter shall not extend, or be deemed to extend, to a Dominion as part of the law of that Dominion unless it expressly declared in the Act that that Dominion has requested, and consented, to its enactment.

In 1951, the South African Parliament purported to pass the Separate Representation of Voters Act, depriving voters in the Cape of the right to vote, disregarding the provisions of section 152 of the South Africa Act. It was argued before the Appellate Division of the Supreme Court of South Africa that the Statute of Westminster had conferred full legislative authority, or sovereignty, on the South African Parliament and that, accordingly, parliament was no longer bound by the South Africa Act 1909. The Supreme Court rejected that argument, stating that the South Africa Act was a constitutional Act whose provisions could not be indirectly amended by the Statute of Westminster. The Court held that the Statute of Westminster was not intended to alter the South Africa Act, but rather to confer additional powers on the legislature. Cantilevres CJ drew a distinction between a truly sovereign legislative body, such as the United Kingdom Parliament, and a legislative body which was less than sovereign: '... a state can be unquestionably sovereign although it has no legislature which is completely sovereign.'

In *Bribery Commissioner v Ranasinghe* (1965), section 55 of the 1946 Constitution of Ceylon (now Sri Lanka) required that the appointment and dismissal of the holders of judicial office be vested in a Judicial Services Commission. Section 29(4) of the Constitution required that amendments to the Constitution required a certificate stating that the amendments had been passed by the requisite two-thirds majority. In 1954, a Bribery Act was passed (with the necessary certificate) giving to the Attorney General powers to investigate and prosecute allegations of bribery. In 1958, a Bribery Tribunal was established, headed by a Bribery Commissioner. No certificate was produced as required under section 29(4). The

---

51 Canada, South Africa, Australia, New Zealand and Eire (the Republic of Ireland).

central issue was whether or not the legislature was free to avoid provisions of the Constitution. The Supreme Court held that it could not: the written Constitution was the determining document and its provisions could not be avoided.

These cases demonstrate one fundamental principle: that legislative bodies do not necessarily enjoy full sovereign power, and that some form of 'higher law' may control their powers. In each of these cases, the powers of the legislatures of New South Wales, South Africa and Ceylon (as it then was) had been established under an Act of the sovereign United Kingdom Parliament. That being so, the legislative bodies had to comply with the constitutional laws in force, and failure to do so would give the courts the jurisdiction to declare a legislative act void.

No one may question the validity of an Act of Parliament

True it is, that what the Parliament doth, no authority on earth can undo.[52]

As has been seen, an Act will be accepted as valid by the courts provided that it has passed through the requisite legislative stages and received royal assent.[53] Regardless of the subject matter of the Act, it will be upheld by the judges.[54] In the time before the 1688 settlement, it was not uncommon for judges to proclaim that an Act of Parliament could be held to be invalid because it conflicted with some higher form of divine law.

In *Dr Bonham's Case* (1610), there is the often-cited *obiter dictum* of Coke CJ to the effect that:

When an Act of Parliament is against common right and reason, or repugnant, or impossible to be performed, the common law will control it, and adjudge such act to be void.

Such views, while appealing to the senses, were of doubtful validity when expressed and have no authority today. The opinion of Lord Reid expressed in *Pickin v British Railways Board* (1974) represents the correct contemporary judicial view on the authority of statute:

In earlier times many learned lawyers seem to have believed that an Act of Parliament could be disregarded in so far as it was contrary to the law of God or the law of nature or natural justice, but since the supremacy of Parliament was finally demonstrated by the revolution of 1688 any such idea has become obsolete.[55]

Non-legal constraints on parliament's powers

Political acceptability to the electorate represents the strongest external basis of restraint. All governments are accountable to the electorate, albeit in terms of a direct vote only periodically. But elections do not of themselves always provide the means of sanctioning governments, nor do they guarantee that government

---

52   Blackstone's *Commentaries on the Laws of England* (1765–69), Vol I.
53   See *The Prince's Case* (1606).
54   But see further below and Chapter 9, on the complexity arising by virtue of membership of the European Community.
55   The case of *Jackson v Attorney General* (2005) represents a recent challenge to the validity of a statute -- the Hunting Act 2004. The case is discussed in detail in Chapter 17.

invariably acts in accordance with the electorate's wishes. Still less can the electorate be regarded as exercising any power to enact law. Whilst the electorate may be correctly regarded as politically sovereign, and can, at the end of the day, oust a government which violates its trust, on the exercise of the franchise the electorate conditionally transfers sovereign legislative power to parliament. As Dicey puts it:

> The electors can in the long run always enforce their will. But the courts will take no notice of the will of the electors. The judges know nothing about any will of the people except in so far as that will is expressed by an Act of Parliament, and would never suffer the validity of a statute to be questioned on the ground of having been passed or being kept alive in opposition to the wishes of the electors. [1885, pp 73–74]

Whereas, therefore, the power of the electorate is great at the time of a general election, it is a more limited power during a government's term of office – most particularly where the government has a strong majority in parliament. It is the task of parliament as a whole, both Commons and Lords, to scrutinise government policy and legislative proposals, and a range of procedural devices exists which facilitate such inquiry. It is through parliament that the will or wishes of the electorate for the most part find expression. Parliament may be seen as the sounding board of the nation. As John Stuart Mill observed:

> Parliament ... [is] at once the nation's Committee of Grievances, and its Congress of Opinions: an arena in which not only the general opinion of the nation, but that of every section of it, and as far as possible of every eminent individual whom it contains, can produce itself in full light and challenge discussion; where every person in the country may count upon finding some body who speaks his mind, as well as or better than he could speak it himself – not to friends and partisans exclusively, but in the face of opponents, to be tested by adverse controversy; where those whose opinion is overruled, feel satisfied that it is heard, and set aside not by a mere act of will, but for what are thought superior reasons, and commend themselves as such to the representatives of the majority of the nation ... [1865, Chapter V, pp 99–100]

No government can afford to ignore parliament and, ultimately, a government can be brought down if its policies are such that it loses the confidence of the House as a whole. If parliament is truly the 'sounding board of the nation', parliament must reflect the political morality within society.[56]

A further political restraint imposed on governments relates to international relations. No state today exists in isolation from its neighbours. The United Kingdom, as with most states, is bound by numerous treaties under international law which impose restrictions on the freedom of government action. Across virtually every aspect of government, such restraints are visible: environmental protection, protection of human rights, the protection of children from abduction, the regulation of currency exchanges, agreements on trade and tariffs and so on. In addition to such treaties, the United Kingdom is bound in practical terms by membership of the European Union and the United Nations. In theoretical terms, therefore, parliament may remain free to enact laws violating any or all of

---

56 See Allan, 1985b; and Lee, 1985.

the United Kingdom's international obligations; in practice, it would not and could not.

ACADEMIC ARGUMENTS AGAINST
THE TRADITIONAL DOCTRINE OF SOVEREIGNTY

We have seen above that there are a number of sophisticated academic arguments concerning the traditional doctrine of sovereignty. In this brief section, the differing approaches are brought together for further consideration.

In *Bribery Commissioner v Ranasinghe* (1965), Lord Pearce had asserted that:

> The proposition which is not acceptable is that a legislature, once established, has some inherent power derived from the mere fact of establishment to make a valid law by the resolution of a bare majority which its own constituent instrument has said shall not be a valid law unless made by a different type of majority or by a different legislative process.

Geoffrey Marshall seizes upon this *dictum* and argues that Lord Pearce:

> ... seemed to imply equally that both non-sovereign and sovereign legislatures may be made subject to procedural rules entrenching parts of the law from simple majority repeal.

Sir Ivor Jennings has also questioned the orthodox Diceyan view. In *The Law and the Constitution*, Jennings distinguishes two situations:

> If a prince has supreme power, and continues to have supreme power, he can do anything, even to the extent of undoing the things which he has previously done. If he grants a constitution, binding himself not to make laws except with the consent of an elected legislature, he has power immediately afterwards to abolish the legislature without its consent and to continue legislating by his personal decree.
>
> But if the prince has not supreme power, but the rule is that the courts accept as law that which is in the proper legal form, the result is different. For when the prince enacts that henceforth no rule shall be law unless it is enacted by him with the consent of the legislature, the law has been altered, and the courts will not admit as law any rule which is not made in that form. Consequently a rule subsequently made by the prince alone abolishing the legislature is not law, for the legislature has not consented to it, and the rule has not been enacted according to the manner and form required by the law for the time being.
>
> The difference is this. In the one case, there is sovereignty. In the other, the courts have no concern with sovereignty, but only with the established law. 'Legal sovereignty' is merely a name indicating that the legislature has for the time being power to make laws of any kind in the manner required by law. That is, a rule expressed to be made by the Queen, 'with the advice and consent of the Lords spiritual and temporal, and Commons in this present Parliament assembled, and by the authority of the same', will be recognised by the courts, including a rule which alters this law itself. If this is so, the 'legal sovereign' may impose legal limitations upon itself, because its power to change the law includes the power to change the law affecting itself. [p 152]

Sir Ivor Jennings then illustrates his thesis by reference to *Attorney General for New South Wales v Trethowan* (1932), *Ndlwana v Hofmeyer* (1937) and *Harris v The*

Minister of the Interior (1952). Jennings concedes that the decisions do not necessarily 'determine the law as it applies in the United Kingdom', and leaps from that proposition to one which claims that Dicey 'failed to prove that that law made the King in Parliament a sovereign law making body' (1959b, p 156). Such a view is unconvincing. The constitutional justification for the decisions examined lay precisely in the fact that the legislatures of both New South Wales and South Africa had legislative powers conferred upon them by a fully sovereign superior sovereign body – the United Kingdom Parliament. Only once such complete sovereignty was conferred would the legislative fetters be removed. No such controlling device pertains to the Parliament of the United Kingdom itself.

Arguing from the proposition that parliament may redefine itself – as in the Parliament Act 1911[57] – and may alter its own composition – as in the Life Peerages Act 1958, Professor JDB Mitchell turns to 'the purported self-limitations of Parliament' (1968, p 78). On section 4 of the Statute of Westminster, Mitchell argues that there are two possible interpretations when looked at from the point of view of the United Kingdom judges. The first is that section 4 amounts to a rule of construction directed to the courts, which does not raise the problem of limitation on parliament. If, however, section 4 is understood to mean that parliament has forfeited its legislative capacity – by conferring that capacity on the recipient legislature – then there 'is quite clearly a purported limitation of the United Kingdom Parliament' (p 79). Parliament has redefined itself in a manner which excludes its power to legislate for the Dominion.

Mitchell cites in support of the argument the *dictum* of Lord Radcliffe in *Ibralebbe v The Queen* (1964) in which Lord Radcliffe argues that while the United Kingdom Parliament has the legal power to legislate for Ceylon (as it then was), to use such power would be 'wholly inconsistent' with the powers of legislation conferred on the legislature of Ceylon.

Further authorities could be offered in support of this view. As seen above, in *British Coal Corporation v The King* (1935), Lord Sankey LC said, in relation to section 4, that:

> ... indeed, the Imperial Parliament could, as a matter of abstract law, repeal or disregard section 4 of the statute. But that is theory and has no relation to realities. [p 20]

Further, in *Ndlwana v Hofmeyer* (1937), Lord Denning asserted that 'freedom once given cannot be revoked'. How should such claims be evaluated? First, as Dicey made clear, the United Kingdom Parliament – in the exercise of its sovereign power – clearly has the power to abolish itself, or to surrender its sovereignty in favour of another legislature, as in grants of independence. In political terms, it is, of course, unthinkable that parliament would attempt to revoke such independence. The more troublesome question is whether parliament retains the capacity to revoke such grants of freedom in legal terms. On this, Dicey was very clear:

---

57 The Parliament Act 1911 reduced the powers of the House of Lords with respect to legislation. See Chapter 17.

'Limited sovereignty', in short, is, in the case of a Parliamentary as of every other sovereign, a contradiction in terms. [1885, p 68]

Professor RVF Heuston has put forward a 'new view' of sovereignty. This view is summarised as follows:

(a) sovereignty is a legal concept: the rules which identify the sovereign and prescribe its composition and functions are logically prior to it;

(b) there is a distinction between rules which govern, on the one hand, (i) the composition and (ii) the procedure, and, on the other hand, (iii) the area of power, of a sovereign legislature;

(c) the courts have jurisdiction to question the validity of an alleged Act of Parliament on grounds b(i) and b(ii), but not on ground b(iii); and

(d) this jurisdiction is exercisable either before or after the royal assent has been signified – in the former case by way of injunction, in the latter by way of declaratory judgment.[58]

To what extent is it correct to state that the judiciary may 'question the validity of an alleged Act of Parliament' on the grounds of the composition and the procedure adopted within parliament? Clearly, as demonstrated by *Attorney General for New South Wales v Trethowan* (1932) and other comparable cases, under certain circumstances, it is within the jurisdiction of the courts to question whether or not an Act is valid. Those circumstances usually arise within jurisdictions having subordinate rather than supreme legislatures.

In this regard, it may be said that the judges are protecting the sovereignty of the United Kingdom Parliament by keeping subordinate legislatures within the powers conferred. In the United Kingdom, however, parliament is distinguishable by the absence of any such controlling powers. The orthodox position is that expressed in *British Railways Board v Pickin* (1974), where the House of Lords, affirming its earlier decision,[59] endorsed the 'enrolled Bill rule'. Thus, once the Bill has proceeded through parliament, either under the normal legislative process or under the Parliament Acts 1911 and 1949, and received royal assent, the Bill becomes a validly enacted Act of Parliament and will not be impugned by the courts. The courts have jurisdiction to determine what is an Act of Parliament. As has been seen earlier, the courts have held, by way of illustration, that mere resolutions of the House of Commons are incapable of having legal effect in the same manner as an Act: *Stockdale v Hansard* (1839) and *Bowles v Bank of England* (1913) are clear authorities for that view.

The central distinguishing feature between the jurisdictions concerned in the 'manner and form' cases and the United Kingdom lies in the existence of a higher legislative authority. In each case, it was the United Kingdom Parliament which defined and limited the powers of a subordinate legislative body. Only once a parliament enjoys full sovereignty can it be free of such constraints. The United Kingdom Parliament, by contrast, is 'uncontrolled': there exists no higher source of legal authority than parliament itself. For this reason, to draw an analogy

---

58 Heuston, 1964a, Chapter I. See also Munro, 1999, Chapter 4. Professor Heuston is supported in his approach by Jennings, 1959b, Chapter 4, Appendix III; Cowen, 1951; Marshall, 1957, Chapters 2–4.

59 *Edinburgh and Dalkeith Railway Co v Wauchope* (1842).

between the legislatures of New South Wales or South Africa and the United Kingdom misses the vital dimension of unlimited power which is enjoyed by the United Kingdom Parliament.

The last words on the manner and form arguments shall be left to Professors Wade (1989) and Munro (1999). Professor Wade summarises his views on manner and form theorists as follows:

> But, in the end, what is the substance of their argument? It is simply their prediction, made with varying degrees of dogmatism, that the judges will, or should, enforce restrictions about manner and form and abandon their clear and settled rule that the traditional manner and form is what counts. But if it is vain for Parliament to command the judges to transfer their allegiance to some new system of legislation if the judges are resolved to remain loyal to the old one, it is still more vain for professors to assert that they should. The judicial loyalty is the foundation of the legal system and, at the same time, a political fact.

Professor Munro finds the arguments as to manner and form equally unconvincing, stating that 'the cases cited by the "manner and form" school do not, in the end, seem very helpful'.

PARLIAMENTARY SOVEREIGNTY AND THE EUROPEAN UNION AND COMMUNITY

In Chapters 8 and 9, the aims, organisation and law making power of the institutions of the European Union are considered, and the relationship between the law of the United Kingdom and European law will become clearer after those chapters have been studied. Nonetheless, it is necessary to consider here, in outline, the impact of membership of the European Union on the doctrine of parliamentary supremacy.

The United Kingdom became a member of the European Communities[60] in 1973. The original Communities – now termed European Community – have their own constitutional structure as defined in the Treaties. The Court of Justice of the Communities has, since the 1960s, asserted the supremacy of Community law over the laws of any Member State.[61] As will be seen later, the Court of Justice has adopted the view that, by becoming signatories to the Treaties, Member States have limited their own legislative competence in Community matters, conferring the supreme power to legislate on these matters on the law making institutions of the Community. Note that, since the European Union was established in 1992, the European Community is but a part, albeit the most significant part, of the European Union.

The laws of the Community – the Treaties, laws enacted by the Commission, Council of Ministers and the European Parliament together with the judicial decisions of the European Court – are binding on all Member States. In the United

---

60 European Economic Community, European Coal and Steel Community, European Community for Atomic Energy.
61 See the early cases of *Costa v ENEL* (1964); *Van Gend en Loos* (1963); *Simmenthal* (1977); *Internationale Handelsgesellschaft* (1972).

Kingdom, the acceptance of Community law is under the European Communities Act 1972 – an Act of the United Kingdom Parliament. Accordingly, all Community law derives its force and authority under this Act, which, as with any Act, has no special legal status within the constitution. However, membership of the Community raises some unique questions for the sovereignty of parliament.

The principal issue for consideration is the attitude of the judges – both domestic and Community – towards Community law. It is clear that, from the perspective of the European Court, Community law prevails over domestic law, and that domestic legislatures have no power to enact binding legislation contrary to the requirements of Community law. From the domestic perspective, however, the issue is not so clear-cut. The issues which require explanation are:

(a) the extent to which the judges are prepared to accept and apply Community law;

(b) the manner in which, and extent to which, inadvertent or deliberate parliamentary Acts are reconciled with the requirements of Community law; and

(c) whether membership of the Community entails an irrevocable relinquishment of parliamentary supremacy.

The application of Community law

Section 2 of the European Communities Act 1972 provides that Community law shall have direct applicability in the United Kingdom:

(1) All such rights, powers, liabilities, obligations and restrictions from time to time created or arising by or under the Treaties, and all such remedies and procedures from time to time provided for by or under the Treaties, as in accordance with the Treaties are without further enactment to be given legal effect or used in the United Kingdom shall be recognised and available in law, and be enforced, allowed and followed accordingly; and the expression 'enforceable Community right' and similar expressions shall be read as referring to one to which this sub-section applies.

Section 2(4) provides for the primacy of Community law, without expressly stating that the law of the Community is supreme:

The provision that may be made under sub-section (2) above[62] includes, subject to Schedule 2 of this Act, any such provision (of any such extent) as might be made by Act of Parliament, and any enactment passed or to be passed, other than one contained in this part of this Act, shall be construed and have effect subject to the foregoing provisions of this section.

Accordingly, all the rights, powers, liabilities, obligations and restrictions provided for under section 2(1) are to be given effect by the courts, and section 2(4) operates as a rule of construction to the courts to interpret law in accordance with the requirements of Community law. The manner in which the courts have achieved the objectives expressed in the European Communities Act 1972 are considered in Chapters 8 and 9, as is the view of the European Court of Justice on the supremacy of Community law. However, it would be misleading to leave this

---

62 Which provides for implementation of Community obligations by secondary legislation.

chapter on the traditional Diceyan theory of sovereignty without giving some introductory overview of the challenge which European Community law has posed. The European Court of Justice (the ECJ) adopts as its guiding principle the supremacy of the law of the Community. In the ECJ's view, a new legal order has been founded, a sovereign legal order within its sphere of competence. The sovereignty of Community law must, according to the ECJ, be respected by Member States, because through accession to the European Community, Member States have 'surrendered' their sovereign power in relation to those matters now regulated by the Community and Union.

The ECJ has adopted several means by which to expand the applicability of Community law and to assert its supremacy. First, the Treaty of Rome, as amended, under Article 10, imposes a duty on all Member States to comply with Community law and not to impede the application of Community law. Secondly, Article 249 of the EC Treaty provides that regulations[63] made under the Treaty (in part) 'shall be binding in its entirety and directly applicable in all Member States'. This principle of 'direct effect' has been adapted and developed by the ECJ to ensure the harmonious application of Community law throughout the legal systems of all Member States. The doctrine of 'indirect effect' is also a concept developed and expanded by the ECJ, and, as will be seen, has far-reaching implications for the courts and legislatures of each Member State. Where provisions of Community law have direct or indirect effect, the individual citizen of that state has a right of redress against the Member State, or against bodies which the ECJ deems to be 'emanations of the state', and, under certain circumstances, the right to compensation from the state. Moreover, while the ECJ does not rule on the validity of domestic legislation, it does rule on the requirements of Community law as interpreted by the Court, and, once that interpretation is received by the domestic courts, that interpretation *must* be given effect – notwithstanding incompatible domestic law.

While it would be premature to reach firm judgment on the fate of conventional Diceyan theory before studying the structure, organisation and objectives of the European Community and Union, some tentative conclusions may be suggested. Without rehearsing the arguments set out above, there are two differing approaches which may be taken to this conundrum. First, it may be argued that unreconstructed Diceyan theory remains unimpaired, despite all appearances and arguments to the contrary, on the basis that the United Kingdom voluntarily acceded to the European Community, the force of Community law within domestic law deriving from the 1972 European Communities Act. That Act, as seen, is consistent with constitutional law and convention – not entrenched (nor could it be) – and remains, in legal theory, repealable. From this perspective, parliamentary sovereignty remains the fundamental rule of the common law, and the key to the source of sovereignty lies with the judges. While the judges continue to cling to the rationale that Community law is given effect – even to the point of setting aside legislation[64] – because of the rule of construction

---

63   A form of secondary legislation.
64   This issue being central to the *Factortame* cases, discussed in Chapter 9.

provided under section 2 of the European Communities Act 1972, judicial loyalty remains unaffected. The clearest evidence for this view is expressed by Lord Bridge in *R v Secretary of State for Transport ex parte Factortame (No 2)* (1991), when he states that:

> By virtue of section 2(4) of the Act of 1972, Part II of the [Merchant Shipping Act 1998] is to be construed and take effect subject to enforceable Community rights – this has precisely the same effect as if a section were incorporated in Part II of the Act 1988 ...

Moreover, it will be seen from the cases of *Macarthys v Smith* (1979) and *Garland v British Rail Engineering Ltd* (1983) that both the Court of Appeal and House of Lords, respectively, endorsed the view that, while effect must, in accordance with section 2(4) of the European Communities Act 1972, be given to Community law, if parliament chose expressly to legislate contrary to Community law, that intention would be given effect by the judges. No more so would this be clearer than if parliament, implausible though this hypothesis may seem, chose to repeal the 1972 Act.

Alternatively, it could possibly be argued, as HWR Wade has argued,[65] that, for the first time in constitutional history, parliament succeeded in 'entrenching' a provision (section 2(4) of the 1972 Act), so as to bind future parliaments. This position, Wade submits, is more than evolutionary: it represents more than a rule of construction to be applied by the courts, and is rather an illustration of the parliament of 1972 imposing 'a restriction upon the Parliament of 1988' (p 570). If this argument had substance, there would indeed have been a 'revolution' in the constitution. However, the argument does not convince in light of the *dicta* of the judges, exemplified by that of Lord Bridge cited above, which confirms the conventional allegiance of the judiciary to the United Kingdom Parliament. Moreover, successive cases raising questions on Community law have come before the Court of Appeal and House of Lords in which the courts have found the requisite interpretative mechanism to accommodate the requirements of Community law as interpreted by the Court of Justice. Judicial interpretative techniques are the essence of the common law, and the essence of the common law is its capacity to evolve in accordance with the socio-political and legal domain within which it resides. In this light, the insistence on the part of the domestic courts that section 2(4) of the European Communities Act 1972 is a rule of construction to be applied to future legislation is hardly 'revolutionary' but rather more a recognition of the requirements of the European legal order and the overriding force of Community law for which the 1972 Act provided. However, as discussed below, there is evidence that some judges are prepared to recognise that certain statutes – including the 1972 Act – have a 'special' constitutional status.

The preoccupation with parliamentary sovereignty is understandable given that sovereignty has conventionally, in the absence of a written constitution, represented the 'cornerstone' or foundation of the British constitution. Membership of the European Community and Union, and the insistence of the

---

65 See Wade, 1996, but see the counter-arguments put forward by Allan, 1997, responding to Wade's analysis.

European Court of Justice on the supremacy of Community law, inevitably challenges traditional understandings of that concept, and raises hitherto unforeseen questions. While traditional Diceyan theory can accommodate membership of the Community and Union, it can do so only by clearly demarcating, as did its author, the realms of the legal and political. Legal theory resides against the backcloth of the political. Political sovereignty, while the United Kingdom remains a member of the Community and Union, may (arguably) lie in the institutions and law making processes of the Community and Union, in which every Member State participates, and which is supported by the political will of the citizens of the Member States. That political sovereignty, while membership continues, has a profound impact on the extent to which the domestic legislature may legislate over areas within the ambit of the treaties establishing the Community and Union. Thus, as Dicey himself argued, back in the nineteenth century under fundamentally different socio-economic and political conditions, the extra-legal may *de facto* limit the exercise of sovereign power. This *de facto* limitation on *legal sovereignty* remains ultimately conditional on the political commitment of the United Kingdom government and people to continued membership of that unique legal order which it voluntarily joined in 1972.

Constitutional reform and parliamentary sovereignty

As noted above, the devolution of power to regional assemblies (in the case of Wales and Northern Ireland) and the Scottish Parliament and the Human Rights Act 1998, which 'incorporates' the European Convention on Human Rights into domestic law, both raise the issue of sovereignty. While full discussion of these matters is found in Chapters 12 and 19 respectively, it is useful here to consider the sovereignty issue.

Devolution

The Scotland Act, Government of Wales Act and Northern Ireland Act 1998 each establish a system of self-government, in differing degrees, for the nations of the United Kingdom other than England. In London, as a pilot project, a new layer of government has been introduced with the Greater London Authority and the office of Mayor of London. Since the powers devolved are the will of parliament, the continued existence of such power remains dependent upon parliament's will. This ultimate power to confer and rescind powers granted to subordinate bodies is nothing new: at a lower governmental level, there is the granting of limited autonomy, defined by Act of Parliament and controlled by the courts, whereby local authorities have long enjoyed a measure of self-governance. This statement, however, and the legal provisions which give it expression, disguise a fundamentally important factor in the devolution debate: the dependence of legal-theoretical sovereignty upon the political sovereignty of the people of the nations.

It is the devolution of legislative power to the Scottish Parliament which illustrates the complexity of the sovereignty issue most starkly. By contrast with Northern Ireland and Wales, Scotland retained a strong sense of national identity since the Union with England in 1707, has a memory of national independence and a distinctive identity expressed through its own legal system.

The Labour government, while enthusiastic about devolution to the regions, was also intent on preserving the United Kingdom and the sovereignty of the United Kingdom Parliament. This was expressed strongly in the government's White Paper, *Scotland's Parliament*:[66] '... the United Kingdom Parliament is and will remain sovereign in all matters.' Section 28(7) of the Scotland Act gives clear expression to this intention: '... this section does not affect the power of the Parliament of the United Kingdom to make laws for Scotland.'

However, while Westminster retains the right to legislate over 'reserved matters', which are adjudged to be of United Kingdom-wide concern rather than national concern, the legislative powers devolved are considerable. The theoretical stance that Westminster remains free to legislate for Scotland over such matters must be in doubt. While Northern Ireland enjoyed devolved power, the convention developed that Westminster would not legislate over areas devolved and, moreover, that domestic affairs of Northern Ireland would not even be debated at Westminster. Were the United Kingdom Parliament to attempt to legislate over Scottish domestic affairs which have been devolved to Edinburgh, against Scottish wishes, real conflict would arise – and no assertions of the sterile sovereignty of Westminster would quell political dissent from north of the border.

This adds up to considerable legislative and political autonomy for Scotland and its people. What, then, is left of 'the sovereignty of the United Kingdom Parliament' in conventional Diceyan terms? *Theoretically*, two aspects of sovereignty remain. The first is the ability – notwithstanding the political unreality – to legislate for Scotland contrary to Scottish wishes. The second is the power to abolish the Scottish Parliament and to reclaim the powers devolved. Given that the government chose first to seek the endorsement of the people for devolution before devolving power, the likelihood of either theoretical power being exercised, *without the support and consent of the people of Scotland*, is negligible. It will be recalled that, in *MacCormick v Lord Advocate* (1953), Lord Cooper questioned the notion that the Treaty of Union resulted in the adoption of the 'distinctively English principle [of sovereignty] which has no counterpart in Scottish constitutional law'. Under Scottish constitutional law, it has always been the case that it is the people, and not a parliament, which is sovereign: the Scottish people exercised their sovereignty in choosing to have their own parliament. Whether the future entails an independent Scotland outside the United Kingdom, or Scotland within some form of quasi-federal relationship with the rest of the United Kingdom, must be a matter for the political judgment of the Scottish people.

---

66   Cm 3648, para 42.

The use of referendums[67]

The use of referendums raises the question of whether or not parliament redefines itself to include the people – in a direct expression of their views – for the purpose of legislating. The referendum has been used in relation to constitutional matters in Northern Ireland in 1973 and 1998; in relation to devolution to Scotland and Wales in 1977 and 1997; in London in 1998 in relation to the establishment of a directly elected mayor and the re-establishment of a London-wide elected authority; and in the United Kingdom as a whole in 1975 in relation to the United Kingdom's continued membership of the European Communities. The Labour government first elected in 1997 is committed to the use of referendums in relation to constitutional reform. Accordingly, further referendums are planned in relation to devolution to English regions, and are expected to be used in relation to reform of the House of Lords and a single European currency. However, referendums, as conceived in the United Kingdom, do not affect parliament's legal sovereignty. While the opinion of the people may be regarded as morally binding on government, parliament's sovereignty is preserved through regarding the result of a referendum as not legally binding the government or parliament.

The Human Rights Act 1998

As with the devolution of power to the nations, the manner in which the government chose to 'incorporate' the European Convention on Human Rights into domestic law is based on the premise of ensuring that parliament retains its sovereignty over law making. Whereas under most constitutions which include fundamental guarantees protecting human rights, those rights are protected from encroachment by the legislature, and the legislature is thereby limited in what it may enact – and is subject to the rulings of a constitutional court – the Human Rights Act 1998 utilises a peculiarly British device which preserves parliament's theoretical sovereignty. The Act provides that judges in the higher courts may issue 'declarations of incompatibility' between statute and the Convention rights incorporated under the Act. Where such a declaration is made, the matter is then referred to the executive, which may choose whether and how to amend the law to bring it into line with Convention rights. Further, where proposals for legislation are introduced into parliament, the relevant minister must declare whether the Bill in question accords with Convention rights. If it does not, an explanation as to the necessity for the legislation must be given. While both of these measures undoubtedly improve the protection of rights and generate a more rights conscious society, they fall far short of making individual rights and freedoms immune from legislative change.

However, the traditional theory of sovereignty, as applied to the Human Rights Act 1998, disguises the importance of the constitutional change which the Act represents. All aspects of policy and practices of public and quasi-public bodies now fall for scrutiny in accordance with Convention requirements. The Human Rights Act has quickly become established at the heart of the legal

---

67   See Butler and Ranney, 1994; Marshall, 1997; Munro, 1997.

system, providing a yardstick against which all actions of government and other public bodies may be judged.

While the government adopted a constitutional mechanism which preserves parliament's sovereignty, and maintains the conventional (and subordinate) role of the judiciary, the working of the Act is more subtle than the restatement of sovereignty implies. The judges are under a duty to interpret legislation in a manner which gives effect to Convention requirements, save where such an interpretation is impossible. Here, there is a significant shift in the process of judicial reasoning which traditionally focuses on interpreting the 'latest will of parliament' as expressed in legislation. The requirement that ministers must state that legislative proposals are in compliance with Convention requirements, coupled with the directive to judges to interpret in line with Convention rights, gives rights a special constitutional and moral status. That the ultimate decision to amend the law in line with a declaration of incompatibility rests with the executive and parliament does not suggest a lessening in the importance of rights so much as an ingenious device by which to keep constitutional fundamentals – sovereignty and separation of powers – intact, rather than turning the constitution on its head by reversing the balance of power between judges and parliament. Nevertheless, the Act does give to judges an unprecedented scope for statutory interpretation and development of the common law in line with Convention rights.

The emergence of the 'constitutional statute'?

It has been seen above that – however significant the subject matter – no Act of Parliament has any formal special status. The effect of this is that no Act may be entrenched: there are no special mechanisms necessary for amendment or repeal of any Act; and that all Acts are subject to implied repeal. However, the courts have long recognised that the European Communities Act 1972, at least, has a special status and that the principle of implied repeal does not apply to the Act.[68]

The constitutional reform programme undertaken since 1997, and most particularly the Human Rights Act 1998, has revived the question whether implied repeal applies to all statutes, or whether some – because of their constitutional importance – may only be expressly repealed. Two cases illustrate this view: *R v Secretary of State for the Home Department ex parte Simms* (2000) and *Thoburn v Sunderland City Council* (2002).

The case of *ex parte Simms* concerned a prisoner's right (under Article 10 of the European Convention) to communicate with journalists with a view to challenging his conviction for a crime. On parliamentary supremacy and the status of the Human Rights Act, Lord Hoffmann was to state that:

> Parliamentary sovereignty means that Parliament can, if it chooses, legislate contrary to fundamental principles of human rights. The Human Rights Act 1998 will not detract from this power. The constraints upon its exercise by Parliament are ultimately political, not legal. But the principle of legality means that Parliament must squarely confront

---

68 See *Garland v British Rail Engineering Ltd* (1983); Lord Denning in *Macarthys Ltd v Smith* (1981).

what it is doing and accept the political cost. Fundamental rights cannot be overridden by general or ambiguous words ... In the absence of express language or necessary implication to the contrary, the courts therefore presume that even the most general words were intended to be subject to the basic rights of the individual. In this way the courts of the UK, through acknowledging the sovereignty of Parliament, apply principles of constitutionality little different from those which exist in countries where the power of the legislature is expressly limited by a constitutional document.

The case of *Thoburn v Sunderland City Council* (2002) concerned the Weights and Measures Act 1985 which authorised both metric and imperial measures for the purposes of trade, and subsequent regulations made under section 2(2) of the European Communities Act 1972, which prohibited dual use and gave priority to the metric system. It was argued that the regulations were inconsistent with the 1985 Act and that this later Act must be taken as having impliedly amended section 2(2) of the European Communities Act 1972. The court held that there was no inconsistency between the 1985 Act and the 1972 Act, so there was no need to discuss implied repeal. Laws LJ, however, chose to consider the issue:

We should recognise a hierarchy of Acts of Parliament: as it were 'ordinary' statutes and 'constitutional' statutes. The two categories must be distinguished on a principled basis. In my opinion a constitutional statute is one which (a) conditions the legal relationship between citizen and state in some general, overarching manner, or (b) enlarges or diminishes the scope of which we would now regard as fundamental constitutional rights. (a) and (b) are of necessity closely related: it is difficult to think of an instance of (a) that is not also an instance of (b). The special status of constitutional statutes follows the special status of constitutional rights. Examples are the Magna Carta, the Bill of Rights 1689, the Act of Union, the Reform Acts which distributed and enlarged the franchise, the Human Rights Act 1998, the Scotland Act 1998 and the Government of Wales Act 1998. The European Communities Act clearly belongs to this family ...

Ordinary statutes may be impliedly repealed. Constitutional statutes may not. For the repeal of a constitutional Act or the abrogation of a fundamental right to be effected by statutes, the court would apply this test: is it shown that the legislature's actual – not imputed, constructive or presumed – intention was to effect the repeal or abrogation? I think that this could only be met by express words in the later statute, or by words so specific that the inference of an actual determination to effect the result contended for was irresistible. The ordinary rule of implied repeal does not satisfy this test. Accordingly, it has no application to constitutional statutes.[69]

---

69   See Campbell and Young, 2002.

PART III

THE EUROPEAN COMMUNITY AND UNION

CHAPTER 8

STRUCTURES AND INSTITUTIONS[1]

A day will come when all the nations of this continent, without losing their distinct qualities or their glorious individuality, will fuse together in a higher unity and form the European brotherhood. A day will come when there will be no other battlefields than those of the mind – open marketplaces for ideas. A day will come when bullets and bombs will be replaced by votes.

Victor Hugo, address to Parliament, 1849

INTRODUCTION

The European Union – of which the European Community is the largest component – now comprises 25 countries with a population of 454 million people.[2] As will be seen below, the original three Communities arose from the desire to put the raw materials of war beyond the control of the nation state once and for all and to unite previously warring nations within a community which would foster not only peace and security but also economic growth and raised standards of living for all its peoples. The Union is based on the rule of law, the protection of individual human rights and a common European citizenship. Originally founded on the goal of achieving a common market for goods and services, the original Communities were based on four freedoms: freedom of movement of persons, goods, services and capital. For over half a century, the European project has fostered political and economic integration, while retaining respect for the individuality and identity of its Member States. Economically nowadays the Union represents a leading trading power – a position which could not be achieved by any of the Member States acting alone. A common currency – the Euro – was introduced in 1999.[3] The ambitions of the Union have extended far beyond the original objectives of a common market for goods and services and now include the aim of developing common foreign and security policies and extensive co-operation between the police and legal systems of the Member States.

To understand the origins of the Union, it is necessary to look back to 1945 and a Europe that had been devastated by war: economically, politically and socially. In the desire to attain some form of harmony in order to guarantee peace and to rebuild Europe, the movement towards the integration of European countries was started. The movement took several forms. In 1948, the Organisation for Economic Co-operation and Development (OECD) was established with financial aid from the United States of America in order to restructure the European

---

1   See, *inter alia*, Hartley, 1998; Mathijsen, 1999; Steiner, 1996, 1995; Craig and de Búrca, 2002; Weatherill and Beaumont, 1999; Shaw, 2000.
2   Enlargement of the Union from 15 to 25 Member States was agreed at the Copenhagen Summit Meeting in 2002. In 2007 Bulgaria and Romania are due to join the Union. Negotiations regarding the accession of Turkey are ongoing.
3   By January 2004, 12 of the then 15 Member States had introduced the Euro.

economies. In 1949, the North Atlantic Treaty Organisation (NATO) was formed as a military alliance between the United States, Canada and Europe.

In 1949, the Council of Europe was established, out of which the European Convention on Human Rights was born. In 1950, under the leadership of the French Foreign Minister, Robert Schuman, a plan was devised whereby the raw materials of war – coal and steel – would be placed under the control of a supra-national organisation and, thus, the European Coal and Steel Community (ECSC) was established under the Treaty of Paris, signed in 1951. The original Member States were Germany, France, Belgium, Italy, Luxembourg and the Netherlands. Initiatives were being introduced to provide supra-national regulation of the non-military use of atomic energy. At the same time, the move towards greater economic co-operation and the creation of a European trading area was underway. The results of these developments took the form of the Treaties of Rome signed in 1957, establishing the European Economic Community (EEC) and the European Atomic Energy Community (Euratom).

The EEC had the broadest aims of the three communities, seeking to create a European common market and close co-operation between Member States. The common market is based on four basic freedoms: persons, goods, capital and services.

The law relating to the European Community is now a wide ranging subject. European Community law intrudes upon, and affects, an ever increasing volume of domestic law and now represents an important source of law in the United Kingdom. The original Treaties establishing the three European Communities have been much amended. Moreover, in 1992, the Treaty on European Union was signed by the heads of the governments of Member States. The 1992 Treaty (in force November 1993) brought into being the European Union, the aims of which go far beyond the original objectives of the European Economic Community and seek to provide the further integration of the laws and policies of Member States.[4] The 1992 Treaty also extended the competence of the institutions of the Community. The Treaty of Amsterdam 1997 amended the EC Treaty and the Treaty on European Union 1992 and represented:

> ... a new stage in the process of European integration undertaken with the establishment of the European Communities. [Preamble]

The Treaty of Amsterdam 1997 confirmed the Union's 'attachment to the principles of liberty, democracy and respect for human rights and fundamental freedoms and of the rule of law'.[5] The political objectives of the Union are extensive, seeking to achieve European economic and monetary union, the promotion of economic and social progress, 'taking into account the principle of sustainable development and within the context of the accomplishment of the

---

4   Article 47 of the Treaty of European Union provides that nothing in that Treaty shall affect the EC Treaty. See *Re Framework Decision on Protection of the Environment Commission v Council* (2005).

5   Note that the Treaty of Amsterdam revises all the Articles of the EC Treaty, and those of the TEU 1992. For the sake of clarity, only the new Treaty provisions are referred to in the text, except in relation to case law relating to EC Treaty Articles before revision of the Treaty, where the old numbers are cited and the new Article numbers are shown in brackets.

internal market and of reinforced cohesion and environmental protection', common defence and foreign policy,[6] and the complete elimination of border controls within the Union.[7]

The current membership of the Union, with dates of accession, is as follows: Austria (1995), Belgium (1957), Denmark (1972), Finland (1995), France (1957), Germany (1957), Greece (1981), Ireland (1972), Italy (1957), Luxembourg (1957), Netherlands (1957), Portugal (1985), Spain (1985), Sweden (1995), United Kingdom (1973). Further expansion of the Union took place in 2004 when the following states became members: Cyprus, the Czech Republic, Estonia, Hungary, Latvia, Lithuania, Malta, Poland, Slovakia, and Slovenia.[8]

EVOLUTION OF THE UNION

The Treaty establishing the ECSC provided for four institutions which today form the nucleus of the institutional framework of the Community/Union: the Commission, being the executive body serving the interests of the Community; the Council, being the executive representing the interests of Member States; the Assembly (a non-elected parliament),[9] and the European Court of Justice (ECJ). On the introduction of Euratom and the EEC, separate Commissions and Councils were established, all three Communities sharing the Assembly and the Court.

Having established three Treaties with different organs and differing powers, the next logical step was to merge the institutions. This merger came about in 1965 (coming into force in 1967), under a Treaty establishing a single Council and single Commission of the European Community: the Merger Treaty. From 1957 until 1987, the EEC Treaty remained unchanged, although membership of the Community expanded from the original six Members to 12.[10]

In 1986, the Single European Act (SEA) was passed.[11] This Act – a European Treaty – provided a timetable for realising the objectives of the original Treaties – namely the free movement of capital, goods, persons and services – by 31 December 1992. In addition, the SEA increased the powers of the European Parliament. The SEA also changed the voting procedure to be adopted in many areas of decision making in Europe. It did this by weakening the requirement of unanimous voting for decisions made by the Council of Ministers and increasing the extent to which the 'qualified majority voting system' would apply. By doing this, the SEA provided that individual Member States could be outvoted in decision making, thus making Europe stronger and the power of the individual Member States to block European legislation weaker.[12] Furthermore, the SEA

---

6   TEU 1997, Article 11.
7   TEU 1997, Article 2.
8   See the European Union (Accessions) Act 2003.
9   Note that the Assembly is now known as the Parliament. It became directly elected in 1979.
10   The United Kingdom, Ireland and Denmark joined in 1973, Greece in 1981, Spain and Portugal in 1986.
11   Given domestic effect under the European Communities (Amendment) Act 1986.
12   See EC Treaty, Article 205.

increased the competence of the Community institutions, including new areas such as the environment and regional development policy,[13] consolidated the legal basis of the European Monetary System,[14] and took steps towards greater political co-operation and foreign policy making.

The Treaty on European Union 1992 (Maastricht)

In December 1991, a new agreement was reached by Heads of Government in Maastricht which significantly expanded the aims and objectives of the Community and marked the creation of the European Union. This agreement resulted in the Treaty on European Union (TEU) – the Maastricht Treaty – which was signed in February 1992. Because of difficulties with ratification,[15] it was to be November 1993 before the Treaty – and the Union it created – became operative.

The Treaty represented a compromise between the federalists (or 'integrationists') and the anti-federalists (or 'inter-governmentalists'). It needs to be understood that, in the development of the Union, there has been exhibited a constant tension between those Member States who see the movement towards almost total political and economic union, whereby the Union would take on the characteristics of a federal state, and those Member States (particularly the United Kingdom) who have reservations about greater fusion in Europe and wish to retain a higher degree of autonomy from Europe than the federalists would wish to see. These Member States, the anti-federalists or inter-governmentalists, accordingly resist the drive towards federalism, preferring development to proceed along more piecemeal lines and to be pursued through inter-governmental agreement rather than movements from the centre of the Union.

As a result of these tensions, rather than drafting a treaty to supplement the existing Treaties and to provide a coherent working 'constitution' for Europe, based on the principle of a more federalist Union, the 1992 Treaty has produced a structure in which the Union was 'founded on the European Community, supplemented by the policies and forms of co-operation'[16] laid down by the TEU. The TEU also provided a framework for co-operation on future developments. The areas concerned were common foreign and security policy and justice and home affairs. There were now three 'pillars' which represent the structure of the Union. The first pillar amended the EEC Treaty (and renamed it the EC Treaty). The second pillar introduced and regulated common foreign and security policy. The third pillar concerned police and judicial co-operation in criminal matters. The Maastricht Treaty involved economic and monetary union as a central process towards further European integration. Jacques Delors, former President of the Commission, envisaged economic and monetary union as the 'left boot and

---

13   See Krämer, 1992; Scott, 1995, 1998.
14   In *de facto* operation since 1979.
15   See *R v Secretary of State for Foreign and Commonwealth Affairs ex parte Rees-Mogg* (1994) and, further, Chapter 6.
16   TEU 1997, Article 1; see Curtin, 1993 for a critical account.

right boot for Europe to wear in its advance towards the ever closer union of the peoples of Europe'.[17]

The Maastricht Treaty also introduced two new Community institutions. The European Central Bank was given law making and other powers[18] and plays a pivotal role in economic and monetary union. The Court of Auditors, having responsibility for scrutinising Community administration, became the fifth institution of the EC, its members having a six year renewable term of office and being under the same requirements of independence from governments as the Commission (Article 246 of the EC Treaty). The European Central Bank is under a duty to 'translate the objective [of economic and monetary union] into monetary targets and to work towards their achievement'. The euro came into existence as a currency in 1999. Notes and coins came into circulation in January 2002. The United Kingdom, while meeting the convergence criteria for joining, opted out of this scheme,[19] but remains free to opt in in the future.

The Treaty of Amsterdam[20]

While the 1992 Maastricht Treaty established the Union and the principles on which it is based, many matters remained unresolved and for future determination. The Treaty of Amsterdam – which resulted from an Inter-governmental Conference – marked significant changes in respect of four principal areas: freedom, security and justice; the Union and the citizen; common foreign and security policy; and the Union's institutions.

The Treaty of Amsterdam introduced significant alterations to the three pillars, in addition to making a number of other important changes which are discussed below. In relation to the structure of the Union, the 1997 Treaty transferred aspects of free movement of persons, asylum and immigration out of the third pillar and into the European Community.

The difficulties experienced in accommodating differing perceptions concerning the Union, and incorporation into domestic systems of all Union and Community measures, led to the adoption of flexibility, under the guise of 'closer co-operation'. Difficulties over the social protocol, European monetary union, border controls and common defence policy represent some of the areas over which a lack of unity exists. The Treaty of Amsterdam formalised the concept by inserting a general flexibility clause into the common provisions of the TEU and also made provision for Member States to avail themselves of Community institutions and procedures, in order to establish closer co-operation between

---

17 Delors Report: *Report on Economic and Monetary Union in the Community* (1989) cited by Dunnett, 'Legal and institutional issues affecting economic and monetary union', in O'Keefe and Twomey, 1994, Chapter 9.

18 EC Treaty, Articles 105–09; Article 237; Article 230; Articles 232–34; Article 288; Protocol 3. Protocol annexed to the EC Treaty on certain provisions relating to the United Kingdom of Great Britain and Northern Ireland, 1997.

19 Protocol annexed to the EC Treaty on certain provisions relating to the United Kingdom of Great Britain and Northern Ireland, 1997, para 1. Denmark and Sweden also remain outside the 'Euro-zone'.

20 See *European Union Consolidated Treaties*, 1997, Luxembourg: Office for Official Publications of the European Communities; Petite, 1998; Editorial (CML Rev), 1997.

themselves, subsequent to authorisation by the Council and under the preconditions laid down in Article 43.

Fundamental rights and freedoms

The Maastricht Treaty had reaffirmed the commitment of the Union to fundamental rights and freedoms as secured under the European Convention on Human Rights. In order further to advance the protection of rights, the Treaty of Amsterdam introduced three new elements. First, the Treaty confirmed that the ECJ has the power to review respect for fundamental rights by the Community institutions. In relation to the European Convention, to which all Member States of the Union, but not the Union itself are signatories, the Treaty provides that Community law is subject to the European Convention. Limited judicial review is also available in respect of the third pillar. In relation to matters pertaining to foreign and security policy, however, judicial review does not lie, this issue having proved too contentious at the Inter-Governmental Conference. In addition to affirming respect for fundamental rights and freedoms, the Treaty of Amsterdam introduced a system of penalties for Member States that fail to respect rights (see below).

The Court of Justice has been emphasising the need to protect rights and freedoms which are common to Member States since the 1960s, and no measure will have the force of law unless it is compatible with the fundamental rights recognised and protected by Member States' constitutions. Among the many freedoms and rights recognised are equal treatment, freedom of trade, human dignity, freedom of association, non-discrimination, freedom of religion, property, freedom of profession, entitlement to fair trial, freedom of competition, respect for freedom of expression and publication, family life and the inviolability of residence. These have all been recognised by the Court of Justice in its case law and many are reflected in the four 'fundamental freedoms' on which the EC is built – free movement of persons, goods, services and establishment.

In 2000 a Charter of Fundamental Rights for the Union was drafted. The EU Charter is based on 'the indivisible, universal values of human dignity, freedom, equality and solidarity' and is divided into seven 'chapters' entitled Dignity, Freedoms, Equality, Solidarity, Citizens' rights, Justice, and General provisions. The Charter was an integral part of the EU Constitutional Treaty which failed to be ratified in 2005 by France and the Netherlands.

Asylum, immigration and law enforcement

Under the 1992 Maastricht Treaty, Justice and Home Affairs represented the third pillar, and were, accordingly, to be regulated under the inter-governmental decision making process, rather than under Community law. However, the 1997 Treaty significantly amended the third pillar, transferring many powers from the Union to the European Community.[21] The transfer meant that this area is regulated under Community law by way of regulations or directives. The ECJ has

---

21   See Title IV of the EC Treaty.

jurisdiction, albeit limited, to review the decisions of domestic courts of last instance, in relation to these matters.[22] Furthermore, the Commission was given the sole right of initiative in respect of such issues, with the exception of matters relating to the abolition of controls at internal borders.

The Schengen Agreement, which provided for the abolition of border controls between the Union and participative Member States, was also formally incorporated into Community law via a protocol annexed to the Treaty of Amsterdam. Special provisions relate to Denmark, Ireland and the United Kingdom. All three countries formally derogated from these measures, because of their special geographical boundaries. Iceland and Norway are associated with the provisions on the basis of their existing agreements with Schengen members, but are free to revoke all or part of the protocol. In relation to Title IV of the EC Treaty, on an area of freedom, security and justice, and on police and judicial co-operation in criminal matters, Denmark, Ireland and the United Kingdom have negotiated special conditions. They may join in the future and may decide to participate in Union initiatives, thereby demonstrating the necessary flexibility which exists in relation to some areas of decision making.

The ECJ has examined the compatibility with Community law of national legislation governing identity checks on citizens when crossing frontiers. It has ruled that the right of freedom of movement is not unconditional, and that, until all Member States are required, through harmonisation of laws provisions, to abolish all controls at frontiers, they are entitled to require that the person seeking entry is able to establish that he or she has the nationality of the Member State.[23] Framework decisions, unlike regulations and directives, do not have direct effect.[24] However, the Court of Justice has ruled that the principle that national law must be interpreted in conformity with Community law is binding in relation to framework decisions.[25] Article 47 of the Treaty of European Union makes it clear that nothing in the TEU was to affect the EC Treaty. Accordingly, framework decisions, being provided for under the TEU, must not seek to regulate matters which fall within the EC Treaty. Should they do so they will be subject to annulment by the Court of Justice.[26]

The third pillar as amended: police and judicial co-operation

In respect of the third pillar, the Treaty of Amsterdam introduced a new form of law making. Formerly, aspects of Justice and Home Affairs were regulated under Conventions signed by the Member States, but rarely ratified, and hence were of limited value. Under the 1997 arrangements, a 'framework decision' is

---

22 On the changing nature of the jurisdiction of the Court in relation to freedom, security and justice and police and criminal matters, see Lyons, 'Variable geometry in the Court of Justice', in de Búrca and Scott, 2000.

23 Case C-378/97, Wijsenbeck J: Press Release of the ECJ No 69/99.

24 Treaty on European Union, Article 34(2)(b).

25 See *Criminal Proceedings against Pupino* (2005).

26 *Re Framework Decision on Protection of the Environment: Commission of the EC v Council of the EC* (2005).

introduced. Similar to a directive, a framework decision is aimed at harmonising laws between Member States, and is binding on the objective to be achieved, whilst leaving a measure of discretion in relation to the methods adopted to achieve the objective. However, unlike directives, the framework decision is stated not to have direct effect – see, further on this, Chapter 9.

The Union and the citizen

The Treaty of Amsterdam reaffirmed citizenship of the Union introduced by the Maastricht Treaty: 'Citizenship of the Union shall complement and not replace national citizenship.'[27] One of the principal concerns over the relationship between the citizen and the Union has been the perception that the Union is remote, lacking in sufficient democracy, and overly complex. The principle of subsidiarity, discussed below, is one means by which Member States may retain a measure of control over decision making in areas which otherwise would fall to Community control. In order to clarify the principle of subsidiarity, and the related concept of proportionality, the Treaty of Amsterdam included a protocol which has legal status. Accordingly, whereas subsidiarity was formerly considered to be a guiding, but non-legal, and unenforceable, principle, it now has legal force.[28]

The Treaty of Amsterdam also strives to promote openness and accessibility for the citizen.[29] A right of access to Council, Parliament and Commission documents has been provided. The right of access to information founded the basis for an application for annulment of a Commission decision in 1996 confirming its refusal to grant access to certain documents.[30] The Code of Conduct drawn up to give effect to the right of access states that 'the public will have the widest possible access to documents held by the Commission and the Council'. The factors which may be relied on for rejecting a request for access include refusal where disclosure would undermine the protection of the public interest.[31] Where exceptions are pleaded by an institution, those exceptions must be interpreted strictly. Further, reasons must be given for the refusal. Merely to state that the institution relies on an exception is inadequate.

Common foreign and security policy

The second pillar of the Union structure established under the Maastricht Treaty 1992 was that of Common Foreign and Security Policy, which represents one of the most politically difficult areas of the Union. Title V of the TEU regulates the matter. Article 13 of the TEU provided, in part, that:

---

27 EC Treaty, Article 17. See *Maria Martinez Sala v Freistaat Bayern* (1998).
28 See de Búrca, 1998.
29 See Dyrberg, 1999.
30 *Interpoc Import und Export GmbH v Commission* (1998).
31 Public security, international relations, monetary stability, court proceedings, inspections and investigations, the protection of the individual and of privacy, the protection of commercial and industrial secrecy, the protection of Community financial interests, and the protection of confidentiality, including the confidentiality of the institutions' proceedings.

1 The European Council shall define the principles of and general guidelines for the common foreign and security policy, including matters with defence implications.

2 The European Council shall decide on common strategies to be implemented by the Union in areas where the Member States have important interests in common.

Decisions are taken by the Council acting unanimously (Article 23(1) of the TEU). However, in light of political sensitivities, the Treaty of Amsterdam also made two concessions to Member States. First, Article 23 of the TEU provided for abstentions, which will not prohibit the Union reaching decisions by a qualified majority. Member States who abstain are under a duty not to impede the action. Secondly, a Member State may attempt to block decisions on the basis of important national interests. Where this occurs, the matter is referred to the European Council for unanimous decision.

The Treaty of Amsterdam also furthered the goal of a common foreign and security policy. The Secretary General of the Council acts as High Representative for foreign and security policy issues. The Secretary General is to continue to be appointed by governments. In relation to security and defence and enforcement capabilities, difficulties arise due to the differing memberships of the European Union, NATO and the Western European Union (WEU). The Amsterdam Treaty enables the Council to take decisions for the Union in relation to humanitarian and rescue tasks and peacekeeping tasks, and enables the Union to avail itself of the WEU to implement the political decisions relating to these tasks.

The Treaty of Nice 2001

The Nice Treaty, like the Amsterdam Treaty, amended the EC Treaty and TEU, reforming the institutions in preparation for the accession of new Member States. The principal changes were to the size and organisation of the Commission, revision of the weighted voting system in the Council, extending qualified majority voting in Council and the power of co-decision of the European Parliament. The Treaty also changed the distribution of seats in the Parliament after enlargement and made changes to the ECJ and the Court of First Instance. Also reformed were the 'enhanced co-operation' procedures which facilitate Member States' co-operation in different areas even though not all Member States wish to take part.[32]

TOWARDS A EUROPEAN CONSTITUTION?[33]

In 2004, membership of the European Union expanded from 15 Member States to 25 States. This major enlargement prompted a revision of the Treaties governing the Union with a view to adapting the institutions and procedures for the future. In 2002, a Convention was established with a view to examining questions raised

---

32 See Treaty of Nice amending the TEU, the Treaties establishing the European Communities and certain related Acts including the Protocols with Final Act and Declarations, Cm 5090, European Community Series No 1 (2001), London: HMSO, and the European Communities (Amendment) Act 2002.

33 See Cm 5897.

by the developing Union.[34] The outcome of the Convention was a draft Constitution of Europe which was designed to replace all the existing Treaties with a single text, thereby clarifying and rationalising the currently complex Treaties. To come into effect the Constitution Treaty had to be ratified by all member states according to their constitutional arrangements. In referendums held in France and Holland the people voted against the Constitution, thereby preventing it from coming into effect.[35]

THE UNITED KINGDOM AND EUROPE

The United Kingdom stood aloof from the early development of the Community, rejecting the call of Sir Winston Churchill in 1949 for a 'United States of Europe'.[36] Instead, Britain formed the European Free Trade Area (EFTA) together with Austria, Denmark, Norway, Portugal, Sweden and Switzerland. In part, EFTA was formed as a defensive action to fend off the potentially adverse effects of the free trading area established under the EEC.

By 1961, the Conservative government of Mr Harold Macmillan had decided to seek entry to the Community, an application which was initially blocked by France. It was not until 1972 that the Final Act was signed containing the instruments of accession of the United Kingdom along with Ireland, Denmark and Norway.[37]

THE EUROPEAN COMMUNITY

Aims and objectives

The original aims of the EEC (now EC) were set out in a Resolution of Foreign Ministers of the ECSC in June 1955 and found expression in Article 2 of the EC Treaty, which provides that:

> The Community shall have as its task, by establishing a common market and an economic and monetary union and by implementing the common policies or activities referred to in Articles 3 and 4, to promote throughout the Community a harmonious and balanced development of economic activities, a high level of employment and of social protection, equality between men and women, sustainable and non-inflationary growth, a high degree of competitiveness and convergence of economic performance, a high level of protection and improvement of the quality of the environment, the raising of the standard of living and quality of life, and economic and social cohesion and solidarity among Member States.

Article 3 of the EC Treaty now provides that the activities of the Community shall include:

---

34 The Convention was chaired by Valerie Giscard d'Estaing and comprised representatives of Member States and candidate countries, and representatives of the European Parliament, Commission and other EU institutions, totalling 105 members. In order to guide the Convention a Praesidium of 12 key persons was established.

35 See Shaw, 2005.

36 Speech at University of Zurich, 19 September 1946.

37 The people of Norway rejected EC membership in a referendum.

(a) the prohibition, as between Member States, of customs duties and quantitative restrictions on the import and export of goods, and of all other measures having equivalent effect;

(b) a common commercial policy;

(c) an internal market characterised by the abolition, as between Member States, of obstacles to the free movement of goods, persons, services and capital;

(d) measures concerning the entry and movement of persons in the internal market as provided for in Title IV;

(e) a common policy in the sphere of agriculture and fisheries;

(f) a common policy in the sphere of transport;

(g) a system ensuring that competition in the internal market is not distorted;

(h) the approximation of the laws of the Member States to the extent required for the functioning of the common market;

(i) the promotion of co-ordination between employment policies of the Member States with a view to enhancing their effectiveness by developing a co-ordinated strategy for employment;

(j) a policy in the social sphere comprising a European Social Fund;

(k) the strengthening of economic and social cohesion;

(l) a policy in the sphere of the environment;

(m) the strengthening of the competitiveness of Community industry;

(n) the promotion of research and technological development;

(o) encouragement for the establishment and development of trans-European networks;

(p) a contribution to the attainment of a high level of health protection;

(q) a contribution to education and training of quality and to the flowering of the cultures of the Member States;

(r) a policy in the sphere of development co-operation;

(s) the association of the overseas countries and territories in order to increase trade and promote jointly economic and social development;

(t) a contribution to the strengthening of consumer protection;

(u) measures in the spheres of energy, civil protection and tourism.

In all the above activities, the Community 'shall aim to eliminate inequalities, and to promote equality, between men and women' (Article 3(2) of the EC Treaty) and take into account the need for environmental protection.

A UNIQUE LEGAL ORDER

The European Community is the creation of the original EEC Treaty, as amended. Community law, however, is not international law as normally understood in the sense of merely establishing mutual obligations between contracting states. Community law involves not only mutual obligations between Member States but also the transfer of sovereign rights to the institutions of that system and the creation of rights and obligations for their citizens, 'who thereby became subjects of the Community' (Mathijsen, 1999). The Community is, therefore, a unique constitutional entity, having its own institutions and law making powers, capable of creating rights and duties within the legal systems of the Member States, and represents far more than a mere form of institutionalised inter-governmental co-operation, the success of which rests on the full approval of each Member State. The law making powers of the Community's institutions, as will be seen below, are far reaching. When duties are imposed on Member States, these may imply rights for individuals which may be enforced in the domestic courts and, in respect of the duties of Member States, also ultimately in the ECJ, the Community's judicial forum.

In constitutional terms, the European Union is not a 'state', neither is it a 'federation', rather it is a unique supranational organisation. When new Member States are admitted to the Union, they become automatically bound by the entire law of the Community – in European terminology, the *acquis communautaire*.[38] Under international law, when a state becomes a signatory to a treaty, it becomes bound by the provisions of that treaty, but not bound by any acts done under the treaty before that state's accession. It is different with the Union, and new Member States become automatically committed to the Treaties, all secondary legislation, judicial and non-judicial decisions made by the institutions of the Union, together with non-binding opinions and resolutions of institutions.

The major constitutional issues

From the constitutional law perspective, the issues which require scrutiny are:

(a) the nature of the European Union, the institutions and their law making powers;

(b) the nature and sources of Community law;

(c) the effect of membership of the Union on the constitution of the United Kingdom;

(d) the relationship between Community law and domestic law.

The allocation of functions between Community institutions and Member States

In any federal or quasi-federal state or organisation, the functions of the federal government and the regional governments must be allocated. As discussed in Chapter 1, the concept of federalism involves the allocation of powers which may reserve some powers to the exclusive competence of the federal government, some powers which will be concurrently held by the federal and regional governments, and some powers over which the regional government has exclusive competence. In the European Union, the manner in which powers are allocated and exercised is largely determined by the Treaty provisions.

The principle of subsidiarity[39]

Subsidiarity is a fundamental concept designed to achieve an appropriate balance between the institutions of the EU and Member States.

Discussion of the principle in the European Union context, even before its incorporation into the Maastricht Treaty, reveal that it is capable of no fewer than 30 different meanings. Designed to determine the appropriate level of action

---

38 Which, literally translated, means 'Community patrimony'. See TEU 1992, Articles 2 and 3.

39 See Emiliou, 1991, and 'Subsidiarity: panacea or fig leaf?', in O'Keefe and Twomey, 1994, Chapter 5; Toth, 1992.

across the whole spectrum of public activity, international (in the widest sense), Community, national, regional and local, it has been invoked in the Community context to assist in determining the exercise of Community powers. In this context, it has been described, variously, as 'the principle of necessity, or proportionality, of effectiveness, an elementary principle of good government, or simply a principle of good sense'. It has been interpreted as meaning that the Community should only act:

(a) where the objective cannot be achieved by regulation at national level;

(b) where the objective can be better, or more effectively, achieved by action at Community level (the 'efficiency by better results' criterion); or

(c) where the matter in question can be more effectively regulated at Community level (the 'administrative efficiency' criterion).[40]

Failure to formulate specific detailed rules regarding subsidiarity led the one time President of the ECJ (1984–88), the late Lord Mackenzie Stuart, in 1991 to argue that the Inter-Governmental Conference at Maastricht should be 'getting down to the detailed rules of detailed competence', rather than leaving subsidiarity as a 'hopelessly ill defined concept',[41] but his words were not heeded. Article 5 of the EC Treaty[42] provides:

The Community shall act within the limits of the powers conferred upon it by this Treaty and of the objectives assigned to it therein.

In areas which do not fall within its exclusive competence, the Community shall take action, in accordance with the principle of subsidiarity, only if and so far as the objectives of the proposed action cannot be sufficiently achieved by the Member States and can therefore, by reason of the scale or effects of the proposed action, be better achieved by the Community.

Any action by the Community shall not go beyond what is necessary to achieve the objectives of this Treaty [the proportionality requirement].

The closely related principles of subsidiarity and proportionality are thus both provided for under Article 5. The Protocol on the Application of the Principles of Subsidiarity and Proportionality restates the principles, listing guidelines to be followed in reaching decisions as to whether action should be taken at Community level or at national level. Now a legal concept, it will be for the ECJ to adjudicate on its scope and application. The Protocol also makes clear that subsidiarity is a concept which is dynamic and flexible, allowing decisions on the appropriate level at which action should be taken to develop on a case by case basis. The doctrine of proportionality is one which is largely alien to – until recently – English lawyers (see also Chapter 27), but one familiar to European lawyers and one utilised by the ECJ. Sir William Wade explains that the principle of proportionality 'ordains that administrative measures must not be more drastic than is necessary for attaining the desired result'.[43] The Protocol on the

---

40 Steiner, 'Subsidiarity under the Maastricht Treaty', and references therein, in O'Keefe and Twomey, 1994.

41 Mackenzie Stuart (Lord), 'Subsidiarity and the challenge of change 1991', in the Proceedings of the Jacques Delors Colloquium, cited in Steiner, fn 38.

42 Inserted by the TEU 1992.

43 Citing Schwarze, 1992, p 680; see also Boyron, 1992.

Application of Subsidiarity also clarifies the distinction between subsidiarity and proportionality.

The application of subsidiarity

Exclusive competence

As the text of Article 5 makes clear, where the Community has 'exclusive competence', the subsidiarity principle has no application. The Community has sole power of decision and therefore no question arises as to whether others share that power, or the extent to which they should be entitled to act. However, many issues remain unclear from the text of the Treaty. For example, there is no definition as to what areas fall within the Community's exclusive competence, and the Commission itself has accepted that there is 'no clear line of demarcation between exclusive and shared power'. On the other hand, it is generally accepted that common agricultural and commercial policies and aspects of common fisheries policies fall within the exclusive competence of the Union. Furthermore, the Commission argued that even where exclusive power exists, it does not mean that 'all responsibility for the activity in question is covered by exclusive competence. The text of the Treaty cannot be interpreted so broadly as to leave common sense out of account'.[44]

Concurrent powers

Where a Member State has a concurrent power, the power to act remains, so long as the Community has not exercised that power. However, if the Community takes action itself, the power of the Member State is pre-empted, and the power to act – once pre-empted – remains with the Community.[45] Where the Community has exclusive power, the Member State has no power to act unless the legislation in question contains a specific authorisation by the Community in favour of the Member States.[46] Secondly, the Court has ruled that, where the Community has exclusive competence to act but has not so acted and urgent action is needed, the Member States may act as 'trustees of the common interest'.[47] Only time, political practice and the jurisprudence of the ECJ will reveal which view is correct. Josephine Steiner provides a further argument for the need for subsidiarity, stating that the principle of subsidiarity is an essential safeguard to protect the interests of differing groups and regions within the Community, and that any transfer of power away from Member States to Europe requires justification:

> ... if competence is to be transferred to centralised authorities, the transfer must be justified. The burden is on the Community institutions to show that there is a real need for Community action, by reference to the scale or effects of the problem, and that the particular action proposed is appropriate and necessary to achieve specific Community goals. [Steiner, 1996, p 63]

---

44 Communication to the Council and Parliament outlining proposals for the Subsidiarity Principle Bulletin EC 10-1992, Pt 2.2.1, cited in *op cit*, Steiner, fn 34.
45 See Weatherill, 'Beyond pre-emption', in O'Keefe and Twomey, 1994.
46 *Donckerwolcke v Procureur de la Republique* (1976).
47 *Commission v United Kingdom* (1981).

Issues of subsidiarity will inevitably fall for the Court to consider. For example, if the Community legislates on a particular area, a Member State may wish to resist that legislation by invoking subsidiarity, and thus the Court will be obliged to make a decision. The power to do so has been criticised on the basis that subsidiarity is a political, rather than a legal concept.[48]

THE INSTITUTIONS OF THE COMMUNITY

The European Commission[49]

Originally called the High Authority, the Commission is centrally concerned with all aspects of Community decision making at all levels and on all fronts: the Commission is the very heart of the Community, exercising both powers of initiative and powers of enforcement. As envisaged by the authors of the original Treaties, the Commission, while acting independently of governments and in pursuit of the objectives of the Community, would help preserve the interests of individual Member States. The Commission was intended to be the engine which drives the Community forward.

Articles 211–19 of the EC Treaty established the powers of the Commission. Article 211 sets out the basic powers:

In order to ensure the proper functioning and development of the common market, the Commission shall:

(a) ensure that the provisions of this Treaty and the measures taken by the institutions pursuant thereto are applied;

(b) formulate recommendations or deliver opinions on matters dealt with in this Treaty, if it expressly so provides or if the Commission considers it necessary;

(c) have its own power of decision and participate in the shaping of measures taken by the Council and by the Assembly [Parliament] in the manner provided for in this Treaty;

(d) exercise the powers conferred on it by the Council for the implementation of the rules laid down by the latter.

The Commission accordingly has powers of initiative and powers of supervision and enforcement.

Commissioners are appointed by the governments of Member States in consultation with one another. The number of Commissioners may be altered by the Council, acting unanimously. Commissioners must be nationals of one of the Member States and no more than two may be nationals of the same Member State. With effect from May 2004 and the accession of the ten new countries, each Member State has one Commissioner. When the Union consists of 27 Member States, the number of Commissioners will be less than the number of Member States, being chosen on a rotation system to be devised, on the principle of equality, by the Council.[50] Commissioners are appointed for a renewable five year

---

48 Mackenzie Stuart (Lord), *The Independent*, 15 June 1992, cited by Emiliou, 1991, p 77.
49 EC Treaty, Articles 211–19.
50 Protocol on the Enlargement of the European Union, Treaty of Nice, Article 4.

term of office, and cannot be dismissed during their term of office by governments.[51] Commissioners remain in office until replaced, or compulsorily retired.[52] Decisions in the Commission are reached by majority voting.

Once appointed, Commissioners must act entirely independently of government: they are not representatives of government. Article 213(2) of the EC Treaty, as revised, provides, in part, that:

> The Members of the Commission shall, in the general interests of the Community, be completely independent in the performance of their duties.
>
> In the performance of these duties they shall neither seek nor take instructions from any government or from any other body. They shall refrain from any action incompatible with their duties. Each Member State undertakes to respect this principle and not to seek to influence the Members of the Commission in the performance of their tasks ...

The Commission is headed by a President, appointed from among the Commission in common agreement with Member States and subject to the approval of the European Parliament. The office is held for a renewable two year term. The Presidency is the most prestigious job in the EC, carrying with it the responsibility for the sense of direction and co-ordination of effort within the Community. The Commission may, under Article 217, appoint a Vice President or two Vice Presidents from among its number. The Treaty of Amsterdam has strengthened the role of the President in several respects. First, in the appointment of Commissioners by Member States, the President has a right to object to a nominee. Secondly, Article 219 of the EC Treaty provides that the Commission shall work under the political guidance of its President.

The European Parliament has the power, under Article 201 of the EC Treaty, to pass a motion of censure to remove the Commission *en bloc*. However, when, in 1999, allegations of waste and mismanagement in the Commission surfaced, Parliament failed to pass a motion of sanction. In the event, the entire Commission, including the President, resigned.

Organisationally, the Commission is divided into Directorates General, each headed by a Director responsible to the relevant Commissioner. Each Commissioner holds one or more portfolios, that is to say, special responsibility for some area of Community policy, and is assisted by a Cabinet of six.

The broad and ill defined power conferred under Article 211 of the EC Treaty and the role of the Commission can only be understood within the framework of the European Union as a whole. It is clear that it is the Commission which is charged with the duty to act in the interests of the objectives of the Community as expressed in the Treaties. It is the Commission which puts forward proposals for decision by the Council of the EU (see below), having negotiated widely with representatives of Member States' governments and with interest groups within

---

51 Commissioners can, however, have their reappointment blocked by a government, as occurred in 1989 when the Prime Minister felt that Lord Cockfield had been over-zealous in his support of the Community.

52 Article 216 provides that, if a Commissioner no longer fulfils the conditions required for the performance of his duties, or if he has been guilty of serious misconduct, the ECJ may, on an application of the Council or the Commission, compulsorily retire him.

the Community. The Council of the EU may, in some instances, request the Commission to draft proposals, and the European Parliament has always been given the right to request the Commission to submit a proposal for legislation. Where the Commission is under an obligation to submit legislative proposals within a certain time laid down in the Treaty, failure to act within that time will render the Commission liable to a challenge before the ECJ. When such proposals assume the force of law, it is again the Commission which is charged primarily with the task of law enforcement.

The Commission's broad powers of initiative should not be understood to mean that the Commission has total freedom of action. The working of the Community depends on a variety of factors, actors and forces. In the final analysis, the Community can only be effective in achieving the goals set out in the Treaties if its proposals can carry the support of the Member States. The effectiveness of Community law within the legal systems of all Member States is ultimately dependent upon the political acceptability of that law. It is for this reason that the role of the Commission is so important, for the Commission – having the sole power to formulate proposals for the implementation of Treaty objectives – is responsible for ensuring that proposals have the support of Member States before they are hardened into law. As originally envisaged by the drafters of the original Treaties, only a body acting with complete independence was competent to negotiate with Member States and formulate acceptable policies. From 2004, the Union comprises 25 states of vastly differing sizes and populations, and within these states there are regions with differing interests and needs. It is vital, therefore, that there is some guarantee that the interests of the smaller Member States, and regions in all Member States, are protected against the power of the larger states. Accordingly, in the process of formulating policies, one of the Commission's principal tasks is to reconcile the differing interests at stake and to make the resulting law acceptable to all.[53]

Where a Member State is in default of Treaty obligations, the Commission has the power to deal with the breach. Article 226 of the EC Treaty, as revised, specifies the procedure to be followed:

If the Commission considers that a Member State has failed to fulfil an obligation under this Treaty, it shall deliver a reasoned opinion on the matter after giving the state concerned the opportunity to submit its observations.

If the state concerned does not comply with the opinion within the period laid down by the Commission, the latter may bring the matter before the Court of Justice.

Most matters are settled at an early stage – infringements being due not to wilful disregard of the law, but rather arising from genuine differences of opinion as to the meaning of requirements, or from administrative delay. Where, however, a Member State fails to fulfil its Community obligations, the Commission will take the case to the ECJ. Where the Court rules that the Member State is in default of

---

53 Temple-Lang, J, 'The European Commission: safeguard for Member States', European Law Lecture (Queen Mary, University of London, 5 June 1995).

its obligations, the Court, at the request of the Commission, may impose a financial penalty on the Member State.[54]

The Council of the EU

Articles 202–10 of the EC Treaty apply here. The Council of the EU has legislative and executive powers and functions. It is the Council which defends the interests of Member States. The Council has no fixed membership and its composition varies depending upon the subject matter under discussion. Each Member State is represented in Council by a government minister.[55] Accordingly, when the subject on the agenda is agriculture, the Council will consist of the Ministers of Agriculture from all Member States; when the subject is transport, the membership will be made up of the respective Ministers of Transport. Article 202 of the EC Treaty, as revised, provides that the Council is to (a) ensure co-ordination of the general economic policies of the Member States; (b) have power to take decisions; and (c) confer on the Commission powers for implementation of rules which the Council lays down.

The Council is the most powerful political institution of the EC, and the Council has interpreted and developed its role in such a manner so as to increase its powers. As seen from Article 203, it is the Council which has power to take decisions, and this represents one of the law making powers in the Community.

When the Communities (now Community) were originally established, it was envisaged that the role of the Council would decline as Member States developed mutual trust, and that much of the running of the Communities would be in the hands of the Commission. It was also felt that governments would become less concerned about their own state's sovereignty and let the Communities grow in a supra-national way under the direction of the Commission. Neither of these two predictions has fully taken place, and the increase in the power of the Council has been at the expense of the power of the Commission.

The voting system for decision making[56]

Central to Community development is the voting system used in the Council. The Treaty provides for three basic methods by which the Council can reach a decision: unanimously, by qualified majority vote or by a simple majority vote. Unanimity is normally required where a new policy is to be initiated or the existing policy framework is to be developed or modified. Unanimity is also required when the Council wishes to amend a Commission proposal against the wishes of the Commission. While the Union and Community rests on consensus, and there is little point in adopting a procedure which will cause national parliaments' resentment or reluctance on the part of state authorities to

---

54 See *Report from the Commission on Monitoring the Appreciation of Community Law*, 21st Annual Report, 2003, Com (2004) 839.

55 EC Treaty, Article 203.

56 See Morner, 'The conflicts inherent in enlargement – is history catching up with the European Union?', in Butterworths, 1994.

implement decisions, a balance is needed between respecting the interests of the Member States while not impeding Community development.

Article 205 of the EC Treaty states that, unless otherwise provided in the Treaty, that is to say under specific articles, the Council shall act by majority vote. In some specific cases the Council is required to act by a qualified majority, for which purpose the votes of Member States are weighted, the largest states having a weighting of ten, the remaining, according to size, eight, five, four, three or two. Where the Council adopts a matter on a proposal from the Commission, 62 votes are required (Article 205). Where unanimity is required, the abstention of a Member State shall not prevent the Council adopting a matter (Article 205). The voting system was designed in order to minimise the circumstances in which one state could block Community progress. It became clear in the 1960s, however, that this was unworkable – most notably when France refused to co-operate in any decisions and caused a constitutional crisis.

The outcome of the crisis was an agreement contained in what is known as the *Luxembourg Accord* of 1966, which provided that:

> Where in the case of decisions which may be taken by majority vote on a proposal from the Commission, very important interests of one or more partners are at stake, the Members of the Council will endeavour, within a reasonable time, to reach solutions which can be adopted by all Members of the Council while respecting their mutual interests and those of the Community in accordance with Article 2 of the Treaty. [*Bulletin of the European Community* 3/66, p 5]

The French government insisted that where very important state interests are at stake, the discussion should continue until unanimous agreement is reached.

This *Accord* had no formal legal status. It was an informal agreement, and probably unlawful. However, the *Accord* profoundly affected decision making, and the French amendment has been interpreted to mean that any state has the right to exercise a veto on questions which affect its vital national interests, and it is for the states themselves to determine when such interests are at stake. However, this does not mean that whenever a Member State asserts that a matter is a 'matter of vital national interest' the Community will accept the statement. For example, in 1982, the United Kingdom was opposed to a decision on agricultural prices, and claimed that this was a matter of vital national interest; the Council, however, refused to accept the plea.[57] Under the Treaty of Amsterdam, however, the issue of important national interests has been resurrected and formalised in the EC Treaty in relation to the provisions for closer co-operation. As noted above, Article 11 of the EC Treaty provides that, in relation to authorisation by the Council for measures aimed at closer co-operation between Member States, where a Member State raises the objection of important national interests, the Council shall refer the matter to the European Council for unanimous decision. It has been noted that 'predictions of the demise of the Luxembourg Compromise were thus distinctly premature: it has been given a

---

57 See *The Times*, 19 May 1982.

new lease of life, no longer in the *demi-monde* of political deals but as part of the legal machinery of the EC Treaty'.[58]

The Treaty of Amsterdam made limited reforms to the voting system. The use of qualified majority voting is extended to most of the new Treaty provisions: those relating to incentives in employment and social matters, equal opportunities, social exclusion, public health, anti-fraud measures, openness and the outermost regions. Of the major existing provisions of the Treaty, the research framework programme is under qualified majority voting, and qualified majority voting may be used in relation to decisions under the second pillar, common foreign and security policy. The Treaty of Nice made provision for the voting in Council with effect from January 2005.[59] To adopt a measure proposed by the Commission there must be at least 232 votes in favour cast by a majority of the Members. In relation to other matters 169 votes are required, cast by at least two-thirds of the Members.[60]

Table 1: Votes in Council from May 2004

Country ....Votes	Country ....Votes
Austria 10	Latvia* 4
Belgium 12	Lithuania* 7
Cyprus* 4	Luxembourg 4
Czech Republic* 12	Malta* 3
Denmark 7	Netherlands 13
Estonia* 4	Poland* 27
Finland 7	Portugal 12
France 29	Slovakia* 7
Germany 29	Slovenia* 4
Greece 12	Spain 27
Hungary* 12	Sweden 10
Ireland 7	United Kingdom 29
Italy 29	**Total** **321**

* = new Member State

With effect from 2009, a qualified majority decision will be one taken by a majority of Member States representing at least 60 per cent of the Union's population.

58 Editorial (CML Rev), 1997, p 769.
59 Protocol on Enlargement, Article 3, amending EC Treaty, Article 205.
60 On co-decision with the Parliament, see below.

The Council, together with the European Parliament, represents a major law making body within the Community. The legislative capacity of Council is limited by the Commission's power of proposal, although Article 208 does provide the means whereby the Council may request the Commission to undertake enquiries the Council considers desirable for the attainment of common objectives, and to submit proposals to the Council.[61]

Because the Council has a fluctuating membership and is not permanently in session,[62] the Committee of Permanent Representatives (COREPER) acts as the permanent body engaged in Council work (Article 207 of the EC Treaty). The Committee is divided into two: the first Committee dealing with social affairs and transport, and the second dealing with foreign affairs, economic and financial affairs. Because agriculture is so central to the Community, it is served by a separate Committee on Agriculture. Beneath this structure is a complex structure of committees, dealing with every subject.

The European Parliament[63]

Originally called the Assembly, Article 189 of the EC Treaty provides that:

> The Assembly which shall consist of the peoples of the states brought together in the Community, shall exercise the advisory and supervisory powers which are conferred upon it by this Treaty.

Members of the Assembly, now Parliament, were initially delegates designated by the parliaments of Member States. In constitutional terms, the delegates had a dual mandate: that of membership of both the domestic and European Parliaments. The Treaty, however, envisaged that the Assembly should draw up proposals for direct elections and that the Council would lay down the appropriate provisions, which it would recommend to Member States for adoption. It was to be in 1976 that agreement could be reached on the proposals drawn up in 1960, and only in 1979 did direct election take place in the United Kingdom. The Council Decision and Act of September 1976 on Direct Elections simply stated that the representatives in the European Parliament of the peoples of the states brought together in the Community shall be elected by direct universal suffrage.[64]

Seats in the European Parliament, the name formally adopted in 1962, are allocated according to the size of population of the Member States, although there

---

61 In *Commission of the EC v Council of the EU* (2005) the Court of Justice ruled that while neither criminal law nor the rules of criminal procedure fell within the competence of the EC, that did not prevent the Community legislature from taking measures related to the criminal law of the member states which it considered necessary in order to ensure that the rules which it laid down on environmental protection were fully effective. Accordingly, it appears that where a matter falls within the competence of the EU, supplementary powers may be implied to ensure that an EU objective is accomplished.

62 Some 80 Council meetings take place each year.

63 EC Treaty, Articles 189–210.

64 Council Decision and Act of September 1976 on Direct Elections, OJ L278, 1976, Article 1.

is no absolute equality in voting powers. Representatives are elected for a term of five years.[65]

However, Community law did not impose any obligation on a member state to bring, for the benefit of one of its citizens, an action against an EC institution under Article 230 of the EC Treaty for annulment of an act adopted by the institution, or under Article 232 EC for failure to act. That did not in principle preclude national law from providing for such an obligation. The Court of Justice so ruled in *Staat der Nederlanden (Ministerie van Landbouw, Natuurbeheer en Visseril) v Ten Kate Holding Musselkanaal BV* (2005).

Table II: Members of the European Parliament from May 2004

Country ......Members	Country ......Members
Austria 18	Latvia* 9
Belgium 24	Lithuania* 13
Cyprus* 6	Luxembourg 6
Czech Republic* 24	Malta* 5
Denmark 14	Netherlands 27
Estonia* 6	Poland* 54
Finland 14	Portugal 24
France 78	Slovakia* 14
Germany 99	Slovenia* 7
Greece 24	Spain 54
Hungary* 24	Sweden 19
Ireland 13	United Kingdom 78
Italy 78	**Total** **732**

* = new Member State

An elected European Member of Parliament may also be a Member of the national parliament. This arrangement has both advantages and disadvantages. On the one hand, it facilitates close links being maintained between the two parliaments; on the other hand, retaining a dual mandate may involve a conflict of interests.[66]

Under the European Parliamentary Elections Act 1999, the United Kingdom is divided into electoral regions. England is divided into nine, Scotland, Wales and

---

65 EC Treaty, Article 190(3). European Union (number of MEPs) (United Kingdom and Gibraltar) Order 2004 (SI 2004/1245).
66 See the House of Lords' Report, *Relations Between the United Kingdom Parliament and the European Parliament After Direct Elections*, HL 256 (1977–78), London: HMSO. In 1997, three Members of Parliament were also Members of the European Parliament.

Northern Ireland each constitute a single electoral region.[67] The Members of Parliament do not sit in groupings organised by nationality but rather by political party groupings. Article 191 of the Treaty recognises the importance of political parties as 'a factor for integration within the Union. They contribute to forming a European awareness and to expressing the political will of the citizens of the Union'. The major political parties are the Socialists, European Peoples' Party, European Democrats, Communists and Liberals. Unless otherwise provided for under the Treaty, the Parliament acts by an absolute majority of the votes cast.[68]

The European Parliament is required to hold an annual session, and may meet in extraordinary session at the request of a majority of its Members or at the request of the Council or of the Commission.[69] In practice, the Parliament meets approximately 12–14 times a year for a few days per session. Members of the Commission may attend all parliamentary meetings and are entitled to address the Parliament.[70] The Parliament holds plenary sessions in Strasbourg, committee meetings and additional plenary sessions in Brussels and has its secretariat based in Luxembourg. Much of the work of Parliament is undertaken by committees on, for example, agriculture, legal affairs and so on. Before a matter goes before Parliament sitting in plenary session, it will normally be considered by the relevant standing committee.

The original intention in relation to Parliament's function was that it would be a 'supervisory and advisory' body, with no legal effect being attached to its deliberations. Under specific Treaty articles, the Council of the EU is obliged to seek the advice of the Parliament, and failure to consider Parliament's view would cause the Council to be in violation of an essential procedural requirement of Community law, and could cause the decision of the Council to be declared void by the ECJ.[71] As will be seen, the powers of the European Parliament have been increasing since 1986 (under the SEA 1986), but even now it remains a very different constitutional institution from that of domestic parliaments.

The European Parliament can adopt its own ideas and try to persuade the Commission to adopt them. Usually this takes the form of an initiative report – around 100 a year are approved by the European Parliament. However, Parliament has no power to insist that the Commission adopt a proposal from Parliament – the right of initiative is firmly in the hands of the Commission itself, other than where the European Parliament or the Council requests a proposal from the Commission.

The European Parliament has decision making powers regarding the annual budget. This power in relation to the Community budget has always been of significance. The revenue of the Community comes primarily from agricultural levies, customs duties on imports from outside the Community and value added

---

67 The European Parliamentary and Local Elections (Pilots) Act 2004 permitted pilot elections for the European Parliament in 2004 by postal vote. Pilot elections were held in four English regions. In all four regions the number of votes more than doubled.

68 EC Treaty, Article 198.

69 EC Treaty, Article 196.

70 EC Treaty, Article 196.

71 *Roquettes Frère SA v Council* (1980); *Maizena GmbH v Council* (1980).

tax (VAT) levied within the Community. When the draft budget is drawn up by the Council, after receiving proposals from the Commission, it is then submitted to Parliament which has power to accept, amend or reject the budget. The right of amendment depends on the type of expenditure proposed. There are two categories of expenditure: compulsory expenditure, which necessarily arises from Treaty provisions, and non-compulsory expenditure. The non-compulsory expenditure can be amended but, in relation to compulsory expenditure, Parliament may suggest amendments but the Council of the EU has the last word.

Parliament has the power to reject the Community budget in total if there are 'important reasons to do so': Article 272 of the EC Treaty. There must be a majority of votes in Parliament and also two thirds of the votes cast. Rejection of the budget occurred in 1979, when a new budget was subsequently drawn up.

Parliament has the right to question the Commission and Council,[72] and replies are given both orally and in writing, and published in the *Official Journal of the European Communities*. Parliament also has the power to dismiss the entire Commission on a vote of censure if the vote is carried by a two thirds majority of the votes cast, a vote which must represent an overall majority of the votes in Parliament.[73] If the vote is carried, the Commission resigns as a body. However, in one sense, the power is too great to be effective, for Parliament has no power to force the incoming Commission to adopt a different policy from that of its predecessor. Under the TEU, however, nominations for appointment to the Commission must hereafter be approved by Parliament.[74]

Extension of Parliament's powers

The powers of the European Parliament have been extended significantly. The legislative process is now more complex and, in specific instances, it is necessary to consult the substantive Articles of the Treaty in order to establish the precise procedure to be followed.

The co-operation and co-decision procedures

The SEA 1986 provided for a new 'co-operation procedure', which applied to many, but not all, instances in which the Treaties require Parliament to be consulted. This procedure, which gave the Parliament the power to propose amendments to legislative proposals, has been largely superseded by the co-decision powers introduced at Maastricht. The co-operation procedure does continue to apply, however, to some issues relating to European monetary union. The TEU 1992 and the 1997 Treaty further extended Parliament's role in the legislative process.[75]

---

72 EC Treaty, Article 197.
73 EC Treaty, Article 201.
74 EC Treaty, Article 214(2).
75 On parliament's powers under the TEU, see Bradley, '"Better rusty than missing"? The institutional reforms of the Maastricht Treaty and the European Parliament', in O'Keefe and Twomey, 1994.

Articles 251 and 252 of the EC Treaty, as revised, define the co-decision procedure to be followed where references are made to it in the substantive Treaty articles.[76] Where Parliament is given a role in the decision making process, Parliament will give an opinion on a Commission reading. The first reading is concluded when the Council adopts a common position. A time limit then applies to Parliament reaching its decision, on the expiry of which the Council may adopt the measure in accordance with its common position. Article 251 requires that, at second reading, Parliament must act by an absolute majority of its Members in order to reject or amend the common position adopted by the Council. If the Parliament rejects the common position, then the measure fails completely. Parliament also has the right to request the Commission to submit legislative proposals, although this power is limited.[77] There is no power given to Parliament to draft a proposal itself if the Commission does not act within the time limit suggested by the Parliament.

The TEU 1992 provided that Parliament shall appoint an ombudsman to inquire into allegations of maladministration within the Community. Article 195 of the EC Treaty, as revised by the Amsterdam Treaty, now regulates this matter. Parliament may also establish committees of inquiry to investigate allegations of maladministration.[78] It was a committee of inquiry which led to the downfall of the Santer Commission in 1999.[79]

The SEA gave the Parliament power to agree or to veto special trade agreements. It also extended Parliament's role in the admission of new Member States, whose admission must be approved by a majority, thus giving the Parliament a power of veto. Where Parliament is given a role in the legislative process under Article 251, as revised, its role is subject to the limitations of being required to act by an absolute majority – rather than simple majority – of its Members, and the time limits imposed, although extendable (Article 249), represent a real restriction on what Parliament may be expected to accomplish – particularly given the relative infrequency of its meetings, and the short duration of its sessions.

With the powers of Parliament enhanced under the SEA and the Treaties on European Union and, most significantly, the extensive increase in the areas over which the Parliament has a right of co-decision with the Council, the European Parliament has gradually been given the powers needed to offset the perception that the Parliament lacked a real role in legislation, including a properly functioning veto power.

The concept of institutional balance

Under any constitution there must be a separation of powers in order to ensure that power is dispersed among the major institutions of the state rather than

---

76 See EC Treaty, Articles 12, 19, 42, 46, 47, 71, 80, 129, 136, 137, 141, 148, 150, 152, 153, 157, 254, 279, 285, 286.
77 EC Treaty, Article 190.
78 EC Treaty, Article 193.
79 See above.

concentrated in one institution. However, as has been seen above, the separation of powers among the EU institutions differs markedly from conventional arrangements. In the first place, it may be noted that the principal institutions, the Council, Commission and Parliament represent different interests: the Council representing the interests of the Member States, the Commission representing the interests of the Community and the Parliament representing the interests of EU citizens. Secondly, there is no 'government' in the normal sense of that word: rather executive powers are shared between the Council and Commission, and the law-making powers shared by the Commission, Council and Parliament. As a result, the arrangements are governed not so much by the concept of separation of powers but by the concept of 'institutional balance'. This is a dynamic concept which has changed over the years – most notably with the increase in power of the European Parliament, but also in the move away from unanimity in decision-making in Council and towards Qualified Majority Voting.[80]

The principle of institutional balance is both political and legal. The case of *Roquettes Frere SA v Commission* (1976), illustrates the principle, the Court of Justice ruling that the requirement of consultation laid down in the EC Treaty 'represents an essential factor in the institutional balance intended by the Treaty'. The failure to consult resulted in a distortion of balance which would be remedied by declaring the relevant measure void. Institutional balance was also central to the case of *Parliament v Council*, the *Chernobyl case* (1990). In that case, although the EC Treaty did not provide that the European Parliament had the right to challenge acts adopted in breach of the Treaty before the Court of Justice, the Court nevertheless ruled that its duty to ensure that the law is observed (Article 220 EC Treaty) entailed the duty to maintain the institutional balance. Accordingly, it ruled that the absence of a right to bring an action was a procedural gap which the Court would not allow to 'prevail over the fundamental interest in the maintenance and observance of the institutional balance laid down in the Treaties ...'.

The European Council[81]

The year 1974 saw the formalisation of an informal arrangement which had pertained from the 1960s. A communiqué was issued at the Paris Summit of Heads of Government and Foreign Ministers of Member States, of which the following is the most important:

> Recognising the need for an overall approach to the internal problems involved in achieving European unity and the external problems facing Europe, the Heads of Government consider it essential to ensure progress and overall consistency in the activities of the Community and in the work on political co-operation.

> The Heads of Government have therefore decided to meet, accompanied by Ministers of Foreign Affairs, three times a year and, whenever necessary, in the Council of the Community and in the context of political co-operation.

---

80 Which in turn affects the ability of a Member State to obstruct developments. See further below.
81 Not to be confused with the Council of the EU.

The constitutional implications of the communiqué are twofold. In the first place, the communiqué represented an adjustment of the institutional arrangements of the Community (now Union) which were brought about without recourse to the formal Treaty-amending provisions, a mechanism demonstrating the dynamic and flexible means by which the Community and Union can evolve. Secondly, the motivation behind the communiqué lay in the perception that the role of the Commission had been reduced by the Member States' insistence on protection of their national interests, as exemplified in the increasing use of the unanimous vote in Council which had the effect of stultifying the growth of the Community. The first official recognition of the communiqué, which had no legal standing, is found in the SEA 1986,[82] which specified the membership of the European Council and reduces the minimum number of annual meetings from three to two. The TEU confirms this arrangement and Article 4 of the Treaty states that:

> The European Council shall provide the Union with the necessary impetus for its development and shall define the general political guidelines thereof ...

> The European Council shall submit to the European Parliament a report after each of its meetings and a yearly written report on the progress achieved by the Union.

The Heads of Government and Foreign Ministers accordingly meet twice a year, together with the President of the Commission, two Members of the Commission and officials. A primary purpose of the meetings is to review economic and social matters such as inflation, economic growth, unemployment, the European monetary system, international political issues, reform of the Common Agriculture Policy and constitutional issues such as applications for membership of the Union and political integration.

The decisions reached are political, the European Council having no law making powers. The impact on the Commission, Council of the EU and Parliament are of constitutional significance. The Commission loses its own power of initiative, the Council of the EU loses power because decisions are reached at Head of State level, and the Parliament is bypassed in the decision making process.

The Court of Auditors

The Court of Auditors comprises one member from each Member State, appointed under similar terms and conditions to judges of the ECJ. The term of years is six, and Members are under a duty to act completely independently in the performance of their duties and to act in the general interests of the Community. A President of the Court, appointed for a renewable term of three years, heads the Court of Auditors. It is the Court of Auditors which has responsibility for monitoring the expenditure of the Community. It carries out audits, examining the accounts of all revenue and expenditure of the Community. At the end of each financial year, the Court of Auditors is under a duty to draw up an Annual Report which is forwarded to the other institutions of the Community and published,

82   EC Treaty, Article 28.

with replies from these institutions, in the *Official Journal of the European Communities*.

The Court of Auditors has the full range of legal remedies available to other institutions, thus reinforcing the safeguards which ensure that it is able to perform effectively. The Court of Auditor's task is to assist the European Parliament and the Council in exercising their powers of control over the implementation of the budget. The Court may also submit observations on specific questions and deliver opinions at the request of one of the European institutions.

The Court of Auditors is required to provide the Council and Parliament with a Statement of Assurance relating to the reliability of accounts and the legality of the underlying transactions. In its auditing function, the Court of Auditors may examine records in the European institutions and the Member States. The Court of Auditors examines the accounts of Community revenue and expenditure and considers whether these have been received and incurred in a lawful manner and whether the financial management has been sound. The Court of Auditors is independent and has the power to carry out its audits at any level. In addition to monitoring the internal revenues and expenditure of the Union, the Court of Auditors also monitors co-operation agreements between the European Union and many developing countries, and the system of Community aid to Central and Eastern Europe.

The Economic and Social Committee

The Economic and Social Committee is appointed by the Council, the number of members being based on the populations of Member States. The Member States submit lists of nominees for appointment, and are required to nominate twice as many persons as will be appointed (Article 259 of the EC Treaty). Members of the Committee are representative of different occupational and social groups. Article 257 of the EC Treaty stipulates that the Committee has advisory status. Article 257 also stipulates that, in particular, the Committee shall have representatives of producers, farmers, carriers, workers, dealers, craftsmen, professional occupations and representatives of the general public.

The Committee of the Regions

The Committee of the Regions comprises representatives of regional and local bodies and has advisbry status (Articles 263–65 of the EC Treaty). It advises the Council and Commission on education, culture and regional development. The Committee, headed by a Chairman, meets at the request of the Council or Commission, and may also meet on its own initiative. The Committee must be consulted by the Council or the Commission where the Treaty so provides.

The European Investment Bank

Established under the TEU 1992 (see Articles 266–67 of the EC Treaty), the European Investment Bank is charged with the task of promoting the 'balanced and steady development of the common market in the interest of the Community'. The Bank operates on a non-profit making basis, and grants loans and can give guarantees which facilitate the financing of a number of projects, including projects for developing less developed regions, modernising or conversion projects and projects of common interest to several Member States.

The European Court of Justice[83]

The judges in the ECJ are appointed by 'common accord of the governments of Member States'. Each state makes one nomination. Unlike superior judges in the United Kingdom, the qualification for appointment to judicial office in the ECJ is that candidates are 'persons whose independence is beyond doubt and who possess the qualifications required for appointment to the highest judicial offices in their respective countries or who are jurisconsults of recognised competence'. Judges are appointed for a six year term of office (Article 223).

The Court is presided over by a President who holds office for a three year term. Assisting the judges are Advocates General, whose duties are defined in Article 222 of the Treaty as 'acting with complete impartiality and independence, to make, in open court, reasoned submissions on cases brought before the Court of Justice ...'. It is the Advocates General who will examine each case and present the legal arguments to the Court for its decision.

Pressure on the ECJ resulted in a Court of First Instance being introduced under the SEA 1986. The majority of cases are heard in Chambers comprising three or five judges. The Court of First Instance is not empowered to hear and determine questions referred for a preliminary ruling under Article 234 of the EC Treaty, on which see further, Chapter 9.

The role of the ECJ is provided for in the most general terms by Article 220 of the EC Treaty: 'The Court of Justice shall ensure that in the interpretation and application of this Treaty, the law is observed.' At first sight, given that the jurisdiction of the Court is derived solely from the Treaties, Article 220 would seem to confine the ECJ to consideration of Community law, a point reinforced by the wording of Article 234 of the Treaty. In the early days, the Court adopted this narrow interpretation of its jurisdiction and rejected any invitation to draw on the law of Member States in the forming of decisions. From the 1970s at least, a change in attitude can be discerned in the reasoning of the Court. From that time, judges felt able, indeed compelled, to make recourse to domestic law of Member States in order to ensure both the effectiveness of Community law within a particular Member State and to produce harmony between the laws of all Member States. The Court accordingly draws particularly on fundamental concepts existing in the laws of Member States in order to enable common legal concepts to be incorporated into Community law.[84] However, the ECJ can only rule on the interpretation and legality of EC/EU law: it has no power to rule on the domestic laws of Member States. It is the need for uniformity of the law within the legal systems of Member States which represents a major function of the Court.

---

83   EC Treaty, Articles 220–24.
84   See Mendelsen, 1981; Dauses, 1985.

Under Article 226 of the Treaty, the ECJ may make rulings on a matter brought before it by the Commission alleging breach of the Treaties by a Member State. Prior to bringing the matter to the ECJ, the Commission exercises a quasi-judicial function. The Commission must first consider that a Member State has failed to fulfil a Treaty obligation and, secondly, give a reasoned opinion to that state and advise as to the action which must be taken, and the time limit for action to be taken to comply with the opinion. Only if a Member State fails to comply with the opinion will the matter be taken to the ECJ. In *Commission v French Republic* (1997), for example, the ECJ ruled that France had failed to fulfil its obligations under the Treaty (Article 28, in conjunction with Article 10), in that it had failed to adopt appropriate measures to prevent farmers and others from obstructing the free movement of fruit and vegetables. The Court ruled that the free movement of goods was one of the fundamental principles of the Treaty. The French government had failed to prevent violent and obstructive behaviour by farmers and others and therefore its failure placed it in breach of the Treaty requirements.[85]

In *Commission v United Kingdom* (2000), the Commission sought a declaration that the United Kingdom had failed fully to comply with a Directive[86] concerning the protection of waters against pollution caused by nitrates from agricultural sources. The United Kingdom authorities had identified only surface waters intended for extraction of drinking water, whereas the Directive also required the identification of surface freshwaters not intended for the abstraction of drinking water which contained excessive nitrate concentrations or could do so. In addition, no 'vulnerable zones' had been identified in Northern Ireland, and those areas which had been designated had been designated on the incorrect criteria, as in the rest of the United Kingdom. The fact that the authorities were now taking action to remedy the failure did not exclude the state's liability for breach of its obligations under the Directive.[87]

Failure to transpose a Directive into national law by the stipulated date will not be excused on the basis that transposition required revision of provisions of a Member State's constitution. The ECJ so held in *Commission v Kingdom of Belgium* (1998), in which an action was lodged under Article 169 of the EC Treaty for a declaration that Belgium had failed to bring into force within the prescribed period the laws, regulations and administrative provisions necessary to comply with Council Directive 94/80/EC, which laid down detailed arrangements for the exercise of the right to vote and to stand as a candidate in municipal elections by citizens of the Union residing in a Member State of which they are not nationals.

Under Article 227 of the Treaty, one Member State may bring a fellow Member State before the Court. Again, a procedure is specified which gives the Commission a quasi-judicial function. Before an action is brought before the Court the aggrieved Member State must bring the matter to the attention of the Commission. Once again, the Commission must give a reasoned opinion, the Member State having been given the opportunity to make oral and written

---

85 See also *National Farmers Union v Secretariat General du Gouvernment* (2002).
86 Council Directive 91/676/EC of 12 December 1991.
87 See also *Commission of the European Union v United Kingdom* (2002).

submissions on the allegation. Once this procedure has been completed, the Member State has a discretion whether or not to bring the matter before the Court. If the Commission fails to act and deliver its opinion within three months from the date of the allegation, then the aggrieved state may proceed with the action before the Court.

Article 228 of the Treaty provides that, if the ECJ finds that a Member State has failed to fulfil its obligations, the state shall be required to take the necessary measures to comply with the judgment of the Court. However, one of the principal defects in the ECJ's power lay in its inability to impose sanctions.

The Treaty of Amsterdam introduced two significant reforms. Regarding policies relating to free movement of persons, visas, asylum and immigration, the ECJ is given jurisdiction to make rulings on questions of interpretation of the relevant Treaty provision and to rule on the validity or interpretation of acts of the institutions of the Community. This right is confined to courts or tribunals against which there is no judicial remedy, and provides that that tribunal or court *must* refer the matter for a ruling. The Court may also give rulings on the interpretation of these matters when requested by the Council, Commission or a Member State. The Court does not have jurisdiction, however, to rule on any measure relating to the maintenance of law and order and the safeguarding of internal security.[88] The Court's jurisdiction is also extended in relation to the third pillar (police and judicial co-operation in criminal matters, formerly justice and home affairs), to give preliminary rulings, in respect of which Member States have made a declaration stating that they accept this jurisdiction. The Court also has jurisdiction to rule on any dispute between Member States or between the Member States and the Commission in respect of the third pillar.

The increasing volume of work undertaken by the ECJ and the Court of First Instance, has led the Court to propose reforms designed to improve efficiency.[89] The Court had advocated a form of accelerated or simplified procedure for dealing with cases of a 'manifestly urgent nature', and for dealing with certain cases on the basis of written procedure alone. In relation to preliminary rulings (under Article 234, on which see below), while the system should remain, the Court has proposed that where an answer to a question is apparent from existing case law, it should rule more frequently by way of simple order, and that Member States could set up judicial bodies with responsibility for dealing with references for preliminary rulings within their territorial jurisdiction.

With the increased membership of the Union, the Court has expressed concern that the increasing number of judges would 'cross the invisible boundary between a collegiate court and a deliberative assembly', a development which could pose a threat to efficiency and the consistency of case law.

---

88 EC Treaty, Article 68.
89 In 2002 the Court celebrated its 50th birthday. In the year to March 2003 the number of cases brought to a close by the ECJ was 513, compared with 434 in 2001. The number of cases brought to a close by the Court of First Instance was 331, compared with 340 in 2001.

Penalties for failure to comply with rulings of the European Court

The TEU empowered the Court to impose a lump sum or penalty payment against a Member State which fails to respect the judgment of the Court.[90] In January 1997, the Commission agreed the procedures for the imposition of fines on Member States who fail to comply with rulings of the ECJ. Where a Member State is in breach of Community law, the Commission will apply to the Court for a determination of the fine. The levels of fines will be relative to the size of the economy of the state.

Article 230 of the EC Treaty provides the ECJ's jurisdiction to review the legality of acts adopted 'jointly by the European Parliament and the Council, of acts of the Council [and] of the Commission ...'. The Court also has jurisdiction to rule on complaints brought by Member States, the Council or the Commission on grounds of 'lack of competence, infringement of an essential procedural requirement, infringement of this Treaty or of any rule of law relating to its application, or misuse of powers'. If an action is well founded, the Court may declare the act concerned to be void.[91] It is by these means that the ECJ controls the exercise of powers by the institutions of the Community.[92]

Article 232 of the Treaty provides the means whereby Member States and institutions of the Community can challenge the Council and Commission on the basis that they have failed to act as required under the Treaty. The use of Article 232 is illustrated by the European Parliament's attempt to push the Council over the implementation of direct elections to Parliament. Article 138(3) of the original EC Treaty (now Article 190(4)) stated that the Assembly shall draw up proposals for direct elections, which it did in 1960. Article 138(3)(2) stated that the Council shall, acting unanimously, lay down the appropriate measures for the elections and make recommendations to Member States for their implementation. The Council failed to act and in 1969 the Assembly again requested action, threatening the Council with an action under Article 175 (now Article 232) for failure to act. Agreement was finally reached and direct elections took place in 1979. Article 138 also provided that the voting procedure employed within Member States for the election of Members of the European Parliament would be 'uniform'. This measure lapsed in 1979, when it became clear that uniformity would not be achievable.[93] Article 190(4) now simply provides that representatives in the European Parliament 'shall be elected by direct universal suffrage'.

Article 234 of the EC Treaty[94]

The single most important jurisdiction in terms of ensuring that Community law is uniformly interpreted within national legal systems is that conferred on the Court to give preliminary rulings under Article 234. The Court may rule on the

---

90 EC Treaty, Article 228.
91 EC Treaty, Article 231.
92 See Steiner, 1995, and references therein. See *European Parliament v Council of the European Union* (1999); *Re Cosmetic Products Directive: France v European Parliament, Council* (2005).
93 Council Decision and Act of 20 September 1976 on Direct Elections.
94 See Arnull, 1988b, 1989 and 1990.

interpretation of the Treaty, and on the validity and interpretation of acts of the institutions of the Community. Article 234 provides that:

> The Court of Justice shall have jurisdiction to give preliminary rulings concerning:
>
> (a) the interpretation of this Treaty;
>
> (b) the validity and interpretation of acts of the institutions of the Community and of the European Central Bank (ECB);
>
> (c) the interpretation of the statutes of bodies established by an act of the Council, where those statutes so provide.
>
> Where such a question is raised before any court or tribunal of a Member State that court or tribunal may, if it considers that a decision on the question is necessary to enable it to give judgment, request the Court of Justice to give a ruling thereon.
>
> Where any such question is raised in a case pending before a court or tribunal of a Member State against whose decision there is no judicial remedy under national law, that court or tribunal shall bring the matter before the Court of Justice.

It is this Article which raises directly the nature of the legal system of the Community and the relationship between Community law, the ECJ and domestic law and the role of judges in national courts. Article 234 is crucial to the development of Community law. The power to interpret the Treaty gives to the Court a dynamic function and the ECJ has a role in the creation of law at least as important as the legislative powers of the Council and Parliament. This power, as utilised, is a matter of some controversy with the European Court, being both criticised and praised for adopting a deliberate policy making stance which goes beyond that of interpretation of the Treaty.[95]

Article 234 envisages a partnership approach between the domestic courts and the ECJ. It is important both as a matter of principle and as a practical matter that the domestic courts are actively involved in the application of Community law, and that a measure of discretion is left to domestic courts in the matter of referring a matter to the ECJ. It must also be recognised, however, that the discretion left to domestic courts carries with it the potential for a distortion of the meaning of Community law within the different legal systems. A particular difficulty faces the courts in the United Kingdom, whose traditional approach to the interpretation of statutes has been one very much constrained by the detailed wording of statutes and the pedantic literal, golden and mischief rules. By contrast, in civil law systems,[96] the judges are experienced in interpreting broadly phrased statutory provisions, using the teleological[97] interpretative method. Lord Diplock explained the approach of the European Court in *Henn and Darby v Director of Public Prosecutions* (1981):

> The European Court, in contrast to English courts, applies teleological rather than historical methods to the interpretation of the Treaties and other Community legislation. It seeks to give effect to what it conceives to be the spirit rather than the letter of the Treaties; sometimes, indeed, to an English judge, it may seem to the exclusion of the letter. It views the Community as living and expanding organisms and the

---

95 See Rasmussen, 1988; Slynn, 1984.

96 Defined as those deriving primarily from Roman law.

97 That is to say, seeking the interpretation which most closely fits the objective sought by the legislature.

interpretation of the provisions of the Treaties as changing to match their growth.
[p 852]

The Court of Justice considered the duty of a national court to refer a question under the discretionary second paragraph of Article 234 in *R (International Air Transport Association and European Low Fares Airline Association) v Department of Transport* (2006). National courts do not have the power to declare acts of the Community institutions invalid, although they had the power to examine the validity of a Community act. Where a party had raised questions on the validity of a Community instrument, before a court against whose decision there was no judicial remedy under national law, which the court considered arguable and not unfounded, that court had a duty to stay proceedings and refer the matter to the Court of Justice for a preliminary ruling on validity.

Under Community law, both the common law and civil law systems must coexist in a manner which best promotes the harmony of the new legal system created by the Treaties. For harmony to be achieved, it is axiomatic that judges with very differing backgrounds and experience adopt a common approach both to interpretation and to the circumstances under which it is appropriate and necessary to refer a matter to the ECJ for interpretation. In order to understand the relationship between the ECJ and national courts, and the issue of the supremacy of Community law, it is first necessary to examine the sources of Community law, and the manner in which Community law comes into effect in domestic law. This matter is discussed in the next chapter.

THE EUROPEAN UNION AND THE EUROPEAN CONVENTION ON HUMAN RIGHTS

The Convention for the Protection of Human Rights and Fundamental Freedoms – drafted and enacted in 1950 under the aegis of the Council of Europe[98] – establishes a charter of rights and freedoms which are protected by the Commission and Court of Human Rights in Strasbourg.[99] The Treaty of Rome 1957 (now Article 303 of the EC Treaty) envisaged close links with the Council of Europe.[100] The Union itself, however, has not as such been bound by the Convention.[101]

In 1979 the Commission of the European Community adopted a Memorandum endorsing the option of accession by the EC to the Convention.[102] A number of obstacles lie in the way of such accession. First, it would enable the rights enshrined in the Convention to enter indirectly into those dualist states[103]

---

98 Of which all Member States of the European Community are members.
99 Institutional changes have been effected to unify the Commission and the Court; see further Chapter 19.
100 Article 230 states that 'The Community shall establish all appropriate forms of co-operation with the Council of Europe'.
101 *Confederation Française Democratique du Travail v European Community* (1979).
102 2/79 Bulletin EC Supp.
103 The United Kingdom, Ireland and Denmark.

which had not incorporated the Convention into domestic law. Secondly, it would further increase the workload of the already stretched Strasbourg machinery. Thirdly, it would pose problems for the enforcement of rights in those states seeking admission to the European Community which do not yet conform to the principle of the rule of law and protection of rights which underlies membership of the European Community and Union.

The Preamble to the SEA 1986 had already made explicit the concern for the protection of human rights within the Community. Article 6 of the TEU states that:

> The Union shall respect fundamental rights, as guaranteed by the European Convention for the Protection of Human Rights and Fundamental Freedoms signed in Rome on 4 November 1950 and as they result from the constitutional traditions common to the Member States, as general principles of Community law.

The original Treaties made no explicit reference to the protection of individual rights in their entirety, although Treaty articles such as Article 141[104] provide for equal treatment of men and women in matters of employment. The manner in which the ECJ has developed the jurisprudence on rights is linked inextricably with its insistence on the supremacy of Community law over the domestic law of Member States. In 1969, the ECJ turned its attention specifically to the status of fundamental individual rights in relation to the principles of Community law. In *Stauder v City of Ulm* (1969), the ECJ stated that it had a duty to protect the rights of individuals as provided for by the constitution of the Member State, and that such provisions formed part of the general principles of Community law. *Internationale Handelsgesellschaft mbH v EVST* (1970) clarified the relationship between domestic constitutional law and Community law in matters of rights. The ECJ expressed its opinion that respect for fundamental rights 'forms an integral part of the general principles of law protected by the Court of Justice. The protection of such rights, whilst inspired by the constitutional traditions common to the Member States, must be ensured within the framework of the structures and objectives of the Community'. In *Nold v Commission* (1974), a case concerning a person's status as a wholesaler, the ECJ ruled that, consistent with its earlier judgment in *Internationale Handelsgesellschaft*, constitutional rights protected under Member States' constitutions must be respected, but also declared that 'international treaties for the protection of human rights' can 'supply guidelines which should be followed within the framework of Community law' (para 13). The European Convention on Human Rights,[105] the International Labour Organisation Treaties,[106] the Council of Europe's European Social Charter, and the International Covenants on Civil and Political and Economic, Social and Cultural Rights[107] have all been cited by the ECJ as aids to the interpretation of Community law.

---

104 Previously Article 119; amended under the TEU.
105 Discussed in Chapter 19. See *Rutili v Ministère de L'Interieur* (1975).
106 See *Defrenne v SABENA* (1978).
107 See *Barber v Guardian Royal Exchange Insurance Company* (1990).

On a piecemeal, case by case basis, the ECJ has gradually and steadily incorporated the protection of individual rights into its case law. However, while all Member States of the Union are signatories to the European Convention on Human Rights (ECHR), the Union is not a party to the ECHR, and the relationship between the Union and ECHR remains indistinct. The ECJ accepts the significance of the ECHR, and regards the ECHR provisions as part of the general principles of Community law. However, that position does not go so far as to amount to the ECHR being regarded as a central, integral part of Community law. Academics disagree as to whether the ECHR is binding on the law of the EC. HG Schermers has argued that the EC is bound by the ECHR.[108] Conversely, A Dremczewski argues that the ECHR does not bind the Union.[109] Whatever the precise status of the ECHR, and its relationship with the Union, it is clear that the ECJ is committed to the protection of rights. What remains unclear is the breadth of the protection which the ECJ will afford to provisions of the ECHR. On the question of whether accession by the Community to the European Convention on Human Rights was compatible with the Treaty establishing the Community, the ECJ has itself ruled that there is no legal basis in the Treaty for such accession, and that accession could only be brought about by amendment of the Treaty.[110]

The Treaty of Amsterdam 1997, reiterating the fundamental commitment of the Union to human rights and fundamental freedoms, introduced the power to issue penalties to Member States who are in breach of rights. Aware of the potential problems entailed in the enlargement of the Union and the admission of Member States with a poor record on human rights, the Treaty provides for a penalty falling short of expulsion from the Union, a penalty which itself could undermine the protection of rights of that Member State's citizens. The principle of respect for human rights is also binding on Member States when acting within the scope of Community law, namely when implementing a Community measure,[111] or seeking to derogate from a fundamental freedom.[112]

---

108 See Schermers, 1990 and 1987.
109 Dremczewski, 1981.
110 Opinion No 2/94 [1996] ECR I-1759.
111 *Wauchauf v Bundescourt für Ernährung und Fortwistschalt* (1989).
112 *ERT v Dimotiki* (1991).

CHAPTER 9

EUROPEAN COMMUNITY LAW AND NATIONAL LAW

SOURCES OF COMMUNITY LAW

Having examined the structure, institutions and law making process of the European Union and Community in the previous chapter, it is now necessary to turn attention to the forms of Community law and the interaction between Community law and domestic law. The primary sources of Community law are the Treaties, as amended. Secondary legislation is law made by the Community institutions, and includes the interpretation of both primary and secondary sources by the European Court of Justice (ECJ). Secondary legislation comprises regulations, directives and decisions. Article 249 of the EC Treaty defines these terms as follows:

> In order to carry out their task, the Council and Commission shall, in accordance with the provisions of this Treaty, make regulations, issue directives, take decisions, make recommendations or deliver opinions ...
>
> - A regulation shall have general application. It shall be binding in its entirety and directly applicable in all Member States;
> - A directive shall be binding, as to the result to be achieved, upon each Member State to which it is addressed, but shall leave to the national authorities the choice of form or methods;
> - A decision shall be binding in its entirety upon those to whom it is addressed;
> - Recommendations and opinions shall have no binding force.

It is clear from Article 249 that regulations and directives have 'binding effect' in all Member States, but, as discussed below, this takes different forms. Decisions and recommendations, on the other hand, have more limited effect, the former binding those to whom they are addressed, the latter having 'no binding force'. There are, however, other 'sources' which, while not having legally binding force, nevertheless have a significant impact on the working of the Community and Union. The institutions of the Union, for example, formulate their own procedures for self-regulation. As will be seen below, the Council has the power to enter into international agreements between the Community and non-EU states on behalf of the Member States of the Union. In addition, there are measures which are labelled 'soft' (as opposed to 'hard') law. As well as recommendations and opinions under Article 249, Jo Shaw (2000) cites 'communications, conclusions, declarations, action programmes and communiqués' as examples of soft law. Joint actions taken by Members States in pursuit of Union objectives also fall within soft law, as do conventions and 'framework decisions' made in relation to policy. While the principal concern in this chapter is with the 'hard law' of the Community and Union, it must also be recognised that these disparate mechanisms exist in order to further European objectives across wide ranging fields of policy on which it may not be possible always to secure complete agreement between all Member States, and therefore translate a soft law measure into hard law which has binding legal effect.

DIRECT APPLICABILITY AND DIRECT EFFECT[1]

The principles of direct applicability and direct effect[2]

As can be seen from the text of Article 249, a regulation is 'binding in its entirety' and has direct applicability. By 'direct applicability' it is meant that the measure leaves no discretion to the Member States but, rather, confers rights and duties within the Member States without further legislative participation. In other words, the provision is self-executing. On the other hand, a directive, whilst binding in its objective, leaves to the Member State some leeway in its introduction and the manner in which a Member State implements and achieves the objectives set by the Council, Commission and European Parliament.

In order to understand the way in which Community law operates within Member States' legal systems, the principle of direct effect must be examined. The basic principle of direct effect of Community measures is that individuals may invoke certain provisions as conferring direct rights, which may be relied on in the national courts. While Article 249 states specifically that regulations are directly applicable, the Article is silent as to the legal *consequence* of this applicability, and as to whether a Treaty provision itself, or regulations or directives, can have direct legal effect on individuals.[3]

The principle of direct effect is linked to Article 10 of the EC Treaty which provides, in part, that:

> Member States shall take all appropriate measures, whether general or particular, to ensure fulfilment of the obligations arising out of this Treaty or resulting from action taken by institutions of the Community. They shall facilitate the achievement of Community tasks. They shall abstain from any measure which could jeopardise the attainment of the objectives of this Treaty.[4]

As can be seen from Article 10, Member States are under a legal duty both to take action to ensure compliance with Community law and to refrain from any action which might impede the application and effectiveness of Community law. Article 10 forms the basis for much of the jurisprudence of the ECJ, and the foundation for the enforcement of individual rights against Member States.

The ECJ reaffirmed the interpretative duty in *Centrosteel Srl v Adipol GmbH* (2000), in which the Court stated that it was well settled that 'in the absence of proper transposition into national law, a directive cannot of itself impose obligations on individuals'. However, the Court went on to state: '... when applying national law, whether adopted before or after the directive, the national court that has to interpret that law must do so, as far as possible, in the light of the wording and the purpose of the directive so as to achieve the result it has in view ...'

---

1   See, *inter alia*, Steiner, 1993; Ross, 1993.
2   The two terms are used synonymously by the ECJ. See Winter, 1972; Eleftheriadis, 1996.
3   See *Consorzio del Prosciutto di Parma v Asda Food Stores Ltd* (1999), in which the Court of Appeal ruled that a regulation did not have direct effect, *inter alia*, since it was not sufficiently clear and precise and itself indicated that it was not intended to have direct effect.
4   See Temple-Lang, 1990.

Direct effect and Articles of the Treaty

In 1963, the ECJ articulated the theoretical basis for the principle of direct effect in *Van Gend en Loos* (1963), a case which involved a reference to the ECJ from the Dutch courts. From this case, many significant later developments of Community law can be seen to originate. Under Article 25 of the EC Treaty (formerly Article 12):

> Customs duties on imports and exports and charges having equivalent effect shall be prohibited between Member States. This prohibition shall also apply to customs duties of a fiscal nature.

Before 1958, and the coming into force of the EC Treaty, the Dutch firm of Van Gend en Loos had been importing glue from Germany, applying a customs duty of three per cent. In 1959, the Dutch government ratified an agreement with other countries establishing an eight per cent duty. The company protested to the Customs Court, relying on the direct effect of Article 12 of the EC Treaty. The Court referred the matter to the ECJ under Article 177 (now Article 234). The principal question for the court was whether, as claimed, Article 12 had direct effect on the legal position on the company. The Treaty Article did not stipulate its legal effect, and Article 189 of the EC Treaty (now Article 249) refers only to regulations having direct applicability. The ECJ held first that, if a Treaty provision is to confer individual enforceable rights, it must indicate that it applies not just to Member States but also to individuals within the state. Secondly, the provision must be clear and precise. Thirdly, the provision must be unconditional and unqualified and not subject to any further measures on the part of Member States. Finally, the provision must be one which does not leave any substantial latitude or discretion to Member States.

Specifically in relation to Article 12, as it then was, the ECJ held that the text was clear and unconditional, that it required no legislative intervention by the Member State and that the Member State had no power to subordinate Article 12 to its own law. Thus, it can be seen that both provisions in the Treaty and regulations are capable of having direct effect if they satisfy the requirements laid down by the ECJ.

The principle of direct effect of Treaty provisions was examined by the House of Lords and the ECJ in *Henn and Darby v Director of Public Prosecutions* (1979–81). In that case, the accused defended a criminal prosecution on the basis that the subject matter of the charge offended against Treaty provisions. The accused were charged with conspiracy to import obscene materials contrary to the law of the United Kingdom. Article 28 of the EC Treaty (formerly Article 30), however, prohibits quantitative restrictions on imports. The House of Lords referred the matter to the ECJ under Article 177 (now Article 234), asking the ECJ to interpret Article 30 (now Article 28) in order to establish whether English law was bound by the restriction in Article 30. In response, the ECJ ruled that English law infringed Article 30 but that lawful restrictions on pornography could be imposed by a Member State under Article 36 of the EC Treaty (now Article 30), which provides that restrictions on imports otherwise contrary to Article 30 are justified on the grounds of, *inter alia*, public morality, public policy or public security.

Accordingly, the prosecution was able to proceed, but the point was established that the defendants could raise the direct effect of Article 30 in their defence.[5]

Directives and direct effect[6]

A further question which arises is whether directives are similarly capable of having direct effect. It has been seen from Article 249 that directives leave no discretion as to their objectives, but do leave some discretion as to manner of implementation. Nevertheless, the ECJ has found provisions of directives to be capable of having direct effect. The reasoning of the ECJ is revealed in *Van Duyn v Home Office* (1975). Article 39 of the EC Treaty (formerly Article 48) provides (in part) that:

1   Freedom of movement for workers shall be secured within the Community.

2   Such freedom of movement shall entail the abolition of any discrimination based on nationality ... as regards employment, remuneration, conditions of work and employment.

3   It shall entail the right, subject to limitations justified on grounds of public policy, public security and public health to accept offers of employment ...

Yvonne Van Duyn, a Dutch national, arrived in England in May 1973, having accepted a job as a secretary with the Church of Scientology. Immigration Officials refused Ms Van Duyn admission to the United Kingdom on the basis that the Secretary of State considered employment with the Church undesirable. In an action against the Home Office, Ms Van Duyn sought to rely on Article 48 of the EC Treaty and a reference was made to the ECJ under Article 177 (now Article 234 of the EC Treaty).

The directive in question was that of the Council[7] which set out the objective of co-ordinating measures concerning movement and residence. The public policy issue, relied on by the Home Office, was regulated by Article 3(1) of Directive 64/221, which stipulates that: '... measures taken on grounds of public policy and public security shall be based exclusively on the personal conduct of the individual concerned.'

The ECJ held that it would be incompatible with the binding effect attributed to a directive to exclude in principle – as the United Kingdom government sought to argue – the possibility that the obligation which it imposed might be invoked by those concerned: that the directive's usefulness would be weakened if an individual could not rely on it before national courts. Since the directive laid down an obligation which was not subject to any exception or condition, and by its nature did not require intervention on the part of the Community or Member States, it followed that the directive was to be regarded as directly effective and conferred enforceable individual rights which national courts must protect.

Thus, it can be seen that, in some cases, directives, as well as regulations and Treaty provisions, may have direct effect – depending on their wording and clarity and whether or not Member State action is required as a prerequisite to

---

5   See also *Erich Ciola v Land Vorarlberg* (1999).

6   See Craig, 1997.

7   64/221/EEC, Article 3.

implementation. The deadline for implementation of the directive must, however, have passed.[8] Where a directive is not precise, and a right insufficiently defined, it will not have direct effect.[9]

Vertical and horizontal effect of Community law

In addition to the concept of direct effect, Community law utilises the notion of vertical and horizontal effect of legal provisions, and this complicating factor is one which is the subject of a good deal of argument. In essence, the concept of vertical effect means that a Community measure – whether a regulation or directive (depending on whether the qualifying criteria are met) – is directly enforceable by an individual against the Member State. In other words, the rights conferred and obligations imposed by Community law are enforceable at the suit of an individual against his or her own Member State, which is responsible for giving effect to the Community provision. For example, in *Van Duyn v The Home Office* (above), the citizen was challenging the decision of a government minister: the action was thus vertical in nature and the directive could be invoked. Of greater difficulty is the question of whether an enforceable obligation exists which entitles an individual to pursue his or her rights, not directly against the Member State, but horizontally against institutions, organisations or individuals within the Member State other than the government of the state and public bodies.

With vertical effect, Community law imposes a duty on the Member State to comply and confers an enforceable right on the citizen. The Member State is thus responsible to the citizen for the enforcement of his or her Community rights. Directives enjoy vertical, but not horizontal, effect and can only be invoked against the state and emanations of the state. The ECJ denies the possibility of horizontal direct effect of directives,[10] which would extend the liability for failure to comply with Community law requirements to non-state bodies or individuals. However, the concept of indirect effect (on which, see below) of directives complicates this theoretically straightforward position. Under the concept of indirect effect, the ECJ insists that national courts have a duty to interpret national law in a manner consistent with Community law directives so far as possible. This doctrine applies even in actions between two individuals, and regardless of whether the directive or national law is earlier in time. Where indirect effect applies, therefore, a directive appears to have been given horizontal effect.

PUBLIC AND QUASI-PUBLIC BODIES

In *Defrenne v SABENA* (1978), the ECJ confirmed the principle of horizontal direct effect of Treaty provisions. Gabrielle Defrenne, an air hostess with the Belgian airline SABENA, was required, under her contract of employment, to retire at the age of 40, whereas men did not have to retire at that age. Moreover, she was paid less than male employees, and would receive a smaller state pension than men.

---

8   See *Pubblico Ministero v Ratti* (1979).
9   See *Gibson v East Riding of Yorkshire Council* (2000).
10 See *Marshall v Southampton and SW Hampshire AHA* (1986); *Faccini Dori* (1994).

The state pension question went to the ECJ, which ruled that Article 119 (now Article 141) of the EC Treaty did not cover state pension rights.[11] Ms Defrenne then commenced actions against her employer, on the issue of equal pay and on the discriminatory retirement ages. In relation to the question of equal pay (but not retirement age), the action was successful.[12] The matter was referred to the ECJ, which ruled that Member States were obliged to implement Article 119 by the end of a transitional period, and that the principle of direct effect of the Article entitled individuals to rely on Article 119, against both public and private sector employers, even where the provisions implementing the principle of equal pay had not been implemented by the state.[13]

The duty imposed on Member States under Article 10 of the EC Treaty is clear, and forms the basis for the ECJ's jurisprudence on direct effect. The question of whether a directive could be relied on by individuals against employers was tested in the English courts in *Marshall v Southampton and South West Hampshire Area Health Authority* (1986). The Sex Discrimination Act 1975 enabled differing retirement ages to be fixed for men and women. Mrs Marshall challenged the legality of the requirement for women to retire at the age of 60, alleging that the Act was contrary to the European Community's Equal Treatment Directive.[14] Two issues, therefore, fell for consideration by the court. First, were different retirements ages in breach of the EC directive and, secondly, if so, could an individual rely on the directive to challenge an Area Health Authority? In other words, the issue was whether the directive was directly effective against an employer in its contractual relationship with an employee or, alternatively, whether the Area Health Authority was an 'emanation of the state'. An Area Health Authority was deemed to be a public (as opposed to a private) body, and accordingly bound by Community law. The ECJ made clear that in principle a directive could not, of itself, create obligations for non-state actors.

In *Foster v British Gas plc* (1991), however, which also entailed differing retirement ages for employees, the Court of Appeal had held that British Gas, a statutory corporation, was not a public body against whom the directive could be enforced. The House of Lords sought clarification on this issue from the ECJ under Article 177 (now Article 234). The ECJ refused to accept British Gas's argument that there was a distinction between a nationalised undertaking and a state agency and ruled that a directive might be relied on against organisations or bodies which were 'subject to the authority or control of the state or had special powers beyond those which result from the normal relations between individuals'. The Court accordingly ruled that a directive might be invoked against 'a body, whatever its legal form, which has been made responsible, pursuant to a measure adopted by the state, for providing a public service under the control of the state and has for that purpose special powers beyond those which result from the normal rules applicable in relations between individuals'.

---

11 *Defrenne v Belgian State* (1971). See now State Social Security Directive 79/7/EEC.
12 *Defrenne v SABENA* (1978).
13 For further discussion of the ECJ's decisions in relations to equality between men and women, see Chapter 20.
14 Directive 76/207/EEC.

Therefore, British Gas was a public body against which a directive might be enforced, a ruling which the House of Lords subsequently accepted. In *Doughty v Rolls Royce plc* (1992), however, the Court of Appeal distinguished *Foster* and held that Rolls Royce plc, although 'under the control of the state', had not been 'made responsible pursuant to a measure adopted by the state for providing a public service'. Rolls Royce was at the time a nationalised body, responsible for providing defence equipment. However the court distinguished between services for the public and services provided to the state, and thereby ruled Rolls Royce not to be a public body for the purposes of the effectiveness of directives. A different result was reached by the Court of Appeal in *National Union of Teachers v Governing Body of St Mary's Church of England (Aided) Junior School* (1997). The court ruled that the governors of a voluntary aided school who had chosen to enter it into the state system were a public body. The powers and duties the Secretary of State for Education and the local education authority amounted to control of the school while it remained in the state system.

The ECJ, in *Faccini Dori v Recreb srl* (1994), re-examined the principle of the horizontal effect of directives. An EC consumer directive,[15] which had not yet been implemented by the Italian authorities, founded a claim against a private undertaking. The Advocate General argued that the ECJ should extend the principle of direct effect of directives to claims against all parties (irrespective of their public or private nature). The ECJ declined to do this, and reasserted its view that directives could not be invoked directly against private bodies. However, the ECJ referred to the possibility that directives could be deemed to be indirectly effective and also that they might be enforceable via the principle of the liability of the state to give effect to Community measures, as seen in *Francovich and Bonifaci v Italy* (1992) (on which, see below).

In relation to directives, the ECJ has ruled that these can, at best, have vertical effect against an emanation of the state – as laid down in *Marshall v Southampton Area Health Authority (No 1)* and subsequently confirmed, as in *Faccini Dori v Recreb srl* (1994) – and not horizontal effect. The role of directives in ensuring the harmonisation and approximation of laws within the legal systems of the Member States of the Union, and the manner in which direct effect ensures harmonisation, is illustrated by the case of *CIA Security International SA v Signalson SA and Securitel SPRL* (1996),[16] which also has significant implications on the direct effect of directives. Involved in this case was the interpretation of Article 30 of the EC Treaty (free movement of goods) and of Directive 83/189/EEC, which came before the ECJ under a reference under Article 177 (now Article 234 of the EC Treaty).[17]

Articles 8 and 9 of Directive 83/189 lay down procedures for the provision of information in the field of technical standards and regulations. Under these provisions, Members States must notify the Commission of all draft technical regulations, and, except in particularly urgent cases, suspend their adoption and

---

15 85/577/EC.
16 See Slot, 1996; Coppel, 1997.
17 The reference was made by the Tribunal de Commerce, Commercial Court, Liège.

implementation for specified periods until the requirement of notification has been complied with. The provisions are unconditional and sufficiently precise in terms of their content to have direct effect and so enable an individual to rely on them before a national court, which *must* decline to apply a national technical regulation which has not been notified in advance in accordance with the directive. The purpose of making such regulations inapplicable is in order to ensure the effectiveness of Community control for which the directive is made. The ECJ ruled that:

> It is settled law that, wherever provisions of a directive appear to be, from the point of view of their content, unconditional and sufficiently precise, they may be relied on against any national provision which is not in accordance with the directive. [*CIA v Signalson* (1996), judgment, para 42]

This decision appears to undermine the clear rule against the horizontal effect of directives as expressed in *Faccini Dori*. Where previously an individual who suffers from the failure of a Member State to implement a directive could resort to a claim for compensation, the decision in *CIA Security* enables an individual to claim in a national court that the directive in question is unenforceable, even in proceedings between private parties.[18] The case of *Unilever Italia v Central Food* (2000) is also relevant. In this case, the Italian government had notified draft labelling rules to the Commission, as required by Directive 83/189. However, rather than delay bringing the draft regulations into force as required by EC law, Italy proceeded to bring them into force. In a dispute between two private organisations, Central Food refused delivery of olive oil because the foods did not comply with Italian labelling legislation. Unilever claimed that the legislation should be inapplicable as contravening EC law, and that the principle of *CIA Security* should extend to a failure to comply with the delay procedure. The ECJ ruled that in civil proceedings between individuals, national courts were required to refuse to apply a national regulation which was adopted during a period of postponement (delay) required under the directive.[19]

The principle of indirect effect

Whereas the principle of direct effect entails rights which are directly enforceable against the Member State or an emanation of the state, indirect effect provides a more subtle mechanism for ensuring compliance with Community law. Indirect effect involves the application of the duty imposed on Member States, including courts of law under Article 10 of the EC Treaty, which provides that:

> Member States shall take all appropriate measures, whether general or particular, to ensure fulfilment of the obligations arising out of this Treaty or resulting from action taken by the institutions of the Community. They shall facilitate the achievement of the Community's tasks. They shall refrain from any measure which could jeopardise the attainment of the objectives of this Treaty.

---

18 See Shaw, 2000, p 451.
19 See Dougan, 2001. Note that the delay is imposed to enable the Commission and other Member States to comment.

In securing the uniformity of the application of Community law within Member States, the ECJ has utilised Article 10 to great effect. National courts are required to interpret all national law in light of Community law, and that duty exists irrespective of whether a Community measure has direct effect.

In *Von Colson v Land Nordrhein-Westfalen* (1984), Article 5 of the EC Treaty (now Article 10) and the Equal Treatment Directive 76/207 fell for consideration by the ECJ (see also *Harz v Deutsche Tradax GmbH* (1984)). As seen above, Article 10 of the Treaty provides that Member States are under a duty to 'take all appropriate measures' to ensure fulfilment of their Community obligations. Ms Von Colson's application for employment in the prison service was rejected. The rejection was based on gender, and was justifiable according to the German court. Under German law, the only compensation payable to Ms Von Colson was her travelling expenses. The question arose as to whether such compensation gave effect to the requirements of Article 5, as it then was. On a reference under Article 177 (now Article 234), the ECJ examined Article 5 (now Article 10) of EC Treaty. The ECJ ruled that Article 5 imposed a duty not just on the governments of Member States, but on all national authorities, including the courts. It is therefore the duty of the domestic courts to interpret national law in such a way as to ensure that the obligations imposed by Community law are achieved. The result is that, although a provision is not directly effective, it may be applied indirectly as law by means of interpretation.[20]

The question of the relationship between domestic law and subsequently introduced Community law came before the ECJ in the *Marleasing* case in 1989. In *Marleasing SA v La Comercial Internacional de Alimentacion SA* (1992),[21] the ECJ, on a reference from a Spanish court, had ruled that, whereas a directive cannot of itself impose obligations on private parties, national courts must as far as possible interpret national law in order to achieve a result pursued by a directive, and that this must be done whether the national provisions in question were adopted before or after the directive. In *Marleasing*, no legislation had been passed to comply with the directive: the duty was nevertheless on the courts to give effect to the *Von Colson* principle, that is to say, the court must interpret domestic law in accordance with Community law. This principle enables directives to have horizontal effect 'by the back door'. A gap in protection, however, still remained. Where there was no domestic law on a Community matter and where, as a result, there was no domestic provision to construe in line with Community law, a problem would remain. The ECJ reaffirmed the interpretative duty in *Centrosteel Srl v Adipol GmbH* (2000), in which the Court stated that it was well settled that 'in the absence of proper transposition into national law, a directive cannot of itself impose obligations on individuals'. However, it went on to state that: '... when applying national law, whether adopted before or after the directive, the national court that has to interpret that law must do so, as far as possible, in the light of the wording and the purpose of the directive so as to achieve the result it has in

---

20 See Drake, 2005.
21 See also *Criminal Proceedings Against Arcaro* (1997); and *Perceval-Price v Department of Economic Development* (2000).

view ...' Note, however, that this is linked to the date on which the implementation period expires. This requirement is designed to frustrate the argument that horizontal effect should not be created on grounds of legal certainty.[22]

The liability of the state

As seen above, Article 10 imposes an obligation on Member States to facilitate and not to impede the objectives of the Community. Where a Member State has failed to undertake its duty, the concept of state liability arises. In *Francovich and Bonifaci v Italy* (1991), employees were seeking compensation against Italy for failure to implement a directive which was designed to guarantee the payment of arrears of wages to employees in the event of their employer's insolvency. The time limit set down by the Community for implementation of the directive had expired and, as a result, Italy was held to be in breach of its Community obligations under Article 5 (now Article 10).[23]

The ECJ held that, while the directive was not sufficiently clear to be directly effective against the state, as regards the identity of institutions responsible for payments, Italy was under an obligation to implement the directive under Article 5 of the EC Treaty. Accordingly, since Italy had failed in its obligation, it was under a duty to compensate individuals for damage suffered as a result of its failure.[24] The ECJ laid down three conditions which applied to the issue of compensation for loss, namely that:

(a) the directive confers individual rights;

(b) the content of those rights can be identified on the basis of the provisions of the directive; and

(c) there is a causal link between the state's failure and the damage suffered by individuals affected.[25]

Under such conditions, an individual may proceed directly against the state. Accordingly, the importance of the principle of direct effect diminishes, and liability falls not on the employer – whether public or private – but on the state, by virtue of its obligations under the Treaty.

However, many questions remained unanswered. Was the state liable only for failure to implement the directive? Was the state liable, irrespective of whether there was any fault involved on the part of the state? Furthermore, was the state liable for loss incurred prior to the ECJ finding the Member State in breach of its obligations? What form of compensation is recoverable? Does it include loss of profits? Is compensation confined to economic loss?

---

22 In *Aannemersbedrijf PK Kraaijeveld BV ea v Gedeputeerde Staten van Zuid-Holland* (1996) and *World Wildlife Fund (WWF) v Autonome Provinz Bozen* (2000) the ECJ considered the question of whether directives could be invoked by individuals in their national courts in the context of judicial review applications, and accepted that this could be the case, without enquiring into their capacity for direct effect. The implication of this is that directives may have an effect distinct from direct effect, which is labelled the 'public law effect'. See Scott, 1998, pp 123, 157.

23 See *Gibson v East Riding of Yorkshire DC* (1999).

24 Cf *Evans v Motor Insurers Bureau* (1999).

25 See also *Marks & Spencer plc v Customs and Excise Commissioners (No 1)* (2000); and *R v Durham County Council ex parte Huddleston* (2000).

In *Brasserie du Pêcheur SA v Federal Republic of Germany* (1996)[26] and *R v Secretary of State for Transport ex parte Factortame Ltd (No 4)* (1996), the ECJ ruled on the principles which regulate the grant of compensation to bodies suffering damage as a result of Member States' breach of Community law. Member States are obliged to make good the loss suffered by individuals when:

- the national legislature, executive or judiciary is responsible for the breach of Community law;
- the rule of law breached is intended to confer rights on individuals;
- the breach is sufficiently serious, defined as a manifest and grave disregard of the limits on the Member State's discretion; and
- there is a direct causal link between the breach of the obligation and the damage suffered.

As to the degree of seriousness of the breach, the considerations to be taken into account by the court considering the issue of compensation, as stipulated by the ECJ, are:

> ... the clarity and precision of the rule breached; the measure of discretion left by that rule ...; whether the infringement and the damage caused was intentional or involuntary; whether any error of law was excusable or inexcusable; the fact that the position taken by a Community institution may have contributed towards the omission, and the adoption or retention of national measures or practices contrary to Community law.

> On any view, a breach of Community law will clearly be sufficiently serious if it has persisted despite a judgment finding the infringement in question to be established, or a preliminary ruling or settled case law of the court on the matter from which it is clear that the conduct in question constituted an infringement. [*Ex parte Factortame (No 4)* (1996)]

Note that *Brasserie* and *Factortame* concerned loss suffered as a result of breaches of Treaty provisions that are directly effective. In other words, the scope of state liability is neither limited to the failure to implement directives nor to the absence of direct effect. Member States must compensate individuals at a level which is commensurate with the loss or damage suffered. Further, if damages could be awarded under English law to similar claims based on domestic law, it is possible to award exemplary damages for the breach of Community law.

The question of compensation was also considered by the ECJ in *R v HM Treasury ex parte British Telecommunications plc* (1996). The United Kingdom had incorrectly transposed a directive into domestic law. The Divisional Court referred the matter to the ECJ which ruled that compensation for loss caused was only payable under the circumstances laid down in *Factortame (No 4)* (above). In the instant case, no reparation was payable because the breach was not sufficiently serious. The directive was imprecisely worded and was reasonably capable of being interpreted in the manner adopted by the United Kingdom.

In *R v Ministry of Agriculture, Fisheries and Food ex parte Hedley Lomas (Ireland) Ltd* (1996), the ECJ ruled that the United Kingdom had an obligation to pay

---

26 For the development of this case, see *R v Secretary of State for Transport ex parte Factortame Ltd (No 1)* (1989); *(No 2)* (1991); *(No 3)* (1992); *(No 5)* (2000).

compensation for damage caused to an individual by its failure to comply with Community law. The United Kingdom authorities decided that they would not issue export licences for the export of live animals intended for slaughter in Spain, on the basis that Spain did not comply with the directive on the welfare of animals and that, if the export licence was granted, the animals would suffer treatment contrary to the directive. However, the export licence was intended to enable the export to a specific slaughterhouse in Spain, which complied with Community directives on animal welfare, and the United Kingdom authorities had no evidence that it did not so comply. As a result, the United Kingdom was in breach of Article 34 of the Treaty (now Article 2a), and its action could not be justified under Article 36 (now Article 30) (justifications for quantitative restrictions on exports). The breach was sufficiently serious and there was a direct causal link between the breach and the damage sustained by the individuals.

In *Dillenkofer v Federal Republic of Germany* (1996), the ECJ ruled, once again, that, if a Member State failed to take 'timeous' (timely) action to implement a Community directive, individuals injured by that failure were entitled to seek reparation from the Member State. Member States had been required to bring a directive[27] into effect before 31 December 1992. Germany brought the directive into effect as from July 1994. Travellers adversely affected by this delay sought compensation for their loss. The ECJ held that:

> The first question to be answered concerned the conditions under which a state incurred liability towards individuals where a directive has not been transposed within the prescribed period.
>
> The crux of that question was whether such a failure was sufficient *per se* to afford individuals who had suffered injury a right to reparation, or whether other conditions had to be taken into account ...

Reciting the precedents, the Court stated that individuals who had suffered damage were entitled to compensation where the three conditions set out above were met. Germany had argued in its defence that the time allowed for full implementation of the directive was too short. This argument, however, did not succeed and the Court ruled clearly that failure to implement a directive within the specified time period *per se* constituted a sufficiently serious breach of Community law.

In *Haim v Kassenzahnärztliche Vereinigung Nordrhein* (2000), the ECJ made it clear that a public law body – as well as the state itself – could be liable for damages for breaches of Community law. Citing *Hedley Lomas*, the Court stated that the same principles applied when considering the liability of the public body as when considering the liability of the state. The question of whether a court of law could be liable to individuals for loss suffered as a result of an error in interpretation was considered by the ECJ in *Köbler v Republic of Austria* (2004). The Court ruled that a Member State's highest court was in principle liable, but only where the court had 'manifestly infringed the applicable law'. All state authorities – legislative, executive and judicial – incurred liability for breach of Community law.

---

27 Council Directive 90/314/EEC of 13 June 1990, Article 9.

THE INTERACTION BETWEEN NATIONAL COURTS AND THE EUROPEAN COURT OF JUSTICE: ARTICLE 234 OF THE EC TREATY[28]

Article 234 represents a vital means by which the harmony of laws between Member States is achieved. The ECJ is insistent both that Community law has supremacy and that it be uniformly applied within Member States. And yet, the treaties establish a partnership between the judges within the national legal systems and the ECJ. It is not difficult to see that the task of uniformity is a difficult one as all nation states adopt and adapt to the requirements of Community law. For optimum effectiveness, a balance needs to be struck between making references to the ECJ where necessary and the domestic courts being able to apply Community law without undue delay or cost.

The text of Article 234 is set out in Chapter 8 (see pp 226–27) and from this it can be seen that courts or tribunals may refer a question, provided that it is a question of Community law – and not national law – which requires interpretation, and provided also that a decision of the ECJ is necessary to enable the national court to reach a decision in the case.[29] A reference becomes mandatory when the question of Community law is before a court or tribunal of last resort, that is to say, a court or tribunal from which there is no further appeal. This does not always mean the House of Lords: in many cases, the appeal structure will end lower in the hierarchy, or leave to appeal may be needed and be refused. Accordingly the court of last resort may effectively be at any level in the judicial hierarchy. If no appeal is possible and the other criteria of a question of Community law and the necessity for interpretation exist, a reference must be made. In *Costa v ENEL* (1964), the reference was from a magistrates' court and involved a claim of less than £2.00 in value: no right of appeal existed because the amount in issue was so small.

The English Court of Appeal, in *Bulmer v Bollinger* (1974), considered the question of when references to the ECJ should be made and Lord Denning laid down the following guidelines for English courts to apply when a reference was a matter of discretion:

(a) the decision must be necessary to enable the court to give judgment – a court must feel that it cannot reach a decision unless a reference is made;

(b) the decision of the question must be conclusive to the case – not just a peripheral issue;

(c) even if the court considers a reference to be necessary, regard must still be paid to the delay involved, the expense, the difficulty of the point of law, and the burden on the ECJ.

These 'guidelines' are questionable in so far as they may impede the willingness of a court to refer matters to the ECJ, and they represent a gloss on the wording of

---

28   See Watson, 1986; Winter, 1972; Curtin, 1990; Pescatore, 1983.

29   The office of immigration adjudicator has been held to be within the meaning of 'court or tribunal' for the purposes of Article 234: *El-Yassini v Secretary of State for the Home Department* (1999).

Article 234. A further impediment to referral may arise from the doctrine of *acte clair* – the concept which states that if a matter is so obvious in its meaning to the domestic court, then no reference need be made. As with the *Bulmer v Bollinger* guidelines, the doctrine of *acte clair* can lead to distortions in interpretation within domestic legal systems. The ECJ has itself considered the circumstances under which courts should refer, and the doctrine of *acte clair*,[30] in the *CILFIT* case of 1983.[31] The Court was asked to consider the meaning of Article 177(3) (now 234(3)) which relates to mandatory references from a court of last resort. The Court ruled that:

(a) there is no duty to refer where a question of Community law was irrelevant – that is, if the interpretation can have no effect on the outcome of the case;

(b) there is no duty of refer when the question is one substantially the same as one previously answered by the ECJ;[32]

(c) there is no need to refer where no real doubt about the law exists. The national court must, however, be satisfied that the matter is equally obvious to courts of other Member States and to the ECJ. To this limited extent, the doctrine of *acte clair* is endorsed.

In *CILFIT*, the ECJ emphasised that the purpose of Article 177 (now Article 234 of the EC Treaty), in general, was to ensure the proper application and uniform interpretation of Community law in all Member States and to prevent divergencies occurring within Member States.

Whereas national courts have some discretion as to whether to refer a matter to the ECJ, the position is different in relation to matters of validity – as opposed to interpretation – of Community law. It is clear that the ECJ has the sole power to rule on whether a measure of Community law is invalid. It is not for national courts to rule on that question. National courts only have the power to uphold the validity of Community legislation.[33]

As seen from the text of Article 234 of the EC Treaty, the questions which may be referred are:

(a) interpretation of the treaties;

(b) the validity and interpretation of acts of institutions of the Community: regulations, directives, etc;

(c) the interpretation of statutes of bodies established by acts of the Council.

Once the ECJ accepts jurisdiction – and a discretion is conferred on the ECJ over whether or not to accept jurisdiction – and gives a ruling, the matter is then returned to the domestic court for application, thus preserving the partnership ideal.

---

30 The concept derives from French law.
31 See Rasmussen, 1984.
32 See *Da Costa en Schaake NV* (1963).
33 See *Henn and Darby v Director of Public Prosecutions* (1981); *Foto-Frost v Hauptzollamt Lubeck Ost* (1987). See also Arnull, 1988a; and Bebr, 1988.

THE QUESTION OF LEGAL SUPREMACY

The question of legal supremacy can be examined both from the standpoint of the Community itself and from that of national law.

The European Court of Justice's view

The ECJ claims that Community law is supreme over national law. This claim carries the following implications:

(a) Community law confers rights on individuals to which national law must give effect;

(b) national law cannot prevail over Community law;

(c) the effectiveness of Community law must be the same in all Member States – it cannot vary in effect from one Member State to another;

(d) courts of Member States must follow the interpretation of laws given by the ECJ or, where there is no authority, and under certain conditions, must refer the matter to the ECJ under Article 234 of the Treaty;

(e) where the ECJ gives a ruling, Member States are under an obligation to amend their national laws so as to conform to Community law.

The ECJ has asserted the supremacy which Community law assumes on many occasions. The early cases lay the foundations for the current relationship between domestic law and Community law. The starting point is once again the case of *Van Gend en Loos v Nederlandse Tariefcommissie* (1963), in which the ECJ enunciated the view that, by signing the treaties, the Member States had created a new legal order, in which individual states had limited their sovereign rights. In *Costa v ENEL* (1964), this view was reaffirmed by the ECJ:

> The transfer by the states from their domestic legal system to the Community legal system of the rights and obligations arising under the Treaty carries with it a permanent limitation of their sovereign rights against which a subsequent unilateral act incompatible with the concept of Community law cannot prevail.

Internationale Handelsgesellschaft mbH v EVST (1970) takes the principle of Community supremacy further. Under Community law, in order to export produce, the company was required to obtain a licence, for which a 'permanent deposit' had to be paid. If the goods were not exported within the licence period, the deposit was to be forfeited. The company paid the deposit, failed to complete the export, and forfeiture was made. The firm sued the agency involved for return of the deposit, arguing that the forfeiture was contrary to the Constitution of the Federal Republic of Germany. The Constitution provided that powers could be transferred to international organisations, but that no transfer could be made of powers which the central government itself did not have. Since the retention of the deposit was contrary to the Federal Constitution, it could not, according to German law, be lawful under the law of the Community. The matter was referred to the ECJ under Article 177 (now Article 234).

The ECJ declared that giving effect to rules or concepts of national law contained even within the constitution of a state, for the purposes of judging the validity of Community measures, would have an adverse effect on the uniformity and efficacy of Community law. The validity of Community measures could be judged only in the light of Community law and could not be affected by allegations that the measures ran counter to fundamental rights as formulated by the constitution of the Member State. Having made this unequivocal and controversial statement, the ECJ softened its tone, ruling that the respect for fundamental rights forms an integral part of the 'general principles of law' protected by the ECJ, and that the protection of such rights, inspired by traditions common to Member States, must be ensured within the framework of the structure and objectives of the Community.

The *Simmenthal* case (1976–80) further developed the jurisprudence of the ECJ in relation to supremacy. Simmenthal imported beef from France into Italy. Under Italian legislation of 1970, fees for veterinary and health checks had to be paid by the importer at the frontier. Simmenthal sued the Italian Minister of Finance for return of the money, arguing that the fee was equivalent to a customs duty and was contrary to Article 12 (now 25) of the Treaty and Community regulations on the common organisation on beef imports. The national court ordered the Ministry to return the money. The minister pleaded that the domestic 1970 Act was binding unless and until set aside by the Italian Constitutional Court.

The Italian court was thus faced with a conflict between Article 12, as it then was, of the Treaty and a later Italian statute. A reference was made under Article 177 (now Article 234), the question at issue being whether directly applicable regulations issued under Article 189 (now Article 249) required national courts to disregard subsequently passed domestic legislation, without waiting for the Constitutional Court to declare it invalid. The ECJ held that regulations take precedence over previous and subsequent domestic legislation and that a national court, whatever its position or role in the national judicial hierarchy, must set aside any provision which conflicts with Community law and apply Community law in its entirety, without waiting until the domestic legislation had been set aside by the Constitutional Court.

The *European Road Transport Agreement (ERTA)* case (*Commission v Council*) (1971) offers another perspective.[34] In 1962, several European states, five of which were EC Member States, others being Eastern European states, signed the European Road Transport Agreement, which sought to establish common rules concerning conditions of work of long distance lorry drivers crossing several state boundaries. As such, the Agreement was not an EC agreement. In 1969, the EC had acted for the (then) six Member States by issuing a regulation covering the same issue. In 1970, the matter was further complicated by the Council meeting to attempt to find a common basis for a new transport agreement. The Commission attempted to have the proceedings of the Council annulled on the basis that the Council was not competent to reach agreements of this kind.[35]

---

34 See Mancini and Keeling, 1991.
35 Acting under the EC Treaty, Article 173 (now Article 230). The power to enter treaties is conferred under Article 310 EC Treaty. In 2006 the Court of Justice reaffirmed the Community's exclusive competence to conclude treaties: see Press Release No 10/06 7 February 2006, Opinion 1/03.

At the heart of the matter lay the question as to who had the power – Member States, the Council or the Commission – to make such 'international' agreements. If Member States retained the power to enter into international agreements (and such a power is a basic attribute of sovereignty), then the Council proceedings were merely recommendatory; if the Council had power then the proceedings took on more of a law making character, which deprived the Member States of competence to act either unilaterally or collectively. The Court held that, having regard to the legal personality of the Community and the exercise of Community competence in 1969, the sole power to enter into such agreements lay with the Community institutions, thus depriving Member States of any capacity in this regard.[36]

In summary, the effect of these early cases is that, since 1962, the ECJ has declared the existence of a new legal order, one to which Member States have limited their sovereign rights by transferring these to the Community. These rights include even the protection of constitutionally guaranteed individual rights. Further, it matters not whether a domestic law in conflict with Community law was passed prior to accession to the EC or subsequently: neither can prevail over Community law. Thirdly, where the Community has the power to act on behalf of Member States in the making of international agreements, Member States have lost that capacity.

Before examining the position of the English courts, it is necessary to consider the means by which Community law is received into English law.

THE RECEPTION OF COMMUNITY LAW INTO THE UNITED KINGDOM

The concepts of monism and dualism

At a conceptual level, the manner in which international law, of which Community law may be regarded as a *sui generis* (that is to say, unique) example, is dependent upon whether a particular state adopts a monist or dualist approach to international law. Monism is the doctrine whereby international law and national law form a single whole, or part of the same conceptual structure, in which international law takes precedence. Under this doctrine, adhered to by, *inter alia*, France and Italy, the obligations of international law, once assumed, enter automatically into the legal system, needing no domestic legislative acts. Once entered, the obligations take precedence over national law.

Dualism, on the other hand, regards the systems of international law and national law as separate: in order for international law to enter into national law, some domestic legislation must be enacted by the national parliament. This is the view adopted by the United Kingdom and is one consistent with the sovereignty of parliament. Treaties are part of international law, and can have no effect in domestic law unless and until a statute of the sovereign United Kingdom Parliament is enacted to give them effect.

---

36 See also *Commission v Finland* (2002).

In 1972, Lord Denning MR confirmed this view in *Blackburn v Attorney General* (1971):

> Even if a Treaty is signed, it is elementary that these courts take no notice of treaties as such. We take no notice of treaties until they are embodied in laws enacted by Parliament, and then only to the extent that Parliament tells us. [p 1382]

Accordingly, the signing of the EC treaties, without any further parliamentary action, had no effect in English law. In order to have effect, it was necessary for parliament to pass the European Communities Act 1972.

The European Communities Act 1972

The most fundamental provisions of the Act can be found in sections 2 and 3(1). Here it is specified that rights and duties which are directly applicable or effective are to be given legal effect within the United Kingdom; that the executive has the power to give effect to Community obligations; that existing and future enactments are to be interpreted and have effect; and that the meaning or effect of Treaty provisions is to be decided according to Community law.

The view of the United Kingdom courts

The manner in which, and extent to which, the United Kingdom courts have accommodated Community obligations requires consideration. First, it should be noted that nothing in the European Communities Act (ECA) 1972 represents an attempt to entrench its provisions, that is to say, to make them immune from amendment or repeal. There is no statement in the Act purporting that EC law is a 'higher form of law', or that the Act cannot be repealed, or could be repealed but only by some specified 'manner and form'. As discussed in Chapter 7, however, it is clear that the doctrine of implied repeal does not operate in relation to the ECA 1972.

Two early challenges were made to the signing of the Treaty on the basis of the potential or actual loss of parliamentary sovereignty. In *Blackburn v Attorney General* in 1971, the plaintiff sought a declaration that the government, by signing the Treaty of Rome, would surrender part of parliament's sovereignty which it could not lawfully do, as no parliament could bind another. In *R v Home Secretary ex parte McWhirter* (1969), the plaintiff adduced that joining the EC was contrary to the Bill of Rights 1689, which declared that all powers of government are vested in the Crown and parliament could not, therefore, by means of a Treaty, transfer those rights.

In both cases, the arguments were disposed of with speed. In *Blackburn*, Lord Denning MR stated that 'even if the Treaty is signed, it is elementary that the courts take no notice of [it] until embodied in an Act of Parliament'. Further, in *McWhirter*, Lord Denning stated that 'even though the Treaty of Rome has been signed, it has no effect as far as the courts are concerned until implemented by Act of Parliament. Until that day, we take no notice of it'.

A challenge to the government's Treaty making power also came in *R v Secretary of State for Foreign and Commonwealth Affairs ex parte Rees-Mogg* (1994). Lord Rees-Mogg sought a declaration from the court to the effect that the government could not lawfully ratify the Treaty on European Union 1992, the Maastricht Treaty, without the consent of parliament. The Court of Appeal gave short shrift to the argument, relying on the earlier precedents, and no appeal was made to the House of Lords.

Conflicts between Community law and domestic law[37]

One area of law which has given rise to an instructive array of case law concerning the relationship between domestic law and Community law is that of sex discrimination. There are, of course, a variety of ways in which discrimination on the basis of sex may arise: in relation to equal pay or equal treatment in respect of access to employment, promotion, training, working conditions, social security and retirement ages. Article 141 and directives[38] form the framework of the law of the Community.

In *Macarthys v Smith* (1981), Mrs Smith was employed by Macarthys as a stockroom manageress. The man who had previously held the position had been paid a higher wage than Mrs Smith. The applicable domestic legislation was the Equal Pay Act 1970, as amended by the Sex Discrimination Act 1975, which provided, *inter alia*, that men and women employed in the same job should be paid equal amounts. The Act was silent, however, as to whether employers were required to pay the same wage to a woman who came to the job after the man had left their employment. The relevant point for interpretation, therefore, was whether men and women, employed at differing times for the same job, were required to be paid equally. However, where women whose work was of equal value to men when employed by a local authority were transferred to another employer by the local authority, the new employer was not obliged to pay the women the same rate as previously. There was no violation of Article 141(1) of the EC Treaty since there was no one body which was responsible for the irregularity and could bring about equal treatment: *Lawrence v Regent Office Care Ltd* (2000).

Article 141 of the EC Treaty provides for equal pay for men and women. This Article is couched in far broader terms than those used by the Equal Pay Act 1970. The matter was referred by the Court of Appeal to the ECJ under Article 177 (now Article 234). The ECJ held that Article 119 required equal pay for men and women whether they were employed contemporaneously or in succession. On receiving the judgment of the ECJ, the Court of Appeal ruled in favour of Mrs Smith. Lord Denning's judgment is of particular significance:

> We should, I think, look to see what those [EC] provisions require about equal pay for men and women. Then we should look at our own legislation on the point – giving it, of course, full faith and credit – assuming that it does fully comply with the obligations under the Treaty. In construing our statute, we are entitled to look to the Treaty as an aid in its construction: and even more, not only as an aid, but as an overriding force. If on close investigation it should appear that our legislation is deficient – or is inconsistent with Community law – by some oversight of our draftsmen – then it is our bounden duty to give priority to Community law. Such is the result of section 2(1) and (4) of the European Communities Act 1972.

---

37 See, *inter alia*, Szyszczack, 1990; de Búrca, 1992a and 1992b.
38 75/117, 76/207, 79/7, 86/378, 86/613.

> Thus far, I have assumed that our Parliament, whenever it passes legislation, intends to fulfil its obligations under the Treaty. If the time should come when our Parliament deliberately passes an Act with the intention of repudiating the Treaty or any provision in it – or intentionally of acting inconsistently with it – and says so in express terms – then I should have thought that it would be the duty of our courts to follow the statute of our Parliament.

Article 119 fell for further consideration in *Garland v British Rail Engineering Ltd* in 1983, this time by the House of Lords. British Rail made concessionary travel facilities available to the children of male employees reaching retirement, but not to the children of women reaching retirement. The question was whether this policy amounted to discrimination contrary to Article 119, as it then was, of the Treaty, and whether the courts in England should construe the Sex Discrimination Act 1975 in a manner so as to make it compatible with the requirements of Article 119. The House of Lords referred the matter to the ECJ, which ruled that the policy amounted to discrimination contrary to Article 119, and that Article 119 must prevail.

In *Duke v GEC Reliance Ltd* (1988), the House of Lords considered the construction of section 6(4) of the Sex Discrimination Act 1975. In the *Duke* case, the plaintiff's claim for damages based on unequal treatment was for a period prior to parliament's amendment of the Sex Discrimination Act to bring English law into line with the requirements of Community law. The House of Lords declined to give retrospective effect to the amendment in light of parliament's express decision not to amend the Act retrospectively. One interpretation of *Duke* is that, being a pre-*Marleasing* case – which makes it clear that the Article 10 duty is imposed on national courts – the House of Lords was in line with the ECJ's interpretation of the Community law at the time.

In *Litster v Forth Dry Dock Ltd* (1990), however, the House of Lords interpreted a domestic regulation contrary to its clear meaning in order to comply with a directive as interpreted by the ECJ. The domestic regulation had been introduced for the purpose of complying with the directive and, accordingly, the House of Lords was complying with its duty under section 2(4) of the ECA 1972 to give effect to Community law.[39] Thus, from the House of Lords' perspective, one important factor in the matter of the interpretation and application of Community law is the response which parliament has made to the Community measure. If parliament had implemented a measure before a directive was made, or if parliament has responded to the requirements of Community law by not amending domestic law in line with Community law, the judges may hold that domestic law prevails over Community law. Where, however, parliament has responded by amending the law, with the intention of bringing English law into line with Community law, the English courts would undoubtedly give effect to the Community law, even where the wording of a domestic regulation required imaginative interpretation to give primacy to Community law.

---

39 See further below on the 1972 Act. See also *Finnegan v Clowney Youth Training Programme Ltd* (1990).

For example, in *Pickstone v Freemans plc* (1989), the applicants were female warehouse workers – operatives – who were paid the same as male operatives but claimed that their work was of equal value to that of warehouse checkers, who were paid more than they were. The Equal Pay Act 1970 did not encompass the concept of equal value, but had been amended in 1983, by statutory instrument under section 2(2) of the ECA 1972, following a ruling by the ECJ that the Equal Pay Act was in breach of a Community directive. The 1983 amendment was intended to bring the Equal Pay Act protection in line with Article 119 and the Community directive, but had been obscurely worded. The result was that the House of Lords was forced to strain to achieve an interpretation which could give effect to what Lord Oliver described as the 'compulsive provision of section 2(4)' of the ECA 1972. The required result was achieved by the House of Lords departing from the strict literal interpretation of the text and implying words to fill the legislative gap in order to reach conformity with Community law.

In *Webb v EMO Cargo (UK) Ltd* (1992), the issue of dismissal on the basis of pregnancy was considered in relation to the EC's Directive on Equal Treatment. The English Trades Union Reform and Employment Rights Act 1993 provides that dismissal on the grounds of pregnancy is unfair.[40] However, in *Webb v EMO Cargo (UK) Ltd* (1992), the Court of Appeal ruled, and the House of Lords affirmed, that a woman who was dismissed from employment because of her pregnancy was not unlawfully dismissed, since – comparing her to a man with a temporary physical disability who would also have been unable to work – the man would also have been dismissed. Under Article 177 (now Article 234), a reference was made to the ECJ. The ECJ ruled that English law was inadequate and held, first, that pregnancy was not a pathological condition to be compared with illness and, secondly, that a pregnant woman's inability to work was temporary and not permanent. Accordingly, the dismissal had amounted to sex discrimination.[41] The Court ruled that the Article 'precludes dismissal of an employee who is recruited for an unlimited term with a view, initially, to replacing another employee during the latter's maternity leave and who cannot do so, because, shortly after recruitment, she is herself found to be pregnant'. The House of Lords, in *Webb v EMO Air Cargo (UK) Ltd (No 2)* (1995) ruled that sections 1(1)(a) and 5(3) of the 1975 Act were to be construed in accordance with the ECJ's ruling and that in the case where a woman was engaged for an indefinite period, the fact that the reason why she would be temporarily unavailable for work at a time when her services would be particularly required was pregnancy was a circumstance relevant to her case, being a circumstance that could not be present in the case of the hypothetical man.[42]

---

40 Trades Union Reform and Employment Rights Act 1993, ss 23–25 and Scheds 2 and 3; EC Pregnancy Directive 92/85.

41 *Dekker v VJV Centrum* (1991).

42 In *Strathclyde Regional Council v Wallace* (1998), the House of Lords ruled that an objectively justifiable employment practice which was not 'tainted' by sexual discrimination, which resulted in unequal pay, did not contravene the Equal Pay Act 1970, relying on *Bilka-Kaufhaus GmbH v Weber von Hartz* (1987), EC Treaty, Article 119 (now Article 141). In a significant ruling by a tribunal on equal pay in March 1998, a former female teacher at an independent school, Eileen Halloran, in an action brought by the Association of Teachers and Lecturers, was found to have been discriminated against in receiving less pay than male teachers.

In *Grant v South West Trains Ltd* (1998), the ECJ apparently reached the limits of its respect for equality. A Southampton employment tribunal had referred a question under Article 234 of the Treaty concerning whether the female partner of a lesbian woman was entitled to the same employment benefits enjoyed by married or cohabiting heterosexual couples. The ECJ ruled that there had been no violation of the Treaty on the basis of sexual inequality.[43]

Undoubtedly, the most constitutionally significant British case revealing the relationship between Community law and domestic law is that *of R v Secretary of State for Transport ex parte Factortame* (1991). In 1970, the Council of Ministers passed a regulation relating to the common organisation of the market in fishery products. The basic principle employed was that, subject to certain exceptions, there should be equal access for the fishing vessels of all Member States to the fishing grounds of fellow Member States. In 1983, due to fears of over-fishing caused by such open access, the Council established, by way of regulation, a system for the conservation and management of resources. This entailed, in part, setting limits to the amount of fish to be caught in certain periods by way of 'total allowable catches' – the allocation of total allowable catches being fairly distributed among the Member States by way of national quotas. The quotas were based on the number of ships flying the flag of a Member State or registered in a Member State.

Spain acceded to the EC in 1986. Before 1986, the extent to which Spanish vessels could ship in British waters was determined under agreements between the Spanish and United Kingdom governments. Under English law, the Merchant Shipping Act 1894 prohibited non-British nationals from owning British fishing vessels but did permit corporate ownership by British companies. Thus, directors/shareholders of Spanish vessels were able to register under the 1894 Act. Some 96 Spanish fishing boats were registered under the Act, and each of these vessels counted as part of the United Kingdom's quota under Community law.

The United Kingdom government, understandably alarmed at the restrictions imposed on the domestic fishing industry and the ability of foreign companies to register and therefore take up part of the United Kingdom's quota, imposed additional conditions for registration which came into force in 1986. The three principal conditions for registration were to be that a proportion of the catch was to be sold in the United Kingdom; that 75 per cent of the crews were to be EC nationals ordinarily resident in the United Kingdom; and that all crew were to be required to contribute to the National Insurance Scheme.

In 1988, the United Kingdom Parliament passed the Merchant Shipping Act and enacted fresh merchant shipping regulations. The new system of registration[44] entailed qualification on the basis of a 'genuine and substantial connection with the United Kingdom'. The revised conditions required that not less than 75 per cent of vessels be owned by United Kingdom citizens resident in

---

43 Note that discrimination on the basis of sexual orientation is now unlawful. See *KB v National Health Service Pensions Agency* (2004).
44 SI 1988/1926.

the United Kingdom; or wholly owned in the United Kingdom, with 75 per cent of shareholders and directors in the United Kingdom; or part owned, with 75 per cent of owners in the United Kingdom; and, further, that vessels be effectively operated from the United Kingdom. Registration would be lost with effect from 31 March 1989 until vessel owners could satisfy the government that they were eligible for registration.

As a result, Factortame, which did not comply with these more stringent requirements, challenged the domestic requirements as incompatible with EC law, claiming discrimination on the grounds of nationality contrary to Article 14 of the Treaty and the rights of companies to establishment under Articles 43–48. The Divisional Court wanted to refer the matter to the ECJ under Article 177 (now Article 234) – a move opposed by the plaintiffs unless the Divisional Court was prepared to grant an interim order protecting their putative Community rights by way of an injunction restraining the government from imposing the requirements of the new regulations. The Divisional Court, in 1990, granted an interim injunction against the government restraining it from applying the Merchant Shipping Act regulations until final judgment was made following a reference to the ECJ under Article 177 (now Article 234).

The government appealed to the Court of Appeal, which ruled that the court had no jurisdiction to grant interim relief disapplying an Act of Parliament. On appeal to the House of Lords, the decision of the Court of Appeal was upheld: injunctive relief against the Crown was not within the court's jurisdiction.

Three constitutionally significant factors arose in *Factortame*. First, whether the court could protect alleged rather than established rights under Community law; secondly, whether – contrary to all previous precedent – the provisions of Community law could confer jurisdiction on the English courts to grant injunctive relief against the Crown; and, thirdly, the conditions under which, should such jurisdiction exist, such relief could be granted.

The ECJ, in its preliminary ruling on the first point (Case 213/89), held that the offending provisions of the Merchant Shipping Act should be suspended, pending a full determination of Factortame's claim, stating that:

> The full effectiveness of Community law would be impaired if a rule of national law could prevent a court seized of a dispute governed by Community law from granting interim relief in order to ensure the full effectiveness of the judicial decision to be given on the existence of rights claimed under Community law.

The ECJ reverted to its decision in *Simmenthal* (1979), reiterating that directly applicable rules were to be fully and uniformly applied in all Member States in accordance with the principle of precedence of Community law over national law. Article 5 of the EC Treaty (now Article 10) imposes an obligation, as has been seen above, to ensure the legal protection which is provided for under the principle of direct effect. The House of Lords in *R v Secretary of State for Transport ex parte Factortame Ltd (No 2)* accepted the ECJ's ruling and granted interim relief.[45]

---

45 On the duty to disapply domestic law in favour of Community law see also *Autologic Holdings plc v Inland Revenue Commissioners* (2004).

While legal action being pursued by Factortame was in progress, a separate action was commenced by the Commission, alleging that the United Kingdom was in breach of its Treaty obligation, and seeking an order that the United Kingdom should suspend the Merchant Shipping Act in respect of fishing vessels.[46] The ECJ held that an interim order could be granted, on the basis that the Act could be in breach of the prohibition against discrimination on the grounds of nationality under Articles 43 and 294.[47]

In *R v HM Treasury ex parte British Telecommunications plc* (1993) (the *BT* case), the applicant sought an interim injunction which would have had the effect – as in *Factortame* – of causing national legislation to be disapplied while the substantive issue was being considered by the ECJ. In *Factortame*, great weight was attached to the very strong *prima facie* case put forward by the applicants. In the *BT* case, the Court of Appeal cautioned against over-reliance on the likelihood of success in the ECJ as a basis for granting relief. In part, this caution was based on the fact that a reference had been made to the ECJ under Article 177 (now Article 234), and that to give great weight to the prognosis for success was to pre-judge the interpretation to be given by the ECJ. The fact that a reference had been made meant that the English court was uncertain as to the question in issue. Accordingly it would be inappropriate to prejudge the issue by granting relief at an interim stage. The Court of Appeal also warned of the difficulties in disapplying domestic legislation. As the court stated, there should be a distinction drawn between a 'major piece of primary legislation' and a 'minor piece of subordinate legislation'. In relation to the former, the court ruled that it would be far more circumspect than in relation to secondary legislation. In the instant case, unlike *Factortame*, the issues were not clear-cut. The court, ruling that it would only grant an interim order 'in the most compelling circumstances', declined to grant the injunction.[48]

The question of the compatibility of domestic law with Community law arose once more in the case of *R v Secretary of State for Employment ex parte Equal Opportunities Commission* (1995) (the *EOC* case). There, the Equal Opportunities Commission had brought an action challenging allegedly discriminatory employment protection provisions in English law, arguing that these contravened European Community legislation. The House of Lords, in a bold decision, granted a declaration to the effect that national law was incompatible with Community law. However, the House of Lords did not go so far as to rule that the English

---

46 *Re Nationality of Fishermen: EC Commission (Spain intervening) v United Kingdom (Ireland intervening)* (1991).

47 In *R v Secretary of State for Transport ex parte Factortame Ltd (No 5)* (2000), the House of Lords ruled that the United Kingdom's breach of Community law was sufficiently serious as to warrant damages. For contrasting interpretations of the *Factortame* case, see Craig, 1991; Wade, 1996; Allan, 1997. See also Williams, 2000.

48 In a challenge to a directive, a company sought to restrain the United Kingdom government from laying before parliament regulations to implement a Council directive. Proceedings were already before the ECJ which was not expected to give judgment until some four months after the time limit for implementation by Member States. The Court of Appeal declined to interfere, stating that interim relief could only be given in cases where there would be irreparable damage and that, in any case, the UK government should not be constrained from making regulations: *R v Secretary of State for Health ex parte Imperial Tobacco Ltd* (2001).

provisions were void; rather, it confined its ruling to the compatibility issue – thus avoiding any potential conflict with parliament and the concept of sovereignty.[49]

In 1994 and 1995, public concern over animal welfare in the export of live animals to Europe for slaughter on the point of destination led to incidents of public disorder and the disruption of exports of animals. In April 1995, the Chief Constable of Sussex decided that no policing would be provided to protect the transport of livestock to the port of Shoreham other than on two consecutive days a week or four consecutive days per fortnight, excluding Fridays, weekends and bank holidays. The Chief Constable later resolved not to change the earlier decision or delay its implementation. International Traders' Ferry Ltd challenged the decision in an application for judicial review.

In *R v Chief Constable of Sussex ex parte International Traders' Ferry Ltd* (1997), the Court of Appeal ruled that the Chief Constable's restrictions on policing could be justified under Article 36 of the EC Treaty (now Article 30), and were proportionate. The export of live animals from the United Kingdom was considered by the ECJ on a reference to the Court by the High Court in *R v Minister of Agriculture, Fisheries and Food ex parte Compassion in World Farming Ltd* (1998). The Royal Society for the Prevention of Cruelty to Animals (RSPCA) and Compassion in World Farming Ltd (CIWF) had asked the minister to prohibit the export of veal calves for rearing in veal crates. They contended that the government had power under Community law to restrict exports to other Member States where the system of rearing calves was contrary to the standards in force in the United Kingdom[50] and the international standards laid down by the European Convention for the Protection of Animals Kept for Farming Purposes, to which all the Member States and the Community had agreed to adhere. Council Directive 91/629/EC laid down minimum standards for the protection of calves, which were lower than the standards laid down by the Convention. CIWF accepted that a ban or restriction on the export of live calves would constitute a quantitative restriction on exports contrary to Article 34 of the Treaty, but nevertheless maintained that such a restriction would be justified having regard to Article 36 (*inter alia*, restrictions justified on the grounds of public morality, public policy or the protection of health or life of animals). The Court ruled that a Member State cannot rely on Article 36 in order to justify restrictions where the Commission has adopted harmonised rules to regulate the area. Directive 91/629/EC laid down standards and, even though these were less stringent than the national provisions, the directive overrode the national requirements.

---

49 See also *Lawrence v Regent Office Care Ltd* (2003); *Armstrong v Newcastle upon Tyne NHS Hospital Trust* (2005).
50 Welfare of Livestock Regulations, SI 1994/2126 and Welfare of Livestock Regulations (Northern Ireland), SI 1995/172.

CONCLUSION

As the discussion of the aims, development and structure of the European Union and Community in Chapter 8 demonstrates, the original aims of the Community established under the Treaty of Rome have been expanded and developed into an ambitious, expansive and vigorous Union and Community, founded on the principles of individual rights and the rule of law. European integration has extended from the limited goals of a common market to incorporate full economic and monetary union and movement towards ever closer co-operation in relation to matters concerning common defence and security policies and matters relating to co-operation in police and judicial matters. As the aims and objectives of the Union have expanded, so too has the law of the Community. The ECJ, through its dynamic approach, has ensured the supremacy of Community law over domestic law, to the extent that the ECJ's early statement that the Community represents a 'unique legal order' is now a reality which touches on increasingly wide aspects of domestic law.

PART IV

CENTRAL, REGIONAL AND LOCAL GOVERNMENT

CHAPTER 10

CENTRAL GOVERNMENT

INTRODUCTION

In this chapter, the structure and roles of the institutions of central government – the Crown, Privy Council, Prime Minister, Cabinet, ministers and government departments – are examined. In Chapter 11, the concept of responsible government is introduced, and the fundamentally important concept of ministerial responsibility is discussed. If government is to be conducted under the law, and in line with the principles of democracy and constitutionalism, it is of the utmost importance that those holding power should be accountable to citizens through their elected legislature. The responsibility of ministers of the Crown is thus fundamental to the constitution, and the more so in the absence of an authoritative constitutional document which defines the scope and limits of ministerial power. Note that the procedural means by which parliament scrutinises government action is considered in Chapter 16.

THE STRUCTURE OF GOVERNMENT

THE CROWN

> It is commonly hidden like a mystery, and sometimes paraded like a pageant, but in neither case is it contentious. The nation is divided into parties, but the Crown is of no party. Its apparent separation from business is that which removes it both from enmities and from desecration, which preserves its mystery, which enables it to combine the affection of conflicting parties – to be a visible symbol of unity to those still so imperfectly educated as to need a symbol.[1]

While the Monarch is titular head of the government and all governmental acts are carried out in the name of the Crown, the role of the Queen is largely, but not completely, formal and ceremonial. In the study of the government it is necessary to bear in mind that the United Kingdom remains a constitutional monarchy and that the Crown is the symbolic head of the executive, legislature and judiciary. The remaining prerogatives of the Crown have been discussed in Chapter 6, which should be referred to for discussion of the Crown's role in the appointment of the Prime Minister and the dissolution of parliament.

Succession to the Crown

The Act of Settlement 1700 provides that succession to the throne is confined to members of the Protestant religion and specifically excludes Roman Catholics, or those married to Roman Catholics, from succession.[2] This religious exclusion has

---

1   Bagehot, 1867, p 90.
2   For this reason, Prince Michael of Kent was excluded from the line of succession upon his marriage to a Catholic in 1978.

been under recent discussion. Any amendment to the Act of Settlement would require the consent of the parliaments of the United Kingdom's Dominions,[3] and may also require the assent of the parliaments of all independent member countries of the Commonwealth which recognise the Queen as Head of State.

The line of succession

Succession to the Crown traditionally devolves according to the principles of *primogeniture*, that is to say that male heirs, and their children (irrespective of sex), take precedence over female heirs. Again, this matter is said to be under current discussion with a view to reform. Because of *primogeniture*, the current line of succession is Prince Charles, his sons Prince William and Prince Henry, Andrew, Duke of York, his daughters, Princess Beatrice and Princess Eugenie, Prince Edward, his daughter Lady Louise Windsor, Princess Anne, the Princess Royal, and then her children, Peter and Zara Phillips, and thereafter to other members of the Royal Family in a predetermined line of succession.

Were the Queen to abdicate, in favour of an early succession by Prince Charles, the assent of the parliaments of the Dominions would be required. The only precedent case is that of King Edward VIII, who abdicated in 1936 in order to avoid the constitutional crisis which was perceived to be imminent if he persisted in his intention to marry the American divorcee, Wallis Simpson.[4]

The Regency Acts

Should the Crown fall 'vacant', through death or (more rarely) abdication, or the Monarch becomes too ill to fulfil his or her constitutional duties,[5] and the successor has not yet reached the age of majority, there will be a need for the appointment of an adult with responsibility for the Crown's duties during the successor's minority. This situation is regulated under the Regency Acts 1937–53.

The Regency Act 1937 provides that the Sovereign may appoint Counsellors of State, charged with the responsibility of carrying out the Sovereign's duties whenever he or she is either absent from the United Kingdom, or suffering from temporary physical or mental illness. Those eligible to be appointed include the Monarch's spouse and the next four persons in line of succession.

Where there is the need to appoint a Regent, the Regency Act 1937 provides that, until the heir to the Throne reaches the age of 18, his or her duties will be carried out by a Regent.[6] The appointment of a Regent continues until it is declared to be no longer necessary by the wife or husband of the Monarch, the Lord Chancellor, the Speaker, the Lord Chief Justice and the Master of the Rolls.

---

3 Statute of Westminster 1931. Australia and Canada have Dominion status. New Zealand ceased to be a Dominion in 1987: see the Constitution Act 1986 (NZ), s 26.
4 See His Majesty's Declaration of Abdication Act 1936.
5 As occurred in the reigns of George III (in 1811) and George VI (in 1938).
6 The 1953 Regency Act provided that if one of Queen Elizabeth II's minor children succeeded to the throne, the Queen and the Duke of Edinburgh would be appointed Regent.

The Royal Titles Act 1953

By statute, the Monarch may assume whatever title she thinks fit, with the assent of member governments of the Commonwealth. The Royal Titles Act provides the title:

> Elizabeth II by the Grace of God of the United Kingdom of Great Britain and Northern Ireland and of her other Realms and Territories Queen, Head of the Commonwealth, Defender of the Faith.

Within the Commonwealth, it was agreed in 1952 that the title of the Monarch within the Commonwealth was for each state to determine.[7] Accordingly, the only title of the Monarch which is uniform throughout the Commonwealth is that of 'Head of the Commonwealth'.

Prince Charles has made it known that he would prefer, on succession, to be known as 'Defender of Faith', rather than Defender of the (Protestant) Faith.

The Civil List

The Civil List is a fund provided by parliament for the financing of expenditure on official business by the Monarch and specified members of her family. The Civil List is designed to offset expenditure incurred on official business, the cost of maintaining royal residences and the salaries and pensions payable to employees of the Crown.[8] The List was established in the reign of George III (1760–1820) and represents an agreement whereby parliament will vote monies for the official business of the Royal Family in exchange for the surrender of hereditary revenues held by the Crown.[9] The revenues are paid directly into the Exchequer and become part of the Consolidated Fund.[10] Payments under the Civil List are provided for by the Civil List Act 1952, as amended.[11] The Civil List Act 1972 made separate provision for the Duke of Edinburgh and other members of the Royal Family who undertake public duties in the name of the Crown. In 1992, the Queen took over financial responsibility for members of the Royal Family, although the Duke of Edinburgh still receives separate provision under the Civil List, as did the late Queen Mother. Financial provision for the Prince of Wales is made from the revenues accruing from the Duchy of Cornwall.

Taxation and the Sovereign

Until 1992, the Sovereign was not liable to pay tax on her private property[12] unless an Act of Parliament so determined. From 1993, the Queen, on her own undertaking, has paid tax on her private income.

---

7 At a meeting of Commonwealth Prime Ministers. See Cmd 8748, 1952, London: HMSO.
8 The amount awarded is variable: see the Civil List Act 1972, which provides that sums may be increased from time to time by statutory instrument, s 6; and the Civil List Act 1975.
9 With the exception of revenues from the Duchies of Cornwall and Lancaster.
10 See further Chapter 15.
11 Civil List Act 1972; Civil List Act 1975.
12 Other than on revenues from Balmoral and Sandringham estates which are liable to tax under the Crown Private Estates Act 1862.

The Crown Estate

Revenues from Crown lands and from other sources are managed by the Crown Estate Commissioners[13] under the authority of the Chancellor of the Exchequer and the Secretary of State for Scotland. The Commissioners lay an annual report before parliament. It is these revenues which are exchanged for provision under the Civil List.

The role of the Monarch in the United Kingdom's constitutional democracy

In Walter Bagehot's often-quoted phrase, the Monarch has the right to 'be consulted, the right to encourage, the right to warn' (1867). As such, the Queen must be fully informed of the actions of her government, and given adequate opportunity to express her views.

If the role of the Monarch is to remain respected by governments of all political persuasions, and the nation, it is axiomatic that the Queen be seen formally to be immune from party-political differences and to fulfil her duties in an even-handed manner. This is not to suggest that the Queen has no views on her government's policies or that she should not express them to the Prime Minister. What is required, however, is the absolute confidentiality of discussions between herself and the Prime Minister, and, should there be a disagreement over policy, it is required that, once the Monarch's views are made known, irrespective of her approval or otherwise, she follows the advice of her Prime Minister on policy matters.[14]

Queen Elizabeth II, since her accession to the throne in 1952, has presided over 35 years of Conservative rule and 19 years of Labour rule. She has thus accumulated a wealth of experience in political matters unmatched by her individual Prime Ministers.

The state opening of parliament

At the start of each new parliamentary session, the Monarch formally opens parliament. The Queen's Speech is formally delivered to the House of Lords with members of the House of Commons having been summoned to the Lords by Black Rod. The Speech outlines the government of the day's proposals for legislation in the forthcoming session. Thereafter, there is a four or five day debate on the Speech in the Commons.

---

13 Crown Estates Act 1961.
14 See the letter to *The Times*, by the Queen's Press Secretary, Sir William Heseltine, 29 July 1986.

THE CHANNELS OF COMMUNICATION
BETWEEN CROWN AND GOVERNMENT

Government papers

The Monarch receives copies of all significant government papers. She also receives copies of reports from ambassadors abroad and Commonwealth High Commissioners. All Cabinet papers and the minutes of Cabinet meetings are received by the Queen.

The weekly prime ministerial audience

Whatever the pressure of work, the Prime Minister attends a weekly half to one hour audience with the Queen. It is at this weekly meeting that issues will be discussed and the Queen's views made known to the Prime Minister.[15] Channels of communication are facilitated by the Queen's Private Secretary, whose appointment is the choice of the Queen, and who on appointment will become a Member of the Privy Council. The Private Secretary may not belong to any political party. Very rarely will the Queen's Private Secretary be drawn into public debate although, in 1986, the then Private Secretary, Sir William Heseltine, wrote to *The Times* (following public claims that the Queen and Prime Minister – then Mrs Thatcher – disagreed on policy matters). In his letter, Sir William Heseltine spelled out three main points concerning the relationship between the Crown and the Prime Minister:

(a) the Sovereign has the right and duty to counsel, encourage and warn her government. She is thus entitled to have opinions on government policy and to express them to the Prime Minister;

(b) whatever the Queen's personal opinions may be, she is bound to accept and act on the advice of her Ministers;

(c) the Sovereign is obliged to treat communications with the Prime Minister as entirely confidential.[16]

THE PRIVY COUNCIL

Historical origins

Since 1066, the Monarch has appointed a Chancellor, who was head of the King's administration and had custody of the Great Seal. The Chancellor had responsibility for the administration of law, drawing up royal writs and exercising judicial powers. The Chancellor has always been a Member of the King's Council. The Privy Council may be viewed as the successor to the *Curia Regis*, the supreme legislative, executive and judicial body. The Council is traceable to the thirteenth century. It was through the Privy Council that monarchs would rule without recourse to parliament. Under Edward I (1272–1307), it was difficult to discern whether legislative acts emanated from the King in Parliament or the King in

---

15 See further Brazier, 1990, Chapter 8 and 1999, Chapter 9.
16 *The Times*, 29 July 1986; see also Marshall, 1986b.

Council.[17] Throughout the fourteenth century, however, there were serious conflicts between the Council and parliament and, in the reigns of Henry IV (1399–1413) and Henry V (1413–22), there is evidence of the Commons petitioning the King against the jurisdiction seized by the Council. The Council by this time was exercising judicial powers in relation to both criminal and civil litigation. Enforcement of the criminal law, where offences against the state were alleged or officers of state were involved, was effected by the feared Court of Star Chamber.[18] To this claim to wide civil and criminal jurisdiction came parliamentary objection on the basis that the Star Chamber was usurping the function of the common law courts. FW Maitland writes of the Council at this time that:

> The Tudor reigns are, we may say, the golden age of the Council: the Council exercises enormous powers of the most various kinds; but it is not an independent body – as against the King it has little power or none at all. [1908, p 256]

By the reign of Henry VIII (1509–47), the Council comprised Privy Councillors – the King's elite advisers – and ordinary Councillors – lawyers and administrators. Over time, the Council fragmented into committees dealing with specified matters. The Council survived the abolition of the Star Chamber, although its powers were much weakened. Following the restoration of the monarchy, it became the body on which the King relied for advice. With the abolition of the Star Chamber, did the Council lose all its judicial powers? From early times the Council had asserted jurisdiction over territory overseas which fell under the suzerainty of the English Crown. With the Channel Islands and the Isle of Man coming under the Crown's protection in the thirteenth century, the seeds were sown for the Privy Council's jurisdiction over civil and criminal appeals from the British Empire and Commonwealth.

With the Glorious Revolution of 1688 and the rise of parliamentary sovereignty, the role of the Council changed. Under William, the inner circle of the Council became known as the Cabinet Council. Through this Cabinet, the King could exercise all his powers, although he had to have recourse to the wider membership of the Privy Council in order to undertake acts which required Orders in Council, the formal means by which such prerogative acts came into effect. It was the Privy Council which determined the summoning and dissolution of parliament, although it seems clear that the King would act through Orders in Council published after consultation with an inner circle of the Privy Council. The early origins of Cabinet government can be seen here. As FW Maitland observed:

> We now see how it is legally possible for the work of government to fall into the hands of a small number of the Council – those Members who hold the high offices of state and who have control over the seals of office. If the King has with him the Chancellor, the Treasurer or First Lord of the Treasury, the Lord Privy Seal, and the Secretaries of State, he can get his work done without consulting the mass of Privy Councillors. If, for any purpose, an Order in Council is required, a meeting of the King with just these few

---

17   Maitland, 1908, p 136.
18   Abolished in 1640.

intimate advisers will be a good enough meeting of the Privy Council at which Orders in Council can be made. So much is the legal possibility of Cabinet government. [1908, p 394]

While King William and Queen Anne attended Council meetings regularly, a change of practice occurred with the reign of George I (1714–27) and George II (1727–60). Neither could speak English, and nor were they particularly concerned with English matters. Accordingly, the Cabinet began to meet without the King. Under George III (1760–1820), the same situation prevailed, the Cabinet meeting without the King and communicating its decision to the King. Again, we find the origins of today's Cabinet, with the three principles of Cabinet government becoming apparent: those of 'political unanimity, common responsibility to parliament and a common leader'.[19] With the rise of the Cabinet system of government in the eighteenth century, the Privy Council gradually lost much of its power.[20]

Composition of the Privy Council

The Privy Council has over 400 members, half of whom are peers, half commoners. There is no fixed number of members. Appointments are made by the Crown, with the advice of the Prime Minister. By convention, all present and past Cabinet members are appointed to the Privy Council. Also included in the membership are members of the Royal Family, senior judges, two Archbishops, British Ambassadors, the Speaker of the House of Commons, present and former leaders of the Opposition, and leading Commonwealth spokesmen and judges. On appointment, a new member of the Council takes the oath of allegiance, or affirms loyalty. The Privy Council oath binds the member to secrecy in relation to any matters discussed in the Council.[21]

Meetings of the Privy Council

The Privy Council may meet wherever the Queen so decides although, normally, the Council will meet at Buckingham Palace. The quorum is three.

FUNCTIONS OF THE PRIVY COUNCIL

Proclamations and Orders in Council

Proclamations are used for the summoning, proroguing and dissolving of parliament and declarations of war and peace. Orders in Council give effect to decisions reached under the royal prerogative and under statute. Orders in Council may be legislative, executive or judicial.

---

19 Maitland, 1908, p 395.
20 See Mackintosh, 1977, Chapter 2. On the constitutional struggles between King, courts and parliament, see Chapter 6.
21 Privy Councillors would in any event be prevented from disclosing confidential information by virtue of the Official Secrets Acts 1911–89.

Committees of the Privy Council

The majority of Privy Council functions are undertaken in committees. Miscellaneous committees have been established. These include committees dealing with scientific research, universities and the granting of charters. The most important committee is the Judicial Committee.

The Judicial Committee was established under statute by the Judicial Committee Act 1833. The Judicial Committee Act 1844 provided that the Queen may, by Order in Council, admit appeals from courts of British colonies or overseas territories. In addition, under the Devolution Acts[22] the Judicial Committee has jurisdiction to determine disputes relating to devolved or reserved powers of the Scottish Parliament, the Northern Ireland Assembly and the Welsh Assembly. Prior to the Constitutional Reform Act 2005, the Judicial Committee was composed of the Lord Chancellor, Lord President and former Lord Presidents of the Council, Lords of Appeal in Ordinary and the Lord Justices of Appeal, former Lord Chancellors and retired Lords of Appeal; senior judges or former judges of those Commonwealth countries from which a right of appeal still lies.[23]

The Constitutional Reform Act 2005 amends the composition and jurisdiction of the Judicial Committee of the Privy Council. In terms of composition, the Lord Chancellor and Lord President of the Council are no longer entitled to sit as members of the Privy Council. In relation to jurisdiction, the power to determine devolution issues is transferred from the Privy Council to the new Supreme Court.[24]

In addition to its appellate jurisdiction, the Judicial Committee has on occasion examined and reported on matters of constitutional importance. It has, for example, examined the legality of telephone tapping, issues of state security, and British policy in relation to the Falkland Islands.

THE OFFICE OF PRIME MINISTER[25]

As with so much of the United Kingdom's constitution the office of Prime Minister is one which developed by convention rather than by law. The office dates from the early eighteenth century,[26] and had become firmly established as a necessary and inevitable post in the latter half of the nineteenth century, when the extension of the franchise combined with the growth of political parties to produce both a (reasonably) accountable government and an opposition party. The first official recognition of the post of Prime Minister derives from the Treaty of Berlin 1878, and statutory and other formal references to the office remain scant.[27]

---

22 Government of Wales Act 1998, Northern Ireland Act 1998, Scotland Act 1998.

23 Appellate Jurisdiction Acts 1876, 1887, 1908; Judicial Committee Amendment Act 1895.

24 See the Constitutional Reform Act 2005, ss 40, 138 and Sched 9.

25 See Blake, 1975. For a listing of prime ministers and their political parties, see Appendix II.

26 Sir Robert Walpole, 1721–42.

27 *Inter alia*, the Chequers Estates Act 1917, Chevening Estate Act 1959, the Parliamentary and Other Pensions Act 1972, the House of Commons Disqualification Act 1975, Ministerial and Other Pensions and Salaries Act 1991.

In 1889, Lord Morley[28] stated that:

> ... the Prime Minister is the keystone of the Cabinet arch. Although in Cabinet all its members stand on an equal footing, speak with an equal voice, and, on the rare occasions when a division is taken, are counted on the fraternal principle of one man, one vote, yet the head of the Cabinet is *primus inter pares*, and occupies a position which, so long as it lasts, is one of exceptional and peculiar authority.

Little has changed over the intervening century and the judgment expressed above remains true today. Contemporary interest focuses on the power of the office, the relationship between the Prime Minister and the Cabinet and the occasional dominance of the Prime Minister over Cabinet colleagues.[29] One question which inevitably arises is whether government has changed from being parliamentary government, through to being best described as Cabinet government and now through to prime ministerial government.[30] The assessment of this question is a matter for evaluation on consideration of the evidence. It must be recognised, however, that the extent to which there exists prime ministerial dominance will depend very much upon the individual personality of the incumbent Prime Minister: there can be no broad generalisations. It must also be recognised that, whatever the personal power of the Prime Minister, he or she is ultimately dependent upon the support of Cabinet, party and parliament; and, in turn, that support is dependent upon the support of the electorate expressed not just through the vote at a general election, but continually expressed in that amorphous concept 'the mood of the people'. As the resignation of Mrs Margaret Thatcher in 1990 demonstrated,[31] even a seemingly invincible Prime Minister, who had enjoyed success at three general elections, can fall victim to the loss of the vital support of Cabinet and consequently the loss of office.

The Prime Minister, in addition to being the figurehead of government both within the United Kingdom and internationally, holds more than one office. The Prime Minister holds office as First Lord of the Treasury[32] and is formally in charge of the Treasury, although in practical terms it is the Chancellor of the Exchequer who runs the Treasury. It is in part because of the role of First Lord of the Treasury that the Prime Minister must be a Member of the House of Commons which has parliamentary supremacy over financial matters.[33] Since 1937, the Ministers of the Crown Act has assumed that the office of Prime Minister and First Lord are held by the same person. Since 1968, the Prime Minister has also held responsibility for the Civil Service as Minister for the Civil Service.[34] On occasions, Prime Ministers will assume other offices. For example,

---

28 Cited in Gwynn, 1932.
29 See Hennessy, 1986b, Chapter 3.
30 See Wolf-Phillips, 1984; Brazier, 1991. On this question and the role of Mrs Thatcher, see Doherty, 1988; Marshall, 1991.
31 See, *inter alia*, Alderman and Carter, 1991; Alderman and Smith, 1990; Marshall, 1991; Blackburn, 'Margaret Thatcher's resignation as Prime Minister', in 1992.
32 Ministerial and Other Salaries Act 1975. As First Lord of the Treasury the Prime Minister has responsibility for the Civil Service which is controlled by the Treasury.
33 No Prime Minister has been a member of the House of Lords since 1902.
34 SI 1968/1656; SI 1971/2099. See *Council of Civil Service Unions v Minister for Civil Service* (1985).

Ramsey MacDonald also held office as Foreign Secretary (Labour government, 1924); Winston Churchill was also Minister of Defence.

The Prime Minister and membership of the House of Commons

Between 1837 and 1902, six Prime Ministers were peers.[35] However, as early as 1839, the Duke of Wellington expressed the view that:

> I have long entertained the opinion that the Prime Minister of this country, under existing circumstances, ought to have a seat in the other House of Parliament, and that he would have great advantage in carrying on the business of the Sovereign by being there.[36]

With the extension of the franchise in 1832, 1867 and 1884, the supremacy of the Commons over the Lords was firmly established and the role of the House of Lords in legislation was reduced significantly by the Parliament Acts of 1911 and 1949. There are good reasons – aside from the office of First Lord of the Treasury – for arguing that the Prime Minister must be a member of the House of Commons. First, he is today the elected leader of the parliamentary party and must lead that party into a general election for an affirmation – or denial – of the party's, and hence his own, mandate. Secondly, the doctrine of individual and collective ministerial responsibility applies to the Prime Minister as it does to all other holders of office. Above all, the doctrines require that a minister is accountable to the electorate through parliament. For the Prime Minister not to be accountable to the democratically elected House of Commons would effectively defeat the concept of collective responsibility and would be an affront to democracy and the very idea of constitutionalism. Certainly, no breach of law would follow if the Queen invited a peer to take office as Prime Minister and First Lord of the Treasury: but it would clearly fly in the face of convention.

The choice of Prime Minister[37]

A change in Prime Minister will be brought about by either resignation or death or – rarely – dismissal of the office holder. Resignation from office may stem from electoral defeat at a general election, from conflict within the government, from losing the support of the party, from losing a vote of confidence in the House, from a challenge to the leadership of the party, from illness or old age, from death, from voluntary retirement or from loss of support of the Cabinet.[38]

Whatever the explanation for a change in Prime Minister, it is for the monarch to appoint the succeeding Prime Minister. It was seen in Chapter 6 that it is the prerogative right of the Crown to appoint whosoever she pleases, but that by

---

35 Lords Melbourne, John Russell, Derby, Aberdeen, Beaconsfield, Salisbury.

36 Parl Debs 3rd Ser Vol 47 Col 1016, cited in Jennings, 1959a, p 21.

37 See, *inter alia*, Jennings, 1959a, Chapter II; Mackintosh, 1977, Chapter 20; Brazier, 1982 and 1990, Chapter 4.

38 Defeat: 1945, 1951, 1964, 1970, 1974, 1979, 1997. Conflict: as in 1931. Loss of party support: Mrs Margaret Thatcher's resignation, 1990. Loss of confidence vote: 1895, 1923, 1979. Leadership challenge: Thatcher, 1990. Illness: Campbell-Bannerman, 1908, Bonar Law, 1923, Eden, 1957, Macmillan, 1963. Old age: Salisbury, 1902, MacDonald, 1935, Churchill, 1955. Voluntary retirement: Baldwin, 1937, Wilson, 1976. Loss of Cabinet support: Mrs Thatcher in 1990.

convention rather than law the Queen appoints as Prime Minister the leader of the political party who can command a majority in the House of Commons. In the days before the major parties chose their leaders by some form of election, some discretion was left to the Queen as to the choice of Prime Minister. Nowadays, such discretion is all but dead, other than where a general election produces a situation where there is no overall majority party in the House of Commons. The actual choice of Prime Minister will thus be dictated by the election process within the major political parties[39] and, where relevant, by the result of a general election.[40]

Formation of Cabinet[41]

Once in office, the first task of the Prime Minister is to form his Cabinet. Constitutionally, the appointment of all ministers is a decision for the monarch but, in practice, it is the Prime Minister who determines who shall be appointed. The Prime Minister decides which government departments should be represented in Cabinet although, by convention, certain Departments are always represented. Thus, the Chancellor of the Exchequer, the Secretary of State for Foreign and Commonwealth Affairs, the Home Secretary, the Secretary of State for Constitutional Affairs and Lord Chancellor, the Secretary of State for Defence, the Secretary of State for Scotland and the Leader of the House of Commons always hold a seat in Cabinet. Further constraints on membership exist. For example, under the Ministers of the Crown Act 1975, certain Cabinet positions are allocated to Members of the House of Lords. Further, under the House of Commons Disqualification Act 1975, the size of Cabinet is effectively controlled – if indirectly – by limiting the number of ministers who may draw a ministerial salary.

It is also for the Prime Minister to decide whether Cabinet Members should remain in office, and he has the right to require a member to resign and, if they refuse, to request the Queen to dismiss them. This form of control was most strikingly seen in 1962 when Harold Macmillan in 'the night of the long knives' removed seven ministers (from a Cabinet of 20) overnight. The Cabinet normally comprises approximately 20 senior members of the government of the day. The actual membership is not fixed, and is (subject to convention) for the Prime Minister to determine.

THE CABINET

The membership of the Cabinet in Tony Blair's government was as follows as at June 2006:

---

39   See Brazier, 1990, Chapter 1.
40   As in 1906, 1918, 1922, 1931, 1935, 1950, 1955, 1959, 1966, October 1974, 1983, 1987, 1992 where the Government was returned with a clear majority in the House of Commons.
41   See Jennings, 1959a, Chapter III.

OFFICE

Prime Minister, First Lord of the Treasury and Minister for Civil Service
Deputy Prime Minister and First Secretary of State
Chancellor of the Exchequer
Secretary of State for Foreign and Commonwealth Affairs
Chancellor of the Duchy of Lancaster
Secretary of State for Constitutional Affairs and Lord Chancellor
Secretary of State for the Home Department
Secretary of State for Education and Skills
Secretary of State for Trade and Industry
Secretary of State for Environment, Food and Rural Affairs
Secretary of State for Defence
Secretary of State for Health
Leader of the House of Commons and Lord Privy Seal
Secretary of State for Culture, Media and Sport and Minister for Women
Secretary of State for Work and Pensions
Secretary of State for Northern Ireland and for Wales
Secretary of State for International Development
Secretary of State for Transport and Secretary of State for Scotland
Leader of the Lords and Lord President of the Council
Parliamentary Secretary to the Treasury and Chief Whip
Chief Secretary to the Treasury
Secretary of State for Communities and Local Government
Minister without Portfolio

Cabinet meetings

The Prime Minister has almost total control over the conduct of Cabinet. The holding and conduct of Cabinet meetings is a matter for the Prime Minister to decide. Traditionally, but not invariably, full meetings of Cabinet are held twice a week. Matters which are to be discussed in Cabinet are for the Prime Minister to determine.[42]

Timing of dissolution of parliament

The timing of the dissolution of parliament is within the Prime Minister's discretion and there is no requirement, either in law or convention, that the Prime Minister submit his choice of date to the Cabinet. On the dissolution of parliament, see further Chapter 6.

---

42 See Mackintosh, 1977, Chapter 21. Cf Wilson, 1976.

Appointments

The Prime Minister has significant powers and influence over the appointment of persons to senior positions. For example, it is the Prime Minister who is responsible for the appointment of a Commission to oversee the work of the Security Service, and his consent is required for the appointment of most senior civil servants. Prime Ministerial nomination leads to the appointment of, *inter alia*, bishops and the Parliamentary Commissioner for Administration. His advice is given to the Queen on honours and on appointments to the Privy Council.

The role and functions of Cabinet[43]

> A Cabinet is a combining committee – a hyphen which joins, a buckle which fastens the legislative part of the state to the executive part of the state. In its origins, it belongs to the one and in its functions, it belongs to the other.[44]

The Cabinet represents the nucleus of government. It is the Cabinet as a whole which, at least in theoretical terms, formulates, initiates and implements the policy of the government. Because there is no written constitution defining and controlling the working of Cabinet, it is not possible to give a fixed picture of its role. The use and working of Cabinets will vary with different governments and the different style and personality of the Prime Minister of the day.

As the central decision making body, the Cabinet has great power in relation to parliament as a whole, in relation to the political party it represents and in relation to the Prime Minister. While the Prime Minister may control the composition and working of Cabinet, no Prime Minister can ultimately survive in office without the support of Cabinet and party.[45] The style of leadership will depend upon the personality of the premier, and an evaluation of whether it is parliamentary government, Cabinet government or Prime Ministerial government will also depend upon the strength of the Prime Minister vis à vis his or her colleagues.

Cabinet committees

In order to facilitate efficiency, the Cabinet is supported by a system of committees which, again, is largely determined by the Prime Minister.[46] Some of these are standing committees which will exist for the life of the government. Ad hoc committees may be established to consider particular matters. In addition, a whole range of official committees staffed by civil servants exist to complement the work of Ministers.

While the use of committees is both necessary and inevitable, it raises important constitutional questions concerning the doctrine of collective responsibility. Collective responsibility requires that each member of Cabinet, and

43 See, *inter alia*, Jennings, 1959a; Mackintosh, 1977; Hennessy, 1986b.
44 Bagehot, 1867, p 68; see also Jones, 'Cabinet government since Bagehot', in Blackburn, 1992.
45 See Brazier, 1999; Alderman and Carter, 1991; Alderman and Smith, 1990.
46 See Jennings, 1959a, Chapter IX; Mackintosh, 1977, Chapter 21; Hennessy, 1986b.

all government ministers and Parliamentary Private Secretaries, is bound by the decisions of the Cabinet. The extent to which the doctrine will in practice be binding will depend upon the extent government members are prepared to maintain confidentiality and unanimity over decisions in which they may have played no part.[47]

The Prime Minister's Private Office

While often mooted, and its absence an apparent anomaly in a sophisticated system of government, there has never been a 'Prime Minister's Department' dedicated to the task of organising, co-ordinating and liaising on behalf of the Prime Minister. Instead, a British Prime Minister's team comprises civil service support and non-civil service political support in the form of a specially appointed team of advisers. Heading the Prime Minister's support system is his Principal Private Secretary who heads the Private Office, who has close relations with both the Cabinet Secretary and the Queen's Private Secretary. A civil servant, usually seconded from the Treasury for a three year period, it is the Private Secretary who co-ordinates the work of the Prime Minister, controlling the flow of paper into Number 10, and prioritising matters for prime ministerial attention. In addition to the Private Secretary, there is a Private Secretary for Overseas and Defence Affairs, Economic and Home Affairs, Europe, Central and Constitutional Affairs and Security and Intelligence. The Private Secretaries link the Prime Minister with Cabinet, other government ministers and civil servants, and attend prime ministerial meetings and Cabinet meetings. The Prime Minister's Diary Secretary – a political appointment since 1979 – also plays a key role in the inner corpus of prime ministerial support, controlling the Prime Minister's time and engagements. A Duty Clerk is responsible for maintaining links between Number 10 and the outside world, and manning the Prime Minister's office in the absence of the Private Secretary. The Prime Minister's secretariat, known as the 'Garden Room Girls' since Lloyd George's premiership, completes the support staff at Number 10. These appointments represent the Prime Minister's staff in his role as head of government. In addition, the Prime Minister must maintain close links with his parliamentary party and with the party in the country. Given the requirement of political neutrality in civil servants, this would be an inappropriate task for the Private Office and, as a result, this responsibility falls on the Prime Minister's Political Secretary, a post funded by the party rather than the taxpayer. Under Tony Blair's leadership a political Chief of Staff has played a central role. Also central to Blair's administration has been the Director of Communications.

---

47   On Cabinet committees under different Prime Ministers see Hennessy, 1986b, pp 100–01.

The Cabinet Office[48]

The daily working of Cabinet is assisted by the Cabinet Office,[49] established in 1917, headed by the Secretary to the Cabinet. It is the Secretary to the Cabinet who is responsible for the recording of Cabinet meetings and circulation of the agreed conclusions. Within the Cabinet Office there exist a number of secretariats, including the Economic Secretariat; Overseas and Defence Secretariat; European Secretariat and Home and Social Affairs Secretariat.[50] There is also a Policy Unit whose function is to serve the Prime Minister rather than Cabinet as a whole.

THE CIVIL SERVICE[51]

A civil servant has been defined as: '... a servant of the Crown, other than holders of political or judicial offices, who is employed in a civil capacity and whose remuneration is paid wholly and directly out of monies voted by Parliament.'[52]

The constitutional relationship between the Civil Service and the government of the day is a matter directly linked to ministers' responsibility to the electorate – through parliament – and the extent to which that responsibility is affected by the role of civil servants. Before considering the relationship between ministers and departments, some preliminary points require attention. Some doubt exists as to the precise number of personnel in the Civil Service, doubts which arise from the difficulties concerning the appropriate classification of some occupations within the public service. For example, employees of the National Health Service are not technically employees of the Crown – and therefore not civil servants – although responsibility for the Health Service lies with the Secretary of State.

One further difficulty in evaluating the operation of the Civil Service arises from the disparity in size between government departments, with some departments having a staff of over 100,000, while others may have less than 10,000. The size of a department has a practical bearing on the extent to which ministers can realistically be said to be making decisions. Added to that difficulty is the preference of some governments for large departments of state. Moreover, recent changes to the structure of the Civil Service to enhance its efficiency have led to a proliferation of government agencies (see below).

When considering responsibility for the Civil Service and accountability to parliament, a further feature of political life must be borne in mind: that of ministerial mobility. The average tenure of responsibility for a department is two years. The Department of Education and Science, between 1944 and 1986, had 21 ministerial heads. During the Thatcher administration (1979–90), Cabinet reshuffles were frequent with several ministers holding a number of portfolios during that government.

---

48 See Wilson, 1976, Chapter 4; Mosley, 1969; Jennings, 1959a, Chapter 9.
49 See Mackintosh, 1977, Chapter 21.
50 See Hennessy, 1990, pp 390–91.
51 See *Report of the Committee on the Civil Service 1966–68*, Cmnd 3638, 1968, London: HMSO; Drewry and Butcher, 1988; Hennessy, 1986b.
52 Report of the Royal Commission on the Civil Service, 1929–31, Cmd 3909, 1931, London: HMSO.

A final practical preliminary point to consider is the sheer volume of work entailed in government. An estimated[53] two-thirds of a minister's working week is taken up by non-departmental business: Cabinet meetings, Cabinet committees, parliamentary party meetings, debates and questions in the House, official visits, and constituency duties. The task of heading a major department of state in addition to all the other duties is a major one, and the practical impact of regular government 're-shuffles', the size of departments and non-departmental duties is great. Such considerations lead the observer to wonder whether ministers, rather than senior civil servants, can truly be said to be in charge of their Departments.

Improving efficiency in the Civil Service

From November 1986 to March 1987, the Efficiency Unit, under the supervision of Sir Robin Ibbs, inquired into the future of the Civil Service.[54] A principal interest of the Unit was expressed to be not so much the detailed working of the Civil Service or its efficiency, but rather the relationship between the Civil Service and ministerial responsibility, and the impact that any recommendations as to the improvement of efficiency within the Civil Service might have on this constitutional relationship.

The report recommended that agencies be established – either within or outside of the departments – charged with the responsibility of overall management of the Department.

The main controls would continue to lie with ministers or the Permanent Secretary but, once policy objectives and budgets had been established, the Agency should have as much independence as possible in deciding how objectives should be met. The crucial question was that of the line of responsibility. The Head of the Agency should be given personal responsibility to achieve the best results. As to the future role of ministers, the report recommended that ministers continue to be wholly responsible for policy but that it was unrealistic to suppose that they could have in-depth knowledge about every operational question:

> ... the convention that they do is part of the cause of the overload which we observed. We believe it is possible for Parliament, through Ministers, to regard managers as directly responsible for operational matters.

The (Social Security) Benefits Agency is the largest. Others include the Child Support Agency, Driver and Vehicle Licensing Agency, Stationery Office, Land Registry, Ordnance Survey, Patent Office and United Kingdom Passport Agency. Issues of responsibility of ministers are also raised in respect of non-departmental public bodies – 'quangos' – whereby state enterprises are privatised.[55] A non-departmental public body is defined as a body 'which has a role in the processes

---

53 Headey, 1974.
54 Report to the Prime Minister, *Improving Management in Government: The Next Steps*, 1988, London: HMSO.
55 See, *inter alia*, Lewis, 'Regulating non-governmental bodies: privatization, accountability and the public-private divide', in Jowell and Oliver, 2000, Chapter 9.

of national government but is not a government department'.[56] The movement towards increased government involvement in commerce and industry stems from 1945, although public corporations had been earlier established.[57] More recently, the movement has been towards privatisation, with, among others, British Rail, British Gas, British Telecom, Her Majesty's Stationery Office, and the Naval Dockyards being sold into private ownership. Accountability for such organisations, when publicly owned, was weak. Today the question is to what extent these organisations are truly private; to what extent ministers exert control over them, whether via financial power or the power to issue policy guidance; and, more importantly, the extent to which parliament assures that ministers are accountable for the implementation of policies.

The Labour government and the Civil Service

When the government entered into office in May 1997, it arrived with not only a radical mandate to reform the constitution, but also one to improve efficiency in the Civil Service. In March 1999, the government published its White Paper, *Modernising Government*, described by Cabinet Secretary Sir Richard Wilson as 'a key document which signals a change of course for the Civil Service for the next ten years as important as Next Steps ten years ago'.[58] The aim, he said, was 'modernisation with a purpose: better policy making, better responsiveness to what people want, and more effective public services'. The White Paper introduced a range of reforms, including the commitment to make public services available on a 24 hour a day, seven day a week basis; removing unnecessary regulation and requiring departments which are preparing policies involving new regulations to submit Regulatory Impact Assessments following consultation with the Cabinet Office; and creating greater incentives for civil servants, which includes considering financial rewards for staff who identify financial savings or service improvements. In Whitehall, all Permanent Secretaries are required to 'ensure that their Department has the capacity to drive through achievement of the key government targets and to take a personal responsibility for ensuring that this happens'. While the focus is on improved management and the delivery of service to the consumer, sight has not been lost of the core civil service values. Selection and promotion will remain based on merit; political impartiality and the giving of best independent advice to government will be maintained.[59]

---

56 *Non-Departmental Public Bodies: Guide for Departments*, 1986, Cabinet Office/MPO, London: HMSO.

57 Eg, the Port of London Authority 1908; Central Electricity Board 1926; London Passenger Transport Board 1933; British Overseas Airways Corporation and British European Airways 1939.

58 Wilson, 1999.

59 The government is committed to introducing a Civil Service Act to place the Service under statutory authority and end regulation under the royal prerogative. In 2004 the Public Administration Select Committee published a Draft Bill for consultation.

CONSTITUTIONAL PRINCIPLES
AND THE CIVIL SERVICE

The role of the Civil Service must be considered against the constitutional features of permanence, political neutrality and anonymity.

Permanence

In many countries, such as the United States of America, the Civil Service is a semi-permanent body, the most senior posts of which change hands with a change in government. A variation on this model, which is employed in Germany and France, involves incoming ministers bringing into the department a small body of hand picked professional advisers. Under the constitution of the United Kingdom, civil servants hold permanent posts, in law 'holding office at the pleasure of the Crown'. Many aspects of employment protection legislation[60] apply to the Civil Service, but such rights as, for example, the right of appeal against unfair dismissal and the right to belong to a trades union, may be revoked under the royal prerogative.[61] Moreover, at common law, the position of civil servants is precarious. Being a servant of the Crown, they may be dismissed with no common law action for wrongful dismissal.[62] However, while the formal position is insecure, in practical terms civil servants enjoy a high degree of security. Terms and conditions of employment are regulated under the prerogative, and the Minister for the Civil Service has power to make regulations relating to the conditions of service of all civil servants.[63]

The constitutional significance of permanency lies in the development of expertise and the natural growth of a Civil Service 'ethos'. Most importantly, permanency ensures the availability of such expertise to governments of differing political persuasions. The Private Secretary is a minister's closest contact with a department, and his adviser.

Political neutrality

The Civil Service owes its loyalty to the government of the day, irrespective of political party, and it is imperative that the Civil Service avoids creating the impression of political bias. While the writings of leading Labour Party politicians referred to above reveal scepticism as to this, its theoretical importance cannot be underestimated.

Following the trial of senior civil servant Clive Ponting for unauthorised disclosure of information to a Member of Parliament,[64] the Head of the Civil Service issued *Notes of Guidance on the Duties and Responsibilities of Civil Servants in Relation to Ministers* (1985, revised 1987) in which it was stated that:

---

60 Employment Protection (Consolidation) Act 1978.
61 *Council of Civil Service Unions v Minister for the Civil Service* (1985), discussed in Chapter 6.
62 *Dunn v R* (1896); *Riordan v War Office* (1959).
63 Civil Service Order in Council 1995.
64 See *R v Ponting* (1985). Ponting was charged under the Official Secrets Act 1911. He was acquitted by the jury.

> The Civil Service has no constitutional personality or responsibility separate from the duly elected government of the day. The rules make it clear that a civil servant who cannot conscientiously comply with his or her official duties because of personal opinions or convictions should take the matter up with his or her superiors, but if unable to carry out instructions should resign from the Service.

The anonymity and political neutrality of civil servants is reinforced by the rules restricting political activity. If the Civil Service is to serve governments of all political persuasions, it is imperative that civil servants, whatever their private political views, should not be seen to be politically active in a manner which would inevitably compromise their neutrality under one political party or another.

The Civil Service is divided, for the purpose of control over political activity, into three groups:

(a) the 'politically free' category which comprises industrial staff and non-officer grades, who may freely engage in either national and local politics;

(b) the 'politically restricted' category, comprising higher staff grades who are debarred from participating in national political activities, but may be permitted to engage in local politics;

(c) an intermediate group which comprises those who are neither employed in the highest or lowest grades.

Political activities which are subject to restriction are divided into activities at both national and local level. Those activities subject to restriction at national level include standing as a candidate for election to the European Parliament; holding office in party political organisations which relate to party politics in relation to the United Kingdom or the European Parliament; and speaking on matters of national political controversy, or expressing such views to the press or in books, articles or leaflets. Canvassing on behalf of a candidate for election to the United Kingdom Parliament or the European Parliament, or on behalf of a political party in respect of such elections, is also prohibited. At local level, civil servants in the restricted category may not stand as candidates for local elections; hold office in party political organisations relating to local government; speak on local politically controversial matters or express such views in the media or other publications; and may not canvass on behalf of either a candidate or a political party in the course of local elections.[65]

Anonymity

In order that the minister be seen to be responsible and accountable for the working of his Department, the Civil Service has traditionally been shielded from the public gaze and protected from public inquiry. By protecting the Civil Service, its impartiality and integrity is enhanced. Further, if civil servants become public figures scrutinised in parliament or the media, their capacity for maintaining the appearance of political impartiality, so important to the concept of permanence, would be damaged.

---

65 *Pay and Conditions of Service Code.*

It has been seen that the minister in charge of a particular government department is absolutely responsible to parliament for the conduct of civil servants, and that this responsibility in turn involves two aspects. The first of these is that the minister has an obligation to explain and answer for the work of his department to parliament; the second is that the minister is responsible in constitutional terms for any failure of departmental policy and administration. As a corollary to ministerial responsibility, the Civil Service is not accountable to parliament and is protected by the concept of anonymity.

While, in theoretical constitutional terms, the anonymity of civil servants is important in buttressing the responsibility of ministers of the Crown, it is becoming, as will be seen below, an increasingly less notable feature of the Civil Service. The explanations for the decrease in anonymity are manifold: the vagaries of individual ministerial responsibility, the increasing strength of departmental select committees and the televising of those proceedings, and recent developments in the management of government departments.

The official *Guidance for Officials Appearing before Select Committees*[66] stressed that civil servants should be 'as helpful as possible' to parliamentary committees, but that advice given to ministers should never be disclosed (in order to protect collective ministerial responsibility), nor should advice given by a Law Officer be revealed. Further, officials should not give evidence about matters of political controversy, or 'sensitive information' relating to commercial or economic matters or related to intergovernmental negotiations. The rules make it clear that civil servants give evidence to committees on behalf of their ministers, and that they are subject to instructions given by ministers.

THE CIVIL SERVICE MANAGEMENT CODE

In 1994, the Treasury and Civil Service Committee reviewed the position of civil servants.[67] In its report, *The Role of the Civil Service*, it concluded that a new Civil Service Code should be drafted to clarify the position of civil servants. The Nolan Committee also recommended clarification in the constitutional framework within which civil servants work and 'the values they are expected to uphold'.[68] The new Code was introduced under the royal prerogative,[69] and came into force in 1996, replacing Sir Robert Armstrong's statement. The *Civil Service Management Code*, as amended, now states that:

> ... the constitutional and practical role of the Civil Service is, with integrity, honesty, impartiality and objectivity, to assist the duly constituted government, of whatever political complexion, in formulating policies of government, carrying out decisions of the government and in administering public services for which the government is responsible.

---

66 Cabinet Office, 1980.
67 HC 27-I (1993–94), London: HMSO.
68 Nolan Report, *Standards in Public Life*, Cm 2850-I, 1995, London: HMSO.
69 See the Civil Service Management Code issued under the Civil Service Order in Council 1995, as amended by the Civil Service (Amendment) Order 1995 and the Civil Service (Amendment) Order 1996.

Civil servants are under a duty to give honest and impartial advice to ministers and to:

> ... endeavour to deal with the affairs of the public sympathetically, effectively, promptly and without bias or maladministration of public money.

They are also required to conduct themselves in such a manner as to:

> ... deserve and retain the confidence of Ministers and to be able to establish the same relationship with those whom they may be required to serve in some future administration.

The *Code* also states that civil servants must not misuse their official position to further their own, or another's, personal interests.

It is expected that a Civil Service Act will incorporate the *Code*.

Special advisers

The appointment of special advisers to ministers blurs the lines of responsibility between ministers and civil servants. The Committee on Standards in Public Life examined a whole tranche of issues in 1999, including the role of special advisers, lobbying, sponsorship and public appointments. On special advisers, the Committee recommended that there be introduced a code of conduct enshrined in a Civil Service Act and that there be a statutory limit to the number of ministerial aides appointed.[70] However, while accepting that there was no evidence that special advisers were 'politicising the civil service', the Committee expressed the concern that 'the considerable increase in numbers, particularly at Number 10, where influential roles are played by special advisers, raises the question of whether their authority outweighs that of objective advisers' and that 'any future growth in numbers would raise questions about a move towards the establishment of a "cabinet system" within departments'.[71]

Special advisers are servants of the Crown. As such there is no entitlement to a period of notice before the termination of employment. However, the *Model Contract for Special Advisers* (May 1997) provides that, other than where employment is terminated by agreement or results from disciplinary proceedings, inefficiency or grounds justifying dismissal at common law, advisers will be given not less than three months' notice in writing. Otherwise employment automatically terminates at the end of the current government administration or when the relevant Cabinet minister leaves the government or moves to another appointment or, in the event of a general election, on the day after polling day. Schedule 1 to the *Model Contract, The Role and Duties of Special Advisers*, states that special advisers 'must always be guided by the basic principle that they are employed to serve the objectives of the government and the department in which they work'. They are exempt from the general civil service requirement that appointments must be made on merit on the basis of fair and open competition, providing that they are appointed 'for the purpose only of providing advice to

---

70 Such limits have already been imposed in relation to the Scottish Parliament and Welsh Assembly.
71 See *Reinforcing Standards*, the Report of the Committee on Standards in Public Life, 2000.

any minister'.[72] Their constitutional position is ambivalent: they are 'servants of the Crown but not a formal part of the departmental hierarchy, do not work directly under a permanent civil servant or have permanent civil servants working for them'. 'Special Advisers are appointed to advise the minister in the development of government policy and its effective presentation.'[73] They do not have any executive powers to instruct civil servants.[74] As Crown employees paid out of public funds, special advisers operate to support the interests of the government rather than the government's political party, although they act as a channel of communication between government and party.[75] Government communications with the media and public is the responsibility of the Government Communication Network, established in 2005 to replace the former Government Information and Communication Service.[76] The Communication Network is headed by a Permanent Secretary of Government Communications.

72 Civil Service Order in Council 1995, Article 3(2), as amended by Civil Service (Amendment) Order in Council 1997. A position affirmed by the Employment Appeal Tribunal, which ruled in *Lord Chancellor v Coker* (2001) that the Lord Chancellor did not discriminate against two women, one of whom was black, on the grounds of sex or race when he appointed as special adviser a white male who was well known to him, without advertising the post. The appointment process with regard to special advisers was not subject to the general rules that applied to the appointment of civil servants since special advisers were not civil servants. In appointing a special adviser, a key quality of the applicant was a commitment to the political understanding of the particular minister.

73 *Model Contract*, Sched 1(iii).

74 See the Report: 'An Independent Review of Government Communcations', January 2004: The Phillis Report.

75 The lack of clarity in responsibilities between civil servants, special advisers and ministers have led to calls for a Civil Service Act to remove ambiguities and provide a statutory basis for the Codes regulating civil servants and advisers. In 2006, a Constitutional Reform (Prerogative Powers and Civil Service etc.) Bill was introduced in the House of Lords.

76 See *Hansard* (HC) 19 January 2004, col 51WS; Cabinet Office Press Notice, CAB 002/05, 20 January 2005. See also the Annual Report 2004 of the Committee on Standards in Public Life.

CHAPTER 11

RESPONSIBLE GOVERNMENT

MINISTERIAL RESPONSIBILITY

The convention of ministerial responsibility is central to the constitution, and plays a fundamental role in the relationship between the executive and parliament. For the doctrine of government under the law to be observed, it is essential that government be accountable to both parliament and the electorate, and that government be conducted in a manner sufficiently open, subject to the requirements of the national interest, to inspire public confidence. The origins of ministerial responsibility are traced by FW Maitland to the principle that 'for every exercise of royal power some minister is answerable' (1908, p 203). Marshall and Moodie describe ministerial responsibility as follows:

> Ministers are responsible for the general conduct of government, including the exercise of many powers legally vested in the Monarch; and ultimately, through Parliament and parties, to the electorate. [1971, Chapter 4]

The doctrine thus has two limbs – individual and collective responsibility. As with so much of the constitution, there is vagueness on occasion as to the distinction between the two limbs which are both closely related and also complementary of one another. In order to facilitate analysis, the topic may be broken down into three aspects:

(a) the collective responsibility of the Cabinet to parliament, and ultimately the electorate, for policy and administration;

(b) the individual responsibility of ministers for the policy and administration of his or her Department;

(c) the individual responsibility of ministers for their personal conduct.

COLLECTIVE RESPONSIBILITY[1]

The convention of collective Cabinet responsibility emphasises the unanimity of government and its accountability to parliament. The classic expression of collective responsibility remains that of Lord Salisbury:

> For all that passes in Cabinet every member of it who does not resign is absolutely and irretrievably responsible and has no right afterwards to say that he agreed in one case to a compromise, while in another he was persuaded by his colleagues ... It is only on the principle that absolute responsibility is undertaken by every member of the Cabinet, who, after a decision is arrived at, remains a member of it, that the joint responsibility of Ministers to Parliament can be upheld and one of the essential principles of parliamentary responsibility established. [*Official Report*, HC Cols 833–34, 8 April 1878]

---

1   See Mackintosh, 1977, Chapter 2; Marshall, 1984, Chapter IV.

The rationale for the convention lies in the need for government to present a united front to parliament and the public in order to maintain confidence. A government which exhibits public disagreements over policy matters is one which will be regarded as weak, and will be subjected to challenges to its authority to continue in office.[2]

Two principal sub-rules underlie collective responsibility. The first rule is that, once an agreement is reached in Cabinet, all members of Cabinet – and many outside Cabinet – are bound to speak in support of the decision. There should be no criticism or dissent from the decision in public – irrespective of whether or not the particular member of Cabinet was party to the discussion. Equally, if a decision is reached by the Prime Minister in Cabinet Committee or the Inner Cabinet when only a small handful of members are present, the decision binds all. The second supporting rule is that records of Cabinet discussions are absolutely secret. The knowledge that Cabinet records are protected by confidentiality enhances the opportunity for members of Cabinet to discuss matters freely, secure in the knowledge that their personal point of view, whatever the decision, will be protected from the public gaze.

These principles are expressed in the Ministerial Code in the following manner:

> Collective responsibility requires that ministers should be able to express their views frankly in the expectation that they can argue freely in private while maintaining a united front when decisions have been reached. This in turn requires that the privacy of opinions expressed in Cabinet and Ministerial Committees should be maintained. Moreover, Cabinet and Committee documents will often contain information which needs to be protected in the national interest. It is therefore essential that, subject to the requirements on the disclosure of information set out in The Freedom of Information Act 2000, ministers take the necessary steps to ensure that they and their staff preserve the privacy of Cabinet business and protect the security of government documents. [Cabinet Office, 1992, 2005, para 6.17]

As with the convention of individual responsibility, there is dispute about the status and scope of collective responsibility. So many exceptions to the classic doctrine can be discerned that it is possible to question whether it is a convention at all within the classical definition, or whether the term convention should be discarded and replaced by the words practice or usage.

Alternatively, it may be argued that the variations which can be observed in the working of the convention merely illustrate one of the greatest strengths of conventional rules – their flexibility.

Agreements to differ

It is possible for the convention of collective responsibility to be waived when the circumstances are such that the political disagreements within Cabinet are of such magnitude that the Prime Minister finds it more expedient to set aside the

---

2   Disagreement over the Iraq War in 2003 led to the resignation of the late Robin Cook, a former Foreign Secretary, and Clare Short, the Secretary of State for International Development.

convention than to have the convention broken by members of Cabinet. Two illustrations of waiver can be given. In 1931–32, the National (coalition) government contained bitterly opposing views over economic policy; in particular, over the levy of tariff duties. Four members of Cabinet handed in their resignations, and withdrew them only after the Prime Minister, Mr Ramsey MacDonald, decided to waive the convention and allow the dissident members to express their views publicly.

In 1975, the Labour government of Mr Harold Wilson was faced with an equally intransigent faction in Cabinet on the matter of the United Kingdom's continued membership of the European Community. The government had decided to put the question to the people in a referendum, although, in advance of the referendum, the government announced that it would not be bound by the result.

Rather than face a public display of disunity in contravention of collective responsibility, Mr Wilson announced a limited waiver of the convention, in the guise of an 'agreement to differ':[3]

> ... those ministers who do not agree with the government's recommendation in favour of continued membership of the European Community are, in the unique circumstances of the referendum, now free to advocate a different view during the referendum campaign.

> This freedom does not extend to parliamentary proceedings and official business ... At meetings of the Council of Ministers of the European Community and at other Community meetings, the United Kingdom position in all fields will continue to reflect government policy.

> I have asked all ministers ... not to allow themselves to appear in direct confrontation, on the same platform or programme, with another minister who takes a different view on the government recommendation.

In the event, one minister (Eric Heffer) flouted the limited waiver, and two senior Cabinet members, Mr Roy Jenkins and Mr Tony Benn, opposed each other in a public televised debate shortly before the referendum took place.

Cabinet papers[4]

The confidentiality of Cabinet discussion is protected by the prohibition against disclosure by members of Cabinet. In addition, the rules regarding the confidentiality of Cabinet papers include the rule that the government of the day may not release the papers of a previous government without the consent of the former Prime Minister.[5] Furthermore, the papers of the previous government may not be disclosed to a government of a different political persuasion. It may at first sight appear curious that an incoming government cannot gain access to the papers of the previous government, and it may be wondered how the government is supposed to act effectively in any policy area if denied so much data. Nevertheless, the rule is justified on the basis that an outgoing government

---

3   HC Deb Col 1745, 23 January 1975; Col 351, 7 April 1975; Cmnd 6003, 1975; Wilson, 1976, pp 194–97.
4   On secrecy in government, see further below.
5   HC Deb Col 1039, 1 July 1982; Cols 468, 8 July 1982; 474; Hunt, 1982.

might be tempted to remove politically sensitive documentation if it feared that a new government would make political capital out of it. Three categories of papers are excepted from the convention:[6]

(a) papers which, even if not publicly available, can be deemed to be in the public domain, for example, letters sent by former ministers to trade associations, trade unions, etc, or to Members of Parliament about constituency cases, or to members of the public;

(b) papers, other than genuinely personal messages, dealing with matters which are known to foreign governments, for example, messages about inter-governmental negotiations;

(c) written opinions of the Law Officers, which are essentially legal rather than political documents.

Ministerial memoirs

The publication of a former minister's memoirs of his political life poses problems for the rules relating to Cabinet secrecy. In 1976, the Radcliffe Committee Report[7] stated that:

> The author should be free to use his ministerial experience for the purpose of giving an account of his own work, subject to restrictions on three separate categories of information:
>
> (a) he must not reveal anything that contravenes the requirements of national security operative at the time of his proposed publication;
>
> (b) he must not make disclosures injurious to this country's relations with other nations;
>
> (c) he must refrain from publishing information destructive of the confidential relationships on which our system of government is based.
>
> The final restriction relates to opinions or attitudes of Cabinet colleagues, advice given to him by colleagues and criticism of those working for him in office.

In *Attorney General v Jonathan Cape Ltd* (1976), the issue of the publication of the diaries of Richard Crossman, a former Labour Cabinet member, was considered. Executors of the estate of Richard Crossman sought to publish his *Diaries*; the government sought an injunction restraining publication. Recognising the convention of collective responsibility, Lord Widgery CJ stated:

> I find overwhelming evidence that the doctrine of joint responsibility is generally understood and practised, and equally strong evidence that it is on occasion ignored.

Having given such ambivalent recognition to the convention, which in any event was not court-enforceable, the injunction was denied.

---

6 Hunt (Lord), 'Access to a previous government's papers', in Marshall, 1989.
7 *Report of the Committee of Privy Councillors*, Cmnd 6386, 1976, London: HMSO, Appendix 2.

INDIVIDUAL MINISTERIAL RESPONSIBILITY[8]

In *Questions of Procedure for Ministers*,[9] individual responsibility is defined as follows:

> The minister in charge of a Department is alone answerable to Parliament for the exercise of the powers on which the administration of the Department depends.

Ministerial responsibility for the department

The classic doctrine of this limb of ministerial responsibility states that a minister is responsible for every action of his department. As AV Dicey expressed it, the responsibility of ministers means, where used in its strict sense, the legal responsibility of every minister for every act of the Crown in which he takes part.

Lord Morrison viewed the doctrine equally strictly:

> ... a minister is accountable to Parliament for anything he or his department does or for anything he has powers to do, whether he does it or not. That is to say, if the action or possible action is within the field of ministerial power or competence, the minister is answerable to Parliament. [1964, p 265]

It is the minister who represents the public face of the department and who speaks for the department in parliament. The doctrine is underpinned by Parliamentary Question Time and in debates in parliament and in committees. During the passage of legislation relating to a particular department's responsibilities, it is the minister who will introduce the Bill and who will defend the Bill throughout its passage through the House of Commons. The minister thus stands as the link between the Civil Service and parliament, assuming full responsibility for the department. As seen in Chapter 10, the conventionally-recognised characteristics of the Civil Service are permanence, political neutrality and anonymity. The civil servant owes his or her duty to the government of the day, and is directly accountable to his or her Secretary of State. The principle of ministerial responsibility to parliament not only underpins the doctrine of democratic responsibility of ministers to the people through parliament, but also facilitates the distinction between the responsibility of elected representatives and the civil servants who are responsible for the practical implementation of policy.

In practical terms nowadays, several factors diminish the extent to which a minister can assume responsibility for every action of the department. The size of departments, the usually short ministerial tenure of office in any one department and the complexity of modern government have long made the pure doctrine unworkable. As a former Home Secretary, Mr Reginald Maudling, stated in 1973, the classic doctrine of responsibility must be viewed in the light of modern conditions, with large departments of state. Furthermore, the complexity of defining the scope of ministerial responsibility must also be seen in light of the rapid and extensive administrative framework under the system of Next Steps

---

8   See Turpin, 'Ministerial responsibility: myth or reality?', in Jowell and Oliver, 2000, Chapter 3.

9   Cabinet Office, 1992, revised 2001, para 33. See also *Civil Servants and Ministers: Duties and Responsibilities*, Cmnd 9841, 1986, London: HMSO, para 11.

agencies which are designed to increase efficiency in administration by establishing specialist agencies, each with its own executive.

Crichel Down

The classic doctrine was seen to operate most clearly in the Crichel Down affair in 1954.[10] Crichel Down, an area of some 725 acres in Dorset, had been compulsorily acquired by the Air Ministry in 1937 for use as a bombing range. After the Second World War, the land was no longer needed and it was transferred to the Ministry of Agriculture and administered by the Agriculture Land Commission. In 1950, the Commission decided that the best way of disposing of the land was to equip it as a single farm unit and lease it.

Three hundred and twenty eight acres of Crichel Down had been part of the Crichel Estates owned by a Mrs Marten. Her husband wanted to reclaim the land. In both 1950 and 1952 he asked the Commission whether he could buy back the land. The Commission wrongly thought that they had no power of sale and declined to investigate his request. Mr Marten raised the matter with his Member of Parliament who referred the matter to the Parliamentary Secretary to the Minister of Agriculture, who requested a report from the Land Commission. The official in charge of making the report was instructed not to approach the previous owners or to inspect the land, and to treat the matter as one of great confidentiality. The resulting report was full of inaccuracies, and went unchecked by the Ministry which decided to adhere to its original plan for the land.

Mr Marten was informed of the decision in 1953, and advised the Ministry that he would rent the whole of the land. Meanwhile, the Ministry had committed itself to another course of action. Mr Marten's letters to the authorities went unanswered and he pressed for a public inquiry. The inquiry found that there had been inaccuracies in the report on the land, muddle and inefficiency in handling the matter and hostility to Mr Marten. In July 1954, the minister Thomas Dugdale accepted responsibility and resigned.[11]

Ministerial responsibility after Crichel Down

It is notable that, between 1954 and 1982, there were no instances of ministerial resignation following allegations of and inquiries into serious defects in departmental administration. In 1959, 52 people were killed by security forces in Nyasaland but the Colonial Secretary Mr Lennox-Boyd did not resign. In 1964, due to a lack of co-ordination within the Ministry of Aviation, an overpayment of some £4 million was made to the Ferranti company, but the minister did not resign. In 1968, the Foreign Secretary, Mr George Brown, did not resign over the Sachsenhausen affair in which 12 former detainees in a Nazi prison camp were wrongly denied compensation under a scheme set up to compensate victims of Nazi persecution.[12]

---

10   Cmnd 9220, 1954, London: HMSO.
11   See, *inter alia*, Nicolson, 1986; Griffith, 1987.
12   *Third Report of the Parliamentary Commissioner for Administration*, HC 54 (1967–68), London: HMSO; *Select Committee Report*, HC 258 (1967–68); Fry, 1970.

In 1971, the Vehicle and General Insurance Company collapsed leaving over a million policy holders uninsured. The Department of Trade and Industry had supervisory responsibility for insurance companies. An inquiry report placed the blame on a civil servant, Mr Jardine, an Under Secretary in the Department, and the minister did not resign.[13] In 1982, the Home Secretary, Mr William Whitelaw, did not resign over a breach of security at Buckingham Palace which resulted in an intruder entering the Queen's bedroom, nor did Mr James Prior (as he then was), the Northern Ireland Minister, resign in 1984, following the escape of terrorists from the Maze Prison. The exchange in parliament revealed divergent views about accountability. In debate, Mr Prior distinguished carefully between responsibility for policy – for which he accepted responsibility – and the failure of officials to follow the correct orders and procedures – for which he denied responsibility:

> However, I do not accept – and I do not think it right for the House to accept – that there is any constitutional or other principle that requires ministerial resignations in the face of failure, either by others to carry out orders or procedures or by their supervisors to ensure that staff carried out those orders ...

Mr Enoch Powell MP was of a different view:

> What happened was an immense administrative disaster. It was not a disaster in a peripheral area of the responsibilities of the Northern Ireland Department. It was a disaster that occurred in an area which was quite clearly central to the department's responsibilities. If the responsibility for administration so central to a department can be abjured by a minister, a great deal of our proceedings in the House is a beating of the air because we are talking to people who, in the last resort, disclaim the responsibility for the administration.[14]

The Falklands War provided the scenario for three ministerial resignations. Lord Carrington, the Foreign Secretary, resigned following allegations, which he denied, over the lack of preparation of the British forces when the Argentinians attacked; Mr Luce and Mr Atkins also resigned from the Foreign Office.[15]

In 1986 came the Westland Helicopter saga.[16] Westland, a helicopter manufacturing company, was threatened with closure. The government sought to promote a rescue bid for the company. Two alternative plans were put forward, one from an American consortium, the other from Europe. Mr Heseltine, Secretary of State for Trade and Industry, wanted the European option to be taken up. Mrs Thatcher, however, favoured the American plan. Mr Heseltine had been informed that he would be able to put his preferred plan to a Cabinet meeting. In the event, however, Mrs Thatcher cancelled that meeting. The conduct of the affair resulted in the resignations of Mr Heseltine, more on the basis of a breakdown in collective responsibility than of individual responsibility, and of Mr Leon Brittan for the breach of convention in the leak of the Solicitor General's letter.

---

13 HL Deb 80; HC Deb 133 (1971–72), para 344.
14 HC Deb Vol 53 Cols 1042, 1060–61, 9 February 1984 and see HM Chief Inspector of Prisons Report, HC 203 (1983–84), London, HMSO.
15 See Cmnd 8787, 1983, London: HMSO.
16 See Oliver and Austin, 1987; Hennessy, 1986a; Marshall, 1989, Chapter 18.

In 1989, Mrs Edwina Currie resigned over the furore caused by her claim that the majority of eggs in the United Kingdom were infected by the salmonella virus and, in 1990, Mr Nicholas Ridley resigned from the Department of Trade and Industry, having accepted responsibility for making intemperate remarks about a fellow Member State of the European Community.

In 1994, the Home Secretary, Michael Howard, faced several calls for his resignation over escapes from Whitemore prison and over the finding of escape equipment and weapons in prisons. Mr Howard refused to resign, citing in his support the precedent set by Mr James Prior (as he then was) over escapes from the Maze prison in Ulster, and the distinction between responsibility for operational matters and matters of policy.[17] In 2002, the Secretary of State for Transport, Stephen Byers, resigned. He had seemed unable to produce progress in transport revitalisation and was perceived by many to be less than straightforward in accounting for the department. He also, fatally, failed to dismiss his special adviser after a callous remark made on 11 September 2001. Also in 2002, the Secretary of State for Education resigned following sustained criticism over examinations.

The Work and Pensions Secretary, David Blunkett, resigned office for the second time in November 2005. He had first resigned his post as Secretary of State for the Home Department in 2004, having had an affair with a married woman and having intervened to have her nanny's application to remain in Britain 'fast-tracked' through the system. The reason given for the second resignation was a three-fold breach of the rule that former ministers should consult the Advisory Committee on Business Appointments about any business appointments they intend to take within two years of leaving office. Mr Blunkett stated that he misunderstood the rule and thought that consultation with the Committee was voluntary. Further allegations were made concerning previously undisclosed financial interests which came to light on the day he resigned.[18]

Evaluating the evidence

From the above evidence, how is the working of the doctrine of individual ministerial responsibility to be evaluated? First, it is arguable that the doctrine represents one of the most significant conventions of the constitution, enhancing the accountability of the government to parliament and the electorate. However, as has been seen above, the existence and acceptance of responsibility does not inevitably lead to the consequence of the resignation of a minister for the failures within his or her department. No hard and fast rules exist which will determine whether and when a minister should resign, and accordingly it cannot clearly be

---

17 In 2006 the Home Secretary, Charles Clarke, refused to resign over the Home Office failure to deport foreign criminals on the expiry of their sentences. Mr Clarke was sacked by the Prime Minister.

18 At the same time as Blunkett resigned, allegations were made that the former Secretary of State for Northern Ireland, Peter Mandelson, had failed to consult the Committee when he resigned 2001. In 2002 he was appointed to the Board of an advertising agency and allegedly took shares in the company.

said that resignation forms a part of the convention itself. On the question of the circumstances under which a minister will resign as a result of departmental mismanagement, Professor SE Finer (1956) considered that:

> ... whether a minister is forced to resign depends on three factors: on himself, his Prime Minister and his party.

> For a resignation to occur, all three factors have to be just so: the minister compliant, the Prime Minister firm, the party clamorous. This conjuncture is rare, and is in fact fortuitous. Above all, it is indiscriminate – which ministers escape and which do not is decided neither by the circumstances of the offence nor by its gravity.

Professor Finer went on to question whether in fact there is a 'convention' of resignation at all, and concluded that the convention is so haphazard in operation that it cannot amount to a rule.[19]

However, in recent years there have been considerable improvements in the system of monitoring the conduct of ministers and members of parliament through the Register of Members' Interests, the Advisory Committee on Business Appointments, the Committee on Standards in Public Life and the Parliamentary Commissioner for Standards. However, as Blunkett's resignation shows (in part), the rules are capable of being misunderstood and there is no automatic sanction for their breach – the issue of resignation remaining firmly in the political arena and dependent upon party political support and most importantly that of the Prime Minister.

THE MORALITY OF PUBLIC OFFICE

Qualification for ministerial office

Given the fundamental importance of ministerial responsibility, it is perhaps surprising that there are neither formal qualifications for office nor formal means by which the suitability for office is scrutinised in advance. Sir Ivor Jennings states that:

> ... the most elementary qualification demanded of a Minister is honesty and incorruptibility. It is, however, necessary not only that he should possess this qualification but also that he should appear to possess it. [1959a, Chapter V, p 106]

Lord Hailsham expresses the same sentiment as follows:

> A politician must be trustworthy, and if he is found out telling a lie or if he is discovered in even a small financial dishonesty, he can only bow himself out of public life. [1975, p 199]

If a minister of the Crown or Member of Parliament conducts his personal or financial affairs in such a manner that falls below an 'acceptable standard', the minister may be required to resign. Finer (1956) describes such conduct as being:

> ... a personal misadventure of the minister which raises such doubt about his personal prudence or integrity as to cause him to resign.

---

19 See also Woodhouse, 1993.

Vetting of prospective ministers?

In the United States of America, appointment to Cabinet office is undertaken only after the 'advice and consent' of the Senate has been obtained.[20] By this means, it is intended to test the suitability of candidates prior to appointment and to avoid the inevitable embarrassment which occurs when resignation is forced through disclosure of some financial, sexual or other impropriety. In the United Kingdom, by contrast, appointment is entirely at the discretion of the Prime Minister and will be made on information which is publicly available and from the personal and political reputation of the candidate. As has been seen above, the standard of conduct required for public life and the reality frequently part company. It is thus at least arguable that some form of 'vetting' – such as occurs with prospective holders of senior Civil Service posts – should be introduced. Professor Rodney Brazier has advocated this course of action,[21] favouring some form of pre-appointment formal inquiry into fitness for office. Such an approach has not found favour with others who have considered it. In the inquiry following the Profumo scandal, Lord Denning stated that there should be no inquiry into politicians' private lives by the security services other than where state security was under threat, a view endorsed by the Security Commission in its report following the resignations of Lords Lambton and Jellicoe.[22] Lord Hailsham has expressed the view that, in a democracy, there should be no such invasive advance inquiries into the private lives of public figures (1975) while recognising the real risks of corruption in public life which 'is hard to define ... harder to detect, and almost as catching as smallpox' (p 201). It must, however, be conceded that when the standard of conduct is lowered and the esteem of a government damaged by lack of integrity, then some action is needed.

INDIVIDUAL RESPONSIBILITY FOR PERSONAL CONDUCT

Personal conduct

While responsibility for the implementation and execution of policy of course entails 'personal conduct', one aspect of ministerial responsibility which has also given rise to particular concern is the conduct of ministers in relation to their private lives. The personal relationships of ministers are also matters which fall under intense public scrutiny. In 1963, the Minister of Defence, Mr John Profumo, was found to have been having a sexual relationship with a prostitute, Christine Keeler. Ms Keeler, it was found, also enjoyed a close personal relationship with a Russian Naval Attaché at the Soviet Embassy. When questioned in the House of Commons about the affair, Mr Profumo lied to the House. When the truth emerged, Mr Profumo resigned office. The cause of his resignation was not so much the sexual affair, but the contempt of the House committed through lying.

---

20   Constitution, Article II, s 2.
21   Brazier, 1998, Chapter 3, and 1994.
22   Lord Denning's Report, Cmnd 2152, 1963, London: HMSO, para 230; Report of the Security Commission, Cmnd 5367, 1973, London: HMSO, para 42.

The potential security aspects of the affair led to a judicial inquiry headed by Lord Denning MR.[23]

In 1973, Lords Lambton and Jellicoe resigned office. Earl Jellicoe, Lord Privy Seal and Leader of the House of Lords, resigned after it had been revealed that he had been associating with prostitutes. Lord Lambton, Parliamentary Under Secretary of State for Defence for the Royal Air Force, resigned over allegations of involvement with illegal drugs. The government requested an inquiry by the Security Commission into any security aspects of the affairs, which resulted in the finding that no classified information had in fact been revealed either directly or indirectly to 'any potentially hostile power'.[24]

In 1983, Cecil Parkinson MP, the Secretary of State for Trade and Industry and Conservative Party Chairman, resigned following revelations about a long standing relationship with his secretary, Sarah Keays, who became pregnant. For some time, the Prime Minister, Mrs Thatcher, and the Party maintained their support for Mr Parkinson,[25] as did his wife throughout the public attention focused on the affair. When Sarah Keays published a series of articles in the national press about the matter, and alleged that Mr Parkinson had said that he wanted to marry her, public and political support began to wane, and Mr Parkinson resigned.

In 1992, Alan Amos MP resigned after allegations of indecency with another man. Also in 1992, the Heritage Secretary David Mellor was forced to resign following revelations of a sexual relationship with an actress (and the receipt of gifts). The majority of the revelations had been brought about through the illicit bugging of an apartment used by Mr Mellor. While this affair alone may not have caused his downfall, the revelation that Mr Mellor and his family had enjoyed the hospitality, while on holiday, of the wife of a Palestinian Liberation Organisation official, sealed his fate. Despite being regarded as an excellent Heritage Secretary, the intense and hostile coverage by the media ensured his resignation.[26] In January 1994, Tim Yeo MP, Minister of State for the Environment, resigned after admitting fathering a child out of wedlock, as did Alan Duncan MP after allegations that he had used the 'right to buy' legislation to make money in property deals with a neighbour. In February 1994, Hartley Booth MP resigned after a 'close relationship' with a research assistant; in May 1994, Michael Brown MP resigned following newspaper reports of a 'friendship' with a male civil servant. In 1998, Ron Davies, the Welsh Secretary, resigned immediately after being discovered in still unexplained but curious circumstances on Clapham Common. The message is, if you are caught out resign sooner rather than later in order to spare the government embarrassment and loss of public confidence.

---

23 Statement to the House 674 HC Deb 809–10, 21 March 1963; Lord Denning's Report, Cmnd 2152, 1963, London: HMSO; Macmillan, 1973, pp 436–41; Denning, 1980, Pt 2, Chapter II; Marshall, 1984, Chapter VI.
24 *Report of the Security Commission*, Cmnd 5367, 1973, London: HMSO, para 5; Marshall, 1984, Chapter VI. On the role of the Security Commission, see further Chapter 25.
25 Thatcher, 1993, pp 310–11; Tebbitt, 1988, pp 205, 208–11.
26 Statement of Resignation 212 HC Deb 139, 25 September 1992.

Financial probity

The personal financial probity of ministers, their Parliamentary Private Secretaries and other Members of Parliament is regarded with seriousness. Under the law and custom of parliament, Members must declare their financial interests in the Register of Members' Interests and make public declarations in debate or committee proceedings of any interests they hold which may affect their impartiality.[27] The holding of directorships, ownership of shares, consultancy positions and receipt of gifts all raise issues concerning integrity and fitness for office. Ministers of the Crown must give up any public appointments or directorships on assuming office. Further, they must divest themselves of any financial interests on assuming office where that interest might give rise to conflict with his or her ministerial responsibilities.[28]

The *Ministerial Code*[29] states that 'Ministers must scrupulously avoid any danger of an actual or apparent conflict of interest between their Ministerial position and their private financial interests'. The *Ministerial Code* also requires that ministers consult the Advisory Committee on Business Appointments about any business appointments they intend to take up within two years of leaving office – a requirement breached by David Blunkett in 2005 (*above*). There is an inherent vagueness in such criteria, yet relatively few ministers and other Members of Parliament have fallen from grace as a result of imprudent (or dishonest) financial dealings. In 1913, the issue of ministers holding shares was raised in debate following allegations of improper ministerial involvement in the Marconi Company.[30] It was rumoured that ministers[31] had used information received as ministers for their own personal advantage. All three ministers involved denied any share dealings. A select committee inquiry exonerated the ministers of all charges of corruption and from charges that they had used their ministerial positions for personal gain.

In 1949, a Tribunal of Inquiry[32] was established to inquire into allegations of payments and other benefits being made to John Belcher MP, Parliamentary Secretary to the Board of Trade. Mr Belcher had received gifts offered with a view to securing favourable treatment in relation to licences granted by the Board of Trade. He resigned office and his parliamentary seat as a result.[33]

Recent ministerial resignations involving allegations of financial imprudence – although in each case there were additional factors involved in the resignations – include, as noted above, David Mellor, the Heritage Secretary, who resigned following a mixture of allegations, one of which involved the receipt of a free holiday from a woman with Palestinian Liberation Organisation associations.[34] In

---

27 On alleged payments for parliamentary questions, see Chapter 18.
28 *Ministerial Code*, Cabinet Office, 2005, para 5.11.
29 Paragraph 113.
30 54 HC Deb 5 Ser 391–514, 543–664. See Donaldson, 1962.
31 Attorney General, Sir Rufus Isaacs, Chancellor of the Exchequer, D Lloyd George, and Postmaster General, Sir Herbert Samuel.
32 Under the Tribunals of Inquiry (Evidence) Act 1921.
33 *Report of the Tribunal*, Cmnd 2616, 1949, London: HMSO.
34 HC Deb Col 139, 25 September 1992.

1992, it was revealed that the Chancellor of the Exchequer, Norman Lamont, had received £4,700 of public money for legal fees involved in the eviction of a tenant from his apartment.[35] In June 1993, the Minister for Northern Ireland, Michael Mates MP, resigned office after it had been revealed that Mr Mates gave to the fugitive businessman Asil Nadir, who faced prosecution on charges of theft and fraud, an inexpensive watch, shortly before Mr Nadir fled the United Kingdom. A subsequent allegation was made that Mr Mates accepted the loan of a car from Mr Nadir for his ex-wife's use and he ultimately resigned despite claiming to have the full support of the Prime Minister.[36] Further embarrassment was caused to the government in 1994, when it was alleged that Jeffrey Archer, former Conservative Party Chairman, had been involved in share-dealing in Anglia Television, on whose Board of Directors his wife held a directorship. Also in 1994, allegations were made that Members of Parliament had accepted payment for asking parliamentary questions. This affair escalated into a full-scale judicial inquiry into 'standards in public life', and to a tightening of the rules regulating the financial interests of all members of the House of Commons.[37] 1998 saw the culmination of the long running inquiry into the financial affairs of Geoffrey Robinson, the former Paymaster General, when in December both Robinson and Peter Mandelson, Secretary of State for Trade and Industry, resigned. Peter Mandelson had been a leading architect in making the Labour Party 'electable' and a pivotal figure in the general election campaign. However, it was revealed that Mandelson had accepted a personal loan from Robinson to finance the purchase of a London home, and that the loan had not been disclosed. While protesting that he had done nothing 'wrong', Mandelson resigned. He returned to ministerial office in 1999 as Secretary of State for Northern Ireland, only to resign again over allegations that he interfered in a passport application of a wealthy Indian businessman who had contributed money to the Millennium Dome for which Mandelson had responsibility at the time. In 2005 the resignation of the Work and Pensions Secretary, David Blunkett, discussed above, was in part prompted by allegations concerning shares in a company which was due to bid for a government contract.

Premature disclosure of confidential information

By convention the contents of the Chancellor of the Exchequer's Budget is kept secret until revealed in Parliament. Traditionally, the rule about secrecy was so strict that the details would not even be revealed to Cabinet before Parliament. Nowadays, however, the rule is much relaxed and it is not uncommon for the Chancellor to discuss proposals prior to formal disclosure.

The Nolan Committee

The result of continued and intensive media interest in ministerial conduct has caused a loss of public confidence in Members of Parliament as a whole, and in

---

35   See Brazier, 1992 and 1993.
36   Interview, *BBC News*, 22 June 1993.
37   On this see Chapter 18.

the conduct and probity of ministers. The Nolan Committee, appointed to inquire into standards in public life, examined in general the standards of conduct expected of ministers. More specifically, the Committee has investigated the question of the rules relating to ministers who retire from office and subsequently take up employment with organisations with whom they had dealings whilst in ministerial office. In addition, the Committee considered the organisation, regulation and personnel employed in non-departmental public bodies (NDPBs or 'quangos').[38]

The conduct of ministers of the Crown

The Nolan Committee endorsed the view that the 'public is entitled to expect very high standards of behaviour from ministers, as they have profound influence over the daily lives of us all'.[39] The Committee distinguished between the need for clear enforceable rules regulating financial conduct and those regulating sexual conduct. In respect of the latter, the Committee, whilst recognising that sexual improprieties may on occasion be relevant to the performance of a minister's public duties, took the view that it was not possible to lay down hard and fast rules to regulate such private conduct. The Committee recommended that the Prime Minister should be given explicit power to determine whether ministers – who are responsible for complying with the standards of conduct – have in fact upheld the required standard (paragraph 13).

Matrix Churchill and Arms to Iraq[40]

Between 1987 and 1989, the Matrix Churchill company exported machine tools to Iraq. It was alleged by Customs and Excise (which brought the prosecution against the directors of the company) that those exports breached the export regulations in place at the time. In defence, it was argued that the government knew about the exports and had in fact authorised them, and that MI6 (the Secret Intelligence Service) was aware of the exports. When the matter came to trial, four government ministers[41] signed public interest immunity certificates (on which see further pp 295 and 306 ff below) refusing disclosure of documents relating to, *inter alia*, records of meetings and communications between the Department of Trade and Industry and the Foreign and Commonwealth Office. The effect of the certificates was to deny to the court the evidence which might have led to the acquittal of the defendants, each of whom was facing a significant term of imprisonment if convicted. The trial of the directors of Matrix Churchill collapsed after a former government minister, Alan Clark, revealed to the court that the government had – as the defence claimed – in fact known of the exports. The Prime Minister

---

38 Quasi-autonomous non-governmental organisations, on which see further below and Chapter 26.
39 Nolan Report, *Standards in Public Life*, Cm 2850-I, 1995, London: HMSO, Chapter 3, para 4.
40 See Leigh, D, 1993; Norton-Taylor, 1995; Tomkins, 1998.
41 Tristan Garel-Jones (Foreign and Commonwealth Office on behalf of Douglas Hurd, the Foreign Secretary); Malcolm Rifkind (Defence Secretary); Michael Heseltine (President of the Board of Trade); Kenneth Clarke (Home Secretary).

established a judicial inquiry the day after the collapse of the trial.[42] The decision to establish a judicial inquiry was brought about in large measure through the failure of select committee inquiries to unravel the full facts surrounding the issue.[43]

Sir Richard Scott's Report represented the most wide ranging judicial inquiry into a number of important constitutional issues, including:

(a) whether the relevant government departments, agencies and responsible ministers operated in accordance with the policies of Her Majesty's government;

(b) an examination of decisions taken by the prosecuting authority and those signing public interest immunity certificates;

(c) an examination of similar cases relevant to the issues of the inquiry and to making recommendations.[44]

The change in policy over exports

In 1989, government minister William Waldegrave, in response to inquiries from Members of Parliament, advised that government policy in respect of exports had not changed. However, in Sir Richard Scott's view, the answers given were not accurate and were apt to mislead albeit unintentionally (para D4.12). In relation to parliamentary questions concerning the policy being applied, Sir Richard found that the government had deliberately failed to 'inform parliament of the current state of government policy on non-lethal arms sales to Iraq' (para D4.25).

The use of public interest immunity certificates

In the Matrix Churchill trial, the government claimed that it had the absolute right, in the name of the public interest, to withhold information which was central to the defendants' case. Furthermore, by relying on immunity from disclosure on the basis of a 'class claim', the government strengthened its case against the duty to disclose.[45] Class claims, are supposedly to do with matters of 'high policy' and yet it was a class claim which the government relied on in the Matrix Churchill case although, in the view of Sir Richard Scott, many of these documents 'could not possibly have been described as relating to "high policy"'.[46]

In Sir Richard Scott's view, 'it had become the practice in the Treasury Solicitor's Department that public interest immunity (PII) class protection for all documents relating directly or indirectly to advice to ministers should be sought, whether in a civil case or in a criminal trial'. Moreover, he found that the documents which the government was so keen to protect caused no damage to the Intelligence and Security Agencies, and that, in any event, if sensitive material was contained within the documents this could have been 'blacked out' on the basis of a contents claim.

---

42 See *Report of the Inquiry into the Export of Defence Equipment and Dual-Use Goods to Iraq and Related Prosecution*, HC 115 (1995–96), 15 February 1996 (the Scott Report).

43 See the Trade and Industry Select Committee, *Second Report, Exports to Iraq: Project Babylon and Long Range Guns*, I IC 86 (1991–92), London: HMSO; see also Tomkins, 1993; Bradley, 1992a.

44 Terms of reference: Scott Report, Vol 1, para A2.2.

45 See *Public Interest Immunity: Government Response to the Scott Report*, February 1996, House of Commons Library. See also Lord Upjohn in *Conway v Rimmer* (1968), pp 993–94.

46 Scott, 1996, p 439.

In 1996, the Attorney General announced that, having reviewed the operation of public interest immunity certificates, the government would no longer utilise the distinction between 'class' and 'contents' claims but rather, in future, it would only claim public interest immunity when the government 'believed that disclosure of a document would cause real harm to the public interest'. The certificate will explain the nature of the harm, and the manner in which disclosure would harm the public interest,[47] thereby allowing for 'even closer scrutiny of claims by the court, which is always the final arbiter'.

The Scott Report and ministerial responsibility

The Arms to Iraq affair resulted in the Scott Report and an in-depth analysis of ministerial responsibility by Sir Richard Scott, the Inquiry chairman. On the question of giving a full and honest account of policy matters to parliament, Sir Richard Scott stated that 'the withholding of information by an accountable minister should never be based on reasons of convenience or for the avoidance of political embarrassment, but should always require special and carefully considered justification'.[48]

In 'Ministerial accountability' (1996), Sir Richard Scott developed the themes analysed by Sir David Maxwell-Fyfe in his report on the Crichel Down affair (see above), and evidence given to the Scott Inquiry by Sir Robin Butler, the Cabinet Secretary. Referring to the distinction increasingly frequently made in recent years between ministerial constitutional responsibility and ministerial constitutional accountability, Sir Richard Scott cited Sir Robin's evidence as follows:

> I am using 'accountability' to mean that the Minister must always answer questions and give an account to Parliament for the action of his department, whether he is 'responsible' in the sense of attracting personal criticism himself, or not. So I am using 'accountability' to leave out, as it were, the blame element of it. The blame element is an open question. There are cases where he is accountable in which he may be personally blameworthy, and there will be occasions when he is not personally blameworthy.[49]

The 'divorce' between the acceptance of responsibility and the consequence of resignation is not, in Sir Richard's expressed view, the 'heart of an effective system of parliamentary accountability' as the Treasury and Civil Service Select Committee regarded it to be.[50] In Sir Richard's view, what does lie at the heart of the constitutional doctrine is rather the:

> ... obligation of ministers to give, or to facilitate the giving, of information about the activities of their departments and about the actions and omission of their civil servants.[51]

This obligation to provide information came into conflict in relation to defence sales with the government's insistence on following the practice of not disclosing

---

47   HL Deb Vol 576 Col 1507–17, and HC Deb Vol 287 Cols 949–58, 18 December 1996.
48   Scott Report, para K8.5.
49   Evidence given to the Inquiry on 9 February 1994: transcript, pp 22–23, cited in the Scott Report.
50   *Fifth Report of the Treasury and Civil Service Committee: The Role of the Civil Service*, HC 27-I (1993–94), London: HMSO, para 133; cited in the Scott Report, p 415.
51   Scott Report, p 415.

to parliament information concerning individual export licensing matters, a practice which did not, in Sir Richard's view, constitute any departure from the practice adopted by all other post-War administrations. However, in 1991, the British government supported the introduction by the United Nations of a voluntary register identifying the movement of, and quantities of, conventional weaponry between supplier and recipient nations. On this basis, Sir Richard Scott called for an abandonment of the blanket refusal to answer parliamentary questions, at least in relation to conventional weaponry.

The refusal to answer questions at all is but part of the problem of the duty to give information. A further cause for concern lay in the failure of ministers to give full answers to questions and, in relation to the Scott Inquiry, in the failure of witnesses to provide the full picture. 'Commercial confidentiality' is an accepted reason for the denial of information, but that, in Sir Richard's view, did not excuse the refusal of information or the provision of information about weapons supply. National security is another justified exception to the duty to make full disclosure. Nevertheless:

> ... setting those rare cases aside, the proposition that it is acceptable for a Minister to give an answer that is deliberately incomplete is one which, in my opinion, is inconsistent with the requirements of the constitutional principle of ministerial accountability. Half the picture can be true ... But the audience does not know that it is seeing only half the picture. If it did know, it would protest.[52]

A strong democracy can only be a legitimate label if the electors are able to express their view on the basis of adequate knowledge of government activities:

> A failure by Ministers to meet the obligations of ministerial accountability by providing information about the activities of their departments engenders cynicism about government and undermines, in my opinion, the democratic process.[53]

The Public Service Committee report: ministerial accountability and responsibility[54]

Reviewing the doctrine of ministerial responsibility from the *Crichel Down* affair in 1954, the Committee produced 34 conclusions and recommendations. In the Committee's view, it was not possible to distinguish absolutely between areas in which a minister is personally responsible (and blameworthy) and areas in which the minister is constitutionally accountable.[55] Further, the Committee concluded that 'proper and rigorous scrutiny and accountability' is a more important feature of ministerial responsibility than parliament's ability to force that minister's resignation.[56] The Public Service Committee had been critical of the fact that the definition and scope of ministerial responsibility was formulated by the

---

52 Scott Report, p 422. See Tomkins, 1996.
53 Scott Report, p 425.
54 *Second Report from the Public Service Committee*, HC 313 (1995–96), London: HMSO.
55 See HC Deb Vol 290 Col 273, 12 February 1997; and *Government Response to the Report of the Public Service Committee on Ministerial Accountability*, HC 67 (1996–97), London: HMSO, November 1996, p vi.
56 See *Government Response to the Report of the Public Service Committee on Ministerial Accountability*, HC 67 (1996–97), London: HMSO.

government of the day, via *Question of Procedures for Ministers*, rather than by parliament, which alone had the right to demand and enforce ministerial responsibility. As a result, and after much inter-Party debate, the House resolved in 1997 that:

> In the opinion of the House, the following principles should govern the conduct of ministers of the Crown in relation to Parliament:
>
> (1) Ministers have a duty to Parliament to account, and be held to account, for the policies, decisions and actions of their departments and next step agencies;
>
> (2) It is of paramount importance that ministers should give accurate and truthful information to Parliament, correcting any inadvertent error at the earliest opportunity. Ministers who knowingly mislead Parliament will be expected to offer their resignation to the Prime Minister;
>
> (3) Ministers should be as open as possible with Parliament, refusing to provide information only when disclosure would not be in the public interest;
>
> (4) Ministers should require civil servants who give evidence before parliamentary committees on their behalf and under their directions to be as helpful as possible in providing accurate, truthful and full information;
>
> (5) The interpretation of 'public interest' in paragraph (3) shall be decided in accordance with statute and the government's Code of Practice on Access to Government Information ...; and compliance with the duty in paragraph (4) shall be in accordance with the duties and responsibilities of civil services set out in the Civil Service Code ...[57]

The Hutton Inquiry[58]

The Iraq War in 2003 was to lead to two judicial inquiries. The first, the *Hutton Inquiry* was prompted by the suicide of Dr David Kelly CMG, a senior government scientist who, inter alia, had been one of the chief weapons inspectors in Iraq on behalf of the United Nations' Special Commission.

Central to the circumstances surrounding Dr Kelly's death was the intelligence relating to weapons of mass destruction (WMD) set out in a government dossier published in September 2002. In May 2003 a journalist, who had met with Dr Kelly, alleged in a radio programme that the government's dossier was wrong in that it claimed that Iraq had WMD which were deployable within 45 minutes and that the government had exaggerated the intelligence to bolster its case to attack Iraq. Dr Kelly acted as an adviser to the Ministry of Defence, the Defence Intelligence Staff and the Secret Intelligence Service (MI6) and part of his role was to speak to the media and other institutions on Iraq issues. The government complained to the BBC about the broadcast. The identity of the journalist's source of information then became of central importance.

Among the several issues which Lord Hutton considered in relation to the government dossier was whether the Prime Minister or officials in 10 Downing Street were responsible for intelligence being set out in the dossier which they knew or suspected was incorrect or misleading. The Inquiry's conclusions

---

57   See HC Deb Vol 292 Cols 1046–47, 19 March 1997. See also Woodhouse, 1997.
58   See Blom-Cooper and Munro, 2004.

regarding the dossier exonerated the government from any attempt to embellish the data relied on. The 45 minute claim at the heart of the controversy had been received by the SIS from a source in Iraq which was regarded as reliable. The allegation that the government 'knew' that the claim was wrong was unfounded. Further the Inquiry found that Downing Street recognised that nothing should be stated in the dossier which was inconsistent with the intelligence received.

The Butler Inquiry

In February 2004 the Prime Minister decided to establish a committee of inquiry to review intelligence on weapons of mass destruction. The Inquiry was chaired by the Rt Hon Lord Butler, a former Cabinet Secretary.[59] The terms of reference of the Inquiry were to investigate the intelligence coverage available in respect of WMD programmes in countries of concern and on the global trade in WMD, taking into account what is now known about these programmes; as part of this work, to investigate the accuracy of intelligence on Iraqi WMD up to March 2003, and to examine any discrepancies between the intelligence gathered, evaluated and used by the Government before the conflict, and between that intelligence and what has been discovered by the Iraq survey group since the end of the conflict; and to make recommendations to the Prime Minister for the future on the gathering, evaluation and use of intelligence on WMD, in the light of the difficulties of operating in countries of concern.

The Inquiry concluded that there had been no wrongdoing on the part of the government. On the '45 minute claim' the Inquiry found that the intelligence report itself was 'vague and ambiguous'.[60] On allegations that the government's motivation for going to war was a desire to control Iraq's oil supplies, the Inquiry found 'no evidence' to support such an allegation.

GOVERNMENT OPENNESS AND GOVERNMENT SECRECY

The issue of the confidentiality of Cabinet papers has been discussed above, pp 283 ff. More generally, the issue of confidentiality of government papers gives rise to questions about the extent to which the government in the United Kingdom operates with an unnecessary degree of secrecy. Secrecy in government raises important questions for the individual citizen concerning the right of access to personal information stored by the government and also to the right of access of citizens more generally to documents concerning government of the state and of access to information about the policies and standards of service of public bodies. The issue of access to personal data held by government is discussed later in this chapter. A further question arises as to the disclosure of government documents to courts of law and the use of public interest immunity certificates by the government to conceal evidence.

---

59 See *Review of Intelligence on Weapons of Mass Destruction*, Report of a Committee of Privy Counsellors, London: The Stationery Office, HC 898, July 2004.
60 *Ibid*, paragraph 507.

STANDARDS OF PUBLIC SERVICE AND
THE OPENNESS OF GOVERNMENT

Access to information[61]

The balance to be struck between the right of authorities to maintain confidential records and the right of individuals to access to that information is increasingly a matter of concern. There is no general right of access to data stored by the state, for example, records maintained by the Police, Inland Revenue, National Health Service and Department of Social Security. Under the Official Secrets Act 1989, categories of information can never be disclosed. A limited right of access to personal files is granted under the Data Protection Act 1984.[62] Citizens in the United Kingdom are entitled to access to official records in certain categories of cases.[63] The information which can be disclosed is currently confined to computerised records, in other words excluding manually created files, although access to these will be introduced in the future.

In any heavily regulated state, government departments will have access to large amounts of personal data on its citizens. Tax authorities, Social Security offices, local authorities and driving licence authorities are but four major holders of personal information. The individual has two interests in personal records. The first is that information held about the individual should be accessible to him or her. The second is that the individual should be protected against disclosure of such personal data to third parties.

The protection of personal data

A range of statutes prohibit the unauthorised disclosure of personal data to third parties. Local authority records (relating to, *inter alia*, adoption, education, child support, housing, medical records and social security) are protected. Equally, in the finance industry, there is protection given to confidential information. In relation to such information, the government does not accept that there is a need to relax the restrictions on disclosure.

Access to personal data

The Data Protection Act 1984 provided that computer-held personal information should be made available to individuals, in order that the person concerned may check the accuracy of the data. The Data Protection Act 1998 replaced and repealed the 1984 Act. The Act applies only to personal data, defined in section 1(1), and confers the right to be informed of whether data is being held and to have that data communicated to the subject. The data covered by the Act is wider than under the 1984 Act and relates to both computer held records and manual files. Disclosure may be refused where it would, *inter alia*, damage national security, or be counter to the interests of the prevention or detection of crime or

---

61 See Savage and Edwards, 1985; Tapper, 1989; Reed, 1993.
62 As extended by the Data Protection (Subject Access Modifications) Health Order, SI 1987/1903.
63 On current proposals for greater access to information, see further below.

the apprehension or prosecution of offenders (sections 28 and 29). A Data Protection Commissioner supervises the operation of the Act, and may issue enforcement notices on any data controller who is not acting in accordance with the principles of the Act (see section 4 and Schedule 1). The Commissioner lays an annual report before parliament. The Access to Personal Files Act 1987 provides that individuals have the right to inspect records relating to social services and housing tenancies. Medical records prepared for insurance or employment purposes are accessible under the Access to Medical Reports Act 1988. The Access to Health Records Act 1990 gives patients the right to see records held by general practitioners, health authorities or NHS trusts.

Access to public records

The Public Records Acts 1958 and 1967 provide for the inspection of public records at the Public Records Office after 30 years, unless there is justification for withholding them. The Lord Chancellor also has the power under the Act to order the release of documents at an earlier period if in the public interest. Under section 5 of the 1958 Act, records may be kept closed for a longer period.[64] The main classes of information not disclosed relate to population census returns, Ministry of Pensions First World War war pensions awards files and the Inland Revenue Stamps and Taxes Division registered files.

The Freedom of Information Act 2000

In 1997, the incoming Labour government promised to inject greater openness into the machinery of government. Towards this end, a White Paper, *Your Right to Know: White Paper on Freedom of Information*, was published in December 1997.[65] The government intended that, for the first time, citizens should have a legal right to information and to the records in which that information is contained. In addition, an independent Information Commissioner would be appointed, who would be answerable not to parliament, but to the courts. The new legal right applies throughout the public sector, as well as to some private organisations carrying out duties on behalf of government and privatised utilities. Citizens are entitled to information, subject to 'harm tests'. The Freedom of Information Act supersedes the Code of Practice on Access to Government Information and amends the Data Protection Act 1998 and the Public Records Act 1958. The Act was fully implemented in 2005, and applies to central government with effect from November 2002. The Act is the culmination of years of attempting to open up the processes of government. There are, however, a number of restrictions imposed on the right to information.

The Freedom of Information Act for the first time confers on citizens a general right of access to data held by public authorities (section 1), including local government, National Health Service bodies, schools and colleges, the police and others. Requests must be in writing, and the authority is under a duty to respond to the request within 20 working days of its receipt. A fee is payable and the duty

---

64 Only one to two per cent of records remain closed for longer periods.
65 Cm 3818, London: HMSO.

to disclose does not arise until the fee is paid. The Act is regulated by a Commissioner to whom the public has a right of direct access (section 18; see further below). A public authority may decline to provide information where the cost exceeds the 'appropriate limit' (section 11; the limits are prescribed and may be changed). The Act also provides a list of exempted information, which considerably weakens the general principle of a 'right to know'.

Information which is exempt from disclosure falls into two categories: that which is absolutely exempt and other information which requires the balancing of the public interest in maintaining the exemption and the public interest in disclosure. The following categories of information are exempt from the duty of disclosure (Part II of the Act):

- information which is accessible by other means or which is to be published;

- information relating to the security services or the royal household;

- personal information or information provided to the authority in confidence;

- information to which professional privilege applies;

- information which might prejudice:

  - national security, defence or the effectiveness of the armed forces;

  - international relations or relations between administrations within the United Kingdom;

  - the country's economic interests;

  - criminal investigations or proceedings;

  - law enforcement;

  - the effective conduct of public affairs;

  - the physical or mental health of any person;

  - trade secrets or commercial interests.

The Act specifies the investigative and enforcement powers of the Commissioner. Where the Commissioner decides that a public authority has failed to communicate information, or to provide confirmation or denial, in a case where it is required to do so, the Commissioner may issue a decision notice specifying the steps which must be taken by the authority in order to comply (section 49(4)). The Commissioner may also issue enforcement notices requiring the authority to take, within a specified time, such steps as are required to comply. Where the Commissioner has issued a decision or enforcement notice in respect of the disclosure of information under section 13, a certificate may be issued by an 'accountable person' as defined in the Act, the effect of which is that a public authority need not comply with the Commissioner's notice (section 52). If an authority fails to comply with the Commissioner's notice, the Commissioner may so certify to the High Court or, in Scotland, the Court of Session, and the court may, having conducted a hearing, deal with the authority as if it had committed a contempt of court (section 53).

Appeals

Either the complainant or the pubic authority may appeal against a decision notice to the Tribunal under section 56. The Tribunal shall either allow the appeal or substitute such other notice as could have been served by the Commissioner, or in other cases must dismiss the appeal. Appeals from the decision of the Tribunal on a point of law lie to the High Court or to the Court of Session in relation to Scotland and to the High Court of Justice in Northern Ireland.

Amendments relating to public records

Part VI of the Act provides a statutory regime for access to public records, replacing the provisions of the Public Records Act 1958 relating to discretionary disclosure. It also provides for increased access to information contained in records more than 30 years old.

Amendments to the Data Protection Act 1998

Part VII extends the Data Protection Act 1998 in relation to subject access and data accuracy on information held by public authorities. Schedule 6 extends the 1998 Act to include relevant personal information processed by or on behalf of both Houses of Parliament. Personal data is, however, exempt if the exemption is required for the purpose of avoiding an infringement of the privileges of either House of Parliament.[66]

THE GOVERNMENT AND THE COURTS

Liability of the Crown[67]

The government, acting in the name of the Crown, has a historic right to privileges and immunities.[68] Before the Crown Proceedings Act 1947, two main principles governed the question of the legal liability of the Crown. The first principle was that 'the King could do no wrong' and, accordingly, could not be held liable for any actions which would be unlawful if committed by individuals. The second rule was that the King could not be sued in his own courts. Designed to protect the unique constitutional position of the Crown, as state regulation increased, Crown privilege extended to a wide range of central government activities, thereby weakening the legal protection given to individuals aggrieved by government action. In 1947, the Crown Proceedings Act extended the liability of the Crown to areas of tort and contract. European Community law, the European Convention on Human Rights and the Human Rights Act have all had an impact on this area of law.

---

66 Freedom of Information Act 2000, Sched 6, inserting s 35A into the Data Protection Act 1998.
67 The law is complex and outside the scope of this text. See Craig, 2003a; de Smith, Woolf and Jowell, 1995; Hogg and Monahan, 2000. See also Fairgrieve, 2002; Sunkin, 2003; Andenas and Fairgrieve, 2003.
68 An aspect of the royal prerogative. See Chapter 6.

The Crown Proceedings Act 1947, section 17, provides that civil proceedings against the Crown must be instituted against the relevant government department, or, if there is no government department which has clear responsibility, the proceedings must be brought against the Attorney General. In Scotland, actions against United Kingdom departments may be instituted against the Advocate General for Scotland, and actions against Scottish devolved bodies instituted against the Lord Advocate.[69]

Section 21 relates to remedies, section 21(1) providing that the court may make such orders as could be made in proceedings between subjects. This is subject to the restriction that the court may not issue injunctions or order specific performance, but may instead grant a declaration. In *M v Home Office* (1994), the House of Lords ruled that an injunction could be granted in an action against a minister personally. Lord Woolf stated:

> There appears to be no reason in principle why, if a statute places a duty on a specified minister or other official which creates a cause of action, an action cannot be brought for breach of statutory duty claiming damages or for an injunction, in the limited circumstances where injunctive relief would be appropriate, against the specified minister personally by any person entitled to the benefit of the cause of action ...

> ... I do not believe there is any impediment to a court making such a finding [of contempt], when it is appropriate to do so, not against the Crown directly, but against a government department or a minister of the Crown in his official capacity.

The House of Lords also ruled in *M v Home Office* that applications for judicial review are not 'proceedings against the Crown' for the purposes of the Crown Proceedings Act 1947: accordingly injunctive relief against a minister or officer of the Crown is available in judicial review.

European Community law requires that rights must be given effective protection, and that any domestic restriction on the grant of a remedy must give way to Community law. As the European Court of Justice stated in *R v Secretary of State for Transport ex parte Factortame Ltd (No 2)* (1991):

> ... a national court, which in a case before it concerning Community law, considers that the sole obstacle which precludes it from granting interim relief is a rule of national law must set aside that rule.

The concept of state liability explained by the ECJ in *Francovich v Italy* (1991) is also relevant. Article 10 of the EC Treaty provides that Member States must do all they can to facilitate the achievement of Community objectives and refrain from actions which obstruct the achievement of Community objectives. In *Francovich* and subsequent cases the ECJ has used Article 10 to impose liability on Member States.[70]

The European Convention on Human Rights, Article 13, requires that everyone whose rights have been violated 'shall have an effective remedy before a national authority notwithstanding that the violation has been committed by persons acting in an official capacity'. Moreover, Article 41 provides that where the Court finds a

---

69 See the Scotland Act 1998, Sched 8.
70 See further Convery, 1997; Downes, 1997.

violation of a Convention right or Protocol and the internal law of a Member State allows only partial reparation to be made, the Court 'shall, if necessary, afford just satisfaction to the injured party'. Section 8 of the Human Rights Act 1998 reflects these provisions, requiring a court which has the power to award damages to make an award where this is necessary to achieve 'just satisfaction' and to have regard to the principles applied by the Court of Human Rights.

Liability in tort

In relation to tortious liability, the Crown is placed in the same legal position as any other adult individual, and has the same liability for the tortious acts of its employees and agents as do private persons and organisations. Two important exceptions to liability remained: liability in respect of actions of members of the armed forces while on duty or on premises used for the purposes of the armed forces, and liability for tortious actions committed by the Post Office.[71] In relation to the armed forces exception, the Crown Proceedings (Armed Forces) Act 1987 abolished the immunity. The Act was not, however, retrospective and the immunity can be revived in times of war or national emergency. In *Matthews v Ministry of Defence* (2002), the Court of Appeal ruled that the immunity was not incompatible with Article 6 of the Convention. These exceptions aside, the Crown is placed in the same position as a private person.

Liability in contract

In principle the liability of the Crown under contract is the same as that of a private person. In practice, however, special considerations apply. The legal status of the Crown has been considered and explained by the judiciary. For example, in *BBC v Johns* (1965) Lord Diplock was to state that the Crown 'personifies the executive government of the country'. In *Town Investments Ltd v Department of the Environment* (1978) Lord Simon of Glaisdale described the Crown as a 'corporation aggregate': a corporation comprising many persons and offices. That description was echoed in part by Lord Woolf in *M v Home Office* (1994) when he said – citing Lord Diplock and Lord Simon of Glaisdale in *Town Investments* – that '… the Crown has a legal personality. It can be appropriately described as a corporation sole or a corporation aggregate … The Crown can hold property and enter into contracts'.

One distinction between contracts between private parties and a contract involving the Crown lies in the sheer scale of government contracts for the procurement of goods and services and the use of standard conditions in government contracts. A further distinction lies in the responsibility of the Crown to act in the public interest. It has been held judicially that:

> the Crown cannot put itself in a position where it is prevented from performing its public duty … If it seeks to make an agreement which has that consequence, that agreement is of no effect.[72]

---

71   The Post Office ceased to be a government department and became a public corporation in 1969. The restrictions on liability were nevertheless retained.

72   Woolf J in *R v IRC ex parte Preston* (1983), p 306.

Two cases illustrate this rule of 'executive necessity'. The first concerns exceptional wartime conditions. A Swedish shipping company had obtained an undertaking by the British government[73] that its ship would be allowed – contrary to government policy – to leave a British port into which it had entered to deliver its cargo without being replaced by a ship of the same tonnage: the 'ship for ship' policy. In breach of this undertaking the ship *Amphitrite* was detained. The owners sold the ship to avoid further loss and claimed damages for breach of contract. The court ruled that, while the government could bind itself through a contract, and be liable for damages for breach of contract, the arrangement in question was not a commercial contract.[74] Rowlatt J stated:

> ... it is not competent for the Government to fetter its future executive action, which must necessarily be determined by the needs of the community when the question arises. It cannot by contract hamper its freedom of action in matters which concern the welfare of the State.[75]

The second case is that of *Crown Lands Commissioners v Page* (1960), in which the Court of Appeal ruled that the exercise of the Crown's discretionary powers in relation to land could not be fettered by an implied covenant in favour of the tenant. Devlin LJ stated the principle:

> When the Crown, in dealing with one of its subjects, is dealing as if it too were a private person, and is granting leases or buying and selling as ordinary persons do, it is absurd to suppose that it is making any promise about the way in which it will conduct the affairs of the nation.

Public interest immunity[76]

The phrase 'Crown privilege' has been superseded by the term 'public interest immunity'. One aspect of the immunity which is of contemporary and continuing concern is the extent to which governments – and agencies of government – may be required to disclose information to a court of law. While the immunity from disclosure of information relates principally to the government, it extends to other persons and organisations. The rules regulating the disclosure of documents in civil and criminal cases vary, but in each case there are common features. First, a document may or may not fall within a category of documents which *prima facie* must be disclosed. Secondly, disclosure may be denied on the basis that the contents of the documents fall within a particular category of disclosure or non-disclosure,[77] or that the documents fall within a class of documents which may or may not be disclosed.[78] Thirdly, disclosure involves the evaluation of the relevance

---

73 Sweden being neutral during the First World War.

74 Contrast this case with that of *Attorney General v De Keyser's Royal Hotel* (1920), discussed in Chapter 6, in which the liability of the Crown to award compensation arose out of statute, and not the royal prerogative.

75 *Rederiaktiebolaget Amphitrite v The King* (1921).

76 See, *inter alia*, Jacob, 1993; Simon Brown, 1994; Zuckerman, 1994.

77 Eg, non-disclosure is in the public interest if the contents reveal the identity of a police informer, or the workings of the security services.

78 Eg, non-disclosure of Cabinet proceedings, or intergovernmental negotiations, or documents relating to military operations. See *Duncan v Cammell Laird* (1942); *Conway v Rimmer* (1968); *Burmah Oil v Bank of England* (1980); *Air Canada* (1983); *R v Chief Constable of West Midlands Police ex parte Wiley* (1995), discussed above.

of the information or documents, which in some cases will be clear, but in other cases less clear until disclosed and evaluated by counsel and the court. Over and above these rules is the public interest immunity certificate. The certificate may be used to claim that it is contrary to the public interest for information or documents to be disclosed irrespective of the first two rules, and may be claimed on the basis of either contents or class. Where the government would prefer not to disclose information, and the information falls into a 'grey area', there is a temptation to claim public interest immunity to protect the information.

Public interest immunity was raised, for example, in *D v NSPCC* (1978)[79] in order to protect the sources of information given to the National Society for the Prevention of Cruelty to Children.

The need for confidentiality was also accepted in *Bookbinder v Tebbit* (1992) in relation to sources of information given to the Audit Commission, which was investigating alleged irregularities in the financial dealings of a local authority. The court must, however, be satisfied that there is a real need to prevent the disclosure of an informant's identity.[80]

Under the Crown Proceedings Act 1947, a court may order the disclosure of documents in the interests of justice. Section 28, however, also provides that the power of the court in civil proceedings does not extend to disclosures which it would not be in the public interest to make.

There are two aspects of public interest entailed within this area of the law: the public interest in the administration of justice and the public interest in non-disclosure of damaging information. The questions which arise are: who has the power to decide whether disclosure would or would not be in the public interest, and on what basis is the 'public interest' to be evaluated?

In *Duncan v Cammell Laird* (1942), dependants of victims who died in the submarine *Thetis*, which sank during trials, sued the builders of the submarine. Disclosure was sought of documents relating to contracts between the Admiralty and the building contractors, and salvage reports on the submarine. The Admiralty refused to disclose the information, relying on national security, and the minister certified that disclosure was against the public interest. The House of Lords held that the minister's certificate was conclusive and could not be questioned. Accordingly, the rule emerged that a court of law could never question a claim of Crown privilege (or public interest immunity), irrespective of the type of documents being sought. The House of Lords ruled that public interest immunity could lie in respect of the contents of a particular document, or to a class of documents which ought to be withheld in the interests of the proper functioning of the public service. This decision altered the law and, in the words of Professor Wade, gave the Crown the right to withhold information and thereby 'to override the rights of litigants not only in cases of genuine necessity but in any case where a government department thought fit'.[81]

---

79 And see *Alfred Crompton Amusement Machines Ltd v Customs and Excise Commissioners (No 2)* (1974).
80 See *Norwich Pharmaceutical Co Ltd v Customs and Excise Commissioners* (1974).
81 Wade and Forsyth, 2004.

In 1957, the Lord Chancellor, Lord Kilmuir, issued a statement.[82] He drew a distinction between documents which were absolutely necessary to protect the 'proper functioning of the civil service', and documents which are relevant to litigation but which do not require 'the highest degree of confidentiality ... in the public interest', and stated that privilege relating to medical and other documents relevant to the defence in criminal proceedings should not be routinely claimed.[83] The rule in *Duncan v Cammell Laird*, however, prevailed until 1967. In *Conway v Rimmer* (1968), the House of Lords took a more robust attitude to a claim of public interest immunity, reversing its own decision in *Duncan v Cammell Laird*. In an action for malicious prosecution against his former Superintendent of Police, the Home Secretary objected to the disclosure of reports made on the former police probationary officer. The court refused to follow the broad ruling in *Duncan v Cammell Laird* and ruled that it was for the court – and not the person seeking to prevent disclosure – to rule on the competing public interests in the administration of justice and confidential information. Accordingly, it is for the person seeking to withhold information to assert – through the use of a public interest immunity certificate – the right to non-disclosure, and for the court to determine whether or not non-disclosure is in the public interest. Lord Reid, in rejecting the claim that the power of decision lay solely with ministers of the Crown, stated that he did not doubt that:

> There were certain classes of documents[84] which ought not to be disclosed whatever their content may be ... To my mind the most important reason is that such disclosure would create or fan ill informed or captious public or political criticism. The business of government is difficult enough as it is, and no government could contemplate with equanimity the inner workings of the government machine being exposed to the gaze of those ready to criticise without adequate knowledge of the background and perhaps with an axe to grind.

In *Burmah Oil Co v Bank of England* (1980), the oil company sought disclosure of information relating to the rescue of the company by the bank, in exchange for low-priced stock in the company. The Attorney General produced a public interest immunity certificate from the Chief Secretary to the Treasury, in which objection was made against producing documents sought on the basis that they related to government policy. The House of Lords inspected the documents, but felt that their disclosure was unnecessary.

A question relating to public interest immunity certificates which assumed particular importance in the Arms to Iraq affair, was whether the minister was under a duty to sign the certificate when advised to do so by the Attorney General. The notion of duty arose in *Air Canada v Secretary of State for Trade* (1983) in which Lord Scarman (in the minority) stated that, whilst it was for the court to accept or deny the claim, in claiming public interest immunity the Crown was not 'claiming a privilege but discharging a duty'. In the *Air Canada* case, the House of Lords ruled, by a majority, that the government was entitled to immunity. At issue

---

82   HL Deb Col 741–48, 6 June 1956.
83   On guidelines issued by the Court of Appeal in relation to disclosure in criminal proceedings, see *R v Keane* (1994).
84   Lord Reid refers here specifically to Cabinet minutes.

were the circumstances under which, in judicial review proceedings, the court would examine documents for which immunity was claimed. No order for disclosure can be made unless the documents are inspected by the court. The majority in the House of Lords ruled that the party seeking disclosure of documents had to show that 'the documents are very likely to contain material which would give substantial support to his contention on an issue which arises in the case' (*per* Lord Fraser, p 917e). It was not sufficient that the documents might reveal information relevant to the case; it had to be established by the person seeking disclosure that it was 'very likely' that the information would assist his case.

The distinction between a right and a duty was also considered in *Makanjuola v Metropolitan Police Commissioner* (1992). In that case, Bingham LJ stated that:

> ... where a litigant asserts that documents are immune from production or disclosure on public interest grounds he is not (if the claim is well founded) claiming a right but observing a duty ...

Bingham LJ went on to state that:

> ... it [the distinction between a right and a duty] does, I think, mean: (1) that public interest immunity cannot in any ordinary sense be waived, since, although one can waive rights, one cannot waive duties; (2) that, where a litigant holds documents in a class *prima facie* immune, he should (save perhaps in a very exceptional case) assert that the documents are immune and decline to disclose them, since the ultimate judge of where the balance of public interest lies is not him but the court; and (3) that, where a document is, or is held to be, in an immune class, it may not be used for any purpose whatever in the proceedings to which the immunity applies, and certainly cannot (for instance) be used for the purpose of cross-examination.

Woolf LJ, while endorsing much of this analysis, noted that *Makanjuola* did not involve a Department of State, represented by a Secretary of State. He stated that:

> If a Secretary of State on behalf of his department, as opposed to any ordinary litigant, concludes that any public interest in the documents being withheld from production is outweighed by the public interest in the documents being available for purposes of litigation, it is difficult to conceive that, unless the documents do not relate to an area for which the Secretary of State was responsible, the court would feel it appropriate to come to any different conclusion from that of the Secretary of State. The position would be the same if the Attorney General was of the opinion that the documents should be disclosed.

However, that situation did not pertain to other bodies or persons, and it could not be left to individuals to decide that documents should be disclosed. The court retained the ultimate right to determine disclosure and would 'intervene to protect the public interest'. The decision in *Neilson*, and those cases in which it had been applied, was wrong and could no longer be justified. It was not, Woolf LJ stated, that 'there had been a change in attitudes since the *Neilson* decision' but rather that 'establishing a class of public interest immunity of this nature was never justified'. In *Wiley*, the House of Lords ruled that in *Neilson* and the subsequent cases in which it had been applied, the law was incorrectly stated. The House of Lords did not, however, go so far as to say that material which came to light in investigations against the police could never be entitled to class immunity.

The House of Lords had the opportunity to re-examine the issue in *R v Chief Constable of West Midlands Police ex parte Wiley; Chief Constable of Nottinghamshire Police ex parte Sunderland* (1995). In that case, the defendant, Mr Wiley, was charged with robbery, but at his trial the prosecution offered no evidence. He subsequently made formal complaints against the police and commenced a civil action against the Chief Constable. Mr Sunderland had been charged with assault but, again, no evidence was offered at trial by the prosecution. He also made a formal complaint against the police. He alleged assault by the police and indicated that he would institute civil proceedings against them. The problem faced by both complainants was that the police had documents which it was thought would attract public interest immunity on behalf of the police, thereby making them unavailable to the complainants. The Chief Constables concerned refused to give undertakings that the documents would not be used to the detriment of the complainants, and the complainants secured a declaration that the Chief Constables had acted unlawfully in refusing to give the undertakings. The Chief Constables appealed against the declarations to the House of Lords. In the earlier case of *Neilson v Laugharne* (1981),[85] the House of Lords had ruled that public interest immunity attached to police complaints documents, on the basis that if it did not the complaints procedure would be damaged. However, the House of Lords ruled that, in principle, documents which are relevant to litigation should be disclosed, unless that disclosure would cause 'substantial harm'. In particular, Lord Templeman stated that 'a rubber stamp approach to public interest immunity by the holder of a document is neither necessary nor appropriate ...'.[86]

---

85 Applied in *Halford v Sharples* (1992) in proceedings alleging unlawful sexual discrimination; distinguished in *Peach v Metropolitan Police Commissioner* (1986) on the basis that the allegation is of a serious crime committed by the police, and *Ex parte Coventry Newspapers Ltd* (1993).

86 At p 281. In *Rowe v United Kingdom* (2000) the European Court of Human Rights has ruled that the use of Public Interest Immunity Certificates which prevent a judge from considering whether or not evidence should be disclosed in the court of a murder trial violates Article 6 of the Convention.

CHAPTER 12

DEVOLUTION AND LOCAL GOVERNMENT

DEVOLUTION

As discussed in Chapters 1 to 3, the constitution of the United Kingdom has traditionally been characterised by the unity of its several parts, with centralised government. Wales became united with England through being conquered in 1262, while the Acts of Union 1706 and 1707 marked the end of the separation of Scotland and England under two sovereign parliaments. Despite the former attempt at devolution of power to both Wales and Scotland in 1978, the population of neither country then expressed – according to the terms of the referendum – the desire for greater separation from centralised government. Two decades later, however, the political position was much changed. A disenchantment with the extent to which the national parliament reflected the views of the people of Scotland, in particular, and Wales, and a rising tide of nationalist regional sentiment, led to change and power being devolved from the centre to the nations. In addition, settlement reached in Northern Ireland under the 1998 Good Friday agreement facilitated the re-establishment of the Northern Ireland Assembly.

NORTHERN IRELAND

The Northern Ireland Act 1998 regulates the Northern Ireland Assembly and Executive. The Act includes many significant distinguishing features unique to the situation pertaining in Northern Ireland. In particular, the Act provides for a power sharing executive, with offices allocated between differing political parties according to their electoral support. The Assembly has statutory power to exclude a minister or junior minister, or a political party, from holding office for a 12 month period if the Assembly resolves that he, she or it no longer enjoys the confidence of the Assembly on the basis that he or she is not committed to non-violence and exclusively peaceful and democratic means. The Act also provides for the protection of all citizens of Northern Ireland from discrimination on the grounds of religious belief and introduces a Human Rights Commission and Equal Opportunities Commission.[1]

The devolution of power to the new Assembly remains conditional under the Belfast Agreement of 1998, and power may be recalled to the United Kingdom Parliament if the terms of the Agreement are not complied with. During a period when power is recalled, the functions of the First Minister and Deputy First

---

1   The Act repeals, *inter alia*, in full, the Government of Ireland Act 1920, Northern Ireland (Temporary Provisions) Act 1972, Northern Ireland Assembly Act 1973, Northern Ireland Constitution (Amendment) Act 1973, Northern Ireland Act 1974, and, in part, the Northern Ireland Constitution Act 1973 and all of the Northern Ireland Act 1982 and the Northern Ireland (Elections) Act 1998.

Minister are undertaken by the Secretary of State, and the functions of Northern Ireland Ministers are exercised by the Northern Ireland Department.

The status of Northern Ireland

Section 1 of the Northern Ireland Act 1998 reiterates earlier pledges regarding the status of Northern Ireland, stating that:

> ... Northern Ireland in its entirety remains part of the United Kingdom and shall not cease to be so without the consent of a majority of the people of Northern Ireland voting in a poll held for the purposes of this section ...

Giving recognition to long held Republican ambitions, section 1 commits the government of the United Kingdom to giving effect to the wishes of the people should a majority express the wish to cease to be part of the United Kingdom and form part of a united Ireland, following such agreement as may be made between the United Kingdom government and the government of Ireland.

The executive

Part III of the Northern Ireland Act 1998 regulates the executive authorities. Within six weeks of the date of the first meeting of the Assembly, the Assembly elected the First Minister and Deputy First Minister. If either the First Minister or Deputy First Minister resigns or otherwise ceases to hold office, the other minister must also cease to hold office at that time, but may continue in office until a new election is held.[2]

Ministerial offices

The number of ministerial offices is determined by the First Minister and Deputy First Minister acting jointly, but may not exceed ten, or such greater number as is approved by the Secretary of State. The allocation of ministerial offices provided for under the Act is designed to achieve power sharing between the political parties, in proportion to the number of seats held in the Assembly. The formula, the 'd'Hondt system' devised by an eighteenth century Belgian political scientist, is the number of seats in the Assembly held by members of the party on the day the Assembly first met following its election, divided by the number of ministerial offices (if any) held by members of the party, plus one. Where this results in the same total for two parties, the party with the bigger number of first preference votes in the Assembly elections has the first choice of offices.[3] An Executive Committee is established, comprising the First Minister, the Deputy First Minister

---

2   Northern Ireland Act 1998, s 16. The leader of the Ulster Unionists, David Trimble, became First Minister and Seamus Mallon, the Social Democratic and Labour Party's (SDLP) deputy leader, became Deputy First Minister.

3   *Ibid*, s 18. In the 1998 elections, the Ulster Unionist Party won 28 seats in the Assembly, the SDLP 24, the Democratic Unionist Party (DUP) 20 and Sinn Fein 18. The formula resulted in the Ulster Unionists having three seats on the executive, the SDLP three, the DUP and Sinn Fein each having two.

and the Northern Ireland Ministers. The First Minister and Deputy First Minister are chairmen of the Committee.[4]

Ministers of Northern Ireland Departments have no power to make, confirm or approve any subordinate legislation, or do any act, so far as the legislation or act is incompatible with Convention rights or Community law, or discriminates against, or aids or incites another person to discriminate against, a person or class of person on the ground of religious belief or political opinion.[5]

Elections

Assembly elections are held every four years. Provision is made for extraordinary elections, whereby, if the Assembly passes a resolution that it should be dissolved, the Secretary of State must propose a date for the election of the next Assembly. The Northern Ireland Assembly (Elections and Periods of Suspension) Act 2003 provides for the postponement of elections to a date to be specified by an order of the Secretary of State. The 2003 Act was passed as a result of the suspension of the Assembly and the perceived breakdown in trust and confidence between the Northern Ireland political parties which made restoration of devolved government impossible. Constituencies are the same as those for parliamentary elections and each constituency returns six members. Voting is by single transferable vote, defined as being a vote:

(a) capable of being given so as to indicate the voter's order of preference for the candidates for election as members for the constituency; and

(b) capable of being transferred to the next choice when the vote is not needed to give a prior choice the necessary quota of votes or when a prior choice is eliminated from the list of candidates because of a deficiency in the number of votes given for him.

The Assembly

The first task of the elected Assembly is to elect from among its members a Presiding Officer and deputies, positions analogous to the Speaker of the House of Commons and his or her deputy.[6] Consistent also with the Scotland Act 1998, there is established a corporate body, known as the Northern Ireland Assembly Commission, comprising the Presiding Officer and members of the Assembly, to perform the functions of providing property, staff and services, and other contractual functions.

Legislation

Section 5 of the Northern Ireland Act 1998 provides for the making of Acts of the Assembly, but reserves to the United Kingdom Parliament the right to make laws for Northern Ireland, subject to the right of the Assembly to modify provisions made by Act of Parliament in so far as it is part of the law of Northern Ireland.

---

4   *Ibid*, s 20.
5   *Ibid*, s 24.
6   *Ibid*, s 39.

The legislative competence of the Assembly is regulated by sections 6 and 7, and section 6(1) states that a provision of an Act is not law if it is outside the legislative competence of the Assembly. Schedule 10 defines and regulates proceedings in relation to disputes over the legislative competence of the Assembly.

Members' interests

A register of members' interests is provided for under section 43. Members having a financial or other interest must declare that interest before participating in Assembly proceedings, and standing orders may include a provision preventing or restricting participation in proceedings by a member with a registrable interest. It is an offence to advocate or initiate any cause, or urge another member to do so, in consideration of any payment or benefit in kind. A person guilty of an offence is liable to a fine not exceeding level five on the standard scale. Proceedings may only be brought with the consent of the Director of Public Prosecutions for Northern Ireland.

Privilege

For the purposes of the law of defamation, absolute privilege attaches to the making of a statement in Assembly proceedings, and to the publication of a statement under the Assembly's authority.[7]

Human rights and equal opportunities

The Act establishes a Human Rights Commission,[8] consisting of a Chief Commissioner and other Commissioners appointed by the Secretary of State.[9] The functions of the Commission include ensuring the adequacy and effectiveness of law and practice in relation to the protection of human rights, and reporting to the Secretary of State such recommendations as are considered necessary to improve law and practice. The Commission has a duty to advise the Assembly on the compatibility of Bills with human rights. The Commission is also under a duty to promote understanding and awareness of the importance of human rights in Northern Ireland.

The Act also establishes an Equality Commission for Northern Ireland, consisting of between 14 and 20 Commissioners appointed by the Secretary of State. The Equality Commission replaces bodies formerly promoting equal opportunities.[10] A statutory duty is imposed on all public authorities to have due regard to the need to promote equality of opportunity between persons of different religious belief, political opinion, racial group, age, marital status or sexual orientation; between men and women generally; between persons with a disability and those without; and between those with dependants and those

---

7   *Ibid*, s 50.
8   See also *ibid*, Sched 7.
9   *Ibid*, s 68. Note that the office of Secretary of State for Northern Ireland is combined with that of the Secretary of State for Wales.
10 *Ibid*, s 74.

without. It is unlawful for a public authority to discriminate, or aid or incite another to discriminate, against a person or class of persons on the grounds of religious belief or political opinion.[11]

North-South Ministerial Council and British-Irish Council

The Belfast Agreement established two new bodies, designed to facilitate and promote co-operative relations between the United Kingdom and the Republic of Ireland. The North-South Ministerial Council comprises representatives of the Irish government and the Northern Ireland Executive with a view to fostering cross-community participation in the Council. The First Minister and Deputy First Minister acting jointly nominate ministers to the Council. Agreements reached by meetings of the North-South Ministerial Council are given effect by the Assembly, and no agreement entered into may come into effect without the approval of the Assembly.[12]

A British-Irish Council is also established, which provides a forum for debate on matters of mutual interest between the British and Irish governments and representatives of the devolved institutions in Northern Ireland, Scotland and Wales, together with representatives from the Isle of Man and the Channel Islands.

SCOTLAND

In 1989, a Scottish Constitutional Convention was set up, following the publication of *A Claim of Right for Scotland* by the Campaign for a Scottish Assembly. It was argued that the people of Scotland had the right to govern themselves, and that the conventional doctrine of parliamentary sovereignty, as understood south of the border, had no basis in Scottish political thought. In Scotland, the preferred view is that the people, not parliament, are sovereign. The final report of the Convention, *Scotland's Parliament, Scotland's Right* was published in November 1995.

While the former Conservative government was opposed to any devolution of power to either Scotland or Wales, the Labour government elected in 1997 declared in its election manifesto that it favoured the devolution of power. In the words of the manifesto, 'our proposal is for devolution not federation. A sovereign Westminster Parliament will devolve power to Scotland and Wales. The Union will be strengthened and the threat of separatism removed'.

The referendum

The Referendums (Scotland and Wales) Act 1997 provided the mechanisms for testing the wishes of the people. The Scottish people were asked to vote both for or against a Scottish Parliament, and for or against the proposition that the Scottish Parliament should have tax varying powers. The referendum in Scotland took place in September 1997. In favour of the establishment of a Scottish

---

11   *Ibid*, s 76.
12   *Ibid*, ss 52, 53.

Parliament were 74.3 per cent of voters, and in favour of tax varying powers, 63.5 per cent.

Devolution and the Treaty of Union

The Union with Scotland Act 1706 and Union with England Act 1707 remain in force and have effect subject to the provisions of the Scotland Act 1998.[13] The government is firmly committed to strengthening the Union, and makes it clear that Scotland continues to form an integral part of the United Kingdom:

> The government want a United Kingdom which everyone feels part of, can contribute to, and in whose future all have a stake. The Union will be strengthened by recognising the claims of Scotland, Wales and the regions with strong identities of their own. The government's devolution proposals, by meeting these aspirations, will not only safeguard but also enhance the Union.[14]

The Scottish Parliament

The Scottish Parliament was established under section 1 of the Scotland Act 1998. The 129 seat parliament is based in Edinburgh. The parliament's first task was to elect a Presiding Officer and two deputies.[15] The Scottish Parliament is unicameral and has a fixed four year term of office, subject to provisions made for the holding of extraordinary general elections under section 3.

The electoral process

In the White Paper, *Scotland's Parliament*,[16] the government recognised the need both for a strong constituency link and for greater proportionality between votes cast and seats won to be achieved through the election of additional members. Members of the Scottish Parliament (MSPs) are elected in two different ways. The majority are elected from individual constituencies. The remaining members – 'additional members' – are selected from party lists drawn up for each of the current European Parliament constituencies. A Clerk of the Parliament, and Assistant Clerks, are appointed by the Scottish Parliamentary Corporate Body, comprising the Presiding Officer and four Members of Parliament. Parliamentary proceedings are regulated by standing orders.[17] The Scottish Parliament has the power to call for witnesses and documents, and provides for criminal penalties in the event of failure to comply with parliament's directions.

Members' interests

Section 39 of the Scotland Act regulates members' interests. It provides for a register of interests and requires members to register financial interests, including

---

13 Scotland Act 1998, s 37.
14 *Scotland's Parliament*, Cm 3658, 1997, London: HMSO, para 3.1.
15 Scotland Act 1998, s 19. Standing orders provide that persons holding office of Presiding Officer or Deputy do not represent the same political party: Sched 3, para 5.
16 See HC Deb Vol 298 Col 1041, 24 July 1997; Vol 299 Col 456, 31 July 1997; HL Deb Vol 581 Col 1526, 24 July 1997; Vol 582 Col 185, 31 July 1997.
17 *Ibid*, s 22.

benefits in kind, and declare interests before taking part in any proceedings in parliament relating to that matter. A Member of Parliament who fails to comply with or contravenes the prohibition is guilty of an offence.

Parliamentary committees

A Parliamentary Bureau is established with the task of proposing the establishment, membership, remit and duration of committees. The Bureau also proposes the political party whose members are eligible to be the convenor (chairperson) and deputy convenor of the committee. The Bureau's proposals are subject to parliamentary approval. A number of mandatory committees have been established, which sit for the duration of a parliamentary session. A number of additional committees have been established, including Education, Culture and Sport, Enterprise and Lifelong Learning, Finance, Health and Community Care, Justice and Home Affairs, Local Government, Procedures, Rural Affairs, Social Inclusion, Housing and Voluntary Sector, Standards, Subordinate Legislation, and Transport and the Environment.

Parliamentary privilege[18]

Section 41 provides that for the purposes of the law of defamation any statement made in proceedings of the parliament and the publication of any statement under the authority of parliament is absolutely privileged.

Maladministration

Section 91 of the Scotland Act makes provision for the investigation of complaints made to members in respect of the exercise of functions by the Scottish Executive.

Legislation

The Scottish Parliament has the power to make Acts of Parliament within the sphere of competence laid down in the Scotland Act. Any Act which is outside the legislative competence of the parliament is not law.[19] Section 28(7) makes clear that the legislative competence of the Scottish Parliament does not affect the power of the parliament of the United Kingdom to make laws for Scotland. The member of the Scottish Executive in charge of a Bill must state, on or before its introduction in parliament, that the provisions of the Bill are within the legislative competence of parliament,[20] and section 29 stipulates that an Act is not law if it is outside the parliament's legislative competence.

Schedule 5: reserved matters

Part I of Schedule 5 lays down five general categories of matters reserved to the United Kingdom Parliament: the constitution; the registration of political parties; foreign affairs; Civil Service, defence and treason. Part II lists specific reservations

---

18   See Munro, 2000.
19   Scotland Act 1998, ss 28, 29.
20   *Ibid*, s 31(1).

under 11 broad heads, namely: financial and economic matters; home affairs; trade and industry; energy; transport; social security; regulation of the professions; employment; health and medicines; media and culture; and miscellaneous. Matters reserved facilitate United Kingdom-wide uniformity, while devolving to the Scottish Parliament the power to regulate non-reserved matters according to national requirements.

The Executive

The Scottish Executive comprises the First Minister, and such ministers as the First Minister appoints, the Lord Advocate, and the Solicitor General for Scotland. The First Minister is appointed by Her Majesty from among members of the parliament, and holds office at Her Majesty's pleasure.[21] Members of the Executive are responsible to the Scottish Parliament.

In *Davidson v Scottish Ministers* (2005) the House of Lords ruled that the Scottish courts had jurisdiction to make coercive orders against ministers of the Scottish Executive in judicial review proceedings. Section 21(1) of the Crown Proceedings Act 1947 should be interpreted so as to ensure that the protection Parliament intended they should have against government ministers was the same as that available in the English courts.

The continuing role of the Secretary of State for Scotland

The Secretary of State for Scotland is responsible for promoting communication between the Scottish Parliament and Executive and between the United Kingdom Parliament and Government on matters of mutual interests, and on representing Scottish interests in reserved matters.[22] The Secretary of State and the Scottish Executive meet in order to monitor progress. From 2003 the office of Secretary of State for Scotland has been combined with that of Secretary of State for Transport.

Law Officers

The Law Officers of the Scottish Executive are the Lord Advocate and the Solicitor General for Scotland. The United Kingdom government also needs advice on Scottish law, and the office of Scottish Law Officer to the United Kingdom government was created to meet this need.[23]

Scottish representation at Westminster

The problematic issue of continued Scottish representation at Westminster after devolution, particularly in relation to matters exclusively English (the 'West Lothian question'),[24] was addressed by initially continuing the same level of Scottish representation as before. However, section 86 of the Scotland Act 1998

---

21 *Ibid*, ss 44 and 45.
22 *Scotland's Parliament*, Cm 3658, 1997, London: HMSO, para 4.12.
23 *Ibid*, paras 4.8, 4.9.
24 On which see the 4th edition of this book, pp 381–84.

amends Schedule 2 to the Parliamentary Constituencies Act 1986 by omitting rule 1(2) requiring Scotland to have not less than 71 constituencies, and providing for Scottish representation in the future to be based on the same electoral quota as for England, the effect of which is to reduce the number of constituencies to 59.

Financial arrangements[25]

The Scottish Parliament has the power to increase or decrease the basic rate of income tax set by the United Kingdom Parliament by up to three pence in the pound. The Inland Revenue continues to administer tax variations.

Since the 1970s, there has existed a 'block formula' system of funding Scotland's public expenditure programmes. There have been adjustments made to this arrangement, and the Scottish Parliament also has tax varying powers which enable it to raise revenue independently. The parliament is entitled to determine its own expenditure priorities. The parliament has powers to control Scottish local government expenditure and to finance local government. It also has control over the form of local taxation, both domestic and non-domestic. There is a statutory duty to maintain effective scrutiny and audit arrangements.

Debating powers

The Scottish Parliament is able to examine devolved matters, and debate all matters irrespective of whether they are devolved or reserved.[26]

Scotland and the European Union

While relations with Europe are the responsibility of the United Kingdom Parliament and government, the Scottish Parliament and Executive play an important role in relation to those aspects of European Union affairs which affect devolved areas. The government has promised to ensure that Scottish Office ministers play a full role in European Union Councils. Scottish Office officials participate in discussions with the relevant Whitehall department. The Scottish Executive and officials are directly involved in the government's decision making and formulation of policy in relation to European Union matters.

The Scottish Parliament scrutinises European Union legislative proposals 'to ensure that Scotland's interests are properly reflected'. Responsibility for ensuring the implementation of European Union obligations lies with the Scottish Executive.

WALES

Rather than devolve legislative power to a Welsh Parliament, the Government of Wales Act 1998 provides for a directly elected Assembly which has the responsibilities formerly exercised by the Secretary of State for Wales. The

---

25 See the Scotland Act 1998, Pts III and IV.
26 *Scotland's Parliament*, Cm 3658, 1997, London: HMSO, para 2.5.

devolution thus conferred administrative rather than legislative power. The government's White Paper, *A Voice for Wales: The Government's Proposals for a Welsh Assembly*,[27] perceived a 'democratic deficit' in the administrative arrangements for Wales. Until devolution, the majority of administrative matters were the responsibility of the Welsh Office. Other bodies, such as health authorities and National Health Service Trusts, and unelected bodies, such as the Welsh Development Agency, Further and Higher Education Funding Councils and *Tai Cymru*, were not accountable to the Welsh people. The only directly accountable bodies were local authorities. The devolution of administrative competence to the Welsh Assembly redresses this lack of local accountability.

The referendum

The result of the referendum held to determine the people's wishes in respect of devolved powers was less clear-cut than that of the Scottish referendum. Only 50 per cent of the electorate voted, as compared with 60 per cent in the Scottish referendum, and 50.3 per cent voted in favour of the establishment of an Assembly. A majority of voters in 11 of the 22 local government areas voted in favour.

The Assembly

Section 1 of the Government of Wales Act 1998 established the 60-member Welsh Assembly, which sits for a fixed four year term of office. Unlike the Scottish Parliament, however, the Assembly has no power to dissolve itself before the end of the four year term of office. The Assembly runs under a committee system. An Executive Committee provides the overall direction for the Assembly and comprises members of the majority party alone. Regional Committees have been established to ensure that the needs of each area of Wales are properly considered. The Regional Committees are advisory bodies only and do not have specific functions or decision making powers. Members of the Assembly are salaried, and allowances are payable.[28]

The electoral system

The additional member electoral system is employed for elections.[29] There are 40 constituency members, elected on the simple majority system, and 20 additional members elected from the party list. Each voter has two votes – one for the constituency member and one for the additional member. The first elections took place in the spring of 1999. Thereafter, elections take place every four years, on the first Thursday in May.[30]

---

27 Debated in the House of Commons, HC Deb Vol 298 Col 753, 22 July 1997, Vol 298 Col 1119, 25 July 1997; HL Deb Vol 581 Col 1322, 22 July 1997. *A Voice for Wales: The Government's Proposals for a Welsh Assembly*, Cm 3718, 1997, London: HMSO.
28 Government of Wales Act 1998, s 16.
29 *Ibid*, s 4.
30 *Ibid*, s 3.

The Leader and Executive Committee

The overall political direction of the Assembly is provided by a Leader of the Assembly, elected by the Assembly, and an Executive Committee (section 56). The Executive Committee, headed by the Leader, comprises leaders of differing subject committees. The Act allows for the Executive Committee to be made up of members of a single political party, and to sit in private. The Committee is thus envisaged to be the equivalent of the British Cabinet. The Leader of the Committee faces questions in the Assembly concerning all issues.

Welsh representation at Westminster

Because the Assembly does not have devolved legislative powers, the West Lothian question does not arise. The Secretary of State for Wales and Welsh Members of Parliament continue to play a full role at Westminster, but one which also involves a new partnership with the Assembly.[31] The number of Welsh members remains unchanged.

The relationship between Westminster and the Assembly

The United Kingdom Parliament at Westminster continues to legislate for Wales. Members of the Assembly need to develop a close partnership with Welsh Members of Parliament. The White Paper stated that the government intended that the Assembly should be able to 'seek to influence legislation which is being considered at Westminster'.[32] The Secretary of State for Wales is under a statutory duty to consult the Assembly about the government's legislative programme, after it has been announced in the Queen's Speech, and the Assembly, following debate, may draft its response. The Secretary of State is able to attend Assembly debates, but is not entitled to vote.

In relation to subordinate legislation, however, the Executive Committee and subject committees have power to prepare secondary legislation for submission to the Assembly for debate and approval. Such pieces of secondary legislation are known as Assembly Orders. A subordinate legislation scrutiny committee has been established to consider draft statutory instruments and report to the Assembly (section 58 of the 1998 Act). The Assembly has the power to revoke, replace or amend such legislation in the same manner as the Secretary of State had formerly been able to do. Proposed Orders relating to Wales are scrutinised by the Assembly's subject committees.[33]

The powers of the Welsh Assembly

As stated above, the Assembly takes over many of the responsibilities which formerly lay with the Secretary of State for Wales. Part II of the Government of

---

31 *A Voice for Wales: The Government's Proposals for a Welsh Assembly*, Cm 3718, 1997, London: HMSO, para 3.33.
32 *Ibid*, para 3.38.
33 *Ibid*, paras 4.22–4.24.

Wales Act 1998 defines the functions of the Assembly. Section 22 provides for the transfer of ministerial functions to the Assembly, by means of Orders in Council.

Members' interests

A register of interests is established, requiring any Assembly member who has a financial or other interest in any matter to be registered and requiring declarations of interests to be made before participating in Assembly proceedings. Under section 72, members are prohibited from advocating any cause on behalf of any person in consideration of payments or benefits in kind. It is an offence to act in violation of the section 72 procedures, and a person found guilty of an offence is liable on summary conviction to a fine. Prosecutions may only be instituted by or with the consent of the Director of Public Prosecutions. Similar provisions to those in the Scotland Act relate to the attendance of witnesses, the giving of evidence and the production of documents.[34]

Privilege

Section 77 provides that any statement made for the purposes of, or for purposes incidental to, proceedings of the Assembly (including committee proceedings), and the publication of reports of such proceedings, are absolutely qualified for the purposes of the law of defamation.

The continuing role of the Secretary of State for Wales

While many of the powers exercised by the Secretary of State are transferred to the Assembly, the Executive Committee and its Subject Committees, the Secretary of State continues to play a pivotal role. The Secretary of State continues to represent Wales in Cabinet, having listened to the views of the Assembly, although he or she is not bound by the Assembly's views. The Secretary of State also meets regularly with the Executive Committee to exchange views about government policy. The Secretary of State is entitled to attend and participate in proceedings of the Assembly, but not to vote or attend committee proceedings. The office of Secretary of State for Wales is now combined with that of the Secretary of State for Northern Ireland.

Resolving disputes about devolution issues

Proceedings to determine a devolution issue may be instigated by the Attorney General, but that right does not preclude the right of any other person to institute proceedings. Where a devolution issue arises in judicial proceedings, a court or tribunal shall order notice of the issue to be given to the Attorney General and the Assembly, unless the Assembly is party to the proceedings. Schedule 7 specifies the court to which a devolution issue will be referred.

---

34   Government of Wales Act 1998, ss 74, 75.

The Welsh Assembly and the European Union

While the United Kingdom government remains responsible for issues arising out of membership of the European Union, it is recognised that Wales needs a strong voice in Europe.[35] The Assembly is able to scrutinise legislative proposals and other European documents. The Assembly also has responsibility for ensuring that European Union obligations are implemented and enforced, and that any financial penalties which may arise out of failure to implement or enforce Union obligations are met. Within the framework of the Council of Ministers, the Secretary of State for Wales participates in meetings of the Council. The Wales European Centre in Brussels continues to act as a facilitator and source of advice on European matters. Members of the Assembly represent Wales on the Committee of the Regions. European Structural Funds are an important source of funding for the regeneration of the Welsh economy.

LONDON: THE GREATER LONDON AUTHORITY AND MAYOR

In addition to the government's firm commitment to devolution to Scotland and Wales, and the future consideration of devolution to the English regions, the government intended to introduce an elected 'strategic authority' for London. As noted below, the Greater London Council (GLC), which formerly represented a centralising focus for the capital city, was abolished in 1985. Many of the GLC's functions reverted to the individual London councils. London was unique in being a capital city without an elected Mayor and centralised area government. The government's White Paper, *A Mayor and Assembly for London*, proposed an elected Mayor and 25 seat Greater London Authority. The Authority does not have direct tax raising powers, but revenue is raised from congestion charging and parking fees. The Greater London Authority Act 1999 establishes and regulates the Authority.

Elections

The first election was held in May 2000, electing an Assembly and Mayor for a four year term of office.[36] Every eligible elector has one vote for the mayoral candidate, one vote for an Assembly member and one vote – a 'London vote' – for a registered political party.

The simple majority voting system is used for the mayoral election unless there are three or more candidates. Where three or more candidates stand, the Mayor is elected under the supplementary vote system, a vote which indicates the voter's first and second preferences from among the candidates.[37] The Assembly members are elected under the simple majority system.[38] 'London members' are

---

35 *A Voice for Wales: The Government's Proposals for a Welsh Assembly*, Cm 3718, 1997, London: HMSO, para 3.46.
36 Greater London Authority Act 1999, s 3.
37 *Ibid*, s 4(2), (3) and Sched 2, Pt 1.
38 *Ibid*, s 4(4).

elected on the party-list system. The qualifications for election to be Mayor or an Assembly member are that the person must be a Commonwealth citizen, citizen of the Republic of Ireland or citizen of the European Union and be over 21 years of age.[39] In addition, the candidate must have demonstrable links with Greater London, either by being a local government elector for Greater London, or through residency or principal employment in Greater London throughout the preceding 12 months.

The Greater London Authority

The general power of the Assembly, as defined in Part II of the Act, is to 'do anything which it considers will further any one or more of its principal purposes', which are defined as:

(a) promoting economic development and wealth creation in Greater London;

(b) promoting social development in Greater London; and

(c) promoting the improvement of the environment in Greater London.

The Secretary of State may issue guidance to the Authority in relation to the above general power.[40] The Authority is required to consult with London councils and representative voluntary bodies (section 32).

The Authority is regulated by Standing Orders defining its procedures, which are made in consultation with the Mayor. The offices of Chair and Deputy Chair of the London Assembly are created. The Local Government Act 1972, Part VA, regulating access to meetings and documents, applies to the Assembly and its committees, with the exception of confidential information and exempt information which may be withheld from the press and the public.

The Assembly is under a statutory duty to keep under review the Mayor's exercise of statutory functions, and has the power to investigate and report on any actions and decisions of the Mayor, actions and decisions of any member of staff of the Authority, matters relating to the principal purposes of the Authority and any other matters which the Assembly considers to be of importance to Greater London. The Assembly may submit proposals to the Mayor, but this function cannot be delegated to a committee or sub-committee.[41]

Bills in parliament

The Authority may promote a local Bill in parliament, or oppose any local Bill which affects the inhabitants of Greater London. The Mayor acts on behalf of the Authority, having consulted the Assembly. In addition, the Mayor on behalf of the Assembly, and following consultation with it, may request a London local authority to include provisions in local Bills. A local Bill promoted in parliament by a London local authority may include provisions which affect the exercise of

---

39 *Ibid*, s 20.
40 *Ibid*, s 30.
41 *Ibid*, ss 59, 60.

statutory functions by the Authority or any of the functional bodies, only if the Authority gives its written consent.[42]

The London Mayor

The Mayor is under a duty to prepare, keep under review and revise strategies relating to transport, the London Development Agency, spatial development (planning),[43] the London Biodiversity Action Plan, municipal waste management, air quality, ambient noise, and culture.[44] In preparing or revising strategies, the Mayor must consult the Assembly, the functional bodies, each London borough council, the Common Council of the City of London and any other 'appropriate person or body'. Adequate publicity must be given to the strategies, and copies provided to the Common Council and each London borough council. The Secretary of State may issue directions to the Mayor to prepare and publish any strategy which the Mayor has not prepared and to stipulate the period in which the strategy must be prepared.[45]

Accountability

The Mayor is under a duty to report to the Assembly, not less than three clear working days before each meeting of the Assembly, on significant decisions taken and the reasons for them, and his response to proposals submitted by the Assembly under section 60. The Mayor must attend every meeting of the Assembly and answer questions put to him about matters relating to his statutory functions.[46] Questions will be answered orally 'so far as practicable to do so', or in writing before the end of the third working day following the day on which the question was asked at the meeting. An Annual Report is to be prepared by the Mayor as soon as practicable after the end of each financial year, reporting on his mayoral activities during the year.

Once in each financial year the Mayor must hold and attend a 'State of London debate', open to all members of the public. In addition, twice in every financial year, a 'People's Question Time' is open to all members of the public, for the purpose of putting questions to the Mayor and Assembly members. People's Question Time must be held within one month of the State of London debate.[47]

The Metropolitan Police

Section 310 of the Act inserts sections 5A and 5B into the Police Act 1996: 'A police force shall be maintained for the metropolitan police district'; 'There shall be a police authority for the metropolitan police district', known as the Metropolitan

---

42 *Ibid*, ss 77–79.
43 Separate provision is made for revision of spatial development strategy under s 340.
44 Greater London Authority Act 1999, ss 41, 142; Regional Development Agencies Act 1998, s 7A(2); Greater London Authority Act 1999, Pt VIII; Greater London Authority Act 1999, ss 352, 353, 362, 370 and 376, respectively.
45 Greater London Authority Act 1999, ss 42–44.
46 Should the Mayor be absent from six consecutive monthly Assembly meetings, he or she is disqualified from office: *ibid*, s 13.
47 *Ibid*, ss 45–48.

Police Authority. Formerly, the Police Authority for the Metropolitan Police District was the Home Secretary. Whereas other police forces in England and Wales were accountable to a local police authority, the Home Secretary's responsibility as police authority meant that London lacked the degree of local accountability existing outside London. The establishment of the Metropolitan Police Authority redresses this lack of accountability, and also ensures that the Mayor and Assembly have a role to play in the combating of crime in the capital. The Metropolitan Police Authority consists of 23 members, 12 of whom are members of the London Assembly appointed by the Mayor, one of whom must be the deputy Mayor, one appointed by the Secretary of State, six appointed by members of the Metropolitan Police Authority from persons on a shortlist prepared by the Secretary of State, and four magistrates for commission areas which are wholly or partly within the metropolitan police district. Members generally serve a four year renewable term. The Authority appoints a chairman from among its members.[48]

The Metropolitan police force is under the direction and control of the Commissioner of Police of the Metropolis,[49] appointed by Her Majesty on the recommendation of the Secretary of State following any recommendations made to him by the Metropolitan Police Authority and representations made by the Mayor.

London Fire and Emergency Planning Authority

The Fire and Emergency Planning Authority replaces the London Fire and Civil Defence Authority as established under the Local Government Act 1985.[50] The reconstituted Authority is responsible to the Mayor. The Fire and Emergency Planning Authority consists of 17 members, of whom nine are Assembly members appointed by the Mayor and the remainder members of London borough councils appointed by the Mayor on the nomination of the London borough councils acting jointly. Members are appointed for a renewable one year term of office. The Mayor is also responsible for appointing a chairman from among the members of the Authority.

LOCAL GOVERNMENT IN
ENGLAND AND WALES: AN OUTLINE[51]

Local government represents both a form of decentralisation of power from central government and a basis for local democracy. Local government predates central government by many centuries. Historically, local government represented an early form of localised self-regulation. The country is divided into local authorities – either county or district – each having law making and

---

48 *Ibid*, Sched 26.
49 *Ibid*, s 314.
50 *Ibid*, s 328.
51 See, *inter alia*, Sharpe, 1970; Byrne, 2000; Stewart and Stoker, 1989; Newton and Karran, 1985; Leach *et al*, 1994; Jones, 1997. Note that local government in Scotland and Northern Ireland is differently arranged.

administrative powers as delegated by parliament. Local authorities nowadays are entirely creatures of statute: accordingly, the only powers which they have are those conferred by the sovereign United Kingdom Parliament. Increasingly, however, the law of the European Union and Community also requires action at local authority level.

The advantages of local government

Central government is ill equipped to deal with many matters which require special local knowledge and regulation on the basis of local needs. The devolution of power to directly elected local authorities enables those with local knowledge and expertise to regulate the provision of services, such as public housing, public sanitation, educational and recreational facilities. Local government, therefore, is justified on the basis of efficiency. Local government also represents the citizen's closest contact with a democratic institution and enables individuals to play a role in the administration of their geographical area. The merits of local government were summarised by the Widdicombe Committee as follows:

> The value of local government stems from its three attributes of:
>
> (a) pluralism, through which it contributes to the national political system;
>
> (b) participation, through which it contributes to local democracy;
>
> (c) responsiveness, through which it contributes to the provision of local needs through the delivery of services.[52]

Regional government for England?

It had been the government's intention to introduce – as a complement to devolution – regional assemblies in England. Regional Development Agencies (RDAs) have been established which are Non Departmental Public Bodies designed to promote economic development in the regions. The government proposed that the regions should also have elected assemblies.[53] Before elections for an assembly could take place, there would be a review to make proposals for wholly unitary authorities. Referendums were to be held where the government believed there was sufficient interest. The Regional Assemblies (Preparations) Act 2002 made the necessary provisions. The Act did not provide for the establishment of the Assemblies, and separate statutes would be needed for that purpose. The introduction of assemblies was dependent upon the results of referendums. In a referendum in the North East in 2004, the electorate voted against the introduction of an assembly.

The structure of local government

In 2000, the structure of local government in England[54] was as follows:

---

52 *The Conduct of Local Authority Business*, Cmnd 9797, 1986, London: HMSO, p 47, and see McAuslan, 1987. See also, *inter alia*, Keith-Lucas and Richards, 1979.

53 See the White Paper *Your Region, Your Choice, Revitalising the English Regions* Cm 5511, May 2002, Cabinet Office/DTLR, available at www.regions.odpm.gov.uk/governance/whitepaperindex.htm.

54 Byrne, 2000, p 56.

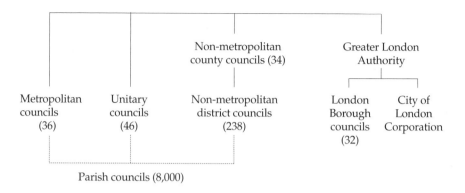

In Scotland – which has its own directly elected Parliament with law making powers – there are 32 unitary councils. In Wales – with its directly elected Assembly – there are 22 unitary authorities. In Northern Ireland there are 26 District Councils and nine Area Boards. Of the latter, four are responsible for health and social services and five for education and libraries.[55]

The size of local government

In comparison with other nations, local government in the United Kingdom is represented by substantially larger units, representing a substantially greater number of people.[56] The figures reveal that whereas the United Kingdom had an average population per local authority of 118,400, the corresponding figure for France is 1,580; Germany 4,925; Norway 9,000; Denmark 18,760, and Sweden 30,040. The population size of authorities naturally affects the number of constituents a local councillor will represent. Accordingly, in France, one elected representative represents 116 people, in Germany 250, in Denmark 783, in Sweden 667 and in the United Kingdom, 2,605.

The functions of local government

Local government has no powers other than those conferred by parliament. The powers conferred must be exercised according to law, and judicial review of local authority decisions may be made to ensure that the rule of law is respected.[57] Some discretion exists, however, as to the means by which local authorities achieve the goals set by central government.

However, the freedom of local authorities to raise finance, undertake expenditure and provide services was substantially reduced under the Conservative government which assumed office in 1979 and lasted until 1997. During that time the government altered the manner in which local taxation was raised, set clear limits on expenditure and imposed sanctions on local authorities who exceeded the expenditure approved by central government. Moreover, the

---

55 Byrne, 2000, p 73.
56 See, more fully, *The Size of Municipalities, Efficiency and Citizen Participation*, Council of Europe: Local and Regional Authorities in Europe, No 56, cited in Jones, 1997, p 9.
57 See Chapters 4, 26 and 27.

provision of services by local authorities has been significantly curtailed. Intent on improving efficiency and on privatising many aspects of government previously performed either by local authorities or by central government, 'market forces' were introduced to many local authority services. Local authorities are now required to put many services out to tender to the private sector, and may provide services themselves only if they can do so in a manner which is competitive with private companies and organisations.

In addition to taxation and the provision of services, local authorities have a regulatory and law making role. Local councils have wide powers to regulate, for example, the granting of licences for taxis and market trading, and the approval of child care facilities and private welfare homes for the elderly, disabled or sick. In relation to law making, local authorities, acting under the authority of Acts of Parliament, have the power to make bylaws – local laws which regulate the area. For example, footpaths, parks and recreational facilities are controlled by local bylaws. In the exercise of all such power, the local authority is subject to control by the courts: all local authorities must act *intra vires* (within their powers), or their decisions will be declared null and void by the courts.

The allocation of functions between authorities in England and Wales

Functions are allocated between local authorities principally on the basis of 'operational efficiency and cost-effectiveness'.[58] The provision of certain services, for example education, is clearly a matter for regulation on a large scale, whereas the provision of local libraries and refuse collection may be appropriate for smaller councils to administer. However, there can be no generalisations about the distribution of functions: there are variations throughout. From the point of view of local democracy, and the accountability and responsiveness of local councillors, however, the larger the local government unit, and the more diffuse the provision of services between differing levels of local government, the more difficult it becomes for the individual to apportion responsibility. In Byrne's analysis, the allocation of responsibilities is made the more complex by the sharing of responsibilities, which of itself takes several forms. Shared responsibilities in this analysis may include *concurrent provision*, whereby all local authorities provide the same service in their area; or *joint provision*, where two or more local authorities combine to provide a common service to all within their common area; or *shared but divided provision*, in which different levels of local authority provide differing aspects of the same service; *reserve powers*, under which larger authorities reserve the power to provide particular aspects of a service otherwise provided by smaller authorities; *claimed powers*, through which individual, small authorities assume responsibility for a service or function formally allocated to a larger authority and *agency powers*, whereby one authority will act as the agent of another authority in the provision of a service or exercise of certain functions.[59]

In addition to the complexity in the allocation of functions between local authorities must be considered the requirement that services be provided in line with the principle of 'best value'.[60] As a result, local authorities nowadays are far less the actual providers of services and more bodies which, through contract, enable services to be provided by those in the private sector. Moreover, no picture of local government can be complete without recognition of the increased, and increasing, functions formerly undertaken by local authorities, which are now undertaken by boards and trusts under provisions introduced by the Conservative government in relation to education and housing which further fragments local government, accountability and democracy.

The Local Government Act 2000 regulates the duty of local authorities to promote the economic, social or environmental well being of the relevant area. Every local authority is to prepare a strategy for promoting or improving the economic, social and environmental well being of their area. The authority must consult or seek the participation of appropriate persons and must have regard to any guidance issued by the Secretary of State. Under section 5 of the Act, the Secretary of State has the power to amend, repeal or revoke enactments relating to the strategy.

The election process

Section 10 of the Representation of the People Act 2000 makes provision for greater flexibility in the voting arrangements for local government elections. A local authority may submit to the Secretary of State proposals for a scheme relating to when, where and how voting is to take place, how the votes cast are to be counted and the sending by candidates of election communications free of postage charges. The scheme may make provision for voting to take place on more than one day, and at places other than polling booths. The Secretary of State has power to approve the proposals either without modification or with such modifications as, after consulting the authority, he considers appropriate. Once elections under the scheme have taken place, the authority concerned must prepare a report on the scheme, detailing its provisions and assessing the scheme's success or otherwise in facilitating voting at the elections in question and, if relevant, the counting of votes, or in encouraging voting at the elections in question or enabling voters to make informed decisions at those elections.

A copy of the report must be sent to the Secretary of State, and published in the relevant area, by the end of a period of three months beginning with the date of the declaration of the result. If it appears to the Secretary of State that it would be desirable for provision to be made to apply generally and on a permanent basis to local government elections in England and Wales, he may by order make such provision as he considers appropriate. Such an order must be made by statutory instrument, and laid before and approved by a resolution of each House of Parliament.[61]

---

60   Local Government Act 1999. See below, pp 345 ff.
61   Representation of the People Act 2000, s 11.

The election of councillors

Councillors are elected for a four year term of office and represent 'wards' within the local government area. In metropolitan districts, one third of councillors retire each year, other than in a year in which there will be county council elections. In other, non-metropolitan districts, councillors retire every four years, or may choose to adopt the metropolitan model. The electoral system reflects that used for general elections, being the simple majority or 'first past the post' system.

Detailed rules regulate election expenditure and, as with general elections, a number of corrupt and illegal practices are proscribed. An election challenge may be presented by way of a petition to the Queen's Bench Division of the High Court.[62] The petition is heard by the election courts which consist of a commissioner appointed by the judges who are nominated to try election petitions.

Qualification and disqualification for election

A candidate must – unlike candidates for parliament – be able to demonstrate a close connection with the locality. Accordingly, he or she must either be on the local register of electors, or have been resident or have occupied property or have had his or her place of employment within the local authority area for a 12 month period preceding 'nomination day'.[63] Bankruptcy, conviction for corrupt or illegal practices, a conviction and sentence of three months' imprisonment within five years of the election or the imposition of a surcharge by the Audit Commission for unlawful local government expenditure[64] will all disqualify a person from standing for election.

The fact of regular local elections during the life of a parliament enables the people not only to express their preferences for those who will govern them until the next set of local elections, but also to express their approval or disapproval of central government policies.

Standards of conduct

The Prevention of Corruption Acts 1906 and 1916[65] made it a criminal offence for a member of the council to accept payments, in money or kind, for services. Under sections 94–98 of the Local Government Act 1972, Councillors must disclose the existence of any direct or indirect financial interest in council business. In 1974, following a scandal involving councillors in the North of England concerning contracts for a private architect, John Poulson, official inquiries were launched into the standard of conduct in public life.[66] While it was

---

62 Representation of the People Act 1983, ss 127–63, as amended.
63 Local Government Act 1972, s 79.
64 Audit of local authority accounts is undertaken under the Local Government Finance Act 1982.
65 And, previously, the Public Bodies Corrupt Practices Act 1889.
66 *Conduct in Local Government,* Cmnd 5636, 1974, London: HMSO; *Report of the Royal Commission on Standards in Public Life 1974–76,* Cmnd 6524, 1976, London: HMSO. See also *The Conduct of Local Authority Business,* Cmnd 9797, 1986, London: HMSO. On the 1994–95 Inquiry into Standards of Conduct in Public Life in relation to Central Government, see Chapters 11 and 16.

found that, in general, local government members' conduct was 'honest', a number of reforms have been introduced.

The conduct of local government came under review from the Committee of Standards in Public Life, chaired by Lord Nolan.[67] The inquiry examined the 'seven principles of public life' – selflessness, integrity, objectivity, accountability, openness, honesty and leadership – identified by the Committee in its inquiries to parliamentary standards. Lord Nolan's frame of reference included the issue of the manner in which, and extent to which, local government operates these principles.

Part III of the Local Government Act 2000 relates to standards of conduct in local government, and requires all local authorities to adopt a code of conduct reflecting the Nolan principles. Every local authority, other than a parish council or community council, must establish a standards committee,[68] the functions of which are to promote and maintain high standards of conduct and assist members of the authority to observe the code of conduct. Every local authority maintains a register of members' interests.[69]

The management of local government[70]

Prior to the reforms introduced by the Local Government Act 2000, the majority of decision making was undertaken by committees, with their decisions being ratified by a meeting of the full council. There were many criticisms of this system, not least that in reality most councils were dominated by one political party, and where the membership of committees reflected the party-political strengths of the council as a whole, opposition councillors had little impact. A further criticism was that the opportunities for holding the majority party to account were weak. The Local Government Act 2000, section 11, provided for new management structures in local government. Three different models were introduced:[71]

- *Mayor and Cabinet Executive:* Here there is a democratically elected Mayor, who then appoints two or more councillors to the executive. The number of members may not exceed ten.
- *Leader and Cabinet Executive:* Under this system the Leader of the council is elected by all members of the council. There are then two options: the Leader will appoint an executive drawn from the council, or the council itself appoints the executive (again drawn from council members). The Leader and executive members may be members of the same political party, thus mirroring the Prime Minister and Cabinet system of central government. The positions are full time and salaried. The number of members may not exceed ten.

---

67   See Nolan (Lord), 'Lord Nolan's shopping list', in Jones, 1997, p 58.
68   Local Government Act 2000, s 53.
69   *Ibid*, s 81.
70   See Oliver, 2003, Chapter 16; Leach *et al*, 1994.
71   See Part II of the Local Government Act 2000. These arrangements are still being introduced and it will be some time before the new structures are fully in place.

- *Mayor and Council Manager Executive:* Under this system there is a democratically-elected Mayor and an officer of the authority appointed as the council manager to the executive by the authority.

In relation to each of these structures the Act provides that the functions of the executive are to carry out any function of a local authority, subject to the power of the Secretary of State to make regulations relating to executive functions.

Every local authority must draw up proposals for the operation of executive arrangements and send a copy of the proposals to the Secretary of State. The proposals must indicate the form the executive is to take, having consulted local government electors and other interested persons. Where the executive arrangement includes a mayor and cabinet executive a referendum is required. In other cases, where a referendum is not required, the authority must implement the proposals in accordance with a timetable included in the proposals. The Secretary of State may direct a local authority to hold a referendum in relation to the election of a mayor and executive cabinet.

The local authority executive may decide whether and which of its meetings are to be held in public or in private. Written records of meetings held in private must be kept, and must include reasons for the decisions to which they relate.

Central government and local government

Parliament is supreme and can control both the structure of local government, and the extent of local government powers and functions. The major forms of control are through primary and delegated legislation. Local authorities have statutory power to make bylaws but these are subject to confirmation by the minister. Central government policy and standard-setting control the manner in which local authorities may exercise their powers. Schemes for town planning, transport and education must have central approval and, in town planning, appeals will ultimately lie to the Secretary of State, and his approval will be needed in relation to compulsory purchase orders. In relation to fire, education and the police, regular inspections are made by central government inspectors.

Local government revenue[72]

Some 75 per cent of local government revenue comes from or via central government; the remaining 25 per cent comes from local taxes. These are either specific grants – for example, for particular services such as fire or police (50 per cent), or general grants – a central government contribution to local authority funds. In addition, local authorities may borrow money, subject to strict control by the Treasury.

The largest grant paid to local government is the Formula Grant, which is made up of the Revenue Support Grant, business rates and the Police Grant. For the year 2003–04 the Formula Grant was allocated using a Formula Spending shares system which is based on a basic 'per client' amount for each service area

---

72 See *Report of the Layfield Committee of Inquiry into Local Government Finance*, Cmnd 6453, 1976, London: HMSO.

with additions to take account of deprivation costs and other area costs. The grant also takes into account each authority's expected ability to collect income from the local council tax.[73]

In relation to sales, fees and charges these vary widely: income is received from, for example, the sale of council properties, planning application fees, transport and parking charges, and library fines. In 2001–02 a total of £8.1 billion was raised from sales, fees and charges.

The financial needs of local government are thus met by a mixture of local and central revenues. In terms of local revenue, from around 1600 until 1988, local domestic rates had been in existence. The rates, calculated according to the value of the property, were cheap and easy to collect, and the public were used to them. Rates applied to a property irrespective of the number of persons living in it. During the 1960s and 1970s, high spending councils led to pressure for reform of the rating system. As the position stood then, a local authority raised the annual local rates and central government, through the Rate Support Grant – a 'top-up' grant, provided the shortfall between revenue and expenditure.

By 1974, the Conservative Party was committed to abolishing local rates. The community charge, or Poll Tax, found favour with the government and was introduced – amid widespread public disorder – under the Local Government Finance Act 1988. The same rate within a local authority area would apply to every person: it was a person-based rather than property-based tax. Accordingly, each resident in a local area would contribute to the costs of services which were enjoyed by all. In addition to that personal tax, the government was keen to reform business rates, and introduced the National Non-Domestic Rate, to be set by government and outside local authority control.

The conflict and disquiet over the introduction of the community charge led to rapid reform.[74] Whilst in principle the tax would serve the needs of fairness and accountability, in practice, the tax was rapidly regarded as iniquitous and, as a result, uncollectable. The backtrack once again centred on property values. From 1993, the council tax is based on values of property within differing price bands and is payable irrespective of the number of people living within a house, although, to mitigate the perceived unfairness of the old rating system, a 25 per cent discount is allowable for single person households.

In 2003–04 council tax revenue rose to £18.9 billion (from £15.2 billion in 2002–03), and council tax bills have increased by 94 per cent since the tax was introduced in 1993–94.

Local authority expenditure

There are three classes of expenditure incurred by local authorities: current expenditure, revenue expenditure and capital expenditure. Current expenditure is the cost of running local authority services. Included in this cost are such matters as staff, heating, lighting, cleaning and the expenditure on goods and services

---

73 Local Government Financial Statistics (England) No 14, 2003, para 2.4.3.
74 Local Government Finance Act 1992.

consumed over the year. Revenue expenditure is expenditure funded by external finance, council tax and local authority reserves.

Irrespective of the class of expenditure, the majority of expenditure goes to education. A miscellany of services ranging from court services, cultural services, housing benefit, planning, parking and public transport fall under the broad heading of Environmental, Protective and Cultural (EPC) which accounts for the second highest category of expenditure. Social services, the police, the fire service and highways all fall within this category.

The abolition of compulsory competitive tendering and the best value concept

The 1999 Local Government Act abolished compulsory competitive tendering for the provision of services, which forced local authorities to compete with the private sector. Tendering, however, while no longer compulsory, continues to form one part of the government's quest for value and efficiency in the provision of local authority services. Section 1 defines the local authorities to which the best value duty will apply, which extends beyond local authorities proper and includes such bodies as the police authorities, Transport for London and other metropolitan transport authorities, waste disposal authorities, fire authorities, and the London Development Agency.

The general duty imposed on best value authorities is to 'make arrangements to secure continuous improvement in the way in which its functions are exercised, having regard to a combination of economy, efficiency and effectiveness'. In deciding how to fulfil its duty under section 3, authorities must consult local tax payers, service users and representatives of persons appearing to have an interest in any area in which the authority carries out functions. The statutory requirement that local authorities operate on 'best value' principles[75] requires local authorities to adopt the most cost-effective method of delivering services to its area, whether undertaking the task themselves, through agreements with private or voluntary bodies, or through partnership agreements with other local bodies via Local Public Service Agreements.

The Secretary of State may specify 'performance indicators' against which to measure an authority's performance and 'performance standards' to be met in relation to the performance indicators. Differing performance indicators or standards may be set for different functions and different functions and may apply at different times.[76] A best value authority must conduct reviews of its functions with the aim to improving the way its functions are exercised, and the Secretary of State may specify matters which an authority must include in a review of functions. In particular an order may require an authority to consider whether it should carry out a particular function, the level at which it should be exercising the function, and its objectives in relation to the exercise of the function.

---

75   Local Government Act 1999, s 3. For the background see the Green Paper *Modernising Local Government: Improving Services through Best Value* (1998); White Paper *Modern Local Government: In Touch with the People*, Cm 1404, 1998; White Paper *Strong Local Leadership – Quality Public Services*, Cm 5237, December 2001.

76   Local Government Act 1999, s 4.

The authority should also assess its performance and the competitiveness of its performance by reference to other best value authorities and commercial or other businesses, and consult other authorities and commercial operations about the exercise of the function. It must also assess its progress towards meeting performance standards, which have been specified.[77]

Each authority must prepare a best value performance plan for each financial year, and the Secretary of State may specify matters which an authority must include in its plan.[78] The performance plan published for a financial year is audited by the authority's auditor.[79] The authority must respond to the auditor's report, and where recommendations have been made, must make a statement of action it intends to take as a result of the report and its proposed timetable, within 30 days of receiving the report or earlier if the report so specifies.[80] The Audit Commission may carry out inspections of an authority's compliance with the requirements, and inspectors have a right of access and may require responsible persons to give such information, explanation or documentation as is required.[81] Where an inspection has been carried out, the Audit Commission must issue a report stipulating areas in which the Commission believes the authority is failing to comply with requirements and may recommend that the Secretary of State give directions to the authority. Where the Commission issues a report stating failure to comply with requirements, the authority must, in its next performance plan, record that fact and any action taken by the authority as a result of the report.[82] Under section 15, the Secretary of State has the power to intervene where he or she is satisfied that an authority is failing to meet the requirements relating to best value. The Secretary of State may require an authority to amend a performance plan, follow specified procedures in relation to the plan and carry out a review of its exercise of specified functions. The Secretary of State may also direct a local inquiry to be held in relation to the exercise of functions.

Section 15 also gives to the Secretary of State the power to direct an authority to take any action which he considers necessary or expedient to secure compliance with best value requirements. The Secretary of State may direct that a specified function of an authority shall be exercised by the Secretary of State or a person nominated by him, thereby removing that function, for the period specified, from the authority.[83] Where the Secretary of State takes over the function of an authority, regulations may be made to avoid the situation where, for example, planning functions have been taken over. The Secretary of State is also the final arbiter of an appeal against that planning decision.[84]

---

77   Local Government Act 1999, s 5.
78   *Ibid*, s 6.
79   *Ibid*, s 7.
80   *Ibid*, s 9.
81   *Ibid*, s 11.
82   *Ibid*, s 13.
83   *Ibid*, s 15(6).
84   *Ibid*, s 15(7), (8).

Audit

The government controls local authorities by way of audit. The Audit Commission[85] of Local Authorities and the National Health Service in England and Wales is the principal body responsible for supervising local government and health service audits. The Commission consists of not less than 15 and not more than 20 members appointed by the Secretary of State.[86] The accounts of bodies subject to the Act are required to be compiled at the end of March annually and audited by auditors appointed by the Commission.[87]

The Commission is responsible for preparing and keeping under review a Code of Audit Practice. An auditor has a right of access to every document relating to a body which appears to him necessary for the purposes of his functions under the Act. It is an offence to fail to comply, without reasonable excuse, with any requirement of the auditor.[88]

If in the course of an audit of a local government body, other than a health service body, it appears that an item of account is contrary to law and has not been sanctioned by the Secretary of State, the auditor may apply to the High Court for a declaration that the item is contrary to law.[89] If the High Court makes such a declaration, it may also require the responsible person to repay the unlawful expenditure in whole or in part. If the unlawful expenditure exceeds £2,000, and at the time the person responsible was a member of a local authority, the court may order him or her to be disqualified from being a member of a local authority for a specified period and may order rectification of the accounts. The High Court must not make an order if it is satisfied that the responsible person 'acted reasonably or in the belief that the expenditure was authorised by law', and in any other case shall 'have regard to all the circumstances, including that person's means and ability to repay the expenditure or any part of it'.[90] If a person has failed to bring into account a sum, and that failure has not been sanctioned by the Secretary of State and a 'loss has been incurred or deficiency caused by the wilful misconduct of any person', the auditor must certify that the sum, or the amount of the loss or deficiency is due from that person.[91] Wilful misconduct has been held to include the failure to collect fees which were due,[92] and a delay in setting the rate resulting in the authority losing interest on money which would otherwise have been collected.[93] A person aggrieved by the auditor's decision to certify a sum or amount due may appeal to the High Court.[94] In relation to health service bodies, section 19 of the Audit Commission Act 1998 provides that if the auditor has reason to believe that the body, or an

---

85 The Audit Commission was established in 1982 to supervise local government audit. Its role was extended to the NHS in 1990.
86 Audit Commission Act 1998, s 1, and see Sched 1.
87 *Ibid*, s 2, and see Sched 2.
88 *Ibid*, ss 4, 6.
89 As in *Hazell v Hammersmith LBC* (1992), discussed above.
90 Audit Commission Act 1998, s 17.
91 *Ibid*, s 18(1).
92 *R v Roberts* (1901).
93 *Lloyd v McMahon* (1987).
94 Audit Commission Act 1998, s 18(10).

officer of the body, has made or is about to make a decision which involves incurring unlawful expenditure, or undertake a course of action which would be unlawful and likely to cause a loss or deficiency, the auditor must refer the matter to the Secretary of State.

In relation to authorities, other than a health service body, the auditor may issue a prohibition notice if he has reason to believe that the body is about to make or has made a decision which involves incurring unlawful expenditure, or has taken, or is about to take, action which is unlawful and likely to cause a loss or deficiency, or is about to enter in the accounts an item of unlawful expenditure.[95] If the authority's chief finance officer has already made a report on unlawful expenditure,[96] no prohibition order may be made in relation to the period covered by the report. Where a prohibition order is issued, it is not lawful for the body concerned to make or implement the relevant decision or undertake the course of action to which the prohibition order relates. The body concerned may appeal against the prohibition order to the High Court.[97] The auditor has power to apply for judicial review of a local authority's, but not a health service body's, decision or failure to act.[98]

The Commission has the power to direct an auditor to undertake an extraordinary audit, and the Secretary of State may require the Commission to direct such an audit.[99]

Under Part III of the 1998 Act, the Commission has responsibility for undertaking or promoting comparative or other studies for the improving economy, efficiency and effectiveness of local authority services and other bodies covered by the Act, and for improving the financial or other management of bodies subject to audit. Bodies subject to the Act may require the Commission to undertake such studies. The right to make studies and receive requests for studies extends to higher education funding councils, the governing bodies of institutions within the higher education sector and further education sector, the Funding Agency for Schools and the governing body of a grant-maintained school. The Secretary of State may request the Commission's assistance in studies designed to improve the economy, efficiency, effectiveness and quality of performance in relation to social services functions of local authorities.[100]

Where a local authority is seen to be failing to achieve 'efficiency and effectiveness' as required by the best value principle, the government may exercise power to intervene and facilitate the takeover of the provision of services.[101]

---

95 Audit Commission Act 1998, s 20.
96 Under the Local Government Finance Act 1988, s 114(2).
97 Audit Commission Act 1998, s 22.
98 *Ibid*, s 24.
99 *Ibid*, s 25.
100 *Ibid*, ss 33–37.
101 See HC Deb, Col 25/26, 15 July 2002; *Tackling Poor Performance in Local Government*, Consultation Paper, Office of Deputy Prime Minister, 2002.

Complaints about local government

Complaints against local government may be made to the authority itself and, if such a complaint does not receive satisfactory treatment, a complaint may be made to the Commissioner for Local Administration. The jurisdiction, role and powers of Commissioners for Administration are considered in Chapter 28.

Local government and Europe

While the role and function of local government is defined, controlled and restrained by central government, local government must also be seen within the wider context of the European Union and Community. Since the United Kingdom acceded to the European Community in 1973, and since the formation of the European Union under the Treaty on European Union 1992, an increasing volume of European law not only affects the legislative sphere of competence of parliament in relation to matters within the competence of the Union, but also affects both national and local policies and standards. The Community was founded on the four freedoms – persons, goods, capital and services – which affect all levels of government. In addition, the community and Union has expanded its sphere of competence over the years to include such diverse matters as environmental protection, health and hygiene standards and weights and measures. Many of the Community laws on these areas fall on local authorities to implement. The freedom of movement and right of establishment of European citizens[102] has implications for local authority housing, as does the European Court of Justice's development of the law of gender equality in the workplace.

The European Union's relationship to local government is not limited to the imposition of regulations and directives imposing duties on local authorities, but extends to the provision of regional aid. The Committee of the Regions of the European Union[103] provides the means by which the views and interests of local authorities may be taken into account. Furthermore, the provision of financial aids and grants through the Social Fund, European Investment Bank and Regional Development Fund provides an additional source of finance for local authorities.

Local government and the courts

Local authorities, being bodies to whom powers are delegated by parliament, may exercise their powers and spend money only for the purposes authorised by statute. In order to ensure that bodies with delegated law making, administrative and/or judicial powers act within those powers (*intra vires*), the courts are seized with jurisdiction to review any action challenged by a person or body aggrieved by that action. Applications for judicial review proceed by way of an application for leave to apply for judicial review. Applicants must have sufficient interest (*locus standi*) in the matter to apply, and the matter challenged must be one falling under public law as opposed to private law. Furthermore, the matter must be one

---

102 Union citizenship was conferred on all nationals of Member States under the Treaty on European Union 1992.

103 Formerly, the Consultative Council of Regional and Local Authorities.

which is justiciable, that is to say, a matter in which the courts deem themselves to be the appropriate body to adjudicate on the matter.[104]

Local government is a regular participant in judicial review proceedings. As seen earlier, all the powers exercised by them are powers delegated by statute; local authorities have no inherent jurisdiction. Accordingly, the courts may rule on the 'vires' of their activities. Judicial review is considered in Chapters 26 and 27 and those chapters should be consulted for discussion of the case law. In relation to control over the exercise of local government powers, the courts employ the concept of fiduciary duty. Local government is in a fiduciary position of trustee of resources to be exercised for the benefit of the consumers of those resources, council tax payers.[105]

104 *Council of Civil Service Unions v Minister for Civil Service* (1985).
105 *Roberts v Hopwood* (1925); *Bromley London Borough Council v Greater London Council* (1982); *Hazell v Hammersmith London Borough Council* (1992).

PART V

PARLIAMENT

CHAPTER 13

THE ELECTORAL SYSTEM

INTRODUCTION

In a democratic state, the electoral process determines who will hold political office. It is the electorate which confers the power to govern and calls government to account. If the electorate is to enjoy true equality in constitutional participation, it is of fundamental constitutional importance that the electoral system ensures four principles:

(a) that there is a full franchise, subject to limited restrictions;

(b) that the value of each vote cast is equal to that of every other vote;

(c) that the conduct of election campaigns is regulated to ensure legality and fairness;

(d) that the voting system is such as to produce both a legislative body representative of the electorate and a government with sufficient democratic support to be able to govern effectively.

It is against these four principal objectives that the law must be evaluated. However, it must be recognised that these elements are in large measure inseparable from each other. Each aspect of the electoral process combines to form a system:

> Any code of electoral law includes a number of essential sections of almost equal importance ... Each of these sections is meaningless in isolation from the others. A wide and equal suffrage loses its value if political bosses are able to gerrymander constituencies so as to suit their own interests; there is no point in having an elaborate system of proportional representation if the electors are all driven in one direction by a preponderance of bribes and threats; legal provisions mean nothing if enforcement is left wholly in the hands of those who profit by breaking it.

> That is why it is right to speak of the 'electoral system'. Procedure for elections is systematic in that its parts are interdependent; it is impossible to advance on one 'front' without regard to others.[1]

THE FRANCHISE[2]

Evolution of the franchise

Prior to the Reform Acts of 1832 and 1867, the right to vote was limited and based on rights in property. The 1832 Act – the Representation of the People Act – increased the franchise by 50 per cent, which represented only seven per cent of the population. The Reform Act of 1867 doubled the number of people entitled to vote.

---

1   Mackenzie, 1967, p 19, cited in Rawlings, 1988, p 2.
2   For a full history of the franchise see, *inter alia*, Anson, 1933; Maitland, 1908, pp 352–64.

The extension of the franchise in 1867 to skilled and unskilled male labourers was not a matter greeted with universal approval. Walter Bagehot retorted that:

> ... no one will contend that the ordinary working man who has no special skill, and who is only rated because he has a house, can judge much of intellectual matters. [(1867) 1993, p 273]

Bagehot feared the potential power of the working class: should they combine as a class, the 'higher orders' might have to consider whether to concede to their demands or 'risk the effect of the working men's combination' (p 278).

Women and the right to vote

Women were to remain disenfranchised until 1928, but the movement for women's right to vote predates the 1867 Act.[3] In 1851, Harriet Taylor Mill had published *Enfranchisement of Women* in the *Westminster Review*. In 1886, John Stuart Mill[4] presented a petition to parliament calling for the enfranchisement of women. The following year, the Manchester Women's Suffrage Committee was formed, soon to be united in a National Committee based in London. When the Reform Bill was before parliament, Mill introduced an amendment – changing the word 'man' to 'person' – thereby entitling women to vote. The amendment was defeated.

A legal challenge to disenfranchisement came in *Chorlton v Lings* (1868). It was argued before the Court of Common Pleas that the Representation of the People Act 1867 had conferred on women a right to vote. The argument centred on the use of the word 'man' in the Act. It was contended that Lord Brougham's Act which stipulated that the word 'man' included 'women' applied to an interpretation of the Representation of the People Act. The court rejected such a view. Willis J declared himself opposed to any view that women were excluded from the franchise on the basis of 'fickleness of judgment and liability to influence', which would be quite inconsistent 'with one of the glories of our civilisation – the respect and honour in which women are held'. However, concerning the prohibition of voting – and the prohibition against peeresses in the House of Lords – Willis J declared that 'out of respect to women, and a sense of decorum, and not from their want of intellect, or their being for any other reason unfit to take part in the government of the country, they have been excused from taking any share in this department of public affairs'.

In 1869, Mill published *The Subjection of Women*. The right to vote was but one campaign. Women were also seeking equal rights in education, in politics and in the medical profession. In 1897, the differing suffrage movements were to be united under the National Union of Women's Suffrage Societies. By 1913, the number of affiliated societies had reached 400. The leadership of Emmeline and Christabel Pankhurst injected new energy into the campaign and the age of militancy in support of the right to vote began. The tide of public opinion started to turn in women's favour in 1909, when the authorities started to force feed

---

3   See Kent, 1987.
4   A Member of Parliament and radical reformer. See, *inter alia, Representative Government* (1865); see also *On Liberty* (1859) and *The Subjection of Women* (1869).

hunger striking suffragettes imprisoned as a result of their campaign. A Bill to give women the right to vote passed second reading in 1910, but was defeated by the Prime Minister, Asquith, acting in concert with Lloyd George, the Opposition Leader. The failure of a second Bill in 1911 sparked violent protest all over London: 217 women were arrested. A Bill of 1913 met with a similar fate and reaction. Fearful of the consequences of imprisonment and hunger strikes, the government passed the 'Cat and Mouse' Act,[5] which enabled the authorities to release hunger striking prisoners who were in medical danger and re-arrest them on their physical recovery.

The persistence of the suffragettes, combined with the involvement of women in industry during the 1914–18 World War, acted as catalysts for winning the right to vote. In 1916, an all-party conference on electoral reform was established under the chairmanship of the Speaker of the House of Commons.

The Representation of the People Act 1918, which implemented the conference's proposals, introduced a full franchise of all men in parliamentary elections and conferred the right to vote in parliament on all women over the age of 30 who were either local government electors or the wives of local government electors.[6] Full equality with men was delayed until 1928. A full franchise, on the basis of equality, and respecting the principle of 'one person, one vote', was finally achieved under the Representation of the People Act 1948.

The current franchise

The right to vote is defined in the Representation of the People Act 1983, as amended. Prior to enactment of the Representation of the People Act 2000, eligibility was based solely on residency in a constituency at a 'qualifying date'.[7] The 2000 Act introduces greater flexibility, allowing registration once resident in a constituency at any date, and supplements the residency requirement with registration on the register of parliamentary electors for that constituency. In addition to residency, a person is eligible to vote once they have made a 'declaration of local connection'.[8] A declaration of local connection must state the name of the declarant and either an address to which election correspondence can be delivered, or that he or she is willing to collect such correspondence periodically from the registration officer's office. The declaration must state the required address and also be dated, and, on the date of declaration, the declarant must also be otherwise qualified to vote by virtue of relevant citizenship and age. A declaration of local connection may be cancelled at any time by the declarant. The declaration is of no effect unless it is received by the relevant registration officer within the period of three months beginning with the date of the declaration.[9]

---

5   Prisoners (Temporary Discharge for Ill Health) Act 1913.
6   In addition, the Parliament (Qualification of Women) Act 1918 provided that: 'A woman shall not be disqualified by sex or marriage from being elected to or sitting or voting as a Member of the Commons House of Parliament.'
7   Representation of the People Act 1983, ss 1, 2.
8   2000 Act, s 6.
9   The Representation of the People Act 2000, Sched 2 extends the parliamentary franchise in relation to overseas voters, amending the Representation of the People Act 1985.

In addition, a person's eligibility depends on citizenship,[10] voting age (now 18 years and over),[11] and not being subject to any legal incapacity — including minors (those under the age of 18), aliens, peers other than Irish peers, mental patients who are compulsorily detained,[12] convicted persons in detention[13] and, for a period of five years, anyone found guilty of election offences.[14] Section 2 of the 2000 Act inserts into section 3 of the 1983 Act provisions relating to the disenfranchisement of offenders detained in mental hospitals.

The disqualification of prisoners was challenged in *R (Pearson) v Secretary of State for the Home Department* (2001). It was held that domestic law disqualifying prisoners from voting at a parliamentary or local government election was not incompatible with the right to vote under the European Convention on Human Rights.[15] However, in *Hirst v United Kingdom* (2004) the European Court of Human Rights ruled that the blanket restriction which deprives all prisoners of the right to vote – irrespective of the length of their sentence or the seriousness of the offence committed – was unlawful. The decision leaves open the question of whether certain prisoners may be subject to restrictions. However, given that disenfranchisement has no relevance to imprisonment – and amounts to a further penalty being imposed – there is a strong case for removing the restriction.[16] [17]

Constituencies

The United Kingdom is divided for electoral purposes into 646 constituencies, or voting areas. Each constituency is represented in parliament by just one member, who has secured a majority of votes in a general election or by-election.[18]

The Boundary Commissions (now Committees)

The principle of 'one man, one vote, one value' is given formal recognition in the rules regulating the work of the Boundary Commissions[19] contained in the Parliamentary Constituencies Act 1986.[20] Equality is not, however, as will be seen below, the sole, or even dominant, criterion. By way of comparison, in the United States of America, the principle was judicially considered by the Supreme Court

---

10 In relation to parliamentary elections, relevant citizenship is British citizenship, a qualifying Commonwealth citizen, or a citizen of the Republic of Ireland. In relation to local government elections, relevant citizens of the European Union are also eligible to vote: Representation of the People Act 1984, ss 1, 2 and 4, as amended by the Representation of the People Act 2000, ss 1, 2 and 4.

11 Representation of the People Act 1983, s 1.

12 *Ibid*, s 7, as substituted by s 4 of the 2000 Act.

13 *Ibid*, s 3, as amended by the Representation of the People Act 1985, Sched 4.

14 *Ibid*, s 60.

15 Article 3 of the First Protocol to the Convention provides for the holding of free elections under conditions ensuring 'the free expression of the opinion of the people in the choice of the legislature'.

16 See also *Matthews v United Kingdom* (1999).

17 The Grand Chamber of the European Court of Human Rights endorsed the decision in *Hirst v United Kingdom (No 2)* (2005).

18 An election in a single constituency, conducted as a result of the seat falling vacant during the life of a parliament.

19 Parliamentary Constituencies Act 1986, Sched 2.

20 As amended by the Boundary Commissions Act 1992.

in *Baker v Carr*, in 1962. In that case, the principle was regarded as of such constitutional importance that the Supreme Court held that the Fourteenth Amendment of the Constitution – the 'equal protection' clause – required that electoral districts had to have an approximately equal number of electors to prevent over- or under-representation and inequality in voting power.

The rules regulating the work of the Commissions are contained in Schedule 2 to the Parliamentary Constituencies Act 1986, from which it can be seen that the principle of 'one man, one vote, one value' is, under the United Kingdom's constitution, but one of several considerations.

The target figure for constituency electorates is based on the simple division of the eligible voting population in the country divided by the number of constituencies. The Commission aims to achieve a result which brings the majority of constituencies within a narrow band of this target figure, bearing in mind the other criteria contained within the rules. Schedule 2 specifies the number of constituencies in Great Britain as a whole, and in Scotland, Wales and Northern Ireland. Parliamentary constituencies are required to respect – as far as possible – local authority boundaries. While constituencies must respect the electoral quota, this may be departed from where there are special geographical considerations which must be respected.

Legal challenges to Boundary Commission reports

The political difficulties – generally the loss of a number of 'safe' seats by one party – which arise from boundary changes have given rise to challenges in the courts. In *R v Home Secretary ex parte McWhirter* (1969), the Labour Party feared the loss of up to ten constituencies as a result of the Commission's recommendations. The Home Secretary laid the report before parliament, without the draft Orders in Council which were necessary to implement the changes. The reason given for failure to produce the draft Orders was that it made little sense to implement changes, given that local government boundaries were under review at the time.

The Home Secretary introduced the House of Commons Redistribution of Seats Bill, implementing some of the recommendations regarding large urban areas, but not the remaining recommendations. The House of Lords introduced amendments, which the Home Secretary rejected. The Home Secretary then suggested compromise amendments, which the House of Lords rejected. Subsequently, the Home Secretary introduced the draft Orders in Council, leaving the Lords' amendments intact, but inviting the House of Commons to reject the Orders. The application for mandamus was withdrawn. In 1970, however, the incoming Conservative government reintroduced and passed the Orders.

In *R v Boundary Commission for England ex parte Foot* (1983), the Labour Party, having been aggrieved by the Boundary Commission's recommendations, sought an order of prohibition and injunctions to restrain the Commission from putting the recommendations to the Home Secretary, alleging that the Commission had misinterpreted the rules.[21] The court rejected the argument, relying on the considerable discretion built into the rules by the Parliamentary Constituencies

---

21 Parliamentary Constituencies Act 1986, Sched 2.

Act. Sir John Donaldson MR, having referred to the constitutional role of judicial review, and accepted that jurisdiction lay to review the decision of the Boundary Commission, stated that unless there was sufficient evidence that the Commission had made recommendations which no reasonable body could make, the court should not intervene.

The reluctant attitude of the courts towards controlling the Boundary Commissions' exercise of power is understandable, given the politically charged nature of the subject matter. Judicial inquiry in this matter comes very close to questioning a matter which is more appropriately dealt with in parliament, and to thereby infringing the privileges of parliament.[22] Nevertheless, such an attitude is thrown into sharp relief when compared with the position in the United States of America, where the constitutional guarantee of 'the equal protection of the law'[23] has been utilised to ensure real equality in voting power.

Electoral Commission

The Political Parties, Elections and Referendums Act 2000 established an Electoral Commission, comprising not less than five but not more than nine Electoral Commissioners, appointed by Her Majesty. The Commission is not to be regarded as the servant or agent of the Crown, or as enjoying any status, immunity or privilege of the Crown. Schedule 1 makes detailed provision for the terms of office. The Commission regulates its own procedure, and may appoint a chief executive and such other staff as the Commission considers necessary.[24]

The Commission's functions include preparing and publishing reports relating to parliamentary general elections and elections to the European Parliament, Scottish Parliament, National Assembly for Wales and Northern Ireland Assembly.[25] The Commission must keep under review matters relating to elections and referendums, including the redistribution of seats at parliamentary elections, the registration of political parties[26] and the regulation of their income and expenditure and political advertising.[27] No nomination may be made in relation to an election in the name of a party unless that party is registered, or the candidate is a person who does not propose to represent any party.[28]

The Commission may provide advice and assistance in relation to elections.[29] The Commission is under a duty to promote public awareness about electoral and democratic systems, including the institutions of the European Union.[30] The Act also provides that the functions of the Boundary Committees are transferred to

22 See Chapter 5 on separation of powers and Chapter 18 on privilege.
23 The Fourteenth Amendment to the Constitution.
24 The chairman of the new Electoral Commission is Sam Younger: the Commission started work on 19 January 2001. The rules relating to disclosure of large donations came into force in February 2001 and will be kept under review by the Commission. The Commission is to consider whether any upper limit should be imposed on donations after the next general election. As from 2002, the maximum allowable expenditure is £20 million.
25 Political Parties, Elections and Referendums Act 2000, s 5.
26 Regulated under the Registration of Political Parties Act 1998.
27 Political Parties, Elections and Referendums Act 2000, Pt II.
28 *Ibid*, s 22.
29 *Ibid*, s 10.
30 *Ibid*, s 13.

the Electoral Commission.[31] The Act provides for 69 offences, with liability ranging from a fine at level five or six months' imprisonment on summary conviction to a fine or one year's imprisonment on conviction on indictment.

There is established a Speaker's Committee, consisting of the Speaker and the Chairman of the Home Affairs Select Committee, the Secretary of State for the Home Department, the minister with responsibilities in relation to local government and five Members of the Commons who are not ministers.[32] The Speaker's Committee scrutinises the annual estimates of the Commission, and decides whether the estimated level of income and expenditure is consistent with the 'economical, efficient and effective discharge' by the Commission of their functions. If the Committee is not satisfied, it may modify the estimates. The estimates are laid before the House of Commons. The Commission also submits to the Speaker's Committee a five year plan, setting out the aims and objectives for the period and estimated requirements for resources. The Speaker's Committee is assisted by the Comptroller and Auditor General, who each year carries out an examination into the economy, efficiency and effectiveness with which the Commission has used its resources in discharging its functions, and reports to the Speaker's Committee, including such recommendations as he considers appropriate.

INITIATING THE ELECTION PROCESS

General elections

General elections must be held every five years, the maximum life of any parliament.[33] Section 7 of the Septennial Act 1715, as amended by the Parliament Act 1911, provides that a parliament shall 'have continuance for five years, and no longer ...'. A royal proclamation dissolves parliament and orders the issue of writs for the election of a new parliament.

The Prime Minister controls the timing of general elections although, in theory, the dissolution of parliament lies within the prerogative of the Crown. For detailed discussion of the dissolution of parliament, see Chapter 6. Within the context of electoral law, what is of significance is the uncertainty relating to the actual date of a general election, and the extent to which Prime Ministers control the timing of elections. While a parliament may run for a full five year term, there are often political reasons against this, which result in Prime Ministers choosing a politically convenient date for his or her own party. Although there is a maximum time limit on the life of a parliament, there is no *minimum* period which a government must serve before calling an election.[34] In 1974, for example, the parliament lasted less

31 Political Parties, Elections and Referendums Act 2000, ss 14–20. The responsibility for constituency reviews is expected to be taken over by the Commission once the latest review is complete. See HL Deb, 3 April 2000, col 1094.

32 *Ibid*, s 2.

33 Parliament Act 1911, s 7.

34 Although, as discussed in Chapter 6, the Crown could, in theory, refuse the dissolution of parliament if it were considered that a second election within a short period of time would run counter to the public interest.

than one year, whereas parliament's life extended to four years and nine months between 1987 and 1992. In the absence of firm rules, Prime Ministers also have latitude over the amount of notice which is given before the election is held.

By-elections

By-elections take place following the death or retirement of a Member of Parliament. Any Member of Parliament may put down a motion to the House, which if successful, requires the Speaker to issue a writ commencing the election procedure. In practice, the Chief Whip of the party which held the seat of the Member moves the motion for a writ. There is a limit laid down by law as to the time period in which a by-election must be held. In 1973, a Speaker's Conference recommended that the motion initiating the by-election process should be moved within three months of the vacancy arising.

Eligibility of candidates

There is no statutory or other authority defining the qualifications for membership of the House of Commons. In order to promote a greater gender balance in parliament, the Sex Discrimination (Election of Candidates) Act 2002 provides that the Sex Discrimination Act 1975 and Sex Discrimination (Northern Ireland) Order 1976 do not apply to the selection of candidates by political parties. Under the House of Commons Disqualification Act 1975, certain categories of persons are eligible for election and others are disqualified under the Act.

Under section 1 of the 1975 Act the following classes of persons are disqualified from membership of the Commons: (a) holders of judicial office;[35] (b) civil servants; (c) members of the armed forces; (d) members of the police; (e) members of non-Commonwealth legislatures; and (f) members of Boards of Nationalised Industries, Commissions, Tribunals and other bodies whose members are appointed by the Crown.[36]

In addition, a number of general restrictions on eligibility apply.

Persons under the age of 21

While the age of majority was reduced in 1969 by the Family Law Reform Act, eligibility for election to parliament does not arise until the age of 21.[37]

Persons suffering from mental illness

Mental illness is a common law disqualification. If an already elected Member of Parliament is authorised to be detained on grounds of mental illness, the Speaker of the House is notified and, following confirmation of the illness, the Member's seat is declared vacant.[38]

---

35 House of Commons Disqualification Act, Sched 1.
36 See *ibid*, Sched 1, Pt II.
37 *Ibid*, Sched 2, para 1.
38 Mental Health Act 1983, s 141.

Peers

Members of the House of Lords, or persons succeeding to a peerage, are not eligible for office. Under the Peerage Act 1963, a person succeeding to a peerage has a limited right to disclaim his peerage. If a member of the House of Commons succeeds to a peerage, he has one month in which to disclaim his peerage or resign from the House of Commons.

Members of the clergy

Formerly, no person who had been ordained 'to the office of priest or deacon' or who was a Minister of the Church of Scotland could stand for election,[39] although a clergyman could relinquish his office and thereby become eligible to stand for election.[40] The House of Commons (Removal of Clergy Disqualification) Act 2001 removes the disqualification, other than for those who hold office as Lords Spiritual in the House of Lords.

Bankrupts

Persons declared bankrupt are ineligible for election to the House of Commons and, if already a Member, may not either sit or vote in parliament until the bankruptcy is discharged by a court or the adjudication annulled.[41]

Treason

Persons convicted of treason are disqualified for election to the House and, if already a Member of the House, may not sit or vote until a pardon has been received or the sentence of the court has expired.[42]

Corrupt practices at elections

Any person found guilty of corrupt practices in the course of an election may be disqualified from membership of the House of Commons. If the corrupt practices come to light only after the election, the Member may be disqualified from sitting in parliament.[43] The disqualification commences from the date of the report of the Election Court on the practices and will last, in relation to any constituency, for a period of five years and, in relation to the constituency in which the practices occurred, for a ten year period.

The conduct of election campaigns

The Representation of the People Act 1983 governs the law relating to election campaigns, controlling both the amount of expenditure and the manner in which

---

39 House of Commons (Clergy Disqualification) Act 1801; Roman Catholic Relief Act 1929; Welsh Church Act 1914.
40 Clerical Disabilities Act 1870.
41 Insolvency Act 1986, s 427.
42 Forfeiture Act 1870, ss 2 and 7.
43 Representation of the People Act 1983, ss 159 and 160. See *Attorney General v Jones* (2000).

it can lawfully be spent, proscribing certain unlawful practices and providing for challenges to the legality of a campaign. Corrupt practices include exceeding the lawful expenditure limits, bribery, treating, and undue influence which includes making threats or attempts to intimidate electors.[44] A bribe is defined as 'any money, gift, loan or valuable consideration, office, place or employment, in order to influence how an elector will cast his or her vote'.[45] 'Treating' occurs where a candidate offers or gives food, drink or entertainment with a view to influencing how the elector will vote.[46] A corrupt practice may be committed by any person, not just the candidate or his or her election agent. While minor infringement of the strict rules may be excused by a court,[47] a finding of corrupt practices may cause the election of the candidate to be invalidated.[48]

It may be noted that, before the Political Parties, Elections and Referendums Act 2000, while the law closely regulated the conduct of constituency campaigns, it virtually ignored regulation of the national political party campaigns. In an age of mass communication, and ever increasing personality politics in terms of political party leaders, the absence of regulation at national level – other than via broadcasting controls – was a matter for concern. On the 2000 Act, see below.

The 2000 Act makes special provision for assistance with voting for persons with disabilities, whether by virtue of partial sight, blindness or other physical incapacity or inability to read.[49]

Expenditure

Section 75 of the Representation of the People Act 1983 provides that no expenditure shall be made other than by the candidate or through his or her election agent. Each candidate is obliged to appoint an election agent.[50] The rationale for this rule lies in establishing and maintaining fairness between candidates and providing a mechanism for accountability as to election expenses. All accounts relating to election expenses must be reported, within 21 days of the election result, to the Returning Officer. Section 76 of the Act[51] permits the Secretary of State to set and raise the permitted amounts of expenditure, in line with inflation, by way of statutory instrument. The allowable amount comprises a fixed sum per constituency plus a sum calculated on the number of voters in a constituency. Any expenditure exceeding the prescribed limits amounts to a corrupt practice under section 75(1). Expenditure on national party election broadcasts is met by central party funds.

---

44 Originally, the Corrupt and Illegal Practices Prevention Act 1883. See now the Representation of the People Act 1983, ss 72–75, 107, 109, 111, 115.
45 *Ibid*, s 113.
46 *Ibid*, s 114.
47 *Ibid*, s 167.
48 *Ibid*, s 159.
49 Representation of the People Act 2000, s 13, amending the 1983 Act, Sched 1, the parliamentary elections rules. The Act also makes provision for the free delivery of election addresses by candidates at the first election for London Mayor: s 14 of the 2000 Act amending the Greater London Authority Act 1999, s 17, on which see Chapter 12.
50 Representation of the People Act 1983, s 67(2).
51 As amended by the Representation of the People Act 1985.

Several challenges to expenditure have been presented to the courts. In *R v Tronoh Mines Ltd* (1952), Tronoh Mines placed an advertisement in *The Times* newspaper urging voters not to vote socialist. The company and *The Times* were charged under the Act. The court held that the expenditure had been incurred with a view to promoting the interests of a Party generally, rather than an individual candidate; that any advantage incurred was incidental and not direct; and that accordingly the expenditure did not fall within section 75. Conversely, in *DPP v Luft* (1977), an anti-fascist group had distributed pamphlets in three constituencies urging voters not to vote for National Front (extreme right wing) candidates. The group was prosecuted under section 75 of the 1983 Act for incurring expenditure with a view to promoting the election of a candidate without the authority of an election agent. It was held that an offence had been committed, even though the promoters were seeking to prevent election of a candidate, rather than directly promote the election of a preferred candidate. In *Walker v Unison* (1995), the court ruled that section 75(1) of the Representation of the People Act 1983 had not been breached. During local elections in Scotland, Unison, a trade union, placed advertisements in national newspapers and on billboards, urging voters not to vote Conservative. The advertisements were placed without the authorisation of an election agent. Two Conservative candidates argued that there had been an illegal expenditure. The court ruled that the advertisements were a generalised attack on a political party, and not a direct attack on the candidates and, accordingly, the advertisements did not contravene the Act.[52]

In *Grieve v Douglas-Home* (1965), Alec Douglas-Home's election was alleged to be void on the basis that he had participated in a national Party Political Broadcast on behalf of the Conservative Party and had not declared the cost of this expenditure within his election expenses. The court held that no offence had been committed either by the candidate or by the broadcasters. The court accepted the contention that the intention behind the broadcast was not to promote the candidature of Douglas-Home in his own constituency but to provide general information about the Party to the general public.

Broadcasting and elections

Broadcasting is controlled by sections 92 and 93 of the 1983 Act and section 37 of the Political Parties, Elections and Referendums Act 2000. Party political broadcasts may be transmitted by the British Broadcasting Corporation and those broadcasters licenced under the Broadcasting Acts 1990 or 1996. There exists a non-statutory body, the Committee on Party Political Broadcasts, which comprises representatives from the broadcasting authorities and from the main political parties. Broadcasting time is allocated on the basis of the number of votes cast for each party at the last general election, and at by-elections between general elections. This arrangement disadvantages the Liberal Democrats, who have wide

---

52 On a challenge to the former £5 limit on expenditure not authorised by the candidate or his/her election agent, see *Bowman v United Kingdom* (1998). The limit operated as a restriction on freedom of expression and violated the Convention. The limit has been raised to £500: see the Representation of the People Act 1983, s 75(1ZA).

popular support throughout the country, and other smaller parties, such as the Scottish National Party and the Green Party, which enjoy much popular support nationwide which rarely – because of the voting system employed – translates into electoral success.

The ITC is under a statutory duty to ensure that news is accurate and impartial, and that political parties are given a fair allocation of time for party political broadcasts and news coverage of their campaigns. The BBC is not controlled by statute, but by Charter, and is under a duty to preserve impartiality. Judicial review will lie if either body infringes the rules. This general duty of fairness was raised by the Rt Hon David Owen MP (now Lord Owen) in *R v Broadcasting Complaints Commission ex parte Owen* (1985). David Owen had complained to the Commission that the allocation of time to various parties, principally the Social Democratic Party, was unjust or unfair under section 54 of the Broadcasting Act 1981. On an appeal to the court, it was held that the Commission had jurisdiction to consider complaints about general fairness, rather than just the unfairness, or otherwise, of particular programmes, but that the Commission had acted lawfully in allocating time on the basis of the number of seats won rather than votes cast. A further challenge to the allocation of broadcasting time came in *R v British Broadcasting Corporation ex parte Referendum Party* (1997). The Referendum Party was founded in 1994 and contested 547 seats at the general election. The broadcasting authorities allocated the party one five minute broadcast on each network. The Conservative and Labour Parties each were allocated four broadcasts. The Referendum Party sought judicial review, claiming that it had three per cent support in public opinion polls and that, given that it was a new party, the broadcasting authorities should not have relied on past electoral support. The Divisional Court held that former electoral support must not be determinative, but that the authorities were allowed to include it as a criterion. The decision was not irrational.

Section 93 of the Representation of the People Act 1983 previously required the consent of participants in broadcasts. In addition to that requirement, if a candidate participated in a broadcast with a view to promoting his own election, every other candidate in the constituency must have consented to the broadcast. This rule was tested in *Marshall v BBC* (1979). The candidate, having refused to participate in a debate, was filmed while canvassing in the streets. On a challenge to the legality of the broadcast, it was held that no offence had been committed. To 'take part' in a constituency item, means to take active part. The effect of section 93 was that one candidate could veto what could be broadcast. The Political Parties, Elections and Referendums Act 2000 replaces section 93 and now requires that broadcasters must comply with a code of practice dealing with the participation of candidates in general and local election campaigns.

The issue of freedom of speech protected under the Human Rights Act 1998 was considered by the House of Lords in *R (ProLife Alliance) v British Broadcasting Corporation* (2003). At issue was the right of a registered political party, the ProLife Alliance, to insist that the BBC and other terrestrial broadcasters transmit its party election broadcast which contravened, in the BBC's opinion, the obligation to ensure that nothing in its programmes, *inter alia*, offended against good taste or decency.[53] In the Court of Appeal, Laws LJ had asserted that the court had a constitutional responsibility to protect political speech, and that while the film was 'graphic and disturbing' that could not justify any restriction. The House of Lords disagreed: the BBC and other terrestrial broadcasters had been entitled to refuse to televise the proposed election broadcast on the ground that it would be offensive to public feeling.

Disputed elections

Any challenge to an election campaign must be made within three weeks of the result being declared. The complaint may be made by a registered elector, by unsuccessful candidates or by their nominees. Since 1868, such challenges go to the Election Court, a Divisional Court of the Queen's Bench Division of the High Court. The court has the power to order a recount; declare corrupt or illegal practices; disqualify a candidate from membership of the House of Commons and declare the runner-up duly elected; or order a fresh election. Two cases illustrate this aspect of the law. In *Re Parliamentary Election for Bristol South East* (1964), Tony Benn MP, who had recently succeeded to a peerage as Viscount Stansgate, stood for re-election. The election was declared void and awarded to the runner-up. In *Ruffle v Rogers* (1982), the election papers were incorrectly counted and affected the outcome of the election. The election was declared void, but the court made clear that had the miscount not affected the result, the election would have been upheld. In *Gough v Local Sunday Newspapers (North) Ltd* (2003), the Court of Appeal ruled that informal counts of ballot papers should not take place in any circumstances. The solicitor to Bedford Borough Council had approved an informal count – in the absence of the candidates and their agents – of postal votes which were discovered after the election had been declared. The rules governing local elections under section 36(2) of the Representation of the People Act 1983 did not provide for a situation where the ballot papers had been overlooked. A fresh election was ordered in 1997, following allegations concerning the accuracy of the count of the vote which returned a Member of Parliament with a majority of just two votes. In *Knight v Nicholls* (2004) it was held that a returning officer had fulfilled his duty to issue ballot papers by delivering them to a carrier (Royal Mail) chosen and paid for the purpose in good time for them to be delivered and returned before the election. At the local election N was elected by a majority of 40 votes over K. The Royal Mail had failed to deliver 110 papers on time for the election. However, since the returning officer had discharged his duty, the election was not invalid.[54]

---

53 Under para 5(1)(d) of the agreement between the BBC and Home Secretary, and in the case of independent broadcasters, the obligation is imposed by s 6(1)(a) of the Broadcasting Act 1990.

54 In *R v Hussain* (2005) the Court of Appeal ruled that it was the duty of the courts to protect the UK's system of democracy and, therefore, those who committed electoral fraud could expect to receive sentences which were designed to deter others from such conduct.

The Registration of Political Parties Act 1998

This Act introduced for the first time a register of political parties. A political party is entitled to be entered on the Register of Political Parties if that party intends to have one or more candidates at parliamentary elections, elections to the European Parliament, Scottish Parliament, National Assembly for Wales, the Northern Ireland Assembly or local government elections. Registration is intended to clarify the identity of *bona fide* political parties and thereby make regulation more certain. Under section 14, no party political broadcast may be made by broadcasters other than on behalf of a registered political party. The responsibility for the register lies with the Electoral Commission.

Political party funding[55]

In the United Kingdom, there is no provision for state aid for political parties for the conduct of election campaigns. Political parties do, however, receive public funds for their parliamentary work. Under the system, generally known as 'Short Money',[56] the money allocated is to be spent exclusively in relation to the party's parliamentary business, and not for election expenses. A similar scheme operates in the House of Lords. Introduced in 1996 by the then Leader of the House of Lords, Viscount Cranborne, 'Cranborne Money' is paid to the first two opposition parties. The Committee on Standards in Public Life has recommended that both the Commons and the Lords consider considerable increases of the amounts paid to opposition parties. In addition to financial support for parliamentary business, candidates at parliamentary elections or elections to the European Parliament are entitled to free postage for one election communication to every elector within the constituency. Candidates are also entitled to the free use of publicly funded premises for an election meeting. Indirect state assistance is provided through political broadcasts during election campaigns.

For election purposes, parties are dependent upon the support of the membership and, more importantly, from companies and trades unions. Approximately 30 per cent of Conservative Party funds come from companies, whereas almost 55 per cent of Labour Party funds have traditionally come from trades union donations, although this pattern has recently changed. In 1976, the Houghton Committee recommended that state aid be given to parties in proportion to the success at the previous election. In 1982, the Commission recommended state funding equivalent to individual contributions to local constituency parties. Neither proposal was adopted.

Concerns over party political funding led to an examination of the matter by the Committee on Standards in Public Life. In November 1997, the Labour Government extended the terms of reference of the Committee to include political party funding. Recognising that 'political parties are essential to democracy', the

---

55 See The Electoral Commission, *The Funding of Political Parties: Report and Recommendations* (2004); Rowbottom, J, (2005).
56 After the Rt Hon Edward Short (now Lord Glenamara), the Leader of the House of Commons in 1975 when the system was introduced.

Committee identified three of the seven 'principles of public life', namely, integrity, accountability and openness, as particularly relevant to the funding of political parties. Increasing election spending by the two main parties, who between them spent some £54 million on the 1997 general election, and the issue of large donations to political parties by persons known or unknown, gave rise to the public perception that election results can be affected by spending and that wealthy organisations or individuals could effectively influence public policy. Undisclosed foreign donations to the Conservative Party also caused concern.

In the Committee's view, it was 'undesirable that a political party should be dependent for its financial survival on funds provided by a few well endowed individuals, corporations or organisations', irrespective of 'whether or not the suspicion [that he who pays the piper calls the tune] is justified'. The problem of public confidence in the political system was compounded when such donations came from undisclosed sources.

Part IV of the Political Parties, Elections and Referendums Act 2000 provides for the control of donations to registered parties and their members, defining permissible donors and providing rules regulating the acceptance or return of donations, and providing for forfeiture of donations by impermissible or unidentifiable donors, under a court order on an application of the Commission. A person commits an offence if he or she knowingly enters into, or does any act in furtherance of, any arrangement which facilitates or is likely to facilitate the making of donations by any person or donor other than a permissible donor. The Act provides for quarterly donation reports to be made, and, in the period of general elections, for weekly reports.[57] Under section 69, the Commission is to maintain a register of donations.

Part V of the Act relates to campaign expenditure. No expenditure may be incurred by or on behalf of the registered party unless it is incurred with the authority of the treasurer or deputy treasurer of the party, or a person authorised by the treasurer or deputy treasurer. Section 74 and Schedule 8 impose limits on campaign expenditure in relation to parliamentary general elections and general elections to the European Parliament, Scottish Parliament, National Assembly for Wales and the Northern Ireland Assembly.[58]

In relation to a general election, Part V of the Political Parties, Elections and Referendums Act 2000 provides that a political party may spend a specified sum per constituency it contests. The overall effect is that a party fielding candidates in every constituency is entitled to spend some £20 million. This figure is quite separate from the allowable expenditure that may be incurred by individual candidates in their constituencies.

In addition to expenditure by political parties, Part VI of the 2000 Act also regulates expenditure by bodies such as companies, trades unions and pressure groups. Section 85 of the Act allows such bodies to incur up to £10,000 in England and £5,000 in each of Northern Ireland, Scotland and Wales for the production of

---

57 Political Parties, Elections and Referendums Act 2000, ss 62, 63, respectively.
58 Part VII and Sched 13 regulate expenditure at referendums.

election material. Any proposed expenditure over these limits requires the body to register with the Electoral Commission as a 'recognised third party'. Once registered, the body may expend prescribed amounts in England, Northern Ireland, Scotland and Wales. Following the election, details of expenditure must be submitted to the Commission.

Financial support and granting of honours

The link between financial donations to political parties and the granting of honours has been a matter of concern since the early twentieth century. In 2006 – in spite of the reforms effected under the Political Parties, Elections and Referendums Act 2000 – fresh allegations of political impropriety were made. The 2000 Act does not regulate the granting of loans to political parties, and accordingly these do not need to be declared. The allegation that the Labour government has been granting peerages to those who have made donations and made loans to the Party came to light when the independent Appointments Commission which scrutinises nominations for life peerages blocked three nominees who allegedly made loans to the Party. In March 2006 both the Constitutional Affairs Committee and the Public Administration Select Committee announced that it would conduct an inquiry into the matter. Moreover the Metropolitan Police have been reported to be investigating whether any offences have been committed under the Honours (Prevention of Abuse) Act 1925.

State funding of political parties?[59]

Any limitation on the rights of parties to accept funds, disclosed or undisclosed, increases the arguments in favour of state funding of political parties. State funding in Europe is an accepted commonplace. Austria, Denmark, France, Germany, Greece, Italy, Portugal and Spain all have publicly funded political parties. This issue is, however, contentious in the United Kingdom on a number of grounds. First, it is argued that state funding potentially undermines the cohesiveness of the party, and introduces the possibility of politically inspired changes to the bases of funding. Moreover, it is argued that state funding would encourage the formation and growth of extremist parties. Opposition is also voiced on the constitutional basis that, to compel citizens to finance political parties, through taxation, especially those with which they have no sympathy, would cause dissent. Set against these objections, however, are the benefits which would accrue from public funding. First, depending on the method used to calculate entitlement, greater equality and fairness would be achieved among the political parties. Secondly, party political finances would become most clearly a matter of open public record. Thirdly, the elimination of contributions from individuals and organisations would eradicate the public's suspicions about the

59 See *Report of the Committee on Financial Aid to Political Parties*, Cmd 6601, 1976, London: HMSO (the Houghton Report); Hansard Society Commission, *The Financing of Political Parties*, 1981; Home Affairs Select Committee, *Funding of Political Parties*, HC 301 (1993–94), London: HMSO.

integrity of party political finance and thus enhance confidence in the political process. Fourthly, the ability of parties to conduct their official duties would be enhanced by improving the level of contributions made. The Houghton Committee commented in its 1976 report that, at a local level, party organisation was weak and 'generally exists on a pitifully inadequate scale of accommodation, equipment, trained staff and resources'. Thus, improved funding would facilitate an enhanced level of efficiency at the grass roots level of democracy.

On the issue of state funding for political parties, the Committee on Standards in Public Life considered the arguments for and against increasing aid. The principal argument in favour was that public funding would 'purify' the political process by eliminating the need for parties to be reliant on donations. State aid would also enable the parties to fulfil their functions more effectively, by ensuring that sufficient funds were available to cover costs and that parties were not reliant on individuals or organisations for finance. On the other hand, it was argued, *inter alia*, that individual taxpayers should not be obliged to contribute to financing political parties with whose views they disagreed. There was also the problem of the criteria for state aid, which, if dependent upon success at elections, could deny new parties access to funding. The Committee found the arguments for and against state funding 'finely balanced', but the arguments in favour were not conclusive. The Committee considered that its proposals for limits on campaign expenditure coupled with the requirements of disclosure and registration would meet the concerns expressed about the current system of party funding.

VOTING SYSTEMS[60]

The first and foremost object of reforming zeal ought, in my opinion, to be the system of parliamentary representation, or rather misrepresentation.[61]

The Labour Government came to power in 1997 committed to major electoral reform, and to holding a referendum to ascertain the people's view. Substantial reform has taken place. The 1999 elections to the new Scottish Parliament employed the additional member system, as did election to the new National Assembly for Wales. The 1999 elections to the Northern Ireland Assembly employed the single transferable vote system, one already utilised for elections in Northern Ireland to the European Parliament and for local elections. The 1999 elections for the European Parliament in the rest of the United Kingdom saw the introduction of a new system of proportional representation based on party lists. Despite these reforms, no move has yet been made to reform the simple majority system employed for election to the United Kingdom Parliament. In this section, the merits and demerits of differing systems are considered.

Vernon Bogdanor categorises voting systems under three heads: plurality systems; majority systems; and proportional systems. Under the heading of proportional systems, there exists a range of differing systems:

---

60 See Finer, 1975; Bogdanor, 1981 and 1983; Bogdanor and Butler, 1983; Chandler, 1982; Oliver, 1983; Butler, 'Electoral reform', in Jowell and Oliver, 2000.
61 Wade, 1989.

'Proportional representation' is in fact a generic term denoting a number of different systems sharing only the common aim of proportionality between seats and votes. This common aim, however, does not prevent the various proportional systems diverging considerably, one from another; and their political consequences, therefore, can be quite different. [Bogdanor and Butler, 1983, p 2]

Despite recent reforms, the United Kingdom is out of step with much of the rest of the world in terms of systems employed for electing its national parliament. As a generalisation, it can be said that those countries influenced by English common law are the countries which retain the majority system of voting. The majority of states on the continent of Europe employ a list system; France by contrast employs a system which involves two ballots. In France, when no candidate wins an absolute majority of the vote in the first ballot, a second ballot is held to determine which of those candidates who have gained 12.5 per cent of the registered electorate in the first ballot are to be elected. In Australia, two electoral systems are employed. For election to the House of Representatives, a system of compulsory preferential voting is used. For election to the Senate, a proportional representation system is employed.

The simple majority system

If it is accepted that a democratic Parliament ought to represent so far as possible the preferences of the voters, this system is probably the worst that could be devised.[62]

For elections to the United Kingdom Parliament, the system of election remains the simple majority (first past the post) system. The origins of the voting system lie in tradition, and the voting system is not a matter of law, but of past political practice. One principal merit of the system lies in its simplicity. The candidate who gains the largest number of votes in the election wins the seat – irrespective of the proportion of votes cast for himself or his opponents. To illustrate, if the votes cast for individual candidates at an election are:

Candidate	Number of votes
Smith	3,200
Jones	2,700
Brown	2,500
Total	**7,400**

Smith wins the election, even though 5,200 voters, or 70 per cent, have voted for the other candidates. This lack of representativeness – when viewed from the perspective of proportionality of votes cast to seats won – is reflected in the results nationwide.

---

62 Wade, 1989, p 9.

The 1997 and 2005 general elections

The general election of 1 May 1997 resulted in a landslide victory for the Labour Party.[63] Tony Blair MP became the youngest Prime Minister, at the age of 43, since 1812, and only the fifth Labour Prime Minister in the twentieth century.[64] The 2005 election results were as follows:

Party	Number of seats	Percentage of seats
Labour	354	54.9%
Conservative	196	30.4%
Lib Dem	61	9.5%
Other	30	4.6%
Speaker & Deputies	4	0.6%
Total	645*	100.0%

* One seat remained vacant

The Electoral Reform Society calculated that had there been a system of proportional representation in place for the 1997 election, the results would have been much different, namely:

Party	Number of seats	Percentage of vote	Percentage of seats
Labour	286	44.4%	43.4%
Conservative	199	31.4%	30.2%
Lib Dem	109	17.2%	16.5%
Other	64	7.0%	9.9%
Speaker	1	-	-
Total	660	100.0%	100.0%

Far from having a commanding majority in the House of Commons, the Labour government would have had 286 seats, the opposition parties 308.

It is figures such as these which explain the demands for reform of the electoral system. Several alternatives present themselves, some of which offer proportional representation, others of which do not, but do represent an improvement of the representativeness of parliament when compared with the simple majority system. The alternative vote, the supplementary vote, the

---

63 The 1997 election resulted in a significant increase in women Members of Parliament. Of 659 Members, 120, or 18.2 per cent.
64 The others being Ramsey MacDonald, 1924, 1929–31, Clement Attlee, 1945–51, Harold Wilson, 1974–76, James Callaghan, 1976–79.

additional member system and the single transferable vote are all alternative systems. The alternative vote and supplementary vote are both majoritarian systems. The latter two – the additional member system and the single transferable vote, along with the party list system – are proportional representation systems. Simply stated, proportional representation means that Members should be elected to parliament on a party basis which reflects the proportion of votes cast for a party in the election: thus, if 40 per cent of the population vote Liberal Democrat, then 40 per cent of the parliamentary seats should be held by that party; not as under the present system, where the 1987 election revealed that 15 per cent of the population voted Liberal Democrat but, in terms of seats in parliament, the party won only three per cent of seats.

Alternative voting systems

The alternative vote

This system retains individual constituencies, but introduces the notion of multiple votes in order of preference. As noted above, it is a majoritarian system, not a proportional representation system. The voter marks his ballot paper with preferences expressed in numerical order. The candidate who wins 50 per cent of the first preference vote is declared elected. Should no candidate achieve 50 per cent, the votes of the candidate who achieves the lowest number of first preference votes are redistributed in accordance with that candidate's supporters' second preferences. The process is continued until one candidate achieves an overall majority of votes compared with all other candidates. Where the system fails is from the point of view of proportional representation, since the overall result will bear little or no resemblance to proportionality. It would also potentially have the effect of returning to parliament candidates who have achieved no clear support (or mandate) from the people. The system does, however, ensure that, within each constituency, the candidate with most support overall is returned to parliament.

The advantages of the alternative vote are, first, that the traditional one member, one constituency principle is retained and, secondly, that the elected candidate has a majority of votes, as compared with other candidates.

The supplementary vote

This system is very similar to the alternative vote system, and is the system recommended by the working party on electoral systems set up by the Labour Party, under the chairmanship of Lord Plant, which reported in 1993.[65] The system allows voters to express a preference through voting for two candidates. If no candidate secures 50 per cent of the vote, the second preferences cast for all candidates other than the top two are redistributed between the two leading candidates until a clear winner emerges. Where there are only three candidates, this system would work smoothly. However, the system becomes more complex in constituencies where a greater number of candidates are standing for election,

---

65 *Report of the Working Party on Electoral Systems*, 1993, London: Labour Party.

for the electorate would not be clear as to who the leading two candidates will be, and may therefore vote tactically in order to ensure, as far as possible, that a candidate who they did not want elected, would not be in either of the two top positions.

The additional member system (AMS)

This is the system adopted for the 1999 elections to the Scottish Parliament and Welsh Assembly. The AMS seeks to combine the advantages of the single member constituency, with overall proportionality between votes and seats. The system is used in Germany. Under AMS, three quarters of the United Kingdom's Members of Parliament (487 seats) would be elected in single member constituencies, using the first past the post system. The remaining quarter (163 seats) would be 'additional members', elected from party lists on a regional party basis, employing a formula based on the largest average of votes cast between the parties. The additional Members thus top up the total for each party in order to give overall proportionality.

Under AMS, each voter would thus have two votes: one for the candidate of his choice in the constituency, one for the party of his choice on a regional basis. It has the advantage of remaining close to the system which is currently in place, while departing from it sufficiently to ensure proportionality. The system would necessitate a reduction of the number of constituency Members of Parliament in order to accommodate the regionally elected Members. If the division between constituency and regional Members is to be equal, this would necessitate doubling the size of current constituencies. However, the AMS also confers wide powers on political parties who would control who is to be included on the regional list, and in what order of priority. For this reason, the Hansard Society Commission on Electoral Reform, chaired by Lord Blake, concluded that the German model of AMS was not suitable for Britain.[66]

A variant of this system is employed in local elections in Germany which avoids the problem of party control. Under this version of AMS, all candidates stand directly as constituency candidates, but only three quarters, or some other proportion, are elected in single member constituencies. The remaining one quarter of seats are allocated to those who were runners up in the election contest, who would sit as additional members.

Single transferable vote (STV)

Employed in the Republic of Ireland and in Northern Ireland for the European Parliament elections and elections to the Northern Ireland Assembly, the STV offers both proportionality between votes and seats and a constituency based, but multi-member, system of election. The STV was recommended for introduction in urban constituencies as long ago as 1917. It would involve a rearrangement of the current single member constituencies into far larger regional units, each returning several Members of Parliament. The method of calculation varies, but is based on

---

66 Hansard Society, *Report of the Commission on Electoral Reform*, 1976, London: Hansard Society, para 93.

a quota of the votes cast that is achieved either by first preference voting producing the required quota or the redistribution of votes cast for losing candidates. The STV offers both proportionality and the greatest range of choice to electors. The system used for local elections and elections to the European Parliament in Northern Ireland[67] requires that the total number of votes be divided by one more than the number of vacant seats, plus one. The current constituencies would require alteration in order to increase their size to accommodate three Members (or four or five, as favoured by the Liberal Democrats),[68] which would require a fresh look at the criteria for constituency boundaries. The current requirement to respect local authority boundaries is the most obvious criterion which would be compromised if such a system were to be adopted.

This is the most complex of alternative systems and, for that reason alone, is not favoured by many, although, despite the complexity, the system works well in Northern Ireland. The voter expresses his or her preferences for candidates in numerical order. A quota is predetermined. Thus, in a five member constituency, the quota would be approximate to one sixth of the votes cast. Successful candidates are those reaching the quota, and those who on a redistribution of second, third and more remote preferences reach the quota. If fewer than the required number of candidates reach the quota figure, then redistribution of second preferences will take place until the required number of elected Members is reached. If, on the other hand, the required number of elected Members is not achieved by the redistribution of second preferences, then a third stage comes into play. The candidate who polls the lowest number of votes is eliminated, and the votes for that candidate distributed among the other remaining candidates in order of preferences expressed. This process of elimination continues until the quota is reached for all five required elected Members.

The party list system[69]

This system requires that a list of candidates be nominated by each political party. The votes for each party's list are calculated on a nationwide basis – rather than a constituency basis – and the parties obtain the number of seats in the legislature in direct proportion to the votes in the country. The party list system is not a serious contender for adoption in the United Kingdom. Two principal defects are perceived with the system: first, it destroys election on the basis of constituencies, and secondly, too much patronage is placed in the hands of party leaders. Within the two principal political parties in the United Kingdom – Conservative and Labour – there exists a broad spectrum of political opinion: from the political left to the political right in each party. To leave the power of nomination, and the positioning of candidates on the 'list', to political leaders would potentially exclude some of the best candidates – most likely, those whose views are incompatible with, or troublesome to, the leadership.

---

67   European Assembly Elections Act 1978, Sched 1, para 2(2)(b).
68   Liberal/SDP Alliance, 1982.
69   Employed in Belgium, Denmark, Greece, Netherlands, Portugal, Spain.

THE CASES FOR AND AGAINST
REFORMING THE SIMPLE MAJORITY SYSTEM

Most of the arguments for reform of the electoral system centre on the alleged defects of the present system. Reformers argue that the status quo results in a government that does not represent the majority of the voters' wishes. Since the Second World War, no government has been elected with a majority of votes overall. The Liberal Democrats have been arguing for reform for many years, and they are not alone in this. Lord Hailsham, former Conservative Lord Chancellor and Cabinet minister, questioned the democratic basis of the current system. Professor SE Finer, Vernon Bogdanor and Professor HWR Wade[70] have all questioned the status quo.

The case for reform therefore centres on the principle of democracy and equality in voting power. For democracy to have real meaning, it is argued that the government of the day, and the composition of the legislature as a whole, must reflect the wishes of the electors. Under such a system, it can be argued that the government would have enhanced authority to pursue its electoral mandate. In answer to the charge that proportional representation can result in weak government, reformers argue that less extreme, rather than weak, government would be the result. Such an outcome would force a 'rethink' in radical politics, with governments being keenly aware that with a slim majority in parliament, and possibly the balance of power being held by a third party (both outcomes being common to proportional representation systems), certain radical policies would have to be modified. Thus many of the more politically contentious subjects, such as education and health, might be largely removed from party political conflict: consensus would become the only way in which to make legislative progress.

Reformers also point to the inequity of the distribution of the vote between the parties under the current system. The simple majority system invariably favours a two party system, and leaves little room for the adequate representation of smaller parties. The Liberal Democrat Party regularly achieves approximately 20 per cent of the popular vote at general elections (and has a high success rate at by-elections), but that overall popularity does not translate into a proportionally related number of parliamentary seats. One explanation for this result is that votes for the Liberal Democrats are spread fairly evenly over the United Kingdom, and not concentrated in one geographic area (although the south west of England is becoming a Liberal stronghold).

The case for the status quo is linked to the point made above. The simple majority system generally, although not invariably, produces a government with a strong parliamentary majority which is able to implement its electoral programme without undue hindrance. This argument requires careful evaluation. One of the often experienced effects of proportional representation systems is that governments are returned with either a very small majority of seats or a minority of seats overall in the legislature. As a result, minority parties with few seats and

---

70 Finer, 1980; Bogdanor, 1983; Wade, 1989.

relatively small electoral support may hold a disproportionate amount of power, making governments dependent upon their wishes in order to implement their legislative programme. As a consequence of this dependence, governments are also subject to the risk of defeats on motions of no confidence,[71] thus producing general political insecurity and the potential for frequent elections.

A further, related effect is that a government may be required to compromise substantially upon its electoral promises in order to govern. Under the current system, it is generally the case that the elected government – always depending upon its majority in parliament – is relatively free to implement its electoral programme. In other words, the voter knows what he or she is getting in terms of policies and proposals for legislation. Under proportional representation, where less strong government is the frequent result, voters can be far less certain either that the policies for which they are voting will be implemented or of the policies which will be pursued after the election.

There also exist doubts as to the effects of a reformed system on the convention of collective ministerial responsibility; see Chapter 11. Under current constitutional arrangements, the convention of collective responsibility requires that the Cabinet 'speaks with one voice' in order to maintain parliamentary, and electoral, confidence. The rule accordingly requires that, where a decision has been made by the Cabinet, each member of Cabinet and non-Cabinet ministers and all their Parliamentary Private Secretaries, adhere to the decision and do not speak out against it. Such a show of unity would prove difficult to sustain in coalition or minority governments. The sister doctrine of individual ministerial responsibility might also prove more difficult to adhere to, particularly where a minister felt unable to support and pursue a policy with which he or she disagreed on political principle. One consequence, therefore, that could flow from the introduction of some form of proportional representation is that governments become less cohesive and, as a result, less commanding of the confidence of the people.

A further argument is put for the status quo: that of the close links currently established between the constituency Member and his or her electorate. Irrespective of the proportion of votes won in an election, the Member of Parliament, once duly elected, and irrespective of political party, represents each and every one of his or her constituents in parliament. Constituencies are relatively small and Members of Parliament are accessible – through surgeries and other contact – to the voters. A Member is thus able to gain a detailed knowledge of his or her constituency, its geography, industry and economy, environment and populace. With large constituencies, such a detailed working knowledge of an area becomes more difficult, with the attendant possibility that a Member is less effective in his representation of that constituency in parliament.

As can be seen, the issue of electoral reform is by no means clear-cut, and real potential constitutional problems could be encountered as a result of its introduction. At the end of the day, the quest for an alternative system is rooted in the paramountcy of the principle of real democracy and equality of representation

---

71   See Chapters 6 and 11.

of the people in parliament. Against that ideal must be set the constitutional implications of introducing reform.

As noted above, one of the manifesto pledges of the Labour Party before the 1997 election was a review of the electoral system for the Westminster Parliament and, once in office, the government appointed Liberal peer Lord Jenkins to review the system. The Jenkins Commission reported in October 1998, and recommended a novel, if complex, solution. The Commission, wanting to retain single member constituencies but also inject a greater degree of proportionality into the system, opted for a 'mixed system' made up of the alternative vote and regional list systems. Constituency members would be elected on the alternative vote system, and comprise 80–85 per cent of members, with additional members, 15–20 per cent elected on the regional list basis. Greater proportionality would be achieved, while the traditional strong link between a member and his or her constituency would be retained. The system would also, the Commission claimed, avoid coalition governments and in its estimation would have produced a single party majority government in three out of the four last general elections.[72]

The current position is that the United Kingdom now employs a number of systems: a system of proportional representation was used in May 1999 for elections to the European Parliament; for elections to the Scottish Parliament and National Assembly for Wales the additional member system was used; and for elections to the Northern Ireland Assembly the single transferable vote system was used. The issue which remains unresolved is the voting system for elections to the United Kingdom Parliament. The government had promised to hold a referendum on that matter and as seen above, the Jenkins Commission recommended a mixed system of voting. The government has however deferred both issues. Despite the experimentation with reform, the government appears unconvinced of wholesale reform of the system employed for elections to the Westminster Parliament.

---

72 Cm 4090-I, para 161. This claim has been disputed by M Pinto-Duschinsky who calculates that coalition would have been the outcome in nine of the last 14 elections: *The Times*, 29 October 1998.

CHAPTER 14

INTRODUCTION TO THE HOUSE OF COMMONS

Parliament is composed of the Crown, the House of Lords and the House of Commons. Its origins lie in the King's Council – the assembly of advisers summoned by the King – and the term 'parliament' can be traced to the thirteenth century.[1]

In order to evaluate parliament, it is necessary to examine its composition and procedure. The former task may be accomplished by either looking at the actual membership of parliament by party allegiance at a fixed point in time or by looking at it in a more sociological manner in order to analyse the class and educational background of Members and their employment status. The undertaking is complicated by the bicameral nature of parliament and the fact that the House of Commons is elected and the House of Lords unelected. The importance of procedure, particularly in the House of Commons, cannot be overemphasised. Only by acquiring an understanding of the procedural rules can sense be made of the functions of parliament and its importance, or otherwise, in the process of government. In the absence of a written constitution which clearly defines and allocates powers and functions, the manner in which the legislative proposals of government are examined, and the administration of the state scrutinised, assumes central importance to the notion of democratic control of the executive. The doctrine of constitutionalism can only be effective if the procedures adopted by parliament are effective in controlling the government.

THE FUNCTIONS OF PARLIAMENT

In *Representative Government* (1861), John Stuart Mill wrote of parliament:

> Instead of the function of governing, for which it is radically unfit, the proper office of a representative assembly is to watch and control the government; to throw the light of publicity on its acts; to compel a full exposition and justification of all of them which anyone considers questionable; to censure them if found condemnable; and if the men who compose the government abuse their trust, or fulfil it in a manner which conflicts with the deliberate sense of the nation, to expel them from office, and either expressly or virtually appoint their successors.

> The House of Commons is the sounding board of the nation – an arena in which not only the general opinion of the nation, but that of every section of it can produce itself in full light and challenge discussion.

Very little has changed. Parliament is not there to govern: that is for the executive. Parliament exists to represent the views and opinions of the people and to influence, constrain and demand justification for the actions of government and to give them legitimacy.

---

1   The role of the sovereign is discussed in Chapter 6. The House of Lords is discussed in Chapter 17.

Accordingly, the functions of parliament may be summarised as being:[2]

(a) to provide the personnel of government;

(b) to legitimise government actions; and

(c) to subject matters of public policy to scrutiny and influence.

As discussed in Chapters 7 and 12, the devolution of legislative power to the Northern Ireland Assembly and Scottish Parliament and, to a lesser extent, the Welsh Assembly affects the scope of the United Kingdom Parliament's role and functions. In terms of debating and scrutinising government policy and administration and the passage of legislation, while the United Kingdom Parliament (Westminster) remains the sovereign legislature in the United Kingdom, there is now a diffusion of power – differing in nature and scope – between Westminster and the devolved institutions.

THE LIFE OF A PARLIAMENT

A parliament is summoned by the sovereign to meet following a general election, and the life of the parliament will run until the subsequent general election. Under section 7 of the Parliament Act 1911, the life of a parliament is restricted to five years from the day on which first appointed to meet, unless previously dissolved. Parliaments are summoned and dissolved by Proclamation of the Crown on the advice of the Privy Council; see Chapter 6. The average life of a parliament is three years, one month.

The parliamentary session

A parliamentary session is the parliamentary year, which commences in November. There is no legal requirement as to the length of a session. At the end of the session, parliament stands 'prorogued' until the new session begins (see below). The significance of prorogation lies in the fact that all business is suspended until the new session.

The number of sitting days per session varies from year to year. The average session length is 168 days. In 2001–02 there were 201 sitting days, averaging seven hours and 40 minutes. In 2004–05, a short session ending in April 2005, there were just 65 sitting days, averaging eight hours and 14 minutes.

Parliamentary sittings

The term 'parliamentary sitting' relates to the daily business of the House. The Commons meets daily from Monday to Friday but is adjourned for three weeks at Christmas, one week at Easter, for the whole of August and for most of September. In emergency situations, the House may be recalled for urgent debate during a recess or at a weekend, as occurred in 1982 for debate on the invasion of the Falkland Islands.[3]

---

2   Norton, 1985a and see 1993.
3   3 April 1982.

The length of parliamentary sittings varies according to the pressure of time on the House. In the 1980s, for example, seven sittings lasted over 24 hours, the longest recorded in that decade being 32 hours and 12 minutes.[4] Where the House sits beyond the normal time of the commencement of business the following day, the business of that day (with the exception of Questions put down for written answer for that day) will be lost. It is a matter of constant concern that parliament sits unsocial hours and, for this reason, reforms have been introduced.

Westminster Hall

In addition to proceedings in the chamber of the Commons, since 1999 Westminster Hall has been used for backbench debates and debates on select committee reports (see Chapter 16). Any member of Parliament may attend. In addition, Westminster Hall sittings are used for the questioning of junior ministers generally on matters which affect more than one government department. In the 2001–02 session, the number of sitting hours in Westminster Hall was 474 and in the short 2004–05 session, just 154 hours.

SUMMONING, ADJOURNMENT, PROROGATION,[5] AND DISSOLUTION OF PARLIAMENT

Summoning

It is within the Crown's prerogative to determine when parliament should be summoned. However, under statute, the Queen is bound to issue writs within three years of the ending of a parliament.[6] In practice, a parliament must be summoned to meet every year in order that approval can be given for monies to be provided for public services. Parliament is summoned to meet by proclamation of the Queen. The proclamation dissolves the previous parliament, orders the issue of writs by the Lord Chancellor and appoints the day and place for the meeting of the new parliament.

Adjournment

During a parliamentary session, parliament will be adjourned on many occasions. The adjournment is no more than an 'interruption in the course of one and the same session'.[7] Up to a quarter of the time in the House of Commons is spent debating the question: '... that this House do now adjourn.'[8] The effect of adjournment is to suspend the sitting of the House for a period but leave unaffected the business of the House. Adjournments take place for a number of reasons and to effect a number of consequences.

---

4   Debate on the Local Government (Interim Provisions) Bill, 22 May 1984.
5   From the Latin, *prorogare*, literally to ask publicly, from *pro* in public and *rogare* to ask.
6   16 Cha 2 c 1 and 6 & 7 Will & Mary c 2.
7   Erskine May, 1997.
8   Silk and Walters, 1987, p 210.

A motion for adjournment can be used in debate to interrupt proceedings. The motion will take the form 'that the debate be now adjourned'. The device may be used as an alternative to moving an amendment to the question before the House, and will be used to determine consideration of the matter in question. The Speaker has a discretion whether to decline to put the matter to the House. The business which has been interrupted can be brought before the House at the next sitting day, provided that notice is given.

Daily adjournment debates

There is a daily motion for adjournment which suspends the day's sitting. Once the motion for adjournment has been moved, the daily adjournment debate takes place.[9] The adjournment debate enables one Member to speak on a topic, previously notified, for 15 minutes, and receive a ministerial reply. Topics may include any matter other than a request for legislation. There is a weekly ballot at which successful Members are chosen for the adjournment debate, other than for the debate on Thursdays when the choice of Member is made by the Speaker.

Adjournment debates before holidays

Adjournment debates also take place before the House adjourns for holidays.[10] No ballot is held for participation: five backbenchers speak for half an hour each and the Leader of the House replies to the debate.

Adjournment debates following consideration of Consolidated Fund Bills

In any session, there will be three Consolidated Fund Bills before parliament. Second reading consideration is purely formal, with no debate. When proceedings are finished, any Member of the government may move a motion 'that this House do now adjourn'.

Adjournments for emergency debates

Provision is made under Standing Orders for urgent matters to be brought to the attention of the House for early debate. A Member may, at the start of business of the day, propose that the House be adjourned for consideration of an urgent matter. It is within the discretion of the Speaker as to whether the matter should be discussed. If satisfied, it is then for the House to give leave for the debate. If refused, the support of not more than 40 Members of the House is required in order for leave to be granted.[11] The debate will take place at the start of business the following day.

---

9   See further Chapter 16.
10 Four times a year.
11 If fewer than 40 Members but not less than ten Members support the motion, the House will determine the matter by a vote.

Prorogation

Prorogation is effected under the prerogative, by the announcement of the Queen's command. The effect of prorogation is that all business before parliament is suspended. Any Bill which has not concluded its parliamentary stages must be brought anew to the future parliament. Parliament will be prorogued until a specified date. The prorogation of parliament has not been effected in person by the Crown since 1854. The period between prorogation and the summoning of a new parliament is known as the 'recess'.

Dissolution

For detailed discussion of dissolution, see Chapter 6. Parliament is dissolved prior to a general election. Under the Parliament Act 1911, the maximum duration of the life of a parliament is five years. Dissolution is therefore required before the expiry of this period. For the most part, the Prime Minister will seek a dissolution – effected by the Crown under the royal prerogative – at a date which is politically favourable to his or her party. The time at which a dissolution is sought is entirely within the Prime Minister's personal discretion. Alternatively, dissolution may be sought when the government loses the support of the House of Commons. Governments may suffer defeats in the Commons on a range of issues which will not force a dissolution. However, if the government is defeated on a motion of confidence on a matter central to its administration a dissolution will be forced.

When a dissolution is granted, the government does not resign until after a defeat in the general election. It was seen in Chapter 6 that, in 1974, the Prime Minister, Edward Heath, did not resign until it was clear that he could not form a pact with the Liberal Party which would secure a working majority in the Commons.

THE ORGANISATION OF BUSINESS

The business in a typical parliamentary session is as follows. The session opens with the State Opening of parliament and the Queen's Speech, which outlines the government's proposals for legislation in the session. The following five days are spent in Debate on the Address, including two days on which the Opposition proposes – 'moves' – amendments to specific areas of policy. The government then introduces the most important Bills and, until Christmas, most of the time of the House will be spent on second reading debates on these Bills. Between Christmas and Easter, the majority of the time of the House will be spent in second reading debates and the committee stage of Bills. Before the end of July, the remaining legislative stages of Bills take place.

PERSONNEL OF THE HOUSE OF COMMONS

The office of Speaker

The office of Speaker is traceable to 1377 and the appointment of Sir Thomas Hungerford, although, from 1258, parliaments had similar officers.[12] The Speaker of the House featured in the constitutional struggles between King and parliament in the seventeenth century. When Charles I arrived in the Commons to arrest the Five Knights, the Speaker declared:

> May it please Your Majesty, I have neither eyes to see, nor tongue to speak in this place, but as the House is pleased to direct me, whose servant I am here, and I humbly beg Your Majesty's pardon that I cannot give any other answer than this to what Your Majesty is pleased to demand of me.

Henceforth, the independence of the Speaker from the Crown was established.

The Speaker regulates the proceedings of the House. The Speaker is a senior Member appointed by common agreement of all Members and is generally a Member of the Opposition Party. The election of the Speaker and Deputy Speakers is the first task undertaken by parliament following a general election. The Speaker acts with political impartiality and controls the business of the House.

The Speaker is the presiding officer of the House and ensures that the rules of conduct and order are observed. The Speaker is also the representative of the Commons in relations with the Crown – it is through the Speaker that the privilege of access to the Sovereign is effected – and the House of Lords and other bodies outside parliament. When the House of Lords amends Commons' Bills, the Speaker checks the amendments to ensure that they do not infringe the financial privileges of the lower House. It is also the function of the Speaker to certify Bills under the Parliament Act 1911.

The Speaker has a discretion in relation to the granting of an application for an emergency debate, whether to allow private notice questions or grant requests for emergency debates, and whether a *prima facie* case of a breach of the privileges of the House has been established. It is also for the Speaker to rule on matters of procedure. Furthermore, the Speaker will decide whether a proposed amendment to a motion will be accepted.

Disciplinary powers of the Speaker

The control of debate lies with the Speaker, who chooses who is allowed to speak. Advance notice of the wish to participate in debate is given and the Speaker calls each side (government and Opposition) alternately, and respects the rights of minority parties to participate. The Speaker has powers under Standing Orders to control the following:

(a) irrelevance or tedious repetition;

(b) minor breaches of order;

(c) the use of disorderly or unparliamentary expressions;

---

12 Known as parlour or prolocutor.

(d) grossly disorderly conduct;

(e) grave disorder;

(f) obstruction of the business of the House by other means.

Disorderly conduct – such as damaging the Mace[13] – may result in the Member, if a suitable apology is not given to the House, being suspended from the House for a period determined by the House on a motion. Suspension from the House in the first instance will be for five sitting days, on a second occasion for 20 days and in the event of a further repetition, for the remainder of the session. Any Member refusing to withdraw from the chamber of the House may be forcibly removed by the Serjeant at Arms.[14] In such an event, the Member will be suspended for the remainder of the parliamentary session. In 2003 the House agreed the proposal that a Member could have his or her salary withheld for a defined period, without suspension.

If a Member persists in a speech after being ordered to discontinue on the basis of irrelevance or tedious repetition, the Speaker may direct him or her to withdraw from the House for the remainder of the sitting, or 'name' him or her for disregarding the authority of the Speaker's Chair. The same penalty may befall a Member who uses unparliamentary language. Unparliamentary language includes:

(a) the imputation of false or unavowed motives;

(b) the misrepresentation of the language of another and the accusation of misrepresentation;

(c) charges of uttering a deliberate falsehood;

(d) abusive and insulting language likely to create disorder.

The Leader of the House

The Leader of the House is responsible to the Prime Minister for the organisation of business in the Commons. It is the function of the Leader of the House to announce the parliamentary business for the following week. The Leader of the House is a minister of the Crown.[15] When the Prime Minister is unavailable, it is the Leader of the House who represents the House of Commons.

The party whips

The party political control of Members of Parliament is in the hands of the party whips. On the government side, all whips receive salaries[16] and are ministers of the Crown. The Chief Whip[17] is assisted by up to 12 other Members. The Chief Whip organises the details of business of the House. The Opposition has a Chief Whip, two salaried assistants and eight to ten non-salaried assistants. The task of

---

13   The ceremonial staff of office of the Commons.
14   An officer of the House responsible for order.
15   House of Commons (Administration) Act 1978, s 1.
16   Ministerial and Other Salaries Act 1975, s 1(1)(a) and Sched 1.
17   Who holds office as Parliamentary or Patronage Secretary to the Treasury.

the government Chief Whip is to act as contact between the Prime Minister, the Leader of the House (to both of whom he is responsible) and Members. The whips (of all parties) keep Members informed about the House's business, and inform Members when they are obliged to attend the House. The degree of coercion of Members will depend on the importance of the matter in hand. When attendance is required – and when political consequences will flow from non-attendance – a 'three line whip' is announced. Where attendance is necessary, but not essential, a 'two line whip' is applied. In order that Members are not unduly pressured by the need for attendance in parliament, 'pairing' is permitted. Pairing is the arrangement whereby Members of government and opposition parties will be linked together: if one is absent the other may abstain from voting. Thus, the non-attendance of one Member will be off-set – in the counting of votes – by the absence of the other. Pairing arrangements must be registered with the Party Whips. Pairing is not permitted in relation to divisions on the most important matters. It is this arrangement which is most frequently threatened when relationships between the government and Opposition break down.

Much of the organisation of the business of the House is in the hands of the whips, including planning the parliamentary timetable and advising on practice and procedure. Whips of all parties are also responsible for recommending candidates for membership of parliamentary committees.

Members of Parliament

Front- and backbenchers

Business in the House is conducted on adversarial lines. The adversarial nature of the Commons is reflected in the layout of the House. The House is divided into two sections which face each other, separated by the Table of the House, behind which the Speaker sits. Each side has a front-bench and several rows of backbenches. On the side to the right of the Speaker sit Members of the government party, ministers of the government occupying the front-bench. Opposite, on the front-bench, will sit the shadow ministers of the Opposition party. All other Members of both the government and Opposition will sit on the backbenches: hence the term 'backbenchers'.

The representation of women in the Commons

The Parliament (Qualification of Women) Act 1918 made women eligible to stand as Members of Parliament. Of 1,613 candidates at the 1918 election, only 17 were women. The first female candidate to take her seat in the House of Commons was Lady Astor, elected in 1919 in a by-election. The representation of women has always been poor in the Commons. In 1918, there was just one woman Member; in 1945, 24 women were elected to parliament. The figures remained between 17 and 29 until 1987, when 41 women were elected. All the major political parties are committed to increasing the representation of women in the Commons. The 1997 general election resulted in a significantly improved proportion of women Members of Parliament. The total number elected was 120 (18 per cent of 659 seats). The 2005 general election returned 126 women members (19.5 per cent of 646 seats).

The first woman to hold ministerial office was Margaret Bondfield. She became the first female Member of Cabinet in 1929. Only one woman has held the office of Speaker: Betty Boothroyd from 1987. The first female Prime Minister was the Rt Hon Margaret Thatcher MP (as she then was), who held office from 1979–90, the longest premiership in the twentieth century.

Salaries and allowances of Members of Parliament

As far back as the thirteenth century, representatives attending parliament were paid – either in cash or kind – and, in addition, could claim travelling expenses. Payment by electors had ceased by the end of the seventeenth century. In the eighteenth and nineteenth centuries, though unpaid, a seat in the House of Commons was valuable, and could attract large sums of money for its purchase. Members of Parliament remained formally unpaid until 1911, despite numerous previous attempts to introduce payment. In 1911, the salary amounted to £400 per annum. In 1996, the Review Body on Senior Salaries, successor to the Top Salaries Review Board, recommended that Members' pay should be increased by 26 per cent to £43,000 per annum. The House also agreed that, from 1997, the yearly rate would be increased by the average percentage of Senior Civil Service pay bands.

Members also receive allowances for secretarial and research assistance, car mileage, and limited travel between the constituency and parliament. In addition, Members whose constituencies are within inner London are entitled to claim a London Supplement payment.

Members' Code of Conduct

Members of Parliament are governed by a Code of Conduct setting out general principles to guide members on the standards of conduct that the House and the public have a right to expect.[18]

The size of the House of Commons

Prior to the 1997 general election, the number of seats in parliament was increased from 651 to 659, as a result of constituency boundary changes. From 2005 the number of seats is 646, reflecting a reduction in Scottish representation at Westminster. If the number of parliamentary representatives is compared with the total population of the country, it can be seen that there is a wide discrepancy in the representativeness of differing legislatures. In Ireland, for example, there are 166 Members of Parliament, each representing 24,000 citizens. By contrast, in Australia, there are 147 Members, each representing 122,000 citizens. In the United Kingdom, there are now 646 Members of Parliament, each representing approximately 93,000 citizens.

---

18 As recommended by the Committee on Standards and Privileges: *Third Report of the Committee on Standards and Privileges*, HC 604 (1995–96), London: HMSO; HC Deb Vol 282 Col 392, 24 July 1996. See further Chapter 16.

Resignation of Members of Parliament

A Member, once duly elected, cannot relinquish his seat.[19] However, provision is made whereby a Member may retire under differing procedures,[20] each of which involves accepting office under the Crown, which obliges the Member to relinquish his seat on the basis of disqualification from membership[21] and a writ to be issued for a by-election. Application for the office is normally granted,[22] although power remains for the application to be refused. The offices are nowadays purely nominal and retained as a device to avoid the absence of any resignation procedure.

The political parties

The major political parties have a similar organisational structure in parliament. The Conservative, Labour and Liberal Democrat Parties have a system of election for the party leader, and are organised into front and backbench Members. Looking at the Commons as a whole, we see that it comprises the government, elected on the basis of the simple majority vote, Her Majesty's Loyal Opposition, being the second largest party in the House, and minority parties – Liberal Democrat, Ulster Unionist, Scottish Nationalist, Plaid Cymru.

Composition of the House of Commons by political party

The 2005 general election resulted in the House of Commons being made up of 354 Labour Members, 196 Conservative Members, 61 Liberal Democrat Members, and 30 Members from other minority parties, plus the Speaker and three deputies.[23]

GOVERNMENT AND OPPOSITION

It is the government which controls the majority of parliament's time. On 75 per cent of sitting days, government business takes priority and it is the government which determines the business to be undertaken (subject to established practices as to Opposition Days, days set aside for Private Members' Bills, etc). From scrutinising the work of parliament, it may be tempting to underplay the importance of parliament as a whole, and the Opposition in particular, in comparison with the power of the government. Such a view is implicit in the pejorative labelling of government as an 'elective dictatorship'.[24] Such charges need to be viewed with some caution. In 1947, Sir Ivor Jennings described the role of the Opposition as 'at once the alternative to the government and a focus for the

---

19 Commons' Journal (1547–1628) 724.
20 Most usually accepting the office of steward or bailiff of Her Majesty's Three Chiltern Hundreds of Stoke, Desborough and Burnham or steward of the Manor of Northstead.
21 Under the House of Commons Disqualification Act 1975, s 4.
22 By the Chancellor of the Exchequer.
23 One seat remained vacant at the 2005 election, due to the death of a candidate.
24 Hailsham, 1978, p 21.

discontent of the people. Its function is almost as important as that of the government'.[25]

In its constitutional role, the Opposition must constantly be questioning, probing and calling government to account. Viewed in this light, notwithstanding the government's control over the timetable and business of the House, it can be said that all parliamentary time is as much 'Opposition time' as 'government time'.

The constitutional importance of the official Opposition is reflected in the fact that the Leader of the Opposition draws a substantial salary in both the House of Commons and Lords, which is drawn on the Consolidated Fund.[26] In addition, since 1975, financial assistance has been provided to all opposition parties to enable them to carry out their role effectively. Each party is entitled to a fixed sum per annum per seat won by the party, plus an amount for every 200 votes cast in the previous election.

The Opposition is allocated 20 days per session in which it can determine the business of the day, representing in an average session 11.6 per cent of parliamentary time. The provision of Opposition Days ensures that the government is obliged to debate matters which it might prefer not to address. Following the Queen's Speech at the opening of a new parliamentary session, the Opposition has the right to determine the subjects for debate on the second of the six days set aside for debate on the speech.

In addition to normal parliamentary procedure for debate, questions, etc, and opposition time, the Opposition has the weapon of the motion of censure – or vote of no confidence. The motion takes the form 'the House has no confidence in Her Majesty's Government'. By convention, the government always makes time for debate on the motion, a three line whip will be employed, and a division (a formal vote – see below) invariably takes place. While fairly infrequent and confined to serious matters of policy, the loss of a motion of confidence can, as in 1979, lead to the resignation of the government, and such motions are always regarded as important parliamentary occasions.

VOTING IN THE COMMONS

A 'division' is the name for the counting of votes on important issues where conflict is apparent. Not every debate will result in a division: divisions are reserved for instances when it is important to register formally the number of votes for and against a particularly important issue. In the 2001–02 session there were 361 divisions and in the short 2004–05 session, 155 divisions were ordered. For the observer, there is something archaic and humourous about the procedure. The Speaker orders 'Division: clear the lobbies'. Division bells sound throughout parliament and in the division district immediately surrounding parliament. Members will interrupt whatever they are doing in response to the bell and return

---

25 Jennings, 1959a, Chapter XV.
26 See Chapter 15.

to parliament for the vote. Members crowd into the 'Aye' or 'Noe' lobby, and as they exit the lobby their attendance is checked. The Speaker then announces the result of the division. Votes are recorded by name in the Official Journal of the House of Commons.

PARLIAMENTARY PUBLICATIONS AND PAPERS

The House of Commons

- *The Commons' Journal:* contains the official record of the proceedings of the House. The Journal dates back to 1547 and is published annually. The Journal contains rulings from the Speaker on procedural matters.
- *The Commons' Official Report:* contains the records of speeches made in the House and written answers to Parliamentary Questions. It is a substantially verbatim report of the proceedings.
- *The Vote:* the collective name of a bundle of papers delivered to Members daily during a parliamentary session. It contains the record of the previous day's proceedings together with the Order Paper for the day which lists the business of the House.
- *The Order Book:* a daily publication setting out the future business of the House.

The House of Lords

- *Minutes of proceedings:* the record of the proceedings in the House of Lords together with details of forthcoming business.
- *The Lords' Journal:* since 1461, the Journals have been kept, providing details of attendance and voting.

Televised proceedings in parliament

Radio broadcasting of Ministerial Question Time (see Chapter 16) began in 1978. Televised broadcasts of the House of Lords have been transmitted since 1985. In 1988, the House of Commons resolved:

> ... this House approves in principle the holding of an experiment in the public broadcasting of its proceedings by television.[27]

The Select Committee on Televising of Proceedings was established to make recommendations as to the rules of coverage.[28] Broadcasting commenced in 1989. The Journals of the House of Commons and Lords remain the official record of proceedings in parliament.

---

27 HC 141 (1988–89), London: HMSO, and *Votes and Proceedings 1988–89*, 12 June 1989. And see Norton, 1991.
28 *Votes and Proceedings 1987–88*, 7 February and 9 March 1988.

CHAPTER 15

THE LEGISLATIVE PROCESS[1]

THE HOUSE OF COMMONS

Approximately two-thirds of the time of the House of Commons is devoted to the consideration of proposals for legislation. In order to effect changes in the law, any proposal must receive the authority of parliament: parliament legitimises policy objectives. A mere decision of parliament, in the form of a Resolution of the Commons, cannot change the law of the land.[2] In order to become law, a legislative proposal must receive the consent of the three component parts of parliament: the Commons, the Lords,[3] and the Crown through the giving of royal assent. In this chapter the process of scrutiny in the House of Commons is considered. Discussion of the legislative role of the House of Lords is to be found in Chapter 17.

Before examining the process of scrutiny in the Commons, the various types of legislation must be considered. Legislative proposals fall under two main categories: primary and delegated (or secondary) legislation. Primary legislation refers to Acts of Parliament. Delegated or secondary legislation refers to legislation drafted by authorised persons or bodies under the authority of a 'parent' statute.

WESTMINSTER AND DEVOLUTION

As seen in Chapter 12, devolution to the Northern Ireland Assembly, Scottish Parliament and, to a lesser extent, the Welsh Assembly (which has no power to enact primary legislation) represents a diminution in Westminster's legislative role. Under devolution, in practical terms, the United Kingdom Parliament retains power to enact primary legislation only to the extent to which this power has not passed to the regional legislature.

PRIMARY LEGISLATION[4]

The classification of Bills

The majority of Bills will be those put forward by the government to implement its policy. Bills fall into four categories: Public Bills, Private Bills, Hybrid Bills and Money Bills. The procedure for passing a Bill depends on its classification. Most attention is here devoted to the legislative procedure for Public Bills.

---

1   See Norton, 1985b, Chapter 5; Miers and Page, 1990; Ryle and Richards, 1988, Chapter 7; Silk and Walters, 1987, Chapter 6; Norton, 1993, Chapter 5; Griffith and Ryle, 2003, Chapter 8.
2   *Stockdale v Hansard* (1839).
3   Other than where the Parliament Act procedure is employed. See Chapter 17.
4   See Rose, 1986; Hansard Society, 1993.

A Public Bill is one which has general application to all members of society, for example, Road Traffic Acts, Environmental Protection Acts, and National Health Service Acts. A Private Bill is one which affects only a particular locality or group or body of persons.

A Hybrid Bill is one of general application, that is to say a Public Bill, which also affects particular private interests in a manner different from the private interests of other persons or bodies of the same category or class. The Bill regulating the development of the Channel Tunnel is an example of a Hybrid Bill, since it affected the private rights of landowners whose land would be compulsorily purchased.[5]

A Money Bill is one which is certified by the Speaker as such, and contains nothing other than financial measures.

A Private Member's Bill is one promoted by an individual Member of Parliament, as opposed to the government[6] or, alternatively, a matter which the government has been unable to fit into its legislative programme but will subsequently adopt and provide time – and support – for the passage of the Bill. Most often, such Bills involve sensitive issues of particular interest to their promoters. The Abortion Act 1967, for example, originated from a Private Member's Bill. Private Members' Bills follow the same legislative process as government Bills, but the time available for their consideration is restricted. Normally, ten (although occasionally more) Fridays each session will be set aside for Private Members' Bills, and it is rare for a Bill to succeed unless the government is prepared to provide additional time for its consideration.

Consolidation Bills represent a re-enactment of legislation in a comprehensive manner and they enable previous legislation – which will generally exist in several statutes – to be repealed. Consolidation Bills do not, for the most part, represent any change in the law; rather, they represent the chance to 'consolidate' all the law on a particular matter within one statute. Consolidation Bills are normally introduced in the House of Lords and then scrutinised by a Joint Committee on Consolidation Bills, comprised of Members of both the House of Commons and the House of Lords. Since there is no change being made in the substantive law, parliamentary time devoted to Consolidation Bills is short and it is rare for a Consolidation Bill to be debated more than briefly on the floor of the Commons. In 1994, the House of Commons agreed that, in order to save further time, Consolidated Bills would no longer require a committee stage. Finally, there are Consolidated Fund and Appropriation Bills which provide statutory authority for government expenditure and which are not debated in parliament.

The legislative picture cannot be complete without consideration of delegated or subordinate legislation. In each parliamentary session an average of 62 Bills are enacted, while the average number of statutory instruments (see further below) amounts to 2,000 per session. In addition, administrative rules drafted by government departments must be considered. These include Codes of Practice,

---

5   See also London (Transport) Bill 1968–69; Norfolk and Suffolk Broads Bill 1986–87.
6   See Griffith and Ryle, 2003; Marsh and Read, 1988.

Circulars and Guidances and, while they do not have the force of law, they nevertheless have an impact on the manner in which laws are implemented.[7]

The origins of legislation

The majority of Bills considered by parliament will be introduced by the government of the day. This does not necessarily mean that the source of the proposal is one emanating from government policy, still less from the party manifesto on which the election was fought.

Consideration of the origins of legislative proposals is important in evaluating the extent to which government and the House of Commons interacts with the society it is elected to serve. JAG Griffith and M Ryle observe:

> It is a central feature of Parliament, however, that it performs a responsive rather than initiating function within the constitution. The government – at different levels – initiates policy, formulates its policy on legislation and other proposals, exercises powers under the prerogative or granted by statute and, in all these aspects, performs the governing role in the state. Both Houses of Parliament spend most of their time responding, in a variety of ways, to these initiatives, proposals or executive actions. [2003, p 5]

The government, however, is not the only source of business for parliament. Much business originates from the Opposition front-bench, and from backbenchers on either side of the two Houses. The inspiration for their input is largely found in general public opinion, outside pressures or interest groups, newspapers, radio and television, and in the minds and attitudes of millions of citizens represented in the Commons by Members.

Parliament therefore finds itself the recipient of a wide range of external pressures and proposals, broadly divided in origin between the government of the day on the one hand and the outside world – the public – on the other.

Professor Finer (1958) labels the forces external to parliament which have an impact on its working as the 'anonymous empire'. Finer is here referring to all those individuals and organisations, lobby groups and interest groups whose aim is to influence the content of legislation. Finer claims that the detailed programme of government legislation 'owes a great deal to sectional groups'. Amongst these groups we can include such organisations as the Confederation of British Industry, Trades Union Congress, National Farmers' Union, National Union of Teachers, British Medical Association and Law Society, each of which is engaged in promoting its own sectional interests. Other pressure groups pursue particular causes: for example, the Royal Society for the Prevention of Cruelty to Animals, JUSTICE (the International Commission of Jurists), Howard League for Penal Reform, Friends of the Earth (environmental issues), and Shelter (housing).

In addition to these and many other groups, the law reform bodies provide a source of legislation. The Law Commission, established under the Law Commissions Act 1965, is under a duty to keep the law under review with a view

---

7   Eg, Guidance to Local Authorities on the Provision of Sites for Gypsies under the Caravan Sites Act 1968; Guidance on Allocation of Local Authority Housing under the Housing Act 1985. See Baldwin and Houghton, 1986; Ganz, 1987.

to its systematic development and reform, including codification of law, and simplification and modernisation of law. If we take, by way of example, the Law Commission's work on family law, the Commission has reviewed the law of legitimacy, custody, wardship, divorce, domestic violence and occupation of the matrimonial home. In conjunction with inter-departmental committees, the Law Commission has also been engaged in a comprehensive review of adoption law.

Commissions of inquiry may be established by the government to examine and report on particular issues, often culminating in a change in the law. For example, the Committee of Inquiry into Child Abuse in Cleveland resulted (in part) in changes implemented in the Children Act 1989 which represented a major overhaul of the law relating to children. The Criminal Law Revision Committee has examined the law relating, *inter alia*, to conspiracy, contempt, arrest and detention, and criminal deception.

Each of these sources may result in proposals for changes in the law. The success of these proposals in terms of becoming law is largely dependent upon the government of the day and its willingness to provide parliamentary time for the consideration of Bills. In any parliamentary session, approximately 50–60 Bills will be introduced, the vast majority of which will reach the statute book.

The preparation of a Bill

Once the government has decided to implement a particular measure, the aims of government must be translated effectively into language which will achieve those objectives. That task is entrusted to parliamentary draftsmen, or parliamentary counsel, attached to the Management and Personnel Office of the Treasury.[8] Drafting involves five stages: understanding, analysis, design, composition and revision.[9] Once a draft Bill is in being, it is examined by the Cabinet Home Affairs Committee before being formally submitted to parliament for scrutiny and enactment.

The structure of a Bill

Each Bill has a short title, for example, the Transport Bill, which indicates the general area of policy involved, together with a long title which summarises the main objectives of the Bill. The Bill is made up of Chapters or Parts which encompass groups of related clauses, and Schedules which contain details supplementary to the primary clauses. The Bill may grant powers to make delegated legislation to ministers or other specified bodies, such as local authorities. There is, necessarily, no uniformity as to the length of Bills, which may range from one clause (Abortion Amendment Bill 1988–89) to 27 Parts, 747 clauses and 25 Schedules (Companies Bill 1985).

---

8   SI 1981/1670.
9   Thornton, 1987, pp 116–17.

Pre-legislative scrutiny

In order to improve the quality of legislation, governments increasingly publish draft Bills for consideration before the Bill is presented in its proposed final form. Since 1997 there has been an increasing use of select committees to scrutinise draft Bills before they are formally presented to Parliament. As will be seen from the discussion in Chapter 16, select committees (unlike normal Standing Committees which examine Bills) have the power to call witnesses and consider documentary evidence. This form of pre-legislative scrutiny enables specialist individuals and groups to contribute to the legislative process and thereby improve the quality of legislation.

Pre-legislative scrutiny may be undertaken by a departmental select committee, a specially convened Committee or a Joint Committee comprising members of both the House of Commons and House of Lords.

The Joint Committee on Human Rights

The Joint Committee on Human Rights comprises six members of the House of Commons and six members of the House of Lords. The Committee examines every Bill which is presented to Parliament with a view to ensuring that the Bill is compatible with human rights.[10] It also examines Draft Bills which have been published for consultation prior to being formally presented to Parliament. The Committee reports to both Houses of Parliament. In 2003 the Committee was critical of the Anti-social Behaviour Bill. The Bill contained a clause amending section 16 of the Public Order Act 1986, which enables the police to impose conditions on public assemblies where the assembly consists of only two – rather than 20 – people. The Committee pointed out that the purpose of section 14 of the 1986 Act was to allow the police to prevent serious public disorder caused by large groups of people: part of that rationale would be lost if conditions could be imposed on only two people. The risk would be that Articles 10 (freedom of expression) and 11 (freedom of peaceful assembly) of the European Convention on Human Rights would be violated if the conditions were not imposed for legitimate purposes and were not proportionate.

The legislative stages: Public Bills

First reading

A Bill which is to be introduced will appear on the Order Paper of the relevant day. The Bill will be presented in 'dummy form' and is deemed to be read a 'first time'. Alternatively, a Bill may be introduced on order of the House, or after having been sent to the Commons following its passage by the House of Lords. Following the purely formal introduction into parliament, a date will be set for second reading and the Bill will be printed and published.

---

10 As guaranteed under the European Convention on Human Rights, now enforceable in the domestic courts by virtue of the Human Rights Act 1998.

Second reading

It is at the second reading that a Bill will receive first in-depth scrutiny. The scrutiny occurs in the form of a debate, generally on the floor of the House, and is confined to matters of principle rather than detail. Exceptionally, the second reading debate may be referred to a committee for consideration, but may only be so referred if 20 or more Members of Parliament do not object and, accordingly, the procedure is reserved for non-controversial matters and not measures 'involving large questions of policy nor likely to give rise to differences on party lines'.[11] Where a Bill has been committed to a second reading committee, the committee considers the principles of the Bill, but the vote on the Bill is taken on the floor of the House. It is at second reading stage that the minister in charge of the Bill must explain and defend the contents of the Bill. The Opposition's task is to probe and question and set out reasons for opposing the Bill. It should not be assumed that the Opposition invariably opposes Bills. In many instances the proposed legislation is uncontroversial and may even be welcomed by the Opposition. The Dangerous Dogs Bill and the Child Support Bill 1990 are illustrations of this phenomenon. If the Bill is opposed, a vote will take place which determines the fate of the Bill. If the vote is lost, the Bill is rejected and the proposed legislation must either be abandoned or the Bill must be reintroduced at a later date.

Once a Bill has successfully completed the second reading stage, it 'stands committed' to a standing committee, unless, exceptionally, the House orders otherwise.[12] Public Bills which are to give effect to proposals contained in a report by either of the Law Commissions, other than a Private Members' Bill or a Consolidation Bill, when set down for second reading will be committed to a second reading committee, unless the House orders otherwise, or the Bill is referred to the Northern Ireland, Scottish or Welsh Grand Committee. If a minister of the Crown moves a motion that a Bill not be referred to a second reading committee, the House will vote on the motion.

Committee stage

Once the second reading has taken place, Bills are sent to a committee for further and detailed consideration. Committee stage may be undertaken by:

- Standing Committee: this is the automatic procedure unless the Commons orders otherwise;
- Committee of the whole House: this is reserved for Bills of constitutional importance. The Human Rights Bill and Northern Ireland, Scotland and Wales devolution Bills were considered by the whole House;
- Committee of the whole House for some parts of the Bill with the remainder being sent to Standing Committee. The Greater London Authority Bill was considered in this way;

---

11 *First Report Select Committee on Procedure*, HC 149 (1964–65), London: HMSO, para 3.
12 In the 2000–01 session, six Bills were considered by a Committee of the Whole House.

- Select Committee;
- Special Standing Committee;
- Joint Committee of both Houses.[13]

Standing committees are designed to scrutinise Bills in detail. The name is in fact a misnomer, for it implies that these are permanent committees, whereas in fact they are not. The committee will be established for the purpose of examining a particular Bill and will then stand down, a feature which, as will be seen, may have implications for the adequacy of scrutiny.

At any one time, there will be eight to ten standing committees in operation. Committees may comprise between 16 and 50 Members of Parliament, and normally between 18 and 25.[14] Membership is drawn from Members of Parliament from all political parties and is proportionate to the overall strength of the party in the House, thus the larger the government's majority in the House, the larger its majority in the standing committee. Appointments are made by a Committee of Selection who will take advice from party whips as to appropriate Members. The Speaker of the House appoints the Chairman of the standing committee, who may be a Member of either side of the House (government or Opposition). Once selected, the Chairman is impartial and enjoys the same powers as the Speaker of the House in relation to selection of amendments for discussion and imposition of the Closure Motion (see further below, p 392).

The function of the standing committee is to examine the Bill clause by clause. The minister in charge of the Bill has the task of steering it successfully through committee, aided by his Parliamentary Private Secretary and civil servants. Amendments may be proposed by Members giving notice to the Public Bill Office of the House of Commons. These amendments may take the form of linguistic details, adding or subtracting a word here or there; alternatively, amendments may be of major substance. Once the clauses of the Bill have been considered, the committee moves to consider any proposed new clauses. Proposals for amendment may be ruled out of order if they are irrelevant, beyond the scope of the Bill, conflict with other proposed amendments, conflict with the principle of the Bill, or are unintelligible, ineffective, vague or spurious.[15]

The proceedings in standing committee are formal and ritualistic. A Member moves an amendment, the minister responds, the Opposition speaks, other Members comment, and debate continues until a decision on a clause – 'that the clause do stand part of the Bill' – is reached. The minister's task is to ensure a smooth passage for the Bill in the fastest possible time. Richard Crossman, Minister of Housing and Local Government in the Labour government of 1974, commented that committee stage is tedious with the minister 'being pinned to the wall' throughout the process.[16] For the most part, deliberations will follow party political lines, and it follows that, provided the government has a majority on the committee, the chances of successfully moving amendments are slight.

---

13 See Griffith and Ryle, 2003, 6-128 – 6-129.
14 Complex Bills may warrant a larger committee membership, as with the Finance Bill 1992.
15 See Erskine May, 1997; Griffith and Ryle, 2003.
16 Crossman, 1977.

The low success rate of backbench proposals for amendment should not be given disproportionate weight. It has been seen above that Standing Orders set out a number of 'inadmissible' categories of proposed amendments. It must also be noted that Members may put forward amendments solely with a view to gaining a clearer picture of the Bill, or for more spurious reasons, such as delaying a Bill or embarrassing the government. Equally, it should be remembered that the composition of the committee reflects that of the House overall: governments with a firm majority will inevitably suffer fewer defeats in committee. Finally, recognition must be given to the fact that the government has gained a mandate in a general election and, whether or not a specific legislative proposal stems from that mandate, the government has a legitimate expectation of getting its legislative programme on the statute book. Equally, the principle of the Bill has been approved on second reading by the House. While parliament as a whole, through its representative committee, has the equally legitimate expectation of being able to give adequate scrutiny to government proposals, that should not necessarily be understood to mean that standing committees should expect to be able to force their views on government.

That said, there have long been criticisms of the effectiveness of standing committees. It has been noted above that the minister in charge of the Bill, together with his civil service advisers, steers the Bill through committee. Any minister not totally in charge of his subject matter will have a short ministerial career, and it is essential that the minister should have a command of his subject and the necessary advice to hand to fend off Opposition attacks. It is inevitable, therefore, that there will be a disparity of information and expertise between the minister and other members of the committee, and that this will affect the adequacy of scrutiny. Further, the shortcomings of standing committees may be exacerbated by their non-specialist composition.

At first sight, it appears anomalous that there is no standing committee system organised on specialist lines. There is a *prima facie* case for committees to be geared to particular subjects, or groups of subjects. On this reasoning, a standing committee could be devised with the remit to consider transport matters, another to consider science and technology Bills, another to consider environmental issues, and so on. If such committees were appointed for the life of the parliament, or for a parliamentary session with Members appointed on the basis of their expertise and interests, the potential for improved scrutiny would be enhanced. However, there is a counter-argument to this. A specialist semi-permanent committee, while having the benefit of expertise, would lose the quality of the assortment of interests which is currently brought to bear on proposals. Members of the committee might become too familiar with each others' attitudes, and ministers and the committee could suffer from becoming inward looking and overly concerned with one subject at the expense of others. Committees are open to the public and their proceedings are recorded in the Official Report of the House, *Hansard*. For debate to become too narrow and technical might disadvantage other Members and the public in their capacity to understand proceedings.

One recognised shortcoming in standing committee procedure is the lack of power to send for 'persons and papers', in other words, witnesses and documents. For Members who are not specialists in the subject matter or in statutory drafting and interpretation, the task of understanding the content of a complex Bill, its implications for other aspects of the law and the relationship between various Parts and Clauses can be daunting. The Procedure Committee[17] examined this perceived difficulty and recommended that a hybrid committee – a Special Standing Committee – displaying the normal features of a standing committee but adopting some of the procedures and powers of select committees be introduced. A Standing Order, passed by the House in 1986, provides that within the first 28 days of a Bill being committed to the Special Standing Committee, written and oral evidence may be taken. A further committee sitting can be devoted to debate on the evidence given to the committee. At this preliminary stage, the committee is acting as a Committee of Inquiry, attempting to see the Bill in its entirety and to evaluate its substance and implications. Following the inquiry period, the committee reverts to ordinary standing committee procedure. In the experimental period from 1980–85, only five Bills were committed to Special Standing Committees. In 1985 in debate, the Leader of the House, Mr John Biffen, reported that the views of ministers on the new procedure were mixed, some finding it helpful, others considering it irksome. In light of the pressure on parliamentary time and the reluctance of ministers to be 'tied up' in committee proceedings, it is unlikely that Special Standing Committees will become the standard form of procedure for the scrutiny of Bills.

Other Bills may be referred to Second Reading Committees, under the procedure outlined above. Neither major nor controversial Bills are referred to Second Reading Committees. Many of these Bills will already have passed through the House of Lords.

Report stage[18]

Once the Bill has been considered in standing committee, the Bill is reported back to the House of Commons as a whole. If amendments have been made in committee, the Bill will be reprinted. Further amendments may be introduced at this stage, but the Speaker will be careful to avoid repetition of the debate in standing committee, so any proposed amendments previously considered will be rejected. The Speaker will accept amendments proposed by the government, proposals representing a compromise and amendments relating to new developments. Generally, the debate at this stage will be brief but, again, this will depend on the importance of the Bill. The Police and Criminal Evidence Bill, for example, was debated for eighteen and a half hours at report stage. Approximately nine per cent of time on the floor of the House is taken up with report.

---

17 See Chapter 16.
18 See Griffith and Ryle, 2003.

Third reading

Third reading represents the last chance for the House of Commons to examine a Bill before it is passed to the House of Lords. At this stage, the Bill cannot be amended, other than to correct small mistakes such as grammatical or printing errors. A Bill may pass through the report and third reading stages at the same time.

PRIVATE MEMBERS' BILLS[19]

Introducing a Private Member's Bill

In addition to Public (and Private and Hybrid) Bills, a number of legislative proposals will be introduced by individual Members of Parliament. In any one session, dozens of Private Members' Bills will be introduced, a minority of which will reach the statute book.

The success of a Private Member's Bill is largely dependent upon it receiving government support. As has been seen in Chapter 14, the government controls the parliamentary timetable, and dominates parliamentary business. Since only six Fridays per session are allocated for consideration of Private Members' Bills, it will be necessary for the government to make additional time for the completion of its parliamentary stages. Whether or not the government is willing to do this will depend upon the political support which the Bill acquires. However, even if a Bill does not successfully pass all its legislative stages, it may have served the useful purpose of heightening parliamentary and public awareness of a particular issue. For example, the Rt Hon Tony Benn MP introduced Private Member's Bills, *inter alia*, on placing the royal prerogative on a statutory basis,[20] and for enacting a written constitution.[21] Neither of these succeeded, but they represent matters in which there is widespread interest.

A Private Member's Bill may be introduced in one of four ways. The first procedure is that of the ballot.

Introduction by ballot

The House will agree, early in the session, for days to be appointed for the purpose of the ballot. Members of Parliament may put their names on the ballot paper on that day. Over 400 Members normally enter the ballot, although many will have no specific proposed legislation in mind. Twenty Members will be successful at the ballot. If successful, the Member must then, within nine days, table the subject matter for his or her Bill. Six Fridays per session are allocated to Private Members' Bills, on which days the Bills take precedence over other parliamentary business.

---

19 See Marsh and Read, 1988.
20 Crown Prerogatives (House of Commons Control) Bill 1988–89.
21 Commonwealth of Britain Bill.

Introduction under Standing Order procedure

Any Member may present a Bill under this procedure by placing the long and short title of the Bill on the Order Paper of the House. The Bill will not be considered, but simply be deemed to have received a first reading and a date set for second reading.

Introduction under the 'Ten Minute Rule'

A Member may give notice of a motion for leave to introduce a Bill. The motions will be considered at specific times allotted by the House, which permits the Member to raise an issue after Question Time on Tuesdays and Wednesdays, thus guaranteeing media attention.[22] Several rules apply. The Member may give one notice at any one time. No notice may be given for leave to bring in a Bill which relates to taxation or expenditure, or to bring in a Bill which covers matters which are substantially the same as those contained in Bills on which the House has already reached a decision in that session.

'Ordinary presentation' of a Bill

Every Member is permitted to introduce a Bill after having given notice. These Bills, however, are not presented until after the Ballot Bills have been presented and put down for second reading. They therefore have little chance of success. Nor do they enjoy the publicity given to Bills introduced under the Ten Minute Rule.

Introduction of a Bill after consideration in the House of Lords

Most Private Members' Bills are introduced in the House of Commons, but a small number in each session may have started their parliamentary life in the Lords. If the Bill passes the Lords, it then comes to the Commons. However, Bills introduced in the Lords are considered only after Bills introduced in the Commons and, accordingly, given the severe time constraints, few are likely even to receive a second reading in the Commons.

'Carry-over' of Bills

It has been noted above the Bills which do not pass all legislative stages within one session will lapse and have to be reintroduced in the following session.[23] In order to avoid duplication of effort and time wastage, the House of Commons agreed[24] that government Bills could be carried over from one session to the next. In 2002 the Commons approved a recommendation that no Bill should be carried over more than once.[25]

---

22 Usually, on Tuesdays or Wednesdays before the start of public business.
23 There are two exceptions to this rule: Bills passed under the Parliament Acts and Private Bills. These may be suspended in one session and revived in the next.
24 Following the recommendation of the Modernisation Committee: Third Report, *Carry-over of Public Bills*, HC 543 of 1997–98.
25 See Standing Order No 80A.

Curtailing debate on legislative proposals

As a result of the pressure on parliamentary time, and the need for a Bill to pass through all its legislative stages in a single session, procedures exist to limit consideration of a Bill.

Closure Motions

The Closure Motion, introduced in 1881, is a means of stopping debate, usually by agreement between government and Opposition, in order to ensure that debates end at times agreed by the parties. The closure can be used in debate on the floor of the House or in standing committee. It is an instrument of control, and one which is used sparingly: rarely will it be used without agreement. In the 1987–88 session, however (a long session), it was used 20 times without inter-party agreement.

In terms of procedure, the motion for closure is put to the Speaker who has discretion whether or not to accept the motion. In addition, at least 100 Members of Parliament must vote in favour of closure.

Selection of amendments

This device is confined to legislative proposals and enables the procedure to be streamlined by the selection of amendments for discussion.

The Allocation of Time Motion

The most extreme form of control is the Allocation of Time Motion, colloquially called the Guillotine Motion, introduced in its present form in 1887. Erskine May (1997) describes Guillotine Motions as representing:

> ... the extreme limit to which procedure goes in affirming the rights of the majority at the expense of the minorities of the House, and it cannot be denied that they are capable of being used in such a way as to upset the balance, generally so carefully preserved, between the claims of business, and the rights of debate.

The device, if approved by the House, enables the government to set a date by which a Bill is to be reported from standing committee to the House, or a date for third reading. If the government puts forward a motion for an Allocation of Time, Standing Orders provide that a debate of up to three hours may take place (which may be extended), unless otherwise proposed in the motion or decided by the Business Committee of the House. Once agreed, the Business Committee of the House, or a business sub-committee of the Standing Committee will determine how many scrutiny sessions are to be held and the date by which the next procedural stage must be accomplished.

In respect of many Bills, the guillotine will be applied more than once, and can apply to any stage of the legislative process. The Dangerous Dogs Bill 1990–91, for example, regarded by the government as an urgent matter, was guillotined twice with the effect that the second reading debate, the committee stage, report and third reading and the consideration of amendments from the House of Lords were all subject to strict time limits. Between 1881 and 1921, 36 Bills were guillotined, between 1921 and 1945, 30. In the 1998–99 session, 12 Bills were subject to the Allocation of Time Motion. The statistics for the 2001–02 session combine the use of the Allocation of Time Motion and the Programme Motion (on which see below). Guillotine or Programme Motions were used 55 times on 23 Bills during the session.[26]

For the most part, the Guillotine Motion is used sparingly and will generally be applied only after a considerable amount of time has been spent on the Bill in committee and the government is at risk of losing the Bill altogether.[27] For example, the Housing Bill of 1979–80 and the Social Security Bill of 1985–86 had both spent over 100 hours in committee before the Allocation of Time Motion was moved. Moreover, the Police and Criminal Evidence Bill 1983–84 had no guillotine applied despite having 59 sittings in standing committee.

If the government chooses to move an Allocation of Time Motion, it is a rare occurrence for it to lose the vote. In 1977, the Labour government moved an Allocation of Time Motion on the Scotland and Wales Bill 1976–77 but, following a six hour debate, the vote was lost by 312 votes to 283 and the government withdrew the Bill.

The use of the guillotine procedure undeniably limits the effectiveness of parliamentary scrutiny of Bills and may result in Bills leaving the House of Commons with significant portions unexamined. This point must be borne in mind when assessing the role and value of the House of Lords in the legislative process.

Programming of Bills

In the 2000–01 session, Orders of the House provided that Programme Motions should be employed to facilitate efficiency in the legislative process. The Modernisation Committee stated that the basic requirements of the reformed system were to ensure that the government gets its legislation through in a reasonable time while allowing Members to have a full opportunity to debate and propose amendments. Further, it was essential that all parts of the Bill be properly considered, and that there should be an improvement in the preparation of Bills so as to reduce the need for amendments.[28]

A motion (request) for a Programme Order is moved directly after the second reading debate and sets out timetabling for further stages in the Commons. Since their introduction, Programme Orders have become a regular feature of the process, replacing Guillotine Motions which are now reserved for the most difficult cases of delay through obstruction by the opposition.[29]

---

26 See the Second Report of the Modernisation Committee, HC 589, 2000, London: The Stationery Office.
27 See Griffith and Ryle, 2003, Chapter 7.
28 See Standing Order No. 83A.
29 In the 2002–03 session a total of 71 Programming Orders were made, with only three Guillotine Motions.

DELEGATED LEGISLATION

The picture of the law making process would be incomplete without a consideration of delegated, or subordinate, legislation.

In 1972, Parliament's Joint Committee on Delegated Legislation described subordinate legislation as covering 'every exercise of power to legislate conferred by or under an Act of Parliament'.[30] Some examples will make the scope of delegated legislation clearer. Delegated legislation may be made by:

(a) *ministers*, in the form of rules and regulations which supplement the provisions of an Act of Parliament;

(b) *local authorities*, in the form of bylaws to regulate their locality according to particular localised needs;

(c) *public bodies*, in the form of rules and regulations. Such bodies include the British Airways Authority, the British Railways Board and the Nature Conservancy Council;

(d) *judges*, in the form of rules of court made under the authority of section 75 of the Supreme Court Act 1981;

(e) *government departments*, in the form of codes of practice, circulars and guidance. These do not contain legal rules, but have a substantive effect on the manner in which the legal rules operate;

(f) *the House of Commons*, in the form of Resolutions of the House. The Provisional Collection of Taxes Act 1968 makes possible the lawful imposition and collection of taxation between the Budget speech and the enactment of the Finance Bill in July/August. Whereas normal Resolutions of the House do not have the force of law, Resolutions enabling the impositions and collections of taxation – being authorised by statute – have legal effect.

The volume of delegated legislation also reveals its importance as a source of law. In any parliamentary year, between 1,500 and 3,000 pieces of delegated legislation will be approved.

The use of delegated law making power is not a purely modern phenomenon, arising from increasing legal regulation of all aspects of life. The power to make subordinate legislation was exercised as early as the sixteenth century.[31] The increase in the volume of delegated legislation derives from the early nineteenth century.

Delegated legislation raises questions about the supremacy of parliament. In *The New Despotism* (1929), Hewart CJ argued that the increased use of delegated legislation, particularly during the First World War under the Defence of the Realm Act 1914, amounted to an effective usurpation of the sovereign law making powers of parliament. Such criticisms led to the appointment, in 1929, of a committee of inquiry[32] to consider the powers exercised by ministers by way of

---

30 *Report of the Joint Committee on Delegated Legislation,* HL 184, HC 475, 1971–72, London: HMSO, para 6.

31 Statute of Proclamations 1539 (31 Hen 8 c 26); and see Allen, 1965.

32 The Donoughmore-Scott Committee.

delegated legislation and to report on safeguards that were desirable or necessary to secure the constitutional principles of the sovereignty of parliament and the supremacy of the law.

The committee's report,[33] while recognising the need for improved parliamentary scrutiny of delegated legislation, nevertheless emphasised its necessity in terms of legislative efficiency. It is efficiency which is the principal justification for the delegation of law making power. Put simply, parliament, as currently constituted, struggles to give adequate scrutiny to primary legislation. To burden parliament with the task of scrutinising every detail of legislation would overload the parliamentary timetable to the extent that the system would break under the strain. A related justification for delegated power lies in the need to supplement or amend the primary rules in light of new developments. Delegated legislation enables the fine tuning of the primary rules to take place, without encumbering parliament as a whole. Further, it may be that the government is clear as to the broad policy to be pursued under an Act, and as to the primary legal rules necessary to achieve a particular goal. There may be less certainty as to the technical, detailed rules necessary: the delegation of law making power enables such rules to be worked out, often in consultation with specialist interest groups outside parliament.

The justifications for subordinate legislation can hold good only if the powers granted are sufficiently clear and precise as to be adjudicated upon by the courts by way of judicial review[34] and if the parliamentary scrutiny accorded to it is adequate.

Under the doctrine of parliamentary sovereignty, the validity of Acts of Parliament cannot be questioned.[35] Subordinate legislation, however, can be reviewed, provided that the jurisdiction of the courts has not been excluded – or 'ousted' – in order to determine its compatibility with the enabling Act. Such exclusion of review is rare and, to ensure immunity from review, the exclusion clause would have to be unambiguous on the face of the parent Act. Of equal importance to the possibility of successful challenge in the courts is the breadth of discretion conferred on the delegate by the Act. If a statute conferred powers on a minister to make regulations 'whenever the minister thinks fit' or (say) to award compensation for injury 'under circumstances to be determined by the minister', the grant of discretion is so wide as to be virtually unreviewable by the courts. Also important is that delegated legislation should not impose retrospective liability on citizens, or be so vague as to be unintelligible. Further, it is necessary that the power granted is conferred on an identifiable delegate in order that the exercise of power be challengeable. On this latter point, the Emergency Powers Act 1939 provided for differing levels of delegation. The Act provided that regulations might empower any authority on persons to make orders, rules and bylaws, for any of the purposes for which the Defence Regulations might themselves be made. Ministerial orders were issued under the regulations,

---

33 *Report on Ministers' Powers*, Cmnd 4060, 1932, London: HMSO.
34 See Chapters 26 and 27.
35 *Pickin v British Railways Board* (1974). See Chapter 7.

directions issued under the regulations and licences issued under the directions. Such subdelegation breaches the rule that a person or body to whom powers are entrusted may not delegate them to another, *'delegatus non potest delegare'*.

The Statutory Instruments Act 1946

The vast majority of delegated legislation is in the form of statutory instruments governed by the Statutory Instruments Act 1946. Section 1 provides that where any Act confers power on His Majesty in Council or on any minister of the Crown, where that power is expressed as a power exercisable by Order in Council or by statutory instrument, the provisions of the Act apply.

Parliamentary scrutiny of delegated legislation[36]

The Statutory Instruments Act 1946 lays down the means by which an instrument may come into effect, but the method adopted will depend on that which is stipulated in the particular enabling Act. First, the parent Act may provide that the instrument be laid before parliament[37] but that no parliamentary action is needed. Secondly, the parent Act may provide that the instrument is subject to the 'negative resolution procedure'.[38] Under this procedure, the instrument can be laid before parliament in its final form and come into immediate effect subject only to there being a successful move to annul the instrument. This move takes the form of a motion, known here as a 'prayer' for annulment of the instrument, which can be made within 40 days of the instrument being laid. Thirdly, the enabling Act may stipulate that the instrument be laid in draft form and that it will come into effect only if a prayer for annulment is not moved successfully. The Statutory Instruments Act also provides for an 'affirmative resolution procedure'. If this is adopted, the instrument may either come into immediate effect, subject to subsequent approval by parliament, or be laid in draft form to come into effect if approved by parliament.

The choice of the procedure to be adopted lies with the government. The problem posed for parliament is again one of time and opportunity. The affirmative resolution procedure is rarely adopted by government; the negative resolution procedure requires that Members of Parliament must be vigilant and astute if they (usually the Opposition) are to be aware that a particular instrument has been laid and are to be able to move a prayer for annulment within the 40 day period. Instruments made under the European Communities Act 1972 to give effect to Community law may be subject to either the affirmative or negative procedure.

Since 1994–95, instruments subject to affirmative resolution are automatically referred to a standing committee, unless the House orders otherwise. Instruments subject to the negative resolution procedure, to which a prayer has been tabled, may be referred to a standing committee on a Motion by a minister of the Crown.

---

36 See Beith, 1981; Hayhurst, and Wallington, 1988; Hansard Society, 1993, Annex A.
37 Statutory Instruments Act 1946, s 4.
38 *Ibid*, s 5.

Supplementing the above scrutiny methods is the Joint Select Committee on Delegated Legislation The Joint Committee comprises seven Members of the House of Commons and seven Members of the House of Lords, and is chaired by a member of the House of Commons. The committee is charged with examining all instruments laid before parliament and those instruments for which there is no laying requirement. The grounds on which the committee will report to parliament are:

(a) that the instrument imposes a tax or charge;

(b) that the parent Act excludes review by the courts;

(c) that the instrument is to operate retrospectively;

(d) that there has been unjustifiable delay in publication or laying;

(e) that the instrument has come into effect in contravention of the rules of notice to the House;

(f) that there is doubt as to whether the instrument is *intra vires*;

(g) that the instrument requires clarification;

(h) that the instrument's drafting is defective.

The committee examines over 1,000 instruments per session. Less than one per cent are reported to parliament and few are debated. The strength of the committee's work lies not in its reports to parliament and any consequent action but rather in its scrutiny of instruments and drawing the relevant government department's attention to defects in instruments.[39]

The Regulatory Reform Act 2001 (formerly the Deregulation and Contracting Out Act 1994) introduced a new form of delegated legislation which is scrutinised by the committee. Under the Act, a minister may issue a Regulatory Reform Order to amend or repeal any enactment of primary legislation with a view to removing or reducing any unnecessary administrative or bureaucratic element. The aim is towards greater efficiency in trade, business and the professions. The power is exercisable provided that no necessary protection is removed from the law. The 1994 Act provided for parliamentary scrutiny. The two-stage process involves, first, the proposal being laid before parliament as a draft order. The Lords' committee and the House of Commons equivalent committee have 60 days in which to report. Secondly, the government then lays a draft order before parliament, either in its original form or amended to take account of the two committees' opinions, for approval by a resolution of each House. The House of Lords can only approve the draft order after the committee has made a second report on the order.

The committee is concerned with four principal matters. First, whether the measure is intra vires; secondly, that the measure removes the relevant administrative burden; thirdly, whether the order removes any required 'necessary protection'; and, fourthly, whether the consultation required under the Act has been adequate. The committee takes oral and written evidence. In

---

39 The House of Lords' Scrutiny Committee for delegated legislation is discussed in Chapter 17. On delegated legislation and the Human Rights Act 1998, see Chapter 19.

January 2006 the government introduced the Legislative and Regulatory Reform Bill, which if passed will significantly alter the balance of power between the legislature and the executive, allowing ministers to amend Acts of Parliament. See further Chapter 5.

The grant of power to ministers to amend primary legislation is known as a 'Henry VIII power': the power to change the law without parliamentary action. These powers have become increasingly common and create concerns over the separation of powers and the reduction in parliamentary control.[40] The Legislative and Regulatory Reform Bill 2006 represents an extension of this form of power. The power will replace the power in the Regulatory Reform Act 2001 and sets out the type of provision that can be made, the conditions and restrictions on the power, and the procedure to be followed.[41] While the Bill is intended to simplify deregulation, the Bill confers unnecessary broad powers. Clause 1 provides that:

> A Minister of the Crown may be order make provision for either or both of the following purposes: (a) reforming legislation; (b) implementing recommendations of any one or more of the United Kingdom Law Commissions, with or without changes.

The only stipulated restrictions relate to taxation and the creation of new criminal offences carrying defined penalties. Nothing in the Bill appears to restrict the government from amending the provisions of the Bill itself.

FINANCIAL PROCEDURES IN THE HOUSE OF COMMONS

Any evaluation of parliament's role and the legislative process must incorporate discussion of the extent to which, and means by which, parliament controls national finance, in terms of both taxation and expenditure. In part, this topic requires consideration in relation to both the legislative process and the scrutiny of the executive.

From a constitutional standpoint, the control over expenditure may be viewed as control over the government of the day and its policies. As WE Gladstone[42] remarked, 'expenditure flows from policy – to control expenditure one must control policy'. Constitutionally, therefore, parliament's role in relation to spending is but one part of its wider role of scrutinising and calling the government to account. Hence, general debates, Question Time, and select committees are all germane to this matter.

Expenditure (supply)

Historically, the need to summon parliament arose from the financial needs of the Crown.[43] The authority of the House of Commons sprang from, and is based on, its power to approve both the raising of taxation and expenditure. The governing

---

40 The European Communities Act 1972 and the Human Rights Act 1998 both contain examples of Henry VIII powers.
41 See *Review of the Regulatory Reform Act 2001*, London: Cabinet Office, 2005.
42 Prime Minister 1868–74; 1880–85; 1886; 1892–94.
43 See Chapters 6 and 7 on the historic struggles between Crown and parliament.

maxim was, and remains, that 'the Crown demands, the Commons grant and the Lords assent to the grant of monies'.[44] The Bill of Rights 1689, Article IV, declared that raising money for the use of the Crown without Parliament's consent was unlawful.

Nowadays, for the 'Crown', must be inserted 'Ministers of the Crown'. Two propositions flow from this situation. First, that all charges – that is, proposals for the expenditure of monies – must be demanded by the Crown before they can be considered by parliament. The demand for approval of monies comes today from ministers, not backbenchers. Secondly, all charges must be considered by the House of Commons before they are approved. The proposals for charges come before the House in the form of resolutions which, once approved, must be embodied in legislation originating in the House of Commons but approved by both Houses.[45]

National revenue to cover the cost of government is derived from three main sources: taxation, borrowing and revenue from Crown lands. All revenue, of whatever kind, is credited to the Exchequer Account at the Bank of England in the form of the Consolidated Fund. All withdrawals must be authorised by statute. Under the Consolidated Fund Acts, approximately one-third of expenditure is authorised in permanent form and does not require annual parliamentary approval. Charges which are immune from this scrutiny are those payments for service which it is deemed should not be constantly drawn into the political arena for debate. For example, payment of interest on the national debt, salaries of judges of superior courts, the Speaker of the House of Commons, Leader of the Opposition, Comptroller and Auditor General and Parliamentary Commissioner for Administration, and payments to meet European Community and Union obligations and the Queen's Civil List all fall under Consolidated Fund Services.

In contrast to Consolidated Fund Services are Supply Services. These cover the bulk of annual public expenditure and cover the needs of all government departments and the cost of the armed forces. Provision for Supply Services require annual approval. The following requirements must be satisfied. The government must lay before the House of Commons each year its estimates for the forthcoming financial year, in the form of resolutions. Once approved, these are translated into Bills – the Consolidated Fund Bills and Appropriation Bills. Money must be appropriated for specific purposes in the same session as that in which it is required by the government: thus, monies voted for one financial year cannot be applied to a subsequent year.

The Voting of Supply is announced in the Queen's Speech at the autumn opening of the parliamentary session: 'Members of the House of Commons, estimates for the Public Service will be laid before you.' The financial year for the purposes of national expenditure runs from 1 April to 31 March.

The Chancellor's Autumn Statement is made to parliament, preceded by preparation of estimates by each government department for the forthcoming

---

44 Erskine May, 1997, and see Standing Order No 46.
45 Subject to the Parliament Acts 1911–49.

financial year, and the Budget announced in the Spring. The timing of the Budget is not, however, fixed and may be timetabled for Spring or Autumn.

Estimates

There exist six classes of estimates.

Ordinary annual estimates

Ordinary annual estimates are the principal estimates. They set out the specific grants of money which will be required to fund the civil service, defence services, the cost of House of Commons administration and the National Audit Office. Control over the form in which estimates are presented is in the hands of the Treasury.[46] Before any change in the form of the estimates is made, approval must be obtained from the Treasury and Civil Service Committee.

Prior to estimates being settled, the Public Expenditure Survey Committee, under the responsibility of the Chief Secretary to the Treasury, will have reported on anticipated needs of departments, and settled any disagreements between departments. Its confidential report is sent to the Cabinet, which formalises expenditure plans.

Votes on account

Votes on account are designed to cover the problem caused by the lapse in time between the end of one financial year and the enactment of legislation authorising expenditure for the forthcoming year. A vote on account authorises up to 45 per cent of projected annual expenditure.

Supplementary estimates

Supplementary estimates may be presented to parliament for approval in relation to increased sums needed for a particular service, or to meet a new situation.

Excess votes

Where a department has exceeded its budget, its administration and expenditure will be audited by the Comptroller and Auditor General who reports to the House. The Committee of Public Accounts will consider the Comptroller's report on the matter, which states its approval or objection to the proposed excess vote. If the Public Accounts Committee approves the additional expenditure, the matter is put to parliament without debate.

Votes of credit

An emergency situation – or unexpected need for supply – may give rise to an application for a vote of credit. Situations of war will give rise to such votes.[47]

---

46 Exchequer and Audit Departments Act 1866.
47 As occurred in both the First and Second World Wars.

Exceptional grants

An exceptional grant is one authorised by parliament for expenditure for some particular objective, such as State funeral expenses or the erection of memorial statues.

Following parliamentary debate and approval, the Appropriation Bill will be drafted authorising withdrawal from the Exchequer Fund. In most parliamentary sessions, three regular Consolidated Fund and Appropriation Bills (and, where necessary, extra Consolidated Fund Bills) are put to parliament for approval.

It will have been noticed that parliamentary approval for these financial Bills is 'without amendment or debate'. Thus far, there seems to be a virtual abandonment of parliament's role in assenting to the 'demands of the Crown'.

Limited time for the scrutiny of expenditure estimates is provided under Standing Orders, which provide for three days per session to be allocated for the consideration of estimates. The estimates to be considered are selected by the Liaison Committee. The estimates selected for debate will generally be those into which the select committee has inquired and reported. Amendments may be tabled, including the reduction in the estimates.

Aside from this limited opportunity, any control which parliament exercises is through the control of policy and the normal parliamentary mechanisms for the scrutiny of government policy and administration. Griffith and Ryle sum up the supply procedure as follows:

> The House has largely abandoned all opportunities for direct control of public expenditure by means of debate and vote on the estimates presented to the House. Except on the three Estimates Days, there is no opportunity to amend or negative any of the individual estimates, and the government secures formal approval for its expenditure, without debate, in three or four block votes each year. In place of formal direct control by Voting Supply, which for many years has become theoretical, the House has increasingly relied on informal indirect control through the exercise of its influence on policy, through scrutiny of policy, administration and expenditure by departmentally related select committees and by *ex post facto* scrutiny of actual spending by the Public Accounts Committee. [2003, pp 357–58]

As the Public Accounts Committee Report to the House in 1987 admits, 'Parliament's consideration of annual estimates – the key constitutional control – remains largely a formality'.[48] The Public Accounts Committee was established in 1861, for the purpose of examining accounts of departments following the submission of reports from the National Audit Office. The work of the Audit Office and the Committee and recent reforms are considered in Chapter 16.

Taxation (ways and means)

In relation to taxation – ways and means – the role of parliamentary scrutiny is rather different. The initiative in tax policies lies with the Treasury, under the political direction of the Chancellor of the Exchequer.[49]

---

48 HC 98 (1986–87), London: HMSO, para 2, cited in Griffith and Ryle, 2003.
49 Nominally, the Prime Minister as First Lord of the Treasury.

The starting point for the annual cycle is the Chancellor's Budget in the Spring or Autumn wherein, as Erskine May points out, 'the Chancellor develops his views of the resources of the country, communicates his calculations of probable income and expenditure and declares whether the burdens upon the people are to be increased or diminished'.

The Budget[50]

The Budget is the annual statement of tax proposals for the forthcoming year, together with the government's expenditure plans for the following three years. At the end of the Budget speech, the ways and means resolutions are tabled. These resolutions form the basis for the main debate on the Budget, which lasts for between three and five days. The Finance Bill is then introduced and, within three to four weeks, will receive its second reading. The Bill then stands committed, in part, to a Committee of the Whole House and to a standing committee. The size of the standing committee for consideration of the Finance Bill is larger than the normal composition, and will have about 30 to 40 Members. The Finance Bill in 1999–2000 illustrates scrutiny. One hundred and fifty clauses were considered in 26 Standing Committee sittings and seven clauses were considered in two days in a Committee of the Whole House.[51] Hundreds of amendments are generally proposed to Finance Bills, although not all of these will be debated.

Income tax rates are effective only until the end of the tax year and require annual renewal under the Finance Act. The authority to collect taxes expires on 5 April each year. The Finance Act becomes law in July. In *Bowles v Bank of England* (1913), the legality of taxation was considered. On 2 April 1912, the House of Commons passed a resolution approving the income tax rate for the year beginning 6 April 1912. The plaintiff had purchased stocks. The Bank deducted income tax from dividends due on 1 July at the new tax rate before the Consolidated Fund Act authorising the new rate had been passed by parliament. The plaintiff sought a declaration that the Bank was not entitled to deduct the tax until approved by parliament. Parker J stated that:

> The question for decision is, does a resolution of the House of Commons authorise the Crown to levy on the subject an income tax assented to by such resolution but not yet imposed by Act of Parliament?

> By the Statute of 1 William and Mary, usually known as the Bill of Rights, it was finally settled that there could be no taxation in this country except under the authority of Act of Parliament. The Bill of Rights remains unrepealed and no practice or custom can be relied on by the Crown as justifying any infringement of its provisions.

> It follows, therefore, that no resolution ... has any legal effect whatsoever ... Such resolutions are necessitated by parliamentary procedure and adopted with a view to the protection of the subject against the hasty imposition of taxes, and it would be strange to find them relied on as justifying the Crown in levying a tax before such tax is actually imposed by Act of Parliament.

---

50 The name derives from French: the *bougette*, or little bag.
51 Griffith and Ryle, 2003, 6–187.

Bowles v Bank of England led to the Provisional Collection of Taxes Act 1913,[52] which gives statutory authority to resolutions, as if imposed by Act of Parliament. In *Attorney General v Wilts United Dairies Ltd* (1921), the Food Controller had, under a regulation of 1919, established a pricing structure for the issue of licences for milk purchase. The company claimed that the Food Controller had no power to impose conditions of payment in granting licences and that the condition amounted to a tax, which could not be imposed without clear and distinct legal authority. Lord Justice Atkin declared that:

> ... in view of the historic struggle of the Legislature to secure to itself the sole power to levy money on its subjects, its complete success in that struggle, the elaborate means adopted by the representative House to control the amount, the conditions and purposes of the levy, the circumstances would be remarkable indeed which would induce the court to believe that the Legislature had sacrificed all the well known checks and precautions and not in express words but, by mere implication, had entrusted a Minister of the Crown with undefined and unlimited powers of imposing charges upon the subject for purposes connected with his department.

The Provisional Collection of Taxes Act 1968 requires that the resolutions passed be confirmed by the second reading of the Bill relating to the tax within 25 days of the House approving the resolution. It also provides that their statutory effect shall continue only until 5 August if passed in April or March, or for four months if passed at any other time. It is this, then, that sets the deadline for the passage of the Finance Act.

Note that the Finance Act is not usually a Money Bill for the purposes of the Parliament Act 1911, since it deals with wider matters than those listed in section 1(2) of the Act. Accordingly, unless certified by the Speaker to be a Money Bill, the Finance Bill will pass through the Lords in the usual manner. By convention, however, in relation to a Finance Bill, the House of Lords has relinquished any effective role in relation to taxation or expenditure.

SCRUTINY OF LEGISLATION BY THE HOUSE OF LORDS

Some Bills will start their life in the House of Lords and, once successfully passed in the Lords, will pass to the Commons for debate and scrutiny. Law Reform Bills, in particular, are regularly introduced in the House of Lords, under the aegis of the Lord Chancellor. The majority of Bills, however, start their parliamentary life in the Commons. Detailed consideration will be given to the House of Lords' role in legislation in Chapter 17. Note, however, that unless the Parliament Act procedure is used (which limits the role of the House of Lords in relation to legislation), Bills which have completed their passage in the Commons are passed to the House of Lords which employs, with some notable differences, the same legislative stages as the House of Commons. The House of Lords may propose amendments to Bills, the acceptance or rejection of which will be a matter for negotiation between the two Houses.

---

52 Now, Provisional Collection of Taxes Act 1968.

THE ROYAL ASSENT

Receiving the royal assent represents the final stage in the enactment of legislation. The royal assent is a prerogative act; for further discussion of this, see Chapter 6. The giving of the royal assent is not a matter which involves the Monarch personally. No monarch since 1854 has given the royal assent, although the power to do so still remains. When royal assent is required, the Lord Chancellor submits a list of Bills ready for the Assent. In the House of Lords, attended by the Commons with the Speaker, the Clerk of the Parliaments reads the title of the Bills for assent and pronounces the assent in Norman French. Once assent has been given, it is notified to each House of Parliament by the Speaker of the House.[53]

PARLIAMENT AND EUROPEAN COMMUNITY LEGISLATION

The manner in which Community law is enacted and takes effect within the United Kingdom is considered in Chapters 8 and 9. Note here that some Community legislation becomes directly applicable within the United Kingdom without any enactment by parliament. Accordingly, it is of particular importance that parliament has the opportunity to scrutinise both proposals for Community legislation and legislation which has been enacted.

In addition to periodic debates on Europe, parliament sets aside time at Question Time for European Community matters to be considered. Furthermore, ministers make regular statements to parliament concerning decisions reached in the Council of Ministers.

The House of Commons has established a select committee on European Legislation. The House of Lords also has a select committee on the European Community. Both committees consider delegated legislation which is being introduced to give effect to Community law and also scrutinise legislative proposals for future European Community law.

In addition to the select committees, the Commons has established two standing committees for the consideration of European matters. The select committee may refer such documentation to the standing committees as it thinks fit. The standing committees, comprising 13 Members, report to the House on matters referred to them.

Finally, successive governments have undertaken not to agree to important European legislative proposals until these have been considered by the committees. However, the effectiveness of these undertakings must be put in doubt by the increasing use of majority voting in the Council of Ministers, which makes it difficult for individual Member States to 'block' any proposed legislation.

---

53 Royal Assent Act 1967.

CHAPTER 16

SCRUTINY OF THE EXECUTIVE

The structure of central government, the concept of ministerial responsibility and the composition of the House of Commons are considered in Chapters 10, 11 and 14 respectively. It will be recalled that the Commons comprises Her Majesty's government, which is drawn from the political party winning the largest number of seats at a general election, government backbenchers, Her Majesty's Loyal Opposition, comprising the Leader of the Opposition and Opposition spokesmen, who comprise the shadow Cabinet, and Opposition backbenchers, and Members of other minority political parties.

In this chapter the procedures by which the House of Commons scrutinises government action are discussed. Consistent with the doctrine of responsible government, the accountability of government towards the democratic legislature is of fundamental importance in ensuring that the government acts under the law and in accordance with the principles of constitutionalism and democracy. In order to evaluate the role of parliament in ensuring compliance with these constitutional doctrines, the procedural mechanisms of the House must be examined.

QUESTION TIME[1]

Question Time in the House of Commons is one of the most publicised features of parliament and represents one of the principal means by which information is obtained from ministers by Members of Parliament and the public, and of underpinning individual ministerial responsibility.

Standing Orders provide that, on Mondays, Tuesdays and Thursdays, the period from 2.35 pm to 3.30 pm is set aside for Question Time.[2] On these days, ministers from several departments may answer Questions, appearing on a rota, determined by the government,[3] which ensures that most departments feature in Question Time at least once every three to four weeks.

The Speaker calls the first Member listed on the Order of Business. The minister then answers the question, and the Member is able to ask a supplementary question. When that has been answered, the Speaker may then call on other Members to ask their supplementary questions. The time allocated to supplementary questions is within the Speaker's discretion. Currently, about 15 to 20 questions are answered orally on each day. The effect of the supplementary is that a Member is able to pose a question for which no notice has been given.

---

1   See Chester and Bowring, 1962; Irwin, 'Opportunities for backbenchers', in Ryle and Richards, 1988; Griffith and Ryle, 2003; Franklin and Norton, 1993; Erskine May, 1997.

2   No question shall be taken after 3.30 pm, other than where the Speaker deems it to be a matter of urgency relating to matters of public importance or to the arrangement of business of the House.

3   HC Deb 898 (1975–76), London: HMSO. See Erskine May, 1997, Chapter 16.

Questions may be put to ministers for either oral or written answers.[4] Questions requiring written answers, which are to be printed in the Official Journal, are marked with a 'W' and are subdivided into those requesting a priority answer and those requesting a non-priority answer. Those questions tabled for oral answer are printed on the Order Paper of the day. Only a few of the many questions put will receive an oral reply. However, those that do not receive an oral reply will receive a written reply published in the Official Report of the House. The number of questions which an individual Member of Parliament may have pending at any one time is eight during a period of ten sitting days, and not more than two on any one day, of which not more than one may be addressed to any one minister.[5]

Question Time is not a spontaneous affair, and it should not necessarily be criticised for not being so. Members wishing to ask questions are required to give up to three sitting days' notice.[6] This time span for notice is designed to ensure both that there is adequate opportunity for ministers to prepare answers and that the issue being raised is still fresh and relevant.

Changes to Question Time agreed by the Commons and implemented in the 2002–03 session include the following:

- a limit of five written questions which may be put by a Member on any one day;
- a reduction in the number of questions for oral answer printed on the Order Paper;
- electronic tabling by Members;
- oral questions being put to junior ministers in Westminster Hall.

As an experiment, MPs may now question several ministers on policy areas for which they have overlapping responsibility. In January 2003, for example, 36 MPs questioned four ministers on youth policy: the Ministers for Home Affairs, Health, Education and Sport.

On occasion – and particularly near the end of a parliamentary session – questions may be answered in the form of 'I will write to the Honourable Member . . .' rather than receiving an oral response. Such replies have not been published in *Hansard* in the past, but placed in the House of Commons' Library for Members' use. These 'Will Writes' have attracted criticism from the Select Committee on Public Administration as being used to avoid answering questions.[7]

Prime Ministerial Question Time

Prime Minister's Question Time has been moved from the conventional 15 minute sessions on Tuesdays and Thursdays, to Wednesdays, when the Prime Minister

---

4   Standing Order No 21.
5   Erskine May, 1997, p 285.
6   The period of notice for questions to the Northern Ireland, Scottish and Welsh Secretaries of State is four working days.
7   See the Committee on Public Administration Second Special Report, HC 853. The Committee also monitors responses to requests for information under the Freedom of Information Act 2000.

answers questions for 30 minutes.[8] It is felt that more meaningful and in-depth scrutiny is facilitated by the reform.

Questions put to the Prime Minister simply request that the Prime Minister list his engagements for the day. Over 100 such questions may appear on the Order Papers; on occasions, this number has risen to over 200. The open question also avoids the possibility – given the rules of notice for questions – that a subsequent question put to the Prime Minister will be politically stale. The open question, therefore, provides a neutral peg on which to hang a supplementary, and real, question. Only two supplementary questions per Member are allowed. Supplementary questions may concern any matter for which the Prime Minister carries responsibility or matters which do not fall within any individual minister's responsibility. For example, if a question is addressed to the Prime Minister which should be addressed to the Secretary of State for Social Security, the Prime Minister will decline to answer and suggest that the matter be referred to the responsible minister. Generally, however, the issue raised will be one of general government policy in relation to matters such as the economy, unemployment, European or other international affairs. The strength of Prime Ministerial Question Time lies in the lack of notice given and the need for the Prime Minister to demonstrate his competence across the full range of government policy.

The Leader of the Opposition does not table questions for oral answer to the Prime Minister. Instead, he is entitled to ask up to six questions to the Prime Minister and may raise virtually any aspect of government policy. For the observer, this is frequently parliament at its best, providing the opportunity – for Question Time is televised – to witness the leaders of the two main political parties in oral combat. As Griffith and Ryle observe:

> ... here is experienced the direct confrontation of the Prime Minister and the Leader of the Opposition in its most concentrated and highly charged form. It is an opportunity no Leader of the Opposition can afford to neglect. It is also the occasion when the Prime Minister can be most critically tested, and various commentators or experienced observers have testified to how carefully the Prime Minister has to prepare for this ordeal. Success or failure on these occasions can greatly strengthen or seriously weaken the political standing of the two protagonists. [2003, pp 501–02]

The role of the Speaker

The rules concerning questions have been developed over time by the Speaker of the House, who is responsible for enforcing them. Only questions on matters which are directly within a minister's responsibility may be put and in addition, by convention, there exists a range of issues which may not form the subject of questions in the House. The following matters are not subject to Question Time:

(a) questions bringing the Sovereign directly before parliament, or questions reflecting on the Sovereign;

(b) questions concerning issues on which the Prime Minister has given advice to the Crown in relation to the royal prerogative: the grant of honours,

---

8   See HC Deb Vol 295 Col 349, 4 June 1997.

ecclesiastical patronage, appointment and dismissal of Privy Councillors or the dissolution of parliament;

(c) questions not relating to the individual responsibility of the relevant minister. Accordingly, questions relating to organisations under the control of authorities other than parliament (for example, the Stock Exchange, trade unions and nationalised industries) are not permitted.[9]

The following subjects are also excluded:

- local authorities and nationalised industries;
- personal powers of the Monarch;
- internal affairs of other countries;
- questions which have previously been put, or on which a minister has previously refused to answer, or to which the answer is a matter of public record;
- defence and national security;
- Cabinet business, and advice given to ministers by civil servants;
- questions seeking legal advice;
- questions which raise issues so broad as to be incapable of reply within the time constraints;
- trivial or irrelevant questions;
- questions aiming to criticise judges;
- questions on matters which are *sub judice*;
- questions posed in unparliamentary language.[10]

The volume of parliamentary questions

The volume of questions put down for oral or written answer on average amount to some 40,000 per parliamentary session. In the 2003–04 session there were 3,687 questions put down for oral answer, and 54,875 put down for written answer, a total of 59,855.[11] In the short 2004–05 session – which lasted only six months – a total of 23,730 questions were put down for oral or written answer, occupying over 10 per cent of the time in the Commons.[12] Figures such as these emphasise one of the most important functions of Question Time: the accountability of government. A superficial observation of Question Time may prompt scepticism about its value. The charge is frequently made that Question Time is no more than a theatrical occasion, with ministers fully briefed by the Civil Service giving prepared answers to questions posed within the rules relating to notice and substance. Questions are not limited to the Opposition parties and may, accordingly, come from the government's own supporters. This feature leads to the comment that questions are planted by government supporters in order to give a minister the opportunity to promote the government's views or boast

---

9   Erskine May, 1997, Chapter 16.
10 Erskine May, 1997, Chapter 17.
11 Of these, 2,206 received oral replies.
12 The session was shortened because of the 2005 General Election.

about its achievements. To exaggerate such claims would be to miss a point of prime importance about Question Time: the provision of information. Every answer given, oral or written, becomes a matter of public record, thus providing a wealth of data about the workings of government.

Urgent Questions

An Urgent Question[13] is an oral question put to a minister without the need to observe the normal rules as to notice. Standing Orders define Urgent Questions as raising matters which are: '... in the Speaker's opinion, of an urgent character, and relate either to matters of public importance or to the arrangement of business.'

Such questions enable a matter of urgency to be raised for immediate discussion in the period following Question Time. Because Urgent Questions take priority over other parliamentary business, rules provide that a Member who wishes to put such a question must give notice to the Speaker before noon on the day he seeks to put the question, and the Speaker has absolute discretion as to whether to allow or disallow the question to be put.[14] Many applications for an Urgent Question are made, but few are granted: in the 2003–04 session there were only 12.

EMERGENCY DEBATES

Under Standing Orders,[15] any Member of Parliament may apply to the Speaker to raise an urgent matter for debate.[16] If granted, the matter will be raised immediately after Question Time and private notice questions, if any. At that time, the matter is briefly introduced and a substantive three hour debate will be arranged for the following day. Because emergency debates disrupt the parliamentary timetable, they are confined to matters deemed to be of urgent national importance, and applications are sparingly granted (normally only one or two per session). In the 2003–04 session there was one unsuccessful application for an emergency debate.

DAILY ADJOURNMENT DEBATES

At the close of the parliamentary day, under Standing Orders, the opportunity is provided for backbenchers to initiate a short debate on a matter of their choosing. Competition for a debate is keen and Members take part in a ballot held in the Speaker's Office for the opportunity. If successful, the Member may speak for 15 minutes on the chosen subject and the relevant minister is given 15 minutes for reply. The subject matter for debate is as varied as are Members' interests. The

---

13 Urgent Questions were previously termed Private Notice Questions.
14 See Erskine May, 1997, p 296.
15 Dating from 1967.
16 See Erskine May, 1997, Chapter 16(3).

matter raised may be one of relevance solely to the Member's constituency or the matter may be related to a particular source of general concern.

Departments can refuse to answer a parliamentary Question if the cost of doing so exceeds the advisory cost limit of £600 for written answers. There is no such limit for oral answers. In 2005, the cost of an answer to an oral question was estimated to be an average of £369, the answer to a written question £134.[17]

EARLY DAY MOTIONS

Behind this curious colloquial term lies one of the least well known or evaluated parliamentary processes. An Early Day Motion (EDM) is a written motion tabled in parliament requesting a debate 'at an early day'. Any Member of Parliament may table an EDM, on any subject matter, subject to a few procedural rules.[18]

EDMs originated in the mid-nineteenth century. Before that time, the parliamentary timetable was relaxed and Members had adequate opportunity to raise matters for subsequent debate in the House. As pressure for time in the House increased, the practice developed of Members giving notice that they intended to raise a particular matter for debate at some future, unspecified, date. These notices were formally recorded from 1865 in the daily papers of the House and today appear on the Motions Notice Paper, which forms part of the daily 'Vote Bundle' – the working papers of the House.

The purpose of tabling an EDM is not only to express a view and request a debate, but also to test the strength of feeling in the House over the matter involved. An EDM may be tabled by one Member or by several, and other Members may add their names in support. Some EDMs are tabled by the Leader of the Opposition: for example, EDM No 351 of 1978–79, supported by five other senior Conservative Members led to a debate on 28 March 1979, which resulted in the resignation of the government and the subsequent general election.

Once tabled, an EDM remains current for the duration of the parliamentary session and may or may not attract considerable support within the House. Between 1948–49 and 1990–91, 29 EDMs attracted over 300 signatures.

The rules and restrictions on EDMs are few, and are consistent with the general rules concerning motions. Thus, the motion must be worded in parliamentary language, must not relate to a matter which is *sub judice* and is limited to 250 words. Within these limits, a Member may table an EDM on any subject. Many EDMs are tabled by Members of all parties on a particular issue, and provide an important outlet for the expression of views across party lines.[19]

In terms of the number of debates which flow from EDMs, their success rate must be regarded as low. The EDM censuring the government tabled by the Rt Hon Mrs Thatcher in 1979 is a rarity, both in terms of securing a debate and in the dramatic effect of signalling the fall of a government. The occasional success of

17 HC Deb 22 March 2005, col 48WS.
18 See Griffith and Ryle, 2003, Chapters 6 and 10.
19 In the 2000–01 session, 1,854 EDMs were tabled.

the EDM was again seen in 1988 in relation to the Education Reform Bill 1988. There, two senior Conservative front-bench Members, Norman Tebbit and Michael Heseltine, tabled a motion calling for the abolition of the Inner London Education Authority: a matter which was contrary to the then policy of the Secretary of State for Education, Kenneth Baker. The EDM was supported by 120 other Conservative backbenchers and caused the Secretary of State to amend the Bill.[20]

Notwithstanding such rare examples of EDMs having important political and legal effects, the overall significance of the EDM should not be underestimated. Depending on the volume of support a particular EDM attracts, it represents an expression of the mood of the House across a whole spectrum of issues which places pressure on the government to respond. Furthermore, where the rules of the House prevent a Member from expressing a view in Debate, perhaps because he cannot catch the Speaker's eye, or by means of a question, perhaps because of ministerial responsibility or because the subject matter falls within one of the excluded categories, the EDM may represent the only vehicle for expression.

SELECT COMMITTEES OF THE HOUSE OF COMMONS

Select committees in the House of Commons are of some antiquity, although the current structure of committees dates back only to 1979. They take several forms and fulfil a number of different functions.[21] Some select committees relate to the running of the House of Commons itself, others relate to the procedures employed by the House, while a third class – the departmentally-related select committees – fulfil an investigative and reporting function. In addition there may at any time be ad hoc select committees established to investigate and report on a specific matter.

The 'domestic' committees include the following: Accommodation and Works; Administration Committee; Broadcasting Committee; Catering Committee; and Finance and Services Committee. The committees relating to procedures include: Modernisation Committee; Procedure Committee; Liaison Committee; and the Information Committee. While the Procedure Committee keeps all Commons' procedures under review, the Modernisation Committee is specifically charged with examining and recommending changes to procedures. The Information Committee advises the Speaker on information technology. The Liaison Committee is made up of the Chairpersons of all the select committees and works to ensure that there is an efficient distribution on the workload of departmentally-related Committees (on this committee see below).

Scrutinising the efficiency and effectiveness with which government Departments and other public bodies have used their resources is the Public Accounts Committee.[22] The Public Administration Committee has the task of

---

20 EDM 563; Notices of Motions, 1987–88, p 3519.
21 For select committees in the House of Lords, see Chapter 17.
22 See further pp 419–20.

examining the reports of the Parliamentary Commissioner for Administration and the Health Service Commissioners for England, Scotland and Wales, and the Parliamentary Ombudsman for Northern Ireland. Additionally the Public Administration Committee also considers matters relating to the Civil Service. Monitoring the privileges of Parliament and the conduct of Members of Parliament is the Committee on Standards and Privileges, discussed in Chapter 18. Examining delegated legislation is the task of the Select Committee on Statutory Instruments, which works closely with the Joint Committee on Statutory Instruments discussed in Chapter 15. There is a European Scrutiny Committee which scrutinises European Union documents, decides which issues require debate and monitors the activities of UK Ministers in the European Council. There is also an Environmental Audit Committee, which has the task of monitoring the contribution made by government departments and public bodies towards environmental protection and sustainable development.

The current system of departmentally related select committees was established in 1979 following recommendations made by the Select Committee on Procedure.[23] In debate, the Leader of the House[24] described the proposals as:

> ... a necessary preliminary to the more effective scrutiny of government ... and opportunity for closer examination of departmental policy ... an important contribution to greater openness in government, of a kind that is in accord with our parliamentary arrangements and our constitutional tradition.

Powers and functions of select committees

The functions of departmentally related select committees are defined as being to examine matters within the Department and to report to the House. To fulfil their tasks Committees have the following powers:

(a) to send for persons, papers and records;

(b) to sit notwithstanding any adjournment of the House;

(c) to adjourn from place to place;

(d) to appoint specialist advisers, either to supply information which is not readily available or to elucidate matters of complexity within the committee's terms of reference.

The majority of Committees have eleven members.[25] The scope of power granted to select committees is very broad. It is for the committee to determine, within the confines of the work of the department, what subject matter to examine and to determine what evidence the committee needs to assist in its examination. To facilitate the working of select committees, each has a permanent staff of some three to four, and some committees have the power, under Standing Orders, to establish sub-committees.

---

23 HC 588 (1977–78), London: HMSO. *First Report of the Select Committee on Procedure* (1977–78), London: HMSO.

24 The Rt Hon Norman St John-Stevas, MP (subsequently, Lord St John of Fawsley).

25 The Environment Food and Rural Affairs Committee has 17 members; the Northern Ireland Affairs Committee has 13.

The committee structure

The departmental select committees and their related departments are as follows:

Select committee	Government departments
Constitutional Affairs	Department for Constitutional Affairs
Culture, Media and Sport	Department for Culture, Media and Sport
Defence	Ministry of Defence
Education and Skills	Department for Education and Skills
Environment, Food and Rural Affairs	Department of Environment, Food and Rural Affairs
Foreign Affairs	Foreign and Commonwealth Office
Health	Department of Health
Home Affairs	Home Office, Attorney General's Office, Crown Prosecution Service, Serious Fraud Office
International Development	Department for International Development
Northern Ireland Affairs	Northern Ireland Office
Office of Deputy Prime Minister: Housing, Planning, Local Government and the Regions	Department for Communities and Local Government*
Science and Technology	Office of Science and Technology
Scottish Affairs	Scottish Office, Lord Advocate's Department
Trade and Industry	Department of Trade and Industry
Transport	Department for Transport
Treasury	Treasury Office, Board of Customs and Excise, Inland Revenue
Welsh Affairs	Welsh Office
Work and Pensions	Department for Work and Pensions

* The office of Deputy Prime Minister was abolished in May 2006. However, the Select Committee name will remain unchanged until the House of Commons' Standing Orders are revised to effect the change.

The Liaison Committee

The task of co-ordinating the work of select committees falls to the Liaison Committee, first established in 1967, the membership of which comprises all the Chairmen of the departmentally-related select committees, and the Chairmen of the Public Accounts Committee and the European Legislation Select Committee. Its role is defined as being:

(a) to consider general matters relating to the work of select committees; and

(b) to give such advice relating to the work of select committees as may be sought by the House of Commons Commission.

In 2003 the Prime Minister agreed to meet twice a year with the Liaison Committee to discuss matters of mutual concern.

Membership of select committees

Membership of select committees, unlike that of standing committees, lasts for the life of a parliament, thus providing stability of membership and the opportunity for Members to develop a degree of expertise in the subject matter. Membership is largely limited, by convention, to backbenchers. The only ministers who are Members are the Leader of the House,[26] the government Deputy Chief Whip[27] and the Financial Secretary to the Treasury.[28] Opposition front-bench spokesmen are not appointed to select committees.

Competition for membership of select committees is keen, particularly for the high profile committees. The political party whips have great influence, if not total control, over membership. The Committee of Selection, itself a select committee, is made up of senior Members of the House drawn from all political parties. The party whips make nominations to the committee which in turn reports to the House for approval. The strength of each political party overall in the House is reflected, largely but not totally accurately, in the membership of select committees, thus giving to the committee a legitimacy approximate to that of the House as a whole.

Committee chairmanship

It might reasonably be assumed that the chairmanship of the committees always fell to Members of the government's own party, but this is not the case, and select committees may be chaired by a Member of any political party. The decision as to which party should chair a particular committee is a matter for negotiation between government and Opposition. Once that decision has been reached, it is for the committee members, under the 'advice' of the whips, formally to elect the chairman.

The significance of the sharing of chairs between government and opposition parties lies in the attempt to minimise party political conflict, in order to increase the effectiveness and efficiency of the scrutiny to be brought to bear on government departments. Once appointed, the chairman acts with complete impartiality. Select committees are designed to operate on the basis of broad consensus as to aims and objectives, and to produce a single authoritative report to parliament as a whole. It is not usual for the committee to vote on party lines

---

26   Services Committee.
27   *Ibid*.
28   Public Accounts Committee.

although, in highly controversial matters, this may occasionally be inevitable. If the committee intends to be critical of the government in its report, it is necessary for at least one Member of the government party to agree with the criticism(s).

The work of select committees illustrated

The inquiries undertaken by select committees are both broad ranging and in depth. It is entirely a matter for the committee to determine what subject to investigate and, accordingly, every aspect of government administration is potentially susceptible to inquiry. In the past, for example, select committees have inquired into the conduct of the Falklands War[29] and the banning of trade union membership at the Government Communication Headquarters (GCHQ).[30] The committees have investigated such matters as the Westland Helicopter affair; Arms to Iraq; salmonella in eggs; and the loss of the Maxwell pension funds, on which see further below. The wide ranging nature of inquiries undertaken is illustrated in the subject matter chosen by the Foreign Affairs Committee in 2004–05:

Reports of the Foreign Affairs Committee, Session 2004–05[31]

- Cyprus;
- Western Balkans;
- Human Rights Annual Report;
- Strategic Export Controls;
- Foreign Policy Aspects of the War Against Terrorism.

The co-operation of government

It has been seen above that committees have the power to send for 'persons and papers'. The work of select committees would be much impaired if the committee was obstructed in its attempt to gain access to evidence. The Select Committee on Procedure had suggested, *inter alia*, that there should be power to compel ministers to attend and to give evidence. That recommendation was rejected by the government, on the basis that select committees should not have power to issue orders to ministers – such a power lay with the House alone. Accordingly, there is no formal requirement that the government co-operate with select committees. However, the Leader of the House has undertaken that:

... every Minister, from the most senior Cabinet Minister to the most junior Under Secretary, will do all in his or her power to co-operate with the new system of committees and to make it a success.[32]

---

29 HC 11 (1984–85), London: HMSO.
30 HC 238 (1983–84), London: HMSO.
31 Paper Nos and government replies: HC 113, Cm 6506; HC 87, Cm 6505; HC 109, Cm 6571; HC 145; HC 36, Cm 6590 respectively.
32 HC Deb Col 45, 25 June 1979; Col 1677, 16 January 1981.

For the most part, governments do co-operate with the committees, but limits to this co-operation can be perceived through an examination of four instances.

The Westland affair

In the aftermath of the Westland Helicopter affair, during which both the Secretary of State for Defence, Michael Heseltine, and the Secretary of State for Trade and Industry, Leon Brittan, resigned,[33] three select committees inquired into the matter.[34] When the Select Committee on Defence announced its intention to inquire into the matter, the government refused to allow witnesses from the Department of Trade and Industry, in particular the Director of Information, to whom a leak of the Solicitor General's letter had been attributed, to give evidence to the committee. The government's justification for this refusal was that the giving of evidence by a senior civil servant to a parliamentary committee would have major implications for the conduct of government and for relations between ministers and their civil servants. This refusal had two implications. First, it meant that parliament was unable to check the accuracy of statements made by the Prime Minister in the House, or those made by Leon Brittan in relation to the leaked letter. The second implication was that the civil servants concerned were neither able to explain nor defend their actions.

Salmonella in eggs

In 1988, a junior Health Minister, Edwina Currie, resigned office, subsequent to public comments made about alleged contamination of eggs. Her remarks that 'most eggs produced in the country' were infected with salmonella had an immediate impact on the sale and consumption of eggs, causing financial damage to egg producers. The Select Committee on Agriculture invited Mrs Currie to give evidence to the committee, but she declined. Following an exchange of letters which involved the select committee chairman insisting that it was for the committee, and not Mrs Currie, to decide whether or not she should give evidence, Mrs Currie grudgingly agreed to appear. In the event, her evidence proved, as she had indicated that it would, unhelpful.

The Maxwell pension fund

During the 1991–92 session, the Social Services Select Committee was enquiring into the mismanagement of pension funds by the Mirror Newspaper Group's recently deceased Chairman, Mr Robert Maxwell. Mr Maxwell's sons, both holding prominent positions in the Group before their father's death, and subsequently assuming control of the companies, were summoned to give evidence. The Maxwells refused, relying on a claimed right to silence in the light of imminent criminal charges and the risk of jeopardising their own fair trial. The

---

33   See the discussion in Chapter 9. See also Hennessy, 1986a; Oliver and Austin, 1987; Linklater *et al*, 1986, Chapter 11; Marshall, 1986a.
34   Defence Committee, HC 518, 519 (1985–86), London: HMSO; Trade and Industry Committee, HC 176 (1986–87), London: HMSO; Treasury and Civil Service Committee, HC 92 (1985–86), London: HMSO.

committee chairman wanted the Maxwells to be charged with contempt of parliament (see Chapter 18), but no action was taken.

Arms to Iraq

In February 1992, the Select Committee on Trade and Industry examined the sale of equipment to Iraq during the conflict in the Gulf.[35] The equipment involved was piping which allegedly could be used to manufacture a missile launcher – a 'supergun'. That inquiry was frustrated by the alleged refusal of the Attorney General and others to give details of the information known to the Department of Trade and Industry when the export licence was granted. Subsequently, three directors of the company Matrix Churchill were prosecuted by Customs and Excise for breach of the restrictions on the export of military equipment contrary to the Import, Exports and Customs Powers (Defence) Act 1939 by obtaining export licences by deception. The prosecution was halted when Alan Clark[36] revealed in court that there had been no deception, since the government was fully aware of the exports and their intended usage. The trial collapsed and prompted a judicial inquiry headed by Sir Richard Scott. The affair involved allegations of a cover up on the part of the government and gave rise to serious questions concerning the role and use of public interest immunity certificates, by the use of which information may be withheld from the courts 'in the public interest'.[37]

Reform of parliamentary evidence rules

The problem of witnesses who attend but who give evidence which is either untruthful or which paints only half the picture – a problem faced by parliament in its committee inquiries into the Arms to Iraq affair, about which Sir Richard Scott was particularly critical – was considered in Chapter 11. In a further attempt to strengthen parliament's powers over its Members, and witnesses giving evidence to its committees, new rules have applied since January 1997. Persons giving evidence are now required to take a formal oath. Anyone found to have lied to parliament may be reported to the Crown Prosecution Service with a view to prosecution for perjury, which, in the event of conviction, could lead to a maximum prison sentence of seven years. Where the person is a Member of Parliament, the committee will ask the Commons to vote to remove the Member's immunity from prosecution.

Select committee reports

At the conclusion of a select committee inquiry, a report will be drawn up. The committee aims to produce an authoritative, unanimous report which is presented to parliament. The degree of consensus over a particular issue within

---

35 See Phythian and Little, 1993.
36 Former Minister of State at the Department of Trade and Industry and Defence Procurement Minister.
37 See further Chapter 11.

the committee membership will dictate the extent to which unanimity can be achieved.

Approximately one-third of all reports published will be debated on the floor of the House. This fact is one which also gives rise to criticism of select committee effectiveness, although it must be conceded that the time given for debate on reports has increased in recent years. Parliamentary procedure does not make specific provision for debate on reports. The Procedure Committee has suggested that eight days per session should be devoted to such debates but this proposal has not been acted upon. Sufficient, but not too much, weight should be attached to this alleged defect, and four arguments may be advanced which limit its impact. The first relates to the commitment undertaken by successive governments to respond to select committee reports. Such an undertaking does not, of itself, ensure that the recommendations of the committee will be implemented but it does ensure that the government will react to any criticisms made and proposals put forward. Members of the committee and other interested Members of Parliament, particularly the Opposition, will be slow to let an opportunity to criticise government pass. The second argument centres on the information gained through the process of the inquiry. It has been seen that ministers may decline or refuse to answer questions fully, and that they can restrict the extent to which civil servants may give evidence. Where a minister refuses to co-operate with a select committee he will inevitably find media attention focused upon him and some cogent justification for his reticence will have to be forthcoming. For the most part, evidence suggests that there is a high degree of ministerial co-operation with committees; this need not be seen as being necessarily willing participation but, rather, a matter of political prudence.

Thirdly, it must be recognised that the reports emanating from select committee inquiries are matters of public record, available both to Members of Parliament and to the interested press and public. The information gathered in the course of an inquiry becomes public information, information which, before the introduction of the new committee structure, was often hidden from the public gaze. Finally, the absence of debate on the floor of the House in many cases will be justified by the pressure on the parliamentary timetable. It may well be the case that debate on all reports is desirable in principle, but, since 1979, over 900 reports have been published by select committees, of varying significance and on a plethora of matters. On many matters, opening debate to all Members of the House may involve a duplication of effort, with non-specialist Members of Parliament inexpertly attempting to re-analyse the information examined by the more specialised select committee Members.

Evaluation

An evaluation of the work of select committees in relation to the fundamentally important question concerning the accountability of government must be approached with caution. The outcome of an appraisal is inevitably related to the expectations which the appraiser holds and, as a consequence, the evaluation of one commentator may not be the same as another's. Caution is also urged against the making of sweeping generalisations as to the effectiveness of select committees which are diverse in nature and operation. Many factors are involved in the analysis: the extent to which media, and hence public, attention is focused on a particular enquiry; the sensitivity of the subject matter; the degree of political consensus within the committee; the extent to which governments are prepared to make time on the floor of the House to debate select committee reports; the extent to which select committee inquiries result in improved efficiency in government; and the extent to which government and other witnesses co-operate with the committees in the provision of information. All of these factors, and more, must be put in the balance before any reasoned conclusions can be reached.

Griffith and Ryle state that:

> ... there are clear indications that the existence of select committees has affected the way government business is conducted ... [2003, 11-054]

> General assessment of the relative success or failure of select committees ... depends on differing expectations. On one matter, however, opinion is almost unanimous: select committees since 1979 have increased the flow of information coming out of Whitehall [ie government departments] and this has resulted to some extent in debates being better informed both inside and outside Parliament. [2003, 11-056]

At the heart of any evaluation must lie the recognition of the inherent tension – already stressed in Chapter 15 in relation to the scrutiny of legislation – between the legitimate right of the government to govern and the equally legitimate right of parliament as a whole to ensure the collective accountability of government and the individual responsibility of ministers.

SCRUTINY OF NATIONAL FINANCE

In Chapter 15, the means by which the House of Commons scrutinises proposals for taxation and expenditure was examined. In this section, the manner in which parliament scrutinises how public money has been spent is discussed. The responsibility for, and control over, expenditure lies with the Chancellor of the Exchequer. The manner in which parliament scrutinises public expenditure is through the Public Accounts Select Committee which examines reports of audits conducted by the Comptroller and Auditor General, who is head of the National Audit Office.[38]

The Public Accounts Committee (PAC)

This committee was first established in 1861. It has the power to examine the accounts 'showing the appropriation of the sums granted by parliament to meet the public expenditure, and of such other accounts laid before parliament, as the committee may think fit'.[39] The committee consists of not more than 15 Members, of whom four represent a quorum. While the composition of the committee represents (as does that of all select committees) the party-political strength of the House, the PAC functions in a non-partisan manner. By convention, the PAC's

---

38 National Audit Act 1983.
39 Standing Order No 122.

Chairman is a Member of the Opposition. The committee has the power to 'send for persons, papers and records' and to report from time to time.[40] The PAC issues approximately 30 to 40 reports per session.[41]

The principal function of the committee is to ensure that money is spent for the purposes intended by parliament, and that money is spent effectively and economically. The committee holds many meetings in public. One day per session is set aside for debate of its reports. By critically examining the expenditure of departments and assessing the extent to which expenditure produces value for money, the PAC exerts considerable influence on government.

The Comptroller and Auditor General (CAG) and National Audit Office (NAO)

The CAG is an officer of the House of Commons, appointed by the Crown, and can be removed from office for misbehaviour only on the successful moving of an address to both Houses of Parliament. As head of the National Audit Office, the CAG's function is to examine the economy, efficiency and effectiveness with which bodies have used their resources in the pursuit of policy.[42] The CAG appoints his own staff, who are not civil servants. The reports of the National Audit Office[43] are recorded in the Weekly Information Bulletin of the House of Commons and are available to the public.

The CAG audits and certifies the accounts of government departments and bodies. Three significant areas of administration lie outside his jurisdiction: nationalised industries, local authorities and private bodies. The independence of the CAG from government, backed by the non-partisan PAC, provides powerful watchdog over the administration of government and the expenditure of public money. The National Audit Office's Annual Report 2005 reveals the scope of the NAO's work. In 2004–05, the Office audited over 570 accounts, auditing over £800 billion of government expenditure and revenue. The Office published 61 major reports for parliament on subjects ranging from Culture, Media and Sport, Defence, Education, Europe, Law and Order, the National Health Service, Overseas Affairs, Revenue, Trade and Industry, Transport and Work and Pensions. National Audit Office reports are presented to parliament and published. Most reports are considered by the Committee of Public Accounts in hearings at which senior official are questioned. The Public Account Committee then publishes detailed recommendations to which the government formally responds. The National Audit Office then monitors the implementation of recommendations.

---

40   Standing Order No 122, para 2.
41   In May 1995, the PAC issued a highly critical report concerning delays and overspending by the Ministry of Defence in relation to defence equipment.
42   National Audit Act 1983, ss 6 and 7.
43   And the corresponding Office for Northern Ireland.

The Government Resources and Accounts Act 2000

Modernisation of the system of controlling the management of public finance was effected with the Government Resources and Accounts Act 2000.[44] In brief, the Act provides for resource accounting and resources budgeting and introduces a system whereby there are consolidated accounts for the whole of the public sector (Whole of Government Accounts). The Act also provides for the Treasury to establish Partnerships UK, a private sector body responsible for the Private Finance Initiative, the system designed to facilitate the injection of private money into government expenditure programmes.

The Act sets out the criteria for the examination of accounts by the Comptroller and Auditor General, who must be satisfied that:

(a) the accounts present a true and fair view;

(b) any money provided has been expended for the purposes intended by parliament;

(c) any resources authorised by parliament have been used for the purposes so authorised; and

(d) the department's financial transactions are in accordance with any relevant authority.

---

44 The Act is complex and its detailed provisions beyond the scope of this book. For analysis, see White and Hollingsworth, 2001.

CHAPTER 17

THE HOUSE OF LORDS

INTRODUCTION

The majority of liberal democracies have bicameral legislatures, or legislatures with two 'chambers' or 'houses'.[1] In the United Kingdom, the second chamber, the Upper House – or House of Lords – is currently an unelected chamber which has judicial, legislative, scrutinising and debating functions.[2] The justifications for, and advantages of, a second chamber, irrespective of the merits of the actual second chamber, are twofold. First, a second chamber provides a forum for reflection, and for 'second thoughts' on policies and legislative proposals. A second chamber provides for a *diffusion* rather than *concentration* of power within parliament. Secondly, depending on the allocation of power between the two chambers, the Upper House plays a valuable role in the revision of legislation which has passed through the Lower House. Such revision is of particular significance where the Lower House is dominated by a government with a strong majority and also when – irrespective of the political make up of the Lower House – procedures for curtailing debate have been employed (see Chapter 15). The scrutiny, and amendment, of Bills is equally important in improving the quality of the statute book. As will be seen below, the House of Lords plays a major role in statute revision. On occasion, such revision is contrary to the wishes of the Commons, which may choose to acquiesce in the Lords' amendments rather than employ the Parliament Act procedure which regulates the respective powers of the two Houses of Parliament. On other occasions, however, the revision undertaken in the Lords is either at the instance of the government itself, which may choose to introduce amendments to Bills in the Lords, or by Members of the House of Lords in order to improve the drafting of the Act.

Until 1999, when the first stage of a major reform to the composition of the House of Lords was implemented, the House of Lords was unique among second legislative chambers. A majority of states have either an elected second chamber or a second chamber which is part elected and part nominated. By contrast, until 1999, the House of Lords was comprised of a majority of unelected hereditary members and a minority of nominated members. In 1999, the right of most hereditary peers to sit and vote in the Lords was abolished, leaving the Lords with a majority of nominated and no democratically elected members. Only Canada and Ireland have a predominantly nominated second chamber. Before the 1997 general election, the Labour Party had pledged to reform the House of Lords, regarding the role of the unelected House as incompatible with modern democracy. Rather than introduce wholesale reform immediately, however, the government decided on a two stage reform. The first, which is largely but not

---

1   Denmark, Sweden and New Zealand have unicameral parliaments.
2   See Bromhead, 1958; Morgan, 1975; Shell, 1992. Under the Constitutional Reform Act 2005, the judicial function will be physically removed from the House of Lords.

wholly accomplished, was to remove the right of the hereditaries to participate in parliament. The second, which remains for the future, was to decide precisely what form of composition was needed – whether fully elected or partly elected and partly nominated – and the powers which the reformed second chamber should have. In order to reach this decision, the government established a Royal Commission, chaired by Lord Wakeham, to consider the issue and make recommendations. While this second stage of reform was expected to be implemented during the Labour government's first parliament, it was decided to postpone the second stage. Details of the reforms, achieved and proposed, are discussed below.

HISTORICAL OVERVIEW[3]

The origins of the House of Lords lie in the councils summoned by English Kings in the eleventh, twelfth and thirteenth centuries, in order to give advice, decide on appeal cases and, under certain circumstances, make financial grants to the King. These 'King's Councils' had developed into a form which is recognisable today by 1295, then being an assembly of the 'three estates of the realm', the clergy, barons and commons – 'those who pray, those who fight, those who work'. From the earliest times, both spiritual and secular hereditary peers formed the membership of the House of Lords, by which name it became known in the sixteenth century. Maitland (1908) asserts that the separation into two Houses occurred around the middle of the fourteenth century, although Stubbs (1880) contends that the two bodies were separate from the earliest time. The functions of the two Houses also differed: it was for the Lords to advise the King, and it was for the Commons to consent to the King's proposals. By 1330, parliament was to meet annually,[4] at least once but more times as summonsed. Nevertheless, as seen in Chapter 6, the sitting of parliament was a matter for the King to determine and, between 1364 and 1689, there were many years in which no parliament met, the longest period being 11 years, during which time Charles I ruled under the prerogative.

The House of Lords, until 1999, comprised a majority of hereditary non-spiritual (secular or temporal) peers, along with life peers (nominated members) and 26 Archbishops and Bishops. Before the seventeenth century, the power of the Lords Spiritual was great. In the 1453–54 parliamentary session, to take but one typical example of historical membership, the membership of the House of Lords was two Archbishops, 18 Bishops, 27 abbots and priors, 5 dukes, 11 earls, three viscounts and 44 barons: a total of 111. With the suppression of the monasteries, spiritual peers were excluded from parliament and, from this time, the Upper House became a predominantly secular body. The growth in the number of secular, or temporal, peers stems from the reign of James I (1603–25), with 96 sitting in his last parliament. By 1685, in the reign of James II, the number had increased to 145. In the brief period of republican rule from 1649 to 1660, following civil war and the execution of Charles I, both the Monarchy and the

---

3   See Powell and Wallis, 1968; Maitland, 1908. See also Chapter 6.
4   4 Edw III c 14.

House of Lords were abolished. Both were restored in 1660. The Acts of Union, with Scotland in 1707 and Ireland in 1800, provided for Scottish and Irish representation in the House of Lords.[5]

THE COMPOSITION OF THE HOUSE OF LORDS

The House of Lords is unelected. While this situation is anomalous, undemocratic and anachronistic in an otherwise democratic society, there are some advantages in the arrangement which are too often overlooked. In essence, the value of an unelected chamber paradoxically lies in its lack of accountability to either the government of the day or the electorate, giving it an independence without which the value of its work would be diminished. However, whether such advantages actually flow from the House of Lords can only be evaluated through examining the impact which the House has, in its revising role, on government legislation. Prior to the removal of the majority of hereditary peers from the House, they represented a majority of peers and, being dominated by Conservative Members, had the ability to act in a party political preferential manner – both to support a Conservative government's legislation and to frustrate that of a Labour government. It was perceptions such as this which caused, in part, the current Labour government to act swiftly to remove the hereditary element as a first stage of reform. In the event, some 92 hereditary peers remained in the Lords, and will so remain until the second stage of reform takes place. Historically, there has also been a political imbalance in the allegiance of life peers, with the Conservative peers outnumbering Labour peers. This imbalance is also being redressed, with the government increasing the number of appointed Labour life peers. However, the uncompleted reform has led to the criticism that the government holds, through its selection of appointees, excessive powers of patronage, capable of undermining the independence of the Lords. A further factor in the composition of the House, which renders evaluation of its work more complex, is the considerable proportion of independent peers, or 'cross benchers', who owe no political allegiance to any party.

The House of Lords has, under the Parliament Act 1911, the power to block any Bill attempting to extend the life of a parliament.[6] This may be seen as no more than a constitutional 'backstop' against a potential abuse of power by government, and the life of a parliament has indeed been extended in recent history in times of national emergency.[7] Such extensions, however, have been with the consent of the Lords. Any attempt by a government to suspend elections in order to protect its own political power would be blocked by the Lords without whose consent such a Bill could not become law. On the other hand, any advantages which flow from the current composition of the Lords must be

---

5   Numbering 16 and 28, respectively. Scottish peers continue to sit in the House; Irish peers continued to sit in the House of Lords after 1922 (see Chapter 3), but were not replaced on their deaths. The last Irish peer entitled to sit in the Lords died in 1961. See Lysaght, 1967.

6   Limited to five years: Parliament Act 1911, s 7, amending the Septennial Act 1715, previously regulated under the Meeting of Parliament Act 1694.

7   Eg, during the two World Wars.

weighed in the balance against the demands of democracy. While an unelected second chamber having no role in the passage of legislation might be acceptable to some, an unelected second chamber with real – although ultimately limited – legislative power represents an affront to the idea of democratic government. It is for this reason that the issue of reform of the House of Lords has been for so long on the political agenda.[8]

Hereditary peers

Hereditary peers are created under the prerogative of the Crown on the advice on the Prime Minister. A peerage is created either by a Writ of Summons to the House or, more recently, under Letters Patent from the Sovereign which will define the line of succession, which invariably falls to the male heirs. A peerage created by a Writ of Summons will devolve to all heirs, thus enabling female successors to the title. Disputes concerning succession to a title are resolved by the House of Lords, through the Committee for Privileges. The evidence of blood tests is admissible in evidence.[9] A peerage cannot be surrendered other than under the disclaimer for life under the Peerage Act 1963,[10] on which, see below. The disclaimer does not prevent the conferment of a life peerage.

In January 1998, there were 759 hereditary peers, out of a total membership of 1,272, comprising just under 60 per cent of the total.[11] All this changed, however, in 1999. Under the House of Lords Act 1999, the rights of most hereditary peers were removed. While it had been intended to remove the rights of all hereditary peers to sit and vote, threats of opposition to the House of Lords Bill from the majority of Conservative hereditary peers persuaded the government to allow 92 peers to remain. In the deal brokered by Viscount Cranborne, the then Conservative Leader in the Lords, the remaining hereditaries would be elected by the hereditary peers themselves. A further seven former hereditary peers were returned to the House of Lords as life peers.

Life peers

Non-judicial life peers were not introduced until the Life Peerages Act 1958. In 1998, there were 461 peers appointed under the 1958 Act: 81 female life peers and 380 male life peers. The award of a peerage is one of the highest honours conferred in the United Kingdom. Approximately one third of former government ministers will receive life peerages. Some former Prime Ministers – such as Sir Winston Churchill and Sir Edward Heath – refused the award of a peerage in order to remain in the House of Commons. Others will decline on point of political principle. Peerages are conferred by the Crown on the advice of the Prime Minister. Twice a year – at New Year and on the Queen's birthday – honours are awarded. There are, occasionally, honours lists announced to mark

---

8   For previous attempts to reform the Lords, and current reform proposals, see below.
9   See *The Ampthill Peerage Case* (1977); *Barony of Moynihan* (1997).
10   *Re Parliamentary Election for Bristol South East* (1964).
11   This figure excludes the 78 peers who had applied for leave of absence and 86 who had not applied for Writs of Summons.

special occasions. Honours are also awarded on the dissolution of parliament and, if there is a change of government, the outgoing Prime Minister will draw up a special honours list. However, there is much evidence to suggest that the system of appointment is used politically by governments, a factor which further undermines the legitimacy of the House of Lords, and there currently exists no formal mechanism by which a balance between the parties can be established and maintained against the wishes of a Prime Minister. If the Prime Minister insists that the working life peers should reflect party-political strength in the House of Commons, as did Margaret Thatcher, and if, as was the case with the Conservative government, that government is in power for a continuous period of 18 years, there is an inbuilt bias in appointments.

This was the legacy inherited by the Labour Government in 1997. In order to redress the political imbalance, the Prime Minister appointed an unprecedented number of life peers, intended to be 'working peers', actively participating in the work of the Upper House.

Once appointed, life peers tend to be more active in the House of Lords – in terms of both attendance in the House and participation in debate – than hereditary peers. Indeed, the Prime Minister made it clear that the appointment of new Labour life peers carried with it the responsibility to attend the House regularly in order to ensure that the government gets its key legislation through parliament. Under current reform proposals, the conferment of a life peerage is to be separated from entitlement to sit in the Lords.[12]

Judicial peers

In 1856, for the first time, a life peerage was granted to a retired judge, although he was allowed neither to sit nor to vote in parliament. In 1876, the Appellate Jurisdiction Act provided that two Lords of Appeal in Ordinary could be appointed as life peers, with both sitting and voting rights. The Lords of Appeal in Ordinary were originally appointed to add legal expertise to the House. In their judicial capacity, the Judicial Committee of the House of Lords represents the highest domestic court for civil appeals in the United Kingdom and for criminal appeals from England, Wales and Northern Ireland.[13] The Law Lords also sit as Members of the Judicial Committee of the Privy Council which has jurisdiction to hear appeals from a limited number of Commonwealth countries. Consideration of the judicial work of the Law Lords should be kept distinct from consideration of their role in the other functions of the House of Lords.

The Law Lords play a role in the legislative and other functions but, by convention, do not participate in purely political debate. To do so would detract from the judicial impartiality which must be evident when acting in a judicial capacity, and would have implications for the delicate balance maintained in the separation of powers.[14]

---

12 See further below. On the whip system, see Chapter 14.
13 No appeal lies from the highest Scottish criminal court, the High Court of Justiciary: Criminal Procedure (Scotland) Act 1887.
14 See Shell, 1992, Chapter 2 and references therein.

The Constitutional Reform Act 2005 reforms the arrangement to reflect a better separation of powers between the legislature an judiciary. As discussed in more detail in Chapter 4, a Supreme Court is to be established in a place physically separated from Parliament. The Law Lords will sit in the Supreme Court and will not be allowed to sit in the House of Lords until they retire from their judicial appointments.

Lords Spiritual

In addition to the hereditary and life peers and Law Lords, 26 Archbishops and Bishops of the Church of England sit in the Lords. The explanation for the presence of Anglican Archbishops and Bishops is historical. As seen above, until the dissolution of the monasteries, spiritual peers represented a majority in the House of Lords. Today, their presence is explained both on the basis of tradition and on the basis of the close links between the established Church of England and the state. There are arguments for reform in this regard, but it should be recognised that the Spiritual Peers owe no allegiance to any political party and, while by convention not speaking or voting on purely political issues, make a significant contribution to debate on many, often sensitive, moral and social issues, such as housing, divorce, abortion, homosexuality, embryology and human fertilisation.

The oath of allegiance

Before becoming a full Member of the House, the new peer is formally introduced and takes the oath of allegiance to the Crown.[15]

Government members in the Lords

The government is represented in the House by the Secretary of State for Constitutional Affairs and Lord Chancellor, Leader of the House (Lord Privy Seal), Lord Advocate, five Ministers of State, seven Under Secretaries of State, the Chief Whip and Deputy Chief Whip and seven whips. The Constitutional Reform Act 2005 provides that the House of Lords will in future make its own arrangements regarding the Speakership, a role traditionally played by the Lord Chancellor. The 2005 Act also provides that in future the holder of the post of Lord Chancellor need not be a member of the House of Lords.

Disqualification from membership of the Lords

Aliens

Aliens are disqualified from membership of the Lords under section 3 of the Act of Settlement 1700. The British Nationality Act 1981, Schedule 7, amends the Act of Settlement to the effect that Commonwealth citizens or citizens of the Republic of Ireland are excluded from its provisions.

---

15 Promissory Oaths Act 1868, s 2; Oaths Act 1978, s 1.

Persons under the age of 21

While the age of majority has been reduced from the age of 21 to the age of 18 years by section 1 of the Family Law Reform Act 1969, no person succeeding to a peerage below the age of 21 may take his or her seat in the House.[16] Technically, persons under the age of 21 are not disqualified, but merely ineligible to take their seats until they reach the age of 21.

Bankrupts

Under the Bankruptcy and Insolvency Acts,[17] no peer may sit whilst adjudicated bankrupt. The disqualification ceases in accordance with the Acts.[18] It is a breach of privilege to sit whilst disqualified.

Treason

Any peer convicted of treason is disqualified from sitting or voting as a Member of the House unless and until he has either completed his term of imprisonment or received a pardon.

The disclaimer of hereditary peerages[19]

Under the Peerage Act 1963, it became possible to disclaim a peerage. A peer who disclaims his or her title does so irrevocably, but the disclaimer will not affect the succession of the title. Under the Act, a peer succeeding to a title before the passing of the Act had 12 months in which to disclaim the title. Peers succeeding to titles subsequently have one year within which to disclaim succession, or, in the case of a person under the age of 21, a year from the date of attaining the age of 21. One exception exists to this rule. If the successor is a Member of the House of Commons, or a candidate for election to the House of Commons, at the date on which he inherits the title, the period for disclaimer is one month (section 2 of the Peerage Act 1963). A total of 11 peers (including Viscount Stansgate, now Tony Benn, Lord Hume and Lord Hailsham) have disclaimed titles under the Act.

Leave of absence

Leave of absence from the House of Lords may be granted at any time during a parliament by applying to the Clerk of the Parliaments. At the start of each new parliament, peers who have previously obtained leave of absence will be asked whether they wish it to continue. Where leave of absence is granted, it is expected that the peer will not attend the House. Should he or she wish to do so, he may give one month's notice of his intention to attend. However, there is no mechanism by which the House can exclude a peer who has leave of absence but nevertheless attends the House.

---

16 Standing Order No 2, 1685. In 1994, the youngest peer was aged five.
17 Bankruptcy Disqualification Act 1871; Bankruptcy Act 1883; Bankruptcy Act 1890; Bankruptcy (Scotland) Act 1913; Bankruptcy Act 1914; Insolvency Act 1986.
18 Insolvency Act 1986, s 427.
19 See Hailsham, 1975; *Report of Joint Committee on House of Lords Reform*, HL 23 (1962–63) and HC 38 (1962–63), London: HMSO.

Attendance in the House

All peers are entitled to attend and vote in the House. Before becoming eligible to
sit in the Lords, it is necessary to apply for and receive a Writ of Summons. It is
expected that Lords who have not taken leave of absence will attend as regularly
as possible. The average daily attendance in 2003–04 was 357.

Membership of the House of Lords: April 1998 prior to reform in 1999

Archbishops and Bishops	26
Peers by succession	750 (16 women)
Hereditary peers of first creation	9
Life peers under the Appellate Jurisdiction Act 1876	26
Life peers under the Life Peerages Act 1958	462 (80 women)
Total	1,273*

*   *This figure included 68 Lords without Writs of Summons and 60 peers on leave of absence.*

Membership of the House of Lords: 1 March 2006

Archbishops and Bishops	26
Peers under House of Lords Act 1999	92
Life peers under the Appellate Jurisdiction Act 1876	27
Life peers under the Life Peerages Act 1958	580
Total	725

Membership of House of Lords by Political Party: 31 March 2004

Conservative	207
Labour	182
Liberal Democrat	64
Crossbench (Independent)	179
Bishops	26
Other	6
Total	**664**

Lords' expenses

No salary is payable to Members of the House of Lords. They are entitled to expenses to cover the cost of travel, overnight accommodation, subsistence and secretarial and other expenses pertaining to their parliamentary duties. One question which remains for future decision is whether, when the final stage of reform takes place, there should be more substantial remuneration for parliamentary work.

Salaried Members of the House of Lords

The Chairman and Principal Deputy Chairman of Committees, government ministers and whips and Lords of Appeal in Ordinary are salaried. The Leader of the Opposition and the Chief Opposition Whip also receive salaries.

Functions of the House of Lords

Until 1911, the powers of the Lords were equal to those of the Commons, with the exception that the Lords recognised – by convention – the supremacy of the Commons in relation to financial matters and accepted that they had no right to initiate or amend Bills relating to finance. The Lords nevertheless claimed the power to reject outright financial legislation, a power which, when exercised, led to a curtailment of their powers.

In the White Paper of 1968,[20] which formed the basis for the Labour government's attempt further to reform the House of Lords, the following functions of the House of Lords were recorded:

(a) the provision of a forum for debate on matters of public interest;

(b) the revision of Bills brought from the House of Commons;

(c) the initiation of Public Bills and Private Members' Bills;

(d) the consideration of delegated legislation;

(e) the scrutiny of the executive;

(f) the scrutiny of private legislation;

(g) select committee work;

(h) the Supreme Court of Appeal.

To this list must now be added the scrutiny and reporting of Bills and draft Bills for their compatibility with Convention rights protected under the Human Rights Act 1998.

The House of Lords contains a wealth of specialism and experience which is unmatched by the House of Commons. It is in part the introduction of life peers which explains the revival of the House of Lords. Perhaps the major factor explaining the resurgence of activity in the Upper House lies in the sheer volume of legislative work introduced by governments in recent years.

---

20 *House of Lords Reform*, Cmnd 3799, 1968, London: HMSO, para 8.

The majority of time in the Lords is devoted to the scrutiny of legislation, both primary and secondary, which in the 2003–04 session occupied 62.2 per cent of the time.[21]

Procedure in the House of Lords

To some extent, the procedure in the House of Lords mirrors that of the Lower House, although significant differences must be noted. The control of procedure lies within the Privileges of the House (see Chapter 18), and is regulated by the Leader of the House, the government Chief Whip and by the House as a whole. The Speaker of the House, currently the Lord Chancellor, has no formal powers to control the House, but is under a duty to attend the House and to sit on the Woolsack. The duty to attend derives from a Standing Order of the House made on 9 June 1660: '... that it is the duty of the Lord Chancellor or the Lord keeper of the great Seale of England ordinarily to attend the Lords house of Parlyament.' His role, as Speaker of the House, however, has been described as 'ornamental and symbolic',[22] for the Lord Chancellor does not have the same powers as the Speaker of the House of Commons. In the passage of legislation, for example, there is no power to select amendments for debate or to curtail debate. Whereas the Speaker in the Commons may rule that certain proposed amendments cannot be debated – perhaps because they are not strictly relevant to the content of the Bill – the House of Lords may decide to debate any and all amendments.

The Leader of the House is a political appointment in the hands of the Prime Minister, and the Leader of the House is a Member of Cabinet. It is his or her principal duty to advise on matters of procedure and order. The government Chief Whip is responsible for the arrangement of government business and consultation with other parties as to its arrangement. As with the Whip in the Commons, the Chief Whip sends out a weekly indication of the need for Members' attendance at particular items of business.

Having examined the composition of the House, the allocation of time and the principal officials of the House, we can now turn our attention to examining the actual business of the House.

GENERAL DEBATES

The importance of debates in the House of Lords, although occupying a decreasing percentage of the time of the House, should not be underestimated. Wednesdays are generally devoted to debates on matters of general public importance. One Wednesday per month is set aside for two short debates limited to two and a half hours, when the subject matter is chosen by backbench peers selected by ballot. Other debates take place as a result of consultation between the political parties, and will be generally timetabled to last for a maximum of either five hours or two and a half hours.

21　House of Lords: Annual Report and Accounts 2003–04.
22　*Report by the Group on the Working of the House*, HL 9 (1987–88), London: HMSO, para 13. But see the discussion of the role of the Lord Chancellor in Chapter 5.

The subject matter for debate is wide ranging, and it is often commented that the quality of debate in the House of Lords attains a higher standard than that in the House of Commons. In part, this is due to the less partisan nature of the House of Lords and, paradoxically, their very lack of accountability enhances their capacity for independence and openness. Since the introduction of life peers in 1958, the quality of debate has been enriched by the diverse backgrounds and experience of Members.

Questions in the House of Lords

Four types of questions are provided for under Standing Orders: starred, unstarred, written and private notice questions.

The daily business of the House commences with up to four starred questions addressed to the government on four days per week. Notice must be given of the question to be asked, and each peer is restricted to two questions per day. The purpose of the question is not to initiate debate but to secure information from the government. Unstarred questions are asked at the end of the day's business and may initiate debate. They may be likened to daily adjournment debates in the Lower House. These are popular with Members, providing an opportunity to initiate debate on a matter of public interest. Questions for written answer are printed on the Order Paper of the day and a government minister will reply within 14 days. The questions and replies are printed in *Hansard*, the official journal of the House. There is no limit on the number of questions which may be asked.

Private notice questions fulfil the same function as in the Lower House, that is, to raise matters for urgent debate without the need to observe the strict rules of notice for other questions. Notice must be given to the Leader of the House by noon on the day on which the question is to be put, and the Leader has absolute discretion as to whether to allow the question to be put.

THE SCRUTINY OF LEGISLATION

The scrutiny of legislation occupies the largest, and an increasing, proportion of the time of the House. Bills, other than financial Bills, which fall within the exclusive powers of the House of Commons, can be introduced in either the Commons or the Lords. The majority of government Bills will be introduced in the Commons and, having passed the Commons' stages of scrutiny, will be passed to the House of Lords, although many Bills are introduced in the Lords. The process of scrutiny in the Lords in some respects mirrors that in the Commons, and Bills receive a formal first reading, followed by the second reading debate and then 'stand committed' for the committee stage, after which the Bill is reported back to the House and then receives its third reading.

Legislative committees in the House of Lords

There are some differences between the two Houses in the scrutiny of legislation. First, in the House of Lords, there is no regular use of standing committees. The House of Lords did make provision for Bills to be read off the floor of the House in Grand Committees. All peers are entitled to attend and participate. The measure facilitates greater efficiency by freeing time in the chamber itself. The use of Grand Committees is increasing, and in the 2002–03 session ten Bills were committed. In 2003–04 some 220 hours of scrutiny took place in Grand Committees. The introduction of Public Bill Committees was also favourably considered in relation to a limited number of Bills and was first used in the 1994–95 session. The procedure reflects that of the special standing committees in the Commons, with a limited period of time set aside for consideration of the Bill, where the committee takes written and oral evidence on the provisions of the Bill. The committee then reverts to standard standing committee procedure and examines the Bill clause by clause. The committees are used to scrutinise Law Commission Bills which are introduced in the House of Lords. Note that select committees may also be used for the committee stage,[23] although this is rare and generally reserved for sensitive issues. Once considered by the committee, the Bill is then recommitted to a committee of the whole House.

Since 2001 there has been a Constitution Committee designed to 'examine the constitutional implications of all Public Bills coming before the House; and to keep under review the operation of the constitution'. The House of Lords also scrutinises Bills for their compatibility with Convention rights.

The pre-legislative scrutiny of Bills by Joint Select Committees is now a regular process. In 2003 a Joint Select Committee was appointed to consider a draft Corruption Bill, another considered the Mental Incapacity Bill and a further Joint Committee considered the draft Civil Contingencies Bill. In 2004 a Joint Committee considered the draft Gambling Bill and another considered the draft Disability Discrimination Bill.

Curtailment of debate

A further difference between procedure in the Commons and the Lords lies in the absence of procedures in the Lords for the curtailment of debate. The absence of the Closure Motion or the Allocation of Time Motion (Guillotine) in the Lords ensures that the contents of Bills are fully debated.

Party discipline in the House of Lords

There exists a system of 'whipping' which ensures some party political control over Members, although the extent of that control is far less than the control exerted by the whips in the Commons. The House of Lords is generally a far less party-political forum than the elected House of Commons. It must also be remembered that the House of Lords contains over 170 cross benchers, or

---

23   House of Lords Procedure Committee, *Third Report*, 1993–94.

independents, who do not owe allegiance to any particular political party. This group represents a potentially significant force in so far as the way in which cross benchers will vote cannot necessarily be foreseen in advance, let alone guaranteed. These factors, together with the independence of the House and not being accountable to an electorate, result in a scrutinising body which can review legislation in depth and largely free from the political and procedural controls which are prevalent in the House of Commons.

THE AMENDMENT OF LEGISLATION

The House of Lords has the power to delay enactment of a Bill under the Parliament Acts 1911–49, but not to veto a Bill. As will be seen, the democratically elected Lower House has the ultimate right to enact legislation in the face of opposition from the Upper House. The House of Lords does, however, have the power to propose amendments to Bills and it is their success or otherwise in this regard which requires examination. At the outset, it must be recognised that amendments proposed are of differing types and are put forward in response to a variety of circumstances. Not all amendments proposed in the Lords and accepted by the House of Commons stem from principled opposition in the House of Lords.

Some amendments are purely technical, amounting to tidying up of statutory language. Others will be the result of government undertakings to implement a proposed Commons' amendment in the Lords. Amendments also arise out of the government's willingness to rethink an aspect of a Bill in light of consideration in the Commons or within the department concerned with the legislation. The Lords here acts as a convenient forum for proposing the relevant amendments.

It may be the case that there has been opposition in the Commons to a particular proposal which the government has resisted, and has used its majority to that effect. If the government is prepared to concede a point, particularly where it foresees opposition in the Lords, it may prefer to give way than to risk losing part of the Bill on a vote in the Lords. Negotiations will frequently take place between the government department and those intending to oppose the measure in order to secure a satisfactory compromise which will ensure the smooth passage of the Bill into law.

Some amendments arise purely as a result of objections voiced in the House of Lords. One example of principled opposition in the Lords, not apparent in the Lower House, is offered by the Child Support Bill 1991.[24] In that Bill, unmarried separated mothers on state benefit were to be placed under a statutory duty to reveal the identity of the fathers of their children in order that the Child Support Agency could enforce the financial duty of fathers to support their children. When the Bill arrived in the Lords, clause 46, which offered no defence to the mother who declined to give the information, was rejected by the Lords. The Bill returned

---

24   See Barnett, 1993.

to the Commons and the government reinstated the clause but made a concession to the Lords and inserted a defence of reasonably withholding information.

The House of Lords is both very active in relation to legislation and makes a substantial impact on many legislative proposals. Most often, the House of Commons will give way to the Lords and accept their amendments, rather than risk losing a Bill for lack of parliamentary time. It must be remembered that, if a Bill fails to pass all of its stages within a session, the Bill will generally be lost and the government must make time to reintroduce it in the next session. Accordingly, the later in a session a Bill is considered by the Lords, the greater will be the inclination of the House of Commons to accept Lords' amendments.

The House of Lords following the 1999 Act

When parliamentary business resumed in January 2000, the majority of hereditary peers had been ousted. It soon became clear, however, that the 'new' House of Lords was not prepared to be more acquiescent towards government legislative proposals. Even before the new year started, the Lords were proclaiming their renewed 'legitimacy' as a revising chamber, and soon made an impact on the government's legislative programme. An example of this was seen in relation to the Criminal Justice (Mode of Trial) Bill, which in part removed the right of defendants charged with 'either way offences', such as theft and burglary, to choose their mode of trial, and which was introduced in the Lords. The Parliament Act procedures do not apply to Bills introduced in the Lords, thus making it easier for the Lords to press home its objections to the Bill successfully. The Lords rejected the Bill, forcing the government to reintroduce the Bill in the Commons where at second reading the government secured a substantial majority. The House of Lords again rejected the Bill and it was withdrawn.

The House of Lords and delegated legislation

The House of Lords' Delegated Powers and Regulatory Reform Committee's principal concern is to scrutinise Bills with a view to establishing the extent of legislative powers which parliament intends to delegate to government ministers. The role of the Committee is 'to report whether the provision of any Bill inappropriately delegates legislative power, or whether they subject the exercise of legislative power to an inappropriate degree of parliamentary scrutiny'. The committee reports to the House, which decides whether or not to accept the committee's recommendations. The committee has eight members and meets as needs require. The committee hears oral evidence in public, and takes evidence in writing on each Public Bill from the relevant government department.

The committee, in the examination of a Bill, considers four principal matters. First, it considers whether the power to make delegated, or secondary, legislation is appropriate, or whether the grant of power is so important that it should only be granted in primary legislation. Secondly, the committee pays special attention to 'Henry VIII powers'.[25] Thirdly, the committee considers which form of

---

25 On which see p 398 above.

parliamentary scrutiny of delegated legislation is appropriate, and in particular whether the power specifies the use of the affirmative or negative resolution procedure.[26] Fourthly, the committee considers whether the legislation should provide for consultation in draft form before the regulation is laid before parliament, and whether its operation should be governed by a Code of Conduct.

THE BALANCE OF POWER BETWEEN THE HOUSE OF LORDS AND THE HOUSE OF COMMONS

The Parliament Acts 1911 and 1949

Before the Parliament Act 1911, the House of Lords enjoyed equal power with the Commons over legislation, with the exception of financial measures which, by convention, the Lords recognised as falling under the authority of the elected Lower House. However, in 1909, the Finance Bill containing Lloyd George's Budget was rejected, in breach of convention, by the House of Lords. As a consequence, the House of Commons passed a Resolution declaring that there had been a breach of the constitution and a usurpation of the rights of the Commons, and calling for the power of the House of Lords to be restricted. King Edward VII was called upon to create sufficient new peers to guarantee the passage of the Finance Bill but refused to do so until the Budget was approved by the electorate. Parliament was dissolved and, in the election of January 1910, the government secured a majority of seats only with the help of minor parties. The House of Lords then passed the Finance Bill.

This conflict between the House of Commons and House of Lords resulted in the Parliament Act 1911, passed by both Houses of Parliament but with the House of Lords being threatened with the creation of more peers to ensure the Bill's safe passage. The Act abolished the Lords' right to reject Money Bills,[27] and imposed a one month time limit during which the Lords may consider such Bills and suggest amendments. If the Bill has not been approved without amendment within one month, provided it has been sent to the Lords within one month before the end of the session, the Bill will proceed to receive the royal assent without the approval of the Lords. Not all financial Bills are Money Bills. Where a Bill contains provisions dealing with other subjects it will not be a Money Bill. The Finance Bill is not automatically a Money Bill, and over half of the Finance Bills sent to the Lords since the 1911 Act have not been certified as Money Bills. While the purpose of the 1911 Act is to prevent amendment or delay in Money Bills, should the Lords propose amendments, these can be either accepted or rejected by the Commons.

Regarding non-Money Bills, the power of the House of Lords was curtailed, their right to reject legislation replaced by a power to delay Bills for a two year period spread over three parliamentary sessions.

Conflict between the two Houses resurfaced over the Labour government's nationalisation programme following the Second World War. The Labour

---

26 See further Chapter 15.
27 Bills certified by the Speaker as Money Bills, defined by the Parliament Act 1911, s 1(2).

government, fearful that the Lords would reject the Iron and Steel Bill, introduced the Parliament Bill in 1947. In 1948, a conference between party leaders from both Houses met to attempt to reach agreement on the terms of the Parliament Bill. In the event, the conference broke down and the Parliament Bill was rejected by the House of Lords at second reading, only to be passed by the Commons under the Parliament Act 1911. The 1949 Act reduced the House of Lords' power of delay over non-Money Bills from two years over three sessions to one year over two sessions. No amendment was made to the provisions of the Parliament Act 1911 regarding Money Bills.

Exclusions from the Parliament Acts

The Parliament Acts do not apply to Private Bills, Bills originating in the House of Lords, Bills containing financial measures but not certified as Money Bills (because they contain other non-money provisions), statutory instruments or Bills purporting to extend the life of a parliament beyond the five years laid down in the Septennial Act 1715, as amended by section 7 of the Parliament Act 1911.

The use of the Parliament Acts

It is notable that the Parliament Acts have been used infrequently. Aside from the Parliament Act 1949, which was passed under the 1911 Act, the Government of Ireland Act 1914, the Welsh Church Act 1914, the War Crimes Act 1991, the European Parliamentary Elections Act 1999 and the Sexual Offences (Amendment) Act 2000 and the Hunting Act 2004 were passed under this procedure. The explanation for the usually low use of the procedure lies largely in conventional practices regulating the relationship between the two Houses. First, as has been seen above, the House of Commons accepts a great many Lords' amendments, for a variety of reasons. Secondly, the House of Lords exercises its delaying powers with some caution. In debate on the War Damage Bill 1965, Lord Salisbury stated that the House of Lords should insist on amendments under two circumstances:

(a) if a matter raises issues important enough to justify such 'drastic' action;

(b) if the issue is such that the electorate can understand it and express approval for the House of Lord's position. In this regard, the House of Lords acts as a 'watchdog of the people'.[28]

Thirdly, if the House of Lords strongly disapproves of a measure but does not wish to defeat the Bill, it may move a resolution deploring parts of the Bill, as occurred in relation to the Immigration Bill 1971 and the British Nationality Act 1981. Fourthly, many disagreements between the House of Commons and the House of Lords will be resolved by negotiations between the two Houses which generally will result in the avoidance of ultimate deadlock. Finally, the Parliament Act procedure may be avoided under the amendment procedure laid down in section 2(4) of the Parliament Act 1911. Under that section, the Acts may only be used if the House of Lords, over two successive sessions, rejects the same Bill. A Bill will be deemed to be the same Bill if it is identical with the former Bill 'or

---

28   See also HL Deb Vol 365 Col 1742, 11 November 1975 (Lord Carrington).

contains only such alterations as are certified by the Speaker to be necessary owing to the time which has elapsed since the date of the former Bill, or to represent any amendments which have been made by the House of Lords in the former Bill in the preceding session'.[29] If amendments have been made which are not agreed to by the Commons, the Bill is deemed to be rejected. This formulation facilitates agreements between the two Houses, yet preserves the ultimate possible use of the Parliament Act procedure.

The Parliament Act procedure and validity

As *Pickin v British Railways Board* (1974) illustrates, the courts are – mindful of parliament's sovereign right to determine its own composition and procedure – reluctant to look at the procedure employed in enacting law. However, the recent case of *Jackson v Attorney General* (2005) provided an opportunity for the House of Lords to consider the validity of an Act which had been passed under the Parliament Act procedure. The claimants argued – unsuccessfully – that the Hunting Act 2004 was invalid because it had been passed under the Parliament Act 1949, which was also invalid. The reason for claiming that the 1949 Act was invalid was because it had been passed under the Parliament Act 1911 without the consent of the House of Lords, a position which contrasts with the 1911 Act, which could only be amended with the consent of the House of Lords.

Central to the argument was whether the Parliament Act 1949 was primary legislation or delegated legislation. It was argued that legislation is not 'primary' where it depends for its validity on a prior enactment. If it was in fact delegated legislation, then the principle came into play that a body which had been delegated power could not, without there being express permission in the delegating (parent) Act, enlarge its own powers. Applying that argument to the Parliament Acts 1911 and 1949, it was argued that the 1911 Act delegated power to the Crown and Commons to enact legislation, under specified circumstances and subject to stated exceptions, without the consent of the House of Lords. It followed that when the Parliament Act 1949 was enacted without the consent of the Lords and reduced the time period during which the Lords could delay legislation, it increased the powers delegated to the Crown and Commons and thereby infringed the principle that a delegate cannot increase its powers. Lord Bingham rejected the view that the 1911 Act delegated legislative power to the House of Commons. The overall objective of the Act, he stated, 'was not to delegate power: it was to restrict, subject to compliance with the specified statutory conditions, the power of the Lords to defeat measures supported by the majority of the Commons . . .'[30]

The House of Lords also took the opportunity to consider the precise *scope* of the power delegated to the Crown and Commons and this in turn entailed two issues. Section 2 of the 1911 Act states two types of Bills which are expressly excluded from passage under the Parliament Act procedure: Money Bills or Bills

---

29   Erskine May, 1997.
30   At p 745, 25.

extending the life of parliament beyond five years. The first question was whether the procedure could be used to amend section 2 itself and thereby extend the life of a parliament.

The Court of Appeal had concluded that there was power under the 1911 Act to make a 'relatively modest and straightforward amendment' to the Act, including the amendment made by the 1949 Act, but not to making 'changes of a fundamentally different nature to the relationship between the House of Lords and the Commons from those which the 1911 Act had made'. Lord Bingham of Cornhill stated in the Lords that that was a proposition which could not be supported in principle. He went on to state that it was unnecessary to resolve the issue whether the 1911 and 1949 Act could be relied on to extend the maximum duration of Parliament beyond five years. However, he did accept that, however academic the point might be, the Attorney General was right in submitting that the 1911 Act and 1949 Act could be used to amend or delete the reference to the maximum duration of Parliament in section 2(1) and that a further measure could then be introduced to extend the maximum duration. The issue was also considered by Lord Nicholls of Birkenhead. He accepted that the express language of the Act prevented the prolonging of the duration of a Parliament beyond five years. On whether the Commons could succeed by a two-stage process as considered by Lord Bingham, Lord Nicholls took the view that it could not be done, stating that the 'express exclusion carried with it, by necessary implication, a like exclusion in respect of legislation aimed at achieving the same result by two steps rather than one. If this were not so the express legislative intention could readily be defeated.'

The second, and related, issue was whether the Parliament Act procedure could be used to effect other fundamental constitutional reform, given that section 2 only made two stipulated exclusions from the use of the procedure: Money Bills and Bills to extend the life of a parliament. In other words, could other exclusions be implied into section 2? Lord Bingham rejected that suggestion. The House of Lords ruled that the purpose of the Parliament Act 1911 was not to enlarge the powers of the House of Commons or to delegate powers to it, but to restrict the powers of the House of Lords to defeat measures supported by the House of Commons. The 1911 Act stated that legislation made under it 'became an Act of Parliament on the Royal Assent being signified' and that there was nothing doubtful or ambiguous about that term.

On a proper interpretation of the 1911 Act, it created a parallel route by which, subject to certain exceptions, 'any' public bill introduced into the Commons could become an Act of Parliament. The term 'any' was to be construed according to its ordinary meaning. There were stated exceptions expressly stated in section 2(1) and there was no scope for introducing or implying further exclusions. Moreover there was no constitutional principle or principle of statutory construction which prohibited a legislature from altering its own constitution. Baroness Hale was forthright, rejecting the Court of Appeal's view that the 1911 procedure could not be used to effect fundamental constitutional change, stating that '... the 1911 Act procedure can be used to effect any constitutional change, with the one exception stated.'

More generally on the contemporary interpretation of parliamentary sovereignty, Lord Steyn, having alluded to the European Union and the European Convention on Human Rights, stated that: '[T]he classic account given by Dicey of the doctrine of the supremacy of Parliament, pure and absolute as it was, can now be seen to be out of place in the modern United Kingdom. Nevertheless, the supremacy of Parliament is still the *general* principle of our constitution. It is a construct of the common law. The judges created this principle.'

Suspension Motions

The Suspension Motion is a device currently available in relation to Private Bills which facilitates their passage through parliament. Where the Suspension Motion is agreed by the House of Commons, a Private Bill may be carried over from one session to another, without the loss of that Bill.

The House of Commons Procedure Committee and House of Lords Procedure Committee agreed to extend the procedure to Public Bills. Where a Bill is in the Commons at the end of one session, and a Suspension Motion is agreed, that Bill will be able to continue its life into the next session. However, the procedure is not designed to 'rescue' contentious Bills over which the two Houses disagree.[31] Rather, the procedure will apply to those Bills which the government notifies to the House of Commons as candidates for the 'carry-over' procedure.[32] It will be for the Commons to agree the motion to suspend the Bill, should the need arise.

SELECT COMMITTEES IN THE HOUSE OF LORDS

The House of Lords has no structured system of select committees as exists in the House of Commons. The House may establish ad hoc committees to consider a matter of public importance.[33] Domestic select committees exist to consider matters of procedure and privileges of the House. In addition, as has been seen, Bills may be committed to select committee for in depth consideration and report.

A number of sessional committees exist. Significant among these are the European Union Committee, the Science and Technology Committee and the Economic Affairs Committee. The former was established in 1974 to consider Commission proposals for European legislation. The committee has acquired a reputation for authoritative scrutiny of the proposals. The committee has a salaried chairman and 18 permanent members, seven sub-committees, and a considerable staff of clerks and legal advisers. It has the right to appoint expert advisers as and when needed. The European Union Committee's terms of reference are:

---

31 Eg, the Crime and Disorder Bill 1998, which provided for the lowering of the age of consent to sexual intercourse between men.
32 The Financial Services and Markets Bill 1999 was passed under the carry-over procedure.
33 For example, Unemployment (1979–82); Overseas Trade (1984–85), Murder and Life Imprisonment (1988–89).

To consider European Union documents and other matters relating to the European Union.

By a Resolution of the House of Lords[34] the government will not, except in special circumstances, agree to any proposal in the Council until it has been cleared by the Committee.

All of the committee's reports (unlike those of the House of Commons) are debated in the Chamber. The government undertakes to respond to the reports within two months of a report's publication.

In the 2000–01 session, three new sessional committees were established. The Select Committee on the Constitution has two main functions. First, it examines the constitutional implications of all Public Bills coming before the House: the scrutiny function. Second, it keeps under review the operation of the constitution: the investigative function. The Committee has 12 members and is assisted by a Legal Adviser. When examining Bills, the Committee considers whether the Bill raises issues of principle affecting the constitution. If it does, the Committee may request information or clarification from the Minister responsible for the Bill or seek other advice. The Committee reports its evidence to the House and publishes any conclusion it has reached. If a Bill is subject to pre-legislative scrutiny, the Constitution Committee may communicate its views on the draft Bill to the Committee. In exercising its investigative function, the Committee may engage specialist advisers, take oral evidence and receive written evidence. The Committee publishes a report and the government is obliged to respond to the report.

Scrutiny reports published in the 2004–05 Session included:

- Inquiries Bill (HL Paper 21);
- Prevention of Terrorism Bill (HL Paper 66);
- Serious Organised Crime and Police Bill (HL Paper 65);
- Identity Cards Bill (HL Paper 82).

The Joint Committee on Human Rights was established, having six members from the House of Lords and five from the House of Commons.[35] The Committee's terms of reference are wide. It has power to consider 'matters relating to human rights' (but not individual cases); to consider proposals for remedial orders, draft remedial orders and those laid before parliament and to consider whether the attention of the House should be drawn to any aspect of them. The Committee has expressed a preference for law reform to be accomplished by primary legislation rather than remedial orders wherever possible in order to ensure adequate parliamentary scrutiny.[36]

The Economic Affairs Committee, having a membership of 13 and supported by a Clerk, a Secretary and a part-time Specialist Adviser, examines economic matters with which parliament should be concerned. The Committee works through formal investigative enquiries hearing oral evidence and examining

---

34   6 December 1999.
35   See Feldman, 2002.
36   See HL 58/HC 473 of 2001–02.

written evidence following which a report will be published, to which the government must formally respond.

The Steering Committee

In order to co-ordinate better the work of committees in the Lords, there is a Steering Committee which serves functions similar to those of the Liaison Committee in the Commons – namely, deciding on subjects for investigation by ad hoc select committees, allocating resources between differing select committees and monitoring the work of the committees.

MEMBERS' INTERESTS IN THE LORDS

In November 1995, a Register of Members' Interests was established, in which a number of interests must be recorded. The requirements are that three categories of interests must be registered, namely:

(a) consultancies or other similar arrangements involving payment or other incentive or reward for providing parliamentary advice or services. Registration under this category is mandatory;

(b) financial interests in businesses involved in parliamentary lobbying on behalf of clients. This requirement is also mandatory;

(c) other particulars relating to matters which the Lords consider may affect the public perception of the way in which they discharge their parliamentary duties. Registration under this category is discretionary.

Interests should be declared in debate whenever Members have a direct financial interest in a subject, along with any other interest which might affect the judgment of the House. The Committee on Lords' Interests has power to investigate allegations of failure to comply with the requirements. The register is published annually.

REFORM OF THE HOUSE OF LORDS

> With a perfect Lower House it is certain that an Upper House would be scarcely of any value ... But though beside an ideal House of Commons the Lords would be unnecessary, and therefore pernicious, beside the actual House a revising and leisured legislature is extremely useful ...[37]

Both the Labour and Liberal Democrat Parties have long had proposals to reform the House of Lords. As seen above, the current Labour government is translating its commitment into reality, as a first step removing the right of the majority of hereditary peers to sit and vote. In the past, the Labour Party has advocated total abolition of the Upper House. Much of the antagonism to the Lords stems from basic principles of democracy, its opponents focusing on the fundamental paradox of a sophisticated democratic state having, as part of its legislative body,

---

37 Bagehot, 1867, pp 133–34.

an unelected and democratically unaccountable institution. The preamble to the Parliament Act 1911 envisaged replacing the House of Lords with an elected House:

> And whereas it is intended to substitute for the House of Lords as it at present exists a Second Chamber constituted on a popular instead of hereditary basis, but such substitution cannot be immediately brought into operation ...

This did not represent the first proposal to reform the House of Lords. As early as 1886 and 1888, debate took place in the House of Commons on the desirability or otherwise of an hereditary element in the legislature. As has been seen above, the constitutional conflict between the House of Lords and Commons in 1908–10 resulted in the restriction on the Lords' powers and the intention to replace the House of Lords.

In 1917, a conference comprising 15 Members of each House was established, under the chairmanship of Viscount Bryce, to consider the composition and powers of the Upper House. Reporting in 1918, the conference recommended that the Upper House should consist of 246 Members indirectly elected by Members of Parliament grouped into regional units, plus 81 Members chosen by a joint standing committee of both Houses of Parliament. The conference regarded the appropriate functions of this revised chamber to be the examination and revision of Commons Bills, the initiation of non-controversial Bills, the discussion of policy, and the 'interposition of so much delay (and no more) in the passing of a Bill into law as may be needed to enable the opinion of the nation to be adequately expressed upon it'. No action was taken on the recommendations.

Following the First World War, reform of the House of Lords remained on the political agenda. A Cabinet committee established to consider the matter rejected the Bryce conference proposals as unacceptable. In 1922, the government put forward proposals for a House of Lords made up of 350 Members. The majority of these were to be either directly or indirectly elected 'from the outside', with the remainder comprising some hereditary peers elected by peers, plus Members nominated by the Crown. The precise numbers of these latter categories were to be laid down in statute. No action resulted from these proposals. Between 1924 and 1935 one further set of Cabinet committee proposals was rejected, as were three Private Members' Bills introduced by Conservative peers in 1929, 1933 and 1935. The Parliament Act 1949, discussed above, was passed by the Labour government and remains the basis for the relationship between the Houses of Commons and Lords today.

Reform remained on the agenda in the 1950s, the Conservative Party manifesto of 1951 promising a further all-party conference on reform. The Labour Party in 1953 declined to co-operate and no further action was taken. In 1958, two significant reforms were introduced by the Conservative government. The first of these related to the problem of the 'backwoodsmen': those peers who make no contribution to the work of the House but nevertheless retain the right to sit and vote when called upon to do so by the government. The report of a House of Lords select committee recommended that Standing Orders be amended to enable those peers who did not regularly attend the House to take leave of absence. This recommendation was adopted but it did not produce an effective solution to the problem posed by the 'backwoodsmen'. The remaining defect lay in the fact that, even where leave of absence was obtained, there was no mechanism existing whereby a peer could be denied the right to enter the House, even if he had not complied with the requirement to give once month's notice of his intention to return to the House.

The Life Peerage Act 1958

The second reform of 1958 was the introduction of the Life Peerage Act. This Act enables the Crown, on the advice of the Prime Minister, to confer peerages for life on men and women who have reached prominence in public life. This single reform has effectively revitalised the Upper House, providing an increased resource of specialisation and experience. By convention, life peerages are conferred on Members of any political party, and on those who have no particular political affiliation. Towards this end, the leaders of the major political parties put forward nominations to the Prime Minister on an annual basis. The Labour Party in the 1980s refused to make any nominations at all, basing their refusal on principled objection to the elitist nature of the House of Lords. This stance has proven to be something of an 'own goal' for the Labour Party, whose membership of the House of Lords is now smaller than it might otherwise have been.

The Peerage Act 1963

In 1963, a more limited, but nonetheless important, reform was implemented. The Peerage Act 1963 has its origins in the succession to a peerage by Anthony Wedgwood-Benn (as he then was), a Member of the House of Commons. As a result of succeeding to the title of Viscount Stansgate, Tony Benn, the Member for Bristol South East[38] was barred from taking his seat in the Commons. A joint committee of the Houses of Commons and Lords reported on this matter in 1962 and recommended reform. As noted earlier, the Peerage Act 1963 provides that a person succeeding to a peerage may disclaim his peerage within one year of his succession,[39] and that a Member of the House of Commons may disclaim within a one month period from succession. The disclaimer is irrevocable, but operates only for the lifetime of the peer disclaiming the title: the title will devolve to his heir upon his death. Section 6 of the the Peerage Act 1963 provides for the first time that peeresses in their own right are entitled to sit and vote in the House of Lords.

The 1968 reform proposals

The Labour government of 1967–69 again turned its attention to reform of the composition of the House of Lords. The party manifesto of 1966 declared the intention to introduce reforms to safeguard measures approved by the House of Commons against delay or defeat in the House of Lords. An all-party conference

---

38   See *Re Parliamentary Election for Bristol South East* (1964).
39   Or on attaining the age of majority.

took place in 1967–68, at which substantial cross-party agreement was reached on the proposals for reform. The resultant government White Paper of 1968[40] proposed that there should be a two tier House. The first tier would consist of 230 voting peers who satisfied a test of attendance on a regular basis. The second tier would consist of peers who remained entitled to attend and to participate in debate, but would not be entitled to vote. The right to a seat in the House of Lords by virtue of succession to a peerage would be removed but existing peers (who did not satisfy the attendance criteria) would either become non-voting peers or might be conferred a life peerage with entitlement to vote. It was recommended that the government of the day should have a small, but not overall, majority of voting peers in the House. The White Paper also recommended that the power of delay by the House of Lords be reduced to a six month period. The White Paper was approved by the House of Lords by 251 votes to 56. An alliance of the far right of the Conservative Party and the left wing of the Labour Party in the House of Commons caused the White Paper to be rejected by 270 votes to 159.

The government proceeded to introduce the Parliament (No 2) Bill 1968 to give effect to the White Paper. The Bill received a second reading by 285 votes to 185, but the committee stage, taken as a committee of the Whole House, became protracted and, after over 80 hours of consideration, the Prime Minister announced the withdrawal of the Bill.

The Labour government's reform agenda

The first commitment made in relation to the House of Lords by the Labour Party before its election to office in 1997 was to abolish, as a first measure, the voting rights of hereditary peers. This was accomplished under the House of Lords Act 1999. Consistent with this proposal is the removal of the right of members of the Royal Family to vote in the House of Lords. The government's ultimate objective, as stated in its election manifesto, was to replace the current House of Lords with a new elected second chamber, elected under a system of proportional representation. The elected House, according to the manifesto, would have the power to delay, for the lifetime of a parliament, changes to 'designated legislation reducing individual or constitutional rights'. However, as will be seen below, the Labour Party's plans for reforming the Lords changed significantly once elected to government.

Once in office, the Labour government moved cautiously. A Royal Commission was established to consider the next phase in reform and to make recommendations. All reform of the House of Lords is problematic. The 1968 reforms failed to be implemented, not because of opposition in the House of Lords, but through opposition in the House of Commons, which crossed party lines. The opposition arose from the Commons' perception that removing the right of hereditary peers to vote would enhance the authority of the House of Lords, and would risk the Lords becoming more bold in its dealing with the House of Commons. One key question for the Royal Commission and the

---

40   Cmnd 3799, 1968, London: HMSO.

government, therefore, was how to move forward to the second reform stage in order to produce an effective and valuable second chamber without threatening the supremacy of the democratically elected House of Commons.

The problem of legitimacy remained after the removal of the hereditary peers' right to vote. Given the fact of political patronage, for services rendered to the Party or country, the life peers have no more constitutional legitimacy than do hereditary peers. Thus, removing the hereditary peers from the House of Lords did not effect any constitutional change of real value, and certainly did not mark a move towards greater democratic legitimacy, but represented no more than a starting point for further, largely undefined, future reform, the consequences of which, in terms of the distribution of power between the two Houses, will depend on both the nature and scope of the reform.

The Royal Commission Report: a House for the future

The Royal Commission Report was published in January 2000. To the disappointment of those advocating radical reform, the Commission recommended that the Upper House, having around 550 members, comprise a majority of nominated members and a minority of selected or elected members representing regional interests. However, despite widespread consultation, the Commission reached no consensus on the most difficult issue: the number of selected or elected members and the method by which members would be selected.

The powers of the second chamber would remain broadly as they are at present, with the second chamber being able to delay, but ultimately not to defeat, primary legislation. The Salisbury convention should continue to be respected. The report recommended that there be greater use of pre-legislative scrutiny of Bills. In relation to secondary legislation, the second chamber should be given power to delay their implementation and to voice its concerns. The power to defeat secondary legislation – in practice, never used – would be removed.

In relation to composition, three options were put forward. Model A provided for 65 members selected by dividing up a regional allocation of seats according to each party's share of the vote in that region at general elections, with one third of the regions selecting regional members at each general election. Model B, supported by a majority of the Commission, proposed 87 members, directly elected at the same time as the European Parliament elections under a system of proportional representation. Model C provided for 195 regional members directly elected at the same time as the European Parliament elections.

On the system of nominations for the House, the Commission recommended that an independent Appointments Commission be established, which would sever the link between the granting of honours and the political patronage of the Prime Minister and government. The Commission also recommended that there should be both gender and ethnic minority representation in the House. The current system of granting of honours would remain, but would not result in membership of the House of Lords.

The Commission recommended that existing life peers, appointed before the publication of the report, who wish to remain in the second chamber should be deemed to have been appointed for life, whereas life peers appointed between the publication of the report and the necessary legislation implementing the report's recommendations should be deemed to be appointed for a 15 year term from the date of the award of the life peerage. On remuneration, the Commission recommended that the financial arrangements be adequate to make regular attendance economically viable, and that remuneration should be linked to attendance in parliament. Payments made, however, for time and lost income should be less than the basic salary of a Member of Parliament over an average session.

The report's recommendations were far removed from the aspirations of those seeking a democratically elected second chamber. That radical option foundered on the problem of the constitutional balance of power between two elected chambers, and the fear – which has always dogged reform of the House of Lords – that the Commons might lose its supremacy. But the Wakeham Report did foresee a second chamber with at least the same powers as the current House of Lords, and one which is broadly representative of British society. In breaking the link between peerages and membership of the second chamber, the Commission removed one of the most contentious aspects of the political honours system in which membership of the second chamber is seen to be conferred for political services to the governing party. Instead, the Commission sought a second chamber which 'should be authoritative, confident, and broadly representative of the whole of British society', its members having a breadth of experience outside the world of politics, skills and knowledge relevant to the careful assessment of constitutional matters. The Commission stated that its intention was to recommend proposals which were not only 'persuasive and intellectually coherent but also workable, durable and politically realistic'.[41]

In 2000, a non-statutory House of Lords Appointments Commission was established as an interim measure, which has the function of making recommendations for non-party-political peerages in the House of Lords.[42] In addition, the Committee vets all nominations for peerages from political parties with a view to assessing their propriety. All nominees are asked to give their consent to the checks to be made by the Commission. Concerns arise over the award of a peerage to persons who have made significant donations to a political party (on which see further page 357–58). Although that does not preclude a peerage being granted, the Commission must be satisfied that the person in question is a credible nominee irrespective of any donations. The Commission takes over the role formerly played by the Prime Minister.[43]

---

41 In 2000 a Private Member's Bill, the Life Peerages (Appointments Commission) Bill, was introduced, detailing the procedure and criteria for appointment to the House of Lords. That Bill failed. On the current arrangements, see below.

42 HL Deb Vol 60 Col WA179, 25 January 2000.

43 The Commission contacted 10,000 organisations, urging them to inform their members and staff, but no public advertisements were placed. The first 15 Members appointed all nominated themselves.

The government's response to the Royal Commission Report

The government signalled its acceptance in principle of the Report. However, the White Paper published in November 2001 made clear that only a minority of peers would be elected.[44] The stated aim was to reduce the size of the House from 700 to 600 members over ten years, with 120 Members directly elected and up to 332 Members nominated by party leaders, with 120 non-party (independent) Members being chosen by the independent Appointments Commission. The number of bishops would be reduced to 16 from 26. The rights of the remaining hereditary peers to sit would be removed. The government rejected the call for more diverse religious representation and the proposal that Members should be salaried.

It was expected that a Draft Bill would be presented in Spring 2002, following the government's consideration of responses to its White Paper. However, that expectation was dashed when disputes arose over the proportion of Members who would be directly elected, with members of the government and the Labour Party opposing the 20 per cent proposal.

In a free vote in February 2003 both the House of Lords and House of Commons voted on a number of reform options: the House of Commons rejected all options while the House of Lords voted to retain a fully-appointed House. A new proposal for reform emerged in 2004, a proposal supported by both the Secretary of State for Constitutional Affairs and the Leader of the House of Commons. It was proposed that a proportion of seats in the Lords should be allocated in proportion to the balance of votes cast for candidates for the House of Commons in a region at a general election. This would achieve a House which is in part indirectly elected: the balance of members would be appointed by the statutory Appointments Commission.

No further action has yet been taken and in 2006 it was proposed that a Joint Committee be established to consider the power and composition of the House of Lords.

Further constitutional reform which affects the House of Lords has been undertaken. The Constitutional Reform Act 2005, discussed further in Chapter 4, reforms the office of Lord Chancellor; makes provision for the House of Lords to make its own arrangements in relation to a Speaker; removes the Appellate Committee of the House of Lords and replaces it with a Supreme Court physically removed from the Houses of Parliament; and establishes a Judicial Appointments Commission.

---

44 *The House of Lords: Completing the Reform*, Cmd 5291, London: HMSO.

CHAPTER 18

PARLIAMENTARY PRIVILEGE

DEFINITION AND CONSTITUTIONAL SIGNIFICANCE OF PRIVILEGE

The privileges of parliament are those rules of both Houses of Parliament which offer protection from outside interference – from whatever source – to the Houses collectively, and to individual members. Erskine May defines privilege as being:

> ... the sum of the peculiar rights enjoyed by each House collectively as a constituent part of the High Court of Parliament, and by Members of each House individually, without which they could not discharge their functions, and which exceed those possessed by other bodies or individuals. Thus, privilege, though part of the law of the land, is to a certain extent an exemption from the general law. [1997, p 69]

Parliamentary privilege provides protection for Members of Parliament against accusations of defamation from outside parliament and also protects the individual member – in the exercise of his or her freedom of speech – from the executive.

Parliamentary privilege presents some intriguing constitutional issues. In some respects, privilege may be compared with the royal prerogative, in so far as both privilege and the prerogative represent a unique aspect of legal power reserved exclusively for a special class of persons. Moreover, parliamentary privilege is a legal power in respect of which the courts – mindful of the doctrine of separation of powers – will be cautious in accepting jurisdiction to regulate. By asserting special powers and immunities for parliament as a whole, and for its members individually, parliament throws around itself a cloak of protection which provides rights and immunities not accorded to individual citizens. The balance which is – and ought to be – struck between legitimate and necessary safeguards for parliament and its members in the exercise of parliamentary duties and the rights of individuals to the protection of the general law is not always satisfactorily achieved.

The law and practice of privilege reveals the extent to which individual members and parliament as a body are free from outside pressure – whether from interest groups, sponsoring bodies and institutions or the media – a freedom which is central to ensure an independent parliament. However, as Marshall and Moodie point out, 'the boundary lines between free comment, legitimate pressure, and improper interference are obviously not easy to formulate in principle' (1971, p 112).

The law and custom of parliament

The privileges enjoyed form part of the 'law and custom of parliament' – *lex et consuetudo parliamenti* – and, as such, it is for parliament to adjudicate on matters of privilege, not the courts.[1] Privileges are embodied in rules of the Houses of

---

1   Coke, 1 Inst 15.

Parliament. The United Kingdom Parliament, however, is not free to extend existing privileges by a mere resolution of the House: only statute can create new privileges.[2] Privileges derive from practice and tradition; they are thus customary in origin. Nevertheless, they are recognised as having the status of law, being the 'law and custom of parliament'. Parliament itself can – in the exercise of its sovereign power – place privileges on a statutory basis. For example, in 1770, the Parliamentary Privilege Act withdrew the privilege of freedom from arrest from servants of Members of Parliament. Further, in 1689, Article IX of the Bill of Rights gave statutory recognition to the freedom of speech in parliament. In 1868, parliament ended its own jurisdiction to determine disputed elections, conferring jurisdiction on the courts by way of the Administration of Justice Act.

The role of the courts

The role of the courts in matters of privilege is confined to determining whether a privilege exists, and its scope. If the court rules that a disputed matter falls within parliamentary privilege the court will decline jurisdiction. This relationship between parliament and the courts may be viewed in two ways. First, it could be viewed as the courts giving recognition to the supremacy – or sovereignty – of parliament. Historically, parliament was established as the High Court of Parliament, having legislative *and* judicial powers.[3] Accordingly, it was appropriate for the ordinary courts of law to defer to the highest court in the land. Nowadays, this justification is less well founded. It is unconvincing to portray parliament, except when exercising its judicial function in enforcing and upholding privilege, as a judicial body.[4] The relationship between parliament and the courts may also be explained by reference to the doctrine of the separation of powers. For the judiciary to rule on the legality of actions of Members of Parliament acting in their parliamentary capacity or on the actions of the House as a whole would, under current constitutional arrangements, place judges in a potentially dangerous position, exercising a controlling power over both the legislature and the executive within it.

THE PRINCIPAL PRIVILEGES

The principal individual privileges are freedom of speech in parliament and freedom of members from arrest in civil matters. The collective privileges of parliament include the exclusive right to regulate composition and procedure, right of access to the Sovereign, and the right to the 'favourable construction' by the Sovereign in relation to its actions. These are formally claimed by the Speaker, in the form of a Speaker's Petition to Her Majesty, at the opening of each new parliamentary session.

The privileges are substantially the same for both Houses of Parliament (though see below on the 'privilege of peerage'). Each House has the sole right to

2   *Stockdale v Hansard* (1839).
3   See McIlwain, 1910.
4   See below for a discussion of recent criticism of the Committee of Privileges and the decision making process of the House of Commons in disciplining members.

regulate the privileges it enjoys – although neither House is free to extend its own privileges other than by statute – and, as a result, some minor differences may be discerned between the two Houses.

Historical overview

Originally designed to protect the right of the King to the services of his advisers, the right to freedom from molestation and arrest was established early. By the sixteenth century, parliament itself was assuming jurisdiction to regulate privilege, and privilege was increasingly being used to protect the fledgling parliament from the power of the Crown. Nowadays, while a few privileges are principally of historical interest, the majority remain central to the working of parliament.

Freedom from arrest

The first recorded statement of the right to freedom from arrest dates from 1340.[5] In 1404, the Commons formally claimed that members were privileged against arrest 'for debt, contract, or trespass of any kind according to the custom of the realm'.[6] The King, however, paid little heed and the matter was not finally resolved. In 1512, Strode, a member of the Commons, was imprisoned under a court order for proposing certain Bills in parliament. Parliament reacted by passing an Act declaring the proceedings against him void, and also that any future proceedings against its members would be void.[7] In 1627, when King Charles I arrested and detained five knights, his action was challenged by an application for habeas corpus. The application failed, the court accepting the certificate of the Crown stating that they had been detained by special order of the King: *per speciale mandatum regis*.[8] In 1629, three members were charged with uttering seditious words in debate and violence against the Speaker of the House. The Crown contended, and the court accepted, that privilege did not attach to seditious words or assault.[9] The Petition of Right 1628 declared the arbitrary power of detention unlawful. In 1640, the Habeas Corpus Act placed protection by writ of habeas corpus from the Crown on a statutory basis and, in 1641, the House declared that arrests of its members were contrary to the law and privilege of parliament.[10]

Freedom of speech

An early example of the Commons protecting its own against the King is the case of Thomas Haxey,[11] who, in 1397, laid a Bill before parliament criticising Richard

---

5   *Bulletin of the Institute of Historical Research*, 1970, Vol 43, pp 214–15, cited in Erskine May, 1997, p 74.
6   *Ibid.*
7   *Strode's Case*; see Maitland, 1908.
8   *Darnel's Case* (the *Five Knights' Case*) (1627).
9   *Eliot's Case* (1629).
10 CJ (1640–42) 203, 3 St Tr 235; 1 Hatsell 250–80, cited in Erskine May, 1997, p 73.
11 (1397) Rot Parl, iii 434.

II. The House of Lords condemned Haxey to die as a traitor, but an Archbishop claimed he was a clerk, thereby giving him the protection of the clergy. He was later pardoned. The Commons subsequently declared that the action against him was contrary to their privileges.

Erskine May reports that the first recorded claim of privilege of speech was contained in the petition of Sir Thomas More in 1523, asking Henry VIII:

> ... to take all in good part, interpreting every man's words, how uncunningly soever they may be couched, to proceed yeat of a good zeale towards the profit of your Realme. [1997, p 72]

This bold assertion met with no recorded reply, but it is thought that Henry was generally tolerant of the Commons since he had little to fear from it. Nevertheless, between that time and 1689, freedom of speech in parliament remained a contended matter. In 1571, Elizabeth I warned the Commons that they would 'do well to meddle with no matters of state but such as should be propounded unto them, and to occupy themselves in other matters concerning the Commonwealth'.[12] Elizabeth maintained her grudging attitude to free speech, reminding the Speaker in 1593 that it was her prerogative not only to summon and dissolve parliament but also to dictate what members could discuss.[13] James I reasserted the supremacy of the Monarchy, stating in 1621 that the privileges of the Commons were derived from the 'grace and permission of our ancestors and us', and that privileges would be respected only to the extent that members acted 'within their duty' – as the King saw it. Parliament's response was to draw up a protestation formally asserting, *inter alia*, that:

> Every Member of the House of Parliament hath, and of right ought to have, freedom of speech, to propound, treat, reason and bring to conclusion the same. [Lockyer, 1985, p 226]

The King's reaction was to remove the protestation from the Commons' Journal and dissolve parliament.

The reign of Charles I (1625–49) was dominated by the struggle between the King and parliament, culminating in the Civil Wars of 1642–48 and the execution of Charles I in 1649. The Petition of Right asserted parliament's power over the King in matters of taxation, imprisonment without good cause and the imposition of martial law. Charles I dissolved parliament in 1629 and ruled for 11 years without a parliament.[14]

The Glorious Revolution of 1688 and the Declaration of Right was finally to settle the conflicts between parliament and the Crown. The issue of free speech in parliament was to be resolved by Article IX of the Bill of Rights 1689 (see further below), which conferred absolute protection – or legal immunity – for words spoken by Members of Parliament during the course of proceedings in parliament.

---

12 Cited in Lockyer, 1985.
13 The penalty for flouting the Queen's will was either to be barred from the House or to be imprisoned: Lockyer, 1985, p 190.
14 On this reign under the royal prerogative, see Chapter 6.

THE CURRENT SCOPE AND ROLE OF PRIVILEGE

Freedom from arrest

For Members of the House of Commons, the freedom extends for 40 days before the start of and 40 days after the end of the session. For peers, the privilege protects from arrest in civil matters at all times. The freedom from arrest does not extend to criminal charges or convictions.[15]

Where the criminal law is concerned, there is no immunity, and the re-arrest of a Member of the House of Commons who had escaped from prison, in the Chamber of the House, was not contrary to privilege.[16] In 1939, a Member of Parliament – Captain Ramsay – was detained under defence regulations. His detention did not amount to a breach of privilege, although it would have done so had he been detained for words spoken in parliament.[17]

Where a member is arrested on a criminal charge, the Speaker of the House is notified and in turn will report to the House either orally or in writing. If a member is detained on grounds of mental illness under the Mental Health Act 1983 then – following specialists' reports to the Speaker confirming the member's illness and detention – his seat will be declared vacant.

Nowadays, the freedom relates only to civil matters and is generally of little significance, given that, with one important exception, imprisonment for debt has been abolished. The exception concerns the availability of imprisonment as a penalty for the non-payment of financial provision during marriage, upon divorce, and for children born outside marriage. In 1963, in the case of *Stourton v Stourton*, a Member of the House of Lords was able to escape the sanction of prison for maintenance default by pleading privilege. It is anomalous that Members of Parliament should be immune from the law in even this limited manner. The Committee on Parliamentary Privilege recommended, in 1967, that the freedom be abolished,[18] but no action was taken.

Freedom of speech and 'proceedings in parliament'

Presently, it is more important to notice that this freedom of speech holds good not only against the Crown, but also against private individuals. A member speaking in either House is quite outside the law of defamation:

> He may accuse any person of the basest crimes, may do so knowing that his words are false, and yet that person will be unable to take any action against him.[19]

The most important privilege claimed by parliament is freedom of speech. Article IX provides that 'freedom of speech and debates in proceedings in parliament ought not to be impeached or questioned in any court or place outside of

---

15 4 Rot Parl 357; 1 Hatsell 17–22, *Thorpe's Case* (1452), cited in Erskine May, 1997, p 75; *John Wilke's Case* (1760–64).
16 Lord Cochrane, 1815: CJ (1814–16) 186; Parl Deb (1814–15) 30, c 309, 336; Colchester ii, 534, 536, cited in Erskine May, 1997, p 95.
17 HC 164 (1939–40), London: HMSO.
18 HC 34 (1967–68), London: HMSO, p xxix.
19 Maitland, 1908, p 375. On the Defamation Act 1996 see further below, p 470.

parliament'. It has been seen above that, if a matter falls within the privileges of parliament, the courts will have no jurisdiction over the matter, other than to determine whether or not a matter of alleged privilege falls within the ambit of privilege. If a positive determination is made, jurisdiction to rule on the matter falls to parliament and not the courts. In order to make such a determination in relation to freedom of speech, the courts are obliged to interpret Article IX of the Bill of Rights, and the phrase 'proceedings in parliament'.

Some matters are settled. The Bill of Rights makes clear that freedom of speech in debate is protected from legal action and redress under the law of defamation. Debates and questions on the floor of the House and in standing and select committees are therefore clearly protected. Other situations are, or have been, less straightforward. For example, what is the situation where a Member of Parliament is discussing parliamentary matters outside the precincts of parliament, or where a Member of Parliament writes to a minister on such a matter? Moreover, what is the position where a member writes to the minister or another member with regard to a matter which he wishes to raise in parliament, or which involves allegations made against bodies or persons outside parliament, on which he requires further information before raising the issue in parliament? Despite numerous suggestions for reform to inject greater clarity into the law, many matters remain unclear. The most recent consideration of the scope of proceedings in parliament is discussed below.

The case law is instructive. In *Rivlin v Bilainkin* (1953), the plaintiff in an action for defamation had been granted an interim injunction to restrain the defendant from repeating the alleged defamation. The defendant repeated the defamatory remarks in letters and took them to the House of Commons, giving one to a messenger to deliver to a Member of Parliament and posting the other four, addressed to other members, in the House of Commons' post office. In an action for an order committing the defendant for a breach of the injunction, the defendant argued that publication of the repetition of the libel was committed within the precincts of the House of Commons and was accordingly not actionable in a court of law. Mr Justice McNair declared himself:

> ... satisfied that no question of privilege arises, for a variety of reasons, and particularly I rely on the fact that the publication was not connected in any way with any proceedings in that House ...

In *Duncan Sandys'* case, in 1938, Mr Duncan Sandys had sent to the Secretary of State for War the draft of a parliamentary question in which he drew attention to a shortage of military equipment. Within the draft, Mr Sandys quoted figures which, in the view of the War Office, could have been obtained only as a result of a breach of the Official Secrets Acts 1911–20. The Attorney General interviewed Mr Sandys, who later complained that he was being threatened with prosecution – in breach of privilege – for failing to disclose the source of his information. A select committee was established to consider the relevance of the Official Secrets Acts to members acting in their parliamentary capacity. The Committee Report considered Article IX of the Bill of Rights, and it observed that:

> ... the privilege is not confined to words spoken in debate or to spoken words, but extends to all proceedings in Parliament. While the term 'proceedings in Parliament' has

never been construed by the courts, it covers both the asking of a question and the giving written notice of such question, and includes everything said or done by a Member in the exercise of his functions as a Member in a committee of either House, as well as everything said or done in either House in the transaction of parliamentary business.

The Committee went on to assert that:

... words spoken or things done by a Member beyond the walls of Parliament will generally not be protected. Cases may, however, easily be imagined of communications between one Member and another, or between a Member and a Minister, so closely related to some matter pending in, or expected to be brought before, the House, that though they do not take place in the chamber or a committee room they form part of the business of the House, as, for example, where a Member sends to the Minister the draft of the Question he is thinking of putting down or shows it to another Member with a view to obtaining advice as to the propriety of putting it down or as to the manner in which it should be framed ...

... on the other hand, a casual conversation in the House cannot be said to be a proceeding in Parliament, and a Member who discloses information in the course of such a conversation would not, in their view, be protected by privilege ...

The Committee ruled that if it were necessary, in order to prove the charge alleged, to produce evidence of what the defendant had said in the House:

... it would be in the power of the House to protect him by withholding permission for the evidence to be given.[20]

The response of the House differed markedly in the case of *Strauss and the London Electricity Board* in 1958.[21] At issue was whether or not communication in written form between a Member of Parliament and a minister was protected by privilege. George Strauss MP had forwarded a letter from a constituent to the relevant minister, in which criticism was made of the manner in which the Board disposed of scrap metal. The minister passed the letter to the Board for comment, whereupon the Board threatened to sue Mr Strauss for libel. The member believed that this was a matter concerned with his parliamentary duties and that he should be covered by privilege. The Committee of Privileges concluded that the letter written was a proceeding in parliament and that, accordingly, the Board had committed a breach of the privilege of the House. The committee was undecided as to whether the Parliamentary Privilege Act 1770 (which provides that legal action taken against members is in itself a breach of the privilege of the House) applied. It was recommended that the House seek a ruling from the Judicial Committee of the Privy Council on the matter. The Judicial Committee ruled that the Act referred only to legal action taken against a member in his private capacity, and not as a result of his conduct as a Member of Parliament. The committee so reported to the House which, following debate, surprisingly rejected the finding of the committee. The London Electricity Board subsequently withdrew its action for libel, and an independent inquiry set up by the minister exonerated the Board.[22]

---

20 *Report from the Select Committee on the Official Secrets Act*, HC 146 (1938–39), London: HMSO.
21 HC 305 (1956–57), HC 227 (1957–58), 591, HC Official Report, 5th Ser, Col 208, London: HMSO; *Re Parliamentary Privilege Act 1770* (1958); Cmnd 431, 1958, London: HMSO; Denning, 1985.
22 Cmnd 605, 1958, London: HMSO.

The case raises two important questions for consideration. First, a great many important negotiations and communications take place through informal discussion between members outside the precincts of the House. Much of this business is as important as matters raised for formal debate in the House, yet it is not covered by parliamentary privilege unless so closely associated to actual or pending proceedings in parliament as to be brought within that phrase.

Secondly, many of the matters dealt with by Members of Parliament involve, as did the *Strauss* case, alleged grievances reported by constituents against government departments and associated public bodies. Inevitably, such grievances may entail actual or potentially libellous statements, but they are not protected by privilege. Where such a matter falls within the jurisdiction of the Parliamentary Commissioner, protection is now afforded by section 10(5) of the Parliamentary Commissioner Act 1967, which provides that such communications are absolutely privileged.[23] Uncertainty remains, however, where it is unclear as to whether or not the matter falls within his jurisdiction. It is unsatisfactory that neither members of the public, nor of parliament, are clear as to the potential scope of liability under the law of defamation.

Two further cases illustrate the scope of the privilege. *R v Rule* (1937) involved a letter written by a constituent to his Member of Parliament complaining about the conduct of a police officer and a magistrate. In an action for libel the court held that, where a communication was one made under a duty or common interest, the matter would attract qualified privilege: that is to say, it would be protected from liability unless malice were proven. A similar conclusion was reached in *Beach v Freeson* (1972), where a Member of Parliament was sued by a firm of solicitors, concerning whom the member had received complaints from a constituent and forwarded the letter, with a covering letter, to the Lord Chancellor and the Law Society. That the letters were defamatory was not contested, but the court nevertheless held that publication of the letters (to the Lord Chancellor and Law Society) was protected by qualified privilege on the basis of public interest.

In *Buchanan v Jennings* (2004)[24] the Privy Council considered the protection from defamation under Article IX of the Bill of Rights 1689.[25] The defendant had made defamatory statements in debate in the New Zealand House of Representatives: these were absolutely privileged and therefore not actionable. Subsequently, however, the defendant was interviewed by a newspaper journalist and stated that he 'did not resile'[26] from the claims made in Parliament. The plaintiff sued: such words were not covered by privilege. Further, nothing in the law of privilege prevented the plaintiff from relying on a record of what was said in parliament as evidence to support an action against the Member based on what

---

23　On the jurisdiction of the Commissioner, see Chapter 28.
24　See Geddis, 2005.
25　Note that decisions of the Privy Council are persuasive rather than binding on the domestic courts.
26　Meaning that he stood by what he had said previously.

he had said outside the House. At common law every republication of a libel was a new libel and a new cause of action. Accordingly, the Member of Parliament could be held liable in defamation if he later adopted or confirmed the original statement, without repeating it, outside parliament.

The protection granted by privilege was considered by the European Court of Human Rights in *A v United Kingdom* (2002). The applicant argued that defamatory remarks made about her and her children in a debate about housing policy which had been reported in local and national newspapers, which she could not challenge in court because of Article IX, violated Article 6 (right to a fair trial), Article 8 (right to respect for private life) and Article 13 (the right to an effective remedy) of the European Convention on Human Rights. The Court of Human Rights found the statements unnecessary and reference to her home 'regrettable', but nevertheless ruled that there was no violation of Convention rights. The rules on privilege were necessary to protect free speech in parliament. Moreover, the British rules were narrower than those operating in several other states.

Freedom of speech: its use and misuse

In the Committee of Privileges report of 1986–87,[27] the Committee had endorsed the view expressed by the Speaker[28] that:

> We should use our freedom of speech ... with the greatest care, particularly if we impute any motives or dishonourable conduct to those outside the House who have no right of reply.

The Committee recognised that there is 'no clear dividing line between statements which represent a legitimate exercise of freedom of speech, on the one hand, and those which constitute an abuse, on the other' and called on members to exercise self-restraint.

In 1955, Kim Philby was named in the House as a Soviet spy, an allegation which surely would not have been made without the protection of privilege. In the 1960s, the Minister of War's association with Christine Keeler, who also had a relationship with a Soviet Attaché, was revealed under the cloak of privilege. Also in the 1960s, a London property racketeer, Peter Rachmann, was identified in the House. In 1980, Jeff Rooker MP made a number of false accusations against a Director of Rolls Royce: the allegations were withdrawn only after the lapse of five weeks. In the 1985–86 session, ministers were accused in parliament of improper involvement with the Johnson Matthey Bank following its collapse. In 1986, Geoffrey Dickins MP accused an Essex doctor of the sexual abuse of children, following a decision of the Director of Public Prosecutions not to prosecute the doctor on the basis that there was insufficient evidence to secure a conviction. Which of these exercises of freedom of speech represented a legitimate exercise of the freedom and which represented an abuse is a matter for individual judgment.

---

27 *Third Report of the Committee of Privileges 1986–87*, HC 604 (1995–96), London: HMSO.
28 HC 110, Official Report, Col 1084.

The House relies heavily on the notion of the self-restraint of its members, and is slow to use its disciplinary powers against offending members. The Committee on Procedure in its First Report urged members to exercise caution, and to avoid misusing their freedom. Where members insist on using privilege as a protective device and cause damage to the reputations and livelihoods of citizens, the advice of the Procedure Committee will give little comfort.[29] Individuals may try to rebut any allegations, may petition parliament and may try to persuade a Member of Parliament to retract a damaging allegation, but such forms of redress are wholly unsatisfactory in comparison with the right to legal redress.

A Joint Committee on Parliamentary Privilege issued its First Report in 1999. In relation to members of the public, the Committee considered whether a 'right of reply' should be introduced but decided against it. A right of reply would do nothing to prove the truth or falsity of any allegation and no financial redress could be made, nor would a statement published in *Hansard* attract the same degree of publicity as the offending allegation.

The courts and privilege

More case law further illustrates the meaning of Article IX and the role of the courts in relation to matters of privilege. In *Rost v Edwards* (1990), a Member of Parliament sued *The Guardian* newspaper for alleged libel.[30] The *Guardian* article had stated that the member, who was a member of the Energy Select Committee and a nominee for selection to the standing committee, considering an Energy Bill, had not registered his interests – as a consultant with two organisations concerned with energy. Subsequent to publication of the article, the member was informed that he was no longer being considered for membership of the standing committee and, further, that he had not been given the chair of the Energy Select Committee. The member instituted libel proceedings, which were adjourned by the court in order to determine the issue of parliamentary privilege. The member wished to adduce evidence before the court which comprised correspondence between himself and a clerk of the House and the Register of Members' Interests.

Mr Justice Popplewell ruled that the correspondence could not be submitted in evidence: that clearly fell within the exclusive domain of parliament and not the court. As to the Register, the judge took the view that it was a public document and, accordingly, could be put in evidence. Mr Justice Popplewell, recognising the respective jurisdictions of parliament and the courts, declared that the courts should nevertheless be slow to refuse to admit in evidence documents which could affect the outcome of legal proceedings and hence individual rights. *Rost v Edwards* was doubted by the Privy Council in *Prebble v Television New Zealand Ltd* (1994). In *Prebble*, a member of the New Zealand House of Representatives sued the television company for libel for publishing an article alleging that state assets had been sold off, contrary to stated policy, and that the

---

29   Given that 'advice' is less compelling than binding rules.
30   See Leopold, 1991.

member had been involved in a conspiracy to effect the sale. In its defence, the company wished to introduce in evidence parliamentary papers which substantiated its claim. The member pleaded privilege. The House of Representatives ruled that it had no power to waive its own privileges and thereby allow the papers to be considered in court. The Privy Council ruled that to adduce such evidence – without the House's waiver of privilege – contravened privilege and the protection given to parliamentary proceedings under Article IX of the Bill of Rights 1689.

In *Pepper v Hart* (1993),[31] the question considered by the House of Lords was whether judges may refer to *Hansard* as an aid to the interpretation of statutes. This issue has long been one of some controversy, and the orthodox view has hitherto been that judges may not under any circumstances refer to *Hansard*. In *Davis v Johnson* (1979), Lord Denning MR stated openly that he privately referred to *Hansard* as an aid to interpretation, only to be criticised for so doing by the House of Lords. However, in *Black-Clawson International Ltd v Papierwerke AG* (1975), all five judges in the House of Lords had agreed that official reports could be consulted to discern the 'mischief' with which the legislation was intended to deal, although their Lordships differed over the extent to which they could be used. Further, in *Pickstone v Freeman* (1988), three members of the House of Lords made reference to a parliamentary speech of the Secretary of State (the other two judges were silent on this matter).

In *Pepper v Hart* (1993), six of the seven judges hearing the case ruled in favour of admitting parliamentary debates before the court in some circumstances (the Lord Chancellor dissented on this point). Arguments were advanced by the Attorney General against such a decision – not least that, by consulting parliamentary debates, the courts would be acting contrary to Article IX of the Bill of Rights 1689, which prohibits the courts from questioning proceedings in parliament. The court rejected those views, concluding that there were no constitutional reasons which outweighed the merits of a 'limited modification' of the rule. Lord Browne-Wilkinson, giving the leading judgment of the court, stated that the rule should be relaxed where:

(a) legislation is ambiguous or obscure, or leads to an absurdity;

(b) the material relied on consists of one or more statements by a minister or other promoter of the Bill together, if necessary, with such other parliamentary material as is necessary to understand such statements and their effect; and

(c) the statements relied on are clear.

The House of Lords in *Pepper v Hart* revealed a marked change in attitude, although the right to refer to *Hansard* is not an unqualified right. The significance of this judgment from the point of view of parliamentary privilege lies in the court's consideration of the scope of Article IX of the Bill of Rights 1689. The Attorney General had argued strongly before the court that for judges to refer to *Hansard* infringed Article IX, amounting to an inquiry into the proceedings in

---

31 See Oliver, 1993.

parliament. This submission was rejected by the court, Lord Templeman declaring that reference to *Hansard*, under limited circumstances, involved no questioning of parliament, but merely clarification as to parliament's intention.[32]

In *R v Deegan* (1998), however, the Court of Appeal ruled that recourse to *Hansard* was not justified. The court below had referred to *Hansard* in order to clarify parliament's intentions as to the meaning of the phrase 'folding pocketknife', the possession of which had led to the appellant's conviction. The Court of Appeal, however, ruled that the conditions laid down in *Pepper v Hart* had not been satisfied, and that for the court to rely on parliamentary records of debate, on a term which was inherently open to interpretation, was unjustified. The appeal was dismissed.

The case of *Prebble v Television New Zealand Ltd* (1995) was reconsidered in *Allason v Haines* (1995). Joe Haines, a political journalist, and Mr Richard Stott, editor of *Today*, applied to have a libel action brought against them by the plaintiff, Mr Rupert Allason MP stayed. The court held that where, in order to defend a libel action, it was necessary to bring evidence of a Member of Parliament's behaviour in the House of Commons, and such a defence would be in breach of parliamentary privilege, the action would be stayed, for it would be unjust to deprive the defendants of their defence. The defendants had sought to show that Early Day Motions were inspired by improper motives. Such evidence would be in contravention of Article IX of the Bill of Rights 1689. To enforce parliamentary privilege in this case would be to cause injustice to the defendants. A stay was granted.

Rost v Edwards was also critically considered by the Joint Committee on Parliamentary Privilege which reported in 1999. The report stated baldly that 'we are in no doubt that if this decision is correct, the law should be changed'.[33] In the Committee's opinion, it is quite wrong for a court of law to be free to investigate and adjudicate upon matters relating to the Register. If there are allegations of wrongful failure to register, that matter should be 'a matter for parliament alone'. The Committee recommended that legislation be introduced to make clear that the Register and matters relating thereto are 'proceedings in parliament'.

Reference to *Hansard* was again considered in *Wilson v First County Trust* (2003). In this case the Court of Appeal referred to *Hansard* not, as in *Pepper v Hart*, to identify the intention of parliament in order to give effect to it, but rather to understand the reason which led parliament to enact a particular provision in the form that it took and to identify whether the statute was compatible with Convention rights. Unusually, legal representation on behalf of the Speaker of the House of Commons and the Clerk of the Parliaments gave evidence concerning the use of *Hansard* by the courts. Lord Nicholls of Birkenhead addressed the constitutional issue in the following way:

---

32 In *Three Rivers District Council v Bank of England (No 2)* and *(No 3)* (1996), it was held that references to ministers' speeches in *Hansard* may be made not only to construe a particular statutory provision whose meaning was ambiguous or unclear, but also in a case where the purpose or object of the statute as a whole is in issue.

33 First Report of the Joint Committee on Parliamentary Privilege, 1999, para 123.

> This House sitting in its judicial capacity is keenly aware, as indeed are all courts, of the importance of the legislature and the judiciary discharging their constitutional roles and not trespassing inadvertently into the other's province. [p 584]

The House of Lords ruled that:

> ... it is a cardinal constitutional principle that the will of Parliament is expressed in the language used by it in its enactments. The proportionality of legislation is to be judged on that basis. The courts are to have due regard to the legislation as an expression of the will of Parliament. The proportionality of a statutory measure is not to be judged by the quality of the reasons advanced in support of it in the course of parliamentary debate, or by the subjective state of mind of individual ministers or other members.

The Defamation Act 1996 and Article IX of the Bill of Rights

The Defamation Act 1996 came into being as a result of the Rupert Allason case and Neil Hamilton's intended libel suit against *The Guardian* newspaper over its allegations that he had accepted rewards in relation to his parliamentary duties.[34] Section 13 of the Defamation Act provides that a person may waive, for the purpose of defamation proceedings in which his conduct in relation to proceedings in parliament is in issue, the protection of any enactment or rule of law which prevents proceedings in parliament being impeached or questioned in any court or place outside parliament. As a result, a Member of Parliament may bring an action for defamation to defend his or her actions, provided that he or she waives the Article IX protection and thereby enables the defence to adduce evidence which otherwise would be excluded on the basis of privilege. If, however, the Member of Parliament is not willing to waive the Article IX privilege, then, on the authority of *Prebble v Television New Zealand Ltd*, the defamation action may be stayed in order to enable the newspaper to adduce evidence which proves the truth of its allegation.

The Hamilton saga continued with Mr Hamilton suing Mohamed Al Fayed for defamation. Mr Al Fayed sought to have the action struck out on the basis that, since the Committee on Standards and Privileges and the Parliamentary Commissioner for Standards had already investigated the allegation, the trial would breach parliamentary privilege. It was argued that section 13 of the Defamation Act 1996 was concerned with the individual privilege of the member concerned and did not apply to parliament's collective privilege of exclusive jurisdiction over its internal regulation. The judge at first instance refused to strike out the action, as did the Court of Appeal. On appeal to the House of Lords, the decision of the Court of Appeal was affirmed. Section 13 applied. Its effect was that the defendant's waiver of his parliamentary protection in relation to the parliamentary inquiry into his conduct overrode any privilege belonging to parliament as a whole and thus allowed the parties in the libel proceedings to challenge the veracity of evidence given to the parliamentary committee.[35]

---

34 *Hamilton v Hencke; Greer v Hencke* (1995), on which see further below.
35 *Hamilton v Al Fayed (No 1)* (1999) and *(No 2)* (2000).

The composition and procedure of parliament

The Houses of Parliament have an inherent right to regulate their own composition and procedure. For example, in *Ashby v White* (1703), the plaintiff – a qualified voter – had been denied the right to exercise his vote by the Mayor of Aylesbury. The House of Lords awarded Ashby damages. The case gave rise to a significant constitutional conflict between parliament and the courts. The House of Commons – which at the time had jurisdiction to hear matters on disputed elections – regarded the decision of the House of Lords as interfering with the exclusive right of the House of Commons to adjudicate on disputed elections. Other voters, similarly denied the right to vote, instigated legal proceedings and were committed to prison by the House of Commons. They brought an application for habeas corpus to test the legality of their detention. In *Paty's Case* (1704) the court refused the writ of habeas corpus. Counsel for the applicants, intending to appeal to the House of Lords, was committed to prison. The majority of the court refused to grant the application, deferring to the Commons.

In *Bradlaugh v Gosset* (1884), Bradlaugh had been duly elected as a Member of Parliament. On arriving to take his seat, Bradlaugh refused to swear the required oath on the Bible, offering instead to swear an oath of allegiance to the Crown. The House of Commons resolved to exclude Bradlaugh from the House. The plaintiff sought a declaration from the court that the resolution was invalid and an injunction to prevent the House of Commons from excluding him. The Court of Queen's Bench declared that it had no jurisdiction to interfere with a matter concerning the internal regulation of parliament's procedures.

The right of the House to regulate its own procedures is further demonstrated in the case of *British Railways Board v Pickin* (1974). There the court declined to inquire into the manner of the passage of a Bill even though the plaintiff alleged that he had been denied his right to make representations on a matter adversely affecting his rights in breach of convention. The Court of Appeal held that the procedure used in relation to a Private – but not Public – Bill could be examined. Lord Denning MR took a bold approach, arguing that it was for the court to ensure that 'the procedure of parliament itself is not abused, and that undue advantage is not taken of it. In so doing, the court is not trespassing on the jurisdiction of parliament itself. It is acting in aid of parliament and, I might add, in aid of justice'. The House of Lords disagreed and adopted its traditional stance: the court will not look 'behind the Parliamentary Roll'.[36] See also the case of *Re Parliamentary Election for Bristol South East* (1964), discussed in Chapter 17. There Mr Tony Benn was refused the right to enter and sit in the Commons, despite being duly elected, because he had succeeded to a peerage on the death of his father, Viscount Stansgate. Only by the passage of the Peerage Act 1963 was Tony Benn able to renounce his peerage and take his seat in the Commons.

On a lighter note, the exclusive rights of the Commons were tested in *R v Campbell ex parte Herbert* (1935). Three members of the Kitchen Committee of

---

36 Following, *inter alia*, *Edinburgh and Dalkeith Rly Co v Wauchope* (1842); *Lee v Bude and Torrington Junction Rly Co* (1871).

the House of Commons were accused of breaching the licensing laws. The action failed, the court holding that the House was not governed by the ordinary laws relating to licensing, which would only apply if it could be shown that they were expressly intended to apply to Westminster. It is for this reason that the House remains free to open its bars at any time of day or night. Sir AP Herbert once speculated whether the immunity conceded in *R v Campbell ex parte Herbert* could be extended by analogy to permit other licentious behaviour in the Commons.

An early conflict between parliament and the courts

In *Stockdale v Hansard* (1839), a prison inspector made a written report to the Secretary of State alleging that 'improper books' were being circulated in Newgate prison. The report was subsequently published by *Hansard*, on order of the House of Commons. Stockdale, the publisher of the 'improper book', sued *Hansard* as publishers of the report, which he regarded as being libellous. In defence, *Hansard* argued that the publication had been by an order of the House of Commons and was, accordingly, covered by the privilege of the House. The Court of Queen's Bench ruled that such publication was not covered by privilege and, moreover, that the House of Commons could not by a resolution deprive the courts of jurisdiction to protect the rights of individuals. Stockdale was awarded damages. The Sheriff of Middlesex levied execution on *Hansard's* property to satisfy the award of damages to Stockdale and the House of Commons responded by passing a resolution to commit the Sheriff for breach of privilege and contempt of parliament. The Sheriff applied for a writ of habeas corpus to test the legality of his detention.[37] The Serjeant at Arms produced a certificate from the Speaker stating simply that the Sheriff was 'guilty of a contempt and a breach of the privileges of this House'. The court refused to examine the lawfulness of the Sheriff's detention, stating that, since the Speaker's warrant did not specify the facts justifying the detention, it was not for the court to inquire into parliament's business. Accordingly, the court conceded jurisdiction to the House of Commons and rendered itself powerless to provide a remedy for a individual who, acting as an agent for the courts in enforcing the court's order for damages, found himself incarcerated on the order of the Commons. While such an outcome hardly inspires confidence in the judicial system, it nevertheless illustrates clearly the judges' reluctance to cross the boundary into matters of privilege.

Breach of privilege and contempt of parliament

A breach of privilege is conduct offending against one of the known privileges of parliament. Contempt is a far wider concept than this and has been defined as:

> ... any act or omission which obstructs or impedes either House of Parliament in the performance of its functions, or which obstructs or impedes any Member or Officer of the House in the discharge of his duty or which has a tendency, directly or indirectly, to produce such results. [Erskine May, 1997, Chapter 9]

---

37 *Sheriff of Middlesex's Case* (1840).

The main types of contempts dealt with by the House of Commons, with illustrations, are listed by Erskine May as being:

(a) Misconduct in the presence of the House or its committees:
- interrupting the proceedings of a committee;
- a witness persistently misleading a committee.

(b) Disobedience to rules or orders of the House or its committees:
- refusal to attend as a witness;
- refusing an order to withdraw from the House.

(c) Presenting a forged or falsified document to the House or its committees:
- forging signatures to petitions.

(d) Misconduct by Members or officers as such:
- deliberately misleading the House;
- corruption by acceptance of bribes.

(e) Constructive contempts:
- speeches or writing reflecting on the House;
- wilful misrepresentation of debates;
- premature disclosure of committee proceedings of evidence;
- other indignities offered to the House, such as fighting in the lobbies, using the badge and the name of the House in connection with an unofficial publication; and serving a writ on a Member in the precincts, while the House was sitting, without leave of the House.

(f) Obstructing Members in the discharge of their duty:
- molesting or insulting Members attending, coming to, or going from the House;
- attempted intimidation of Members, including publishing threatening posters regarding Members voting in a forthcoming debate and threatening to stop public investment in a Member's constituency if that Member persisted in making speeches of the kind he had made in a recent debate;
- molesting Members on account of their conduct in parliament, for example, by inciting newspaper readers to telephone a Member to complain of a question he had tabled;
- speeches or writings reflecting on Members' conduct in the House, for example, accusing the Speaker of partiality in the Chair.

(g) Obstructing officers of the House while in the execution of their duty:
- resisting the Serjeant at Arms when enforcing an order of the House.

(h) Obstructing witnesses:
- calling a person to account or censuring him for evidence given by him to a committee of the House.

The 1999 Report of the Joint Committee on Parliamentary Privilege recommended that contempt of parliament be defined in statute as part of its proposal for a new Parliamentary Privileges Act and an accompanying code.[38]

---

38 See further below.

MEMBERS' INTERESTS AND MEMBERS' INDEPENDENCE

Freedom from interference in parliament's work is a foundational principle of privilege. Accordingly, it is essential that all Members of Parliament are under no external pressure which could pose an actual or potential threat to their independence. However, from a constitutional standpoint, this issue represents one of the most troublesome aspects of privilege. It remains a topic of much contemporary significance and raises difficult questions. In 1994, this issue came to the fore and, as a result of a number of allegations concerning members' interests, an inquiry headed by Lord Justice Nolan was established by the Prime Minister to examine the issue.[39] The findings of the inquiry are discussed below.

A majority of members of the House of Commons are in paid employment in addition to being salaried members of the House.[40] Many members are also sponsored by outside bodies who contribute to their election expenses and may contribute towards the cost of secretarial and/or research staff employed by a member.[41] It may be argued as a point of principle that Members of Parliament should not receive any financial or other assistance from any outside party, whether a company or a trades union, since the very fact of receipt of such support potentially undermines the independence and integrity of the recipient.[42] This is not, however, the view adopted by the House of Commons itself although, from time to time, the House is troubled by such issues. The traditionally accepted view is that such sponsorship or remuneration is perfectly proper, provided that it does not impede the member's independence in the actual exercise of his parliamentary duties.

However, there is a fine line to be drawn between legitimate payments to members and payments designed to impede a member's independence, which may amount to bribery and corruption.

Rules regulating members' interests

In 1695, by a resolution of the House, the 'offer of money or other advantage' to a Member of Parliament for the purpose of persuading him or her to promote any matter in parliament was ruled to be 'a high crime and misdemeanour'. Further, in 1858, a resolution declared it to be 'improper for any member to promote any matter' in relation to which he or she had received a financial reward.[43] Specifically in relation to the asking of parliamentary questions, the Committee of Privileges in 1945 ruled that it was a breach of the privileges of the House to 'offer money or other advantage' to induce members to take up questions with

---

39 Committee of Inquiry on Standards in Public Life.
40 Non-ministerial salaries have only been payable since 1911. For the background, see Erskine May, 1997, Chapter 1.
41 The trade unions have a statutory right to sponsor Members of Parliament from separate political funds (Trade Union and Labour Relations (Consolidation) Act 1992).
42 A view expressed by Dennis Skinner MP: 'One Member, one salary' (*BBC Television News*, 20 April 1995).
43 CJ (1857–58) 247.

ministers.[44] Members of Parliament found guilty of corruption may be expelled from the House.

When speaking in debate or in any proceedings in the House or its committees, or when communicating with other members or ministers, a resolution of 1974 requires that members shall disclose 'any relevant pecuniary interest or benefit ... whether direct or indirect, that he may have had, may have or may be expecting to have'.[45]

In 1947, the Committee of Privileges had the opportunity to examine the issue of contracts made between members and outside bodies. Mr WJ Brown was elected the Member for Rugby in 1942. He had previously held the post of General Secretary of the Civil Service Clerical Association and, following his election, agreed to become its Parliamentary General Secretary. Following disagreements between Mr Brown and the Association, it was resolved that Mr Brown's appointment should be terminated. The matter was raised in the Commons, the argument being advanced that the Association's threat to terminate Mr Brown's contract was calculated to influence the member in the exercise of his parliamentary duties and, accordingly, amounted to a breach of privilege.

On the facts of the case, the Committee ruled that the making of such payments in itself did not involve any breach of privilege, and that:

> On the other hand, your committee regard it as an inevitable corollary that if an outside body may properly enter into contractual relationships with and make payments to a Member as such, it must in general be entitled to terminate that relationship if it lawfully can where it considers it necessary for the protection of its own interest so to do. What, on the other hand, an outside body is certainly not entitled to do is to use the agreement or the payment as an instrument by which it controls, or seeks to control the conduct of a Member or to punish him for what he has done as a Member.[46]

A further instance of alleged improper pressure being brought to bear on Members of Parliament occurred in 1975. The Yorkshire Area Council of the National Union of Mineworkers who sponsored a number of Labour Members of Parliament, resolved that it would withdraw its sponsorship from any member who voted in the House in a manner which conflicted with Union policy. The Committee of Privileges found this threat to be a serious contempt of the House, amounting as it did to an attempt to force a member to vote in a particular way and thus threatening a member's freedom of speech.[47] In the event, the National Executive of the Union nullified the resolution and no action was taken against the Union.

The Register of Members' Interests

On the wider question of the financial interests of Members of Parliament, under the rules of the House, all members are required to declare their interests, these

---

44 *Henderson's Case*, HC 63 (1944–45), London: HMSO.
45 Adopting recommendations of the Select Committee on Members' Interests (Declaration), HC 57 (1969–70), London: HMSO.
46 See HC Deb 15 Col 284, July 1947; HC 118 (1946–47), London: HMSO.
47 See HC 634 (1974–75), London: HMSO.

being recorded in the Register of Members' Interests. A resolution of the House of Commons provided that:

> ... in any debate or proceeding of the House or its committees or transactions or communications which a Member may have with other Members or with Ministers or servants of the Crown, he shall disclose any relevant pecuniary interest or benefit of whatever nature, whether direct or indirect, that he may have had, may have or may be expecting to have. [22 May 1974]

The practice was considered by the Select Committee on Members' Interests in 1968–69 and 1969–70. On the relevance of interests, the Committee reported that:

> The judgment on whether an interest is relevant and should be declared is in the first instance a matter for the Member concerned ... The main criterion for declaration should be relevant to debate or other activity in which a Member is taking part. An interest should be declared whenever a specific and relevant financial connection exists which might reasonably be thought to affect the expression of a Member's views on the matter under debate or other activity ... If the interest is not relevant there is no need to declare it. Nor need an interest be declared which does not entail an actual or potential benefit.[48]

The Register of Members' Interests is published annually.[49] The following classes of interests are required to be registered:[50]

(a) remunerated directorships of companies, public or private;

(b) remunerated employments, trades, professions, offices or vocations;

(c) the names and details of clients of a lobbying company in relation to which a Member plays a parliamentary role;

(d) gifts, benefits or hospitality received. Sums in excess of £125 cash or material benefit must be registered, as must hospitality over £160;

(e) financial sponsorships either as a parliamentary candidate where, to the knowledge of the Member, the sponsorship in any case exceeds 25 per cent of the candidate's election expenses; or as a Member of Parliament, by any person or organisation, stating whether any such sponsorship includes any payment to the Member or any material benefit or advantage, direct or indirect, such as the services of a research assistant;

(f) overseas visits, relating to or arising out of membership of the House, where the cost of any such visit has not been borne wholly by the Member or by public funds;

(g) any payments or any material benefits or advantages received from or on behalf of foreign governments, organisations or persons;

(h) land or property of substantial value (excluding a Member's home) or from which a substantial income is derived;

(i) names of companies or other bodies in which a Member has, to his knowledge, either himself or with or on behalf of his spouse or infant children, a beneficial interest in share holdings of a nominal value greater than one hundredth of the issued share capital;

---

48   See HC 57 (1969–70), London: HMSO, pp viii–x.
49   See below for data published in the *First Report of the Committee on Standards in Public Life* (the Nolan Report), Cm 2850-I, 1995, London: HMSO.
50   1995 revised Register.

(j) miscellaneous and unremunerated interests. Registration of such interests is voluntary.[51]

Failure to register an interest may be regarded as a contempt of the House. The only member who consistently refused to enter any interests on the Register was Mr Enoch Powell. Mr Powell adopted the constitutional stance that, since only statute could impose legal duties on individuals, the House could not – through the use of resolutions – lawfully require him to register. The select committee, having tried persuasion and inviting the House to take action to enforce the duty to register, took no further action.

The rules relating to ministers are more strict than those relating to ordinary Members of Parliament.[52] Ministers are required to resign directorships in all companies other than those dealing with family estates, to divest themselves of any investments which might involve a conflict of interest with their ministerial position, and to avoid speculative investments which might be seen to be made with the benefit of information acquired as a result of their ministerial office. A minister may only continue to act as a Member of Lloyd's with Prime Ministerial permission.[53]

The seriousness with which the House regards matters of interests which come to its attention may be seen in the case of Michael Mates, a senior Conservative Party member. Mr Mates was chairman of the Select Committee on Defence, which was considering low flying exercises by the airforce, which entailed consideration of the use of flight simulation equipment. Mr Dale Campbell-Savours MP complained to the select committee that Mr Mates had failed properly to register and declare certain financial interests in the defence industry. Mr Mates had financial interests in a defence consultancy business, and in a manufacturer of flight simulation equipment, for whom Mr Mates acted as general adviser. It was not disputed that Mr Mates had never spoken on behalf of either company in the House or in committee, and there was no allegation that Mr Mates had used his parliamentary position to further the interests of either company.

Mr Mates's defence was that his interests had no relevance to the deliberations of the committee and that, in any event, the interests' appearance on the Register of Members' Interests ensured that members of the select committee were fully aware of his interests. The select committee was highly critical of Mr Mates's conduct, asserting that 'we do not believe that Mr Mates's judgement was sound on this point'.[54]

The committee took the view that Mr Mates was in error in not declaring his interests when asking, as Chairman of the Defence Select Committee, questions relating to flight simulators. It was accepted that Mr Mates had made no personal

---

51 The Register of Members' Interests can be viewed at www.parliament.the-stationery-office.co.uk.
52 See *Questions of Procedure for Ministers*, 1992, London: Cabinet Office, para 8.
53 *Ibid*, paras 118–23. See further Chapter 11 on the issue of ministerial conduct.
54 *Second Report of the Select Committee on Members' Interests*, HC 506, July 1990, London: HMSO, para 20.

gain nor had he made any effort to conceal his interests. Nevertheless, his conduct fell below the high standard of disclosure expected by the select committee. In the event, the committee decided not to ask the House to take any action, but recommended that all Members of Parliament take serious note of the findings in the report.

Cash for questions[55]

The cash for questions affair began in 1993, when political lobbyist Ian Greer advised Mohamed Al Fayed to bribe Members of Parliament to pursue his interests in parliament. In 1994, Al Fayed publicly claimed that Tory MPs were paid to plant questions. The *Guardian* newspaper pursued the story, leading to a libel action by Mr Hamilton and Mr Greer. That action was dropped when it became apparent that the *Guardian* had damning evidence which would cause the action to fail.[56]

In 1994, a number of allegations were made against Members of Parliament in relation to accepting money for the tabling of parliamentary questions to ministers. Allegations were also made in relation to improper payments being accepted by members from outsiders, in the form of payment for hotel bills. Further allegations were made in respect of the failure of a number of Members of Parliament who allegedly failed to record benefits received and other relationships in which members received financial reward for services in the Register of Members' Interests.

In 1994, two Parliamentary Private Secretaries resigned (from the government but not from parliament) following allegations that they had received money in exchange for tabling parliamentary questions. Furthermore, in 1994, two Junior Ministers faced allegations that they received payments and/or gifts in exchange for tabling parliamentary questions. On 20 October 1994, *The Guardian* alleged that Tim Smith MP and Neil Hamilton MP had each received £2,000 for tabling questions in parliament concerning the takeover of Harrods by the Al Fayed brothers. Tim Smith resigned on the day of the report. Neil Hamilton remained in office, claiming that he enjoyed the continued support of the Prime Minister. On 21 October, however, *The Guardian* newspaper published details of a bill from the Ritz Hotel in Paris, totalling an estimated £4,000, paid for by Mr Al Fayed. The then Prime Minister subsequently demanded Mr Hamilton's resignation.

The matter was referred to the Committee of Privileges. The rapidly accelerating and intensifying atmosphere of suspected corruption – or 'sleaze' – in public life caused the Prime Minister to appoint a judicial inquiry to be carried out by the Committee on Standards in Public Life.

The cash for questions affair also raises issues concerning the press. Journalists from *The Sunday Times*, working undercover, offered a payment of £1,000 to two Conservative Parliamentary Private Secretaries, Graham Riddick and David Tredinnick. The offers were made by telephone and the conversations recorded by

---

55   See also Chapter 11 on fitness for public office.
56   For an entertaining account, see Leigh and Vulliamy, 1997.

the journalists. The Committee of Privileges inquired into the allegations in July 1994 and, in April 1995, recommended that the two members be suspended from parliament for 20 days and 10 days respectively for conduct which 'fell below the standards of the House'. In April 1995, the House, following debate, adopted the committee's recommendation. The members also lost their parliamentary salaries for the periods of suspension. Concerning the role of *The Sunday Times*, the committee was highly critical of the manner in which their investigation was conducted, but no action has been taken against the newspaper.

The Committee on Standards in Public Life: the Nolan Inquiry

The Committee on Standards in Public Life, chaired by Lord Nolan, was established as a standing body, with membership being held for three years. The Committee's terms of reference were:

> To examine current concerns about standards of conduct of all holders of public office, including arrangements relating to financial and commercial activities, and to make recommendations as to any changes in present arrangements which might be required to ensure the highest standards of probity in public life.

> For these purposes, public life should include Ministers, civil servants and advisers, Members of Parliament and United Kingdom Members of the European Parliament, members and senior officers of all non-departmental public bodies and of national health service bodies, non-ministerial office holders, members and other senior officers of other bodies discharging publicly funded function, and elected members and senior officers of local authorities.

Individual allegations of impropriety do not fall within the committee's terms of reference.[57]

In May 1995, the committee published its First Report, the Nolan Report. While finding that, in general, 'there is no evidence ... of a growth in actual corruption' (paragraph 6), the committee recorded a widespread loss of public confidence in the probity of Members of Parliament. Evidence to the committee revealed that 64 per cent of the public believed that Members of Parliament made money by using their office improperly, a figure which had risen from 46 per cent in 1984.[58]

The committee set out the general principles of conduct which apply to public life as being selflessness, integrity, objectivity, accountability, openness, honesty and leadership.

Members of Parliament

The Nolan Report recorded that the 1995 Register of Members' Interests suggested that 26 members had entered into agreements with public relations or lobbying firms. A further 142 members had consultancies 'with other types of company or with trade associations'. The 168 members between them held a total

---

57   See Doig, 2002. In this chapter, the findings relating to Members of Parliament are discussed. The conduct of ministers and civil servants is considered in Chapter 11.

58   Professor Ivor Crewe citing a Gallup survey.

of 356 consultancies. When ministers and the Speaker are excluded from the analysis, almost 30 per cent of Members of Parliament held some form of consultancy agreement. In relation to associations with trades unions, a total of 184 members had sponsorship agreements, 27 had paid consultancies, and a further ten received some form of financial assistance from trade unions. Accordingly, the committee concluded that almost 70 per cent of Members of Parliament (excluding ministers and the Speaker) had some form of financial relationship with outside bodies.

Despite the evidence of witnesses and persons writing to the committee, the committee did not conclude from this evidence that such arrangements should be banned. Indeed, the involvement of Members of Parliament in outside work was regarded by the committee as a benefit to parliament as a whole. As the committee viewed the matter:

> ... a Parliament composed entirely of full time professional politicians would not serve the best interests of democracy. The House needs if possible to contain people with a wide range of current experience which can contribute to its expertise. [para 19]

The committee was also concerned that a ban on outside financial interests would act as a deterrent to people who would otherwise stand for election to parliament. The committee recommended, therefore, that Members of Parliament should continue to have the right to engage in outside employment. The matter which remained was how best to protect the integrity of members and the House as a whole in light of such continuing outside employment.

Having reviewed the early resolutions of the House, and the later resolution of 1947,[59] and the rules regulating the registration of members' interests, the committee found that the Register had worked unsatisfactorily. The committee invited the House of Commons to review the statement of principle which governed the registration of interests.

Paid consultancies

Three fifths of all members of the House have arrangements with clients or sponsors. While appreciating that paid consultancies enable 'many entirely respectable, and in some cases highly deserving, organisations' to 'gain a voice in the nation's affairs',[60] the committee recognised that there was a fine – and difficult – line to be drawn between paid advice and paid advocacy, the latter of which is a matter of concern. To remove the right to engage in such arrangements would be 'impracticable' and was, accordingly, not recommended. There was, however, one area – the issue of 'general consultancies' – in which the committee wanted to see firm and immediate action.

General consultancies

Public relations and lobbying firms are engaged in acting as advisers and advocates to a wide range of clients, all of which pursue their own objectives in

---

59 See the case of Mr Brown, discussed above, p 475.
60 Nolan Report, para 46.

terms of exerting pressure on parliament. The problem posed by such companies is that registration of an agreement with the company does not necessarily disclose the actual client for whom, in fact, the member is acting in a parliamentary capacity. The committee recommended that there be an immediate ban introduced on such relationships; parliament did not act specifically on this proposal but, rather, tightened the rules relating to registration and the declaration of interests.

Clarifying the Register of Members' Interests

The committee acknowledged that the 1995 Register was an improvement on previous Registers. However, there still remained areas of doubt and uncertainty as to the precise requirements of disclosure of interests, and an unacceptable degree of laxity in the enforcement of registration. The committee recommended that the entry requirements be clarified. Since the beginning of the 1995 session, members have been required to deposit in full any contracts which involve the member acting in a parliamentary capacity on behalf of any organisation, and these contracts are available for public inspection. In addition, members are required to reveal their annual remuneration, and also estimated monetary benefits received of any kind. Furthermore, all agreements which do not involve the member acting in a parliamentary capacity for an organisation and, therefore, do not need to be deposited, should contain clear terms stating that the agreement does not involve the member acting for the organisation in a parliamentary capacity.[61]

The committee also emphasised the requirement that Members of Parliament disclose their interests on 'each and every occasion when a member approaches other members or ministers on a subject where a financial interest exists'.[62] The onus is on the members to disclose the interest, and he or she should not assume that the interest is one known about by the other party.

The rules on conflicts of interest should be further developed, and clarification provided on the circumstances under which a member of Parliament should withdraw from, or refrain from taking part in, proceedings in parliament.

Gifts and hospitality

In relation to gifts and hospitality, the committee found that the rules set out in *Questions of Procedure for Ministers*[63] were sufficiently detailed and that no further elaboration was required. The committee endorsed the important principle set out in *Questions of Procedure*:

> It is a well established and recognised rule that no Minister or public servant should accept gifts, hospitality or services from anyone which would, or might appear to, place him or her under an obligation.[64]

---

61   Nolan Report, para 70.
62   *Ibid*, para 63.
63   *Ibid*, paras 80–81.
64   At paragraph 126. See Chapter 3, para 40 of the report.

Enforcing members' obligations

The Nolan Committee considered that Members of Parliament are insufficiently aware of the binding nature of resolutions of the House, and that this climate of laxity is one of the contributory factors to poor compliance. Furthermore, the committee regarded the respective roles of the Select Committee on Members' Interests and the Committee of Privileges of the House as unclear. The committee proposed the appointment of an independent Parliamentary Commissioner for Standards, responsible for maintaining the Register of Members' Interests and for providing guidance on standards of 'conduct, propriety and ethics'. The Commissioner fulfils a similar function to that of the Comptroller and Auditor General and the Parliamentary Commissioner for Administration.[65] The Commissioner has power to receive and investigate complaints concerning members' conduct.

In relation to ministers, the Nolan Report was critical of the position whereby ministers may leave government office and assume senior positions with – in particular – companies which have recently been privatised by the government.

In response to aspects of the Nolan Report, the House approved a Code of Conduct, incorporating the key principles of conduct in public life.[66] Ministers leaving office are no longer permitted to take employment in the private sector without the appointment being vetted by an independent committee. From the parliamentary session 1995–96, all Cabinet Ministers have to wait at least three months before taking outside paid employment. In addition, a two year waiting period may be imposed. In relation to appointments to non-governmental public bodies, a Commissioner for Public Appointments has been established to ensure that there is no political bias in such appointments.

The House of Commons also passed resolutions which (a) introduce a rule against paid advocacy and (b) require members entering into agreements for the provision of services in their capacity as members to deposit the terms of their agreements with the Parliamentary Commissioner for Standards at the same time as they are registered in the Register of Members' Interests. Furthermore, the House resolved to revise the 1947 resolution by inserting the requirement that no Member of Parliament (nor member of his or her family) shall receive remuneration of any kind in relation to raising an issue in parliament by means of any speech, question, motion, introduction of a Bill or amendment to a motion or Bill. In addition, the House resolved that the rules on declaration of interests be amended to make it clear that members are required to declare any relevant interest when tabling questions for oral or written answer or when preparing amendments to a Bill. Further, the Committee of Standards and Privileges and the office of Parliamentary Commissioner for Standards were established.

The first *Report of the Parliamentary Commissioner for Standards* (the Downey Report) was published in July 1997. The 898 page report, which had taken ten months to complete, made it clear that the five former ministers and Members of

---

65   See Chapters 16 and 28, respectively.
66   HC 688 (1995–96).

Parliament involved in accusations of accepting financial rewards, which were not recorded as required in the Register of Members' Interests and were denied by the MPs, were guilty of breaking the parliamentary rules.[67] The Downey Report found the evidence against Neil Hamilton 'compelling':

> The evidence that Mr Hamilton received cash payments from Mr Al Fayed in return for lobbying services is compelling: and I so conclude.

The insistence that parliament remain a self-regulatory body has come under question in light of the Downey Report. While early analyses of the Downey Report all praised the painstakingly detailed approach of the Commissioner, there were suggestions that such allegations should perhaps be investigated by a statutory tribunal, headed by a judge, and holding public, rather than private, hearings.[68] The ability of parliament to remain a self-regulatory body was thrown into further doubt by the circumstances surrounding the departure of the Commissioner for Standards, Elizabeth Filkin, who left having been told that she would not be automatically reappointed for a further term of office and would need to reapply through open competition. At root, the problem appeared to be that the Commissioner was too rigorous in her enquiries. The Commissioner accused ministers, Members of Parliament and civil servants of undermining her position.[69]

The Parliamentary Commissioner for Standards is to investigate allegations that lobbyists have influenced the work of independent all-party groups of MPs.[70] There are 370 all-party groups, 102 of which focus on particular countries while the others focus on subjects. The groups comprise mainly backbenchers from the Commons and Lords. They are not an official part of the parliamentary process, but since their formal recognition in 1985 have been regulated by standing orders and must be formally recorded in a register supervised by the Committee on Standards and Privileges. All-party groups do not receive public funding and the organisational costs and costs of drafting reports is met by special interest groups such as companies, trade associations and charities.

Penalties for breach of privilege and contempt

Historically, the most important power available to the House was to commit the offender to prison. Erskine May describes this power as the 'keystone of parliamentary privilege', but it is little used and has not been used since *Bradlaugh's Case* in 1884.[71] The House can vote to allow the offender to be

---

67 Lady Olga Maitland, Norman Lamont, Nirj Deva and Gerald Malone, all of whom were defeated at the General Election, and Sir Peter Hordern who stood down before the election.

68 See Professor Vernon Bogdanor, *The Guardian*, 4 July 1997.

69 The post of Commissioner in future is to be part time and at a lower rate of pay. In *R v Commissioner for Standards and Privileges ex parte Al Fayed* (1998) the Court of Appeal ruled that the court had no jurisdiction to review decisions of the Commissioner, on the basis that the Commissioner was concerned with activities within parliament, and the Commissioner was accountable to the special standing committee in the House of Commons, which alone had the power to perform supervisory functions over the Commissioner.

70 *The Times* 14 January 2006. See www.timesonline.co.uk/politics.

71 The Joint Committee on Parliamentary Privilege recommended in 1999 that the power to imprison should be abolished, except for the power to detain persons temporarily who disrupt the proceedings of either House.

prosecuted by the police, as happened in 1970, when a stranger threw a CS gas canister into the Chamber.[72] The most regularly employed sanction is the reprimand. The House may order that a member be suspended from the House or expelled. In 1948, Garry Allighan MP was found to have lied to a committee, falsely accusing other members of taking money. The House ordered his expulsion from parliament.[73] In 1988, Ron Brown MP was suspended from the House for the contempt of damaging the Mace. In 1994, the House suspended two members, with loss of salary, for 20 days and 10 days respectively, for accepting payment for putting down parliamentary questions. Following a report from the Standards and Privileges Committee,[74] a Member of Parliament, the Member for Liverpool (Mr Wareing) was also suspended for failing to register a shareholding interest in the Register of Members' Interests. In 2004 a Labour Minister was required by the Standards and Privileges Committee to apologise to the House of Commons for failing to register her earnings as a presenter of a television show.

The House of Lords has the power to impose fines on offenders. Curiously, the House of Commons does not have that power although, historically, it did. The last occasion on which a fine was imposed was in 1666.[75] The power to impose fines was denied in *R v Mead* (1762). Recommendations of the Select Committee on Parliamentary Privilege in 1967 and 1977 that such a power be introduced by statute have not been implemented. Where newspapers breach the rules of privilege or commit contempt of parliament, the editor may be called to the Bar of the House to explain and apologise, and journalists may be excluded from the precincts of the House for a specified period.

With regard to maintaining order in the House, the Speaker has a range of available disciplinary powers. The Speaker will firstly warn a member about his conduct. If this does not ensure order, the Speaker may request the member to leave the Chamber. If the member refuses to leave, the Speaker may direct him to withdraw[76] immediately, and the member must leave the precincts of parliament for the remainder of the day. In the rare event that a member refuses to comply with the order to withdraw, the Speaker may formally 'name' the member[77] and put down a motion that the member be suspended from the service of the House. The suspension on a first offence will last for five sitting days, on a second occasion, for 20 sitting days and on any subsequent occasion, for as long as the House shall determine.

There has always been uncertainty over whether the bribery of a member of either House is an offence under common law which is enforceable by the courts.[78]

---

72 CJ (1970–71).
73 HC Deb Vol 443 Cols 1094–1198, 30 October 1947.
74 HC 182 (1997–98), London: HMSO; and see the MP's complaint concerning procedure, HC Deb Vol 299 Col 1051, 30 October 1997.
75 *White's Case* (1666).
76 Standing Order No 42.
77 Standing Order No 43.
78 *Upholding Integrity: The Prevention of Corruption* – the Government's Proposals for Reform of the Criminal Law of Corruption in England and Wales, Cm 4759. See also the Report of the Joint Committee on Parliamentary Privilege, HL 43, HC 214 of 1998–99.

The Code of Conduct for Members of Parliament

The Code of Conduct sets out the general principles to guide members on standards of conduct that the House and the public have a right to expect, together with a *Guide to the Rules relating to the Conduct of Members*.[79] These include matters relating to the registration of interests and their declaration and the advocacy rule. In relation to registration, interests to be registered are directorships; remunerated employment; sponsorships which amount to 25 per cent or more of election expenses, or other funds related to a candidate's election campaign; free or subsidised research assistance; gifts, benefits or hospitality; overseas visits; overseas gifts and benefits; land and property; shareholdings; and miscellaneous interests. Where members have entered into agreements which are relevant to their parliamentary duties, these are to be deposited with the Parliamentary Commissioner for Standards in addition to being registered. Where an informal, unwritten agreement, has been entered into, it must also be deposited with the Commissioner in written form. In relation to paid advocacy, this is banned in relation to a number of important matters. In particular, paid advocacy is banned in relation to initiating parliamentary proceedings, including the presentation of Bills, presentation of petitions, the asking of parliamentary questions, tabling or moving motions, or moving amendments to Bills. Any Member of Parliament, or member of the public, may lay a complaint, alleging breach of the Code, with the Commissioner for investigation. The Commissioner has a discretion whether or not to investigate. The Commissioner reports his findings to the Select Committee on Standards and Privileges, which examines the findings. If no *prima facie* case is disclosed, this is reported to the Commons. If there is a *prima facie* case disclosed, the committee, following its examination, will report to the Commons, detailing its findings. The final decision on the matter lies with the House of Commons.

Subsequent to the *cash for questions* affair, the House of Commons re-stated the resolution of 1947[80] and added the following:

> ... in particular, no Member shall, in consideration of any remuneration, fee, payment, reward or benefit in kind, direct or indirect ...
>
> (a) advocate or initiate any cause or matter on behalf of any outside body or individual; or
>
> (b) urge any other Member of either House ... including Ministers, to do so, by means of any speech, question, motion, introduction of a Bill or amendment to a motion or Bill.[81]

PUBLICATION OF PARLIAMENTARY PROCEEDINGS

The publication of proceedings in parliament is covered by the same rules as the reporting of proceedings in court. The underlying principle is that publication is in the public interest and generally outweighs any disadvantage to individuals.

---

79 HC Deb Vol 282 Col 392, 24 July 1996.
80 HC Deb Col 284, 15 July 1947; HC 118 (1946–47), London: HMSO.
81 HC Deb Cols 604, 661, 6 November 1995.

On the extent to which the reporting and publication of parliamentary proceedings is protected, section 1 of the Parliamentary Papers Act 1840 provides that, where civil or criminal proceedings are commenced, the defendant may present to the court a certificate stating that the publication in question was made under the authority of the House of Lords or House of Commons, and that the 'judge or court shall thereupon immediately stay such civil or criminal proceeding'.

Section 2 provides that similar protection exists for correct copies of official reports and authorised papers. Section 3 provides that extracts or abstracts from such reports or papers, for example in newspapers, are protected provided that such extracts are published *bona fide* and without malice. Thus papers of the House, or papers ordered to be published by the House, plus fair and accurate, but unauthorised, reports of proceedings are covered by qualified privilege, and an action for damages for injury allegedly caused by their publication would only lie if malice could be proven.

The Parliamentary Papers Act was passed as a direct result of two cases in which the courts and parliament came into conflict, namely *Stockdale v Hansard* (1839) and the *Sheriff of Middlesex's Case*. While the passing of the Parliamentary Papers Act 1840 gives statutory authority to publication of official papers and authorised reports, uncertainty still remains as to the scope of the protection.

Privilege and the media

Publications which reflect on the dignity of the House as a whole are classified as 'constructive contempts', as are reflections on individual members.[82] Illustrations of adverse comments published in the press include that of the *Sunday Express* which, in 1953, commented that two members were asleep during an all night sitting of the House. Further, in 1956, the *Sunday Express* criticised Members of Parliament for exempting themselves from the petrol rationing which had been imposed as a result of the Suez crises. The report of the Committee of Privileges held that the editor had been:

> ... guilty of a serious contempt in reflecting upon all Members of the House and so upon the House itself by alleging that Members of the House had been guilty of contemptible conduct in failing, owing to self interest, to protest at an unfair discrimination in their favour. Such an attack on Members is calculated to diminish the respect due to the House and so to lessen its authority.[83]

The issue of media pressure again fell for consideration by the Committee of Privileges in 1956. A Member of Parliament, Mr Arthur Lewis, gave notice of a forthcoming Prime Ministerial parliamentary question, which asked:

> ... whether he will arrange for part of the money contributed by the government for relief in Hungary to be allocated to the relief of the several thousand Egyptian people who have been rendered homeless and destitute by British shelling and rocket fire in Egypt.

---

82 Erskine May, 1997, p 121.
83 *Second Report from the Committee of Privileges*, HC 38 (1956–57), London: HMSO.

In a scathing editorial in the *Sunday Graphic*, readers were invited to telephone Mr Lewis and give him their views. To assist this task, the newspaper published the member's telephone number. As a consequence, the member received thousands of irate telephone calls before the Post Office was able to change his number. In both cases, the editors were called to the Bar of the House and apologised.

Unauthorised disclosure of parliamentary proceedings

The unauthorised disclosure of proceedings conducted in private and of draft reports of committees which have not been reported to the House is governed by a resolution of the House of 1837, as amended in 1980. The resolution makes such disclosure a contempt of the House.[84] The House resolved in 1978 that its penal jurisdiction should only be used where the action complained of was likely to cause a 'substantial interference' with a committee's work.[85] The Committee of Privileges recommended in its 1985 report that 'substantial interference' with regard to leaked documents should be confined to confidential or classified information or deliberate attempts to undermine the work of the committee.[86]

Between 1971 and 1988, six incidents of unauthorised disclosure were recorded.[87] In no case was the source of the leak – presumed to be a member of the select committee – identifiable and, in each case, the journalists concerned had refused to reveal their sources. The House has shown itself to be unwilling to punish publishers when it cannot identify and punish the source of the leak.

In 1985, *The Times* newspaper published a leaked draft report of the Home Affairs Select Committee and a draft report of the Environment Select Committee on the disposal of radioactive waste. The Committee of Privileges recommended that both the member responsible for the leak and the journalist should be punished but, when the matter was put to the House, it declined to follow the committee's recommendation.[88]

A fresh issue arose in 1999 with the leak of select committee reports to ministers. In July 1999, a senior Labour MP, Earnest Ross, was forced to resign from the Foreign Affairs Select Committee after he had been found responsible for leaking a critical report over the Foreign Office's role in allegedly breaching a United Nations arms embargo in Sierra Leone to the Foreign Secretary, Robin Cook. The leak had the potential, if used by the Foreign Secretary, of interfering with the work of the select committee. After criticism by the Standards and Privileges Committee, Mr Ross apologised to the House and was suspended for ten days. Subsequently, two Labour Members, one who had leaked a Social Security Select Committee Report and one who had received the report, were suspended from the Commons for three and five days, respectively. The Prime Minister and the Cabinet Secretary then issued directions to ministers and senior civil servants that any leaked documents were to be returned immediately and

---

84   See Leopold, 1980.
85   HC Deb Vol 943 Col 1198, 6 February 1978.
86   *Second Report from the Committee of Privileges: Premature Disclosure of Proceedings of Select Committee*, HC 555 (1984–85), London: HMSO, paras 51–55.
87   Griffith and Ryle, 2003.
88   HC Deb Vol 98 Cols 293–330, 20 May 1986.

without use having been made of them, and that the Ministerial Code of Practice would be amended to cover the leaking of such reports which potentially undermine the authority of select committees.

The procedure for determining issues of privilege and contempt

If an allegation of breach of privilege or contempt is made, the complaint is communicated to the Speaker. The member will be given written notice of the complaint. The Speaker must be satisfied, first, that the matter is one involving privilege and, secondly, that the complaint is substantial. If he or she so finds, the Speaker advises the complainant that he may put down a Motion which will be debated the following day. For the most part, the matter will then be referred by the House to the Committee on Standards and Privileges (formerly the Committee of Privileges). The committee is made up of 11 senior members of the House from all political parties, chaired by the Leader of the House. The Committee has the power to call for persons, papers and records. It also has the power to compel members to attend. Although acting in a quasi-judicial capacity, the committee is not bound to follow strict rules of procedure. The legal rules of evidence do not apply and there is normally no legal representation. The Committee sits in private (but may sit in public).[89] If the Committee finds that there has been a breach, it will make recommendations as to punishment, but has no power to apply the sanction: that is for the House as a whole, who will vote on the matter following a debate. The House is not bound by the Committee's recommendations and may, as happened in the case of *Strauss* (1985), reject them.

The manner in which parliament regulates aspects of privilege gives rise to questions concerning the right to fair trial protected under Article 6 of the European Convention on Human Rights, incorporated under the Human Rights Act 1998. Parliament is exercising a form of penal jurisdiction when punishing Members.[90]

Members' interests in the House of Lords

Privilege in the House of Lords

The House of Lords enjoys the same privilege of freedom from arrest[91] and freedom of speech as the Commons. Freedom of access to the Sovereign is enjoyed by the House collectively and by each peer individually. This privilege of peerage extends to all peers, irrespective of whether they sit in the House of Lords. The House of Lords has the same right as the Commons to determine its own procedure. In the event of a disputed peerage, the House of Lords has jurisdiction to determine the matter.[92] The House of Lords has the power to

---

89 Demands by the Rt Hon Tony Benn MP that the Committee sit in public were rejected in 1994. Moreover, his announced intention to disclose details of the Committee's hearings resulted in his deselection from the Committee.

90 See Report of the Joint Committee on Parliamentary Privilege (HL 43-I, HC 214-I, 1998–99), paras 271–314.

91 *The Sunday Times*, 16 July 1995.

92 See *Stourton v Stourton* (1963).

commit persons for breach of privilege or contempt and also the power to impose fines. The House of Lords may also summon judges to attend in order to give advice on points of law.

Members' interests

In July 1995, Lord Griffiths published his report on outside interests of peers. The report was submitted to the Lords' Procedure Committee. The recommendations included the introduction of a Register of Members' Interests on which all remunerated positions must be declared. Peers are no longer permitted to act as advocates for companies or organisations from whom they receive remuneration. They are, however, allowed to act as advisers to outside groups. Peers are no longer free to ask questions or to table amendments where their sponsoring organisation stands to gain benefit.

In 1996, in response to increased concerns over members' interests, a Register of Members' Interests was established in the House of Lords. In addition, the House has approved a motion that Lords should always act on their personal honour and should never accept any financial inducement as an incentive or reward for exercising parliamentary influence.

Further reform of parliamentary privilege

In addition to the reforms considered above, there remains a need to clarify the definition given to the phrase 'proceedings in parliament' in Article IX of the Bill of Rights in order that both members and other individuals may better understand the scope of the protection given by privilege.

The Joint Committee on Parliamentary Privilege considered the question of the definition of parliamentary proceedings in its 1999 report. The Committee recommended that there should be enacted a Parliamentary Privileges Act to cover this and a number of other reforms.

Defining 'proceedings in parliament'

Rejecting earlier suggested definitions of parliamentary proceedings as too wide, the Committee proposed the following statutory definition:

(1) For the purposes of Article IX of the Bill of Rights 1689 'proceedings in Parliament' means all words spoken and acts done in the course of, or for the purposes of, or necessarily incidental to, transacting the business of either House of Parliament or of a committee.

(2) Without limiting (1), this includes:

    (a) the giving of evidence before a House or a committee or an officer appointed by a House to receive such evidence;

    (b) the presentation or submission of a document to a House or a committee or an officer appointed by a House to receive it, once the document is accepted;

    (c) the preparation of a document for the purposes of transacting the business of a House or a committee, provided any drafts, notes, advice or the like are not circulated more widely than is reasonable for the purposes of preparation;

    (d) the formulation, making or publication of a document by a House or a committee;

    (e) the maintenance of any register of the interests of the members of a House and any other register of interests prescribed by resolution of a House.

(3) A 'committee' means a committee appointed by either House or a joint committee appointed by both Houses of Parliament and includes a sub-committee.

(4) A document includes any disc, tape or device in which data are embodied so as to be capable of being reproduced therefrom.

In addition, there should be a statutory definition of 'place out of parliament', and the scope of the prohibition on 'questioning'. Article IX should not apply to court proceedings in so far as they relate to interpretation of Acts of Parliament or subordinate legislation (the *Pepper v Hart* principle), or to judicial review. Tribunals appointed under the Tribunals of Inquiry (Evidence) Act 1921 could also be excluded from Article IX. The legislation should make it clear that the application of Article IX extends to Scotland and Northern Ireland. Disputes as to the meaning of 'proceedings in parliament' arising in court proceedings should continue to be resolved by the trial judge, whereas those arising in the House should be dealt with there.

In relation to the question of bribery and corruption of Members of Parliament, which was the subject of enquiry by the Committee on Standards on Public Life[93] and the Joint Committee on Parliamentary Privilege,[94] the government published its proposals to reform the law and stated that it intended to introduce legislation when parliamentary time allows.[95] The government's proposals were based on the recommendations of the Law Commission.[96] The government accepts the need to modernise the law[97] and to provide a statutory definition clarifying the meaning of 'acting in a corrupt manner'. The Act will apply to both the public and private sectors. Liability would extend to extraterritorial offences committed by British nationals. The Act will make it clear that the changes in the law apply to members of both Houses of Parliament. A draft Corruption Bill was published in 2003. It was scrutinised by a Joint Committee of both Houses of Parliament, which was highly critical of the Bill and invited the Home Office to draft a revised Bill.

---

93 *Sixth Report*, Cm 4557, 2000, London: HMSO.

94 *Report*, 30 March 1999 (HL Paper 43-1, HC 214-1).

95 See *Raising Standards and Upholding Integrity: The Prevention of Corruption*, 2000.

96 *Legislating the Criminal Code: Corruption*, No 248, Report, 1998. See www.open.gov.uk/ lawcomm.

97 Principally, the Public Bodies Corrupt Practices Act 1889, the Prevention of Corruption Act 1906 and Prevention of Corruption Act 1916.

PART VI

THE INDIVIDUAL AND THE STATE

CHAPTER 19

THE PROTECTION OF HUMAN RIGHTS

INTRODUCTION

In Chapter 4, the rule of law, a concept which portrays the idea of governmental power limited by law and the democratic process, was discussed. It was seen that from early times the sovereignty of law over man was proclaimed in order to safeguard citizens from the abuse of power by monarchs and governments. The protection of individual rights and freedoms by the state is an essential feature of the rule of law.

THE ORIGINS OF THE IDEA OF RIGHTS: EARLY CONCEPTIONS OF LIMITED GOVERNMENTAL POWER

John Locke

In *Two Treatises of Government*, John Locke claimed that sovereign power was limited and that the people had the right to resort to revolution against the sovereign if power was abused. Such writing was both revolutionary and seditious – challenging the very basis of state authority. Locke went into exile in 1683.[1] With the accession of William of Orange to the throne in 1689, Locke returned to England and his work – previously unpublished – reached the light of day, albeit anonymously. The timing of publication could not have been more forceful. An historic settlement between parliament and Crown had finally and recently been reached, resulting in the Bill of Rights 1689, thus ending centuries of conflict. However, Locke's writing presented a theory which challenged the basis of sovereign power by asserting the rights of man against the sovereign. Much of the first *Treatise* is an argument directed against absolute monarchical power and the use of the prerogative. By insisting that government held its power on trust, Locke was indirectly claiming the sovereignty of the people over the sovereignty of government. Government had a legitimate right to rule, and to use the law for the good of the people; but that right was conditional and limited by the ultimate power of the people to overthrow a government which violated its trust. As Locke observed:

> ... acting for the preservation of the community, there can be but one supreme power, which is the legislative, to which all the rest are and must be subordinate, yet the legislative being only a fiduciary power to act for certain ends, there remains still in the people a supreme power to remove or alter the legislative, when they find the legislative acts contrary to the trust reposed in them. For all power given with trust for the attaining an end being limited by that end, whenever that end is manifestly neglected or opposed, the trust must necessarily be forfeited, and the power devolve

---

1 The *Treatises* were assumed to have been in manuscript form by 1683. Whilst in exile, Locke wrote *Essay Concerning Human Understanding* and *Letter on Toleration*.

into the hands of those that gave it, who may place it anew where they shall think best for their safety and security. And thus the community perpetually retains a supreme power of saving themselves from the attempts and designs of anybody, even of their legislators, whenever they shall be so foolish or so wicked as to lay and carry on designs against the liberties and properties of the subject. For no man or society of men having a power to deliver up their preservation, or consequently the means of it, to the absolute will and arbitrary dominion of another, whenever any one shall go about to bring them into such slavish condition, they will always have a right to preserve what they have not a power to part with, and to rid themselves of those who invade this fundamental, sacred, and unalterable law of self-preservation for which they entered into society. And thus the community may be said in this respect to be always the supreme power, but not as considered under any form of government, because this power of the people can never take place till the government be dissolved. [*Two Treatises of Government*, 1690, Bk II, Chapter XIII, para 149]

Thomas Paine

Thomas Paine (1737–1809), who claimed not to have read Locke's works, was to echo many of Locke's radical and revolutionary sentiments. Paine was involved in two revolutions: that of the United States of America in 1775, and that of France in 1789 – an involvement which he claimed made his life 'truly useful'. The background of the two men could not have been more different. Whereas John Locke had a privileged upbringing, being educated at Westminster School and Christ Church, Oxford, where he remained for some 15 years before entering into service with the Earl of Shaftsbury,[2] Thomas Paine was largely self-educated. In 1773, he issued a pamphlet,[3] the radical nature of which caused him to be discharged from his position as an exciseman (customs officer). In the course of his political lobbying for higher pay for fellow excise officers, he met Benjamin Franklin.[4] With Franklin's support, Paine emigrated to North America.

While John Locke had been writing against the background of the constitutional struggles in the United Kingdom, which were to culminate in the assertion of parliament's sovereignty over the King, Paine was writing in the midst of the struggle for independence in America against the sovereign English King George III. In 1775, Paine, working as a journalist on the *Pennsylvania Journal*, was supporting the right of colonists to control their own affairs. In criticising England for her treatment of, among others, American Indians and black slaves, Paine predicted the eventual separation of America from Britain. In 1776 he published *Common Sense*, which not only attacked the policy of the King towards the colony, but also attacked the institution of monarchy itself. *Common Sense* exerted a profound influence on the course of political events, and the Declaration of Independence (4 July 1776) echoed Paine's sentiments. In both *Common Sense* and *Rights of Man*, arbitrary power is decried and the freedom of the individual declared to be sovereign. Paine distinguished between the natural and civil rights of individuals:

---

2   Lord Ashley, one of the most powerful figures in the court of Charles II.
3   The Case of the Officers of the Excise.
4   1706–90. American statesman; a draughtsman of the American Constitution and Ambassador to France 1776–85.

Natural rights are those which appertain to man in right of his existence. Of this kind are all the intellectual rights, or rights of the mind, and also those rights of acting as an individual for his own comfort and happiness, which are not injurious to the natural rights of others. Civil rights are those which appertain to man in right of his being a member of society. Every civil right has for its foundation, some natural right pre-existing in the individual, but to the enjoyment of which his individual power is not, in all cases, sufficiently competent. [*Rights of Man* (1791–92), Part II, p 90]

Civil rights, for Paine, are entailed in, and grow out of, individual natural rights, and are accordingly antecedent to any form of government. When man entered into society:

... the individuals themselves, each in his own personal and sovereign right, entered into a compact with each other to produce a government: and this is the only mode in which governments have a right to arise, and the only principle on which they have a right to exist. [p 92]

Furthermore:

The rights of men in society, are neither devisable, nor transferable, nor annihilable, but are descendable only; and it is not in the power of any generation to intercept finally, and cut off the descent.

The American constitution reflected these views, the preamble declaring:

We the People of the United States, in order to form a more perfect Union, establish Justice, ensure Domestic Tranquillity, provide for the Common Defence, promote the general Welfare, and secure the Blessings of Liberty to ourselves and our Posterity, do ordain and establish this CONSTITUTION for the United States of America.

THE EMERGENCE OF THE
CONSTITUTIONAL PROTECTION OF RIGHTS

These early expressions of an emergent notion of individual rights can be seen today in most written constitutions in the world, whether or not the constitution is 'autochthonous'.[5]

The attempt to protect human rights on an international level began with the founding of the League of Nations after World War I and the imposition of certain safeguards of human rights in peace treaties negotiated after the war for the protection of minorities. It was not, however, until after the Second World War that the international community became convinced of the real and pressing need to protect and promote human rights as an integral and essential element for the preservation of world peace and co-operation. The United Nations[6] provided the appropriate forum for international quasi-legislative activity. In 1948, the Universal Declaration on Human Rights was adopted, supplemented by two implementing international covenants in 1966: the International Covenant on

---

5   Defined as a constitution originating from, and having the authority of, the people it
     governs: it springs from the people and is not conferred upon the people from any higher
     authority. See Wheare, 1966.
6   Which superseded the League of Nations in 1945.

Civil and Political Rights and the International Covenant on Economic, Social and Cultural Rights. Taken together, these documents represent an international Bill of Human Rights. Inspired by the United Nations Declaration and Covenants, many other regional conventions were drafted, for example the European Convention on Human Rights and Fundamental Freedoms 1950, the American Convention of Human Rights 1969 and the African Charter of 1987.[7]

Natural law and positive law[8]

The ancient concept of natural law, as discussed in Chapter 4, concerns an evaluation of the validity of human law against some higher source of authority, whether theological or secular, which is both eternal and universal. The demands of natural law challenge the law of human rulers – demanding that law conform to higher principles. One such principle is the respect for individual rights and freedoms, and it may therefore be argued that the protection of human rights is a natural law concept. It should not be assumed, however, that the assertion that the rights of man derive from natural law has been completely or unequivocally accepted.

In the nineteenth century, for example, the rise of nationalism in the West challenged doctrines of natural law. The same century also witnessed the rise of positivism – the legal-theoretical schools of thought concerned solely to identify and define the concept of valid human law. These two developments – nationalism and positivism – shifted the focus of attention away from individual rights towards an analysis of state power. By way of illustration, Hegel's *Philosophy of Right* (1821) portrayed the state as absolutely sovereign, its form and content being determined by history, but its existence and power being unrestricted by any form of natural law.

In the United Kingdom, the Scottish philosopher David Hume laid the foundations for positivism.[9] Positivism, in its many forms, concerns the endeavour of isolating the law laid down by human superior (the sovereign power) to human inferior (the subject).[10] In essence, Hume's thesis was that, in logic, it is not possible to derive a statement of fact (an existential statement) from a statement of what ought to be (a normative statement). By this reasoning, only by keeping statements of fact and statements of 'ought' – or moral statements – separate can there be a true understanding of reality, and law. The implication of such a distinction for law and legal theory is that no moral statement as to what 'ought to be' can be inferred from a purely factual statement. This essential logical separation of the factual from the normative underlies the positivist endeavour: the attempt to provide a coherent logical structure of legal rules, and legal rules alone, unaffected by morality. For the positivist, whatever is enacted according to the accepted constitutional procedure employed within the state is valid law and entails an absolute obligation of obedience. As such, there can be no claim to

---

7   See also the Hong Kong Bill of Rights based on the UN Covenant on Civil and Political Rights.
8   See Finnis, 1980; Hart, 1961.
9   See *An Enquiry Concerning the Principles of Morals* (1751), *Political Discourses* (1752).
10 See eg Austin, 1832; Hart, 1961, Chapters 1–4.

freedoms or human rights which are capable of overriding the positive law. According to positivist theories of law, while in a perfect world the positive law may – and ideally should – conform to moral precepts, should it fail so to do, the individual is powerless to confront the law.

The nineteenth century rise in positivism represented both an attack on the claims of natural law and an attempt to analyse scientifically the law as it exists in fact. The doctrine of natural law for which so much had been claimed in relation to human rights and freedoms was placed on the defensive. The protection of rights based on natural law was further damaged by the utilitarians. Having rejected natural law as providing the lodestar for enactment of positive law, the utilitarians adopted the principle of utility. By utility is meant that the proper guidance in the formation of laws is the overall effect of a legislative proposal on society as a whole. A proposal for legislation will be in conformity with the doctrine of utility if it increases the sum of happiness in society overall. The leading exponent of the utilitarian school was Jeremy Bentham (1748–1832) whose *An Introduction to the Principles of Morals and Legislation* was to exert enduring influence. Bentham dismissed the idea of natural law and natural rights: natural rights were 'nonsense' – and worse – 'nonsense on stilts'.

Despite the attacks from nationalists, positivists and utilitarians, the quest for the protection of rights – from wheresoever derived – continued; a quest which became reinvigorated by the horrors of the Second World War.

Rights and freedoms in Britain

It has long been a paradox that the United Kingdom – viewed as a liberal democratic state – should have no comprehensive written Bill of Rights.[11] This is especially so given that the United Kingdom has been responsible for restoring independence to many former colonies and dominions and, in so doing, has conferred upon those states both a written constitution and a Bill of Rights. The Human Rights Act 1998 marks a significant constitutional change in relation to citizens' awareness about rights, and their protection by judges in the domestic courts.[12] The Act and its implications are considered later in this chapter. Prior to incorporation of Convention rights, the judges used the Convention as an aid to interpretation to assist in resolving ambiguities in domestic law. However, given the supremacy of parliament, the judges previously had no jurisdictional basis on which they could employ the Convention to protect rights. The Human Rights Act confers this jurisdiction, requiring the courts not only to protect Convention rights, but to make 'declarations of incompatibility' wherever domestic law is judicially seen to conflict with Convention rights. By this means, parliament preserves its supremacy over changes in the law which may be required by judicial evaluation of domestic law against the provisions of the Convention. Before considering the

---

11 The Bill of Rights 1689, it will be recalled, was concerned with constitutional arrangements between the Crown and parliament, not with the rights of individuals.

12 See the Consultation Paper, *Bringing Rights Home: Labour's Plans to Incorporate the European Convention on Human Rights into United Kingdom Law*, 1996, London: Labour Party. Note that technically the Human Rights Act 1998 does not incorporate the Convention, but rather makes Convention rights enforceable before the domestic courts.

Human Rights Act, however, it is necessary to understand the status and working of the European Convention and the scope and application of the Convention rights which the Act incorporates.

THE EUROPEAN CONVENTION ON HUMAN RIGHTS[13]

Introduction

Europe was one of the principal theatres of the Second World War, following which there was felt to be a great need for European political, social and economic unity. Those objectives were perceived to be promoted, in part, by the adoption of a uniform Convention designed to protect human rights and fundamental freedoms.[14] In 1949, the Council of Europe was established and the Convention on Human Rights ratified by Member States in 1951, coming into force in 1953.[15] Despite having been instrumental in the drafting of the text of the Convention, the British government had strong reservations about the Convention and its impact on British constitutional law. As a result of such reservations, it was not until 1965 that the government gave individuals the right to petition under the Convention.

The influence of the Convention before the Human Rights Act 1998[16]

The attitude of the United Kingdom courts towards the Convention was, in the past, the traditional one adopted in relation to treaties. Treaties form part of international law and have no place within the domestic legal order unless and until incorporated into law.[17] The courts regarded the Convention as an aid to interpretation but had no jurisdiction directly to enforce the rights and freedoms under the Convention.[18] This could, however, of itself be significant. For example, in *Waddington v Miah* (1974), Lord Reid stated – having referred to Article 7 of the Convention which prohibits retrospective legislation – that 'it is hardly credible that any government department would promote, or that parliament would pass, retrospective criminal legislation'.[19]

R v Secretary of State for the Home Department ex parte Brind (1991) also illustrates the influence of the Convention. The Home Secretary had exercised his discretionary power under section 19(3) of the Broadcasting Act 1981 to issue a notice prohibiting the broadcasting on television or radio of the voices of any person speaking on behalf of an organisation proscribed under the Prevention of Terrorism (Temporary Provisions) Act 1974. The words used could be reported

---

13 The literature on the Convention is extensive. See, *inter alia*, Fawcett, 1987; Jacobs, 1975; Van Dijk and Van Hoof, 1990; Palley, 1991; Harris, O'Boyle and Warbrick, 1995.
14 See Robertson and Merrills, 1993.
15 For a succinct history of the Convention, see Lester (Lord), 'European human rights and the British constitution', in Jowell and Oliver, 2000.
16 See Browne-Wilkinson, 1992; Bingham, 1993; Laws, 1993.
17 See *Kaur v Lord Advocate* (1980).
18 *Waddington v Miah* (1974).
19 See further below for the (retrospective) War Crimes Act 1991.

through the medium of an actor, provided that the voice of the spokesperson was not broadcast. The challenge to this prohibition was, in the House of Lords, based primarily on the argument that it was contrary to the United Kingdom's obligations under Article 10 of the Convention, guaranteeing freedom of expression. It was argued that the Home Secretary should have had regard to the Convention in exercising his discretion under the Broadcasting Act.

The House of Lords was prepared to accept that there was a presumption that parliament would enact laws that were in conformity with the Convention. Accordingly, it was accepted that where a statute permits two interpretations, one in line with the Convention, the other contrary to it, the interpretation which fitted with the Convention should be preferred. In *Brind*, the court could find no ambiguity in section 29(3) of the Broadcasting Act.[20] The only basis for challenge therefore was that the Home Secretary's decision was unreasonable in the *Wednesbury*[21] sense: that the decision was so irrational or unreasonable that no rational or reasonable person could have reached the same decision.

A rather different approach to the Convention was adopted in *Derbyshire County Council v Times Newspapers Ltd* (1993), concerning the question of whether a local council could bring an action in libel against newspapers (see further below). In the Court of Appeal, Butler-Sloss LJ was forthright in declaring that 'where there is ambiguity, or the law is otherwise unclear as so far undeclared by an appellate court, the English court is not only entitled but ... obliged to consider the implications of Article 10'. The House of Lords, however, while arriving at the result achieved in the Court of Appeal – namely that local authorities enjoyed no standing to sue in defamation – did so without relying on Article 10 of the Convention, but relying on the common law.

Accordingly, there existed (before the Human Rights Act 1998 came into force) no obligation on courts to rely on the Convention if a source of authority could be found within domestic law. Increasingly, however, it appeared that – within certain limits – the judiciary expressed willingness to protect individual liberties and, where a statute was ambiguous, or silent, to construe the statute strictly and in favour of the liberty of the citizen.

However, there were limits to the extent to which judges were able to protect rights, as the case of *R v Inland Revenue Commissioners ex parte Rossminster Ltd* (1980) revealed.[22] In *Rossminster*, the House of Lords ruled that, where the meaning of a statute is clear and unambiguous, the court possessed no jurisdiction to go against its unambiguous words, and was under a duty to uphold the will of parliament by giving effect to its words.[23] In both *Attorney General v BBC* (1981) and *Attorney General v Guardian Newspapers (No 2)* (1990), however, the House of Lords confirmed that it was the duty of the courts to have

---

20 On the post Human Rights Act 1998 position and ambiguity, see Lord Irvine, 1998.
21 *Associated Provincial Picture Houses Ltd v Wednesbury Corporation* (1948). See further Chapter 27.
22 See also *R v Kelly, R v Sandford* (1998); and *R v Secretary of State for the Home Department ex parte Hussain Ahmed* (1998).
23 See also *R v DPP ex parte Kebeline* (1999).

regard to the international obligations assumed under the Convention, and to interpret the law in accordance with those obligations.

Institutions and procedure under the Convention

The Council of Europe, under which the Convention operates, is constitutionally distinct from the European Union. The Council was founded in 1949, inspired by the United Nation's Universal Declaration of Human Rights of 1948. The Committee of Ministers is the political body, consisting of one representative from each state government (usually Foreign Ministers). The Court of Human Rights – elected by the Consultative Assembly of the Council of Europe – represents the judicial body. Judges are elected for a renewable six year term of office, and need not be drawn exclusively from the judiciary in Member States. To qualify for appointment, a person must be 'of high moral character' and must either possess the qualifications required for appointment of high judicial office or be a jurisconsult of recognised competence.

The right of application

Applications may be brought by Member States or by individuals. The right of individual petition to a body outside the jurisdiction of states was a constitutional innovation. As noted above, the British government was exceedingly cautious about conceding such a right and only in 1965 did the right of individual application become available to citizens of the United Kingdom. Applications may come from individuals, groups of individuals or non-governmental organisations. The applicant(s) must be personally affected by the issue: complaints involving alleged conduct which does not personally affect the individual complainant are not admissible.[24]

With the Human Rights Act 1998 fully in force, individuals will only make an application to the Court of Human Rights if they fail to secure an effective remedy before the domestic courts.

The procedure

Exhaustion of domestic remedies

Any domestic remedies which are available must be exhausted.[25] Thus, if a remedy is available within domestic law, it must first be sought. Only where there exists no remedy in law, or where the pursuit of a remedy would be unequivocally certain to fail,[26] may an individual lodge a petition.

---

24   *X v Norway* (1960). See also *Vijayanathan v France* (1991).
25   ECHR, Article 35.
26   Eg, where there are strong precedents established.

The time limit

The application must be made within six months of the final decision of the highest court having jurisdiction within the domestic legal system.[27]

Admissibility

A number of hurdles face the applicant in having his application declared admissible:

(a) a complaint must not constitute an 'abuse of right of complaint'. In essence, this means that the complainant should not be pursuing a remedy out of improper motives – such as political advantage. In short, the complaint must be brought for genuine reasons;

(b) a complaint must not be anonymous;

(c) a complaint must not relate to a matter which has been investigated and ruled upon previously;

(d) a complaint must relate to a right which is protected under the Convention;

(e) a complaint is inadmissible if, although the application relates to a protected right, the state against which the complaint is made has derogated from that provision, or lodged a reservation (see below for further discussion of derogations and reservations);

(f) the application must relate to violation of the Convention by a state which is bound by the Convention, or to an organisation for which the state has responsibility;

(g) the application must not be such that it represents an attack on another right protected by the Convention. Article 17 provides that there is no right to 'engage in any activity or perform any act' which is aimed at the destruction of protected rights;

(h) a complaint must not be 'manifestly ill founded'. By this is meant that the application must be plausible – there must be *prima facie* evidence of a violation.

Once an application is declared admissible, the examination of the merits will commence. The complainant has a limited right to appear where the Court requires further evidence. The Court's decision must be reasoned and, if not unanimous, individual judges may give a separate opinion. Under Article 43(1) of the Convention, any party to the case may, within three months from the date of the judgment of a Chamber (effectively the 'court of first instance' hearing the case), request that the case be referred to the Grand Chamber. If it is not so referred, the judgment becomes final. Alternatively, if referred, the judgment of the Grand Chamber is final and Member States undertake to abide by the decision of the Court. Compensation can be awarded by the Court.

---

27 ECHR, Article 35.

Enforcing the judgment

The task of ensuring that the judgment is complied with lies with the Committee of Ministers: the matter is thus returned to the political arena. If a state refuses to comply with the judgment, its membership of the Council of Europe can be suspended or, ultimately, it may be expelled from the Council. Where exercised, this ultimate power has regrettable implications and would remove the protection of the Convention from individuals within the state and thus further damage the protection of rights. Greece withdrew from the Council of Europe following five allegations of persecution against it between 1967 and 1970. In 1974, a new Greek government ratified the Convention once more. However, failure to comply with a judgment will cause adverse publicity for the state and there is thus great political pressure to conform. Following the judgment in *Brogan v United Kingdom* (1988), concerning the seven day detention provisions in the Prevention of Terrorism Acts, however, the British government announced its intention to derogate from the protection given in Article 5 to the right to liberty and freedom and access to a court of law for the determination of the legality of detention.

The 'margin of appreciation'

In respect of almost all Articles of the Convention, there is an area of discretion as to the means by which they protect the substantive rights. This margin of appreciation is necessary in order that the Convention can apply in a workable fashion in very diverse societies. It also means, however, that application of the Convention will not be uniform throughout the legal systems and that states may be able to deviate from the protection given.

Whether the state has a margin of appreciation – and the scope of it – is a matter to be determined under the Convention. The doctrine is unpredictable in operation and has become, over the years, applicable to all Articles. Accordingly, it is a concept which is capable of significantly undermining the protection given by the Convention, and has been criticised for so doing.[28]

Derogation and reservation

Where a state finds it impossible or undesirable to comply with specific Articles, it is possible for the state to derogate, or enter a reservation as to the matter.[29] No derogation is permitted in relation to Article 2 (the right to life), other than in war situations. Derogation is not allowed in respect of Articles 3 (freedom from torture), 4(1) (slavery or servitude), and 7 (freedom from retrospective criminal liability).[30] The right of derogation is limited. Article 15 provides that:

> In time of war or other public emergency threatening the life of the nation any High Contracting Party may take measures derogating from its obligations under this Convention to the extent strictly required by the exigencies of the situation,

---

28 See Van Dijk and Van Hoof, 1990, p 604.
29 ECHR, Articles 15 and 64, respectively.
30 Note, however, the War Crimes Act 1991, s 1 of which provides for the prosecution of war crimes committed between 1939 and 1945.

provided that such measures are not inconsistent with its other obligations under international law.

A challenge can be made to the lawfulness of derogation. Following the United Kingdom's derogation after the decision in *Brogan v United Kingdom* (1988), a challenge was lodged, but failed when it was held that the situation in Northern Ireland did amount to a public emergency[31] and was thus within the terms of Article 15.[32]

The substantive rights

Article 1 provides that states will 'secure to everyone within jurisdiction the rights and freedoms defined in Section 1 of this Convention'.

Article 2: the right to life

Article 2 guarantees the right to life. There is no violation of Article 2 where loss of life is caused by reasonable self-defence against unlawful violence or use of necessary force to effect a lawful arrest or to quell civil unrest. The scope of this Article is broad but vague. It is, for example, unclear as to the duty, if any, which is imposed on states to sustain life by providing the economic and social conditions under which the right to life is meaningfully upheld. In *Simon-Herald v Austria* (1971), for instance, allegations that the state had failed to provide adequate medical care to prisoners was ruled admissible, although a friendly settlement was reached thus avoiding the need for a judicial analysis. The Court of Human Rights ruled, in *Evans v United Kingdom* (2006) that an embryo has no right to life. English law which required the consent of both parties to fertility treatment and which could be withdrawn up to the point of implantation of an embryo did not violate Article 2.

The allowable exceptions to the protection of Article 2 are designed to excuse unintentional causes of death in violent situations. Thus the use of plastic bullets in a riot will not violate Article 2,[33] nor will measures taken to prevent possible future terrorist activities.[34] There are, however, limits to the lawful use of force. The killing of three Irish Republican Army members by members of the SAS in Gibraltar[35] was challenged under the Convention. In *McGann, Farrell and Savage v United Kingdom* (1995), the Court ruled that, given the information which the security forces had received regarding the movements of the suspected terrorists, their shooting did not violate Article 2 of the Convention. Nevertheless, the Court ruled that there had been inadequate control over the security forces operation and that, as a result, the killing of the suspected terrorists was 'more than absolutely necessary' as provided within Article 2. Thus the action taken, to be lawful, must be proportionate to the circumstances of the case.[36] A violation of

---

31 *Brannigan and McBride v United Kingdom* (1993).
32 See further below on derogation under the Human Rights Act 1998.
33 *Stewart v United Kingdom* (1985).
34 *Kelly v United Kingdom* (1993).
35 For further details on the circumstances, see Chapter 25.
36 Compare *Kelly v United Kingdom* (1993).

Article 2 was also found in *Andronicus v Cyprus* (1996), a case arising when the police, in a siege operation, fired at the hostage taker but killed the hostage. It was held that the number of bullets fired reflected a lack of caution in the operation.

In *Jordan v United Kingdom* (2001), the families of men shot dead by the SAS and Royal Ulster Constabulary in three incidents between 1982 and 1992 were each awarded £10,000 compensation by the Court. It ruled that the authorities had failed to conduct a proper investigation into the circum-stances of the persons killed in the fight against terrorism. The required investigation had to be independent and effective in the sense that it was capable of leading to a determination of whether the force used was or was not justified in the circumstances and to the identification and punishment of those responsible: there is thus a procedural aspect to Article 2.[37] See also *Edwards v United Kingdom* (2002), where the United Kingdom was found to have violated Article 2 through its failure to protect the life of a prisoner who was killed in his cell.

Article 3: freedom from torture, inhuman and degrading treatment

Article 3 states that 'no one shall be subjected to torture or to inhuman or degrading treatment or punishment'. In *Ireland v United Kingdom* (1978), the Republic of Ireland[38] alleged that the United Kingdom had, *inter alia*, violated Article 3 of the Convention, which proscribes 'inhuman or degrading treatment or punishment'. In 1966, the United Kingdom had declared that there was a state of emergency in Northern Ireland. In 1971, acting under the Civil Authorities (Special Powers) Act 1922,[39] the government introduced new powers of detention and internment of suspected Irish Republican Army terrorists. Fourteen suspects were subjected to such techniques as hooding, wall-standing for between 23 and 29 hours, noise intrusions and deprivation of sleep, food and water. There was evidence that the men subjected to these practices suffered weight loss and pain.

The treatment fell within the meaning of inhuman treatment; it was also degrading, arousing feelings of fear, anguish and inferiority capable of humiliating and debasing the prisoners and breaking their physical or moral resistance. To amount to torture, however, comparison must be made with inhuman and degrading treatment. The distinction, ruled the Court, derives from the difference in the intensity of suffering inflicted. In this case it did not occasion suffering of a particular intensity and cruelty implied by the word torture as understood by the Court.[40]

In *Tyrer v United Kingdom* (1978), the Court ruled on the compatibility of birching as a judicial punishment in the Isle of Man with the requirements of Article 3. Tyrer, then aged 15, was given three strokes of the birch as punishment

---

37 See also *McShane v United Kingdom* (2002).
38 Under ECHR, Article 24, which provides for inter-state applications.
39 See now the Northern Ireland (Emergency Provisions) Act 1991, Pt IV and Sched 3.
40 There was no violation of Article 14 (the harsher treatment given to the IRA suspects was justified by their greater menace), and no violation of Article 1 (which cannot be a head for a separate breach of the ECHR).

for an assault on a school prefect. The question raised was whether the punishment amounted to a violation of Article 3. The Court held that, while a conviction for a criminal offence itself could humiliate, for a finding to be sustained under Article 3, there needed to be found a humiliation deriving from the execution of punishment imposed. The mere fact that the punishment being inflicted was distasteful was not enough. Under the circumstances, with the victim having to undress, the treatment reached a level of degrading punishment.[41] Issues are also raised as to the lawfulness of the conditions under which a prisoner is detained.[42] In *Price v United Kingdom* (2001), the Court of Human Rights ruled that the detention of a severely disabled person in unsuitable conditions at a police station and subsequently detention in prison in similar conditions amounted to degrading treatment contrary to Article 3.[43]

The law relating to immigration, race and citizenship has also been tested under Article 3. In *East African Asians v United Kingdom* (1973), legislation restricted immigration of British passport holders in East Africa, preventing those who had neither a parent nor grandparent born or naturalised in the United Kingdom from entering the country. The Commission ruled that racial discrimination of this type constituted a form of affront to human dignity and amounted to degrading treatment. More recently, the treatment of asylum seekers by the state has given rise to allegations of violations of Article 3. This issue is further discussed in Chapter 24.[44]

To return a person to his or her country of nationality will raise Article 3 if the person is liable to suffer ill-treatment by state officials. This issue was tested in *Chahal v United Kingdom* (1997). Mr Chahal, a Sikh, had been politically active in Sikh affairs. In 1990, the Home Secretary decided to deport him from the United Kingdom on grounds of national security and the international fight against terrorism. The Court of Human Rights ruled, by twelve votes to seven, that the United Kingdom violated Article 3 of the Convention and – unanimously – that there had been a violation of Article 13 in conjunction with Article 3, in that effective remedies did not exist before the courts in England. Mr Chahal had been subjected to torture in India on a visit in 1984. The Court was appraised of substantiated allegations of torture by the authorities in India. In addition, there was a violation of Article 5(4), in that Mr Chahal had been denied the opportunity to have the lawfulness of his detention decided by a national court.[45]

---

41 See also *Costello-Roberts v United Kingdom* (1993); *A v United Kingdom* (1998).
42 See *Krocher and Moller v Switzerland* (1984).
43 See also *Z v United Kingdom* (2001): a violation of Article 3 through failure of the state to protect children from long-term neglect and abuse. See *X v Bedfordshire County Council* (1995). Compare *Hill v Chief Constable of West Yorkshire* (1988) and *Osman v United Kingdom* (2000). See also *E v United Kingdom* (2002). In *Z v United Kingdom*, the children were awarded, in total, £192,000 as pecuniary damage, £32,000 each for non-pecuniary damage and a total of £39,000 for costs and expenses.
44 See *Soering v United Kingdom* (1989); *Vilvarajah v United Kingdom* (1991).
45 See also *D v United Kingdom* (1997): a violation of Article 3 arose from the threat to remove the defendant from the UK to his country of origin when he was terminally ill and there was no one to care for him in his own country.

Article 4: freedom from slavery

Article 4 states that no one shall be held in slavery or servitude, and no one shall be required to perform forced or compulsory labour. The term 'forced or compulsory labour' does not include any work required to be done in the ordinary course of lawful detention or during conditional release from such detention; or military service recognised in states of emergency or which forms a part of normal 'civil obligations'. This provision has little relevance in the majority of Western democracies and has given rise to little case law. Challenges have been made relating to the requirement that German lawyers undertake compulsory legal aid work, but these have failed.[46]

Articles 5 and 6: right to liberty and to fair trial

Article 5 provides that everyone has the right to liberty and security of person and that no one shall be deprived of his liberty other than in accordance with lawful arrest or detention. The right includes the right to be informed of reasons for an arrest and of any charges being brought. It also includes the right to be brought 'promptly' before a court to determine the lawfulness of the detention, and the right to a trial within a reasonable time or to release pending trial.

This long and intricate Article has provided the platform for many challenges on behalf of persons detained and is in many cases linked to Article 6. The first requirement to be met in relation to Article 5 is that, where a person is deprived of his liberty, the deprivation must be in consequence of a lawful detention.

The following cases illustrate the protection given by Article 5.

- The arrest and detention of protesters violated Article 5(1) on the grounds that the protest was entirely peaceful and there had been no obstruction or provocation: *Steel v United Kingdom* (1998).[47]

- A two year delay between reviews by the Parole Board of detention was unreasonable and made the continued detention unlawful: *Oldham v United Kingdom* (2001).[48]

- Detention for up to seven days, at the Home Secretary's discretion, under the Prevention of Terrorism (Temporary Provisions) Act 1974 violated Article 5: *Brogan v United Kingdom* (1988).[49]

- The failure of the police to bring an arrested person before a judge promptly violated Article 5: *O'Hara v United Kingdom* (2001).[50]

---

46 *Van der Mussele v Belgium* (1983).
47 See also *Weeks v United Kingdom* (1987); *Johnson v United Kingdom* (1997).
48 See also *Wemhoff v Federal Republic of Germany* (1979); *Neumeister v Austria* (1968); and *Stogmuller v Austria* (1969).
49 See also *Brannigan and McBride v United Kingdom* (1994). The government in response issued a derogation notice and re-enacted the provisions. See also *Yagci and Sargin v Turkey* and *Mansur v Turkey* (1995).
50 See also *Murray v United Kingdom* (1996); *Benham v United Kingdom* (1996); *Hussain v United Kingdom* (1996); *Curley v United Kingdom* (2001); *Blackstock v United Kingdom* (2005); *Kolanis v United Kingdom* (2005).

- The power of a Mental Health Tribunal to review the detention of a patient but not to order his release – a power which lay with the executive – violated Article 5: *Benjamin v United Kingdom* (2002).

- The lack of formal rules regulating the admission and detention of compliant incapacity patients, notwithstanding the need for protective detention, violated Article 5(1) and the absence of procedures to determine the lawfulness of continued detention violated Article 5(4) *L v United Kingdom* (2004).[51]

Article 6: the right to fair trial

Article 6 provides for the right of fair trial before an independent and impartial tribunal, and for the presumption of innocence. In addition, Article 6 requires that those accused of a criminal offence are informed promptly of the charges, have adequate time to prepare a defence, have a right to be represented by a lawyer and have free legal assistance 'when the interests of justice so require'. The right to examine witnesses is also included. Article 6 is the most frequently cited Article. The protection given relates to the 'determination of ... civil rights and obligations' and 'of any criminal charge'. The Court has had to determine the meaning and scope of these phrases. A 'criminal charge' has been interpreted to mean 'the official notification given to an individual by the competent authority of an allegation that he has committed a criminal offence'.[52]

The phrase 'civil rights and obligations' has given rise to extensive interpretation. As a general principle, where the consequence of an administrative decision is one which affects the civil rights of individuals, then Article 6 may be held to apply.[53] For example, in *Konig* (1980), Dr Konig's licence to practise as a doctor in his own clinic was withdrawn. The Court ruled that the decision affected Dr Konig's civil rights and that, therefore, the protection of Article 6 applied.[54]

Article 6 was also instrumental in *T and V v United Kingdom* (1999). The Court ruled that the setting of the tariff period to be served by juveniles convicted of murder for retribution and deterrence by the Home Secretary deprived the applicants of the opportunity to have their detention reviewed by a judicial body. Furthermore, being tried in an adult court violated the right to fair trial.

Particular difficulties arise in disciplinary proceedings for criminal offences in the armed forces. The consequence of trying the matter under disciplinary regulations rather than a court of law is to remove the normal application of Article 6. The Court has ruled that whether an offence is classified as criminal or disciplinary is less important than the nature of the offence. Article 6.1 was violated where the applicant, an army officer, had been detained before trial on the instruction of his commanding officer who then played a role in hearing the

---

51 See also *Blackstock v United Kingdom* (2005); *Kolanis v United Kingdom* (2005).
52 *Eckle v Federal Republic of Germany* (1982), para 73.
53 *Konig v Federal Republic of Germany* (1980). *Ringeisen v Austria* (1971).
54 See also *Devlin v United Kingdom* (2002); and *Devenney v United Kingdom* (2002).

case against the applicant: *Hood v United Kingdom* (1999).[55] Royal Navy courts martial violated Article 6 in that the judge advocates were serving naval officers appointed by a naval officer. Furthermore, where there was no independent, full-time, permanent president of the court Article 6 was violated: *Grieves v United Kingdom* (2004).[56]

In *Campbell and Fell v United Kingdom* (1984), following involvement in a prison riot, the applicants had been punished by the Board of Prison Visitors with loss of remission of sentence. The Court held that Article 6 applied to the decision making process of the Board of Visitors.[57] Article 6 has also been used to protect the rights of prisoners. The determination of charges relating to breach of prison rules being decided by those who were appointed by the Home Office and who had investigated those charges could not be said to be independent. Furthermore, in *Whitfield v United Kingdom* (2005) Article 6 was violated by denying the applicants legal representation.

A 'fair and public hearing' includes the right to legal advice before the judicial hearing: *Golder v United Kingdom* (1975). The applicant, who was serving a prison sentence, wanted to sue a prison officer for defamation. His request to the Home Secretary to consult a solicitor was denied. The Court held that Article 6 had been violated. The Court has further ruled that not only must access to law not be impeded (by the denial of legal advice or other means), but the state has a duty to ensure effective access to law.[58] The right of access to law is not absolute, but any restrictions which are imposed must not be such as to impair 'the very essence of the right'. Limitations will be incompatible with the Convention if they do not pursue a legitimate aim and are not proportional to the objective being sought.[59]

Article 6(1) also requires that the hearing take place 'within a reasonable time'. The reasonableness of the length of the proceedings will depend upon their complexity.[60]

Being compelled to answer questions by the investigating authorities under threat of contempt of court violates the right not to incriminate oneself: *Saunders v United Kingdom* (1996).[61] Article 6 protects the right to legal advice. The right is not expressly stated and may be subject to restrictions for good cause. Being detained for over 48 hours without access to legal advice, which resulted in the

---

55 See also *Findlay v United Kingdom* (1997); *Jordan v United Kingdom* (2001). In *Coyne v United Kingdom* (1996), a court martial conducted before the Armed Forces Act 1996 came into force was not an independent and impartial tribunal. See now the Armed Forces Discipline Act 2000.

56 See also *Cooper v United Kingdom* (2004). Cf *R v Spear* (2001).

57 Cf *Engel et al v Netherlands* (1976).

58 *Airey v Ireland* (1979). See also *P, C and S v United Kingdom* (2002).

59 *Ashingdane v United Kingdom* (1985). See also *Ezeh and Connors v United Kingdom* (2003).

60 See *Davies v United Kingdom* (2002); *Mitchell v United Kingdom* (2002).

61 See *IJL, GMR and AKP v United Kingdom* (2000): the Court of Human Rights in 2000 found a violation of Article 6(1) through the use of the applicants' statements at trial which they had been compelled under statute to give to inspectors appointed by the Department of Trade and Industry. The Court awarded a total sum of £40,000 for costs and expenses. See also *Averill v United Kingdom* (2000).

applicant signing a confession statement violated Article 6: *Magee v United Kingdom* (2000).[62] Where the conviction of the applicants had been upheld as safe by the Court of Appeal, the applicants having exercised their right to silence on the advice of their solicitor, and the trial judge had failed accurately to instruct the jury as to the inferences to be drawn from the right to silence, a violation of Article 6 occurred: *Condron v United Kingdom* (2000).[63] The presence of police officers within hearing during an accused's interview with his solicitor violated Article 6: *Brennan v United Kingdom* (2001). The denial of legal aid where the interests of justice required legal representation violates Article 6: *Granger v United Kingdom* (1990); *Benham v United Kingdom* (1996). The failure of the prosecution to lay Public Interest Immunity Certificates (which preclude evidence being given in court) before the judge violated Article 6. While there was no absolute right to disclosure it was for the judge to control the release or otherwise of material: *Rowe v United Kingdom* (2000).[64]

Judicial impartiality is central to Article 6. The requirement of judicial impartiality was tested before the Court of Human Rights, in a judgment which had implications for the role of Lord Chancellor. In *McGonnell v United Kingdom* (2000), a case relating to the position of the Deputy Bailiff of Guernsey as President of the States of Deliberation, Guernsey's legislative body, and subsequently as the sole judge of law in proceedings relating to the applicant's planning application which had been refused, the Court of Human Rights held that the Deputy Bailiff's position was 'capable of casting doubt' as to his 'impartiality' and, as a result, was in violation of Article 6(1) of the European Convention on Human Rights, which guarantees 'a fair and public hearing ... by an independent and impartial tribunal established by law'.[65]

Article 6 has been held not to be violated where state immunity had prevented the applicants from pursuing cases in domestic court proceedings.[66] The three applicants each sought redress for the actions of British, Kuwaiti and United States' authorities for, respectively, an alleged assault, wrongful imprisonment and torture, and discrimination. The respondent governments pleaded state immunity. The Court ruled that in each case the doctrine of state immunity, designed to promote comity between nations, applied.

Article 7: non-retrospectivity

Article 7 prohibits retrospective criminal law. It is an accepted presumption of statutory interpretation under English law that parliament does not intend – in the absence of clear words – to legislate with retrospective effect, and Article 7 reflects this approach.

---

62 Compare *Murray (John) v United Kingdom* (1996), and see Munday, 1996.
63 See also *Beckles v United Kingdom* (2003), *Cuscani v United Kingdom* (2002).
64 In *CG v United Kingdom* (2002), the Court of Human Rights ruled that excessive and undesirable interruptions by a judge did not necessarily render a trial unfair.
65 See also *Sander v United Kingdom* (2001).
66 *McElhinney v Ireland* (2001), *Al-Adsani v United Kingdom* and *Fogarty v United Kingdom* (2000).

A challenge lodged under the Convention, claiming a violation of Article 7, for a penalty imposed which could not have been foreseen occurred in *Harman and Hewitt v United Kingdom* (1989). Ms Harman showed confidential documents to a journalist after they had been read out in court, as a result of which she was found guilty of contempt. Previously, no liability had been imposed in such situations – the information had been regarded as having entered the 'public domain' through disclosure in court. Ms Harman's application was ruled admissible, but a friendly settlement was reached with the government.

The European Court of Human Rights has ruled on the compatibility of a conviction for marital rape with Article 7 of the Convention: *SW v United Kingdom; CR v United Kingdom* (1995). In *R v R* (1992), the House of Lords ruled that the exemption of husbands from the law of rape against their wives was obsolete. Two men were convicted of rape or attempted rape of their wives in 1989 and 1990, following the decision in *R v R*. The applicants alleged that their conviction amounted to a violation of Article 7 which prohibits a retrospective change in the criminal law. The Court ruled that the convictions did not violate the Convention: the judicial decisions had done no more than continue a line of reasoning which diminished a husband's immunity; the decisions had become a reasonably foreseeable development of the law and the decisions were not in contravention of the aims of Article 7.[67]

Article 8: privacy

Article 8 provides the right to respect for private and family life, home and correspondence. The right is not absolute and may be restricted by law in the interests of national security, public safety or the economic well being of the country, for the prevention of disorder or crime, for the protection of health or morals, or for the protection of the rights and freedoms of others.

Article 8 has provided the legal means by which to challenge domestic law and practice in two principal areas – respect for privacy and non-intervention by the state (including the keeping of personal records), and respect for the individual's private life in terms of his or her own personal relationships.

Respect for individual privacy

As can be seen from the text of Article 8, the right to privacy is subject to several exceptions, and the protection which can in fact be accorded to privacy is limited.

The interception of communications has given rise to challenges under the Convention. In *Foxley v United Kingdom* (2001),[68] the Court of Human Rights ruled that Article 8 was violated by the interception of correspondence which included correspondence between the applicant and his solicitors. The legal basis for the interception was the Insolvency Act 1986, under which a court ordered the redirection of the applicant's mail to a trustee in bankruptcy. However, the intercepts continued after the expiry of the court order and involved

---

67 See also *Welch v United Kingdom* (1995).
68 See also *PG and JH v United Kingdom* (2001).

communications between the applicant and his lawyer. That was unjustified and violated Article 8.

In *Malone v United Kingdom* (1984), the Court found that the law was unclear, and that, accordingly, 'the minimum degree of legal protection to which citizens are entitled under the rule of law in a democratic society is lacking' (paragraph 79). The government's response to the judgment was to introduce the Interception of Communications Act 1985 (see Chapter 25), which placed the granting of warrants for interception of communications on a statutory basis.[69]

Covert surveillance by the police prior to the enactment of the Police Act 1997, which provided for statutory authority for such surveillance, violated the right to respect for private and family life, as guaranteed by Article 8. The Court of Human Rights so held in *Khan v United Kingdom* (2000). The applicant had been convicted for drug dealing, on the basis of evidence improperly obtained by a secret listening device installed by the police. The evidence so gained was the sole evidence against the accused. There was a violation of Article 8: since there was an absence of statutory authority for the intercept, the interference could not be considered to be in accordance with law.[70] In *Wood v United Kingdom* (2004) the Court of Human Rights ruled that the covert recording of a burglary suspect while in police custody violated his right to privacy. The suspects had been arrested and detained in a police cell fitted with audio equipment. The recorded conversation formed the basis of the prosecution. There was no legal basis for the recording and no effective remedy for the violation.

In *Halford v United Kingdom* (1997), Alison Halford, a former Assistant Chief Constable, won a significant victory in the European Court of Human Rights. Whilst in her post in Merseyside, Ms Halford's telephone calls were intercepted by senior police officers. The Court of Human Rights ruled that there had been a violation of the Convention. The Court also ruled that domestic law provided no avenue for a complaint such as this to be determined. Ms Halford was awarded £10,000 compensation. This case raised, for the first time, the issue of the right to privacy of employees at work. Government lawyers had argued, unsuccessfully, that there was no protection under the Convention on the basis that the telephones which had been tapped were government property.

The Grand Chamber of the Court of Human Rights ruled, unanimously, that there had been a violation of Article 8 in *Roche v United Kingdom* (2005). The applicant had joined the Army in 1953 and had participated in mustard gas and nerve gas tests conducted under the auspices of the Army at Porton Down in 1962–63. He later suffered a number of health problems which he attributed to his participation in the tests. From 1987 he sought access to his service medical

---

69 See also *McLeod v United Kingdom* (1999); *Armstrong v United Kingdom* (2002); *Taylor-Satori v United Kingdom* (2002). The refusal of a local authority to disclose its full secrets in relation to a person who had been in its care as a child amounted to a failure to fulfil the positive obligation to protect a person's private and family life: see *MG v United Kingdom* (2002).

70 On the admissibility of evidence gained through foreign intercepts and consideration of *Khan v United Kingdom*, see *R v X, Y and Z* (2000), Court of Appeal, Criminal Division. On the disclosure of CCTV footage to the media, see *Peck v United Kingdom* (2003).

records with limited success. The Court ruled that the state had a positive obligation to provide an effective and accessible procedure enabling an applicant to have access to all records, and that an individual should not be required to litigate to obtain disclosure.

Privacy of the family

In *Hoffman v Austria* (1994), the Court ruled that Ms Hoffman had been discriminated against (contrary to Article 14) and her respect for family life violated (Article 8) by the Supreme Court of Austria, which had denied her the custody of her children on divorce, principally because she had become a Jehovah's Witness. In *Marckx v Belgium* (1979), a complaint was lodged on the basis that Articles 12 and 14 had been violated by discriminatory inheritance rules for illegitimate children.[71] English law relating to care proceedings and the powers of local authorities to control access of parents to children in local authority care have also been successfully challenged under the Convention, leading to changes to the rights of parents to access to a court of law in order to challenge a local authority's decision to terminate contact between children and their parents.[72]

In *G v United Kingdom (Minors: Right of Contact)* (2000), there was no violation of Article 8 with regard to the alleged failure of the English and Scottish courts to enforce access arrangements between the applicant and his children, following his wife's refusal to comply with court orders. Compare *TP and KM v United Kingdom* (2001), in which a violation of Articles 8 and 13 was held to have been committed by the authorities. A mother and daughter had been separated for nearly a year by the local authority as a result of allegations that the child had been sexually abused by the mother's partner. The local authority had withheld evidence from the mother and failed to submit the issue to court, and had thereby excluded the mother from the decision-making process.[73]

The rights of Gypsies to live on their own land without planning permissions was considered by the Court of Human Rights in *Buckley v United Kingdom* (1997).[74] The Court ruled that the United Kingdom authorities had not violated Article 8 or Article 14 (enjoyment of substantive rights without discrimination) of the Convention. Mrs Buckley had purchased land, and had sought and been refused planning permission. The Court ruled, by a majority, that the protected right to a home may be limited 'in accordance with law' as 'necessary in a democratic society'. However, the Court ruled that the measures taken by national authorities must be proportionate to the legitimate aim pursued. Two dissenting judges ruled that there was a violation of Article 8 and one dissenting judge held that there had also been a violation of Article 14 of the Convention.

---

71 See the Family Law Reform Act 1987; see also the Inheritance (Provision for Family and Dependants) Act 1975 and the Fatal Accidents Act 1976, as amended, both of which place the illegitimate child in the same position as legitimate children.
72 *WRO v United Kingdom* (1988), which resulted in the Child Care Act 1980, s 12.
73 The Court awarded each applicant £10,000 for non-pecuniary damage and £25,000 for costs and expenses.
74 See Barnett, 1996.

See also *Chapman v United Kingdom* (2001), which followed *Buckley* in holding that there was no violation of Article 8, but by a narrower majority of ten votes to seven.

In a significant case relating to the responsibility of the state towards citizens affected by industrial and manufacturing hazards, the Court of Human Rights ruled in *Guerra v Italy* (1998) that the failure of state authorities to advise citizens of the threat posed by environmental pollution violated their right of enjoyment of their homes in such a way as to affect their private and family life adversely.

Respect for private sexual life

In *Dudgeon v United Kingdom* (1982), the right to respect for privacy was examined against the claim that legislation in force in Northern Ireland prohibited homosexual conduct between adult males. As a result, the Homosexual Offences (Northern Ireland) Order 1982 was passed to bring domestic law into line with the requirements of the Convention. See also *Lustig-Praen and Beckett v United Kingdom* and *Smith and Grady v United Kingdom* (2000), in which the Court of Human Rights ruled that the ban on homosexuals in the armed forces violated Article 8 of the Convention.

The prosecution and conviction of a man, for engaging in non-violent homosexual acts in private with up to four other men, was a violation of Article 8. The Court of Human Rights so held in *ADT v United Kingdom* (2000). The Court ruled that the applicant was a victim of an interference with his right to respect for his private life, both as to the existence of legislation prohibiting consensual sexual acts between more than two men in private, and as to the conviction for gross indecency. The interference was not justified as being 'necessary in a democratic society' in the protection of morals and rights and freedoms of others.

Article 9: freedom of thought, conscience and religion

This Article has founded the basis for few cases under the Convention. Applications which have been made under this Article relate primarily to the conditions under which an individual may exercise his rights. In the case of prisoners detained following a criminal conviction, the prison authorities are entitled to prescribe limits to the exercise of religious and other rights, simply because such restrictions represent 'an inherent feature of lawful imprisonment'. In *X v Austria* (1965), refusal by prison authorities to allow a Buddhist prisoner to grow a beard was held not to violate the Convention.[75]

Article 10: freedom of expression

Freedom of expression includes freedom to hold opinions and to receive and impart information and ideas without interference by public authority and regardless of frontiers. The right is not absolute and may be restricted by law – to

---

75 Note that in *R (Shabina Begum) v Denbigh High School* (2006), the House of Lords ruled that a school's uniform policy did not violate Article 9.

the extent necessary in a democratic society – in the interests of national security, territorial integrity or public safety, for the prevention of disorder or crime, for the protection of health or morals, for the protection of the reputation or rights of others, for preventing the disclosure of information received in confidence, or for maintaining the authority and impartiality of the judiciary. The case law is discussed in Chapter 21.

Article 11: peaceful assembly and association

The right to freedom of peaceful assembly and to freedom of association with others includes the right to form and join trade unions. The rights are not absolute and may be restricted by law. The right to peaceful assembly is more limited than a right to assemble. Where a state seeks to regulate assemblies which are not peaceful – or unlikely to be peaceful – no violation of the right occurs.

The right to join a trade union has been interpreted to incorporate the right not to join a trade union. In *Young, James and Webster* (1981), the Court interpreted Article 11 to mean that there is a measure of choice left to individual workers whether or not to join a trade union.

Deprivation of the right to be a member of a trade union was considered by the Court in *Council of Civil Service Unions v United Kingdom* (the *GCHQ* case) (1985).[76] The Minister for the Civil Service, the Prime Minister, had, following industrial unrest, by Order in Council ruled that workers at Government Communications Headquarters (GCHQ) would no longer be entitled to membership of a trade union. The ban was challenged by judicial review proceedings, which were ultimately unsuccessful in the House of Lords. The applicants argued that their rights under Article 11 had been infringed, and also rights under Article 13, which provides for an effective domestic remedy. In answer, the government argued that the order was justified, *inter alia*, under Article 11(2) on the basis of the protection of national security. The Commission found a clear violation of Article 11. However, the ban on union membership was justifiable under Article 11(2) and therefore there was no violation of the Convention.

In *Wilson v United Kingdom* (2002), the Court of Human Rights held that financial incentives offered by employers to employees in exchange for employees giving up trade union protection for collective bargaining purposes violated Article 11. The applicants had applied to employment tribunals, arguing that the requirement to sign contracts giving up their rights was contrary to the Employment Protection (Consolidation) Act 1978, section 23(1)(a). Those proceedings culminated in the House of Lords, which ruled against them. The Court of Human Rights ruled that while the state was not directly involved, the responsibility of the state was engaged where it failed to secure to the applicants the rights conferred under Article 11. On the case law relating to the right to assembly, see Chapter 22.

---

76   For further discussion of this case, see Chapters 6 and 23.

Article 12: the right to marry

Article 12 provides that 'men and women of marriageable age have the right to marry and to found a family, according to the national laws governing the exercise of this right'.

The right of transsexuals to marry was previously denied by the Court of Human Rights; see *Rees v United Kingdom* (1987) and *Cossey v United Kingdom* (1992). In 2002, however, in *Goodwin v United Kingdom,* the Court found that English law, which prohibits transsexuals from marrying on the basis that a person's sex determines gender identity for marriage purposes and cannot be changed, violated both Articles 8 (the right to privacy) and 12. The Court ruled that the law placed transsexuals in a position where they could 'experience feelings of vulnerability, humiliation and anxiety' and that the 'very essence of the Convention was respect for human dignity and human freedom'. On the right to marry, the Court held that the matter could not be left entirely within the state's margin of appreciation and there was no justification for denying transsexuals the right to marry. In the earlier case of *B v France* (1992), the Court had ruled that French law violated Article 8, in that official documentation could not be altered, thereby causing the applicant distress and humiliation.[77] Following the *Goodwin* case, the House of Lords ruled in *Bellinger v Bellinger* (2003) that English law which prevented transsexuals from entering a valid marriage was incompatible with the Convention. As a result of these two cases, the Gender Recognition Act 2004 provides transsexual people with legal recognition of their acquired gender. Once legal recognition has been granted, a new birth certificate can be granted and the person will be eligible to marry someone of the opposite sex (see further pp 550–51 below).

The right to marry and found a family does not entail a right to a termination of marriage by divorce. In *Johnston v Ireland* (1987), the applicant claimed that his right under Article 12 was violated by the government through its failure to provide for divorce in Ireland which would enable him to marry and found a family with the woman with whom he was now living. The Court of Human Rights ruled, in *B and L v United Kingdom* (2005), that the ban on in-law marriages (Marriage Act 1949, as amended by the Marriage (Prohibited Degrees of Relationship) Act 1986) violated Article 12. There was an inconsistency between the legal impediment to such marriages and the possibility of removing the incapacity by a private Act of Parliament and that made the ban irrational, illogical and a violation of the right to marry.

Article 13: remedies

Article 13 imposes a duty on Member States to provide effective remedies for any violation of the substantive rights protected by the Convention. Article 13 has been interpreted to mean that an effective remedy before a national authority is

---

77 See also *X, Y and Z v United Kingdom* (1997); *AV v United Kingdom* (1998); Leach, 1998.

guaranteed to 'everyone who claims that his rights and freedoms under the Convention have been violated'.[78]

Judicial review[79] provides an effective means by which to ensure that government complies with the procedural requirements of the law.[80] However, judicial review may not give the degree of protection required under the Convention. As will be seen in Chapter 26, judicial review is concerned with the procedural correctness of a decision, not with the merits of that decision. The adequacy of judicial review as a remedy was considered by the Court of Human Rights in *Kingsley v United Kingdom* (2002). There, the Gaming Board had revoked the applicant's licence. The applicant claimed that the Board was biased against him. The Court of Appeal held that even if there had been some form of bias, the decision on the licence had to be taken by the Board because there was no other body with jurisdiction to make the decision, and that as efforts had been made to minimise the effect of any potential bias, the decision could not be impugned for bias. The Court of Human Rights ruled that the Gaming Board did not present the 'necessary appearance of impartiality' and that 'the subsequent judicial review was not sufficiently broad to remedy that defect'.

The failure to provide abused children with a procedure whereby their allegations that the local authority had failed to protect them from serious ill-treatment or the possibility of obtaining an enforceable award of compensation for the damage suffered through abuse amounted to a violation of Article 13. The Court of Human Rights so held in *DP and JC v United Kingdom* (2002).

Article 14: non-discrimination

Article 14 provides for non-discrimination in the enjoyment of the substantive rights and freedoms protected by the Convention. There is not, therefore, a right to non-discrimination *per se* but, rather, a right not to be discriminated against in relation to any of the other rights and freedoms. Thus, Article 14 enjoys no independent existence; it is tied to other Articles in the Convention.[81] However, it is possible that a violation of Article 14 is found even where a claim that a breach of another Article has occurred fails. For example, in *Abdulaziz, Cabales and Balkandali* (1985), three foreign wives residing in England complained that their husbands were not allowed to enter the country. The applicants alleged a violation of Articles 8 and 14. The Court rejected the complaint concerning Article 8, adopting the view that the right to family life does not entail the right to establish a home wheresoever people choose. However, there was a violation of Article 14, in so far as the rules provided easier conditions under which men could bring in their wives than those which existed for wives trying to bring their husbands into the country.[82]

---

78 *Klass v Federal Republic of Germany* (1978); see also *Bubbins v United Kingdom*: the absence of a *judicial* determination over the liability of the police in damages violated Article 13.
79 See Chapters 26 and 27.
80 *Vilvarajah and Four Others v United Kingdom* (1991); and see *Leander v Sweden* (1987).
81 *X v Federal Republic of Germany* (1970).
82 The Immigration Rules were amended in 1985 as a result of this case.

Article 16: aliens[83]

Article 16 authorises restrictions on the political activity of aliens. This provision affects all Articles in the Convention in so far as they relate to the political activities of aliens. Article 16 does not mean that there can be no violation of other substantive Articles in respect of aliens.

The Convention protocols

In addition to the substantive Articles of the Convention, there exists a series of Protocols on matters ranging from the right to peaceful enjoyment of possessions (First Protocol, Article 1),[84] education (First Protocol, Article 2), the holding of regular free elections (First Protocol, Article 3), freedom of movement (Fourth Protocol), abolition of the death penalty (Sixth Protocol), appeals in criminal cases and sexual equality (Seventh Protocol), procedural matters under the Convention (Ninth Protocol) and minority rights (Tenth Protocol). The Eleventh Protocol abolished the Commission and provided new procedures for applying directly to the court. The United Kingdom is not a party to the Fourth, Sixth or Seventh Protocols. In relation to Article 2 of the First Protocol, the government has entered a reservation to the effect that the rights of parents to determine the education of their children are respected in the United Kingdom only to the extent that such respect is compatible with the requirements of the Education Acts.[85]

Protocol 1

In *JA Pye (Oxford) Ltd v United Kingdom* (2005) the European Court of Human Rights ruled that a provision of English land law which enabled squatters – under the doctrine of adverse possession – to deprive the applicant companies of their title to land, imposed on them an excessive burden and upset the fair balance between the demands of the public interest and the applicants' right to the peaceful possession of their property.

THE HUMAN RIGHTS ACT 1998

The incorporation of Convention rights into domestic law under the 1998 Act put an end, finally, to the debate over whether or not to incorporate, which had endured for decades. That long-running debate focused on three principal

---

83   Article 15 provides for derogation. For discussion see pp 496–97 above.
84   See *Stretch v United Kingdom* (2003).
85   On 4 November 2000, Protocol 12 opened for signature. The Protocol prohibits arbitrary discrimination. The year 2000 marked the 50th anniversary of the Convention. Article 14, which provides that the substantive rights guaranteed by the Convention are to be enjoyed without discrimination, is weak and there exists no free-standing right to non-discrimination. Protocol 12 introduces an independent right to equality, stating that the 'enjoyment of any right set forth by law shall be secured without discrimination, on any arbitrary ground'.

concerns, namely the criticism that the Convention is outdated and not tailored specifically to British conditions; that the judiciary was ill equipped to assume the mantle of guardian of individual rights in the face of executive power and the concept of parliamentary sovereignty;[86] and concerns over the manner in which 'incorporation' would affect the conventional balance of power between judges and parliament. There was also the argument that the House of Commons, as the democratically-elected representative of the people, was best equipped to respond to the better protection of rights.

In order to enable all public authorities (including the courts) to adapt to the Act's requirements in order to minimise the number of challenges for violations of Convention rights, in England and Wales there was a delay imposed between the Act being passed and its coming into effect.[87]

The Act provides a charter of rights now enforceable before the domestic courts. The effectiveness of the Human Rights Act 1998 rests on three foundations:

- the willingness of the judges robustly to defend rights and to interpret Convention rights in a manner favouring individual protection against governmental encroachment;

- parliament's willingness to amend the law to ensure compliance with declarations of incompatibility with Convention rights; and

- the energy with which individual citizens are prepared to assert their rights in courts of law.

The effect of the Act is such that three avenues for challenging public bodies arise. First, a failure to comply with Convention rights now forms the basis for legal action; secondly, a new ground for judicial review has been introduced, namely the failure to comply with the Convention; and, thirdly, Convention rights may be used as a defence against actions brought by public bodies against private bodies or individuals. It has been held by the Court of Appeal that the protection of the Act extends beyond the territory of the United Kingdom and is capable of applying to actions of officials in British Consulates.[88] In relation to British armed forces occupying overseas territory the position was different. In *R (Al-Skeini) v Secretary of State for Defence* (2006) the Court of Appeal ruled that it was clear that when a citizen of Iraq was in the custody of British soldiers in a military detention centre that the detainee was within the jurisdiction of the United Kingdom and therefore protected by Convention rights. However, in relation to Iraqi civilians killed in Basra city, it was impossible to hold that the United Kingdom was in effective control of Basra city for the purposes of Convention jurisprudence.[89]

---

86 See Griffith, 1997; but cf Lester, 1994 and 1997.
87 The Act came into effect in Scotland in 1998; in England and Wales in 2000.
88 *R (B) v Secretary of State for Foreign and Commonwealth Affairs* (2005).
89 In *R (Quark Fishing Ltd) v Secretary of State for Foreign and Commonwealth Affairs* (2005) the House of Lords ruled that since provision protecting property rights guaranteed under the Convention had not been expressly extended by the United Kingdom to the British Overseas Territory of South Georgia, no claim for damages could be brought in respect of a violation of such rights there.

The manner in which the Act was drafted raises a number of questions:

- the meaning of 'public authorities' for the purposes of the Act;
- whether the Act has solely 'vertical' effect – binding only those bodies for which the state is accountable to Strasbourg – or is capable of also having 'horizontal' effect, and being enforceable against bodies for which the state is not accountable to Strasbourg;
- the extent to which judicial interpretative techniques relating to statutes will change, and the extent to which the judges will develop the common law to give effect to Convention rights.

As will be seen below, the emerging case law is clarifying these issues.

The status of the Human Rights Act

As discussed in Chapter 7, under the constitution of the United Kingdom, and consistent with the doctrine of parliamentary sovereignty, legislation cannot be entrenched. That is to say, it cannot be given a 'special' or 'higher' status than other Acts of Parliament. This traditional doctrine has been preserved in relation to the Human Rights Act. In its White Paper, the government announced that it did not intend to permit the courts to strike down Acts of Parliament, whether that legislation preceded the Act or was introduced subsequently. Thereby, parliament's sovereignty and, to the extent possible, the separation of powers, are preserved. The Act, in the government's view, was 'intended to provide a new basis for judicial interpretation of all legislation, not a basis for striking down any part of it'.[90]

However, notwithstanding the careful drafting of the Human Rights Act in order to preserve sovereignty, the judges appear to be developing the concept of the 'constitutional statute',[91] one consequence of which is that the doctrine of implied repeal does not operate and only an express intention to amend or repeal the Act will have effect.

Section 2 of the Human Right Act requires the domestic courts to take into account, *inter alia* judgments of the Court of Human Rights. This does not, however, mean that the courts are bound to follow slavishly such judgments. The issue was central to the case of *Kay v Lambeth LBC; Leeds City Council v Price* (2006) in which the House of Lords considered both sections 2 and 6 of the Human Rights Act 1998. In the *Leeds* case before the Court of Appeal, the court concluded that the decision of *Connors v United Kingdom* (2004) was inconsistent with the earlier decision of the House of Lords in *Harrow LBC v Qazi* (2004) and that they were bound to follow the House of Lords. Lord Bingham of Cornhill recognised that effective implementation of the Convention depended upon 'constructive

---

90 White Paper, *Rights Brought Home: The Human Rights Bill*, Cm 3782, 1997, London: HMSO, para 2.14. However, the courts are given power over delegated, or secondary, legislation.

91 See *R v Secretary of State for the Home Department ex parte Simms* (2000); *Thoburn v Sunderland City Council* (2002).

collaboration' between the Court of Human Rights and national courts. He also, however, insisted that adherence to precedent was a 'cornerstone of the legal system' which ensured a degree of certainty. The substantive issue related to a public authority's right to possession under domestic law in light of an occupier's right to respect for his home under Article 8. The Court referred to the margin of appreciation accorded to national authorities and ruled that domestic law would automatically justify the interference with an occupier's Article 8 rights unless it could be shown that domestic law was not Convention compatible, which in turn would involve an assessment of an individual's personal circumstances.

The meaning of public authorities[92]

The Human Rights Act 1998 provides that public authorities exercising executive powers must comply with the requirements of the Convention. The European Convention imposes responsibilities on signatory states to protect rights, and as such it is the state and its agencies which are the defendants in allegations of Convention violations before the Court of Human Rights. The emphasis on public bodies/authorities under the Human Rights Act reflects this now traditional form of state liability.[93] As will be seen, however, the impact of the Human Rights Act is extending beyond the sphere of public bodies for which the state is responsible.

Section 6(3)(b) of the Act provides that a public authority includes 'any person certain of whose functions are functions of a public nature'. The test, therefore is not state ownership, funding or control *per se* but rather the functions which a body performs. The position is complicated by section 6(5) which provides that a person is not a public authority (applying the functions test) 'if the nature of the act is private'. Accordingly, the Act recognises that some authorities may, notwithstanding their ownership or control or funding by the state, be public on the functions test, but will not be treated as public bodies in relation to some actions which are deemed to be private. An example given in debate was that of Railtrack, which is a public authority when exercising its function as a safety regulator, but acts privately in its role as property developer.[94]

The definition of 'public body' was considered by the Court of Appeal in *R (Heather) v Leonard Cheshire Foundation* (2002). The Foundation is a private charity which provides accommodation for the disabled, some of which is funded by the local authority pursuant to its statutory duty under the National Assistance Act 1948, as amended. The court made it clear that residents of the home funded by the local authority could rely on their Convention rights against the authority but not against the charity, since it was not exercising public functions. Aside from the funding being provided by the state, there was no other evidence 'of there being a public flavour to the functions of the foundation or the foundation itself.

---

92 See Oliver, 2004; Sunkin, 2004.
93 See Oliver, 2000.
94 See HC Deb Vol 314 Cols 406–414, 17 June 1998, and Col 1231 16 November 1997. The Home Secretary in debate stated that the British Broadcasting Corporation is a public authority but that independent television companies are not, whilst the Independent Television Commission is: *Hansard* Col 778, 16 December 1998.

The foundation was not standing in the shoes of the local authorities'.[95] In *Billesley Parochial Church Council v Wallbank* (2001), the House of Lords ruled that a Parochial Church Council which had statutory duties to enforce parish church repairs was not a public authority for the purposes of the Human Rights Act. The Court ruled that although the Church of England had special links with central government and performed certain public functions, it was not a core public authority.

However, the classification of bodies (public or private) does not exhaust the potential for the Act to develop the protection of Human Rights, because according to section 6 the courts themselves are public authorities and are under a statutory duty to give effect to Convention rights. Accordingly, the courts may, in complying with their section 6 duty, enforce Convention rights against private – or non-state – bodies.[96]

The interpretative duty: section 3[97]

Section 3 of the Human Rights Act 1998 requires that primary and secondary legislation, whenever enacted, must be interpreted and applied in a manner consistent with Convention rights. However, section 3(2) makes it clear that this requirement does not affect the validity, continuing operation or enforcement of any incompatible primary legislation, and does not affect the validity, continuing operation or enforcement of incompatible subordinate legislation, if the primary legislation prevents removal of the incompatibility.[98] The definition of primary legislation is provided in section 21 of the Act, which in part provides that primary legislation includes any 'public general Act, local and personal Act, private Act ... and Order in Council made in exercise of Her Majesty's Royal Prerogative'. It was seen in Chapter 6 that Acts of Parliament have always been deemed to have superior force to acts of the prerogative,[99] and that where a claimed prerogative power is held to exist, if it is not expressly overruled by statute, it will be held to be 'in abeyance' and the statute will prevail. The Human Rights Act 1998, however, appears to elevate Orders in Council to the same status as Acts of Parliament, thereby making them immune from invalidation by the courts. Accordingly, whereas the courts may set aside secondary legislation which is incompatible with the Convention – unless the parent Act makes this impossible – Orders in Council regulating the exercise of the prerogative may not be so set aside.[100]

---

95 See also *Poplar Housing and Regeneration Community Association Ltd v Donoghue* (2001): a housing association performing functions analogous to the local authority was a public authority for the purposes of the Act.

96 See Wade, 2000, p 223; cf Hunt, 1998. There is an analogy here with Article 10 of the EC Treaty, which the Court of Justice has used to great effect in extending the liability of Member States. See further Chapter 9.

97 See Lord Irvine, 2003.

98 See Feldman, 2002.

99 See *Attorney General v de Keyser's Royal Hotel Ltd* (1920); *R v Secretary of State for the Home Department ex parte Fire Brigades' Union* (1995).

100 See Allen and Sales, 2000.

Declarations of incompatibility are regulated under section 4, which provides that if a court is satisfied that a provision of primary or subordinate legislation is incompatible with one or more Convention rights, it may make a declaration of incompatibility. The courts with the jurisdiction to make declarations of incompatibility are the House of Lords, the Judicial Committee of the Privy Council, the Courts-Martial Appeal Court; in Scotland, the High Court of Justiciary, sitting as a court of criminal appeal, or the Court of Session; and, in England, Wales and Northern Ireland, the High Court or Court of Appeal. Section 4(6), however, contains a vital limitation, in that a declaration of incompatibility does not affect the validity, continuing operation or enforcement of the provision in question, and is not binding on the parties to the proceedings in which it is made. However, where the court finds a violation of a Convention right, it has the power under section 8 to grant a remedy to the victim. The power to amend the law has thereby been preserved for the government and parliament.[101]

In the exercise of the interpretative duty under section 3 of the Human Rights Act 1998, the courts have rapidly adapted to the approach of the Court of Human Rights in employing the concepts of proportionality and necessity, which give greater scope for the protection of rights than the conventional concepts employed in judicial review under the umbrella of the *Wednesbury*[102] unreasonableness test, which spans 'illegality, impropriety and procedural irregularity'. Even before the Human Rights Act 1998 came into effect, the courts were developing a more vigorous approach to the protection of rights. In *R v Ministry of Defence ex parte Smith* (1996), it was recognised that in judicial review proceedings, where human rights were in issue, the courts should 'anxiously scrutinise' executive decisions. That approach, however, did not satisfy the interpretative duty according to Lord Steyn in *R (Daly) v Secretary of State for the Home Department* (2001), where he stated that while there was an overlap between the traditional *Wednesbury* grounds for review and the proportionality approach, there was nevertheless 'a material difference between the *Wednesbury* and *Smith* grounds of review and the approach of proportionality applicable in respect of review where Convention rights are at stake'.

In *Wilson v First County Trust Ltd (No 2)* (2003), the House of Lords took the opportunity to examine the structure and workings of the Human Rights Act. The House of Lords ruled that there was no power to grant a declaration under section 4 of the Human Rights Act unless the interpretative duty under section 3 had been engaged. There was a powerful presumption against the retrospective application of the Act, and, in relation to transactions which had taken place prior to the coming into force of the Act, there could be no question of interpretation under section 3 and accordingly no power to grant a declaration under section 4.

---

101 See below on declarations made under the 1998 Act.
102 *Associated Provincial Picture Houses Ltd v Wednesbury Corporation* (1948).

Convention rights, section 3 and statute[103]

Section 3 of the Human Rights Act requires the courts to interpret primary and subordinate legislation in a way which is compatible with Convention rights, 'so far as it is possible to do so'.[104] The House of Lords in *R v A (Complainant's Sexual History)* (2002)[105] gave guidance as to the correct approach. At issue was whether the statutory restrictions on the admissibility of evidence prejudiced the right to fair trial.[106] The Court ruled that it first had to consider whether a legislative provision interfered with a Convention right. If there was an interference, then the court had to look at the legislative purpose of the provision and employ the concept of proportionality. Three issues had to be considered:

- First, was the legislative objective sufficiently important to justify limiting a fundamental right?

- Secondly, were the measures adopted to meet that objective rationally connected to it?

- Thirdly, the court must be satisfied that the means used to impair the right or freedom were no more than necessary to accomplish the objective (the proportionality test).

Section 3 of the Human Rights Act 'went further than requiring the court to take the Convention into account: the court had a duty to strive to find a possible interpretation compatible with Convention rights'. Lord Steyn stated that this might even require the courts 'to adopt an interpretation which may appear linguistically strained'.[107]

Section 3 provided the basis for the reinterpretation of a statutory provision to make it compatible with Convention rights in *Ghaidan v Godin-Mendoza* (2004). The Rent Act 1977[108] provided that on the death of a protected tenant his or her surviving spouse, if then living in the house 'as his or her wife or husband', became a statutory tenant by succession. The House of Lords in *Fitzpatrick v Sterling Housing Association Ltd* (2001) had ruled that this provision did not include same-sex relationships. In *Ghaidan*, however, the House of Lords used Article 3 as a remedial section and reinterpreted the provision to read 'as if they were his wife or husband' and thereby protected the tenancy. Lord Steyn stated that it was necessary '. . . to emphasise that interpretation under section 3(1) is the prime remedial remedy and that resort to section 4 must always be an exceptional course.'

---

103 See Klug and Starmer, 2001.
104 See Bennion, 2000.
105 On the joinder of the Home Secretary under s 5 see *R v A* (2001).
106 Under consideration was the Youth Justice and Criminal Evidence Act 1999, s 41(3)(c), which precluded evidence and questioning about a complainant's sexual history in an attempt to redress the problems of low conviction rates and outmoded stereotypes of women.
107 See also *R v Ashworth Special Hospital Authority ex parte N* (2001) and *R v Secretary of State for the Home Department ex parte Mellor* (2001), discussed below.
108 Schedule 1, para 2.(2).

The limits of interpretation

Strive as the judges may to interpret statutes compatibly, there are limits. First, it is clear that the 1998 Act is not retrospective. For example, in *R v Kensal (No 2)* (2001), the House of Lords ruled that it should follow its previous decision notwithstanding that a majority of the House now believed the precedent case to have been wrongly decided. Note, however, that this case involved a pre-Human Rights Act precedent. The court ruled that if parliament had intended convictions valid before the Act came into force to be re-opened on the basis of rights conferred by the 1998 Act, it would have said so clearly.[109]

In *Pearce v Governing Body of Mayfield School* (2001), the Court of Appeal considered the issue of gender orientation in relation to discrimination under the Human Rights Act 1998. Disruptive pupils abused a lesbian teacher at the school in the early 1990s. Such conduct was not discriminatory under the Sex Discrimination Act 1975. Since the Human Rights Act was not in force at the time of the conduct in question, the applicant could not seek compensation under that Act. In *Secretary of State for the Home Department v Wainwright* (2002), the Court of Appeal affirmed that there was no tort of invasion of privacy at common law, and that because the conduct complained of occurred in 1997, before the Human Rights Act came into force, section 3(1) of the Act did not apply to introduce a right to privacy retrospectively. Mrs Wainwright and her son had been strip-searched by prison officers,[110] having been told that they were under suspicion of bringing drugs into the prison when visiting an inmate. They consented to the searches. The county court judge ruled that the tort of trespass to the person had been committed and awarded damages. The claimants relied on section 3 of the 1998 Act, arguing that once the Act was in force the court a the duty to comply with it even though the matters complained of took place before the Act came into force.[111] The Lord Chief Justice stated that the 1998 Act could not change substantive law by introducing a retrospective right to privacy which did not exist at common law.

The second limitation lies in the distinction between legitimate interpretation and the 'redrafting' of statutes. For example, in *In re W and B (Children: Care Plan)* (2002), the Court of Appeal considered the interpretive duty and held that the duties of local authorities under the Children Act 1989 should be subject to a system of 'starred milestones' which require authorities to implement care plans within time limits. No such provision had been made by parliament in the Children Act. In the House of Lords Lord Nicholls ruled that section 3 of the 1998 Act maintained the constitutional boundary between interpretation by the courts and the enactment and amendment of statutes by parliament, and that an interpretation of an Act which departed from an essential feature of an Act of Parliament was likely to have crossed the boundary. Here, parliament had entrusted local authorities with responsibility for looking after children in

---

109 See also *R v Secretary of State for the Home Department ex parte Mahmood (Amjad)* (2001).
110 Under r 86(1) of the Prison Rules (SI 1964/388), made pursuant to the Prison Act 1952, s 47.
111 *R v Kensal (No 2)* (2001) did not decide this point.

care. The House of Lords ruled that the Court of Appeal's interpretation went beyond the boundary of interpretation and exceeded its judicial jurisdiction.[112] Although the line between legislating and interpreting may appear to be fine, it is nevertheless understood by the judges.

Convention rights, interpretation and common law

The Lord Chancellor in debate stated that:

> ... it is right as a matter of principle for the courts to have the duty of acting compatibly with the Convention not only in cases involving other public authorities but also in developing the common law in deciding cases between individuals. Why should they not?[113]

While section 3 does not refer to common law, as seen above, the Act requires that the common law be developed consistently with Convention rights, and section 6, which includes courts and tribunals as public bodies, underpins the jurisdiction. Development of the common law has been seen most clearly in relation to privacy, which engages three issues. First, there is no common law right to privacy: as Glidewell LJ stated in *Kaye v Robertson* (1991), 'It is well-known that in English law there is no right to privacy'. Secondly, privacy rights under common law derive from a relationship of confidence and breach of that confidentiality. Thirdly, Article 8 protects privacy rights in relation to family life, the home and correspondence. In *Venables v News Group Newspapers Ltd* (2001), an injunction was granted which prevents, indefinitely, the media from revealing the identity and whereabouts of the applicant. Butler-Sloss LJ recognised that the defendant newspapers were not within the definition of public authorities, but nevertheless asserted that the court – as a public authority – must itself act compatibly with the Convention. Article 8 of the Convention thus prevailed over Article 10 (freedom of expression) and was applied against a private body, thereby giving horizontal effect to the right.[114]

The doctrines of proportionality and necessity, developed by the Court of Human Rights, have been accepted as judicial tools in the enforcement of Convention rights. In *R (Daly) v Secretary of State for the Home Department* (2001), for example, in the House of Lords, in declaring the prison policy of requiring prisoners to leave their cells for the purpose of searches, including searches of privileged legal correspondence, unlawful, Lord Bingham of Cornhill stated that his conclusions had been reached 'on an orthodox application of common law principles' but stated that the same result would yield by reliance on the Convention. However, he recognised that this coincidence between common law and Convention might not always occur. Lord Steyn was more explicit regarding the requirements of proportionality. Citing Lord Clyde in *De Freitas v Permanent*

---

112 See *Poplar Housing and Regeneration Community Association Ltd and Secretary of State for the Environment v Donoghue* (2001).
113 *Hansard* 583 HL Deb 783, 24 November 1997. And see Lord Irvine, 1998, in which the Lord Chancellor stated that 'the Convention rights must pervade all law and all courts systems' (at p 232).
114 See also *Campbell v MGN Ltd* (2002) and *Douglas v Hello! Ltd* (2002), and Chapter 21.

Secretary of Ministry of Agriculture, Fisheries, Lands and Housing (1999), Lord Steyn declared that the criteria to be applied are 'more precise and more sophisticated than the traditional grounds of review', and that under the proportionality approach 'the intensity of review is somewhat greater'. Where there has been an infringement of a right, it must be established that the limitation of the right 'was necessary in a democratic society, in the sense of meeting a pressing social need, and the question whether the interference was really proportionate to the legitimate aim being pursued'.

Section 5 of the Human Rights Act

Section 5 of the Human Rights Act 1998 confers on a minister the right to be heard. The purpose of section 5(2) is to ensure that the appropriate minister has an opportunity to address the court on the objects and purposes of the legislation in question and any other matters which might be relevant. In *R v A (Joinder of Appropriate Minister)* (2001), the House of Lords ruled that where an issue was raised in criminal proceedings which might lead to the House of Lords considering making a declaration of compatibility, it was appropriate to join the Crown in advance of the appeal hearing. Where the Crown was already represented by the Director of Public Prosecutions, his role as prosecutor was different from that of a government minister in the discharge of executive responsibilities. The House granted the application for joinder made by the Home Secretary, who bore responsibility for promotion of the legislation in question. See also *Wilson v First County Trust Ltd (No 2)* (2003) (discussed above) in which the Attorney General appeared on behalf of the Speaker of the House of Commons and the Clerk of the Parliament intervened.

Declarations of incompatibility

Where the superior courts[115] are unable to interpret statutes in a manner which makes them compatible with Convention rights, a declaration of incompatibility may be issued. This puts the government and parliament 'on notice' that the statute requires amendment.[116] The Court of Appeal has ruled that a declaration should not be granted to a claimant who had not been, and could not be adversely affected by, impugned legislation in *Lancashire County Council v Taylor* (2005).

There are a number of explanations for the relatively low number of declarations which have been issued. First, as *Wilson v First County Trust Ltd* (2003) makes clear, the power to make a declaration only arises where the duty of interpretation is engaged, and that cannot be engaged where the facts occurred before the Human Rights Act came into force. Secondly, there have been several cases in which the High Court has issued a declaration but this has been overturned on appeal. Thirdly, where there are defects in procedures or administrative practices, the courts will generally hold that these are cured by the

---

115 The High Court and above.
116 See *R (D) v Secretary of State for the Home Department* (2002).

supervisory jurisdiction of the courts. Finally, there is emerging from the case law a 'doctrine of deference'.

The doctrine of deference[117]

It is apparent from the case law that the judges are very conscious of the invisible boundary line between those matters on which they regard themselves as competent to adjudicate and those matters which should be left for the democratically elected government. This is the doctrine of deference. The doctrine may be compared with that of justiciability under judicial review. The principal distinction lies in the fact that whereas courts will rule on justiciability in order to decide whether to review, with deference the courts conduct an examination and then decide that they should defer to the elected government and/or parliament on the grounds of competence and/or democratic principle. The concept is also similar to the concept of margin of appreciation, which is used by the Court of Human Rights and which confers on states an area of discretion with which the Court will not interfere.[118] 'Deference' may also be expressed in the form of competence – in the form of the question: 'Is this matter within the competence of the courts to decide or for Parliament and/or the executive?' Underlying the concept is the desire to preserve the separation of powers between the judiciary, executive and legislature and to protect the judges from charges that they are interfering in another institution's legitimate sphere of power. Notwithstanding the legitimacy of the objective, there is a fine line to be drawn between deferring to another institution and failing adequately to protect human rights – the duty which has been conferred on the judges by the Human Rights Act.

The doctrine can be illustrated by reference to a number of cases. For example, in *R v Secretary of State for the Environment ex parte Holding and Barnes plc* (2001) (the *Alconbury* case) – in which it was argued that the Secretary of State's power to rule on planning matters contravened the requirements of a fair and independent tribunal – the House of Lords held that decisions relating to planning were best made by the executive. In *R v Lichniak* (2002) the House of Lords ruled that the imposition of a mandatory life sentence on all convicted murderers did not violate Articles 3 and/or 5 and was a matter of policy best determined by the democratically-elected Parliament. In *ProLife Alliance v BBC* (2003) the House of Lords overturned the decision of the Court of Appeal which had ruled that freedom of political expression overrode the duty of the BBC not to broadcast material which was offensive. Lord Hoffmann – in the course of criticising the term 'deference' – argued that the decision was one 'within the proper competence of the legislature' – not the courts. Furthermore, in *R v Lambert* (2001) Lord Woolf stated that the courts:

---

117 See Jowell, 2003; Jowell, 'Judicial deference and human rights: a question of competence', in Craig and Rawlings, 2003; Edwards, 2002; Oliver, 2003, Chapter 6; Steyn, 2005.

118 The margin of appreciation is a concept derived from international law: it has no application within domestic law.

... should as a matter of constitutional principle pay a degree of deference to the view of Parliament as to what is in the interest of the public generally when upholding the rights of the individual under the Convention.

Making an application under the Act

Section 7(3) of the Act provides that an individual may make an application to the courts if, and only if, he or she 'is, or would be, a victim of an unlawful act'. A person claiming that a public authority has acted, or proposes to act, in a way made unlawful by section 6(1) may bring proceedings against the authority, or may rely on the Convention right concerned in any legal proceedings. In relation to judicial review proceedings, the victim test is also applied, giving a narrower meaning to 'sufficient interest' (or 'standing') than that applied under other judicial review proceedings.

The definition of standing follows the approach of the Court of Human Rights. A victim or potential victim has standing, as does a person who, while not the immediate victim of an alleged violation, is nevertheless affected. An example is a family member of a person deported or threatened with deportation where this violates the Article 8 right to family life. The position of third parties who are not directly affect is more complex and gives rise to differing tests to be applied depending on the type of proceedings being brought. The sufficient interest – or standing – requirements in judicial review proceedings allow 'public interest' organisations to bring proceedings. Help the Aged, the Child Poverty Action Group and the Joint Council for the Welfare of Immigrants have all been taken to have standing.[119] Standing for the purposes of the Human Rights Act, however, excludes interest groups unless they can establish that their members are actual or potential victims. Interest groups whose members are not victims, but who have special expertise in an area (for example, environmental groups such as Greenpeace or Friends of the Earth), will not have standing. They will, however, be permitted to make submissions to the court on matters within their expertise. In debate, the Lord Chancellor, referring the practice before the Court of Human Rights, stated that '... our courts will be ready to permit *amicus* written briefs from non-governmental organisation; that is to say briefs, but not to treat them as full parties', and further that '... I dare say that the courts will be equally hospitable to oral interventions, provided that they are brief'.[120]

Proceedings must be brought within one year of the date on which the act complained of took place, but this limit may be extended by the court if it considers it 'equitable', having regard to any stricter time limit imposed on the proceedings in question (section 7(5) of the Act). 'Legal proceedings' is defined to mean proceedings brought by a public authority and appeals against the decision of a court or tribunal (section 7(6)).

---

119 See *R v Sefton Metropolitan Borough Council ex parte Help the Aged* (1997); *R v Secretary of State for Social Security ex parte Joint Council for the Welfare of Immigrants* (1997); and *R v Lord Chancellor ex parte Child Poverty Action Group* (1998).

120 *Hansard* HL Deb Col 834, 24 November 1997.

Remedies

Article 13 of the Convention, which provides that everyone shall have an effective remedy before a national authority, has not been incorporated. Instead, section 8 of the Human Rights Act regulates remedies. Section 8 provides that, where a court finds that a public authority has acted unlawfully, it may grant 'such relief or remedy, or make such order within its jurisdiction as it considers just and appropriate'. Accordingly, courts and tribunals may only award a remedy which is within their statutory powers.

Damages may only be awarded by a court which has power to award damages or to order the payment of compensation in civil proceedings, and no award of damages is to be made unless, taking into account all the circumstances of the case and any other relief or remedy available, the court is satisfied that the award is necessary to afford just satisfaction to the complainant. The court must take into account the principles applied by the Court of Human Rights in relation to the award of compensation under Article 41. In many instances, a finding of a violation may be deemed to be a sufficient remedy. However, the full range of remedies – declarations, injunctions and the prerogative orders of certiorari (quashing orders), mandamus (mandatory orders) and prohibition (prohibitory orders) – are also available to those courts and tribunals with the power to grant them.

One question which arises is the issue whether or not section 8 provides an adequate remedy according to the jurisprudence of the European Court of Human Rights.[121] The courts are under a duty, under section 2, to take into account the case law developed in Strasbourg. Accordingly, there is the potential for considerable case law on the relationship between section 8 of the Human Rights Act 1998 and Article 13 of the Convention.

Ensuring legislative conformity with Convention rights

Ensuring that domestic legislation conforms to Convention requirements involves two procedures. The first relates to the enactment of legislation generally, and the second relates to legislative action taken after a declaration of incompatibility has been issued by the courts.

In relation to legislative proposals, the Act provides for declarations to be made to parliament that the proposed legislation conforms to Convention requirements. Section 19 requires that a minister in charge of a Bill in either House of Parliament must, before second reading, make a statement to the effect that either a Bill does comply with Convention rights or that, although such a statement cannot be made, the government nevertheless wishes to proceed with the Bill.

In relation to remedial legislation, the Act introduces a special legislative procedure for reform. While this mechanism preserves the principle that it is parliament, as the democratically elected legislature, which is sovereign in

---

121 See *Chahal v United Kingdom* (1996), discussed above, p 499.

making and reforming law, it also opens the door to the possibility that governments of differing political persuasions may react with greater or lesser enthusiasm to declarations of incompatibility. The extent to which successive governments respond to the ruling of the courts thus lies in the *moral* rather than *legal* authority of the Convention.

The fast track legislative procedure

Where a higher court[122] makes a declaration of incompatibility, or where the Court of Human Rights in Strasbourg declares that the Convention has been violated, the relevant government minister will have power to enact amending legislation by Order in Council (a 'remedial order'). Other than where it is necessary for the Order to have immediate effect, the Order will be subject to the approval of both Houses of Parliament, and will only come into effect once approval has been secured. Section 10 and Schedule 2 regulate remedial action and remedial orders.

Two procedures are provided for. Under the standard procedure,[123] a draft of the order must be laid before parliament for a 60 day period before it is approved by resolution of each House. When laying the draft instrument, the minister must also provide the 'required information', which entails an explanation of:

> ... the incompatibility which the proposed order seeks to remove, including particulars of the court declaration, finding or order which caused the minister to propose a remedial order; and a statement of the reasons for proceeding under section 10 and for making an order in the terms proposed.[124]

During the period in which the draft is laid before parliament, representations may be made to the minister, either by parliament or by any other person. If representations are made, the draft must be accompanied by a statement containing a summary of the representations and details of any changes introduced into the proposed order as a result of the representations.[125] Section 10 and Schedule 2 also provide that, if a minister considers that there are 'compelling reasons', he may make such amendments to legislation as he considers necessary to remove the incompatibility, by means of a statutory instrument. The power applies to both primary and subordinate legislation, thus conferring on the executive potentially wide law making power – subject ultimately to parliament's approval. In debate on the Bill, the Lord Chancellor stated that 'if legislation has been declared to be incompatible, a prompt parliamentary remedy should be available'.[126]

---

122 As interpreted by the Human Rights Act 1998, s 6.
123 *Ibid*, Sched 2.
124 *Ibid*, Sched 2, para 3.
125 *Ibid*, Sched 2, para 2.
126 *Hansard* HL Col 1231, 3 November 1997.

Derogations and reservations

The Human Rights Act 1998 makes provision for derogations and reservations in sections 14 to 17. Derogations are discussed on pp 496–97 above.

In relation to reservations, section 15 provides in part that:

(1) In this Act, 'designated reservation' means:

    (a) the United Kingdom's reservation to Article 2 of the first protocol to the Convention [the right to education in conformity with parents' religious and philosophical convictions]; and

    (b) any other reservation by the United Kingdom to an Article of the Convention or of any protocol to the Convention, which is designated for the purposes of this Act in an order made by the Secretary of State.

Case law under the Human Rights Act 1998

While there have been few declarations of incompatibility, there have been numerous challenges under the 1998 Act, some successful but many more unsuccessful. 'Catalogues' of cases briefly digested are inherently unsatisfactory. It is, however, important to appreciate the scope of the Act as applied in its early years.

Article 2: the right to life

A court making a declaration of lawful withdrawal of treatment in a case where a patient was in a permanent vegetative state does not infringe the right to life. The court applied the principle established in *Airedale National Health Trust v Bland* (1993) in *NHS Trust A v M; NHS Trust B v H* (2001). In the high profile case of Diane Pretty, the paralysed victim of motor neurone disease, the House of Lords ruled, *inter alia*, that Article 2 was directed towards protecting the sanctity of life and did not entail a right to terminate one's own life.[127] Where there was a serious risk to life to former soldiers through their giving evidence before a tribunal enquiring into the shootings in Northern Ireland on 'Bloody Sunday', the Court of Appeal ruled that the evidence should be given elsewhere.[128] In *R (Amin) v Secretary of State for the Home Department* (2003) the House of Lords emphasised the requirement that the state fulfil its procedural duty to establish an independent public investigation into the death of a prisoner in prison.

Article 3: freedom from torture, inhuman and degrading treatment

In *Napier v Scottish Ministers* (2001), the Court of Session ruled that Article 3 was violated by the conditions in prisons. The court ordered the executive to transfer the applicant to conditions of detention which complied with Article 3. In *N v Secretary of State for the Home Department* (2005) the House of Lords ruled that the removal of a seriously ill illegal immigrant to a country where it was alleged that her life expectancy would be reduced would violate Article 3 only in exceptional

---

127 *R (Pretty) v Director of Public Prosecutions* (2001). Mrs Pretty subsequently lost her appeal to the Court of Human Rights.
128 In *R (A) v Lord Saville of Newdigate* (2000).

circumstances. The European Court of Human Rights' decision in *D v United Kingdom* should be 'very strictly confined' (*per* Laws LJ). In *R (Limbuela) v Secretary of State for the Home Department* (2005), the House of Lords ruled that Article 3 may be violated if the state denies the barest necessities of life for an asylum seeker: the case is discussed at p 658.

There was no infringement of Article 3 or 5 through the imposition of a life sentence on a mentally ill offender rather than the making of a hospital order. The Court of Appeal (following the approach taken in *R v Offen*, below) so held in *R v Drew* (2002), in which the offender presented a serious and continuing danger to the safety of the public and a hospital order would not have ensured adequate security. The imposition of a mandatory life sentence was held to be compatible with Articles 3 and 5 in *R v Lichniak* (2002).[129]

Article 5: the right to liberty[130]

Article 5 was employed to test the compatibility of an automatic life sentence imposed on a defendant who had committed two serious offences. The Court of Appeal ruled that if the offender was a significant risk to the public the court could impose a life sentence under section 2 without contravening the Convention.[131] In *Anderson v Scottish Ministers* (2001), the Privy Council ruled that the continued detention of mental patients on grounds of public safety did not infringe Article 5 of the Convention, even where there was no medical treatment for the condition. The House of Lords in *R v Leeds Crown Court ex parte Wardle* (2001) ruled that continued detention in custody where the accused was charged with a second offence while in custody on the first charge did not infringe the Convention. The fresh time limit was justified by the need to give the prosecutor sufficient time to prepare the evidence relating to each offence.

In *R (C) v Mental Health Review Tribunal* (2001) the Court of Appeal ruled that the listing of all hearings by the Mental Health Review Tribunal in a uniform specified period after a request for review had been made was unlawful in that it did not ensure that individual applications were heard as soon as reasonably practicable. In *In re K (A Child) (Secure Accommodation Order: Right to Liberty)* (2000) the Court of Appeal ruled that a secure accommodation order, while a deprivation of liberty, was justified as 'being detention of a minor by lawful order for the purpose of educational supervision' under Article 5(1)(d).

A declaration of incompatibility was made by the Court of Appeal in *R (H) v Mental Health Review Tribunal, North and East London Region* (2001). At issue was Article 5 of the Convention, which guarantees the right to liberty and the right to take proceedings to determine the lawfulness of detention. The applicant was detained under the Mental Health Act 1983, section 73 of which provides, inter alia, that in order to satisfy a mental health review tribunal that he was entitled to

---

129 Article 4 provides protection from slavery. There is no domestic case law: see p 500 above.

130 The case of *A v Secretary of State for the Home Department* (relating to the indefinite detention of non-British suspected terrorists is discussed in Chapter 25).

131 *R v Offen* (2001). At issue was the Crime (Sentences) Act 1997, under which an automatic life sentence could be imposed on a defendant who had committed two serious offences.

discharge, the burden of proof fell on the restricted person to show that he was no longer suffering from a mental disorder warranting detention. Section 73 could not be given an interpretation which was compatible with the Convention. The Secretary of State for Health then made a remedial order amending section 73 in order to make it compatible with Article 5. The House of Lords overturned a declaration of incompatbility in *R (MH) v Secretary of State for Health* (2005). The claimant was severely mentally disordered and had been admitted for assessment to hospital under section 2 of the Mental Health Act 1983. She was not competent to take legal proceedings. However, the scheme of the 1983 Act was such that even if judicial proceedings could not be undertaken for some reason, there was access to a tribunal which could be initiated by a representative of the patient. Alternatively, the Secretary of State had power to refer under section 67, and that decision was judicially reviewable. There was sufficient protection in the Act to make it compatible with Article 5(4).

Article 6: the right to fair trial[132]

As expected, Article 6 has generated a wealth of case law. It is clear that the courts are following the approach of the Court of Human Rights in looking less at detailed irregularities in trial procedures and more to the overall fairness of the criminal process. In *R (Dudson) v Secretary of State for the Home Department* (2005) the House of Lords ruled that the requirement of a 'fair and public hearing' under Article 6 did not require that there always be an oral hearing at every stage in criminal proceedings. Here the process of reviewing the claimant's tariff which he was required to serve for retribution and deterrence, undertaken by the Lord Chief Justice, disclosed all relevant material and there had been a sufficient opportunity to make representations in writing. It was not a situation where procedural fairness required there to be an oral hearing before a final decision could be made.[133] Where there are alleged defects in the process, the courts will only rule that a violation of Article 6 has occurred where the cumulative effect is to render the trial unfair. Furthermore, where there are defects identified, if these are remedied by the appeal process, or through judicial review proceedings, then the courts will be slow to find a violation of Convention rights. Article 6 comprises a number of rights relating to differing aspects of judicial decision making.

Substantive issues and Article 6 protection

Article 6 does not apply where a prisoner serving a mandatory life sentence is accused of breaching prison rules. That is not a criminal charge and therefore the guarantees of Article 6 do not apply.[134] Similarly, the House of Lords ruled that the giving of a warning to a 15 year old boy did not involve the determination of a

---

132 See Craig, 2003b.

133 However, in *R (Hammond) v Secretary of State for the Home Department* (2005) the House of Lords ruled that the right to a fair and public hearing under Article 6 may necessitate a judge exercising his discretion and deciding to conduct an oral hearing.

134 *Matthewson v The Scottish Ministers* (2001); see also *R (Tangney) v Secretary of State for the Home Department* (2005).

criminal charge. Accordingly no issue arose under Article 6.[135] In *Matthews v Ministry of Defence* (2003)[136] the House of Lords ruled that section 10 of the Crown Proceedings Act 1947, which exempted the Crown from liability in tort for injuries suffered by members of the armed forces, operated as a bar to litigation. The Secretary of State had substituted a no-fault system of compensation for a claim for damages in such cases. The combined effect of these two factors was that the claimant had no civil rights to which Article 6 might apply.

Article 6 does not apply to proceedings relating to an accused's fitness to plead. The applicants in *R v M, R v Kerr, R v H* (2001) had argued that Article 6 applied because it was unfair to try someone under a disability which prevented him from participating in proceedings because of a mental handicap. The Court of Appeal stated that the proceedings could not result in a conviction and therefore the argument failed.

Child law and the powers and duties of local authorities in relation to housing law have also given rise to challenges. The Court of Appeal has held that secure accommodation orders against children, although not criminal proceedings, attract rights to fair trial.[137]

In *R (Anderson) v Secretary of State for the Home Department* (2002), the House of Lords, convened as a panel of seven, removed the power of the Home Secretary to determine the tariff term to be served for punitive purposes by defendants convicted of murder and sentenced to life imprisonment. The House of Lords made a declaration under section 4 of the Human Rights Act 1998 that section 29 of the Crime (Sentences) Act 1997, which conferred on the Home Secretary control of the release of mandatory life sentence prisoners, was incompatible with the right under Article 6 to have a sentence imposed by an independent and impartial tribunal.

Lord Bingham of Cornhill stated that the court 'would not without good reason depart from the principles laid down in a carefully considered judgment of [the Court of Human Rights] sitting as a grand chamber'. Referring to *Stafford v United Kingdom* (2002),[138] the court accepted the view there expressed that 'the imposition of what was in effect a substantial term of imprisonment by the exercise of executive discretion ... lay uneasily with ordinary concepts of the rule of law'. The Court also considered *Benjamin and Wilson v United Kingdom* (2002), in which the Court of Human Rights ruled that the Home Secretary's role remained objectionable despite his showing that he always acted in accordance with the recommendations of the Mental Health Review Tribunal. In that case it had been observed that this impinged on the fundamental principle of separation of

---

135 *R (R) v Durham Constabulary* (2005).
136 See Hickman, 2004.
137 *In re M* (2001).
138 The Court of Human Rights ruled that the Home Secretary's powers relating to sentencing were incompatible with Article 6. *V v United Kingdom* (2000). *A Practice Statement: Life Sentences* (2002) replaces the term 'tariff' with 'minimum term'. The sentencing judge should indicate the appropriate determinate sentence suitable for punishment and retribution. He should then calculate the minimum term to be served before the prisoner's case should be referred to the Parole Board. Differing considerations apply to adult and juvenile cases.

powers. The functional separation of the judiciary from the executive was 'fundamental' since the rule of law depended on it.

Disclosure of informants' identity

When considering whether to disclose whether a person was a police informer, the court had to balance the need to protect the informer and the requirements of fair trial. The court would not be constrained by precedent which identified possible exceptions to the rule of non-disclosure.[139]

Temporary judges

Article 6 was also invoked in *Millar v Dickson* (2002). There, the defendants were tried by temporary sheriffs. The decision follows that of *Starrs v Ruxton* (2000), where it was held that temporary sheriffs were not an independent and impartial tribunal within the meaning of Article 6 of the Convention. The right to fair trial was of the utmost importance to citizens. By continuing prosecution of the accused before temporary sheriffs, the Lord Advocate had violated the right of the accused to the protection of Article 6.[140]

Article 6 was examined by the High Court of Justiciary in *Hoekstra v Her Majesty's Advocate* (2001). In that case, the right to an impartial tribunal was violated by a judge sitting in a case of criminal appeal, who wrote a newspaper article strongly critical of the Convention. The article, which *inter alia* suggested that persons suspected of drug dealing should not have the right to privacy (under Article 8) against covert surveillance, would create in the mind of an informed observer 'an apprehension of bias' on the part of its author against the Convention and its rights. The court ordered that fresh appeal proceedings should be heard by three different judges.

Evidence and Article 6[141]

The question of admitting evidence of previous sexual relations at trial came before the Court of Appeal in *R v A (No 2)* (2001). In *R v Botmeh, R v Alami* (2001), the Court of Appeal ruled that there was nothing 'unlawful or unfair' in the court considering an *ex parte* application to withhold evidence on the ground of public interest immunity where that evidence had not been subject to a public interest immunity application to the trial judge. The court ruled that the defence had no absolute right to disclosure of relevant evidence and that 'strictly necessary measures restricting the rights of the defence were permissible, provided they were counterbalanced by procedures followed by the judicial authority'.

The Court of Appeal in *R v Looseley* (2001) ruled that an accused's right to a fair trial was not prejudiced by admitting evidence obtained through the use of undercover police officers. At the start of his trial, the accused alleged that the police officers had incited him to commit the offence. The correct test was:

---

139 *D v National Society for the Prevention of Cruelty to Children* (1978) at 218.
140 See also *Scanfuture United Kingdom Ltd v Secretary of State for Trade and Industry; Link v Same* (2001).
141 On evidence and Article 8, see below.

... whether the officers did no more, whether than by active or passive means, than to afford the accused the opportunity to offend of which he freely took advantage in circumstances where it appeared that he would have behaved in a similar way if offered the opportunity by someone else; or whether, on the other hand, by means on unworthy or shameful conduct, they had persuaded him to commit an offence of a kind which otherwise he would not have committed.

The fact that a trial had been found to be unfair by the Court of Human Rights did not, of itself, make the conviction unsafe. The Court of Appeal so ruled in *R v Lewis* (2005). The Court of Human Rights in *Edwards and Lewis v United Kingdom* (2003) had ruled that Article 6 had been violated, the appellant being deprived of a fair trial in that proceedings had not been stayed as an abuse of process on the ground of entrapment by police officers. The Court of Appeal found that there had been overwhelming incontrovertible evidence, and that the appellant – following legal advice – had pleaded guilty.

Remedial proceedings

In *Taylor v Lawrence* (2002), the Court of Appeal ruled that if it was established that a significant injustice had occurred, the court could re-open an appeal after its final judgment had been delivered and there was no alternative remedy. When the alternative remedy would be an appeal to the House of Lords, the Court of Appeal could only re-open a case where it was satisfied that no leave to appeal would be given by the House of Lords. Similarly, defects at trial which were capable of being reviewed by the Court of Appeal did not violate Article 6.[142] The Court of Appeal has also considered the procedures under the Housing Act 1996 in relation to decisions as to the suitability of accommodation for the homeless and declared that the right to appeal to the county court, which granted full jurisdiction to that court, satisfied the requirements of the 'developing domestic law of human rights'.[143] Article 6 was considered in tandem with Article 8 (the right to respect for private and family life) by the Court of Appeal in *St Brice v Southwark London BC* (2002). The court ruled that where a local authority, acting on a possession order granted by a county court, evicted a tenant without notice, it did not infringe the tenant's rights under the Convention. Those rights had already been protected by the hearing in the county court.

Time lapses in proceedings

On the reasonableness of time lapses between charge and trial, the Court of Appeal in *Dyer v Watson; HM Advocate v K* (2002) ruled that it would be a breach of Article 6 for a boy charged with serious sexual offences when aged 13 to be tried some 28 months later, when he would be a youth of 16. However, a delay of 20 months between charging police officers with perjury and the date of trial was not such a delay as to violate Article 6.

---

142 *R v Smith (Joe)* (2001); *R v Craven* (2000).
143 *Runa Begum v Tower Hamlets LBC* (2002).

The fixing of a penalty by tax commissioners in relation to a defaulting taxpayer amounted to the determination of a criminal offence and Article 6 of the Convention applied. The Chancery Division of the High Court so ruled in *King v Walden (Inspector of Taxes)* (2001). Accordingly, the taxpayer was entitled to have his case determined 'within a reasonable time'. Here there was a delay of five years, which the court stated was 'marginally, but only just' acceptable. Article 6 applies to the determination of civil penalties pursuant to criminal charges brought under the Value Added Tax Act 1994 and the Finance Act 1994.[144] In *Attorney General's Reference (No 2 of 2001)* (2001), the Court of Appeal ruled that, in considering whether a criminal charge had been determined within a reasonable time for the purposes of Article 6 of the Convention, the relevant time normally started to run when the defendant was charged by the police or served with a summons, rather than when he was first interviewed by the police.[145]

Equality between defence and prosecution

The Court of Appeal ruled that the equality of arms between prosecution and defence in criminal proceedings did not require representation of the defendant by Queen's Counsel merely because the Crown was so represented.[146] In *R v Weir* (2001), the House of Lords ruled that it had no power to extend the time allowed for a prosecutor to apply for leave to appeal from the Court of Appeal. The right to fair trial guaranteed under Article 6 did not require that the prosecution be given an equal right to the defence: that 'would stand the Convention on its head'.

The presumption of innocence

The presumption of innocence has fared badly. Making the assumption that property or expenditure by a person convicted of a drug trafficking offence was the proceeds of drug trafficking was not incompatible with the presumption of innocence: *HM Advocate v McIntosh* (2001). Admitting, under statutory compulsion, to being the driver of a motor vehicle did not violate the right not to incriminate oneself, provided the overall fairness of trial was not compromised: *Brown v Stott* (2001). The reversal of the burden of proof in the Drug Trafficking Act 1994 did not contravene Article 6, given the powers of review held by the Court of Appeal: *R v Benjafield* (2002). See, however, *Sheldrake v Director of Public Prosecutions* (2003), in which the House of Lords ruled that the reversal of the burden of proof under the Road Traffic Act 1988 should be interpreted so as to reduce the burden of proof from a legal burden to an evidential burden.[147]

---

144 *Han and Yau t/a Murdishaw Supper Bar v Commissioners of Customs and Excise* (2001).
145 See also *HM Advocate v R* (2003).
146 *R v Lee (Attorney-General's Reference No 82 of 2000)* (2002).
147 See also *Davies v Health and Safety Executive* (2003). On the secrecy of jury deliberations see *R v Mirza; R v Connor and Pollock* (2004).

Article 7: the prohibition against retrospectivity

In *Gough v Chief Constable of Derbyshire* (2001), the Queen's Bench Division ruled that banning orders which prevented UK nationals from leaving the country in order to attend regulated international football matches were lawful and a proportionate restriction on freedom of movement under EC law. Further, such an order imposed after a conviction of a public order offence was not a penalty and there was no violation of Article 7 of the Convention.

In *R v C* the Court of Appeal dismissed an appeal against conviction for the rape of a wife in 1970. In 2002 the defendant had been convicted of a number of sexual and violent offences including the rape of his wife over 30 years previously. The defendant alleged a violation of Article 7. The Court applied the cases of *R v R* (1992) and *SW v United Kingdom* (1995). There was no abuse of process in prosecuting for an offence committed before the immunity from prosecution was lifted. Further, Article 7(2) provided 'ample justification' for trial and punishment 'according to the general principles recognised by civilised nations'.

Article 7 was also central to the case of *R (Uttley) v Secretary of State for the Home Department* (2004). In this case a prisoner who had committed serious sexual offences, including rape, before 1983 was convicted and sentenced in 1995 to 12 years' imprisonment. Had he been convicted and sentenced in 1983 he would have been released (subject to good behaviour) on remission after serving two-thirds of his sentence. However, the Criminal Justice Act 1991 came into effect in 1992. Under that Act the prisoner was released after two-thirds of his sentence, but released on licence, the terms of which would remain in force until he had served three-quarters of his sentence. He was placed under supervision and restrictions imposed on his freedom. If he failed to comply with the conditions he would be recalled to serve the rest of his sentence. Further, if he committed a further imprisonable offence before the 12 year term expired, the court could add all or part of the remaining sentence to any new sentence imposed. The applicant sought a declaration that the post-1992 scheme amounted to a violation of Article 7, in that he was treated more severely as a result of the 1991 Act. The House of Lords ruled that there was no violation. The decisive point was that the maximum sentence which could have been imposed on the defendant in 1983 was life imprisonment: the sentence of 12 years imposed was manifestly a less heavy penalty than could have been imposed.

Article 8: the right to privacy

The Convention right to privacy, discussed here, must also be considered in relation to freedom of expression, with which it may conflict. It will be seen from the case law on Article 10, discussed in Chapter 21, that the restrictions imposed on freedom of expression are having the effect of substantially promoting privacy, at least when considered within the context of protection from intrusion by the media. As can be seen from the following, Article 8 has been invoked in relation to unmarried couples,[148] mental patients, prisoners, the evidence of defendants in

---

148 *M v Secretary of State for Work and Pensions* (2004).

criminal proceedings, planning law and the making of possession orders over a home. It has also been raised in matters relating to deportation orders and electoral law.

Mental patients

In *R v Ashworth Special Hospital Authority ex parte N* (2001), the High Court ruled that the right to privacy was not violated through the random monitoring of telephone calls of mental patients classified as having dangerous, violent or criminal propensities. Provision had been made to gather information on escape plans, disturbances and arrangements to bring in illicit substances, threats to others and behaviour presenting security implications. There was evidence that patients were likely to abuse the use of telephones unless prevented from doing so. Random monitoring interfered with Article 8 no more than was necessary to achieve the permitted purpose.

Prisoners

The House of Lords considered both common law and Article 8 of the Convention in *R (Daly) v Secretary of State for the Home Department* (2001). It was Home Office policy that prisoners should be required to leave their cells during searches conducted by prison officers. The search included the scrutiny of privileged legal correspondence. The House of Lords ruled that the policy infringed the common law right to legal professional privilege in communications with legal advisers. The court ruled that the policy interfered with Article 8. Lord Bingham stated that:

> ... the policy interfered with Mr Daly's exercise of his right under Article 8(1) to an extent much greater than necessity requires. In this instance, therefore, the common law and the Convention yield the same result ...

Article 8 was invoked alongside Article 12 (the right to marry and found a family) in *R v Secretary of State for the Home Department ex parte Mellor* (2001). A prisoner, who was sentenced to life imprisonment, claimed that he was entitled to facilities to enable him and his wife to have a child through the use of artificial insemination. The Court of Appeal ruled that imprisonment was incompatible with the exercise of conjugal rights and that the restrictions in Article 8(2) applied. The restrictions were necessary for the maintenance of security in prison. Prisoners inevitably forfeited aspects of their rights. It did not follow, however, that prisoners would always be prevented from inseminating their wives artificially, or naturally. The interference with the fundamental human rights in question involved an exercise in proportionality. Exceptional circumstances could require the restriction to yield. In this case, however, they did not.

Evidence and Article 8[149]

The question of the admission of illegally obtained evidence into court was considered in *R v Loveridge* (2001). In that case, contrary to section 41 of the

---

149 On evidence and Article 6 see above.

Criminal Justice Act 1925, the police had filmed defendants at a magistrates' court in order to compare the pictures with pictures previously taken by closed circuit television cameras, in order to link the defendants to a robbery. The Court of Appeal ruled that the filming had been unlawful and in breach of Article 8. However, their Lordships were satisfied that the breach of Article 8 did not interfere with the fairness of the hearing. The appeals against conviction were dismissed. In *R v X, Y and Z* (2000), the Court of Appeal ruled that there was no violation of Article 8 through the admission of evidence resulting from telephone intercepts lawfully made according to the country in question. Although such evidence of the result of intercepts made in the United Kingdom would not be admissible by virtue of the Interception of Communications Act 1985, that did not preclude the admission of evidence from outside the United Kingdom.[150]

Planning law and possession orders

In *South Buckinghamshire District Council v Porter, Chichester District Council v Searle, Wrexham Borough Council v Berry and Hertsmere Borough Council v Harty* (2003), the power to issue injunctions to restrain the breach of planning control was in issue in relation to Gypsies. In an unusually sympathetic decision in relation to Gypsies, the Court of Appeal ruled that the power to grant the injunction should not be used to evict Gypsies from their mobile homes unless the need for such a remedy to protect the environment outweighed the Gypsies' rights under Article 8. The precedents, *Mole Valley DC v Smith* (1992), *Guildford BC v Smith* (1994) and *Hambleton DC v Bird* (1995), could not be considered consistent with the court's duty under section 6(1) of the Human Rights Act 1998 to act compatibly with Convention rights. Proportionality required not only that the injunction be appropriate and necessary for the attainment of the public interest objective sought, but also that it did not impose an excessive burden on the individual whose private interests – here the Gypsy's private life and home and the retention of his ethnic identity – were at stake.[151] Gypsy rights were also at issue in *Clarke v Secretary of State for the Environment, Transport and the Regions* (2002). In this case, the Queen's Bench Division ruled that in deciding whether to grant planning permission to a Gypsy to station a caravan on land for his residential use it could be a breach of Articles 8 and 14 (the right to enjoyment of Convention rights without discrimination) to take into account the fact that he had refused the offer of alternative, conventional housing accommodation as being contrary to his culture as a Gypsy.[152]

Electoral law

Article 8 of the Convention was violated by the refusal of an electoral registration officer to allow an elector to have his name removed from an electoral register

---

150 See also *R (P) v Secretary of State for the Home Department; R (Q) v Same* (2001); *R (S) v Chief Constable of South Yorkshire* (2002).

151 See also *First Secretary of State v Chichester DC* (2004) in which Article 8 rights prevailed over any harm to the public interest which could be offset by imposing conditions.

152 See also *Poplar Housing and Regeneration Community Association Ltd v Donoghue* (2001).

before that register was sold to a commercial firm for marketing purposes. The Queen's Bench Division so held in *R (Robertson) v Wakefield Metropolitan District Council* (2001). No provision had been made in the Representation of the People (England and Wales) Regulations for the editing of the register following requests to be excluded and this breached the EC Directive. Article 8 was violated, since the sale of the register to marketing organisations increased the likelihood of infringement of a person's privacy.[153]

Deportation

In *R (Samaroo) v Secretary of State for the Home Department* (2001), the Court of Appeal ruled that where a decision had to be made in relation to whether to deport a person on the grounds of the prevention of crime and disorder (in this case conviction for importing Class A drugs), a fair balance had to be struck between the legitimate aim and the affected person's fundamental rights. The Secretary of State was entitled to regard drug trafficking as very serious and there was no violation of Article 8.[154]

Article 9: freedom of religion, etc

Article 9 was not violated by the prohibition in the Misuse of Drugs Act 1971 in relation to the supply of cannabis which it was claimed was for use in acts of religious worship (Rastafarianism). The Court of Appeal so held in *R v Taylor (Paul Simon)* (2000). In *R v Secretary of State for Education and Employment ex parte Williamson* (2005), the House of Lords held that a genuine belief in corporal punishment in schools was not a manifestation in practice or observance of a religion or belief. Nor was it a religious or philosophical conviction for the purposes of the right to education in Article 2 of the First Protocol. An employee who was unable to accept an employer's change in working hours to include working on Sundays which interfered with the employee's manifestation of his religion was free to resign in order to manifest those beliefs. Therefore Article 9 was not engaged. In *R (Shabina Begum) v Denbigh High School* (2006) the House of Lords ruled that there was no violation of Article 9 where a school adopted a policy relating to permissible uniforms which prohibited the wearing of a jilbab. The school was sensitive to the needs of its pupils and provided a choice of uniforms.

Special considerations apply to the position of religion and the churches. Section 13 of the Act provides for freedom of thought, conscience and religion, and states:

13(1) If a court's determination of any question arising under this Act might affect the exercise by a religious organisation (itself or its members collectively) of the Convention right to freedom of thought, conscience and religion, it must have a particular regard to the importance of that right.

---

153 In addition, there was a failure by domestic law to comply with EC Directive 95/96/EC of October 24 1995, OJ 1995 L281/31 which required that an individual could object to the processing of personal data which the data controller anticipated would be processed for the purposes of direct marketing.

154 See *R v Secretary of State for the Home Department ex parte R* (2000); *R (Grant) v Lambeth LBC* (2004).

The section was included to protect the churches from liability under the Convention. Thus, for example, if a person alleges that he or she is the victim of a breach of the Convention right to marry (Article 12) or the right to respect for private and family life (Article 8) by the beliefs, rules and practices of a religious faith, the court, in determining the issue, must have special regard to the importance of those beliefs and practices.

Article 10: freedom of expression

The case law under this Article is discussed in Chapter 21.

Article 11: freedom of association

Article 11 was considered in *Royal Society for the Prevention of Cruelty to Animals v Attorney General* (2002). The Chancery Division ruled that the RSPCA had the right to exclude applicants whom the Society thought in good faith were likely to damage its objectives. In question was the right of the Society to exclude current members and deny membership to applicants who sought to reverse the Society's policy against hunting with dogs. However, the court ruled that the Society should adopt a procedure through which any potentially excluded person should have the opportunity to make representations. Freedom of association in relation to demonstrations and police powers was considered by the Court of Appeal in *R (Laporte) v Chief Constable of Gloucestershire Constabulary* (2004). The case is discussed in Chapter 22 at p 587.

Article 12: The right to marry

See p 509 above, and further pages 550–51 below.

Protocol 1: the right to enjoyment of possessions[155]

The Court of Appeal in *Lindsay v Commissioners of Customs and Excise* (2002) ruled that the policy of seizing motor vehicles belonging to people who evaded duty on tobacco and alcohol, and refusal to restore the vehicle save in exceptional circumstances, fettered the discretion of officers. It failed to distinguish between commercial smuggling and importation for distribution among family and friends. Under Article 1 of Protocol 1, deprivation of possessions could only be justified if it was in the public interest. There had to be a reasonable relationship of proportionality between the means employed and the aim pursued. Here there was not.

A child's right to education under Article 2 of Protocol 1 to the Convention was not violated by enforcement of immigration control which involved the removal of a child settled in a school in England after her parents' application to

---

155 In *R (Quark Fishing Ltd) v Secretary of State for Foreign and Commonwealth Affairs* (2005) the House of Lords ruled that since provisions protecting property rights guaranteed under the Convention had not been expressly extended by the United Kingdom to the British Overseas Territory of South Georgia, no claim for damages could be brought in respect of a violation of such rights there.

remain in the United Kingdom had been rejected. The Court of Appeal so held in *R v Secretary of State for the Home Department ex parte Holub* (2001). Article 2 did not confer a right to education in any particular country and was accordingly limited in scope.[156]

CONCLUSION

The European Convention on Human Rights has provided vital protection for citizens against the power of the state. As has been seen, the case law against the United Kingdom is substantial and, in many instances, has led to considerable reform of the law. Nevertheless, the right of individual petition, conferred in 1965, meant long delays and high costs for litigants. The Convention has for the most part, and despite its limitations in scope, served individuals well in the protection of fundamental rights. The incorporation of Convention rights into domestic law under the Human Rights Act 1998 was a logical step forward for a government seriously committed to individual rights and freedoms and represents a significant extension of the rule of law. Incorporation may also change the traditional public conception of individual freedoms in favour of rights, and bring a greater clarity to the law relating to both civil liberties and human rights.

The absence of an authoritative body dedicated to ensuring compliance with the Human Rights Act gave rise to criticism. That deficiency has now been remedied under the Equality Act 2006 which establishes a Commission for Equality and Human Rights. The Commission is discussed in the next chapter.

---

156 See also *Wilson v First County Trust Ltd (No 2)* (2003), discussed above.

CHAPTER 20

FREEDOM FROM DISCRIMINATION

The common law proved inadequate to protect individuals against discrimination on the basis of race, gender or disability. Parliament intervened and there is now a statutory framework. The Acts employ similar concepts and are enforced by similar machinery.[1]

The Human Rights Act 1998 incorporates Article 14 of the European Convention on Human Rights, which provides for non-discrimination on the grounds of sex, race, colour, language, religion, political or other opinion, national or social origin, association with a national minority, property, birth or other status. However, Article 14 protects against discrimination only in respect of 'the enjoyment of the rights and freedoms set forth in [the] Convention': it is not, therefore, a blanket prohibition on discrimination in all circumstances.

The right to equal treatment under the law is a fundamental human right. The law has responded to demands for protection against discrimination in a piecemeal manner as those who have suffered discrimination have pressed their claim to equal treatment. Legislation prohibiting racial discrimination was first introduced in the 1960s, equal treatment for women in the 1970s and the right not to be discriminated against on the grounds of disability in the 1990s. Most recently rules have been introduced to make discrimination on the grounds of sexual orientation and religion or belief in employment or vocational training unlawful and discrimination on the grounds of age is to be legislated against.

In relation to racial, sexual and disability discrimination the governing legislation established a statutory Commission to combat discrimination. The Race Relations Act 1976 established the Commission for Racial Equality (CRE);[2] the Sex Discrimination Act 1975 established the Equal Opportunities Commission (EOC) and the Disability Rights Commission Act 1999 established the Disability Rights Commission (DRC). In 2003 the government announced its intention to introduce a single body to regulate equality legislation,[3] and the Equality Act 2006 now provides for the setting up of a Commission for Equality and Human Rights (CEHR) which will assume responsibility for promoting equality and combating unlawful discrimination on racial, sexual and disability grounds as well as sexual orientation, religion or belief, and age. The Commission will also have responsibility for the promotion of human rights and ensuring that public bodies comply with the Human Rights Act 1998. The CEHR will take over the work of the CRE, the EOC and the DRC with transitional provisions in place to ensure

---

1   See Hale, 2005.
2   *R v Commission for Racial Equality ex parte Hillingdon Council* (1982); *Race Relations Board v Dockers' Labour Club* (1976); *Council for Racial Equality v Amari Plastics* (1982).
3   See HC Vol 412, col 17WS, 20 October 2003. See also the White Paper, Cm 6185, *Fairness for All: A New Commission for Equality and Human Rights*, Stationery Office, 2004.

continuity. The CEHR will also be responsible for the new equality strands of sexual orientation, religion or belief and age.[4]

The Equality Act 2006 and the Commission will be discussed further later in this chapter.

RACIAL DISCRIMINATION

Race Relations Acts

In 1965, parliament, for the first time, considered legal protection against racial discrimination to be necessary. The Race Relations Act 1965, however, proved to provide only limited value in protection.[5] The Act provided not for access to the courts for protection from discrimination, but for an application to be made to the Race Relations Board established under the 1965 Act. The Race Relations Act 1968 strengthened the powers of the Board, but protection from discrimination remained limited. The law is now found in the Race Relations Act 1976, as amended by the Race Relations (Amendment) Act 2000 and the Equality Act 2006.

Racial discrimination is defined under the Act as being discrimination based on the grounds of colour, race, nationality, ethnic or national origins. Discrimination may be direct or indirect. The Act did not, however, prohibit all forms of racial discrimination, and confined protection to discrimination in the field of employment, including service of the Crown, such as the armed forces,[6] the police and local authorities, and to education, housing and the provision of goods and services.

The Race Relations (Amendment) Act 2000[7] extends the range of public bodies subject to the Act and imposes a statutory duty on public authorities[8] to eliminate discrimination and to promote equality of opportunity and good relations between racial groups.[9] Section 19B defines public authorities in line with the Human Rights Act 1998, section 6. Accordingly, a public authority is a body carrying out functions of a public nature, and the Act does not apply where the functions being carried out are private in nature. The Act also provides for codes of practice. The duties may be enforced by compliance notices issued by the Commission for Equality and Human Rights (CEHR) and where necessary

---

4   The Race Relations Act, Sex Discrimination Act, Religion or Belief Regulations and Sexual Orientation Regulations 2003 provide for limited forms of positive discrimination, labelled 'positive action'. There are two forms of permissible positive action: affording members of a group access to facilities for training which would help fit them for particular work, and encouraging members of a group to take advantage of opportunities for doing particular work: Race Relations Act, s 25; Sex Discrimination Act, s 48; Religion and Belief Regulations, reg 26; Sexual Orientation Regulations.

5   The Race Relations Act 1968 extended the 1965 Act, but effectiveness remained unsatisfactory.

6   See *R v Army Board of Defence Council ex parte Anderson* (1992).

7   Amending the Race Relations Act 1976, s 71(1).

8   Specified in Sched 1A, which lists 60 authorities including ministers, government departments, the armed forces, health authorities, local authorities, police authorities, probation and magistrates' committees.

9   See O'Cinneide, 2001.

enforced by a court order.[10] The Act also makes the police subject to the Race Relations Act 1976 and makes chief officers of police vicariously liable for acts of discrimination by police officers.[11] Excluded from the Act are immigration authorities, the security services, Parliament and the Scottish Parliament and Welsh Assembly, and acts of the judiciary.[12]

The definition of racial discrimination

The courts have encountered problems with the definition of racial discrimination which is linked to discrimination of the grounds of colour, race, nationality, ethnic or national origins. In *Seide v Gillette Industries* (1980) it was held that people of Jewish origin and culture fell within the definition. In *Mandla v Dowell Lee* (1983), the House of Lords ruled that Sikhs fell within the definition of a racial group and were thus protected under the Act.[13] The characteristics of an ethnic group included a long shared distinctive history and a distinctive cultural tradition. Further common characteristics included a common geographical origin, common language and religion, common literature, and being a minority within a larger society.

In *Commission for Racial Equality v Dutton* (1989), the Court of Appeal had to decide whether Gypsies constituted a racial group. The court reviewed the variety of meanings given to 'Gypsies'. Applying the tests propounded by the House of Lords in *Mandla v Dowell Lee*, Nicholls LJ stated that:

> ... Gypsies are a minority, with a long shared history and a common geographical origin ... having certain, albeit limited, customs of their own ... a distinctive style of dressing, ... a language or dialect, ... a repertoire of folktales and music passed on from one generation to the next.

The court accepted that many Gypsies no longer derive from a 'common stock', but that of itself did not prevent them from being a racial group within the wide definition in the Act.[14] By distinction, the court ruled in *Dawkins v Department of Environment* that Rastafarians, while enjoying distinctive cultural features, having their own music and hair styles, do not fall within the meaning of a racial group, for their 'shared history' is only of some 60 years' duration (compared with that of Gypsies, whose history is of over 700 years' duration).

Direct and indirect discrimination

Direct discrimination

Under section 1(1) of the Act, direct discrimination involves the treatment of a person less favourably than another, on the basis of race. For an offence to

---

10   Race Relations (Amendment) Act 2000, ss 71C–71E.
11   In response to the findings of the Macpherson Inquiry into the death of black teenager Stephen Lawrence. See *Report of the Stephen Lawrence Inquiry*, Cm 4262-I, February 1999, and Chapter 23.
12   In *British Telecommunications plc v Reid* (2004) the Court of Appeal ruled that an award of compensation totalling £8,000, made under the Race Relations Act 1976 to an employee for injury to feelings and aggravated damages that related to a single direct incident of racial discrimination, was neither wrong in principle nor excessive in amount.
13   Race Relations Act 1976, s 3(1).
14   At p 27G. See Barnett, 1995 and 1994.

be proven, there is no need to establish that the person discriminating on racial grounds intended so to do.[15] Direct discrimination includes segregation on the grounds of race, and to provide separate facilities for differing races, irrespective of the quality of the facilities, is an offence.[16] Proving direct discrimination – whether on grounds of race or sex – is difficult: there will usually be a number of other grounds for, say, rejecting an application for employment, other than pure racial or sexual discrimination.[17] In order to minimise the difficulties of proof, it has been established that, once the inference has been raised that discrimination has occurred, the burden of proof shifts to the alleged discriminator to prove that the decision was not racially or sexually discriminatory.[18] In *Sidhu v Aerospace Composite Technology Ltd* (2000), the Court of Appeal ruled that an employer's policy in relation to violence and abusive language which applied to all employees, irrespective of race, was not direct discrimination when applied to an employee who had suffered racial abuse and retaliated with violence.

In *Nagarajan v London Regional Transport* (2000), the House of Lords considered the meaning of discrimination by way of victimisation under section 2 of the Race Relations Act 1976. The issue turned on whether or not it was necessary to establish that there was conscious motivation to discriminate, as was held by the appeal tribunal and the Court of Appeal. The House of Lords ruled that conscious motivation was not a prerequisite for a finding of direct discrimination under section 1 of the Act, and that section 2 had to be read in that context. If a job applicant's previous complaint under the Race Relations Act had a significant influence on the decision not to offer him a job, the case fell within section 2(1), even though the interviewee did not consciously realise that he was prejudiced by that knowledge.[19]

In *Chief Constable of the West Yorkshire Police v Khan* (2001), the House of Lords ruled that where a chief constable had refused a reference for a police officer who had brought proceedings against him in an employment tribunal, the refusal was not 'by reason that' the officer had brought proceedings but because of the existence of the proceedings and the chief constable's need to preserve his legal position in relation to them. Accordingly, the officer's complaint of victimisation under section 2(1)(a) of the Race Relations Act 1976 failed.

The House of Lords clarified the question whether former employees could rely on the Discrimination Acts[20] once their period of employment had terminated in *Rhys Harper v Relaxion Group plc* (2003). It had been held by the Court of Appeal in *Post Office v Adekeye* (1997) that once a period of employment had ended, the former employee had no remedy. The House of Lords in *Rhys Harper* disapproved this decision. The obligation not to discriminate arose from

---

15   *R v Council for Racial Equality ex parte Westminster City Council* (1984).
16   Race Relations Act 1976, s 1(2).
17   See Cotterrell, 1981; Millar and Phillips, 1983.
18   *Dornan v Belfast County Council* (1990).
19   See also *Redfearn v Serco Ltd* (2005).
20   Sex Discrimination Act 1975, s 6(2); Race Relations Act 1976, s 4(2); Disability Discrimination Act 1995, s 4(2); Equality Act 2006.

the employer-employee relationship and accordingly the right to a remedy did not disappear once the employment ceased.

In *Wong v Igen Ltd* (2005) the Court of Appeal considered changes in the law relating to the burden of proof in direct discrimination cases. Regulations implementing European Directives amended the Discrimination Acts.[21] The new provisions reverse the burden of proof and provide that if an applicant showed that he or she had been treated less favourably than others in circumstances which were consistent with that treatment being based on grounds of race or sex, the tribunal should draw an inference that such treatment was discrimination *unless* the respondent could satisfy the tribunal that there was an innocent explanation.[22]

Indirect discrimination

Indirect discrimination occurs when a person conducts him or herself in a manner which is not directly discriminatory, but which has the indirect effect of being discriminatory. Indirect discrimination may affect individuals or a group of persons. Accordingly, if, for example, an employer attaches conditions of employment to an advertised post which a member of a particular racial group cannot fulfil, there will be indirect discrimination. The proof of indirect discrimination is again a difficult one to establish. Once a *prima facie* case of discrimination has been made out, it is for the defendant to rebut the presumption that there has been discrimination. To do so, the defendant must establish to the satisfaction of the court that any conditions of employment are justifiable. By way of example, in *Mandla v Dowell Lee* (1983) the House of Lords ruled that the rules relating to school uniform, which prohibited the wearing of a turban, which the pupil was required to wear on religious grounds, were discriminatory. The House of Lords ruled that the statutory words 'can comply' meant 'can in practice comply' or 'can consistently with customs and cultural conditions of the racial group comply', not 'can physically comply' (pp 565–66, *per* Lord Fraser). Conversely, in *Singh v British Railway Engineers* (1986), a condition of employment was the wearing of protective headgear – a condition with which the applicant could not comply by virtue of wearing a turban in accordance with the requirements of his faith. The court here held that the condition was justifiable on the basis of the requirements of safety. In *Bilka-Kaufhaus GmbH v Weber von Hartz* (1986), however, the European Court of Justice ruled that conditions of employment must be justifiable, *inter alia*, according to the extent to which they are appropriate to achieving a necessary objective.[23] This test has made it more difficult for employers to argue that conditions are non-discriminatory.

---

21 Disability Discrimination Act 1995 (Amendment) Regulations 2003; Employment Equality (Religion or Belief) Regulations 2003; Employment Equality (Sexual Orientation) Regulations 2003; Race Relations Act 1976 (Amendment) Regulations 2003, inserting new s 54A into the 1976 Act.

22 A manager was jointly and severally liable for damages together with the employer where she had encouraged a discriminatory culture at work by behaviour and example. The Employment Appeal Tribunal so ruled in *Miles v Gilbank* (2005), in which the employee had been subjected to bullying and discrimination at work following the disclosure that she was pregnant.

23 See *Hampson v Department of Education and Science* (1991).

Section 33(1) of the Race Relations Act 1976 provides that a person is to be treated as a person committing an unlawful act if that person knowingly aids another person to do an unlawful act. In *Anyanwu v South Bank Students' Union* (2000), two students had been expelled from the university and debarred from entering university premises, including the Students' Union, by which they were employed. The Union then dismissed the students from their employment. The students brought proceedings alleging that they had been discriminated against on racial grounds by the Union and that the university had knowingly aided the Union in their unlawful dismissal. The Court of Appeal held by a majority that, although the university had taken action against the students, and that action brought about their dismissal from employment, the university had not aided or helped the Union to dismiss the students. In *Hallam v Avery* (2001), the House of Lords considered the meaning of aiding another to commit an unlawful act under the Race Relations Act 1976. Police officers told a local authority that a reception booked at its premises was to be a Gypsy wedding with a potential risk of disturbance. Acting on that advice, the council imposed additional booking conditions which amounted to unlawful discrimination contrary to sections 20 and 21 of the 1976 Act. The officers, however, who took no part in the council's decision, could not be shown to have aided it to do that unlawful act.

Where there is an allegation of unfair dismissal by virtue of racial discrimination, what had to be compared was how the employer had treated the complainant and how that employer would have treated another employee, not how a hypothetical reasonable employer would have treated another employee. The House of Lords so ruled in *City of Glasgow Council v Zafar* (1988), holding that it was not legitimate to infer from the unreasonableness of the dismissal that it had been racially motivated.[24]

Exceptions to protection

Exceptions are made to the protection of the Act. Residential accommodation in small premises is excepted, as is foster accommodation for the care of children.[25] Businesses with less than six partners are also exempted, as are associations with less than 25 members. Further limitations in the protection given lie in the areas of employment. For example, it is justifiable for an employer to insist on candidates for employment being of a particular race in order to ensure authenticity. Accordingly, it is lawful for an Indian restaurant to advertise for, and employ, only Indian staff.[26]

---

24   In *British Telecommunications plc v Reid* (2004) the Court of Appeal ruled that an award of compensation totalling £8,000, made under the Race Relations Act 1976, to an employee against an employer for injury to feelings and aggravated damages that related to a single direct incident of racial discrimination, was neither wrong in principle nor excessive in amount.

25   Race Relations Act 1976, s 23(2).

26   *Ibid*, s 29.

SEXUAL DISCRIMINATION

Sexual equality[27]

Factual and legal inequalities between the sexes have bedevilled history.

The 'feminist campaign' began in the eighteenth century. Mary Wollstonecraft (1759–97) argued for equality in treatment between men and women. In *The Vindication of the Rights of Women*, Wollstonecraft argued for educational and political equality. Socio-economic changes in the eighteenth century resulted in the emergence of middle class society, in which women became a 'leisured class'. Thus, the differences between men and women became more, rather than less, defined. Excluded from public affairs and the world of work, femininity became an objective and a goal. It was a dangerous development for women, for femininity emphasised the idea of both difference and fragility – and dependence.

The legal disabilities under which women laboured, analysed by John Stuart Mill over a century ago in *The Subjection of Women* (1869), have been slow to pass. On marriage, a wife traditionally and effectively became the property of the husband: the doctrine was that of 'one flesh' created by the spiritual, legal and physical union within – in the United Kingdom – a Christian marriage. Three consequences, at least, flowed from this doctrine. First, a married woman was, until 1882, effectively incapable of owning property. Secondly, by marriage, a woman impliedly consented to sexual intercourse with her husband whenever he so required. It was, until the House of Lords' decision in *R v R* in 1991, impossible in law for a married man to rape his wife. As Archbold stated: 'It is a clear and well settled law that a man cannot rape his wife.'[28]

Thirdly, the husband had sole control, or custody, of the children of the marriage. Mothers, until 1839, had no custody rights whatsoever – and then only to the age of seven years. The 'right', such as it was, would be lost through committing adultery. Equality in parental rights was not to be achieved until 1973.[29]

Statutory protection from sexual discrimination

In 1919, parliament enacted legislation to remove some legal disabilities in the field of property and contract, the vote and employment.[30] However, in the field of employment, many exceptions existed to a right to equal treatment. The Sex Discrimination Act 1975 attempted to redress the factual inequalities which remained. Much still remains to be achieved: the average pay for women has traditionally been lower than that of men; women form the majority of part time,

---

27 But note that Plato argued for equality in relation to employment!
28 See Naffine, 1994; Report No 205, *Rape Within Marriage*, 1992. The Criminal Justice and Public Order Act 1994, s 142(1)(2), defines rape, in part, as: (a) sexual intercourse with a person (whether vaginal or anal) who at the time of the intercourse does not consent to it; and (b) at the time he knows that the person does not consent to the intercourse or is reckless as to whether that person consents to it. Section 142(1)(1) makes it an offence for a man to rape a woman or another man.
29 Guardianship Act 1973.
30 Sex Disqualification (Removal) Act 1919.

low paid workers.[31] Moreover, the demands of child care continue to reduce the opportunities for women in employment, and the state has not been robust in insisting that employers provide child care facilities. The law of the European Community has had a significant impact on the issue of equal pay for women, and domestic legal protection must be seen nowadays in light of Community law.[32]

The Equal Pay Act 1970 and Sex Discrimination Act 1975[33]

Employment and dismissal

Contractual employment rights are regulated under the Equal Pay Act 1970, whilst other aspects of employment are governed by the Sex Discrimination Act 1975. The two Acts are thus designed to provide protection in all fields of employment. It is unlawful to discriminate on the basis of sex or marital status in the context of employment, education and the provision of goods and services.[34] The Court of Appeal, in *Nelson v Carillion Services Ltd* (2003), considered whether the burden of proof lay on the person discriminated against, or the alleged perpetrator of the discrimination. The court ruled that under both the Equal Pay Act 1970 and the Sex Discrimination Act 1975 the burden of establishing discrimination rested on the complainant. Sexual discrimination – as with racial discrimination – may be direct or indirect. Indirect discrimination may arise through unjustified conditions of employment, for example through stipulating that applicants be of a certain height or age, where height or age is irrelevant to the particular job. On the other hand, some conditions of employment will be fully justified, for example particular academic qualifications. The issue of justifiable qualifications arose in *Price v Civil Service Commission* (1978), where a condition was applied that applicants be under the age of 28 years. Mrs Price, aged 35, alleged discrimination and her claim was upheld. However, in *Saunders v Richmond upon Thames LBC* (1978), a female qualified applicant was refused employment as a golf professional, although her qualifications were higher than those of the man who was appointed. Despite her qualifications, the Employment Appeal Tribunal ruled that there was insufficient evidence that she had in fact been discriminated against on the basis of her sex.[35]

In order to establish sexual discrimination, a women must prove that – but for her sex – she would have been treated more favourably. In order to establish this

---

31 See eg *R v Secretary of State for Employment ex parte Equal Opportunities Commission* (1994), in which English employment legislation was declared to be incompatible with the requirements of European Community law (see further Chapter 9).

32 EC Treaty, Article 119; Equal Pay Directive 75/117; Equal Treatment Directive 76/207; Pregnancy Directive 92/85; Parental Leave Directive 96/34/EC (OJ L145/4, 1996) and see 96/34/EC (OJ L19/24, 1998); Working Time Directive 93/104/EC (OJ L307/18, 1993).

33 The domestic employment legislation must be viewed in light of the substantial development of case law under the law of the European Community, discussed in Chapters 8 and 9.

34 Sex Discrimination Act 1975, ss 6, 22 and 29.

35 A manager was jointly and severally liable for damages together with the employer where she had encouraged a discriminatory culture at work by behaviour and example. The Employment Appeal Tribunal so ruled in *Miles v Gilbank* (2005), in which the employee had been subjected to bullying and discrimination at work following the disclosure that she was pregnant.

requirement, the 1975 Act provided that a woman's treatment must be evaluated against that of a 'comparable man'.[36] Accordingly, the curious and regrettable consequence arises whereby, if an employer only employs women – and does so at a lower rate of pay than he would have paid to men – no discrimination can be proven, for there is no comparator.

In *Shamoon v Chief Constable of the Royal Ulster Constabulary* (2003) the House of Lords dismissed an appeal by a former female chief inspector who claimed sexual discrimination. On the comparator, Lord Hope said that it 'had been one of the most problematic and limiting aspects of direct discrimination. The choice of comparator required that a judgment be made as to which of the differences between any two individuals were relevant and which were irrelevant'.

In *Glasgow City Council v Marshall* (2000), the House of Lords had to determine whether employers who paid employees different rates in respect of their duties as teachers and instructors (the teachers being paid more) had acted lawfully. Proceedings were brought under the Equal Pay Act 1970 by one male and seven female instructors, claiming that they were entitled to equal pay. The employers relied on the absence of sexual discrimination. The House of Lords ruled that the employer had established a defence under section 1(3) of the Act, and that the inequality of pay was due not to sexual discrimination but to some other material fact.[37]

In *Ratcliffe v North Yorkshire County Council* (1995), the House of Lords ruled that the County Council had violated section 1 of the Equal Pay Act 1970. The action had been brought by Unison, the public service union, on behalf of 1,300 dinner ladies employed by the Council, whose pay had been reduced from £3.31 per hour to £3.00 per hour, a rate below that of dustmen, gardeners, cleaners and street sweepers, with whom they had been compared for equal pay purposes. Section 1 of the Equal Pay Act 1970[38] provides that: 'An equality clause shall not operate in relation to a variation between the women's contract and the man's contract if the employer proves that the variation is genuinely due to a material factor which is not the difference of sex ...' Under the Local Government Act 1988, local councils were obliged to put the provision of school meals out to tender, and could only lawfully continue to provide such services if their own tender was accepted. In order to render its bid competitive, the Council had made a number of women redundant and re-employed them at lower hourly rates of pay. The House of Lords ruled that the Council 'had paid women less than men engaged on work rated as equivalent'. There was no material difference between the case of the women and that of their male comparators and, accordingly, the Council had discriminated against the women.

The Equal Opportunities Commission welcomed the decision, pointing out that women still received wages which on average were only 79 per cent of those

---

36 Sex Discrimination Act 1975, s 5; and see *James v Eastleigh Borough Council* (1990).
37 *Allonby v Accrington and Rossendale College* (2001); *Whiffen v Milham Ford Girls' School* (2001); *Home Office v Bailey* (2005); and *Cadman v Health and Safety Executive* (2004). See also *Strathclyde Regional Council v Wallace* (1998).
38 Substituted by the Equal Pay (Amendment) Regulations, SI 1983/1794, reg 2.

earned by men, and that any clarification which would eliminate inequalities was a step forward.[39]

The position of pregnant women in employment causes particular difficulties and, again, the idea of the comparator was utilised.[40] The Trade Union Reform and Employment Rights Act 1993 provides that dismissal on the grounds of pregnancy is unfair.[41] However, in *Webb v EMO Cargo (UK) Ltd* (1992), the Court of Appeal ruled, and the House of Lords affirmed, that a woman who was dismissed from employment because of her pregnancy was not unlawfully dismissed, since – comparing her to a man with a temporary physical disability who would also have been unable to work – the man would also have been dismissed.[42] The House of Lords, referred the issue to the European Court of Justice for a ruling on the requirements of EC law.

The Court of Justice ruled in favour of the appellant on two grounds. First, it ruled that pregnancy could not be compared with a male illness, since pregnancy was not pathological. Secondly, the appellant could not be dismissed, because her inability to perform the terms of her employment was temporary, not permanent. The dismissal of the appellant therefore constituted sex discrimination.[43] *Webb v EMO Air Cargo* was followed in *Alabaster v Woolwich plc* (2005). The appellant was entitled to maternity pay. She had received a pay rise, but that increase was not reflected in her maternity pay. She complained of sex discrimination contrary to the Equal Pay Act 1970 and of unauthorised deductions from wages under the Employment Rights Act 1996. The Court of Appeal ruled that in order to give effect to Article 141 of the EC Treaty and the EC principles of 'equality, equivalence and effectiveness' it was necessary to disapply those parts of section 1 of the 1970 Act which imposed the requirements for a male comparator. The right to return to work was further protected by the Court of Appeal in *Crees v Royal London Mutual Insurance Society Ltd* and *Greaves v Kwik Save Stores Ltd* (1998).

Two employees had been dismissed because, being unwell, they had failed to return to work following maternity leave on the due date. The Court of Appeal ruled that they had been unfairly dismissed. Under the Employment Protection (Consolidation) Act 1978,[44] the employees were entitled to return to work and had given the necessary notice that they would do so. There would be circumstances where it would be impossible to be present on the return date and

---

39 See also *Magorrian v Eastern Health and Social Services Board* (1998) and *Marschall v Land Nordrhein-Westfalen* (1997). See also *Armstrong v Newcastle Upon Tyne NHS Hospital Trust* (2005).
40 See eg *Turley v Allders* (1980); *Hayes v Malleable WMC* (1985).
41 Trade Union Reform and Employment Rights Act 1993, ss 23–25 and Scheds 2 and 3; EC Pregnancy Directive 92/85.
42 *Dekker v VJV Centrum* (1991). On the European Court's ruling in *Webb*, see [1994] 2 CMLR 729.
43 *Webb v Emo Cargo (UK) Ltd (No 2)* (1995).
44 As amended by the Trade Union Reform and Employment Rights Act 1993, s 23.

to require the physical presence of the employee in order for the right to return to work to remain would result in absurdities.[45]

The right to non-discrimination applies equally to men and women.[46] The Court of Appeal so confirmed in *Hammersmith and Fulham London Borough Council v Jesuthasan* (1998). In this case, a part time worker employed in the public sector was held to be equally entitled as a female employee to claim redundancy payments and compensation for unfair dismissal. Jesuthasan had originally alleged that he had been the victim of racial discrimination. He subsequently sought to amend his original application to include claims for unfair dismissal and redundancy. The Employment Appeal Tribunal refused to allow him to amend his application.[47] The Employment Protection (Consolidation) Act 1978 had been amended by the 1995 Employment Protection (Part-time Employees) Regulations (SI 1995/31), in order to conform to the House of Lords' decision in *R v Secretary of State for Employment ex parte Equal Opportunities Commission* (1995) (the *EOC* case is discussed in Chapter 9). The novel point for decision was whether a male part time worker employed in the public sector was entitled to claim a redundancy payment and compensation for unfair dismissal, in relation to a dismissal occurring before the 1978 Act was amended. It was common ground that, had the employee been a female part time worker, she could have claimed redundancy payment and compensation for unfair dismissal. In the *EOC* case, the House of Lords had ruled that the qualifying periods for entitlement[48] were incompatible with European Community law. In the present case, the employee was in exactly the same position as the female employee in the *EOC* case. It was argued for the Council that the *EOC* case was distinguishable, in that the objective of Community law was to protect women against indirect discrimination arising out of the fact that more women than men were part time workers. Mummery LJ was unable to accept that proposition. The general proposition of law in the *EOC* case was that discriminatory provisions should be disapplied irrespective of sex and, further, the employee did not complain of sexual discrimination but unfair dismissal and redundancy under the 1978 Act, subject to the disapplication of qualifying provisions declared in the *EOC* case to be incompatible with European Community law. The employer was an 'emanation of the state' and bound by the direct effect of Article 119 (now Article 141 of the EC Treaty) and relevant directives. The appeal was allowed.[49]

European Community law now makes provision for sexual orientation in employment. For example, Council Directive 2001/78/EC requires equal

---

45 [1998] ICR 629. On equality of treatment in relation to redundancy payments, see *Barry v Midland Bank plc* (1999). See also *Halfpenny v IGE Medical Systems Ltd* (2001).

46 Sex Discrimination Act 1975, preamble.

47 [1996] ICR 991.

48 Namely, two years of continuous employment for employees who worked for 16 or more hours a week, and five years of continuous employment for employees who worked between eight and 16 hours a week.

49 See also *Hill and Stapleton v Revenue Commissioners and the Department of Finance* (1998) and *London Underground v Edwards* (1999). On pensions entitlement for part time workers see *Preston v Wolverhampton Healthcare NHS Trust (No 2)* (2001); *Preston v Wolverhampton NHS Trust Ltd* (2000); *Powerhouse Retail Ltd v Burroughs* (2006).

treatment in employment in relation to sexual orientation. The Employment Equality (Sexual Orientation) Regulations 2003 implement this directive, and make discrimination on grounds of sexual orientation unlawful.[50]

There has been a gradual improvement in the protection given to transsexual people in the field of employment.[51] In *Chief Constable of West Yorkshire Police v A* (2004), for example, the House of Lords ruled that A – a sex-changed male to female transsexual – had to be regarded as a woman for the purposes of employment. Accordingly, the Chief Constable had not been entitled to refuse to employ A as a woman police constable on the basis that she could not carry out searches on female suspects: following the sex-change A was in law a woman and accordingly the justification provided by the Sex Discrimination Act 1975, section 7(2), that employment could be refused on the basis of preservation of privacy or decency where a man might object to physical contact with a woman, was not applicable. However, the most significant improvement in the position of transsexuals comes from the Gender Recognition Act 2004, discussed below.[52]

The Gender Recognition Act 2004

In the cases of *Goodwin v United Kingdom* and *I v United Kingdom* (2002) the European Court of Human Rights held, for the first time, that the law prohibiting a transsexual person from marrying violated the Convention rights to respect for private life (Article 8) and the right to marry (Article 12). However, in *Bellinger v Bellinger* (2003), in which the 'wife' was seeking legal recognition of her marriage to a man, the House of Lords ruled that the marriage between a man and a male-to-female transsexual person was void. The Court declared that section 11 of the Matrimonial Causes Act 1973[53] was incompatible with the Human Rights Act 1998, which incorporates Convention rights into domestic law.

The Gender Recognition Act 2004 establishes Gender Recognition Panels, comprising legal and medical members, appointments to which are made by the

---

50 The court ruled that *Burton v DeVere Hotels Ltd* (1997), in which it was held that an employer could be liable for discriminatory acts of employees in circumstances where the employer could control the employees, was wrongly decided. See, however, *Chief Constable of Kent County Constabulary v Baskerville* (2003), in which the Court of Appeal – in a decision made after the House of Lords' decision in *Macdonald and Pearce* – ruled that a Chief Constable was liable under the Sex Discrimination Act for discriminatory treatment by fellow police officers: the Police Act 1996, s 10, stated that a police force was under the direction and control of the chief constable. See also *Mendoza v Ghaidan* (2002). See further Chapter 9 on EC law and sexual equality

51 However, in *Croft v Royal Mail Group* (2003) it was held that it was not unlawful for an employer to require an employee, who intended to undergo gender reassignment surgery and who dressed as a woman, to use the unisex disabled toilet rather than the female toilets.

52 In relation to same-sex couples, in *Ghaidan v Godin-Mendoza* (2004) the House of Lords ruled that none of the distinctions between cohabiting heterosexual couples and same-sex couples withstood scrutiny. Accordingly, the Rent Act 1977 was to be read to include the surviving same-sex partner within the provisions relating to persons living with the original tenant 'as his or her wife or husband'.

53 Which requires that parties to a marriage be male and female respectively, a provision interpreted by the courts as requiring parties to a marriage to be of the same biological sex as they were at birth, thereby precluding any recognition of gender change.

Lord Chancellor.[54] A Gender Recognition Panel will determine applications for gender recognition certificates. An application may be made by a person of either gender, who is aged at least 18, who is either (a) living in the other gender, or (b) having changed gender under the law of a country outside the United Kingdom.[55] Section 2 stipulates the criteria which must be satisfied and requires that where satisfied, the Gender Recognition Panel must grant a certificate.[56] The recognition is not retrospective, although it does apply to the interpretations of enactments, instruments and documents made before as well as after the issue of a certificate.[57]

Once a full certificate has been granted, the person's gender becomes for all purposes the acquired gender.[58] Section 12, however, states that the fact that a person's gender has become the acquired gender under the Act does not affect the status of that person as the father or mother of a child, thereby ensuring the continuity of parental rights and responsibilities and avoiding confusion within the family. Section 10 and Schedule 3 regulate registration.[59] The respective Registrars General for England and Wales, Scotland and Northern Ireland must maintain a Gender Recognition Register which is not open to public inspection. The person is then entitled to a new birth certificate reflecting the acquired gender. The new certificate will not reveal the fact that there has been a change of gender.

Sexual harassment

Sexual harassment is defined as 'conduct of a sexual nature or other conduct based on sex affecting the dignity of men and women at work'.[60] Section 6(6)(b) of the Sex Discrimination Act 1975 and section 4 of the Race Relations Act 1976 refer to conduct which has detrimental effect on the victim. In *Hereford and Worcester County Council v Clayton* (1996), it was held that a sexist comment directed against a woman firefighter was detrimental to women in the message which it conveyed. The European Commission has drafted a Code of Practice on sexual harassment giving guidance to employees and employers.[61] Sexual harassment, as a form of sexual discrimination, is, again, difficult both to define and to prove.

However, the Court of Appeal took a robust approach to the issue of harassment in *Tower Boot Company v Jones* (1997), holding that employers were under a duty to make themselves aware of any harassment in the workplace and take steps to prevent harassment.

---

54 Gender Recognition Act 2004, Sched 1(1).
55 *Ibid*. Section 1(1).
56 Note that there is also provision for interim recognition certificates: see s 4 and Sched 2.
57 Section 9(2).
58 For example, marriage law, social security and pensions, inheritance, succession to peerages etc. The general principle is subject to limited exceptions in the Act. The Act makes the necessary amendments to marriage law and the Sex Discrimination Act 1975 and Sex Discrimination (Northern Ireland) Order 1976 (N.I.15).
59 Part I relates to England and Wales; Part 2 to Scotland and Part 3 to Northern Ireland.
60 OJ C157/2.
61 *On the Protection of the Dignity of Men and Women at Work*, 35 OJ L49/3, 1992.

The Protection from Harassment Act 1997 provides for civil remedies for harassment. The Act provides that a person must not pursue a course of conduct which amounts to harassment of another, and which he knows, or ought to know, amounts to harassment.[62] Harassment is not further defined. The Act creates a criminal offence of harassment in addition to providing for civil remedies in the form of a restraining order.[63] The Act is not designed to inhibit journalists or photographers, but is aimed to stop 'stalking'. However, where an individual reporter or photographer repeatedly follows and causes harassment, that conduct may fall within the scope of the Act.

Formerly, the courts had found difficulty in protecting individuals from harassment where they fell outside the scope of the domestic violence legislation. The former legislation provided for relief only where the parties were either married to each other, or living together as husband and wife in a cohabiting relationship.[64] In *Patel v Patel* (1988), for example, the courts were powerless to grant relief in a situation where a family member (a father in law) was being harassed by another family member (his son in law), because the relationship fell outside the definitions of the domestic violence legislation. In *Khorasandjian v Bush* (1993),[65] however, the Court of Appeal controversially extended the law of tort to provide a remedy against unwanted intrusions into privacy through persistent telephone calls. In that case, a former boyfriend was unable to accept that the relationship was over. There had been no cohabitation. While it is unclear whether there existed a separate head of tortious liability for harassment, the court ruled that the occupier of property, in addition to the owner of the property, had the right to relief under the law of nuisance.[66]

Religious discrimination in employment

The Employment Equality (Religion or Belief) Regulations 2003 make it unlawful to discriminate on grounds of religion or belief in employment and vocational training. They prohibit direct discrimination, indirect discrimination, victimisation and harassment.[67] Religion or belief is defined as meaning any religion, religious belief or similar philosophical belief. An exception is made in relation to national security. An exception is also made to protect Sikhs in connection with requirements as to the wearing of safety helmets. Regulations 27 to 34 provide remedies for individuals, including compensation by way of proceedings in employment tribunals and in the county or sheriff courts.

---

62 Protection from Harassment Act 1997, s 1 and, in relation to Scotland, s 8(1).

63 *Ibid*, s 3.

64 The 1978 Act covered only married couples. See now the Family Law Act 1996 as amended by the Domestic Violence, Crime and Victims Act 2004.

65 See, however, *Hunter v Canary Wharf* (1997).

66 On the Protection from Harassment Act 1997, see further Chapter 22.

67 The Regulations are made under s 2(2) of the European Communities Act 1972 to give effect to Council Directive 2000/78/EC of 27 November 2000 establishing a general framework for equal treatment in employment (OJ L 303, 2.12.2000).

EQUALITY AND DISABILITY

In 1995, parliament passed the Disability Discrimination Act, under which the National Disability Council was established as an advisory body. The Council had no investigative powers in relation to allegations of discrimination nor did it have enforcement powers. The Disability Rights Commission Act 1999 amended the 1995 Act and provides for the establishment of the Disability Rights Commission, modelled on the EOC and the Commission for Racial Equality. The Equality Act 2006 provides that the Commission for Equality and Human Rights (CEHR) will take over the role of the Disability Rights Commission.

Under the 1995 Act, a person has a disability for the purposes of the Act if he or she has a physical or mental impairment which has a substantial and long term adverse effect on his or her ability to carry out normal day to day activities.[68] The provisions of the Act relate both to persons with a current disability and to persons who have previously suffered a disability. It is unlawful for an employer to discriminate against a disabled person in relation to arrangements for interviews, the terms of an offer of employment, or refusing to offer or deliberately not offering the disabled person employment. It is equally unlawful to discriminate against a disabled employee. The meaning of discrimination in section 5 is modelled on the Race Relations Act 1976 and Sex Discrimination Act 1975.[69] Where any arrangements made by the employer, or any physical feature of the relevant premises place the disabled person at a 'substantial' disadvantage, the employer is under a duty to make adjustments to premises, reallocate work, transfer the employee to another post, alter working hours, assign him or her to a different place of work,[70] allow him or her to be absent for the purposes of rehabilitation, assessment or treatment, provide training, acquire or modify equipment or instruction or reference manuals, modify procedures for testing or assessment, provide a reader or interpreter and provide supervision.[71] Section 7 makes detailed provision for matters to be taken into consideration when determining whether an employer has complied with the duty imposed, and provides for the making of regulations to amplify the specific requirements of the Act.

Complaints under the Act are made to an employment tribunal, which has the power to make a declaration as to the rights of the complainant and the respondent in relation to the complaint, to order the respondent to pay compensation to the complainant and to make recommendations to the respondent as to the actions required to be taken to obviate or reduce the adverse effect on the complainant. Compensation is calculated by applying the principles

---

68 Disability Discrimination Act 1995, s 1.
69 *Clark v TDG Ltd* (1999).
70 See *Beart v Prison Service* (2003); *Collins v Royal National Theatre Board Ltd* (2004).
71 Disability Discrimination Act 1995, s 6. In order to improve access to education for disabled children, the Education (Disability Strategies and Pupils' Educational Records) (Scotland) Act 2002 provides that all schools must keep under review their strategies for improving access.

applicable to the calculation of damages in claims of tort or, in Scotland, reparation for breach of statutory duty, and may include compensation for injury to feelings.[72]

Part III of the Act relates to discrimination in other areas, including the provision of goods or services, accommodation and facilities.[73] Part V regulates public transport and provides that the Secretary of State may make regulations relating to the accessibility of taxis, public service vehicles and rail vehicles. The Private Hire Vehicles (Carriage of Guide Dogs etc) Act 2002 amends the Disability Discrimination Act 1995 by extending the duty to carry disabled people accompanied by guide dogs to operators and drivers of private hire vehicles.

Section 55 of the Act makes it unlawful to discriminate against another by way of victimisation. Victimisation is interpreted as meaning treating a disabled person less favourably than another person because the disabled person has brought proceedings under the Act. It is unlawful for a person to knowingly aid another person to do an act made unlawful under the Act.[74]

The original DDA has already been significantly extended. In response to the Disability Rights Task Force recommendations, the Disability Rights Commission was established in 2000.[75] The Special Educational Needs and Disability Act 2001 reflected recommendations of the Commission and made it unlawful to discriminate against disabled pupils and students seeking access to education in schools and colleges. The Disability Discrimination Act 1995 (Amendment) Regulations 203 implement aspects of the EC Employment Directive 2000/78/EC. The Regulations end the exemption of small employers from the scope of the DDA and remove the excluded occupations, bringing the police, fire-fighters, prison officers and partners in business partnerships within its ambit.

The Disability Discrimination Act 2005[76] extends the definition of disabled person to include people who suffer from HIV, multiple sclerosis and cancer as from the point of diagnoses as opposed to from the point at which the condition starts to affect their day to day activities.[77] The 2005 Act also extends the scope of the Act to local government and other public authorities. It introduces a new duty to require public authorities to tackle harassment and discrimination and to promote positive attitudes. The Act brings previously exempted transport services within the ambit of the Act. It also extends the Act to private clubs with 25 or more members and imposes a duty on landlords and others who manage property to make reasonable adjustments to property.

---

72 Disability Discrimination Act 1995, s 8.
73 See *Manchester CC v Romano* (2005), discussed below.
74 Disability Discrimination Act 1995, s 57.
75 See the Disability Rights Commission Act 1999.
76 The Disability Discrimination Act 2005 received the Royal Assent on 7 April 2005. The Bill was given pre-legislative consideration by a Joint Committee of both Houses.
77 Disability Discrimination Act 2005, s 18.

In *Manchester City Council v Romano (Disability Rights Commission intervening)* (2004) the claimant was a local authority landlord which was seeking possession against two defendants who were secure tenants on the ground that they had been guilty of conduct causing a nuisance to their neighbours.[78] Each of the defendants was suffering from a recognised mental illness. The Court of Appeal dismissed the appeals of the defendants, holding that the claimant's conduct was justified and did not amount to unlawful discrimination. While the defendants had a mental impairment within the meaning of section 1(1) of the Disability Discrimination Act 1995, nevertheless that impairment did not have a substantial effect on their ability to carry out normal day to day activities and that therefore there was no discrimination.

In *Archibald v Fife Council* (2004) the House of Lords ruled that an employer was acting lawfully when – because of an employee's disability – transferring her to a sedentary post at a higher grade without requiring her to compete with other applicants. The applicant had been employed as a road sweeper, but following surgery became unable to continue in that post. The council retrained her and shortlisted her for a number of vacancies. However, after applying unsuccessfully for over one hundred posts, she was dismissed on the ground of her inability to carry out her employment as a road sweeper. Interpreting the Disability Discrimination Act 1995, Lady Hale held that while section 6(7) did not *require* an employer to treat a disabled employee more favourably than others, it did not preclude such treatment. The Local Government and Housing Act 1989, section 7, required that all staff be appointed on merit: that section however was subject to the 1995 Disability Act. Accordingly, appointments were to be made on merit, subject to reasonable adjustments.

AGE DISCRIMINATION

The principle of non-discrimination is a general principle of European Community law.[79] In *Werner Mangold v Rudiger Helm* (2006) the Court of Justice ruled that legislation which authorised, without restrictions, the conclusion of fixed-term employment contracts for all workers over the age of 52 was unlawful. In the United Kingdom, in 2006, draft Employment Equality (Age) Regulations were published.[80] The Age Regulations will cover both established and new concepts and will prohibit direct and indirect age discrimination, subject to a justification defence, harassment and victimisation. Employers will be under a duty to consider an employee's request to continue working after the age of 65. Furthermore, the upper age limit for unfair dismissal and redundancy rights will be removed.[81]

---

78 Under ground 2 of Sched 2 to the Housing Act 1985.
79 See Council Directive 2000/78/EC of 27 November 2000 (OJ 2000 L 303, p 16).
80 See www.dti.gov.uk/er/equality/age.htm.
81 Amending s 109 of the Employment Rights Act 1996.

THE EQUALITY ACT 2006

Section 1 of the Equality Act 2006 establishes the Commission for Equality and Human Rights (CEHR).[82] The general duty of the CEHR is set out in section 3:

> The Commission shall exercise its functions under this Part with a view to encouraging and supporting the development of a society in which –
>
> (a) people's ability to achieve their potential is not limited by prejudice or discrimination,
> (b) there is respect for and protection of each individual's human rights,
> (c) there is respect for the dignity and worth of each individual,
> (d) each individual has an equal opportunity to participate in society, and
> (e) there is mutual respect between groups based on understanding and valuing of diversity and on shared respect for equality and human rights.

The Act imposes duties on the CEHR in respect of promoting understanding of and good practice in relation to equality and diversity, to promote equality of opportunity, the awareness and understanding of rights, to enforce equality law and to work towards the elimination of unlawful discrimination and unlawful harassment.[83] The CEHR is also charged with promoting human rights and encouraging public bodies to comply with the Human Rights Act 1998. It is also under a duty to promote understanding and encourage good practice in respect of members of different groups. The Commission will play a monitoring and advisory role in respect of equality and human rights, making recommendations to government in relation to amendment of equality and human rights law.

The Commission is also empowered to undertake investigations where it suspects that a person may have acted unlawfully and violated human rights.[84] Where an unlawful act has been committed the CEHR may issue an 'unlawful act notice' which may require a person to prepare an action plan to avoid repetition or continuation of the unlawful act or recommend action to be taken for that purpose.[85] An appeal lies against the unlawful act notice to an employment tribunal, county court or sheriff in Scotland. Similar provisions apply in relation to the assessment of public bodies' compliance with their duties in relation to gender, race and disability and to discrimination on grounds of religion or belief. The provisions on religion and belief include direct discrimination, indirect discrimination and victimisation. Religion is defined in line with Article 9 of the Convention on Human Rights.[86]

---

82 The Commission shall not take human rights action in relation to a matter if the Scottish Parliament has legislative competence over that matter: s 7.
83 Equality Act 2006, s 8.
84 *Ibid*, s 20.
85 *Ibid*, s 21.
86 See *ibid*, s 44.

CHAPTER 21

FREEDOM OF EXPRESSION AND PRIVACY

FREEDOM OF EXPRESSION

Freedom of expression entails many aspects: an individual's freedom to express any view he or she wishes, however offensive to others, in private or public; freedom of the press to express any view; freedom of authors to write and publish; and freedom of film makers to record and distribute films/videos for private and public consumption. From the standpoint of democracy, freedom of speech is crucial to the exchange of political ideas and to the formation of political opinions. The freedom of speech guaranteed to Members of Parliament under Article IX of the Bill of Rights 1689 reflects the constitutional importance of political debate, as does the right of newspapers and broadcasters to publish fair and accurate reports of parliamentary proceedings.[1]

Blackstone, in his *Commentaries*, said of freedom of the press that:

> ... the liberty of the press is indeed essential to the nature of a free state. Every free man has an undoubted right to lay what sentiments he pleases before the public; to forbid this is to destroy the freedom the press; but if he publishes what is improper, mischievous or illegal, he must take the consequences of his own temerity.

Freedom of expression is essential in a free and democratic society, and restrictions which inhibit criticism of public authorities, in particular, undermine the potential for scrutiny of official action. For this reason, in *Derbyshire County Council v Times Newspapers* (1993), the House of Lords ruled that neither local nor central government had standing to sue for defamation. Lord Keith stated that 'it is of the highest importance that a democratically elected governmental body ... should be open to uninhibited public criticism'.

In the United Kingdom, until recently, there was no right to free speech but, in a negative way, there was a freedom of expression subject to the limitations imposed by law. Freedom of expression is now regulated under Article 10 of the European Convention on Human Rights, now incorporated into domestic law under the Human Rights Act 1998. However, the right is limited by restrictions.

Freedom of expression under Article 10 includes the 'freedom to hold opinions and to receive and impart information and ideas without interference by public authority and regardless of frontiers'.[2] The right is subject to such legal restrictions as are 'necessary in a democratic society in the interests of national security or public safety, for the prevention of disorder or crime, for the protection of health or morals or for the protection of the rights and freedoms of others'.[3]

---

1   The Parliamentary Papers Act 1840. See Chapter 18.
2   But does not prevent state licensing of broadcasting, television or cinemas.
3   The issue of whether to order the postponement of reporting of a trial until after the conclusion of a second related trial came before the Court of Appeal in *R v Sherwood ex parte Telegraph Group plc* (2001). The court ruled that the ban was necessary in the interests of justice. See further p 573 below.

Legal restrictions on the exercise of the right by members of the armed forces, police or administration of the state are permitted. The effect of Article 10 is that all restrictions on the right must be justified, in common with other restricted Articles, according to these criteria: they must be both *necessary* and *proportionate*.[4]

The Article 10 right is also regulated by section 12 of the Human Rights Act 1998, which was drafted so as to prevent claims to privacy[5] restricting freedom of the press. Section 12(4) provides that:

> The court must have particular regard to the importance of the Convention right to freedom of expression and, where the proceedings relate to material which the respondent claims, or which appears to the court, to be journalistic, literary or artistic material (or to conduct connected with such material), to –
>
> (a) the extent to which –
>
>   (i)   the material is, or is about to, become available to the public;[6] or
>
>   (ii) it is, or would be, in the public interest for the material to be published;
>
> (b) any relevant privacy code.[7]

The House of Lords upheld the right of prisoners to freedom of expression in *R v Secretary of State for the Home Department ex parte Simms* (1999). The court ruled that an indiscriminate ban on all visits to prisoners by journalists or authors in their professional capacity was unlawful. A prisoner had a right to seek, through oral interviews, to persuade a journalist to investigate his allegations of miscarriage of justice in the hope that his case might be re-opened. The applicants were serving life sentences for murder and, having had their renewed applications for leave to appeal against conviction turned down, continued to protest their innocence. The Home Office had adopted a blanket policy that no prisoners had a right to oral interviews with journalists. Lord Steyn stated that the applicants wished to challenge the safety of their convictions, and that, 'in principle, it was not easy to conceive of a more important function which free speech might fulfil'. His Lordship was satisfied that it was administratively workable, and consistent with prison order and discipline, to allow prisoners to

---

4   On the meaning of these terms, see Chapter 19.

5   Protected under Article 8.

6   In *Attorney General v Times Newspapers* (2001) the government lost its appeal to restrain publication of Richard Tomlinson's *The Big Breach: From Top Secret to Maximum Security*, which the government alleged would damage national security. The Court of Appeal ruled that if the material was already in the public domain, whether at home or abroad (the book had been published in Moscow), then there should be no restraint on freedom of expression.

7   See *R v Advertising Standards Authority Ltd ex parte Matthias Rath BV* (2001), in which adjudications published by the Advertising Standards Authority under its non-statutory code were held to be 'prescribed by law' within the meaning of Article 10. The Codes of Advertising and Sales Promotion had the 'underpinning' of subordinate legislation which gave recognition for the statutory recognition of means of dealing with complaints. The Code of Practice was readily accessible and therefore prescribed by law, its provisions being sufficiently clear and precise to enable any person to know the acceptable limits of advertisements and the consequences of infringing the provisions. The rights of children to freedom of expression and participation in family life was recognised by the Court of Appeal in *Mabon v Mabon* (2005). The Court recognised that in the case of articulate teenagers, it must accept that their rights outweighed the paternalistic judgment of the welfare of the child. 'There was a growing acknowledgment of the autonomy and consequential rights of children.'

be interviewed for the purpose here at stake. The Home Secretary's policy and the governor's administrative decisions pursuant to that policy were unlawful.

Freedom of expression was also at issue in *R (Nilsen) v Governor of Full Sutton Prison* (2004). The Court of Appeal ruled that a prison rule preventing a prisoner from publishing material about his offences did not violate the right to freedom of expression and its application was proportionate and justified on the facts. In 1983 Nilsen had been sentenced to six life sentences for six murders, the details of which were horrifying. He intended to publish details in an autobiography. The Home Secretary had exercised powers under the Prison Act 1952 to withhold the work. The restriction was a legitimate exercise of power: it could not be argued that a prisoner should be permitted to publish an article 'glorifying in the pleasure that his crime had caused him'. The restriction was not disproportionate and it was legitimate to have regard to the effect the exercise of freedom of expression would have in the world outside the prison.

Freedom of expression does not necessarily include the right to access to information. In *R v Secretary of State for Health ex parte Wagstaff; R v Secretary of State for Health ex parte Associated Newspapers Ltd* (2001), the High Court ruled that the holding in private of the inquiry into the multiple murders committed by Dr Harold Shipman contravened Article 10. It constituted unjustified governmental interference with the reception of information that others wish or may be willing to impart. Compare *R (Persey) v Secretary of State for Environment, Food and Rural Affairs* (2002), in which the High Court distinguished *Wagstaff* and ruled that Article 10 did not impose a positive obligation on government to provide an 'open forum'. The applications related to the Secretary of State's decision to hold three separate, independent inquiries into the outbreak of foot and mouth disease with the evidence for the most part to be heard in private. The court distinguished between the right to freedom of expression and access to information: Article 10 prohibited interference with freedom of expression, it did not require its facilitation. Equally, the High Court ruled in *R (Hard) v Secretary of State for Health* (2002) that there was no presumption one way or the other as to whether an inquiry should be held in public. There was no right of access to information conferred by Article 10. However, in *Open Door Counselling and Dublin Well Woman v Ireland* (1992), the Court of Human Rights ruled that restrictions – an injunction – placed on the dissemination of any information regarding the availability of abortion advice and treatment represented an unlawful restriction and was therefore contrary to Article 10.

RESTRICTIONS ON FREEDOM OF SPEECH

Defamation[8]

Defamation – slander or libel – may be defined as the publication, whether oral or written, of a falsehood which damages the reputation of the person concerned and lowers the victim's reputation in the eyes of 'right thinking members of

---

8   For details, see textbooks on the law of tort.

society generally'.[9] Slander is defamation in the form of the spoken word; libel is defamation in some permanent form, such as publication in books or newspapers. Publication via radio or television broadcasting, or in the course of public theatre performances, is defined as libel rather than slander.[10]

Defamation may attract criminal or civil liability. Criminal libel[11] is rare, and proceedings may not be brought without leave of a High Court judge, which will be granted only where the libel is *prima facie* very serious and the public interest justifies the prosecution. In 1976, a private prosecution was brought against the publishers of *Private Eye* in respect of allegations that Sir James Goldsmith was involved in a conspiracy to obstruct the course of justice.[12] The Law Commission has recommended that criminal libel should be abolished.[13]

Civil liability for defamation is more frequent and poses difficult questions concerning the extent to which freedom of expression is to be balanced against protection of the reputation of others – whether individuals or organisations. Relaxation of the restrictions on reporting imposed by the law of defamation in the United Kingdom were considered, but rejected, by the Faulks Committee.[14]

Technological advances in communications have prompted further regulation. The European Community Directive on Electronic Commerce (the E-Commerce Directive)[15] is given effect in the United Kingdom by the Electronic Commerce (EC Directive) Regulations 2002,[16] the effect of which is to make internet defamation law broadly consistent with the Defamation Act. Defamatory statements in newsgroup postings, e-mails or on web pages are regarded as libel. Defamatory statements made in the course of internet relay chat, internet phone or video teleconferencing are regarded as slander. The practical distinction between the two concepts is that in an action for slander the claimant must prove that he or she has suffered some actual financial losss, but this is not necessary in the case of libel.

Article 14 of the Directive provides that an Internet Service Provider (ISP) is immune from libel actions if it does not have actual knowledge of illegal activity or knowledge of facts or circumstances from which it is apparent that the activity or information is illegal. Where an ISP obtains knowledge of illegal activity, it must act expeditiously to remove or to disable access to the information. Member States must encourage industry self-regulation, including the establishment of codes of conduct. To protect intermediaries who unknowingly disseminate defamatory statements on the internet, it is a defence to show that he or she was not the author, editor or publisher of the statement; took reasonable care in relation to its

---

9　*Sim v Stretch* (1936), p 671.
10　Theatres Act 1968, s 4; Broadcasting Act 1990, s 166.
11　An offence at common law but partly regulated by statute: Libel Act 1843, Law of Libel Amendment Act 1888.
12　*Goldsmith v Pressdram Ltd* (1977) (the prosecution was withdrawn after a settlement was reached with the publishers). See also *Desmond v Thorne* (1982).
13　Working Paper No 84, 1982, London: HMSO. See also Report of the Committee on Defamation, Cmnd 5909, 1975, London: HMSO.
14　Cmnd 5909, 1975; cf the Justice Report, *The Law and the Press*, 1965.
15　Directive 2000/31/EC.
16　SI 2002/2013.

publication and did not know, and had no reason to believe, that what he or she did caused or contributed to the publication of the defamatory statement.[17]

Defences to an action for defamation

The defence of truth

If a statement is damaging to the reputation of another but nevertheless justified on the basis that it is true, no liability will arise. It is not essential that every aspect of a statement must be absolutely true, but it must be true in most material respects.[18] Section 5 of the Defamation Act 1952 provides a statutory defence of truth.[19]

Fair comment

Expressions of opinion on matters of public interest – even though unfair or biased – may be protected under the defence of fair comment. The defence will not succeed if there are factual inaccuracies in the statement or if the statement was motivated by malice. The defence is important in giving limited protection to the publication of comments about public figures whose actions are matters of public interest.[20]

Unintentional defamation

Under section 4 of the Defamation Act 1952, the unintentional, or innocent, publication of statements which are defamatory may be defended. It must be shown that the publisher of the defamation has genuinely tried to make amends either by way of an apology or by correcting the false statement.

Absolute privilege

Some speech is absolutely privileged. That is to say, the words, however libellous, are protected from the law of defamation. An example of such protection is parliamentary privilege; see Chapter 18 on this. As we have seen, Article IX of the Bill of Rights 1689 gives absolute protection to words spoken in proceedings in parliament. Statements made in the course of judicial proceedings also attract absolute privilege; as do statements by the Parliamentary Commissioner for Administration.[21]

Qualified privilege

This offers a more limited protection. A statement will attract qualified privilege provided that the defamatory statement is made without malice. The

---

17 Defamation Act 1996, s 1(1)(a),(b),(c).
18 See eg *Bookbinder v Tebbit* (1989).
19 The protection is not absolute and is restricted, for example, in relation to publications regarding records of former (spent) criminal convictions: Rehabilitation of Offenders Act 1974, s 8.
20 See *Silkin v Beaverbrook Newspapers Ltd* (1958); *Slim v Daily Telegraph Ltd* (1968).
21 Parliamentary Commissioner Act 1967, s 10(5).

Parliamentary Papers Act 1840 gives privilege from defamation laws to fair and accurate reports of proceedings in parliament. Qualified privilege has been held to attach to a communication between a Member of Parliament – who forwarded a constituent's complaint – and the Lord Chancellor and the Law Society where the matter is held to be in the public interest.[22]

Newspapers, radio and television broadcasts also attract qualified privilege. Under the Defamation Act 1952, protection extends to fair and accurate reports of judicial proceedings and international organisations; fair and accurate reports of public meetings; local authority meetings; meetings of public companies; proceedings before statutory tribunals and inquiries; and public election meetings.[23]

Qualified privilege was considered by the House of Lords in *Reynolds v Times Newspapers Ltd* (2001). The former Prime Minister of the Republic of Ireland brought libel proceedings against *The Times* newspaper in relation to an article which, he alleged, suggested that he had lied to parliament and to Cabinet colleagues. No account of the Prime Minister's explanation was given. On qualified privilege, the House of Lords ruled, *inter alia*, that there should be no defence of generic qualified privilege for political information. The article had made serious allegations without giving the former Prime Minister's explanation, and the defence of qualified privilege was not made out and could not be argued by the defendants at the re-trial of the issue.

In *Loutchansky v Times Newspapers Ltd* (2001), the Court of Appeal reconsidered qualified privilege, following the approach laid down in *Reynolds v Times Newspapers Ltd*. In 1999, *The Times* had published two articles in which it accused Grigor Loutchansky of involvement in international criminal activities. The public interest in a democratic society necessitated freedom of expression and the promotion of a free and vigorous press. However, there was a corresponding duty to act responsibly, and no privilege arose unless the press was seen to be acting responsibly. Where that was made out, and there was no malice, the publisher acquired an immunity from legal liability for the publication of statements the truth of which could not be fully proven. Brooke LJ stated that 'the court had to balance the powerful interests of the media in the right to freedom of expression against the interest of an individual who complained that he had been wrongfully defamed'. There was, however, no unfettered right to publish whatever a newspaper believed to be in the public interest. The publication must be consistent with the restriction in Article 10(2) of the Convention on Human Rights.[24]

Qualified privilege came before the Court of Appeal in *Galloway v Telegraph Group Ltd* (2006). The claimant, George Galloway MP, had been awarded damages for libellous articles. The newspaper had to tried to justify the statements as true, but argued that the public had a right to know the contents of the documents even if they were defamatory and irrespective of whether the factual content

---

22   *Beach v Freeson* (1972).
23   Defamation Act 1952, ss 7 and 10.
24   See also *Green v Associated Newspapers Ltd* (2004) and *Jameel (Mohammed) v Wall Street Journal Europe Sprl* (2005).

was true or not. At issue was whether the coverage amounted to 'reportage' – the neutral reporting of allegations – which it was entitled to publish notwithstanding the rule against repetition of a libel. While freedom of expression was of fundamental importance, it had to be balanced against the rights of the individual. In this case the newspaper was not merely reporting what the documents said, but had adopted and embellished them and that was fatal to the defence of qualified privilege.

Sedition, incitement to disaffection and treason[25]

Sedition

Sedition includes words or conduct directed against the peace or authority of the state. Sedition is a common law offence which may involve the spoken word or written materials which are libellous. The intention which must be proven in relation to sedition is that the accused intended to bring 'into hatred or contempt', or 'excite disaffection' against, the Crown or government.[26] The words used must be such that they are intended to promote violence or public disorder. Merely strong criticism, therefore, which is not intended to be inflammatory will not result in liability. Recent use of the law of sedition is seen in *R v Chief Metropolitan Stipendiary Magistrate ex parte Choudhury* (1991), in which the Divisional Court,[27] adopting the test laid down by the Canadian Supreme Court,[28] ruled that the correct test for seditious intention is 'an intention to incite to violence or to create public disturbance or disorder against His Majesty or the institutions of government'.

Incitement to disaffection

The Incitement to Disaffection Act 1934 provides that it is an offence intentionally to attempt to dissuade a member of the armed forces from complying with his duty. It is also an offence to aid, counsel or procure commission of the principal offence. In *R v Arrowsmith* (1975), the defendant was accused and convicted for distributing leaflets to soldiers urging them not to serve in Northern Ireland, and the conviction was upheld by the Court of Appeal.[29] A similar offence exists in relation to causing disaffection within the police force.[30] There also remains on the statute book the Aliens Restriction (Amendment) Act 1919, as amended, section 3 of which prohibits aliens from causing sedition or disaffection among the population and the armed forces, and makes it a summary offence to

---

25 See Robertson, 2001, Chapter 4.
26 *R v Burnes* (1886).
27 On an application for judicial review of a magistrate's refusal to issue summonses against Mr Salman Rushdie, author of *The Satanic Verses*.
28 *Boucher v R* (1951).
29 An application under the European Convention on Human Rights failed: see *Arrowsmith v United Kingdom* (1978).
30 Police Act 1997, s 91.

cause industrial unrest in an industry in which he has not been employed for two years.

Treason

The Treason Act 1351 made it a capital offence to give 'aid and comfort to the King's enemies'. In *Joyce v Director of Public Prosecutions* (1946), William Joyce was convicted of making propaganda broadcasts on behalf of the Nazis during the Second World War. The death penalty for treason and piracy with violence was abolished by the Crime and Disorder Act 1998, section 36. Section 21(5) of the Human Rights Act 1998 abolishes the death penalty for military offences.

Incitement to racial hatred

The first attempt at protecting persons from racial hatred was contained in the Race Relations Act 1965. The justification for restricting offensive racist speech – and hence freedom of expression – lies in the greater need to protect individual minority groups from demeaning and discriminatory speech. Incitement to racial hatred is now regulated under sections 17 to 23 of the Public Order Act 1986.[31] Section 17 defines racial hatred as meaning 'hatred against any group of persons in Great Britain defined by reference to colour, race, nationality (including citizenship) or ethnic or national origins'.

There are two basic requirements which relate to the offences in the Act. First, that the words used, or behaviour, must be 'threatening, abusive or insulting'. Secondly, the words or behaviour must either have been intended to incite racial hatred or be likely to do so. Under the Act, it is an offence to use words or behaviour, or display written material, which have the above elements. Publication of or distributing such material is also an offence.[32] The performance of plays, showing of films or videos or playing of records or broadcasts intended to or likely to incite racial hatred is an offence.[33] The Act, in section 23, also creates the offence of possession of such materials. Prosecutions may only be commenced with the consent of the Attorney General.

Racial abuse at football matches is a criminal offence.[34] The Crime and Disorder Act 1998 extends the law to include racially aggravated offences,[35] a reform prompted by the findings of the inquiry into the death of Stephen Lawrence.[36] The offences of racially aggravated assault, criminal damage, public disorder and harassment are created. In addition, higher sentences may be imposed in relation to any other offences found to be racially motivated.

---

31   As amended by the Criminal Justice and Public Order Act 1994, s 155.
32   Public Order Act 1986, s 19.
33   *Ibid*, ss 20–22.
34   Football (Offences) Act 1991, s 3.
35   Sections 28–32, 82.
36   *The Macpherson Report*, Cmnd 4262.

The Racial and Religious Hatred Act 2006[37]

The Racial and Religious Hatred Act 2006 amends the Public Order Act 1986. Part 3A of the Public Order Act defines religious hatred as being 'hatred against a group of persons defined by reference to religious belief or lack of religious belief'. It is an offence to use threatening words or behaviour, or to display any written material which is threatening, if the person intends to stir up religious hatred. It is also an offence to publish or distribute written material which is threatening if the person intends to stir up religious hatred.[38] The 2006 Act also makes it an offence to present or direct a play which involves the use of threatening words or behaviour if there is intent to stir up religious hatred. The distribution, showing or playing of a recording of visual images or sounds which are threatening is also an offence. It is also an offence to have such materials in one's possession if there is the intention to stir up religious hatred.[39] No proceedings may be brought without the consent of the Attorney General.

The concerns of those who opposed the Bill on the grounds that it would restrict freedom of expression by criminalising discussion or criticism or ridicule of religions or beliefs or practices were met with the insertion of section 29J to the Public Order Act 1986, which now provides that:

> Nothing in this Part shall be read or given effect in a way which prohibits or restricts discussion, criticism or expressions of antipathy, dislike, ridicule, insult or abuse of particular religions or the beliefs or practices of their adherents, or of any other belief system or the beliefs or practices of its adherents, or proselytising or urging adherents of a different religion or belief system to cease practising their religion or belief system.

Obscenity, indecency, censorship and pornography[40]

The Obscene Publications Act 1959

The Obscene Publications Act 1959 creates the offence of publication of an obscene article, whether or not for gain. Further, it is an offence to have such articles in ownership, possession or control for the purpose of publication for gain or with a view to publication.[41] An article[42] is 'obscene' if 'its effect ... is ... such as to tend to deprave and corrupt persons who are likely, having regard to all relevant circumstances, to read, see or hear the matter contained or embodied in it'.[43]

---

37 The Racial and Religious Hatred Act was passed following considerable controversy over the provisions in the Bill. The government had intended to outlaw 'abusive and insulting language and behaviour' and to make it a criminal offence to be 'reckless' in actions that incite religious hatred. However, those provisions were defeated in the House of Commons by 283 to 282 votes. The Act does not extend to Northern Ireland or Scotland.

38 Racial and Religious Hatred Act 2006, Schedule, inserting ss 29A, 29B and 29C respectively to the Public Order Act 1986.

39 *Ibid,* inserting ss 29D, 29E and 29F to the 1986 Act.

40 See Robertson, 2001, Chapter 5. On feminist arguments against pornography, see Smart, 1989, especially Chapter 6; Itzin, 1992; Barnett, 1998, Chapter 12.

41 Obscene Publications Act 1959, s 2(1), as amended.

42 Which covers books, pictures, films, records and video cassettes.

43 Obscene Publications Act 1959, s 1(1).

An article will be 'published', according to section 1(3), if a person:

(a) distributes, circulates, sells, lets on hire, gives or lends it, or who offers it for sale or for letting on hire; or

(b) in the case of an article containing or embodying matter to be looked at or a record, shows, plays or projects it.

The Criminal Justice and Public Order Act 1994 amends section 1(3) by adding the words 'or where the matter is stored electronically, transmits that data'.[44]

The tendency to 'deprave and corrupt'

It is not sufficient that an article disgusts, or is 'filthy', 'loathsome' or 'lewd'.[45] What must be established is that the article will 'deprave or corrupt'.[46] Nor is it sufficient that the article is capable of depraving or corrupting just one person: the test is whether or not a significant proportion of persons likely to read or see the article would be depraved or corrupted by it.[47] The fact that the persons likely to read the article regularly read such materials is irrelevant to whether or not the material can deprave or corrupt,[48] although the same argument may not hold if the likely audience is police officers experienced with dealing with pornography.[49]

In *Handyside v United Kingdom* (1976),[50] in which a publication entitled *The Little Red Schoolbook* had been seized under the Obscene Publications Act 1959, the Court of Human Rights ruled that there was no violation of Article 10.[51] The publishers claimed that the Obscene Publications Act represented a violation of Article 10 in several respects. The Court ruled that there was no breach of the Convention. The 'protection of morals' clause in Article 10(2) entitled the government to impose restrictions on freedom of expression, provided that the restrictions were proportionate to the aim pursued. It was for the Court to decide whether the restrictions were necessary and sufficient. In this case, the book was aimed at under 18 year olds and encouraged promiscuity.

There exists a defence of public good[52] but the defence is interpreted narrowly.[53] For example, in *Director of Public Prosecutions v Jordan* (1977),[54] where the defendant argued the psychotherapeutic benefit of 'soft porn' for the consumer, the judge rejected the defence, holding that what was for the public good was art, literature or science. It is an offence to send or attempt to send

---

44   Criminal Justice and Public Order Act 1994, s 84. See *R v Fellows and Arnold* (1997).

45   *R v Anderson* (1972).

46   *R v Martin Secker and Warburg* (1954).

47   *DPP v Whyte* (1972), *per* Lord Wilberforce.

48   *Shaw v DPP* (1962).

49   *R v Clayton and Halsey* (1963).

50   See also *Muller v Switzerland* (1991).

51   See also *Wingrove v United Kingdom* (1996) and *Otto-Preminger Institut v Austria* (1994) on the law of blasphemy. On public order, see *Steel v UK* (1998) and *Hashman and Harrup v UK* (2000).

52   Obscene Publications Act 1959, s 4.

53   See eg *R v Penguin Books Ltd* (1973).

54   And see *Attorney General's Reference (No 3 of 1977)* (1978).

indecent or obscene materials through the post.[55] It is also an offence to import indecent or obscene materials. Such materials may be forfeited.[56]

Indecency and pornography

While offences relating to obscenity requires proof relating to its tendency to 'deprave and corrupt', indecency requires no such proof and is of a lesser order. Lord Parker in *R v Stanley* (1965) stated that indecency was 'something that offends the ordinary modesty of the average man . . . offending against recognised standards of propriety at the lower end of the scale.'[57]

Pornography is not a legal concept. There is no legal prohibition against pornography as such – rather prosecutions will be brought under the headings of obscenity and/or indecency. Pornography does, however, raise a number of issues which are of particular concern to feminists and the literature is now extensive. The pornography industry is both global and vast. Concerns about pornography include the protection of women who work in the industry, and the impact that pornographic representations of women has on the status of women in society. However, the attempt in the United States to outlaw pornography on the grounds – *inter alia* – that it undermines women's equality, failed: freedom of expression prevailed.[58]

Broadcasting, cinemas, theatres and video recordings

Section 2 of the Theatres Act 1968 prohibits obscenity in theatrical performances. The law relating to obscenity applies to live performances, subject to the defence of public good. Legal regulation of live performances also exists in the form of section 20 of the Public Order Act 1986, which prohibits the use of threatening, abusive or insulting words or behaviour intended or likely to stir up racial hatred. Section 6 of the Theatres Act prohibits words or behaviour likely to cause a breach of the peace. In order to avoid frivolous or censorious legal action, the consent of the Attorney General is required in relation to prosecutions under the Theatres Act, Public Order Act and Sexual Offences Act.

The Broadcasting Act 1990 and Video Recordings Act 1984 each prohibited obscenity on local radio services, television and video. In relation to broadcasting, the British Broadcasting Corporation (BBC), established under the royal prerogative,[59] is under a duty not to adopt its own political stance on current affairs, and may only broadcast party political programmes with the consent of the major political parties.

---

55 Post Office Act 1953, s 11.
56 Customs Consolidation Act 1876 and Customs and Excise Management Act 1979, s 49.
57 See Robertson, 1979, Chapter 7.
58 See Dworkin, 1981.
59 The BBC was established by Royal Charter. Its chairman and governors are appointed by the Crown on the advice of the Prime Minister. The BBC operates under licence from the government issued under the Wireless Telegraphy Acts 1904–67.

The Office of Communications (OFCOM)

The Office of Communications Act 2002 established OFCOM in preparation for the transfer of regulatory functions from the former broadcasting regulators.[60] The Communications Act 2003 provided for the transfer of functions from five bodies or office holders to OFCOM. The relevant bodies and offices are:

- the Broadcasting Standards Commission;
- the Director General of Telecommunications who had responsibilities for regulating Oftel, a non-ministerial government department which regulated the telecommunications operators in the United Kingdom;
- the Independent Television Commission;
- the Radio Authority, which had regulatory and licensing powers in relation to all non-BBC radio services broadcasting in the United Kingdom, whose powers derived from the Broadcasting Acts 1990 and 1996;
- the Secretary of State with regulatory powers in respect of radio exercised through the Radiocommunications Agency, an executive agency of the Department of Trade and Industry.

The general duties of OFCOM are set out in section 3 of the Communications Act 2003. OFCOM's principal duty is to further the interests of the public and to further consumer interests where appropriate through promoting competition. OFCOM is required to act in accordance with European Community requirements as laid down in EC Communications Directives which were adopted in 2002 and which provide for a common regulatory framework for electronic communications networks and services. The 2003 Act is designed to ensure that EC requirements are met. OFCOM is required to ensure a wide availability of a range of television and radio services and maintain a sufficient plurality of providers. It is also required to protect members of the public from offensive and harmful material and to apply standards in television and radio services which protect people from unfair treatment and infringements of privacy. In exercising its functions, OFCOM is to have regard to the principles of transparency, accountability and proportionality.[61]

The Secretary of State for Trade and Industry and Secretary of State for Culture, Media and Sport each has responsibilities in relation to OFCOM. OFCOM is accountable to Parliament through select committees and the National Audit Office.

Film and video

The regulation of films falls to the British Board of Film Classification (BBFC), and their availability for viewing by the public controlled by local authorities. The

---

60 See the White Paper, *A New Future For Communications* (Cm 5010).

61 The OFCOM board does not meet in public to reach decisions, in part to protect commercial confidentiality. According to Lord Currie of Marylebone, OFCOM's Chairman, the Board will be open and transparent in its consultation processes and in the giving of reasons for its decisions: see the Minutes of Evidence taken before the Select Committee on Culture, Media and Sport, 16 December 2003, HC 132-i.

BBFC operates a system of classification by age: 'U' for general circulation, 'PG' (parental guidance), 12, 12A (children under 12 accompanied by an adult), 15, and 18 certificate films, and R18 films which are for restricted viewing only on segregated premises. The BBFC may refuse a certificate if the film contravenes the Obscene Publications Act 1959, and may insist on cuts to a film before a certificate is granted. Local authorities exercise control through the granting of licences for a particular film to be shown in its area.[62]

The BBFC also classifies videos for private viewing. The Video Recordings Act 1984 requires that the BBFC should have 'special regard to the likelihood of video works being viewed in the home' (section 4). The BBFC must also pay 'special regard' to the harm caused to potential viewers by the depiction of criminal activity, illegal drugs, violence and sexual behaviour.[63] The growth of the internet led to the transmission of electronically stored data being included within the Obscene Publications Act 1959 definition of 'publication'.[64] However, the likelihood of enforcement is slim, given the nature of the internet and the ability of anyone, worldwide, to place items on it.

Conspiracy to corrupt public morals

Under the common law, publishers may be liable for the offence of conspiracy to corrupt public morals. In *Shaw v Director of Public Prosecutions* (1962), Shaw, the publisher of a directory giving the names and details of prostitutes, was prosecuted for conspiracy to corrupt public morals.[65] The House of Lords (Lord Reid dissenting) held that the courts have a 'residual power to enforce the supreme and fundamental purpose of the law, to conserve not only the safety and order but also the moral welfare of the state'.[66]

Shaw v Director of Public Prosecutions was upheld in *Knuller Ltd v Director of Public Prosecutions* (1973). The publishers had produced a magazine containing advertisements for male homosexuals. The House of Lords upheld *Shaw*, rejecting as a defence the fact that the Sexual Offences Act 1967 provided that homosexual acts between adult males, in private, were no longer an offence. The use of this common law offence is rare; nevertheless, it remains an available offence which enables the state to avoid statutory offences which provide defences such as that of the 'public good'.[67]

Blasphemy and blasphemous libel[68]

Blasphemy is a common law offence which prohibits words which cause outrage to the feelings of a Christian by abusing Christ or by denying or attacking the

---

62 Under the Cinemas Act 1985.
63 Under the Criminal Justice and Public Order Act 1994, s 90.
64 *Ibid*, s 168.
65 Shaw was also found guilty of an offence under the Obscene Publications Act 1959. See further above.
66 Seaborne Davies, 1962.
67 Obscene Publications Act 1959, s 4.
68 See Kenny, 1992.

established church. Between 1922 and 1977, there were no prosecutions brought and it was thought that the offence had fallen into disuse. In 1976, however, the magazine *Gay News* published a poem and illustration depicting Christ at the Crucifixion. A private prosecution against the editor and publisher was instigated,[69] alleging that the poem and illustration 'vilified Christ in His Life and His Crucifixion'. The resulting case was *R v Lemon* (1979), in which the jury, by a majority verdict, found the words and drawing blasphemous.[70] On appeal to the House of Lords, the question of law concerned the mental element required for a conviction of blasphemy. By a majority, the House of Lords held that there was no need to prove an intention to blaspheme, but rather that it was sufficient to prove that a blasphemous libel – a publication calculated to outrage and insult a Christian's religious beliefs – had been published. The majority[71] dismissed the appeal against conviction, holding that the law required no more than an intention to publish words found by the jury to be blasphemous. It was unnecessary to hold[72] that there was an intention to offend, or reckless indifference as to whether or not offence was caused.

In Lord Scarman's opinion, the law should be extended to protect the religious beliefs and feelings of non-Christians. Lord Scarman stated that:

> ... the offence belongs to a group of criminal offences designed to safeguard the internal tranquillity of the kingdom. In an increasingly plural society such as that of modern Britain it is necessary not only to respect the differing religious beliefs, feelings and practices of all but also to protect them from scurrility, vilification, ridicule and contempt. [p 658]

This view was not to prevail, however. In *R v Chief Metropolitan Stipendiary Magistrate ex parte Choudhury* (1991), it was held that blasphemy remained confined to protection of the Christian religion as exemplified by the established Church of England, and did not extend to the protection of the Islamic faith. That the law should offer such limited and discriminatory protection is both anachronistic and offensive to the principle of equality in a pluralistic society. The Law Commission in 1985 recommended that the offence be abolished,[73] but the government has not acted on this recommendation.[74]

The European Court of Human Rights upheld the state's right to control blasphemous materials in *Wingrove v United Kingdom* (1996). The British Board of Film Classification refused to issue a certificate for *Visions of Ecstasy*, on the ground that the film blasphemed Jesus Christ. The Court ruled that the restriction on freedom of expression was justified under Article 10(2).[75]

---

69 By Mrs Mary Whitehouse.
70 See also *Gay News Ltd v United Kingdom* (1982).
71 Lords Scarman, Dilhorne and Russell.
72 As did Lords Diplock and Edmund-Davies.
73 See Report No 145; also Working Paper No 79, *Offences Against Religion and Public Worship* (1981), and Robilliard, 1981.
74 HC Deb Col 395, 27 June 1989.
75 On the Racial and Religious Hatred Act 2006 see p 565 above.

Contempt of court

The law relating to contempt of court developed in order to protect the judiciary and judicial proceedings from actions or words which impede or adversely affect the administration of justice, or 'tends to obstruct, prejudice or abuse the administration of justice'.[76] Contempt of court, under English but not Scottish law, may be criminal or civil. In relation to criminal contempt, which may be dealt with in both the civil and criminal courts, the action relates to conduct which is designed to interfere with the administration of justice, which may of itself involve a criminal offence. The court has the power to rule on the existence of a contempt and to punish the guilty party. Where the judge finds the person guilty of contempt, he may commit the person instantly to prison. Two principal forms of criminal contempt exist.

Scandalising the court

The need to maintain public confidence in the judiciary underpins this offence. Criticism of a judge, or a court's decision, may be a contempt if it suggests bias or unfairness on the part of the judge or court.[77]

Contempt in the face of the court

Conduct in court which impedes the judicial process may be a contempt. A demonstration which interrupts proceedings,[78] or insulting behaviour, or refusal of a witness to answer questions or give evidence or comply with a court order to disclose information, may amount to contempt.[79]

Publications prejudicing the course of justice

The balance to be struck between freedom of expression and the protection of judicial proceedings is a matter for debate. The Contempt of Court Act 1981, which reformed the common law of contempt, sought to achieve the appropriate balance. Before that Act, the law relating to contempt proved capable of inhibiting freedom of the press for an extensive period of time, where judicial proceedings became protracted. The leading case which presaged reform of the law is that of *Sunday Times v United Kingdom* (1979). In 1974, the House of Lords restored an injunction[80] prohibiting *The Sunday Times* from publishing articles relating to the drug Thalidomide, manufactured by Distillers Ltd, which, it was alleged, caused serious deformities in babies. The parents of the affected children intended to sue Distillers for compensation. The company entered into protracted negotiations

---

76 Report of the Phillimore Committee on Contempt of Court, Cmnd 5794, 1974, p 2. See Dhavan, 1976.
77 See *R v New Statesman (Editor) ex parte DPP* (1928); *Ambard v Attorney General for Trinidad and Tobago* (1936); *R v Metropolitan Police Commissioner ex parte Blackburn (No 2)* (1968).
78 See *Morris v Crown Office* (1970).
79 See *Attorney General v Mulholland and Foster* (1970); *British Steel Corporation v Granada Television Ltd* (1963).
80 *Attorney General v Times Newspapers Ltd* (1974). The injunction had been discharged by the Court of Appeal.

with the families' solicitors. The injunction restrained any further publication on the matter by the newspaper. *The Sunday Times* made an application under Article 10 of the European Convention on Human Rights, which protects freedom of expression, alleging that the common law of contempt violated Article 10. The European Court of Human Rights held that there had been a violation of Article 10. As a result, the Contempt of Court Act 1981 was enacted, clarifying the law on pre-trial publicity.[81]

The Contempt of Court Act 1981

Section 1 of the Contempt of Court Act provides for the 'strict liability rule'. The rule is defined as 'the rule of law whereby conduct may be treated as a contempt of court as tending to interfere with the course of justice in particular legal proceedings *regardless of intent to do so*' (emphasis added). In order for the strict liability rule to be established, a number of issues need to be satisfied. First, the test relates only to publications falling within section 2 of the Act. Publications are defined in section 2(1) as including 'any speech, writing [programme included in a programme service][82] or other communication in whatever form, which is addressed to the public at large or any section of the public'. Secondly, the publication must be such that it 'creates a substantial risk that the course of justice in the proceedings in question will be seriously impeded or prejudiced'.[83] Thirdly, the strict liability rule applies only if the proceedings in question are 'active', as defined by Schedule 2 to the Act. In relation to appellate proceedings, these are active from the time they are commenced, by an application for leave to appeal or apply for review, or by notice of appeal or of application to review or by other originating process, 'until disposed of or abandoned, discontinued or withdrawn'.[84] In relation to criminal proceedings, the starting point is the issue of a warrant for arrest, arrest without warrant or the service of an indictment.[85] The end point is acquittal, sentence, any other verdict or discontinuance of the trial. In relation to civil proceedings, the start point is when the case is set down for a hearing in the High Court. The end point is when the proceedings are disposed of, discontinued or withdrawn.[86]

It is a defence to prove that, at the time of publication, or distribution of the publication, he or she does not know, and has no reason to suspect, that relevant proceedings are active.[87] Fair and accurate reports of legal proceedings, held in public and published 'contemporaneously and in good faith' do not attract the strict liability rule.[88] In addition, if publication is made as, or as part of, a discussion in 'good faith of public affairs or other matters of general public

---

81   See further Chapter 22 on Article 10 and rights of protest.
82   Added by the Broadcasting Act 1990, s 203.
83   See *Re Lonrho* (1990).
84   Contempt of Court Act 1981, Sched 2, para 15.
85   *Ibid*, Sched 1, para 4.
86   *Ibid*, Sched 1, paras 12 and 13. See *Attorney General v Hislop and Pressdam* (1991).
87   *Ibid*, s 3(1), (2).
88   *Ibid*, s 4.

interest', it is not to be treated as contempt of court, 'if the risk of impediment or prejudice to particular legal proceedings is merely incidental to the discussion'.[89]

The issue of whether to order the postponement of reporting of a trial in the interests of justice, until after the conclusion of a second related trial was considered in *R v Sherwood ex parte The Telegraph Group plc* (2001). The Court of Appeal dismissed an appeal against an order made under section 4(2) of the Contempt of Court Act 1981 during the trial of a police constable for murder. The order prevented reporting on that trial until after the conclusion of a second trial against three other defendants who were originally co-defendants of the accused. The jurisdiction to make a postponement order under the 1981 Act operated in light of Articles 6 (right to fair trial) and 10 (right to freedom of expression) of the Convention. The 1981 Act required the court to consider whether a ban was necessary to avoid the perceived risk of prejudice. Even if such a risk was not demonstrated, however, it did not follow that an order had to be made. The next question to address was whether such an order was 'necessary' within the meaning of Article 10(2) of the Convention.[90]

Section 10 of the Contempt of Court Act regulates the disclosure of sources. The court may not require disclosure, and a person will not be guilty of contempt as a result of non-disclosure unless the court is satisfied that 'disclosure is necessary in the interests of justice or national security or for the prevention of disorder or crime'. The leading case is *X Ltd v Morgan Grampian* (1991), in which the House of Lords ruled on the decision making process entailed in section 10. In that case, a confidential plan was stolen from the plaintiffs and information from the plan given to a journalist. The plaintiffs applied for an order requiring the journalist, William Goodwin, to disclose the source and sought discovery of his notes of the telephone conversation in order to discover the identity of the source. The House of Lords, in balancing the competing interests – the applicant's right to take legal action against the source and the journalist's interest in maintaining confidentiality with the source – held that the interests of the plaintiffs outweighed the interests of the journalist. This decision led to an application under Article 10 of the European Convention – the right to freedom of expression. In *Goodwin v United Kingdom* (1996), the Court ruled that the order against the journalist violated his right to freedom of expression which was central to a free press.[91]

It is for the court to determine whether a particular decision making forum is a 'court' for the purposes of the law of contempt of court. In *General Medical Council v British Broadcasting Corporation* (1998), the Court of Appeal ruled that the Professional Conduct Committee (PCC) of the General Medical Council was not part of the judicial process of the state and accordingly was not subject to

---

89 See *Attorney General v English* (1983); *Attorney General v TVS Television*; *Attorney General v HW Southey & Sons* (1989); *Pickering v Liverpool Daily Post and Echo Newspapers plc* (1991). See also the Public Interest Disclosure Act 1998, which amends the Employment Rights Act 1996 and provides protection for employees who disclose wrongdoing by his or her employer.

90 The disclosure of jury discussions, for the purpose of prompting an official investigation into the facts, to an unauthorised person, is contempt of court. The House of Lords so ruled in *Attorney General v Scotcher* (2005).

91 On freedom of expression under the Convention, see also Chapter 19.

the Contempt of Court Act 1981. The PCC was a statutory committee under the Medical Act 1983, which exercised a sort of judicial power, but it was not the judicial power of the state. It had a recognisable judicial function, but was not part of the judicial system of the state.

Where the judge considers that disclosure is necessary in the interests of justice, a discretion remains as to whether disclosure should be ordered. That involved weighing up the competing interests of the need for disclosure and the need for protection of sources. In *John v Express Newspapers* (2000), the Court of Appeal ruled that the need to protect journalistic sources overrode the need for disclosure of the source of a confidential document which had come into the hands of a journalist by a breach of confidentiality in relation to legal advice given by a firm of solicitors.[92] However, the exercise of discretion led to a different conclusion in *Camelot Group plc v Centaur* (1999). In that case, a disloyal employee of Camelot sent a copy of draft accounts to a journalist employed by the defendant. The Court of Appeal ruled that the public interest in enabling the plaintiffs to discover a disloyal employee who leaked confidential information was greater than the public interest in enabling the employee to escape detection. The order for disclosure was upheld.

Contempt of court and Article 10 of the European Convention

The impact of the Human Rights Act 1998 is being felt in this area of law. In *Ashworth Security Hospital v MGN Ltd* (2002), the *Mirror* newspaper had published verbatim extracts from hospital medical records of information concerning a convicted murderer who was detained at the hospital. The information had been supplied to the newspaper, in breach of confidence and breach of contract, by a hospital employee through an intermediary. The Contempt of Court Act 1981, section 10, provided for orders of disclosure of sources of information only where it was established that 'disclosure is necessary in the interests of justice or national security or for the prevention of disorder or crime'. The hospital had failed to identify the informant and sought an order that MGN identify the intermediary as the only likely means of discovering the source's identity. MGN argued that such an order would contravene Article 10 of the Convention. The Court of Appeal ruled that unless the source was identified and dismissed, there was a significant risk that there would be further selling of confidential information, and that such disclosures amounted to an attack on confidentiality which should be safeguarded in any democratic society. Where a person against whom disclosure was sought – in this case the intermediary – had 'become mixed-up in wrongful, albeit not tortious, conduct that infringed a claimant's legal rights', the court had jurisdiction to order disclosure. The decision was affirmed by the House of Lords. In *Interbrew SA v Financial Times* (2002), the court declared itself bound by the decision in *Ashworth*. A claimant was entitled to an order for delivery up of leaked

---

92 See also the Court of Appeal's refusal to order disclosure to the police of supposed evidence relating to former MI5 officer, David Shayler, held by *The Guardian* and *The Observer* newspapers: *The Guardian*, 21 July 2000.

and partly forged documents held by publishers in order to enable him to ascertain the proper defendant to a breach of confidence action. The 'public interest in protecting the source of a leak was not sufficient to withstand the countervailing public interest in letting Interbrew seek justice in the courts against the source'.[93]

However, the importance of protecting journalistic sources was recognised in *Mersey Care NHS Trust v Ackroyd* (2006), the sequel to *Ashworth Hospital Authority v MGN Ltd (supra)*. The Hospital Trust had commenced an action against the journalist identified as a result of the order of disclosure, Mr Ackroyd, in the attempt to compel the journalist to reveal the source of his information. The High Court ruled that in balancing conflicting rights – the right to privacy and the right to freedom of expression – it was necessary to apply the guidelines set out in *Campbell v Mirror Group Newspapers plc* (2004)[94]. Applying those guidelines, the court came to the opposite conclusion to that reached in the *Ashworth Hospital* case. Here an order for disclosure would not be proportionate to the hospital's legitimate aim to seek redress against the source, given 'the vital public interest in the protection of a journalist's source'.

In *Attorney General v Punch Ltd* (2002), the former editor of *Punch*, and the publishers, had been fined for being in contempt of court. At issue was the publication by *Punch* of an article by David Shayler, the former MI5 officer. The Attorney General had been granted injunctions on the basis that revelations by David Shayler about matters relating to his employment would be contrary to national security. The question was, where a court ordered that specified material was not to be published, would a third party who, with the knowledge of the order, published the specified material automatically commit a contempt of court, or would contempt only occur if the third party thereby knowingly defeated the purpose for which the order was made? The House of Lords ruled that the editor must have known that by publishing the article he was doing 'precisely what the court order was intended to prevent, namely, pre-empting the court's decision on the confidentiality issues relevant to trial'.

In *Cream Holdings Ltd v Banerjee* (2004) the claimants sought an interim injunction to restrain publication of confidential information supplied by a former employee of the claimants who had obtained the information without permission. This raised the issue of the freedom of the press in relation to section 12(3) of the Human Rights Act 1998, which provides that no injunctive relief should be granted so as to restrain publication unless the court is satisfied that the applicant is likely to establish that publication should not be allowed. The House of Lords ruled that the principal purpose for which section 12(3) was enacted was to protect freedom of speech by setting a higher threshold for the granting of interlocutory injunctions against the media.

---

93 The restriction on publication of information which would lead to the identification of an HIV healthcare workers (here a dentist) was justified under Article 10(2) according to the Court of Appeal in *H v N (A Health Authority); H v Associated Newspapers Ltd* (2002).

94 Discussed below at p 578.

The House of Lords ruled that to construe the word 'likely' as to mean 'more likely than not' in all situations would impose too high a test; that there could be no single rigid standard governing all applications and some flexibility was needed. All the circumstances of the case had to be taken into consideration. Generally, the court should not make an interim restraint order unless it was satisfied 'that the applicant's prospects of success at trial were sufficiently favourable to justify the order being made in the light of all the other circumstances of the case'. In the instant case, the disclosures were matters of serious public interest and the claimants' prospects of success at trial were not sufficiently high to justify making an interim order.[95]

In *In re S (A Child) (Identification: Restrictions on Publication)* (2004), the House of Lords considered the basis of the courts' jurisdiction to restrain publicity to protect a child's private and family life by way of injunction. The Court ruled that jurisdiction derived from Convention rights rather than the inherent jurisdiction of the High Court. At issue here was the conflict between the child's right to private and family life under Article 8 and the right of freedom of expression (of the press) under Article 10.

The House of Lords stated that:

> . . . neither Article as such had precedence over the other, the correct approach being to focus on the comparative importance of the specific rights claimed in the individual case, with the justifications for interfering or restricting each right being taken into account and the proportionality test applied to each . . .

On the fact of this case, the Court declared that:

> . . . although the ordinary rule was that the press could report everything that took place in a criminal court, it was the duty of the court to examine with care each application for a departure from the rule by reason of Article 8, but in so doing the court was not . . . . to create further exceptions by a process of analogy save in the most compelling circumstances. . . .

The freedom of the press to report criminal proceedings would be inhibited by an extension of the protection of Article 8 and there should be no injunction granted.

Law of confidence

Injunctions are orders of a court, which can be either permanent or interim. Injunctions impose what is called a 'prior restraint', that is to say, they prevent disclosure of information in advance to avoid publication. An injunction can be granted on the basis that the proposed item is libellous (defamatory) or in breach of the common law duty of confidence. In the case of alleged libel, judges are reluctant to impose a 'prior restraint' if the defendant swears that he or she can prove the truth of the defamatory statement or can defend it on the basis of 'fair comment'. In cases of breach of confidence, the judges are more willing to grant the injunction. An example of this is seen in *Schering Chemical v Falkman Ltd* (1981). In *Schering*, a Thames Television documentary about a pregnancy drug was

---

95   On prior restraint see also *Martha Greene v Association Newspapers Ltd* (2004).

scheduled for transmission. The programme's producer had been engaged as a consultant to the drug manufacturers and the programme revealed material obtained by him during his consultancy. The court held that a duty of confidence existed, which should be enforced by injunction. In 1987, the BBC intended to transmit a television documentary *My Country Right or Wrong* in which former security officers were interviewed. An injunction was granted on the basis that there had occurred a breach of confidence in the course of the interviews.[96] The BBC was vetted by the Attorney General, who then withdrew the action but, nevertheless, the transmission of the programme had been delayed for six months. The book *Spycatcher,* written by a former member of the Security Services, was also restrained by way of an injunction based on breach of confidence owed to the Service. See Chapter 25 for a discussion of *Spycatcher*. One objectionable aspect of the use of such prior restraint is that there exists no trial of the merits of the work which is being restrained: an injunction is issued, and the trial of the facts may occur much later, when it may transpire that there has been an unjustified, and often lengthy, restriction on freedom of expression.

The notion of breach of confidence, originally relevant mainly to trade secrets and unfair competition and industrial espionage, has expanded in no particularly logical way, proceeding on a case by case basis. Disclosure of information may amount to breach of confidence if the relationship is based on marriage,[97] contracts of employment, consultancies and potentially any situation involving a 'confidential relationship'. A duty of confidence is owed to Cabinet by individual ministers,[98] and by members of the Security Services and civil servants to the Crown.[99] Where such a relationship is held to exist, an obligation is imposed to keep information confidential and a proposed disclosure will found an action for breach of confidence.

However the law relating to breach of confidence has been expanded to a degree which suggests that, while there is no right to privacy under common law, privacy claims are being given greater protection than was the case prior to the Human Rights Act 1998. In *Douglas v Hello! Ltd* (2001), the Court of Appeal ruled that individuals had a right of personal privacy which was grounded in the equitable doctrine of breach of confidence.[100] Michael Douglas and Catherine Zeta Jones had granted *OK!* magazine exclusive rights to publish photographs of their wedding. *Hello!* magazine had obtained photographs of the wedding and had been subjected to an interim injunction restraining publication before the trial of the substantive issues.[101] In this case, the claimants had lessened the degree of privacy concerning their wedding by allowing *OK!* magazine to publish photographs, thereby affecting the balance between their rights (to privacy) and

---

96 *The Times,* 5 and 18 December 1987.
97 See *Duke of Argyll v Duchess* (1967).
98 See Chapter 11.
99 See Chapters 25 and 11, respectively.
100 See also *Earl Spencer v United Kingdom* (1998), in which the Court of Human Rights stated, *inter alia,* that the claim to breach of privacy could have been adequately protected under the common law of breach of confidence.
101 Breach of confidence, malicious falsehood and interference with contractual relations.

the rights of others to freedom of expression. The court discharged the injunction. However, in a strong statement of principle, Sedley LJ said that 'we have reached a point at which it can be said with confidence that the law recognises and will appropriately protect a right of personal privacy'.

In *Campbell v Mirror Group Newspapers (MGN) Ltd* (2002), the model Naomi Campbell was awarded damages, albeit minimal, by the High Court for the disclosure of information relating to her attending meetings for the treatment of drug addiction. By a majority of three to two, the House of Lords held that the 'broad test' to be applied was 'whether disclosure of the information ... would give substantial offence to a reasonable person of ordinary sensibilities assuming that the person was placed in similar circumstances'. Lord Hope stated that the right to privacy (which lies at the heart of an action for breach of confidence) had to be balanced against the right of the media to publish information. Conversely, the media's freedom of expression had to be balanced against the respect which had to be given to private life. In this case, Lord Hope said that had it not been for the publication of photographs of Ms Campbell leaving the place of treatment, the balance between the competing rights would have been 'about even'. However, the photographs 'added greatly' to the intrusion of the claimant's private life and their publication outweighed the defendants' right to freedom of expression.[102]

Campbell may be compared with *A v B plc* (2002). The Court of Appeal ruled that any interference with freedom of the press had to be justified, and could not be limited because there was no identifiable public interest in the material being published. The court distinguished between the confidentiality which attached to sexual relations within marriage 'or other stable relationships' and the confidentiality which attached to transient relationships. Here, a footballer, A, had had sexual relationships with C and D. He did not want his wife to find out. C and D, however, had no interest in maintaining confidentiality. The Lord Chief Justice recognised that the Convention provided 'new parameters within which the court would decide in an action for breach of confidence whether a person was entitled to have his privacy protected', or 'whether the intrusion into freedom of information which such protection involved could not be justified'. In this case, it was not obvious why an injunction should be granted: A's relationships were not in the categories of relationships which the court should be astute to protect when other parties did not want them to remain confidential. Freedom of the press should prevail, and regulation of reporting in the press should be a matter for the Press Council, not the courts.

---

102 In *Campbell v Mirror Group Newspapers Ltd (No 2)* (2005) the House of Lords ruled that where a successful claimant in a libel action had entered into a conditional fee arrangement which included a percentage uplift as a success fee, the newspaper's liability in costs to pay that success fee was not incompatible with its right to freedom of expression, even though the claimant might have sufficient resources to be able to fund her own litigation without resorting to such an agreement. The newspaper had argued that the threat of liability to pay a large sum by way of costs was just as likely to inhibit freedom of expression as the threat of liability to pay a large sum by way of damages. The House of Lords disagreed: the Access to Justice Act 1999 provided that all costs were recoverable from the unsuccessful party and conditional fee arrangements were available to everyone, irrespective of their personal resources.

In exceptional circumstances, where individuals are at serious risk of injury or death if their identity or whereabouts become known, the law of confidence can be applied to protect them. The Family Division of the High Court so held in *Venables v News Group Newspapers* (2001). In exceptional circumstances, taking into account the Human Rights Act 1998, the court had jurisdiction to extent the protection of confidentiality where 'not to do so would be likely to lead to serious physical injury, or the death of the person seeking that confidentiality', and there was no other way to protect the applicant other than seeking injunctive relief.

Defences to an action for breach of confidence include the following:

Staleness

In *Attorney General v Jonathan Cape Ltd* (1976) (the *Crossman Diaries* case) the information disclosed in breach of confidence was some ten years old and no harm would follow from its publication. Accordingly, the court held that, in the absence of a breach of national security, further restraint was not justified. However, in the *Spycatcher* case, *Attorney General v Guardian (No 2)* (1990), while the injunction was eventually lifted, the government claimed that the duty of former Security Service personnel is lifelong and that no publication of any matter concerning their employment may be disclosed. Section 1 of the Official Secrets Act 1989 now reflects this duty and imposes criminal sanctions on any revelations made in relation to security matters.

The material is in the public domain

While there may be found to be a duty of confidence, this duty does not necessarily result in an injunction being permanently imposed to restrain publication. In addition to the material being 'stale', it may be that the material has already been published elsewhere, and is thus in the 'public domain'. In relation to the book *Spycatcher*, this matter weighed with the court. The book had been published in Australia and the United States of America and was, in fact, freely available anywhere outside the United Kingdom. In *Attorney General v Times Newspapers Ltd* (2001) the Court of Appeal ruled that it was the responsibility of the newspaper's editors to form a judgment about whether material had been brought sufficiently into the public domain. The editor was not required to seek confirmation from either the Attorney General or the court that this was the case. Such an approach, the court ruled, was 'consonant with Article 10 of the European Convention on Human Rights and section 12 of the [Human Rights] Act'.

Revealing true information to correct falsity

Irrespective of the existence of a duty of confidence, there may be situations where material has been published which is false and which justifies a breach of confidence in order to rectify the falsehood. In *Woodward v Hutchins* (1977), for example, a falsehood concerning a pop star had been published. Notwithstanding a duty of confidence, there was a justified and legitimate need for rebuttal of the untruths.

Iniquity: to reveal evidence of crime/fraud

Breach of confidence may be excused by the court if the defence of revealing criminal or fraudulent activities is made out.

Public interest

The defence of public interest was considered in *Lion Laboratories v Evans and Express Newspapers* (1984). The *Express* newspaper revealed information concerning faulty intoximeters used to measure the extent of alcohol in an individual's bloodstream. Deficiencies in the breathalyser equipment could have resulted in wrongful convictions for driving under the influence of alcohol. The disclosure of confidential information was justified. There was no question of the manufacturer having been guilty of any 'iniquity' or wrongdoing. However, the matter was one of public interest which overrode any claim to confidentiality of the information. Public interest disclosures by employees are now protected under the Public Interest Disclosure Act 1998 which amends the Employment Rights Act 1996.

PRIVACY

The idea that individuals have a 'right to privacy' has a strong and intuitive hold on the popular imagination: the autonomous human being claims a protective personal and family sphere into which others may not intrude without permission. Privacy is inextricably linked to liberty: the freedom from restriction on lawful activities whether by the state, its agents, or private bodies or individuals. As John Stuart Mill wrote in *On Liberty*:

> ... the sole end for which mankind are warranted, individually or collectively, in interfering with the liberty of action of any of their number, is self-protection. [That] the only purpose for which power can be rightfully exercised over any member of a civilised community, against his will, is to prevent harm to others. His own good, either physical or moral, is not a sufficient warrant.

The idea of privacy rights is inherent in the criminal law and the law of property. The right to personal safety and the peaceful enjoyment of personal possessions is reflected in the law detailing offences against the person and the law relating to theft. The right to exclude uninvited visitors from one's home is reflected in the laws relating to trespass and the requirements of lawful authority to enter private property.[103] Identity forms a key element in private life and reflects the individual's liberty to adopt an identity and lifestyle without interference from others. Accordingly, measures which intrude on this aspect of privacy require justification. In the United Kingdom the idea that individuals should have and carry identity cards has long been resisted;[104] the use of closed circuit television (CCTV) recorders is regarded with suspicion; and all forms of surveillance and interceptions of communications by state agencies require lawful authority.

---

103 Note, however, that rights of entry are accorded to the police under common law and statute in defined circumstances and by statute to assorted utility companies.
104 But see now the Identity Card Bill 2006, discussed in Chapter 25.

There has never, however, previously been a legal right to privacy in the United Kingdom. The principal reason for this lies in the difficulties of defining the full scope of privacy and its relationship with competing concepts and interests. The privacy of the individual, for example, competes with the right to freedom of expression of the press. The need for the state to keep official records also competes with individual privacy. Privacy may compete also with the powers of the police to investigate crime and the powers of the security forces to combat terrorism. Increasingly as criminal activities such as drug trafficking, trafficking in human beings and international money laundering are globalised, there is a need for the police and security agencies to co-operate with European and international forces. Article 8 of the European Convention on Human Rights, now incorporated under the Human Rights Act 1998, provides that everyone has the right to respect for 'his private and family life, his home and his correspondence'.[105]

In *Secretary of State for the Home Department v Wainwright* (2003), the House of Lords ruled that there was no general common law tort of invasion of privacy. The claimants had visited a relative in prison, and been told by a prison officer that they would have to be strip searched. They reluctantly agreed. They claimed damages for trespass to the person which infringed their right to privacy. The claimants argued – *inter alia* – that in order to conform to the Convention on Human Rights, the House of Lords should declare that there was a tort of invasion of privacy under which the searches were actionable and damages for emotional distress recoverable. They relied on *Douglas v Hello! Ltd* (2001), where Sedley LJ had discussed the way in which the law of confidence had developed, reducing the need for a relationship of confidence between the recipient of the confidential information and the person from whom it was obtained, and that the basic value protected by the law was privacy. However, Lord Hoffmann in *Wainwright* stated that he did not understand Sedley LJ to 'have been advocating the creation of a high-level principle of invasion of privacy ...'. He went on to state that there was 'a great difference between identifying privacy as a value which underlay the existence of a rule of law, and might point the direction in which the law should develop, and privacy as a principle of law in itself'.

Lord Hoffmann also argued that the coming into force of the Human Rights Act 1998 weakened – rather than strengthened – the argument for the creation of a tort of invasion of privacy. That submission was based on the fact that sections 6 and 7 of the Act are 'in themselves substantial gap-fillers'. Furthermore, a general tort of invasion of privacy would 'pre-empt the controversial question of the extent, if any, to which the Convention required the state to provide remedies for invasions of privacy by persons who were not public authorities'.

Privacy and the media

The invasion of privacy by the media has also become a matter of rising concern. In 1953, the Press Council was established.[106] This self-regulatory body proved

---

105 The powers of the police and security forces are considered in Chapters 23 and 25 respectively.
106 The Broadcasting Complaints Commission plays a similar role in relation to broadcasting: Broadcasting Act 1990, s 142.

woefully inadequate at controlling the press, not least because it had no powers to fine newspapers. In 1972, the Younger Committee was established to consider reforms in relation to press freedom. The Committee recommended that a tort of disclosure of information unlawfully acquired and a tort and crime of unlawful surveillance by technical devices be introduced.[107] The proposed reforms were not implemented. Concern over intrusions into individual privacy increased with the media attention given to the Royal Family in recent years. The case of *Kaye v Robertson* (1991) heightened public interest in the respective right of an individual to privacy and the right of the public to information. In *Kaye*, journalists entered a hospital room in which the well known actor, Gordon Kaye, was being treated for severe injuries sustained in a car accident. Kaye agreed neither to be photographed nor interviewed. An injunction was sought, and granted, to restrain the newspaper from publishing the 'interview' and photographs. On appeal, the Court of Appeal ruled that there was no right to privacy under English law which could found the basis for an injunction.

In 1990, the Committee on Privacy and Related Matters (the Calcutt Committee) was established, which led to the creation of another self-regulatory body in 1991, the Press Complaints Commission.[108] A review of the workings of the Commission by Sir David Calcutt[109] found the protection accorded to individuals inadequate. It was recommended, therefore, that a statutory body be established, but no action has been taken.

The Press Complaints Commission administers a Code of Practice, drafted by the industry, which regulates accuracy of reporting and personal privacy. In relation to the latter, the Code provides that:

> Everyone is entitled to respect for his or her private and family life, home, health and correspondence. A publication will be expected to justify intrusions into any individual's private life without consent.

> The use of long lens photography to take pictures of people in private places without their consent is unacceptable.

The Press Complaints Commission Annual Report 2002 revealed that 2,630 complaints were received in 2002. Fifty one per cent of complaints concerned national daily and Sunday newspapers. The majority of individual complaints related to accuracy in reporting (56 per cent) while 23.5 per cent related to invasions of privacy. Of the 1,799 complaints which fell inside the Code, the Commission ruled that in 711 cases there was no breach of the Code, while 1,052 cases were either resolved or not pursued. Of the 36 cases adjudicated, 17 were upheld and 19 not upheld. The Commission stated that 91 per cent of complaints were made by 'ordinary men and women', not just the 'rich and famous'.

---

107 *Report of the Younger Committee*, Cmnd 5012, 1972; and see MacCormick, 1973.
108 *Report of the Committee on Privacy and Related Matters*, Cmnd 1102, 1990. See Munro, 1991.
109 *Review of Press Self-Regulation*, Cmnd 2135, 1993, London: HMSO.

CHAPTER 22

FREEDOM OF ASSOCIATION AND ASSEMBLY

While the detection and prosecution of crime and the preservation of public order are of first importance in any state, the extent to which police powers reflect a legitimate interference with the liberty and security of citizens is a problematic question which involves evaluating the balance struck between the rights of the individual and the powers of the police. In this chapter, the manner in which law regulates associations and assemblies – whether meetings or processions – is examined. In addition, it is necessary to consider the manner in which law regulates an individual's freedom to move around, and the conditions under which it is or is not lawful to enter into and remain on land, both private and public.

The law of association and assembly must now be evaluated against Article 11 of the European Convention on Human Rights, incorporated under the Human Rights Act 1998. Article 11 provides that 'everyone has the right to freedom of peaceful assembly and to freedom of association with others, including the right to form and to join trade unions for the protection of his interests'. Article 11, however, is subject to a number of lawful exceptions. The rights may be restricted on the basis that they are 'necessary in a democratic society in the interests of national security or public safety, for the prevention of disorder or crime, for the protection of health or morals or for the protection of the rights and freedoms of others'. In addition, Article 11 does not prevent lawful restrictions being imposed by the state on members of the armed forces, or the police or the civil service. Accordingly, while all domestic law must be compatible with Article 11, a great deal of discretion is accorded to the state.

Freedom of assembly and association, protected by Article 11, must also be viewed in relation to freedom of expression guaranteed by Article 10 of the Convention and considered in the previous chapter.

FREEDOM OF ASSOCIATION

While citizens are generally free to join any club, society or trades union, two statutory restrictions exist. The first restriction relates to membership of military or quasi-military organisations. The Public Order Act 1936 provides, in part, that the wearing of uniforms in public with the intention of promoting a political objective is unlawful, and that membership of groups organised and trained for the purpose of displaying physical force is unlawful. To be a member of such a group, or to solicit or invite financial or other support for the group, is an offence.

In *R v Jordan and Tyndall* (1963), the defendants were members of a fascist group, Spearhead. They exercised in military fashion and were known to be storing chemicals capable of being used for the manufacture of bombs. They were convicted under section 2(1)(b) of the Public Order Act 1936. In *Director of Public Prosecutions v Whelan* (1975), the defendants were charged under section 1 of the 1936 Act. Participating in a Sinn Fein march in Northern Ireland, the defendants wore black berets, dark clothing and carried the Irish flag. It was held that the wearing of similar clothing could amount to a 'uniform'. Specific groups are proscribed under the Terrorism Acts.[1]

FREEDOM OF ASSEMBLY

... it can hardly be said that our constitution knows of such a thing as any specific right of public meeting.[2]

An individual is free to assemble with others to the extent that the law does not prohibit such assemblies or the assembly does not involve unlawful actions. In 1885, Dicey was to record that 'the police have with us no special authority to control open air assemblies'. Today much has changed. Under common law, a number of restraints were placed on this freedom, and the Public Order Acts 1936 and 1986 and the Criminal Justice and Public Order Act 1994 restrict rights of assembly. While there is a general freedom to assemble on private property or on public land, in the case of the former, it will be a trespass to do so without the consent of the landowner. In relation to land to which the public have a right of access, the right of assembly is controlled by local authority bylaws, and a criminal offence is committed if these are breached. Further, the right of assembly may be controlled by statute. By way of example, the right to assemble in Trafalgar Square is regulated under statute, under which permission must be granted by the Secretary of State for the Environment.[3] Hyde Park is equally regulated.[4]

The duty to facilitate meetings

The constitutional importance of freedom of expression and involvement in civic life is reflected in the right to use schools and other public rooms for meetings in local elections, by-elections and general elections.[5] In addition, under the Education (No 2) Act 1986, the governing bodies of universities and colleges are under a duty to 'take such steps as are reasonably practicable to ensure that freedom of speech within the law is secured for members, students and employees of the establishment and for visiting speakers'.[6] This requirement gave rise to a challenge in *R v University of Liverpool ex parte Caesar-Gordon* (1991). In that case, the university had refused permission for a meeting at which two diplomats from the South African Embassy were due to speak. The decision was based on the fear that the meeting would cause public unrest in the surrounding area. The Divisional Court ruled that the university had acted *ultra vires* its

---

1   See further Chapter 25.
2   Dicey, 1885, p 271.
3   SI 1952/776. See also the Metropolitan Police Act 1839, s 52, which provides for police enforcement of access to parliament by its members.
4   Royal and Other Parks and Gardens Regulations 1988, SI 1988/217, and see *Bailey v Williamson* (1873).
5   Representation of the People Act 1983, as amended by the Representation of the People Act 1985 and Greater London Authority Act 1999, s 17.
6   Education (No 2) Act 1986, s 43.

powers. The university authorities were not entitled to take into account threats of violence outside its precincts. Only where the risk of violence would relate to university precincts, would the university be justified in imposing restrictions.

The meaning of 'public meeting' was considered by the House of Lords in *McCartan (Turkington Breen) v Times Newspapers Ltd* (2000). At issue was whether a meeting, in this case a press conference, held on private premises, to which members of the press had been invited and others also attended without an invitation but without any restriction, was a 'public meeting'.[7] A meeting was public if those who arranged it opened it to the public, or by issuing a general invitation to the press showed an intention that the proceedings of the meeting should be communicated to a wider public.

INDIRECT RESTRICTIONS ON THE RIGHT OF ASSEMBLY

A number of indirect means may be employed in order to restrain public meetings. Such means include breach of the peace, obstruction of police officers and obstruction of the highway.

Breach of the peace

In *Beatty v Gillbanks* (1882), the Salvation Army met knowing that there would be an opposing meeting. The magistrates' court issued an order preventing the meeting. When the meeting assembled in defiance of the order, the police ordered the meeting to disband and arrested one of the members. On the defendant's appeal against conviction, the Queen's Bench Division refused to accept the restriction on freedom of assembly based on the threatened unlawful acts of others. A person acting lawfully was not responsible for the unlawful reaction of others. Where, however, participants in a meeting engage in unlawful conduct which provokes others and results in a breach of the peace – or a reasonable apprehension of a breach of the peace – the meeting may be held to be unlawful. Further, if the meeting is conducted lawfully and yet provokes an actual breach of the peace, the police may order the meeting to disband. Failure to comply with an order to leave an assembly on the grounds of an officer's reasonable belief that it is necessary to avoid a breach of the peace is a criminal offence.[8]

Breach of the peace is a concept which traditionally has involved a degree of proximity and immediacy between the conduct of individuals and the anticipated breach of the peace. However, in *Moss v McLachlan* (1985), in the course of the miners' strike 1984–85, the defendants were ordered to turn back on a journey to another colliery some four miles away. The police suspected that they were intending to join the picket line in support of fellow miners and that a breach of the peace might occur. When the miners refused to obey the order to turn back, they were arrested for obstruction. The judge conceded a wide discretion to the police and ruled that, provided a senior police officer 'honestly and reasonably

---

7   For the purposes of a claim to privilege under the Defamation Act (Northern Ireland) 1955, s 7.

8   *Duncan v Jones* (1936): see below.

formed the opinion' that there was a real risk of a breach of the peace, in an area proximate to the point of arrest, they could take whatever measures were reasonably necessary to prevent it. This decision, whilst understandable from the police's point of view, is regrettable for it introduces a dangerous breadth to the offence. Furthermore, uncertainty is created as to the precise scope of the police's power to interfere with freedom of movement.

The *Beatty v Gillbanks* principle has been undermined in a number of cases. In *Jordan v Burgoyne* (1963), the court ruled that a person addressing an audience would be found guilty of a breach of the peace if his or her words were likely to inflame the audience and lead to violence. Equally, in *Percy v Director of Public Prosecutions* (1995), the court ruled that conduct which was not itself unlawful could amount to a breach of the peace if the words spoken were likely to cause disorder among those listening, even if members of the audience had attended with the express intention of causing trouble. Further, in *Morpeth Ward Justices ex parte Ward* (1992), the issue was not so much the conduct of the protesters but, rather, whether or not the conduct had the effect of provoking violent behaviour, even where the reaction to the protest was unreasonable. However, in *Nicol v Director of Public Prosecutions* (1996), the court adopted a more restrictive approach. The protest in question concerned an attempt to stop anglers from fishing. The protesters blew horns and provoked the anglers. It was held that, although there was nothing unlawful in the protesters' actions, the provocation of the anglers was likely to cause a breach of the peace because it was unreasonable action.

A more liberal approach was taken in *Redmond-Bate v Director of Public Prosecutions* (1999). Three women preachers, who were preaching on the steps of a cathedral, were approached by a police constable and warned not to stop people. Later, he returned to find that a crowd had gathered, some of whom were hostile to the speakers. The constable asked the women to stop preaching, but when they refused arrested them for a breach of the peace. They were convicted of obstructing a police officer in the execution of his duty. On appeal, it was held that there was no lawful basis for the arrest. Free speech, provided that it did not tend to provoke violence, irrespective of its content (unless contrary to law), was to be respected. There were no grounds on which the constable could apprehend a breach of the peace, much less one for which the preachers would be responsible.

The European Convention on Human Rights is making an impact on the law of protest, in terms of both the right to liberty (Article 5) and the right to freedom of expression (Article 10). In *Hashman and Harrup v United Kingdom* (2000), the issue was freedom of expression relating to hunt saboteurs. The applicants were bound over 'to be of good behaviour' for one year. The applicants claimed that the concept of behaviour *contra bona mores* was so broadly defined that it did not comply with Article 10(2) of the Convention, the requirement that any interference with freedom of expression be 'prescribed by law'. The Court of Human Rights ruled that the definition of *contra bona mores*, as behaviour which was 'wrong rather than right in the judgment of the majority of contemporary fellow citizens', was particularly imprecise and failed to give the applicants sufficiently clear guidance as to how they should behave in future. Accordingly, the interference with freedom of expression was not 'prescribed by law' and there had been a violation of Article 10.[9]

In *Appleby v United Kingdom* (2003), the Court of Human Rights ruled that campaigners against building on a playing field did not suffer a deprivation of their right to freedom of speech or assembly when the owners of a shopping centre prevented them from meeting on their premises to exchange information and ideas about the proposed building plans. While freedom of expression was an important right it was not unlimited. Nor was it the only Convention right at stake. Regard must also be given to the property rights of the owner of the shopping centre under Article 1 of Protocol No 1. In the present case the restriction on the applicants' ability to communicate their views was limited to the entrance areas and passageways of the shopping centre. It did not prevent them from expressing their views elsewhere, including the public access paths into the area.

The Court of Appeal considered police powers in relation to demonstrations in *R (Laporte) v Chief Constable of Gloucestershire Constabulary* (2004). The claimant was a member of an activist group which, according to its website, promoted anarchist ideas. The police received intelligence that three coaches, carrying items and equipment, were en route from London towards the airbase where a demonstration against the Iraq war was due to take place. The police stopped, boarded and searched four vehicles, including the claimant's coach. There were items of clothing and a few items capable of being used offensively. None of the passengers acknowledged ownership.

The Chief Constable decided that it was impracticable to arrest all the passengers, but that it was necessary to prevent them from getting to the demonstration where, in his view, the passengers intended to cause a breach of the peace. He then ordered the driver of the coach to return to London, escorted by police riders who prevented the coach from stopping. In effect the passengers were 'imprisoned' in the coach for two and a half hours.

Lord Woolf CJ stated that the case raised an issue of importance, namely the ability of the police to take action to avoid a breakdown in law and order as a result of a demonstration. In part this involved the police's duty to prevent breaches of the peace, the 'limits [of which] power are by no means clear'. The Court of Appeal took the view that the police's apprehension of a breach of the peace was reasonable, as was the decision to prevent the claimant and others from proceeding to the airbase. The apprehension of a breach of the peace was a justification for finding that he acted in the execution of his duty. The Court endorsed the decision of *Moss v McLachlan* (1985). The Court also stated that had the police done no more than direct the passengers to reboard the coach and instructed the driver not to proceed to the airbase, that would have been an appropriate response that was both necessary and proportionate. However, the passengers were 'virtual prisoners' for the length of the journey: the order to

---

9   See also *Steel v United Kingdom* (1998).

return to London without stopping was disproportionate and not justifiable at common law and violated Article 5 of the European Convention.

By contrast, the High Court ruled that the police were justified in holding demonstrators and passers-by within a cordon for seven hours for public order reasons during a large May Day demonstration in London in *Austin v Commissioner of Police of the Metropolis* (2005). The claimants argued that their detention for seven hours amounted to a violation of Article 5 of the Convention because they were neither threatening the peace themselves, nor by their unreasonable actions provoking others to violence. They also claimed false imprisonment and damages for distress. The police had cordoned exits to Oxford Circus, where 3,000 people had gathered. No one was allowed to leave without police permission. The police did not intend to arrest the whole crowd. They were using measures short of arrest for the preservation of order, provided for under sections 13 to 14 of the Public Order Act 1986. The police believed the claimants to be demonstrators and that they were about to commit a breach of the peace. The Court ruled that the measures were necessary to prevent disruption and that there was no unlawful false imprisonment, the containment being justified under the doctrine of necessity.

Obstructing the police

Under the Police Act 1996,[10] it is a criminal offence to obstruct the police in the execution of their duty. Section 89 provides that:

> (1) Any person who assaults a constable in the execution of his duty, or a person assisting a constable in the execution of his duty, shall be guilty of an offence ...
>
> (2) Any person who resists or wilfully obstructs a constable in the execution of his duty, or a person assisting a constable in the execution of his duty, shall be guilty of an offence ...

In *Duncan v Jones* (1935), the defendant had intended to hold a public meeting at a place previously used for that purpose. The police, aware that a disturbance had previously occurred in that place, instructed Mrs Duncan to hold the meeting on an alternative site. Mrs Duncan refused and started the meeting on the highway. She was arrested and charged under section 51 of the Police Act. The defendant could have been charged with obstruction of the highway (see below) or with inciting a breach of the peace. However, in the alternative the police charged her with obstructing a police officer. The court held that, once the police officer reasonably considered that a breach of the peace could occur, any action which impeded him in the course of preventing such an occurrence amounted to an obstruction of the police. In *Piddington v Bates* (1960), in the course of an industrial dispute, the police directed that no more than two pickets should be allowed at each entrance to the factory. The defendant joined the picket line in defiance of the order, regarding the restriction as unreasonable, and was charged with obstruction. On appeal, the Divisional Court upheld his conviction.

10　Formerly, Police Act 1964, s 51.

Obstructing the highway: the Highways Act 1980

A citizen is free to move along the highway. It is, however, a criminal offence to obstruct the highway. Obstructing the highway also represents a public nuisance, which may be prosecuted on indictment under common law.[11] Under section 137 of the Highways Act 1980, 'if a person, without lawful authority or excuse, in any way wilfully obstructs the free passage along a highway he is guilty of an offence'.[12] In *Hirst v Chief Constable for West Yorkshire* (1986), animal rights demonstrators protesting outside a store selling animal fur products were charged with obstructing the highway. The magistrates' court convicted them of obstruction. However, on appeal, the Divisional Court held that the justices should have considered the reasonableness of the action and weighed in the balance the right to protest and demonstrate and the need for public order. The magistrates' court had failed to consider this and, accordingly, failed to respect the freedom to protest on matters of public concern. This approach was echoed in *Director of Public Prosecutions v Jones* (1999), in which the House of Lords ruled that – provided a highway was not in fact obstructed – it could be lawful to use it for protest.

PUBLIC ORDER

The Public Order Act 1986 was passed after growing concern over demonstrations, industrial disputes, riots and football hooliganism.[13] The Act had two principal objectives. The first was to provide a comprehensive code as to the organisation and control of processions and demonstrations. The second was to provide a code relating to disorderly conduct, which can range from behaviour which causes alarm or distress to riot. In addition, the Act created offences relating to football hooliganism and to control of persons unlawfully camping on private land.

The law relating to public order was further reformed substantially by the Criminal Justice and Public Order Act 1994.[14] This Act made major reforms across a wide spectrum of criminal justice matters and matters relating to sexual offences. New sentences for young offenders were introduced; the right to silence of defendants was curtailed; and the powers of police to take body samples increased. In relation to public order, the Act increased the powers of the police and local authorities in respect of trespass, 'rave parties', squatters and campers, and marked a significant shift away from individual liberties towards increasing state regulation in favour of maintaining public order. The Crime and Disorder

11 *R v Clark (No 2)* (1964).
12 The Police and Criminal Evidence Act 1984, s 25(3)(d)(v) provides for a power of arrest.
13 See *Report on the Red Lion Square Disorders*, Cmnd 5919, 1975, London: HMSO; *Report on the Brixton Disorders*, Cmnd 8427, 1981, London: HMSO; *Criminal Law: Offences Relating to Public Order*, Law Com No 123, 1983, London: HMSO; *Review of Public Order Law*, Cmnd 9510, 1985, London: HMSO.
14 *Implementing the Report of the Royal Commission on Criminal Justice*, Cmnd 2263, 1993, London: HMSO.

Act 1998 introduces new criminal offences where conduct contrary to public order is racially aggravated.[15]

The regulation of processions

A procession is not defined in the Public Order Act. Processions were originally regulated under the Public Order Act 1936 and the powers were extended under the Public Order Act 1986. In *Flockhart v Robinson* (1950), a procession was said to be 'not a mere body of persons: it is a body of persons moving along a route'. Accordingly, a procession must involve more than one person. To be regulated by the Act, a procession must be public. A public place is defined in section 16 as being:

(a) any highway ...; and
(b) any place to which at the material time the public or any section of the public has access, on payment or otherwise, as of right or by virtue of express or implied permission.

The requirement of notice

Under section 11, notice must be given to the police of a procession which is designed to express or oppose the views of another, to publicise or encourage support for a campaign, or to commemorate an event. Processions which are regularly held within a particular area need not be notified to the police. Where it is impracticable to give notice in advance, the requirement may be waived. This exception enables spontaneous demonstrations to take place.

Six clear days' notice must be given, except where it is impracticable to do so.[16] Failure to give notice, or organising a procession different from the one notified, is a summary offence. In Scotland, similar requirements exist. Under the Civil Government (Scotland) Act 1982, as amended,[17] the police must receive at least seven days' notice. Where a ban is imposed on a particular march, a right of appeal exists.[18]

The power to impose conditions

Where notice has been given in accordance with section 11, then a senior police office (Chief Constable or Commissioner) may impose conditions, under section 12. If a procession is under way, then a senior officer on the scene may impose conditions. The basis on which conditions may be attached include situations where the senior police officer reasonably believes that a procession may result in serious public disorder, serious damage to property or serious disruption of the life of the community.[19] An alternative basis for conditions is where it is reasonably believed that the procession is taking place for an illegitimate purpose. Intimidation, for example, would be an 'illegitimate purpose'. Under section 14 of

---

15   The Anti-Social Behaviour Act 2003 amends both the 1986 and 1994 Acts.
16   Public Order Act 1986, s 11(6).
17   By the Local Government (Scotland) Act 1994.
18   Civil Government (Scotland) Act 1982, ss 62 and 64.
19   Public Order Act 1986, s 12(1).

the Act, conditions may also – on the same grounds as those stated in section 12 – be imposed on assemblies.

If the requirements for the imposition of conditions are met, the senior officer has a wide discretion as to the conditions which may in fact be imposed. Section 12(1) merely states that he may impose conditions 'as appear to him necessary'. Under section 12, there is power to impose conditions as to the route to be followed, and to prohibit entry into particular public places. Failure to comply with the conditions, or to incite others not to comply, is an offence.[20]

The power to ban processions

Under section 13, the Chief Officer of Police[21] may issue a banning order, which may only be issued if the power to impose conditions is insufficient to prevent serious public disorder. In London, the banning order must have the consent of the Home Secretary, and elsewhere the consent of the local authority. The power to ban processions represents a power to ban all processions, rather than to ban a particular procession, and can cover all or part of a police area and last for up to three months.[22] Organising or participating in, or inciting participation in, a banned procession is a summary offence.[23]

The power to enter meetings on private premises

Where a private meeting is held, the police have power to enter and remain on the premises under certain circumstances. A meeting is defined as a private meeting if it is held in entirely enclosed premises. Thus, even if the meeting is held in publicly owned and managed premises, such as a school or town hall, it will be a private meeting. In *Thomas v Sawkins* (1935), a police officer entered a private meeting which was held to protest against the Incitement to Disaffection Bill. The organiser of the meeting brought an action based on trespass, and argued that, as a result of trespass by the police, he had the right to evict the officers. The meeting had not given rise to a breach of the peace. However, the court held that notwithstanding its peaceful nature, the police had grounds for reasonably suspecting that a breach of the peace might occur and were therefore entitled to enter and remain on the premises.

The regulation of public assemblies[24]

While there is power to regulate a public assembly, there was no power to issue a banning order under the 1986 Act. However, section 70 of the Criminal Justice and Public Order Act 1994 inserted section 14A into the 1986 Act, which provided a power to ban assemblies. A public assembly is defined as 'an assembly of two or

20 Public Order Act 1986, s 12(4), (5).
21 In London, the Commissioner for the City of London or Commissioner for the Metropolis.
22 The power to ban a procession is subject to judicial review: *Kent v Metropolitan Police Commissioners* (1981).
23 Public Order Act 1986, s 13(7), (8), (9).
24 See Bonner and Stone, 1987.

more persons in a public place which is wholly or partly open to the air'.[25] However, an individual who disobeys an order, even where he or she does not actually join the assembly, is liable under the Act.[26] The basis on which the conditions which may be attached[27] are the same as those for conditions imposed on processions. Intimidation, as a ground for imposing a condition, has been interpreted to mean more than 'causing discomfort'.[28]

The Serious Organised Crime and Police Act 2005 (SOCPA) regulates demonstrations in designated areas. Under section 132 SOCPA it is an offence to organise a demonstration, take part in a demonstration or demonstrate on one's own without having obtained authorisation before the start of the demonstration.[29] Section 138 provides that a designated area is to be defined by order of the Home Secretary, but that no point in the designated areas may be more than one kilometre from Parliament Square (Westminster).

A person seeking authorisation from the Commissioner of Police for a demonstration must given written notice, not less than six clear days before the day on which the demonstration is to start or, if that is not practicable, then as soon as it is and in any event not less than 24 hours before the time the demonstration is to start. Where notice is given, with the specified details as to date, time, place, duration, name and address of person giving notice and in the required time, the Commissioner must give authorisation for the demonstration. However, the Commissioner may impose conditions as to place, time, duration, number of persons, number and size of banners and placards and maximum permissible noise levels. Conditions may also be specified for the purpose of preventing any of the following:

(a) hindrance to any person wishing to enter or leave the Palace of Westminster,
(b) hindrance to the proper operation of Parliament,
(c) serious public disorder,
(d) serious damage to property,
(e) disruption to the life of the community,
(f) a security risk in any part of the designated area,
(g) risk to the safety of members of the public (including any taking part in the demonstration.

Trespassory assemblies

A Chief Officer of Police may apply for a banning order if he reasonably believes that an assembly is likely to involve trespass or might result in serious disruption to community life or cause damage to buildings and structures. This power must be seen within the context of section 14(c) of the Public Order Act 1986,[30] which confers power on the police to stop persons within a five mile radius of the

---

25 Public Order Act 1986, s 16, as amended by the Anti-Social Behaviour Act 2003, s 57.
26 *Broadwith v Chief Constable of Thames Valley Police* (2000).
27 Public Order Act 1986, s 14(1).
28 *Police v Reid* (1987).
29 See *R (Haw) v Secretary of State for the Home Department* (2006).
30 Inserted by the Criminal Justice and Public Order Act 1994, s 71.

assembly, if the police reasonably believe that they are on their way to the assembly, and the assembly is subject to a section 14A order.

In _Director of Public Prosecutions v Jones_ (1999), section 14 was considered. A section 14A order had been issued, which prohibited the holding of a trespassory assembly within a four mile radius of Stonehenge. The assembly was heading for Stonehenge, and was within the four mile radius, and on the public highway. The court held that the highway was for passing and repassing only, and that assembling on the highway was outside the purpose for which the implied licence to use the highway was granted. The respondents argued that they were both peaceful and not obstructive and were making 'reasonable use' of the highway. The House of Lords ruled, by a majority of three to two, that the public had the right to use the highway for such reasonable and usual activities, _inter alia_ including peaceful assembly, as was consistent with the primary use for passage and repassage. It was a question of fact and degree in each case whether the user was reasonable and not inconsistent with that primary right.

The right to move freely along the highway, for a minority group such as Gypsies, entails the need for a lawful place to stop. While local authorities had been under a duty to provide sites under the Caravan Sites Act 1968,[31] the government has now removed that statutory duty.[32] This is of particular concern, given that Gypsies – a recognised racial group protected under the Race Relations Act 1976 and under international law[33] – traditionally travel with caravans from area to area, usually in search of seasonal work.

The problems encountered in the 1970s and 1980s with groups of New Age Travellers meeting for the summer solstice at Stonehenge and the problems caused by 'rave parties' resulted in the criminalisation of trespass for the first time under English law. Section 39 of the Public Order Act 1986 provided the police with powers to direct persons to leave land where they had entered land as trespassers, with a common purpose of remaining there, where steps had been taken by the occupier[34] to ask them to leave. A further requirement under section 39 was that the trespasser had caused damage to property on the land or had used threatening, abusive or insulting words or behaviour towards the occupier and his associates, or that the trespassers had brought 12 or more vehicles onto the land. Failure to obey the instruction of the police to leave the land as soon 'as reasonably practicable'[35] amounted to a criminal offence. A number of difficulties arose with the interpretation of section 39, and that section has been repealed and replaced by section 61 of the Criminal Justice and Public Order Act 1994. A number of significant amendments have been made to the powers of the police.

First, whereas under the 1986 Act persons could be directed to leave where they had entered the land as trespassers, the 1994 Act makes it possible to remove persons who are in fact trespassing, whether or not they entered the land as

---

31 Caravan Sites Act 1968, s 6.
32 Criminal Justice and Public Order Act 1994, s 80.
33 _Commission for Racial Equality v Dutton_ (1989).
34 Or on behalf of the occupier.
35 Public Order Act 1986, s 39(2).

trespassers.[36] Thus, even where persons originally entered land at the invitation of the occupier, if they have subsequently become trespassers they can be directed to leave the land. Secondly, whereas the 1986 Act provided for damage to property on land as a criterion for a direction to leave, the 1994 Act extended the concept of damage to include damage to the land itself. Thirdly, the 1986 Act applied in relation to persons having 12 or more vehicles on the land: the 1994 Act reduced the number of vehicles to six. This is a major change and one of great disadvantage for the minority Gypsy population which traditionally migrates in convoys of caravans.

Fourthly, the Act extended the land to which the provisions apply. Common land[37] is now included, as are footpaths, bridleways, byways, public paths and cycletracks.[38] Fifthly, section 62 of the 1994 Act gave the police new powers to remove 'vehicles and other property' on land. The police must be satisfied that there are alternative caravan sites available to the trespassers to move to.[39] The power to seize vehicles and property arises where the trespasser fails to comply with a direction to leave within a reasonable time. Reasonableness is an objective test and will depend on all the circumstances of the case, including the roadworthiness of vehicles.[40] Where vehicles are seized, powers are given for the safe keeping, disposal and destruction of the vehicles, the powers to be exercised according to Regulations to be drafted by the Secretary of State.[41]

Rave parties

The Criminal Justice and Public Order Act 1994 introduced new police powers to order persons to leave gatherings, created a new criminal offence of failing to leave within a reasonable time and provided for arrest without warrant. The provisions govern open air gatherings of 20 or more persons, where amplified music is played at night time.[42] Failure to comply with a police direction may result in the power to seize and remove vehicles and sound equipment.[43]

The Act gives the police power to regulate the movement of persons to a gathering. Where a direction has been made under section 63, the police may stop persons and order them not to proceed to the gathering. The exercise of this sweeping power is confined to an area within a five mile radius of the gathering.

Other public order offences under the 1986 Act

The Act replaces a number of common law offences. The Law Commission considered, for example, that the offence of breach of the peace was too vague a

---

36 Criminal Justice and Public Order Act 1994, s 61(2).
37 As defined in the Commons Registration Act 1965, s 22.
38 Criminal Justice and Public Order Act 1994, s 61(9)(b)(i).
39 *Ibid*, s 62A, as amended by the Anti-Social Behaviour Act 2003, s 60.
40 See *Krumpa v Director of Public Prosecutions* (1989).
41 Public Order Act 1986, s 67(3).
42 Criminal Justice and Public Order Act 1994, s 63, as amended by the Anti-Social Behaviour Act 2003, s 58.
43 *Ibid*, s 64.

concept and that it should be replaced with more specific offences. In its place, the concept of unlawful violence is used, which encompasses a number of situations. Violent conduct is defined as meaning any violent conduct, whether or not intended to cause injury or damage.[44]

Riot

Riot is the most serious offence under the Act. 'Riot' is defined in section 1 as being where 12 or more persons who are present together use or threaten unlawful violence for a common purpose and the conduct of them (taken together) is such as would cause a person of 'reasonable firmness' present at the scene to fear for his personal safety; each of the persons using unlawful violence for the common purpose is guilty of riot.

Under section 1, a riot may be committed in private as well as public places. The common purpose may be inferred from the conduct, and does not need to be articulated. The purpose itself need not be unlawful – a perfectly legitimate demonstration may turn into a riot if the conditions for a riot are satisfied, namely the use of unlawful violence for a common purpose which is such as to cause persons of reasonable firmness present to fear for their personal safety, although it is not necessary that such persons actually be present at the scene. The mental element required for liability, under section 6(1), is that a person 'intends to use violence or is aware that his conduct may be violent'. The seriousness with which the offence is viewed is reflected in the requirement of trial on indictment (trial by jury) and liability on conviction to imprisonment for a term not exceeding ten years or a fine, or both.[45]

Violent disorder

Section 2 of the Public Order Act 1986 created a new statutory offence of violent disorder, which replaced the common law offence of unlawful assembly. The offence shares similarities with the offence of riot, but differs in several respects. First, for the offence to be committed, there need to be only three people, rather than 12 as required for a riot, involved in the violent conduct. Secondly, there needs to be no common purpose, as is required for the offence of riot. It is sufficient for an offence of violent disorder to be committed that the persons be involved in the use or threat of violent conduct. It is necessary that the conduct be such that it causes a person 'of reasonable firmness' to 'fear for his personal safety', although such persons need not actually be present.[46] The offence can be committed in private or in public.[47] The mental element required under section 6 is that the person intends to use or to threaten violence, or is aware that his conduct may be violent or threaten violence. Self-induced intoxication, other than through prescribed medication in a course of medical treatment, is not an excuse.

---

44 Public Order Act 1986, s 8.
45 *Ibid*, s 1(6).
46 *Ibid*, s 2(3).
47 *Ibid*, s 2(4).

The requirement of three persons' involvement in the violent disorder has caused difficulties. In *R v Fleming* (1989), for example, four persons were charged, one was acquitted and the jury failed to reach a decision on a second. Accordingly, the conviction of the remaining two defendants was quashed.[48] The Court of Appeal in *Fleming* noted that it was possible for fewer than three persons to be convicted where, for example, there was sufficient evidence as to the involvement of more than three persons but some of the greater number evaded arrest or lacked the required mental element for the offence. The jury must be correctly directed on the matter, and failure to direct appropriately will cause a conviction to be quashed. This occurred in *R v Whorton* (1990), where there was evidence that eight to ten people were involved in the violence, but only four were charged and only two convicted. Their appeal against conviction was successful, on the basis that the judge had not directed the jury that they could only convict if there were either three defendants before them or, if a lesser number, a greater number had in fact been involved in the violent disorder.

The offence is triable on indictment (by the Crown Court) or summarily (by a magistrates' court), and carries a term of imprisonment of up to five years on indictment, a fine or both and, on summary conviction, imprisonment of up to six months or a fine, or both.[49]

Affray

A person is guilty of an affray if he uses or threatens unlawful violence towards another and his conduct is such as would cause a person of reasonable firmness present at the scene to fear for his personal safety.[50]

Two or more persons may be involved in the offence, in which case it is necessary that their conduct be considered together for the purpose of section 1. A verbal threat of unlawful violence is not sufficient for the offence to be committed. The offence may take place in private or in public and, again, the test for unlawful violence is whether a person of reasonable firmness, who need not in fact be present, is put in fear of his personal safety. The mental element is the same as that required for violent disorder. Police constables may arrest without warrant, and the offence is triable on indictment or summarily. On indictment, the offence carries a term of imprisonment not exceeding three years or a fine or both; on summary conviction, there is liability to imprisonment of up to six months or a fine or both.[51]

The definition of affray was considered by the Court of Appeal in *R v Sanchez* (1996). On the charge of affray, the trial judge directed the jury on the requirement for a 'person of reasonable firmness' and said that the victim was such a person and that he was to be believed when he said that he was frightened. The Court of Appeal held that there was a misdirection, in that the judge's directions

---

48   See also *R v Abdul Mahroof* (1988).
49   Public Order Act 1986, s 2(5).
50   *Ibid*, s 3.
51   *Ibid*, s 3(7).

overlooked the need to direct the jury to consider not only the victim but also the putative third person, the hypothetical bystander; affray was a public order offence and there were other offences for the protection of persons at whom the violence was aimed.

Fear or provocation of violence

Under section 4 of the Public Order Act 1986, a person is guilty of an offence if he:

(a) uses towards another person threatening, abusive or insulting words or behaviour; or

(b) distributes or displays to another person any writing, sign or other visible representation which is threatening, abusive or insulting, with the intent to cause that person to believe that immediate unlawful violence will be used against him or another by any person, or to provoke the immediate use of unlawful violence by that person or another, or whereby that person is likely to believe that such violence will be used or it is likely that such violence will be provoked.

The offence is one which may be committed by a single person. For a prosecution to succeed, it is necessary to establish that threatening, abusive or insulting words or behaviour have been directed towards a specific person. Rude or offensive words or behaviour may not necessarily be insulting, and swearing may not be abusive.[52] It is also necessary to establish that the person affected is caused to believe that immediate unlawful violence is about to be used against him. In *Horseferry Road Metropolitan Stipendiary Magistrate ex parte Siadatan* (1990), it was held that the violence feared must be both immediate and unlawful.[53] A threat of violence at some future time will not suffice for this offence to be proven. The mental element required under section 6 is that the person intends his words or behaviour (or signs, etc) to be threatening, abusive or insulting or that he is aware that it may be threatening, abusive or insulting.

Harassment, alarm or distress[54]

Under sections 4A[55] and 5 of the Act, a person is guilty of an offence if he:

(a) uses threatening, abusive or insulting words or behaviour, or disorderly behaviour; or

(b) displays any writing, sign or other visible representation which is threatening, abusive or insulting, thereby causing ... harassment, alarm or distress or within the hearing or sight of a person likely to be caused harassment, alarm or distress thereby.

The introduction of these offences, and the use to which they are put by the police, raises controversy. The offence was designed to provide powers to deal with relatively minor acts of antisocial, unruly or disorderly conduct which, while

---

52   *R v Ambrose* (1973).
53   See further below, pp 598–99. On the Racial and Religious Hatred Act 2006 see Chapter 21.
54   See *Criminal Law: Offences Relating to Public Order*, Law Com No 123, 1983, and Williams, 1984. See Geddis, 2004.
55   Introduced by s 154 of the Criminal Justice and Public Order Act 1994.

of itself not serious, causes fear in others. In its White Paper, the government illustrated the sort of behaviour that was being targeted:[56]

    (a) hooligans on housing estates causing disturbances in the common parts of blocks of flats ...;

    (b) groups of youths persistently shouting abuse and obscenities or pestering people waiting to catch public transport or to enter a hall or cinema; someone turning out the lights in a crowded dance hall, in a way likely to cause panic;

    (c) rowdy behaviour in the streets late at night which alarms local residents.

For the offence to be proven, it is necessary that the words or behaviour, or signs etc, are uttered or displayed within the sight of a person who is likely to be harassed or alarmed or distressed – it is not necessary to prove actual harassment, alarm or distress. However, the mental element required is that the person using the words, behaviour or signs either intended his conduct to be threatening, abusive or insulting or be aware that it might be. Thus, words uttered in a public place (for example, by demonstrators or persons attending football matches) which might in fact be threatening or abusive, and might in fact cause alarm or distress to someone hearing the words, will not be sufficient for a prosecution to succeed.[57]

In *Jordan v Burgoyne* (1963), the accused made an inflammatory racist speech in Trafalgar Square. He was prosecuted under the forerunner to section 4 of the Public Order Act 1986, section 5 of the Public Order Act 1936. It was held that the speech went beyond the limits of tolerance. The defendant could not argue that the words used were not likely to cause ordinary persons to commit breaches of the peace. The defendant had to 'take his audience as he found them'. If the words used were likely to provoke that audience, or part thereof, to commit a breach of the peace, the defendant was guilty of an offence.

Insulting words were the subject of judicial scrutiny in *Brutus v Cozens* (1973). In *Brutus*, the defendant and other anti-apartheid protesters interrupted play at a Wimbledon tennis match. The audience resented the interruption. Brutus was charged with insulting behaviour likely to cause a breach of the peace. In the Divisional Court, it was held that an offence occurred where the behaviour affronted other people, and reflected a contempt for their rights. The House of Lords, however, allowed Brutus's appeal. Not all speech or conduct fell within the meaning of the section. It must be conduct or speech which the ordinary person would recognise as insulting – a term which was deemed incapable of precise definition. The mere resentment of the crowd, as opposed to violence, did not suffice to make the actions insulting.

The issue of violent reaction to provocative words was considered in *R v Horseferry Road Magistrate ex parte Siadatan* (1991). The case concerned Salman Rushdie's novel, *The Satanic Verses*. In an application laid against the publishers and the author, it was argued that distribution of the book offended against section 4 of the 1986 Act, in so far as it contained abusive and insulting language which was likely to provoke violence amongst devout Muslims. The magistrate

---

56 *Review of Public Order Law*, Cmnd 9510, 1985, London: HMSO, para 3.22. On Anti-Social Behaviour Orders see Chapter 23.

57 See *Director of Public Prosecutions v Clarke* (1992).

refused to issue a summons. The issue went to the Divisional Court for judicial review. It was there held that the violence which was apprehended by the words must be immediate violence, not some distant act of violence.

In *R v Stephen Miller* (1999), the defendant appealed against sentence for racially aggravated threatening words. The defendant had pleaded guilty to two offences: first, aggravated threatening words and behaviour contrary to section 4 of the Public Order Act 1986, as amended by section 31 of the Crime and Disorder Act 1998; and secondly, travelling on a railway without a ticket. He was sentenced to 18 months' imprisonment, and appealed. The Court of Appeal dismissed his appeal. His conduct towards the conductor on the train was particularly bad. The sentence was designed to reflect public concern about conduct which damaged good racial relations within the community.[58]

The mental element on the part of the accused must be satisfied. KA Ewing and CA Gearty provide illustrations of the uses to which section 5 has been put.[59] The Act has been used to curb the wearing of obscene T-shirts and hats; to suppress a satirical poster of the former Prime Minister Mrs Thatcher; and to prosecute protesters outside abortion clinics in Ireland.[60] In Gearty and Ewing's assessment, section 5 of the Act represents a 'mechanism for punishing non-violent non-conformity for the crime of being itself'.[61] It must be conceded that section 5 represents a serious, and hitherto uncontemplated, limitation of freedom of expression and an alteration of the balance between individual liberty and the legitimate expectations of citizens to be protected from the consequences of another person's words and actions.

However, Article 10 proved constructive in relation to section 5 of the Public Order Act 1986 in *Percy v Director of Public Prosecutions* (2002). In this case, Ms Percy had been convicted under section 5 in relation to her protest against American military policy at an American air base. In the course of her protest Ms Percy defaced and trampled on an American flag. On appeal, it was held that too much reliance had been placed by the trial judge on the fact that her behaviour towards the flag – which was insulting to Americans at the base – was avoidable, at the expense of the defendant's right to freedom of expression. Her conviction was incompatible with Article 10 and was quashed.

Harassment[62]

The Protection from Harassment Act 1997 makes it a criminal offence to pursue a court of conduct which amounts to harassment of another and which that person

---

58 In *R v Rogers (Philip)* (2005), the Court of Appeal ruled that using the words 'bloody foreigners' was capable of amounting to the offence of using racially aggravated abusive or insulting words with the intent to cause fear or provoke violence. However, prosecutors should not bring charges (under s 31(1) of the Crime and Disorder Act 1998) unless satisfied that the facts truly suggested that the offence charged was aggravated by racism.
59 Ewing and Gearty, 1990, Chapter 4.
60 *Director of Public Prosecutions v Fidler* (1992); *Director of Public Prosecutions v Clarke* (1992).
61 Ewing and Gearty, 1990, p 123.
62 On sexual harassment see further Chapter 20.

knows amounts to harassment of the other.[63] Section 3 provides a civil remedy which enables an individual to seek an injunction against a person who is harassing them or may be likely to do so. In order to secure a conviction under section 2, the following requirements must be met:

- there must be a 'course of conduct'
- the conduct must take place on at least two occasions[64]
- the course of conduct must take place against 'another person'
- the conduct must harass or alarm another or cause that person distress.

In *Dalichi UK Ltd v Stop Huntingdon Animal Cruelty* (2004), the High Court ruled that the Protection from Harassment Act 1997 was intended to protect individuals and not corporate victims of harassment. However, individuals who were non-corporate claimants were entitled to protection. Stop Huntingdon Animal Cruelty was an unincorporated association whose stated objective was the closure of laboratories run by Huntingdon Life Sciences, which conducted research using live animals. As a result of a campaign of harassment and intimidation, Huntingdon Life's insurance brokers had ceased to act for them. In addition, its auditors withdrew their services. The claimants, their directors and employees had 'unquestionably been subject to harassment of a very serious nature intended to intimidate and terrify'. Granting the injunctive relief, Owen J ruled that the 'balance of justice and convenience weighed heavily in favour of granting interlocutory injunctive relief' bearing in mind 'the rights to freedom of speech and of assembly and association'.[65]

The courts have interpreted the 1997 Act strictly, requiring that 'another person' be a specific individual. As a result, it was unclear whether protection could be given to the employees of an organisation who had not been personally harassed, even though another employee had been. The Serious Organised Crime and Police Act 2005 (SOCPA) amends the 1997 Act to cover this situation. Section 125 SOPCA amends section 1 of the 1997 Act. Section 1A of the 1997 Act provides (in part) that:

> A person must not pursue a course of conduct –
>> (a) which involves harassment of two or more persons, and
>> (b) which he knows or ought to know involves harassment of those persons, and
>> (c) by which he intends to persuade any person –
>>> (i) not to do something that he is entitled to do, or
>>> (ii) to do something that he is not under any obligation to do.

---

63 Protection from Harassment Act 1997, s 2. The exercise by an individual of his right to freedom of expression and the instigation of secret surveillance of another person were capable to constituting a course of conduct amounting to harassment: *Howlett v Holding* (2006).

64 See *Banks v Ablex Ltd* (2005).

65 See also *Hall v Save Newchurch Guinea Pigs (Campaign)* (2005). An employer can be vicariously liable under s 3 of the 1997 Act for breach of a statutory duty imposed only on his employee for harassment committed by one of its employees in the course of his or her employment. The Court of Appeal so ruled in *Majrowski v Guy's and St Thomas's NHS Trust*, (2005).

The provision is not intended to criminalise peaceful protesting but will be engaged where there are threats and intimidation which seek to force others to do something or not to do something. Section 125(5) SOCPA inserts a new section 3A into the 1997 Act which allows for an injunction to be sought where there is an actual or apprehended breach of section 1(1A). Section 125(7) amends the definition of course of conduct in section 7(3) of the 1997 Act stating that in the case of conduct in relation to two or more persons, a course of conduct means conduct on at least one occasion in relation to each person.[66]

The Crime and Disorder Act 1998

Sections 28 to 32 of the Crime and Disorder Act 1998 extend the law to encompass racially aggravated offences. It is an offence under sections 4 and 5 of the Public Order Act 1986 (fear of provocation of violence, intentional harassment, alarm or distress) to engage in racially aggravated conduct. Section 32 makes it an offence to act in a racially aggravated manner in relation to sections 2 and 4 of the Protection from Harassment Act 1997. Under section 28(1), an offence is racially aggravated if:

(a) at the time of committing the offence, or immediately before or after doing so, the offender demonstrates towards the victim of the offence hostility based on the victim's membership (or presumed membership) of a racial group; or

(b) the offence is motivated (wholly or partly) by hostility towards members of a racial group based on their membership of that group.[67]

Section 28(3) provides that:

It is immaterial ... whether or not the offender's hostility is also based, to any extent, on –

(a) the fact of presumption that any person or group of persons belongs to any religious group ...

Under section 82, the court may impose a higher penalty for racially aggravated offences.

---

66 On harassment of a person in his or her home see SOCPA 2005, s 126.

67 In *DPP v M* (2004), the High Court ruled that the use of the phrase 'bloody foreigners' was contrary to s 28(1)(a) in that the word 'foreigners' was capable of describing a racial group and the word 'bloody' was capable of demonstrating hostility.

CHAPTER 23

THE POLICE AND POLICE POWERS

THE ORGANISATION OF THE POLICE[1]

The United Kingdom has no national police force. Instead, the police are organised on a basis which links them to the locality. In England and Wales, there now exist 43 police forces: the City of London Police, the Metropolitan Police and 41 forces outside London. Scotland has six forces and Northern Ireland one. The Police Act 1996 provides that the Home Secretary may alter police areas 'in the interest of efficiency or effectiveness'.[2] In 1962, a Royal Commission examined the question whether there should be a national police force under central government control, but concluded that the status quo should be maintained, subject to supervision by central government.[3] The regulation of the police represents a tri-partite arrangement involving the Secretary of State for the Home Department (the Home Secretary), local police authorities and Chief Constables of Police. Each of the local police forces has its own police authority, the role of which is discussed below.

The Home Office

The Home Office is one of the largest departments of state. In April 2005 it had a total staff of 73,306.[4] It has national responsibility for the police service in England and Wales. It also has responsibility for the National Offender Management Service (NOMS) which includes the prison[5] and probation services. The Immigration and Nationality Directorate (IND) is also within the Home Office's responsibility. Smaller organisations such as the Passport Service, the Criminal Records Bureau and the Forensic Science Service are within the Home Office's remit, together with a number of non-departmental public bodies including the Criminal Injuries Compensation Authority and Youth Justice Board. The new Serious Organised Crime Agency (SOCA)[6] which brings together the National Criminal Intelligence Service and the National Crime Squad is also within the Department's responsibility.

The Home Secretary has a number of powers in relation to local forces. The Home Secretary may, in consultation with the police authority and Chief Constable, determine policy objectives for the police authority.[7] The Home Secretary may issue Codes of Practice which regulate the manner in which the

---

1   See Uglow, 2002, Chapter 2; Newburn, 2003, Chapter 4.
2   Police Act 1996, s 32. Note that in 2006 there are mergers planned for many police forces.
3   *Ibid*, s 37.
4   *Home Office: Departmental Report 2004–05*, p 130.
5   With a staff of 48,000.
6   Under the Serious Organised Crime and Police Act 2005, on which see further below.
7   Police Act 1996, s 39, as amended by the Police Reform Act 2002, s 6.

police authority pursues policy objectives,[8] may direct the authority to establish performance targets and may impose conditions on police authorities.[9] In addition, the Home Secretary has powers to provide and maintain 'such organisations, facilities and services' as the Home Secretary thinks necessary for promoting the efficiency and effectiveness of the police.[10] The Police Act 1996 also extended the powers of the Home Secretary, and provided that the Home Secretary may make regulations for the government, administration and conditions of service of police forces.[11]

Police authorities are funded by central government. The annual grant is determined by the Home Secretary with the approval of the Treasury. The Home Secretary has a wide discretion, under section 46 of the 1996 Act, as to the amount of the grant. The efficiency of police forces is under the jurisdiction of Her Majesty's Inspectors of Constabulary appointed by the Home Secretary and accountable to him.[12] The Home Secretary is under a duty to prepare an Annual National Policing Plan and to lay it before parliament.[13] The Plan sets out the strategic policy priorities for England and Wales for the forthcoming three years and describes the objectives being set.

The Metropolitan Police Authority

Until 1999, the Home Secretary was the police authority for the Metropolitan Police. Under the Greater London Authority Act 1999 (on which see Chapter 12), there is established a Metropolitan Police Authority, which replaces the Home Secretary as police authority.[14] The 1999 Act amends the Police Act 1996, introducing a Police Authority for the Metropolitan Police District and specifying membership of the Authority. The Authority is headed by the Commissioner of Police of the Metropolis, appointed by the Crown and holding office at Her Majesty's pleasure.[15] The Metropolitan Police Force is under the direction and control of the Commissioner. There is a Deputy Commissioner who has the power to exercise any or all of the powers and duties of the Commissioner during any absence from duty of the Commission, any vacancy in the office of the Commissioner or at any other time with the consent of the Commissioner.[16]

---

8   Police Act 1996, s 39.
9   See *R v Home Secretary ex parte Northumbria Police Authority* (1989).
10   Police Act 1996, s 50.
11   *Ibid*, s 54.
12   Police Reform Act 2002, s 1, inserting s 36A into the Police Act 1996. The Police and Justice Bill 2006 will establish Her Majesty's Chief Inspector for Justice, Community Safety and Custody which will replace Her Majesty's Chief Inspector for Prisons, HM Inspectors of Constabulary, HM Chief Inspector of the Crown Prosecution Service, HM Inspectorate of the National Probation Service for England and Wales and HM Inspectorate of Court Administration.
13   Cmd 1728. The Human Rights Act 1998 imposes additional duties on the police. See below.
14   Greater London Authority Act 1999, ss 310, 312.
15   *Ibid*, ss 314 and 315 amending the Police Act 1996, ss 9 and 9A.
16   *Ibid*, s 316 amending the Police Act 1996, s 9.

The proposed restructuring of police forces

In 2005 Her Majesty's Inspector of Constabulary (HMIC) identified problems relating to the ability of local forces to deliver effective policing of serious crime and major incidents. The response of the Home Secretary was to propose the restructuring of police forces. Following the responses of police forces, HMIC drew up 'protective services assessments' identifying those forces which could be merged. In a Statement to the House of Commons, the Home Secretary reported that mergers would take place in the West Midlands, North East, North West and Wales, the effect of which would be a reduction from 16 forces to six.[17] Further amalgamations will take place once the detailed proposals have been finalised.

The functions of police authorities

Local police authorities are responsible for setting policy objectives for the police, subject to the Home Secretary's power to determine the objectives.[18] The general function is 'to secure the maintenance of an efficient and effective police force for its area'. The police authority is responsible for ensuring the efficiency of the local force.[19] The composition of the police authority is now regulated by the Police Act 1996. The standard membership of the authority is 17, of which nine are local authority councillors. Five further members are appointed from a shortlist drawn up by the Home Secretary. The remaining three members are local magistrates and appointed by the magistrates collectively. The police authority has control over the police budget.

The police authority has the power to order a Chief Constable or Assistant Chief Constable to retire 'in the interests of efficiency and effectiveness', following consultation with, and the approval of, the Home Secretary.[20] The Home Secretary also has power to require a police authority to exercise the powers. The police authority reports annually to the Home Secretary.[21]

Chief Constables of Police

Outside the Metropolitan area, which is headed by the Metropolitan Commissioner of Police, police forces are under the operational control of Chief Constables.[22] The Chief Constable is responsible for recruitment and promotions to the ranks below that of Assistant Chief Constable, and exercises disciplinary powers over the police. The Chief Constable makes annual reports to the police

---

17 House of Commons, *Hansard*, 6 February 2006, cols. 39–42. All four of Wales' police forces are to merge.
18 Police Act 1996, s 37.
19 *Ibid*, s 6.
20 *Ibid*, ss 11 and 12.
21 *Ibid*, s 9.
22 *Ibid*, s 10.

authority,[23] and the Home Secretary can require the Chief Constable to submit reports.[24]

A police officer is a servant of the state.[25] He or she is not employed under a contract of employment, but is a holder of public office.[26] Police officers are not servants of the Chief Constable.[27]

Prior to the enactment of section 88 of the Police Act 1996, the liability of a police officer for wrongful actions was personal. Whilst a servant of the Crown, the Crown was not, at common law, vicariously liable for wrongful actions of officers because, being neither appointed nor paid by the Crown, the officer was not 'in the employment of the Crown'.

Section 88 of the Police Act 1996 makes it clear that Chief Constables are liable for torts committed by constables under their direction and control:

> The chief officer of police for a police area shall be liable in respect of torts committed by constables under his direction and control in the performance or purported performance of their functions in like manner as a master is liable in respect of torts committed by his servants in the course of their employment, and accordingly shall in respect of any such tort be treated for all purposes as a joint tortfeasor.

Where damages or costs are ordered in a legal action, these are awarded against the Chief Constable and paid out of the local police budget.

The police were formerly also exempt from the legislation regulating racial discrimination, the Race Relations Act 1976 previously only applying to *employers* and *employees*, not office holders. The Race Relations (Amendment) Act 2000 reformed the law, following the recommendation of the Report of Inquiry into the death of Stephen Lawrence (the Macpherson Report), which stated:

> ... the full force of the Race Relations legislation should apply to all police officers, and Chief Officers of Police should be made vicariously liable for the acts and omissions of their officers relevant to that legislation.[28]

The police are liable in law in actions for assault, wrongful arrest,[29] false imprisonment, trespass, public misfeasance, negligence or an action for the return of property which has been wrongfully taken. An action for malicious prosecution is available where a person believes that the police have maliciously and without reasonable cause abused their powers in recommending prosecution to the Crown Prosecution Service. Further, the police are liable in law for the care of those in their custody.[30]

---

23 Police Act 1996, s 22.
24 *Ibid*, s 44.
25 *Fisher v Oldham Corporation* (1930).
26 See *Attorney General for New South Wales v Perpetual Trustee Company Ltd* (1955).
27 *White v Chief Constable of South Yorkshire* (1999).
28 To give effect to these recommendations, s 4 of the 2000 Act inserts new ss 76A and 76B into the 1976 Act.
29 See eg *Wershof v Metropolitan Police Commissioner* (1978).
30 See *Kirkham v Chief Constable of Greater Manchester* (1990); *Treadaway v Chief Constable of West Midlands* (1994).

The Police Reform Act 2002 provides a legal basis for civil liabilities arising from operations of joint investigation teams involving police officers from different forces and from abroad. Under the 2000 Convention on Mutual Assistance in Criminal Matters between Member States of the European Union, there is a requirement to provide arrangements for civil claims against joint forces. Section 103(1) of the 2002 Act extends the liabilities of chief officers of police by providing that they are liable for any unlawful conduct of members of international joint investigation teams. The liabilities of the Directors General of the National Criminal Intelligence Service and the National Crime Squad (from 2006 united under the Serious Organised Crime Agency), Scottish chief constables and the chief constable of the Police Service of Northern Ireland are extended in the same manner.

Police officers hold office under statute, and are subject to the police disciplinary code. They are not allowed to belong to trade unions, or any other association concerned with levels of pay or conditions of employment. Police Federations represent police officers in matters relating to welfare, and have restricted powers in relation to police discipline.[31] Police officers are not permitted to take any active part in politics, nor participate in any other activity which could actually impede, or give the suggestion that it could impede, the officer's impartiality.[32]

Police civilians

The Police Reform Act 2002 enables chief officers of police to employ suitably skilled and trained civilians to exercise functions as Community Support Officers, investigating officers, detention officers and escort officers.[33] A civilian officer is entitled to use reasonable force in the exercise of his or her functions. In relation to authorised forced entry into property, a civilian officer must be accompanied by a constable, unless the entry is required to save life or prevent injury, or to prevent serious damage to property.

Community Support Officers (CSOs) have the power to issue fixed penalty notices for certain offences.[34] The Secretary of State may add to or remove from the list of offences for which Community Support Officers may not issue fixed penalty notices.

The Serious Organised Crime and Police Act 2005[35] confers new powers on Community Support Offices. These powers include a power to direct traffic and place traffic signs on road, power to deal with begging, power to search detained persons for items that could cause injury or assist escape, power to enforce certain licensing offices, power to enforce byelaws, power to search persons for alcohol and tobacco in certain circumstances and a power to deal

---

31 Police Act 1996, s 59.
32 Police Regulations 1995, SI 1995/215.
33 Police Reform Act, s 38 and Sched 4. Schedule 4 provides detailed rules relating to civilian officers.
34 Including those listed in s 1(1) of the Criminal Justice and Police Act 2001.
35 Schedule 8, amending Sched 4 to the Police Reform Act 2002.

with possession of controlled drugs. Chief officers of police are also given power to designate CSOs with the power to require a name and address. It is a criminal offence not to comply with the request for a name and address. Where the CSO has reasonable grounds for believing that the information is false or inaccurate the CSO may detain the person for up to 30 minutes pending the arrival of a constable.

Codes of Practice, notes for guidance and Home Office circulars

Under the Police and Criminal Evidence Act 1984, a number of Codes of Practice have been issued. The Codes do not have the force of law, but represent an administrative means of regulating differing aspects of police powers. Breach of the Codes does not give rise to civil or criminal liability.[36] Under the 1984 Act, there are seven Codes of Practice. Code A relates to stop and search procedures; Code B to the search of premises; Code C to interviews and conditions of detention; Code D regulates identification procedures; and Code E and F regulate the tape and visual recording of interviews. Code G regulates the exercise of statutory powers of arrest. The notes for guidance are not part of the Codes, but represent interpretative guidelines. Home Office circulars are designed to supplement the provisions of the Police and Criminal Evidence Act and other statutes.

Judicial control and police policy

The exercise of police discretion is reviewable by the courts, although the courts confer a great deal of latitude in relation to that discretion. In *R v Commissioner of Police for the Metropolis ex parte Blackburn (No 1)* (1968), the Court of Appeal made it clear that an order of mandamus would lie against the Metropolitan Police Commissioner. The Commissioner had issued a policy statement in which he made it clear that supervision of gambling clubs would not take place, other than where there was a suspicion that the clubs were being frequented by criminals. The applicant, Blackburn, claimed that illegal gambling was taking place and applied to the courts for an order of mandamus to compel the Commissioner to reverse his policy. The court insisted that the Commissioner had a public duty to enforce the law, and that his discretion could be controlled by the courts. Nevertheless, since the Commissioner had undertaken to reverse his former policy, the order would not be granted. Neither was mandamus ordered in *R v Commissioner of Police for the Metropolis ex parte Blackburn (No 3)* (1973). In that case, the applicant sought to compel, by order of the court, enforcement of the Obscene Publications Act 1959. However, the Chief Officer had increased the numbers in the vice squad, and reorganised its working methods.

Police discretion returned for consideration in *R v Chief Constable of Sussex ex parte International Traders' Ferry Ltd* (1997). In that case, animal rights protesters, concerned about the welfare of live animal exports, blockaded ports in order to stop the exports. To assist the exporter, the police deployed 1,125 officers, a level of policing which was maintained for some ten days. In order to maintain the

---

36   PACE 1984, s 67(10).

operation, seven other police forces assisted.[37] The cost of the operation amounted to £1.25 million. The Home Office refused to make a special grant to assist with the financial cost of the operation. In April, the Chief Constable indicated that new arrangements would have to be made, which would involve the company having to reduce its shipments. The company sought judicial review of the Chief Constable's decision. The Court of Appeal upheld the Divisional Court's refusal to interfere with the decision of the Chief Constable. In light of the circumstances, the Chief Constable's decision could not be 'regarded as so unreasonable as to enable a court to interfere'. The court approved the statement of Neill LJ in *Harris v Sheffield United Football Club Ltd* (1987):

> I see the force of the argument that the court must be very slow before it interferes in any way with a decision of a chief constable about the disposition of his forces.

The House of Lords affirmed the decision of the Court of Appeal.

In *R (Tucker) v Director General of the National Crime Squad* (2003), the Court of Appeal ruled that the police are entitled to run their affairs concerning operational or management decisions without the intervention of the courts, and therefore those matters, as distinct from disciplinary issues, were not amenable to judicial review.

Complaints against the police

The Police Reform Act 2002 establishes a new system for handling complaints against the police and introduces a new body – the Independent Police Complaints Commission (IPCC) – to oversee the system.[38] The IPCC is a non-departmental public body.

The IPCC consists of a chairperson appointed by the Crown and not less than ten other members appointed by the Secretary of State. The functions of the Commission are set out in section 10 of the Police Reform Act 2002 as being:

(a) the handling of complaints made against the police;

(b) recording police conduct which may constitute a criminal offence or behaviour justifying disciplinary proceedings.

Complaints against the police may be made by a member of the public who claims to be the person in relation to whom the conduct took place, or a person who, while not being the direct victim, claims to have been adversely affected by the conduct. A person who witnesses the conduct may complain, as may a person acting on behalf of one of the people within the above categories.[39] Police conduct which has not been the subject of a complaint, but which involves a criminal offence or behaviour justifying disciplinary proceedings, must be referred to the IPCC. Where the IPCC considers that a matter requires investigation, it may choose to conduct one of four types of investigation:

---

37 Under the Police Act 1964 (now the Police Act 1996, s 24).

38 The Independent Police Complaints Commission replaced the Police Complaints Authority originally established under the Police and Criminal Evidence Act 1984. See *Complaints Against the Police: Framework for a New System*, available through the Home Office website at www.homeoffice.gov.uk.

39 Police Reform Act 2002, s 12.

- a police investigation on behalf of the appropriate police authority;
- a police investigation supervised by the IPCC;
- a police investigation managed by the IPCC;
- an investigation by the IPCC independent of the police.[40]

The Act imposes a duty on all police authorities, chief officers of police forces and Directors General of the National Criminal Intelligence Service and National Crime Squad to co-operate and assist in investigations and to provide information.[41] Independent IPCC investigations will take place in relation to the most serious complaints or conduct matters and those of the highest public interest.[42] Once the investigation is complete, the results must be reported. If the report indicates that a criminal offence may have been committed by a police officer, the IPCC must notify the Director of Public Prosecutions to decide whether criminal proceedings are to be brought against the officer. The complainant and other interested persons[43] must be informed of the outcome of an investigation.

The 2002 Act introduces a right of appeal for the complainant. In relation to an investigation undertaken on behalf of the appropriate authority or one supervised by the Commission, the complainant may appeal to the Commission against the finding of the investigation, or against the proposal to take, or not to take, action in respect of matters dealt with in the report, or on the basis that he or she has not been given adequate information either about the findings or about the action which the authority proposes.

The European Convention on Human Rights and the police[44]

The Human Rights Act 1998 incorporates Convention rights. The Convention had already had an impact on the liability of police. The European Court of Human Rights ruled, in *Osman v United Kingdom* (1998), that Article 6 had been violated in respect of the effect of the police's immunity from civil actions under the rule formulated in *Hill v Chief Constable of West Yorkshire Police* (1989). The applicant alleged that there had been violations relating to Articles 2, 6 and 8 of the Convention. The applicant's son had become the object of attachment on the part of a schoolteacher, and the family had suffered criminal damage to their home: the police visited the school but took no further action. Subsequently, the teacher was questioned by police in relation to missing school files. Following damage to the family's home and other incidents, the police again questioned the teacher. In 1988, the teacher went to the Osmans' home, where he shot and killed the applicant's husband and injured her son. He then shot and injured the deputy headmaster and shot and killed his son.

---

40 *Ibid*, Sched 3, para 15(4).
41 *Ibid*, ss 15, 17.
42 Such investigations are entirely new and result from recommendations of the Home Affairs Committee and the Inquiry into the death of Stephen Lawrence: See the Macpherson Report, available through www.official-documents.co.uk.
43 As defined in s 21.
44 See further Chapter 19.

In 1989, the applicant commenced a civil action against the police. In 1992, the Court of Appeal upheld the request of the police that the statement of claim be struck out, on the basis that, according to the ruling in *Hill*, no action could lie for public policy reasons against the police for their negligence in the investigation and suppression of crime.

The Court of Human Rights ruled that, in relation to Article 2, there was no violation of the Convention, *inter alia*, because of the difficulty in policing modern societies, the unpredictability of human conduct and the operational choices which the police had to make. Any obligation to protect the right to life of the applicant's husband had to be interpreted in a way which did not impose an impossible or disproportionate burden on the authorities. In respect of Article 8, which was allegedly breached by the failure of the police to protect the family, no violation was found. The Court ruled that, given the finding in relation to Article 2, it followed that there had been no violation of any implied positive obligation under Article 8. In relation to Article 6, however, the Court ruled unanimously that the application of the exclusionary rule constituted a disproportionate restriction on the applicant's right of access to a court.

In *Price v United Kingdom* (2001), the Court of Human Rights ruled that the detention of a severely disabled person in unsuitable conditions at a police station and subsequent detention in prison in similar conditions amounted to degrading treatment contrary to Article 3. The authorities admitted that they were unable to cope with the applicant's special needs. There was no evidence of any positive intention to humiliate or debase the applicant. However, to detain a seriously disabled person in such conditions which risked her health constituted a violation of Article 3. See also *Edwards v United Kingdom* (2002), in which the United Kingdom was found to have violated Article 2 through its failure to protect the life of a prisoner killed in his cell by a fellow inmate who had a history of violence and had been diagnosed schizophrenic. There had been a failure on the part of the agencies involved to pass on information about the victim, and failures in the mechanisms designed to protect prisoners. A private, non-statutory inquiry had been established to investigate and report on the death, the proceedings of which were defective and violated the procedural obligation of Article 1 to hold an effective investigation into the victim's death. There was also a violation of Article 13, in that the victim's parents had no avenue through which to secure an enforceable award of compensation for the damage suffered.

Notwithstanding the critical stance of the Court of Human Rights, the decision of *Hill v Chief Constable of West Yorkshire* (1989) was applied by the House of Lords in *Brooks v Commissioner of Police of the Metropolis* (2005). The claimant and his friend L, who were black, were attacked by a group of white youths and L was killed. The claimant's treatment by the police was the subject of severe criticism in the report of an inquiry established to look into the matter. He brought an action against the police and Crown Prosecution Service, claiming damages for negligence, false imprisonment and misfeasance in public office and racial discrimination. While other actions were discontinued or struck out, the Court of Appeal had allowed his appeal in relation to his claim in negligence against the Commissioner in respect of three duties of care that he alleged had been owed to him by the police (in relation to protecting, supporting and assisting a victim/eye-witness of a serious crime and to give reasonable weight to the account given to the police and act upon it).

The House of Lords ruled that as a matter of public policy the police generally owed no duty of care to victims or witnesses in respect of their activities when investigating suspected crimes. Since the duties of care alleged by the claimant had been inextricably bound up with the investigation of a crime, his claim based on those duties should be struck out. Lord Steyne stated that the prime function of the police is the 'preservation of the Queen's peace'. The 'police must concentrate on preventing the commission of crime; protecting life and property; and apprehending criminals and preserving evidence . . . retreat from the principle in *Hill's* case would have detrimental effects for law enforcement . . . placing general duties of care on the police to victims and witnesses the police's ability to perform their public functions in the interests of the community, fearlessly and with despatch, would be impeded. It would, as was recognised in *Hill's* case, be bound to lead to an unduly defensive approach in combating crime.'

POLICE POWERS IN RELATION TO THE DETECTION AND INVESTIGATION OF CRIME

Questioning by the police

It is a fundamental rule that the citizen is not obliged to answer police questions, unless there is lawful justification for official interference with the citizen's liberty. The rule was endorsed in *Rice v Connolly* (1966). There, the appellant was questioned by the police. He refused to answer questions and was, accordingly, arrested for obstructing a police officer in the execution of his duty contrary to section 51(3) of the Police Act 1964.[45] On appeal, Lord Parker CJ stated that a citizen has every right to refuse to answer questions; generally the citizen has a 'right to silence'.

In *Kenlin v Gardiner* (1967), the issue in question concerned whether a person could lawfully be stopped in the street by the police. Police officers attempted to question two boys. One of the boys tried to run away, whereupon a police constable tried physically to stop him and a scuffle broke out. The boys were charged with assaulting a police constable in the execution of his duty. There was no question that an assault on the police had occurred. The question for decision was whether the assault by the boys was justified. The Divisional Court held that the attempt to restrain the boy amounted to an assault by the police officer, and was, accordingly, an unlawful attempt to detain him. As such, the police officer was not acting in the course of his duty and, as a result, the boys were not guilty of assaulting a police officer 'in the execution of his duty'. A distinction must be made between a refusal to answer questions and conduct which amounts to obstruction of the police; see further below.

---

45 Now, Police Act 1996, s 89.

There are, however, situations in which a citizen is under a duty to answer questions. For example, under road traffic law,[46] there is a duty to give one's name and address, and a refusal to do so and to give up one's driving licence and other motoring documents is an offence. Other than under statutory authority, however, there is a right to silence.[47]

Power exists to stop motorists on any ground, and failure to stop is an offence.[48] A police officer is entitled to immobilise a car by removing the ignition keys. The vehicle owner may be detained in order to allow the officer sufficient time to determine whether an arrest is to be made, to effect arrest, and to give reasons for the arrest. Moreover, the police have the power to detain a motorist in order to administer a breathalyser test.[49] Powers also exist under the Official Secrets Act 1911 whereby the Home Secretary can grant the police permission to question suspects. Refusal to answer questions in respect of inquiries made in respect of investigations into fraud and drug trafficking can amount to a criminal offence, as can refusal to disclose information under the Terrorism Acts.[50]

Stop and search powers

Under the Police and Criminal Evidence Act 1984, the police have been given the power to stop and search a person reasonably suspected of carrying prohibited articles such as offensive weapons and/or housebreaking equipment or stolen goods. The Criminal Justice Act 2003 extends the list of prohibited articles to include an article made, adapted or intended for use in causing criminal damage.[51] The police also have the power to set up road blocks if there are reasonable grounds for suspicion that a person in the area has committed a serious arrestable offence (see further below), or that a serious arrestable offence is about to be committed, or that a person is unlawfully 'at large'.[52] Section 60 of the Criminal Justice and Public Order Act 1994 provides that powers may be given to the police, by a police officer of the rank of superintendent or above, to stop and search persons and vehicles, where that officer reasonably believes that incidents involving serious violence may take place in any locality in his area, and that it is expedient so to do to prevent their occurrence. The authorisation lasts for up to 24 hours. If no superintendent is available, a Chief Inspector or Inspector may grant authorisation for the stop and search if 'he reasonably believes that incidents involving serious violence are imminent'.[53]

---

46   See the Road Traffic Act 1988, s 163, as amended by the Serious Organised Crime and Police Act 2005.
47   *Lodwick v Sanders* (1985), but see below.
48   Road Traffic Act 1988, s 163.
49   *Lodwick v Sanders* (1985).
50   See Chapter 25. See also the Official Secrets Act, s 6, which imposes a duty to provide information as to offences under the 1911 Act.
51   PACE 1984, s 1, as amended by the Criminal Justice Act 2003.
52   Road Traffic Act 1988 and PACE 1984, s 4.
53   PACE 1984, s 60(2).

The Police Act 1997

Article 8 of the European Convention on Human Rights provides for respect for private and family life, home and correspondence. Surveillance operations and interception of communications are intrinsic aspects of policing. There being no common law or statutory right to privacy under domestic law, such techniques were not unlawful, as confirmed by Sir Robert Megarry VC in *Malone v Metropolitan Police Commissioner* (1979). However, in *Malone v United Kingdom* (1984) the Court of Human Rights ruled that there was insufficient protection given by law. The Interception of Communications Act 1985 was passed to remedy the defects in domestic law. The legal framework is now set out in the Regulation of Investigatory Powers Act 2000 (on which see Chapter 25). The Police Act 1997 places the power of the police to interfere with property and plant surveillance devices on a statutory basis. Modelled on the Interception of Communications Act 1985,[54] the Act provides that authorisation for the bugging of property may be given on the basis that it would facilitate the 'prevention and detection of serious crime' which cannot 'reasonably be achieved by other means'.[55] No exemptions from the provisions are made: thus, solicitors' offices, doctors' surgeries and even Roman Catholic confessionals may fall victim to bugging by the police. Authorisation must be given by the Chief Officer of Police[56] or, if he is unavailable, by an officer of Chief Constable rank.[57] Written authorisations remain in effect for three months whereas, in cases of emergency, oral authorisation may be made which will remain in force for 72 hours. Following opposition to the Bill, the government accepted that independent commissioners[58] should review the authorisations. Such review does not, however, necessarily precede police action on the warrant. In cases where private dwellings, hotel bedrooms or offices are involved, a commissioner's prior approval for the authorisation is required. Prior approval is also required where the surveillance may result in the revealing of confidential personal information, confidential journalistic material or matters which are subject to legal privilege.[59]

THE PROTECTION OF SUSPECTS

Helping the police with inquiries[60]

In law, the police have no power to detain a person in order to make inquiries. Section 29 of the Police and Criminal Evidence Act clarifies this rule. A person is either free to leave a police station where he voluntarily attends to assist the police, or the police must arrest him. If a person is detained by the police, he must be informed immediately that he is under arrest and be given reasons for the arrest, the absence of which may render the arrest unlawful.

---

54 See now the Regulation of Investigatory Powers Act 2000, discussed in Chapter 25.
55 Police Act 1997, s 93(2).
56 *Ibid*, s 93(5).
57 *Ibid*, s 94.
58 *Ibid*, s 91(1).
59 *Ibid*, s 97.
60 See Zander, 1997; Clarke and Feldman, 1979.

The identification of suspects

One of the principal causes of wrongful conviction lies in the wrongful identification of suspects.[61] Identification may take place by witnessing, or by fingerprinting and the taking of bodily samples. Code of Practice D governs the procedures to be followed, although Code D does not regulate those detained as terrorist suspects under the Terrorism Acts, save for the provisions relating to fingerprinting and bodily samples.

Identification by identity parade is the most reliable means of identification, and will be carried out if the defendant requests it or consents to it. If it is impracticable to hold an identity parade,[62] perhaps because there are a large number of suspects or because there are insufficient people with similar characteristics to the suspect,[63] the police may then turn to alternative means of identification. Identification by witness may be effected by arranging for the witness to see the suspect in a group, generally in a public place away from the police station. The consent of the suspect is required, but his or her failure to consent does not prohibit the use of group identification. Alternatively, video identification may be used. Face to face confrontation of the witness and accused may take place provided identification is not possible by any other means.

Search of the person

Before 1984, there was considerable doubt about the breadth of power to search an arrested person. The police had a common law power to search a person if they reasonably believed that he was carrying a weapon or evidence relevant to the crime of which he was suspected. Resisting a lawful search would amount to obstruction of the police. In *Lindley v Rutter* (1980), the police, having arrested the defendant while drunk, insisted on searching her person and attempted to remove her bra. Ms Lindley resisted the attempt and scratched and bit a police woman. On a charge of obstruction of the police, the magistrates' court convicted Ms Lindley. On appeal, however, the conviction was quashed. While it was conceded that the police were under a duty not to allow a person to escape, or to destroy evidence, the lawfulness of their action depended upon the circumstances of the case. This personal search, which was highly unlikely to yield any evidence, required strong justification. Under the circumstances the police had exceeded their powers. In *Brazil v Chief Constable of Surrey* (1983), the police also attempted to search a woman, in the course of which she assaulted the officers. The police claimed that the search was necessary, first, to ensure the detainee's own safety, and secondly, to discover whether she was carrying drugs. The search was ruled unlawful. There was no need for the search and, in relation to the search for drugs, the detainee had not been informed of the police's reasons for the search. Her conviction for assaulting a police officer in the execution of his duty was quashed.

---

61 *Report of the Criminal Law Revision Committee*, Cmnd 4991, 1972, London: HMSO, para 196.
62 Cf *R v Ladlow, Moss, Green and Jackson* (1989) and *R v Penny* (1991).
63 See *Campbell* (1993).

Search of an arrested person under the Police and Criminal Evidence Act 1984

The Police and Criminal Evidence Act 1984, as amended, provides that searches may be made of an arrested person, the premises on which he or she was arrested and any vehicle in which the suspect was arrested. The grounds for the search are for evidence relating to any offence, or for evidence which may assist the escape of the suspect.[64]

Intimate body searches are also permitted under the 1984 Act. The search must be carried out by a doctor, unless a senior officer believes that that is impracticable. The search may only be made for articles which may cause injury or for class 'A' drugs.[65] The powers to search the person and take personal samples were extended by the Criminal Justice and Public Order Act 1994, section 58, which defines both intimate and non-intimate samples.

The Criminal Justice Act 2003 extends police powers, authorising the police to take electronic fingerprints and a DNA sample. Electronic fingerprinting enables the police to confirm the identity of a suspect within minutes where that person's fingerprints are already held on the National Fingerprint Database. The DNA sample will be entered onto the National DNA Database. Both databases enable speculative searches to be made to see whether a suspect is linked to any unsolved crime. The Criminal Justice Act 2003 amends PACE 1984 section 61 in relation to the taking of fingerprints without the consent of a person detained at a police station. Non-intimate samples may be also be taken without consent where an arrested person has not yet had such a sample taken, or where the samples prove insufficient.[66]

The conditions of interviews

The Code of Practice on the Detention, Treatment, and Questioning of Persons by Police Officers (Code C) provides that a suspect should be given eight hours in any 24 hours free of questioning. Breaks for refreshment should be given regularly (every two hours), unless such breaks would adversely affect the inquiries. Persons who are mentally disordered and children should be interviewed in the presence of a competent adult. The detention must be reviewed regularly, the first taking place after six hours from the time of lawful detention; subsequent reviews to be conducted at intervals of no more than nine hours.

Tape recording of interviews[67]

The tape recording of police interviews acts as protection for the person being questioned, and as protection for the police against accusations of oppression.

---

64 PACE 1984, s 32(2).
65 The Criminal Justice Act 2003 extends the power to test for special Class A drugs to persons aged 14 and over.
66 Criminal Justice Act 2003, ss 9 and 10.
67 See Baldwin, 1985.

Tape recording is regulated by a code of practice.[68] Both the defence and prosecution have the right to listen to tape recordings, although the police provide summaries of the recordings.[69] The police must maintain proper records of any interview, including the time of commencement and ending and any breaks in questioning. The person interviewed must be allowed to read the record.

The caution

The caution to be administered is laid down in the Criminal Justice and Public Order Act 1994, and reads:

> You do not have to say anything. But, if you do not mention now something which you later use in your defence, the court may decide that your failure to mention it now strengthens the case against you. A record will be made of anything you say and it may be given in evidence if you are brought to trial.[70]

Arrest

A lawful arrest is an arrest for which there is legal authority. Three categories of lawful arrest exist: arrest under warrant, arrest without warrant under common law and arrest without a warrant under statute. Where a person has been wrongly arrested and detained under statute,[71] the person detained is entitled to damages: *Roberts v Chief Constable of Cheshire Constabulary* (1999); *Woodward v Chief Constable, Fife Constabulary* (1998).

Arrest under warrant

Section 1(1) of the Magistrates' Courts Act 1980 provides that a warrant for arrest may be made on the basis that a 'person has, or is suspected of having, committed an offence'. The warrant should not be issued unless the offence is indictable[72] or punishable by imprisonment.[73] The warrant is issued by a magistrate after a written application by a police officer has been substantiated on oath. The warrant may be executed even if the police officer does not have it in his or her possession at the time, but the warrant must be shown to the person arrested as soon as possible.[74] When an arrest warrant has been issued, a constable may enter and search premises to make the arrest, using such reasonable force as is necessary. Where a constable executes a warrant in good faith believing it to be valid, he or she is protected from liability under the Constables' Protection Act 1750. The magistrate may endorse the warrant for bail.

---

68 Code of Practice for the Detention, Treatment and Questioning of Persons by Police Officers, Code C.
69 See Baldwin and Bedward, 1991.
70 Criminal Justice and Public Order Act 1994, s 34, as amended by the Criminal Justice Act 2003, Code C, para 10.4.
71 PACE 1984, s 34; Criminal Justice (Scotland) Act 1980.
72 A serious offence triable by jury in the Crown Court.
73 Criminal Justice Act 1967, s 24(1).
74 Magistrates Courts Act 1980, s 125(3).

Arrest without warrant: common law

The only common law power to arrest without warrant is where there are reasonable grounds for suspicion that a breach of the peace is about to occur, or has been committed and is likely to continue or to reoccur.[75] If violence has occurred or is about to occur to persons or property, a police officer may reasonably believe that a breach of the peace is about to occur. If a breach of the peace has occurred, but has ceased, the power to arrest ceases.

In *Trevor Foulkes v Chief Constable of Merseyside Police* (1998), the Court of Appeal considered the issue of reasonable grounds in law for the arrest and subsequent detention of a person in relation to an apprehended breach of the peace. The police officer had arrested the appellant in the course of a domestic incident, honestly believing that arrest was necessary to prevent a breach of the peace. The Court of Appeal ruled that, where there was no actual breach of the peace but only an apprehended breach, the power of arrest was only to be exercised in the clearest of circumstances where the officer was satisfied that a breach of the peace was imminent. The arresting officer in this case acted honestly but did not have reasonable grounds for the arrest. Arrest was an inappropriate management of a dispute between husband and wife in the family home.

An apprehended breach of the peace was also central to the decision in *Bibby v Chief Constable of Essex Police* (2000). A bailiff had gone to a debtor's premises for the purpose of seizing assets due under a liability order issued by a magistrates' court. The debtor threatened to call his friends to prevent the removal of goods. Fearing a breach of the peace, a police constable, who had been called to the premises, ordered the bailiff to leave. When the bailiff refused, he was arrested and led away to the police station in handcuffs. He was later released without charge. The bailiff sued the police for assault and wrongful imprisonment. The Court of Appeal considered the conditions to be met in order to exercise the 'now exceptional' common law power of arrest. These included the following:

- There must be the clearest of circumstances and a sufficiently real and present threat to the peace to justify the extreme step of depriving of his liberty a citizen who is not at the time acting unlawfully.[76]
- The threat must be coming from the person who is to be arrested.[77]
- The conduct must clearly interfere with the rights of others.
- The natural consequence of the conduct must be violence from a third party.
- The violence from the third party must not be wholly unreasonable.
- The conduct of the person to be arrested must be unreasonable.[78]

In the instant case, the bailiff was acting lawfully and attempting to enforce an order of a court. Although the constable reasonably came to the conclusion that a breach of the peace was imminent he had failed to consider where the threat was

---

75 See *R v Howell* (1982).

76 *Foulkes v Chief Constable of Merseyside Police* (1998).

77 *Redmond-Bate v Director of Public Prosecutions* (1999). The following three points are taken from this case.

78 *Nicol v Director of Public Prosecutions* (1996).

coming from. Accordingly, neither the arrest nor the use of handcuffs was justified.[79]

Arrest without warrant under statute

The powers of arrest provided under sections 24 and 25 of the Police and Criminal Act 1984 (PACE) are based on the concept of the seriousness of the offence in question. Sections 110 and 111 of the Serious Organised Crime and Police Act 2005 (SOCPA) amend these powers. Section 110 provides a replacement section 24 of PACE. The power of arrest without warrant for an arrestable offence is replaced with the power of arrest without warrant for an 'offence'. Under the new section 24(1), a constable has the power of arrest without a warrant in relation to:

    (a) anyone who is about to commit an offence;

    (b) anyone who is in the act of committing an offence;

    (c) anyone whom he has reasonable grounds for suspecting to be about to commit an offence;

    (d) anyone whom he has reasonable grounds for suspecting to be committing an offence.

Under section 24(2) a constable may arrest without a warrant anyone whom he has reasonable grounds to suspect is guilty of an offence which the constable has reasonable grounds to suspect has been committed. If an offence has been committed, a constable may arrest without warrant anyone who is guilty of the offence or anyone whom he has reasonable grounds for suspecting to be guilty of it (section 24(3)). However, the exercise of the power of arrest under subsections (1), (2) or (3) is exercisable only if the constable has reasonable grounds for believing that it is *necessary* to arrest the person in question for any of the reasons specified in subsection (5). These are:

    (a) to enable the name of the person in question to be ascertained (in the case where the constable does not know, and cannot readily ascertain, the person's name, or has reasonable grounds for doubting whether a name given by the person as his name is his real name);

    (b) correspondingly as regards the person's address;

    (c) to prevent the person in question –

        (i) causing physical injury to himself or any other persons;

        (ii) suffering physical injury;

        (iii) causing loss of or damage to property;

        (iv) committing an offence against public decency (subject to subsection (6)); or

        (v) causing an unlawful obstruction of the highway;

    (d) to protect a child or other vulnerable person from the person in question;

    (e) to allow the prompt and effective investigation of the offence or of the conduct of the person in question;

    (f) to prevent any prosecution for the offence from being hindered by the disappearance of the person in question.

---

79 See also *Redmond-Bate v Director of Public Prosecutions* (1999), above.

Section 24(6) provides that subsection (5)(c)(iv) applies only where members of the public going about their normal business cannot reasonably be expected to avoid the person in question.

A new section 24A of PACE relates to the power of persons other than police constables to make an arrest without a warrant. That right is now limited to the power of arrest for indictable offences, and the power may only be exercised on the basis of *necessity*, and in the absence of a constable who could make the arrest. The reasons making an arrest necessary are stipulated as being to prevent the person in question –

  (a) causing physical injury to himself or any other person;
  (b) suffering physical injury;
  (c) causing loss of or damage to property; or
  (d) making off before a constable can assume responsibility for him.

Section 110(2) SOCPA provides that section 25 of PACE setting out the general arrest conditions shall cease to have effect.

Giving reasons for the arrest

A failure to give reasons for an arrest will cause the arrest to be unlawful. In *Christie v Leachinsky* (1947), the House of Lords ruled that a person must be told of the fact of his or her arrest and the grounds for arrest, although this need not be done if the circumstances are obvious or it is difficult to communicate with the arrested person. Section 28 of the Police and Criminal Evidence Act 1984 places the requirements on a statutory basis and makes them more stringent. Subject to a person escaping before the information can be communicated, section 28 requires that:

  (a) the person making the arrest must inform the arrested person of the fact of, and reasons for, arrest, either immediately or as soon as is reasonably practicable afterwards;
  (b) a police officer making an arrest must inform the person arrested of these matters even if they are obvious.

No particular form of words need be used, but they must be in sufficient detail to enable the arrested person to understand the issue and, if possible, to deny the allegation and be released. Where it is not possible to state reasons immediately, for example because the arrestee is reacting violently, reasons must be stated as soon as practicable. This requirement is illustrated in *Director of Public Prosecutions v Hawkins* (1988). In that case, a violent struggle prevented reasons being given immediately. However, when the arrestee was subdued, reasons for the arrest were still not given. The arrest became unlawful when the opportunity to give reasons arose, and reasons were not given. A sympathetic attitude to the arresting authorities was seen in *Lewis v Chief Constable of the South Wales Constabulary* (1991). There, two people were arrested and not immediately informed of the reasons for arrest. In an action for false imprisonment, the Court of Appeal upheld the decision of the circuit judge, that the arrests were unlawful until the reasons were given but, once the reasons were given, the arrests became lawful. In *Taylor v Chief Constable of Thames Valley Police*

(2004), the Court of Appeal ruled that in a case of violent disorder an arrest was lawful provided that the arrested person was informed that he was being arrested on suspicion of violent disorder. However, in *Ghagar v Chief Constable of West Midlands Police* (2000), the Court of Appeal took a strict view in relation to a motoring offence, stating that a police officer must state both the offence which a person is suspected of committing and the power to request a name and address.

The giving of reasons for arrest is also a requirement under the European Convention on Human Rights. In *Fox, Campbell and Hartley v United Kingdom* (1990), the applicants were arrested on suspected terrorist offences, but were not informed of the reason for the arrest, although they were told they were being arrested under a specified statutory provision. When later interviewed, they were asked about specific criminal offences. The Court of Human Rights held that paragraph 5(2) of Article 5 had not been satisfied at the time of the arrest, but that the defect was later rectified. In *Murray v United Kingdom*, the Court again found no breach of Article 5. Although the applicant was denied reasons for some half an hour, she was eventually informed of the reason for arrest during interrogation.

Detention following arrest

Once a person has been arrested, he or she may be detained by the police for questioning before a charge is laid. There exists a fine balance to be achieved here between permitting the police to question a suspect in order to determine whether there exist sufficient grounds on which to make a charge, and the need to protect persons from unwarranted detention by the police. As a general rule, where a person has been charged with an offence he or she must be brought before a magistrates' court 'as soon as practicable'.[80] This provision gives effect to the requirements of the European Convention on Human Rights. The Police and Criminal Evidence Act 1984, as amended, provides that a person may be detained, under the authority of a superintendent, for a maximum of 36 hours for any indictable offence. The time runs from the time of the person's arrest or, in the case of a person's arrest outside the relevant police area, from the time he arrives in the police station.[81]

The period is extendable. The grounds on which extended detention may be authorised are as follows. For authorisation by a senior officer of police, there must be reasonable grounds for believing that the detention is necessary in order to secure or preserve evidence or obtain evidence by questioning; that the offence in question is indictable'; and that the police investigation is being conducted 'diligently and expeditiously'.[82] A review of detention must be made after 24 hours.[83] The police may apply to a magistrates' court for a further period of

---

80 PACE 1984, s 46.
81 *Ibid*, s 41(2)(a)(i), (ii).
82 *Ibid*, s 42(1)(a), (b), (c).
83 *Ibid*, s 42(4).

detention which, if granted, may extend the period of detention to a possible maximum of 96 hours.[84]

Bail

The Criminal Justice Act 2003 amends the Bail Act 1976 in order to ensure that the law is compliant with the European Convention on Human Rights. Article 5 of the Convention provides that 'Everyone has the right to liberty and security of the person and ... no one shall be deprived of his or her liberty except, *inter alia*, where lawfully arrested and detained'. Article 5(3) specifically provides for entitlement to trial within a reasonable time or to release pending trial.

Section 41(7) provides that, if a person has not been charged at the expiry of 36 hours, he shall, subject to sub-section 8, be released, either on bail or without bail.[85] The time limit does not apply to persons whose extended detention has been authorised by a senior officer[86] or where a successful application has been made to a magistrates' court by the police for continued detention.[87] Bail may be subject to conditions, such as reporting to a police station. Exceptionally – as in the case of a Class A drug user whose drug taking contributed to the offence or where he or she has been assessed and refuses to undergo treatment – bail may be denied.[88]

The Criminal Justice Act 2003 enables the police to make an immediate grant of bail ('street bail') where there is no need to deal with the arrested person at a police station.[89]

Conditions of detention

The Codes of Practice detail the conditions under which persons may be held. These include no more than one person in a cell, access to toilet and washing facilities, the provision of adequate food and daily exercise. The police may not use more than 'reasonable force' in relation to detainees in preventing escape or causing damage to property. Appropriate medical treatment must be given where necessary. Article 3 of the European Convention on Human Rights, incorporated into domestic law under the Human Rights Act 1998, prohibits torture and inhuman or degrading treatment or punishment.[90]

In *R v Commissioner of Police of the Metropolis* (1999), the House of Lords ruled that authorities, such as the police or prison service, who were entrusted with holding prisoners in custody, had a duty to take reasonable care to prevent them from harming themselves or committing suicide. Where there was a breach of that duty and a suicide occurred, the authorities were not entitled to rely on the

---

84   PACE 1984, s 43 as amended by the Serious Organised Crime and Police Act 2005, and s 44.
85   Bail Act 1976, as amended.
86   PACE 1984, s 42(1).
87   *Ibid*, s 43.
88   Criminal Justice Act 2003, s 19, amending the Bail Act 1976, s 3.
89   *Ibid*, Part 1, amending PACE 1984, s 30.
90   See *Price v United Kingdom* (2001), discussed on p 499, and *Napier v Scottish Ministers* (2001), on p 525.

defences of *volenti non fit injuria* or *novus actus interveniens* in an action for negligence brought by the estate of the deceased.

The right to legal advice[91]

Under section 58(1) of the Police and Criminal Evidence Act 1984, 'a person arrested and held in custody in a police station or other premises shall be entitled, if he so requests, to consult a solicitor privately at any time'. The right to legal advice is also protected under Article 6 of the European Convention on Human Rights. See the discussion of *Magee v United Kingdom* (2000), *Condron v United Kingdom* (2001) and *Murray v United Kingdom* (1996) in Chapter 19.

Delay in complying with a request to consult a lawyer is only permitted where the person is being held in connection with a serious arrestable offence and where a senior officer has authorised the delay. The grounds on which delay may be authorised include reasonable grounds for believing that there will be interference with or harm to evidence; that exercising the right would lead to alerting other suspects who have not yet been arrested; or that exercising the right would hinder the recovery of any property obtained as a result of the offence.[92]

Legal representation may be crucial to the protection of the suspect from oppressive questioning by the police. Where confessions are obtained by oppression, a guilty verdict may subsequently be set aside.[93] Guidelines laid down for solicitors who attend interviews are published by The Law Society. The guidelines for intervening in questioning include, *inter alia*, the following:

> ... you may need to intervene if the questions are: ... oppressive, threatening or insulting;
>
> ... you should intervene if the officer is not asking questions but only making his/her own comments ...
>
> ... if questions are improper or improperly put, you should intervene and be prepared to explain your objections ...
>
> ... if improprieties remain uncorrected or continue, advise the suspect of his/her right to remain silent.[94]

When a person has been arrested and is being held in custody at a police station, he or she has the right to communicate with one other person 'as soon as practicable'.[95] A delay is only permitted where an officer of the rank of superintendent authorises it, on the basis that 'he has reasonable grounds to believe' that the communication will lead to interference with evidence connected with a serious arrestable offence, or physical injury to other persons, or will lead to alerting of other suspects connected with the offence, and will hinder the recovery of property obtained as a result of the offence.[96] Section 58(1) of the Police and Criminal Evidence Act 1984 also provides that a person who is in police detention 'shall be entitled, if he so requests, to consult a solicitor privately at any time'. In

---

91 See Baldwin, 1993.
92 PACE 1984, s 58(8) and see Code C.
93 See *R v Paris, Abdullahi and Miller* (1992).
94 *Guidelines*, 1991, London: The Law Society, para 6.
95 PACE 1984, s 56.
96 *Ibid*, s 56(5)(a), (b), (c).

addition, section 59 inserts into the Legal Aid Act 1982 a provision which is capable of preventing a solicitor from providing advice and legal representation under the legal aid scheme if 'they do not also provide advice and assistance ... for persons ... held in custody'. Under Code of Practice C,[97] a detainee is to be informed of the right to legal advice,[98] and given the name of a duty solicitor if he or she requires it.[99] The detainee is also entitled to have a solicitor present during questioning.[100] However, where a person is arrested for a serious arrestable offence, and an officer of the rank of superintendent or above so authorises, access to a solicitor may be delayed for up to 36 hours. Such a delay may be authorised where the officer is concerned that there is a risk to witnesses or to evidence relating to the case, or where immediate access would hinder the recovery of any property obtained as a result of the offence.[101] In cases of suspected terrorism, the right to consult a solicitor is conditioned by the requirement that the interview is conducted within 'the sight and hearing' of a uniformed officer.[102] The Court of Appeal has construed section 58(8) narrowly. In *R v Samuel* (1988), it was held that delay in access to legal advice can only be justified on specific grounds which must be substantiated to the satisfaction of the court.

The right to inform someone of arrest and detention

A person held in a police station is entitled to inform a relative or friend 'or other person concerned with his welfare' of his arrest without delay, unless such notification would prejudice the investigation of crime or the arrest of other suspects.[103]

The right to silence[104]

In relation to the right to silence, the position of a person who has been arrested is different from that of a citizen before arrest. The reforms introduced under the Criminal Justice and Public Order Act 1994 are amongst the most controversial reforms to the protection of an accused for many years. Those who oppose a weakening of the right to silence base their arguments on the relative vulnerability of the accused, and the need to protect the accused from making statements which might falsely incriminate him or her.[105] Against this concern must be set the argument that when individuals are permitted to remain silent when questioned by the police, advantage of this right is taken by 'professional criminals' who are familiar with the process. The concern has been that such

---

97   PACE 1984, Code C.
98   *Ibid*, para 3.1(ii).
99   *Ibid*, Note 6B.
100 *Ibid*, para 6.5.
101 *Ibid*, s 58(8).
102 *Ibid*, s 58(15).
103 *Ibid*, s 56.
104 See McConville and Hodgson, 1993.
105 The reform was opposed by, *inter alia*, the Law Society, the Bar Council and the Magistrates' Association. Those in favour included the Police Service, the Crown Prosecution Service, HM Council of Circuit Judges and many senior judges.

persons will conceal information under questioning and then 'ambush' the prosecution by revealing the information in court.[106]

Sections 34 to 38 of the Criminal Justice and Public Order Act 1994 effected the reforms. Under section 34, where an accused is being questioned under caution and fails to mention any fact later relied on in his evidence or, where the accused has been officially charged with an offence[107] or officially informed that he might be prosecuted for it,[108] he fails to mention any fact which in the circumstances existing at the time 'the accused could reasonably have been expected to mention' when questioned, charged or informed, then the court, in determining whether there is a case to answer,[109] and the court of jury, in determining whether the accused is guilty of the offence charged,[110] may 'draw such inferences from the failure as appear proper'. Following the case of *Murray v United Kingdom* (1996),[111] such inferences may only be drawn when the accused has consulted a lawyer before exercising the right to silence.[112]

Section 35 relates to the accused's silence at trial. Other than where a person's guilt is not in issue, or where the court considers that the physical or mental condition of the accused 'makes it undesirable for him to give evidence', the court must satisfy itself that the accused is aware that the stage has been reached where he or she can give evidence in defence. If the accused then chooses not to give evidence, or without good cause refuses to answer questions, it is permissible for the court or jury to draw such inferences 'as appear proper from his failure to give evidence or his refusal, without good cause, to answer any question'.[113] Section 35 relates to persons who have attained the age of 14 years[114] and, where the age of the person is 'material', his age 'shall for those purposes be taken to be that which appears to the court to be his age'.[115]

Section 36 relates to the effect of an accused's failure to account for objects, substances or marks. Where a person has been arrested by a constable, and the police reasonably believe that the presence of the object, substance or mark may be attributable to the accused participating in the commission of a specific offence, the police are entitled to ask for an explanation as to the object, etc.[116] If the person fails to account for it, then the court, when (a) considering whether to dismiss the charge, or (b) deciding whether there is a case to answer, or (c) deciding whether the accused is guilty of the offence charged, is entitled to 'draw such inferences from the failure or refusal as appear proper'.[117]

---

106 See *R v Zuckerman* (1989).
107 Criminal Justice and Public Order Act 1994, s 34(1)(a). For judicial guidance see *R v Argent* (1997). See also *R v Cowan* (1996); *R v Friend* (1997); *R v Morgan* (2001).
108 *Ibid*, s 34(1)(b).
109 *Ibid*, s 34(2)(c).
110 *Ibid*, s 34(2)(d).
111 See also *Re Bowden* (1999); *Condron v UK* (2000).
112 Youth Justice and Criminal Evidence Act 1999, s 58.
113 Criminal Justice and Public Order Act 1994, s 35(2).
114 *Ibid*, s 35(1).
115 *Ibid*, s 35(6).
116 *Ibid*, s 36(1).
117 *Ibid*, s 36(2).

Section 37 relates to the accused's failure to account for his or her presence at a particular place. If a person arrested by a constable was found at a place where the offence was committed, and the officer reasonably believes that his presence was attributable to participation in the offence, and the constable requests him to account for his presence, then, if that person fails to do so, a court, or court or jury, in circumstances (a), (b) and (c) in relation to section 36, may draw 'such inferences from the failure or refusal as appear proper'.[118]

The right to silence and serious fraud trials

Different provisions apply to serious fraud trials. Under the Criminal Justice Act 1987, where the Serious Fraud Office issues a 'section 2 notice', the person to whom the notice is addressed commits a criminal offence if he or she does not attend for interview and answer questions. In addition, under section 432(2) of the Companies Act 1985, where a company is under investigation, a person is under a legal obligation to answer questions. By these means, any 'right to silence' is effectively negatived.[119] In *Saunders v United Kingdom* (1996), the Court of Human Rights ruled that the provisions were in violation of Article 6 of the European Convention on Human Rights.[120]

The reliability of evidence[121]

It is central to the protection of the individual that evidence be obtained in a lawful manner. The question arises as to how the law can secure a balance between ensuring that the police operate within the law and the Codes of Practice which supplement the law, and allowing evidence to be used which may have been obtained in a manner not strictly in accordance with the rules but which does prove that a suspect committed a particular crime. If evidence is made inadmissible on the basis of a procedural irregularity, a guilty suspect may go free. On the other hand, if the evidence – however obtained – is admitted, and proves false, there is a danger of innocent suspects being wrongfully convicted. The use of telephone intercepts by the police is authorised under the Police Act 1997, which makes it clear that such intercepts are lawful provided they are authorised under the Act. In addition, the Regulation of Investigatory Powers Act 2000 provides statutory authority for interceptions by the security forces. On this aspect of the law see Chapter 25.

Prior to the Police and Criminal Evidence Act 1984, the admissibility of evidence was regulated under the common law. A distinction was drawn between illegally obtained evidence which was admissible, and involuntary confessions which were inadmissible on the basis that they might be unreliable.[122] The Police and Criminal Evidence Act 1984 placed the admissibility of evidence on a

---

118 Criminal Justice and Public Order Act 1994, s 37(1), (2), (3).

119 See *Director of the Serious Fraud Office ex parte Smith* (1993); *R v Saunders* (1995).

120 See also *IJL, CMR and AKP v United Kingdom* (2000) and, further, Chapter 19.

121 The law of evidence is complex and outside the scope of this chapter other than by way of introduction. See Fenwick, 2002, Chapter 14.

122 See *R v Isequilla* (1975); *R v Ping Lin* (1976); *R v Sang* (1980).

statutory basis. In relation to confessions, there are four criteria to be employed in determining whether they should be admissible in court. Section 76 regulates confessions.[123] Confessions are admissible into court unless the confession has been obtained by (a) oppression,[124] or (b) in consequence of anything said or done which was likely, in the circumstances existing at the time, to render unreliable any confession which might be made by him in consequence thereof.[125] In those circumstances, the court 'shall not allow the confession to be given in evidence against him except in so far as the prosecution proves to the court beyond reasonable doubt that the confession (notwithstanding that it may be true) was not obtained as aforesaid'.[126] Moreover, in any case where the prosecution proposes to give in evidence a confession, the court may, of its own motion, require the prosecution to prove that the confession has not been obtained in the circumstances above.[127] However, where a confession has been partly or wholly excluded on the grounds above, that fact does not affect the admissibility in evidence (a) of any facts discovered as a result of the confession, or (b) where the confession is relevant as showing that the accused speaks, writes or expresses himself in a particular way, of so much of the confession as is necessary to show that he does so.[128]

In relation to the exclusion of 'unfair evidence', section 78 of the Police and Criminal Evidence Act 1984 provides that:

> In any proceedings, the court may refuse to allow evidence on which the prosecution proposes to rely to be given if it appears to the court that, having regard to all the circumstances, including the circumstances in which the evidence was obtained, the admission of the evidence would have such an adverse effect on the fairness of the proceedings that the court ought not to admit it.[129]

Section 78 of the Police and Criminal Evidence Act 1984 is far wider than section 76, and may be relevant to confessions obtained which do not fall within the requirements of section 76.[130] Thus, for example, if a confession is fabricated, the defence will argue that the accused did not make a confession and, accordingly, that 'confession' could not fall under section 76. The power to refuse to allow evidence is discretionary. Where there has been a breach of the rules under the Police and Criminal Evidence Act, and that breach is substantiated to the satisfaction of the court, the question to be determined is whether the breach is substantial or significant,[131] other than where the police have acted in bad

---

123 Confessions are defined to include 'any statement wholly or partly adverse to the person who made it, whether made to a person in authority or not and whether made in words or otherwise': PACE 1984, s 82.
124 'Oppression' is defined to include torture, inhuman or degrading treatment, and the use or threat of violence (whether or not amounting to torture): PACE 1984, s 76(8).
125 PACE 1984, s 76(1)(a), (b).
126 *Ibid*, s 76(2).
127 *Ibid*, s 76(3).
128 *Ibid*, s 76(4).
129 *Ibid*, s 82(3), preserves the common law power to exclude evidence at the court's discretion.
130 *R v Mason* (1987). See *R v Khan* (1997); *Khan v UK*, discussed in Chapter 19. See also *R v Chalkley* (1998).
131 *R v Keenan* (1989).

faith.[132] Having established whether a breach of the rules is substantial or significant, the court will then look to the nature of the rule in question in relation to the circumstances of the case. Thus, for example, the right to have a legal adviser present will be deemed the more important in relation to a vulnerable suspect who could be easily confused by police questioning.

Alternatives to prosecutions

The identification of the offender and having sufficient evidence to instigate a prosecution does not mean that a prosecution will inevitably follow. The police may decide to take no further action or to give an informal warning. Alternatively they may administer a formal caution which diverts the offender away from the criminal justice system.[133] A caution may only be given where the offender admits the offence, there is sufficient evidence to prosecute and the offender gives informed consent to the caution.[134] Once these conditions are satisfied, consideration must also be given to the public interest, taking into account the nature of the offence, the likely penalty if convicted, the age and health of the offender, previous criminal history and the offender's attitude to the offence. The caution is formally recorded and subsequently may be disclosed in court. There are potential difficulties with the caution: for example in relation to sex offenders, who will be entered on to the register of sex offenders and required by the police to fulfil certain requirements even though the offender has not been formally convicted of the offence.

The Criminal Justice Act 2003 introduced the Conditional Caution, which is defined as 'a caution which is given in respect of an offence committed by the offender and which has conditions attached to it'. If an offender fails, without reasonable excuse, to comply with any of the conditions the Caution will be cancelled and the offender prosecuted for the original offence. In order for a Conditional Caution to be given, three criteria must be satisfied. First the offender must be aged 18 or over. Second, the offender must admit the offence to an 'authorised person' and third, the prosecutor must consider that there is sufficient evidence to charge the offender with the offence.[135]

Conditions attached to a Caution fall into two main categories: rehabilitation and reparation. Rehabilitation conditions may relate to treatment for drug or alcohol dependence, or anger management courses. They may also involve restorative justice processes whereby the offender and victim are brought together with a view to helping reduce the victim's fear of crime and overcome the trauma caused by the crime and also to reduce reoffending.[136] Reparation conditions may include making good any damage caused, restoring stolen goods, paying modest

---

132 *R v Walsh* (1989).

133 See *The National Standards Home Office Circular* 18/1994.

134 The Crime and Disorder Act 1998, s 65 introduces a statutory scheme of reprimands and final warnings which replace cautions for young offenders.

135 See www.cps.gov.uk/publications/docs/conditionalcautioningcode2004.pdf.

136 See *Conditional Cautioning: Criminal Justice Act 2003, sections 22–27. Code of Practice and associated annexes*, London: Home Office.

financial compensation or in some cases a simple apology to the victim. The involvement of the victim is entirely voluntary.[137]

Habeas corpus

The ancient writ of habeas corpus is available to test the legality of a person's detention. The writ can be issued either by the person imprisoned or by someone acting on his behalf. If it is established that there is a *prima facie* ground for believing the detention to be unlawful, the writ will be issued. Habeas corpus is used in several areas of law where acts of the executive result in detention. Its use can be seen in, for example, immigration and asylum law and mental health law. In *Nikonovs v Governor of Brixton Prison* (2005), the Court of Appeal stated that the right to habeas corpus could only be restricted by express statutory language and could not be implied into an Act

Originally a common law power, the right to a writ was placed on a statutory basis under the Habeas Corpus Act 1679. The Act of 1679 relates to persons imprisoned on a criminal charge. The Habeas Corpus Act 1816 relates to persons detained other than on a criminal charge.[138] AV Dicey instructed that:

> ... if, in short, any man, woman, or child is deprived of liberty, the court will always issue a writ of habeas corpus to any one who has the aggrieved person in his custody to have such person brought before the court, and if he is suffering restraint without lawful cause, set him free.[139]

In the case of *Wolfe Tone* (1798), Tone was tried and found guilty of high treason by a court-martial and sentenced to death. A writ was issued on the basis that, since Wolfe Tone was not under commission to the English army, but rather held a commission from the French Republic, there was no jurisdiction for his trial by court-martial in Ireland. The Lord Chief Justice instructed the sheriff to go immediately to the army barracks and demand that Tone not be executed. When the officers refused to comply with the order, the Lord Chief Justice ordered that Tone, and the detaining officers, be taken into the custody of the sheriff. On seeking to recover Tone from detention, it was found that he had cut his throat and could not be moved. On this case, Dicey wrote, seemingly without irony, that 'it will be admitted that no more splendid assertion of the supremacy of law can be found than the protection of Wolfe Tone by the Irish Bench'.[140]

The writ has also been used to test the legality of detention of slaves: *Sommersett's Case* (1771) and of students: *Ex parte Daisy Hopkins* (1891). In *Board of Control ex parte Rutty* (1956), a writ was issued to test the legality of the detention of a mentally defective patient who had been detained for eight years without an order of a court. Nowadays, the writ of habeas corpus is most often used to test the legality of the detention of immigrants. However, in *R v Home Secretary ex*

---

137 See further www.homeoffice.gov.uk/justice/victims/personal/index.html.
138 The Habeas Corpus Act 1862 prohibits the courts from issuing writs in respect of colonies or dominions where those jurisdictions have power to issue the writ.
139 Dicey, 1885, p 219.
140 Dicey, 1885, p 294. See also Heuston, 1964, Chapter 2; *Stockdale v Hansard* (1839); and *Sheriff of Middlesex's* case (1840), discussed in Chapter 18.

parte Mughal (1974) and *R v Home Secretary ex parte Zamir* (1980), the court refused to allow habeas corpus to be used to question the decision to remove an illegal immigrant from the country. Conversely, in *R v Home Secretary ex parte Khawaja* (1984), the House of Lords ruled that the question as to whether a person was an illegal immigrant was not within the exclusive jurisdiction of the Home Secretary to decide. Rather it was a matter of fact, which the courts would decide. Before Khawaja could be removed from the country, the court had to be satisfied on the evidence that he was in fact an illegal immigrant. Only if he was an illegal immigrant would the court permit deportation.

There exists an overlap between habeas corpus and judicial review which causes uncertainty: see Chapters 26 and 27. In *R v Home Secretary ex parte Cheblak* (1991), the Court of Appeal held that habeas corpus is not a substitute for judicial review proceedings. However, where an application for judicial review is pending, a writ may be used to ensure that the applicant is not prematurely removed from the country.[141]

The use of habeas corpus is supplemented by the European Convention on Human Rights, Article 5 of which provides that every person who is detained is entitled to take proceedings by which the lawfulness of the detention is decided speedily by a court and release ordered if the detention is not lawful. See further Chapter 19.

PROTECTION OF PERSONAL PROPERTY

In *Semayne's Case* (1605), the principle that an 'Englishman's home is his castle' was judicially declared. Two early cases reveal judicial boldness in the protection from unlawful entry into property. In *Wilkes v Wood* (1763), an Under Secretary of State, accompanied by police, entered Wilkes's home, broke open his desk and seized papers. In an action for trespass against the Under Secretary, Lord Pratt CJ stated that the power claimed would affect 'the person and property of every man in this kingdom, and is totally subversive of the liberty of the subject'. Moreover, such action, being without justification and unlawful, was 'contrary to the fundamental principles of the constitution'.

In the seminal case of *Entick v Carrington* (1765), the Secretary of State, under a general warrant, authorised the entry into property and the seizure of property belonging to Entick, who was suspected of publishing seditious literature. In an action for trespass against Carrington, Lord Camden CJ declared:

This power, so claimed by the Secretary of State, is not supported by a single citation from any law book extant ...

If it is law, it will be found in our books. If it is not to be found there, it is not law.

By the laws of England, every invasion of private property, be it ever so minute, is a trespass. No man can set his foot upon my ground without my licence, but he is liable to an action, though the damages be nothing ...

---

141 *R v Home Secretary ex parte Muboyayi* (1991).

Every entry into the property of the citizen must be authorised by law. However, such freedom from arbitrary intrusion is – in the absence of a written guarantee of rights – subject always to the sovereignty of parliament. It may also be that the royal prerogative will confer legitimacy on what might otherwise be deemed an invasion of property. The principle that 'a man's home is his castle' has many exceptions. For example, statutory rights of entry are conferred on employees of public authorities. In addition to rights of physical entry into property, the issue of warrants to intercept communications[142] authorises a non-physical but nevertheless real intrusion into a person's private property.

Rights of entry under common law

The courts have considered rights of entry under common law. In *Thomas v Sawkins* (1935), it was held that the police are entitled to be present at a public meeting on private premises even where organisers asked them to leave. The officers had reasonably believed that a breach of the peace would occur and that they were therefore justified in remaining and were not trespassing.[143] In *R v Inland Revenue Commissioners ex parte Rossminster Ltd* (1980), however, the House of Lords ruled that clear wording in a statute would override the individual's right to privacy in the home.

Police powers of entry came into conflict with Article 8 of the European Convention in *McLeod v United Kingdom* (1998). The applicant was required by a court order to surrender certain items to her former husband. The former husband entered the premises, with members of his family and a solicitor's clerk, with the permission of the applicant's mother, but in the applicant's absence. The police had been called because of fears of a breach of the peace and entered the premises and checked the list of items to be removed. Following the applicant's return, the police insisted that the husband leave with the property. The applicant's action against the police was dismissed by the Court of Appeal. The Court of Human Rights ruled that although the police's action was lawful and had the legitimate aim of preventing a breach of the peace, their entry in the applicant's absence and their failure to check the terms of the court order rendered their conduct disproportionate and in violation of the right to privacy.

Police powers of entry, search and seizure

The police have special powers of entry and search, recognised under common law, but now clarified under the Police and Criminal Evidence Act 1984. For the most part, entry is authorised under a warrant authorised by a magistrate.[144] Where a warrant is issued, any constable may execute it and any person authorised to accompany a constable has the same powers as that constable.[145] A warrant must be executed within one month and entry and search must be undertaken at a reasonable time, unless the purpose of the search would be

---

142 Under the Regulation of Investigatory Powers Act 2000. See further Chapter 23.
143 See Goodhart, 1936–38.
144 PACE 1984, s 8.
145 *Ibid*, s 16, as amended by the Criminal Justice Act 2003, s 2.

frustrated by entry at a reasonable time. Over and above entry under warrant, however, there exists a class of cases under which the police may enter without warrant under sections 17 and 18 of the Act. Included in this class are entry to arrest for an indictable offence or for offences under the Public Order Act 1936, or Criminal Law Act 1977. Entry without warrant is also lawful if exercised to recover a prison, court or mental hospital detainee and to save life or prevent serious damage to property.

Under sections 18 and 19 of the Police and Criminal Evidence Act 1984, the police have the power to seize and retain a vehicle and not just parts of it or its contents, although those sections relate to 'premises'. The Court of Appeal so held in *Cowan v Commissioner of Police of the Metropolis* (2000). The court also ruled that a vehicle was 'premises' for the purpose of the Act and the Act did not give power to seize premises but only contents, and that rule applied where the premises were immovable and could not physically be removed. Where premises were moveable there was no reason not to interpret 'anything' in sections 18 and 19 as including 'everything'. When exercising a search warrant under section 8(1) of the Police and Criminal Evidence Act 1984, however, a police officer was not entitled to remove items from the premises in order to sift through them for the purpose of deciding whether they fell within the scope of the warrant.[146] In *Webb v Chief Constable of Merseyside Police* (2000), the Court of Appeal ruled that there was no statutory power for the police to retain money seized by the police in the investigation of drug trafficking, where the person entitled to possession of the money was not convicted of a drug trafficking offence and there was no general power to retain the money on public interest grounds. It might be lawful for the police to retain goods of a kind that it was unlawful to deal in them at all, but money was not of this character.

Where police exercise statutory powers of entry by the use of reasonable force, unless circumstances make it impossible, impracticable or undesirable, the police should give any occupant present the reason for his seeking to exercise that power of entry. In *O'Loughlin v Chief Constable of Essex* (1998), the police had entered premises under section 17 of the Police and Criminal Evidence Act 1984, for the purpose of arrest. The Court of Appeal, dismissing an appeal by the Chief Constable of Essex against an order of the county court, granted damages and costs to the defendant for, *inter alia*, assault by the defendant's officers.

Under section 32 of the Police and Criminal Evidence Act 1984, where a person is arrested at a place other than a police station, a police constable may search the arrested person for anything which might assist him to escape from lawful custody or for anything which might be evidence relating to an offence, and to enter and search any premises in which he was when arrested or immediately before he was arrested for evidence relating to the offence for which he has been arrested.[147] The power is subject to the requirement that the 'constable has reasonable grounds for believing that the arrested person may

---

146 *R v Chesterfield Justices ex parte Bramley* (1999).
147 PACE 1984, s 32(2).

present a danger to himself or others'.[148] The power to search is limited to what is 'reasonably required' for the purpose of discovery.[149] Search of the person is restricted: a person may not be required to remove any of his or her clothing in public, other than an outer coat, jacket or gloves, and the search may only be conducted if the constable 'has reasonable grounds for believing' that the person concerned has concealed on his or her person anything for which a search is permitted.[150] If the permitted search discloses anything which might be used to cause physical injury to the person or any other person, the officer may seize and retain anything found, other than an item subject to legal privilege, if there are reasonable grounds for believing that the item may be used to assist escape from lawful custody, or is evidence of an offence, or has been obtained in consequence of the commission of an offence.[151]

Searching a suspect's property

At common law, the legality of searches of a person's property was doubtful. In *Ghani v Jones* (1969), police officers investigating a woman's disappearance searched, without a warrant, her father-in-law's house. At the request of the police, passports and documents were handed over. When the return of the passports was requested, the police refused. The court ruled that where no one had been arrested, the police were justified in taking an article if, first, 'there were reasonable grounds for believing that a serious offence had been committed'; secondly, there were reasonable grounds 'for believing that the article in question is either a fruit of the crime ... or is the instruments by which the crime was committed ... or is material evidence to prove the commission of the crime'; thirdly, the police must reasonably believe that the person in possession of the article has 'himself committed the crime, or is implicated in it, or is accessory to it, or at any rate his refusal must be quite unreasonable'; fourthly, the police must not keep the article longer than reasonably necessary; and finally, the 'lawfulness of the conduct of the police must be judged at the time, and not by what happens afterwards'. This decision tipped the balance very much in favour of the powers of the police, to the detriment of individual citizens. However, in *Jeffrey v Black* (1978), where the defendant was arrested for allegedly stealing a sandwich, and the police subsequently searched his home and found drugs, the court ruled that, whereas the search might have been lawful if the police were looking for evidence connected with the theft, it was unlawful to search for evidence of another offence. In *McLorie v Oxford* (1982), the court disapproved of lenient attitudes to police searches. Lord Justice Donaldson confirmed that there was no common law right to enter into a dwelling house to search for 'the instruments of crime, even of serious crime'. The police are entitled, when searching premises and its occupiers for controlled drugs under a warrant, to restrict the movement of persons to one room while another room is being searched.[152]

---

148 PACE 1984, s 32(1).
149 *Ibid*, s 32(3).
150 *Ibid*, s 32(4), (5).
151 *Ibid*, s 32(8), (9).
152 See *Director of Public Prosecutions v Meaden* (2004).

Police powers to enter property other than after arrest

At common law, the police have no right to enter into private property without a warrant. Accordingly, if they so enter and are asked to leave – even where reasonable force is used to evict them – the police are not acting in the execution of their duty and an individual cannot be convicted for assaulting a police officer executing his duty.[153] There are a number of conditions under which a police officer might enter property, each of which is founded on the basis of a 'lawful excuse'. In the absence of a lawful excuse for entry, the police committed a trespass. At common law, entry was lawful to prevent a breach of the peace,[154] or in the case of actions designed to save life or prevent injury. Under the Criminal Law Act 1967, there was statutory power to enter premises in order to execute an arrest.

In *Khazanchi v Faircharm Investments Ltd; McLeod v Butterwick* (1998), the Court of Appeal held that the police have no right to forcibly enter property for lawful purposes, even where the owner had previously consented to their entry, when the owner, not aware of the police's intention to visit at a particular time, locked his house on leaving.

The right to search premises under the Police and Criminal Evidence Act 1984

Under section 18, a police officer may enter premises of a person arrested for an indictable offence and search for evidence of the offence for which he has been arrested or for related offences. There must be reasonable grounds for believing that the evidence is on the premises. Authorisation for the search must be given by a senior officer, and a written record of the grounds for the search and the evidence sought must be made.[155]

THE CRIMINAL JUSTICE AND POLICE ACT 2001[156]

The 2001 Act provides statutory authority for giving penalty notices under a range of legislation governing minor offences. The effect of complying with the penalty notice is to discharge any liability to be convicted of the offence to which the notice relates.[157] As an alternative, the person concerned may choose to be tried for the offences.

Problems are encountered by the police in the seizure of materials which might be legally privileged, namely correspondence between a client and his or her lawyer. Where the police seize such material and the owner claims that it is

---

153 *Davis v Lisle* (1936).
154 See *Thomas v Sawkins* (1935), above.
155 Special powers also arise under the Terrorism Acts: see Chapter 25. Problems arise with the search of prisoners' property when the claim to legal privilege arises: see *R (Daly) v Secretary of State for the Home Department* (2001), in which the House of Lords ruled that prison officers could not exclude prisoners from their cells in order to effect a search. See Chapter 19.
156 The Act amends the Police and Criminal Evidence Act 1984, the Police and Criminal Evidence (Northern Ireland) Order 1989 and the Terrorism Act 2000.
157 Criminal Justice and Police Act 2001, ss 1 and 2, as amended by the Licensing Act 2003 and Anti-social Behaviour Act 2003.

privileged, the position of the police has proved uncertain.[158] In order to remedy the difficulties, the Criminal Justice and Police Act 2001 provides statutory authority for the removal of property for examination elsewhere and authorises the removal of material which is intrinsically related (such as computer disks), where it is not reasonably practicable for the property to be separated from that which it would otherwise be unlawful to remove.[159] Where property is found to be privileged, it must be returned as soon as is practicable.[160] Any person from whom property is seized may apply to the Crown Court for the return of the property.[161]

THE ANTI-SOCIAL BEHAVIOUR ACT 2003

Tackling antisocial behaviour became a key policy for the Labour government first elected in 1997.[162] The Crime and Disorder Act 1998[163] provided for Anti-social Behaviour Orders (ASBOs) to be granted by Magistrates' Courts or County Courts on the application of the local authority or chief officer of police for the area.[164] In addition British Transport police, registered social landlords, housing action trusts (HATS) and English county councils may apply for ASBOs.[165] The grounds for making an order under section 1 of the Crime and Disorder Act 1998 – which can be made in respect of any person aged ten or over – are:

(a) that the person has acted, since the commencement date [of the Act], in an anti-social manner, that is to say, in a manner that caused or was likely to cause harassment, alarm or distress to one or more persons not of the same household as himself; and

(b) that such an order is necessary to protect persons in the local government area in which the harassment, alarm or distress was caused or was likely to be caused from further anti-social acts by him.[166]

An ASBO prohibits the defendant from doing anything described in the order. Section 1(6) provides that the prohibitions in the order:

are those necessary for the purpose of protecting from further anti-social acts by the defendant –

(a) persons in the local government area; and

(b) persons in any adjoining local government area specified in the application for the order.

---

158 See *R v Chesterfield Justices ex parte Bramley* (2000), in which police seized large amounts of material in order to search it elsewhere, not knowing whether or not any of the material was privileged.

159 Criminal Justice and Police Act 2001, s 50.

160 *Ibid*, s 54.

161 *Ibid*, s 59.

162 See the White Paper *Respect and Responsibility – taking a stand against anti-social behaviour*.

163 As amended by the Police Reform Act 2002 and Anti-social Behaviour Act 2003.

164 Since their introduction in 1999 until the end of June 2005 a total of 4,649 ASBOs had been issued, of which 2,057 had been applied to children aged 10 to 17.

165 Anti-social Behaviour Act 2003, s 13. The section also amends ss 152 and 153 of the Housing Act 1996.

166 Crime and Disorder Act 1998, s 1(1). For the equivalent provision in relation to Scotland see s 19.

The order has effect for a minimum period of two years and will last for a period specified in the order or until further order.[167,168]

The Anti-social Behaviour Act 2003 significantly increased the powers available to local authorities, social housing landlords and the police to deal with a range of anti-social behaviour.[169] Social housing landlords are under a statutory duty to prepare and publish policies and procedures on anti-social behaviour and to make them available to the public.[170,171] The conduct need not cause a nuisance or annoyance to any specific person: it is sufficient that the behaviour could have that effect.[172] The Anti-social Behaviour Act 2003, section 87, extends the scheme to 16 and 17 year olds and provides power to extend it to a lower age group. Where a penalty notice is given, the parent or guardian is liable to pay the penalty.[173]

The legal issues relating to ASBOs[174]

There are several aspects of the ASBO law and procedure which give rise to concern. It can be seen from section 1 above that whereas an order may be based on actual anti-social conduct, it can also be granted where the conduct was 'likely to cause harassment, alarm or distress . . .'. By what criteria are the courts to reach decisions about the likelihood of harassment, alarm or distress? What may cause harassment etc. to one person may cause no reaction in another. If the court is always to gear its decision-making to the weakest victim the scope for making orders rises considerably. In *Chief Constable of Lancashire v Potter* (2003) Auld LJ considered the difficulty in deciding the 'likely' effect of conduct. He took the view, in the instant case relating to prostitution and heroin addiction that the defendant's conduct had to be taken into account together with all the circumstances of the case. 'Likely', he stated, meant 'more probable than not'.

Even where conduct has caused, or is deemed likely to cause harassment etc., no order may be made unless it is 'necessary to protect relevant persons from

---

167 Crime and Disorder Act 1998, s 1(4)(7).

168 The Crime and Disorder Act 1998, section 8, granted the courts power to make 'parenting orders' to provide guidance and counselling to parents of children displaying anti-social behaviour. The Anti-social Behaviour Act 2003 extends the law. Section 19 enables schools and local authorities to enter into parenting contracts where a child has been excluded from school or has failed to attend school regularly. Such contracts are voluntary. A parenting order can be made in relation to parents convicted of school attendance offences: section 20 of the 2003 Act enables local education authorities to apply to Magistrates' Courts for parenting orders for parents of children who have been excluded from school.

169 See Macdonald, 2006.

170 Anti-social Behaviour Act 2003, s 12.

171 An injunction may be granted against any person whose behaviour could cause nuisance or annoyance to anyone listed in s 153A Housing Act 1996, including residents, neighbours, visitors and staff.

172 The 2003 Act also amends the Housing Act 1985 and Housing Act 1988 in relation to secure tenancies which can be demoted on the grounds of anti-social behaviour and for possession proceedings to be brought on the same basis.

173 The law is further extended by the Serious Organised Crime and Police Act 2005, which provides for the lifting of reporting restrictions on juveniles following an ASBO breach, and the Drugs Act 2005, which provides for intervention orders to be attached to an ASBO.

174 See Samuels, 2005; Padfield, 2004; Ashworth, 2004.

further anti-social acts by him'. Here again the court is engaged in a speculative exercise, but nevertheless one which should provide some protection for defendants whose conduct has been anti-social on one occasion but which is not likely to be repeated.

The penalties for contravention of the conditions of an ASBO are severe. On summary conviction, the penalty of a term of imprisonment not exceeding six months or a fine or both, and on conviction on indictment, to imprisonment not exceeding five years or a fine or both. The Criminal Justice and Police Act 2001 introduced a penalty notice scheme for disorderly behaviour.[175]

Anti-social Behaviour Orders are civil, not criminal, orders. An order being imposed involves no prosecution, no formal trial, no conviction or criminal record. None of the rights protected under Article 6 of the European Convention automatically apply.[176] However, breach of the order is a criminal offence carrying heavy penalties. The conditions which may be attached to an ASBO are not limited to prohibitions against repetition of the behaviour which formed the basis for the application. Accordingly, a defendant who breaches one of the conditions may find him or herself facing a heavy penalty for conduct which was not of itself unlawful and which was not the cause of the ASBO. Such penalties suggest retrospectivity in a manner attracting the protection of Article 7 of the Convention on Human Rights. Alternatively, it could be argued that the tough penalties for breaching an ASBO could be used to increase the courts' powers of sentencing for other offences carrying lesser penalties.

The case law is now clarifying some of these issues. For example, in *W v Director of Public Prosecutions* (2005) the Court of Appeal ruled that an ASBO which was drafted so as to prevent an individual from committing any criminal offence was too widely drafted and was unenforceable. W had been convicted of theft, thereby breaching the ASBO. The Court of Appeal ruled that while the ASBO could have been drafted to prohibit theft (or other specific offences) it was too wide and did not specify precisely what an individual could, or could not do. Further in *R v Lee Kirby* (2005) the Court of Appeal ruled that an ASBO should not be made where the underlying objective was to give the court higher sentencing powers in the event of similar offending (in this case dangerous driving and driving whilst disqualified). Nor should an ASBO be a normal part of the sentencing process where the case did not involve intimidation, harassment and distress.[177] In *R v Lamb* (2005) the Court of Appeal ruled that where the breach of an ASBO did not involve harassment, alarm or distress, community penalties should be considered in order to help the offender live within the terms of the

---

175 The Domestic Violence, Crime and Victims Act 2004 provides for a Commissioner for Victims and Witnesses to be appointed by the Secretary of State, in consultation with the Attorney-General and the Lord Chancellor. The Commissioner's primary functions are to promote the interests of victims and witnesses of crime and anti-social behaviour. The Commissioner is also to keep under review the Code of Practice issued in relation to the services provided to victims of crime.

176 See *Carl Wareham v Purbeck Council* (2005), in which the defendant was held not to have the right under Articles 6 or 8 to be heard or consulted in relation to an ASBO appliction.

177 See also *R v Paul Rush* (2005): the imposition of a ten year ASBO to protect the defendant's parents from harassment was excessive and would be reduced to five years.

order. Where such penalties were available, and a custodial sentence imposed, it should be kept as short as possible. In *Chief Constable of West Mercia Constabulary v Boorman* (2005) the High Court ruled that evidence of events which took place more than six months before an application for an ASBO was admissible both for the purposes of proving that a person acted in an antisocial manner within the six-month period and that such an order was necessary. In *R v Boness, R v Bebbington* (2005) the Court of Appeal ruled that an Antisocial Behaviour Order had to be proportionate in relation to the risk to be guarded against. The order had to be tailor-made for the offender, not designed for use in every case. In the instant case the orders were excessive and disproportionate and would be quashed. In *Manchester City Council v Higgins* (2005) the Court of Appeal ruled that a local authority was entitled to immediate possession of a council house tenanted by a mother whose son aged 13 was subject to an ASBO, and subsequently given a secure unit order together with intensive supervision, for his behaviour which made life intolerable for neighbours. The boy had victimised a widow caring for three children each with disabilities. The boy's mother had personality problems and lacked parenting skills. There was little prospect of the boy reforming and no remorse: it would be disproportionate not to make an order for immediate possession.

The ABSO process operates between the civil and the criminal spheres as some form of hybrid process involving elements of each. Being civil proceedings, the standard of proof ought to be that of the balance of probabilities rather than the criminal standard of beyond reasonable doubt. In the case of *Clingham v Kensington and Chelsea Royal LBC; R (McCann) v Crown Court at Manchester* (2003) the House of Lords upheld the classification as civil. Accordingly hearsay evidence could be admissible. The purpose of the order was preventative rather than punitive and did not result in a penalty or criminal record. The Court, however, modified the standard of proof.[178] Lord Steyn endorsed the view of Lord Bingham of Cornhill in *R v Chief Constable of Avon and Somerset Constabulary* (2001) that the heightened civil standard and the criminal standard were virtually indistinguishable.

In order for Anti-social Behaviour Orders (ASBOs) to be effective and enforceable, publicity is necessary. This, however, raises the issue of the rights of those subject to ASBOs to privacy under Article 8 of the Convention on Human Rights, now protected by the domestic courts under the Human Rights Act 1998. The issue cam before the courts in *R (Stanley) v Metropolitan Police Commissioner* (2004).[179] The local authority had applied for ASBOs and the proceedings received extensive publicity. The authority had used photographs obtained under powers conferred by the Police and Criminal Evidence Act 1984 and posted details of the proceedings on its community website. The claimants sought a declaration that the publicity was unlawful and in breach of Article 8.

---

178 See Ramsay, 2004; Beattie, 2005.
179 See Ashworth, 2005.

The Court dismissed the application. It recognised, however, that such publicity could infringe Article 8 and emphasised that local authorities should consider Article 8 before embarking on a publicity campaign. The publicity given should be both proportionate and necessary to the legitimate aims of the ASBO – namely enforcing existing orders, controlling conduct and deterring others. The degree of publicity needed would vary from case to case, but had to be sufficient to enable the public to know against whom the orders had been granted and to avoid any mis-identification.

The Crime and Disorder Act 1998 also introduced 'local child curfew schemes' which enabled a local authority or chief officer of police to ban children of specified ages (under ten) being in a public place within a specified area for specified hours (between 9am and 6am) other than where they are under the effective control of a parent or responsible person aged 18 or over. The ban may not exceed a period of ninety days. If the ban is contravened a police constable may 'remove the child to the child's place of residence unless he has reasonable cause to believe that the child would, if removed to that place, be likely to suffer significant harm.' The 1998 Act was supplemented by the 2003 Anti-social Behaviour Act, section 30, which confers powers on the police to disperse groups of two or more and return young people under the age of 16 who are unsupervised in public places after 9pm to their homes. The police, however, have no power to forcibly remove a young person to his or her home if he/she is unwilling to go: the power granted under section 30(6) of the Anti-social Behaviour Act 2003 is permissive rather than coercive.[180] However, in *R (W) v Richmond upon Thames LBC* (2005) a 15-year-old boy challenged the use of a dispersal zone. In judicial review proceedings the High Court ruled that the law did not give the police a power of arrest and that the police could not force someone to go with them.

THE SERIOUS ORGANISED CRIME AND POLICE ACT 2005

The Serious Organised Crime and Police Act 2005 (SOCPA) establishes the Serious Organised Crime Agency (SOCA) which brings together the National Crime Squad (NCS), the National Criminal Intelligence Service (NCIS), the investigative and intelligence work of Her Majesty's Customs and Excise (HMCE) on serious drug trafficking and the Immigration Service's responsibilities in relation to organised immigration crime. Special arrangements are made for Scotland and Northern Ireland, in relation to which the Agency will work in partnership with the Scottish Drug Enforcement Agency and the Police Service of Northern Ireland respectively.

The Act also reforms police powers following a review of the Police and Criminal Evidence Act 1984 carried out by the Home Office and Cabinet Office,[181] and strengthens the law in relation to public order.

---

180 *R (W) v Commissioner of Police of the Metropolis* (2005).
181 See www.homeoffice.gov.uk/docs/pacereview2002.pdf.

The Serious Organised Crime Agency

Section 1 of SOCPA establishes the Agency and provides for the abolition of the National Criminal Intelligence Service and the National Crime Squad.[182] The Agency is an executive Non-Departmental Public Body. Schedule 1 provides that there shall be a Board of SOCA, consisting of a chairman and ordinary members appointed by the Secretary of State, the Director General and ex-officio members appointed by the Director General after consulting the chairman. The term of office is five years, which is renewable. The Director General is responsible for general operational control, including deciding which operations should be mounted and how they should be conducted.[183] The Home Secretary is responsible for setting the strategic priorities of SOCA, and the Board also has a role in priority setting. Neither the Home Secretary nor the Board, however, may interfere with the operational independence of the Director General.[184]

The functions of SOCA are defined in section 2 as being the prevention and detection of serious organised crime and contributing to the reduction of such crime and to the mitigation of its consequences. In relation to serious fraud which is primarily the responsibility of the Commissioners for Revenue and Customs, SOCA's powers are restricted and the agency may only act with the agreement of the Director of the Serious Fraud Office or if the Serious Fraud Office declines to act in relation to it. Section 60 of the 2005 Act, as amended by section 33 of the Terrorism Act 2006, confers investigatory powers on the Director of Public Prosecutions, the Director of Revenue and Customs Prosecutions and the Lord Advocate in respect of offences listed in section 61 and in relation to terrorist investigations.

A primary function of SOCA relates to intelligence: section 3(1) providing for the 'gathering, storing, analysing and disseminating' of information relating to the 'prevention, detection, investigation or prosecution of offences or the reduction of crime . . .'. Such information may be disseminated to police forces and law enforcement agencies. The Agency may also institute criminal proceedings in England and Wales or Northern Ireland at the request of chief officers of a police force or a law enforcement agency. It may also enter into arrangements for cooperating with bodies or persons in the United Kingdom or elsewhere in relation to its functions.

Members of SOCA staff may be designated as a person having the powers of a police constable, the powers of an officer of Revenue and Customs, and/or the powers of an immigration officer.[185] The Director General may confer some or all of the powers on a member of staff according to the needs of the Agency. Where a person becomes a member of SOCA, having previously held powers in their capacity of a police constable, an officer of revenue and Customs or immigration officer, those powers are no longer exercisable and are replaced by the powers conferred by the Director General.

---

182 Established by the Police Act 1997.
183 SOCPA, s 21.
184 *Ibid*.
185 SOCPA, s 43. Details of the designated powers are specified in ss 44–49.

The Act imposes a general duty on police forces (including special police forces)[186] to furnish the Agency with relevant information relating to crime and to assist the Agency in the exercise of its functions.[187]

Protection of animal research organisations

SOCPA 2005 creates criminal offences relating to actions taken against animal research establishments. Under section 145 it is an offence to do or threaten to do an act amounting to a criminal offence, or a tortious act causing the organisation loss or damage with the intention of harming an animal research organisation in circumstances where it is intended or likely to cause the organisation to withdraw from a contract, decide not to enter a contract or fail to perform a contractual duty. A further criminal offence is created under section 146. This relates to person A threatening another person, 'B', that he will commit a crime to do a tortious act causing loss or damage to B because of B's connection with an animal research organisation. On summary conviction a person is liable to imprisonment for a term not exceeding 12 months or a fine not exceeding the statutory maximum (currently £5,000), or to both. On conviction on indictment a person is liable to imprisonment for a term not exceeding five years or to an unlimited fine, or to both.

---

186 The British Transport Police, Ministry of Defence Police, Civil Nuclear Constabulary and the Scottish Drug Enforcement Agency.
187 SOCPA, ss 36 and 37.

CHAPTER 24

CITIZENSHIP, IMMIGRATION AND ASYLUM[1]

CITIZENSHIP

The concept of citizenship is fundamental to the question of rights of residence and freedom of movement of the individual. An individual's right to enter and remain in a country depends upon his or her status. Under international law no state may deny entry to its own nationals where they are not entitled to enter or remain in other states. However, subject to international obligations, states may by law determine which non-nationals may enter and remain within their territory, and may remove those who enter and remain unlawfully. In recent decades the increasing number of refugees and other migrants have required new laws to regulate entry and entitlement to remain. In this chapter a broad overview of the law is given.

Historically, at common law, any individual lawfully within the realm owed a duty of allegiance to the Crown, in return for which the Crown owed a duty of protection to the individual.[2] This reciprocal relationship, in the eighteenth century, came to be dubbed the social contract under which citizens conceded power to government to rule, the government holding its powers as a trustee of the individual's rights and freedoms.[3] The Crown had the right to control rights of entry to the country, and the duty to protect the country's borders.

Magna Carta of 1215 recognised the right of merchants, other than those from enemy countries in time of war, to enter, leave, stay and travel in England. The Magna Carta also expressed the right of other individuals who owed allegiance to the King, to enter, leave and re-enter the realm.[4] In times of emergency, the King could prevent persons from leaving the realm.[5] Classes of persons could be denied entry and those already present ordered to leave the land, where their remaining constituted a perceived threat to the 'public good'. In 1530, for example, a statute[6] provided that Gypsies could no longer enter the country and, in 1547, statute provided that Gypsies over the age of 14 born in England had one month in which to leave the realm.[7] In the Victorian era, immigration was legally uncontrolled. From the 1880s, large numbers of East European Jews fleeing from persecution entered the country, and a political campaign for restrictions to be introduced resulted in the enactment of the Aliens Act 1905. Not all aliens were

---

1   See Macdonald and Webber, 2001; Supperstone and Cavanagh, 1994.
2   See Chitty, 1820.
3   See Locke, 1690; Paine, 1791; Rousseau, 1762.
4   Excepting those who had been lawfully convicted, or outlawed, or who were enemy aliens: Chapter 42. The right to leave one's country is an international law right under the International Covenant on Civil and Political Rights, Article 12(2), which provides that 'everyone shall be free to leave any country, including his own'.
5   Under the prerogative writ of *ne exeat regno*.
6   'An Act concerning outlandifh People, calling themfelves Egyptians'.
7   The Act of Elizabeth 1547. See Barnett, 1995.

barred, and controls were aimed at those arriving at certain ports and travelling on the cheapest class of ticket. The Act also introduced power to curb the entry of certain groups – powers which were on one occasion used to restrict entry of Chinese and Gypsy people. The aliens inspectorate was the forerunner to the immigration service, and came under the control of the Home Office. The First World War marked a tightening of immigration control under the Aliens Restriction Act 1914 and the Defence of the Realm Acts. From 1919, all aliens were subject to controls on entry. The Aliens Restriction (Amendment) Act 1919 confirmed the restrictions and remained in force until 1973.

With the expansion of the British Empire, the status of British subject was conferred on all citizens within the Empire. With the growth in independence of formerly dependent territories, the newly independent states exerted their own right to control nationality and immigration. In 1948, the British Nationality Act created a new classification – that of citizen of the United Kingdom and Colonies. All such citizens, and citizens of other Commonwealth nations, became British subjects or Commonwealth citizens, and continued to enjoy the same rights of entry and residence in the United Kingdom. These extensive rights to enter and reside were, by the 1960s, put under great strain as increasing numbers of overseas subjects sought to enter and reside in the United Kingdom. The Commonwealth Immigrants Acts of 1962 and 1968 imposed restrictions on entry. Discrimination entered into the law.[8] Under the Commonwealth Immigrants Act 1962, controls were introduced which distinguished between the rights of entry of citizens from Commonwealth countries who had familial and ancestral links with the United Kingdom and those who did not. The 1968 Act further tightened rights of immigration, limiting the rights of entry of those who had no parental or grandparental links with the United Kingdom. The Immigration Act 1971 further distinguished between subjects who were free to enter the United Kingdom and those who needed permission to enter. The 1971 Act also provided the criteria for rights of residence in the United Kingdom. Under the Act, the distinction between aliens and Commonwealth citizens was reduced, and the important distinction became those with rights of abode in the United Kingdom as against others, whether aliens or Commonwealth immigrants, who were subject to immigration control and required permission to enter and remain. Also in 1973, the United Kingdom became a member of the European Communities, now the European Community and Union, and distinctions arose between the rights of citizens of Member States of the Community and citizens from non-EC countries. Section 1 of the Act lays down general principles. Section 1(1) of the Immigration Act 1971 provides that:

> All those who are in this Act expressed to have the right of abode in the United Kingdom shall be free to live in, and to come and go into and from, the United Kingdom without let or hindrance except such as may be required under and in accordance with this Act to enable their right to be established or as may be otherwise lawfully imposed on any person.

---

8   See Martin, 'Racism in immigration law and practice', in Wallington, 1984, pp 245–57.

Section 2 of the 1971 Act stipulates who has the right of abode. A person has a right of abode in the United Kingdom if (a) he is a British citizen; or (b) he is a Commonwealth citizen who (i) immediately before the commencement of the British Nationality Act 1981 was a Commonwealth citizen having the right of abode in the United Kingdom by virtue of section 2(1)(d) or section 2(2) of the Act as then in force, and (ii) has not ceased to be a Commonwealth citizen in the meanwhile.

The 1971 Act also created the status of patriality and non-patriality – non-patrials having lesser rights of entry than patrials. The classification scheme was complex and much criticised. One consequence of the concept was that some Commonwealth and United Kingdom citizens were not conferred a right of entry by virtue of patriality, notwithstanding that they had no other country to go to. The rules worked particularly harshly in relation to East African Asians, and this fact resulted in condemnation by the Commission of Human Rights on the basis that it represented degrading treatment contrary to Article 3 of the European Convention on Human Rights.[9]

British citizenship

British citizenship may be acquired by birth, adoption, descent, registration or naturalisation.

Birth

A legitimate child born in the United Kingdom, one of whose parents is a British citizen or is 'settled'[10] in the United Kingdom at the time of its birth assumes British citizenship. A child born outside marriage acquires citizenship through his or her mother, unless the child is legitimated by the subsequent marriage of his or her parents. Prior to the 1981 Act, any person (with minor exceptions) born in the United Kingdom became a British citizen.

The Nationality, Immigration and Asylum Act 2002, section 9, now removes from nationality legislation the distinctions between legitimate and illegitimate children and repeals section 47 of the 1981 Act. The 2002 Act inserts a new definition of father into section 50 of the 1981 Act, stipulating that a father is either the husband at the time of the child's birth of the woman who gives birth to the child, a person who is treated as a father under the Human Fertilisation and Embryology Act 1990 or, where neither of those categories apply, any person who satisfies the prescribed requirements as to proof of paternity.

---

9 The *East African Asian* cases (1973). The matter was referred to the Committee of Ministers which failed to reach a decision by the required two-thirds majority.
10 Being ordinarily resident in the United Kingdom and not subject to restrictions on the time a person may remain under immigration law: Immigration Act 1971, s 33.

Adoption and legitimation

A child[11] adopted by a British citizen becomes a British citizen from the date of the adoption order. Where the adopters are married, the child becomes a British citizen provided that one of the adoptive parents is a citizen.

Descent

A child born outside the United Kingdom becomes a citizen if one of his or her parents is a British citizen, provided that that parent has not also acquired citizenship through descent. Where the child is born to a parent who acquired citizenship through descent, the child will only acquire citizenship if the parent is an employee of the Crown, or other designated services.[12]

Registration

After a period of residence in the United Kingdom, a person may acquire citizenship through registration. Children born in the United Kingdom who are not automatically entitled to citizenship through birth, have a right to be registered as citizens at the age of ten, provided that the child has not been absent from the United Kingdom for more than 90 days in each of the first ten years.[13] A child is also entitled to registration if one of his or her parents acquires citizenship or becomes settled in the United Kingdom during his or her minority.[14] British Dependent Territories citizens, British Overseas citizens and British Protected Persons[15] resident for five years in the United Kingdom are also entitled to registration.[16] The Home Secretary has a general discretion to register any child as a British citizen.[17] Under the Immigration, Asylum and Nationality Act 2006, section 58, applicants for nationality by registration must satisfy the Secretary of State that they are of 'good character'.

Naturalisation

Naturalisation as a British citizen is regulated by section 6 of and Schedules 1 and 5 to the British Nationality Act 1981. A five year residence period is a precondition for applying for naturalisation, which is granted at the discretion of the Home Secretary. The Home Secretary, in deciding whether to grant naturalisation, must be satisfied that the applicant is of 'good character', has a command of the English, Welsh or Gaelic language, and intends to have his or her principal residence in the United Kingdom, unless employed in a designated form of employment as specified in the Act.[18] Naturalisation may also confer citizenship

---

11   Under the age of 18 years: Family Law Reform Act 1969.
12   British Nationality Act 1981, ss 14 and 2(1)(b), (c).
13   *Ibid*, s 1(4).
14   *Ibid*, s 1(3).
15   A British Protected Person is one so declared by Order in Council or by virtue of the Solomon Islands Act 1978.
16   British Nationality Act 1981, s 4.
17   *Ibid*, s 3(1).
18   *Ibid*, s 6(1) and Sched 1.

on the spouse of a British citizen. Section 42 of the British Nationality Act 1981 provides that no certificate of naturalisation may be granted unless the applicant has made the necessary oath and pledge. Schedule 5 to the Act requires those attaining citizenship to swear an oath of allegiance and pledge loyalty to the United Kingdom, upholding its democratic values and obeying its laws.

The Nationality, Immigration and Asylum Act 2002 lays down further requirements in relation to acquiring citizenship through naturalisation. In the attempt to encourage assimilation of members of ethnic minority communities into British life, the Act amends the British Nationality Act 1981 and provides for citizenship 'ceremonies' and a pledge of allegiance.[19] The Act further requires that the applicant has sufficient knowledge about life in the United Kingdom.[20]

British Overseas Territories citizenship

Part II of the 1981 British Nationality Act, as amended by the British Overseas Territories Act 2002, governs Overseas Territories[21] citizenship. A person may acquire citizenship through birth, adoption, descent, registration as a minor or naturalisation, concepts which follow the same formula as that discussed above.[22] Section 3 of the Act confers British citizenship on any person who was a British overseas territories citizen immediately before section 3 of the 2002 Act came into force.

The Falkland Islands

The British Nationality (Falkland Islands) Act 1983 confers British citizenship on persons born in the Falklands to parents who are settled there.

Hong Kong

The Hong Kong Act 1985 created the status of British Nationals (Overseas) for Hong Kong citizens after the transfer of sovereignty from the United Kingdom to China in 1997. Under the British Nationality (Hong Kong) Act 1990, the Home Secretary could confer citizenship on up to 50,000 Hong Kong residents and their families, nominated by the Governor of Hong Kong, to enable them to live in the United Kingdom in the future if they wished to leave Hong Kong after the transfer of power.[23]

---

19 Nationality, Immigration and Asylum Act 2002, s 3 and Sched 1, inserting s 42 into the British Nationality Act 1981.
20 *Ibid*, s 1, inserting the requirement into Sched 1, para 1(1)(c) of the 1981 Act as sub-para (ca).
21 Overseas Territories are Anguilla, Bermuda, British Antarctic Territory, British Indian Ocean Territory, Cayman Islands, Falkland Islands and Dependencies, Gibraltar, Montserrat, Pitcairn, Henderson, Ducie and Oeno Islands, St Christopher and Nevis, St Helena and Dependencies, the Sovereign Base areas of Akrotiri and Dhekelia (Cyprus), Turks and Caicos Islands, Virgin Islands: *ibid*, Sched 6.
22 British Nationality Act 1981, ss 15, 16, 17, 18, as amended.
23 British Nationality (Hong Kong) (Selection Scheme) Order 1990, SI 1990/14. The British Nationality (Hong Kong) Act 1997 provides that the Secretary of State shall on application register as a British citizen any person who was ordinarily resident in Hong Kong and satisfied certain conditions immediately before 4 February 1997.

Commonwealth citizenship

Every person who is a British citizen, British overseas territories citizen or British subject, or a subject in a country listed in Schedule 3,[24] has the status of a Commonwealth citizen.[25]

Deprivation of citizenship

The British Nationality Act 1981, as amended,[26] provides for the deprivation of citizenship and for a right of appeal against a decision to deprive a person of his or her citizenship. Section 40(1) of the 1981 Act now provides that those liable to deprivation are British citizens, British Overseas Territories citizens, British Overseas citizens, British Nationals (Overseas), British subjects and British protected persons. The grounds on which citizenship may be deprived are that:

.... the Secretary of State is satisfied that deprivation is conducive to the public good.[27]

Furthermore, a person may be deprived of citizenship status if the Secretary of State is satisfied that the registration or naturalisation was obtained by means of (a) fraud, (b) false representation, or (c) concealment of a material fact.[28] A person may not be deprived of citizenship under section 40(2) if this would make him or her stateless. The Secretary of State does not have the power to deprive a person of British citizenship based on acts done before that person became a British citizen: *R (Hicks) v Secretary of State for the Home Department* (2005). The claimant, who was entitled to registration, had been detained by US authorities at Guantanamo Bay following allegations that he had given active support to and been involved in activities with Al-Quaeda. The Home Secretary did not have power to deprive the claimant of citizenship and the argument based on public policy could not succeed.

There is a right of appeal against a deprivation order to an adjudicator, and a right of appeal for both parties to appeal to a tribunal from the adjudicator on a point of law. A further appeal, on a point of law, lies to the Court of Appeal or the Court of Session (if the adjudicator's decision was in Scotland). The right of appeal does not apply where the Secretary of State has certified that his decision was reached on information which should not be disclosed – on the basis of national security, in the interests of relations with another country or 'otherwise in the public interest'.[29]

---

24 Antigua and Barbuda, Australia, Bahamas, Bangladesh, Barbados, Canada, Republic of Cyprus, Dominica, Fiji, The Gambia, Ghana, Grenada, Guyana, India, Jamaica, Kenya, Kiribati, Lesotho, Malawi, Malaysia, Malta, Mauritius, Mozambique, Nauru, New Zealand, Nigeria, Pakistan, Papua New Guinea, Saint Lucia, Saint Vincent and the Grenadines, Seychelles, Sierra Leone, Singapore, Solomon Islands, Sri Lanka, Swaziland, Tanzania, Tonga, Trinidad and Tobago, Tuvalu, Uganda, Vanuatu, Western Samoa, Zambia, Zimbabwe.

25 British Nationality Act 1981, s 36.

26 By the Nationality, Immigration and Asylum Act 2002, the Immigration and Asylum Act 1999 and the Immigration, Asylum and Nationality Act 2006.

27 British Nationality Act 1981, s 40(2), as amended by s 56 of the Immigration, Asylum and Nationality Act 2006.

28 *Ibid*, s 40(3).

29 *Ibid*, s 40A, introduced by s 4 of the Nationality, Immigration and Asylum Act 2002.

The Immigration, Asylum and Nationality Act 2006 provides for the deprivation of rights of abode. Section 57 confers on the Home Secretary the power to remove a right of abode where such a right derives from possession of citizenship of another Commonwealth country and it is conducive to the public good to remove or exclude the person from the United Kingdom.

European Union citizenship

The Treaty on European Union 1992, as amended by the Treaty on European Union 1997, confers Union citizenship on the citizens of all Member States.[30] Under the 1992 Treaty, asylum policy, immigration, control over external borders and policies relating to nationals of third countries, were one of the designated areas of common interest between Member States, and fell within the Justice and Home Affairs pillar.[31] Member States are under a duty to co-operate in these matters, and to act in compliance with the European Convention on Human Rights and the 1951 Convention on the Status of Refugees. There was common agreement that the working of third pillar of the Union structure – Justice and Home Affairs – was unsatisfactory. As a result, under the Treaty on European Union 1997 (the Treaty of Amsterdam), all issues relating to the free movement of persons within the Union, including asylum, visas and immigration, have been placed under Community law and its law making processes, while issues relating to crime and the police remain in the third pillar.

Freedom of movement and rights of establishment are a central feature of the European Union and Community. The elimination of border controls between Member States further extends the freedom of movement for persons within the territorial boundaries of the European Union. It has been agreed, however, that the United Kingdom may retain its border controls.

Article 4(4) of Council Directive of 1968, on the abolition of restrictions on movement and residence within the European Community for workers of Member States and their families,[32] provides that:

> A member of the family who is not a national of a member state shall be issued with a residence document which shall have the same validity as that issued to the worker on whom he is dependent.

Article 2 of the Amsterdam Treaty reaffirms the concept of citizenship. It states that among the objectives of the Union is the aim to:

> ... strengthen the protection of the rights and interests of nationals of its Member States through the introduction of a citizenship of the Union.

Articles 17 and 18 of the EC Treaty provide that:

> Citizenship of the Union is hereby established. Every person holding the nationality of a Member State shall be a citizen of the Union. Citizenship of the Union shall complement and not replace national citizenship.

> Citizens of the Union shall enjoy the rights conferred by this Treaty and shall be subject to the duties imposed thereby.

---

30 See further Chapter 8.
31 It was thus outside the European Community structure. See further Chapter 8.
32 68/360/EEC (OJ Special English edn, 11, 1968, p 485), as amended by Dec 95/1/EC (OJ L1/1, 1995).

> Every citizen of the Union shall have the right to move and reside freely within the
> territory of the Member States, subject to the limitations and conditions laid down in
> this Treaty and by the measures adopted to give it effect.

In addition to rights of residence, every citizen of the Union has the right to stand as a candidate and to vote in municipal elections in the Member State in which he or she resides,[33] and to stand as a candidate and vote in elections for the European Parliament.[34] Union citizens are entitled to protection from the diplomatic or consular authorities of any Member State.[35] Citizens of the Union have the right to petition the European Parliament under Article 194 of the Treaty, and have the right also to apply to the European Union Ombudsman under Article 195.[36]

The free movement of persons provisions under the EC Treaty founded the basis for the development of the idea of European citizenship. The ideas of free movement of persons and rights of establishment within the common market were essentially linked to the economic aspects of the Community. The concept of citizenship now adopted under the Amsterdam Treaty is far broader than this, and reflects the wider political and social union which is aspired to. The Commission has the duty to develop further the concept of citizenship and to report to the European Parliament and the Council on developments. The Council has the power to adopt the proposals of the Commission, following consultation with the European Parliament, and acting unanimously, which the Council will recommend for adoption by Member States.

Under the Schengen Agreement of 1985, several Member States agreed to remove all forms of border controls between their countries. This agreement is now formally incorporated, under the Amsterdam Treaty, into the EC Treaty. In respect of the United Kingdom and Ireland, however, opt outs were negotiated, in order to allow these Member States to preserve border controls, in light of their particular geographical characteristics.[37] By 2001 only Britain and Ireland remained outside the Schengen Agreement.

Rights of entry and residence

Rights of entry and residence are inextricably linked to the question of citizenship. The United Nations International Covenant on Civil and Political Rights, to which the United Kingdom is a party, provides that 'No one shall be arbitrarily deprived of the right to enter his own country'.[38] The United Kingdom entered a reservation in respect of this broadly phrased right under international law, by which it reserved the right to 'continue to apply such immigration legislation governing entry into, stay in and departure from the United Kingdom' as it deems necessary.[39]

---

33 EC Treaty, Article 19.
34 *Ibid*, Article 19.
35 *Ibid*, Article 20.
36 *Ibid*, Article 21.
37 Special arrangements also exist in relation to Denmark. See also the Schengen Implementation Convention 1990.
38 Article 12(4).
39 Reservation of 20 May 1976.

Establishing the right to enter

The holding of a valid British passport identifying that person as a British citizen or as a citizen of the United Kingdom and Colonies having the right of abode in the United Kingdom, or travel document of a European Union Member State entitles the holder to entry. Passports are issued under the royal prerogative through the Passport Agency. The case of *R v Secretary of State for Foreign and Commonwealth Affairs ex parte Everett* (1989) established that the decision to revoke or refuse a passport is subject to judicial review. Passports are only issued once the Passport Agency is satisfied as to the accuracy of the application and supporting documentation. Section 3 of the Immigration Act 1971[40] provides:

(8) When any question arises under this Act whether or not a person is a British citizen ... it shall lie on the person asserting it to prove that he is.

(9) A person seeking to enter the United Kingdom and claiming to have the right of abode there shall prove that he has that right by means of either:

(a) a United Kingdom passport describing him as a British citizen or as a citizen of the United Kingdom and Colonies having the right of abode in the United Kingdom; or

(b) a certificate of entitlement.

The holding of a passport, however, is not conclusive proof of the right to enter. Where a passport has been obtained as a result of fraud or theft, an immigration officer who suspects that this is the case is entitled to require that the passport holder substantiate his or her claim to be the legitimate holder of the passport. In these situations, therefore, the burden of proof as to identity rests with the passport holder. However, where the Passport Agency has indisputably issued a passport to the holder, albeit one of a limited duration, the question arises – should a dispute occur over the matter – as to where the burden of proof lies over the issue of the validity of that passport and the right of its holder to enter.

IMMIGRATION LAW

Whereas citizenship entitles a person to enter and remain in the country of citizenship, non-citizens have no automatic right of entry into another country, nor does a state have any duty to admit aliens. Every state has the right – subject to international treaty obligations – to control who enters the state and the conditions which apply to that entry, as for example the right to work and the length of stay. Furthermore, the state has the right to deport aliens from its territory, provided that the person's removal would not infringe international law obligations. As will be seen below, the 1951 Geneva Convention, for example, prohibits the return of a refugee to a country where 'his life or freedom would be threatened on account of race, religion, nationality, membership of a particular social group or political opinion'. The powers to control immigration are under the responsibility of the Secretary of State for the Home Office (the Home Secretary), but in practice are entrusted to immigration officers subject to review by the courts. Power to give leave to remain in the United Kingdom, or to vary

---

40 As amended by the British Nationality Act 1981, the Immigration and Asylum Act 1999 and the Nationality, Immigration and Asylum Act 2002.

conditions of leave, are exercisable by the Home Secretary.[41] Deportation orders are also the responsibility of the Home Secretary.

Immigration law is contained in a complex web of statutes, with Acts of Parliament being enacted in piecemeal fashion and no attempt being made to consolidate the law in a manageable, comprehensive form. The first modern statutory control over immigration was provided by the Aliens Act 1905, which permitted the refusal of entry to persons regarded as 'undesirable'. By the Commonwealth Immigrants Act 1962, more favourable treatment was given to descendants of white immigrants than to citizens of the New Commonwealth.[42] The Immigration Act 1971, as amended, together with the Immigration Rules, provides the structure of immigration law. Rights of entry are determined by citizenship status under the British Nationality Act 1981. As noted above, section 1 of the Immigration Act 1971 provides that those who 'have a right of abode shall be free to live in, and to come and go into and from, the United Kingdom without let or hindrance' subject to restrictions enabling their status to be determined.[43] Those who do not have the right of abode may live, work and settle in the United Kingdom 'by permission and subject to such regulation and control of their entry into, stay in and departure from the United Kingdom'.[44]

A person who has the right of abode is a person who is a British citizen, or a Commonwealth citizen who was a Commonwealth citizen having the right of abode immediately before the commencement of the British Nationality Act 1981, and who has not ceased meanwhile to be a Commonwealth citizen.[45] Under the British Overseas Territories Act 2002, a right of abode was conferred on those who were formerly British Dependent Territories citizens. All European Union citizens, plus nationals of Iceland, Norway and Liechtenstein (which are not EU members but have special status under the Agreement on the European Economic Area), are entitled to enter the United Kingdom under the freedom of movement provisions of the European Union treaties.[46] Citizens of the Republic of Ireland also have the right to enter free of immigration controls, as do people arriving from the Channel Islands and the Isle of Man.

Where a person does not have a right of entry and abode, section 3 states that a person 'shall not enter the United Kingdom unless given leave to do so under this Act'.[47] Leave may be given to enter the United Kingdom either for a limited

---

41   Immigration Act 1971, s 4.

42   See Evans, 1983, p 3.

43   Immigration Act 1971, ss 1–3. The Immigration, Asylum and Nationality Act 2006, s 30, amends s 3(9) of the 1971 Act.

44   *Ibid*, s 1(2).

45   *Ibid*, s 2.

46   See the European Economic Area Act 1993; Immigration (EEA) Regulations 2000, SI 2000/2326.

47   In *R v Secretary of State for the Home Department ex parte Rahman* (1997), the Court of Appeal ruled that, where a court had to establish the truth relating to a fact in the light of which the Secretary of State had decided that a person had entered the country by deception and was an illegal entrant, the court was entitled to take into account all the material on which the decision maker had relied, even though that might be hearsay. The onus was on the Secretary of State to establish, to a level of proof appropriate to a crime in civil proceedings, that the person was an illegal entrant. On the facts, by a majority, the court ruled that the Secretary of State had done so.

period or for an indefinite period. Where limited leave is given for entry into the United Kingdom, the leave may be subject to conditions restricting an individual's right of employment or occupation, or requirements to register with the police, or both. The leave to enter may be varied. The leave may be restricted, enlarged or added to by varying or revoking conditions.

The general provision relating to regulation and control is section 3 of the Immigration Act 1971, as amended, which provides in part that:

(1) Except as otherwise provided by or under this Act, where is person is not [a British citizen]:

(a) he shall not enter the United Kingdom unless given leave to do so in accordance with this Act;

(b) he may be given leave to enter the United Kingdom (or, when already there, leave to remain in the United Kingdom) either for a limited or for an indefinite period;

(c) if he is given limited leave to enter or remain in the United Kingdom, it may be given subject to all or any of the following conditions, namely –

(i) a condition restricting his employment or occupation in the United Kingdom;

(ii) a condition requiring him to maintain and accommodate himself, and any dependants of his, without recourse to public funds; and

(iii) a condition requiring him to register with the police.

The Home Secretary has the power to lay down rules for the regulation of entry and stay in the United Kingdom, and these must be laid before parliament. The rules are subject to nullification by parliament within 40 days of being laid.[48]

The Labour government sought to reform the law in the face of substantial pressure imposed on the administrative system by escalating numbers of persons seeking asylum in the United Kingdom. The Home Secretary stated that the Immigration and Asylum Act 1999 was intended to make the 'system fairer, faster and firmer'.[49] The 1999 Act makes provision covering most areas of immigration and asylum. The Act is intended to enable genuine travellers to enter more quickly whilst also combating illegal entry and strengthening powers to deal with other persons not entitled to enter or remain in the United Kingdom.

Section 1 of the 1999 Act amended section 3 of the Immigration Act 1971, and is designed to make more flexible and streamlined the granting of leave to enter. Leave to enter may now be granted, refused or varied outside the United Kingdom, thus relieving the pressure on immigration officers at points of entry and giving greater certainty to travellers intending to enter the United Kingdom. Conditions may be imposed on the right to enter. Leave to enter for a limited time is renewable and continues until the application is determined or until the end of the appeal period.[50]

---

48 Note that if a person is detained by immigration officials unlawfully, the officers have no immunity from a claim for damages for wrongful imprisonment: *D v Home Office* (2005).
49 *Hansard*, HC Vol 326 Col 37.
50 Immigration and Asylum Act 1999, s 3.

The Immigration Services Commissioner

The Immigration and Asylum Act 1999 introduces an Immigration Services Commissioner, appointed by the Secretary of State in consultation with the Lord Chancellor and Scottish Ministers.[51] It is the general duty of the Commissioner to promote good practice by those who provide immigration advice or immigration services.[52] The Commissioner issues a Code of Standards and rules. The Commissioner has responsibility for registering those persons or bodies qualified to provide immigration advice or services.[53]

REFUGEES AND ASYLUM

A refugee is a person who leaves his or her homeland because of a fear of or actual persecution and seeks refuge – asylum – in another country. This area of the law is regulated by both international and national law.

Under the 1951 Convention Relating to the Status of Refugees,[54] which came into force in 1954, the United Kingdom has undertaken certain obligations. The United Nations' Office of High Commissioner for Refugees is the umbrella office responsible for providing advice and guidance as to the interpretation and implementation of the Convention.[55] A person is defined under the Convention as a refugee if he:

(a) is outside the country of his nationality or habitual residence;

(b) has a well founded fear of being persecuted for reasons of race, religion, nationality, membership of a particular social group, or political opinions; and

(c) is unable or, because of that fear, unwilling to avail himself of the protection of that country.[56]

A person is precluded from asylum if he or she 'acts contrary to the purposes and principles of the United Nations' which includes involvement in terrorist activities, whether committing, preparing or instigating terrorism or encouraging others to do so.[57]

Protection is also afforded by the Human Rights Act 1998. Article 3 of the European Convention on Human Rights – now incorporated into domestic law under the 1998 Act – imposes a duty on states to protect people from torture, inhuman or degrading treatment. Furthermore, Articles 5 and 8 relating to the right to liberty and right to respect for private and family life may also be invoked to protect asylum seekers. As will be seen, the effect of this is that states may not

---

51 Immigration and Asylum Act 1999, s 83.
52 On functions see also Sched 5.
53 See the Immigration and Asylum Act 1999, s 84.
54 Cmd 9171, 1951, London: HMSO; and Cmnd 3906, 1967, London: HMSO. See UK Treaty Series No 39, Cmnd 9171, 1954, London: HMSO. The Convention was amended in 1967 by the Protocol Relating to the Status of Refugees.
55 There is, however, no permanent judicial body scrutinising and enforcing the Convention. As a result, the courts in different signatory states may take different approaches to the Convention.
56 Convention Relating to the Status of Refugees, Article 1A(2).
57 Immigration, Asylum and Nationality Act 2006, s 54.

remove a person from its territory to a country where the person is at real risk of being tortured or being subjected to inhuman or degrading treatment.

A claim for asylum is defined under section 18(3) of the Nationality, Immigration and Asylum Act 2002 as being a 'claim by a person that to remove him from or require him to leave the United Kingdom would be contrary to the United Kingdom's obligations' under the Geneva Convention or Article 3 of the European Convention on Human Rights. In *R (Ullah) v Special Adjudicator; Do v Immigration Appeal Tribunal* (2004) the claimants alleged that they were at risk of religious persecution if returned to their own countries. The House of Lords ruled that there might be cases in which anticipated ill-treatment would infringe Articles other than Article 3 in particular, Articles 2, 5, 6 and 8 and possibly Article 9. Article 8 of the European Convention – the right to respect for private and family life, home and correspondence – was employed in *R (Razgar) v Secretary of State for the Home Department* (2004). The Secretary of State ordered the removal of an asylum seeker, an Iraqi of Kurdish origin, to Germany as a safe third country and the country from which he had come, having rejected his human rights claim as 'manifestly illfounded'. In judicial review proceedings, the claimant adduced evidence from a psychiatrist that he suffered from psychological illness and that if he was returned to Germany he might kill himself. In addition, there was a risk that he would not receive appropriate treatment in Germany. The House of Lords upheld the order quashing the Secretary of State's decision: there was no basis on which the claim could be dismissed as manifestly ill-founded.[58,59,60]

Where a person makes a claim for asylum or a 'human rights claim' – a claim that one or more of his or her Convention rights would be infringed if the claim for asylum was rejected and the person threatened with removal from the United Kingdom – the claimant's credibility is a key issue. Asylum seekers often arrive in the United Kingdom without documentation and/or evidence that the state from which they have fled was subjecting them to, or threatening to, persecute them or fail to protect them from persecution by non-state agents. In terms of procedure, the asylum seeker must make a formal application for asylum status, the content of which will be checked against Home Office information on countries of origin. The applicant is then invited for an asylum interview at which the facts are presented to an asylum case worker. The record of that meeting is then referred to

---

58 In *R (Rodriguez-Torres) v Secretary of State for the Home Department* (2005), the Court of Appeal ruled that it was only in the most exceptional cases that the removal of a person from the United Kingdom in the course of immigration control would involve a violation of rights under the European Convention. The medical evidence relating to sever depression with an increased risk of suicide if returned fell short of the high threshold laid down in *Razgar*.

59 In *R (G) v Immigration Appeal Tribunal* (2004) the Court of Appeal ruled that the rights of asylum seekers were adequately protected by the statutory review process which was both adequate and proportionate and that the courts should not grant leave for judicial review which amounted to an attempt to 'buy time'.

60 In *R (Rashid) v Secretary of State for the Home Department* (2005) the Court of Appeal ruled that the Home Secretary's failure to apply to one applicant for asylum a policy which had been applied to two other applicants in an identical position had been so unfair as to amount to a misuse of power requiring the court to declare that the applicant should be granted indefinite leave to remain in the United Kingdom.

a senior immigration officer to make a decision whether to refuse or allow the application.

The Asylum and Immigration (Treatment of Claimants etc.) Act 2004 (the 2004 Act) makes provision for determining the credibility of applicants. Section 8 applies to immigration officers, the Secretary of State, the Asylum and Immigration Tribunal or the Special Immigration Appeals Commission and provides a wide range of 'behaviour' which is regarded as damaging to the claimant's credibility and must be taken into account in reaching a decision. In addition to the eight specified acts, ranging from failure without reasonable explanation to produce a passport to failure to make an asylum or human rights claim before being arrested under an immigration provision, section 8(12) provides a catch-all criteria, namely that the deciding authority may consider any behaviour to which section 8 does not apply.

Credibility is therefore central to the decision, but it turns on circumstances for which there may be no clear evidence and on the ability of claimants – generally from very different cultural, political, racial and social backgrounds and lacking fluency in English – to present their case convincingly at the hearing. There is no guarantee that the applicant will have received legal advice, nor is legal representation available at the hearing. If their claim is rejected, an appeal lies to the Asylum and Immigration Tribunal (the AIT). However, there is no appeal available on the facts of the case. Moreover, the AIT is staffed by a single person, thereby depriving the applicant of consideration by a panel. It is questionable whether this process amounts to a fair trial compatible with Article 6 of the European Convention.

In order to give some protection to the asylum applicant, the Court of Appeal in *R (Dirshe) v Secretary of State for the Home Department* (2005) ruled that he or she should be permitted to make a tape recording of the interview with the immigration officer to ensure that the procedure meets the standard of fairness required. The court accepted that the interview was a critical part of the procedure for determining asylum decisions. The immigration official created a record of the interview: it was essential that the applicant have an adequate opportunity to challenge its adequacy.

Support for asylum seekers

The Immigration and Asylum Act 1999, the Nationality, Immigration and Asylum Act 2002 and the Asylum and Immigration (Treatment of Claimants, etc.) Act 2004 regulate support for asylum seekers and their dependants. Asylum seekers are taken out of the benefits system[61] and detailed provision is made for their support under the Act. The National Asylum Support Service has responsibility for support. Support may be given through the provision of accommodation which is 'adequate', providing for the essential living needs of the supported person, enabling the person to meet expenses (other than legal and other

---

61　The exclusion from benefits covers jobseeker's allowance, attendance allowance, severe disablement allowance, invalid care allowance, disability living allowance, income support, working families' tax credit, disabled persons' tax credit, social fund payments, child benefit, housing benefit, council tax benefit.

prescribed expenses) in relation to asylum claims, and enabling the asylum seeker to attend bail proceedings.[62] If the circumstances of a particular case are 'exceptional', the Home Secretary may provide such support as he considers necessary to enable the person to be supported.[63] Local authorities may also provide support in accordance with arrangements made by the Home Secretary.[64] The Act introduces a number of offences relating to support. It is an offence to make false representations, dishonest representations, or to delay or obstruct, without reasonable excuse, a person exercising functions relating to support, or to refuse or neglect to undertake an obligation to maintain a supported person, having given a written undertaking to do so.[65]

Concern over the escalating number of asylum seekers and the need to process their applications speedily led to the Nationality, Immigration and Asylum Act 2002.[66] Sections 16 and 17 of the Act provide for accommodation centres to house asylum seekers and their dependants or those who are destitute.[67] Asylum seekers may be detained at Reception Centres for a short period in order to process their applications without engaging the prohibition against denying a person his or her liberty under Article 5 of the European Convention on Human Rights.[68] Centres may offer facilities and services including food and essential items, money, assistance with transport and other activities, facilities for religious observance, healthcare, and education and training. Reporting and residence requirements may be imposed on asylum seekers, and those who fail to comply with the requirements may have their support discontinued. Section 55 of the 2002 Act provides that a person shall not be given support[69] where a claim for asylum has been made but the Home Secretary is not satisfied that the claim was made as soon as reasonably practicable after the person's arrival in the United Kingdom. Support may also be refused where the Home Secretary is satisfied that information provided by the applicant is false or incomplete.[70] In order to avoid a potential violation of Article 3, section 55(5) provides that the Home Secretary or an authority may provide assistance 'to the extent necessary' for the purpose of avoiding a breach of a person's Convention rights.

---

62 Immigration and Asylum Act 1999, s 96, specifying the types of support which may be given to eligible persons defined in s 95.

63 *Ibid*, s 96(2).

64 *Ibid*, s 99. On accommodation and local connection see *Al Ameri v Royal Borough of Kensington and Chelsea* and *Osmani v London Borough of Harrow* (2004) and s 11 of the Asylum and Immigration (Treatment of Claimants, etc.) Act 2004.

65 *Ibid*, ss 106, 107, 108, respectively.

66 In 2002 there were 103,100 applications for asylum in the United Kingdom. In 2003 there was a 41% decrease, the number of applications being 61,100. In France there were 58,100 applications in 2002 and 69,300 in 2003, a 19% increase. In Germany there were 71,100 applications in 2002 and 50,400 in 2003. Source: UNHCR IGC Secretariat provisional figures.

67 Defined in s 19 as a person who does not have and cannot obtain both adequate accommodation and food and other essential items.

68 See *R (Saudi) v Secretary of State for the Home Department* (2002): conditions of detention reasonable and period of detention not excessive. See p 659 below.

69 Under ss 4, 95 and 98 of the Immigration and Asylum Act 1999 and ss 17 and 24 of the 2002 Act; Housing (Scotland) Act 1987; Housing Act 1996; Local Government Act 2000, s 2.

70 Nationality, Immigration and Asylum Act 2002, s 57, amending the Immigration and Asylum Act 1999, Sched 8, para 12.

The denial of support has been challenged in the courts. In *Westminster City Council v National Asylum Support Service* (2002) the House of Lords ruled that a local authority was obliged to provide accommodation for a destitute asylum seeker who was in need of care and attention and whose need for accommodation arose from infirmity as well as destitution.[71] In *R (S) v Secretary of State for the Home Department* (2003) the court ruled that section 55(1) required that assistance be given to asylum seekers faced with destitution to avoid a breach of Article 3 of the Convention.

There is no simple test applicable to determine whether the decision of the Home Secretary to refuse to provide support to an asylum seeker amounted to inhuman or degrading treatment in breach of Article 3 of the European Convention: each case has to be judged in relation to all the circumstances which are relevant to it. The Court of Appeal so ruled in *R (S) v Secretary of State for the Home Department* (2003). In *R (Q) v Secretary of State for the Home Department* (2003), the Court of Appeal held that denial of support was 'treatment' within Article 3. The House of Lords considered the issue in *R (Limbuela) v Secretary of State for the Home Department* (2005). Lord Bingham stated that 'Treatment was inhuman or degrading if, to a seriously detrimental extent, it denied the most basic needs of any human being'. The Home Secretary's duty to provide support '. . . arose when it appeared on a fair and objective assessment of the facts and circumstances that an individual applicant faced an imminent prospect of serious suffering caused or materially aggravated by denial of shelter, food or the most basic necessities of life'.[72] In *R (Morris) v Westminster City Council* (2005) the Court of Appeal ruled that a statutory provision requiring a British citizen's dependent child, subject to immigration control, if both were habitually resident in the United Kingdom, to be disregarded when determining whether that citizen had a priority need for accommodation was discriminatory and in breach of the right to family life. Section 185(4) of the Housing Act 1996 had been declared incompatible with Articles 8 and 14 in October 2003. The Court stated that it was a perfectly legitimate policy objective to reduce the incentive for people to come to Britain for the purpose of claiming benefits or services. Its application to an adult who was in the UK as of right, and who had her child with her, was not justifiable.[73]

The Asylum and Immigration Act (Treatment of Claimants etc.) 2004, sections 9 and 10[74] provides that support may be withdrawn from failed asylum seekers who have failed to leave the country voluntarily. Before a decision to refuse support is made, an interview will be held where the family may explain why they have not left and what steps they are taking to leave. Those who cooperate with the authorities will not have support withdrawn.[75] The 2004 Act, section 12, provides that there shall be no back-dating of benefits.

---

71 See also *R (Limbuela) v Secretary of State for the Home Department* (2004).
72 On support for disabled children see *Westminster City Council v National Asylum Support Service* (2002); *R (A) v National Asylum Support Service* (2003).
73 See also *Szoma v Secretary of State for Work and Pensions* (2005).
74 Amending Sched 3 to the Nationality, Immigration and Asylum Act 2002.
75 *Per* Lord Bassam, *Hansard*, HL, vol 661, col 701.

On the other hand, in *R (Gezer) v Secretary of State for the Home Department* (2004) the Court of Appeal ruled that while the Secretary of State had a duty not to act in such a way as to cause a person to suffer conditions which would violate Article 3, the Secretary of State did not have a duty – when offering assistance in the form of housing – to make special inquires to save the applicant from harm. In the instant case the harm came from violent and abusive treatment from the local population.

The Nationality, Immigration and Asylum Act 2002, section 71, provides for reporting requirements and residence requirements. Failure to comply with the requirements makes a person liable for detention under Schedule 2 to the Immigration Act 1971. The 2002 Act, section 70, also provides for residency requirements for a period of up to 14 days associated with induction. The induction process is intended to explain the procedures involved in the asylum application and the requirements which they must satisfy. The residence restriction can be imposed irrespective of whether the asylum seeker has alternative available accommodation. In *R (Saudi) v Secretary of State for the Home Department* (2002) the House of Lords ruled that the policy of detaining asylum seekers at Oakington Reception Centre for a short period in order to ensure speedy and efficient processing of their applications was lawful and did not infringe Article 5(1) of the European Convention on Human Rights.

The Geneva Convention 1951

If a person is found to be a refugee, that person is entitled not to be expelled or returned to the country from which he fears persecution by agents of the state. If, however, the person has come to the United Kingdom from a third country, he may be returned to that third country.[76] In reaching decisions as to whether to return an asylum seeker to a third country, the Home Secretary has to be satisfied that the third country presents no risk which would breach international obligations, namely that the third country would not send the detainee to another country, other than in accordance with the Convention.[77] In *Gardi v Secretary of State for the Home Department* (2002), the Court of Appeal ruled that ethnic Kurds who had a safe and autonomous region to return to (the Kurdish Autonomous Region in Iraq), and an undertaking by the Home Secretary that the claimant

---

76 See *R v Secretary of State for the Home Office ex parte Bugdaycay* (1987).
77 See *R (Lika) v Secretary of State for the Home Department* (2003), where the Court of Appeal ruled that an asylum seeker could not apply for asylum in Germany and subsequently seek asylum in the United Kingdom on the ground that Germany was not a safe country for him when Germany was still considering his application. Therefore the Home Secretary's refusal of the asylum application was lawful under the Dublin Convention Determining the State Responsible for Examining Applications for Asylum Lodged in One of the Member States of the European Communities signed in June 1990, which was partly incorporated by the Asylum and Immigration Act 1996.

would not be removed from the United Kingdom until a supervised and safe method of travel could be arranged, did not establish refugee status.[78]

If a person is deemed to be a refugee, and has not come from a safe third country, he is entitled to remain. However, he may be deported on the basis of the requirements of national security or public order, although only if some country in which he would be safe will accept him.[79] However, the protection of the Refugee Convention will not apply where a person has been involved in terrorist activities (see above) or on the grounds of national security.[80] A person is not a refugee for the purposes of the Convention on the sole ground that he or she is stateless, being unable to return to the country in which he or she is habitually resident. To bring a person within the Convention, it must be established that there is a well founded fear of persecution on Convention grounds.[81] The Convention also imposes a duty on states not to prosecute as illegal entrants those who claim asylum without delay, a requirement reflected in section 31 of the Immigration and Asylum Act 1999.[82]

Article 32 of the Convention which prevents a refugee being returned to a place where their life or freedom is threatened does not apply where a refugee has been convicted of a particularly serious crime and is a danger to the community.[83]

The test for deciding whether a person has a well founded fear is both subjective and objective. In *R v Secretary of State for the Home Department ex parte Sivakumaran* (1988), the House of Lords ruled that, whilst the fear is subjective, the reasonableness of that fear is an objective test. Moreover, the House of Lords ruled that the test was one to be applied by the Home Secretary. If the Home Secretary decides that there is a 'reasonable chance', a 'serious possibility' or 'substantial grounds for thinking' that the person will be persecuted, the objective test will be satisfied.

In *R v Secretary of State for the Home Department ex parte Gashi (Besnik)* (1999), the Secretary of State made an order to return the applicant to Germany, from where he had previously been required to leave, having fled there from Kosovo. The Court of Appeal ruled that the Home Secretary was not entitled to assume that Germany properly applied the Refugee Convention, and evidence suggested

---

78 In *R (Khadir) v Secretary of State for the Home Department* (2005) the House of Lords ruled that a failed asylum seeker who was admitted into the UK under restricted terms of a temporary admission order pending his removal could not claim that the continued failure of the Home Secretary to establish a safe route for his return meant that his removal was no longer pending so as to require the grant of exceptional leave to enter, provided the Home Secretary remained intent on removing him and there was some prospect that could happen.

79 Convention Relating to the Status of Refugees, Articles 32, 33(2).

80 See Immigration, Asylum and Nationality Act 2006, s 55.

81 *Revenko v Secretary of State for the Home Department* (2000).

82 See *R v Uxbridge Magistrates' Court ex parte Adimi* (2001).

83 Interpreted as being sentenced to a term of imprisonment of at least two years: s 72 of the 2002 Act.

disparities in treatment between asylum seekers which the Home Secretary had a duty to investigate.[84]

In determining whether a person is suffering a well founded fear of persecution, past persecution is relevant for the purposes of determining a person's refugee status.[85] It is a question of fact and degree whether a single beating amounts to persecution and, in that determination, a court or tribunal should consider not only the seriousness of the beating but also the risk of repetition if that person was returned to his or her country of origin.[86] A person does not forfeit the right to the protection of the Convention on the Status of Refugees even where an asylum seeker had in bad faith and for the sole purpose of obtaining refugee status acted in such a manner in this country as to put himself at risk of persecution in his country of origin. While his claim would need careful scrutiny and his credibility would be low, nevertheless he would still be entitled to protection in this country if he could establish a genuine and well founded fear of persecution if returned to his home country.[87] Moreover, it did not follow that an asylum seeker must be refused asylum because he, albeit unreasonably, would engage in certain political or religious activities on his return which would put him or her at greater risk. The Court of Appeal insisted that a single question arose in all asylum cases: 'Was there a serious risk that on return the applicant would be persecuted?'[88] The adequacy of the protection which state authorities would provide for a person if returned to his or her country, from the activities of third parties who posed a risk to a person or group, is also a relevant consideration in determining whether a person should be granted asylum. Where the state was unwilling or unable to protect the person from acts of ill treatment, that factor formed part of the consideration as to whether the applicant's fear of persecution was well founded.[89]

In *R (Bagdanavicius) v Secretary of State for the Home Department* (2005) the House of Lords ruled that where an asylum-seeker sought to enter in reliance on the ill treatment provisions of the European Convention on Human Rights, it was necessary for him to show that the state he fled from did not provide a reasonable level of protection against such harm by non-state agents. The Court ruled that any harm inflicted by non-state agents would not constitute Article 3 ill treatment unless in addition the state had failed to provide reasonable protection. By contrast, in *R (Atkinson) v Secretary of State for the Home Department* (2004) the Court of Appeal ruled that where a state was willing but unable to protect an

---

84 See also *R (Yogathas and Thangarasa) v Secretary of State for the Home Department* (2002). The Court of Appeal, upheld the entitlement of the Secretary of State to determine the credibility of any fresh evidence adduced by an applicant for asylum in *R v Secretary of State for the Home Department ex parte Nkereuwen* (1999).

85 But see *R (Hoxha) v Special Adjudicators* (2005) in which past persecution did not suffice to satisfy the Convention.

86 *Demirkaya v Secretary of State for the Home Department* (1999).

87 *Danian v Secretary of State for the Home Department* (2000).

88 *Ahmed (Iftikhar) v Secretary of State for the Home Department* (1999).

89 *Horvath v Secretary of State for the Home Department* (2001); see also *Suarez v Secretary of State for the Home Department* (2002) in which the Court of Appeal ruled that the unlawful activities of agents of the state were capable of giving use to a fear of persecution. See also *Krotov v Secretary of State for the Home Department* (2004).

asylum seeker from ill treatment, Article 3 was engaged and he could succeed in his claim. Furthermore, the Court of Appeal, in *Hysi v Secretary of State for the Home Department* (2005) ruled that a decision to return an 18 year old son of a gypsy mother to Kosovo on the basis that he could relocate to a part of the country where he could conceal his mixed ethnicity ought not to have been taken without consideration whether it would be unduly harsh to do so.

In *Adan v Secretary of State for the Home Department* (1998), the House of Lords ruled that it was insufficient for an asylum seeker to ground his or her claim to asylum on potential persecution if returned to his or her home country, unless that claim could demonstrate that that person would be specifically discriminated against. Accordingly, where the applicant claimed that he or she would be persecuted because of membership of a particular group involved in a civil war – in this case in Somalia – the applicant was not to be accorded refugee status. Unless the applicant could prove that he or she was in particular danger, over and above others in society, the claim would fail. In this case, every person claiming refugee status had to demonstrate a 'well founded fear of persecution, above the risk to life and liberty involved in being caught in a civil war'. Additionally, the House of Lords ruled, the fear of persecution must exist at the time they apply for asylum – a fear founded on the time at which they left the country was not sufficient.[90]

The House of Lords also considered the meaning of 'particular social group' in *Islam v Secretary of State for the Home Department* (1999). The asylum applicants, who were citizens of Pakistan and had suffered violence there as a result of allegations of adultery, sought asylum on the basis that, if they returned to Pakistan, they would suffer persecution and would be unprotected by the authorities, and might be liable to death by stoning. They argued that their return would be contrary to the Convention, and that the persecution they would suffer would be 'for reasons of membership of a particular social group'. The House of Lords held that a particular social group had to exist independently of the Convention. Women in Pakistan constituted a particular social group because they were discriminated against as a group and the state gave them no protection. In *Liu v Secretary of State for the Home Department* (2005) the Court of Appeal ruled that the actions of persecutors might suffice to identify or create a 'particular social group' for the purposes of establishing a well-founded fear of persecution under the 1951 Geneva Convention. The applicant, a citizen of China, was married with two female children. She had become pregnant, contrary to China's reproduction control laws, and was taken to hospital where her eight-month foetus was forcibly removed. She refused sterilisation and attempts to return her to hospital and escaped. At issue was whether the applicant's fear of persecution was for reasons of 'membership of a particular social group'. The applicant's appeal was allowed and the matter remitted for rehearing by a differently constituted appeal tribunal.

Liu's case compares favourably with that of *Fornah v Secretary of State for the Home Department* (2005). Fornah, a 15 year old girl, was refused asylum in the United Kingdom. She had sought refuge because she feared that if she returned to

---

90 See also *Omoruyi v Secretary of State for the Home Department* (2001).

Sierra Leone she would have to undergo circumcision. The Court of Appeal ruled, Arden LJ dissenting, that, given that the practice was widely accepted and that circumcision would result in full acceptance in society, the threatened genital mutilation did not constitute persecution by reason of membership of a particular social group.

R v Secretary of State for the Home Department ex parte Canbolat (1997) the court ruled that it was not for the court to assess the merits of the case – that was for the Home Secretary. Only if the Home Secretary had reached a decision to which he could not properly have come, on the material before him, could the court interfere.[91]

The House of Lords reconsidered the Geneva Convention in *Januzi and Others v Secretary of State for the Home Department* (2006). The Court ruled that when deciding whether it would be reasonable to expect an asylum seeker to relocate to an area within his country of nationality rather than seek protection abroad, it was not relevant to consider whether the quality of life in the place of relocation met the basic norms of civil, political and socio-economic rights. The Convention did not expressly address the relocation issue. The relevant test was reasonableness and that did not involve comparison between the conditions prevailing in the place of relocation and the country where asylum was sought.[92] Persecution apart, the Convention was not directed to the level of rights prevailing in the country of nationality.[93]

The issue of discrimination within the immigration system was considered by the House of Lords in *R (European Roma Rights Centre) v Secretary of State for the Home Department* (2004). A pre-entry clearance system operated at Prague airport under which Roma gypsies were questioned at greater length than other potential immigrants. This had been ruled not to be a violation of the 1951 Geneva Convention, the claimants neither being outside their own country of nationality nor within the United Kingdom. It was, however, contrary to the Race Relations Act 1976. Immigration officers treated the claimants more sceptically than other claimants: they did so solely on the basis of race and the reason for so acting was irrelevant. The system was inherently and systematically discriminatory and unlawful.[94]

---

91 See also *R v Secretary of State for the Home Department ex parte Abdi; Secretary of State for Home Affairs ex parte Gawe* (1996); *R v Secretary of State for the Home Department ex parte Launder* (1997); *Kriba v Secretary of State for the Home Department* (1998). On the Human Rights Act 1998, see below.

92 The House of Lords considered and rejected the approach taken in the New Zealand case of *Butler v Attorney General* (1999) and *Refugee Appeal No 71684/99* (2000), preferring the Canadian apprach taken in *Thirunavukkarasu v Canada (Minister of Employment and Immigration)* (1993) pp 687–88.

93 In *Huang v Secretary of State for the Home Department* (2005) the Court of Appeal ruled that where a claimant who had no entitlement to enter or remain who appealed on the ground that his removal would constitute a disproportionate interference with his right to private and family life under Article 8, the adjudicator's duty was only to see whether an exceptional case had been made out such that proportionality required a departure from the normal rule.

94 The fast-track scheme to deal with unmeritorious asylum claims was not unfair and unlawful so long as Home Office officials were willing to operate the scheme with flexibility on a case by case basis. The Court of Appeal so ruled in *R (Refugee Legal Centre) v Secretary of State for the Home Department* (2004).

In *R (Sivakumar) v Secretary of State for the Home Department* (2003), the House of Lords was called on to consider whether a person who had been tortured by security forces in his home country as a suspected terrorist might be entitled to refugee status. The applicant was a Tamil from the north of Sri Lanka, who claimed that he had been detained and ill-treated by authorities in Sri Lanka. There was evidence of widespread torture of persons and most victims were Tamils. The Sri Lankan authorities had subjected the applicant to 'sustained, exceptionally sadistic and humiliating torture'. The applicant's stated belief that he was in daily fear was not surprising: there was a reasonable likelihood of persecution on grounds of race.[95]

Section 31 of the 1999 Act reflects the prohibition in Article 31(1) of the 1951 Convention against penalising refugees for their method of entry to a country to seek asylum,[96] and provides that it is a defence for a refugee charged with an offence to which this section applies to show that, having come to the United Kingdom directly from a country where his life or freedom was threatened, he presented himself to the authorities in the United Kingdom without delay, showed good cause for his illegal entry or presence and made a claim for asylum as soon as was reasonably practicable. If the refugee has stopped in a third country in transit from a country where his life or freedom was threatened en route to the United Kingdom, the defence in sub-section (1) only applies if he shows that he could not reasonably have expected to be given protection under the Refugee Convention in that other country.[97]

IMMIGRATION AND ASYLUM APPEALS[98]

The Nationality, Immigration and Asylum Act 2002 restructured the appeal system. In turn, the Asylum and Immigration (Treatment of Claimants, etc.) Act 2004 amends the 2002 Act, replaces the two-tier system of appeal with a single tribunal, the Asylum and Immigration Tribunal. The Immigration Appeal Tribunal is abolished.[99] A party to an appeal to the Tribunal may apply to the High Court (in Scotland the Outer House of the Court of Session; in Northern Ireland the High Court) for an order requiring the Tribunal to reconsider its decision on the grounds that the Tribunal made an error of law.[100] Where an appeal has been reconsidered, section 103B of the 2004 Act provides for a party to bring a further appeal on a point of law to the Court of Appeal (in Scotland the Inner House of the Court of Session; in Northern Ireland the Court of Appeal). An appeal may only be brought with the permission of the Tribunal, or if the Tribunal

---

95 A conscientious objection to compulsory military service did not entitle a person to refugee status: *Sepet v Secretary of State for the Home Department* (2003).

96 See *Adimi, Sorani and Kaziu* (1999).

97 Immigration and Asylum Act 1999, s 31(2).

98 The Immigration, Asylum and Nationality Bill 2006 makes a number of reforms to the appeal process.

99 Asylum and Immigration (Treatment of Claimants, etc.) Act 2004, s 26, providing that ss 100–103 of and Sched 5 to the Nationality, Immigration and Asylum Act 2002 shall cease to have effect.

100 2004 Act, s 103A.

refuses permission, the appropriate appellate court. Decisions which may be appealed are stated in section 82(2) of the 2002 Act:

> refusal of leave to enter the United Kingdom; refusal of entry clearance; refusal of a certificate of entitlement under section 10 (the right of abode certificate); refusal to vary leave to enter or remain; revocation of indefinite leave to enter or remain (under section 76); a removal decision under section 10(1)(a)(b) or (c) of the Immigration and Asylum Act 1999; decision to remove an illegal entrant and dependants under Immigration Act 1971; decision to make a deportation order under section 5(1) of the 1971 Act and refusal to revoke a deportation order under section 5(2) of the 1971 Act.

Section 83 of the Act relates to appeals against the refusal of an asylum claim where the Secretary of State has granted leave to enter or remain for a period exceeding one year.

Section 84 specifies the grounds for appeal. These are:

(a) that the decision is not in accordance with immigration rules;

(b) that the decision is unlawful by virtue of section 19B of the Race Relations Act 1976 (discrimination by public authorities);

(c) that the decision is unlawful under section 6 of the Human Rights Act 1998 as being incompatible with the appellant's Convention rights;

(d) that the appellant is an European Economic Area national or a member of the family of an European Economic Area national and the decision breaches the appellant's rights under the Community treaties in respect of entry to or residence in the United Kingdom;

(e) that the decision is otherwise not in accordance with the law;

(f) that the person taking the decision should have exercised differently a discretion conferred by immigration rules;

(g) that the removal of the appellant would breach the United Kingdom's obligations under the Refugee Convention or would be unlawful under section 6 of the Human Rights Act 1998.

Under section 92, a person may not appeal under section 82(1) while he or she is in the United Kingdom unless the appeal relates to matters specified in (c), (d), (e), (f) and (g) above, or is an appeal against refusal of leave to enter where the appellant is in the UK and has entry clearance or a work permit; or if the appellant has made an asylum claim, or a human rights claim while in the United Kingdom, or is an European Economic Area national and claims that the decision breaches the appellant's rights under Community law. Similar provision is made for those in relation to whom an order has been made under section 11(2) or 12(2) of the 1999 Act removing him or her to a third country. Section 94 of the 2002 Act, as amended by section 27 of the Asylum and Immigration (Treatment of Claimants, etc.) Act 2004, relates to unfounded human rights or asylum claims and to such claims made where the claimant is entitled to reside in a state listed in section 94(4). Section 94 provides that a person may not bring an appeal while in the United Kingdom solely by virtue of having made an asylum or human rights claim where the Secretary of State certifies that claim as clearly unfounded. It also provides that where the Secretary of State is satisfied that an asylum or human rights claimant is entitled to live in a state listed in subsection (4) he shall certify the claim as clearly unfounded unless he is satisfied that it is not.

Section 97 relates to national security and prevents a person from appealing if the Secretary of State certifies that the person's exclusion or removal from the United Kingdom is in the interests of national security or in the interests of the relationship between the United Kingdom and another country. Section 98 makes similar provision in relation to certification that the exclusion or removal of a person is conducive to the public good. Where a certificate has been issued and an appeal is pending, that appeal shall lapse.[101]

THE CRIMINAL LAW

The Immigration Act 1971, section 24, makes it a criminal offence for a non-British citizen to enter the United Kingdom in breach of a deportation order or without leave; or to remain beyond the permitted time limit where leave to enter and remain is limited; or to fail to observe any conditions of leave. Schedule 1 to the British Nationality Act 1981, as amended by the Nationality, Immigration and Asylum Act 2002, makes further provision concerning those who are in breach of immigration laws and therefore unlawfully present in the United Kingdom. Part 7 of the 2002 Act repeals section 25 of the 1971 Act and replaces it with four new sections.[102] Section 25[103] makes it an offence knowingly to assist a person in breaching the immigration laws of the United Kingdom and that of any Member State of the European Union. Under section 25A it is an offence to knowingly, and for gain, assist an asylum seeker to enter the United Kingdom, and under section 25B it is an offence to assist a person to enter in breach of a deportation or exclusion order. Where a person is convicted under sections 25, 25A or 25B, section 25C provides for the forfeiture of vehicles, ships or aircraft involved in the offence(s). Section 145 of 2002 Act creates the criminal offence of trafficking of people for the purposes of prostitution.

The Asylum and Immigration (Treatment of Claimants etc.) Act 2004 (hereafter the 2004 Act) extends the law by introducing a new criminal offence of trafficking people into, within or out of the United Kingdom for the purposes of exploitation. Exploitation is defined as behaviour contravening Article 4 of the Convention on Human Rights (slavery or forced labour), or relating to an offence concerning organ removal, or being subjected to force, threats or deception to induce a person to provide services or benefits, or inducing a persons to do something which because of illness, disability or youth that person is unlikely to resist. The 2004 Act and Immigration, Asylum and Nationality Act 2006 regulate employment of illegal immigrants and those subject to immigration control.

The Immigration, Asylum and Nationality Act 2006, sections 15–20, introduce a penalty scheme in relation to the employment of those subject to immigration control. The Secretary of State is given the power to issue a penalty notice stating why he or she believes the employer is liable, the amount of the penalty, arrangements for its payment and information relating to objections and appeals.

---

101 Asylum and Immigration (Treatment of Claimants, etc.) Act 2004, s 99.
102 Section 143 of the 2002 Act, introducing new ss 25, 25A, 25B and 25C.
103 As amended by s 1 of the Asylum and Immigration (Treatment of Claimants, etc.) Act 2004.

Section 149 of the 2002 Act inserted section 26B into the Immigration Act 1971 which provides that it is an offence to possess ink stamps, both genuine and replica, without reasonable excuse. Section 3 of the 2004 Act extends the offence to include possession of cards or stickers which are increasingly being used instead of ink stamps.[104]

The 2004 Act makes it an offence, at a leave or asylum interview, without reasonable excuse, not to have with him or her an immigration document which is in force and which satisfactorily establishes his or her, or any dependent child's, identity and nationality or citizenship.[105]

Powers of arrest, search and fingerprinting

The Immigration Acts 1971 to 2006 govern the powers of immigration officers in relation to entry of premises, arrest and search of suspects and the fingerprinting of persons suspected of immigration offences. Power of arrest without warrant is available in respect of offences under the 1971 Immigration Act for illegal entry, assisting illegal entry, deception and obstruction of an immigration officer.[106] Section 14 of the 2004 Act provides for arrest without warrant where an immigration officer – in the course of exercising a function under the Immigration Acts forms a reasonable suspicion that a person has committed or attempted to commit one or more of a list of specified offences. The power of entry and search for the purpose of arrest or following arrest is subject to the requirement that the power be exercised only to the text that is reasonably required.[107]

Fingerprinting is regulated by section 141 of the 1999 Act, as amended by sections 28 and 29 of the 2006 Act. Fingerprints may be taken from adults arriving without proof of identity, those granted temporary entry where there is a suspicion that they may break entry conditions, illegal entrants subject to removal, a person who has been detained or arrested about whom a decision to give leave to enter has not yet been reached, asylum seekers and dependants of the above. The fingerprinting of children under the age of 16 is subject to restrictions. Where there is doubt as to the age of the person, fingerprints may be taken if a senior officer (Chief Constable, Chief Immigration Officer, Prison Governor) reasonably believes that the person is aged 16 or over. Provision is made for requiring attendance for fingerprinting, and for the subsequent destruction of fingerprints.[108] Codes of Practice, based on the Codes issued under the Police and Criminal Evidence Act 1984, must be complied with by immigration officers and those authorised to take fingerprints. An immigration officer exercising any power conferred under the 1971 Act or the 1999 Act may, if necessary, use reasonable force.[109] The Nationality,

---

104 Section 3 amends s 5 of the Forgery and Counterfeiting Act 1981 by extending the interpretation of 'immigration documents'.
105 Section 2. Section 3 of the 2004 Act amends s 5 of the Forgery and Counterfeiting Act 1981 (offences relating to documents) to include immigration documents.
106 Sections 24 and 25.
107 Immigration Act 1971, s 28, as amended by s 14 of the 2004 Act.
108 Immigration and Asylum Act 1999, ss 142 and 143, as amended by the Immigration, Asylum and Nationality Act 2006, s 29.
109 *Ibid*, s 146.

Immigration and Asylum Act 2002, section 126, extends the law, requiring those applying for immigration to provide information about his or her external physical characteristics. Such data may also be provided voluntarily in support of an application (section 127). Section 128 amends section 144 of the Immigration and Asylum Act 1999 by including in the definition of external physical characteristics, features of the iris or any other part of the eye.

Carriers' liability

The Immigration and Asylum Act 1999, as amended by the Nationality, Immigration and Asylum Act 2002, imposes civil liability on persons responsible for the transportation of 'clandestine entrants' to the United Kingdom. The law was amended following the case of *International Transport Roth GmbH v Secretary of State for the Home Department* (2002). The Court of Appeal considered the provisions of the Immigration of Asylum Act 1999 which made carriers liable to a fixed penalty of £2,000 for every clandestine entrant found concealed in a vehicle. Once a penalty notice had been issued by the Secretary of State, a senior immigration officer could detain the vehicle if he considered that there was a serious risk that the penalty would not be paid and no satisfactory alternative security had been given. The owner or driver could apply to the court for the release of the vehicle. The Court of Appeal ruled that the scale and inflexibility of the penalty without the possibility of mitigation or the right for the penalty to be determined by an independent tribunal were factors which made the scheme unfair. The scheme also imposed an excessive burden on the carriers which was disproportionate to the objective to be achieved and was in breach of Article 1 of the First Protocol to the European Convention on Human Rights.

Civil liability covers all vehicles, trains, rail freight wagons, ships or aircraft bringing clandestine entrants to the United Kingdom, and provides power to detain such vehicles, ships or aircraft as security until all charges for the carriage of illegal entrants have been paid.

The 'responsible person' is liable to a penalty for each clandestine entrant, irrespective of whether the responsible person knew or suspected that a clandestine entrant was concealed in the transporter, or that there were one or more other persons concealed with the clandestine entrant in the same transporter.[110] It is a defence for the carrier to show that he or an employee was acting under duress, and for the carrier to show that he did not know and had no reasonable grounds for suspecting that a clandestine entrant was or might be concealed in the transporters or that an effective system for preventing the carriage of clandestine entrants was in operation and that, on the occasion in question, the responsible person was operating that system properly. If the Secretary of State decides that a person is liable, he must issue a penalty notice stating the reasons for deciding that the person is liable, the amount of the penalty or penalties, the date before which the penalty must be paid, and include an explanation of the steps to be taken if the person objects to the penalty.

---

110 Defined as a ship, vehicle or aircraft: Immigration and Asylum Act 1999, s 43.

There is a statutory right of appeal against the imposition of a penalty: a county court (or equivalent in Scotland) may cancel or reduce the penalty or dismiss the appeal.[111] The Secretary of State must issue a Code of Practice specifying matters to be considered in determining the amount of a penalty.[112] If a penalty notice has been issued, a senior officer (which means an officer not below the rank of Chief Immigration Officer) may detain the relevant vehicles until all penalties have been paid, but the power may only be exercised if there is a significant risk that the penalty will not be paid in the prescribed time if the transporter is not detained, and may not be exercised if alternative security has been given. The detention of the transporter is lawful, even though it is subsequently established that the penalty notice was ill founded, unless the Secretary of State was acting unreasonably in issuing the penalty notice. Where a transporter is detained, the owner or responsible persons or any person with an interest in the transporter may apply to the court for its release. The court may order its release if satisfactory security has been tendered, there is no significant risk that the penalty will not be paid or there is significant doubt whether the penalty is payable. If the court does not order release, the Secretary of State may sell the transporter if the penalty is not paid before the end of a period of 84 days beginning on the date on which the detention began. Provision is also made for the detention of carriers following the arrest of a person in connection with offences relating to assisting illegal entry and harbouring an unlawful entrant.[113]

The Nationality, Immigration and Asylum Act 2002 provides for the introduction of an Authority-to-carry (ATC) scheme which requires carriers to check the details of passengers against a Home Office database to confirm that they pose no known immigration or security risk. The Immigration, Asylum and Nationality Act 2006, section 31, amends the Immigration Act 1971 in respect of the provision of information by those responsible for ships and aircraft relating to passengers and crew. The 2006 Act also extends police powers in relation to information relating to passengers, crew and freight, and section 34 creates a criminal offence of failing to comply with requirements relating to the disclosure of information.

Marriage regulations

The Asylum and Immigration (Treatments of Claimants, etc.) Act 2004 amends the law relating to marriages involving persons who are subject to immigration control. Where the marriage is to take place in the United Kingdom,[114] section 19 of the 2004 Act provides that notices under section 27 of the Marriage Act 1949 are to be given only at a designated registration centre. Notice must be given together and in person. The superintendent registrar may not enter in the marriage notice book notice of a marriage unless satisfied that the party who is subject to immigration control has entry clearance granted for the purpose of enabling him to marry in the United Kingdom and has written permission of the Secretary of

---

111 Immigration and Asylum Act 1999, s 35A.
112 *Ibid*, s 32A.
113 See *ibid*, ss 34–38.
114 Under a superintendent registrar's certification under Part III of the Marriage Act 1949.

State to marry in the United Kingdom. Similar provision is made in respect of marriage which are intended to be solemnised in Scotland.[115]

DEPORTATION

Deportation is the act of removing a person from the country. A British citizen cannot be deported. Most non-citizens can be subject to deportation. Section 3(5) of the Immigration Act 1971 provides:

> A person who is not a British citizen is liable to deportation from the United Kingdom if:
>
> (a) the Secretary of State deems his deportation to be conducive to the public good; or
>
> (b) another person to whose family he belongs is or has been ordered to be deported.

Furthermore, section 3(6) provides that:

> Without prejudice to the operation of subsection (5) above, a person who is not a British citizen shall also be liable to deportation ... if, after he has attained the age of seventeen, he is convicted of an offence for which he is punishable with imprisonment and on his conviction is recommended for deportation by a court empowered by this Act to do so.

The Immigration Act 1971 provides that a person who has been notified that the Secretary of State intends to make a deportation order against him or who has been recommended for deportation by a court may be detained pending deportation.[116] A person may be bailed pending deportation. In order to avoid the situation where a court grants bail in ignorance of actual or impending deportation action, the Asylum and Immigration (Treatment of Claimants, etc.) Act 2004, section 34, amends the 1971 Act and provides that an application for bail may only be made to the Immigration Service or immigration appellate body.

The Asylum and Immigration (Treatment of Claimants, etc.) Act 2004, section 35, provides that the Secretary of State may require a person to take specified action in order to obtain a travel document which will facilitate that person's deportation or removal from the United Kingdom. Such action may involve the provision of information or documents, fingerprinting, cooperating with officials, attending interviews etc. A person who fails, without reasonable excuse, to comply with the Secretary of State's requirement commits an offence. Section 36 of the 2004 Act makes provision for the electronic monitoring of persons subject to immigration control where a residence restriction is in place, or a reporting restriction could be imposed and where immigration bail is granted.

Immigration officers have the power to direct the removal of a person who is not a British citizen under the following circumstances:

(a) having only a limited leave to enter or remain, he does not observe a condition attached to the leave or remains beyond the time limited by the leave;

(b) he uses deception in seeking (whether successfully or not) leave to remain;

(ba) his indefinite leave to enter or remain has been revoked under section 76(3) of the Nationality, Immigration and Asylum Act 2002; or

---

115 Asylum and Immigration (Treatment of Claimants, etc.) Act 2004, s 20. These provisions have been challenged successfully before the High Court. See *R (Baiai and Trzcinska) v Secretary of State for the Home Department* (2005).

116 Immigration Act 1971, Sched 3.

(c) directions ... have been given for the removal, under this section, of a person ... to whose family he belongs.[117]

There are a number of exemptions to the power to deport. Section 7 of the Immigration Act 1971[118] provides that a Commonwealth citizen or citizen of the Republic of Ireland shall not be liable to deportation on the order of the Home Secretary or recommendation of a court following conviction for a criminal offence, if he or she has been ordinarily resident in the United Kingdom and Islands for a period of five years immediately prior to the Home Secretary's decision or the date of his or her conviction. Under the Nationality, Immigration and Asylum Act 2002, section 77, an asylum seeker cannot be removed before notice of the Secretary of State's decision on the application is given.[119] Equivalent provisions apply to those subject to appeal proceedings. There is a right of appeal against a deportation order being made.[120, 121] However, under the Immigration, Asylum and Nationality Act 2006, section 7, a person subject to deportation on national security grounds may only appeal against the decision to deport from outside the United Kingdom. An in-country appeal is available on human rights grounds unless the Home Secretary has certified that removal would not breach the European Convention on Human Rights. An in-country appeal against certification lies with the Special Immigration Appeals Commission.[122]

The Asylum and Immigration (Treatment of Claimants, etc.) Act 2004, section 33 and Schedule 3 replace and extend the provisions contained in section 11 and 12 of the Immigration and Asylum Act 1999 relating to the removal of asylum seekers to a safe third country without substantive consideration of the asylum claim. The United Kingdom is under an obligation under the 1951 Convention on the Status of Refugees and the Human Rights Act 1998 not to remove persons who would be at risk in another country. Under section 11 and Schedule 3 certain countries are deemed safe for Refugee Convention purposes, being regarded as a place:

(a) where a person's life and liberty are not threatened by reason of his race, religion, nationality, membership of a particular social group or political opinion,

(b) from which a person will not be sent to another State in contravention of his Convention rights, and

---

117 Immigration and Asylum Act 1999, s 10, as amended by the Nationality, Immigration and Asylum Act 2002.

118 As amended by the Nationality, Immigration and Asylum Act 2002, s 75.

119 However, interim or preparatory action may be taken with a view to deportation once the decision is given: s 77(4).

120 Nationality, Immigration and Asylum Act 2002, s 79.

121 In *R (N, Kenya) v Secretary of State for the Home Department* (2004) the Court of Appeal dismissed an appeal against deportation which had been challenged on the basis of a prospective breach of Article 8 of the Convention. The appellant had been sentenced to 11 years' imprisonment after being convicted of abduction, threats to kill, three rapes and false imprisonment. The Court of Appeal ruled that in the first instance the public interest factor was a matter for the Home Secretary, whose view should be taken into account by the adjudicator.

122 Section 7, inserting a new s 97A into the Nationality, Immigration and Asylum Act 2002.

(c) from which a person will not be sent to another State otherwise than in accordance with the Refugee Convention.[123]

A person who is to be removed to one of the safe countries may not challenge their removal on Refugee Convention grounds. They may challenge their removal on the basis that their European Convention rights would be infringed, but where the Secretary of State certifies that a human rights claim is clearly unfounded, any appeal on this ground can only be pursued from abroad. In addition to the deemed safe countries, other countries can be certified as safe for a given individual. Furthermore, in relation to certain countries claims based on human rights grounds will be certified as clearly unfounded unless the Home Secretary is satisfied that they are not clearly unfounded.

Removal centres for detained persons

The Immigration and Asylum Act 1999, as amended, provides for the management of centres for the accommodation of immigration and asylum detainees, and provides for the contracting out of the provision and running of centres.

Judicial review

Immigration raises difficult questions for the courts, particularly in light of the wide powers conferred on the Home Secretary. Judicial criticism of the exercise of the Home Secretary's powers occurred in *M v Home Office* (1992). The Home Secretary, Kenneth Baker, had ignored an order of the court that M should not be returned to Zaire, where he feared torture. Immigration officials put M on a plane, which the Home Secretary refused to have turned back. The House of Lords held that an injunction could lie against ministers of the Crown, and that they would be guilty of contempt of court for defiance of orders of the court.

Where the Home Secretary has rejected an application for asylum, and the applicant submits a fresh application based on 'new, apparently credible evidence', the Home Secretary has a duty to consider that application afresh: *R v Secretary of State for the Home Department ex parte Boybeyi* (1997). An unsuccessful application for asylum does not preclude the making of a second application, based on fresh evidence.[124] However, where no fresh application is submitted, there is no right of appeal against the Home Secretary's decision to deny asylum: *R v Special Adjudicator ex parte Secretary of State for the Home Department* (1999).[125] In *R v Home Secretary ex parte Bugdaycay and Musisi* (1987), the House of Lords took a more robust approach. In judicial review proceedings, it ruled that the

---

123 Asylum and Immigration (Treatment of Claimants, etc.) Act 2004, Sched 3, para 3. The Schedule lists countries which are deemed safe. These are all countries bound by the EU Council Regulation EC No 343/2003 or the Dublin Convention, being all members of the enlarged European Union together with Norway and Iceland.
124 *R v Secretary of State for the Home Department ex parte Onibiyo* (1996).
125 See also *R v Special Adjudicator ex parte Secretary of State for the Home Department* (1997); *R v Secretary of State for the Home Department ex parte Cakabay* (1988); *R v Secretary of State for the Home Department ex parte Salem* (1999).

Home Secretary had failed to take into account relevant considerations in his decision to deport a Ugandan refugee to Kenya (where the applicant had lived previously). Evidence existed that Kenya had previously returned refugees to Uganda. The court had the aid of the Refugee Convention (discussed above), Article 33 of which provides that no one should be returned to a territory where his life or freedom would be threatened, which the court held should govern the interpretation of the Immigration Rules.

In *R (Anufrijeva) v Secretary of State for the Home Department* (2003) the House of Lords ruled that an adverse administrative decision had to be communicated to the relevant individual before it could take legal effect, in order that the individual could challenge the decision in the courts. The claimant was therefore entitled to receive social security payments for the period preceding the proper notification of the decision of the Home Secretary that her claim to asylum had failed.

On the other hand, judicial review should be granted sparingly. For example, the Court of Appeal ruled that the rights of asylum seekers were adequately protected by the statutory process and that the courts should not grant leave for judicial review of a refusal of permission to appeal to the Immigration Appeal Tribunal from the decision of an adjudicator in *R (G) v Immigration Appeal Tribunal* (2004). The statutory review procedure was adequate and proportionate and asylum seekers should not be able to buy time by applying for permission to seek judicial review.

The Human Rights Act 1998 requires that the courts enforce the Convention rights incorporated under the 1998 Act. The Act also requires new modes of interpretation which extend far beyond the limited *Wednesbury* test, and now include an evaluation as to whether in reaching decisions which restrict Convention rights the executive has acted in a manner which is proportionate to the objective being pursued and has taken only such measures as are necessary in relation to the permitted limitations of rights, as stipulated in Convention Articles (for example, *inter alia*, in the interests of national security, public safety and public order).

National security and the public interest

In 1962, Dr Soblen, an American citizen who had been convicted of espionage in the United States, fled from the country before being sentenced. Whilst on an aeroplane, Dr Soblen cut his wrists, and was landed in London for hospital treatment. The Home Secretary issued a deportation order on the basis that his continued presence was 'not conducive to the public good'. When Dr Soblen applied for habeas corpus, the Court of Appeal ruled that Dr Soblen had no right to make representations, and that deportation was an administrative matter for the Home Secretary.[126]

In *R v Home Secretary ex parte Hosenball* (1977), two American journalists, Philip Agee and Mark Hosenball, were detained with a view to deportation, on the basis

---

126 See *R v Home Secretary ex parte Soblen* (1963). See also Thornberry, 1963.

that their work involved obtaining and publishing information prejudicial to national security. There was no appeal against the Home Secretary's decision where national security was pleaded.[127] Instead, there was a right to a hearing before a panel of three advisers to the Home Secretary. When Hosenball tried to challenge the Home Secretary's decision in the courts, the Court of Appeal upheld the deportation order. While recognising that the rules of natural justice[128] had not been complied with in the decision to deport Hosenball, the Court of Appeal nevertheless ruled that the requirements of national security prevailed and that, in matters of national security, the Home Secretary was responsible to parliament, and not to the courts.

In *Rehman v Secretary of State for the Home Department* (2003), the House of Lords considered the Secretary of State's decision to refuse an application for indefinite leave to remain in the United Kingdom on the basis that the applicant represented a threat to national security, in that he was allegedly involved in an Islamist terrorist organisation. The Special Immigration Appeals Commission (SIAC) had ruled that the conduct relied on by the Secretary of State had to be conduct targeted at the United Kingdom or its citizens. The House of Lords upheld the Secretary of State's appeal: action against a foreign state could indirectly affect the security of the United Kingdom, and preventative or precautionary action might be justified. While there had to be material from which the Secretary of State could proportionately and reasonably conclude that there was a real possibility of actions harmful to national security, deciding whether deportation would be conducive to the public good was a matter of executive judgment.

The case of *R v Home Secretary ex parte Cheblak* (1991) also reveals the extensive powers of the Home Secretary to detain persons 'in the interests of national security'. During the Gulf War, 160 Iraqi and Palestinian citizens were detained with a view to deportation, on the basis that their presence was not 'conducive to the public good'. Abbas Cheblak and his family had been resident in the United Kingdom for 16 years. In an application for habeas corpus, the Court of Appeal accepted the Home Secretary's explanation that Cheblak had associations with an unspecified organisation which supported the Iraqi government, and refused to press the Home Secretary for further information.[129]

EXTRADITION

Extradition is the process by which a person who has been accused or convicted of a crime in another country is returned to that country to face trial or serve his or her sentence. Extradition may be contrasted with deportation: deportation is the process instigated by the government of a state to expel a non-national from its territory. Extradition, on the other hand, is a process initiated by another state

---

127 Immigration Act 1971, s 15(3). See Chapter 25 on national security.
128 See Chapter 27. The rules of natural justice apply to immigration decisions: *Re HK* (1967).
129 Mr Cheblak was subsequently released from detention following a hearing before the Home Secretary's panel. See also *R v Secretary of State for the Home Department ex parte Jahromi* (1995) and *Chahal v UK* (1997).

requesting a person's return to face trial or, where that person has already been convicted of a crime, to serve his or her sentence.

The Extradition Act 1989 was repealed by the Extradition Act 2003. The 1989 Act was a consolidation of three earlier pieces of legislation.[130] As crime has become increasingly international in nature and co-operation between states to tackle international crime increases, it was felt that the law needed review and reform. The 2003 Act was passed in order to modernise the law, to give effect to European Community legislation,[131] to ensure that the process is quick and effective, and to ensure that extradition law is compatible with human rights. The Act also provides for a single, simplified appeal process.[132]

The 2003 Act distinguishes between two categories of countries: those which do not have the death penalty as a punishment and those which retain the death penalty. The former territories are designated as Category 1, the latter as Category 2. It is for the Secretary of State to designate countries with which Britain has extradition arrangements to the appropriate category.[133] When a requesting country issues a warrant, that warrant must state whether it has been issued for the purpose of arrest and prosecution for a specified offence, or whether the person is unlawfully at large after having been convicted of a specified offence. In both cases, the sentence that could be imposed on conviction or the sentence that has already been imposed must be stated.[134]

Extradition may be sought of persons who are accused of an extradition crime but not yet convicted of an offence and persons who have been convicted but not yet sentenced. Section 64 of the Extradition Act 2003 defines types of conduct which constitutes extradition offences in relation to category 1 countries. In relation to cases where a person has been accused but not yet convicted, conduct constitutes an extradition offence if:

- the conduct occurred in the category 1 territory;

- a certificate has been issued in the category 1 territory confirming that the offence falls within the 'European framework list';[135] and

---

130 Criminal Justice Act 1988, Part I; Fugitive Offenders Act 1967; Extradition Act 1870, as amended.

131 Council Framework Decision of 13 June 2002 on the European arrest warrant and surrender procedures between Member States: 2002/584/JHA.

132 See *Cartwright v Superintendent of Her Majesty's Prison* (2004).

133 See the Extradition Act 2003, Sched 1; Extradition Act 2003 (Designation of Part 1 Territories) Order (SI 2003/3333); Extradition Act 2003 (Designation of Part 2 Territories) Order 2003 (SI 2003/3334).

134 Extradition Act 2003, s 2. The courts are vigilant to ensure that extradition procedures are strictly observed: see *R (Guisto) v Governor of Brixton Prison* (2003); *R (Bleta) v SS Home Department* (2005); *R (Castillo) v Kingdom of Spain* (2005). On the enforceability of a European arrest warrant for the surrender of a fugitive whose criminal conduct took place partly in the state issuing the warrant and partly in the United Kingdom see *King's Prosecutor, Brussels v Cando Armas* (2005). The House of Lords was required to consider s 65 of the Extradition Act 2003 in light of the European Council Framework Decision of 2002 on European arrest warrant and surrender procedures between Member States (2002/584/JHA; OJ 18 July No L190/1).

135 See s 215: the list is set out in Article 2.2 of the framework decision of the Council of the European Union of 13 June 2002 on the European arrest warrant and surrender procedures (2002/584/JHA). The list is reproduced in Sched 2 to the 2003 Act.

- the offence is punishable with detention for a period of three years or more.

In relation to persons convicted of the offence, conduct constitutes an extradition offence if the same circumstances as those above are present, other than in relation to sentence. Section 65 provides that a sentence of detention of 12 months or more must have been imposed.

Part 2 of the 2003 Act regulates extradition to category 2 territories. In relation to persons accused or convicted of an offence, but not yet sentenced, section 137 provides that conduct is an extradition offence if:

- the conduct occurred in the category 2 territory;

- the conduct would amount to an offence punishable with detention for a period of 12 months or more if it occurred in the United Kingdom; and

- the conduct is similarly punishable under the law of the requesting category 2 territory.[136]

In addition to the extradition conditions above, the 2003 Act also provides that genocide, crimes against humanity, war crimes and related offences are extradition offences. Conduct that would be punishable in the United Kingdom under these heads amounts to an extradition offence even if that conduct would not have been an offence at the time and place it occurred.[137]

The Act retains a number of bars to extradition provided under the 1989 Act and the judge considering the application for extradition must decide whether any of these bars prevent extradition: if any bar is applicable the person must be discharged.[138] In addition to these statutory bars, a person may not be extradited if his or her extradition would violate that person's human rights.[139] Accordingly, having considered the section 11 bars, the judge must then decide whether the person's extradition would be compatible with his or her human rights as protected under the European Convention on Human Rights incorporated into domestic law under the Human Rights Act 1998.[140]

The Extradition Act 2003, Part 4, makes detailed provision in relation to police powers. The scope of police powers to deal with arrest, search and seizure in extradition cases, either under common law or under the Police and Criminal Evidence Act 1984, had been questioned in the case of *R (Rottman) v Commissioner of Police for the Metropolis* (2002). The House of Lords ruled that the common law power of search and seizure was not extinguished by the Police and Criminal

---

136 In relation to offences over which the requesting state claims extra-territorial jurisdiction, ss 64 and 137 provide the conditions under which extradition may be granted. See *R (Al-Fawwaz) v Governor of Brixton Prison* (2001).

137 Extradition Act 2003, s 196. See *R v Bow Street Metropolitan Stipendiary Magistrate ex parte Pinochet Ugarte (No 3)* (1999).

138 The bars are: the rule against double jeopardy, extraneous considerations, the passage of time, the person's age, hostage-taking considerations, speciality, the person's earlier extradition to the United Kingdom from a category 1 or 2 territory: ss 11, 12–19. See *Jaffar v Governor of Brixton Prison* (2003) on the time bar.

139 See *Asian v Republic of Germany* (2006).

140 Extradition Act 2003, s 21.

Evidence Act and that the police officers were entitled to exercise their powers of entry, search and seizure.[141] Section 161 provides for entry and search for the purposes of arrest, while section 162 makes it clear that there is power to enter and search premises where the person is arrested, or in which he was immediately before arrest, where there are reasonable grounds to believe that there is evidence on the premises of the relevant offence or of the person's identity. The power of search is limited to searching for evidence 'so far as reasonably necessary'. Section 162(6) authorises the seizure and retention of evidence.[142]

In *Woodcock v Government of New Zealand* (2003) the High Court considered an application for a writ of habeas corpus in respect of the applicant's detention pending a decision to return him to New Zealand. He had left New Zealand in 1987. In 2002 he was arrested following an extradition request in relation to a number of sexual offences, the majority of which were alleged to have been committed between 1982 and 1985. The applicant claimed that to return him would be unjust or oppressive because of the passage of time. The court ruled that the questions for decision under section 11(3)(b) of the Extradition Act 1989 was not whether – given the passage of time – it would be unjust to try the accused, but whether it would be unjust to return him. The court had to consider the safeguards that existed in the domestic law of the requesting state to ensure that there would be no unjust trial. The New Zealand courts had satisfactory procedures to guard against unjust trial and it would not be unjust to return him.[143]

In *R (Bleta) v Secretary of State for the Home Department* (2004) the Home Secretary certified that the Albanian Government's request for extradition was valid under section 70 of the Extradition Act 2003. The request was valid if it contained a statement that the person was unlawfully at large after conviction by a court. Neither the request nor the Home Secretary's certificate contained any explicit statement to that effect. In the absence of clear words to the effect that a person was not only at large but unlawfully at large, it would be unsafe so to conclude and therefore the Secretary of State's certificate would be quashed.

Where a person has been convicted in another country in his absence, and the conviction was based on evidence which rendered the trial unfair and in breach of Article 6 of the European Convention, it would not be in the interests of justice to extradite that person. The High Court so ruled in *Migliorelli v Government of Italy* (2006). However, in *R (Bermingham) v Director of the Serious Fraud Office, Bermingham v Government of the United States* (2006) it was held that where a criminal case was triable in either of two jurisdictions, there was no requirement

---

141 See the Extradition Act 2003 (Police Powers) Order (SI 2003/3106). See also *R (Hewitson) v Chief Constable of the Dorset Police* (2004). Note, however, that in *R (Hewitson) v Chief Constable of the Dorset Police* (2004) the Divisional Court ruled that the decision in *Rottman* could not be extended to legitimise search and seizure when the accused had been arrested (under the Extradition Act 1989, s 8(1)(b)) a short distance from the relevant premises.
142 On international terrorism and the detention of non-British suspects see Chapter 25.
143 On extradition and judicial review see *R (Okandeji) v Bow Street Magistrates' Court* (2005).

that the decision maker decide the place of trial to protect a defendant's Convention rights. The Court ruled that the 2003 Act gave no discretion to either the court or Minister: if the statutory conditions were met the Secretary of State must order extradition. The Secretary of State had no statutory discretion to refuse extradition. Moreover, the prosecutor was not required to establish a *prima facie* case on the evidence.[144]

---

144 See also *R (Norris) v Secretary of State for the Home Department* (2006).

CHAPTER 25

STATE SECURITY[1]

INTRODUCTION

The security of the state is of the utmost importance to the integrity and well being of a nation and to individual citizens whose rights and freedoms are protected by the security of the state.[2] On the other hand, the rights of citizens may be adversely affected by the exercise of such powers and there exists the potential for governments to hide behind the doctrine of national security in order to prevent scrutiny of executive action. Two principal constitutional questions arise from state security. The first concerns the extent to which arrangements secure some form of balance between the competing needs of state security and protection of the individual. The second issue relates to the manner in which – and extent to which – the government is held accountable for powers exercised in the name of state security, either through supervision of the courts or through the democratic process.

Legal regulation of state security matters is relatively recent. Although the original Official Secrets Act dates from 1911, it has only been in the past two decades that statute has regulated the interception of communications,[3] and the Security and Intelligence Services, MI5 and MI6, and the government's signals intelligence organisation, Government Communications Headquarters. Incorporation of Convention rights under the Human Rights Act 1998 necessitated further clarity in the law, provided by the Regulation of Investigatory Powers Act 2000, the main purpose of which is to ensure that relevant investigatory powers are used in accordance with human rights.

The terrorist bombings in the United States of America in September 2001 ushered in unprecedented international co-operation to combat terrorism. In Britain, the government reacted swiftly to introduce tighter anti-terrorism laws. The Anti-Terrorism, Crime and Security Act 2001 was a reaction to the attacks.

THE SECURITY SERVICES

The terminology

The United Kingdom's internal Security Service is known as MI5 (MI stands for Military Intelligence). The Security Service dealing with matters overseas is the Secret Intelligence Service, or MI6. The government's signals intelligence gathering headquarters is Government Communications Headquarters, or GCHQ. Special Branch is part of the police forces and has special duties in

---

1   See, *inter alia*, Bulloch, 1963; Deacon, 1969 Pincher, 1981; West, 1981, 1983; Williams, 1965; Andrew, 1985; Lustgarten and Leigh, 1994; Garton Ash, 1997.
2   On the Racial and Religious Hatred Act 2006 and the Identity Card Bill, see Chapter 21.
3   Interception of Communications Act 1985, Security Services Act 1989, Intelligence Services Act 1994.

relation to public order, the gathering of intelligence and combating subversion and terrorism. The operations of MI5 and MI6 are co-ordinated by the Intelligence Co-ordinator, based in the Cabinet Office. In addition, there is the armed forces wing of military intelligence which, nowadays, is operative principally, but not exclusively, in Northern Ireland.

The Security Service (MI5)

Until 1989, MI5 was unknown to law. It was not regulated by statute and did not enjoy any special common law powers. MI5 was established in 1909[4] under the royal prerogative as part of the defence forces of the realm. The Service is headed by a Director General who is responsible to the Secretary of State for the Home Office. It is not, however, formally a part of the Home Office and thus occupies a curious constitutional status. The Director General has access to the Prime Minister on matters of importance. Since the ending of the Cold War, approximately 70 per cent of MI5's resources are devoted to gathering intelligence about terrorism.[5] Moreover, the Security Service Act 1996 now extends the role of MI5 in relation to investigations relating to 'serious crime', particularly the drugs trade.

Functions of the Service

In 1952, the then Home Secretary, Sir David Maxwell-Fyfe, issued a directive to the Director General outlining the functions of the Service:

> The Security Service is part of the defence forces of the country. Its task is the defence of the Realm as a whole, from external and internal dangers arising from attempts at espionage and sabotage, or from actions of persons and organisations whether directed from within or without the country, which may be judged to be subversive of the state.[6]

The Profumo affair[7]

In 1963 the Secretary of State for War, the Rt Hon John Profumo, resigned from office as a result of his lying to the House of Commons over press disclosures concerning an alleged affair with Christine Keeler, who had associations with a Russian Naval Attaché. The Prime Minister, Harold Macmillan, appointed Lord Denning to inquire into the security aspects of the affair. In his report, Lord Denning stressed that the function of the Security Service:

> ... is to defend the Realm from dangers which would threaten it as a whole, such as espionage on behalf of a foreign power, or internal organisations subversive of the state. For this purpose it must collect information about individuals and give it to those concerned. But it must not, even at the behest of a Minister or a government

---

4 As part of the War Office. MI5 was originally known as MO5.
5 The Home Secretary revealed in July 1998 that MI5 holds approximately 440,000 files, but that only 13,000 are 'active' dossiers on British citizens, over half of whom were suspected of terrorist activities. Of the remainder, 35,000 files related to MI5's administration; 40,000 related to subjects and organisations studied by MI5; 290,000 files related to individuals who had been the subject of an MI5 inquiry in the past 90 years. A further 230,000 files were 'closed'. Active files included about 20,000, of which one-third related to foreign nationals: *Hansard*, HC Vol 317 Col 251.
6 Reproduced in Lord Denning MR's judgment in *R v Home Secretary ex parte Hosenball* (1977).
7 See Denning, 1980, Chapter 3.

department, take part in investigating the private lives of individuals except in a matter bearing on the defence of the Realm as a whole.[8]

Further judicial expression of the role of MI5 is found in the judgment of Taylor J in *R v Secretary of State for the Home Department ex parte Ruddock* (1987).

> The function of the Security Service is the defence of the realm as a whole from, *inter alia*, the actions of persons who and organisations which may be subversive of the state ... A warrant to intercept should only issue where there is reasonable cause to believe that major subversive activity is already being carried on and is likely to injure the national interest. The material reasonably likely to be obtained by the interception must be of direct use to the Security Service in its functions ...

> Normal methods of investigation must either have failed or be unlikely to succeed. Interception must be strictly limited to what is necessary to the Security Service's defined functions and must not be used for party political purposes ...

Despite such strictures, there have been many charges made against MI5 from journalists and from members of MI5 itself.[9]

Spycatcher[10]

The most celebrated exposure of MI5 came in the form of Peter Wright's book, *Spycatcher* (1987). Among many allegations made by Wright in *Spycatcher* was the claim that MI5 had 'bugged and burgled its way across London' without lawful authority.

As an electrical engineer with MI5, Peter Wright's expertise included bugging embassies, diplomatic residences and international conferences. In 1963, Wright was promoted to an interrogator and to the post of Chairman of an internal committee inquiring into Soviet infiltration of the Security Services. Wright believed that MI5's perceived poor performance in the Cold War years of the 1950s and 1960s was in part due to Soviet infiltration at the highest point of MI5. The defections of two security agents, Donald Maclean and Guy Burgess, in 1951, and the confession and defection of Kim Philby in 1963,[11] gave added weight to the security fears. Wright was further convinced that the then head of MI5, Roger Hollis, was a Soviet agent: a matter officially denied.[12] The revelation in 1979 that Anthony Blunt, surveyor of the Queen's art collection and knight of the realm, had been a KGB[13] spy since his recruitment by the Russians whilst a student at

---

8 The *Report on the Security Aspects of the Circumstances Leading up to the Resignation of Mr JD Profumo*, Cmnd 2152, 1963, London: HMSO, caused disquiet. One outcome was the establishment of the Security Commission in 1964. See Leigh and Lustgarten, 1991.

9 See, *inter alia*, Pincher, 1981; West, 1983.

10 See Watt, 1988; Pannick, '*Spycatcher*: two years of legal indignation', in Kingsford-Smith and Oliver, 1990.

11 An MI6 officer, appointed to MI6 Head of Station in Washington. See Trevor-Roper, 1968; Philby, 1968.

12 See Pincher, 1981. Pincher relied heavily on information obtained from Wright. An official inquiry chaired by Lord Trend in 1974–75 failed to establish Hollis's innocence. See HC Deb Vol 1 Cols 1079–85, 26 March 1981. Hollis retired from MI5 in 1965. The Security Commission investigated the charges: its report was never published. Instead, a government statement was issued outlining measures taken as a result of the report: see Cmnd 8450, 1982, London: HMSO.

13 The Russian secret service.

Cambridge University[14] revealed the extent to which the Security Services had become vulnerable to Russian infiltration.

In 1976, Wright retired and Lord Rothschild introduced him to the journalist Chapman Pincher. In collaboration with Pincher, *Spycatcher* was written: a book which launched one of the most farcical chapters in recent legal and political history, revealing as much about the secrecy of government as about the workings of MI5. In *Spycatcher,* Wright alleged that MI5 had, over the years, in addition to 'bugging and burglary', interrogated and hounded hundreds of individuals in an inquiry into the membership of the Communist Party rivalling that of the McCarthy Inquiry in the United States of America in the 1930s. The allegations made by Wright became a matter of intense political and legal interest.

The government, intent on stopping circulation of *Spycatcher*, sought an injunction to restrain publication.[15] The litigation against *Spycatcher* commenced in Australia in 1985, and ultimately failed.[16] In 1986 the Attorney General was granted injunctions to restrain publication – injunctions which were to endure for some four years.[17] In 1990, however, the House of Lords held that the wide availability of the information and the public interest in freedom of speech and the right to receive information outweighed the interests of the Crown in preserving government secrecy.[18] The issue of the temporary injunctions was taken to the European Court of Human Rights, wherein it was held that the injunctions granted violated Article 10 of the Convention.[19]

One outcome of the *Spycatcher* affair was the enactment of the Security Service Act 1989, which placed MI5 on a statutory basis. The Regulation of Investigatory Powers Act 2000 reforms the law relating to the Security Services and the interception of communications.

The Security Service Act 1989[20]

The Act defined the functions of MI5 and placed the issuing of warrants under statutory authority. Section 3 of the Act empowered the Home Secretary to issue warrants authorising 'entry on or interference with property'. This power is now contained in sections 5 and 6 of the Intelligence Services Act 1994. The Act also provided, for the first time, a complaints procedure for individuals who are

---

14 From 1926. Following Blunt's exposure, Blunt was stripped of his knighthood.
15 See Turnbull, 1988; on the *Attorney-General v Jonathan Cape Ltd* (1976) see Young 1976, particularly Chapters 2 and 11.
16 (1987) 8 NSWLR 341; HC of Australia (1988) 165 CLR 30.
17 *Attorney General v Guardian Newspapers Ltd* (1987).
18 *Attorney General v Guardian Newspapers Ltd (No 2)* (1990).
19 *The Observer, The Guardian and The Sunday Times v United Kingdom* (1991). See Bindman, 1989. See further Chapter 19; and see Leigh, 1992. In *Attorney General v Blake* (1996), Sir Richard Scott VC ruled that the Crown was not entitled to the profits gained by Blake, a former Secret Intelligence Officer who became a Soviet Agent in 1951 through the publication of his autobiography. By 1989, when the autobiography was published, none of the information was any longer confidential and, therefore, there was no breach of the lifelong duty imposed on former security service officers not to disclose confidential information. Furthermore, it was ruled that to grant relief would entail an infringement of Blake's rights under ECHR, Article 10.
20 See Leigh and Lustgarten, 1989.

aggrieved by actions of MI5 and a Commissioner charged with the task of reviewing the procedure by which the Home Secretary issues warrants. Section 1 defines the functions of MI5 as being:

(2) ... the protection of national security and, in particular, its protection against threats from espionage, terrorism and sabotage, from the activities of agents of foreign powers and from actions intended to overthrow or undermine Parliamentary democracy by political, industrial or violent means.

(3) It shall also be the function of the Service to safeguard the economic well being of the United Kingdom against threats posed by the actions or intentions of persons outside the British Islands.

In 1992, MI5 assumed responsibility for terrorism related to Northern Ireland. This had previously been under the jurisdiction of Special Branch.

MI5 itself is not defined in the Act. The Secret Intelligence Service – MI6 – did not fall under the control of the Act. Other agencies, such as Special Branch, which carries out many of the functions of MI5 (see below), and GCHQ, are not mentioned in the Act.[21] National security is not defined in the Act. In debate on the Bill, the Home Secretary stated that the 'phrase refers – and can only refer – to matters relating to the survival or well being of the nation as a whole, and not to party-political or sectional or lesser interests'.[22]

The duties of the Director General of MI5 are set out in section 2. These are primarily the responsibility 'for the efficiency of the Service', and for ensuring that the Service only collects information necessary for the proper discharge of its functions, and that it does not take any action to further the interests of any political party. The Director General is required to report annually to the Prime Minister and the Secretary of State for the Home Department, and may otherwise report to them at any time the Director General so decides.

While the Director General is under a duty to report to the Prime Minister, there is no duty imposed on the Prime Minister to lay that report before parliament. There is thus no parliamentary scrutiny of the Director General's exercise of power. Attempts in both the House of Commons and the House of Lords to introduce such scrutiny failed. However, the Intelligence Services Act 1994,[23] for the first time, introduced parliamentary scrutiny to the work of the Security Services – both MI5 and MI6 – and to GCHQ. Under the Act, a Parliamentary Intelligence and Security Committee is established. As discussed below, the Committee is not a select committee, and is not given the powers of a select committee. Furthermore, under the Act, information may be withheld from the Committee on the basis that 'the Secretary of State has determined that it should not be disclosed'.[24]

The 1989 Act also introduced a Security Services Commissioner to keep under review the procedure by which warrants were issued by the Home Secretary. The office of Security Services Commissioner was abolished by the Regulation of

21 This omission is remedied by the Intelligence Services Act 1994, on which see further below.
22 *Hansard*, HC Vol 143 Col 1113; see also Vol 145 Col 217, and see HL Vol 357 Col 947.
23 See Supperstone, 1994.
24 Intelligence Services Act 1994, Sched 3, para 3(1)(b)(ii).

Investigatory Powers Act 2000. It has been replaced by the Intelligence Services Commissioner. See further below.

The Security Service Act 1996

The Security Service Act 1996 extended the function of MI5 to matters concerning 'serious crime'. The government's objective was to enable MI5 to investigate 'organised crime' and 'drug trafficking, money launderers and racketeers'. MI5 acts in a supportive role, and the principal responsibility lies with the conventional law enforcement agencies.[25] However, 'serious crime' is not itself defined in the Act. Nor is the scope of MI5's jurisdiction entirely clear. Moreover, it remains under the operation control of the Director General, and is not accountable to local police authorities, nor are its operations supervised by the Police Complaints Authority.

The Secret Intelligence Service (MI6)[26]

MI6 is the branch of the Security Services which deals with information gathering and operations outside the United Kingdom. Whereas a degree of openness has been established concerning the work of MI5, the work of MI6 remains closely guarded. It was only in 1992 that the Prime Minister acknowledged publicly for the first time that MI6 existed. It is MI6 operations – together with military intelligence and the work of GCHQ – which gathers intelligence from around the world through espionage and covert action. In times of war – whether 'hot' or 'cold' – the Service is of inestimable value to the protection of the state against outside threats.[27] MI6 is under the control of the Foreign and Commonwealth Office, and requires its approval before launching operations. Any politically sensitive matters require the personal approval of the Foreign Secretary. While, in theory, MI6 is confined to operations outside the United Kingdom, and hands responsibility over to MI5 once a matter becomes 'internal', there have been doubts expressed as to whether the boundaries are, or indeed can be, so clearly drawn.

The functions of MI6

The Intelligence Services Act 1994 defined, for the first time, the statutory functions of MI6. Section 1 provides that its function is to obtain and provide information relating to the actions or intentions of persons outside the British Islands, and to perform other tasks relating to the actions or intentions of such persons. Such actions must be related to the objectives defined in the Act, namely in the interests of national security 'with particular reference to defence and foreign policies', in the interests of the national's economic well being, and assisting in the 'prevention or detection of serious crime'.[28] The Intelligence Services Act 1994 provides for the

---

25 See HL Deb Cols 398–99, 14 May 1996.
26 See West, 1981; Bloch and Fitzgerald, 1983.
27 It was with MI6 that Paul Henderson, Managing Director of Matrix Churchill worked during the Iran-Iraq War – a matter which led to a judicial inquiry. See further Chapter 11.
28 Intelligence Services Act 1994, s 2.

issue of warrants. Authorisation given by the Secretary of State excludes criminal or civil liability for acts done under the authorisation. The Secretary of State may only grant an authorisation if he is satisfied that the operation is necessary for the 'proper discharge of a function of the Intelligence Service or GCHQ'. The authorisation may relate to particular acts or acts undertaken in the course of a specified operation. It may be limited to a particular person or persons and be subject to conditions. The authorisation must be signed by the Secretary of State or, in an urgent case, a senior official where the Secretary of State has expressly authorised it to be given. Where the authorisation is signed by the Home Secretary it will expire at the end of a six month period, subject to renewal by the Home Secretary for a further six month period. Any other authorisation ceases to have effect at the end of the second working day following the day on which it was given.

Operations are authorised by the Secretary of State for Foreign and Commonwealth Affairs, and agents' activities are regulated by administrative internal rules. Where action within the British Islands is required, MI5 may apply to the Home Secretary for a warrant to carry out operations on behalf of MI6. The Terrorism Act 2006 amends the 1994 Act to extend protection for action taken within the British Islands under a warrant authorising action in relation to property outside the British Islands where the property is believed to be outside the British Islands or where there is a mistaken belief as to whether it is within the British Islands and action is taken in respect of that property within five days from the day on which the presence of the property became known.[29]

Government Communications Headquarters (GCHQ)[30]

GCHQ at Cheltenham[31] was established under the royal prerogative, as part of the Foreign and Commonwealth Office.[32] The principal tasks of GCHQ include the security of military and official communications and the provision of signals intelligence (SIGINT) for the government. GCHQ has an annual budget of about £500 million and a staff of some 4,500 personnel, making it the largest of the three intelligence services in the United Kingdom.

Legal authority for the interception of international communications was first provided under the Official Secrets Act 1920, section 4 of which provided for the interception of 'telegrams' under the warrant of the Home Secretary on the basis of the public interest. The Intelligence Services Act 1994 placed GCHQ on a statutory basis.[33] The statutory duty of MI6 and GCHQ is to exercise its functions 'in the interests of national security, with particular reference to the defence and foreign policies of Her Majesty's government in the United Kingdom; in the interests of the economic well being of the United Kingdom in relation to

---

29 Terrorism Act 2006, s 31.
30 See Andrew, 1985; West, 1986; Lustgarten and Leigh, 1994.
31 GCHQ has stations abroad including Cyprus.
32 Its original title was the Government Code and Cipher School.
33 The Australian and Canadian equivalents, the Defence Signals Directorate and Communication Security Executive respectively, remain regulated under the prerogative.

the actions or intentions of persons outside the British Islands; or in support of the prevention or detection of serious crime'.[34] The Director of GCHQ is responsible for the 'efficiency of the agency'[35] and has a right of access to the Prime Minister and Secretary of State for Foreign and Commonwealth Affairs. The Director is under a duty to report annually to the Prime Minister.

The Intelligence Services Act 1994, sections 5–7, provide statutory authority for warrants issued by the Secretary of State. No warrant may be issued for interference with individual communications within the United Kingdom, unless the interception is designed to uncover information relating to the prevention or detection of terrorism. GCHQ co-operates in signals intelligence matters with its counterparts in Australia, Canada, New Zealand and the United States.

From 1947 until 1984, employees at GCHQ were entitled to belong to trade unions. In January 1984, the Foreign Secretary announced, without warning, that this right was to be removed. GCHQ had experienced disruption for some two years, with a loss of 10,000 working days. In 1983, a GCHQ employee, Geoffrey Prime,[36] was arrested and convicted of spying for the Soviet Union. Both factors – and the government's general desire to curb the power of trade unions – contributed to the banning of unions at GCHQ.[37] The legal outcome of the exercise of the prerogative[38] in banning union membership at GCHQ led to *Council of Civil Service Unions v Minister for the Civil Service* (1984), in which the House of Lords ruled in favour of the government on the basis of national security.[39]

Special Branch[40]

Established in 1883 to deal with problems of security in relation to Ireland, Special Branch rapidly expanded to deal with many security matters. Originally, Special Branch was confined to the Metropolitan Police Force; from 1945, other police forces established Special Branches. Nowadays, each provincial force has its own Special Branch. Special Branch is staffed by ordinary police officers under the direction of the Chief Constable. Much of their work is related to Security Service matters. The principal task of Special Branch is to counter threats of terrorism. Other functions include jury vetting in cases involving national security or terrorism, providing personal protection and assisting with immigration matters, including keeping watch at airports and seaports.

---

34 Intelligence Services Act 1994, ss 1(2)(a) and 3(2)(a).
35 *Ibid*, s 4.
36 See *Report of the Security Commission: GA Prime*, Cmnd 8876, 1981, London: HMSO.
37 See Young, 1989, Chapter 16.
38 Under the Civil Service Order in Council 1982, Article 4, which empowers the minister to make regulations and issue instructions regarding the conditions of service of civil service employees. See Forsyth, 1985; cf Wade, 1985.
39 See, further on this case, Chapters 6 and 19. In 1995, the government amended the terms and conditions of employment of staff at GCHQ. Staff are to be restricted to membership of a body whose officers and representatives are appointed from, and answerable only to, GCHQ staff. The conditions of service continue to exclude any form of industrial action: HL Deb Vol 567 Col 147, 20 December 1995. Note that in 1997 the Labour government restored trade union rights to employees at GCHQ.
40 See Bunyan, 1977; Allason, 1983.

Military intelligence and the armed forces

In 1940, the Special Operations Executive (SOE) was formed to supplement the work of MI5 and MI6, which were geared principally to work in peace time. Subsequently, the need for special units to operate under military command, and under cover, became perceived as imperative. Originally known as L Detachment, Special Air Service Brigade and, later, simply SAS, the service was introduced on the initiative of David Stirling of the Scots Guards, and approved by the Commander-in-Chief. Members of the SAS were recruited primarily from commandos. A parallel organisation, the Special Boat Service (SBS), was established to complement the work of the SAS.

The SAS has been involved in many operations overseas, in Northern Ireland and on the mainland, principally working against terrorism. It was, for example, the SAS which stormed the Iranian Embassy in London in 1980 to free hostages from terrorists who had occupied the Embassy and, as discussed below, it was the SAS which was dispatched to Gibraltar to arrest suspected IRA terrorists.

The SAS is controlled at both a political level and a practical, operational level. In relation to terrorism, a special committee, known as COBRA and chaired by the Home Secretary, meets with representatives from the Ministry of Defence, MI5, the Foreign and Commonwealth Office and the SAS to decide the appropriate political and military response. In relation to operational matters, a special unit within the Ministry of Defence, the Joint Operations Centre (JOC), comprising the Foreign Office, Home Office, intelligence services and the SAS, activates the SAS at home or overseas. Exceptionally, the Prime Minister may personally activate the SAS, as in the Iranian Embassy siege. When the SAS is operational, it exercises the powers of the police, although formal authority remains with the police, and the police resume their normal functions once the operation is complete.

Defence intelligence

The Ministry of Defence has its own Defence Intelligence Staff, DIS, which is the main provider of strategic defence intelligence to the Ministry of Defence and the armed forces. The Chief of DIS, a serving three star officer drawn from any of the three services, reports to the Chief of the Defence Staff and the Permanent Secretary of the Ministry of Defence, and is a member of the Joint Intelligence Committee (on which see further below). DIS is divided into two main parts: the Defence Intelligence Analysis Staff (DIAS) and the Intelligence and Geographic Resources Staff (IGRS). DIAS is responsible for providing global defence intelligence assessments and strategic warning, and draws on classified information provided by GCHQ. IGRS has six discrete policy branches, including the Joint Air Reconnaissance Intelligence Centre, and the Defence and Security Centre and Military Survey.

DIS analyses GCHQ's signals intelligence with a view to assessing the strength of foreign armies and weaponry, including chemical weapons. Defence attachés at foreign embassies act as information gatherers in the field. During the Cold War, the role of DIS was principally intelligence analysis. In times of war, however, that function changes from intelligence gathering and analysis to the provision of information for use of troops on the ground.

The Joint Intelligence Committee[41]

The Joint Intelligence Committee (JIC) co-ordinates the work of MI6 and GCHQ, and agrees intelligence requirements. The head of the JIC reports to the Cabinet Secretary and, through him, to the Prime Minister. The JIC has around 30 members, drawn on secondment from the Foreign Office and Ministry of Defence. Membership of the JIC includes the Director of GCHQ, the Chief of MI6, Chief of Defence Intelligence Staff and the Director General of MI5. Divided into geographic areas and by functions, the JIC meets weekly to review assessments.

MI5 contributes intelligence to the JIC on national matters. The JIC also makes international assessments, drawing on intelligence from other agencies such as the United States' Central Intelligence Agency (CIA). The intelligence requirements are reviewed annually by the Intelligence Co-ordinator. Close links are maintained between the JIC and MI5, with its Director General being a member of JIC. MI5 and MI6 also co-operate to avoid duplication and their financial resources in some areas are shared. MI5 also contributes intelligence to the JIC Assessments Staff, and is a major customer for intelligence produced by SIS and GCHQ, particularly in relation to terrorism.

The Security Commission[42]

In 1964, following the Profumo affair, the Prime Minister, Sir Alec Douglas-Home announced the creation of a Security Commission. The Commission investigates and reports upon the circumstances in which a breach of security is known to have occurred in the public service, and upon any related failure of departmental security arrangements or neglect of duty; and, in the light of any such investigation, advises whether any change in security arrangements is desirable.[43]

The Commission meets at the request of the Prime Minister, who consults the Leader of the Opposition and the Chairman of the Commission before making a reference to the Commission. The Commission has no power of initiative in relation to the matters it investigates. The Chairman of the Commission is a senior judge, and the Commission has seven members. The Commission has undertaken inquiries, *inter alia*, into the conduct of former ministers,[44] into allegations about the Head of MI5, Roger Hollis,[45] into investigations of security matters in Signals and Communication Units, and into the circumstances surrounding the conviction of Geoffrey Prime for espionage.[46] The Commission has power to call whomsoever it wishes as witnesses, and to summon documents. Prior to its

---

41 See Adams, 1994, and Urban, 1997.
42 On the role and work of the Commission, see Leigh and Lustgarten, 1989.
43 See HC Deb Cols 1271–75, 23 January 1964.
44 *Earl Jellicoe and Lord Lambton,* Cmnd 5367, 1973, London: HMSO.
45 The report remained unpublished.
46 Cmnd 9923, 1986, London: HMSO; Cmnd 8876, 1985, London: HMSO, respectively.

hearings, the Commission will frequently have availed itself of the Security Services to investigate allegations. No legal representation is allowed for witnesses before the Commission. The Commission reports, with recommendations, to the Prime Minister.

THE INTERCEPTION OF COMMUNICATIONS[47]

The government's response to the outcome of *Malone v United Kingdom* (1984), in which the absence of statutory authority for intercept warrants was held to have violated Article 8 of the Convention on Human Rights, was to pass the Interception of Communications Act 1985. The Interception of Communications Act 1985 made it a criminal offence to intentionally intercept a communication and provided statutory power to the Secretary of State to issue warrants 'in the interests of national security, or for the purpose of preventing or detecting serious crime or for the purpose of safeguarding the economic well-being of the United Kingdom'.

The provisions relating to interception of communications under the 1985 Act were repealed and replaced by the Regulation of Investigatory Powers Act 2000 (RIPA), which also amends the Police Act 1997 and the Intelligence Services Act 1994. The 2000 Act was prompted by two major concerns. The first was that the 1985 Act regulated intercepts of communications transmitted via mail and by a public telecommunications system, which at the time of the legislation covered most data transmissions. Technological advances since 1985, however, have expanded communications systems – through the internet and email and through telecommunication systems not provided by public telecommunications providers. Also falling outside the 1985 Act was data which was 'encrypted' and required a 'key' to unlock it. The second motivation for reform was the influence of the European Convention on Human Rights and the Human Rights Act 1998. As discussed in more detail in Chapter 19, cases such as *Halford v United Kingdom* (1997) and *Khan v United Kingdom* (2000) had successfully challenged domestic law.

The Act relates to powers concerning the interception of communications, intrusive surveillance on residential premises and in private vehicles, covert surveillance in the course of specific operations, the use of covert human intelligence sources (agents, informants, undercover officers), the acquisition of communications data and access to encrypted data.[48] The Act is intended to ensure that the law clearly states the purposes for which such powers may be used; which authorities may exercise the powers; who should authorise the use of

---

47 See *Report of the Committee on the Interception of Communications* (the Birkett Report), Cmnd 283, 1957, London: HMSO; *The Interception of Communications in Great Britain*, Cmnd 7873, 1980, London: HMSO; *The Interception of Communications in Great Britain* (the Diplock Report), Cmnd 8191, 1981, London: HMSO; Williams, 1979; Lambert, 1980; *The Interception of Communications in the United Kingdom*, Cmnd 9438, 1985, London: HMSO; Leigh, 1986; *Interception of Communications in the United Kingdom*, Cm 4368, 1999, London: HMSO.

48 Section 15 of the Terrorism Act 2006 amends the penalties relating to encryption offences in s 53 of RIPA 2000.

power; the use that can be made of material gained; independent judicial oversight of the exercise of powers; and a means of redress for aggrieved individuals.

The powers of the police to conduct surveillance was given statutory force by the Police Act 1997. Part I established a National Criminal Intelligence Service Authority to provide criminal intelligence to other police and law enforcement agencies, and placed surveillance techniques under statutory authority.[49] The Act was modelled on the Interception of Communications Act 1985, and placed the Home Secretary's Guidelines on a statutory basis. Authorisation may be given, under section 93(2), for the use of surveillance devices if surveillance will be of substantial value in the prevention and detection of serious crime, and the objective cannot reasonably be achieved by other means. Serious crime is defined as including crimes of violence, crimes involving financial gain and crimes involving large numbers of persons, or crimes for which a person with no previous conviction could expect to receive a prison sentence of three or more years. Authorisation is given by a Chief Officer of Police, or an officer of the rank of Assistant Chief Constable.[50] Prior authorisation by a commissioner appointed under section 91 of the Act must be obtained if the property involved is a private dwelling, a hotel bedroom or office premises, and also where the surveillance may result in the acquisition of confidential knowledge, or journalistic or other matters subject to legal privilege.[51]

Section 1 of RIPA 2000 creates the offence of unlawful interception and a separate tort of unlawful interception. Unlawful interceptions relate to any communication in the course of its transmission by means of a public postal service or public telecommunications system. Intercepts are lawful only if authorised under the Act. Conduct which has lawful authority is lawful for all other purposes. A person having the right to control the operation or use of the system which is intercepted, or having the express or implied consent of such a person to make the interception, is excluded from criminal liability.[52]

An intercept will be lawful under section 3(1) if the person intercepting has the consent of the sender and recipient of the communication, or has reasonable grounds for believing that they have consented. Section 3(2) provides that an intercept will be lawful if the communication is one sent by or intended for a

---

49 The Act also established a National Crime Squad and a Police Information Technology Organisation. It also made provision for access to criminal records for employment and licensing purposes. Note that the Serious Organised Crime and Police Act 2005 amalgamates agencies to form the Serious Organised Crime Agency.

50 Police Act 1997, ss 93(5) and 94. Minor amendments to the Act are introduced under the Regulation of Investigatory Powers Act 2000.

51 For an unsuccessful attempt to challenge the legality of telephone interceptions, see *R v Secretary of State for the Home Department ex parte Ruddock* (1987): the decision was reached prior to the Interception of Communications Act 1985. But compare *Halford v United Kingdom* (1997), discussed in Chapter 19.

52 A person found guilty of an offence is liable on conviction on indictment to a term of imprisonment not exceeding two years, or to a fine, or to both. On summary conviction, there is liability to a fine not exceeding the statutory maximum. Proceedings may only be instituted with the consent of the Director of Public Prosecutions or, in Northern Ireland, with the consent of the Director of Public Prosecutions for Northern Ireland.

person who has consented to the intercept and surveillance conducted via the intercept has been authorised under Part II of the Act, which regulates surveillance and the use of undercover agents. Section 4 provides lawful authority for intercepts of communications between the United Kingdom and other countries, where the interceptor overseas is required by law to intercept the communication.

Section 5 regulates interceptions under warrant. The Secretary of State may issue a warrant authorising or requiring interceptions only where he believes that the warrant is necessary in the interests of national security, or for the purpose of preventing or detecting serious crime, or for the purpose of safeguarding the economic well being of the United Kingdom. The warrant may be issued only if the Secretary of State also believes that the conduct authorised is *proportionate* to what is sought to be achieved by that conduct. In considering whether to issue a warrant, the Secretary of State must take into account whether the information which it is thought necessary to obtain could reasonably be obtained by other means.

Warrants may be issued only on the application of persons specified under the Act. The warrant must be issued under the hand of the Secretary of State or, in certain circumstances, by a senior official,[53] who must be expressly authorised by the Secretary of State to do so. A warrant issued by a senior officer ceases to have effect at the end of the fifth working day following the day of the warrant's issue, but is renewable. A warrant renewed under the signature of the Secretary of State has effect for six months.

Section 15 is intended to minimise the disclosure of intercepted material. It is the duty of the Secretary of State to ensure that the number of persons to whom the material may be disclosed and the extent to which material may be disclosed or copied is limited to the minimum that is necessary for the authorised purposes.

Section 16, as amended by the Terrorism Act 2006, provides additional safeguards in relation to the disclosure of information obtained under a section 8(1) warrant which identifies the material to be examined but does not identify the name or premises which are subject to the intercept. Section 17 prevents the disclosure of specified[54] information relating to intercepts in any legal proceedings. Exceptions to this prohibition are provided by section 18.[55]

Authorisation of surveillance and human intelligence sources

Part II of the Regulation of Investigatory Powers Act 2000 provides a statutory basis for the authorisation and use of covert surveillance agents, informants and undercover officers. It is intended to regulate the use of such techniques and 'safeguard the public from unnecessary invasions of their privacy'.

Conduct is lawful for all purposes once authorised, provided that the conduct of the authorised person is in accordance with the authorisation, and no civil

---

53 RIPA 2000, s 7. The Terrorism Act 2006, s 32, amends RIPA 2000, s 9 in relation to warrants.
54 See *ibid*, s 17(1)(a)–(g).
55 On the admissibility of evidence obtained by interception, see *Attorney General's Reference (No 5 of 2002)* (2003).

liability attaches to any conduct which is incidental to any conduct which is lawful. The conduct authorised includes conduct outside the United Kingdom. Authorisations may only be granted where necessary in the interests of national security and related purposes specified by the Act, and the authorised conduct must be proportionate to what is sought to be achieved.[56]

Section 30 specifies the persons entitled to grant authorisations and includes the Secretary of State and senior officers of relevant public authorities. In relation to Northern Ireland, the grant of authorisations is also exercisable by the First Minister and Deputy First Minister acting jointly.

Investigation of electronic data protected by encryption

Part III of RIPA 2000 provides for the interception of data protected by encryption. The Home Secretary, commenting on the Act, stated that it:

> ... will ensure that the United Kingdom's law enforcement and security agencies have the power they need to do their job effectively in a changed technological world. New communications tools such as the internet offer up huge legitimate benefits for us all. But serious criminals too have always been quick to jump on the latest technological bandwagon in their efforts to evade detection. The 'e' prefix can apply to today's criminals as well as to commerce ...[57]

THE INTELLIGENCE SERVICES COMMISSIONER AND THE TRIBUNAL[58]

The Intelligence Services Commissioner is appointed by the Prime Minister.[59] A person may only be appointed as Commissioner if he or she holds or has held a high judicial office.

The Regulation of Investigatory Powers Act 2000, section 65, establishes a Tribunal. The Tribunal has a duty to investigate allegations against the Security Services and to hear and determine any proceedings brought. The Tribunal is not under a duty to hear or determine any complaint which is frivolous or vexatious. Complaints must be brought within one year after the taking place of the conduct to which it relates, but the Tribunal may, if it is equitable to do so, extend the time. The Tribunal has the power to make an award of compensation. In addition, the Tribunal may order the quashing or cancelling of any warrant or authorisation and/or the destruction of any records of information. The Commissioner assists the Tribunal in connection with the investigation of any matter by the Tribunal. The Tribunal is the only tribunal to which proceedings under section 7 of the Human Rights Act 1998 may be brought against any of the intelligence services, or any other person in relation to conduct by or on behalf of any of those

---

56 See RIPA 2000, s 29(5).
57 Home Office, *News Release*, 28 July 2000.
58 RIPA 2000 repeals s 5 of and Sched 1 to the Security Service Act 1989 which provided for a Tribunal to investigate complaints. Section 9 of and Scheds 1 and 2 to the Intelligence Services Act 1994, which also provided for a Tribunal, are repealed and replaced by RIPA 2000, Part IV.
59 Under the Intelligence Services Act 1994.

services.[60] The conduct in question must have been conduct by or on behalf of a person holding any office, rank or position with any of the intelligence services, any of Her Majesty's forces, any police force, the National Criminal Intelligence Service, National Crime Squad or Commissioners of Customs and Excise. All persons employed by the Security and Intelligence Services and police are under a duty to disclose or provide to the Commissioner all documents and information as he or she may require for the purposes of an investigation. The Commissioner makes an annual report to the Prime Minister, which is to be laid before each House of Parliament. If it appears to the Prime Minister, after consultation with the Commissioner, that the publication of any matter in an annual report would be contrary to the public interest or prejudicial to national security, the prevention or detection of serious crime or the economic well being of the United Kingdom, the Prime Minister may exclude that matter from the report laid before each House.

The extent to which the Commissioner is able to exercise any effective control over the Secretary of State is unclear. The weakness of the whole basis of the Tribunal's jurisdiction is reinforced by the absence of any appeal therefrom and the prohibition against questioning of the Tribunal and Commissioner before any court of law. With the exclusion of any form of judicial scrutiny of the Commissioner's and Tribunal's findings, the danger for the individual is all too apparent. This arrangement is far different from that pertaining in the United States, where security matters are regarded as being within the competence of the courts. In *United States v United District Court* (1972), the Supreme Court, in a unanimous judgment, declared:

> We cannot accept the government's argument that internal security matters are too subtle and complex for judicial evaluation. There is no reason to believe that federal judges will be insensitive to or uncomprehending of the issues involved in domestic security cases ... If the threat is too subtle or complex for our senior enforcement officers to convey its significance to a court, one may question whether there is probable cause for surveillance.

The Canadian Security Intelligence Service Act 1984 involves judges and the Solicitor General in the process of granting warrants.[61]

PARLIAMENTARY SCRUTINY OF THE SECURITY SERVICES

National security and the work of the Security Services have traditionally been matters on which governments have declined to provide information to parliament. Parliamentary Committees repeatedly have been denied the right to investigate MI5[62] although, since 1979, the Defence Committee has considered aspects of security. In 1994, however, the Intelligence and Security Committee was established with limited powers to investigate security matters. The Committee,

---

60 Section 7 proceedings relate to applications brought by victims of an alleged violation of Convention rights by a public authority.
61 See Burns, 1976; Hazell, 1989; Hutchinson and Petter, 1988.
62 See HC 773 (1979–80); HC 242 (1982–83); HC Deb Col 444, 12 May 1983.

which has a membership of nine, is established to 'examine the expenditure, administration and policy of the Security Service, the Intelligence Service and GCHQ'.[63] Membership is confined to non-ministerial Members of the House of Lords and House of Commons. Members are appointed by the Prime Minister, after consultation with the Leader of the Opposition.[64] The Committee, which is based in Whitehall rather than parliament, brings both MI6 and GCHQ under a weak form of quasi-parliamentary scrutiny although, operating *ex post facto* and lacking the openness of a select committee, its constitutional effectiveness must be questionable. The Committee must make an annual report to the Prime Minister, which must be laid before parliament. However, should the Prime Minister feel that publication of any matter would be 'prejudicial to the continued discharge of the functions of the Services, or GCHQ', the Prime Minister may exclude such matters from the report.[65]

The Committee determines its own procedure.[66] Where the Committee requests information from the Director General of MI5, the Chief of MI6 or the Director of GCHQ, that information must be supplied unless the relevant person informs the Committee that it cannot be disclosed on the basis of sensitivity, or where the Secretary of State has determined that it should not be disclosed. Schedule 3 defines sensitive information as being:

(a) information which might lead to the identification of, or provide details of, sources of information, other assistance or operational methods available to the Security Service, the Intelligence Service or GCHQ;

(b) information about particular operations which have been, are being or are proposed to be undertaken in pursuance of any of the functions of those bodies; and

(c) information provided by, or by an agency of, the government of a territory outside the United Kingdom where that government does not consent to the disclosure of the information.

OFFICIAL SECRECY[67]

The Official Secrets Acts 1911–89

The first Official Secrets Act arrived on the statute book in 1889. The latest Act is that of 1989. The 1911 Act – which survived virtually untouched until 1989 – was passed through parliament with one hour's debate and within 24 hours. Motivation for the 1911 Act lay in alleged enemy agent activity in the country.[68] The motives behind the 1989 Act were formed largely from the failure of the earlier Act. As will be seen, section 2 of the 1911 Act provided for numerous offences based on vague criteria of disclosure of information and juries have on occasion refused to convict, even where it was clear from the facts and the law

---

63   Intelligence Services Act 1994, s 10.
64   *Ibid*, s 10(3).
65   *Ibid*, s 10(5), (6), (7).
66   *Ibid*, Sched 3, para 2.
67   See Robertson and Merrills, 1993; Hooper, 1988; Ewing and Gearty, 1990.
68   See Andrew, 1985; French, 1978; Le Queux, 1915.

that a guilty verdict should have been returned.[69] Official inquiries into the working of the Act revealed deficiencies.[70]

The *Spycatcher* case also provided motivation for the government to reform the law. In the government's view, members and ex-members of the Security Services should be under a lifelong duty of confidentiality in respect of their work. One defect in the 1911 Act lay in the duty of – and hence liability for – non-disclosure enduring only for the duration of employment.

Section 1 of the 1911 Act provides penalties for spying. It is an offence to enter into top-secret establishments or to collect, publish or communicate any official document (which includes official code words, passwords, sketches, plans, models, articles or notes) or information which might be useful to a potential enemy, if the actions are carried out 'for any purpose prejudicial to the safety or interest of the state'. The accused has no 'right to silence' and a trial may be held in secret, or partly in secret. Section 2 of the Act reversed the normal burden of proof from the prosecution to the defence. It was not necessary for the prosecution to prove that the accused was guilty of any particular act 'tending to show a purpose prejudicial to the safety or interest of the state'. Guilt could be established if 'from the circumstances of the case, or his conduct, or his known character as proved, it appears that his purpose was a purpose prejudicial to the safety or interest of the state'. Moreover, any information or document handed over to another person, without lawful authority, could 'be deemed to have been made, obtained, collected, recorded or communicated for a purpose prejudicial to the safety or interests of the state unless the contrary is proved'. Penalties for espionage are swingeing. George Blake, a former MI6 officer convicted of espionage, was sentenced to 42 years' imprisonment.[71] In 1985, Michael Bettany, a former MI5 officer, was convicted of attempting to pass official information to the Russians and sentenced to 23 years' imprisonment. Geoffrey Prime was sentenced to 35 years for disclosing material whilst employed at GCHQ.[72] Not all offences will lead to a prosecution. Neither Kim Philby nor Anthony Blunt was prosecuted. Instead, each was offered immunity from prosecution in return for a confession, an offer declined by Kim Philby, who fled to Moscow.

Section 2 of the 1911 Act (now reformed under the Official Secrets Act 1989) prohibited the disclosure of any official information without authorisation to anyone not authorised to receive it, and covered some one million public servants and a further one million government contractors. It also covered the retention of any document by a person not entitled to retain the same, failure to take reasonable care of a document, and receiving any document without authority. Section 2 was capable of generating over 2,000 different criminal offences,

69 See *R v Ponting* (1985), discussed below.
70 See *Departmental Committee on Section 2 of the Official Secrets Act 1911*, Cmnd 5104, 1972, London: HMSO; White Paper, *Reform of Section 2 of the Official Secrets Act 1911*, Cmnd 7285, 1978, London: HMSO.
71 Blake subsequently escaped from prison after 25 years, with the help of friends.
72 *R v Prime* (1983).

including the disclosure of the number of cups of tea consumed in the MI5 canteen.[73]

Reform of the Official Secrets Act 1911[74]

A Committee of Inquiry, headed by Lord Franks was established to review the working of section 2. The Committee was highly critical of section 2 and recommended that it be reformed.[75] It was not, however, until 1989 that reform took place.[76]

The major provisions of the Official Secrets Act 1989

Section 2 of the Official Secrets Act 1911 was repealed and replaced by the 1989 Act. Rather than the catch-all section 2 of the 1911 Act, the 1989 Act created offences directed to specific groups of people and information. In relation to most areas, the prosecution must prove both that the information has been unlawfully transmitted and that the disclosure of the information is 'damaging'. The concept of 'damaging disclosure' has, however, not been incorporated into section 1 which relates to security and intelligence matters. With this exception, there is a presumption of harm built into the Act. A further exception relates to those who are not Crown servants or government contractors in relation to whom the prosecution will have to prove – in addition to the harm test – that the defendant knew or had good reason to know that the specific harm was likely to have been caused. In relation to such information, the disclosure in itself is an offence. There is no longer a defence of 'public good' which applied under section 2 of the 1911 Act.

Security and intelligence

Under section 1 of the 1989 Act, any person who is, or has been, a member of the Security and Intelligence Services, and any other person who is informed that the provision of the Act applies to him, is guilty of an offence if 'without lawful authority' he discloses 'any information, document or other article related to security or intelligence'. The offence is committed irrespective of whether or not the disclosure is damaging. A person who is, or has been, a Crown servant or government contractor will be guilty of an offence if he makes a 'damaging disclosure of any information, document or other article relating to security or intelligence'. In *R v Shayler* (2001), the House of Lords ruled that a former member

---

73 *Departmental Committee on Section 2 of the Official Secrets Act 1911*, Cmnd 5104, 1972, London: HMSO, para 16, and see Robertson and Merrills, 1993. See *Chandler v Director of Public Prosecutions* (1964); *R v Aitken* (1971). For an account, see Aitken, 1971.

74 See, *inter alia*, Hooper, 1988; White Paper, *Reform of Section 2 of the Official Secrets Act 1911*, Cm 408, 1988, London: HMSO. See also the White Paper, *Open Government*, Cm 2290, 1993, London: HMSO, discussed in Chapter 11.

75 *Departmental Committee on Section 2 of the Official Secrets Act 1911*, Cmnd 5104, 1972, London: HMSO.

76 See the White Paper, *Reform of Section 2 of the Official Secrets Act 1911*, Cmnd 7285, 1978, London: HMSO; Green Paper, *Freedom of Information*, Cmnd 7520, 1979, London: HMSO; White Paper, *Reform of Section 2 of the Official Secrets Act 1911*, Cm 408, 1988, London: HMSO.

of the Security Services was not entitled to rely on the defence that the disclosure was made in the public or national interest. There was no contravention of Article 10 of the European Convention through the restriction of members and former members of the security forces disclosing information.

Security and intelligence are defined as being the work of, or work in support of, the Security and Intelligence Services. A disclosure is defined as damaging if 'it causes damage to the work of, or of any part of, the Security or Intelligence Services' or if unauthorised disclosure would be likely to cause such damage. A charge may be defended if the person in question can prove that, at the time of the alleged offence, 'he did not know, and had no reasonable cause to believe' that the unauthorised disclosure related to security or intelligence or, in the case of an offence under sub-section (3), he did not know, or had no reasonable cause to believe, that the disclosure would be damaging.

Defence

Any unauthorised damaging disclosure of information, documents or other articles relating to defence is an offence.[77] A disclosure is damaging if 'it damages the capability of any part of the armed forces, or leads to loss of life or injury to the forces, or endangers the interests of the United Kingdom abroad, or obstructs the promotion or protection of those interests, or is likely to have any of these effects'. It is a defence to prove that the person did not know, and had no reasonable cause to believe, that such disclosure would be damaging.

Section 4 defines 'defence' as including the 'size, shape, organisation, logistics, order of battle, deployment, operations, state of readiness and training of the armed forces of the Crown; weapons, stores or other equipment of those forces; defence policy and strategy, and military planning and intelligence; and plans and measures for the maintenance of essential supplies and services that are, or would be, needed in time of war'.

International relations

Under section 3 of the 1989 Act, an unauthorised damaging disclosure, by a person who is or has been a Crown servant or government contractor, of any information, document or other article relating to international relations, or confidential information obtained from another state or international organisation is an offence. A disclosure is damaging if it 'endangers the interests of the United Kingdom abroad, or seriously obstructs the promotion or protection of those interests or endangers the safety of British citizens abroad', or 'is likely to have any of those effects'. It is a defence to prove that the accused did not know, and had no reasonable cause to believe, that the information fell within sub-section (1), or that its disclosure would be damaging.

---

77   Official Secrets Act 1989, s 2.

Crime and special investigation powers

Section 4 of the Act makes it an offence to disclose, without lawful authority, information, documents or other articles which result in the commission of an offence, or facilitate an escape from legal custody or impede the prevention or detection of offences or the apprehension or prosecution of suspected offenders, or disclosures which are likely to have those effects. It is a defence to a charge to prove that the person did not know, and had no reasonable cause to believe, that the disclosure related to prohibited materials or that disclosure would have any of the damaging effects mentioned.

Authorised disclosures under the Act

A disclosure by a Crown servant (or other notified person) is authorised if it is made with lawful authority and if (and only if) the disclosure is made in accordance with a person's official duty.[78] In relation to government contractors, a disclosure is lawful only if it is made with official authorisation or for the purposes of his functions relating to the contract and without contravening an official restriction. In relation to any other person, a disclosure is lawful only if it is made to a Crown servant for the purposes of his functions as such, or in accordance with official authorisation. It is a defence to a charge to prove that, at the time of disclosure, the person believed that he had lawful authority to make the disclosure in question.

The duty to safeguard information

Under section 8, Crown servants and government contractors are under a duty to protect any information, document or other article which it would be an offence to disclose under the Act. It is an offence for a Crown servant to retain an article contrary to his or her official duty, and for a government contractor to fail to comply with a request for the return or disposal of the information or document, or to fail to take such care of the information or document as 'a person in his position may be reasonably expected to take'. It is a defence for a Crown servant to prove that he believed he was acting in accordance with his official duty and 'had no reasonable cause to believe otherwise'.

Prosecutions

No prosecution may be instituted other than with the consent of the Attorney General.[79]

Penalties

A person convicted of an offence under the Act, other than under section 8(1), (4) or (5), shall, on indictment, be liable to imprisonment for a two year term, or a fine, or both. On summary conviction, a person is liable to up to a six month term

78 Official Secrets Act 1989, s 7.
79 Official Secrets Act 1989, s 9.

of imprisonment, or a fine, or both. A person convicted under section 8(1), (4) or (5) is liable, on summary conviction, to a term of imprisonment of up to three months, or a fine, or both.

The catch-all nature of section 2 of the Official Secrets Act 1911 has thus been reformed. Whether, in fact, the 1989 Act is less swingeing in scope is another matter. Geoffrey Robertson QC states that the scope of the 1989 legislation, 'while not the theoretical dragnet of the old section 2, is none the less considerable'.[80]

Restrictions on the media: Defence Advisory Notices[81]

The Official Secrets Acts of course apply to information which might be revealed by the press, and the doctrine of breach of confidence also represents a fetter on freedom of information. A further restriction on press freedom is the 'DA' (Defence Advisory) Notice system. The basis for the system is entirely extralegal and voluntary. No formal sanction exists for failure to comply with a DA Notice. The system was established in 1912. A DA Notice Committee was established, chaired by a Permanent Under Secretary of the Ministry of Defence, which comprised both newspaper editors and civil servants.[82] At the request of a government department, the committee will draft a Notice, and advice as to its scope and meaning will be given to the press by the committee's secretary. Compliance with a DA Notice will not affect any right to bring legal action against a newspaper,[83] and neither will non-compliance. The system is vague and defective. It is also contrary to principle to have a non-statutory system which effectively fetters the freedom of the press. The system was reviewed in both 1962 and 1980, when retention of the system was recommended. The 1980 inquiry by the Defence Committee of the House of Commons nevertheless expressed reservations about retaining the system.[84] A further review was conducted in 2000. The current DA Notices cover Military Operations, Plans and Capabilities; Nuclear and Non-nuclear Weapons and Equipment; Ciphers and Secure Communications; Sensitive Installations and Addresses; and British Security and Intelligence Services and Special Forces.

Judicial attitudes to pleas of national security

Where national security is pleaded by the government in judicial review proceedings, the courts are exceedingly reluctant to challenge the executive. Whilst this is, *prima facie*, regrettable from the point of view of the aggrieved

---

80   Robertson and Merrills, 1993. See also Palmer, 1990.
81   See *The 'D' Notice System*, Cmnd 3312, 1967, London: HMSO; *Report of the Committee of Privy Councillors Appointed to Inquire into 'D' Notice Matters*, Cmnd 3309, 1967, London: HMSO; *Third Report of the Defence Committee: The 'D' Notice System*, HC 773 (1979–80), London: HMSO; *Ministry of Defence: The Defence Advisory Notices: A Review of the 'D' Notice System*, MOD Open Government Document 93/1993.
82   Then known as the Admiralty, War Office and Press Committee; now the Defence Press and Broadcasting Advisory Committee.
83   As occurred in 1970 when *The Sunday Telegraph* was prosecuted under the Official Secrets Act 1911 for disclosure of material supplied by Jonathan Aitken.
84   HC 773 (1979–80), London: HMSO, and see Jaconelli, 1982.

citizen, it is explained – although not necessarily justified – by the relationship between the executive, legislature and judiciary. As seen in Chapter 5, the doctrine of separation of powers, whilst not strictly adhered to under the United Kingdom's constitution, is respected by the courts. In no area of policy is this respect more clearly demonstrated than in matters of national security, which will frequently, but not inevitably, be linked to the exercise of the royal prerogative. In Chapter 6, the judiciary's cautious approach to review of the prerogative was examined, and it was there seen that the prerogative ensures for the executive a wide and inadequately defined area of power which is largely immune from judicial review. It will be recalled that in *Council of Civil Service Unions v Minister for Civil Service* (1985) (the GCHQ case) the House of Lords ruled that the courts have jurisdiction to review the exercise of executive power irrespective of whether the source of power was statutory, or under the common law prerogative.

Notwithstanding that claim, the House of Lords conceded that matters of national security fell within the class of powers deemed 'non-justiciable' by the courts (by which is meant that the subject matter is one more appropriately controlled by the executive accountable to parliament rather than the courts of law).[85] However the incorporation of Convention rights under the Human Rights Act 1998 extends judicial protection. The Convention protects, *inter alia*, the right to liberty and the right to fair trial. In *A v Secretary of State for the Home Department* (discussed at page 710) the House of Lords took a robust approach to the power of the executive to detain non-British terrorist suspects, declaring that the relevant statutory provision was incompatible with the right to liberty protected under Article 5.

Detention in wartime

In *Liversidge v Anderson* (1942), the House of Lords refused[86] to review the Home Secretary's power of detention under the Defence of the Realm Acts. It will be recalled from Chapter 6 that the regulation provided that the minister had power to order the detention of persons whom he 'had reasonable cause to believe' to be of hostile origin or associations and 'in need of subjection to preventative control'.[87]

EMERGENCY POWERS

While, in peace time, the responsibility for maintaining order and detecting crime lies with the police forces, in times of emergency, further assistance will be needed if order is to be restored.

The Civil Contingencies Act 2004 confers on the executive wide-ranging powers to deal with emergency situations. The Act is separated into two main parts: Part

---

85   On the definition of harm to national security see *Secretary of State for the Home Department v Rehman* (2001).

86   Lord Atkin dissenting. Note that Lord Atkin's dissent was accepted as a correct statement of common law in *R v Inland Revenue Commissioners ex parte Rossminster Ltd* (1980).

87   On deportation and extradition, see further Chapter 24.

1 making provision for local arrangements for civil protection and Part 2 providing for emergency powers. An 'emergency' is broadly defined.[88] In relation to Part 1 of the Act, it is defined as 'an event or situation' which threatens serious damage to human welfare, serious damage to the environment of a place in the United Kingdom, or war or terrorism which threatens serious damage to the security of the United Kingdom. In relation to Part 2, an emergency is defined in the same way but relates to emergencies in the United Kingdom or in a part or region rather than a 'place'. In both Parts of the Act, an event or situation which threatens damage to human welfare only if it involves loss of human life; human illness or injury; homelessness; damage to property; disruption of a supply of money, food, water, energy or fuel; disruption of a system of communication; disruption of facilities for transport, or disruption of services relating to health. An event or situation threatening damage to the environment involves contamination of land, water or air with biological, chemical or radioactive matter, or disruption or destruction of plant life or animal life.

The Act confers on the executive the power to amend the definition of an emergency by amending, by order, the list of events or situations which may threaten damage to human welfare. Any such orders are subject to the affirmative resolution procedure. Under Part 2, section 20, emergency regulations may be made by Order in Council if the conditions in section 21 are satisfied. Those conditions are that an emergency has occurred, is occurring or is about to occur; that it is necessary to make provision for the purpose of preventing, controlling or mitigating an aspect or effect of the emergency and that the need for such provision is urgent. Emergency regulations lapse 30 days after they are made unless an earlier date is specified. The regulations are renewable.[89] They must be laid before parliament as soon as reasonably practicable and lapse at the end of seven days unless each House of Parliament passes a resolution approving them.

The Act imposes duties on public authorities to assess and make provision for emergencies, and to provide information and assistance to the public.

The use of the armed forces in times of unrest

The use of troops in 1911 in South Wales is the only occasion on which troops have been brought in to assist the police. During the miners' strike 1984–85, the troops were not called in. Instead, the police forces co-ordinated their operations in order to contain the situation successfully. Where troops are deemed necessary to aid the police, it is the Home Secretary, acting on the request of the Chief Officer of police, who has responsibility. As was seen in Chapter 6, the Home Secretary has the power to issue weapons to police forces for the quelling of civil disturbance.[90]

In time of war

The Defence of the Realm Acts 1914–15 conferred wide powers on the Crown to make Regulations for ensuring public safety and defence of the realm. The courts

---

88 Civil Contingencies Act 2004, ss 1 and 19.
89 *Ibid*, s 26.
90 See *R v Secretary of State for the Home Department ex parte Northumbria Police Authority* (1988).

have ruled that these broad powers include the power to detain a person without trial on the basis of his or her hostile associations.[91] The power to regulate supplies does not, however, include the power to impose a tax upon produce.[92] Specific power to impose charges in relation to matters regulated under Defence Regulations was conferred under the Emergency Powers (Defence) Act 1939. Under the regulations, the Home Secretary was given power to detain persons whom he had reasonable cause to believe came within certain categories. The power was regarded by the courts as reviewable.[93] Under the Emergency Powers (Defence) (No 2) Act 1940, powers were conferred compulsorily to direct labour in support of the war effort. Compulsory military service was introduced under National Service Acts.

Special powers in relation to Northern Ireland[94]

In Chapter 3, an outline history of the troubles in Northern Ireland is provided. It will be recalled that the partition of Ireland, with six counties of Ulster being separated from the rest of Ireland and becoming the newly-created state of Northern Ireland, did not quell the centuries of disturbances between the mainly Catholic South of Ireland and the mainly Protestant newly created Northern Ireland. In order to contain the terrorist activities of the Irish Republican Army, in 1922 the Civil Authorities (Special Powers) Act[95] was passed by the Northern Ireland Parliament. From 1969, British troops have been used in Northern Ireland in support of the civil authorities. In 1971 – under this Act – the internment of suspected terrorists was introduced. In 1973, the Northern Ireland (Emergency Provisions) Act was passed at Westminster, amended in 1975 and re-enacted in 1978, 1987, 1991 and 1996.[96] In 1974, the Prevention of Terrorism (Temporary Provisions) Act was passed, initially for a five year renewable term. The Act was subsequently renewed, although the 1989 Act was not subject to the five year term, but was subject to annual renewal by parliament, as are parts of the Northern Ireland (Emergency Provisions) Act 1996. The Prevention of Terrorism (Additional Powers) Act 1996, the Terrorism Act 2000, the Anti-Terrorism, Crime and Security Act 2001 and the Terrorism (Northern Ireland) Art 2006, discussed below, supplement the law.

---

91 See *R v Halliday ex parte Zadig* (1917).
92 See *Attorney General v Wilts United Dairies Ltd* (1921) and the War Charges Validity Act 1925.
93 See *Liversidge v Anderson* (1942).
94 See Calvert, 1968; Macdermott, 1972.
95 Walsh, 1983; Lord Diplock, *Report of the Commission to Consider Legal Procedures to Deal with Terrorist Activities in Northern Ireland*, Cmnd 5185, 1972, London: HMSO; Lord Gardiner, *Report of a Committee to Consider, in the Context of Civil Liberties and Human Rights, Measures to deal with Terrorism in Northern Ireland*, Cmnd 5847, 1975, London: HMSO.
96 Scarman J, *Government of Northern Ireland: Report of a Tribunal of Inquiry into Violence and Civil Disturbances in Northern Ireland in 1969*, (NI) Cmd 566, 1972, London: HMSO; Earl Jellicoe, *Review of the Operation of the Prevention of Terrorism (Temporary Provisions) Act 1976*, Cmnd 8803, 1983, London: HMSO. See, *inter alia*, Bell, 1979; Bishop and Maillie, 1987; Lord Shackleton, *Review of the Operation of the Prevention of Terrorism (Temporary Provisions) Acts 1974 and 1976*, Cmnd 7324, 1978, London: HMSO.

TERRORISM

The Terrorism Act 2000 reformed and extended existing terrorist legislation.[97] Whereas the Prevention of Terrorism (Temporary Provisions) Act 1989 required annual renewal, the Terrorism Act has permanent status. In relation to Northern Ireland, it had been hoped that special provision would no longer be required following the peace settlement. However, in light of the problems implementing full devolution to Northern Ireland, special provisions were included in Part VII of the Terrorism Act 2005 which were time-limited to five years and required annual orders to continue in force. The Terrorism (Northern Ireland) Act 2006 provides that the Part VII provisions remain in force until 2007 and for the Secretary of State to extend that period by order until 2008.

The terrorist attacks on New York and Washington in September 2001 prompted a swift response from the British government. The Anti-Terrorism, Crime and Security Act 2001 builds on existing legislation in order to ensure that the security forces have the necessary powers to combat terrorist threats to the United Kingdom. The 2001 Act aims to cut off terrorist funding and to enable government departments and agencies to collect and share information in the attempt to avert threats. The Act also altered immigration procedures, and provided additional powers for the detention of suspected international terrorists who have been certified by the Secretary of State as a threat to national security. The Act also enhanced the security of nuclear and aviation industries and aimed to improve the security of dangerous substances which may be used by terrorists. It extended police powers and facilitated greater co-operation between police forces. Controversially, the Act also provided for extended powers of disclosure of information by public authorities to the police and security agencies involved in criminal investigations.

The law relating to terrorism must be seen within the wider geographical context as the world seeks to counter the globalisation of terror. In 2001 the United Nations (UN) adopted Security Council Resolution 1373 on the fight against terrorism and there are 12 UN terrorism conventions setting standards for international action:

- to prevent and combat terrorist acts such as bombing, hijacking and hostage-taking;

- to prevent and combat terrorist financing, recruitment and supply of weapons; and

- to extradite or prosecute terrorists and deny them safe haven.

Within the European context, both the Council of Europe and the European Union have been active. In 2003 the Council of Europe set up the Committee of Experts

---

97 It repeals the Prevention of Terrorism (Temporary Provisions) Act 1989, the Prevention of Terrorism (Additional Powers) Act 1996, the Northern Ireland (Emergency Provisions) Act 1996 and the Northern Ireland (Emergency Provisions) Act 1998, and makes minor amendments to other relevant Acts. See *Inquiry into Legislation Against Terrorism*, Cm 3420, 1996, London: Stationery Office; *Legislation Against Terrorism*, Cm 4178, 1998, London: Stationery Office.

on Terrorism (CODEXTER) with the responsibility of coordinating and monitoring terrorism. Under the auspices of the Committee of Experts two new Conventions against terrorism have been drafted and opened for signature by member states: the *Council of Europe Convention on the Prevention of Terrorism* and the *Council of Europe Convention on the Laundering, Search, Seizure and Confiscation of the Proceeds from Crime and on the Financing of Terrorism*.[98] In 2002 the Council of the European Union adopted Council Framework Decision on Combating Terrorism.[99] Article 1 of the Framework Decision requires all Member States to take the necessary action to ensure that terrorist acts committed with the aim of seriously intimidating a population, or unduly compelling a Government or international organisation to perform or abstain from performing any act, or seriously destabilising or destroying the fundamental political, constitutional, economic or social structures of a country or international organisation are defined as criminal offences under domestic law.

Defining terrorism

Whereas under the Prevention of Terrorism (Temporary Provisions) Act 1989, terrorism was defined as the 'use of violence for political ends, and included the use of violence for the purpose of putting the public or any section of the public in fear',[100] the Terrorism Act 2000 adopts a wider definition, namely:

> In this Act 'terrorism' means the use or threat, for the purpose of advancing a political, religious or ideological cause, of action which –
>
> (a)   involves serious violence against any person or property,
>
> (b)   endangers the life of any person, or
>
> (c)   creates a serious risk to the health or safety of the public or a section of the public.[101]

Action includes action outside the United Kingdom, and references to any person or to property mean any person or property wherever situated, and a reference to the public includes a reference to the public of a country other than the United Kingdom.[102] This definition is intended to cover not just terrorism for political ends, as in the case of Northern Ireland, but terrorism undertaken for religious or ideological motives, which, while not necessarily violent in themselves, are capable of having widespread adverse affects. Examples cited are of disruption to key computer systems or interference with the supply of water or power where life, health or safety may be put at risk. In *Secretary of State for the Home Department v Rehman* (2002), it was held that the promotion of terrorism against any state by an individual in the United Kingdom was capable of being a threat to the national security of the United Kingdom, and accordingly deportation in the interests of national security for terrorist activities which were not targeted against the United

---

98   Council of Europe Treaty Series 196 and 198 respectively (2005).
99   2002/475/JHA.
100 Prevention of Terrorism (Temporary Provisions) Act 1989, s 20.
101 Terrorism Act 2000, s 1. The Terrorism Act 2006 extends the definition of actions and threats designed to influence a government to international governmental organisations.
102 *Ibid*, s 1(2).

Kingdom or its citizens was lawful under the Immigration Act 1971. Lord Hoffmann expressed the view that judges should respect the decisions of Ministers of the Crown in relation to whether national security is threatened.

Proscribed organisations

The Terrorism Act 2000 governs proscribed organisations, listed under Schedule 2. Part II of the Terrorism Act 2006 amends the 2000 Act to cover organisations which promote or encourage terrorism. The 2006 Act also provides that an organisation listed in Schedule 2 which is operating under a different name shall be treated as the listed organisation (section 22). The Secretary of State may add or remove an organisation from the list, but may only add an organisation if he believes that the organisation is concerned in terrorism.[103] An organisation is concerned in terrorism if it commits or participates in acts of terrorism, prepares for terrorism, promotes or encourages terrorism, or is otherwise concerned in terrorism.[104] The Act introduces a Proscribed Organisations Appeal Commission (POAC),[105] to which individuals or organisations may appeal, having first applied to the Secretary of State for deproscription and been refused.[106]

The Commission must allow an appeal if it considers that the Secretary of State's decision was flawed when considered in the light of the principles applicable on an application for judicial review.[107] If the appeal is allowed, the Secretary of State must lay a draft order before parliament or, in urgent cases, make an order removing the organisation from the list.[108] Appeals from the POAC, on a question of law, lie to the Court of Appeal, Court of Session or Court of Appeal in Northern Ireland. An appeal may only be brought with the consent of the Commission or, where the Commission refuses permission, with the permission of the relevant court.[109] If an appeal to the POAC is successful, and an order made deproscribing the organisation, any individual convicted of an offence in relation to the organisation, provided the offence was committed after the date of the Secretary of State's refusal to deproscribe, may appeal against his conviction to the Court or Appeal or Crown Court.[110] In order that individuals seeking deproscription should not be deterred from pursuing an appeal or from instituting proceedings under section 7 of the Human Rights Act 1998, through a risk of prosecution for offences in relation to a proscribed organisation, section 10 of the Terrorism Act provides that evidence cannot be relied on in criminal proceedings for such an offence except as part of the defence case. In *R v Z*

---

103 Terrorism Act 2000, s 3.

104 Terrorism Act 2000, s 3(5).

105 *Ibid*, s 5, as amended by s 22 of the Terrorism Act 2006.

106 *Ibid*, s 4, as amended by s 22 of the Terrorism Act 2006.

107 See Chapter 27.

108 Terrorism Act 2000, s 5.

109 *Ibid*, s 6.

110 *Ibid*, s 7, as amended by s 22 of the Terrorism Act 2006. Section 8 makes equivalent provision for Scotland and Northern Ireland. Section 9 makes provision for the Human Rights Act 1998, s 7, to apply to appeal proceedings brought before the POAC, in relation to s 5(4) and (5), ss 6 and 7 (appeals to a court of law from a decision of the POAC), and paras 4–8 of Sched 3 (relating to procedure before the POAC).

(*Attorney General for Northern Ireland's Reference*)(2005) the House of Lords considered the definition of a proscribed organisation under the 2000 Act. Z and others had been charged with belonging to a proscribed organisation, being an organisation listed in Schedule 2 or, by section 3(1)(b) one that operated 'under the same name as an organisation listed in that Schedule'. Z belonged not to the Irish Republican Army listed in the Schedule, but to the Real Irish Republican Army, a splinter group formed in 1997, and was convicted. The Court of Appeal dismissed Z's appeal, ruling that in the interpretation of a controversial provision in a statute, it had to be read in the context of the statute as a whole and the historical context of the situation which led to its enactment. Faced with rival claims as to who represented the IRA, a blanket description had been adopted to embrace all 'emanations, manifestations and representations of that organisation': accordingly the term IRA encompassed the Real Irish Republican Army.

Sections 11 to 12 relate to offences concerning membership of and support for a proscribed organisation. A person guilty of an offence under these sections shall be liable, on conviction on indictment, to a term of imprisonment not exceeding ten years, to a fine or to both, and on summary conviction, to a term of imprisonment not exceeding six months, to a fine not exceeding the statutory maximum or to both. It is a defence for a person charged with an offence under section 11(1) to prove that the organisation was not proscribed on the last occasion on which he became a member or began to profess to be a member, and that he has not taken part in the activities of the organisation at any time while it was proscribed. Section 12 relates to the support for a proscribed organisation and makes it an offence to invite support and/or to arrange, manage or assist in arranging or managing a meeting and/or to address such a meeting. A 'meeting' means a meeting of three or more persons, whether or not the public are admitted.

The wearing of an item of clothing, or wearing, carrying or displaying an article in a public place, in such a way or in such circumstances as to arouse reasonable suspicion that that person is a member or supporter of a proscribed organisation is an offence. On summary conviction, a person guilty under section 13 is liable to six months' imprisonment, a fine not exceeding level five on the standard scale or both.

Terrorist property

Part III of the Terrorism Act 2000 relates to terrorist property, defined under section 14 to mean money or other property which is likely to be used for the purposes of terrorism (including any resources of a proscribed organisation) and proceeds of acts of terrorism. It is an offence to partake in fundraising for the purposes of terrorism. In relation to inviting support from others or receiving money or other property, there must be an intention that it should be used, or reasonable cause to suspect that it may be used, for terrorist purposes. The use or possession of money for terrorist purposes is an offence under section 16, and involvement in funding arrangements with knowledge or reasonable cause to suspect that it will be used for terrorist purposes is an offence under section 17. The concealment, removal, transfer or other mechanism for controlling terrorist property ('money laundering') is an offence under section 18. It is a defence to prove that the person did not know and had no reasonable cause to suspect that the arrangement related to terrorist property. Persons guilty of an offence under sections 15 to 18 are liable, on conviction on indictment to imprisonment for a term not exceeding 14 years, to a fine or to both or, on summary conviction, to a term of imprisonment not exceeding six months, to a fine not exceeding the statutory maximum, or to both.[111] A court before which a person is convicted of an offence under sections 15 to 18 may make a forfeiture order under section 23.

Section 19 imposes a duty on banks and other businesses to report any suspicion that someone is laundering terrorist money or committing any other terrorist property offence to the police. Sub-section (5) exempts professional legal advisers in relation to information obtained in privileged circumstances. Section 20 relates to information disclosures to the police, and provides that a person so disclosing is not liable for breaching legal restrictions on disclosure. Section 21 covers those co-operating with the police, and provides that a person does not commit an offence under sections 15 to 18 if he is acting with the express consent of a constable.

Part III of the 2000 Act introduced powers for the police, customs officers and immigration officers to seize cash[112] at borders and to seek forfeiture of cash in civil proceedings. The Anti-Terrorism, Crime and Security Act 2001 extended the law in order to prevent terrorists gaining access to their money. The police may require financial institutions to provide information on accounts of up to 90 days and it is an offence for such institutions not to report where there are reasonable grounds for suspicion that funds are being used by terrorists. In order to prevent the use or removal of funds, cash and assets may now be seized by enforcement agencies whenever an investigation is started, rather than when a person is about to be charged. The 2001 Act also provides for the assets of overseas governments or residents who have taken, or are likely to take, action threatening the economy or a threat to life or property of a UK national or resident to be frozen by the Treasury.

Terrorist investigations

Part IV of the Terrorism Act 2000 regulates powers in relation to terrorist investigations, defined to include the commission, preparation or instigation of acts of terrorism, an act which appears to have been done for such purposes, the resources of a proscribed organisation, the possibility of making a proscription or deproscription order under section 3(3), or the commission, preparation or instigation of an offence under the Act.[113] Sections 33 to 36 give power to the police to designate and demarcate a specified area by cordons for the purposes of a terrorist investigation. It is an offence to fail to comply with an order.

---

111 Terrorism Act 2000, s 22.
112 Defined as coins and notes in any currency, postal orders, travellers' cheques, bankers' drafts and such other kinds of monetary instrument as the Secretary of State may specify by order: Terrorism Act 2000, s 24.
113 *Ibid*, s 32.

Under section 39, it is an offence to disclose to another anything which is likely to prejudice a terrorist investigation or to interfere with material which is likely to be relevant to the investigation.[114]

Counter-terrorist powers

A terrorist for the purposes of Part V of the Terrorism Act 2000 is a person who has committed an offence under the Act, or is or has been concerned in the commission, preparation or instigation of acts of terrorism.[115] A constable may arrest without a warrant a person who he reasonably suspects to be a terrorist.[116] A constable may apply for a warrant relating to specified premises if he is satisfied that there are reasonable grounds for suspecting that a person suspected of terrorism is to be found there. The warrant authorises entry and search for the purpose of arresting the person in question.[117]

The 2000 Act provides powers for the entry, under warrant, into specified premises in order to search for evidence. The Terrorism Act 2006 extends the power of entry, and search into one or more sets of premises or *any* premises under a persons occupation or control. An all premises warrant may relate only to non-residential premises and the powers must be exercised within 24 hours of the warrant being issued.[118] Powers of search, seizure and forfeiture of terrorist publications are amended and extended under section 28 of the Terrorist Act 2006.

Stop and search powers relating to suspected terrorists include the power to stop and search the person for evidence of being a terrorist, and an arrested person may be searched. Anything discovered in the course of a search which the constable reasonably suspects of being evidence that the person is a terrorist may be seized.[119] Specified senior police officers may authorise any constable in uniform to stop a vehicle in an area or at a place specified in the authorisation and to search the vehicle, its driver, a passenger and anything in the vehicle or carried by the driver or a passenger, and may also be granted to stop pedestrians.[120] The power may only be used for the purpose of searching for articles which could be used in connection with terrorism, and may be exercised whether or not the constable has grounds for suspecting the presence of articles of that kind. Where suspected items are discovered in the course of a search, they may be seized and

---

114 Terrorism Act 2000, s 39(7). It is also an offence for a person to collect, make a record of, publish, communicate or attempt to elicit information which is useful to a person committing or preparing an act of terrorism, or to possess a document or record containing information which would be useful (*ibid*, s 103). The offence is confined to a person who is or has been a constable, a member of Her Majesty's Forces, the holder of a judicial office, an officer of any court or a full time employee of the prison service in Northern Ireland. It is a defence to prove that he had a reasonable excuse for his action or possession.

115 Terrorism Act 2000, s 40.

116 *Ibid*, s 41, Sched 8 relating to detention, treatment, review and extension applies.

117 *Ibid*, s 42.

118 *Ibid*, Parts 1 and 2 of Schedule 5 as amended by Terrorism Act 2006 sections 26 and 27.

119 *Ibid*, s 43.

120 *Ibid*, s 44. Authorisation may also be granted for the control of parking: ss 48–52.

retained.[121] Authorisations are for a maximum, renewable, 28 days.[122] It is an offence to fail to comply with an order to stop a vehicle, or to stop or wilfully obstruct a constable in his exercise of the power conferred by an authorisation under section 44.

The powers of stop and search were tested to the limit in *R (Gillan and Another) v Commissioner of Police of the Metropolis* (2006). An authorisation – lasting 28 days and covering the whole of the London Metropolitan District – had been made allowing police officers to stop and search members of the public at random for articles that could be used in connection with terrorism.[123] There had been successive authorisations in place since 2001. In 2003, an arms fair was being held in Docklands, East London, which attracted opposition and a demonstration. The claimants – one a student, the other a journalist – were stopped and searched. Nothing incriminating was found. Their application for judicial review was unsuccessful and their appeal was considered by the House of Lords. The House of Lords ruled that the powers were subject to effective restraints and that there had been justification for the authorisations made since 2001 and that they were lawful. Moreover, there was no violation of Article 5(1) of the Convention, in that they were merely kept from proceeding or kept waiting rather than deprived of their liberty.

The Act makes weapons training for terrorist purposes an offence. Formerly relating only to Northern Ireland under the Northern Ireland (Emergency Provisions) Act 1996, the 2000 Act extended this prohibition throughout the United Kingdom. The Act covers conventional firearms and explosives and extends to cover chemical, biological and nuclear weapons and materials.[124] It is an offence to provide or receive instruction or invite another to receive instruction in the making or use of defined weapons. It is a defence to prove that the action or involvement was wholly for a purpose not concerned with terrorism.

It is an offence to possess articles in circumstances which give rise to a reasonable suspicion that such possession is for a purpose connected with the commission, preparation or instigation of an act of terrorism. Section 57 replicates section 16A of the Prevention of Terrorism (Temporary Provisions) Act 1989 and reverses the onus of proof, sub-section (2) providing that it is a defence for a person charged to prove that his possession of an article was not for a purpose connected with terrorism. The Terrorism Act 2006, section 13, increases the penalty for possession for terrorist purposes from ten to 15 years. Article 6(2) of the European Convention on Human Rights provides for the presumption of innocence of the defendant in criminal trials, and presumes that the prosecution will need to prove guilt. However, the reversal of the burden of proof does not *per se* indicate a violation of the right to a fair trial.[125]

---

121 Terrorism Act 2000, s 45.
122 *Ibid*, s 46. Authorisations must be confirmed or amended by the Secretary of State within 48 hours of their being made, or they cease to have effect.
123 Under sections 44 and 45 of the Terrorism Act 2000. The authorisation had been confirmed by the Home Secretary pursuant to section 46.
124 Terrorism Act 2000, s 54.
125 The government certified that the Bill complied with the Convention.

The Anti-Terrorism, Crime and Security Act 2001 also made provision for the extended detention of suspected international terrorists.[126] Where the Secretary of State certified that a person is a threat to national security and cannot be deported within a reasonable time, the suspect could be detained. The Act required the government to derogate from Article 5(1) of the European Convention on Human Rights.[127] The Special Immigration Appeals Commission (SIAC)[128] reviewed such detention regularly, and its decisions were excluded from judicial review. An appeal from the Commission on a point of law lay to the Court of Appeal.

In *A v Secretary of State for the Home Department* (2004) a panel of nine Law Lords (Lord Walker dissenting) ruled that measures empowering the Home Secretary to detain indefinitely, without charge or trial, non-nationals whom he suspected of international terrorist activity, but whom he could not deport, were incompatible with the United Kingdom's European Convention obligations. The House of Lords made a declaration of incompatibility under section 4 of the Human Rights Act that section 23 of the Anti-terrorism, Crime and Security Act 2001 was incompatible with Articles 5 and 14 of the Convention.

Lord Bingham stated that great weight had to be given to the judgment of the Home Secretary in relation to matters of national security which involved political judgment. However, he did not accept that the courts must always defer to the executive. Lord Bingham viewed the issue as one of separation of powers: the more purely political the question the more appropriate it was for political resolution. The greater the legal content of any issue, the greater 'the court's potential role because under our constitution and subject to the sovereign power of Parliament it was the function of the courts and not of political bodies to resolve legal questions'. His Lordship further recognised the different functions of the executive and the courts, stating that 'the function of independent judges charged to interpret and apply the law was universally recognised as a cardinal feature of the modern democratic state, a cornerstone of the rule of law itself'.

The right to liberty was a fundamental Convention right. Detaining foreign nationals without trial – but not nationals suspected of terrorist offences – was not justified and infringed both Article 5 and 14. The Derogation Order (Human Rights Act 1998 [Designated Derogation] Order SI 2001 No 3644) was disproportionate and could not be justified.

Lord Hoffmann specifically addressed the question of whether there was a public emergency within the meaning of Article 15 of the Convention. He recognised 'the power of fanatical groups of terrorists to kill and destroy' but did not consider that they threatened 'the life of the nation'. Lord Walker, dissenting, stated that while detention without trial was a grave matter, it was for parliament and the Secretary of State to judge the necessary measures, and the 2001 Act contained important safeguards. The Home Secretary's powers were subject to judicial review by the statutory commission (the Special Immigration Appeals

---

126 Part 4, ss 21–32.
127 See further Chapter 19.
128 The Act makes the SIAC a superior court of record. Three members hear appeals, one of whom holds or has held high judicial office and one of whom is or has been an immigration judge.

Tribunal which is chaired by a High Court judge); the legislation was temporary in nature and while in force there was detailed scrutiny of the operation of sections 21 to 23. In nearly three years no more than 17 individuals had been certified under section 21: the number of persons actually detailed was relevant to the issue of proportionality.[129]

Police powers are enhanced under the 2001 Act. Part 10 extends the power to search for identity. The Act authorises the fingerprinting, photographing and ordering the removal of face coverings worn to conceal identity. The Act also provides for the British Transport Police, UK Atomic Energy Authority officers and Ministry of Defence Police to operate outside their own jurisdiction to assist local police forces. The 2001 Act strengthens security powers in relation to the nuclear industry and aviation and in relation to chemical and biological weapons.[130]

Terrorism overseas

The Terrorism Act 2000 also regulates terrorism overseas. Under section 59, it is an offence to incite another person to commit an act of terrorism wholly or partly outside the United Kingdom, if that act would constitute an offence listed in sub-section (2) in England and Wales, namely, murder, wounding with intent, and offences involving poison, explosions and endangering life by damaging property. A person found guilty shall be liable to any penalty to which he would be liable on conviction of the relevant offence. Sections 60 and 61 make equivalent provision in relation to Scotland and Northern Ireland. Section 62 regulates acts of terrorism outside the United Kingdom involving causing explosions[131] and the use of biological or chemical weapons, and provides that a person committing such an act is guilty of an offence. Equally, it is an offence to do anything outside the United Kingdom which would amount to an offence under sections 15 to 18 if it had been done in the United Kingdom.

Port and border controls

Section 53 and Schedule 7 to the Terrorism Act 2000 regulate border controls. An 'examining officer', being a constable, immigration officer or customs officer designated for the purposes of Schedule 7 by the Secretary of State and Commissioners of Customs and Excise, has the power to stop, question and detain a person, at an airport, hoverport or port or border area, for the purposes of determining whether he or she is a person suspected of being concerned in the

---

129 See also *A v Secretary of State for the Home Department* (No 2) (2005) in which the House of Lords ruled that evidence obtained by torture by foreign state officials was inadmissible in court.

130 See the Nuclear Material (Offences) Act 1983 as amended by the Terrorism Act 2006, section 14 which provides for life imprisonment on conviction on indictment. On the Terrorism Acts and the European Convention on Human Rights, see *Brogan v United Kingdom* (1989), *McGann, Farrell and Savage v United Kingdom* (1995), which are discussed in Chapter 19.

131 An offence under the Explosive Substances Act 1883, s 2, 3 or 5; an offence under the Biological Weapons Act 1974, s 1; an offence under the Chemical Weapons Act 1996, s 2.

commission, preparation or instigation of acts of terrorism.[132] A place is within a border area if it is no more than one mile from the border between Northern Ireland and the Republic of Ireland.[133] In relation to a train travelling from the Republic of Ireland to Northern Ireland, the first place in Northern Ireland at which it stops for the purpose of allowing passengers to leave is within the border area. Owners or agents of ships or aircraft employed to carry passengers for reward on journeys between Great Britain, the Republic of Ireland and Northern Ireland must not dock or land for the purposes of embarking or disembarking passengers at any place other than a designated port as listed in the Act.[134] The Secretary of State may designate control areas in any port, and specify conditions for or restrictions on the embarkation or disembarkation of passengers in a control area. The captains of ships or aircraft travelling between Great Britain, the Republic of Ireland, Northern Ireland or any of the Islands are under a duty to ensure that passengers and members of crew do not disembark other than in accordance with arrangements approved by an examining officer. Section 16 introduces carding arrangements, which require persons embarking or disembarking in relation to journeys between Great Britain, the Republic of Ireland, Northern Ireland or any of the Islands to provide such information as the Secretary of State, by order, may require.

A person questioned is required to provide any information requested, and produce a valid passport or other document establishing his or her identity. A person may be removed from a ship, aircraft or vehicle for the purpose of detaining for questioning. A person detained for questioning must be released no later than the end of a nine hour period beginning with the time when the questioning begins, unless otherwise detained under any other power.[135]

Powers of search are granted to examining officers. The examining officer may 'for the purpose of satisfying himself whether there are any persons who he may wish to question' search a ship or aircraft. In relation to the person questioned, the examining officer may search the person, his possessions or a ship or aircraft. In relation to questioning in border areas, the examining officer has the power to search vehicles. The search of a person in border searches must be carried out by a person of the same sex.[136] Property may be detained, for a period of seven days, for the purpose of deciding whether it may be needed for use as evidence in criminal proceedings, or in connection with decisions concerning deportation to be taken by the Secretary of State.[137]

---

132 Defined in the Terrorism Act 2000, s 40(1)(b) and 40(2), as including a person who has been, whether before or after the passing of the Act, concerned in the commission, preparation or instigation of acts of terrorism within the meaning given in s 1.
133 *Ibid*, s 40(1).
134 *Ibid*, Sched 7, para 12.
135 Terrorism Act 2000, Sched 7, para 6.
136 *Ibid*, Sched 7, paras 7 and 8.
137 *Ibid*, para 11.

THE PREVENTION OF TERRORISM ACT 2005

The Prevention of Terrorism Act 2005 was a response to the House of Lords' decision in *A v Secretary of State for the Home Department supra*. The 2005 Act provides for the making of 'control orders' over terrorist suspects. These are preventative in nature and may impose any conditions necessary to prevent or restrict an individual's further involvement in terrorist-related activities.

There are two forms of control order. There are non-derogating orders which may be made by the Secretary of State having acquired the permission of the court. In urgent cases, the control order may be made without prior permission, but must then be confirmed by the court. When considering whether to grant permission for a non-derogating order to be made, and when considering whether to confirm a non-derogating order, the court may hold an *ex parte* hearing and must consider whether the Secretary of State's decision is obviously flawed. If it was, the order may be refused or quashed. If it was not, the court must refer the control order to a full *inter partes* hearing which will apply judicial review tests to the control order to decide whether it should continue in force. At the full hearing the court must consider whether any of the following decision were flawed:

the decision that there are reasonable grounds for suspecting that the person is involved in terrorist-related activity;

the decision that a control order is necessary to protect the public from the risk of terrorism; and

the decision on the imposition of each of the obligations imposed by the order.

A non-derogating control order may be renewed for 12 months. Where a non-derogating order is renewed, the order must specify the expiry date of the renewed order.

The second type of order is a derogating control order, made by the court itself on the application of the Home Secretary. All control orders will be subject to full hearings by the High Court or Court of Session and there is a right of appeal on a point of law from the High Court or Court of Session.

In relation to derogating control orders, at a preliminary hearing – which can be *ex parte* – the court will decide if there is a *prima facie* case for the order. If there is then the order will be made and a full *inter partes* hearing arranged. At the full hearing the court will confirm the derogating control order if:

on the balance of probabilities it is satisfied that the controlled person is or has been involved in terrorist-related activity;

it considers the obligations imposed necessary for the purpose of protecting the public from the risk of terrorism;

it appears that the risk arises out of or is associated with a public emergency in respect of which there is a designated derogation from the whole or a part of Article 5;

the obligations imposed are in a list of derogating obligations set out in the designation order.

A derogating control order lasts for six months, unless revoked. It can continue for more than six months if the court renews it. A renewed order will be valid for a further six months. The court has the power to quash a control order, modify the obligations it imposes, or in the case of non-derogating control orders, give directions to revoke or modify the order.

Section 1, subsections (4) to (8) sets out illustrations of obligations which may be imposed. These include requiring a person to stay at a particular place generally or at particular times; wearing and maintaining apparatus; providing advance notice of proposed movements or activities. Breach of an obligation imposed by a control order, without reasonable excuse, is a criminal offence punishable, following conviction on indictment, with a prison sentence of up to five years, or a fine, or both; or, following summary conviction, to a prison sentence of up to 12 months (six months in Scotland or Northern Ireland), or a fine, or both. The civil standard of proof is to be applied to the question of involvement in terrorism-related activity in hearings related to derogating control orders.

The operation of the Act is to be reviewed after nine months, with subsequent reviews carried out annually. The Home Secretary must report to Parliament every three months on the exercise of control order powers during that period.

THE TERRORISM ACT 2006

The Terrorism Act 2006 was introduced to tighten the law following two attacks on London in July 2005. The Act introduces new criminal offences in relation to terrorism, amends the definition of terrorism, increases the penalties available, extends the grounds for detention and extends the period of detention and makes other miscellaneous changes to the law. Section 36 provides that the Secretary of State must appoint a person to review the operation of the Terrorism Act 2000 and Part I of the 2006 Act. The review must be carried out every 12 months and the report made to the Secretary of State must be laid before Parliament.

The definition of terrorism is extended to include actions and threats or using noxious substances or things to influence a government or intimidate to international governmental organisations.[138]

Section 1 creates the offence of encouragement of terrorism, and applies to a statement 'that is likely to be understood by some or all of the members of the public to whom it is published as a direct or indirect encouragement or other inducement to them to the commission, preparation or instigation of acts of terrorism or Convention offences.' It is an offence to publish such a statement, or cause another to publish such a statement with the intention that members of the public 'be directly or indirectly encouraged to commit, prepare or instigate acts of terrorism or Convention offences'.[139] It is also an offence to be 'reckless as to whether members of the public will be directly or indirectly encouraged etc.' An indirect encouragement is defined as being a 'statement describing terrorism in

138 Amending section 1(1)(b) of the Terrorism Act 2000 and section 113(1)(c) of the Anti-terrorism, Crime and Security Act 2001.
139 Convention offences are those listed in Schedule 1 to the Act.

such a way that the listener would infer that he should emulate it.' Section 2 creates the offence of disseminating a terrorism publication with the intention, or being reckless, of directly or indirectly encouraging or inducing the commission, preparation or instigation of acts of terrorism.[140] The criminal offences under sections 1 and 2 extend to internet activity.[141]

The Act extends the law to cover *any* conduct undertaken in preparation for committing, or assisting another to commit, acts of terrorism. Conviction carries a sentence of life imprisonment. Providing training or instruction for, or receiving instruction or training in, skills relating to terrorism is a criminal offence carrying a sentence on conviction on indictment to a term of imprisonment of up to ten years or a fine, or both. If tried summarily, the offences carry a term of imprisonment of up to 12 months, a fine not exceeding the statutory maximum, or both.[142] The same penalties apply to the offence of attendance at a place used for terrorist training.[143] The making and possession of radioactive material or devices, or the misuse of devices or material, or demands or threats relating to such items are criminal offences punishable with life imprisonment.[144] Conduct outside the United Kingdom is a criminal offence in the United Kingdom if it would amount to an offence listed in section 17(2). Prosecutions may be instituted in England and Wales only with the consent of the Director of Public Prosecutions and in Northern Ireland with the consent of the Director of Public Prosecutions for Northern Ireland.

The Terrorism Act 2006 extends the period in which a terrorist suspect may be held in detention without charge to 28 days. The extension of detention must be authorised by a High Court or High Court of Justiciary judge. It had been the government's aim to have a period of detention of up to 90 days.[145] That proposal, however, was rejected by the House of Commons and replaced by 28 days. The grounds on which detention may be extended are set out in the Terrorism Act 2000.[146] The Terrorism Act 2006 amends those provisions to include continued detention pending the result of an examination or analysis of relevant evidence, to obtain relevant evidence whether by questioning or otherwise and to preserve relevant evidence.

---

140 The Terrorism Act 2006, section 28 provides for warrants to enter and search and seize terrorist publications and for forfeiture.
141 Terrorism Act 2006 Section 3.
142 In Scotland or Northern Ireland, on summary conviction to imprisonment for a term not exceeding six months or a fine not exceeding the statutory maximum, or both.
143 Terrorism Act 2006 Section 8.
144 *Ibid* sections 9–11.
145 In France suspects can be held for up to four years for offences punishable by more than ten years; in Germany suspects must be brought to court the day after their arrest; in Italy foreign terror suspects can be expelled immediately if they pose a security risk; in Canada non-citizens can be detained with the case being reviewed every six months.
146 See Schedule 8.

IDENTITY CARDS

In 2003 the government published the findings from a consultation exercise on the introduction of Identity Cards.[147] The Identity Cards Act 2006 will introduce a scheme which will operate on a United Kingdom-wide basis. The Act provides for a National Identity Register, the purpose of which is the provide a 'convenient method for individuals to prove their identity' and to provide a 'secure means of identifying individuals where that is in the public interest', defined as being for the purposes of national security, prevention and detection of crime, enforcement of immigration controls, enforcements on prohibitions on unauthorised working or employment and the efficient and effective provision of public services. The scheme will initially be voluntary, although anyone applying for renewal of a passport will have their biometric details entered on the new register. From 2010 it will be compulsory for anyone renewing their passport to buy an ID card.[148]

---

147 See *Identity Cards: a Summary of Findings from the Consultation on Entitlement Cards and Identity Fraud* (CM 6019). See also *Identity Cards: the next steps* (Cm 6020).
148 Or other 'designated document', such documents are to be determined by the Secretary of State.

PART VII

INTRODUCTION TO ADMINISTRATIVE LAW

CHAPTER 26

JUDICIAL REVIEW: INTRODUCTION, JURISDICTION AND PROCEDURE[1]

THE CONSTITUTIONAL ROLE OF JUDICIAL REVIEW

Judicial review represents the means by which the courts control the exercise of governmental power. Government departments, local authorities, tribunals, state agencies and agencies exercising powers which are governmental in nature must exercise their powers in a lawful manner. Judicial review has developed to ensure that public bodies which exercise law making power or adjudicatory powers are kept within the confines of the power conferred. In one sense, therefore, judicial review is relevant to most aspects of the constitution. The Human Rights Act 1998 extends the scope of judicial review in that any failure on the part of a public body to respect human rights will be subject to review by the courts.

Judicial review is concerned with the legality of the decision made, not with the merits of the particular decision. Accordingly, the task of the judges is to ensure that the exercise of any power which has been delegated to ministers and administrative and adjudicatory bodies is lawful according to the power given to that body by Act of Parliament. As will be seen below, there is academic debate concerning the appropriate basis on which the courts exercise their supervisory jurisdiction. The traditional view has been that the judge's task is to ensure that public bodies act within their powers – or *intra vires* – and that, provided that the body has acted within its powers as defined by statute, and according to the common law based rules of natural justice, the body's decision will not be challengeable under the public law process of judicial review.[2]

From this traditional perspective, judicial review is principally concerned with questions of jurisdiction and natural justice. The primary question to be asked is whether a particular person or body with delegated law making or adjudicatory powers had acted *intra vires* or *ultra vires*, and whether the decision making process entailed the application of natural justice. If the person or body was acting within its jurisdiction, and respecting the demands of natural justice, the courts would not interfere with the decision – even if the decision was in some respect wrong. Nowadays, although the judges still express their role in the traditional language of '*vires*', the approach taken is more robust than before. If a public body, as defined in law, makes an error of law, the courts – through the process of judicial review – will intervene to ensure that the body in question reconsiders a matter and acts in a procedurally correct manner.[3]

The uncertain and expanding role of judicial review causes controversy.[4] Simply expressed, in any society regulated by a complex administrative

---

1   See Craig, 2003a; Wade and Forsyth, 2000.
2   See Chapter 27 on natural justice.
3   See Chapter 27 for further discussion of the concept of *ultra vires*.
4   See eg the differing views of Stephen Sedley J and Professor Ross Cranston expressed in Richardson and Genn, 1994, Chapters 2 and 3, respectively.

machinery, an essential feature of that society is that administrators have a sphere of power within which, in the interests of certainty and efficiency, they should be free to operate. The doctrine of ministerial responsibility, discussed in Chapter 11, ensures that accountability for policy and administration lies with the relevant Secretary of State, who is accountable to the electorate through parliament. However, against that argument for non-interference with matters of administration must be set the demands of individual justice and fairness. If an individual, or a body of persons, is aggrieved by an administrative decision, and their rights adversely affected, there is a requirement that procedures exist whereby such decisions may be challenged in the courts. It is through judicial review that the requirements of legality of the exercise of powers by public bodies is tested. From this perspective, judicial review exemplifies the application of the rule of law[5] in a democratic society.[6] This raises a further question of constitutional significance. To what extent is it legitimate for a non-elected judiciary to intervene to correct the administrative process which is controlled through powers granted by the democratically elected parliament? One response to this question is that judicial review – with respect to the review of delegated law making and adjudicatory powers – ensures that parliament's will is observed, and judicial review may thus be regarded as an aspect of parliamentary sovereignty.[7]

As a result of extensive regulation, powers have been conferred by parliament upon various government departments, administrative bodies and tribunals – powers which must be exercised within the 'four corners' of the legislation. Traditionally, judicial review has been regarded as unconcerned with the merits of a particular case, or with the justice or injustice of the rules which are being applied, but rather as being concerned with the manner in which decisions have been taken: has this decision maker acted within the powers given? Most of the rules applied by administrators will be statutory, but the courts have also – under common law – developed rules which will apply to decision makers over and above the statutory rules. Thus, decision makers must not only exercise their powers in the correct manner as prescribed by the statute, but must also comply with the rules of reasonableness, natural justice and fairness. In addition, due to the Human Rights Act 1998 the courts now have the additional task of ensuring – in part through judicial review – that public authorities do not violate protected Convention rights. The Human Rights Act has profound implications for judicial review, affecting not only an expansion in the role of the courts but also requiring different modes of interpretation than hitherto. These issues will be discussed in the next chapter.

In essence – and subject to changes which have been brought about by the Human Rights Act 1998, devolution to regional assemblies and the proposed Freedom of Information Act – the courts seek, by judicial review, to ensure four principal objectives:

---

5   For an early expression of this view, see Dicey, 1885, Appendix 2.
6   See Allan, 2001.
7   See Chapter 7. See also Craig, 1999, and Jowell, 1999.

(a) that Acts of Parliament have been correctly interpreted;

(b) that discretion conferred by statute has been lawfully exercised;

(c) that the decision maker has acted fairly;

(d) that the exercise of power by a public body does not violate human rights.

THE GROWTH IN PUBLIC ADMINISTRATION[8]

Judicial review derives from the historical power of the courts to keep inferior bodies within their legal powers. While 'public administration' may be traced back to Elizabethan times,[9] it was in the mid-nineteenth century that government expanded its legislative and administrative functions into areas hitherto untouched. The growth in the nineteenth century of industrialisation resulted in central regulation, for example of town and country planning, the provision of housing and housing improvement,[10] public health, regulation of the railways and factory management and schemes for compensation for injury.[11] One consequence of such regulation was the need for mechanisms for resolving disputes between individuals and the regulatory bodies. Statutory inquiries became the formal mechanism by which disputes were to be resolved.

The early twentieth century laid the foundations for the Welfare State. The introduction of health insurance[12] and measures to combat unemployment[13] led to the establishment of tribunals of administration and adjudication. The major reform came with the publication of the Beveridge Report,[14] which set out radical proposals for extensive reforms in social welfare and led to the introduction of the National Health Service.

To portray succinctly the administrative system existing nowadays is not an easy task. As with so much of the institutional framework of the state, developments have proceeded in a pragmatic, ad hoc fashion. In 1980, the *Report on Non-Departmental Public Bodies*[15] classified administrative bodies into executive bodies, advisory bodies and tribunals. The Report cited 489 executive bodies. The work of tribunals and inquiries had earlier been investigated by the Franks Committee, whose report[16] led to the passing of the Tribunals and Inquiries Act 1958. Today, over 40 different tribunals exist, with jurisdiction over such diverse subject matters as commerce, economic matters, education, employment, Foreign Compensation, housing, physical and mental health, immigration, the National Health Service, pensions and residential homes.

---

8   See, *inter alia*, Dynes and Walker, 1995.

9   Eg, the Poor Relief Act 1601.

10 Artisans' and Labourers' Dwelling Improvement Act 1875; Housing of the Working Classes Act 1890.

11 Public Health Acts 1848, 1872, 1875; Factory Act 1833; Workmen's Compensations Acts 1897 and 1906, respectively.

12 National Insurance Act 1911.

13 Labour Exchanges Act 1909 and National Insurance Act 1911.

14 *Social Insurance and Allied Services*, Cmnd 6404, 1942, London: HMSO.

15 Cmnd 7797, 1980, London: HMSO.

16 *Report of the Committee on Administrative Tribunals and Enquiries*, Cmnd 218, 1957, London: HMSO.

What is a 'public body' for the purposes of judicial review?

Judicial review is only available to test the lawfulness of decisions made by public bodies. If judicial review is applied for, and the court rules that the body whose decision is being challenged is a private body, then the remedy of the aggrieved individual will lie in private law, not public law, proceedings. In determining whether or not the body whose decision is being challenged on an application for judicial review is a public as opposed to private body, the court will look at its functions. The test is not whether or not the authority is a government body as such but, rather, whether it is a body exercising powers analogous to those of government bodies. National public agencies have been a feature of administration since the Reform Act of 1832. The Poor Law Commissioners established in 1834, for whom there was no responsible Minister in Parliament (until 1847) are an early example of such an agency. The post-Second World War nationalisation programmes of the Labour government between 1945 and 1951 and the expansion of welfare provision, both then and subsequently, resulted in numerous public bodies being established which were not government bodies, nor were they part of local government. Examples of such bodies include the British Broadcasting Authority, Legal Aid Board (now the Legal Services Commission), Atomic Energy Authority and British Airports Authority. It was estimated that by 1991 there were some 1,444 public bodies which were not related to government departments.[17] In 1979, the incoming Conservative government was firmly committed to privatisation. British Gas, British Airways, British Rail, British Telecom, the water supply industry and electricity industry were all privatised.[18] The drive towards privatisation and reduced state holdings in many other enterprises[19] has not, however, reduced the number of public bodies. Parallelling the privatisation movement has been the growth in standard setting and regulatory bodies designed to ensure appropriate accountability of providers to consumers. The Police Complaints Authority, Lord Chancellor's Advisory Committee on Legal Education and Conduct, Higher Education Funding Council, and Human Fertilisation and Embryology Authority are all examples of bodies created under statute.[20] Furthermore, there have been a number of regulatory bodies established on a voluntary basis. The Press Complaints Commission, City Panel on Takeovers and Mergers, Advertising Standards Authority, Jockey Club and Football Association are all examples of such bodies. One question which arises is how the courts determine whether a body – howsoever established – is a public body and thus amenable to judicial review of its decisions. The City Panel on Takeovers and Mergers provided an opportunity for judicial analysis of public and private bodies.

---

17 *Public Bodies*, 1991, London: HMSO.
18 Gas Act 1986, Civil Aviation Act 1980, Water Act 1989, Electricity Act 1989. Plans to privatise the Post Office were abandoned in 1994 after a backbench revolt against the plans.
19 Eg, British Petroleum, British Nuclear Fuels Ltd, Cable and Wireless, Rolls Royce, Jaguar.
20 Police and Criminal Evidence Act 1984, Courts and Legal Services Act 1990, Higher Education Act 1992, Human Fertilisation and Embryology Act 1990.

THE COURTS' INTERPRETATION OF PUBLIC BODIES

In *R v City Panel on Takeovers and Mergers ex parte Datafin Ltd* (1987), the Takeover Panel had dismissed a complaint made by a bidder of 'acting in concert' contrary to the rules on takeovers. The bidder applied for judicial review. The court declined to grant the application on the basis that there were no grounds for judicial review (on which, see below) but, nevertheless, rejected the claim made by the City Panel that the court had no jurisdiction to consider the application. The Panel was subject to judicial review, despite its lack of statutory or prerogative source of power, because it was a body exercising public functions analogous to those which could be, or could have been in the absence of the Panel, exercised by a government department. Lord Justice Lloyd stated that, for the most part, the source of the power will be decisive. Accordingly, if a body is set up under statute or by delegated legislation, then the source of the power brings the body within the scope of judicial review. However, Lloyd LJ also recognised that in some cases the matter would be unclear. Where that situation existed, it was necessary to look beyond the source of the power and consider the 'nature of the power' being exercised. In Lloyd LJ's view, '[i]f a body in question is exercising public law functions, or if the exercise of its functions have public law consequences, then that may be sufficient to bring the body within the reach of judicial review'.

By contrast with the *City Panel on Takeover and Mergers* case, in *R v Disciplinary Committee of the Jockey Club ex parte Aga Khan* (1993), the Aga Khan sought judicial review of the Jockey Club's decision to disqualify his winning horse from a race for failing a dope test, the court ruled that the relationship between racehorse owners and the Club, and the powers of the Club, derived from agreement between the parties and was a matter of private rather than public law.[21]

More recently, in *R (on the application of Julian West) v Lloyd's of London* (2004) the Court of Appeal ruled that decisions taken by Lloyd's of London were not amenable to judicial review either on the basis that it was performing a governmental function or because it was a public authority within the meaning of section 6(1) of the Human Rights Act 1998. The decisions were solely concerned with the commercial relationship between the applicant and Lloyd's and were governed by the contracts into which the applicant had entered. Accordingly the decision were of a private and not a public nature. The same principle will be applied whenever a matter is regulated by contract between two private parties – the matter is one of private and not public law. There is a fine distinction to be drawn here. The regulation of a private school, for example, has been held to be a matter of private law, whereas the regulation of City Technical Colleges, non-fee paying publicly funded institutions, is a matter of public law. However, where a pupil attends a private school under a publicly funded assisted places scheme,

---

21   See also *R v Chief Rabbi ex parte Wachmann* (1993); and Barendt *et al*, 1993. See also *R (Mullins) v Appeal Board of the Jockey Club* (2004).

that school falls within the jurisdiction for judicial review in relation to the school's decision, in particular, the decision to expel a pupil.[22]

Under section 6 of the Human Rights Act 1998, public authorities are defined as including courts and tribunals and 'any person certain of whose functions are functions of a public nature'. In *Marcic v Thames Water* (2003), for example, a privatised water and sewerage company was held to be a public body for the purposes of the Act. See further Chapter 19. The Act excludes both Houses of Parliament and those acting in connection with parliamentary proceedings. For the purposes of judicial review, section 7 provides that an applicant is only to have sufficient interest if he or she is a victim of the unlawful act. In relation to proceedings relating to judicial acts, these may be brought only by exercising a right of appeal or by an application for judicial review.[23]

Review and appeal[24]

Judicial review must be distinguished from an appeal against a decision. The court and tribunal structure provides a more or less rational appeal structure for those aggrieved by a judicial decision. The appellate court will have the power to reconsider the case and to substitute its own decision for that of the lower court. An appeal may be made on both the law and the facts of the case, so that a full re-hearing may take place. Judicial review, by contrast, is concerned solely with the manner in which the decision maker has applied the relevant rules: it is thus procedural in nature. It is not for the court – in judicial review proceedings – to substitute its judgment for that of the decision making body to which powers have been delegated but, rather, to ensure that the adjudicator has kept within the rules laid down by statute and the common law. In short, the role of the courts in judicial review is to exercise a supervisory, not an appellate, jurisdiction. Judicial review 'is not an appeal from a decision, but a review of the manner in which the decision was made'.[25]

The question of whether judicial review or the appeal mechanism was the appropriate method of challenging a judicial decision was considered by the Court of Appeal in *R (Sivasubramaniam) v Wandsworth County Court* (2003). The Court of Appeal ruled that the High Court ought not to entertain an application for permission to apply for judicial review of the decision of a judge in the county court where the applicant had failed to pursue the alternative available remedy of an appeal, or where a county court judge had refused permission to appeal against the decision of a district judge, save in the exceptional circumstances of clear want of jurisdiction, or procedural irregularity amounting to a denial of a fair hearing.

Two issues arose, according to the Master of the Rolls:

1   If an unsuccessful party to a decision by a county court judge sought judicial review of the decision, rather than pursuing the alternative remedy of appeal

---

22   See *R v Governors of Haberdashers' Aske's Hatcham College Trust ex parte T* (1994), *per* Dyson J.
23   Human Rights Act 1998, s 9.
24   See *Chief Constable of the North Wales Police v Evans* (1982).
25   *Per* Lord Brightman in *Chief Constable of the North Wales Police v Evans* (1982), p 1174.

to the High Court, or in the case of a second appeal to the Court of Appeal, should that application be entertained?

2   Where an appeal court had refused permission to appeal against a decision of the lower court and the unsuccessful party then sought judicial review, should that application be entertained?

The Master of the Rolls recalled that 'authority showed that judicial review was customarily refused as an exercise of judicial discretion where an alternative remedy was available'. The Access to Justice Act 1999 had introduced a new system of appeals in civil cases. The 1999 Act provided 'a coherent statutory scheme' governing appeals at all levels short of the House of Lords. To allow an applicant to pursue a claim for judicial review was to defeat the object of access to justice and should not be permitted unless there were exceptional circumstances.

Judicial review derives from the courts' inherent powers to keep decision making bodies within the bounds of their powers, and to provide remedies for abuse of power, and its purpose is not to substitute a decision of the court for the decision of the administrative body.

It should be noted that seeking judicial review is not the only avenue for those complaining about public bodies. The case of *Marcic v Thames Water Utilities Ltd* (2004) illustrates the courts' approach. The appellant sought an injunction to restrain Thames Water from permitting the use of its sewerage system in such a way as to cause flooding to his property, and a mandatory order compelling Thames Water to improve the sewerage system, and damages. Thames Water operates its system under statutory powers and subject to statutory duties. The Water Industry Act 1991 provides for a Director General of Water Services with wide ranging powers and duties, not least of which the power to make Enforcement Orders requiring providers to comply with the requirements of the Act. The House of Lords ruled that the appellant had chosen to side-step the statutory scheme by pursuing judicial review proceedings against the Secretary of State rather than seeking to enforce the statutory duty of the water authority. The House of Lords emphasised that the courts were ill-equipped to deal with statutory undertakings which involved large scale capital expenditure: parliament had entrusted that function to the Director.

The outcome of judicial review

Differences also exist in the respective outcomes of appeal and judicial review. In the case of appeals, where the appeal is successful, it will usually result in a new decision being substituted for the previous decision.[26] In the case of review, a successful case will usually result in the previous decision being nullified – or quashed – but no new decision will be put in its place. Instead, the body in relation to which a successful application for judicial review has been made will be directed to redetermine the case according to the correct rules and

---

26   In some instances, a new trial may have to be ordered in order for a fresh decision to be reached.

procedure, and it is by no means inevitable that the decision reached according to the lawful procedure will be more favourable to the individual than the original decision.

Furthermore, there is no automatic right to a remedy in judicial review proceedings: the remedy is discretionary. This matter is contentious.[27] In some cases, the court will decline to grant a remedy. The court may hold, for example, that while the decision making process was defective, nevertheless the applicant has suffered no injustice, or that even if a remedy were granted, the decision maker would reach the same conclusion on the merits, or that the impact on administration would be too great if a remedy were granted.

Applying for leave for judicial review

It must be noted here that there is no unfettered right to judicial review. The aggrieved individual must seek leave to apply for judicial review, and a number of criteria, which are discussed below, govern the exercise of the discretion to grant or refuse the application for judicial review.

The requirement to seek leave for judicial review is controversial, and there are cogent arguments for its reform. For example, the JUSTICE-All Souls Report[28] argued for its repeal on the basis, first, that the leave requirement is discriminatory; secondly, that the justification for leave based on eliminating 'groundless, unmeritorious or tardy harassment' on the part of applicants can be dealt with in the same manner as in ordinary litigation;[29] and, thirdly, that the issue of standing is no longer finally determined at the stage at which the application for leave is considered; see further below. However, there is support for the view that, while the need to seek leave represents a procedural hurdle which does not exist in other areas of the law, there remains a need to filter out unmeritorious cases at an early stage. The Law Commission re-examined the question of application for leave and concluded that it remains 'essential to filter out hopeless applications for judicial review by a requirement such as leave'.[30]

When seeking leave to apply the application must be served on the defendant and unless the court orders otherwise, any person the claimant considers to be an interested party. Permission will be granted where an arguable case has been shown. If permission is refused the claimant can request reconsideration at a hearing. Further a dissatisfied claimant may apply to the Court of Appeal for permission to appeal against the refusal of permission.[31]

---

27 See Bingham, 1991.
28 *Administrative Law: Some Necessary Reforms*, 1988. See also Law Commission, *Administrative Law: Judicial Review and Statutory Appeals*, Consultation Paper No 226/HC 669.
29 As provided for by RSC Ord 18, r 19.
30 Law Commission, *Administrative Law: Judicial Review and Statutory Appeals*, Consultation Paper No 226/HC 669.
31 See Bridges, Meszaros and Sunkin, 2000 and Cornford and Sunkin, 2001.

THE CONCEPT OF JUSTICIABILITY

Justiciability is a concept which defines the judges' view of the suitability of the subject matter to be judicially reviewed. There are some matters in relation to which the courts – mindful of the doctrine of separation of powers – prove to be exceedingly reluctant to review. Matters such as the exercise of prerogative power and, most importantly, issues of national security, and matters of high policy, the courts may regard as non-justiciable.

Matters of public policy not for judicial review

Where a matter complained of involves issues of high policy, the courts will decline to exercise a supervisory function over such decisions. Matters of public policy are for determination by the executive, and not the judiciary, and any purported attempt to control the decision will be regarded as a violation of the separation of powers and an intrusion into the proper decision making sphere of the executive. For example, in *Nottinghamshire County Council v Secretary of State for the Environment* (1986), it was held that the court should not intervene to quash guidance drafted by the Secretary of State, on the authority of parliament, setting limits to public expenditure by local authorities. Lord Scarman ruled that:

> Unless and until a statute provides otherwise, or it is established that the Secretary of State has abused his power, these are matters of political judgment for him and for the House of Commons. They are not for the judges or your Lordships' House in its judicial capacity.

Similarly, in *Hammersmith and Fulham London Borough Council v Department of the Environment* (1991), concerning the lawfulness of 'charge capping' local authorities (penalising local authorities for exceeding their budgets), the House of Lords ruled that the decision was not open to challenge on the grounds of irrationality 'short of the extremes of bad faith, improper motive or manifest absurdity'. Lord Bridge went on to rule that such decisions, relating to national economic policy, 'are matters depending essentially on political judgment' and that, in the absence of any evidence of bad faith or abuse of power, the courts would be 'exceeding their proper function if they presumed to condemn the policy as unreasonable'. In *R v Parliamentary Commissioner for Administration ex parte Dyer* (1994), Simon Brown LJ held that matters of national policy were not open to challenge before the courts other than on the basis of bad faith, improper motive or manifest absurdity. Matters of national economic policy were for political – not judicial – judgment.

Judges also adopt a cautious attitude when it comes to reviewing the exercise of the royal prerogative and will decline so to do in particular where issues of national security are involved. Many of the matters which the courts regard as non-justiciable – that is to say, not within judicial competence to determine – fall within the royal prerogative. However, as discussed in Chapter 6, the courts will not decline to judicially review a matter simply because the source of the power exercised is the royal prerogative. The House of Lords made it clear in *Council of Civil Service Unions v Minister for Civil Service* (1985) that the source of the power was not determinative of whether the courts would review, but rather the matter to be decided was whether the subject matter of the application was justiciable or not.[32]

LIMITATIONS ON JUDICIAL REVIEW

It is a first principle of justice and the rule of law that public bodies are required to act within the scope of the powers allocated to them by parliament and, accordingly, in principle, judicial review should lie wherever the *vires* of administrative action is in question. However, that principle must be set in the balance against the needs of certain administration, and the necessary restrictions which may be imposed on individuals or bodies seeking to disrupt the administrative process, without good cause. The balance to be struck between these often competing principles is a difficult matter. Where parliament limits the availability of judicial review, the courts will adopt a restrictive interpretation to the statutory words, employing the presumption that parliament did not intend – save in the most express manner – to exclude the jurisdiction of the courts. A number of different statutory means are employed in the attempt to limit the availability of judicial review. In summary, parliament may adopt the following means:

(a) the general requirement that applications for judicial review are brought within three months of the challenged decision;

(b) clauses which are intended to prevent any challenge;

(c) clauses which are designed to limit review to a specified time period in relation to particular matters where delay needs to be avoided;

(d) 'conclusive evidence' clauses.

Attempts to exclude judicial review totally

In *R v Medical Appeal Tribunal ex parte Gilmore* (1957), the statute provided that 'the decision on any medical question by a medical appeal tribunal ... is final'. Under an industrial injuries scheme, compensation for accidental industrial injuries was set under a tariff. Gilmore went blind in both eyes in two accidents and was assessed at a disablement of 20 per cent. The tariff provided that the loss of sight in both eyes entitled the applicant to a 100 per cent assessment. The tribunal had, accordingly, made an error of law. However, the opportunity for the court to redress the wrong turned on the exclusion of review in the statute. The Court of Appeal held that the jurisdiction of the court was not ousted by the statutory words, Denning LJ stating that:

> ... the remedy of certiorari is never to be taken away by any statute except by the most clear and explicit words. The word 'final' is not enough. That only means 'without appeal'. It does not mean 'without recourse to certiorari'. It makes the decision final on the facts, but not final on the law. Notwithstanding that the decision is by a statute made 'final', certiorari can still issue for excess of jurisdiction or for error of law on the face of the record ... [p 583]

---

32 See also *Attorney General v de Keyser's Royal Hotel Ltd* (1920); *Laker Airways v Department of Trade* (1977); *R v Secretary of State for the Home Department ex parte Fire Brigades' Union* (1995); *M v Home Office* (1993).

However, in *South East Asia Firebricks v Non-Metallic Mineral Products Manufacturing Employees' Union* (1981), an 'ouster clause' succeeded. The Malaysian Industrial Court, in a successful legal challenge by trades unions, had ordered employers to take back employees after a strike. Statute[33] provided that an award of the court was 'final and conclusive' and that '... no award shall be challenged, appealed against, reviewed, quashed or called into question in any court of law'.

The Privy Council, citing *Gilmore* with approval, nevertheless distinguished between an error which affected the jurisdiction of the court to make a determination[34] and decisions which, whilst in error, were not of such a fundamental nature as to deprive the court of jurisdiction. In this case, the error was within the jurisdiction of the court and, accordingly, the ouster clause was effective. According to Lord Fraser of Tullybelton:

> ... the Industrial Court applied its mind to the proper question for the purpose of making its award. The award was accordingly within the jurisdiction of that court, and neither party has contended to the contrary ... the error or errors did not affect the jurisdiction of the Industrial Court and their Lordships are therefore of the opinion that section 29(3)(a) effectively ousted the jurisdiction of the High Court to quash the decision by certiorari proceedings ... [pp 373–74]

The seminal case on ouster clauses is *Anisminic v Foreign Compensation Commission* (1969). In 1956, property in Egypt belonging to an English company was sequestrated by the Egyptian authorities and subsequently sold to an Egyptian organisation, TEDO. Anisminic then sold to TEDO its mining business. In 1959, a Treaty signed by the United Kingdom and the United Arab Republic provided for the return of sequestrated property, other than property sequestrated in a period during which Anisminic's property was taken over. The Foreign Compensation Commission (FCC), established to make awards of compensation to companies adversely affected by sequestration of property, ruled that Anisminic did not qualify for compensation. The Foreign Compensation Order 1962,[35] Article 4(1)(b)(ii), provided that that both the applicant and the successor in title be British nationals. TEDO – the successor in title – was not a British national and, accordingly, Anisminic's claim failed. The Foreign Compensation Act 1950 provided that the decisions of the FCC 'shall not be called in question in any court of law'.[36]

Anisminic sought judicial review of the FCC's decision. The question for the court was whether the phrase 'shall not be questioned' succeeded in ousting the jurisdiction of the courts, or whether, notwithstanding that section, the courts had the power to rule on the lawfulness of the FCC's decision. The House of Lords ruled that the jurisdiction of the courts was not ousted. Accordingly the court had power to review the FCC's decision, which it declared to be null and void. The FCC had acted outside its jurisdiction by misinterpreting the Order in Council

---

33 Industrial Relations Act 1967, s 29(3)(a).
34 Relying on *Anisminic v Foreign Compensation Commission* (1968).
35 Egypt: Determination and Registration of Claims. An Order in Council.
36 Foreign Compensation Act 1950, s 4(4).

and reached a decision based on a ground which it was not entitled to take into account, namely the nationality of the successor in title. The nationality of the successor in title, according to the House of Lords, was not a relevant consideration when the applicant was the original owner of the sequestered property. The House of Lords ruled unanimously that section 4(4) did not protect decisions which were taken outside of jurisdiction.

The *Anisminic* decision raises complex issues. The House of Lords appeared to destroy the distinction between errors of law within the jurisdiction of the decision making body, which had previously been regarded as non-reviewable, and errors of law which took the decision maker outside its jurisdiction and were therefore reviewable. In effect, clauses which attempted to oust the jurisdiction of the courts appeared to have been rendered meaningless. The problem which remains is whether *Anisminic* provides clear guidelines as to how to distinguish between those elements of a tribunal's decision which, if decided incorrectly, cause the tribunal to exceed its jurisdiction, and those aspects of a tribunal's decision which, although decided incorrectly, do not cause the tribunal to exceed its jurisdiction – in other words the error is 'within jurisdiction'. The decision also reveals judicial emphasis on the rule of law – even in the face of apparently clear words that parliament does not intend review to take place. In the view of Wade and Forsyth (2004), the judges in *Anisminic* have ensured that the courts are 'the exclusive arbiters on all questions of law'.

In *Pearlman v Keepers and Governors of Harrow School* (1979), the Court of Appeal ruled that the misinterpretation of provisions in the Housing Act 1974 by the county court amounted to a 'jurisdictional error' which nullified the court's decision. Lord Denning MR stated that the distinction between errors which entail an excess of jurisdiction and an error made within jurisdiction should be abandoned.

The question of exactly which errors of law are 'jurisdictional' was considered in *Re Racal Communication Ltd* (1981). In *Racal*, the Director of Public Prosecutions (DPP) sought an order of the court[37] in order to obtain evidence relating to an alleged offence. The order was refused. Section 441(3) of the Companies Act provided that no appeal lay from a decision of the judge hearing the application. Nevertheless the DPP appealed, and the Court of Appeal allowed the appeal, relying on *Anisminic* and *Pearlman*. Lord Denning ruled that the 'no appeal' clause was of no effect, for the judge had misconstrued the words in section 411 of the Act. The House of Lords overturned the Court of Appeal's decision, approving of Geoffrey Lane LJ's dissenting judgment in *Pearlman*, in which he had held that the judge had done nothing which was outside his scope of inquiry. A distinction was drawn between errors made by a tribunal or other administrative bodies, which would be reviewable, and errors made by a court of law. Lord Diplock, in *Racal*, supported the view expressed by Lord Denning MR in *Pearlman*, stating:

> The breakthrough made by *Anisminic* was that, as respects administrative tribunals and authorities, the old distinction between errors of law that went to jurisdiction and errors of law that did not was for practical purposes abolished. [p 383]

---

37 Under the Companies Act 1948, s 411.

A further distinction, and limitation to the *Anisminic* principle, is to be seen in *R v Lord President of the Privy Council ex parte Page* (1992). There, the issue concerned a decision made by a university Visitor, and whether such a decision was reviewable on the basis of *Anisminic*. The House of Lords ruled that it was not. The powers of Visitors were established by the founder of the university, who had established a body of law and the office of Visitor to enforce that 'domestic' law. Accordingly, *per* Lord Browne-Wilkinson, the Visitor could not 'err in law in reaching his decision since the general law is not the applicable law'. Accordingly, the Visitor could not act *ultra vires* by applying his interpretation of the rules of the university. Jurisdiction to review did lie in cases where the Visitor acted outside his jurisdiction, or where he acted without regard to the rules of natural justice. However, there was no jurisdiction to review decisions taken within jurisdiction.

Time limits on judicial review

In the attempt to protect decisions from challenges which may impede or otherwise affect their implementation, statute may provide that there should be no challenge by way of judicial review other than within a specified time period. *Smith v East Elloe Rural District Council* (1956) illustrates the attitude of the courts to such time limits. In *Smith*, a challenge to the validity of a compulsory purchase order was limited, under statute, to a six week period following the date of confirmation of the order. If not challenged within that period the order 'shall not ... be questioned in any legal proceedings whatsoever'. Mrs Smith did not challenge the order within the time limit but, some six years later, sought to challenge the order on the basis that the clerk to the council had acted in bad faith, and that bad faith was a ground on which – despite the clear wording of the time limit in the statute – the order's validity could be impugned. The House of Lords, by a majority, rejected this view. It was, however, unanimously agreed that Mrs Smith could proceed against the clerk to the council for damages, on the basis of bad faith in procuring the order. Viscount Simonds explained the attitude of the court:

> My Lords, I think that anyone bred in the tradition of the law is likely to regard with little sympathy legislative provisions for ousting the jurisdiction of the court ... But it is our plain duty to give the words of an Act their proper meaning, and ... I find it quite impossible to qualify the words ... in the manner suggested ... What is abundantly clear is that words are used which are wide enough to cover any kind of challenge which an aggrieved person may think fit to make. I cannot think of any wider words ... I come, then to the conclusion that the court cannot entertain this action in so far as it impugns the validity of the compulsory purchase order ... [pp 750–52]

The Court of Appeal in *R v Secretary of State for the Environment ex parte Ostler* (1976) followed the reasoning in *Smith*. In *Ostler*, the Highways Act 1959[38] provided that an aggrieved person had the right to challenge the validity of a compulsory purchase order – on the basis of *ultra vires* – within six weeks from the date of publication of the order. Subject to that right, the order 'shall not be

---

38 Schedule 2, paras 2 and 3.

questioned in any legal proceedings whatsoever'. The proposed road building scheme had two stages. The first involved the acquisition of the land for the main road; the second related to the acquisition of land for the side roads which would give access to the main road. Two public inquiries were held, at the first of which there were allegations that an officer of the Department of the Environment had given assurances that vehicular access would be gained by a widening of the access road during the second phase of the development. Ostler's business would be affected by the widening of the access road, but he was unaware of the assurance allegedly given at the inquiry and did not challenge the decision. At the second inquiry, Ostler wished to object to the road widening, and wanted to give evidence that he would have objected at the first inquiry had he known of the secret undertaking. He was refused permission to give evidence on the basis that his objection related to the first stage of the development. Ostler subsequently learned of the undertakings and sought to challenge the compulsory order on the ground that natural justice had been denied and that the order had been made in bad faith amounting to fraud. The court accepted that, had Ostler challenged the order within six weeks, the court would have considered his complaint. The court was faced with the question of whether *Anisminic* applied, or whether the decision in *Smith v East Elloe* was the relevant precedent. Lord Denning MR considered the two precedent decisions and distinguished between them in three respects. First, the limitation in the *Smith* case amounted to a time limitation for review, as opposed to a purported total ouster of jurisdiction as in *Anisminic*. Secondly, the decision by the Foreign Compensation Board in *Anisminic* was a 'truly judicial' decision, whereas that in *Smith* was an administrative decision. Thirdly, in *Anisminic,* the court was required to consider the 'actual determination of the tribunal', whereas in *Smith* the court was considering the process by which the decision was reached. Lord Denning concluded:

> ... the policy of the 1959 Act is that when a compulsory purchase order has been made, then if it has been wrongly obtained or made, a person aggrieved should have a remedy. But he must come promptly. He must come within six weeks. If he does so, the court can and will entertain his complaint. But if the six weeks expire without any application being made, the court cannot entertain it afterwards. The reason is because, as soon as that time has elapsed, the authority will take steps to acquire property, demolish it and so forth. The public interest demand that they should be safe in doing so. [pp 95–96]

Exclusion of review by 'conclusive evidence clauses'

Parliament may effectively oust the jurisdiction of the courts by inserting a clause into statute which provides that a subordinate piece of legislation shall have effect 'as if enacted in this Act', or that confirmation of an order by a designated minister shall be 'conclusive evidence that the requirements of this Act have been complied with, and that the order has been duly made and is within the powers of this Act'. Such clauses were strongly criticised in 1932 by the Committee on Ministers' Powers[39] but, nevertheless, they continue to be used and have been effective in ousting judicial review. In *R v Registrar of Companies ex parte Central*

---

39 Cmd 4060, 1932, London: HMSO.

Bank of India (1986), for example, a clause in the Companies Act 1985 effectively ousted the jurisdiction of the courts. Nevertheless, the potential for their use, and their effectiveness, provides the basis for a damaging exclusion of judicial review.

THE BASIS FOR JUDICIAL REVIEW

The Supreme Court Act 1981

The basis for review today lies in section 31 of the Supreme Court Act 1981 and the Civil Procedure Rules 1998.

> Section 31 provides, in part, that:
>
> (1) An application to the High Court for one or more of the following forms of relief, namely:
>   (a) an order of mandamus, prohibition or certiorari;
>   (b) a declaration or injunction under sub-section (2); or
>   (c) an injunction under section 30 restraining a person not entitled to do so from acting in an office to which that section applies,
>
>   shall be made in accordance with rules of court by a procedure to be known as an application for judicial review.
>
> (2) A declaration may be made or an injunction granted under this subsection in any case where an application for judicial review, seeking that relief, has been made and the High Court considers that, having regard to:
>   (a) the nature of the matters in respect of which relief may be granted by orders of mandamus, prohibition or certiorari;
>   (b) the nature of the persons and bodies against whom relief may be granted by such orders; and
>   (c) all the circumstances of the case,
>
>   it would be just and convenient for the declaration to be made or for the injunction to be granted, as the case may be.
>
> (3) No application for judicial review shall be made unless the leave of the High Court has been obtained in accordance with rules of court; and the court shall not grant leave to make such an application unless it considers that the applicant has a sufficient interest in the matter to which the application relates.

Under the Civil Procedure Rules 1998, an action must be brought within three months of the decision against which review is sought. However, shorter time periods may be specified in statute and these must be complied with.

STANDING TO APPLY FOR JUDICIAL REVIEW

The 'sufficient interest' test[40]

The Supreme Court Act 1981 provides that the court must not grant leave for an application for judicial review 'unless it considers that the applicant has a sufficient interest [otherwise expressed as "standing" or *locus standi*] in the matter to which the application relates'. The justification for such a requirement lies in the need to limit challenges to administrative decision making to genuine cases of

---

40   Supreme Court Act 1981, s 31(3).

grievance and to avoid unnecessary interference in the administrative process by those whose objectives are not authentic. The applicant may be an individual whose personal rights and interests have been affected by a decision, or an individual concerned with official decisions which affect the interests of society as a whole. Alternatively, the application may be brought by an interest or pressure group desiring to challenge a decision which affects the rights and interests of members of that group or society at large.

The manner in which the test is applied

The test of 'sufficient interest' was provided in *R v Inland Revenue Commissioners ex parte National Federation of Self-Employed and Small Businesses* (1982). The House of Lords' approach was as follows. The question of whether there is standing should be examined in two stages. At the first instance, standing should be considered when leave to apply is sought. At that stage, the court is concerned, according to Lord Scarman, to ensure that 'it prevents abuse by busybodies, cranks and other mischief makers'. If leave is granted, the court may – at a second stage, when the merits of the case are known – revise its original decision and decide that after all the applicants do not have sufficient interest. The effect of this is to reduce the issue of sufficient interest and to elevate the question of the merits of the case.

Individual standing: personal rights and interests

Given the breadth of administrative decision making in a heavily regulated society, individuals may have their rights or expectations affected in multifarious ways, as has been seen above. Two further examples from the case law illustrate the concept of individual standing. In *Schmidt v Secretary of State for Home Affairs* (1969), students who had entered the country as 'students of scientology' challenged the decision of the Home Office not to allow them to remain once the permitted period of stay had expired. The students had a 'legitimate expectation' (see below) that they would be allowed to make representations to the Home Office, which they were denied, over a matter affecting their individual liberty. The students had 'sufficient interest' for leave to be granted.

In the case of *R v Secretary of State for the Environment ex parte Ward* (1984) a Gypsy living on a caravan site was held to have standing to apply for an order requiring that the Secretary of State should direct the local authority to fulfil its statutory duty to provide an adequate site. Standing was also granted to Mrs Gillick, the mother of several daughters, who wished to challenge a Health Authority over its policy relating to contraception for young girls,[41] and to a journalist acting in the public interest.[42] By contrast, in *Holmes v Checkland* (1987) an opponent of cigarette smoking was deemed not to have standing to seek to restrain the BBC from broadcasting a snooker championship sponsored by a tobacco company on the ground that he had no more interest than any other

---

41 *Gillick v West Norfolk and Wisbech Area Health Authority* (1986).
42 *R v Felixstowe Judges ex p Leigh* (1987).

member of the public and accordingly could only proceed with the aid of the Attorney-General.[43]

In *R v Secretary of State for Foreign and Commonwealth Affairs ex parte Rees-Mogg* (1994), the applicant sought judicial review of the government's ratification of the Treaty on European Union without parliamentary consent. Rees-Mogg was held to have sufficient standing, but the application was dismissed on the basis that the issue was non-justiciable.[44]

The Human Rights Act 1998 introduced a new basis for 'standing'. Section 7 of the Act provides that only a 'victim' of an act of a public body may make a claim. That test – which is the same as the test applied under the European Convention on Human Rights – is narrower than standing in other judicial review proceedings. It also excludes representative bodies and interest groups taking action on behalf of their members.

The standing of interest and pressure groups

Actions in defence of the group's own interests

A group may have its interests adversely affected by administrative decision making. By way of illustration, in *R v Liverpool Corporation ex parte Liverpool Taxi Fleet Operators' Association* (1972), Liverpool Corporation had the duty of licensing taxis and fixing the number of licences to be granted. When the Corporation announced that the number of licences was to be increased, without consulting the Operators' Association, leave to apply for judicial review was sought. The Association had sufficient standing. Equally, in *Royal College of Nursing v Department for Health and Social Security* (1981), the Royal College had standing to challenge a departmental circular concerning the role of nurses in abortions.

Both these cases involve organisations seeking to challenge decisions which affect their own members. Accordingly, the standing requirement is relatively easy to satisfy, since each of their members would have individual standing. The position is less straightforward where a group seeks to defend what it regards as the wider interests of society.

The standing of interest and pressure groups acting in the public interest

Inland Revenue Commissioners v National Federation of Self-Employed and Small Businesses (1982) provided the test for standing. The facts, in brief, entailed the employment of casual labour on newspapers, where the workers frequently adopted false names and paid no income tax. The Inland Revenue Commissioners (IRC) entered into an agreement with the relevant trades unions, workers and employers to the effect that if the workers filled in tax returns for the previous two years, the IRC would not pursue tax due for previous years. The National Federation (an association of taxpayers) argued that the IRC had no power to enter into this agreement and sought judicial review. The IRC defended the action on the

---

43   Note that the Attorney General's decision whether to bring a relator action cannot be challenged in court: *Gouriet v Union of Post Office Workers* (1978).

44   For the meaning of 'justiciability', see above. See also *Blackburn v Attorney General* (1971), wherein a challenge to accession to the Treaty of Rome was unsuccessful.

basis that the National Federation did not have sufficient interest – or standing (*locus standi*) – to apply for judicial review. The court upheld the IRC's claim. The House of Lords ruled that the court had been correct in granting leave at the first stage, but that on the facts – the second stage – the National Federation lacked sufficient interest to challenge the legality of the agreement. The House of Lords ruled that there was no standing to challenge the particular wrongdoing alleged but that, if the Revenue had in fact been acting with impropriety, there would have been standing in a taxpayer to challenge its unlawful acts. In *R v Her Majesty's Treasury ex parte Smedley* (1985), the applicant for review sought to challenge the decision of the Treasury to pay a sum of money from the Consolidated Fund, without express parliamentary approval, to meet European Community obligations. Smedley was thus applying in his own interest and in the interests of all British taxpayers and electors.[45] The court held that he had standing, although the challenge failed on its merits. A case to be distinguished from the *National Federation* case is that of *R v Attorney General ex parte ICI plc* (1986). The application was based on a complaint that four competitor companies had been assessed at too lenient a rate, contrary to the Oil Taxation Act 1975. The court held that the company had standing: it had a genuine and substantial complaint.

The judges are, however, not united in their approach to the 'sufficient interest' test, which confers on the courts a great deal of discretion. In *R v Secretary of State for the Environment ex parte Rose Theatre Trust Company Ltd* (1990), Schiemann J cited a number of propositions which he deduced from the *IRC* case. The *Rose Theatre* case concerned the question of whether a company which had been incorporated for the purpose of campaigning to save the historic Globe Theatre site in London had sufficient interest, or *locus standi*. Included in the guidelines were that the question of whether sufficient interest exists is not purely a matter within the discretion of the court; that sufficient interest did not necessarily entail a direct financial or legal interest; that the assertion of an interest by a person or a group does not mean that sufficient interest exists; and that, even where thousands of people joined together in a campaign, that was not conclusive that sufficient interest existed. The court ruled that the company did not have sufficient interest. However, in *R v Poole Borough Council ex parte BeeBee* (1991), the same judge ruled that two pressure groups, the World Wildlife Fund (WWF) and the British Heperetological Society (BHS), had sufficient interest to challenge a decision of the Council which had granted planning permission to itself for the development of a heathland with designated 'special scientific interest' status. The BHS had a financial interest in the site, and the WWF had undertaken to pay any legal costs if necessary.[46]

A liberal approach to sufficient interest was also taken in *R v Secretary of State for the Environment ex parte Greenpeace Ltd (No 2)* (1994). Greenpeace applied for judicial review to challenge the decision of the Inspectorate of Pollution to allow the siting of a nuclear reprocessing plant (THORP) at Sellafield. It was held that the Inspectorate had not abused its powers in varying British Nuclear Fuel plc's licence. However, while Greenpeace lost the case, the court nevertheless ruled

---

45　*Per* Sir John Donaldson MR.
46　But for another decision denying sufficient interest to interest groups see *R v Darlington Borough Council ex parte Association of Darlington Taxi Owners* (1994).

that Greenpeace did have standing to challenge the decision. It was in the interests of justice to allow Greenpeace – an organisation with over 400,000 supporters in the United Kingdom – to bring an action on behalf of all concerned with the project. The court declined to follow the *Rose Theatre* decision, but warned that it should not be assumed that Greenpeace or other pressure groups would automatically be held to have sufficient interest in any future case.

Further cases involving successful challenges by pressure groups include *R v Secretary of State for Foreign and Commonwealth Affairs ex parte World Development Movement Ltd* (1995), *R v Secretary of State for Employment ex parte Equal Opportunities Commission* (1995) (the *EOC* case) and *R v Secretary of State for the Environment ex parte the Royal Society for the Protection of Birds* (the *RSPB* case) (1995). In the first case, the World Development Movement (WDM) sought judicial review of the Foreign Secretary's decision to grant financial aid to Malaysia for the building of the Pergau dam. The WDM argued that the Secretary of State had exceeded his powers. The court held that the WDM had sufficient interest. The WDM played a prominent role in giving advice and assistance in relation to aid and had consultative status with the United Nation's bodies. Further, it was unlikely that there would be any other person or body with sufficient interest to challenge the decision. In the *EOC* case, the Equal Opportunities Commission (EOC) sought a declaration that the United Kingdom was in breach of European Community law obligations in relation to Article 119 (now Article 141) of the EC Treaty and the Equal Pay and Equal Treatment Directives of the Community. The alleged breach concerned the Employment Protection (Consolidation) Act 1978, which discriminated between full time and part time employees in relation to redundancy pay and compensation for unfair dismissal. The House of Lords confirmed that the EOC had sufficient interest and, moreover, that English law was incompatible with the requirements of European Community law. In the *RSPB* case, the Royal Society had sufficient interest to challenge the decision of the Secretary of State's decision affecting the development of land which had hitherto been a special site for the conservation of birds.

THE EXISTENCE OF ALTERNATIVE REMEDIES

The availability of alternative remedies is a relevant factor in deciding whether leave will be granted for judicial review. In *R v Inland Revenue Commissioners ex parte Preston* (1985), Lord Templeman stated that leave for an application for judicial review should not be granted 'where an alternative remedy was available'. Thus, by way of example, where parliament has set up under statute a comprehensive appeals structure, judicial review cannot be used as a means of circumventing this.[47] Moreover, the statutory rights of appeal must be exhausted.[48] If, however, there are exceptional circumstances – for example if inordinate delays are experienced in the proceedings – the court may grant leave to apply for judicial review.[49]

---

47 *R v Secretary of State for Social Services ex parte Connolly* (1986).
48 *R v Secretary of State for the Home Department ex parte Swati* (1986).
49 *R v Chief Constable of Merseyside Police ex parte Calveley* (1986).

A MATTER OF PUBLIC – NOT PRIVATE – LAW

Judicial review is confined to matters of public – as opposed to private – law. The courts will not seize jurisdiction to review an administrative action or decision if the matter involved is one of private law. Accordingly, the respondent must be a public authority, and the right at issue must be a public right. If the matter is one of public law, the aggrieved person must apply by way of judicial review and not under any other procedure.

The 'exclusivity principle'

In *O'Reilly v Mackman* (1983), the applicants had taken part in a prison riot at Hull gaol and the Board of Visitors (who exercise disciplinary powers over prisoners) reduced the remission of sentence as punishment. The applicants tried to establish that the Board of Visitors had acted contrary to the rules of natural justice. This they attempted to do by means of an originating summons or writ.[50] It was not contested that the issue was a matter of public law and that they could have employed the judicial review procedure, provided that they applied for leave within the requisite three months. No leave from the court is needed in relation to private law proceedings. The issue for the court was whether it was an abuse of the process of the court to use the alternative basis to bring the action. Lord Diplock stated:

> If what should emerge is that his complaint is not of an infringement of any of his rights that are entitled to protection in public law, but may be an infringement of his rights in private law and this is not a proper subject for judicial review, the court has power under rule 9(5), instead of refusing the application, to order the proceedings to continue as if they had begun by writ ... [pp 283–84]

Referring to the procedural disadvantages which had existed prior to the reforms introduced in 1977 by Order 53,[51] Lord Diplock went on to state:

> ... now that those disadvantages to applicants have been removed and all remedies for infringement of rights protected by public law can be obtained upon an application for judicial review, as also can remedies for infringements of rights under private law if such infringement should also be involved, it would in my view as a general rule be contrary to public policy, and as such an abuse of the process of the court to permit a person seeking to establish that a decision of a public authority infringed rights to which he was entitled to protection under public law to proceed by way of an ordinary action and by this means evade the provisions of Order 53 for the protection of such authorities. [p 285]

The decision in *O'Reilly* has been trenchantly criticised by Professor HWR Wade.[52] The 'exclusivity principle' – keeping public and private law rigidly distinct – was introduced by Lord Diplock in *O'Reilly*, notwithstanding the Law Commission's intention that procedural reforms introduced in 1977 were not intended to create a rigid distinction between public and private law

---

50 The means by which private law proceedings are initiated.
51 Now replaced by the Civil Procedure Rules 1998.
52 Wade and Forsyth, 2004.

proceedings.[53] Before that time, although the distinction between public and private law was drawn, the system was not exclusive. Professor Wade regards the exclusivity principle, declared in *O'Reilly*, as amounting to a 'serious setback for administrative law'. He goes on to state that:

> ... it has caused many cases, which on their merits might have succeeded, to fail merely because of choice of the wrong form of action ... It has produced great uncertainty, which seems likely to continue, as to the boundary between public and private law, since these terms have no clear or settled meaning ... [Wade and Forsyth, 1994, p 682]

Professor Wade regards this as an unnecessary restriction on access to the courts, a restriction which has been avoided in Scotland, Australia, New Zealand and Canada. His assessment of the House of Lords' decision in *O'Reilly* is that:

> ... the House of Lords has expounded the new law as designed for the protection of public authorities rather than of the citizen. Such are the misfortunes which can flow from the best intentioned reforms.

Exceptions to the exclusivity principle

The harshness with which the exclusivity principle could operate led Lord Diplock in *O'Reilly* to state that exceptions to the rule would exist where the case involved both public and private law elements, particularly where the public law element was collateral (auxiliary or secondary) to the private law element. What is evident in this matter is that a balance needs to be struck between too rigid a rule, which denies individuals the protection of judicial review, and too lax an approach, which would enable individuals either to pursue a remedy in judicial review when other procedures are in fact more appropriate or, conversely, to pursue other remedies when judicial review would be appropriate, in order to evade the requirements of judicial review. It is also evident that the judges are struggling to find the correct balance.

A public law issue used in defence in private law proceedings

In *Wandsworth London Borough Council v Winder* (1985), the House of Lords allowed a matter of public law (the lawfulness of the council's decision) to be used as a defence to private law proceedings (possession proceedings). Winder was a tenant of the local authority, which gave notice that rents were to be raised. Winder claimed that the increase was unreasonable and contrary to law. The local authority brought an action for possession of the premises. Winder defended this action on the basis that the rent increase was outside the powers of the local authority and void for unreasonableness. On appeal to the House of Lords, the question for the court was whether Winder could challenge the local authority's action by way of a defence based on judicial review grounds, or whether he should have instigated separate judicial review proceedings by way of an application to the High Court. The local authority submitted that Winder should have used judicial review but that, since he was by then out of time to do so, he

---

53   Cmnd 6407, 1976, London: HMSO.

could not challenge their decision by way of a defence to the possession proceedings.

Lord Fraser of Tullybelton, citing *O'Reilly*, acknowledged that it was in the interests of good administration to protect authorities from unmeritorious or late challenges, but that this factor had to be weighed in the balance against the argument for preserving the ordinary rights of private citizens to defend themselves against unfounded claims. In his opinion, Winder's action could not be described as an abuse of the process of the court. Winder had not selected the procedure, he was merely seeking to defend himself. If the public interest required that people should not have the right to defend themselves, then that was a matter for parliament, not the courts.

Cases involving both public and private law issues

In *Roy v Kensington and Chelsea and Westminster Family Practitioner Committee* (1992) a further exception to the exclusivity principle emerged, whereby the House of Lords ruled that the principle did not apply where the proceedings involved matters of both public and private law. In *Roy*, a Family Practitioner Committee was responsible for making payments to general practitioners in respect of their National Health Service work.[54] Dr Roy's allowance was reduced by the committee on the basis that he had reduced the amount of his time spent on National Health Service work. Dr Roy litigated to recover the sum reduced. At first instance, the judge decided that the decision to reduce his payments was a matter of public law to be challenged under judicial review proceedings. On appeal to the House of Lords, it was held that, when a litigant had a private law right – in relation to a matter which involved an issue of public law – he was not precluded from pursuing his private law right. Accordingly, the fact that the public law issue could have been determined under judicial review proceedings was not held to deny him a remedy under private law. In *Andreou v Institute of Chartered Accountants in England and Wales* (1998), the applicant had been granted leave to bring judicial review to challenge the validity of a bylaw of the Chartered Institute, but failed to observe the time limit. He then commenced a private law action alleging breach of contractual duty to exercise its bylaw making powers fairly and to act fairly in its disciplinary proceedings. The Court of Appeal ruled that the Institute was, in part, a public body. However, here it was appropriate to proceed under private law since there was a private law right at issue, even though there was also a public law issue involved.

In *R v Peter Edward Wicks* (1997), the House of Lords ruled that the validity of an enforcement notice under the Town and Country Planning Act 1990 could not be impugned in criminal proceedings, but only by the High Court on an application for judicial review. The defendant appealed against the Court of Appeal decision dismissing his appeal against conviction for failure to comply with the enforcement notice. So long as the enforcement notice was not a nullity or patently defective on its face, it was valid and would remain so until quashed. No criminal court had the power to quash, and it was not open to the defence to

---

54 Under the National Health Service (General Medical and Pharmaceutical) Regulations 1974.

go behind the notice and seek to investigate its validity. The proper course to take was to apply for an adjournment of the criminal proceedings and apply to the High Court for judicial review in which the validity of the notice could be attacked.[55]

A challenge to the *vires* of subordinate legislation or an administrative act can be raised in criminal proceedings. The House of Lords so held in *Boddington v British Transport Police* (1998). The defendant, in criminal proceedings on charges of smoking a cigarette in a railway carriage where smoking was prohibited, sought to argue that the Network South Central's decision to post notices banning smoking was *ultra vires* its powers to bring the relevant bylaw into force. On appeal, the court had ruled that it was not open to the defendant to raise that public law defence in criminal proceedings against him. The House of Lords, however, stated that a defendant was so entitled, and that if the defendant managed to rebut the presumption in favour of the lawfulness of the subordinate legislation or administrative act, the legislation or act had no legal effect at all and could not found a prosecution. In the instant case, there was nothing in the bylaws or the relevant Act to rebut the presumption that the defendant was entitled to defend himself against a criminal charge on the basis of the validity of the decision to put no smoking notices in carriages. However, the manner in which the relevant bylaw had been brought into force was not *ultra vires* and accordingly the appeal was dismissed.

Broad versus restrictive approaches to standing

O'Reilly and *Winder* were both considered extensively in *Roy v Kensington and Chelsea and Westminster Family Practitioner Committee* (above), in which Lord Lowry examined the 'broad' or 'liberal' approach to judicial review and the 'narrow' or 'restrictive' approach. A broad approach lessens the importance of the distinction between public and private law and would allow either the Order 53 procedure to be used or the pursuit of a private law remedy. A narrow approach, however, would dictate that if the matter is primarily a matter of private law then the judicial review procedure is inappropriate. While Lord Lowry 'disclaimed any intention of discussing the scope of the rule in *O'Reilly*', he nevertheless went on to make a case for a more liberal approach. Lord Lowry stated that:

> ... the Law Commission, when recommending the new judicial review procedure, contemplated the continued co-existence of judicial review proceedings and actions for a declaration with regard to public law issues ...

> ... this House has expressly approved actions for a declaration of nullity as alternative to applications for certiorari to quash, where private law rights were concerned: *Wandsworth London Borough Council v Winder* (1992), p 655, *per* Robert Goff LJ.

Citing Goff LJ, Lord Lowry continued:

> The principle remains in fact that public authorities and public servants are, unless clearly exempted, answerable in the ordinary courts for wrongs done to individuals.

---

55 See also *Steed v Secretary of State for the Home Department* (2000); *R v Falmouth and Truro Port Health Authority ex parte Southwest Water Ltd* (2000); *Wandsworth LBC v A* (2001).

> But by an extension of remedies and a flexible procedure it can be said that something resembling a system of public law is being developed. Before the expression 'public law' can be used to deny a subject a right of action in the court of his choice it must be related to a positive prescription of law, by statute or by statutory rules. We have not yet reached the point at which mere characterisation of a claim as a claim in public law is sufficient to exclude it from consideration by the ordinary courts: to permit this would be to create a dual system of law with the rigidity and procedural hardship for plaintiffs which it was the purpose of the recent reforms to remove': *Davy v Spelthorn Borough Council* (1984), *per* Lord Wilberforce.

> In conclusion, my Lords, it seems to me that, unless the procedure adopted by the moving party is ill suited to dispose of the question at issue, there is much to be said in favour of the proposition that a court having jurisdiction ought to let a case be heard rather than entertain a debate concerning the form of the proceedings.

Lord Slynn advanced the argument for a more flexible approach to the choice of proceedings in *Mercury Communications Ltd v Director General of Telecommunications* (1996). In that case, the effect of *O'Reilly v Mackman* was further limited. A dispute arose between Mercury Communications and British Telecom (BT), both of which are public limited companies licenced by the Secretary of State under the Telecommunications Act 1984. Mercury Communications was dependent upon the rental of part of BT's network. The Director General, exercising powers under the 1984 Act, determined the dispute, and his decision affected the terms of the contract between Mercury and BT. Mercury initiated private proceedings in the Commercial Court by originating summons. At first instance, the Director General and BT failed to have the proceeding struck out, the court applying the *O'Reilly* principle. On appeal, however, it was argued, successfully, that this was an abuse of process. The case went to the House of Lords, which reversed the decision of the Court of Appeal. Lord Slynn emphasised that when determining the issue of the choice of private or public law proceedings, flexibility must be retained. It was recognised that the Director General had statutory functions and performed public duties. However, this did not eliminate the possibility of private law proceedings. Since the Director General's decision had been imposed as part of a contract, this could be regarded as a contractual dispute. Accordingly, the commencement of private law proceedings was equally well suited to determine the issue as judicial review proceedings. The issue of the appropriateness of proceedings was a matter to be determined by the courts on a case by case basis. Lord Slynn stated that:

> ... when it comes to a question of striking out for abuse of process of the court the discretion exercised by the trial judge should stand unless the arguments are clearly and strongly in favour of a different result to that to which he has come. [p 59]

The House of Lords reconsidered the question of the appropriate form of proceedings once more in *O'Rourke v Camden London Borough Council* (1997). In this case, the plaintiff had applied to the local authority for accommodation, under the Housing Act 1985, on his release from prison. Section 63(1) of the Housing Act provides that a local authority is under a duty to provide accommodation in respect of those who are 'homeless and [have] a priority need', and that includes persons who are 'vulnerable as a result of ... physical disability or other special reason'. Initially, the authority refused him accommodation, but subsequently provided accommodation for a 12 day period, after which the plaintiff was evicted and no alternative accommodation offered. The plaintiff brought a private action against the council for wrongful eviction without providing alternative accommodation, and claimed damages. The House of Lords ruled that the question of whether section 63 of the Housing Act gave rise to public or private law proceedings depended on the intention of parliament. The duty to provide accommodation was a matter of public law and the Act 'was a scheme of social welfare, intended on grounds of public policy and public interest to confer benefits at the public expense not only for the private benefit of people who found themselves homeless but also for the benefit of society in general'. The provision of accommodation, and the type of accommodation, was 'largely dependent on the housing authority's judgment and discretion'. Accordingly, it was 'unlikely' that parliament had intended section 63 to give rise to a private action.

The issue of the choice between public and private proceedings returned to the courts in *Trustees of the Dennis Rye Pension Fund v Sheffield City Council* (1997). The plaintiffs were required by the local council to carry out repairs to certain houses to make them fit for human habitation,[56] and applied for improvement grants from the council under the Local Government and Housing Act 1989. When the work was complete, the council refused to pay the grant, on the basis that, *inter alia*, the repairs had not been carried out to the required standard. The plaintiff then commenced private law proceedings for recovery of the money due. The council, however, argued that if there were any grounds for complaint, the appropriate process was an application for judicial review. Accordingly, the council sought to have the plaintiff's claim struck out, on the grounds that the private law proceedings were an abuse of process. The issue went to the Court of Appeal. Lord Woolf MR regretted that the 'tactical' issue of the choice of proceedings had inevitably led to very substantial costs being incurred 'to little or no purpose'. He further criticised the narrow approach taken by the House of Lords in *O'Rourke v Camden London Borough Council*.

The Court of Appeal considered the choice between judicial review proceedings and other legal action against a public authority. In determining that question, the court should not be overly concerned with the distinction between public and private rights, but look to the practical consequences of pursuing the alternative actions. The court accepted that when a council was performing its role in relation to the making of grants, it was performing a public function which did not give rise to private rights. If the choice made had 'no significant disadvantages' for the parties, the public or the courts, it should not normally be regarded as an abuse of process. The court applied *O'Reilly v Mackman* (1982) and *Roy v Kensington and Chelsea and Westminster Family Practitioner Committee* (1992). Lord Woolf MR, after a consideration of these and other cases, ruled that as a general rule it is contrary to public policy, and as a result an abuse of the process of the court:

---

56 Under the Housing Act 1989, s 189.

... to permit a person seeking to establish that a decision of a public authority infringed rights to which he was entitled to protection under public law to proceed by way of an ordinary action and by this means to evade the provisions of Order 53 for the protection of such authorities.

However, Lord Woolf made three 'pragmatic suggestions' and stated that it is to be remembered that:

If it is not clear whether judicial review or an ordinary action is the correct procedure it will be safer to make an application for judicial review than commence an ordinary action since there then should be no question of being treated as abusing the process of the court by avoiding the protection provided by judicial review ...

If a case is brought by an ordinary action and there is an application to strike out the case, the court should, at least if it is unclear whether the case should have been brought by judicial review, ask itself whether, if the case had been brought by judicial review when the action was commenced, it is clear leave would have been granted. If it would, then that is at least an indication that there has been no harm to the interests judicial review is designed to protect ...

Finally, in cases where it is unclear whether proceedings have been correctly brought by an ordinary action, it should be remembered that, after consulting the Crown Office, a case can always be transferred to the Crown Office List as an alternative to being struck out.[57]

The more liberal approach to procedure was evident in *Clark v University of Lincolnshire and Humberside* (2000) in which a student sued her University for breach of contract after having been failed in her examination following unproven allegations of plagiarism. She was outside the three month time limit for judicial review and the University argued that this would have been the appropriate form of proceeding. The Court of Appeal disagreed, stating that the distinction between judicial review and private actions was now limited and that a claim would not be struck out on the basis that the applicant had proceeded under contract rather than judicial review.

It must also be recognised that the courts are keen to ensure that the parties have made use of any alternative suitable remedies. In the case of *R (Cowl) v Plymouth City Council (Practice Note)* (2001) the Court of Appeal was critical of litigation which raised to no point of legal principle but which the claimants nevertheless appealed against the decision of the Council. Lord Woolf CJ, having reviewed the facts and the alternative remedy of having the matter determined by a complaints panel stated that:

The courts should not permit, except for good reason, proceedings for judicial review to proceed if a significant part of the issues are limited. If subsequently it becomes apparent that there is a legal issue to be resolved, that can thereafter be examined by the courts which may be considerably assisted by the findings made by the complaints panel.

This case will have served some purpose if it makes clear that the lawyers acting on both sides of a dispute of this sort are under a heavy obligation to resort to litigation only if it is really unavoidable. If they cannot resolve the whole of the dispute by the use

---

57 *Trustees of the Dennis Rye Pension Fund v Sheffield City Council* (1997), p 755.

of the complaints procedure they should resolve the dispute so far as is practicable without involving litigation.[58]

REMEDIES[59]

Introduction

The granting of a remedy in judicial review proceedings is at the discretion of the court. Even where the applicant establishes his or her case, the court may refuse a remedy if there has been a delay in commencing proceedings, or if the applicant has acted unreasonably, or where the public interest in efficient administration could be damaged by the granting of a remedy. The available remedies under public law are the 'prerogative remedies': quashing orders, prohibiting orders and mandatory orders. In addition, under private law there are the remedies of declaration and injunction, which may also be granted under judicial review proceedings.

Quashing order (formerly certiorari)

This remedy overlaps with that of prohibition (below). A quashing order is one which 'quashes', or sets aside as a nullity, the original decision: accordingly it is both negative and retrospective in nature: *R v Criminal Injuries Compensation Board ex parte Lain* (1967); *O'Reilly v Mackman* (1983). The classic *dictum* is that of Lord Atkin:[60]

> ... whenever any body of persons having legal authority to determine questions affecting the rights of subjects, and having the duty to act judicially, act in excess of their legal authority, they are subject to the controlling jurisdiction of the King's Bench Division exercised in these writs.

If only part of a decision is *ultra vires* that part may be severed from the good and the order of certiorari granted to quash the bad part of the decision. A quashing order is similar to a prohibiting order, the quashing order operating retrospectively, the prohibiting order operating prospectively.

Prohibiting order (formerly prohibition)

Prohibition is an order which prevents a body from making a decision which would be capable of being quashed by certiorari. It is thus protective in nature. Neither quashing orders nor prohibiting orders lie against decisions of the higher courts.

Lord Atkin explained the relationship between certiorari and prohibition in the *London Electricity case*:[61]

---

58   *R (Cowl) v Plymouth City Council (Practice Note)*, paras 14 and 27.
59   The orders were renamed under the Civil Procedure Rules 1998, r 54.1. See Oliver, 2001.
60   *R v Electricity Commissioners ex parte London Electricity Joint Committee Company (1920) Ltd* (1924).
61   *Ibid* [1924] 1 KB 171 at p 206.

> I see no difference in principle between certiorari and prohibition, except that the latter may be invoked at an earlier stage. If the proceedings establish that the body complained of is exceeding its jurisdiction by entertaining matters which would result in its final decision being subject to being brought up and quashed on certiorari, I think that prohibition will lie to restrain it from exceeding its jurisdiction.

Prohibition will prevent a public body from acting unlawfully in the future. It may also be used to prevent a body from implementing a decision which has already been taken which was itself *ultra vires*. A failure to comply with an order amounts to a contempt of court.

Mandatory order (formerly mandamus)

This order is one which compels an authority to act. A mandatory order does not lie against an authority which has complete discretion to act. A failure to comply with the order amounts to a contempt of court. Mandatory orders do lie against the Crown, and may be used to enforce action by a minister or official, as for example in *Padfield v Minister of Agriculture Fisheries and Food* (1968) in which a minister was compelled to refer a complaint to a statutory committee.

Whereas prohibition prevents a future unlawful act, a mandatory order prevents an unlawful failure to act. Whenever a public body is under a duty to act, and fails to comply with that duty, a citizen with sufficient interest may seek an order which compels the authority to act. A mandatory order and a quashing order may work together. For example, if an authority has abused its power, a quashing order may be issued together with a mandatory order requiring the authority to act according to law. On the other hand, a mandatory order alone implies that the authority has acted *ultra vires* and therefore operates like a quashing order to nullify the defective decision.

Declarations

A declaration is a statement of the legal position of the parties, and is not accordingly a remedy *per se*. Although lacking coercive force, public bodies will respond to a declaration and comply with its terms by rectifying its actions. Declarations are available against the Crown.

Injunctions

Injunctions may be interim or permanent, and positive or negative. Injunctions may be used to prevent a minister or administrative body from acting unlawfully. In *M v Home Office* (1993), the House of Lords held that injunctions could lie against ministers of the Crown, and that breach of an injunction could lead to a minister, in his official capacity as representative of the Crown, being held in contempt of court. See further Chapters 6 and 11.

Damages

An applicant for judicial review may be awarded damages in conjunction with one of the other remedies. Damages will only be awarded if they would have been recoverable had the applicant begun an action by writ (that is, a private law action).

DEFAULT POWERS

Statute may provide that a minister has powers to act in order to oblige a decision making body to comply with their statutory duty. For example, section 9 of the Caravan Sites Act 1968 provided that the Secretary of State had the power to give directions to local authorities to comply with their statutory duty to provide adequate sites for Gypsies residing in, or resorting to their area.[62] Other examples of similar powers are found in the Public Health Act 1936, the Education Act 1944, the National Health Service Act 1977, the Housing Act 1985, the Local Government Act 1985 and the Town and Country Planning Act 1990. In respect of the Housing Act provisions, in *R v Secretary of State for the Environment ex parte Norwich City Council* (1982), the Secretary of State had the power to act as he 'thinks necessary' to ensure that tenants are able to exercise their 'right to buy' from local authorities. His failure to enforce the local authorities' duty was itself subject to the control of the courts through judicial review. Default powers are a backstop, but an important weapon in ensuring that local authorities and other bodies comply with the requirements of statute.

Remedies and the Human Rights Act 1998

Section 8 of the Human Rights Act 1998 authorises a court to 'grant such relief or remedy, or make such order, within its powers as it considers just and appropriate'. Accordingly, any remedies which a particular court may award are available for breaches of Convention rights. Declarations, damages, injunctions or the prerogative orders are available. When awarding damages, the courts must take into account the principles applied by the European Court of Human Rights in relation to awards of compensation. Claims for damages do not lie against the decision of a court which has breached the Convention, even though courts are defined as public bodies under the Act. Section 9 of the 1998 Act requires that proceedings against a first instance court be brought by way of appeal or by judicial review. An exception to this is provided in section 9(3) and (4), which provide for awards of damages against the Crown where any judicial body has been guilty of a breach of Article 5 (the right to liberty). Where there has been a breach of a Convention right caused by an Act of Parliament, damages cannot be awarded. In this situation, the consequence will be the making of a declaration of incompatibility. Only the High Court and courts above have the power to issue declarations of incompatibility.

---

62   The duty to provide sites has been repealed: Criminal Justice and Public Order Act 1994, s 80.

CHAPTER 27

THE GROUNDS FOR JUDICIAL REVIEW

With the procedural aspects of judicial review proceedings in mind, attention can now be turned to the grounds on which judicial review may be sought. Two principal classes of action may be pursued: those which allege that there has been a breach of statutory requirements, and those alleging that a decision has been reached in an unreasonable manner or in disregard of the rules of natural justice. These broad headings have traditionally been divided into a number of subheadings. In *Council of Civil Service Unions v Minister of State for Civil Service* (1985) (the *GCHQ* case), the House of Lords took the opportunity to offer a rationalisation of the grounds for judicial review and ruled that the bases for judicial review could be subsumed under three principal heads, namely, illegality, irrationality and procedural impropriety. It was accepted that further grounds for review, such as 'proportionality' might emerge. Lord Diplock elucidated the concepts:

> By 'illegality' as a ground for judicial review, I mean that the decision maker must understand correctly the law that regulates his decision making power and give effect to it. Whether he had or not is par excellence a justiciable question to be decided, in the event of dispute, by those persons, the judges, by whom the judicial power of the State is exercisable.

> By 'irrationality', I mean what can now be succinctly referred to as *Wednesbury* unreasonableness.[1] It applies to a decision which is so outrageous in its defiance of logic or of accepted moral standards that no sensible person who had applied his mind to the question to be decided could have arrived at it. Whether a decision falls within this category is a question that judges by their training and experience should be well equipped to answer ...

> I have described the third head as 'procedural impropriety' rather than failure to observe basic rules of natural justice or failure to act with procedural fairness towards the person who will be affected by the decision. This is because susceptibility to judicial review under this head covers also failure by an administrative tribunal to observe the procedural rules that are expressly laid down in the legislative instrument by which its jurisdiction is conferred, even though such failure does not involve any denial of natural justice.

> That is not to say that further development on a case by case basis may not in course of time add further grounds. I have in mind particularly the possible adoption in the future of the principle of 'proportionality' which is recognised in the administrative law of several of our fellow members of the European [Economic] Community ... [pp 410–11]

The traditional approach to judicial review – outlined below – is changing markedly, led by the influence of European law under the law of the European Community and by the Convention on Human Rights. Depending particularly on how the law develops under the Human Rights Act 1998, it may well prove that judicial review, as hitherto understood, is undergoing fundamental change.

---

1   *Associated Provincial Picture Houses Ltd v Wednesbury Corporation* (1948). See further below.

THE TRADITIONAL DOCTRINE OF *ULTRA VIRES*

Ultra vires refers to action which is outside – or in excess of – powers of decision making bodies. While judges continue to use the term *ultra vires*, it is nowadays too limited a term to encompass the whole ambit of judicial review. It may be preferable, therefore, to regard judicial review as the control of discretion and the regulation of the decision making process by the courts. By way of example, in *R v Hull University Visitor ex parte Page* (1993), Lord Browne-Wilkinson adopted the traditional language of *ultra vires*:

> If the decision maker exercises his powers outside the jurisdiction conferred, in a manner which is procedurally irregular or is *Wednesbury* unreasonable, he is acting *ultra vires* his powers and therefore unlawfully.

Two cases illustrate this rule. In *R v Richmond upon Thames Council ex parte McCarthy and Stone Ltd* (1992), the local planning authority implemented a scheme of charging £25.00 for informal consultation between corporation officers and property developers. The House of Lords held that the imposition of the charge was unlawful. Such a charge was neither incidental to the planning function of the local authority, nor could a charge be levied on the public without statutory authority. The council had misconstrued its powers and, accordingly, acted *ultra vires*. Further, in *Hazell v Hammersmith and Fulham Council* (1992), the council attempted to increase its revenue through financial investments which, for success, were dependent upon the fluctuation in interest rates. The House of Lords ruled that the council had no power to enter into 'interest rate swaps' which were purely speculative in nature. Such speculation was inconsistent with the statutory borrowing powers conferred on local authorities and neither conducive to nor incidental to the exercise of those powers.

Difficulties with the traditional *ultra vires* doctrine

The *ultra vires* principle is consistent with the doctrine of parliamentary sovereignty and, to some extent, with the concept of the rule of law. However, there are objections to the courts holding so tenaciously to a concept which, in some respects, is inappropriate to describe what the courts actually do in the control of administrative powers. The judges cling to the *ultra vires* doctrine as a means of protecting their constitutional position. As has been seen in Chapters 5 and 7, the judges are not entrusted with constitutional powers to invalidate Acts of Parliament, and judicial decisions are susceptible to being overruled by Acts of Parliament.[2] With the supremacy of parliament in mind, the judges exercise care to maintain a sufficient separation of powers. It is for this reason that judges are cautious about reviewing the exercise of prerogative powers and limit their role in relation to parliamentary privileges to ruling on the existence and scope of privilege. Keen awareness of this constitutional position explains the hold which the traditional doctrine of *ultra vires* has for judges. *Ultra vires* is entirely consistent with the supremacy of parliament and the rule of law.

---

2   See eg *Burmah Oil v Lord Advocate* (1965) and the War Damage Act 1965.

However, the doctrine of *ultra vires* cannot explain adequately the judges' power to rule, as they do, on certain aspects of decision making. While the judges declare that matters of 'high policy' are not for them to decide, when judges rule on 'unreasonableness' or, as Lord Diplock classifies the concept, 'irrationality', the judges come close to ruling on the merits of a particular decision. Furthermore, as shall be seen below, the concept of 'error of law' fits uneasily with the concept of *ultra vires*.

For reasons such as these, the concept of *ultra vires* is nowadays regarded by many as an inadequate rationale for judicial review. The preferred view is that the courts need not resort to fictions such as the 'intention of parliament' or the technicalities of 'jurisdictional facts' and 'errors of law' (on which, see below), but that rather the courts will intervene wherever there has been an unlawful exercise of power. As Dawn Oliver expresses the matter, 'judicial review has moved on from the *ultra vires* rule to a concern for the protection of individuals, and for the control of power'.[3]

Traditional terminological and classificatory difficulties in judicial review

While Lord Diplock, in the *GCHQ* case, offered a rationalisation of the headings of review, the question of terminology and classification remains difficult and sometimes obscure. This problem should be recognised at the outset. It should also be borne in mind that the categories are by no means watertight and discrete: in many instances, there will appear overlaps between the headings. By way of illustration, a decision maker may act *ultra vires* by taking into account irrelevant considerations. Depending upon the magnitude of the irrelevant consideration, he or she may also be acting irrationally.

Irrationality: *Wednesbury* unreasonableness

'Irrationality' is a concept which takes the courts further from reviewing the procedures by which a decision has been made and testing its legality, and closer to substituting the court's own view of the merits of the decision. The terms 'irrationality' and '*Wednesbury* unreasonableness' appear to be used at the judge's own preference.[4] Alternative expressions such as 'arbitrary and capricious', 'frivolous or vexatious' and 'capricious and vexatious' are also used on occasion to express the same concept.[5] 'Acting perversely' has also been used to judicially express the idea of unreasonableness.[6] The term 'unreasonableness' may thus be seen as an 'umbrella concept' which covers most of the major headings of review.

---

3   Oliver, 1987.
4   See eg Lord Donaldson MR in *R v Devon County Council ex parte G* (1989), p 577.
5   *Per* Wade and Forsyth, 2004 and references therein.
6   *Per* Lord Brightman in *R v Hillingdon London Borough Council ex parte Pulhofer* (1986). The test of *Wednesbury* unreasonableness is the foundation of the jurisdiction of University Visitors, who should only intervene in academic matters in exceptional circumstances: *Jhamat v Inns of Court School of Law (Visitors to the Inns of Court)* (1999).

Early expression was given to the concept in two cases, *Rooke's Case* (1598) and *Keighley's Case* (1609). In *Rooke's Case*, Coke LJ proclaimed:

> ... and notwithstanding the words of the commission give authority to the commissioners to do according to their discretions, yet their proceedings ought to be limited and bound with the rule of reason and law. For discretion is a science or understanding to discern between falsity and truth, between wrong and right, between shadows and substances, between equity and colourable glosses and pretences, and not to do according to their wills and private affections ...

The classic case of more recent times is that of *Associated Provincial Picture Houses Ltd v Wednesbury Corporation* (1948). The local authority had the power to grant licences for the opening of cinemas subject to such conditions as the authority 'thought fit' to impose. The authority, when granting a Sunday licence, imposed a condition that no children under the age of 15 years should be admitted. The applicants argued that the imposition of the condition was unreasonable and *ultra vires* the corporation's powers. The authority argued that there were no limits on the conditions which could be imposed in the statute. Lord Greene MR alluded to the many grounds of attack which could be made against a decision, citing unreasonableness, bad faith, dishonesty, paying attention to irrelevant circumstances, disregard of the proper decision making procedure and held that each of these could be encompassed within the umbrella term 'unreasonableness'. The test propounded in that case was whether an authority had acted, or reached a decision, in a manner 'so unreasonable that no reasonable authority could ever have come to it':

> ... a person entrusted with a discretion must, so to speak, direct himself properly in law. He must call his own attention to the matters which he is bound to consider. He must exclude from his consideration matters which are irrelevant to what he has to consider. If he does not obey those rules, he may truly be said, and often is said, to be acting 'unreasonably'. Similarly, there may be something so absurd that no sensible person could ever dream that it lay within the powers of the authority ...

> The court is entitled to investigate the action of the local authority with a view to seeing whether they have taken into account matters which they ought not to take into account, or, conversely, have refused to take into account and once that question is answered in favour of the local authority, it may still be possible to say that, although the local authority have kept within the four corners of the matters which they ought to consider, they have nevertheless come to a conclusion so unreasonable that no reasonable authority could ever have come to it. In such a case, again, I think the court can interfere. [p 229]

'Unreasonableness' was employed to challenge a bylaw which prohibited singing 'in any public place or highway within fifty yards of any dwelling house' although, on the merits of the case, the challenge failed.[7] In *Roberts v Hopwood* (1925), the council, in adopting a policy of paying higher wages than the national average for its workers, was unreasonable, for the discretion of the council was limited by law – it was not free to pursue a socialist policy at the expense of its rate payers. The House of Lords ruled that, irrespective of the wording of the

---

7   *Kruse v Johnson* (1898).

statute, the council had a duty to act 'reasonably'; its discretion was limited by law.[8]

The standard of reasonableness imposed by the courts is high: to impose too low a standard would in effect mean the substitution of judicial discretion for administrative discretion. It is for this reason that Lord Greene, cited above, states that a decision is unreasonable if it is 'so absurd that no sensible person could ever dream that it lay within the powers of the authority', and Lord Diplock, in *Council of Civil Service Unions v Minister for the Civil Service* (1985), regarded unreasonableness as entailing a decision '... so outrageous in its defiance of logic or of accepted moral standards that no sensible person who had applied his mind to the question to be decided could have arrived at it'.

In *Secretary of State for Education and Science v Tameside Metropolitan Borough Council* (1977), the Secretary of State for Education directed a newly elected local authority to implement plans, devised by the predecessor council, to introduce comprehensive schooling and abolish grammar schools.[9] At the election, there had been a change in the political composition of the council, which resulted in the change of policy. The Secretary of State's power was to direct an authority as to the exercise of its powers if he was satisfied that the authority was acting unreasonably. The Secretary of State argued that the new council would not be able to organise the necessary system of selective entry required for grammar schools in time for the new academic year, and that the authority was therefore unreasonable.

The matter went to the House of Lords. The court had to determine the extent of the Secretary of State's discretion under section 68 of the Education Act. The wording of the section was subjective: '... if the Secretary of State is satisfied.' It fell to the court to determine whether, in the circumstances of the case, the Secretary of State had acted lawfully according to the court's interpretation of whether the Secretary of State did in fact have reasonable grounds for believing that the authority had acted unreasonably. Applying the *Wednesbury* reasonableness test to the decision of the local authority to retain grammar schools, the House of Lords ruled that the authority had not been unreasonable and, as a result, the Secretary of State's directions were unlawful.

In *R v Secretary of State for the Home Department ex parte Brind* (1991), the House of Lords re-examined the reasonableness of the exercise of the Home Secretary's discretion to issue a notice banning the transmission of speech by representatives of the Irish Republican Army and its political party, Sinn Fein. Despite the issue involving a denial of freedom of expression, the court ruled that the exercise of the Home Secretary's power[10] did not amount to an unreasonable exercise of discretion.[11]

---

8 See Lord Wrenbury's judgment [1925] AC 578, p 613.
9 Under powers conferred by the Education Act 1944, s 68.
10 Under the Broadcasting Act 1981. See further Chapter 19.
11 *R v Radio Authority ex parte Bull* (1995).

The doctrine of proportionality[12, 13]

The Human Rights Act provides an additional basis on which the legality of actions of public authorities will be tested. The Human Rights Act 1998 provides for judicial review to extend to the review of administrative action to determine its compatibility with Convention requirements. As has been seen above, a fundamental concept utilised in domestic judicial review cases has conventionally been that of 'reasonableness'.[14] At issue is whether a public body, in its exercise of administrative discretion, has acted within the bounds of reasonableness conferred by the legislation, under which are subsumed the concepts of illegality, irrationality and procedural impropriety. Both the European Court of Justice of the European Community and the European Court of Human Rights – which are separate institutions and operate under separate jurisdictions[15] – have long employed the concept of 'proportionality', and it is this concept – traditionally been regarded with some suspicion by domestic judges – which has now become applicable.[16]

The doctrine of proportionality is one which confines the limits of the exercise of power to means which are proportional to the objective to be pursued. The doctrine has taken firm roots in the jurisprudence of, for example, the United States of America, Canada and the law of many continental European countries. Both the European Court of Justice of the European Community[17] (ECJ) and the European Court of Human Rights[18] adopt proportionality as a test against which to measure the legality of actions of authorities.[19] In *R v Home Secretary ex parte Brind* (1991), the House of Lords was not yet prepared to accept that the concept represented a separate and distinct head of judicial review.

Where issues of European Community law or the European Convention on Human Rights are involved, the doctrine is one which must be considered if the English interpretation of European law is to be consistent with that of the European Court of Justice and the Court of Human Rights. In *Stoke-on-Trent City Council v B & Q plc* (1984), for example, Hoffmann J was prepared to adopt the ECJ's proportionality test when considering the compatibility of the Shops Act 1950 and the free trade provisions of the EC Treaty.

Consistent with the requirements of the Convention, any action which *prima facie* violates protected rights, must be justified on the basis that the infringement is justifiable on the grounds set out in the Convention Articles: thus, the action taken must be judged according to whether or not that action was proportionate

---

12   See Jowell and Lester, 'Proportionality: neither novel nor dangerous', in Jowell and Oliver, 1988; Jowell, 2000.
13   On the status of the Convention before the Human Rights Act came into force, see Chapter 19. See also *R v Secretary of State for the Home Department ex parte Hussain Ahmed* (1999).
14   See *Associated Provincial Picture Houses Ltd v Wednesbury Corporation* (1948).
15   See further Chapter 8.
16   Proportionality has, however, been recognised by the Court of Appeal in the past. See eg *R v Barnsley Metropolitan BC ex parte Hook* (1976); *Attorney General v Jonathan Cape Ltd* (1976).
17   See Chapters 8 and 9.
18   See Chapter 19.
19   See eg *Dudgeon v United Kingdom* (1982), discussed in Chapter 19.

to the objective behind the action. The Convention is replete with state discretion – the 'margin of appreciation' – allied to criteria such as 'necessary in a democratic society in the interests of national security, public safety or the economic well being of the country, for the prevention of disorder or crime for the protection of health or morals, or for the protection of rights and freedoms of others'.[20]

The doctrine of proportionality has now been adopted in domestic courts of law. In *Brind*, Lord Ackner asked pithily whether the Secretary of State had 'used a sledgehammer to crack a nut'. In several pre-Human Rights Act cases, it is clear that the courts have been using the doctrine of proportionality but without making explicit references thereto. For example, in *R v Barnsley Metropolitan Borough Council ex parte Hook* (1976), a market stall holder had had his licence revoked for urinating in public. Lord Denning MR quashed the decision, partly on the basis that the penalty – the loss of the licence – was disproportionate to the 'offence'.[21]

Proportionality was also evident in *R v Chief Constable of Sussex ex parte International Trader's Ferry Ltd* (1999). In that case, judicial review had been sought regarding the Chief Constable's decision to restrict the deployment of police officers to assist the exporters, who were being obstructed by demonstrators. In the House of Lords, Lord Slynn stated that when answering the question of whether 'appropriate measures' had been taken, the correct approach was to ask 'whether the steps taken were proportionate', and that the Chief Constable had 'shown here that what he did in providing police assistance was proportionate to what was required'. In his judgment, Lord Cook took the opportunity to consider proportionality and the *Wednesbury* test of unreasonableness, stating that 'the European concepts of proportionality and margin of appreciation produce the same result as what are commonly called *Wednesbury* principles', and re-defined the reasonableness test to the more simple formula of 'whether the decision in question was one which a reasonable authority could reach'.

With the Human Rights Act 1998, proportionality moves centre stage. In interpreting the Act, section 2 requires that domestic courts and tribunals 'must take into account' the judgments and decisions of the Court of Human Rights. Under section 6, courts and tribunals are public authorities under the Act and are therefore under a duty not to violate Convention rights. Furthermore, most Convention rights are not absolute and unqualified, but allow states to impose limitations on specified grounds, commonly in the interests of 'public safety' or 'national security'. Restrictions on the exercise of rights – derogations – must also commonly be 'prescribed by law' and 'necessary in a democratic society'.[22] The combined effect of these provisions necessitates that courts follow the reasoning of the Court of Human Rights, and that includes the doctrine of proportionality. The domestic courts have traditionally been wary of the doctrine, on the basis that it requires judges to go beyond an analysis of the legality of the decision making process on the grounds of legality, rationality and procedural propriety, and to

---

20 ECHR, Article 8(2).
21 Also consider *Wheeler v Leicester City Council* (1985), discussed below.
22 See Chapter 19 for the text of Convention Articles.

address two further questions. The first is, where a breach of a right is found to have occurred, was the offending action justified as being both necessary and proportionate to the objective being sought? This requires the courts not only to look at the processes involved in reaching decisions, but to evaluate whether on the facts the decision maker adopted the approach which least undermined the right in question. That exercise involves the judges looking to the merits of decisions, rather than the process of decision making – which has been the conventional concern of judicial review – and blurs the line between review and appeal. Constitutionally, that alters the position of the judges vis à vis the executive.

The decision of the House of Lords in *R (Daly) v Secretary of State for the Home Department* (2001) is also important in demonstrating the movement away from the traditional test of *Wednesbury* unreasonableness towards the doctrines of necessity and proportionality. The House of Lords ruled that the policy of excluding prisoners from their cells while prison officers conducted searches – which included scrutinising privileged legal correspondence – was unlawful. Lord Bingham stated that the conclusion had been reached according to common law principles, but accepted that the same result could have been achieved if the analysis had proceeded on the basis of the European Convention.[23] Lord Cooke was explicit in recognising the limitations of the traditional *Wednesbury* approach, stating that before long it would be accepted that the *Wednesbury* case was an unfortunately retrogressive decision in English law.

However, the question arises as to whether the doctrine of proportionality applies only where fundamental human rights are in issue, or whether it will come to pervade all aspects of judicial review. This issue was addressed by Lord Slynn in *R (Alconbury Developments Ltd) v Secretary of State for the Environment, Transport and the Regions* (2001), where he stated that:

> I consider that even without reference to the Human Rights Act the time has come to recognise that this principle [proportionality] is part of English law, not only when judges are dealing with [European] Community acts, but also when they are dealing with acts subject to domestic law. *Trying to keep the* Wednesbury *principle and proportionality in separate compartments seems to me to be unnecessary and confusing.* [emphasis added]

Whether proportionality will ultimately supersede the concept of reasonableness or rationality was also considered by Dyson LJ in *R (Association of British Civilian Internees (Far East Region) v Secretary of State for Defence* (2003) in which he stated that:

> ... we have difficulty in seeing what justification there now is for retaining the *Wednesbury* test ...

> But we consider that it is not for this court to perform its burial rites. The continuing existence of the *Wednesbury* test has been acknowledged by the House of Lords on more than one occasion.

---

23   The relevant Convention right being the right to privacy under Article 8.

On the other hand, Jeffrey Jowell QC has stated that 'The new constitutional approach will not affect all our judicial review. There will no doubt remain areas where traditional techniques of reasoning and justification will suffice to ensure standards of legal, fair and reasonable administration based upon the practical morality familiar to our common law' (2000, p 682).

The former Lord Chancellor, moreover, has expressed constitutional objections to the introduction of proportionality:

> ... it invites review of the merits of public decisions on the basis of a standard which is considerably lower than that of *Wednesbury* unreasonableness and would involve the court in a process of policy evaluation which goes far beyond its allotted constitutional role. [Irvine, 1996]

The difficulty with proportionality from the traditional approach to judicial review is that it comes close to ruling on the substance, or merits, of a case and thereby risks the judges becoming embroiled in the administrative process in a manner which might be seen as infringing on the separation of powers between the executive and the judiciary. It also, at a conceptual level, raises the question of whether – and under what circumstances – differing levels of judicial scrutiny are required. Unreasonableness and irrationality are terms imbued not only with familiarity but with the comfort of a degree of objectivity which can (generally) be applied without a deep analysis of the merits of the case in hand. Proportionality, on the other hand, is more sensitive to the context of the case and requires the court to consider whether the decision reached or action taken is restricted to what is strictly required (proportionate) to the objective being sought which it cannot do without considering both the policy and the means adopted to achieving it.

In *R (Daly) v Secretary of State for the Home Department* (2001) Lord Steyn examined the differences between reasonableness and proportionality, identifying the following differences:

- the doctrine of proportionality may require the reviewing court to assess the balance which the decision maker has struck, not merely whether it is in the range of rational or reasonable decisions;
- the proportionality test may go further than the traditional grounds of review in as much as it may require attention to be directed to the relative weight accorded to interests and considerations;
- even the heightened scrutiny test (the *Smith and Grady* test) is not necessarily appropriate to the protection of human rights.

What has become clear from the case law is that there are now differing levels of review being applied, depending on the nature of the case in hand, ranging from non-justiciable issues on which the courts will not adjudicate,[24] from areas of policy where the judges will defer to the executive,[25] the conventional

---

24 As in *Council for Civil Service Unions v Minister for the Civil Service* (1985).
25 See, for example, *A v Secretary of State for the Home Department* (2004).

reasonableness test,[26] human rights issues where the courts will give 'anxious scrutiny' to the matter[27] and finally the proportionality test.[28]

Illegality

Acting for improper motives, failing to take account of relevant considerations, failing to respect the requirements of natural justice and fettering a discretion by adopting a rigid policy will all amount to unreasonableness – and hence illegality – as understood by the courts.

While the terms 'unreasonableness' and 'illegality' are frequently and confusingly used interchangeably, illegality most accurately expresses the purpose of judicial review: to ensure that decision makers act according to the law. In the following section, illegality is examined under the following headings:

- Errors of law and fact
- Onerous conditions
- Using powers for the wrong purpose
- Relevant and Irrelevant considerations
- Acting in bad faith
- Fettering discretion
- Unauthorised delegation
- Failure to act.

Errors of law

The problem concerning the role of the courts and the extent to which it is appropriate for there to be judicial intervention in administration, discussed in Chapter 26, is clearly illustrated in relation to errors of law and errors of fact. The question for determination is whether, and to what extent, administrators enjoy a measure of discretion in decision making, which empowers them to make determinations of fact which are immune from judicial review. Before considering the courts approach, it is necessary to define the terms error of law and error of fact.

An error of law may take several forms. An authority may wrongly interpret a word to which a legal meaning is attributed. For example, where an authority is under a duty to provide 'accommodation', the question arises as to whether the quality of what they have, in fact, provided amounts, in law, to accommodation. Does the accommodation have to be of a particular quality, or be particularly suited to what the applicant needs?[29] Questions may also arise as to whether there has been a legal exercise of power in relation to the objectives of relevant legislation, or whether a discretion has been properly exercised, or whether

---

26 See *Associated Provincial Picture Houses Ltd v Wednesbury Corporation* (1948).
27 *R v Ministry of Defence ex parte Smith* (1995).
28 *R v Secretary of State for the Home Department ex parte Daly* (2001). See Le Sueur, 2005 and Olley, 2004.
29 See *R v Hillingdon London Borough Council ex parte Pulhofer* (1986).

relevant considerations have been taken into account, or irrelevant considerations excluded from the decision making process.

Historically, the judges have assumed the power to adjudicate on matters which are termed 'errors on the face of the record'. Errors on the face of the record – that is to say, evidence from the documentation that the decision maker has made a wrong decision in law – will cause the judges to rule that the decision was defective, even if the decision maker was acting inside jurisdiction (*intra vires*). Such a power does not sit easily alongside the concept of *ultra vires*, the very basis of which is to strike down decisions which have been taken *ultra vires* (outside jurisdiction).

As has been seen, if an authority is to act *intra vires*, it must conduct itself according to a correct interpretation of the law. However, what is of the essence in relation to error of law is that the authority misinterprets or misunderstands the powers which it has been granted and, accordingly, acts *ultra vires* whereas, when an authority uses powers for the wrong purpose, the authority has correctly interpreted its powers but used them towards the wrong objective. As has been said, an error of law may manifest itself in several ways. It may be that an authority misinterprets its legal powers, as in *Perilly v Tower Hamlets Borough Council* (1973), where the local authority believed – erroneously – that it was obliged to consider applications for stall licences in a street market in the order in which they were received. The effect of this was to deny a licence to Perilly even though his mother, by then deceased, had held a licence for some 30 years. The licence granted to an incoming applicant in preference to Perilly was set aside by the court.

The seminal case is that of *Anisminic Ltd v Foreign Compensation Commission* (1969), discussed in Chapter 26. It will be recalled that the House of Lords held the decision of the Commission to be *ultra vires*. The decision made by the Commission was so wrong that, in law, it did not amount to a decision at all. As a result, the section preventing the questioning of the Commission's decision in a court of law was not relevant or binding on the court, for the ruling of the Commission – being so wrong in law – resulted in the Commission acting outside its jurisdiction, and nothing in the Act prohibited a court of law from reviewing what was, in law and in effect, a nullity.

The House of Lords ruled that:

> If the inferior tribunal, as a result of its misconstruing the statutory description of the kind of case in which it has jurisdiction to inquire, makes a purported determination in a case of a kind into which it has no jurisdiction to inquire, its purported determination is a nullity.

Anisminic Ltd v Foreign Compensation Commission destroyed the distinction between errors of law which 'went to jurisdiction' (that is, deprived the decision making body of power to determine the question) and errors of law within jurisdiction. In *Anisminic*, the House of Lords ruled that, in effect, the old distinctions were obsolete in relation to the decisions of administrative and other bodies (but not necessarily inferior courts of law).[30] Lord Diplock has reasserted his support for

30   See Diplock, 1974; Wade, 1969; Gould, 1970; Gordon, 1971.

this view in *Re Racal Communications Ltd* (1981) and *O'Reilly v Mackman* (1983). In the former case, Lord Diplock confirmed the 'breakthrough' achieved in *Anisminic*. In *O'Reilly*, Lord Diplock went further and asserted that the distinction had been rendered obsolete in relation both to tribunals and inferior courts. This approach was confirmed by the House of Lords in *R v Hull University Visitor ex parte Page* (1993). Professor HWR Wade's evaluation of these cases is that 'it is clear now that they made an important extension of judicial review in English law ...'.[31]

The House of Lords returned to the questions of jurisdictional errors in *R v Monopolies and Mergers Commission ex parte South Yorkshire Transport Ltd* (1993). Under section 64(1)(a) of the Fair Trading Act 1973, the Secretary of State has power to refer a merger of companies to the Monopolies and Mergers Commission (MMC). The jurisdiction of the MMC was to consider mergers which result in more than 25 per cent of services being supplied by one company 'in a substantial part of the United Kingdom'. Two merged bus companies sought judicial review of the MMC's investigation, on the basis that the land area did not amount to a 'substantial part of the United Kingdom'. The court ruled that the MMC had directed itself properly as to the meaning of 'substantial'. However, it was also recognised that what amounted to 'substantial' could be interpreted in different ways, and that persons might reasonably disagree about that interpretation. Lord Mustill ruled that, in such a situation, a decision would only be ruled unlawful if the decision 'is so aberrant that it cannot be classed as rational'. Thus, where the statute provides broad criteria, over the meaning of which reasonable persons might reasonably disagree, the court will be slow to step in and substitute its judgment, unless the decision maker's decision falls outside what the court regards as a reasonable interpretation of a word which is essentially imprecise.[32]

Errors of fact[33]

An error of law will be reviewed by the courts. An error of fact is an error which the courts will be more reluctant to review. Administrators are given powers to exercise in relation to their specialised area, and it is the decision maker who has all the factual information to hand on which to base a decision. For the courts to intervene in this matter, would – unless some caution is exercised – amount to the courts taking over the very role of the administrators. Nevertheless, there may be some errors of fact which are of such a fundamental nature that they cause a decision to be unlawful. Ian Yeats offers the following illustrative example of the role of fact in administrative decision making. He writes:

> In the simplest situations, the facts which have to be found and the law which has to be determined can be presented as a series of preconditions which have to exist before the duty can be performed or the power exercised. A board is empowered (or obliged) to take some action in respect of 'dilapidated dwelling houses in Greater London'. The

31 Wade and Forsyth, 2004.
32 See also *R v Ministry of Defence ex parte Walker* (1999).
33 See Jones, 1990; Yeats, I, 'Errors of fact: the role of the courts law', in Richardson and Genn, 1994; Craig, 2004.

ability (or duty) to act in respect of a particular building depends on establishing that it is (1) in Greater London, (2) a dwelling house and (3) dilapidated. If the board finds that the three conditions are satisfied, it may (or must) proceed. If it finds that any one of them is not satisfied, then it cannot.

A disgruntled property owner invites a court to review the board's findings: the court has to decide whether, and how far, it should defer to the board's views. If the complaint is that the premises are not in Greater London, the court is likely to intervene. The question defines in the most literal way the area in which the board has competence, can easily be resolved by a court, and is unlikely to occur frequently. The question is not about the correctness of the decision on the building's fate, but about whether the board whose decision is under review had the function of determining it. If the complaint is that the house is not dilapidated, the court will be reluctant to intervene. That is a question involving elements of judgment which naturally appear to have been remitted to the board and which it, rather than the court, has the facilities and probably the specialised expertise to answer; if the court were to agree to answer it, every decision of the board would be potentially reviewable. If the complaint is that the premises do not constitute a dwelling house, the issue is less clear-cut. The court might think it proper to impose its view, partly because the problem might be posed in a narrowly legal form, that of identifying the correct sense in which the expression 'dwelling house' was used in the legislation. [pp 131–32]

When the court considers whether there has been an error of law, it is seeking to discover the correct definition of the legal words in the relevant statute. When the court is considering whether there has been an error of fact, the court is trying to determine whether the facts of the case 'fit' with the interpretation of the statute.

Errors of fact raise difficult questions. As has been seen, an error of law will be made when the decision maker acts contrary to the requirements of legality – or, in other words, he has broken one of the rules for lawful decision making. Errors of fact are more complex. If a decision maker bases his decision on a misunderstanding of the factual situation of the case, he will reach a decision which is wrong. The question which then arises is whether the courts will review such an error in judicial review proceedings. In general, the answer to that question is that the courts will be very cautious. After all, the courts will often not have the expertise to assess the factual situation, and may have great difficulty in deciding whether a factual error has resulted in the wrong decision. The courts have traditionally approached this matter by dividing errors of fact into two categories. The first relates to reviewable errors of facts, which are jurisdictional, and the other category is that of non-reviewable, non-jurisdictional facts.

Professor Wade illustrates a jurisdictional fact as follows:

A rent tribunal ... may have power to reduce the rent of a dwelling house. If it mistakenly finds that the property is a dwelling house when in fact it is let for business purposes, and then purports to reduce the rent, its order will be *ultra vires* and void, for its jurisdiction depends upon the facts which must exist objectively before the tribunal has power to act. [Wade and Forsyth, 2004]

On the other hand, other mistakes will not have this effect. Professor Wade illustrates as follows:

Many facts on the other hand will not be jurisdictional, since they will have no bearing on the limits of the power. A rent tribunal's findings as to the state of repair of the property, the terms of the tenancy, and the defaults of landlord or tenant will probably not affect its jurisdiction in any way and will therefore be immune from jurisdictional challenge.

The question to be asked, therefore, is whether the mistake of fact is one which is central to the decision maker's power of decision. Only such crucial errors of fact will be reviewed by the court. In addition, if a decision is reached on the basis of facts for which there is no evidence, or based on essential facts which have been proven wrong, or been misunderstood or ignored, the court will quash the decision (p 320).

Two cases further illustrate the courts' approach to law and fact, and demonstrate that the judges will – depending upon the circumstances of the case – adopt either a strict approach or a more lenient approach to the matter. In *R v Secretary of State for the Home Department ex parte Khawaja* (1984), the House of Lords was required to rule on two questions. The first question was whether the phrase 'illegal immigrant' in the Immigration Act 1971, covered a person who had been granted permission to enter the country through fraud or deception as well as a person who secretly entered the country without any leave. On this point, the House of Lords held that it could. The second question concerned the standard of proof which the immigration officer had to apply. It was argued that the correct standard to be applied was whether the immigration officer had reasonable grounds for his decision. The House of Lords rejected that view, holding that, because the liberty of the person was involved, the standard of proof that deception had taken place was one of a high degree of probability.

In *R v Hillingdon London Borough Council ex parte Pulhofer* (1986), the House of Lords approached the matter rather differently. Under the Housing Act 1985,[34] local authorities are under a duty to provide accommodation for homeless persons as defined by the Act. For the purposes of their decision, the House of Lords had to interpret the meaning of 'accommodation'. The House of Lords adopted a very broad interpretation of the word, refusing to import a standard of reasonableness of accommodation which would protect the individual from being placed in unsuitable housing. Unlike the decision in *Khawaja,* where the House of Lords introduced a standard of proof which was protective of the individual against the administration, in *Pulhofer,* the court's ruling protected the administration – the housing authority – and not the individual. The Housing and Planning Act 1986 reverses the House of Lords' decision in *Pulhofer*, and requires that 'accommodation' be accommodation which it is reasonable for a person to continue to occupy. It can be seen from these two cases, that the interpretation of the question of law can dictate a very different outcome, depending upon the judicial approach taken.

When the issue concerns individual rights, for example, the courts will be slow to adopt an approach which has the effect of delimiting those rights. *Tan Te Lam v Superintendent of Tai A Chau Detention Centre* (1996), decided by the Privy Council, illustrates the point well.[35] The applicants were detainees in Hong Kong,

---

34 Originally, the Housing (Homeless Persons) Act 1977.
35 Following the transfer of sovereignty in 1997, appeals no longer lie to the Privy Council from the Hong Kong courts.

having arrived there by boat from Vietnam. They were detained in detention centres, pending decisions as to whether to grant or refuse permission to remain in Hong Kong, or, if a decision to refuse permission were made, pending their removal from Hong Kong and repatriation to Vietnam. The applied for writs of habeas corpus to test the legality of their detention. By the time the appeal reached the Privy Council, the applicants had been detained for long periods of time, the longest being 24 months, pending determination of refugee status, followed by a further 44 months. The Privy Council stated, first, that the power to detain could only be exercised during the period necessary, in all the circumstances, to effect removal; secondly, that, if it becomes clear that removal is not going to be possible within a reasonable time, further detention is not authorised; thirdly, that the person seeking to exercise the power of detention must take all reasonable steps to ensure removal within a reasonable time.

In *Khawaja v Secretary of State for the Home Department* (1984), discussed above, the House of Lords had earlier considered the legality of a detention order pending removal, as an illegal immigrant, from the United Kingdom.[36] There was a dispute of fact as to whether the applicant had obtained leave to enter as a result of fraud. The House of Lords ruled that the issue of whether the applicant was an illegal immigrant was a matter which had to be established before it could be determined whether there was any power to detain with a view to deportation. That question 'was a precedent or jurisdictional fact which, in the case of deprivation of liberty, had to be proved to exist before any power to detain was exercisable at all'.

E v Secretary of State for the Home Department (2004) provided the opportunity for the Court of Appeal to reconsider the review of fact. The applicants claimed that the Immigration Appeal Tribunal (IAT) which had refused leave to appeal to the Court of Appeal had erred in not taking account evidence which had become available since the hearing before the IAT but before making the decision whether to allow an appeal. The evidence supported the applicants' claims that they would be at risk if returned to their country of origin. The Court of Appeal ruled that the IAT should reconsider the decision to take account of the evidence where there was a serious risk of injustice because the evidence had not been considered.

Onerous conditions attached to decision

A decision by an authority may also be unreasonable and unlawful if conditions are attached to the decision which are difficult or impossible to perform. For example, in *Pyx Granite Co Ltd v Ministry of Housing and Local Government* (1958), Lord Denning MR in the Court of Appeal held that planning conditions '... must fairly and reasonably relate to the permitted development' and must not be so unreasonable that it can be said that parliament clearly cannot have intended that they should be imposed.

Accordingly, in the *Pyx Granite* case, the condition that permission be conditional upon the company constructing a road ancillary to the development

---

36   The power to detain in *Khawaja* arose from the Immigration Act 1971, Sched 2, paras 9 and 16.

at its own expense when so required by the authority and to grant a public right of passage over it was *ultra vires*. *Pyx Granite* was followed in *Hall and Co Ltd v Shoreham-by-Sea Urban District Council* (1964). The defendant council granted planning permission for a development, subject to conditions, which included the requirement to construct an ancillary road over the entire frontage of the site and subject to the right of public passage. While the objective of the council was viewed as 'reasonable', the terms of the conditions requiring the plaintiffs to construct a road at their own expense, for public use and without compensation, were not reasonable. The *ultra vires* conditions were fundamental to the whole planning permission which was, accordingly, void. Equally, in *R v Hillingdon London Borough Council ex parte Royco Homes Ltd* (1974), planning permission was also tied to conditions. The conditions were that Royco Homes make properties constructed available for occupation by those on the council's housing waiting list and, further, that for ten years the houses be occupied by persons subject to security of tenure under the Rent Acts. The conditions were *ultra vires*.

According to Lord Widgery CJ, the conditions represented:

> ... the equivalent of requiring the applicants to take on at their own expense a significant part of the duty of the council as housing authority. However well intentioned and however sensible such a desire on the part of the council may have been, it seems to me that it is unreasonable ... [p 732]

Where an authority makes a decision which is in part good, but in part bad – perhaps because of attaching onerous conditions to planning permission – the court may either invalidate the entire decision or sever the bad part of the decision from the good. The decision in *Agricultural Horticultural and Forestry Industry Training Board v Aylesbury Mushrooms Ltd* (1972) illustrates the principle. There, the Training Board was under a mandatory statutory duty to consult certain organisations and trades unions before reaching a decision. The Board failed to consult the Mushroom Growers Association. The court held that the decision was good, and could remain, in relation to those associations which had been consulted, but bad in relation to the Mushroom Growers Association, and that the Board had a duty to reconsider their decision after consultations with the Association.

In some cases, it will not be possible to sever a part of a decision from the whole decision, in which case, the entire decision may be invalidated.[37] For example, in *Director of Public Prosecutions v Hutchinson* (1990), the local authority passed a bylaw which prohibited unauthorised access to Greenham Common air force base. The Act of Parliament, under which the authority purported to exercise its powers, provided that no bylaw should be passed which affected the rights of registered commoners in the area. In an action for trespass against anti-nuclear protesters, the defendants pleaded the invalidity of the bylaw. The House of Lords ruled that the bylaw was invalid and, as a result, the protesters escaped conviction for trespass.

---

37 As in *Hall and Co Ltd v Shoreham-by-Sea Urban District Council* (1964) discussed above.

Using powers for the wrong purpose

Powers conferred must be used for the purpose for which they were granted. In *Attorney General v Fulham Corporation* (1921), the authority was empowered under statute to establish washhouses for the non-commercial use of local residents. The Corporation decided to open a laundry on a commercial basis. The Corporation was held to have acted *ultra vires* the statute. *Westminster Corporation v London and Northern Western Railway Company* (1905), however, represents a case where a charge of wrong purpose failed. The Corporation had power, under section 44 of the Public Health Act 1891, to provide public conveniences and had constructed them midway under the street with access gained by means of a subway. The Railway Company which owned stock in adjacent buildings claimed that the power had been used improperly. The House of Lords disagreed, stating that 'the primary object of the council was the construction of the conveniences with the requisite and proper means of approach thereto and exit therefrom'.

Thus, where a public authority uses a power for the purpose intended by parliament and reasonably provides a facility incidental to – or complementary to – the power conferred, the authority is acting within its powers. It can of course be argued that the Corporation's prime objective was, in fact, the provision of a subway; nevertheless, that objective – if it was the primary objective – did not invalidate the action.

The *Westminster Corporation* case was further considered in *R v Inner London Education Authority ex parte Westminster City Council* (1986), which provided an opportunity for the Divisional Court to consider the issue of two purposes being pursued under one power. On the facts of the case, it was held that, in pursuing two purposes in relation to education funding, the Council had allowed an 'irrelevant consideration' to dominate its decision making and that, accordingly, it had acted *ultra vires*.

The test which Professor Evans prescribes is: 'What is the true purpose for which the power was exercised? If the actor has in truth used his power for the purposes for which it was conferred, it is immaterial that he was thus enabled to achieve a subsidiary object ...'

Acting in a manner inconsistent with the purpose of an Act was seen in *Padfield v Minister for Agriculture, Fisheries and Food* (1968). Under the Agricultural Marketing Act 1958, a Committee of Investigation was established to make inquiries, if the minister 'so directed', into complaints made to the minister concerning the operation of, amongst other products, milk. South Eastern dairy farmers complained that the Milk Marketing Board had fixed prices in a manner prejudicial to farmers in the South Eastern region of the country. The minister refused to refer the matter to the Committee of Investigation. The farmers challenged the minister's decision. The House of Lords granted an order of mandamus, requiring the minister to consider properly whether he should exercise his discretion to refer. The House of Lords ruled by a majority[38] that, while the minister was not obliged to refer every complaint made, he did not have an unfettered discretion to refuse to refer a case. The result was something of a

---

38 Lord Morris of Borth-y-Gest dissenting.

hollow victory for the farmers, since the incoming minister, having referred the matter to the committee, which upheld the complaint, rejected the committee's recommendations.

In *R v Secretary of State for Foreign and Commonwealth Affairs ex parte World Development Movement* (1995), the government was held to have acted unlawfully in relation to aid money paid to Malaysia. In 1988,[39] the United Kingdom government signed an agreement with the Malaysian Prime Minister, Mahathir Mohamed, for the sale of arms valued at £1.3 billion.[40] In 1989, Britain offered £234 million towards the building of the Pergau Dam. In 1991,[41] the deal went ahead, despite warnings from officials that the project was uneconomic and a waste of public funds. The monies were paid out of the Overseas Development Administration (ODA) budget. Under international law, any linkage between aid monies and arms sales is prohibited. While the government denied any such link, a House of Commons Foreign Affairs Committee inquiry concluded that the government had, in effect, made such a link. Furthermore, under section 1 of the Overseas Development and Co-operation Act 1980, the Foreign Secretary is empowered to authorise payments only 'for the purpose of promoting the development or maintaining the economy of a country or territory outside the United Kingdom or the welfare of its people'. The High Court ruled that the Foreign Secretary had acted unlawfully, in part because the project was 'economically unsound', and also because the aid did not promote the development of a country's economy as required by law. As a result, some £55 million already spent on the project had to be returned to the ODA.[42]

In *Porter v Magill* (2002), the House of Lords ruled that the power to sell property to tenants in the hope of gaining party political advantage at an election was unlawful. It was argued that provided some proper purpose was being pursued, the decision was not unlawful. The House of Lords disagreed: the power had to be used for its intended purpose – and that was not to secure an electoral advantage.

Relevant and irrelevant considerations in decision making

The following section considers relevant and irrelevant considerations which are taken into account in decision making. To a large extent, there is at best a fine line between using powers for the wrong purpose and the relevancy of considerations. Categorisation is a limited, although organisationally useful, device: the essential point to remember is that the heart of the matter lies in whether or not discretionary powers have been exercised lawfully or not, irrespective of the headings under which cases may be grouped. One case which straddles the boundaries of using powers for an improper purpose and taking irrelevant considerations into account is that of *R v Somerset County Council ex parte Fewings* (1995). The local authority decided to ban stag hunting on land

---

39   When Baroness Thatcher was Prime Minister.
40   The agreement being signed by the then Secretary of State for Defence, George Younger.
41   Under the premiership of John Major.
42   See also *R v Secretary of State for the Environment ex parte Spath Holme Ltd* (2000).

owned by the council and designated for recreational purposes.[43] Laws J accepted that, in some circumstances, stag hunting could legitimately be banned – for example, where the hunt would damage rare flora, or if the animals themselves were rare. Here, however, the motivation behind the ban was the moral objection of the councillors to hunting. Laws J ruled that:

> If the activity in question is permissible under the general law, as is the practice of deer hunting, it is by no means to be prohibited on grounds only of the decision maker's distaste or ethical objection where the reach of his statutory function on its face requires no more than the making of objective judgments for the management of a particular regime. [p 530]

On appeal to the Court of Appeal, the decision was upheld, but on narrower grounds. The Court ruled that the Council's mind had not been directed to relevant statutory provisions, and it had not considered, as it was required to do, whether a ban of hunting would be for the general public benefit.

A case which illustrates the intermingling of grounds for review is that of *Wheeler v Leicester City Council* (1985). In *Wheeler*, the House of Lords thoroughly examined the concepts of unreasonableness and of fairness, and here the interaction between bad faith, unreasonableness and procedural impropriety can be discerned. In 1984, the Rugby Football Union announced a tour to South Africa, with a team including three members of the Leicester Football Club. At the time, the government was opposed to any sporting links with South Africa. Leicester City Council – with a 25 per cent immigrant population – was virulently opposed to the proposed tour. The Leicester Club secretary attended a meeting with the leader of Leicester Council, at which he was asked to support the government's – and the council's – policy of opposition to the South African regime of apartheid. The club's response was to assert its opposition to apartheid but to stress that they were not constrained from playing in South Africa as a result of governmental opposition, which had neither made such tours illegal nor subject to sanctions on those who visited South Africa. As a result of the club's refusal to comply with the City Council's request that they withdraw from the tour, Leicester City Council resolved that the club would be suspended from using a local playing field for a 12 month period, the ban to be reviewed after a year and a new decision to be taken based on the club's attitude to South Africa at that time. The House of Lords ruled that a political policy – however morally justified – could not provide the lawful basis on which to deprive the club of engaging in its lawful activities.

As can be seen, the two purposes tests involves the issue of irrelevant considerations. That is to say, a subsidiary or secondary purpose being pursued may – if it dictates the decision making process – invalidate that process. Here, attention is turned to situations where an authority fails to take account of relevant considerations, or takes into account irrelevant considerations which materially affect the decision reached, and may be held to be acting *ultra vires*. Many of the cases involve the fiduciary duty which is owed by local authorities to their rate payers. In *Roberts v Hopwood* (1925), for example, the local authority was

---

43 Under the Local Government Act 1972, s 120.

empowered by statute to pay its workers 'as it thought fit'.[44] Nevertheless, when the council decided to pay wages which were higher than the national average and to pay men and women equally, it was held to have been acting beyond its powers. Its duty to its ratepayers overrode its desire to better the lot of its workers.[45] The court held that the council was pursuing a policy of 'philanthropic socialism' which was inconsistent with its duties to its ratepayers. Compare *Roberts v Hopwood* with *Pickwell v Camden London Borough Council* (1983), in which the council had paid additional monies to its manual workers in order to secure settlement of an industrial dispute. It was held that the payments were reasonable.

Similar considerations applied in *Bromley London Borough Council v Greater London Council* (1983). There, the Greater London Council, wishing to increase passenger numbers – and thereby reduce the traffic congestion on the roads – by decreasing fares on public transport, sought to pay for this by seeking a higher level of subsidy for London Transport by increasing the rates payable by ratepayers, the burden of which would fall on the residents of London boroughs. The House of Lords held the Greater London Council to be acting *ultra vires*. The House of Lords ruled that, whilst section 3 of the Transport (London) Act 1969 conferred a wide discretion on the authority, and that grants could be levied to supplement the income from transport fares, that discretion was limited by London Transport's basic obligation to run its operations on ordinary business principles, which their fare reduction policy contravened. As in *Roberts v Hopwood* (1925), the council could not use its grant making powers to achieve a social policy which was inconsistent with those obligations: the Greater London Council (GLC) was using its powers for the wrong purpose. Moreover, the rate reduction was also invalid in so far as it involved a breach of fiduciary duty owed by the council to its rate payers. The fact that the policy had been part of an election mandate was not sufficient justification for the policy. The members of the council were representatives of the people, not delegates thereof. Accordingly, they were not irrevocably bound to fulfil election promises but, rather, must act in the interests of all constituents – not just those constituents who were users of London Transport.

This view on the doctrine of mandate – or responsibility to electors – may be contrasted with the decision in *Secretary of State for Education v Tameside Metropolitan Borough Council* (1977). The Labour controlled Council in March 1975 proposed a scheme of comprehensive education to come into effect in 1976. In 1976, a Conservative Council was elected. The Party had conducted its election campaign in large part on the education platform. On entering office, the council reversed the education policy of the previous administration. The Secretary of State issued a direction under section 68 of the Education Act 1944, ordering the council to implement the comprehensive schooling policy of the previous local council. The House of Lords laid much emphasis on the wishes of the electorate. Lord Wilberforce declared:

---

44 Under the Metropolis Management Act 1855, s 62.
45 See also *Prescott v Birmingham Corporation* (1955); *Taylor v Munrow* (1960).

... if he [the Secretary of State] had exercised his judgment on the basis of the factual situation in which this newly elected authority were placed – with a policy approved by the electorate, and massively supported by the parents – there was no ground, however much he might disagree with the new policy and regret such administrative dislocation as was brought about by the change, on which he could find that the authority were acting or proposing to act unreasonably ...

Where an irrelevant consideration does not affect the outcome of a decision, the court may hold that the authority is acting *intra vires*. For example, in *R v Broadcasting Complaints Commission ex parte Owen* (1985), the Broadcasting Authority – with the statutory responsibility of ensuring fairness in the allocation of broadcasting time for political parties at election time – refused to consider a complaint that a political party had been given too little broadcasting time. That decision was challenged in the courts. However, while the Commission had some good reasons for not considering the complaint, it had also erred by giving weight to an irrelevant consideration, namely, that the task would be burdensome. The court nevertheless held that the Commission was acting within its lawful discretion.

Whether or not a local authority may not take into account considerations relating to financial resources when assessing an individual's needs was considered by the Court of Appeal and House of Lords in *R v Gloucestershire County Council ex parte Barry; R v Lancashire County Council ex parte Royal Association for Disability and Rehabilitation* (1997).[46] Under the Chronically Sick and Disabled Persons Act 1970, a local authority is under the duty to identify the needs of disabled persons, and to meet such needs. The House of Lords ruled that the resources of the authority were a relevant consideration. Lord Nicholls of Birkenhead conceded that the argument put forward by Lord Lloyd, dissenting, that a person's needs were unaffected by local authority resources was an 'alluring argument', but one which he could not accept. The argument, he stated, was flawed by a 'failure to recognise that needs for services cannot sensibly be assessed without having some regard to the cost of providing them'.

The reasoning of the majority in the House of Lords in *Barry*, was followed in *R v Sefton Metropolitan Borough Council ex parte Help the Aged* (1997). In that case, the needs of an elderly woman who was admitted to a nursing home, and the cost of meeting those needs, were in issue. Having considered the case of *Barry*, the Court of Appeal ruled that a local authority was entitled to have regard to its own limited financial resources. However, where a need existed, the authority was under a statutory duty to make arrangements to meet that need and lack of resources was no excuse. The authority could not, from the time that a person was assessed as being in need, fail to meet their statutory duty. Financial considerations were uppermost in the decision in *R v Cambridge Health Authority ex parte B* (1995), in which the Court of Appeal held that the courts could not make judgments about how health authorities decide to allocate a limited budget. The health authority had refused to fund further chemotherapy or a second bone marrow transplant for a ten year old girl with only a few weeks to live.

---

46   See also *R v Liverpool Crown Court ex parte Luxury Leisure Ltd* (1998).

Notwithstanding that decisions relating to human life had to treated with the greatest seriousness, the court could not substitute its judgment about the allocation of financial resources for that of the authority.[47]

The Home Secretary was held to have taken irrelevant considerations into account, and failed to give weight to relevant considerations, in *R v Secretary of State for the Home Department ex parte Venables* (1997). In this case, when the Home Secretary decided to impose a tariff (the minimum sentence to be served to reflect retribution and deterrence) on the teenage killers of a young child, he took into account public opinion demanding that they be detained for life and failed to consider the progress which the killers had made in detention.

Acting in bad faith

To some extent, any decision which is *ultra vires* may involve 'bad faith' whenever there has been a failure to decide a case in the manner required by law. Some decisions however, may have inadvertently breached the requirements of legality, whereas others will reveal an improper motive and unreasonableness, and more clearly demonstrate that the decision maker acted in 'bad faith'.

Fettering discretion

An authority may act *ultra vires* if, in the exercise of its powers, it adopts a policy which effectively means that it is not truly exercising its discretion at all. This principle is explained in *R v Port of London Authority ex parte Kynoch* (1919), in which it was held that an authority could not adopt a rigid policy which had the effect of ensuring that applications of a certain category would invariably be refused. In *Kynoch*, the applicant sought judicial review of the decision of the Port of London Authority to refuse him permission to construct a wharf on land he owned adjoining the Thames river. Permission was refused on the basis that the Authority itself had a duty to provide the facilities. The challenge to the Authority's decision failed, on the basis that it appeared to the court that the Authority had given genuine consideration to the application on its merits.

Compare *Kynoch* with *British Oxygen Co v Board of Trade* (1971) in which *Kynoch* was judicially considered. In *BOC*, the House of Lords upheld the right of the Board of Trade to have a general policy, provided that the policy did not preclude the Board from considering individual cases. Lord Reid considered the scope of discretion, asserting that:

> There are two general grounds on which the exercise of an unqualified discretion can be attacked. It must not be exercised in bad faith, and it must not be so unreasonably exercised as to show that there cannot have been any real or genuine exercise of the discretion. But, apart from that, if the minister thinks that policy or good administration requires the operation of some limiting rule, I find nothing to stop him ... What the authority must not do is to refuse to listen at all.

---

47 See also *R v East Sussex County Council ex parte Tandy* (1998); *B v Harrow London Borough Council* (2000); *R v Camden and Islington Health Authority ex parte E* (2001).

The application failed. The Board of Trade had not adopted a rigid and invariable policy which rendered the consideration of applications a mere sham exercise in which there was no possibility of a fair consideration of the merits because of the adoption of a rigid policy.

However, in *H Lavender & Sons Ltd v Minister of Housing and Local Government* (1970), a different conclusion was reached. Lavender had applied for planning permission to extract sand and gravel from high grade agricultural land. The local planning authority refused permission and Lavender appealed to the Minister of Housing and Local Government. The appeal was dismissed, the Minister of Housing and Local Government being persuaded by the Minister of Agriculture that such land should be preserved for agricultural purposes. Accordingly, the minister ruled that:

> It is the minister's present policy that land should not be released for mineral working unless the Minister of Agriculture is not opposed. In the present case, the agricultural objection has not been waived and the minister has therefore decided not to grant planning permission for the working of the site.

The decision was set aside. The minister was entitled to have a policy but, in reality, in this instance, the minister's decision had been based solely on another minister's objection. The minister, therefore, did not open his mind to Lavender's application and thereby fettered his discretion. In reality, the decision to refuse planning permission was that of the Minister of Agriculture who had no power to determine such matters.

In *Stringer v Minister of Housing and Local Government* (1970), the court considered the legality of a minister's policy to restrict development of land which could interfere with the Jodrell Bank telescope. The court held that the minister's general policy was lawful, provided that the policy did not result in his failing to take into account relevant issues in each individual application for planning permission. In *Sagnata Investments v Norwich Corporation* (1971), the council had a policy never to grant permits for amusement arcades in Norwich. There was no objection to Sagnata Investments itself; rather, no application – whatever its merits – would have succeeded because of the council's policy. The court held that the council had paid no regard whatsoever to the merits of the application. The council's decision was therefore quashed.[48]

In *R v Chief Constable of North Wales Police ex parte AB* (1997),[49] the Queen's Bench Division ruled that the policy of the North Wales police to disclose information to members of the public concerning the presence of a former paedophile offender was not unlawful. The court recognised that, in general, good public administration involved not disclosing damaging information about individuals unless there was sound justification for so doing. The applicants for judicial review, who were married, had both been convicted of serious sexual offences against children, and had served long prison sentences. The Lord Chief Justice recognised the tension between the rights of former offenders and the

---

48 See also *Stringer v Minister of Housing and Local Government* (1970) on fettering discretion.
49 See *R (H) v Ashworth Hospital Authority; R (Ashworth Health Authority) v Mental Health Review Tribunal for West Midlands and North West Region* (2002).

interests of the community. The police had not adopted a policy of blanket disclosure, but had carefully considered the case on its merits, and accordingly had not fettered its discretion. The decision was upheld by the Court of Appeal.[50]

The House of Lords' decision in *R v Secretary of State for the Home Department ex parte Simms* (1999) is also significant in demonstrating the courts' refusal to allow a strict policy to undermine individual rights. The decision in *Simms* was reached on common law principles and before the Human Rights Act 1998 came into force, but nevertheless the approach taken is consistent with post-Human Rights Act cases. It may be compared with the House of Lords' decision in *Daly*, discussed below, in which a prison policy was held to violate a Convention right.[51] In *Simms*, the applicants had been convicted of murder but continued to plead their innocence; they had been refused permission to appeal against their convictions. The prisoners wished to pursue their claim to justice through the press. The Home Secretary had adopted a policy which imposed a blanket ban on journalists interviewing prisoners with a view to publication, on the basis that such publicity could undermine prison control and discipline. The House of Lords overruled the Court of Appeal's decision upholding the ban. Lord Steyn concluded – in the language of proportionality and human rights[52] – that 'these provisions are exorbitant in width in so far as they would undermine the fundamental rights invoked by the applicants in the present proceedings and are therefore *ultra vires'*.

Unauthorised delegation

Where powers are conferred by statute, the general rule is that they may not be delegated unless that delegation is authorised by law. Not all delegations will be unlawful. The courts will not hold, for instance, that a minister must exercise each and every power personally. It is accepted that, where statute confers powers on ministers, the powers are, in fact, exercisable on his behalf by the personnel of his department. As explained in *Local Government Board v Arlidge* (1915), 'a minister cannot do everything himself'.[53] In *Arlidge* – an early and seminal case which ensured the conduct of government under the supervision of the courts – the court held that, whilst a minister could lawfully delegate his power of determination to a subordinate, he, nevertheless, remained constitutionally and personally accountable to parliament for the conduct of his department.[54]

---

50 Reported as *R v Chief Constable of North Wales Police ex parte Thorpe* (1998), and see the government's proposals for arrangements on release of paedophiles from prison, HL Deb, Vol 589, Col 479, 5 May 1998. See also *R v Secretary of State for the Home Department ex parte Dinc* (1998); *R v North West Lancashire Health Authority ex parte A* (2000). On judicial review of immigration and asylum decisions, see Chapter 24.

51 In *Daly*, the right in question was the right to privacy. In *Simms* – had it been heard after the Human Rights Act 1998 came into force, the issue would have been freedom of expression under Article 10.

52 On which see below.

53 Note also that this case is also an early authority for the proposition that the rules of natural justice do not necessarily require an oral hearing in every case: *per* Taylor LJ in *R v Army Board of the Defence Council ex parte Anderson* (1991).

54 See Dicey, 1885, Appendix 2.

This principle was well illustrated in *Carltona v Works Commissioners* (1943). The Commissioners were given powers, under wartime regulations, to requisition property. Carltona's property was requisitioned, the order for requisition being signed, for and on behalf of the Commissioners, by a civil servant with the rank of assistant secretary. Lord Greene MR stated:

> It cannot be supposed that the particular statutory provision meant that in every case the minister in person should direct his mind to the matter. Constitutionally the decision of such an officer is the decision of the minister; the minister is responsible to Parliament. If the minister delegated to a junior official then he would have to answer to Parliament ...

The decision in *Arlidge* may be compared with that of *Barnard v National Dock Labour Board* (1953). In *Barnard*, disciplinary powers delegated by statute to the London Dock Board were subdelegated to a port manager. That delegation was held to be *ultra vires*, on the basis that such a disciplinary function could not lawfully be delegated to another and must be exercised by the Board to whom the power was granted. Similarly, in *R v Talbot Borough Council ex parte Jones* (1988), where a local councillor applied for local authority housing. The housing tenancy committee resolved that the applicant should be given priority status and that her rehousing, subsequent to divorce, should be decided by the chairman and vice chairman of the committee, according to the Council's Standing Orders,[55] in consultation with the Borough Housing Officer. In 1986, the Housing Officer allocated her a house. In proceedings for judicial review, it was held that the decision to allocate housing could not lawfully be subdelegated from the chairman and vice chairman of the committee to the Housing Officer. The decision was also void on the grounds that irrelevant considerations had been taken into account and that relevant considerations – the needs of others on the waiting list – had been ignored.[56]

Failure to act

An authority may be under a statutory duty to take action and, depending upon the specificity of that duty, may be held to be acting unlawfully if it fails to act. This is a difficult area of law, in that some duties imposed by statute are clear and precise, and hence enforceable by the courts, whereas others may be of a general, non-specific nature and thus not court-enforceable: all will turn on the wording of the statute. Statute may stipulate the objective to be achieved but leave it to a local authority or other public body to determine the manner in which the objective should be achieved. Furthermore, in many cases, statute will provide that the Secretary of State shall have default powers, by the use of which he can compel a local authority to act should it fail so to do, in which case, the courts may be reluctant to permit the pursuit of an alternative remedy. In *R v Secretary of State for the Environment ex parte Norwich City Council* (1982), the authority had the duty to

---

55 Under the Local Government Act 1972, s 101.
56 In *R v Home Secretary ex parte Oladehinde* (1991), the House of Lords ruled that the Immigration Act 1971 provided specific matters which could not be delegated by the minister, and the court would not infer further restrictions.

sell council housing to tenants[57] at a discounted rate. If a tenant exercised his or her right to buy, and the council did not respect that right, the minister could exercise his powers to ensure compliance with the legislation, if satisfied that a tenant's right had 'not effectively and expeditiously' been recognised. The council argued that this policy was reasonable. However, the Court of Appeal rejected that argument, since the council had no discretion in light of the statutory right to buy. The failure of the council to implement the 'right to buy' legislation was to be controlled by the minister. Should the minister, in the exercise of his powers, act *ultra vires*, the court will control the exercise of power by judicial review. However, the courts may not be willing to rule against the minister merely because the court takes a different view of the merits of the case (*per* Lord Denning).[58]

PROCEDURAL IMPROPRIETY

Under statute

Failure to comply with procedures laid down by statute may invalidate a decision. The courts distinguish between those procedural requirements which are mandatory, the breach of which will render a decision void, and those which are directory, which may not invalidate the decision taken. In *London and Clydesdale Estates Ltd v Aberdeen District Council* (1979), the House of Lords emphasised the inherent vagueness in the distinction and stressed that the court would not draw a hard and fast line: it is all a matter of degree and the particular circumstances of the case must be examined.[59] However, in some cases, the requirement to adhere to procedural correctness is clear. For example, in *Bradbury v Enfield London Borough Council* (1967), the Education Act 1944 provided that, if a local education authority intends to establish new schools or cease to maintain existing schools, notice must be given to the minister, following which, public notice must be given in order to allow interested parties to comment.[60] The Council breached the requirement of public notice and the plaintiffs sought an injunction. The Council claimed that educational chaos would occur if they were required to comply with the procedural requirements. That plea met with little sympathy in court. Lord Denning stated that:

> ... if a local authority does not fulfil the requirements of the law, this court will see that it does fulfil them. ... I can well see that there may be a considerable upset for a number of people, but I think it far more important to uphold the rule of law. Parliament has laid down these requirements so as to ensure that the electors can make their objections and have them properly considered. We must see that their rights are upheld. [p 1324]

Further, as has been seen earlier, in the *Aylesbury Mushroom* case,[61] the court ruled that the statutory requirements of consultation[62] with organisations or

---

57 Housing Act 1980. The Housing Act 1985 confers default powers on the minister to act where a local council fails to comply with the policy of the Act.
58 See further the case law on resource allocation at pp 771–72 above.
59 See also *Wang v Commissioner of the Inland Revenue* (1994).
60 Education Act 1944, s 13.
61 *Agricultural, Horticultural and Forestry Industry Training Board v Aylesbury Mushroom Ltd* (1972).
62 Under the Industrial Training Act 1964, s 1(4).

associations which represented substantial numbers of people could not be avoided by consultation with the largest representative body of all agricultural horticultural and forestry industry, workers – the National Farmers' Union. For true consultation to take place in accordance with law, there must be communication with the representative organisations and the opportunity given of responding thereto, without which 'there can be no consultation'.

However, on occasion, although an authority is under a duty to act, and fails to act, the court may nevertheless uphold the decision made, provided that the decision making process was otherwise fair and the failure to act does not affect the quality of the decision reached. This was the position in *Berkeley v Secretary of State for the Environment* (2000). In this case, in a planning application by Fulham Football Club to redevelop part of its land to provide apartments and a riverside walk, the Secretary of State was required[63] to consider the environmental impact of the proposed development, and to issue an 'environmental statement'. The Court of Appeal ruled that the Secretary of State's failure to act did not invalidate the decision. The planning application had been referred to the Secretary of State who had appointed an inspector. A public hearing had been held, at which the applicant had been heard and at which the environmental impact of the proposed development had been fully considered. The court found that 'the procedures adopted, although flawed, had been thorough and effective [so as] to enable the inspector to make a comprehensive judgment on all the environmental issues'.[64]

Breach of natural justice

The rules of natural justice are common law rules – although, in many instances, their requirements may be made statutory. The fundamental dictate of justice is that those affected by decision makers should be dealt with in a fair manner. In order for this to be achieved, there may be several requirements which must be fulfilled. As Lord Lane CJ stated in *R v Commission for Racial Equality ex parte Cottrell and Rothon* (1980):[65]

> As has frequently been said, and there is no harm in repeating it, all that the rules of natural justice mean is that the proceedings must be conducted in a way which is fair ... fair in all the circumstances.

That the rules of natural justice are not rigid and determinate is emphasised by Lord Bridge in *Lloyd v McMahon* (1987):

> ... the so called rules of natural justice are not engraved on tablets of stone. To use the phrase which better expresses the underlying concept, what the requirements of fairness demand when any body, domestic, administrative or judicial, has to make a decision which will affect the rights of individuals depends on the character of the decision making body, the kind of question it has to make and the statutory or other framework in which it operates.

---

63 Under the Town and Country Planning (Assessment of Environmental Effects) Regulations, SI 1988/1199, reg 4.

64 See also *R v Secretary of State for the Home Department ex parte Jeyeanthan; Ravichandran v Secretary of State for the Home Department* (1999).

65 At p 1586.

The requirements of fairness are reflected in Article 6 of the European Convention on Human Rights, now enforceable in the domestic courts under the Human Rights Act 1998. Article 6 requires a 'fair and public hearing within a reasonable time by an independent and impartial tribunal established by law'.

The rule against bias: *nemo iudex in causa sua*[66]

The essence of justice lies in a fair hearing. The rule against bias is strict: it is not necessary to show that actual bias existed, the merest appearance or possibility of bias will suffice: '... justice should not only be done but should manifestly and undoubtedly be seen to be done.'[67] The suspicion of bias must, however, be a reasonable one. Both financial or personal interest in a case may disqualify a person from adjudicating.

Financial bias

A financial interest in the outcome of a case will automatically disqualify a judge from hearing a case. In *Dr Bonham's Case* (1609), Lord Coke held that members of a board which determined the level of physicians' fines could not both impose and receive the fines, thus giving early judicial expression for the requirement of freedom from bias. An early expression of the absolute requirement not only to be impartial in fact, but also to be demonstrably and clearly free from the merest suspicion of bias is found in *Dimes v Grand Junction Canal Ltd* (1852). In *Dimes*, Lord Cottenham LC held shares in the canal company involved in litigation. The House of Lords set aside the decision in which he had adjudicated despite the fact that:

> No one can suppose that Lord Cottenham could be in the remotest degree influenced by the interest ... It is of the last importance that the maxim that no man is to be judge in his own cause should be held sacred.

Thus, the mere existence of a financial interest, even where it does not, in fact, result in actual bias but may present the appearance of bias will be sufficient to disqualify a judge from adjudication.

In *R v Sussex Justices ex parte McCarthy* (1924), the applicant had been charged with dangerous driving and convicted. On discovering that the clerk to the magistrates' court was a solicitor who had represented the person suing McCarthy for damages, McCarthy applied for judicial review based on bias on the part of the clerk. The clerk had retired with the magistrates when they were considering their verdict. It was accepted that the magistrates neither sought advice nor were given advice by the clerk during their retirement. Nevertheless, McCarthy's conviction was invalidated on the basis of the possibility of bias.

The question of financial bias again arose in *Metropolitan Properties Co v Lannon* (1969), where an application was lodged by a property company in order to

---

66 On the independence of the judiciary see Chapter 5.
67 See *R v Sussex Justices ex parte McCarthy* (1924), p 259, discussed below.

challenge a decision of a rent assessment committee on the basis that Lannon, a member of the committee had, in his professional capacity as a solicitor, given advice to tenants of a close business associate of the property company. Lord Denning MR ruled that, while there was no actual bias:

> ... the court looks at the impression which would be given to other people. Even if he was as impartial as could be, nevertheless, if right minded persons would think that, in the circumstances, there was a real likelihood of bias on his part, then he should not sit. And, if he does sit, his decision cannot stand ...

> The court will not inquire whether he did, in fact, favour one side unfairly. Suffice it that reasonable people might think he did. The reason is plain enough. Justice must be rooted in confidence: and confidence is destroyed when right minded people go away thinking: 'The judge was biased.' [p 599]

A financial interest in a case which does not go beyond the financial interest of any citizen does not disqualify judges from sitting. Thus, for example, in *Bromley London Borough Council v Greater London Council* (1983), the fact that all the judges in the Court of Appeal were themselves both taxpayers and users of public transport in London did not disqualify them from hearing the case.

The same position prevails in the United States of America[68] but, there, the issue of the financial interests of federal judges is expressly covered by statute. The Ethics in Government Act 1978 requires that Supreme Court and Federal judges must make a public declaration of 'income, gifts, shares, liabilities and transactions in securities and real estate'.[69]

Other bias

Judges – as with any other person – may exhibit bias by virtue of race, sex, politics, background, association and opinions.[70] When adjudicating, however, they must be demonstrably impartial. This impartiality involves:

> ... the judge, listening to each side with equal attention, and coming to a decision on the argument, irrespective of his personal view about the litigants ...

and, further, a requirement that:

> Whatever his personal beliefs, the judge should seek to give effect to the common values of the community, rather than any sectional system of values to which he may adhere.[71]

Where a judge feels that he has a bias against one of the parties to litigation he may disqualify himself from sitting on the case, as did Lord Denning MR in *Ex parte Church of Scientology of California* (1978). There, counsel for the Church requested that he disqualify himself as a result of eight previous cases involving the Church on which he had sat. In *R v Bow Street Metropolitan and Stipendiary Magistrate ex parte Pinochet Ugarte* (1999), extradition proceedings against the

---

68   28 USC S455(b).
69   See Cranston, 1979.
70   See Griffith, 1997; Devlin, 1978.
71   Bell, 1983, pp 4 and 8.

former Chilean Head of State were challenged on the basis that one of the Law Lords, Lord Hoffmann, had links with Amnesty International, the charitable pressure group which works on behalf of political prisoners around the world, which had been allowed to present evidence to the court. It was accepted that there was no actual bias on the part of Lord Hoffmann, but there were concerns that the public perception might be that a senior judge was biased. As a result, the proceedings were abandoned and re-heard by a new bench of seven judges.

The Court of Appeal has jurisdiction to re-open proceedings if it is clearly established that a significant injustice has probably occurred and that there is no alternative effective remedy. Before exercising such a power, the court considers the effect of re-opening the appeal on others and the extent to which the complaining party is the author of his own misfortune. Where a remedy lies in an appeal to the House of Lords, the Court of Appeal will only give permission to re-open an appeal if it is satisfied that leave to appeal to the House of Lords will not be given.[72]

There has been uncertainty and inconsistency in the interpretation of 'bias'. In *R v Gough* (1993), opposing counsel presented two different tests for bias. The first suggested criterion was whether a reasonable and fair minded person sitting in the court and knowing all the relevant facts would have had a reasonable suspicion that a fair trial of the defendant was not possible – the 'reasonable suspicion' test. The second suggested test was whether there was a real likelihood of bias. The question to be asked is whether there was a 'real danger' that a trial may not have been fair as a result of bias – the 'real likelihood' test.[73] The House of Lords declared that the correct test was whether there was a real likelihood, in the sense of a real possibility, of bias of the part of a justice or member of a tribunal. The *Gough* test must now be considered in light of *Porter v Magill* (2002 discussed below), which provides the definitive test.

The Court of Appeal reconsidered judicial bias in the *Locabail (UK) Ltd v Bayfield Properties Ltd* (2000) cases. The court distinguished the two rules relating to disqualification, the first being where the judge had an interest in a case which he decided, as in *Dimes v Grand Junction Canal* (1852), and where he would be automatically disqualified. The second rule was that based on examination of all the relevant circumstances, where there was a real danger or possibility of bias, as in *R v Gough* (1993). In relation to the circumstances surrounding *Timmins v Gormley*, one of the *Locabail* cases, which concerned the publication, by the Recorder who adjudicated in a personal injury case, of articles which were allegedly biased in favour of claimants and against insurers, the court ruled that, taking a broad common sense approach, a lay observer with knowledge of the facts could not have excluded the possibility that the Recorder was biased. While it was not inappropriate for a judge to publish in his area of expertise, and that such contributions could further rather than hinder the administration of justice, nevertheless, it was always inappropriate for a judge to use intemperate language

---

72   See *Taylor v Lawrence* (2002).
73   At p 727; see also *R v Spencer* (1987).

about subjects on which he had adjudicated or would have to adjudicate. The appeal was allowed and a retrial ordered.[74]

In *Porter v Magill* the Leader of Westminster Council had allegedly adopted a policy of selling certain properties to tenants who would then be disposed to vote Conservative in a forthcoming election. The issue of bias arose through the role of the district auditor, Magill. There were allegations that the auditor had acted as investigator, prosecutor and judge. Moreover, it was alleged that he had prejudged the issue. The common law rule against bias came under fresh scrutiny. Uncertainty had arisen due to a divergence between the English and Scottish courts, the fact that some Commonwealth jurisdictions did not follow the *Gough* test, and that the test also diverged from the approach used by the Court of Human Rights in Strasbourg. Lord Hope stated that the question of bias should be phrased in the following manner:

> The question is whether the fair-minded and informed observer, having considered the facts, would conclude that there was a real possibility that the tribunal was biased.[75]

The House of Lords considered the issue of bias in *Gillies v Secretary of State for Work and Pensions* (2006). A Disability Appeal Tribunal consists of a legally qualified chairman and two other members, including a medical member. The medical member of the tribunal in question was a doctor who for a number of years had been providing reports for the Benefits Agency as an examining medical practitioner. The appellant, whose application for renewal of a disability living allowance had been refused argued that there was a reasonable apprehension that the medical member had been biased. Referring to *Porter v Magill* (2002) the House of Lords ruled that a fair minded observer would have had no reason to suppose that the doctor would not act impartially towards the claimant. Her experience in the preparation of reports was an asset and the bringing of experience to bear when examining evidence and reaching a decision had nothing to do with bias.

The right to a fair hearing: *audi alteram partem*

It is a fundamental requirement of justice that, when a person's interests are affected by a judicial or administrative decision, he or she has the opportunity both to know and to understand any allegations made, and to make representations to the decision maker to meet the allegations. As noted above, the right to fair trial is protected under Article 6 of the European Convention on Human Rights. The case law of the Court of Human Rights and the domestic courts is discussed in Chapter 19. By way of example, a fair determination of a case may involve one or more of the following:

(a) the right to being given notification of a hearing;

(b) the right to be given indications of any adverse evidence;

---

74 See also *R v Local Commissioner for Administration ex parte Liverpool City Council* (1999), discussed in Chapter 28.

75 See also *Secretary of State for Work and Pensions v Cunningham* (2004); *AWG Group Ltd v Morrison* (2006).

(c) the right to be given an opportunity to respond to the evidence;

(d) the right to an oral hearing;

(e) the right to legal representation at a hearing;

(f) the right to question witnesses.

The basic requirement is that – irrespective of the decision making body, whether 'judicial', 'quasi-judicial' or 'administrative' – the individual should be treated fairly in the decision making process.

'Judicial', 'quasi-judicial' and 'administrative' functions: the distinctions

An early expression of the requirement of a hearing is to be found in *Cooper v Wandsworth Board of Works* (1893). There, Cooper had – without giving notice to the Board, as required by law – started to erect a house. The Board had the power to demolish buildings built without the requisite permission, and exercised their power so to do. Cooper applied for – and recovered – damages from the Board for trespass to his property. Byles J held that the plaintiff should have been given a hearing before the Board exercised their powers, even though there was no express statutory requirement that they do so:

> ... although there are no positive words in a statute requiring that the party shall be heard, yet the justice of the common law shall supply the omission of the legislature.[76]

Ridge v Baldwin (1964) represents a classic case which reveals judicial insistence on procedural fairness.[77] Ridge, the Chief Constable of Brighton, had been suspended from duty following charges of conspiracy to obstruct the course of justice. Despite Ridge having been cleared of any allegations against him, the judge made comments which were critical of Ridge's conduct. Subsequently, Ridge was dismissed from the force.[78] Ridge was not invited to attend the meeting at which the decision to dismiss him was reached, although he was later given an opportunity to appear before the committee which confirmed its earlier decision. Ridge appealed to the Home Secretary,[79] who dismissed his appeal. Ridge then sought a declaration that the dismissal was *ultra vires,* on the basis that the committee had violated the rules of natural justice. The following extract is taken from Lord Reid's judgment, in which the opportunity was taken to review the doctrine.

> The principle of *audi alteram partem* goes back many centuries in our law and appears in a multitude of judgments of judges of the highest authority. In modern times opinions have sometimes been expressed to the effect that natural justice is so vague as to be almost meaningless ... It appears to me that one reason why the authorities on natural justice have been found difficult to reconcile is that insufficient attention has been paid to the great difference between various kinds of cases in which it has been sought to

---

76 See *Steeple v Derbyshire County Council* (1984); but cf *R v Amber Valley District Council ex parte Jackson* (1984). See also *R v Hendon Rural District Council ex parte Chorley* (1933).

77 See, on this point, *R v Hillingdon Borough Council ex parte Royco Homes Ltd* (1974); *R v Commission for Racial Equality ex parte Cottrell and Rothon* (1980).

78 Under the Municipal Corporations Act 1882, s 191(4), which provides that a constable may be dismissed on the basis of either negligence in the discharge of his duty or being 'otherwise unfit' for duty.

79 Under the Police (Appeals) Act 1927.

apply the principle. What a minister ought to do in considering objections to a scheme may be very different from what a watch committee ought to do in considering whether to dismiss a chief constable ... [p 64]

... I would think that the authority was wholly in favour of the appellant, but the respondent's argument was mainly based on what has been said in a number of fairly recent cases dealing with different subject matter. Those cases deal with the decisions of ministers, officials and bodies of various kinds which adversely affected property rights or privileges of persons who had no opportunity or no proper opportunity of presenting their cases before the decisions were given ... [p 68]

The right to a hearing founded a challenge in *Re Pergamon Press Ltd* (1971),[80] in which the directors of two companies refused to answer questions unless given a judicial-style hearing. The court ruled, however, that, although the inspectors appointed to investigate the companies were under a duty to act fairly, this must be weighed against the interests of good administration.

Impartiality was scrutinised by the European Court of Human Rights in *Kingsley v United Kingdom* (2001). The Court ruled that the applicant's right to fair trial, guaranteed by Article 6, had been violated. The applicant had been refused a certificate to hold a management position in the gaming industry, by the Gaming Board of Great Britain. He sought judicial review, alleging bias on the part of a supervisory board. The Court examined the composition of the panel which decided that the applicant was not a fit and proper person to hold a certificate, and concluded that it did not present the necessary appearance of impartiality to amount to an independent and impartial tribunal. However, the Court went on to assert that even where an adjudicatory body did not comply with the requirements of Article 6, there would be no breach of the Article if the proceedings were subject to 'subsequent control by a judicial body that had full jurisdiction and did provide the guarantees of Article 6(1)'. The Court of Appeal accepted that the applicant had an arguable case, and that there was a real risk of bias, but had concluded that the decision had to stand, since the decision could only be made by the board and could not be delegated to an independent tribunal. The Court of Human Rights ruled that where a complaint was made about a lack of impartiality, the concept of full jurisdiction required that the 'reviewing court not only considered the complaint but had the ability to quash the impugned decision and to remit the case for a new decision by an impartial body'. In the present case, the domestic courts were unable to remit the case to an impartial tribunal; neither the High Court nor the Court of Appeal had 'full jurisdiction' within the meaning of Article 6 and there was a violation of the Convention.

However, the Court of Appeal in *R (Beeson) v Dorset County Council* (2003) affirmed the view that the availability of judicial review satisfied the requirements of Article 6 of the European Convention on Human Rights regarding an independent and impartial tribunal. Even where the first instance decision maker lacked the necessary element of impartiality (here the tribunal had two members who were local councillors in a dispute over the now-deceased's entitlements regarding residential care and the value of his property), the availability of

---

80   See also *Maxwell v Department of Trade* (1974).

judicial review would remedy that defect 'unless there was some special feature of the case to show the contrary'. In the instant case there was no special feature and there was no evidence that the panel had not arrived at a fair and reasonable recommendation.

The duty to act 'fairly' and concept of 'legitimate expectation'[81]

Irrespective of the labelling attached to the body in question, there exists a duty to 'act fairly'. The principles of fairness have not been given either universal or consistent interpretations. For example, in *McInnes v Onslow Fane* (1978), Megarry VC stated:

> ... the further the situation is away from anything that resembles a judicial or quasi-judicial decision, and the further the question is removed from what may reasonably be called a justiciable question, the more appropriate it is to reject an expression which includes the word justice and to use instead terms such as 'fairness' or the 'duty to act fairly'. [p 1530]

In *Council of Civil Service Unions v Minister for the Civil Service* (1985), the House of Lords once again turned to the apparent differences in the concepts, Lord Roskill seemingly rejecting the phrase 'natural justice' in favour of the duty to 'act fairly'. Lord Roskill asserted that:

> The phrase [natural justice] might now be allowed to find a permanent resting place and be better replaced by speaking of a duty to act fairly. But the latter phrase must not in its turn be misunderstood or misused. It is not for the courts to determine whether a particular policy or particular decisions taken in fulfilment of that policy are fair. They are only concerned with the manner in which those decisions have been taken and the extent of the duty to act fairly will vary greatly from case to case as indeed the decided cases since 1950 consistently show. [p 414]

The principle of fairness can be clearly seen in the case of *Re HK (An Infant)* (1967), wherein it was held that, whilst immigration officers were not obliged to hold a hearing before deciding an immigrant's status, they were nevertheless under an obligation to act fairly. The duty to give a hearing will be higher if a 'legitimate expectation' has been created in the mind of the complainant by the public body concerned.[82]

A legitimate expectation will arise in the mind of the complainant wherever he or she has been led to understand – by the words or actions of the decision maker – that certain procedures will be followed in reaching a decision. The complainant may have been led to believe, for example, that there would be an oral hearing, or that he would be able to make formal representations. Where such expectations have been created, the decision maker is not free simply to ignore the procedures which have been indicated. Two considerations apply to legitimate expectations.

---

81 See Sales and Steyn, 2004.
82 The courts are also concerned to ensure that government proposals which will affect individual citizens are fairly presented in order to enable objectors to address the issue in question. In *R v Secretary of State for Transport ex parte Richmond upon Thames London Borough Council (No 4)* (1994), the Court of Appeal ruled that the government's proposals to restrict night flights at Heathrow, Gatwick and Stansted had been fairly set out in consultations documents. On this issue see further Chapter 19. See also *R v National Lottery Commission ex parte Camelot Group plc* (2001).

The first is where an individual or group has been led to believe that a certain procedure will apply. The second is where an individual or group relies upon a policy or guidelines which have previously governed an area of executive action.

The principle of the protection of legitimate expectations was recognised under English law in the 1970s in *R v Liverpool Corporation ex parte Liverpool Taxi Fleet Operators' Association* (1972) (discussed below),[83] and it is one of the major principles of European Community law.[84] The concept is one which has given rise to judicial disagreement. The central difficulty with legitimate expectation is whether an individual affected by an administrative decision has a legitimate expectation that the correct procedure will be followed, or whether the expectation to be protected can also be substantive. The debate as to whether legitimate expectations are confined to procedure and do not extend to substance was considered in *R v Ministry of Agriculture ex parte Hamble Fisheries* (1995) in which Sedley J stated that the applicants had a legitimate expectation on the basis of the Ministry's previous policy and accepted that substantive as well as procedure legitimate expectations could be protected. Conversely in *R v Secretary of State for the Home Department ex parte Hargreaves* (1996), in the Court of Appeal Hirst LJ rejected Sedley J's approach and stated that in relation to matters of substance the test was that of *Wednesbury* unreasonableness – not legitimate expectation.

The Court of Appeal ruled in *R (Bibi) v Newham LBC* (2001) that a local authority which made promises which gave rise to legitimate expectations that the applicants would be provided with accommodation with security of tenure had to be honoured to the extent that the expectation was taken into account when allocating the applicants' position on the housing list. The applicants were refugees and accepted by the authority as homeless. The authority wrongly thought that it was under a duty to provide accommodation with security of tenure. However, the promise that such accommodation would be provided founded a legitimate expectation which had to be considered.[85]

However, while the concept of legitimate expectation has, according to the Court of Appeal, achieved an important place in developing the law of administrative fairness, whether such an expectation has been raised is dependent upon the circumstances in which statements are made, and whether in an instant case they could be taken as propounding a policy or merely statements applicable to particular cases. In *R v Secretary for the Home Department ex parte Behluli* (1998), the Home Secretary had ordered the removal of the applicant to Italy under section 2 of the Asylum and Immigration Act 1996. The applicant argued that he had a legitimate expectation that his case would be dealt with in accordance with the Dublin Convention.[86] The Court of Appeal ruled, however, that the statements relied on by the applicant fell short of the requirements necessary to establish to the requisite degree of clarity and certainty that the Secretary of State

---

83 See also *Council for Civil Service Unions v Minister for Civil Service* (1984).
84 See Usher, 2005.
85 See also *Henry Boot Homes Ltd v Bassetlaw DC* (2002).
86 Relating to the removal of persons to safe third countries.

would deal with all applications for asylum in accordance with the Convention and not in accordance with the Asylum and Immigration Act 1996 and rules made thereunder.

Legitimate expectations were again considered by the Court of Appeal in *R (Nadarajah) v Secretary of State for the Home Department, R (Abdi) v Same* (2005). Lord Justice Laws stated that the theme running through the legitimate expectation cases was that 'where a public authority had issued a promise or adopted a practice which represented how it proposed to act in a given area, the law would require the promise or practice to be honoured unless there was good reason not to do so'. The principle underlying that requirement was one of good administration which was a legal standard which although not articulated in the Convention on Human Rights nevertheless took its place alongside such rights as the right to fair trial and no punishment without law. The principle of good administration would be undermined 'if the law did not insist that any failure or refusal to comply was objectively justified as a proportionate measure in the circumstances'. Moreover, that approach made 'no distinction between procedural and substantive expectations'.

The giving of assurances

In *Attorney General for Hong Kong v Ng Yuen Shiu* (1983), the applicant had been an illegal immigrant for some years. He was eventually detained and an order was made for his deportation. The Director of Immigration had given a public undertaking that illegal immigrants such as Ng Yuen Shiu would not be deported without first being interviewed. The assurance was also given that 'each case would be treated on its merits'. Lord Fraser of Tullybelton in the Privy Council ruled that there was no general right in an alien to have a hearing in accordance with the rules of natural justice. Nevertheless, a 'legitimate expectation' had been created in the mind of the immigrant and, accordingly, breach of the requirement of fairness justified the order for his removal from Hong Kong to be quashed.[87] A public body cannot give undertakings which conflict with its statutory duty. In *R v Inland Revenue Commissioners ex parte Preston* (1985),[88] the House of Lords ruled that if it should do so, it was in principle entitled to go back on its undertaking. However, if the authority made an assurance and then exercised its statutory power in a manner which caused unfairness, that exercise could be viewed as an abuse of power and the undertaking upheld by the courts.

Fairness may involve the due consultation of interested parties before their rights are affected by decisions. For example, in *R v Liverpool Corporation ex parte Liverpool Taxi Fleet Operators Association* (1972), the corporation had given undertakings to the taxi drivers to the effect that their licences would not be revoked without prior consultation. When the corporation acted in breach of

---

87 See also *R (Zegiri) v Secretary of State for the Home Department* relying on *R v Secretary of State for the Home Department ex parte Besnik Gashi* (1999).
88 See also *R v Inland Revenue Commissioners ex parte MFK Underwriting Agencies Ltd* (1990).

this undertaking, the court ruled that it had a duty to comply with its commitment to consultation.[89]

The Court of Appeal in *R v North and East Devon Health Authority ex parte Coughlan* (1999)[90] ruled that a decision by a health authority to close a home for the severely disabled at which the applicant resided, and to transfer her to the care of a local authority, was unlawful. The applicant had been assured by the predecessor to the health authority that the home was her home for life, thus creating a legitimate expectation which no public interest overrode. Furthermore, under Article 8 of the Convention on Human Rights, everyone had a right to respect for his home and the judge had been entitled to treat the case as one in which there would be an unjustifiable breach of Article 8.

The *Coughlan* decision has significant implications for judicial review. The Court of Appeal moved beyond the traditional test of procedural impropriety, thereby developing the law relating to legitimate expectations. The Court identified three differing situations which would give rise to differing approaches to review. The first related to a public body which had to consider previous policy or representations before changing that policy. Here, review on *Wednesbury* grounds was appropriate. The second class of case concerned the legitimate expectation of being consulted, in which case the court would look closely at the reasons for the change of policy and whether that decision was fair. The third class of case is where a promise by a public body had brought about a 'substantive legitimate expectation' on the part of the applicant. Here the court's approach would be more intensive. It would, in Craig and Schonberg's analysis, 'decide whether the frustration of the expectation was so unfair that to take a new and different course of action would amount to an abuse of power', and once the legitimate expectation had been established, 'the court would have the task of "weighing the requirements of fairness against any overriding interest relied upon for the change of policy"'.[91] Accordingly, there are two standards of review, one where the decision was irrational in the *Wednesbury* sense, and one on the basis of abuse of power, which was for the court to determine. Policy changes on the part of public authorities are not unusual nor unlawful in the general case, nor should the courts, as the Court of Appeal recognised, jeopardise 'the important principle that the executive's policy making powers should not be trammelled'. Where, however, a substantive legitimate expectation has arisen – as in *Coughlan* – through the express promise made in precise terms, and was relied on by the applicant, the decision was unlawful.

---

89 See also *R v Ministry of Defence ex parte Walker* (2000) in which the House of Lords ruled that a soldier injured in action in the former Yugoslavia was not entitled to compensation under the Criminal Injuries Compensation Scheme. A policy adopted in 1994 excluding compensation for death or injury resulting from war operations or military action in peacekeeping operations in Bosnia was not irrational. The applicant had been given no assurances and the only legitimate expectation he had was that the Ministry of Defence would apply the policy in force at the time of his injury.

90 See Craig and Schonberg, 2000; Roberts, 2001; Elliott, 2000; Hilson, 2002.

91 *Coughlan*, para 57, cited in Craig and Schonberg, 2000.

Acting in a manner so as to create an expectation

A public body may act in a manner which creates an expectation in the mind of a person or body. For example, in *R v Secretary of State for Health ex parte US Tobacco International Inc* (1992), the company had opened a factory in 1985, with a government grant, for the production of oral snuff. The government made the grant available notwithstanding its awareness of the health risks of the product. In 1988, however, the government – having received further advice from a committee – announced its intention to ban snuff. The company sought judicial review, relying on a legitimate expectation based on the government's action. The court ruled, however, that, even though the applicant had a legitimate expectation, that expectation could not override the public interest in banning a harmful substance.

The existence of policies and/or guidance

In *R v Secretary of State for the Home Department ex parte Asif Mahmood Khan* (1984), the Home Office had published a circular stating the criteria to be used for determining whether a child could enter the United Kingdom. When the applicant sought to bring his nephew into the United Kingdom from Pakistan, entry was refused. In judicial review proceedings, it was established that the immigration rules did not specify any particular criteria, but that the Home Department's circular did so specify. It was also established that the criteria used in determining whether to allow the child into the country were different from that provided under the circular. The Home Secretary had acted *ultra vires*: he had created legitimate expectation and was not free to employ different criteria.[92]

A further challenge to the powers of the Home Secretary can be seen in *R v Secretary of State for the Home Department ex parte Ruddock* (1987). The Home Secretary had authorised the interception of telephone calls without statutory authority.[93] The basis on which the Home Secretary decided to intercept calls was provided in a circular. The applicant claimed that the Home Secretary had failed to follow the criteria laid down in the circular. The court held that the applicant had a legitimate expectation that the criteria would be followed but, nevertheless, the applicant lost the case because it was held that the minister could have come to the judgment that the criteria were applied and that he was not acting unreasonably. The decision, which appears to weaken the binding nature of legitimate expectations, is explainable in light of the alleged national security aspects of the case. The applicant had been a leading member of the Campaign for Nuclear Disarmament, which the government feared was being influenced by the Communist Party.

A change made to a policy which had been embedded in an agreement between prison inmates and prison authorities was considered by the Court of

---

92 Cf *Re Findlay* (1985), wherein the doctrine was limited merely to an expectation that prisoners would have their cases individually considered according to whatever policy the minister chose to adopt.

93 The case was decided before the Interception of Communications Act 1985 was implemented.

Appeal in *R v Secretary of State for the Home Department ex parte Hargreaves* (1996). The agreement stated that prisoners could apply for home leave after serving one third of their sentence, subject to good behaviour. The Secretary of State decided, however, that only prisoners who had served half their sentence could apply for home leave. Hargreaves and others unsuccessfully applied for judicial review. They subsequently appealed to the Court of Appeal.

The Court of Appeal held that the agreement between the prison inmates and the prison authorities did not give rise to a legitimate expectation which could be enforced by judicial review. Furthermore, the Home Secretary's decision to change the policy was not to be tested against the overall fairness of that decision, but rather whether the policy was unreasonable in the *Wednesbury* sense. On that test, the Home Secretary's decision was not unlawful. The Court of Appeal expressed regret, however, that the documents on which the prisoners relied were 'other than completely clear and unambiguous', and called for greater clarity in the future.

The right to make representations

Inevitably, the extent to which the individual is enabled to make representations to a decision making body will be inextricably linked to the question of the right to a hearing. Where there exists no right to an oral hearing, the question becomes one of the extent to which – and means by which – the view of the individual can be put to the decision making authority. It may well be the case that the opportunity to make written submissions will satisfy the requirements for justice and fairness. For example, in *Lloyd v McMahon* (1987), local government councillors were in breach of their statutory duty to set the level of local rates. When the district auditor came to determine the issue, the applicants claimed the right to an oral hearing, and that the absence of such a hearing amounted to a breach of the rules of natural justice and was, accordingly, *ultra vires*. The court disagreed, holding that, since the auditor had given notice of the case against them and had considered written representations from them, he had acted fairly and, accordingly, lawfully.

The requirements of fairness mean that where a body was exercising penal powers which involved the imposition of a penalty which was more severe than would normally be expected, it had to give the person affected the opportunity of making representations on the issue. The High Court so held in *R (Gutta) v General Medical Council* (2001). The Medical Council had found Dr Gutta guilty of serious professional misconduct and resolved to have her name erased from the register and that her suspension should take effect immediately, rather than after an appeal had been heard, as was normal. The Council was under a duty to give notice of its intention to make such an order, give the opportunity to make representations and give adequate reasons for reaching its conclusion.

The right to question the 'other side'

It is not invariably the case that, where there is to be an oral hearing, it should be conducted according to the strict rules which would apply in a court of law. Accordingly, it should not be assumed that a party will be entitled to cross-examine the 'other side'. However, in *Errington v Wilson* (1995), it was made clear that Justices of the Peace must observe the rules of natural justice and, in particular, allow cross-examination under certain circumstances. A food authority had seized batches of cheese which it believed to be contaminated with listeria monocytogenes. The authority then sought a destruction order from the justice of the peace. The magistrate refused to allow cross-examination of witnesses called by the authority. The court held that, given the nature of the proceedings, the magistrate was required to allow cross-examination if the proceedings were to be fair; and that, given the difference of opinion between experts on crucial points, Errington had been denied natural justice.

The admissibility of evidence and attendance of witnesses

In *R v Board of Visitors of Hull Prison ex parte St Germain (No 2)* (1979), prisoners who had been involved in a prison riot were charged with breaches of the Prison Rules. In the course of the hearing, hearsay evidence was given to the court on behalf of a number of officers who were unable to attend the hearing. The decision of guilt on the charges was challenged by judicial review proceedings, on the basis that the Board of Visitors had breached the rules of natural justice. Lane LJ, while not ruling that hearsay evidence could never be admissible, nevertheless ruled that, in the particular circumstance of the case, the Board should have ruled the hearsay evidence inadmissible. The decision of the Board was quashed by order of certiorari. Similar issues were under scrutiny in *R v Commissioner for Racial Equality ex parte Cottrell and Rothon* (1980). The Commissioner had received a complaint of unlawful discrimination by Messrs Cottrell and Rothon, a firm of estate agents. The company had been given the opportunity to make representations – both written and oral – to the commissioners. No witnesses were available at the hearing. Nevertheless, the Commission issued a non-discrimination notice.[94] The company sought to have the decision quashed, relying in part on *R v Board of Visitors of Hull Prison ex parte St Germain (No 2)* (1979). Noting the absence of any statutory requirement to provide an opportunity to cross-examine witnesses in the course of a hearing, and distinguishing between the facts of *St Germain*, the Court of Appeal ruled that there was no breach in the rules relating to fairness.

In *R v Panel on Takeovers and Mergers ex parte Guinness plc* (1990), the Takeover Panel refused to grant an adjournment of the inquisitorial proceedings in order to allow witnesses to attend. The court expressed anxiety about this refusal, but declined to hold that the Panel had acted unlawfully.

A different conclusion was reached, in *R v Army Board of the Defence Council ex parte Anderson* (1991). The applicant for judicial review had made allegations of racial discrimination[95] which resulted in him taking absence without leave. Members of the Board considered his allegation of discrimination on the basis of circulated papers, and did not meet for the purpose of reaching its decision. The complainant had requested, but been refused, an oral hearing, and had also

---

94   Under the Race Relations Act 1976, s 58(5).
95   *Ibid.*

requested, but been refused, the disclosure of documents relating to his case. The Board decided that whilst there was some *prima facie* evidence of discrimination, it was insufficient to warrant either an apology or an award of compensation. Anderson sought judicial review of the Army Board's decision. Counsel for the Board reverted to the distinction between administrative and judicial functions. Taylor LJ, in the course of ruling that such a distinction was unnecessary, held that, should the distinction have been a necessary one, he would characterise the role of the Army Board, in connection with the complaint, as judicial rather than administrative. Applying the principles established in *Lloyd v McMahon* (1987), Taylor LJ ruled that four principles applied to the standard of fairness required in a hearing such as that of the Board:

(1) There must be a proper hearing of the complaint in the sense that the board must consider ... all the relevant evidence and contentions before reaching its conclusion. This means, in my view, that the members of the Board must meet ...

(2) The hearing does not necessarily have to be an oral hearing in all cases ... Provided that they [the board] achieve the degree of fairness appropriate to their task it is for them to decide how they will proceed and there is no rule that fairness always requires an oral hearing ...

    What it [the board] cannot do ... is to have an inflexible policy not to hold oral hearings.

    The board fettered its discretion and failed to consider the requirements for an oral hearing in the present case on its own merits.

(3) The opportunity to have the evidence tested by cross-examination is again within the Army Board's discretion. The decision whether to allow it will usually be inseparable from the decision whether to have an oral hearing. The object of the latter will usually be to enable witnesses to be tested in cross-examination, although it would be possible to have an oral hearing simply to hear submissions.

(4) Whether oral or not, there must be what amounts to a hearing of any complaint under the 1976 Act. This means that the Army Board must have such a complaint investigated, consider all the material gathered in the investigation, give the complainant an opportunity to respond to it and consider his response.

On the duty of disclosure of documents, Taylor LJ ruled that:

> Because of the nature of the Army Board's function pursuant to the 1976 Act, ... I consider that a soldier complainant under that Act should be shown all the material seen by the board, apart from any documents for which public interest immunity[96] can properly be claimed.

The decision of the board was quashed.

The rights of prisoners have also been scrutinised in relation to the requirement that they have sufficient information in order to challenge a Home Secretary's decision as to their detention or release. Under the Criminal Justice Act 1991, the Home Secretary has a statutory duty to release, on the direction of the Parole Board, discretionary life prisoners after they have served a 'tariff period' (section 34). The period to be served is considered by the trial judge. In *R v Secretary of State for the Home Department ex parte Doody* (1993), the House of Lords ruled that the prisoner was entitled to know the length of the tariff period recommended by the trial judge, and other relevant factors, in order that he may

---

96 On public interest immunity, see Chapter 11.

make written representation to the Home Secretary concerning the date fixed for consideration by the Parole Board of his sentence.[97] The failure to respect the entitlement to know the period recommended in order to make written submissions led to the Home Secretary's decision being quashed.[98]

The availability of legal representation

Whether or not legal representation is available as of right will also depend upon the nature of the hearing and the nature of the rights affected. There is no general right to legal representation and, in some cases, it may prove to be either unnecessary or counterproductive to the proceedings and, accordingly, the courts have been unwilling to concede a general right to representation.[99] Where the proceedings are before a tribunal, the right to be represented is at the discretion of the tribunal. The general principle, according to the Royal Commission on Legal Services, is that 'it is desirable that every applicant before any tribunal should be able to present his case in person or to obtain representation'.[100]

Whereas legal representation is rarely denied before tribunals,[101] such representation is inextricably linked to the financial means of the applicant or to the availability of Legal Aid (now referred to as Legal Help). It may be more appropriate, in many instances, for applicants to be represented by non-lawyers. A range of organisations offer representation. The Citizens Advice Bureaux, trades unions, social workers, specialist agencies,[102] the Free Representation Unit, friends or relatives may all be allowed to appear before tribunals. The essential criterion for representation is that the tribunal should not adopt a rigid policy, but rather should exercise a genuine discretion in relation to the availability of representation.[103]

Failure to give reasons

According to Lord Denning MR, the giving of reasons is 'one of the fundamentals of good administration'.[104] Unless a decision maker provides adequate information as to the basis on which a decision has been reached, any possible protection which could be given to an aggrieved person is adversely affected.

Under the Tribunals and Inquiries Act 1992, there exists a statutory duty to give reasons, on request, where decisions are reached by tribunals, public inquiries, or under specific statutes. Under common law, however, there is no

---

97 Where the trial judge does not make a recommendation, the Home Secretary may certify the length of the period of sentence which must be served: Criminal Justice Act 1991, Sched 12, para 9. See *R v Home Department ex parte McCartney* (1993).

98 See also *R v Secretary of State for the Environment ex parte Slot* (1997); *R v Secretary of State for the Home Department ex parte McAvoy* (1998).

99 See, *inter alia*, *R v Secretary of State for the Home Department ex parte Tarrant* (1985); *R v Board of Visitors of HM Prison, The Maze ex parte Hone* (1988).

100 *Report of the Royal Commission*, 1979, Vol I, para 15.11, p 169.

101 Proceedings before the Family Practitioner Committee is an exception; National Health Service (Service Committees and Tribunal) Regulations, SI 1974/455, reg 7.

102 Eg, the Child Poverty Action Group; the United Kingdom Immigration Advisory Service.

103 *Per* Lord Denning MR in *Pett v Greyhound Racing Association (No 2)* (1970).

104 *Breen v AEU* (1971), p 191.

such duty,[105] although the argument that there should be such a duty is strong. A decision making body is under a 'general duty' to give reasons, and any departure from the requirement to give reasons will require sound justification. Where an authority fails to give reasons for a decision which is challenged subsequently by judicial review proceedings, the failure to give reasons may cause the court to consider that there were no good reasons whatsoever for the decision. Lord Keith expressed it thus:

> ... if all other known facts and circumstances appear to point overwhelmingly in favour of a different decision, the decision maker who has given no reasons cannot complain if the court draws the inference that he has no rational reason for his decision.[106]

The courts have developed a number of exceptions to the general rule that no reasons need be given at common law. The courts may hold, for example, that a failure to give reasons will prejudice an applicant's chances of successfully applying for judicial review,[107] or that a failure to give reasons amounts to arbitrariness,[108] or that legitimate expectations have been created which demand that any departure from that expectation be explained or, more sweepingly, that in the interests of fairness, reasons must be given.

In *R v Civil Service Appeal Board ex parte Cunningham* (1991), for example, the Court of Appeal, while again stating that there was no general duty to give reasons, held that the Civil Service Appeal Board – which determined the applicant's compensation for unfair dismissal – was under a duty to give reasons, for its powers were analogous to the judicial powers of an industrial tribunal. Fairness demanded that the Board give reasons, in the same manner as required for tribunals.[109]

The duty to give reasons must now be evaluated in light of the House of Lords' decision in *R v Secretary of State for the Home Department ex parte Doody* (1993). As seen above, in *Doody*, the applicants, who were serving mandatory life sentences, sought information as to the basis on which the decision concerning the period for their mandatory detention had been reached. The House of Lords laid down two justifications for the requirement that information be given. First, if reasons were not given to the applicants, the possibility of their successfully applying for judicial review would be frustrated. Secondly, a failure to give reasons adversely affected the concept of fairness. Lord Mustill, while acknowledging that there remained no general duty to give reasons, stated that a duty would be implied under certain circumstances. Where, as in *Doody*, the applicant did not know the reasons for a decision, it was impossible to make any effective representations in support of his case. Without the knowledge of any case against him, the applicant was denied the very information which would found the basis of making representations in support of his case. The Home

---

105 See *R v Secretary of State for the Home Department ex parte Doody* (1993).
106 *R v Trade Secretary ex parte Lonrho plc* (1989), p 620. See Bradley, 1986; and Herberg, 1991.
107 As in *Doody's* case (1993).
108 See *Padfield v Minister of Agriculture, Fisheries and Food* (1968).
109 See also *R v Parole Board ex parte Wilson* (1992); *Selvanathan v General Medical Council* (2001); *Baird v Thurrock Borough Council* (2005).

Secretary was, accordingly, under a duty to provide reasons both on the basis that the giving of reasons was a prerequisite to an application for judicial review, and on the basis of requirements of fairness.

In *R v Ministry of Defence ex parte Murray* (1998), the Divisional Court ruled that, although there was no general overriding principle of law which required decision makers to give reasons for their decisions, the duty of fairness required that reasons be given, where demanded by the circumstances of the case. The applicant had been convicted by court martial of wounding. The court martial reached its conclusion and passed sentence without giving reasons. The applicant's conduct, which was 'entirely out of character', and to which he pleaded guilty, was caused by ingestion of an anti-malarial drug. Where there was no explicit duty of fairness in statute, the courts would require that reasons be given where fairness demanded it. In this case, the applicant, his regiment and his family were entitled to reasons.

In *R v Criminal Injuries Compensation Authority ex parte Leatherland* (2000), the High Court ruled that the Criminal Injuries Compensation Authority was obliged as a matter of procedural fairness to provide proper reasons, together with at least the gist of any supporting evidence, for its decisions to reduce or refuse claims for compensation. A practice of withholding such material until the day of any appeal hearing was bad administration and unfair.

However, not all bodies will be under a duty to give reasons on the basis of fairness. In *R v Universities Funding Council ex parte Institute of Dental Surgery* (1994), for example, the Divisional Court ruled that the Higher Education Funding Council was not under a duty to give reasons as to why an academic institution was given a downgraded research grading which resulted in a loss to the Institute of research funds. Such matters were, in the court's opinion, matters of academic judgment, and a duty to give reasons for a decision could not, in this case, be founded on the requirements of fairness alone.[110] Sedley J stated that there were two classes of case emerging. The first class was exemplified in the *Doody* case, where the nature of the process requires, in the interests of fairness, reasons to be given. The second class is illustrated by *Ex parte Cunningham* (1991), in which the majority of the court held that there was something peculiar to the case which required reasons to be given in the interests of fairness. In the *Institute of Dental Surgery* case, provided the decision was based purely on academic judgment, and did not involve any irrelevant or improper factors being taken into account, the decision would not be impugned on the basis that reasons had not been given for the decision. TRS Allan is critical of the decision. In his view, 'if the requirement of reasons, where it exists, reflects the demands of fairness and reasonableness, its denial in the present case must cause one to doubt whether the Institute was treated either fairly or reasonably' (1994, p 210).

---

110 See also *R v University College London ex parte Idriss* (1999), in which it was held that it was 'very doubtful' whether a university's refusal to admit an applicant for entry to a course was susceptible to judicial review and that there was no duty to give reasons either at common law or under the university's own statutes.

The duty of the Crown Prosecution Service to give reasons for its decisions was considered by the Divisional Court in *R v Director of Public Prosecutions ex parte Manning* (2000). The applicant's brother had died of asphyxia while being restrained by prison officers whilst on remand in prison. At a coroner's inquest, the jury returned a verdict of unlawful killing. However, the Crown Prosecution Service concluded that, while there was a *prima facie* case against a prison officer, there was no realistic prospect of a successful prosecution. The applicant then requested the reasons for the Crown Prosecution Service's decision, but was refused. He then sought judicial review. It was held that while there was no absolute obligation on the Service to give reasons for a decision not to prosecute, a violent death in custody gave rise to great concern. Further, since a jury had returned a verdict of unlawful killing implicating an identifiable person, there was an expectation of a plausible explanation for the decision and of solid grounds to support the decision.

In *R v Secretary of State for the Home Department ex parte Al Fayed* (1997), the Court of Appeal ruled that the Home Secretary had a duty to indicate to the applicant the area(s) of concern on which he was basing his refusal to grant naturalisation in order that the applicant may have an opportunity to allay the Home Secretary's concerns. The Home Secretary's decision was quashed. In *R v Secretary of State for the Home Department ex parte Moon* (1995), the court ruled that the Secretary of State's refusal to explain his reasons for concluding that the entry of the Reverend Sun Myung Moon would not be conducive to the public good was unfair and contrary to the rules of natural justice.

The duty of a professional judge to give reasons was upheld by the Court of Appeal in *Flanner v Halifax Estate Agencies Ltd* (2000). In general, it was the duty of a judge to give reasons; the extent of the duty would depend on the circumstances, but, where the dispute involved opposing reasons and analysis, the judge must explain why he preferred one case over the other.[111] In *Stefan v General Medical Council* (1999), the health committee of the General Medical Council had suspended the applicant indefinitely because of her medical condition. No reasons were given. The court stated that the common law rule against a general duty to give reasons was changing and might have to be reconsidered in light of the Human Rights Act 1998 (on which, see below). Although there was no general duty to give reasons, nevertheless, in light of the nature of the appeal and the importance for the practitioner, they ought to have done so.[112]

The giving of reasons, whether by courts or administrative bodies, assumes increased importance in light of the Human Rights Act 1998. Article 5 of the Convention (the right to liberty and security) expressly states that persons arrested shall be informed promptly, in a language which he or she understands, of the reasons for the arrest. Article 6 of the Convention protects the right to a fair trial in the determination of civil rights and obligations or of criminal charges. While the giving of reasons is not an explicit requirement in Article 6, it is implicit in facilitating the right of appeal.

---

111 See *Practice Direction* (1999).
112 See also *R (I) v Independent Appeal Panel for G* (2005).

In *South Buckinghamshire District Council v Porter (No 2)* (2004) the House of Lords gave guidance concerning the adequacy of reasons given in planning decisions. The applicant, a gypsy, had purchased land in a Green Belt area in 1985 and stationed her mobile home on it. She applied for, but was refused, planning permission to remain on the site and enforcement notices were issued by the Council. In 2000 the applicant reapplied, but was refused, permission. On appeal the inspector ruled that there were material changes in the circumstances since the previous application. There was now no alternative council site available for her and her health had deteriorated considerably. He concluded that these circumstances were sufficient to override Green Belt policies. He granted personal planning permission to the applicant, meaning that she could remain there as long as she wished, but that thereafter the permission would lapse. The Court of Appeal ruled that the inspector had failed to give adequate reasons for his decision and that he had failed to have regard to the fact that continued occupation of the site was unlawful and in persistent breach of planning control.

The House of Lords allowed the applicant's appeal. Summarising the law, Lord Brown of Eaton-under-Heywood stated that:

> The reasons for a decision must be intelligible and they must be adequate. They must enable the reader to understand why the matter was decided as it was and what conclusions were reached on the "principal important controversial issues", disclosing how any issue of law or fact was resolved. Reasons can be briefly stated, the degree of particularity required depending entirely on the nature of the issues falling for decision. The reasoning must not give rise to a substantial doubt as to whether the decision-maker erred in law, for example by misunderstanding some relevant policy or some other important matter or by failing to reach a rational decision on relevant grounds. . . . A reasons challenge will only succeed if the party aggrieved can satisfy the court that he has genuinely been substantially prejudiced by the failure to provide an adequately reasoned decision.

The Freedom of Information Act 2000

As discussed in Chapter 11, the Freedom of Information Act gives legislative force to the Labour government's commitment to more open government. An Information Commissioner has been appointed, with jurisdiction to investigate allegations that public authorities and bodies have failed to provide information and documents requested. The Act, it will be recalled, introduces the principle that information and documents will be disclosed, subject to a test of harm which justifies official non-disclosure. The Commissioner's decisions are published and are subject to judicial review. The effect of the Freedom of Information Act on judicial review will, however, arguably be to reduce the number of applications for judicial review, in particular on the basis of failure to give reasons. This appears to be supported by the government's announcement that it did not intend to appeal against the decision in the *Al Fayed* case, but rather indicated that it would give reasons for refusing citizenship. Judicial review, as seen in the previous chapter, is concerned with the decision making process rather than the merits of the decision, and provides a discretionary remedy, which requires the decision maker to reconsider the matter in accordance with the correct procedure. Provided that the decision making process is in accordance with the requirements of law and the principles of natural justice, the decision will not be impugned. Under the Freedom of Information Act, however, where a public body – which is widely defined – fails to give reasons for its decision, recourse may be had to the Commissioner who has wide ranging powers to investigate, and has the power to order disclosure. Where a public body refuses to supply, for example, reasons for its decision, and the Commissioner orders it to disclose reasons, should the public body then continue to refuse to disclose, with no justification, that refusal may be deemed to be analogous to contempt of court. Furthermore, should the body concerned reveal to the Commissioner that it had no rational basis for its decision, that decision may then be impugned on the basis of irrationality. The citizen may, accordingly, find a more efficient and effective remedy under the jurisdiction of the Commissioner than the courts.

CHAPTER 28

COMMISSIONERS FOR ADMINISTRATION: OMBUDSMEN

INTRODUCTION

In the United Kingdom, the past 40 years have seen a major expansion in mechanisms for citizens to complain against government departments and other public bodies. When a citizen has a complaint against the administration of government, that complaint could be pursued in courts or tribunals or through parliament via the constituency Member of Parliament. However, these means for the redress of grievances have been proven inadequate and, as a result, alternative and additional mechanisms have been introduced.

The word 'ombudsman' is Swedish, and means a representative of the people. In Sweden, the office of *Justitieombudsman* was established in 1809. Finland introduced a similar office in 1919, as did Denmark in 1955. In 1963, Norway followed, with a parliamentary ombudsman, the model which had been adopted by New Zealand in 1962. During the 1970s, countries throughout the world adopted some form of office of ombudsman.

COMMISSIONERS FOR ADMINISTRATION IN THE UNITED KINGDOM

The existing scheme of Commissioners for Administration is given overleaf. Note that in addition, there exist a number of ombudsmen in the private sector, for example, the Banking Commissioner, Building Societies Commissioner, Corporate Estate Agents Commissioner, Pensions Commissioner,[1] Personal Investment Authority Ombudsman, Prisons Ombudsman, Investment Commissioner, Insurance Commissioner, Commissioner for Trades Union Members and the press and media and telephone information services.

---

1   It has been held that the Pensions Ombudsman is required to observe the statutory procedure within the Pensions Schemes Act 1993 and the rules of natural justice: see *Seifert v Pensions Ombudsman; Lynch v Pensions Ombudsman* (1997). See also *Miller v Stapleton* (1996); *Hamar v Pensions Ombudsman* (1996).

Commissioners for Administration

	Date of introduction
Parliamentary Commissioner for Administration[2]	1967
Parliamentary Commissioner for Administration[3] and Commissioner for Complaints (Northern Ireland)[4]	1969
Health Service Commissioners: England, Wales and Scotland[5]	1972
Local Government Commissioners: England, Wales[6] and Scotland[7] (Scotland 1975)	1974
Legal Services Commissioner[8]	1990
European Union and Community Ombudsman[9]	1992
Scottish Parliamentary Commissioner[10]	1998
Welsh Administration Ombudsman[11]	1998
Public Services Ombudsman for Wales[12]	2005

THE PARLIAMENTARY COMMISSIONER FOR ADMINISTRATION[13]

The movement towards establishing a Parliamentary Commissioner for Administration (or ombudsman) began in 1959. In that year, the British section of the International Commission of Jurists, JUSTICE, established an inquiry into grievances against the administration. The resultant report[14] advocated setting up an additional avenue for the redress of grievances, the office being modelled on

---

2   Parliamentary Commissioner Act 1967. As amended by the Parliamentary and Health Service Commissioner Act 1987; Parliamentary Commissioner Act 1994.
3   Parliamentary Commissioner (Northern Ireland) Act 1969.
4   Commissioner for Complaints (Northern Ireland) Act 1969.
5   National Health Service (Scotland) Act 1972; National Health Service Reorganisation Act 1973; Parliamentary and Health Service Commissioners Act 1987; Health Service Commissioners Act 1993; Health Service Commissioners (Amendment) Act 2000.
6   Local Government Act 1974; Local Government and Housing Act 1989, s 23.
7   Local Government (Scotland) Act 1975.
8   Courts and Legal Services Act 1990.
9   EC Treaty, Article 195, introduced under the Treaty on European Union 1992.
10 Scotland Act 1998. See Scotland Act 1998 (Transitory and Transitional Provisions) (Complaints of Maladministration) Order 1999, SI 1999/1351.
11 Government of Wales Act 1998.
12 Public Services Ombudsman Wales Act 2005
13 See Pugh, 1978. See also Clothier, 1984.
14 *The Citizen and the Administration* (the Whyatt Report), 1961.

the same lines as those of the ombudsmen in Scandinavian jurisdictions. As the report stated, there appeared to be:

> ... a continuous flow of relatively minor complaints, not sufficient in themselves to attract public interest, but nevertheless of great importance to the individuals concerned, which give rise to feelings of frustration and resentment because of the inadequacy of the existing means of seeking redress.[15]

The existing machinery was found wanting: parliamentary Question Time was inadequate to deal with the volume of problems arising; if a complaint was made directly to the government department, the department investigated the complaint; if a Member of Parliament attempted to investigate, he could not gain access to all departmental documentation. Accordingly, the report advocated establishing a permanent office, independent of the executive and accountable only to parliament, removable from office only after a successful address had been moved to both Houses of Parliament. The report recommended that a select committee should be established to consider the Commissioner's reports and to give parliamentary authority to the work of the Commissioner. The report also recommended that the Parliamentary Commissioner for Administration's office should be one which supplemented, rather than undermined, existing procedures for complaint. Complaints, at least initially, concerning maladministration[16] should be routed through Members of the House of Commons, rather than directly addressed to the Parliamentary Commissioner. This would preserve to Members of Parliament the opportunity to resolve a matter of complaint but, failing their ability to do so, confer the right to refer the matter to the Parliamentary Commissioner for investigation and report.

The government's response to the report was cautious. Concern was expressed as to the interference in the running of government,[17] and that the Commissioner's role would be incompatible with the doctrine of ministerial responsibility. Furthermore, the government felt that:

> ... there is already adequate provision under our constitution and Parliamentary practice for the redress of any genuine complaint of maladministration, in particular by means of the citizen's rights of access to Members of Parliament.[18]

The incoming Labour government, however, accepted the need for an office to complement the existing complaints machinery.[19] Thus, in 1967, the Parliamentary Commissioner Act was passed. Being a constitutional innovation, the provisions as to procedure, jurisdiction and powers of enforcement were restrictive.

Appointment

The Parliamentary Commissioner for Administration is appointed by the Crown on the advice of the government, following consultation with the Chairman of the

---

15   *The Citizen and the Administration*, 1961, para 76.
16   On which, see below.
17   Lord Chancellor, HL Deb Vol 244 Cols 384–85.
18   Attorney General, 666 HC Col 1125.
19   *The Parliamentary Commissioner for Administration*, Cmnd 2767, 1965, London: HMSO.

House of Commons' Select Committee on the Parliamentary Commissioner for Administration. The post is held 'during good health and behaviour' and is effectively until retirement. The Office of Parliamentary Ombudsman and Health Service Ombudsman for England is held by the same person.

The constitutional position of the Commissioner

By 1983, the office of Parliamentary Commissioner for Administration had been operative for 15 years, and the Commissioner[20] took the opportunity to review the working of his office in his annual report. He described his office in the following manner:

> The office of Parliamentary Commissioner stands curiously poised between the legislature and the executive, while discharging an almost judicial function in the citizen's dispute with his government, and yet it forms no part of the judiciary. It is from the centre of that triangle that I have been able to appreciate the virtues of our unwritten and therefore flexible constitutional arrangements and still more the goodwill of those men and women, legislators and administrators who govern us.

Aims and objectives

The purpose of the Office of Parliamentary and Health Service Ombudsman (OPHSO) is:

(a) to consider and resolve complaints impartially and promptly and to achieve appropriate redress of grievances;

(b) to report the results to complainants, Members of Parliament and the bodies complained about; and

(c) to promote improvements in public services by feeding back the lessons learned from casework to policy makers and providers.[21]

THE COMPLAINTS PROCEDURE

Complaints must be in writing, and made to the constituency Member of Parliament (ie a member of the House of Commons).[22] The complaint must be made within 12 months of the day on which the person became aware of the matters alleged, unless the time period is extended by the Commissioner, on the basis that an investigation is necessary.[23] There is no change involved in making a complaint, or for any investigation which is undertaken. The complaint must relate to maladministration and not the merits of a decision or the policy being pursued. This restriction has led to some 43 per cent of complaints made being rejected by the Commissioner.

The requirement that complaints be made initially to Members of Parliament reinforces the view that the Commissioner is a supplement to the parliamentary

---

20 Sir Cecil Clothier who held office from 1979–85.
21 OPHSO, *Business Plan 2003–04*.
22 Parliamentary Commissioner Act 1967, s 5(1)(a).
23 *Ibid*, s 6(3).

process rather than a substitute. This restricted right of access, however, causes difficulties for complainants, and is not a model adopted elsewhere.[24] In the majority of countries having some form of parliamentary ombudsman, complaints are made directly to the ombudsman. Moreover, this filter mechanism has not been adopted in relation to the Health Service Commissioner, the Commissioners for Local Government or the Complaints Commissioner for Northern Ireland.[25]

Jurisdiction

Section 5(1) of the Parliamentary Commissioner Act 1967 provides that a member of the public may make a complaint and the Commissioner may investigate that complaint where, subject to the rules on jurisdiction, the person 'claims to have sustained injustice in consequence of maladministration'.[26] Before examining that concept, it must be noted that there are a number of restrictions to the jurisdiction of the Parliamentary Commissioner, which result in a large number of complaints each year not being investigated.

Excluded matters

The work of the police,[27] of nationalised industries, the Cabinet Office, Prime Minister's Office, Parole Board, tribunals, Bank of England, Criminal Injuries Compensation Board and government commercial and contractual transactions are all excluded.[28] The Commissioner may not investigate any matter where the complainant has a right of 'appeal, reference or review' to a tribunal, or a remedy in any court of law, unless it would be unreasonable to expect the complainant to have resort to such a remedy.[29] The Commissioner thus has a discretion as to whether or not a complaint should be accepted. It has been indicated that, where the legal process would be too cumbersome, slow or expensive in relation to the objective to be gained, the complaint will be accepted.[30]

The interaction between legal proceedings and complaints to the Commissioner was well illustrated in 1975. The government decided to increase the licence fee for television sets. In advance of the fee increase, individuals renewed their licences at the existing rate. The Home Office then decided to revoke the 36,000 licences issued at the cheaper rate. A number of complaints were referred to the Commissioner, who found maladministration on the part of government, *inter alia*, for not giving sufficient warning of the increases and for inefficiency. The Commissioner, however, ruled that the government was acting

---

24 See the JUSTICE Report, *Our Fettered Ombudsman*, 1977, and the Select Committee Report, *Parliamentary Commissioner for Administration (Review of Access and Jurisdiction)*, HC 615 (1978–79), London: HMSO.
25 There is, however, a 'filter' procedure for the Parliamentary Commissioner for Northern Ireland.
26 See below for the meaning of 'maladministration'.
27 Which has its own internal complaints procedures.
28 See HC 322 (1983–84), London: HMSO.
29 Parliamentary Commissioner Act 1967, s 5(2).
30 See McMurtie, 1997.

on legal advice and therefore should not be sanctioned. Judicial review proceedings were commenced to determine the lawfulness of the Home Secretary's decision, as a result of which the complainants established a legal remedy.[31] It may be argued that the Commissioner was wrong in exercising his discretionary jurisdiction in this case, since it should have been foreseen that an action in judicial review would lie.

The departments and matters which the Commissioner is precluded from investigating are wide ranging. Schedule 3 of the Parliamentary Commissioner Act 1967 sets out the excluded matters, the most significant of which are:

- Action taken in matters certified by a Secretary of State or other Minister of the Crown to affect relations or dealings between the government of the United Kingdom and any other government or any international organisation of States or government.

- Action taken in connection with the administration of the government of any country or territory outside the United Kingdom which forms part of Her Majesty's dominions or in which Her Majesty has jurisdiction.

- Action taken by the Secretary of State under the Fugitive Offenders Act 1967 or the Extradition Act 1989.

- Action taken by or with the authority of the Secretary of State for the purposes of investigating crime or of protecting the security of the State, including action so taken with respect to passports.

- The commencement or conduct of civil or criminal proceedings before any court of law in the United Kingdom.

- Any exercise of the prerogative of mercy.

- Action taken in matters relating to contractual or other commercial transactions ... being transactions of a government department.

- Action taken in respect of appointments or removals, pay, discipline, superannuation or other personnel matters, in relation to:
  the armed forces, any office or employment under the Crown.[32]

- The grant of honours, awards or privileges within the gift of the Crown, including the grant of Royal Charters.

Departments and matters within the Commissioner's jurisdiction

Schedule 2 of the Act lays down those Departments subject to the jurisdiction of the Commissioner. The Parliamentary and Health Service Commissioners Act 1987 extended the Commissioner's jurisdiction to cover some non-departmental bodies, and the complete list of Departments and bodies within the Commissioner's jurisdiction is now found in Schedule 1 to the 1987 Act, as amended by the Parliamentary Commissioner Act 1994.

The Commissioner's discretion

Where a matter falls within the Commissioner's jurisdiction, the Commissioner has discretion as to whether to accept the complaint.[33] Section 5(5) provides that

---

31 *Congreve v Home Office* (1976).
32 Commissioner for Complaints (Northern Ireland) Act 1969, s 5(1), provides that the Commissioner has jurisdiction over matters of employment in the public sector.
33 Parliamentary Commissioner Act 1967, s 5(1).

the Commissioner shall act 'in accordance with his own discretion'. Because of the breadth of discretion conferred on the Commissioner, both in relation to accepting complaints and in the conduct of investigations, judicial review of his or her decisions is unlikely to succeed. For example, in *Re Fletcher* (1970), the applicant sought an order of mandamus to force the Commissioner to investigate a complaint. The House of Lords refused, relying on the broad discretion conferred on the Commissioner by statute. In *R v Parliamentary Commissioner for Administration ex parte Dyer* (1994), the applicant sought judicial review of the Commissioner's investigation into her complaints against the Department of Social Security. The applicant was dissatisfied with a report of the Commissioner and sought judicial review on four grounds. The allegations were, first, that the Commissioner had not investigated all her complaints; secondly, that she had not been given the opportunity to comment on the draft reports; thirdly, that the Commissioner, having heard her complaints, refused to reopen the investigations; and, fourthly, that the Commissioner was wrong in holding that he could not reopen the inquiry. The Queen's Bench Division held that it had jurisdiction to review the work of the Commissioner. Lord Justice Simon Brown declared that he could see nothing in the Commissioner's role or the statutory framework in which he operated which is 'so singular as to take him wholly outside the purview of judicial review'. Nevertheless, the court would be slow to review given the breadth of discretion conferred under the Act.[34]

The meaning of 'maladministration'

Maladministration is the key concept relating to the Commissioner's jurisdiction, but it is not defined in the Act. The concept derives from the Whyatt Report of 1961, where it was described as a term which 'was not of precise meaning'. The failure to define the concept in the Act was deliberate. The minister responsible for introducing the legislation, Mr Richard Crossman, felt that the Act was of such an innovatory nature that time would be needed to adjust to the Act's introduction and that no rigid criteria should be set. In the House of Commons, Mr Crossman described maladministration as including 'bias, neglect, inattention, delay, incompetence, ineptitude, perversity, turpitude, arbitrariness and so on'.[35]

The meaning of maladministration can best be understood when placed in the context of actual investigations undertaken by the Ombudsman. Among its many cases undertaken in one year, the *Annual Report 2004–2005: A Year of Progress* presents the following examples:

> The Ombudsman found that a General Practitioner had failed to provide an adequate standard of care and treatment through delay and obstruction.
>
> The Ombudsman upheld a complaint concerning informed consent to surgery. The patient required treatment for cancer of the oesophagus. The Ombudsman found that the brief 'mention' of the surgery procedure was unacceptable and meant that informed

---

34 Cf *R v Parliamentary Commissioner for Administration ex parte Balchin* (1998) and *Balchin (No 2)* (2000), in which judicial review was granted, and the Parliamentary Commissioner found to have fallen into error.
35 *Official Report* HC 734 Col 51.

consent was not given. Poor documentation was also found. It was also unacceptable that the task of obtaining signed consent was given to a junior doctor.

Jobcentre Plus had incorrectly advised a couple over their eligibility to income support. The couple had moved in together and the man had reduced his working hours as a result of the advice. They then suffered a loss of income. They complained to Jobcentre Plus which admitted the mistake but refused to pay any compensation for their loss which was exacerbated by the man's deterioration in health as a result of stress.

The Ombudsman found maladministration on the part of the Legal Services Commission which had failed to provide an appropriate level of service; as a result of the mistakes interest had accrued on her statutory charge liability. The Commission apologised and arranged for her statutory charge account to be reimbursed and for an *ex gratia* payment to compensate for the distress suffered as a result of the Commission's failings.

The courts have examined the concept of maladministration in relation to the work of Local Government Commissioners. For example, in *R v Commissioners for Local Administration ex parte Bradford Metropolitan Borough Council* (1979), maladministration was described as 'faulty administration' and 'bad administration', whereas, in 1980, Lord Donaldson MR explained that maladministration is primarily concerned with the manner in which authorities reach or implement decisions, and is not concerned with the quality of the decision itself.[36] In *R v Local Commissioner for Administration ex parte Liverpool City Council* (1999), the Court of Appeal ruled that the failure of local councillors to follow the National Code of Local Government Conduct, and failure to observe the requirement to declare financial interests when taking part in decisions relating to planning, was maladministration.

Maladministration is a more restrictive concept than is employed in other jurisdictions. In Denmark, for example, the ombudsman may examine 'mistakes' and 'unreasonable decisions' and, in Norway, the ombudsman can investigate decisions which are 'clearly unreasonable'. In the United Kingdom, being tied to the concept of maladministration, the Commissioner is not concerned with the merits of any decision taken, nor the fairness or otherwise of the rules governing any situation, but rather with the manner of the application of the rules.

The Commissioner's investigation and report

In the exercise of his or her jurisdiction, the Commissioner is vested with strong powers by the Parliamentary Commissioner Act 1967. The Commissioner has the same powers as a court in respect of requiring the attendance of witnesses and the right of examination, and the production of documents, subject to the protections of Cabinet proceedings and documents and such information as a person would not be compelled to disclose to a court of law (section 8). To obstruct the Commissioner in the performance of his duties under the Act, without lawful excuse, may be certified as a contempt.

Under section 10, where the Commissioner accepts jurisdiction and investigates a complaint, a report of the findings is sent to the complainant and

---

36 *R v Commissioners for Local Administration ex parte Eastleigh Borough Council* (1980).

the principal officer of the department concerned. If the matter has not been remedied, or is unlikely to be, he or she may lay a special report before each House of Parliament. The Commissioner's *Annual General Report* is laid before parliament. The Commissioner has no power to grant a remedy or to grant compensation. He or she does, however, make recommendations as to the appropriate remedy, and as to levels of suitable compensation.

The volume of complaints[37]

Complaint	2001–02	2002–03	2004–05
PCA	2,139	1,973	2,728*
AOI	33	42	—
HSC	2,662	3,999	2,478
TOTAL[38]	4,834	6,014	

* The Access to Information cases in 2004–05 are included in the figure for the PCA.

There are three categories of complaint: those made to the Parliamentary Commissioner and referred by a Member of Parliament; those referred by a Member of Parliament relating to the withholding of information contrary to the Code of Practice on Access to Government Information (AOI complaints); and those made to the Health Service Commissioner (HSC complaints). In 2004 the Commissioner's responsibilities as Welsh Administration Ombudsman were transferred to the Public Service Ombudsman for Wales. With effect from January 2005 the responsibility for access to government information is transferred to the Information Commissioner.

The evidence indicates that, whilst a high number of complaints are rejected (either because they relate to matters not within the Commissioner's jurisdiction, whether relating to an excluded department or relating to matters of policy, or because they reveal no *prima facie* case of maladministration), once a complaint is admitted for investigation, the prospect of a finding of maladministration – at least in part – is high.

In the year 2004–05 the bodies most frequently complained about were the Department for Work and Pensions with 860 complaints received, Inland Revenue (348 received) and the Home Office (166 received). Of the problems encountered in terms of maladministration, these are put down to the sheer scale of the administrative function and the necessary complexity of laws. The impersonal nature of services, the forms and lack of access to administrators and problems of delay also feature highly.

37 Source: Parliamentary and Health Service Ombudsman *Business Plan 2003–2004*.
38 During 2002–03 the Parliamentary Commissioner completed investigations into 2,234 complaints; in 2004–05, 2,886 cases were completed.

THE PROBLEM OF ACCESSIBILITY
AND PUBLIC AWARENESS

On accessibility, the Commissioner has questioned his own position.[39] As seen, prior to reform, discussed below, access to the Commissioner could only be gained through a Member of Parliament, and not directly. Of the 100 plus national ombudsmen around the world, the British Commissioner was unique in having no powers of initiative, being dependent upon references from the MP 'filter'. In the report for 1988, the Commissioner considered the difficulties in increasing public awareness about the Commissioner's role and powers,[40] despite regular press notices, press and radio and television interviews and the booklet available from Citizens Advice Bureaux and public libraries. In the Commissioner's report of 1990,[41] the problem of public awareness was again alluded to.

The Commissioner himself has noted that public awareness is most usually raised through some major issue or scandal. Two illustrations may be cited. The first major investigation arising out of a number of complaints was into the non-payment of compensation by the Foreign Office to 12 persons who had been prisoners of war in the Sachsenhausen camp.[42] Monies had been made available by the German government and distributed by the Foreign Office to former detainees. The Commissioner found there had been maladministration[43] and the government awarded compensation to the complainants.

The Barlow Clowes affair resulted in hundreds of complaints being made to the Commissioner concerning the collapse of the Barlow Clowes company.[44] In 1988, the group of companies collapsed, causing significant losses to shareholders. The Department of Trade and Industry has responsibility for licensing such investment companies.[45] Following the company's collapse, numerous shareholders complained to Members of Parliament, 159 of whom referred the complaints to the Parliamentary Commissioner. The Commissioner made five findings of maladministration on the part of the Department of Trade and Industry, including errors, lack of information before making decisions, delay in instigating a formal inquiry, a failure to appreciate that auditors would not find the relevant information and insufficient rigour in exercising its regulatory role – all of which resulted in injustice.

---

39 *Parliamentary Commissioner for Administration Annual Report for 1983* (1983–84), London: HMSO. And see *Report of the Select Committee on the Parliamentary Commissioner for Administration: The Powers, Work and Jurisdiction of the Ombudsman* (1992–93), London: HMSO.

40 *Parliamentary Commissioner for Administration Annual Report for 1988* (1988–89), London: HMSO.

41 *Parliamentary Commissioner for Administration Annual Report for 1990* (1990–91), London: HMSO.

42 See Bradley, 1992b.

43 *Third Report of the Parliamentary Commissioner for Administration*, HC 54 (1967–68), London: HMSO; and see Gregory and Drewry, Part I and Part II, 1991.

44 See Gregory and Drewry, Part I and Part II, 1991.

45 Under the Prevention of Fraud (Investment) Act 1958; now Financial Services Act 1986.

The government initially rejected the Commissioner's findings and recommendations as to compensation, arguing both that no investment is free of risk and that those with larger amounts of money should accept a higher level of responsibility and therefore loss. The Commissioner expressed disappointment that the government did not unreservedly accept his report. His recommendation was that compensation should be payable to investors at a rate of 90 per cent for losses incurred under £50,000, and 85 per cent for losses under £100,000. The Secretary of State for Trade and Industry accepted the recommendations, but maintained that the government had no legal liability to compensate investors, and claimed that the Department's handling of the case was 'within acceptable range of standards reasonably to be expected of regulators'. The Secretary of State went on to say that compensation was being made only because of the Parliamentary Commissioner's recommendations.[46]

The losses caused to egg manufacturers over allegations made by officials concerning the salmonella virus resulted in charges of maladministration and compensation of £600,000 being paid by the Ministry of Agriculture, Fisheries and Food.[47] The Animal Health Act 1981[48] provided that, where the salmonella virus was found in flocks, the flock should be slaughtered and compensation paid for the loss of the healthy birds. No compensation was payable for the diseased birds. The Ministry fixed the level of compensation – irrespective of the proportion of the flock infected by the virus – at 60 per cent of the value of the healthy birds. On investigation, the Commissioner found that inadequate compensation had been paid.[49]

It has been seen above that the government is, in general, prepared to accept the findings of the Commissioner and to implement his or her recommendations. In December 1991, the Financial Secretary to the Treasury[50] stated that 'I am not aware of any circumstances in which [the Parliamentary Ombudsman's] recommendations have been ignored. This is the basis on which the government has tended to work – and has, as far as I am aware, always worked – in that we do accept and implement the recommendations that are made'.[51] This commitment was reiterated by the Chancellor of the Duchy of Lancaster[52] in 1993, when he stated that 'invariably, in the end, [the government] accepted the Commissioner's say-so'.[53] However, it has also been seen above that, in relation to the Barlow Clowes affair, the government deviated from this normally accepted practice and, while prepared to offer compensation, did so 'without admission of

---

46   In total, £150 million was paid in compensation.
47   HC 947 (1992–93), London: HMSO.
48   Animal Health Act 1981, Sched 3, para 5(2).
49   *Fourth Report: Compensation to Farmers for Slaughtered Poultry,* HC 519 (1992–93), London: HMSO.
50   Mr Francis Maude MP.
51   *Second Report from the Select Committee on the PCA: The Implications of the Citizen's Charter for the Work of the Parliamentary Commissioner for Administration,* HC 159 (1991–92), London: HMSO, Q 11.
52   Then the Rt Hon William Waldegrave MP.
53   *First Report from the Select Committee on the PCA: The Powers, Work and Jurisdiction of the Ombudsman,* HC 33 (1993–94), London: HMSO, Q 733.

fault or liability'.[54] The government has proved to be more obdurate in relation to the 1995 report of the Commissioner, relating to financial damage caused by the prolonged plans to build the Channel Tunnel Rail Link.

The Channel Tunnel Rail Link (the CTRL) is a stretch of railway line, designed to take high speed cross-channel trains. The government's original intention was that the CTRL would be financed by the private sector. However, when private funding was not forthcoming, the project could not proceed. In 1990, the Secretary of State for Transport announced that the route was to be reconsidered. The project was thus kept alive, but uncertainty surrounded the area of south east England in which it was to be built. As a result, thousands of properties were 'blighted' and owners unable to sell their homes. The route was finally decided in 1994.

In February 1995, the Commissioner[55] laid a special report before the House.[56] The special report was only the second such report to be made in the history of the office of Commissioner.[57] The basis for the laying of a special report is that the Commission considers that injustice has been caused to persons as a result of maladministration and that the injustice has not been, or will not be, remedied. In the Commissioner's report on the CTRL project, the Commissioner considered that maladministration had occurred in the Department of Transport between June 1990 and April 1994. The Commissioner's view was that the Department of Transport 'had a responsibility to consider the position of ... persons suffering exceptional or extreme hardship and to provide for redress where appropriate'[58] and that the government had a duty to consider the position not just of all citizens, but also of individual citizens harmed by its action. The Commissioner found that 'no special consideration was given to that aspect of good administration and it is on that basis that I criticise the department'.[59] The Commissioner recommended that individuals who had suffered exceptional hardship should receive compensation from the government. The government's reaction was to state that it was not its policy to compensate those affected by generalised blight, and that, in relation to those individuals who had suffered exceptional hardship, it was too difficult to define criteria to identify such individuals. With this, the Commissioner disagreed. While he accepted that there were definitional difficulties, he did not 'accept at all that it is technically beyond a government department's capabilities' to establish the relevant criteria.[60]

The Commissioner's report and the government's response was considered by the Select Committee on the Parliamentary Commissioner for Administration (see

---

54 Observations by the government to the *Report of the PCA on Barlow Clowes*, HC 99 (1989–90), London: HMSO, para 43.
55 Mr William Reid CB.
56 Pursuant to the Parliamentary Commissioner Act 1967, s 10(3).
57 The first was in 1977–78, which also involved the Department of Transport.
58 *Fifth Report of the PCA: The Channel Tunnel Rail Link and Blight*, HC 193 (1994–95), London: HMSO, para 46.
59 *Ibid*, Q 1.
60 *Ibid*, Q 1.

further below). In its report,[61] the committee agreed with the Commissioner's assessment of the evidence. The committee stated that:

> The department failed to provide any material to contradict this finding when invited to do so by the committee. At no point was direct and comprehensive consideration given to the question of whether it was either desirable or possible to offer *ex gratia* compensation to those exceptionally afflicted by the generalised blight of the CTRL project.

The committee considered that at the heart of the matter lay the definition of maladministration. In his annual report for 1993, the Commissioner included in his definition 'failure to mitigate the effects of rigid adherence to the letter of the law where that produces manifestly inequitable treatment'.[62] Endorsing this definition, the committee stated that the definition implies:

> ... an expectation that when an individual citizen is faced with extraordinary hardship as a result of strict application of law or policy, the executive must be prepared to look again and consider whether help can be given. That the department did not do. It never considered the possibility of distinguishing cases of extreme hardship from the mass of those affected adversely by blight.[63]

The committee concluded that:

> 1(i) ... the Department of Transport should have considered whether any *ex gratia* payments were due when the CTRL project entered the period of uncertainty caused by problems of funding between June 1990 and April 1994;
>
> (ii) ... it is desirable to grant redress to those affected to an extreme and exceptional degree by generalised blight, in line with the principle that maladministration includes a failure to mitigate the effects of rigid adherence to the letter of the law where that produces manifestly inequitable treatment;
>
> (iii) ... it should be possible to distinguish a small number of cases of exceptional hardship.

This highly critical report on the actions of the Department of Transport and the government's failure to respond positively to the Commissioner's report represents a landmark case in the complex tri-partite constitutional relationship between the Commissioner, his select committee and parliament, and the executive. In 1997, the government finally agreed to pay compensation of £5,000 to property owners whose property value had been adversely affected by the delay in reaching decisions over the routing of the CTRL.[64]

---

61 *Sixth Report of the PCA: The Channel Tunnel Rail Link and Exceptional Hardship*, HC 270 (1994–95), London: HMSO.
62 *Report of the Parliamentary Commissioner for Administration: Annual Report for 1993*, HC 345 (1993–94), London: HMSO, para 10.
63 *Sixth Report*, fn 58, para 20.
64 See James and Longley, 1996. The Child Support Agency also attracted a significant volume of complaints. The number of complaints was such that, in 1994, the Commissioner took the 'unprecedented step of declining to investigate fresh individual complaints' other than where they concerned aspects of the Agency's work which the Commissioner had not yet inquired into. In 1995, complaints against the Child Support Agency amounted to one quarter of all cases referred to the Commissioner. See *Sixth Report*, paras 17–18 and *Parliamentary Commissioner for Administration Annual Report for 1995*, Cm 296; and see HC 193 (1994–95), London: HMSO.

The select committee

The Parliamentary Commissioner is aided by a select committee, which considers the annual and special reports of the Parliamentary Commissioner and Health Service Commissioner and takes evidence from the Commissioners and others, including government departments and health authorities, on matters arising from reports in order to ensure that all reasonable efforts are made to tighten up procedures, prevent the repetition of faults and provide any appropriate remedies.

The select committee represents the formal link between the Commissioner and parliament. The committee is able to exert pressure on government departments to comply with the recommendations of the Commissioner.

The Parliamentary Commissioner and ministerial responsibility

One aspect of the office of Commissioner which caused concern when the office was proposed was the relationship between the Commissioner and ministers, and the impact of the Commissioner's office on the doctrine of ministerial responsibility.

Ministerial responsibility[65] is a fundamental constitutional principle. Separated into the collective responsibility of the Cabinet and the individual responsibility of Ministers for their conduct and that of their department, the concept underpins the idea of governmental accountability to parliament and to the electorate. Accordingly, where a person has a grievance against a government department or other public body which is not resolved to the complainant's satisfaction, responsibility falls on the relevant Minister and it is for the Minister to account to parliament for any wrongdoing by a body under his responsibility. The view of the government at the time was that ministerial responsibility and the office of the Commissioner were irreconcilable. As noted above, in the Attorney General's view, there already existed 'adequate provision' under the constitution for the redress of grievances.

JUSTICE replied:

> The Commissioner would help to make ministerial responsibility more effective. He would penetrate the screen which Ministers interpose between Members of Parliament and government departments and he would keep Parliament informed about administrative practices which were open to criticism. The responsibility of the Minister would remain as it is – neither more nor less.

The government's policy of making administration more open and accessible has an impact on the work of the Parliamentary Commissioner. Three major developments reflected this commitment. The Citizen's Charter provided that public bodies must state their objectives, must publicise the standards of service to be expected by consumers and establish complaints procedures for dissatisfied

---

65   It will be recalled from the discussion in Chapters 2 and 11.

customers.[66] Specific services must publish their own individuated Charter. The establishment of 'Next Step Agencies',[67] the task of which is to achieve greater efficiency in the delivery of public services, also affects the role of the Commissioner. The setting up of Agencies, the head of which are responsible for operational matters and accountable to parliament through select committee inquiries, has the effect of reducing the size of the central Civil Service and introducing greater management efficiency and accountability. The minister remains responsible to parliament for policy matters. In relation to the Parliamentary Commissioner,[68] his powers of investigation, report and recommendation continue to extend to Agencies. However, complaints made by the public to Members of Parliament about operational matters are to be directed to the chairman of the board of the Agency. Complaints regarding matters of policy remain within the political domain and the responsibility of ministers.

REFORM OF THE OFFICE OF PARLIAMENTARY COMMISSIONER

The office of Commissioner suffers from a number of drawbacks. Individuals have – unlike in most other jurisdictions – no right of direct access to the Parliamentary Commissioner. The concept of maladministration is relatively narrow and is linked to injustice suffered as a result of a decision. Furthermore, while the 1987 Act has extended the bodies into which the Commissioner has jurisdiction to investigate, there remain a significant number of matters outside his jurisdiction. Many of these relate to matters which fall under the royal prerogative,[69] which, as has been seen, is subject to inadequate parliamentary scrutiny and to limited judicial review.

The question of direct access to the Commissioner was again considered by the select committee in 1993–94.[70] The committee conducted a survey of Members of Parliament in order to ascertain their views on the filter. Of the 333 Members who responded, the committee reported that 38.4 per cent were in favour of direct access to the Commissioners, whereas 58.0 per cent were against direct access. The committee commented that:

> It is clear that many Members value their role as champions of their constituents' complaints and are unwilling to see this constitutional function in any way bypassed or diminished.[71]

The Commissioner himself, however, argued forcibly that the filter was 'potentially disadvantageous to complainants', in part because individuals may

---

66 In the six months from July 2001 to January 2002, the Commissioner upheld complaints against a number of public bodies over the refusal to disclose information: *Access to Official Information: Fifth Report*, HC 585 (2002), London: HMSO. See www.ombudsman.org.uk.

67 See *Improving Management in Government: The Next Steps*, 1988, London: HMSO.

68 And Commissioner for Local Administration.

69 See Chapter 7.

70 HC 33 (1993–94), London: HMSO, paras 53–77.

71 HC 33 (1993–94), London: HMSO, para 58.

feel that their Member of Parliament would be unwilling to help them and because of the administrative burden on Members of Parliament in transmitting material to the Commissioner. JUSTICE and the National Consumer Council also argued for reform of the system. The committee summarised the objections to the MP filter as follows:

(a) The public should have direct access to the Commissioner as a matter of right.

(b) The filter is an anomaly, almost unknown in other ombudsman systems.[72] No such requirement exists, for instance, in the case of the Health Service Commissioner.

(c) Individuals with complaints may be unwilling to approach an MP, while desiring the ombudsman's assistance.

(d) The filter means that the likelihood of individuals' cases being referred to the Commissioner will largely depend on the views and practice of the particular constituency MP. Some look with more favour on the Office of the Commissioner than others.

(e) The filter acts as an obstacle to the Commissioner effectively promoting his services.

(f) The filter creates an unnecessary bureaucratic barrier between the complainant and the Commissioner, involving considerable paperwork for MPs and their offices.[73]

The committee concluded, however, that the advantages of retaining the filter system outweighed these significant disadvantages. The committee was particularly concerned to retain the role of the Member of Parliament in the investigation of complaints, and about the potentially vast increase in the number of complaints being received by the Commissioner if the filter was removed.

The question of the jurisdictional basis of maladministration has also been subject to consideration. The JUSTICE-All Souls Report of 1988[74] recommended no change to the definition. In 2000 a Cabinet review of Ombudsmen concluded that there should be major reform aimed at simplifying the arrangements for complaints and removing the 'MP filter'. The review recommended that the offices of Parliamentary, Local Government and Health Service Commissioners should be restructured into one single Public Service Commissioner able to receive complaints about any matter within jurisdiction.[75]

COMMISSIONERS FOR NORTHERN IRELAND, SCOTLAND AND WALES

Northern Ireland, Scotland and Wales each have a Parliamentary Commissioner for Administration with similar powers and functions as the United Kingdom Parliamentary Commissioner. In Northern Ireland there is also a Police Ombudsman.[76]

---

72 Only Sri Lanka and France employ similar filters.

73 HC 33 (1993–94), London: HMSO, para 65.

74 JUSTICE-All Souls, *Administrative Law: Some Necessary Reforms*, 1988, London: HMSO.

75 Cabinet Office, *Review of Public Sector Ombudsmen in England*, 2000. In 2000 a Parliamentary Commissioner (Amendment) Bill, removing the MP filter, was passed by the House of Lords but rejected by the Commons.

76 Respectively, Parliamentary Commissioner (Northern Ireland) Act 1969; Scotland Act 1998; Government of Wales Act 1998; Police (Northern Ireland) Act 1997.

THE HEALTH SERVICE COMMISSIONERS

The National Health Service (Scotland) Act 1972 and National Health Service Reorganisation Act 1973[77] introduced separate Health Service Commissioners for England, Wales and Scotland. The Parliamentary Commissioner for Administration undertakes the role of Health Service Commissioner. The Commissioner reports directly to the Secretary of State for Health, but his reports are laid before both Houses of Parliament and will be considered by the Parliamentary Commissioner Select Committee.

Jurisdiction

Section 109 of the Health Service Act 1977 provides that the following are subject to investigation by the Health Commissioner: regional, district and special health authorities; family health services authorities; Mental Health Act Commission; Dental Practice Board; and National Health Service Trusts.

The Commissioner may investigate any matter relating to an alleged failure to provide a service it is meant to provide, and any other action taken by or on behalf of the authority. The jurisdiction is thus much broader than 'maladministration'. However, the complaint must be one which involves injustice or hardship suffered as a result of failures under the two headings for complaint. Individuals have the right of direct access to the Commissioner.

Excluded matters

Section 116(2)(b) of the Health Service Act 1977 provides that the Commissioner shall not investigate complaints about services provided by family doctors, dentists, opticians and pharmacists. This broad exclusion was justified on the basis that the services provided are provided independently, under contracts with local family health services authorities which have jurisdiction to adjudicate on complaints. The most significant exclusion from jurisdiction related to clinical decisions. The Health Service Commissioners (Amendment) Act 1996, however, extends the jurisdiction of health service commissioners. Section 6 removed the statutory bar which prevented the Commissioner from investigating complaints concerning clinical judgment, thus correcting one of the most significant former jurisdictional exclusions.

Service committees which consider allegations against doctors, dentists, opticians and pharmacists originally could not be investigated by the Commissioner, under Schedule 13, paragraph 19 of the National Health Service Act 1977. Personnel matters were also excluded, as are commercial transactions, and inquiries set up by the Secretary of State into aspects of the National Health Service. Sections 1 and 2 of the Health Service Commissioners (Amendment) Act 1996, however, now bring the providers of general medical, dental, ophthalmic and pharmaceutical services and people in the independent sector who provide services to NHS patients within the Commissioners' jurisdiction.

---

77   As amended by the National Health Service Act 1977, Pt V. See now the Health Service Commissioners Act 1993.

LOCAL GOVERNMENT COMMISSIONERS[78]

The Local Government Act 1974 established Commissioners for Local Administration, for England and Wales. England is divided into three areas, each represented by one or more Commissioners.[79] The Scottish system is established under Part II of the Local Government (Scotland) Act 1975. Commissioners are appointed by the Crown and hold office 'during good behaviour'.

Jurisdiction

The Commissioners have jurisdiction to investigate any complaint of maladministration involving council committees, their Members and officers of the council. Police authorities and water boards are also subject to investigation.[80] The Local Government Act 1988[81] brings development corporations and the Commission for New Towns within the Commissioner's jurisdiction. Since 1989, the public has the right of direct access to the Commissioner, a reform which resulted in a 44 per cent increase in complaints by the year ending March 1989 and by March 1990 in a further 25 per cent increase in complaints.

Maladministration causing injustice

The concept of maladministration used for the Parliamentary Commissioner is adopted for the Local Commissioners. Maladministration resulting in injustice has been found to include incomplete record keeping and the failure to give reasons for decisions, and a finding of maladministration may be made where an authority fails to have adequate complaints procedures. Inadequate school places, and unreasonable delays in processing applications for improvement grants have also been found to amount to maladministration. Shortages of staff and financial resources will not excuse a council from a finding of maladministration.

Section 31 of the Act provides that an authority need only consider a Commissioner's report if it has been found that the maladministration in question has resulted in injustice. Mere maladministration is not enough.

Remedies

Where a finding of maladministration resulting in injustice has been made, section 31 of the Local Government Act 1974 imposes a duty on authorities to consider the report and to advise the Commissioner of any action taken to comply with the findings, or proposed action. Section 31 of the 1974 Act has been amended to provide that authorities may make 'any payment' to the aggrieved person that it thinks appropriate.

---

78 Recommended by the JUSTICE Report, *The Citizen and His Council: Ombudsmen for Local Government?*, 1969; and see the White Paper, *Reform of Local Government in England*, 1970, London: HMSO.
79 Local Government Act 1974, s 23.
80 *Ibid*, ss 25, 34(1).
81 Local Government Act 1988, s 29, Sched 3.

Not every decision of the Commissioners will be accepted. In 1986, for example, the Select Committee on the Parliamentary Commissioner noted that 19 per cent of local authorities who had adverse reports made by the Commissioners had ignored the recommendations.[82] The Local Government and Housing Act 1989 provides that local authorities have three months in which to respond to the Commissioner's report and that they should notify the Commissioner of any action taken, or action which they are proposing to take in response to his report.[83] If the Commissioner is not satisfied with the response he may issue a further report. Where the local authority proposes not to act in response to the report, the matter must be referred to a full council meeting; see further Chapter 10.

Excluded matters

Schedule 5 to the Local Government Act excludes matters relating to the internal regulation of schools, personnel matters, action taken concerning the commencement of legal proceedings and criminal investigations, commercial and contractual matters.

Complaints

Housing matters form the basis for approximately 40 per cent of complaints each year, with complaints about planning accounting for approximately 30 per cent of complaints. Education, social services, local taxation and environmental health each comprise approximately five per cent of complaints.

Judicial review and Commissioners for Administration

Judicial review of decisions of Commissioners is an available form of redress, although the breadth of discretion conferred on Commissioners often renders their decisions beyond challenge. In *Law Debenture Trust Group plc v Pensions Ombudsman* (1999), the Chancery Division allowed an appeal against a finding of maladministration by the Pensions Ombudsman. The complainant had applied to trustees of his pension scheme for early retirement following an injury. The trustees concluded that he was not incapacitated, having carried out video surveillance. The court ruled that the only basis available to the Ombudsman for overturning the decision of the trustees was on the ground of perversity, and that such a finding would have to be expressed in clear terms in the Ombudsman's decision, which had not been done. Further, a finding of perversity could only be made after consideration of the *Wednesbury* criteria with respect to unreasonableness. The Ombudsman was wrong to find that surveillance *per se* amounted to maladministration.

---

82 *Third Report from the Select Committee on the Parliamentary Commissioner for Administration: Local Government Cases: Enforcement of Remedies*, HC 448 (1985–86), London: HMSO.
83 Local Government and Housing Act 1989, s 26(2)–(2)(c).

In *R v Parliamentary Commissioner for Administration ex parte Balchin* (1998), the Queen's Bench Division quashed a decision of the Parliamentary Commissioner. The Commissioner had found maladministration in relation to property blighted by a road scheme in Norfolk, but following judicial review his decision was quashed, whereupon a second ombudsman investigated the matter. The second decision included fresh findings based on new evidence. It was disputed whether the Commissioner had made a finding as to whether, if there had been any maladministration, that had caused any injustice to the applicants. The court held that the decision on maladministration was flawed since his reasoning was inadequate, and that there had been a failure to give reasons for findings on the principal controversial issues. The application was granted and certiorari ordered.

THE INFORMATION COMMISSIONER

The Freedom of Information Act 2000, discussed in Chapter 26, represents a step in the direction of more open government by conferring on citizens a legal right, subject to limited exceptions, to access to information held by public bodies. An Information Commissioner has been appointed who is independent of parliament and accountable to the courts. The Commissioner's jurisdiction comes into play after there has been a complaint made to a department or other public body, and that body has conducted an internal inquiry which produces no satisfactory outcome. Complaints are made by the public via a Member of Parliament. The Commissioner has wide powers to investigate complaints, including the right of access, under warrant, to enter and search the records of public authorities and, where it is suspected that information is being, or will be, suppressed, to remove that information. There is no right of appeal from the Commissioner to the courts, but his or her decisions are amenable to judicial review. The Commissioner lays an annual report before parliament, and issues reports on investigations undertaken.

EUROPEAN UNION AND COMMUNITY OMBUDSMAN[84]

The Treaty on European Union 1992 introduced the office of ombudsman, appointed by the European Parliament. Under Article 195, the ombudsman is appointed for the life of a Parliament, and may be removed by the Court of Justice, at the request of the Parliament, on the basis that 'he no longer fulfils the conditions required for the performance of his duties or if he is guilty of serious misconduct'. The ombudsman is completely independent in the exercise of his duties, and may not seek or take instructions from any body.

Citizens of the European Union have the right of direct access to the ombudsman, and complaints may be referred by a Member of the European Parliament. The ombudsman has jurisdiction to hear complaints relating to institutions of the Union and to require national government bodies to provide

---

84   On the institutions of the Community, see Chapter 8.

information relating to complaints. Where a finding of maladministration is made, the matter is referred to the relevant institution which has a period of three months in which to respond. The ombudsman submits an annual report to the European Parliament. The complaint must relate to maladministration on the part of institutions of the Union. The European Court of Justice and the Court of First Instance, acting in their judicial role, are excluded from the ombudsman's jurisdiction.[85]

---

85   See Lord Millett, 2002.

APPENDIX I

MONARCHS OF BRITAIN

Name	Lived	Reigned
William the Conqueror	1027 – 1087	1066 – 1087
William II	1056 – 1100	1087 – 1100
Henry I	1068 – 1135	1100 – 1135
Stephen	?1097 – 1154	1135 – 1154
Henry II	1133 – 1189	1154 – 1189
Richard I	1157 – 1199	1189 – 1199
John	1167 – 1216	1199 – 1216
Henry III	1207 – 1272	1216 – 1272
Edward I	1239 – 1307	1272 – 1307
Edward II	1284 – 1327	1307 – 1327
Edward III	1312 – 1377	1327 – 1377
Richard II	1367 – 1400	1377 – 1399
Henry IV	1367 – 1413	1399 – 1413
Henry V	1387 – 1422	1413 – 1422
Henry VI	1421 – 1471	1422 – 1461
Edward IV	1442 – 1483	1461 – 1470
		1471 – 1483
	(Henry VI briefly restored to the throne in 1470)	
Edward V	1470 – ?1483	1483
Richard III	1452 – 1485	1483 – 1485
Henry VII	1457 – 1509	1485 – 1509
Henry VIII	1491 – 1547	1509 – 1547
Edward VI	1537 – 1553	1547 – 1553
Mary I	1516 – 1558	1553 – 1558
Elizabeth I	1533 – 1603	1558 – 1603
James I	1566 – 1625	1567 – 1625 (James VI of Scotland)
		1603 – 1625 (England)
Charles I	1600 – 1649	1625 – 1649
Interregnum	1649 – 1660	–
Charles II	1630 – 1685	1660 – 1685
James II	1633 – 1701	1685 – 1688
William and Mary	1650 – 1702	1689 – 1702
Anne	1665 – 1714	1702 – 1714
George I	1660 – 1727	1714 – 1727
George II	1683 – 1760	1727 – 1760
George III	1738 – 1820	1760 – 1820
George IV	1762 – 1830	1820 – 1830
William IV	1765 – 1837	1830 – 1837
Victoria	1819 – 1901	1837 – 1901
Edward VII	1841 – 1910	1901 – 1910
George V	1865 – 1936	1910 – 1936
Edward VIII	1894 – 1972	1936 (abdicated)
George VI	1895 – 1952	1936 – 1952
Elizabeth II	1926 –	1952 –

APPENDIX II

PRIME MINISTERS OF THE UNITED KINGDOM

Name	Party	Dates
Sir Robert Walpole		3 April 1721 – 11 February 1742
The Earl of Wilmington		16 February 1742 – 2 July 1743
The Hon Henry Pelham		25 August 1743 – 10 February 1746
The Earl of Bath		10 – 12 February 1746
The Hon Henry Pelham		13 February 1746 – 6 March 1754
The Duke of Newcastle		6 March 1754 – 26 October 1756
William Pitt (the elder)		16 November 1756 – 6 April 1757
The Duke of Devonshire		6 April – 8 June 1757
Earl Waldegrave		8 – 12 June 1757
The Duke of Devonshire		12 – 29 June 1757
William Pitt (the elder)		19 June 1757 – 5 October 1761
The Duke of Newcastle		5 October 1761 – 26 May 1762
The Earl of Bute		26 May 1762 – 8 April 1763
George Grenville		10 April 1763 – 10 July 1765
Marquess of Rockingham		10 July 1765 – 12 July 1766
William Pitt (the elder)		30 July 1766 – 12 March 1767
The Duke of Grafton		12 March 1767 – 28 January 1770
Lord North		28 January 1770 – 20 March 1782
Marquess of Rockingham		27 March 1782 – 1 July 1782
The Earl of Shelburne		3 July 1782 – 24 February 1783
The Duke of Portland		2 April 1783 – 19 December 1783
The Hon William Pitt (the younger)	Tory	19 December 1783 – 14 March 1801
Henry Addington	Tory	14 March 1801 – 10 May 1804
The Hon William Pitt (the younger)	Tory	10 May 1804 – 23 January 1806
Lord Grenville	Whig	31 March 1807 – 6 September 1809
The Duke of Portland	Tory	31 March 1807 – 6 September 1809
Spencer Perceval	Tory	4 October 1809 – 11 May 1812
The Earl of Liverpool	Tory	8 June 1812 – 17 February 1827
George Canning	Tory	10 April 1827 – 8 August 1827
Viscount Goderich	Tory	31 August 1827 – 8 January 1828
The Duke of Wellington	Tory	22 January 1828 – 15 November 1830
Earl Grey	Whig	16 November 1830 – 9 July 1834
Viscount Melbourne	Whig	16 July 1834 – 17 November 1834
The Duke of Wellington	Tory	17 November 1834 – 10 December 1834
Sir Robert Peel	Conservative	10 December 1834 – 8 April 1835
Viscount Melbourne	Whig	18 April 1835 – 30 August 1841
Sir Robert Peel	Conservative	30 August 1841 – 30 June 1846
Lord John Russell	Whig	30 June 1846 – 23 February 1852
The Earl of Derby	Conservative	23 February 1852 – 19 December 1852
The Earl of Aberdeen	Coalition	19 December 1852 – 1 February 1855
Viscount Palmerston	Whig-Liberal	6 February 1855 – 19 February 1858
The Earl of Derby	Conservative	26 February 1858 – 10 June 1859
Viscount Palmerston	Whig-Liberal	12 June 1859 – 18 October 1865
Earl Russell	Whig-Liberal	29 October 1865 – 26 June 1866
The Earl of Derby	Conservative	6 July 1866 – 25 February 1868
Benjamin Disraeli	Conservative	28 February 1868 – 3 December 1868

William Gladstone . . . . .Liberal . . . . .3 December 1868 – 17 February 1874
Benjamin Disraeli . . . . .Conservative . . . . .20 February 1874 – 18 April 1880
William Gladstone . . . . .Liberal . . . . .23 April 1880 – 23 June 1885
Marquess of Salisbury . . . . .Conservative . . . . .23 June 1885 – 27 January 1886
William Gladstone . . . . .Liberal . . . . .1 February 1886 – 20 July 1886
Marquess of Salisbury . . . . .Conservative . . . . .25 July 1886 – 11 August 1892
William Gladstone . . . . .Liberal . . . . .15 August 1892 – 3 March 1894
Earl of Rosebery . . . . .Liberal . . . . .5 March 1894 – 25 June 1895
Marquess of Salisbury . . . . .Conservative . . . . .25 June 1895 – 12 July 1902
Arthur Balfour . . . . .Conservative . . . . .12 July 1902 – 4 December 1905
Sir Henry . . . . .Liberal . . . . .5 December 1905 – 7 April 1908
Campbell-Bannerman
Herbert Asquith . . . . .Liberal . . . . .7 April 1908 – 26 May 1915
Herbert Asquith . . . . .Coalition . . . . .26 May 1915 – 7 December 1916
David Lloyd George . . . . .Coalition . . . . .7 December 1916 – 19 October 1922
Andrew Bonar Law . . . . .Conservative . . . . .23 October 1922 – 20 May 1923
Stanley Baldwin . . . . .Conservative . . . . .22 May 1923 – 22 January 1924
James Ramsey MacDonald . . . . . . .Labour . . . . .22 January 1924 – 4 November 1924
Stanley Baldwin . . . . .Conservative . . . . .4 November 1924 – 5 June 1929
James Ramsey MacDonald . . . . . . .Labour . . . . .5 June 1929 – 24 August 1931
James Ramsey MacDonald . . . . . . .National . . . . .25 August 1931 – 7 June 1935
. . . . .Government
Stanley Baldwin . . . . .National . . . . .7 June 1935 – 28 May 1937
. . . . .Government
Neville Chamberlain . . . . .National . . . . .28 May 1937 – 10 May 1940
. . . . .Government
Winston Churchill . . . . .Coalition . . . . .10 May 1940 – 23 May 1945
Winston Churchill . . . . .Conservative . . . . .23 May 1945 – 26 July 1945
Clement Attlee . . . . .Labour . . . . .26 July 1945 – 26 October 1951
Winston Churchill . . . . .Conservative . . . . .26 October 1951 – 5 April 1955
Sir Anthony Eden . . . . .Conservative . . . . .6 April 1955 – 9 January 1957
Harold Macmillan . . . . .Conservative . . . . .10 January 1957 – 13 October 1963
Sir Alec Douglas-Home . . . . .Conservative . . . . .18 October 1963 – 16 October 1964
Harold Wilson . . . . .Labour . . . . .16 October 1964 – 19 June 1970
Edward Heath . . . . .Conservative . . . . .19 June 1970 – 3 March 1974
Harold Wilson . . . . .Labour . . . . .3 March 1974 – 16 March 1976
James Callaghan . . . . .Labour . . . . .5 April 1976 – 28 March 1979
Margaret Thatcher . . . . .Conservative . . . . .4 May 1979 – 22 November 1990
John Major . . . . .Conservative . . . . .27 November 1990 – 2 May 1997
Anthony Blair . . . . .Labour . . . . .2 May 1997 to present

APPENDIX III

MEMBERSHIP OF THE COMMONWEALTH

Member country ....**Status**

Antigua and Barbuda ....Monarchy under Queen Elizabeth II
Australia ....Monarchy under Queen Elizabeth II
The Bahamas ....Monarchy under Queen Elizabeth II
Bangladesh ....Republic
Barbados ....Monarchy under Queen Elizabeth II
Belize ....Monarchy under Queen Elizabeth II
Botswana ....Republic
Britain ....Monarchy under Queen Elizabeth II
Brunei Darussalam ....National Monarchy
Cameroon ....Republic
Canada ....Monarchy under Queen Elizabeth II
Cyprus ....Republic
Dominica ....Republic
Fiji ....Republic
The Gambia ....Republic
Ghana ....Republic
Grenada ....Monarchy under Queen Elizabeth II
Guyana ....Republic
India ....Republic
Jamaica ....Monarchy under Queen Elizabeth II
Kenya ....Republic
Kiribati ....Republic
Lesotho ....National Monarchy
Malawi ....Republic
Malaysia ....National Monarchy
Maldives ....Republic
Malta ....Republic
Mauritius ....Republic
Mozambique ....Republic
Namibia ....Republic
Nauru ....Republic
New Zealand ....Monarchy under Queen Elizabeth II
Nigeria ....Republic (Membership suspended 1995)
Pakistan ....Republic
Papua New Guinea ....Monarchy under Queen Elizabeth II
St Kitts and Nevis ....Monarchy under Queen Elizabeth II
St Lucia ....Monarchy under Queen Elizabeth II
St Vincent and the Grenadines ....Monarchy under Queen Elizabeth II
Samoa ....Republic
Seychelles ....Republic
Sierra Leone ....Republic
Singapore ....Republic

Solomon Islands .Monarchy under Queen Elizabeth II
South Africa . . . . .Republic
Sri Lanka . . . . .Republic
Swaziland . . . . .National Monarchy
Tanzania . . . . .Republic
Tonga . . . . .National Monarchy
Trinidad and Tobago . . . . .Republic
Tuvalu . . . . .Monarchy under Queen Elizabeth II
Uganda . . . . .Republic
Vanuatu . . . . .Republic
Zambia . . . . .Republic
Zimbabwe . . . . .Republic

BIBLIOGRAPHY

Adams, J, *The New Spies: Exploring the Frontiers of Espionage*, 1994, London: Hutchinson

Aitken, J, *Officially Secret*, 1971, London: Weidenfeld & Nicolson

Alderman, RK and Carter, N, 'A very Tory coup: the ousting of Mrs Thatcher' (1991) 44 Parl Aff 125

Alderman, RK and Smith, MJ, 'Can prime ministers be pushed out?' (1990) 43 Parl Aff 260

Allan, TRS, 'Legislative supremacy and the rule of law: democracy and constitutionalism' [1985] CLJ 111 (1985a)

Allan, TRS, 'The limits of parliamentary sovereignty' [1985] PL 614 (1985b)

Allan, TRS, 'Law, convention, prerogative: reflections prompted by the Canadian constitutional case' [1986] CLJ 305

Allan, TRS, *Law, Liberty and Justice*, 1993, Oxford: Clarendon

Allan, TRS, 'Requiring reasons for reasons of fairness and reasonableness' [1994] CLJ 207

Allan, TRS, 'Parliamentary sovereignty: law, politics and revolution' (1997) 113 LQR 443

Allan, TRS, *Constitutional Justice: A Liberal Theory of the Rule of Law*, 2001, Oxford: OUP

Allason, R, *The Branch: A History of the Metropolitan Police Special Branch 1883–1983*, 1983, London: Secker & Warburg

Allen, CK, *Law and Orders*, 3rd edn, 1965, London: Stevens

Allen, R and Sales, P, 'The impact of the Human Rights Act 1998 upon subordinate legislation promulgated before October 2, 2000' [2000] PL 358

Andenas, M and Fairgrieve, D, 'Reforming Crown immunity: the comparative law perspective' [2003] PL 730

Andrew, C, *Secret Service: The Making of the British Intelligence Community*, 1985, London: Heinemann

Anson, W (Sir), *Law and Custom of the Constitution*, 4th edn, 1933, Oxford: Clarendon

Archbold: Criminal Pleading, Evidence and Practice 2003, 2002, London: Sweet & Maxwell

Aristotle, *The Politics*, 1962, Sinclair, TA (trans), Harmondsworth: Penguin

Arnull, A, 'National courts and the validity of Community acts' (1988) 13 EL Rev 125 (1988a)

Arnull, A, 'The scope of Article 177' (1988) 13 EL Rev 40 (1988b)

Arnull, A, 'The uses and abuses of Article 177 EEC' (1989) 52 MLR 622

Arnull, A, 'References to the European Court' (1990) 15 EL Rev 375

Ashworth, A, 'Involuntary confessions and illegally obtained evidence in criminal cases – Part I' [1963] Crim LR 15 (1963a)

Ashworth, A, 'Involuntary confessions and illegally obtained evidence in criminal cases – Part II' [1963] Crim LR 77 (1963b)

Ashworth, A, 'Excluding evidence and protecting rights' [1977] Crim LR 723

Ashworth, A, 'Social control and "anti-social behaviour": the subversion of Human Rights?' (2004) 120 LQR 263

Ashworth, AJ, 'Anti-social Behaviour Orders' (2005) Crim LR 292

Atkins, E and Hoggett, B, *Women and the Law*, 1984, Oxford: Basil Blackwell

Aubert, V, *In Search of Law*, 1983, Oxford: Martin Robertson

Austin, J, *The Province of Jurisprudence Determined* (1832), 1954, London: Weidenfeld & Nicolson

Bacon, F, *Advancement of Learning* (1605), 1951, Oxford: OUP

Bagehot, W, *The English Constitution* (1867), 1993, London: Fontana

Bailey, SH et al, *Smith, Bailey and Gunn on The Modern English Legal System*, 4th edn, 2002, London: Sweet & Maxwell

Baldwin, J and Bedward, J, 'Summarising tape recordings of police interviews' [1991] Crim LR 671

Baldwin, J, 'The police and tape recorders' [1985] Crim LR 659

Baldwin, J, *The Role of Legal Representatives at the Police Station*, RCCJ Research Study No 3, 1993, London: HMSO

Baldwin, R and Houghton, J, 'Circular arguments: the status and legitimacy of administrative rules' [1986] PL 239

Barber, NW, 'Privacy and the police: private right, public right or human right? *R v Chief Constable of the North Wales Police ex parte AB*' [1998] PL 19

Barendt, E, Baron, A, Herberg, JW and Jowell, J, 'Public law' (1993) 46 CLP Annual Review 101

Barker, R, *Political Legitimacy and the State*, 1990, Oxford: Clarendon

Barnett, H, 'A privileged position? Gypsies, land and planning law' [1994] Conveyancer 454

Barnett, H, 'Reflections on the Child Support Act' (1993) 5 J of Child Law 77

Barnett, H, 'The end of the road for Gypsies?' (1995) 24 Anglo-American L Rev 133

Barnett, H, '*Buckley v United Kingdom*: landmark or signpost?' (1996) 146 NLJ 1628

Barnett, H, *Introduction to Feminist Jurisprudence*, 1998, London: Cavendish Publishing

Barron, A and Scott, C, 'The Citizen's Charter programme' (1992) 55 MLR 526

Bates, St JT, *Devolution to Scotland: The Legal Aspects*, 1997, Edinburgh: T & T Clark

Beattie, K, 'Control orders and ASBOs: taking liberties?' (2005) Legal Action, April 7

Bebr, G, 'The reinforcement of the constitutional review of Community acts under Article 177 EEC Treaty' (1988) 25 CML Rev 667

Beith, A, 'Prayers unanswered: a jaundiced view of the parliamentary scrutiny of statutory instruments' (1981) 34 Parl Aff 165

Bell, J, *Policy Arguments in Judicial Decisions*, 1983, Oxford: Clarendon

Bell, JB, *The Secret Army: The IRA 1916–79*, 1979, Dublin: Academy

Bennion, F, 'What interpretation is "possible" under section 3(1) of the Human Rights Act 1998?' [2000] PL 77

Bindman, G, '*Spycatcher*: judging the judges' (1989) 139 NLJ 94

Bingham, TH (Sir), 'Should public law remedies be discretionary?' [1991] PL 64

Bingham, TH (Sir), 'The European Convention on Human Rights: time to incorporate' (1993) 109 LQR 390

Birch, D, 'Excluding evidence from entrapment: what is a "fair cop"?' (1994) 47 CLP 73

Birch, D, 'The pace hots up: confessions and confusions under the 1984 Act' [1989] Crim LR 95

Birkenhead (Lord), *Points of View*, Vol 1, 1922, London: Hodder & Stoughton

Bishop, P and Maillie, E, *The Provisional IRA*, 1987, London: Heinemann

Blackburn, R, 'Monarchy and the Personal Prerogatives' (2004) PL 546

Blackburn, RW and Kennon, A, with Sir Michael Wheeler-Booth, *Parliament: Functions, Practice and Procedures*, 2nd edn, 2003, London: Sweet & Maxwell (referred to as Griffith and Ryle, 2003 in the text)

Blackburn, RW, *Constitutional Studies*, 1992, London: Mansell

Blackstone, W (Sir), *Commentaries on the Laws of England* (1765–69), 2001 edn, Morrison, W (ed), London: Cavendish Publishing

Blake (Lord), *The Office of Prime Minister*, 1975, Oxford: OUP

Bloch, J and Fitzgerald, P, *British Intelligence and Covert Action*, 1983, Dingle, Co Kerry: Brandon

Blom-Cooper, L and Drewry, G, *Final Appeal*, 1972, Oxford: Clarendon

Blom-Cooper, L and Munro, C, 'The Hutton Report' (2004) PL 472

Bogdanor, V and Butler, D, *Democracy and Elections*, 1983, Cambridge: CUP

Bogdanor, V, *Devolution*, 1979, Oxford: OUP

Bogdanor, V, 'The forty per cent rule' (1980) 33 Parl Aff 249

Bogdanor, V, *The People and the Party System*, 1981, Cambridge: CUP

Bogdanor, V, *Multi-Party Politics and the Constitution*, 1983, Cambridge: CUP

Bogdanor, V (ed), *Constitutions in Democratic Politics*, 1988, London: Policy Studies Institute

Bogdanor, V, *Power and the People*, 1997, London: Gollancz

Bogdanor, V, *Devolution in the United Kingdom*, 1999, Oxford: OUP

Bolingbroke, H, *Remarks on the History of England*, 3rd edn, 1748, London: Francklin

Bonner, D and Stone, R, 'The Public Order Act 1986: steps in the wrong direction' [1987] PL 202

Bowen, CD, *The Lion and the Throne*, 1957, London: Hamish Hamilton

Boyle, K, Hadden, T and Hillyard, P, *Law and State*, 1975, Oxford: Martin Robertson

Boyron, S, 'Proportionality in English administrative law: a faulty translation?' (1992) 12 OJLS 237

Bracton, H, *The Laws and Customs of England* (1200–68), 1968–77, Thorne, SE (trans), Cambridge, Mass: Harvard UP

Bradley, AW and Ewing, KD, *Constitutional and Administrative Law*, 13th edn, 2003, Harlow: Longman

Bradley, AW, 'Openness, direction and judicial review' [1986] PL 508

Bradley, AW, 'Good government and public interest immunity' [1992] PL 514 (1992a)

Bradley, AW, 'Sachsenhausen, Barlow Clowes – and then' [1992] PL 353 (1992b)

Bradney, A, 'The judicial activity of the Lord Chancellor 1946–87' (1989) 16 JLS 360

Brazier, M, 'Judicial immunity and the independence of the judiciary' [1976] PL 397

Brazier, R, 'Choosing a prime minister' [1982] PL 395

Brazier, R, 'Government and the law' [1989] PL 64

Brazier, R, *Constitutional Texts*, 1990, Oxford: Clarendon

Brazier, R, 'The downfall of Margaret Thatcher' (1991) 54 MLR 471

Brazier, R, 'Regulating ministers' and ex-ministers' finances' (1992) 43 NILQ 19

Brazier, R, 'Ministers in court: the personal legal liability of ministers' (1993) 44 NILQ 317

Brazier, R, 'It is a constitutional issue: fitness for ministerial office in the 1990s' [1994] PL 431

Brazier, R, *Constitutional Reform*, 2nd edn, 1998, Oxford: Clarendon

Brazier, R, *Constitutional Practice*, 3rd edn, 1999, Oxford: Clarendon

Bridges, L, Meszaros, G and Sunkin, M, 'Regulating the Judicial Review Caseload' (2000) PL 651

Bromhead, PA, *The House of Lords and Contemporary Politics*, 1958, London: Routledge and Kegan Paul

Brookfield, FM, 'The courts, Kelsen, and the Rhodesian revolution' (1969) 19 Toronto ULJ 326

Browne-Wilkinson (Lord), 'The independence of the judiciary in the 1980s' [1988] PL 44

Browne-Wilkinson (Lord), 'The infiltration of a Bill of Rights' [1992] PL 405

Bulloch, J, *MI5: The Origin and History of the British Counter-Espionage Service*, 1963, London: Arthur Barker

Bunyan, T, *The History and Practice of the Political Police in Britain*, 1977, London: Quartet

Burns, P, 'The law and privacy: the Canadian experience' (1976) 54 Canadian Bar Rev 1

Butler, D and Ranney, A (eds), *Referendums around the World*, 1994, Basingstoke: Macmillan

Butler, D, 'The Australian crisis of 1975' (1976) 29 Parl Aff 201

Butler, D, *Governing Without a Majority: Dilemmas for Hung Parliaments in Britain*, 1983, London: Collins

Butler, D, *British General Elections since 1945*, 1989, Oxford: Blackwell

Butterworths European Information Services, *Butterworths' Annual European Review*, 1994, London: Butterworths

Byrne, A, *Local Government in Britain*, 7th edn, 2000, Harmondsworth: Penguin

Cabinet Office, *An Independent Review of Government Communications (The Phillis report)*, 2004, London: The Cabinet Office

Cain, M and Hunt, A, *Marx and Engels on Law*, 1979, London: Academic

Callaghan, J, *Time and Chance*, 1987, London: Collins

Calvert, H, *Constitutional Law in Northern Ireland*, 1968, London: Stevens

Campbell, D and Young, J, 'The metric martyrs and the entrenchment jurisprudence of Lord Justice Laws' [2002] PL 399

Chambers, G, *Equality and Inequality in Northern Ireland, Part 2: The Workplace*, 1987, London: Policy Studies Institute

Chandler, JA, 'The plurality vote: a reappraisal' (1982) 30 Political Studies 87

Chester, N and Bowring, N, *Questions in Parliament*, 1962, Oxford: OUP

Chitty, J, *Law of the Prerogatives of the Crown*, 1820, London: Butterworths

Clarke, DN and Feldman, D, 'Arrest by any other name' [1979] Crim LR 702

Clayton, R and Tomlinson, H, *Civil Actions against the Police*, 2nd edn, 1992, London: Sweet & Maxwell

Clothier, C (Sir), 'Legal problems of an ombudsman' (1984) 81 Law Soc Gazette 3108

Coke, E (Sir), *Institutes of the Laws of England; Concerning the Jurisdiction of the Courts*, 1644

Collins, H, *Marxism and Law*, 1982, Oxford: Clarendon

Connolly, M and Loughlin, J, 'Reflections on the Anglo-Irish Agreement' (1986) 21 Government and Opposition 146

Convery, J, 'State liability in the United Kingdom after *Brasserie du Pêcheur*' (1997) 34 CML Rev 603

Coppel, J, 'Horizontal effect of directives' [1997] Industrial LJ 69

Cornford, T and Sunkin, M, 'Bowman, Access and the Recent Reforms of Judicial Review Procedure' (2001) PL 11

Cotterrell, RBM, 'The impact of sex discrimination legislation' [1981] PL 469

Cowen, DV, *Parliamentary Sovereignty and the Entrenched Sections of the South Africa Act*, 1951, Cape Town: Juta

Craig, P and de Búrca, G, *European Community Law*, 2nd edn, 2002, Oxford: OUP

Craig, P, 'Judicial Review, Appeal and Factual Error' (2004) PL 788

Craig, PP and Rawlings, R (eds), *Law and Administration in Europe*, 2003, Oxford: OUP

Craig, PP and Schonberg, S, 'Substitute legitimate expectations after *Coughlan*' [2000] PL 684

Craig, PP, 'Dicey: unitary, self-correcting democracy and public law' (1990) 106 LQR 105

Craig, PP, 'Sovereignty of the United Kingdom after *Factortame*' (1991) 11 YBEL 221

Craig, PP, 'The common law, reasons and administrative justice' [1994] CLJ 282

Craig, PP, 'Directives: direct effect, indirect effect and the construction of national legislation' (1997) 22 EL Rev 519

Craig, PP, 'Competing models of judicial review' [1999] PL 428

Craig, PP, 'The courts, the Human Rights Act and judicial review' (2001) 117 LQR 589

Craig, PP, *Administrative Law*, 5th edn, 2003, London: Sweet & Maxwell (2003a)

Craig, PP, 'The Human Rights Act, Article 6 and procedural rights' [2003] PL 753 (2003b)

Cranston, R, 'Disqualification of judges for interest or opinion' [1979] PL 237

Crossman, R, *The Diaries of a Cabinet Minister*, 1977, London: Jonathan Cape

Crossman, R, *Introduction to the English Constitution*, 1993, London: Fontana

Curtin, D, 'The province of government: delimiting the direct effect of directives in the common law context' (1990) 15 EL Rev 195

Curtin, D, 'The constitutional structure of the Union: a Europe of bits and pieces' (1993) 30 CML Rev 17

d'Entrèves, AP, *Natural Law*, 2nd edn, 1970, London: Hutchinson

Dale, W, *The Modern Commonwealth*, 1983, London: Butterworths

Dauses, M, 'The protection of fundamental right in the Community legal order' (1985) 10 EL Rev 398

David, R and Brierley, JEC, *Major Legal Systems*, 3rd edn, 1985, London: Sweet & Maxwell

de Búrca, G and Scott, J (eds), *From Uniformity to Flexibility*, 2000, London: Hart

de Búrca, G, 'A community of interests? Making the most of European law' (1992) 55 MLR 346 (1992a)

de Búrca, G, 'Giving effect to European Community directives' (1992) 55 MLR 215 (1992b)

de Búrca, G, 'The principle of subsidiarity and the Court of Justice as an institutional actor' (1998) 36(2) JCMS 217

de Smith, SA, *The New Commonwealth and its Constitutions*, 1964, London: Stevens

de Smith, SA and Brazier, R, *Constitutional and Administrative Law*, 8th edn, 1998, Harmondsworth: Penguin

de Smith, SA, Woolf, H and Jowell, J, *Judicial Review of Administrative Action*, 5th edn, 1995, Harmondsworth: Penguin

Deacon, R, *A History of the British Secret Service*, 1969, London: Frederick Muller (updated, 1980, London: Panther)

Denning (Lord), *The Discipline of Law*, 1979, London: Butterworths

Denning (Lord), *The Due Process of Law*, 1980, London: Butterworths

Denning (Lord), *What Next in the Law?*, 1982, London: Butterworths

Denning (Lord), 'The *Strauss* case' [1985] PL 80

Devlin (Lord), 'Judges, government and politics' (1978) 41 MLR 501

Dhavan, R, 'Contempt of court and the *Phillimore Committee Report*' (1976) 5 Anglo-American L Rev 186

Dias, RWM, 'Legal politics: norms behind the grundnorm' [1968] CLJ 233

Dicey, AV, *Introduction to the Study of the Law of the Constitution* (1885), 10th edn, 1959, London: Macmillan

Dickson, B, 'Northern Ireland's emergency legislation: the wrong medicine' [1993] PL 592

Diplock (Lord), 'Administrative law: judicial review reviewed' [1974] CLJ 223

Doherty, M, 'Prime ministerial power and ministerial responsibility in the Thatcher era' (1988) 41 Parl Aff 49

Doig, A, 'Sleaze fatigue: the House of Ill-Repute' (2002) 55 Parliamentary Affairs 389

Donaldson, F, *The Marconi Scandal*, 1962, London: R Hart-Davis

Dougan, M, 'Case comment' (2001) 38 CML Rev 1503

Downes, A, 'Trawling for a remedy: state liability under Community law' (1997) LS 286

Drake, S, 'Twenty Years after Von Colson: The Impact of "Indirect Effect" on the Protection of the Individual's Community Rights' (2005) 30 EL Rev 329

Dremczewski, A, 'The domestic application of the European Human Rights Convention as European Community law' (1981) 30 ICLQ 118

Drewry, G and Butcher, T, *The Civil Service Today*, 1988, Oxford: Blackwell

Drewry, G, 'The Lord Chancellor as judge' (1972) 122 NLJ 855

Drewry, G (ed), *The New Select Committees*, 1989, Oxford: OUP

Drewry, G, 'Judicial inquiries and public reassurance' [1996] PL 368

Dworkin, A, *Pornography: Men Possessing Women*, 1981, London: Women's Press

Dworkin, R, *Taking Rights Seriously*, 1977, London: Duckworth

Dworkin, R, *A Matter of Principle*, 1986, Oxford: OUP

Dynes, M and Walker, D, *The Times Guide to the New British State: The Government Machine in the 1990s*, 1995, London: Times Books

Dyrberg, P, 'Current issues in the debate on public access to documents' (1999) 24 European L Rev 157

Editorial, 'The Treaty of Amsterdam: neither a bang nor a whimper' (1997) 34 CML Rev 767

Edwards, R, 'Judicial deference under the Human Rights Act' (2002) 65 MLR 859

Electoral Commission: *The Funding of Political Parties: Report and Recommendations* (2004)

Eleftheriadis, P, 'The direct effect of Community law: conceptual issues' (1996) 16 YBEL 205

Elliott, M, '*Coughlan*: substantive protection of legitimate expectations revisited' (2000) 5 JR 27; (2000) 59 CLJ 421

Emiliou, N, 'Subsidiarity: an effective barrier against "the enterprises of ambition"?' (1991) 17 EL Rev 383

Erskine May, T, *Parliamentary Practice*, 22nd edn, 1997, London: Butterworths

Esher, RBB, *The Influence of King Edward: and Essays on Other Subjects,* 1915, London: John Murray

European Commission, 'Report from the Commission on monitoring the application of Community law (2003) 21st Annual Report Com(2004) 839

Evans, JM, *Immigration Law*, 2nd edn, 1983, London: Sweet & Maxwell

Ewing, KD and Gearty, CA, *Freedom Under Thatcher*, 1990, Oxford: Clarendon

Ewing, KD, *The Funding of Political Parties*, 1987, Cambridge: CUP

Ewing, KD, 'The Futility of the Human Rights Act' (2004) PL 829

Fairgrieve, D, 'Pushing back the boundaries of public authority liability: tort law enters the class-room' [2002] PL 288

Fawcett, J, *The Application of the European Convention on Human Rights,* 1987, Oxford: Clarendon

Feldman, D, 'Parliamentary Scrutiny of Legislation and Human Rights' (2002) PL 323

Fenwick, H, *Civil Liberties & Human Rights*, 3rd edn, 2002, London: Cavendish Publishing

Fine, R, *Democracy and the Rule of Law: Liberal Ideals and Marxist Critiques*, 1984, London: Pluto

Finer, SE, 'The individual responsibility of ministers' (1956) 34 Public Admin 377

Finer, SE, *Anonymous Empire*, 1958, London: Pall Mall

Finer, SE, *Adversary Politics and Electoral Reform*, 1975, London: Anthony Wigram

Finer, SE, *The Changing British Party System*, 1980, Washington: AEI Studies

Finnis, JM, *Natural Law and Natural Rights*, 1980, Oxford: Clarendon

Forsyth, C, 'Judicial review, the royal prerogative' (1985) 36 NILQ 25

Foster, RF (ed), *The Oxford History of Ireland*, 1989, Oxford: OUP (1989a)

Foster, RF, *Modern Ireland 1600–1972*, 1989, Harmondsworth: Penguin (1989b)

Franklin, M and Norton, P, *Parliamentary Questions*, 1993, Oxford: Clarendon

Fredman, S, *Women and the Law*, 1997, Oxford: Clarendon

French, D, 'Spy fever in Britain 1900–15' (1978) 21 Historical Journal 355

Fry, GK, 'The Sachsenhausen concentration camp case and the convention of ministerial responsibility?' [1970] PL 336

Fuller, L, 'Positivism and fidelity to law – a reply to Professor Hart' (1958) 11 Harv L Rev 630

Fuller, L, *The Morality of Law*, 1964, New Haven: Yale UP

Galligan, DJ, 'The nature and functions of policies within discretionary power' [1976] PL 332

Ganz, G, *Quasi-legislation: Some Recent Developments in Secondary Legislation*, 1987, London: Sweet & Maxwell

Garton Ash, T, *The File: A Personal History*, 1997, London: HarperCollins

Gearty, G, *Terror*, 1991, London: Faber & Faber

Geddis, A, 'Free Speech Martyrs on Unreasonable Threats to Social Peace' (2004) PL 853

Geddis, A, 'Parliamentary Privilege: *Quis custodiet ipsos custolies?*' (2005) PL 696

Gibb, F, 'The Law Lord who took the rap over Pinochet' (1999) *The Times*, 19 October, p 3

Gilvarry, E, 'Selection changes to be urged' (1991) 88 Law Soc Gazette 6

Goodhart, AL, '*Thomas v Sawkins*: a constitutional innovation' [1936–38] CLJ 22

Goodhart, AL, *Essays in Jurisprudence and the Common Law*, 1931, Cambridge: CUP

Gordon, DM, 'What did the *Anisminic* case decide?' (1971) 34 MLR 1

Gould, BC, '*Anisminic* and judicial review' [1970] PL 358

Gregory, R and Drewry, G, 'Barlow Clowes and the ombudsman: Part I' [1991] PL 192 (1991a)

Gregory, R and Drewry, G, 'Barlow Clowes and the ombudsman: Part II' [1991] PL 408 (1991b)

Griffith, JAG and Ryle, M, *Parliament: Functions, Practice and Procedures*, 2nd edn, 2003, London: Sweet & Maxwell

Griffith, JAG, 'Crichel Down: the most famous farm in British constitutional history' (1987) 1 Contemporary Record 35

Griffith, JAG, *The Politics of the Judiciary*, 5th edn, 1997, London: Fontana

Guest, AG (ed), *Oxford Essays in Jurisprudence*, 1961, Oxford: OUP

Gwynn, SL, *The Life of Walpole*, 1932, London: Butterworths

Hadfield, B, 'The Anglo-Irish Agreement 1985 – blue print or green print' (1986) 37 NILQ 1

Hadfield, B, *The Constitution of Northern Ireland*, 1989, Belfast: SLS

Hailsham (Lord), *The Door Wherein I Went*, 1975, London: Collins

Hailsham (Lord), *The Dilemma of Democracy*, 1978, London: Collins

Hale (Baroness), 'The Quest for Equal Treatment' (2005) PL 571

Hale, B (Dame), 'Equality and the judiciary – why should we want more women judges?' [2001] PL 489

Hale, M (Sir), *The History of the Pleas of the Crown*, 1736, Emlyn, S (ed), London: E and R Nott and R Gosling

Hamilton, E and Cairns, H (eds), *Plato's Collected Dialogues*, 1989, Ewing, New Jersey: Princeton UP

Hanks, PJ, *Constitutional Law in Australia*, 2nd edn, 1996, Sydney: Butterworths

Hansard Society, *Making the Law*, 1993, London: Hansard

Harlow, C (ed), *Public Law and Politics*, 1986, London: Sweet & Maxwell

Harris, DJ, O'Boyle, M and Warbrick, C, *Law of the Convention on Human Rights*, 1995, Edinburgh: Butterworths

Harris, J, *Legal Philosophies*, 1980, London: Butterworths

Hart, HLA, 'Positivism and the separation of law and morals' (1958) 71 Harv L Rev 593

Hart, HLA, *The Concept of Law*, 1961, Oxford: Clarendon

Hartley, T, *The Foundations of European Community Law*, 4th edn, 1998, Oxford: Clarendon

Harvey Cox, W, 'The Anglo-Irish Agreement' (1987) 40 Parl Aff 80

Hayhurst, JD and Wallington, P, 'The parliamentary scrutiny of delegated legislation' [1988] PL 547

Hazell, R, 'Freedom of information in Australia, Canada and New Zealand' (1989) 67 Public Admin 189

Headey, BW, *British Cabinet Ministers: The Roles of Politicians in Executive Office*, 1974, London: Allen & Unwin

Hennessy, P, 'Helicopter crashes into Cabinet: Prime Minister and constitution hurt' (1986) 13 JLS 423 (1986a)

Hennessy, P, *Cabinet*, 1986, Oxford: Blackwell (1986b)

Hennessy, P, *Whitehall*, 1990, London: Fontana

Herberg, JW, 'The right to reasons – palm trees in retreat?' [1991] PL 340

Heuston, RFV, *Essays in Constitutional Law*, 2nd edn, 1964, London: Stevens (1964a)

Heuston, RFV, *Lives of the Lord Chancellors, 1885–1940*, 1964, Oxford: Clarendon (1964b)

Heuston, RFV, *Lives of the Lord Chancellors, 1940–70*, 1987, Oxford: Clarendon

Hewart, CJ, *The New Despotism*, 1929, London: Benn

Heydon, JD, 'Illegally obtained evidence' [1973] Crim LR 690

Hickman, TR, 'The uncertain shadow ...' [2004] PL 122

Hickman, TR, 'Between Human Rights and the Rule of Law: Indefinite Detention and the Derogation Model of Constitutionalism' (2005) MLR 655

Hilson, C, 'Judicial review, policies and the fettering of discretion' [2002] PL 111

HMSO, *Review of Intelligence on Weapons of Mass Destruction: Report of a Committee of Privy Counsellors*, 2004, London: The Stationary Office, HC 898

HMSO, 'Your Region, Your Choice, Revitalising the English Regions' (2002) Cm 5511

Hobbes, T, *The Leviathan* (1651), 1973, London: JM Dent

Hogg, PW and Monahan, P, *Liability of the Crown*, 3rd edn, 2000, London: Carswell

Holdsworth, W, 'The treaty making power of the Crown' (1942) 58 LQR 177

Holt, J, *Magna Carta*, 1965, Cambridge: CUP

Hooper, D, *Official Secrets: The Use and Abuse of the Act*, 1988, Sevenoaks: Coronet

Hughes, M, *Ireland Divided: The Roots of the Modern Irish Problem*, 1994, Cardiff: Wales UP

Hume, D, *An Enquiry Concerning the Principles of Morals* (1751), 1957, Indianapolis: Bobbs-Merrill

Hume, D *Political Discourses* (1752), 1769, Edinburgh: Kineald and Donaldson

Hunt, M, 'The "horizontal effect" of the Human Rights Act' [1998] PL 423

Hunt (Lord), 'Access to a previous government's papers' [1982] PL 514

Hutchinson, A and Petter, A, 'Private rights/public wrongs: the liberal lie of the Charter' (1988) 38 Toronto ULJ 278

Hutchinson, AP and Monahan, P (eds), *The Rule of Law: Ideal or Ideology*, 1987, Toronto: Carswell

Identity Cards: a Summary of Findings from the consultation on Entitlement Cards and Identity Fraud (CM 6019)

Identity Cards: the next steps (CM 6020)

Irvine of Lairg (Lord), 'Judges and Decision-Makers: The Theory and Practice of Wednesbury Review' (1996) PL 59

Irvine (Lord), 'The development of human rights under an incorporated Convention on Human Rights' [1998] PL 221

Irvine (Lord), 'The impact of the Human Rights Act: parliament, the courts and the executive [2003] PL 308

Itzin, C (ed), *Pornography: Women, Violence and Civil Liberties*, 1992, Oxford: OUP

Iyer, TKK, 'Constitutional law in Pakistan: Kelsen in the courts' (1973) 21 AJCL 759

Jackson, P and Leonard, P, *Constitutional and Administrative Law*, 8th edn, 2001, London: Sweet & Maxwell

Jacob, JM, 'From privileged Crown to interested public' [1993] PL 121

Jacobs, FG and White, RCA, *The European Convention on Human Rights*, 2nd edn, 1996, Oxford: Clarendon

Jaconelli, J, 'The "D notice" system' [1982] PL 37

Jalland, P, *The Liberals and Ireland: The Ulster Question in British Politics to 1914*, 1980, Hemel Hempstead: Harvester

James, R and Longley, D, 'The Channel Tunnel Rail Link, the Ombudsman and the Select Committee' [1996] PL 38

Jennings, I (Sir), *Cabinet Government*, 3rd edn, 1959, Cambridge: CUP (1959a)

Jennings, I (Sir), *The Law and the Constitution*, 5th edn, 1959, London: Hodder & Stoughton (1959b)

Jennings, I (Sir), *Parliament,* 2nd edn, 1969, Cambridge: CUP

Jones, G (ed), *The New Government Agenda*, 1997, Hemel Hempstead: ICSA

Jones, T, 'Mistake of Fact in Administrative Law' (1990) PL 507

Jowell, J and Oliver, D (eds), *New Directions in Judicial Review*, 1988, London: Stevens

Jowell, J and Oliver, D (eds), *The Changing Constitution*, 4th edn, 2000, Oxford: OUP

Jowell, J, 'Of *vires* and vacuums: the constitutional context of judicial review' [1999] PL 448

Jowell, J, 'Beyond the rule of law: towards constitutional judicial review' [2000] PL 671

Jowell, J, Judicial deference: servility; civility or institutional capacity? [2003] PL 592

Kafka, F, *The Trial*, Muir, E and Muir, W (trans), 1956, London: Secker & Warburg

Keedy, ER, '*R v Sinnisiak*: a remarkable murder trial' (1951) 100 Pennsylvania UL Rev 48

Keith, B, *The King, the Constitution, the Empire and Foreign Affairs: Letters and Essays 1936–37*, 1936, London: Longmans, Green

Keith-Lucas, B and Richards, PG, *A History of Local Government in the Twentieth Century*, 1979, London: Allen & Unwin

Kelsen, H, *The General Theory of Law and State*, 1961, New York: Russell

Kelsen, H, *The Pure Theory of Law,* 1967, Berkeley: California UP

Kenny, CS, 'The evolution of the law of blasphemy' [1992] CLJ 127

Kent, SK, *Sex and Suffrage in Britain 1860–1914*, 1987, Ewing, New Jersey: Princeton UP (rep 1990, London: Routledge)

King, ML, *Why We Can't Wait*, 1963, New York: Signet

Kingsford-Smith, D and Oliver, D (eds), *Economic With the Truth: The Law and Media in a Democratic Society*, 1990, Oxford: OUP

Klug, F and Starmer, K, 'Incorporation through the "front door": the first year of the Human Rights Act' [2001] PL 654

Krämer, L, *The EEC Treaty and Environmental Protection*, 1992, London: Sweet & Maxwell

Lambert, J, 'Executive authority to tap telephones' (1980) 43 MLR 59

Laski, H, *Reflections on the Constitution*, 1951, Manchester: Manchester UP

Laslett, P (ed), *Philosophy, Politics and Society*, 1975, Oxford: Blackwell

Laws, J (Sir), 'Is the High Court the guardian of fundamental constitutional rights?' [1993] PL 60

Le Queux, W, *German Spies in England*, 1915, London: S Paul

Leach, P, 'Birth certificates, privacy and human rights' (1998) 142 SJ 628

Leach, S, Stewart, J and Walsh, K (eds), *The Changing Organisation and Management of Local Government*, 1994, Basingstoke: Macmillan

Lee, HP, 'Reforming the Australian Constitution – the frozen continent refuses to thaw' [1988] PL 535

Lee, JJ, *Ireland 1912–85: Politics and Society,* 1990, Cambridge: CUP

Lee, S, 'The limits of parliamentary sovereignty' [1985] PL 633

Lee, S, 'And so to school' (1987) 103 LQR 166

Lee, S, *Judging Judges*, 1989, London: Faber & Faber

Legg, T (Sir), 'Judges for the new century' [2001] PL 62

Leigh, D and Vulliamy, E, *Sleaze: The Corruption of Parliament*, 1997, London: Fourth Estate

Leigh, D, *Betrayed: The Real Story of the Matrix Churchill Trial*, 1993, London: Bloomsbury

Leigh, I and Lustgarten, L, 'The Security Services Act 1989' (1989) 52 MLR 801

Leigh, I and Lustgarten, L, 'The Security Commission: constitutional achievement or curiosity?' [1991] PL 215

Leigh, I, 'A tapper's charter?' [1986] PL 8

Leigh, I, '*Spycatcher* in Strasbourg' [1992] PL 200

Leigh, I, 'Matrix Churchill, supergun and the Scott Inquiry' [1993] PL 630

Leigh, I, 'By Law Established? The Crown, Constitutional Reform and the Church of England' (2004) PL 266

Leopold, P, 'Leaks and squeaks in the Palace of Westminster' [1980] PL 368

Leopold, P, 'Freedom of speech in Parliament: its misuse and proposals for reform' [1981] PL 30

Leopold, P, '"Proceedings in Parliament": the grey area' [1991] PL 475

Lester (Lord), 'Fundamental rights' [1994] PL 70

Lester (Lord), 'First steps towards a constitutional Bill of Rights' (1997) 2 EHRLR 124

Lester, A, 'The Utility of the Human Rights Act: a Reply to Keith Ewing' (2005) PL 249

Le Sueur, A, 'The Rise and Ruin of Unreasonableness' (2005) Judicial Review 32

Linklater, M, Leigh, D with Mather, I, *Not Without Honour: The Inside Story of the Westland Scandal*, 1986, London: Sphere

Locke, J, *Two Treatises of Government* (1690), 1977, London: JM Dent

Lockyer, R, *Tudor and Stuart Britain 1471–1714*, 2nd edn, 1985, Harlow: Longman

Lustgarten, L and Leigh, I, *In From the Cold: National Security and Parliamentary Democracy*, 1994, Oxford: Clarendon

Lustgarten, L, *The Legal Control of Racial Discrimination*, 1980, London: Macmillan

Lustgarten, L, 'Racial inequality and the limits of law' (1981) 44 MLR 68

Lustgarten, L, 'Socialism and the rule of law' (1988) 15 JLS 25

Lysaght, CE, 'Irish peers and the House of Lords' (1967) 18 NILQ 277

MacCormick, DN, 'A note on privacy' (1973) 84 LQR 23

MacCormick, N, 'Does the United Kingdom have a constitution? Reflections on *MacCormick v Lord Advocate*' (1978) 29 NILQ 1

MacCormick, N, *Questioning Sovereignty*, 2001, Oxford: OUP

Macdermott (Lord), 'Law and order in times of emergency' [1972] Juridical Review 1

Macdonald, IA and Webber, F, *Macdonald's Immigration Law and Practice*, 5th edn, 2001, London: LexisNexis UK

Macdonald, S, 'A Suicidal Women, Roaming Pigs and a Noisy Trampolinist: Refining the ASBO's Definition of Anti-social Behaviour' (2006) 69 MLR 183

Mackay (Lord), *The Administration of Justice*, 1994, London: Stevens

Mackenzie, R, *Free Elections*, 1967, London: Allen & Unwin

Mackintosh, JP, *The British Cabinet*, 3rd edn, 1977, London: Stevens

MacMillan, CA, 'Burying treasure trove' (1996) 146 NLJ 1346

Macmillan, H, *At the End of the Day* (1961–63), 1973, London: Macmillan

Maitland, FW, *The Constitutional History of England*, 1908, Cambridge: CUP

Mancini, G and Keeling, D, 'From *CILFIT* to *ERTA*: the constitutional challenge facing the European Court' (1991) 11 YBEL 1

Markesinis, BS, *The Theory and Practice of Dissolution of Parliament*, 1972, Cambridge: CUP

Marsh, D and Read, M, *Private Members' Bills*, 1988, Cambridge: CUP

Marsh, NS, 'The declaration of Delhi' (1959) 2 J of the International Commission of Jurists 7

Marshall, G and Moodie, G, *Some Problems of the Constitution*, 5th edn, 1971, London: Hutchinson

Marshall, G, *Parliamentary Sovereignty and the Commonwealth*, 1957, Oxford: Clarendon

Marshall, G, *Constitutional Theory*, 1971, Oxford: Clarendon

Marshall, G, *Constitutional Conventions*, 1984, Oxford: Clarendon

Marshall, G, 'Cabinet Government and the Westland affair' [1986] PL 181 (1986a)

Marshall, G, 'The Queen's press relations' [1986] PL 505 (1986b)

Marshall, G (ed), *Ministerial Responsibility*, 1989, Oxford: Clarendon

Marshall, G, 'The end of prime ministerial government?' [1991] PL 1

Marshall, G, 'The referendum: what? when? how?' (1997) 50 Parl Aff 307

Martin, FX (ed), *Leaders and Men of the Easter Rising: Dublin 1916*, 1967, London: Methuen

Mathijsen, PSRF, *A Guide to European Union Law*, 7th edn, 1999, London: Sweet & Maxwell

McAuslan, P and McEldowney, JF, *Legitimacy and the Constitution: The Dissonance between Theory and Practice in Law*, 1985, London: Sweet & Maxwell

McAuslan, P, 'The Widdicombe Report: local government business or politics?' [1987] PL 154

McConville, M and Baldwin, J, 'Confessions: the dubious fruit of police interrogation' (1980) 130 NLJ 993

McConville, M and Hodgson, J, *Custodial Legal Advice and the Right to Silence*, RCCJ Research Study No 16, 1993, London: HMSO

McGarry, J, 'The Anglo-Irish Agreement and the prospects for power sharing in Northern Ireland' (1988) 59 Political Quarterly 236

McIlwain, CH, *The High Court of Parliament and its Supremacy*, 1910, New Haven: Yale UP

McIlwain, CH, *Constitutionalism, Ancient and Modern*, 1958, Ithaca, New York: Great Seal

McMurtie, SN, 'The waiting game – the Parliamentary Commissioner's response to delay in administrative procedures' [1997] PL 159

Mendelsen, M, 'The European Court of Justice and human rights' (1981) 1 YBEL 126

Miers, DR and Page, AC, *Legislation*, 2nd edn, 1990, London: Sweet & Maxwell

Mill, JS, *On Liberty* (1859), 1989, Cambridge: CUP

Mill, JS, *Representative Government* (1861), 1958, Indianapolis: Bobbs-Merrill

Mill, JS, *The Subjection of Women* (1869), 1989, Cambridge: CUP

Millar, E and Phillips, P, 'Evaluating anti-discrimination legislation in the United Kingdom: some issues and approaches' (1983) 11 Int J Soc L 417

Millett (Lord), 'The right to good administration in Europe' [2002] PL 309

Mitchell, JDB, 'Sovereignty of Parliament – yet again' (1963) 79 LQR 196

Mitchell, JDB, *Constitutional Law*, 2nd edn, 1968, Edinburgh: Green

Montesquieu, C, *De l'Esprit des Lois* (1748), 1989, Cambridge: CUP

Morgan, JP, *The House of Lords and the Labour Government 1964–1970*, 1975, Oxford: OUP

Morrison (Lord), *Government and Parliament*, 3rd edn, 1964, Oxford: OUP

Morton, G, *Home Rule and the Irish Question*, 1980, Harlow: Longman

Mosley, RK, *The Story of the Cabinet Office*, 1969, London: Routledge and Kegan Paul

Mummery, DR, 'The privilege of freedom of speech in Parliament' (1978) 94 LQR 276

Munday, R, 'Inferences from silence and European human rights law' [1996] Crim LR 370

Munro, CR, 'Laws and conventions distinguished' (1975) 91 LQR 224

Munro, CR, 'Press freedom: how the beast was tamed' (1991) 54 MLR 104

Munro, CR, 'Power to the people' [1997] PL 579

Munro, CR, *Studies in Constitutional Law*, 2nd edn, 1999, London: Butterworths

Munro, CR, 'Privilege at Holyrood' [2000] PL 347

Naffine, N, 'Windows on the legal mind: evocations of rape in legal writing' (1992) 18 Melbourne UL Rev 741

Naffine, N, 'Possession: erotic love in the law of rape' (1994) 57 MLR 10

Neumann, F, *The Rule of Law: Political Theory and the Legal System in Modern Society*, 1986, Leamington Spa: Berg

Newburn, T, *The Settlement of Claims at the Criminal Injuries Commission Compensation Board*, Home Office Research Study No 112, 1989, London: HMSO

Newburn, T, *Crime and Criminal Justice Policy*, 2003, Harlow: Longman

Newton, K and Karran, TJ (eds), *The Politics of Local Expenditure*, 1985, London: Macmillan

Nicolson, IF, *The Mystery of Crichel Down*, 1986, Oxford: Clarendon

Norton, P, *Parliament in the 1980s*, 1985, Oxford: Blackwell (1985a)

Norton, P, *The Commons in Perspective*, 2nd edn, 1985, Oxford: Blackwell (1985b)

Norton, P, 'Televising the House of Commons' (1991) 44 Parl Aff 185

Norton, P, *Does Parliament Matter?*, 1993, Hemel Hempstead: Harvester

Norton-Taylor, R, *Truth is a Difficult Concept: Inside the Scott Inquiry*, 1995, London: Fourth Estate

Nozick, R, *Anarchy, State and Utopia*, 1974, Oxford: Blackwell

O'Cinneide, C, 'The Race Relations (Amendment) Act 2000' [2001] PL 220

O'Connor, U, *The Troubles: The Struggle for Irish Freedom 1912–1922*, 1989, London: Mandarin

O'Halpin, E, *The Decline of the Union: British Government in Ireland 1892–1920*, 1987, Dublin: Gill and Macmillan

O'Keefe, D and Twomey, PM (eds), *Legal Issues of the Maastricht Treaty*, 1994, London: Chancery

Oliver, D and Austin, R, 'Political and constitutional aspects of the *Westland* affair' (1987) 40 Parl Aff 20

Oliver, D, 'Reform of the electoral system' [1983] PL 108

Oliver, D, 'Is the *ultra vires* rule the basis of judicial review?' [1987] PL 543

Oliver, D, '*Pepper v Hart*: a suitable case for reference to *Hansard*?' [1993] PL 5

Oliver, D, 'The frontiers of the state: public authorities and public functions under the Human Rights Act' [2000] PL 476

Oliver, D, 'Public law procedures and remedies – do we need them?' [2001] PL 91

Oliver, D, *Constitutional Reform in the United Kingdom*, 2003, Oxford: OUP

Oliver, D, 'Functions of a Public Nature under the Human Rights Act' (2004) PL 329

Olley, K, 'Proportionality at Common Law' (2004) 9 Judicial Review 197

Olowofoyeku, AA, 'The *nemo judex* rule: the case against automatic disqualification' [2000] PL 456

Owen Dixon, J, 'The law and the constitution' (1935) 51 LQR 611

Padfield, N, 'The Anti-social Behaviour Act 2003: the ultimate nanny-state Act?' (2004) Crim LR 712

Paine, T, *Rights of Man* (1791, Pt I), 1984, rep 1998, Collins, H (ed), New York: Penguin

Paine, T, *Rights of Man* (1792, Pt II), 1984, rep 1998, Collins, H (ed), New York: Penguin

Palley, C, 'The evolution, disintegration and possible reconstruction of the Northern Ireland Constitution' (1972) 1 Anglo-American L Rev 368

Palley, C, *The United Kingdom and Human Rights*, 1991, London: Sweet & Maxwell

Palmer, S, 'Tightening secrecy law' [1990] PL 243

Pannick, D, *Sex Discrimination Law*, 1985, Oxford: Clarendon

Pennock, JR and Chapman, JW (eds), *Political and Legal Obligation*, 1970, New York: Atherton

Pescatore, P, 'The "doctrine of direct effect": an infant disease of Community law' (1983) 8 EL Rev 155

Petite, M, 'The Treaty of Amsterdam' (www.law.harvard.edu/programs/JeanMonnet/papers/98/98-14-The.html)

Philby, K, *My Silent War*, 1968, London: MacGibbon and Kee

Phythian, M and Little, W, 'Parliament and arms sales: lessons of the Matrix Churchill affair' (1993) 46 Parl Aff 293

Pincher, C, *Their Trade is Treachery*, 1981, London: Sidgwick and Jackson

Plamenatz, J, *Man and Society*, 1963, New York: Longman

Plucknett, TFT, '*Dr Bonham's Case* and judicial review' (1926) 40 Harv L Rev 30

Poole, KP, 'The Northern Ireland Commissioner for Complaints' [1972] PL 131

Powell, E and Wallis, K, *The House of Lords in the Middle Ages*, 1968, London: Weidenfeld & Nicolson

Priestley, J, *An Essay on the First Principles of Government; and on the Nature of Political, Civil, and Religious Liberty, including remarks on Dr Brown's Code of Education, and on Dr Balguy's Sermon on Church Authority*, 2nd edn, 1771, London: J Johnson

Pugh, I (Sir), 'The ombudsman – jurisdiction, power and practice' (1978) 56 Public Admin 127

Ramsay, P, 'What is anti-social behaviour?' (2004) Crim LR 908

Ranelagh, J, *A Short History of Ireland*, 1983, Cambridge: CUP

Rasmussen, H, 'The European Court's *acte clair* strategy in *CILFIT*' (1984) 9 EL Rev 242

Rasmussen, H, 'Between self-restraint and activism; a judicial policy for the European Court' (1988) 13 EL Rev 28

Rawlings, HF, *Law and the Electoral Process*, 1988, London: Sweet & Maxwell

Rawls, J, *A Theory of Justice*, 1973, rev edn 1999, Oxford: OUP

Raz, J, *The Authority of Law*, 1979, Oxford: OUP

Reed, C (ed), *Computer Law*, 2nd edn, 1993, London: Blackstone

Reid (Lord), 'The judge as lawmaker' [1972] JSPTL 22

Richardson, G and Genn, H (eds), *Administrative Law and Government Action*, 1994, Oxford: OUP

Riddell, P, 'Quality control deficiency that lets down the law' (1994) *The Times*, 16 December

Ridley, FF, 'There is no British Constitution: a dangerous case of the Emperor's clothes (1988) 41 Parl Aff 340

Roberts, M, 'Public law representations and substantive legitimate expectations' (2001) 64 MLR 112

Roberts-Wray, K, *Commonwealth and Colonial Law*, 1966, London: Stevens

Robertson, AH and Merrills, JG, *Human Rights in Europe*, 3rd edn, 1993, Manchester: Manchester UP

Robertson, G, *Obscenity*, 1979, London: Weidenfeld

Robertson, G, *Freedom, the Individual and the Law*, 7th edn, 2001, Harmondsworth: Penguin

Robilliard, StJ, 'Offences against religion and public worship' (1981) 44 MLR 556

Rose, R, 'Law as a resource of public policy' (1986) 39 Parl Aff 297

Ross, M, 'Beyond *Francovich*' (1993) 56 MLR 55

Rousseau, J, *The Social Contract and Discourses* (1762), 1977, London: JM Dent

Rowbottom, J, 'The Electoral Commission's Proposals on the Funding of Political Parties' (2005) PL 468

Ryle, M and Richards, G (eds), *The Commons Under Scrutiny*, 3rd edn, 1988, London: Routledge and Kegan Paul

Sales, P and Steyn, K, 'Legitimate Expectations in English Public Law: An Analysis' (2004) PL 564

Sampford, CJG, '"Recognize and declare": an Australian experiment in codifying constitutional conventions' (1987) 7 OJLS 369

Samuals, A, 'Anti-social Behaviour Orders: Their legal and jurisprudential significance' (2005) 69 J. Crim L 223

Savage, N and Edwards, C, *A Guide to the Data Protection Act 1985*, 1985, London: Financial Training

Sawer, G, *Australian Federalism in the Courts*, 1967, Melbourne: Melbourne UP

Sawer, G, *Federation Under Strain*, 1977, Melbourne: Melbourne UP

Schermers, HG, *Judicial Protection in the European Community*, 4th edn, 1987, Dordrecht: Kluwer

Schermers, HG, 'The European Community bound by fundamental human rights' (1990) 27 CML Rev 249

Schwarze, J, *European Administrative Law*, 1992, Luxembourg: Office for Official Publications of the European Communities

Scott, J, *Development Dilemmas in the EC: Rethinking Regional Development Policy*, 1995, Milton Keynes: OU Press

Scott, J, *European Community Environmental Law*, 1998, London: Longman

Scott, R (Sir), 'Ministerial accountability' [1996] PL 410

Seaborne Davies, D, 'The House of Lords and the criminal law' (1962) 6 JSPTL 104

Sharpe, LG, 'Theories and values of local government' (1970) 18 Political Studies 153

Shaw, J, *Law of the European Union*, 3rd edn, 2000, Basingstoke: Palgrave

Shaw, J, 'Europe's Constitutional Future' (2005) PL 132

Shell, D, 'The House of Lords and the Thatcher government' (1983) 38 Parl Aff 16

Shell, D, *The House of Lords*, 2nd edn, 1992, London: Harvester

Silk, P and Walters, R, *How Parliament Works*, 1987, London: Longman

Simmonds, KR, 'The British Islands and the Community: II Isle of Man' (1970) 7 CMLR 454

Simmonds, KR, 'The British Islands and the Community: III Guernsey' (1971) 8 CMLR 475

Simon Brown LJ, 'Public interest immunity' [1994] PL 579

Slapper, G and Kelly, D, *The English Legal System*, 8th edn, 2006, Abingdon: Routledge-Cavendish

Slot, PJ, 'Case C-194/94: *CIA Security International SA v Signalson SA and Securitel SPRL*' (1996) 33 CML Rev 1035

Slynn, G, 'The Court of Justice of the European Community' (1984) 33 ICLQ 409

Smart, C, *Feminism and the Power of Law*, 1989, London: Routledge

Smith, ATH, 'Dicey and civil liberties: comment' [1985] PL 608

Smith, DJ, 'Policy and research: employment discrimination in Northern Ireland' (1988) 9(1) Policy Studies 41

Spalin, E, 'Abortion, speech and the European Community' [1992] J of Social Welfare and Family Law 17

Spjut, RJ, 'Internment and detention without trial in Northern Ireland' (1986) 49 MLR 712

Steiner, J and Woods, L, *Textbook on EC Law*, 8th edn, 2003, Oxford: OUP

Steiner, J, 'From direct effects to *Francovich*: shifting means of enforcement of Community law' (1993) 18(3) EL Rev 3

Steiner, J, *Enforcing EC Law*, 1995, London: Blackstone

Stephens, L, *The Science of Ethics* (1882), 1972, Newton Abbot: David and Charles

Stewart, J and Stoker, J (eds), *The Future of Local Government*, 1989, Basingstoke: Macmillan

Steyn (Lord), 'Deference: a Tangled Story' (2005) PL 346

Stubbs, W, *The Constitutional History of England: In its Origin and Development*, 1880, Oxford: Clarendon

Sunkin, M, 'Crown immunity from criminal liability in English law' [2003] PL 716

Sunkin, M, 'Pushing Forward the Frontiers of Human Rights Protection' (2004) PL 643

Supperstone, M and Cavanagh, J, *Immigration*, 3rd edn, 1994, London: Longman

Supperstone, M, 'The Intelligence Services Act 1994' [1994] PL 329

Szyszczack, E, 'Sovereignty: crisis, compliance, confusion, complacency?' (1990) 15(6) EL Rev 483

Tebbitt, N, *Upwardly Mobile*, 1988, London, Weidenfeld & Nicolson

Temple-Lang, J, 'Community constitutional law: Article 5 EC Treaty' (1990) 27 CML Rev 645

Thatcher, M, *The Downing Street Years*, 1993, London: HarperCollins

Thompson, WI, *The Imagination of an Insurrection: Dublin, Easter 1916*, 1967, Oxford: OUP

Thoreau, HD, *Resistance to Civil Government* (1848), 2nd edn, 1992, Rossi, W (ed), London: Norton

Thornberry, CHR, 'Dr Soblen and the alien law of the United Kingdom' (1963) 12 ICLQ 414

Thorne, SE, *'Dr Bonham's Case'* (1938) 54 LQR 543

Thornton, GC, *Legislative Drafting*, 3rd edn, 1987, London: Butterworths

Tomkins, A, 'Public interest immunity after Matrix Churchill' [1993] PL 650

Tomkins, A, 'Government information and Parliament: misleading by design or by default?' [1996] PL 472

Tomkins, A, *The Constitution after Scott: Government Unwrapped*, 1998, Oxford: Clarendon

Tomkins, A, 'Readings of *A v Secretary of State for the Home Department*' (2005) PL 259

Toth, AG, 'The principle of subsidiarity in the Maastricht Treaty' (1992) CML Rev 1079

Trevor-Roper, H, *The Philby Affair: Espionage, Treason and Secret Service*, 1968, London: Kimber

Tur, R and Twining, W (eds), *Essays on Kelsen*, 1986, Oxford: Clarendon

Turnbull, M, *The Spycatcher Trial*, 1988, London: Heinemann

Uglow, S, *Criminal Justice*, 2002, London: Sweet & Maxwell

Urban, M, *UK Eyes Alpha: The Inside Story of British Intelligence*, 1997, London: Faber & Faber

Usher, J, 'The Reception of General Principles of Community Law in the United Kingdom' (2005) 16 European Business Law Review 489

Van Dijk, P and Van Hoof, G, *Theory and Practice of the European Convention on Human Rights*, 2nd edn, 1990, Deventer, Netherlands: Kluwer

Vile, MJC, *Constitutionalism and the Separation of Powers*, 1967, Oxford: Clarendon

von Hayek, F, *The Road to Serfdom* (1944), 1994, London: Routledge and Kegan Paul

von Hayek, F, *The Constitution of Liberty*, 1960, London: Routledge and Kegan Paul

Wade, ECS, 'Act of State in English law' (1934) 15 BYIL 98

Wade, HWR and Forsyth, CF, *Administrative Law*, 9th edn, 2004, Oxford: OUP

Wade, HWR, 'The basis of legal sovereignty' [1955] CLJ 177

Wade, HWR, 'Constitutional and administrative aspects of the *Anisminic* case' (1969) 85 LQR 198

Wade, HWR, 'Procedure and prerogative in public law' (1985) 101 LQR 180

Wade, HWR, *Constitutional Fundamentals*, rev edn, 1989, London: Stevens

Wade, HWR, 'Sovereignty – revolution or evolution' (1996) 112 LQR 568

Wade, HWR, 'Horizons of horizontality' [2000] LQR 217

Wagner, A and Squibb, GD, 'Precedence and courtesy titles' (1973) 89 LQR 352

Walker, C, 'Review of the prerogative' [1987] PL 63

Wallington, P (ed), *Civil Liberties*, 1984, Oxford: Martin Robertson

Walsh, D, *The Use and Abuse of Emergency Legislation in Northern Ireland*, 1983, London: The Cobden Trust

Wasserstrom, R, 'The obligation to obey the law' (1963) California UL Rev 780

Watkins, A, *A Conservative Coup*, 1992, London: Duckworth

Watson, J, 'Experience and problems in applying Article 177 EEC' (1986) 23 CML Rev 207

Watt, D, 'Fallout from treachery: Peter Wright and the *Spycatcher* case' [1988] Political Quarterly 206

Weatherill, S and Beaumont, P, *EU Law*, 3rd edn, 1999, Harmondsworth: Penguin

West, N, *MI5: British Security Service Operations 1909–45*, 1981, London: Bodley Head

West, N, *A Matter of Trust: MI5 1945–72*, 1983, London: Hodder & Stoughton

West, N, *GCHQ: The Secret Wireless War 1900–86*, 1986, London: Weidenfeld & Nicolson

Wheare, KC, *The Constitutional Structure of the Commonwealth*, 1960, Oxford: Clarendon

Wheare, KC, *Federal Government*, 4th edn, 1963, Oxford: OUP

Wheare, KC, *Modern Constitutions*, 2nd edn, 1966, Oxford: OUP

White, F and Hollingsworth, K, 'Public finance reform: the Government Resources and Account Act 2000' [2001] PL 50

White paper: *A New Future For Communication* (CM SOLO)

White paper: *Respect and Responsibility – taking a stand against anti-social behaviour*

Williams, DGT, *Not in the Public Interest*, 1965, London: Hutchinson

Williams, DGT, 'Telephone tapping' [1979] CLJ 225

Williams, DGT, 'Public order and common law' [1984] PL 12

Williams, G, *Learning the Law*, ATH Smith (ed), 12th edn, 2002, London: Sweet & Maxwell

Williams, L, 'Defining a sufficiently serious breach of Community law: the House of Lords casts its net into the waters' (2000) 25(4) EL Rev 452

Wilson, H, *The Labour Government 1964–70: A Personal Record*, 1971, London: Weidenfeld & Nicolson

Wilson, H, *The Governance of Britain*, 1976, London: Weidenfeld & Nicolson

Wilson, R (Sir), *The Civil Service in the New Millennium*, May 1999 (www.cabinetoffice.gov.uk/1999/senior/rw_speech.htm)

Winter, T, 'Direct applicability and direct effect: two distinct and different concepts in Community law' (1972) 9 CML Rev 425

Wolf-Phillips, L, 'A long look at the British Constitution' (1984) 37 Parl Aff 385

Woodhouse, D, 'Ministerial responsibility in the 1990s: when do ministers resign?' (1993) 46 Parl Aff 277

Woodhouse, D, 'Ministerial responsibility: something old, something new' [1997] PL 262

Wormald, J, 'James VI and I: two Kings or one?' (1983) 68 History 187

Wright, P, *Spycatcher: The Candid Autobiography of a Senior Intelligence Officer*, 1987, New York: Viking

Young, H, *The Crossman Affair*, 1976, London: Hamish Hamilton

Young, H, *One of Us*, 1989, London: Macmillan

Zander, M, 'When is an arrest not an arrest?' (1997) 147 NLJ 379

Zander, M, *Cases and Materials on the English Legal System*, 9th edn, 2003, London: Butterworths

Zellick, GJ, 'Government beyond law' [1985] PL 283

Zuckerman, AAS, 'Public interest immunity – a matter of prime judicial responsibility' (1994) 57 MLR 703

INDEX